LET'S

Alas

& the Pacific

"Lighthearted and sophisticated, informative and fun to read. *[Let's Go]* helps the novice traveler navigate like a knowledgeable old hand."
—*Atlanta Journal-Constitution*

"The guides are aimed not only at young budget travelers but at the independent traveler, a sort of streetwise cookbook for traveling alone."
—*The New York Times*

■ Let's Go writers travel on your budget.

"Retains the spirit of the student-written publication it is: candid, opinionated, resourceful, amusing info for the traveler of limited means but broad curiosity."
—*Mademoiselle*

"The writers seem to have experienced every rooster-packed bus and lunar-surfaced mattress about which they write."
—*The New York Times*

"All the dirt, dirt cheap."
—*People*

■ Great for independent travelers.

"A world-wise traveling companion—always ready with friendly advice and helpful hints, all sprinkled with a bit of wit."
—*The Philadelphia Inquirer*

"Lots of valuable information for any independent traveler."
—*The Chicago Tribune*

■ Let's Go is completely revised each year.

"Unbeatable: good sight-seeing advice; up-to-date info on restaurants, hotels, and inns; a commitment to money-saving travel; and a wry style that brightens nearly every page."
—*The Washington Post*

"Its yearly revision by a new crop of Harvard students makes it as valuable as ever."
—*The New York Times*

■ All the important information you need.

"Enough information to satisfy even the most demanding of budget travelers...*Let's Go* follows the creed that you don't have to toss your life's savings to the wind to travel—unless you want to."
—*The Salt Lake Tribune*

"Value-packed, unbeatable, accurate, and comprehensive."
—*The Los Angeles Times*

Let's Go Publications

Let's Go: Alaska & the Pacific Northwest 1998
Let's Go: Australia 1998 **New title!**
Let's Go: Austria & Switzerland 1998
Let's Go: Britain & Ireland 1998
Let's Go: California 1998
Let's Go: Central America 1998
Let's Go: Eastern Europe 1998
Let's Go: Ecuador & the Galápagos Islands 1998
Let's Go: Europe 1998
Let's Go: France 1998
Let's Go: Germany 1998
Let's Go: Greece & Turkey 1998
Let's Go: India & Nepal 1998
Let's Go: Ireland 1998
Let's Go: Israel & Egypt 1998
Let's Go: Italy 1998
Let's Go: London 1998
Let's Go: Mexico 1998
Let's Go: New York City 1998
Let's Go: New Zealand 1998 **New title!**
Let's Go: Paris 1998
Let's Go: Rome 1998
Let's Go: Southeast Asia 1998
Let's Go: Spain & Portugal 1998
Let's Go: USA 1998
Let's Go: Washington, D.C. 1998

Let's Go *Map* Guides

Berlin
Boston
Chicago
London
Los Angeles
Madrid
New Orleans
New York City
Paris
Rome
San Francisco
Washington, D.C.

Coming Soon: Amsterdam, Florence

About Let's Go

THIRTY-EIGHT YEARS OF WISDOM

Back in 1960, a few students at Harvard University banded together to produce a 20-page pamphlet offering a collection of tips on budget travel in Europe. This modest, mimeographed packet, offered as an extra to passengers on student charter flights to Europe, met with instant popularity. The following year, students traveling to Europe researched the first, full-fledged edition of *Let's Go: Europe,* a pocket-sized book featuring honest, irreverent writing and a decidedly youthful outlook on the world. Throughout the 60s, our guides reflected the times; the 1969 guide to America led off by inviting travelers to "dig the scene" at San Francisco's Haight-Ashbury. During the 70s and 80s, we gradually added regional guides and expanded coverage into the Middle East and Central America. With the addition of our in-depth city guides, handy map guides, and extensive coverage of Asia and Australia, the 90s are also proving to be a time of explosive growth for Let's Go, and there's certainly no end in sight. The first editions of *Let's Go: Australia* and *Let's Go: New Zealand* hit the shelves this year, expanding our coverage to six continents, and research for next year's series has already begun.

We've seen a lot in 38 years. *Let's Go: Europe* is now the world's bestselling international guide, translated into seven languages. And our new guides bring Let's Go's total number of titles, with their spirit of adventure and their reputation for honesty, accuracy, and editorial integrity, to 40. But some things never change: our guides are still researched, written, and produced entirely by students who know first-hand how to see the world on the cheap.

HOW WE DO IT

Each guide is completely revised and thoroughly updated every year by a well-traveled set of over 200 students. Every winter, we recruit over 140 researchers and 60 editors to write the books anew. After several months of training, Researcher-Writers hit the road for seven weeks of exploration, from Anchorage to Adelaide, Estonia to El Salvador, Iceland to Indonesia. Hired for their rare combination of budget travel sense, writing ability, stamina, and courage, these adventurous travelers know that train strikes, stolen luggage, food poisoning, and marriage proposals are all part of a day's work. Back at our offices, editors work from spring to fall, massaging copy written on Himalayan bus rides into witty yet informative prose. A student staff of typesetters, cartographers, publicists, and managers keeps our lively team together. In September, the collected efforts of the summer are delivered to our printer, who turns them into books in record time, so that you have the most up-to-date information available for your vacation. And even as you read this, work on next year's editions is well underway.

WHY WE DO IT

We don't think of budget travel as the last recourse of the destitute; we believe that it's the only way to travel. Living cheaply and simply brings you closer to the people and places you've been saving up to visit. Our books will ease your anxieties and answer your questions about the basics—so you can get off the beaten track and explore. Once you learn the ropes, we encourage you to put *Let's Go* down now and then to strike out on your own. As any seasoned traveler will tell you, the best discoveries are often those you make yourself. When you find something worth sharing, drop us a line. We're Let's Go Publications, 67 Mount Auburn Street, Cambridge, MA 02138, USA (email fanmail@letsgo.com).

HAPPY TRAVELS!

Contents

WASHINGTON AND OREGON 306

APPENDIX 507

INDEX 513

Maps

Researcher-Writers

Yukiko "The Yukon" Bowman *Northern BC, Yukon Territory, Interior Alaska*

Yuki had to go to the Yukon. It was fate—written in the stars—inscribed in her very name. So she set off, stuffed in her tin-can two-wheel-drive, armed only with bottles of DEET, carrot sticks, and a phenomenal enthusiasm for the road and her copy. She sent back mountains of revolutionary wisdom, infused with a new perspective on the dirt roads of the Great White North and their inescapable run-of-the-mill gas stations and greasy spoons. Although she says she wants to spend a winter in the Yukon someday, she's spending the next one in Japan. Keep on truckin', Yuki.

Allen "Dollar-a-Day" Chen *Southern BC, Alberta*

Allen was the Energizer Bunny of the Pacific Northwest. With his native Californian pizzazz, he bungee jumped, kayaked, surfed, sailed, and climbed his way through Western Canada, inserting enthusiasm, refreshing opinions, and dead mosquitoes (!) into his exhaustive copy. From the glaciers and treeline trails of Yoho National Park to the pubs of Vancouver, Allen discriminatingly combed through listings without spending much more than a red cent. Wow. Next year, he's moving on to meander through more mountains, this time in Colorado. We wish him luck.

Lauren "Iron Woman" Klein *Southwestern and Southcentral Alaska Northwestern BC*

Hailing from the urban wilds of New Jersey, Lauren convinced us that she's actually a Panhandle native at heart...and a tough one, at that. Now forever a part of Prince Rupert history, she won the Prince Rupert Triathalon *on a work day,* then moved on to do some darn fine writing. Always on the lookout for another room with a view or campground-by-the-sea, Lauren kept us smiling. All the while, she basked in an aura of good luck—free tickets to a Jewel concert in Anchorage and free rides from friendly families on the Queen Charlotte Islands made her trip a watery triumph.

Abigail "Jah Lives!" Mnookin *Oregon*

Abby sent back pages and pages of near perfect copy, so smoothly polished we could see our faces. We considered ditching the computers and pasting her work directly into the book, which would have suited our most eco-friendly researcher-writer just fine. Abby's disdain for chain motels and touristy tack meant her chapter would be chock full of yummy campgrounds and budget restaurant goodness. Along the way she caught up with Ani diFranco in Jacksonville and Elvis in Portland. Read all about it—Abby tells no lies.

Daniel "USS" Silverberg *Washington*

Lover of all things nuclear and naval, Daniel was the only researcher-writer with a double-0 licence. His mission was to infiltrate the Evergreen state, and he succeeded with James Bond style and Jack Ryan cool. He went deep undercover in Washington's nightlife, finding the deffest pubs, the phattest clubs, and the dopest dives from Seattle to Spokane. "This beats the hell out of pinball," Daniel wrote. Or, even more succinctly, "Juan de Fuca kicks ass." So do you, Agent Silverberg. Chapter Eight will self-destruct in five seconds.

Sarah "Sourdough" Thomas *Southcentral and Interior Alaska*

"Top of the world, Ma!" From Anchorage to well beyond the Arctic Circle, Sarah proved she was cut from the same cloth as Alaska's hardy pioneers. Wrapped in polar fleece, she mushed far into the wilderness, conquering mighty Denali, falling in love with Wrangell-St. Elias, and boggling at Barrow. Our soon-to-be-a-sourdough blazed new trails for the book and struck the mother lode of earnest, loving copy. A Colorado native, it seems Sarah can't get enough of the ice and snow—she's even considering selling ice cream in Wrangell.

Let's Go Picks

In Alaska and the Pacific Northwest, every turn, town, or truck stop boasts a superlative. Everything is the largest, the oldest, the most breathtaking, or has more vegan options. So we've picked out some bests and biggests of our own, and here are the results—our favorites.

Best Greasy Spoons: Our best greasy spoon is not a greasy spoon. *Quel* paradox. The **PaRaDoX Palace Cafe,** in Portland, OR, is a vegetarian's version of Mel's Diner, complete with turquoise vinyl seats and tofu burritos (p. 415). For the real deal, order "burgers by the bagful" at **Dick's,** in Spokane, WA (p. 399). They cost 55¢ a piece. No kidding.

Best Dose of History: Victoria, BC, remembers who was here first at the **Royal British Columbia Museum** (p. 202). Fantastic, and fantastically thorough exhibits on native culture, history, and everything else.

Best Views: Alaska is basically one huge view. Ask at the visitors center. Or putt to the **Eagle Quality Center,** in Homer, AK, where you can gaze at glorious Kachemak Bay from the most scenic parking lot in the world (p. 78). At the other end of the book, climb the neo-gothic tower on the hill in Seattle's **Volunteer Park,** for a look at Puget Sound and the city below (p. 325). Only the boldest budget travelers bring their binoculars to **Wreck Beach** in Vancouver, BC, where everyone else basks in the buff (p. 192). That's right—we're talkin' naked!

Best Place to Take a Shower While Eating Pizza and Downing a Beer: Well, the only place, really, other than the privacy of your own home. **Hungry Beaver Pizza,** in Wrangell, AK, is a one-stop night-on-the-town, combining a bar, a pizza joint, and public access showers in inimitable Alaskan fashion (p. 138).

Best Drives: Dempster Highway, from Dawson City, YK, to Inuvik, NWT. The Dempster takes the hardest of the hardcore on an incredible wilderness journey to the top of the world (p. 272). **Route 20,** part of the Cascades Loop through North Cascades National Park, WA, proves you don't need to subject your hatchback to whiteouts and washboard gravel (Dempster Highway, we're looking your way!) for jaw-dropping views of rugged, snow-covered peaks (p. 391).

Best Places to Party: Get good and rowdy at the raging **Howling Dog Saloon,** in Fairbanks, AK (p. 118). Mellow out at **The King's Head Pub,** Vancouver, BC (p. 193). Clean yourself off at **Sit and Spin,** Seattle's grooviest laundromat (p. 331).

Best Big-Ass Mountains: Denali, AK, 20,320 ft. of solid rock and glacier ice, sometimes hides under the name Mt. McKinley. Whatever it's called, it's still the biggest, baddest peak in North America (p. 101). Mighty **Mt. Rainier,** WA (p. 381). is smaller than the champ at 14,411 ft., but this active volcano is nonetheless a scrappy challenger with an attitude and some of the most beautiful alpine hiking in the Northwest. Disqualified for unsportsmanlike conduct: **Mount St. Helens,** WA (p. 376).

Best Place to Meddle with the Laws of Physics: Oregon Vortex, Gold Hill, OR (p. 469). Balls roll uphill, pendulums hang at bizarre angles, and the harsh mistress of gravity takes a holiday at the original "magnetic vortex." Accept no imitations.

Best Big Chunks of Ice: The far north is lousy with glaciers, but the overgrown ice cubes aren't always easy to get to. By car: drive to **Salmon Glacier,** near Hyder, BC (p. 252). By foot: hike the **West Glacier Trail,** near Juneau, AK (p. 154). By sea: set sail for the **Sawyer Glaciers,** in Tracey Arm, AK (p. 153). Say hello to some bona fide glacier magic.

Best Places to Get Up Close and Personal with the Animals: Perch on a seaside rock and watch pods of orcas frolic in Puget Sound at **Lime Kiln State Park,** on San Juan Island, WA (p. 354). In Haines, AK, watch thousands of bald eagles—the world's largest annual concentration—converge on an out-of-season Salmon Run at **Chilkat Bald Eagle Preserve** (p. 159). For porcine proximity, head to **Kate's Roadhouse** near Seward, AK, where a full-sized pig lives in the TV room, watching *Friends* with the guests (p. 67). Hey, those nachos were for *sharing!*

Acknowledgments

Thanks, thanks, and more thanks (and a few more thanks—why not) to Rob MacDougall, who made the conquering of this great white whale-of-book fun, funny, frenzy-free (well, relatively), and full of Canadian hijinks. Also special thanks to the god of alliteration. Kate—you wizard of pacing, running headers, and grammar—you paved our road and paved it well. Thank you. As for the other domestics, you kept us sane and happy, giggling away to the tunes of neverending Scott Brown™ impersonations, and, if we were lucky, Prince. Office gurus Anne, Dave, Krzys, Jake, and Melanie, thanks for the smooth sailing. Ian—what a pal you are. Joanna and Anna P., you're the greatest, inside and out (of the office, that is). Lisa, thanks for the friendship, love of lists, and the original deadline fun. Liz, you left us in great hands. Chris, Jarrett, Lauren, and Seth, thanks for the phone calls, emails, and Friday nights. Thanks, Mom, for listening ad infinitum, Dad, for telling me to look for rust under the mats in the trunk, and Anna, for playing Beaver to my Wally. And finally, my eternal thanks to Tim for being there even when I wasn't and reminding me that there's an outside world, too (and for doing the dishes). Now I'm goin' back to Cali.

—LMT

Numero Uno: To the incomparable Lindsey M. Turrentine, who did it all and made it look good. Bagfuls of thanks. In my world, your name would be on the cover, above the title, in 48pt. GillSans. *Numero Dos:* To the indestructible Kate Galbraith, who feigned surprise when everything came out peachy in the end, as if she hadn't been making it so all along. To the rest of the domestic room: Feh on the Eurotrash upstairs; our Moms know we're cool. And so do I. To my fellow Centurions for something. Damned if I can remember what. Extracurricular love and thanks to Mom and Dad and Jamie and Amy and Beth and Scott, for being the best family, ever, in the history of the world. Bar none. 6 Marie and entourage: I love you all. (Bet you were expecting distancing irony.) To the Dog from Outer Space, wherever you are: thanks for the phlegm. Thanks to Sarah, for being better to me than she had any right to be. To my crack trivia squad of droogs and gits: for Bob Izumi, Snidely Whiplash, and 93,000,000 Yankee miles. Thank you, INS, for not reading the fine print. Bubbly thanks to the Cadbury Bottling Company (and to Lindsey) for the champagne of ginger ales. All together now, people: push out the jive, bring in the love.

—RDM

How to Use This Book

As the Bible of the budget traveler, *Let's Go: Alaska and the Pacific Northwest* preaches a simple faith. Commandment 1: Things change, people change. Call ahead. Commandment 2: The best way to travel is tough and cheap. You can't buy the joys of an out-of-the-way budget find. Commandment 3: Thou shalt plan ahead. Any good trip begins with a healthy dose of planning: never fear, we're here to help you. Commandment 4: This hallowed volume covers a tremendous portion of North America. We do not pretend to do it all. You will sometimes have to forge into unknown territory. Commandment 5: Buy maps. Use them a lot. Commandment 6: The faithful follower's best tool is, in the end, not this trusty yellow volume; it is a sense of adventure that will take him or her off the beaten path and into uncharted waters.

That said, we'll give it to you straight: this book has 9 chapters that pave the intrepid traveler's way from north to south, beginning in Alaska and ending in Oregon. They are preceded by the **Essentials** chapter, at the beginning of the book, which provides information on trip planning, how to enter and leave the grand old U.S. of A. and Canada, and how to get around once you're there. We also cram in heaps of no-nonsense advice on safety and packing.

The journey begins in the urban sprawl of **Anchorage,** in **Southcentral Alaska,** and includes access points to glaciers, fjords, mountain ranges, and tremendous marine life. In Chapter Two, the **Interior,** you'll find Alaska's infamous highway system. These roads are not for the timid, but along them you can access **Denali,** the tallest peak in North America, and the city of **Fairbanks,** a major stopping point for those planning a trip in Alaska's rugged inland wilderness. Chapter Three follows **Southeastern Alaska,** better known as the Panhandle, north along Alaskan waterways from **Ketchikan** to **Skagway,** including **Juneau,** the capital of Alaska. Chapter Four is the final chapter on Alaska and covers the massive Alaskan **Bush,** the expanses of wilderness in northern and western Alaska, inaccessible except by plane (never a true budget option). Chapters Five through Seven cover Western Canada. **Southern British Columbia** begins with the province's most accessible destination, **Vancouver,** and proceeds north through **Vancouver Island.** If you have a taste for the open road, the company of Winnebagos, or you're heading for Alaska, then move on to Chapter Six, **Northwestern Canada,** the birthplace of the **Alaska Highway** and the home of the **Yukon Territory.** Chapter Seven delves deep into the prairies of **Alberta** and the Canadian Rockies, including **Banff** and **Jasper National Parks.** The last two chapters of our sacred tome will lead you back to the northwestern corner of the U.S. Chapter Eight, **Washington,** begins with **Seattle,** and Chapter Nine whoops it up in **Oregon,** starting with **Portland.**

For each area, we list Practical Information and Orientation, Accommodations, Food, Sights, Entertainment, and often, Outdoors. It may be useful to flip through a few sections to familiarize yourself with the book; understanding its structure will help you make the most of the information it contains.

A NOTE TO OUR READERS

The information in this book is gathered by *Let's Go*'s researchers from late May through August. Each listing is derived from the assigned researcher's opinion based upon his or her visit at a particular time. The opinions are expressed in a candid and forthright manner. Other travelers might disagree. Those traveling at a different time may have different experiences since prices, dates, hours, and conditions are always subject to change. You are urged to check beforehand to avoid inconvenience and surprises. Travel always involves a certain degree of risk, especially in low-cost areas. When traveling, especially on a budget, always take particular care to ensure your safety.

ESSENTIALS

PLANNING YOUR TRIP

When to Go

Traveling is like comedy—timing is everything. In Alaska and the Pacific Northwest, the tourist season and the weather are the major timing concerns. In general, summer is high season; between June and August expect to share the warm weather with crowds of fellow tourists. In the off-season, crowds are smaller and rates are lower, but it's called the off-season for a reason—some of the sights and attractions you came to see may be closed, and winter travel can be treacherous and unpleasant. Snow, icy roads, and prohibitively cold weather (especially in northern Canada and Alaska) will limit both your movement and your desire to be outdoors.

Major holidays may also affect travel plans. On the biggest holidays, such as Independence Day (July 4) in the U.S. and Canada Day (July 1) in Canada, nearly every town has a celebration of some sort. Businesses and services may be closed, and both transportation and accommodation should be arranged some time in advance (see **Appendix: Holidays and Festivals,** p. 507).

CLIMATE

In Alaska and the Yukon, the weather varies from the coast inland. In general, summer and early fall are the warmest and sunniest times of year; however, wet, windy, and cold days, even during the summer, should be no real surprise. In Alaska's interior, the temperature ranges from around 70°F in summer to -30°F and below in winter. As you progress farther north, summer days and winter nights become longer. North of the Arctic Circle, the sun does not set at all on the nights around the summer solstice in July—or rise on the days around the winter solstice on December.

In British Columbia, Washington, and Oregon, the key weather-making factor is the mountains. West of the mountains it rains. A lot. To the east it is relatively dry. In general, temperatures west of the mountains are more moderate than east—cooler in the summer and warmer in the winter. Winters in coastal Washington and Oregon are soggy but not extremely cold. East of the Rockies, Alberta's temperatures are more extreme, with fine summers but harsh winters (see **Appendix: Weather,** p. 508, for more temperature information).

Useful Information

GOVERNMENT INFORMATION OFFICES

Each state and province has its own travel bureau (listed below) which can recommend other useful organizations, send brochures and maps, and answer questions about the region. Contact the tourist bureau (often called the "Visitors Information Center") in any city you plan to visit for more than a few days. Ask them anything. We dares ya. Addresses for local tourist offices throughout Alaska and the Pacific Northwest appear in the **Practical Information** section for each town or region.

Alaska Division of Tourism, 33 Willoughby St., 9th floor; P.O. Box 110801, Juneau, AK 99811-0801 (907-465-2010; fax 465-2287).

Travel Alberta, Commerce Place, 10155 102 St. 3rd floor, Edmonton, AB T5J 4G8 (800-661-8888 or 403-427-4321; fax 427-0867).

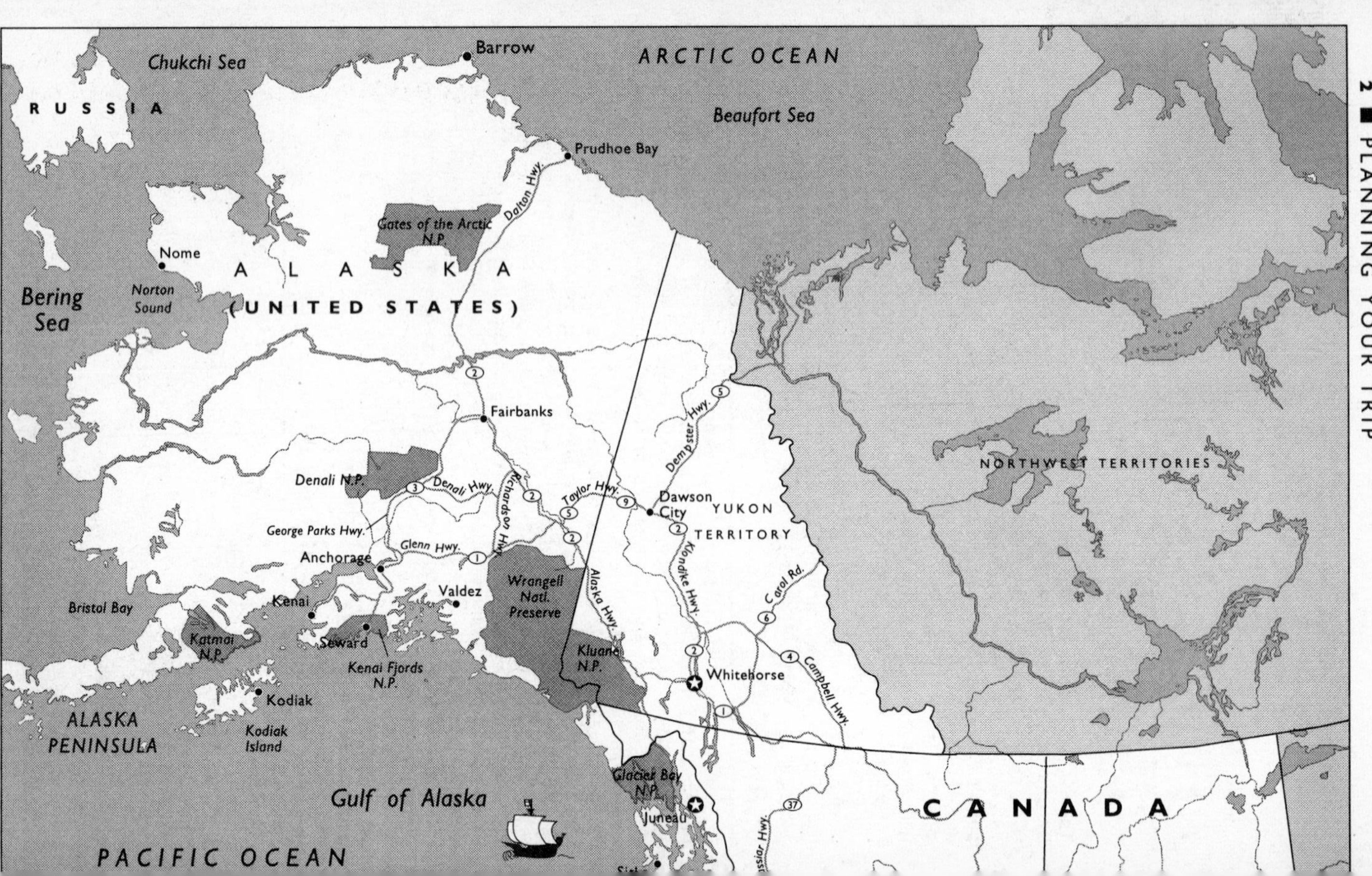
Chukchi Sea
Barrow
ARCTIC OCEAN
RUSSIA
Beaufort Sea
Prudhoe Bay
Dalton Hwy.
Gates of the Arctic N.P.
Nome
ALASKA
(UNITED STATES)
Bering Sea
Norton Sound
Fairbanks
Denali N.P.
Denali Hwy.
Richardson Hwy.
Taylor Hwy.
Dawson City
YUKON TERRITORY
Dempster Hwy.
NORTHWEST TERRITORIES
George Parks Hwy.
Glenn Hwy.
Anchorage
Wrangell Natl. Preserve
Alaska Hwy.
Klondike Hwy.
Carol Rd.
Valdez
Bristol Bay
Kenai
Katmai N.P.
Seward
Kenai Fjords N.P.
Kluane N.P.
Whitehorse
Campbell Hwy.
Kodiak
ALASKA PENINSULA
Kodiak Island
Glacier Bay N.P.
Gulf of Alaska
Juneau
CANADA
PACIFIC OCEAN

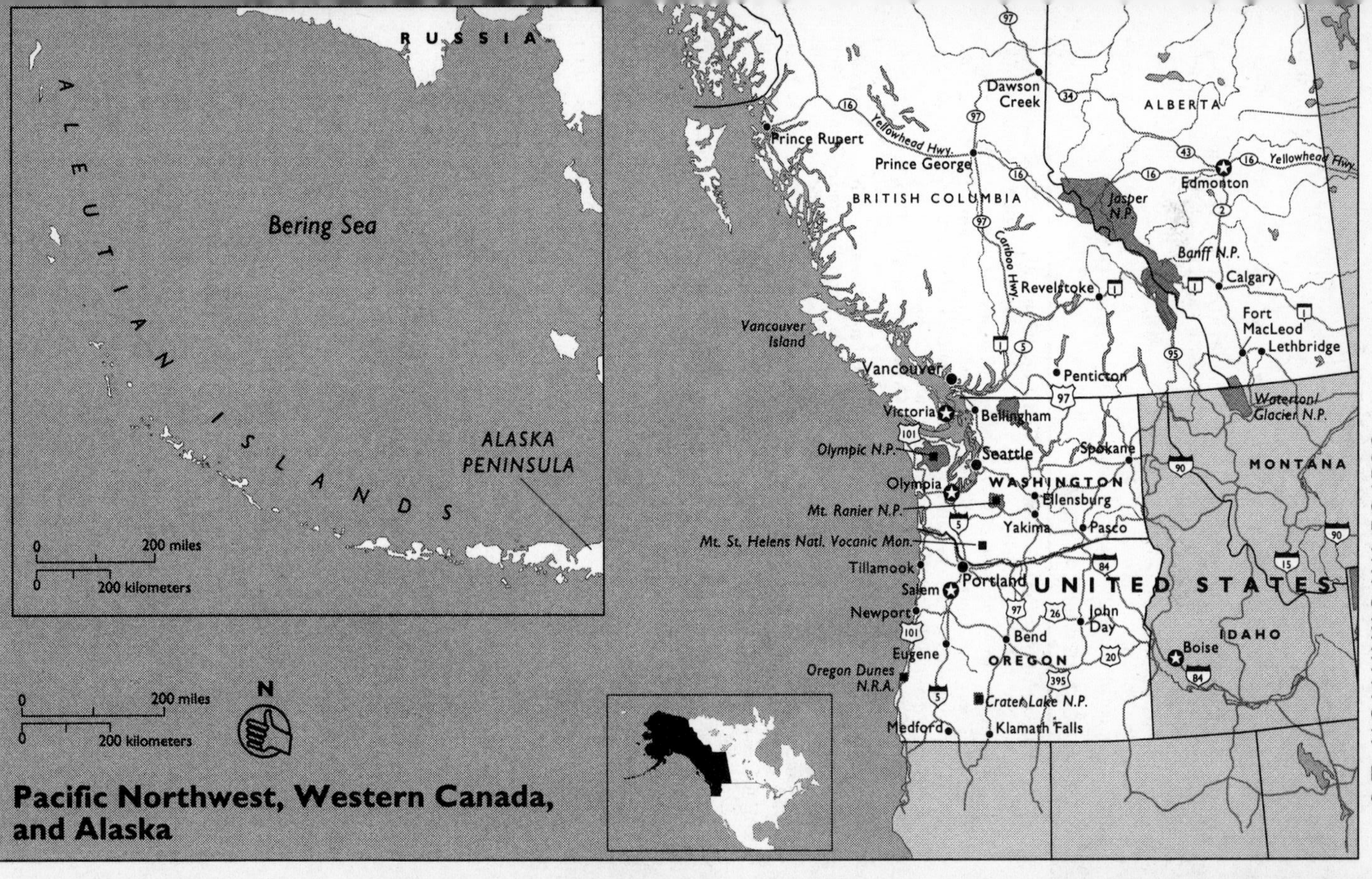
RUSSIA
Bering Sea
ALEUTIAN ISLANDS
ALASKA PENINSULA
200 miles
200 kilometers
Dawson Creek
ALBERTA
Prince Rupert
Yellowhead Hwy.
Prince George
BRITISH COLUMBIA
Jasper N.P.
Edmonton
Banff N.P.
Calgary
Fort MacLeod
Lethbridge
Revelstoke
Cariboo Hwy.
Penticton
Vancouver Island
Vancouver
Waterton/Glacier N.P.
MONTANA
Victoria
Bellingham
Olympic N.P.
Seattle
Spokane
WASHINGTON
Olympia
Ellensburg
Mt. Ranier N.P.
Yakima
Pasco
Mt. St. Helens Natl. Vocanic Mon.
Tillamook
Portland
UNITED STATES
Salem
Newport
Bend
John Day
IDAHO
Boise
Eugene
OREGON
Oregon Dunes N.R.A.
Crater Lake N.P.
Medford
Klamath Falls
N
200 miles
200 kilometers
Pacific Northwest, Western Canada, and Alaska

Tourism British Columbia, 1117 Wharf St., Victoria, BC V8W 2Z2. (800-888-8835 in Canada; 800-663-6000 in the U.S.; 604-387-1642 elsewhere; http://www.tbc.gov.bc.ca/tourism/tourismhome.html).

Oregon Tourism Commission, 775 Summer St. NE, Salem, OR 97310 (800-547-7842; fax 503-234-6762).

Washington State Tourism, Dept. of Community, Trade and Economic Development, P.O. Box 42500, Olympia, WA 98504-2500. Call 800-544-1800 for a general state tourism travel packet, or 206-586-2088 to reach the State Department of Tourism with questions.

Tourism Yukon, P.O. Box 2703, Whitehorse, YT Y1A 2C6 (403-667-5340; fax 667-3546; email yktour@yknet.yk.ca; http://www.touryukon.com).

TRAVEL ORGANIZATIONS

Council on International Educational Exchange (Council), 205 East 42nd St., New York, NY 10017-5706 (888-COUNCIL/268-6245; fax 212-822-2699; http://www.ciee.org). Administers work, volunteer, academic, internship, and professional programs world-wide. Also offers identity cards, including the ISIC and the GO25, and a range of publications, among them the useful (and free) magazine *Student Travels.* Call or write for more information.

Federation of International Youth Travel Organizations (FIYTO), Bredgade 25H, DK-1260 Copenhagen K, Denmark (tel. (45) 33 33 96 00; fax 33 93 96 76; email mailbox@fiyto.org; http://www.fiyto.org). An international organization promoting educational, cultural, and social travel for young people. Member organizations include language schools, educational travel companies, national tourist boards, accommodation centers and other suppliers of travel services to youth and students. FIYTO sponsors the GO25 Card (http://www.go25.org).

International Student Travel Confederation, Herengracht 479, 1017 BS Amsterdam, The Netherlands (tel. (31) 20 421 2800; fax 20 421 2810; email istcinfo@istc.org; http://www.istc.org) Nonprofit confederation of student travel organizations whose focus is to develop, promote, and facilitate travel among young people and students.

HITTING THE BOOKS

On the road, knowledge is power. The mail-order travel shops listed below offer books with the scoop on specific travel issues. Some sell travel supplies as well.

Adventurous Traveler Bookstore, P.O. Box 1468, Williston, VT 05495 (800-282-3963; fax 677-1821; email books@atbook.com; http://www.adventuroustraveler.com). Outdoor adventure travel books and maps for the U.S. and abroad. Their web site offers extensive browsing opportunities. Free 40-page catalogue.

Rand McNally, 150 S. Wacker Dr., Chicago, IL 60606 (800-333-0136; http://www.randmcnally.com). Publishes one of the most comprehensive road atlases of the U.S., Canada, and Mexico, available for $10 in their stores throughout the country, and most other bookstores. Phone orders also available.

Specialty Travel Index, 305 San Anselmo Ave. #313, San Anselmo, CA 94960 (415-459-4900; fax 459-4974; email spectrav@ix.netcom.com; http://www.spectrav.com). Extensive listing of "off the beaten track" and specialty travel opportunities. $6, one-year subscription (2 copies) $10.

Superintendent of Documents, U.S. Government Printing Office, P.O. Box 371954, Pittsburg, PA 15250-7954 (202-512-1800; fax 512-2250; email gpoaccess@gpo.gov; http://www.access.gpo.gov/su_docs). Open Mon.-Fri. 7:30am-4:30pm. Publishes *Your Trip Abroad* ($1.25), *Health Information for International Travel* ($14), and "Background Notes" on all countries ($1). Postage is included in the prices.

Travel Books & Language Center, Inc., 4931 Cordell Ave., Bethesda, MD 20814 (800-220-2665; fax 301-951-8546; email travelbks@aol.com). Sells over 75,000 items, including books, cassettes, atlases, dictionaries, and a wide range of specialty travel maps. Free comprehensive catalog upon request.

Wide World Books and Maps, 1911 N. 45th St., Seattle, WA 98103 (206-634-3453; fax 634-0558; email travel@speakeasy.org; http://www.travelbooksandmaps.com/travelbk). Stocks travel guides, travel accessories, and hard-to-find maps.

INTERNET RESOURCES

We've come a long way since the world of *Tron.* Today, people can make their own airline, hotel, hostel, or car rental reservations on the Internet, and connect personally with others abroad, allowing people to become their own budget travel planners. There are a number of ways to access the **Internet.** Most popular are commercial internet providers, such as **America Online** (800-827-6394) and **CompuServe** (800-433-0389). Many employers and schools also offer gateways to the Internet, often at no cost (unlike the corporate gateways named above). The Internet itself can be used in many different forms, but the most useful to net-surfing budget travelers are the World Wide Web and Usenet newsgroups. For information on Internet access during your travels, see **Keeping in Touch: Email,** p. 47.

Student and Budget Travel Guide (http://asa.ugl.lib.umich.edu/chdocs/travel/travel-guide.html). A great place to start surfing, with links to the CIA world factbook, consular information sheets, state travel advisories, Amtrak train schedules, a subway navigator, a jet lag diet, and more.

Internet Guide to Hostelling (http://www.hostels.com). Just what it sounds like.

Rent-A-Wreck's Travel Links (http://www.rent-a-wreck.com/raw/travlist.htm). Surprisingly complete page of links.

Big World Magazine (http://www.paonline.com/bigworld). A budget travel 'zine with a web page and a great collection of links to travel pages.

Shoestring Travel (http://www.stratpub.com). Another budget travel 'zine, with feature articles, links, user exchange, and accommodations information.

In addition to the web sites above, we also list relevant web sites throughout different sections of the Essentials chapter. Web sites come and go very rapidly; a good web site one week might disappear the next, and a new one might quickly take its place.

Documents and Formalities

When traveling, always carry on your person two or more forms of identification, including at least one photo ID. A passport combined with a driver's license or birth certificate usually serves as adequate proof of identity and citizenship. Many establishments, especially banks, require several IDs before they will cash traveler's checks. Never carry all your forms of ID together, however; you risk being left entirely without ID or funds in case of theft or loss. If you plan an extended stay, register your passport with the nearest embassy or consulate.

PASSPORTS

Before you leave, photocopy the page of your passport that contains your photograph, passport number, and other identifying information; this will help prove your citizenship and facilitate the issuing of a new passport if your old one is lost or stolen. Carry one photocopy in a safe place apart from your passport, and leave another copy at home. If you do lose your passport, notify the local police and the nearest embassy or consulate of your home government immediately.

Canadian and U.S. citizens may cross the U.S./Canada border with only proof of citizenship (e.g. a birth certificate or a voter's registration card along with a photo ID; a driver's license alone will not be enough). U.S. citizens under 18 need the written consent of a parent or guardian; Canadian citizens under 16 need notarized permission from both parents.

Australian citizens must apply for a passport at a post office, a passport office, or an Australian diplomatic mission. An appointment may be necessary. A parent may file an application for a child who is under 18 and unmarried. A 32-page adult passport costs AUS$120 and is valid for 10 years; a child's costs AUS$60 and is valid for 5 years. For more info, call toll-free (in Australia) 13 12 32.

British citizens can apply in person or by mail to a passport office for a full passport, which costs UK£18 and is valid for 10 years (five years if the applicant is under 16). Children under 16 may be included on a parent's passport. Processing by mail usually takes 4-6 weeks. The London office offers same-day, walk-in rush service; arrive early. The **U.K. Passport Agency** can be reached by phone at (0990) 21 04 10, and information is available on the Internet at http://www.open.gov.uk/ukpass.

Irish citizens can apply for a passport by mail to either the **Department of Foreign Affairs,** Passport Office, Setanta Centre, Molesworth St., Dublin 2 (tel. (01) 671 16 33), or the Passport Office, Irish Life Building, 1A South Mall, Cork (tel. (021) 27 25 25). Obtain an application at a local Garda station. Passports cost IR£45 and are valid for 10 years. The new Passport Express Service allows citizens to get a passport through the post office in 2 weeks for an extra IR£3. Citizens under 18 or over 65 can request a 3-year passport that costs IR£10.

New Zealand citizens can obtain passport application forms in New Zealand from travel agents or a **Department of Internal Affairs Link Centre.** Applications may also be forwarded to the Passport Office, P.O. Box 10526, Wellington, New Zealand. Standard processing time is 10 working days for correct applications. Adult passports, valid for 10 years, cost NZ$80. Children's passports, valid for 5 years, cost NZ$40. An urgent passport service is available for an extra NZ$80. Overseas, forms and passport services are provided by New Zealand embassies, high commissions, and consulates. Different fees and processing times apply.

South African citizens can apply for a passport at any **Home Affairs Office** or **South African Mission.** Tourist passports, valid for 10 years, cost SAR80. Children under 16 must be issued their own passports, valid for 5 years, which cost SAR60. Time for the completion of an application is normally 3 months or more from the time of submission. If a passport is needed in a hurry, an **emergency passport** may be issued for an extra SAR50.

EMBASSIES AND CONSULATES

Contact your nearest embassy or consulate to obtain information regarding visas and passports to the United States and Canada. For embassies and consulates of other countries in Canada and the U.S., see p. 34.

U.S. Embassies: In **Australia,** Moonah Place, Canberra, ACT 2600 (tel. (02) 6270 5000; fax 6270 5970); in **Canada**, 100 Wellington St., Ottawa, ON K1P 5T1 (613-238-5335 or 238-4470; fax 238 5720); in **Ireland,** 42 Elgin Rd., Ballsbridge, Dublin 4 (tel. (01) 668 71 22); in **New Zealand,** 29 Fitzherbert Terr., Thorndon, Wellington (tel. (04) 472 20 68; fax 472 35 37); in **South Africa,** 877 Pretorius St., Arcadio 0083; P.O. Box 9536, Pretoria 0001 (tel. (012) 342 10 48; fax 342 22 44); in the **U.K.,** 24/31 Grosvenor Sq., London W1A 1AE (tel. (0171) 499 90 00; fax 409 1637).

U.S. Consulates: In **Australia,** MLC Centre, 19-29 Martin Place, 59th Fl., Sydney, NSW 2000 (tel. (02) 9373 9200; fax 9373 9125); in **Canada,** P.O. Box 65, Postal Station Desjardins, Montréal, QC H5B 1G1 (514-398-9695; fax 398-0973); 360 University Ave., Toronto, ON M5G 1S4 (416-595-1700; fax 595-0051); 1095 W. Pender St., Vancouver, BC V6E 2M6 (604-685-4311); in **New Zealand,** 4th Fl., Yorkshire General Bldg., corner of Shortland and O'Connell St., Auckland (tel. (09) 303 27 24; fax 342 22 44); in **South Africa,** Broadway Industries Centre, Heerengracht, Foreshore, Capetown (tel. (021) 21 42 80; fax 25 41 51); in the **U.K.,** Queen's House, 14 Queen St., Belfast, N. Ireland, BT1 6EQ (tel. (0123) 232 82 39); 3 Regent Terr., Edinburgh, Scotland EH7 5BW (tel. (0131) 556 8315; fax 557 6023).

Canadian Embassies and High Commissions: In **Australia,** Commonwealth Ave., Canberra ACT 2600 (tel. (02) 6273 3844); in **Ireland,** Canada House, 65 St. Stephen's Green, Dublin 2 (tel. (014) 78 19 88; fax 478 12 85); in **New Zealand,** 61 Molesworth St., Thorndon, Wellington (tel. (04) 473 95 77; fax 471 20 82); in **South Africa,** Private Bag X14, Hatfield 0028 (tel. (012) 422 30 00; fax 422 30 53); in the **U.K.,** MacDonald House, 38 Grosvenor Square, W1X 0AA (tel. (0171) 258 66

00); in the **U.S.,** 501 Pennsylvania Ave., Washington, D.C. 20001 (202-682-1740; fax 682-7689).

Canadian Consulates: In **Australia,** Level 5, Quay West Bldg., 111 Harrington St., Sydney NSW 2000 (tel. (02) 9364 3000; fax 9364 3098); in **New Zealand,** Level 9, Jetset Centre, 44-48 Emily Place, Auckland (tel. (09) 309 36 90); in **South Africa,** Reserve Bank Building, 19th Fl., 360 St. George's Mall St., Capetown 8001 (tel. (021) 23 52 40; fax 23 48 93); in the **United Kingdom,** 3 George St., Edinburgh EH2 2XZ (tel. (0131) 220 43 33; fax 245 60 10); in the **U.S.,** 22nd Floor, 1251 Ave. of the Americas, New York, NY 10020-1175 (212-596-1600; fax 596-1791); 300 S. Grand Blvd., 10th Fl., Los Angeles, CA 90071 (213-346-2700); 412 Plaza 600, 6th and Stewart St., Seattle, WA 98101-1286 (206-443-1372; fax 441-7838).

U.S. AND CANADIAN ENTRANCE REQUIREMENTS

Foreign visitors to the United States and Canada are required to have a **passport** (see above) and **visa/proof of intent to leave.** To visit either country, you must be healthy and law-abiding, and demonstrate the ability to **support yourself financially** during your stay. A visa, stamped into a traveler's passport by the government of a host country, allows the bearer to stay in that country for a specified purpose and period of time. To obtain a U.S. or Canadian visa, contact the nearest embassy or consulate.

United States Travelers from certain nations may enter the U.S. without a visa through the **Visa Waiver Pilot Program.** Visitors qualify as long as they are traveling for business or pleasure, are staying for 90 days or less, have proof of intent to leave (e.g. a returning plane ticket), have a completed I-94W, and enter aboard particular air or sea carriers. Participating countries include Australia, France, Germany, Ireland, Italy, Japan, New Zealand, and the UK. Contact a U.S. consulate for more info; countries are added frequently.

Most visitors from elsewhere obtain a **B-2,** or "pleasure tourist," visa at the nearest U.S. consulate or embassy, which normally costs $20 and is usually valid for six months. Don't lose your visa. If you do lose your I-94 form (arrival/departure certificate attached to your visa upon arrival), you can replace it at the nearest **U.S. Immigration and Naturalization Service (INS)** office, though it's very unlikely that the form will be replaced within the time of your stay. **Extensions** for visas are sometimes attainable with a completed I-539 form; call the forms request line at (800) 870-3676. For more info, contact the INS at (800) 755-0777 or (202) 307-1501 (http://www.ins.usdoj.gov). The **Center for International Business and Travel (CIBT),** 25 W. 43rd St. #1420, New York, NY 10036 (800-925-2428 or 212-575-2811), secures travel visas for a variable service charge.

Canada Citizens of Australia, France, Germany, Ireland, Mexico, New Zealand, the U.K., and the U.S. may enter Canada without visas as long as they plan to stay for 90 days or fewer and carry proof of intent to leave. South Africans do need a visa to enter Canada. Citizens of all other countries should contact their Canadian consulate for more information. Write to **Citizenship and Immigration Canada** for the booklet *Applying for a Visitor Visa* at Information Centre, Public Affairs Branch, Journal Tower South, 365 Laurier Ave. W., Ottawa, Ontario K1A 1L1 (613-954-9019; fax 954-2221), or consult the electronic version at http://cicnet.ingenia.com/english/coming/imm5256e.html. **Extensions** are sometimes granted; phone the nearest Canada Immigration Centre listed in the phone directory.

CUSTOMS: ENTERING

Unless you plan to import a BMW or a barnyard beast, you will probably pass right through customs with minimal ado. The U.S. and particularly Canada restrict the importation of firearms, fireworks, and obscene literature and films. It is also illegal to import many perishable foods, including most fruits, vegetables, and meat products, because many carry pests. Officials may also seize articles made from certain protected species, so be ready to part with your illegal powdered rhino horn or snake-skin boots. (See **Health,** p. 13, for information on carrying prescription drugs.)

United States You may bring the following into the U.S.: $100 in gifts and $200 in personal merchandise, 200 cigarettes (1 carton) and 50 cigars (no Cubans!), and personal belongings such as clothes and jewelry. Travelers age 21 and over may also bring up to 1 liter of alcohol, although state laws may further restrict this amount. Money (cash or traveler's checks) can be transported, but amounts over $10,000 must be reported. Customs officers may ask how much money you are carrying and your planned departure date in order to ensure that you'll be able to support yourself while in the U.S.

The **U.S. Customs Service,** 1301 Constitution Ave., Washington, D.C. 20229 (202-927-5580; http://www.customs.ustreas.gov), publishes a brochure with the snappy title *Customs Guidelines for Visitors to the United States,* detailing everything the international traveler needs to know about American customs.

Canada Besides personal items, the following things may be brought in free of duty: up to 1.14L of alcohol or a 24-pack of beer (as long you are of age in the province you are visiting), 50 cigars, 200 cigarettes (1 carton), 400g of manufactured tobacco, and gifts valued less than CDN$60. As in the U.S., if you exceed the limited amounts, you will be asked to pay a fine. For detailed info on Canadian customs and booklets on other Canadian travel information, write **Canada Customs,** 2265 St. Laurent Blvd., Ottawa, ON K1G 4K3 (800-461-9999 or 613-993-0534 outside Canada; fax 991-9062; http://www.revcan.ca).

CUSTOMS: RETURNING HOME

Upon returning home, you must declare all articles you acquired abroad and must pay a duty on the value of those articles that exceed the allowance established by your country's customs service. Goods and gifts purchased at duty-free shops abroad are not exempt from duty or sales tax at your point of return; you must declare these items as well. Restrictions generally apply to items such as alcohol, tobacco and tobacco products, and perfume. Contact the authorities listed below for your own country's specifics.

Australia: Australian Customs Service, GPO Box 8, Sydney NSW 2001 (tel. (02) 9213 2000; fax 9213 4000).

Canada: Canada Customs, 2265 St. Laurent Blvd., Ottawa, Ontario K1G 4K3 (613-993-0534). Phone the 24hr. Automated Customs Information Service at 800-461-9999, or visit Revenue Canada at http://www.revcan.ca.

Ireland: The Revenue Commissioners, Dublin Castle (tel. (01) 679 27 77; fax 671 20 21; email taxes@iol.ie; http://www.revenue.ie) or **The Collector of Customs and Excise,** The Custom House, Dublin 1.

New Zealand: New Zealand Customs, 50 Anzac Ave., Box 29, Auckland (tel. (09) 377 35 20; fax 309 29 78).

South Africa: Commissioner for Customs and Excise, Private Bag X47, Pretoria 0001. South Africans residing in the U.S. should contact the **Embassy of South Africa,** 3051 Massachusetts Ave., NW, Washington DC 20008 (202-232-4400; fax 244-9417).

U.K.: Her Majesty's Customs and Excise, Custom House, Nettleton Road, Heathrow Airport, Hounslow, Middlesex TW6 2LA (tel. (0181) 910 37 44; fax 910 37 65).

U.S.: U.S. Customs Service, Box 7407, Washington D.C. 20044 (202-927-6724; http://www.customs.ustreas.gov). Ask for the brochure *Know Before You Go.*

YOUTH, STUDENT, AND TEACHER I.D.

Many U.S. establishments will honor an ordinary university student ID for student discounts. Still, the following two main forms of student and youth identification are extremely useful, especially for the accompanying insurance packages (see p. 15).

International Student Identity Card (ISIC): Flash this card and be showered with discounts for sights, theaters, museums, accommodations, train, ferry, and airplane travel, and other services. Ask about discounts even when none are advertised. Applicants must be at least 12 years old and degree-seeking students at a secondary or post-secondary school. Because of the proliferation of phony ISICs, many airlines and some other services require other proof of student identity; an official letter from your school registrar and/or your school ID card should do the trick. The card provides accident insurance of up to US$3000 and US$100 per day in-hospital care for up to 60 days. In addition, cardholders have access to a toll-free 24hr. **Traveler's Assistance hotline** (800-626-2427 in U.S. and Canada, elsewhere call collect 713-267-2525), whose multilingual staff can provide help in case of medical, legal, and financial emergencies overseas. Most budget travel agencies (see p. 23) issue the ISIC. The card is valid from September to December of the following year and costs US$19 or CDN$15. An *ISIC Handbook,* which comes with membership, lists some of the discounts available. The **International Teacher Identity Card (ITIC)** costs US$20 and offers the same insurance coverage, as well as similar but limited discounts. For more information consult the organization's web site at http://www.istc.org.

International Youth Discount Travel Card or **GO25 Card:** Issued by the **Federation of International Youth Travel Organizations** (see **FIYTO,** p. 4). A discount card for all travelers under 26 (not just students). This one-year card offers many of the same benefits as the ISIC, and most organizations that sell the ISIC also sell the GO25 Card. The fee is US$19, CDN$15, or UK£5. A brochure that lists discounts is free when you purchase the card. Information is available from FIYTO headquarters in Denmark, on the web at http://www.fiyto.org or http://www.go25.org, or by contacting Travel CUTS in Canada, STA Travel in the U.K., or Council Travel in the U.S. (see **Budget Travel Agencies,** p. 23).

Money Matters

Staying in the cheapest accommodations possible and preparing their own food from time to time, budget travelers in the Pacific Northwest can expect to spend anywhere from $10 to $60 per person per day. Transportation will increase these figures. Don't sacrifice health or safety for a cheaper tab—no trip is fun if you're sick, hungry, or getting mugged.

CURRENCY AND EXCHANGE

It is cheaper to buy domestic currency than to buy foreign, so as a rule you should convert money to U.S. or Canadian dollars once there. It's a good idea, however, to convert enough money before you leave to last a couple of days; this prevents problems if you arrive after banking hours or on a holiday. You should also convert to the local currency before visiting little-touristed areas where bank tellers may not recognize or be willing to exchange foreign currencies. Wholesale rates offered at banks will be lower than those offered by other exchange agencies. If the bank has a surcharge for every exchange, you'll lose money with every transaction, so convert in large sums. Most international airports in Canada and the U.S. have currency exchange booths.

The Greenback (The U.S. Dollar)

CDN$1 = US$.73	**US$1= CDN$1.39**
AUS$1 = US$0.76	**US$1 = AUS$1.32**
IR£1 = US$1.51	**US$1 = IR£0.66**
NZ$1 = US$0.69	**US$1 = NZ$1.45**
UK£1 = US$1.63	**US$1 = UK£061**

The main unit of currency in the U.S. is the dollar; the dollar is divided into 100 cents. The color of paper money is green in the U.S; bills come in denominations of $1, $5, $10, $20, $50, and $100. The U.S. has 1¢ (penny), 5¢ (nickel), 10¢ (dime), and 25¢ (quarter) coins.

The Loonie (The Canadian Dollar)

US$1 = CDN$1.39	**CDN$1 = US$0.73**
AUS$1 = CDN$1.05	**CDN$1 = AUS$0.95**
IR£1 = CDN$2.10	**CDN$1 = IR£0.48**
NZ$1 = CDN$0.95	**CDN$1 = NZ$1.04**
UK£1 = CDN$2.27	**CDN$1 = UK£0.44**

The main unit of currency in Canada is the **dollar,** which is identical to the U.S. dollar in name only. Most Canadian businesses cheerfully accept U.S. currency, their cheer fuelled by the substantial hike they'll take out of the going exchange rate. Paper money comes in denominations of $5, $10, $20, $50, and $100, which are all the same size but color-coded. Coins come in denominations of 1¢, 5¢, 10¢, 25¢, $1 and $2. The $1 coin is known as the **loonie** for the loon on one face; its recently introduced $2 counterpart has been dubbed the **"twoonie"** for reasons unknown.

SALES TAX AND TIPPING

State or provincial **sales taxes** are added to virtually all purchases in Canada and the U.S. Groceries are usually the sole exception. Oil-rich Alaska and Alberta have no local sales taxes, but Alberta, like all of Canada, has a 7% federal **goods and services tax (GST).** Visitors can claim a rebate of the GST they pay on short-term accommodations (less than one month) and on most goods they buy to take home. This can be a significant amount, so be sure to save your receipts and pick up a GST rebate form while in Canada. The total claim must be at least CDN$14 of GST (equal to $200 in purchases; each individual receipt must exceed CDN$50) and must be made within one year of the date of purchase. Further information is available from local tourist offices or through **Revenue Canada, Visitor's Rebate Program,** 275 Pope Rd., Summerside, PEI C1N 6C6 (800-668-4748 in Canada or 902-432-5608 outside Canada).

In both Canada and the U.S., it is customary to **tip** waitstaff 15% on sit-down meals and cab drivers 15% on the fare. At the airport, try to carry your own bags; porters expect a customary $1 per bag tip. **Bargaining** is generally fruitless and frowned upon.

TRAVELER'S CHECKS

Traveler's checks are one of the safest and least troublesome ways to carry large sums of money, as they can be refunded if lost or stolen. Several agencies and banks sell them, usually for a small percentage commission. Keep some cash on hand in less-touristed regions, since smaller establishments may not accept traveler's checks.

You should expect a fair amount of red tape and delay in the event of theft or loss of traveler's checks. Ask for a list of refund centers when you buy your checks. To expedite the refund process, keep your check receipts separate from your checks and store them in a safe place or with a traveling companion. Record check numbers when you cash them and leave a list of check numbers with someone at home. Keep a separate supply of cash or traveler's checks for emergencies, and never countersign your checks until you are prepared to cash them. The following companies sell traveler's checks denominated in U.S. and Canadian dollars:

American Express: (800) 221-7282 in the U.S. and Canada; in New Zealand (0800) 44 10 68; in the U.K. (0800) 52 13 13. Elsewhere, call U.S. collect (801) 964-6665 or visit the AmEx online travel offices at http://www.aexp.com. American Express traveler's checks are the most widely recognized worldwide and the easiest to replace if lost or stolen. Checks can be purchased for a small fee at American Express Travel Service Offices, banks, and American Automobile Association offices (AAA members can buy the checks commission-free). Cardmembers can also purchase checks at American Express Dispensers at Travel Service Offices at airports and by ordering them via phone (800-ORDER-TC/673-3782). **Cheques for Two** can be signed by either of two people traveling together.

Thomas Cook MasterCard: Call (800) 223-9920 in the U.S. and Canada; from the U.K. call (0800) 622 101 free or (1733) 502 995 collect or (1733) 318 950 collect; elsewhere call U.S. collect (609) 987-7300. Commission 1-2% for purchases. Thomas Cook offices may sell checks for lower commissions and will cash checks commission-free.

VISA: (800) 227-6811 in the U.S.; in the U.K. (0800) 895 492; from anywhere else in the world call (011 01733) 318 949 and reverse the charges. Any of the above numbers can tell you the location of their nearest office. All Visa traveler's checks can be reported lost at these numbers.

CREDIT CARDS

Credit cards can be invaluable in the U.S. and Canada, and are sometimes expected or required (for example, many car rental agencies require that you have a credit card). Credit cards are also useful when an emergency, such as an unexpected hospital stay, leaves you temporarily without other resources. In addition, some cards carry services for users which may range from personal or car rental insurance to emergency assistance. Major credit cards can be used to extract cash advances from associated banks and ATMs; this can be a good bargain for foreign travelers because credit card companies get the wholesale exchange rate, which is generally 5% better than the retail rate used by banks. However, you will be charged ruinous interest rates if you don't pay off the bill quickly, so be careful when using this service. **American Express** cards also work in some ATMs, as well as at AmEx offices and major airports.

MasterCard (outside North America, "EuroCard" or "Access") and **Visa** ("Carte Bleue" or "Barclaycard") are the most widely accepted. Both sell credit cards through banks. For lost or stolen cards call Visa (800-336-8472); Mastercard (800-999-0454). **American Express** cards carry a hefty annual fee ($55, unless you are a student, in which case you have the option of obtaining the free Optima card), but offer extensive travel-related services (800-THE-CARD/843-2273).

ATM CARDS

There are tens of thousands of ATMs (automatic teller machines) everywhere in the U.S. and Canada, offering 24-hour service in banks, airports, grocery stores, gas stations, etc. ATMs allow you to withdraw local currency from your bank account wherever you are. There is often a limit on the amount of money you can withdraw per day (usually about US$500, depending on the type of card and account), and computer network failures are not unknown. The two major ATM networks in North America are **Mastercard/Cirrus** (800-4-CIRRUS/424-7787) and **PLUS/Visa** (800-843-7587), slightly more common in Western Canada. Inquire at your bank about fees charged for ATM transactions.

EMERGENCY CASH

If you run out of money on the road, you can have more mailed to you in the form of traveler's checks bought in your name, a certified check, or through postal money orders, available at post offices (85¢ fee; $600 limit per order; cash only). Certified checks are redeemable at any bank, while postal money orders can only be cashed at post offices upon display of two IDs (one of which must be a photo ID). Keep receipts, since money orders are refundable if lost. **Personal checks** from home will probably not be acceptable no matter how many shiny ID cards you have.

Wiring money can cost from $15 (for domestic service) to $35 (international), depending on the bank, as well as an added fee ($7-15) for receiving the money. Once you've found a bank that will accept a wire, write or telegram your home bank with your account number, the name and address of the bank to receive the wire, and a routing number. Also notify the bank of the form of ID that the second bank should accept before paying the money. As a very last resort, consulates will wire home for you and deduct the cost from the money you receive.

Western Union (800-CALL-CASH/225-5227) is a well-known and expensive service that can be used to cable money within the domestic United States with your Visa, Discover, or MasterCard. You or someone else can phone in a credit card number or bring cash to a Western Union office for pick-up at another Western Union location. The rates for sending cash are generally $10 cheaper than with a credit card. You will need ID to pick up the money.

American Express is one of the easiest ways to get money from home. AmEx allows Green Card holders to draw cash from their checking accounts at any of its major offices and many of its representatives' offices, up to $1000 every 21 days (no service charge, no interest). Unless using the AmEx service, avoid cashing checks in foreign currencies; they usually take weeks and a $30 fee to clear.

Safety and Security

For emergencies in the U.S. and Canada, dial **911.** This number works in most places. If it does not, dial 0 for the operator and request to be connected with the appropriate emergency service (i.e., police, fire, ambulance, etc.).

HELP LINES

United States Department of State issues travel advisories on the U.S. and/or Canada, including crime and security, on their 24hr. hotline (202-647-5225) and web site (http://travel.state.gov).

Travel Assistance International by Worldwide Assistance Services, Inc. 1133 15th St. NW #400, Washington, D.C. 20005-2710 (202-828-5894 or 800-821-2828; fax 202-828-5896). Provides its members with a 24hr. hotline for emergencies and referrals. Year-long frequent traveler package (US$235-$295) includes medical and travel insurance, financial assistance, and help in replacing lost documents.

United States Center for Disease Control and Prevention (404-332-4559; fax 332-4565; http://www.cdc.gov). Excellent source of general information on health for travelers, and maintains a travelers hotline (see **Health,** p. 13).

American Automobile Association (AAA), 1050 Hingham St., Rocklin, MA 02370 (800-AAA-HELP/222-4357 in the U.S.; in Canada 800-337-4357). Offers members emergency road service and free towing (for more benefits, see p. 29).

Traveler's Assistance Hotline (800-626-2427 in U.S. and Canada, elsewhere call collect 713-267-2525). Available to ISIC holders (see p. 9).

STREET SMARTS

Trust your instincts—they are your most valuable assets. The gawking camera-toter is a more obvious target than the low-profile local look-alike. Try to look like you know what you are doing and where you are going, even if you don't. Walking into a cafe or shop to check your map beats checking it on a street corner; better still, look over your map before leaving the hotel room. Do not keep money or anything precious in your back pocket or a fanny pack; use a neck pouch or money belt instead. Sleeping in a car or van parked in the city is *extremely* dangerous—even the most dedicated budget traveler should not consider it an option. Be aware of your surroundings: a single block can separate safe and unsafe areas. If you feel uncomfortable, leave as quickly and directly as you can, but don't allow fear to close off whole worlds to you. Careful exploration will build confidence and make your travels that much more rewarding.

A good self-defense course will give you concrete ways to react to different types of aggression. Community colleges frequently offer such courses inexpensively. **Impact, Prepare,** and **Model Mugging** can refer you to local self-defense courses in the United States (800-345-KICK/345-5425). Course prices vary from US$50-400. Women's and men's courses are offered.

ALCOHOL AND DRUGS

If you carry **prescription drugs** while your travel, it is vital to have a copy of the prescriptions themselves readily accessible at the U.S. and Canadian borders. The importation of **illegal substances** into Canada or the U.S. is, needless to say, illegal, and a punishable offense. Away from borders, police attitudes vary widely across the region, but the old standards—marijuana, LSD, heroin, cocaine—are illegal in every province and state. If you are arrested for drug possession in the U.S. or Canada you can be subject to a wide range of charges.

In Oregon, Washington, and Alaska, the **drinking age** is 21. British Columbia and the Yukon Territory prohibit drinking below the age of 19, while in Alberta you can drink at age 18. In both the U.S. and Canada, the law is strictly enforced. Particularly in the U.S., be prepared to show a photo ID (preferably some government document—driver's license or passport) if you look under 30. Sixty-five years after Prohibition, some areas of the U.S. are still "dry," meaning they do not permit the sale of alcohol at all, while other places prohibit the sale of alcohol on Sundays. Officials on both sides of the border take **drunk driving** very seriously—don't do it.

Health

Common sense is the simplest prescription for good health while traveling: eat well, drink and sleep enough, and don't overexert yourself. Travelers complain most often about their feet and their gut, so take precautionary measures. Drinking lots of fluids will prevent dehydration and constipation, and wearing sturdy shoes, clean socks, and using talcum powder can help keep your feet dry and happy. To minimize the effects of jet lag, "reset" your body's clock by adopting the time of your destination immediately upon arrival. Most travelers feel acclimatized to a new time zone after two or three days.

BEFORE YOU GO

A good rule of thumb: if you can't live without something, bring a spare or make a backup plan. If you wear **glasses** or **contact lenses,** carry an extra prescription and arrange to have your doctor or a family member send a replacement pair in an emergency. In your **passport** or other document, write the names of any people you wish to be contacted in case of a medical emergency and list any allergies or medical conditions which doctors should be aware of. Bring any **medication** you regularly take and may need while traveling, as well as a copy of the **prescription** and a statement of any preexisting medical conditions you may have, especially if you will be bringing insulin, syringes, or any narcotics into the USA or Canada.

Those with medical conditions (e.g. diabetes, allergies to antibiotics, epilepsy, heart conditions) may want to obtain a **Medic Alert** identification tag (US$35 the first year, and $15 annually thereafter), which identifies the condition and gives a 24-hour collect-call information number. Contact Medic Alert at 800-825-3785, or write to Medic Alert Foundation, 2323 Colorado Ave., Turlock, CA 95382. Diabetics can also contact the **American Diabetes Association,** 1660 Duke St., Alexandria, VA 22314 (800-232-3472) to receive copies of the article *Travel and Diabetes* and a diabetic ID card, which carries messages in 18 languages explaining the carrier's diabetic status.

For more general health information, contact the **American Red Cross.** The ARC publishes a *First-Aid and Safety Handbook* (US$5) available for purchase by calling or writing to the American Red Cross, 285 Columbus Ave., Boston, MA 02116-5114 (800-564-1234). Finally, the **United States Center for Disease Control and Prevention,** Travelers' Health, 1600 Clifton Rd. NE, Atlanta, GA 30333 (404-332-4559 for traveler's hotline; 404-639-3311 for public inquiries; 800-227-8922 for STD hotline; 800-342-2437 for AIDS/HIV hotline; 800-243-7889 for TTY; fax 332-4565; http://www.cdc.gov) is an excellent source of general information on health for travelers.

COMMON WOES

For minor health problems, bring a compact **first-aid kit**, including bandages, aspirin or other pain killer, antiseptic soap or antibiotic cream, a thermometer, a Swiss Army knife with tweezers, moleskin, a decongestant for colds or allergies, motion sickness remedy, medicine for diarrhea or stomach problems, sunscreen, and insect repellent with DEET. If you suffer from any of the following ailments in a severe or prolonged form, seek medical help as soon as possible.

Altitude: Travelers to high altitudes must allow their bodies a couple of days to adjust to the lower levels of oxygen in the air before engaging in strenuous activities. Expect some drowsiness, and an amplification of the effects of alcohol.

Bee Stings: Can be potentially fatal if you are allergic; always be prepared if you are. If you suffer from restricted breathing after a sting, seek medical attention.

Diarrhea: Traveler's diarrhea is very common. Many people take over-the-counter remedies (such as Pepto-Bismol or Immodium) to counteract it, but be aware that such remedies can complicate serious infections. The most dangerous side effect of diarrhea is dehydration. Drink plenty of non-alcoholic, non-caffeinated beverages, eat salty foods, and rest. This too shall pass.

Frostbite: Skin affected by frostbite turns white, then waxy and cold. Victims should drink warm beverages, stay dry, and *gently and slowly* warm the frostbitten area with dry fabric or, better, with steady body contact. *Never* rub or pour hot water on frostbite; skin is easily damaged when frozen.

Giardia: Found in many rivers and lakes, *giardia lamblia* is a bacteria that causes gas, painful cramps, loss of appetite, and violent diarrhea. To protect yourself, bring your water to a rolling boil for several minutes or purify it with iodine tablets before drinking or cooking with it.

Heatstroke: Heatstroke is preceded by the dizziness and nausea of **heat exhaustion**, which is less serious and can be treated with rest, water, and salty foods. When sweating stops and body temperature rises, more dangerous heatstroke has begun. Cool the victim immediately with liquids, wet towels, and shade, and consider medical attention.

Hypothermia: Hypothermia results from exposure to cold and is a real danger in Alaska and the Pacific Northwest, even in summer. The signs are easy to detect: shivering, slurred speech, loss of coordination, exhaustion, hallucinations, or amnesia. *Do not let victims of advanced hypothermia fall asleep*—their body temperatures will drop further, and if they lose consciousness, they may die. To avoid hypothermia, keep dry and out of the wind. Dress in layers; wool keeps insulating even when wet as do pile fleece jackets and Gore-Tex rain gear. Never rely on cotton for warmth; this "death cloth" will make you colder when wet.

Lyme Disease: Tick-borne diseases, such as Lyme disease, can be very serious. Lyme disease is not known to exist in Alaska, but may be a problem for travelers in the Pacific Northwest. Lyme is characterized by a circular rash of two inches or more that looks like a bull's eye. Other symptoms are flu-like: fever, headache, fatigue, or aches and pains. Untreated, Lyme disease is very dangerous. There is no vaccine, but Lyme can be treated with antibiotics if caught early. Removing a tick within 24 hours greatly reduces the risk of infection. Wear bug repellent when hiking, and periodically stop and check for ticks; they are brownish and about the size of the head of a pin. To be super-cautious (and a bit dorky looking), pull your socks up over your pant legs.

Mosquitoes: Perhaps Alaska's greatest threat to your *mental* health are the incredible swarms of mosquitoes which descend on humanity every summer. Backcountry mosquitoes scoff at any insect repellent less potent than 95% **DEET** (not available in Alaska, so stock up down south), or (for reasons unexplained by modern science) **Avon Skin-so-Soft** hand cream. After-bite products with ammonium hydroxide will ease your pain.

Poison Ivy, Poison Oak, Poison Sumac: These plants secrete oils that can cause unbearable itchiness, hives, and sometimes inflammation of the affected areas. Some people have allergic reactions that cause serious asthma-like symptoms; find medical help if this occurs. If you think you have come into contact with one of these plants, wash your skin in soap and cold water (heat dilates the pores, driving the poison deeper). An excellent soap is **Fels Naptha,** available at any well stocked drug store. If rashes occur, calamine lotion, topical cortisones (like Cortaid©), or antihistamines may stop the itching. Fight the near-irresistible urge to scratch; it will only spread the oil.

Rabies: Can be fatal if untreated. If you are bitten by any wild animal, clean your wound thoroughly and seek medical help.

Sunburn: Carry sunscreen and apply it liberally and often. You may not have gone to Alaska in search of a tan, but in summer the sun will be up for 20 or more hours a day. Sunscreens of Sun Protection Factor (SPF) 20 are strong enough for the fairest skin; higher ratings won't help and are more expensive.

AIDS, HIV, STDS

Acquired Immune Deficiency Syndrome (AIDS) is a growing problem around the world. The World Health Organization estimates that there are around 13 million people infected with the HIV virus. The easiest mode of HIV transmission is through direct blood to blood contact with an HIV+ person; *never* share intravenous drug, tattooing, or other needles. The most common mode of transmission is sexual intercourse. Well over 90% of adults newly infected with HIV acquired their infection through heterosexual sex, and women now represent 50% of all new HIV infections. To lessen your chances of contracting any sexually transmitted disease (STD), use a latex condom every time you have sex. Condoms are widely available in Canada and the U.S., but it doesn't hurt to stock up before you set out. The **U.S. Center for Disease Control** (see p. 13) can provide more info.

Insurance

Beware of offers for unnecessary coverage—your current policies might well extend to many travel-related accidents. **Homeowners' insurance** often covers theft during travel and loss of travel documents (passport, plane ticket, railpass, etc.), while many types of **medical insurance** (especially university policies) cover medical costs incurred abroad. Check with your provider for details.

ISIC, and **ITIC,** (see p. 8) provide $3000 worth of accident and illness insurance and $100 per day for up to 60 days of hospitalization. Cardholders have access to a toll-free 24-hour helpline whose multilingual staff can provide assistance in medical, legal, and financial emergencies overseas. **Council** (see p. 4) offers a range of plans to supplement basic insurance coverage, with options covering medical treatment and hospitalization, accidents, baggage loss, and even charter flights missed due to illness. Most **American Express** cardholders (customer service 800-528-4800) receive automatic car rental (collision and theft, but not liability) insurance and travel accident coverage (US$100,000 in life insurance) on flight purchases made with the card.

Insurance companies usually require a copy of the police report for thefts, or evidence of having paid medical expenses (doctor's statements, receipts) before they will honor a claim. They may have time limits on filing for reimbursement. Always carry policy numbers and proof of insurance. Check with each insurance carrier for restrictions and policies. Most of the carriers listed below have 24-hour hotlines.

Access America, 6600 West Broad St., PO Box 11188, Richmond, VA 23230 (800-284-8300; fax 804-673-1491). Covers trip cancellation/interruption, on-the-spot hospital admittance, emergency medical evacuation, sickness, and baggage loss.

The Berkeley Group/Carefree Travel Insurance, 100 Garden City Plaza, P.O. Box 9366, Garden City, NY 11530-9366 (516-294-0220 or 800-323-3149; fax 516-294-1096). Offers two comprehensive packages including coverage for trip cancellation/interruption/delay, accident and sickness, medical, baggage loss, bag delay, accidental death and dismemberment, and travel supplier insolvency. Trip cancellation/interruption may be purchased separately at US$5.50 per $100 of coverage.

Globalcare Travel Insurance, 220 Broadway, Lynnfield, MA 01940 (800-821-2488; fax 617-592-7720; email global@nebc.mv.com; http://www.nebc.mv.com/globalcare). Complete medical, legal, emergency, and travel-related services. On-the-spot payments and special student programs, including benefits for trip cancellation and interruption. Waives pre-existing medical conditions and provides coverage for the bankruptcy or default of cruiselines, airlines, or tour operators.

Travel Guard International, 1145 Clark St., Stevens Point, WI 54481 (800-826-1300; fax 715-345-0525; http://www.travel-guard.com). Comprehensive insurance programs starting at US$40. Programs cover trip cancellation/interruption, medical coverage abroad, emergency assistance, and lost baggage.

Alternatives to Tourism

There's no better way to immerse yourself in a culture than to become part of its economy. Finding a job is often a matter of timing and luck. Job leads may come from local residents, hostels, employment offices, and chambers of commerce. Temporary agencies often hire for non-secretarial placement as well as for standard typing assignments. Marketable skills, i.e., touch-typing, dictation, computer knowledge, and experience with children will prove very helpful in your search for a temporary job. Volunteer (unpaid) jobs are readily available almost everywhere in Canada and the U.S; some provide room and board in exchange for labor. Consult newspapers and bulletin boards on college campuses for job listings.

WORKING FOR A LIVING

You **must** apply for a work visa to work in the U.S. Working or studying in the U.S. with only a B-2 (tourist) visa is grounds for deportation. The first step toward acquiring a work visa begins at the U.S. consulate or embassy nearest you. **Council Travel** (see p. 23) runs a summer travel/work program which lets students spend their summers working in the U.S.; check your local Council agency for details.

If you intend to work in Canada, you will need an **Employment Authorization,** obtained before you enter the country; visitors are not ordinarily allowed to change status once they have arrived. Residents of the U.S., Greenland, and St. Pierre/Miquelon may apply for Employment Authorization at a port of entry. Your potential employer must contact the nearest **Canadian Employment Centre (CEC)** for approval of the employment offer. For more information, contact the consulate or embassy in your home country. **Travel CUTS,** Council's Canadian analogue, will also have useful information (see **Budget Travel Agencies,** p. 23).

Canneries

Seafood harvesting and processing jobs are no bed of oysters. While it is possible to earn a lot of cash in a little time, you must be willing to put in long, hard hours at menial and unrewarding tasks. As the **Alaska Employment Service** eloquently states, "Most seafood processing jobs are smelly, bloody, slimy, cold, wet, and tiring because of manual work and standing for many hours. The aroma of fish lingers with workers throughout the season. Most get used to it. Those who can't generally leave." If you're still interested, the Alaska Employment Service (part of the Department of Labor) is a good source of information: c all (Alaska area code 907) Kodiak 486-3105, Anchorage 269-4800, Petersburg 772-3791, Sitka 747-3347, Ketchikan 225-5500, Homer 235-7791, Kenai 283-4304, Seward 224-5276, or Valdez 835-4910.

Treeplanting

Planting trees is the Canadian equivalent of work in the canneries—the smell is better, but the hours are long and hard, and the bugs can be indescribable. Canada requires its lumber companies to reforest the areas they log. Whether the planting can recreate Canada's old-growth forests is a question of some debate; what the policy has created, though, is an intense and potentially lucrative job opportunity in the forests of northern British Columbia and Alberta. Planters are usually paid between ten and thirty cents per tree; an experienced planter can plunk enough trees in the ground to earn as much as $200 a day. Most treeplanters are university students who work from late spring to mid-summer. The companies that hire them range from well-run, professional organizations to ragtag hippie collectives to exploitative rip-off operations. To gather information on treeplanting in Western Canada, contact **Forestry Canada** at (250) 363-0600. Treeplanting is not for everyone; ask plenty of questions so you know what you're getting into before you go.

STUDY OPPORTUNITIES

If you are interested in studying in the Pacific Northwest or Alaska, contact the universities listed below directly for information about enrolling. As a first step, however, the **Institute of International Education (IIE)** (809 United Nations Plaza, New York, NY 10017-3580; 212-984-5413 for recorded information; fax 984-5358), which administers many exchange programs, is an excellent source of information. IIE publishes *Academic Year Abroad,* which details semester and academic-year programs offered worldwide (US$43, plus $4 shipping), and *Vacation Study Abroad,* with information on short-term programs including summer and language schools (US$37, plus $4 shipping).

Lewis & Clark College, 615 SW Palatine Hill Rd., Portland, OR 97219-7899 (503-768-7040 or 800-444-4111; fax 503-768-7055; email admissions@lclark.edu; http://www.lclark.edu).

Oregon State University, 104 Kerr Administration Bldg., Corvallis, OR 97333-2106 (541-737-4411; fax 541-737-2482; email osuadmit@ccmail.orst.edu; http://www.orst.edu).

Simon Fraser University, Office of the Registrar, Burnaby, BC V5A 1S6 (604-291-3224; fax 291-4969; http://www.sfu.ca); branch downtown at Harbor Center, 515 West Hastings, Vancouver, BC V6B 5K3 (604-291-5040).

University of Alaska Anchorage, 3211 Providence Dr., Anchorage, AK 99508-8046 (907-786-1480; fax 786-4888; http://www.uaa.alaska.edu).

University of Alaska Fairbanks, Office of Admissions, P.O. Box 757480, Fairbanks, AK 99775-7480 (800-291-4192 in Alaska; 907-474-7500 elsewhere; fax 474-5379; email fyapply@aurora.alaska.edu; http://zorba.uafadm.alaska.edu).

University of Alberta, 120 Administration Bldg., Edmonton, AB T6G 2M7 (403-492-3113; fax 492-7172; email registrar@ualberta.ca; http://www.registrar.ualberta.ca).

University of British Columbia, Office of the Registrar, 2016-1874 East Mall, Vancouver, BC V6T 1Z1 (604-822-3159; fax 604-822-5945; http://www.ubc.ca).

University of Calgary, 2500 University Dr. NW, Calgary, AB T2N 1N4 (403-220-6645; fax 289-1253; http://www.ucalgary.ca).

University of Oregon, Office of Admissions, 240 Oregon Hall, 1217 University of Oregon, Eugene, OR, 97403-1217 (541-346-3201; fax 346-5815; TTY 346-1323; email uoadmit@oregon.uoregon.edu; http://www.uoregon.edu).

University of Victoria, Admission Services, P.O. Box 3025, Victoria, BC V8W 3P2 (250-721-8119; fax 721-6225; http://www.uvic.ca).

University of Washington, Office of Admission, Schmitz Hall Room 320, Box 355840, Seattle, WA 98195-5840 (206-543-9686; fax 685-3655; http://www.washington.edu)

Washington State University, 370 Lighty Student Services Bldg., Pullman, WA 99163-1067 (509-335-5586; fax 335-4902; email admiss@wsu.edu; http://www.wsu.edu).

U.S. Student Visas Foreign students who wish to study in the United States must apply for either an **M-1 visa** (vocational studies) or an **F-1 visa** (for full-time students enrolled in an academic or language program). An F-1 allows you to work part-time in an on-campus position. For information on how to obtain and submit the proper forms, and how to acquire an on-campus job, contact the international student office at the institution you will be attending.

Canadian Student Visas To study in Canada you will need a **Student Authorization.** To obtain one, contact the nearest Canadian consulate or embassy. Be sure to apply at least four months ahead of time; it can take a long time to go through, and there is a processing fee. You will also need to prove to the Canadian government that you are able to support yourself financially. A student authorization is good for one year. If you plan to stay longer, it is extremely important that you do not let it expire before you apply for renewal. Canadian immigration laws permit full-time students to seek on-campus employment. For specifics, contact a Canadian Immigration Center (CIC) or consulate. Residents of the U.S., Greenland, and St. Pierre/Miquelon may apply for Student Authorization at a port of entry.

Packing

Pack lightly...that means you. Even if you have a car. The more you bring, the more you have to worry about. A good rule is to lay out only what you absolutely need, then take half the clothes and twice the money.

THE BACKPACK

If you plan to cover most of your itinerary on foot, a sturdy **frame backpack** is unbeatable. **Internal-frame packs** mold better to your back, keep a lower center of gravity, and can flex adequately on difficult trails that require a lot of bending and maneuvering. **External-frame packs** are more comfortable for long hikes over even terrain since they keep the weight higher and distribute it more evenly. Before you buy any pack, try it on and imagine carrying it, full, a few miles up a rocky incline. Make sure it has a strong, padded hip belt that transfers weight from your shoulders to your hips and legs. Any serious backpacking requires a pack of at least 4000 cubic inches. Allow an additional 500 cubic inches for your sleeping bag in internal-frame packs. Good packs cost anywhere from $150 to $500. Be wary of excessively low-end prices and don't sacrifice quality. See **Camping and Hiking Equipment,** p. 40.

DRESS FOR SUCCESS

The clothing you bring will, of course, depend on when and where you're planning to travel. In general, **dressing in layers** is best when traveling; if you're hot, peel off a shirt, and if you're cold, add a layer.

Summer: Stick to natural fibers and lightweight materials. Start with a few t-shirts; they take up virtually no space and you can wear a sweatshirt or sweater over them on a chilly night. Pack a couple of pairs of shorts and jeans, as well as underwear, socks, a towel, and swimwear.

Winter: Warm winter clothing is obviously a must. Bring heavier layers, including at least one that insulates while wet, such as polypropylene, polar fleece, or wool. Never rely on cotton for warmth.

Rain: A waterproof jacket and a backpack cover will take care of you and your stuff at a moment's notice. Gore-Tex® is a miracle fabric that's both waterproof and breathable; it's all but mandatory if you plan on hiking. Avoid cotton as outer-wear, especially if you will be outdoors a lot.

Footwear: My god, your feet are what you walk on! Well-cushioned athletic shoes or lace-up leather shoes are good for general walking, but for serious hiking a good pair of water-proofed hiking boots is essential: they're lightweight, rugged, and dry quickly. *Break in your shoes before you leave home.* A double pair of socks—light absorbent cotton inside and thick wool outside—will cushion feet, keep them dry, and help prevent blisters. Talcum powder in your shoes and on your feet can prevent sores, and moleskin is great for blisters. Bring a pair of **flip-flops** for the fungal floors of communal showers.

RANDOM USEFUL STUFF

Sleepsacks: If planning to stay in **youth hostels,** make the requisite sleepsack instead of paying the hostel's linen charge. Fold a full size sheet in half the long way, then sew it closed along the open long side and one of the short sides.

Toiletries: soap, shampoo, toothpaste, deodorant, razors, toilet paper, tampons, condoms, birth control, vitamins, sunscreen, lip balm, and insect repellent. Pack spillables in plastic bags to prevent chemical slicks within your luggage. Bring whatever you need to keep your contact lenses happy.

More useful than random: alarm clock, batteries, waterproof matches, sun hat, needle and thread, safety pins, sunglasses, pocketknife, plastic water bottle, compass, towel, padlock, whistle, flashlight, earplugs, duct tape (for patching tears in anything), clothespins, maps, tweezers, garbage bags.

More random than useful: notebook with pens, harmonica, bandanas, string, rubber bands, very small rocks, personal stereo (Walkman) with headphones, and a lead-lined pouch (for protecting film or Kryptonite from airport x-rays).

Specific Concerns

WOMEN TRAVELERS

Women exploring on their own inevitably face additional safety concerns, but these warnings and suggestions should not discourage women from traveling alone. Be adventurous, but avoid unnecessary risks. Trust your instincts: if you'd feel better somewhere else, move on. Always carry extra money for a phone call, bus, or taxi. You might consider staying in hostels which offer single rooms that lock from the inside or in religious organizations that offer rooms for women only. Stick to centrally located accommodations and avoid solitary late-night treks or metro rides. **Hitching** is never safe for lone women, or even for two women traveling together.

Your best answer to verbal harassment is usually no answer at all. Don't hesitate to seek out a police officer or a passerby if someone is giving you a hard time. In emergencies, a toll-free call to 911 should result in immediate assistance. See **Street Smarts,** p. 12, for more safety advice.

The **National Organization for Women (NOW)** can refer women travelers to crisis centers and counseling services and provide lists of feminist events. Contact NOW through a local branch or at 3543 18th St., San Francisco, CA 94110 (415-861-8960; fax 861-8969; email sfnow@sirius.com; http://www.sirius.com/~sfnow/now.html).

Handbook For Women Travellers, by Maggie and Gemma Moss (UK£9). Encyclopedic and well-written. Available from Piatkus Books, 5 Windmill St., London W1P 1HF (tel. (0171) 631 07 10).

A Journey of One's Own, by Thalia Zepatos (US$17). Interesting and full of good advice, with a bibliography of books and resources. Available from The Eighth Mountain Press, 624 Southeast 29th Ave., Portland, OR 97214 (503-233-3936; fax 233-0774; email eightmt@aol.com).

A Foxy Old Woman's Guide to Traveling Alone, by Jay Ben-Lesser (Crossing Press, US$11). Info, informal advice, and a resource list on solo travel on a low-to-medium budget.

OLDER TRAVELERS

Senior citizens are eligible for a wide range of discounts on transportation, museums, movies, theaters, concerts, restaurants, and accommodations. If you don't see a senior citizen price listed, ask and you may be pleasantly surprised. (For information on the **Golden Age Passport,** honored at all U.S. national parks, see p. 39).

American Association of Retired Persons (AARP), 601 E St. NW, Washington, D.C. 20049 (202-434-2277). Members 50 and over receive benefits and services including the AARP Motoring Plan from AMOCO (800-334-3300), and discounts on lodging, car rentals, cruises, and sight-seeing. Annual fee US$8 per couple, US$20 for three years, lifetime membership US$75.

Elderhostel, 75 Federal St., 3rd Fl., Boston, MA 02110-1941 (617-426-7788, fax 426-8351; http://www.elderhostel.org). For those 55 or over (spouse of any age). Programs at colleges, universities, and other learning centers in over 70 countries on varied subjects lasting one to four weeks.

National Council of Senior Citizens, 8403 Colesville Rd., Silver Spring, MD 20910-31200 (301-578-8800; fax 578-8999). Memberships cost US$13 per year, US$33 for 3 years, or US$175 for a lifetime. Individuals or couples can receive hotel and auto rental discounts, a senior citizen newspaper, and use of a discount travel agency.

Unbelievably Good Deals and Great Adventures That You Absolutely Can't Get Unless You're Over 50, by Joan Rattner Heilman. After you finish reading the title page, check inside for some great tips on senior discounts and the like. Contemporary Books, US$10.

BISXUAL, GAY, AND LESBIAN TRAVELERS

Prejudice against bisexuals, gays, and lesbians still exists in Canada and the U.S., but acceptance is growing. In the larger cities of the Pacific Northwest, and in major tourist and college towns, you will not generally need to compromise your freedom to enjoy your trip. Outside these areas, however, gay and lesbian travelers must regrettably be advised to watch their step to avoid possible harassment or aggression.

Most major cities in both Canada and the U.S. have large, active gay and lesbian communities. Wherever possible, *Let's Go* lists local gay and lesbian information lines and community centers, as well as local hot spots.

Damron Travel Guides, P.O. Box 422458, San Francisco, CA 94142 (800-462-6654 or 415-255-0404; fax 703-9049; email damronco@ud.com; http://www.damron.co). Publishes the *Damron Address Book* (US$15), which lists bars, restaurants, guest houses, and services in the United States, Canada, and Mexico catering to gay men. The *Damron Road Atlas* (US$15) contains color maps of 56 major U.S. and Canadian cities and gay and lesbian resorts and listings of bars and accommodations. *The Women's Traveller* (US$12) includes maps of 50 major U.S. cities and lists bars, restaurants, accommodations, bookstores, and services catering to lesbians. *Damron's Accommodations* lists gay and lesbian hotels (US$19). Mail order available for an extra $5 shipping.

Ferrari Guides, P.O. Box 37887, Phoenix, AZ 85069 (602-863-2408; fax 439-3952; email ferrari@q-net.com; http://www.q-net.com). Gay and lesbian travel guides: *Gay Travel A to Z* (US$16), *Men's Travel in Your Pocket* (US$14), *Women's Travel in Your Pocket* (US$14), and more. Available in bookstores or by mail order. Postage/handling $4.50 for the first item, $1 for each additional item mailed within the US. Overseas, call or write for shipping cost.

Gayellow Pages, P.O. Box 533, Village Station, New York, NY 10014. (212-674-0120; fax 420-1126; email gayellow_pages@juno.com; http://gayellowpages.com). An annually updated listing of accommodations, resorts, hotlines, and other items of interest to the gay traveler. USA/Canada edition US$16.

Women Going Places (Inland Book Company, US$14). An international women's travel and resource guide emphasizing women-owned enterprises, geared toward lesbians. Available in bookstores.

TRAVELERS WITH DISABILITIES

Hotels and motels in Alaska and the Pacific Northwest have become increasingly accessible to disabled persons, and many national parks are trying to make exploring the outdoors more feasible. (For information on the **Golden Access Passport,** honored at all U.S. national parks, see p. 39). Call ahead to restaurants, hotels, parks, and other facilities to find out about accessibility.

Arrange transportation well in advance to ensure a smooth trip. A number of major **car rental agencies** have hand-controlled vehicles at some locations (see **By Car: Renting,** p. 30). **Amtrak, VIA Rail** and virtually all major **airlines** will accommodate disabled passengers if notified at least 72 hours in advance. **Greyhound** buses will provide free travel for a companion; if you are without a fellow traveler, call Greyhound (800-752-4841) at least 48 hours before you plan to leave and they will make arrangements to assist you. For transportation information in individual U.S. and Canadian cities, contact the local chapter of the Easter Seals Society.

American Foundation for the Blind, 11 Penn Plaza, New York, NY 10011 (212-502-7600), open Mon.-Fri. 8:30am-4:30pm. Provides information and services for the visually impaired. For a catalogue of products, contact Lighthouse Enterprises, 36-20 Northern Boulevard, Long Island City, NY 10011 (800-829-0500).

Facts on File, 11 Penn Plaza, 15th floor, New York, NY 10001 (212-967-8800). Publishers of *Disability Resource,* a reference guide for travelers with disabilities (US$45 plus shipping). Available at bookstores or by mail order.

Mobility International, USA (MIUSA), P.O. Box 10767, Eugene, OR 97440 (514-343-1284 voice and TDD; fax 343-6812; email info@miusa.org; http://miusa.org). International Headquarters in Brussels, rue de Manchester 25, Brussels, Belgium, B-1070 (tel. (332) 410 62 97; fax 410 68 74). Contacts in 30 countries. Information on travel programs, international work camps, accommodations, and organized tours for those with physical disabilities. Membership US$30 per year. Sells *A World of Options: A Guide to International Educational Exchange, Community Service, and Travel for Persons with Disabilities* (US$30, nonmembers $35).

Society for the Advancement of Travel for the Handicapped (SATH), 347 Fifth Ave., #610, New York, NY 10016 (212-447-7284; fax 725-8253; email sathtravel@aol.com; http://www.sath.org). Publishes a quarterly travel magazine, *Open World* (free for members, US$13 for nonmembers) and a wide range of information sheets with advice on trip planning for people with disabilities. Annual membership US$45, students and seniors US$30.

Twin Peaks Press, P.O. Box 129, Vancouver, WA 98666-0129 (MC and Visa orders call 800-637-2256; otherwise 360-694-2462; fax 360-696-3210; email 73743.2634@compuserve.com; http://netm.com/mall/infoprod/twinpeak/helen.htm). Publishers of *Travel for the Disabled,* which provides travel tips, lists of accessible tourist attractions, and advice on other resources for disabled travelers (US$20). Also sells *Directory for Travel Agencies of the Disabled* (US$20), *Wheelchair Vagabond* (US$15), *Directory of Accessible Van Rentals* (US$10), and damn fine coffee. Postage $3.50 for first book, $1.50 for each additional book.

Tours or Trips for Disabled Travelers:

Directions Unlimited, 720 N. Bedford Rd., Bedford Hills, NY 10507 (800-533-5343; in New York 914-241-1700; fax 241-0243). Specializes in arranging individual and group vacations, tours, and cruises for the physically disabled.

Flying Wheels Travel Service, 143 W. Bridge St., Owatonne, MN 55060 (800-535-6790; fax 451-1685). Arranges trips in the U.S. and abroad for groups and individuals in wheelchairs or with other sorts of limited mobility.

The Guided Tour Inc., Elkins Park House, Suite 114B, 7900 Old York Road, Elkins Park, PA 19027-2339 (800-783-5841 or 215-782-1370; fax 635-2637). Organizes travel programs for persons with developmental and physical challenges and those requiring renal dialysis. Call, fax, or write for a free brochure.

TRAVELERS WITH CHILDREN

Family vacations can be recipes for disaster—unless you slow your pace and plan ahead. When deciding where to stay, remember the special needs of young children. If you pick a B&B, call ahead and make sure it's child-friendly. If you rent a car, make sure the rental company provides a car seat for younger children. Consider using a papoose-style device to carry your baby on walking trips. Be sure that your children carry some sort of ID in case of an emergency, and arrange a reunion spot in case of separation when sight-seeing.

Restaurants often have children's menus and discounts. Virtually all museums and tourist attractions have a children's rate, as do most airlines, trains, and bus companies. Finding private spaces for breast-feeding is sometimes a problem while traveling; pack accordingly or search for mother-friendly spots wherever you end up.

Some of the following publications offer tips for adults traveling with children or distractions for the kids themselves. You can also contact the publishers to see if they have other related publications that you might find useful.

Backpacking with Babies and Small Children (US$10). Published by Wilderness Press, 2440 Bancroft Way, Berkeley, CA 94704 (800- 443-7227 or 510-843-8080; fax 548-1355; email wpress@ix.netcom.com).

Kidding Around (US$8). Illustrated series of books for children about cities across the U.S. Educational (and distracting) books that could prove invaluable for keeping little ones happy on long trips. Published by John Muir Publications, P.O. Box 613, Santa Fe, NM 87504 (800-285-4078; fax 505-988-1680; contact Kathleen Chambers).

Travel with Children by Maureen Wheeler (US$12, postage $1.50). Published by Lonely Planet Publications, Embarcadero West, 155 Filbert St., #251, Oakland, CA 94607 (800-275-8555 or 510-893-8555; fax 893-8563; email info@lonelyplanet.com; http://www.lonelyplanet.com). Also at P.O. Box 617, Hawthorn, Victoria 3122, Australia.

DIETARY CONCERNS

Travelers who keep **kosher** should contact synagogues in larger cities for information on kosher restaurants; your own synagogue or college Hillel should have access to lists of Jewish institutions across the nation. **The Jewish Travel Guide** lists synagogues, kosher restaurants, and Jewish institutions in over 80 countries. It is available in the U.S. from Sepher-Hermon Press, 1265 46th St., Brooklyn, NY 11219 (718-972-9010; US$13.95 plus $2.50 shipping), and in the U.K. from Ballantine-Mitchell Publishers, Newbury House 890-900, Eastern Ave., Newbury Park, Ilford, Essex, U.K. IG2 7HH (tel. (0181) 599 88 66; fax 599 09 84).

Vegetarian food is gaining acceptance in even the staunchest ranching communities in Alaska and the Pacific Northwest. *Let's Go* often notes restaurants with good vegetarian selections in city listings. The **North American Vegetarian Society,** P.O. Box 72, Dolgeville, NY 13329 (518-568-7970), sells several titles related to travel in the U.S. and Canada.

GETTING THERE AND GETTING AROUND

Budget Travel Agencies

Council Travel, the travel division of Council, is a full-service travel agency specializing in youth and budget travel. They offer discount airfares, railpasses, hostelling cards, guidebooks, budget tours, travel gear, and international student (ISIC), youth (GO25), and teacher (ITIC) identity cards. U.S. offices include: Emory Village, 1561 N. Decatur Rd., **Atlanta,** GA 30307 (404-377-9997); 729 Boylston St., **Boston,** MA 02116 (617-266-1926); 1153 N. Dearborn, **Chicago,** IL 60610 (312-951-0585); 10904 Lindbrook Dr., **Los Angeles,** CA 90024 (310-208-3551); 205 E. 42nd St., **New York,** NY 10017 (212-822-2700); 3606A Chestnut St., **San Diego,** CA 92109 (619-270-6401); 530 Bush St., **San Francisco,** CA 94108 (415-421-3473); 1314 N.E. 43rd St., **Seattle,** WA 98105 (206-632-2448); 3300 M St. NW, **Washington, D.C.** 20007 (202- 337-6464). **For U.S. cities not listed,** call 888-COUNCIL (268-6245) or visit their web site at http://www.ciee.org.

STA Travel, 6560 Scottsdale Rd. #F100, Scottsdale, AZ 85253 (800-777-0112; fax 602-922-0793; http://sta-travel.com). A student and youth travel organization with over 150 offices worldwide offering discount airfares for young travelers, railpasses, accommodations, tours, insurance, and ISICs. Sixteen offices in the U.S. including: 297 Newbury Street, **Boston,** MA 02115 (617-266-6014); 429 S. Dearborn St., **Chicago,** IL 60605 (312-786-9050); 7202 Melrose Ave., **Los Angeles,** CA 90046 (213- 934-8722); 10 Downing St., Suite G, **New York,** NY 10003 (212-627-3111); 4341 University Way NE, **Seattle,** WA 98105 (206-633-5000); 2401 Pennsylvania Ave., **Washington, D.C.** 20037 (202-887-0912); 51 Grant Ave., **San Francisco,** CA 94108 (415-391-8407). In the U.K., 6 Wrights Lane, **London** W8 6TA (tel. (0171) 938 47 11 for North American travel). In New Zealand, 10 High St., **Auckland** (tel. (09) 309 97 23). In Australia, 222 Faraday St., **Melbourne** VIC 3050 (tel. (03) 9349 6911).

Let's Go Travel, Harvard Student Agencies, 17 Holyoke St., Cambridge, MA 02138 (617-495-9649; fax 496-7956; email travel@hsa.net; http://hsa.net/travel). Railpasses, HI-AYH memberships, ISICs, ITICs, FIYTO cards, guidebooks (including every *Let's Go*), maps, bargain flights, and a complete line of budget travel gear. All items available by mail; call or write for a catalogue.

Campus Travel, 52 Grosvenor Gardens, London SW1W 0AG (http://www.campustravel.co.uk). Forty-six branches in the U.K. Student and youth fares on plane, train, boat, and bus travel. Skytrekker, flexible airline tickets. Discount and ID cards for students and youths, travel insurance for students and those under 35, and maps and guides. Puts out travel suggestion booklets. Telephone booking service: in Europe call (0171) 730 34 02; in North America call (0171) 730 21 01; worldwide call (0171) 730 81 11.

Travel CUTS (Canadian Universities Travel Services Limited), 187 College St., Toronto, Ont. M5T 1P7 (416-979-2406; fax 979-8167; email mail@travelcuts). Canada's national student travel bureau and equivalent of Council, with 40 offices across Canada. Also in the U.K., 295-A Regent St., **London** W1R 7YA (tel. (0171) 637 31 61). Discounted domestic and international airfares open to all; special student fares to all destinations with valid ISIC. Issues ISIC, FIYTO, GO25, and HI hostel cards, as well as railpasses. Offers free *Student Traveller* magazine, as well as information on the Student Work Abroad Program (SWAP).

Usit Youth and Student Travel, 19-21 Aston Quay, O'Connell Bridge, Dublin 2 (tel. (01) 677-8117; fax 679-8833). In the U.S.: New York Student Center, 895 Amsterdam Ave., New York, NY, 10025 (212-663-5435; email usitny@aol.com). Specializes in youth and student travel. Low-cost tickets and flexible travel arrangements all over the world. Supplies ISIC and FIYTO-GO 25 cards in Ireland only.

By Air

The **airline industry** attempts to squeeze every dollar from customers; finding a cheap airfare will be easier if you understand the airlines' systems. To obtain the best fare, buy a round-trip ticket, stay over at least one Saturday, and travel during off-peak times (Mon.-Thurs. morning) and hours (overnight **"red-eye"** flights can be cheaper and faster than primetime). Call every toll-free number and don't be afraid to ask about discounts; if you don't ask, it's unlikely they'll be volunteered. Students and others under 26 should never need to pay full price for a ticket. Seniors can also get great deals; many airlines offer senior traveler clubs or airline passes with few restrictions and discounts for their companions as well. Outsmart airline reps with Michael McColl's *The Worldwide Guide to Cheap Airfare* (US$15), an incredibly useful guide for finding cheap airfare.

Since travel times peak June to August and around holidays, reserve a seat several months in advance for these times. Call the airline the day before your departure to confirm your flight reservation, and get to the airport early to ensure you have a seat; airlines often overbook. (Of course, being "bumped" from a flight doesn't spell doom if your travel plans are flexible—you will probably leave on the next flight and receive a free ticket or cash bonus. If you would like to be bumped to win a free ticket, check in early and let the airline officials know.)

The commercial airlines' lowest regular offer is the **Advance Purchase Excursion Fare (APEX);** specials advertised in newspapers may be cheaper, but have more restrictions and fewer available seats. APEX fares provide you with confirmed reservations and allow "open-jaw" tickets (landing in and returning from different cities). Call as early as possible; these fares often require a two- to three-week advance purchase. Be sure to inquire about any restrictions on length of stay.

MAJOR AIRLINES

Within North America Given the large distances between points within the United States and Canada, North Americans travel less on buses and trains and more in airplanes or cars when traversing long distances. Buses and trains take much longer and do not always confer a savings equal to the added trouble (a cross-country trip will take three to five days, compared with seven hours by plane).

Many U.S. and Canadian airlines offer special air passes and fares to international travelers. You must purchase these passes outside of North America, paying one price for a certain number of flight vouchers. Each voucher is good for one flight on an airline's domestic system; typically, all travel must be completed within 30-60 days. The point of departure and destination for each coupon must be specified at the time of purchase, but dates of travel may be changed once travel has begun, usually at no extra charge. **US Airways** offers such packages from US$309. **United, Continental, Delta,** and **TWA** sell vouchers as well. TWA's **Youth Travel Pak** offers a similar deal to students 14-24, including North Americans. **Greyhound Air of Canada** (800-661-8747; http://www.greyhound.ca) offers inexpensive student packages for trips all over Canada, but seats can only be reserved 48 hours before departure (fares range from CDN$115 to $165). Available only to travelers who are not citizens in any North American country, **Canadian Regional Airlines** and its affiliate **Horizon Air** (England office tel. (01737) 55 53 00; fax 55 53 00; email airpass@aol.com) offer unlimited flight air passes for Western Canada (1-week WestPass UK£145, 2-week £UK195, 3-week UK£245); the Western United States (includes 4 cities in Canada; 1-week AirPass UK£139, 2-week UK£175, 3-week UK£259); and the entire Canadian Regional network (1-week NationalPass UK£199, 2-week UK£249, 3-week UK£299).

Air Canada (800-776-3000; http://www.aircanada.com). Discounts for students ages 12-24 on stand-by tickets for flights within Canada; still, advance-purchase tickets may be cheaper.

Alaska Airlines, P.O. Box 68900, Seattle, WA 98168 (800-426-0333; http://www.alaska-air.com).

America West Air, 4000 E. Sky Harbor Blvd., Phoenix, AZ 85034 (800-235-9292; http://www.americawest.com).
American, P.O. Box 619612, Dallas-Ft. Worth International Airport, TX 75261-9612 (800-433-7300; http://www.americanair.com).
Continental, 2929 Allen Parkway, Houston, TX 77210 (800-525-0280; http://www.flycontinental.com).
Delta, Hartsfield International Airport, Atlanta, GA 30320 (800-241-4141; http://www.delta-air.com).
Northwest, 5101 Northwest Dr., St. Paul, MN 55111-3034 (800-225-2525; http://www.nwa.com). Occasional student rates.
TWA, 1 City Center, 515 N. 6th St., St. Louis, MO 63101 (800-221-2000; http://www.twa.com).
United, P.O. Box 66100, Chicago, IL 60666 (800-241-6522; http://www.ual.com).
US Airways, Crystal Park Four Dr., Arlington, VA 22227 (800-428-4322; http://www.usair.com).

From Europe Travelers from Europe will experience the least competition for inexpensive seats during the off-season; but "off-season" need not mean the dead of winter. Peak-season rates generally take effect from mid-May until mid-September. Don't count on getting a seat right away during these months. The worst crunch leaving Europe takes place from mid-June to early July; August is uniformly tight for returning flights. Take advantage of cheap off-season flights within Europe to reach an advantageous point of departure for North America, if you can. (London is a major connecting point for budget flights to the U.S.; New York City is often the destination.) Once in the States, you can catch a coast-to-coast flight to make your way out West; see **Within North America,** above for details.

If you decide to fly with a commercial airline rather than through a charter agency or ticket consolidator (see below), you'll be purchasing greater reliability, security, and flexibility. Many major airlines offer reduced-fare options, such as three-day advance purchase fares: these tickets can only be purchased within 72 hours of the time of the departure, and are restricted to youths under a certain age (often 24). Check with a travel agent for availability. Seat availability is known only a few days before the flight, although airlines will sometimes issue predictions.

Some airlines with cheaper international flights are: **British Airways** (800-247-9297), **Continental** (800-525-0280), **Northwest** (800-225-2525), **TWA** (800-221-2000), and **United** (800-538-2929). Smaller, budget airlines often undercut major carriers by offering bargain fares on regularly scheduled flights. Competition for seats on these smaller carriers can be fierce—book early. Other trans-Atlantic airlines include **Virgin Atlantic Airways** (800-862-8621) and **IcelandAir** (800-223-5500).

From Asia, Africa, and Australia While European travelers may choose from a variety of regular reduced fares, Asian, Australian, and African travelers must rely on APEX (see p. 24). A good place to start searching for tickets is the local branch of an international budget travel agency (see **Budget Travel Agencies,** p. 23). **STA Travel,** with offices in Sydney, Melbourne, and Auckland, is probably the largest international agency you will find.

Qantas (800-227-4500), **United** (800-241-6522), and **Northwest** (800-225-2525) fly between Australia or New Zealand and the United States. Advance purchase fares from Australia have extremely tough restrictions. If you are uncertain about your plans, pay extra for an advance purchase ticket that has only a 50% penalty for cancellation. Many travelers from Australia and New Zealand take **Singapore Air** (800-742-3333) or other East Asian-based carriers for the initial leg of their trip. **Delta Airlines** (800-241-4141), **Japan Airlines** (800-525-3663), **Northwest** (800-225-2525) and **United Airlines** (800-538-2929) offer service from Japan. A round-trip ticket from Tokyo to L.A. usually ranges from US$1250-2500. **South African Airways** (800-722-9675), **American** (800-433-7300), and **Northwest** connect South Africa with North America.

CHARTER FLIGHTS AND TICKET CONSOLIDATORS

Charters are flights a tour operator contracts with an airline to fly extra loads of passengers to peak-season destinations. They are often cheaper than flights on scheduled airlines, although fare wars, consolidator tickets, and small airlines can beat charter prices. Delays are not uncommon, and companies reserve the right to change the dates of your flight or even cancel the flight a mere 48 hours in advance. To be safe, get your ticket as early as possible, and arrive at the airport several hours before departure time. Think carefully when you book your departure and return dates; you will lose all or most of your money if you cancel your ticket. Restrictions on the length of your trip and the time frame for reservations may also apply. Prices and destinations will change drastically from season to season, so be sure to contact as many organizations as possible in order to get the best deal. Try **Interworld** (305-443-4929); **Travac** (800-872-8800), or **Rebel** (800-227-3235), or book through a travel agent.

Ticket consolidators resell unsold tickets on commercial and charter airlines for very low prices, but deals include some risks. Tickets are sold on a space-available basis which does not guarantee you a seat; you get priority over those flying stand-by but below regularly-booked passengers. The earlier you arrive at the airport the better, since passengers are seated in the order they checked in. There are rarely age constraints or stay limitations, but unlike tickets bought through an airline, you won't be able to use your tickets on another flight if you miss yours. This may be a good route to take if you are traveling: on short notice (you bypass advance purchase requirements, since you aren't tangled in airline bureaucracy); on a high-priced trip; to an offbeat destination; or in the peak season, when published fares are jacked way up. Not all consolidators deal with the general public; many only sell tickets through travel agents. **Bucket shops** are retail agencies that specialize in getting cheap tickets. Look for their tiny ads in the travel section of weekend papers—the *Sunday New York Times* is a good source. Be a smart shopper; among the many reputable and trustworthy companies are, unfortunately, some shady wheeler-dealers. Before committing, contact the local Better Business Bureau to find out your company's track record. Get the company's policy in writing, and insist on a **receipt** that gives full details about the tickets, refunds, and restrictions, and record who you talked to and when. **NOW Voyager,** 74 Varick St. #307, New York, NY 10013 (212-431-1616; fax 334-5243; http://www.nowvoyagertravel.com), does consolidation with reliability which rivals that of most charter companies (97% of customers get on flights the first time) and prices which are considerably lower. For more consolidators and other useful information, consult Kelly Monaghan's *Consolidators: Air Travel's Bargain Basement* (US$7 plus $2 shipping) from the Intrepid Traveler, P.O. Box 438, New York, NY 10034 (email intreptrav@aol.com).

COURIERS

Those who travel light should consider flying as a **courier.** The company hiring you will use your checked luggage space for freight; you're only allowed to bring carry-ons. You are responsible for the safe delivery of the baggage claim slips (given to you by a courier company representative) to the representative waiting for you when you arrive—don't screw up or you will be blacklisted as a courier. You will probably never see the cargo you are transporting—the company handles it all—and airport officials know that couriers are not responsible for the baggage checked for them. **Restrictions** to watch for: you must be over 18, have a valid passport, and procure your own visa (if necessary); most flights are round-trip only with short fixed-length stays (usually 1 week); only single tickets are issued (but a companion may be able to get a next-day flight); and most flights are from New York. For a practical guide to the air courier scene, check out Kelly Monaghan's *Air Courier Bargains* (US$15 plus $3 shipping), available from Upper Access Publishing (UAP), P.O. Box 457, Hinesburg, VT 05461 (800-356-9315; fax 242-0036; email upperacces@aol.com), or consult the *Courier Air Travel Handbook* (US$10 plus $3.50 shipping), published by Bookmasters, Inc., P.O. Box 2039, Mansfield, OH 44905 (800-507-2665; fax 419-281-6883).

STANDBY

Flying **standby** will add a certain thrill to the prospects of when you will leave and where exactly you will end up. Standby brokers do not sell tickets but the promise that you will get to a destination near where you want to go, within a window of time (usually 5 days), from a location in a region you've specified. You call in before your date-range to hear all of your flight options for the next seven days and your probability of boarding; then you decide which flights you want to try to make and present a voucher at the airport which grants you the right to board a flight on a space-available basis. This procedure must be followed again for the return trip. Flexibility of schedule and destination is often necessary, but all companies guarantee you a credit or refund if the available flights that fit your date and destination range were full. **Airhitch** (800-326-2009 or 212-864-2000 on the East Coast; 310-726-5000 on the West Coast; tel. 1 47 00 16 30 in Europe) and **Air-Tech Ltd.** (212-219-7000; fax 219-0066) are two prominent standby brokers.

Be sure to read all the fine print in your agreements with either of the above companies—a call to the Better Business Bureau may be worthwhile. Be warned that it is difficult to receive refunds and that clients' vouchers will not be honored when an airline fails to receive payments in time.

By Train

Amtrak (800-USA-RAIL (872-7245); http://www.amtrak.com) is the main provider of passenger train service in the U.S. Most cities have Amtrak offices which directly sell tickets, but tickets must be bought through an agent in some small towns. The informative web page lists up-to-date schedules, fares, arrival and departure info, and allows reservations. **Discounts on full rail fares:** senior citizens get 15% off; students, 15% off with a Student Advantage Card (call 800-96-AMTRAK/26-8725) to purchase a card for US$20); travelers with disabilities, 15% off; current members of the U.S. armed forces, active-duty veterans, and their dependents, 25% off; children under 15 accompanied by a parent, 50% off; children under age two ride free on the lap of an adult. Circle trips and holiday packages can also save money. Call for up-to-date info and reservations.

The **USA Rail Pass** is a discount option available only to those who aren't citizens of North America; it allows unlimited travel and unlimited stops over a period of either 15 or 30 days. A 30-day nationwide travel pass sells for US$480 during peak seasons (mid-June to mid-Aug. and mid-Dec. to early Jan.) and US$350 during the off-season; a 15-day nationwide pass is US$375/$260. Less expensive regional passes are also available; call Amtrak for details.

VIA Rail, P.O. Box 8116, Station A, Montreal, QC H3C 3N3 (800-561-3949; http://www.viarail.ca), is Amtrak's Canadian analogue. **Discounts on full fares:** students with ISIC card and youths under 24 get 40% off full fare; seniors (60 and over) get 10% off; children under 15 get 50% off when accompanied by an adult; children under two ride free on an adult's lap. Reservations are required for first-class seats and sleeping car accommodations. Call for details. The **Canrail Pass** allows unlimited travel on 12 to 15 days within a 30-day period. Between early June and mid-October, a 12-day pass costs CDN$540, senior citizens, students and youths under 24 pay CDN$586. Off-season passes cost CDN$369, seniors and youths pay CDN$332. Add $35 for each additional day of travel desired. Call for information on seasonal promotions, such as discounts on Grayline Sightseeing Tours.

For Alaskans in the most isolated regions, the only link to civilization is the **Alaska Railroad.** North America's northernmost railroad covers 470 mi. of land—connecting Seward and Whittier in the south with Anchorage, Fairbanks, and Denali National Park farther north. In 1984, the railroad, one of the last nationally owned railroads in the country, was sold into private hands, changing its name to the **Alaska Railroad Corporation (ARRC),** P.O. Box 107500, Anchorage, AK 99510-7500 (800-478-2467 in Alaska; 800-544-0552 in the lower 48; 907-265-2494 elsewhere; fax 907-265-2323;

email reservations@akrr.com; http://www.alaska.net/~akrr). See specific locations for fares, details and additional rail options.

By Bus

Buses generally offer the most frequent and complete service between the cities and towns of the Pacific Northwest and Alaska. Often a bus is the only way to reach smaller locales without a car. *Russell's Official National Motor Coach Guide* (US$14.45 including postage) contains schedules of every bus route (including Greyhound) between any two towns in the United States and Canada. Russell's also publishes two semiannual *Supplements,* one which includes a *Directory of Bus Lines and Bus Stations* (US$6), and one which offers a series of Route Maps (US$6.45). To order any of the above, write Russell's Guides, Inc., P.O. Box 278, Cedar Rapids, IA 52406 (319-364-6138; fax 364-4853).

Greyhound (800-231-2222; http://www.greyhound.com), operates the largest number of routes in the U.S., though local bus companies may provide more extensive services within specific regions. Schedule information is available at any Greyhound terminal or by calling the 800 number. Reserve with a credit card over the phone at least 10 days in advance, and the ticket can be mailed anywhere in the U.S. Fares are reduced for tickets purchased more than 21 days in advance. You can buy your ticket at the terminal, but arrive early. *Advance purchase is cheaper, so make reservations early.* **Discounts on full fares:** senior citizens, 10% off; children ages two to 11, 50% off; travelers with disabilities or special needs and their companions ride together for the price of one. If boarding at a remote **"flag stop,"** be sure you know exactly where the bus stops. It's a good idea to call the nearest agency and let them know you'll be waiting and at what time. Catch the driver's attention by standing on the side of the road and flailing your arms wildly—better to be embarrassed than stranded. If a bus passes, it is probably because of overcrowding—a later, less-crowded bus should stop. Whatever you stow in compartments underneath the bus should be clearly marked; be sure to get a claim check for it, and watch to make sure your luggage is on the same bus as you.

Ameripass: Allows adults unlimited travel for 7 days (US$189), 15 days (US$299), 30 days (US$409), or 60 days (US$599). Prices for students with a valid college ID, and senior citizens are slightly less: 7 days (US$169), 15 days (US$269), 30 days (US$369), or 60 days (US$539). Children's passes are half the adult price. Before purchasing an Ameripass, total up the separate bus fares between towns to make sure that the pass is really more economical, or at least worth the unlimited flexibility it provides. Most bus companies in the U.S. honor Ameripasses, but check for specifics.

International Ameripass: For travelers from outside North America. Primarily sold in foreign countries, they can also be purchased in either of Greyhound's International Offices, located in New York City and Los Angeles (800-246-8572). A 4-day pass, which cannot be used during a weekend, is US$109, 5-day pass US$129, 7-day pass US$159, 15-day pass US$239, 30-day pass US$319, 60-day pass US$499.

Greyhound Lines of Canada (800-661-TRIP/661-8747 in Canada or 403-265-9111 in the United States; http://www.greyhound.ca) is the main intercity bus company; note that it has no affiliation with the Greyhound in the U.S. The British Columbia **Student Pass** (CDN$119) allows four one-way trips anywhere in the province; a similar pass exists for Alberta (CDN$99). For North American residents, the **Canada Pass** offers unlimited travel on all routes, including limited links to northern U.S. cities (7 day pass CDN$199; 15 day pass CDN$259; 30 day pass CDN$349; 60 day pass CDN$449). For foreign visitors, the **International Canada Pass** offers a similar deal with slightly lower prices (7 day pass CDN$189; 15 day pass CDN$259; 30 day pass CDN$339; 60 day pass CDN$439). This pass can only be purchased overseas at select travel agencies, including those listed above for Greyhound Lines.

Green Tortoise, 494 Broadway, San Francisco, CA 94133 (800-867-8647 or 415-956-7500; http://www.greentortoise.com), has "hostels on wheels" in remodeled diesel buses done up for living and eating on the road; meals are prepared communally. Green Tortoise's charm lies in its price and personality, not in its luxury. Prices include transportation, sleeping space on the bus, and tours of the regions you pass through. Deposits ($100 most trips) are generally required as space is tight.

By Car

BEFORE YOU STEP ON IT

American Automobile Association (AAA), 1050 Hingham St., Rocklin, MA 02370 (800-AAA-HELP/222-4357; to sign up call 800-JOIN-AAA/564-6222; http://www.aaa.com). The best-known of the auto clubs. Offers free trip-planning services, road maps and guidebooks, emergency road service anywhere in the U.S., free towing, and commission-free traveler's cheques from American Express with over 1,000 offices scattered across the country. Discounts on Hertz car rental, Amtrak tickets, and various motel chains and theme parks. AAA has reciprocal agreements with the auto associations of many other countries which often provide you with full benefits while in the U.S. Basic membership fees are US$55 for the 1st year with $39 annual renewal; US$23 yearly for additional family members.

AMOCO Motor Club, P.O. Box 9049, Des Moines, IA 50368 (800-334-3300). Services include trip-planning and travel information, 24hr. towing (free for 5 mi. or back to the tower's garage), and emergency road service. Two memberships available: **AARP** (gives car rental discounts at Avis, Hertz, and National) costs US$40 for one person, $48 for two, family memberships $68; **AMOCO** (discounts at Alamo, Avis, and Hertz) costs US$60 for a couple, $85 for a family. Premier memberships (US$68-$110) entitle you to 50 mi. free towing.

Canadian Automobile Association (CAA), 1145 Hunt Club Rd., #200, Ottawa, Ontario K1V 0Y3 (800-CAA-HELP/222-4357; to sign up call 800-JOIN-CAA/564-6222; http://www.caa.ca). Affiliated with AAA (see above), the CAA provides nearly identical membership benefits, including 24hr. emergency roadside assistance, free maps and tour books, route planning, and various discounts. Basic membership is CDN$53 and $34 for family members.

Montgomery Ward Auto Club, 200 N. Martingale Rd., Schaumburg, IL 60173-2096 (800-621-5151). Provides 24hr. emergency roadside assistance for any car, unlimited trip routing, and up to US$1500 for travel emergencies. US$79 monthly membership fee. Associate memberships available for driving-age children 16-23 for US$24 annually.

UNDER THE HOOD AND ON THE INTERSTATE

If you are driving in America, a road atlas is your best friend. **Rand McNally's Road Atlas,** covering all of the USA and Canada, is one of the best resources for maps (available at bookstores and gas stations, US$10).

Tune up the car before you leave, pack an easy-to-read manual, and learn a bit about minor automobile maintenance and repair—it may at least help you keep your car alive long enough to reach a reputable garage. Your trunk should contain the following necessities: a **spare tire** and **jack, jumper cables, extra oil, flares,** a **flashlight,** and **blankets** (in case you break down at night or in the winter). In the summer, carry extra **water** for you and your radiator. If there's a chance you may be stranded in a remote area, keep emergency food and water on hand. Always have plenty of **gas** and check road conditions ahead of time when possible, particularly during the winter. Gas is generally cheaper in towns than at interstate service stops. The enormous travel distances of North America will require you to spend more on gas than you might at first expect. To burn less fuel, make sure your tires have enough air, check the oil, and avoid running the air-conditioner unnecessarily.

Be sure to **buckle up**—seat belts are required by law in many regions of the U.S. and Canada. The **speed limit in the U.S.,** thanks to recent legislation devolving power to the states, varies considerably from region to region and road to road. Most urban highways retain a limit of 55 miles per hour (88 km/hr), while rural routes range from 65 to 80 mph (104 to 128 km/hr). The **speed limit in Canada** is generally 100 km/hr (63 mph).

In the 1950s, President Eisenhower envisioned an **interstate system,** a federally funded network of highways designed primarily to subsidize American commerce. Thanks to Ike's vision, there is a simple, consistent system for numbering interstates. Even-numbered interstates run east-west and odd ones run north-south, decreasing in number toward the south and west. If the interstate has a three-digit number, it is a branch of another interstate (i.e., I-285 is a branch of I-85), and is often a bypass skirting around a large city. An even digit in the hundreds place means the branch will eventually return to the main interstate; an odd digit means it won't.

RENTING

While the cost of renting a car for long distances is often prohibitive, renting for local trips may be reasonable. National chains usually allow cars to be picked up in one city and dropped off in another (for a hefty charge). By calling a toll-free number you can reserve a reliable car anywhere in the country. Drawbacks include steep prices and high minimum ages for rentals (usually 25). Many branches rent to ages 21-24 with an additional fee, but policies and prices vary from agency to agency. **Alamo** (800-327-9633; http://www.goalamo.com) rents to ages 21-24 with a major credit card for an additional US$20 per day. Some branches of **Avis** (800-331-1212; http://www.avis.com) and **Budget** (800-527-0700) rent to ages 21-24 with a credit card, but it's not the norm. **Hertz** (800-654-3131; http://www.hertz.com) enforces a minimum age of 25, unless the renter has a corporate account. Most **Dollar** (800-800-4000) branches and some **Thrifty** (800-367-2277; http://www.thrifty.com) locations allow ages 21-24 to rent for an additional daily fee of about US$20. **Rent-A-Wreck** (800-421-7253; http://www.rent-a-wreck.com) specializes in supplying vehicles that are past their prime for lower-than-average prices; a bare-bones compact less than eight years old rents for around US$20. There are also local agencies which serve a specific city or region, and these sometimes offer better deals.

Most rental packages offer unlimited mileage, although some allow you only a certain number of miles free before a charge of 25-40¢ per mile takes effect. Most quoted rates do not include gas or tax, so ask for the total cost before handing over the credit card; many large firms have added airport surcharges not covered by the designated fare. Return the car with a full tank unless you sign up for a fuel option plan that enables stipulates otherwise. When dealing with any car rental company, be sure to ask whether the price includes insurance against theft and collision. There may be an additional charge, the collision and damage waiver (CDW), which usually comes to about $12-15 per day. If you use **American Express** to rent the car, they will automatically cover the CDW; call AmEx's car division (800-338-1670) for more information.

AUTO TRANSPORT COMPANIES

These services match drivers with car owners who need cars moved from one city to another. Would-be travelers give the company their desired destination and the company finds a car which needs to go there. The only expenses are gas, tolls, and your own living expenses. Some companies insure their cars; with others, your security deposit covers any breakdowns or damage. You must be at least 21, have a valid license, and agree to drive about 400 mi. per day on a fairly direct route. Companies regularly inspect current and past job references, take your fingerprints, and require a cash bond. Cars are available between most points, although it's easiest to find cars for traveling from coast to coast; New York and Los Angeles are popular transfer points. If offered a car, look it over first. Think twice about accepting a gas guzzler since you'll be paying for the gas. With the company's approval you may be able to share the cost with several companions.

Auto Driveaway, 310 S. Michigan Ave., Chicago, IL 60604 (800-346-2277; http://www.autodriveaway.com).

A. Anthony's Driveaway, 4391 NW 19th Ave., Pompano Beach, FL 33064 (954-970-7384; fax 970-3881).

Across America Driveaway, 3626 Calumet Ave., Hammond, IN 46320 (800-619-7707 or 219-852-0134; fax 800-334-6931; http://www.schultz-international.com).

NORTHCOUNTRY DRIVING

Many major roads in Alaska and Northwestern Canada are still in **desperately bad shape.** Dust and flying rocks are major hazards in the summer, as are the road construction crews, which interrupt long-distance trips with miserable 10- to 30-mi. patches of gravel as they repave the road. Traveling on a sturdy set of wheels will more than double the area you can reach without hitchhiking. Many of the worst roads in Alaska have been treated with calcium chloride to minimize the dust flying up from the road. It can be very hard on your car's paint, though, and you should take every opportunity to wash your car. *Drive slowly;* it will make the trip much easier on your car. Melting and contracting permafrost in the north causes "frost heaves," creating dips and Dali-esque twists in the road. Radiators and headlights should be protected from flying rocks and swarming bugs with a **wire screen** and/or plastic **headlight covers;** good **shocks** and a functional **spare tire** are absolutely essential. Wintertime snow cover can actually smooth your ride a bit: the packed surface and the thinned traffic can create easier driving (although the dangers of avalanches and driving on ice offer a different set of concerns). Check **road conditions** before traveling. A number of information hotlines exist for just this purpose: for British Columbia highways, call (900) 451-4997; for the Alaska Highway, call (250) 774-7447 in BC, (403) 667-8215 in the Yukon.

Two guides which include maps and detailed routes are available from **Vernon Publications, Inc.,** 3000 Northup Way, #200, Bellevue, WA, 98004 (800-726-4707 or 425-827-9900; fax 425-822-9372; http://www.alaskainfo.com). *The MILEPOST* (US$21.95) is a guide to the highways of Alaska and northwestern Canada. *The Alaska Wilderness Guide* covers the bush communities and remote areas of back-country Alaska (US$16.95).

On Two Wheels

Before you rush onto the byways of the Pacific Northwest pedaling furiously away on your banana-seat Huffy Desperado, remember that safe and secure cycling requires a quality helmet and lock. A good **helmet** costs about $40—much cheaper than critical head surgery. U-shaped **Kryptonite** or **Citadel** locks run about $30 and carry insurance against theft for one or two years if your bike is registered with the police.

There are a ton of publications that will help you get the most out of your bicycle. *Cuthbertson's All-in-One Bike Repair Manual* (US$12 plus $3.50 shipping) available from **Ten Speed Press,** Box 7123, Berkeley, CA 94707 (800-841-2665; fax 510-559-1629), provides vital information on repair and maintenance during long-term bike sojourns. **Rodale Press,** 33 E. Minor St., Emmaus, PA 18098-0099 (800-848-4735; 610-967-5171), publishes a number of books for the intrepid would-be cyclist, including *Cycling for Women* (US$9 plus $3.50 shipping), *Mountain Biking Skills* (US$18 plus shipping) and the popular *Bicycle Maintenance and Repair* ($20 plus shipping). **Umbrella Books,** a subsidiary of Epicenter Press, at P.O. Box 82368 Kenmore, WA 98028 (206-485-6822), sells a number of regional guides, including *Bicycling the Oregon Coast,* by Robin Cody (US$11), and *Alaska's Wilderness Highway, Traveling the Dalton Road,* by Mike Jensen. More specific information about cycling in the Northwest is available from tourist bureaus, which often distribute free maps.

CYCLING TOURS AND ASSOCIATIONS

Adventure Cycling Association, P.O. Box 8308-P, Missoula, MT 59807 (406-721-1776; fax 721-8754; email acabike@aol.com; http://www.adv-cycling.org). A national, non-profit organization that maps long-distance routes and organizes bike tours for members. Membership US$28 in the U.S., US$35 in Canada and Mexico.

The Canadian Cycling Association, 1600 James Naismith Dr., #212A, Gloucester, ON K1B 5N4 (613-748-5629; fax 748-5692; email leisure@canadian-cycling.com; http://www.canadian-cycling.com). Distributes *The Canadian Cycling Association's Complete Guide to Bicycle Touring in Canada* (CDN$24), plus guides to specific regions of Canada, Alaska and the Pacific Coast. Also sells maps and books.

Rocky Mountain Cycle Tours, 333 Baker St., Nelson BC V1L 4H6 (800-661-2453; fax 250-354-2058), organizes summer bicycle tours in Alberta and BC.

Backroads, 801 Cedar St., Berkeley, CA 94710-1800 (800-462-2848; fax 510-527-1444; http://www.backroads.com). Offers tours in 23 states, including Alaska and parts of British Columbia. Trips range from a weekend excursion (US$299) to a 9-day extravaganza (US$1098).

BY MOTORCYCLE

Another two-wheel option, motorcycling is cheaper than driving a car, but it takes a tenacious soul to pull off the trip. Those considering a long journey should contact the **American Motorcyclist Association,** 33 Collegeview Rd., Westerville, OH 43801 (800-AMA-JOIN/262-5646 or 614-891-2425; fax 891-5012; email ama@ama-cycle.org; http://ama-cycle.org), the linchpin of U.S. biker culture. A full membership (US$29 per year) includes discounts on insurance, rentals, and hotels, a subscription to *American Motorcyclist*, and a kick-ass patch for your riding jacket. For an additional $25 members benefit from emergency roadside assistance, including pick up and delivery to a service shop.

By Ferry

Along the Pacific coast, ferries are an exhilarating and often unavoidable way to travel. Practically none of southeast Alaska (the Panhandle) is accessible by road; most of this area can be reached only by the **Alaska Marine Highway** (see below). In addition to basic transportation, the ferry system gives travelers the chance to enjoy the beauty of the water and the coast, one of the Northwest's finest outdoor experiences. Ferry travel, however, can become quite expensive when you bring a car along. In Alaska, schedule an overnight ferry ride and sleep free in on the top deck or in the lounge. Free showers are also a bonus on all but the smallest boats.

ALASKA MARINE HIGHWAY

The **Alaska Marine Highway,** P.O. Box 25535, Juneau, AK 99802-5535 (800-642-0066; TTD 800-764-3779) consists of two unconnected ferry systems administered by one bureaucracy. The **southeast** system runs from Bellingham, WA and Prince Rupert, BC up the coast to Skagway, stopping in Juneau, Ketchikan, Haines, and other towns. The **southcentral/southwest** network serves Kodiak Island, Seward, Homer, Prince William Sound, and, occasionally, the Aleutian Islands. For both systems, the ferry schedule is a function of tides and other navigational exigencies. There is a slight additional charge for stopovers, and should be reserved at the same time as the rest of your itinerary. Write ahead for all schedules, rates, and information.

Those who intend to hit the ground running, and keep running, would be smart to check out the **AlaskaPass.** The pass offers unlimited access to Alaska's railroad, ferry, and bus systems; a 15-day pass sells for US$649, a 30-day pass for $899. A pass allowing travel on 21 non-consecutive days over a 45-day period costs US$949. The fare may seem expensive, but with a network that extends from Bellingham, WA to Dutch Harbor on the Aleutian Islands, the pass is a good deal for those who want to see a lot of Alaska in a short amount of time. If you're interested, contact AlaskaPass

Inc., P.O. Box 351, Vashon, WA 98070-0351 (800-248-7598 or 206-463-6550; fax 800-488-0303 or 206-463-6777; http://www.alaskapass.com).

The full trip from Bellingham to Skagway takes three days—an adventure in itself, peppered with whales, bald eagles, and the majesty of the Inside Passage. (*The Love Boat*'s notorious Alaskan voyages took this same route.) All southeast ferries have free showers, cafes, and a heated top-deck "solarium" where cabinless passengers can sleep (bring a sleeping bag); some boats offer lectures on history and ecology.

PLANNING YOUR FERRY TRIPS

Information about fares, reservations, vehicles, and schedules varies greatly throughout the year (see sections on Seattle, southwestern BC, and Alaska). Be sure to consult each ferry company when constructing your itinerary in order to clear up any additional questions before finalizing your plans.

The **Alaska Northwest Travel Service, Inc.,** 3303 148th St. SW, Suite 2, Lynnwood, WA 98037 (206-787-9499 or 800-533-7381, fax 206-745-4946), is an agent for Alaska and British Columbia ferries, as well as a full service travel agency specializing in Alaska; they can book ferries, cruise ships, and airline reservations. They will also plan individualized itineraries. Ferry scheduling information can also be found in *The MILEPOST* (see p. 31).

BC Ferries, 1112 Fort St., Victoria, BC V8V 4V2 (888-223-3779 in BC; 250-386-3431 elsewhere; fax 250-381-5452; http://bcferries.bc.ca/ferries) Passenger and vehicle ferry service throughout coastal British Columbia. Special facilities for passengers with disabilities. Service is frequent, and reservations are only required on the longer routes: Tsawwassen/Gulf Islands, Inside Passage, Discovery Coast Passage, and Queen Charlotte Islands.

Black Ball Transport, Inc., 430 Belleville St., Victoria, BC. V8V 1W9 (604-386-2202); Foot of Laurel, Port Angeles 98362 (360-457-4491 fax 604-386-2207). Ferries daily between Port Angeles, WA and Victoria, with a crossing time of 95 min. US$6.75 each way, car and driver $27.25, motorcycle and driver $16.50. Bicycles US$3.25 extra. Advance reservations not accepted.

Washington State Ferries, 801 Alaskan Way, Seattle, WA 98104-1487 (800-84-FERRY/843-3779 or 206-464-6400 for schedule information; http://www.wsdot.wa.gov/ferries/). Ferries to Sidney, BC, and throughout Puget Sound. No reservations, except for travel to the San Juan Islands or British Columbia. Service is frequent, but traffic is heavy, especially in summer, when waits of over an hour to board a ferry are not uncommon. Fares fluctuate, but are reasonable.

By Thumb

Let's Go urges you to consider the risks and disadvantages of hitchhiking before thumbing it. Hitching means entrusting your life to a stranger who happens to stop beside you on the road. While this may be comparatively safe in some areas of Europe and Australia, it is **NOT** so in the United States. We do **NOT** recommend it. We strongly urge you to find other means of transportation. Do not put yourself in a situation where hitching is the only option.

If you feel you have no other alternative, if you *insist* on ignoring our warnings, and decide to hitchhike anyway, there are many precautions that must be taken. First, assess the risks and your chances of getting a ride. **Women traveling alone should never hitch in the United States. Never.**

Never hesitate to refuse a ride if you will feel at all uncomfortable alone with the driver. If at all threatened or intimidated, experienced hitchers ask to be let out no matter how uncompromising the road looks, and they know *in advance* where to go if stranded and what to do in emergencies. In rural areas, hitching is reportedly less risky than in urban areas. Hitching is much more common in Alaska (see below) and the Yukon than farther south. All states prohibit hitchhiking while standing on the roadway itself or behind a freeway entrance sign; hitchers more commonly find rides near intersections where many cars converge. The information provided below is not intended as an endorsement of hitching.

HITCHING IN ALASKA

Many people hitchhike instead of depending on buses in Alaska, but it is not unusual to find yourself stranded on a sparsely traveled route. A wait of a day or two between rides is not unusual on certain stretches of the Alaska Highway. Alaska state law prohibits moving vehicles from not picking up stranded motorists, as the extreme weather conditions can be life-endangering. However, hitchhiking backpackers may only legally thumb for rides on the on-and-off ramps of major highways—not on the highways themselves.

Carrying a large cardboard sign clearly marked with your destination can improve your chances of getting a ride. Drivers may not want to stop if they don't know where you're going. When it gets particularly tough, hitchers add "SHARE GAS."

Catching a ride from Canada into Alaska on the Alaska Highway involves crossing the **Alaska-Yukon border,** which is a series of questions about citizenship, insurance, contraband, and finances, followed by an auto inspection. Hitchers should walk across the border to avoid hassle.

ONCE THERE

Embassies and Consulates

For a more extensive list of embassies and consulates in the U.S., consult the web site http://www.embassy.org. A similar compilation for the neighboring maple leafs can be found at http://www.impactconsulting.com/embassyott. (For U.S. and Canadian embassies and consulates overseas, see p. 6.)

Embassies in U.S.: Australia, 1601 Massachusetts Ave. NW, Washington, D.C. 20036 (202-797-3000); **Canada,** 501 Pennsylvania Ave. NW, Washington, D.C. 20001 (202-682-1740); **Ireland,** 2234 Massachusetts Ave. NW, Washington, D.C. 20008 (202-462-3939); **New Zealand,** 37 Observatory Circle NW, Washington, D.C. 20008 (202-328-4800); **South Africa,** 3051 Massachusetts Ave. NW, Washington, D.C. 20008 (202-232-4400); **United Kingdom,** 3100 Massachusetts Ave. NW, Washington, D.C. 20008 (202-462-1340).

Consulates in U.S.: Australia, 630 5th Ave., New York, NY 10111 (212-245-4000) and 611 N. Larchmont Blvd., Los Angeles, CA 90004 (213-469-4300); **Canada,** 1251 Ave. of the Americas, Exxon Building, 16th floor, New York, NY 10020-1175 (212-596-1600) and 550 S, Hope St., 9th floor, Los Angeles, CA 90071 (213-346-2711); **Ireland,** 345 Park Ave., 17th Floor, New York, NY 10154 (212-319-2552) and 44 Montgomery St., Suite 3830, San Francisco, CA 94101 (415-392-4214); **New Zealand,** 12400 Wilshire Blvd., Suite 1150, Los Angeles, CA 90025 (310-207-1605); **South Africa,** 333 E. 38th St., 9th Floor, New York, NY 10016 (212-213-4880) and 50 N. La Cienega Blvd., # 300, Beverly Hills, CA 90211 (310-657-9200); **United Kingdom,** 845 3rd Ave., New York, NY 10022 (212-752-8400); 11766 Wilshire Blvd., #400, Los Angeles, CA 90025 (213-385-7381).

Embassies in Canada: Australia, 50 O'Connor St., #710, Ottawa, ON K1P 6L2 (613-236-0841); **Ireland,** 130 Albert St., #1105, Ottawa, ON K1P 5G4 (613-233-6281); **New Zealand,** 99 Bank St., #727, Ottawa, ON K1P 6G3 (613-238-5991); **South Africa,** 15 Sussex Dr., Ottawa, ON K1M 1M8 (613-744-0330); **United Kingdom,** 80 Elgin St., Ottawa, ON K1P 5K7 (613-237-1530); **United States,** 100 Wellington St., Ottawa, ON K1P 5T1 (613-238-4470).

Consulates in Canada: Australia, 175 Bloor St. East, suite 314, Toronto, ON M4W 3R8, (416-323-1155); **New Zealand,** 888 Dunsmuir St., #1200, Vancouver, BC V6C

3K4 (604-684-7388); **South Africa,** 1 Place Ville Marie, #2615, Montreal, QC H3B 4S3 (514-878-9217) and Stock Exchange Tower, #2300, 2 First Canadian Place, Toronto, ON M5X 1E3 (416-364-0314); **United Kingdom,** 1000 de la Gauchetiere West, Suite 4200, Montreal, QC H3B 4W5 (514-866-5863) and 1111 Melville St., #800, Vancouver, British Columbia V6E 3V6 (604-683-4421); **United States,** 2 Place Terrasse Dufferin, CP 939, Québec City, QC G1R 4T9 (418-692-2095), 1095 West Pender St., Vancouver, British Columbia V6E 2M6 (604-685-4311).

Accommodations

Always make reservations, especially if you plan to travel during peak tourist seasons. The local crisis center hotline may have a list of persons or groups, as well as local shelters, who will house you in an emergency.

HOSTELS

Youth hostels offer unbeatable deals on indoor lodging ($5-25 per night), and they are great places to meet traveling companions from all over the world. Many hostels even have **ride boards** to help you hook up with other hostelers going your way. As a rule, hostels are dorm-style accommodations where the sexes sleep apart, often in large rooms with bunk beds. (Some hostels allow families and couples private rooms, often for an additional charge.) You must bring or rent your own sleep sack (see **Packing,** p. 18). Sleeping bags are often not allowed. Hostels frequently have kitchens and utensils available, and many have storage areas and laundry facilities. Some also require you to perform a communal chore daily.

The Hostel Handbook for the U.S.A. & Canada (Jim Williams, Ed.; available for $4 ($6 outside the U.S.) from Dept: IGH, 722 Saint Nicholas Ave., New York, NY 10031; email InfoHostel@aol.com; http://www.hostels.com/handbook), lists over 500 hostels. If you have Internet access, check out the **Internet Guide to Hostelling** (http://hostels.com). Reservations for over 300 **Hostelling International (HI)** hostels (see listing below) may be made via the International Booking Network (IBN), a computerized system which allows you make hostels reservations months in advance for a nominal fee (202-783-6161). If you plan to stay in hostels, consider joining one of these associations:

Hostelling International-American Youth Hostels (HI-AYH), 733 15th St. NW, #840, Washington, D.C. 20005 (202-783-6161; fax 783-6171; email hiayhserv@hiayh.org; http://www.hiayh.org). Maintains 34 offices and over 150 hostels in the U.S. Membership can be purchased at many travel agencies (see p. 23) or the HI-AYH national office in Washington, D.C. 1-year membership US$25, under 18 $10, over 54 $15, family cards $35; includes *Hostelling North America: The Official Guide to Hostels in Canada and the United States*. Reserve by letter, phone, fax, or through the International Booking Network (see above). Basic rules (with much local variation): check-in 5-8pm, check-out 9:30am (although most urban hostels have 24 hr. access), max. stay 3 days, no pets or alcohol allowed on the premises. Fees US$5-22 per night.

Hostelling International-Canada (HI-C), 400-205 Catherine St., Ottawa, Ontario K2P 1C3, Canada (613-237-7884; fax 237-7868). Maintains 73 hostels throughout Canada. IBN booking centers in Edmonton, Montreal, Ottawa, and Vancouver; expect CDN$9-22.50/night. Membership packages: 1-yr. CDN$25, under 19 $12; 2-yr. $35; lifetime $175.

Rucksackers-AAIH North America, 250 W. 77th St., #906, New York City, NY 10024 (212-769-3286; fax 877-5733). The *Rucksackers Accommodations Booklet* includes maps and description of the over 300 affiliated hostels worldwide, which is available free at any member hostel, or by mail with a double-stamped self-addressed envelope to the address above.

HOTELS AND MOTELS

Many visitors centers, especially ones off major thoroughfares entering a state, have hotel coupons that can save you a bundle; if you don't see any, ask. Budget motels are often clustered off the highway several miles outside of town, but the carless may do better to try the hostels, YMCAs, YWCAs, and dorms downtown. The annually updated *National Directory of Budget Motels* (US$6, plus $2 shipping), from **Pilot Books,** 103 Copper St., Babylon NY 11702 (516-477-1095; fax 422-2227), covers over 2200 low-cost chain motels in the U.S. Pilot Books also publishes *The Hotel/Motel Special Program and Discount Guide* (US$6, plus $2 shipping), which lists hotels and motels offering special discounts. Also look for the comprehensive *State by State Guide to Budget Motels* (US$13), from Marlor Press, Inc., 4304 Brigadoon Dr., St. Paul, MN 55126 (800-669-4908 or 612-484-4600; fax 612-490-1182; email marlor@ix.netcom.com).

It is fortunate that the Canadian hostel system is somewhat more extensive than that of the U.S. because of that country's dearth of cheap motels. U.S. budget motel chains cost significantly less than the chains catering to the next-pricier market, such as Holiday Inn. Chains usually adhere more consistently to a level of cleanliness and comfort than locally operated budget competitors; some even feature heated pools and cable TV. Contact these chains for free directories, and always inquire about discounts for seniors, families, frequent travelers, groups, or government personnel: **Motel 6** (800-466-8356), **Super 8 Motels** (800-800-8000, 605-229-8708; fax 605-229-8900; http://www.super8motels.com/super8.html), **Choice Hotels International** (800-453-4511), **Best Western International** (800-528-1234 or 602-957-4200; fax 602-957-5505).

BED AND BREAKFASTS

As alternatives to impersonal hotel rooms, bed and breakfasts (private homes with spare rooms available to travelers, abbreviated **B&Bs**) range from the acceptable to the sublime. B&Bs are an excellent way to explore an area with the help of a knowledgeable host, and some hosts go out of their way to be accommodating—accepting travelers with pets or giving personalized tours. Often the best part of your stay will be a home-cooked breakfast (and occasionally dinner). Many B&Bs do not provide phones or TVs, and bathrooms must sometimes be shared.

Prices vary widely. B&Bs in major cities are usually more expensive than those in out-of-the-way places. Doubles can cost anywhere from $20-300 per night; most are in the $30 to $50 range. Some homes give special discounts to families or seniors. Reservations are almost always necessary, although in the off-season (if the B&B is open), you can frequently find a room on short notice.

Several travel guides and reservation services specialize in B&Bs. Among the more extensive guides are *The Complete Guide to Bed and Breakfasts, Inns and Guesthouses in the U.S. and Canada* (US$17), which lists over 11,000 B&Bs plus inns (available through Lanier Publications, P.O. Box D, Petaluma, CA 94953; 707-763-0271; fax 763-5762; email lanier@travelguides.com; http://www.travelguides.com), and *America's Favorite Inns, B&Bs, and Small Hotels* (US$20). Both can be found in bookstores (see **Hitting the Books,** p. 4). The **National Network of Reservation Services,** P.O. Box 4616, Springfield, MA 01101, can book reservations at over 7000 B&Bs throughout America and Canada (800-884-4288; fax 401-847-7309; email annas@wsii.com; http://www.tnn4bnb.com). The **Northern Network of Bed and Breakfasts** (867-993-5644; fax 993-5648) Box 954, Dawson City, YK Y0B 1G0 serves the same function for Alaska and northern Canada.

YMCAS AND YWCAS

Young man, young man: not all **Young Men's Christian Association (YMCA)** locations offer lodging; those that do are often located in urban downtowns, which can be convenient but a little gritty. YMCA rates are usually lower than a hotel's but higher than a hostel's and may include use of libraries, pools, and other facilities. Many YMCAs accept women and families (group rates often available), but some will not lodge people under 18 without parental permission. All reservations must be made and paid for in advance, with a traveler's check (signed top and bottom), money order, certified check, Visa, or Mastercard. Call the local YMCA in question for fee information. For information or reservations (reservation fee US$3, $6 overseas), contact **Y's Way International,** 224 E. 47th St., New York, NY 10017 (212-308-2899; fax 212-308-3161; http://www.ymca.int for links to branches worldwide). For Y's in **Canada,** contact the Montréal YMCA at 1450 Stanley St., Montréal, QC H3A 2W6 (514-849-8393; fax 849-8017) or the YMCA of Greater Toronto, 42 Charles St., Toronto, ON M4Y 1T4 (416-928-9622 or 800-223-8024; fax 416-928-2030).

Most **Young Women's Christian Associations (YWCAs)** accommodate only women or, sometimes, couples. Nonmembers are often required to join when lodging. For more information or a world-wide directory ($10), write **YWCA-USA,** 726 Broadway, New York, NY 10003 (212-614-2700).

DORMS

Many **colleges and universities** in the U.S. and Canada open their residence halls to travelers when school is not in session—some do so even during term-time. No general policy covers all of these institutions, but rates tend to be low, and college campuses can be some of the best sources for information on things to do, places to stay, and possible rides out of town. College dorms are popular with many travelers, especially those looking for long-term lodging, so reserve ahead. Some schools require that you at least feign an interest in attending their institution. To contact colleges and universities in Alaska and the Pacific Northwest, see **Study Opportunities,** p. 17.

HOME EXCHANGE AND RENTALS

Home exchange offers the traveler with a home the opportunity to live like a native, and to dramatically cut down on accommodation fees—usually only an administration fee is paid to the matching service. Once the introductions are made, the choice is left to the two hopeful partners. Most companies have pictures of member's homes and information about the owners (some will even ask for your photo!). A web site listing many exchange companies can be found at http://www.aitec.edu.au/~bwechner/Documents/Travel/Lists/HomeExchangeClubs.html. Renting a home may also be a good deal for some: depending on the length of stay, and the desired services.

Barclay International Group, 150 W 52nd Street, New York, NY 10022 (212-832-3777 or 800-845-6636; fax 212-753-1139; email Barcintl@ix.netcom.com; http://www.barclayweb.com). Arranges hotel alternative accommodations (apartment, condo, cottage, B&B or villa rentals) in over 20 countries, including the U.S. and Canada. Most are equipped with kitchens, telephones, TV, and concierge and maid service. Rentals are pricey, starting around $700 per week off-season. Less expensive than hotels with comparable amenities, these accommodations may suit families with children, business travelers, or Kosher or vegetarian travelers.

The Invented City: International Home Exchange, 41 Sutter St., #1090, San Francisco, CA 94104 (800-788-CITY/2489 in US or 415-252-114 elsewhere; fax 252-1171; email invented@aol.com). Listing of 1700 homes worldwide. For $50, you get your offer listed in one and receive three catalogues. It works via a simple swap; details are worked out between members.

Camping and the Outdoors

USEFUL PUBLICATIONS

A variety of publishing companies offer hiking guidebooks to meet the educational needs of novice or expert. For information about camping, hiking, and biking, write or call the publishers listed below to receive a catalogue.

Family Campers and RVers/National Campers and Hikers Association, Inc., 4804 Transit Rd., Bldg. #2, Depew, NY 14043 (716-668-6242; fax same). Membership fee (US$25) includes their publication *Camping Today.*

Sierra Club Bookstore, 85 Second St. 2nd Fl., San Francisco, CA 94109 (800-935-1056 or 415-977-5600; fax 923-5500). Books on many national parks, several series on different regions of the U.S., as well as *Learning to Rock Climb* (US$14), *The Sierra Club Family Outdoors Guide* (US$12) and *Wildwater* (US$12).

The Mountaineers Books, 1001 SW Klickitat Way, #201, Seattle, WA 98134 (800-553-4453 or 206-223-6303; fax 223-6306; email mbooks@mountaineers.org). Many titles on hiking (the *100 Hikes* series), biking, mountaineering, natural history, and conservation.

Wilderness Press, 2440 Bancroft Way, Berkeley, CA 94704-1676 (800-443-7227 or 510-843-8080; fax 548-1355; email wpress@ix.netcom.com). Publishes over 100 hiking guides and maps for the western U.S. including *Backpacking Basics* and *Backpacking with Babies and Small Children* (each US$11).

Woodall Publications Corporation, P.O. Box 5000, 13975 W. Polo Trail Dr., Lake Forest, IL 60045 (800-323-9076 or 847-362-6700; fax 362-8776; http://www.woodalls.com). Covering the U.S., Mexico, and Canada, Woodall publishes the ever-popular and annually updated *Woodall's Campground Directory* (US$20) and *Woodall's Plan-it, Pack-it, Go!: Great Places to Tent, Fun Things To Do* (US$13), which are generally available in American bookstores.

For **topographical maps** of the U.S., write the **U.S. Geological Survey,** Branch of Information Services, P.O. Box 25286, DFC, Denver, CO 80225 (800-435-7627; fax 303-202-4693); for Canada, contact the **Canada Map Office,** 130 Bentley Ave., Ottawa Ont., K1A 0E9 (613-952-7000; fax 613-957-8861), which distributes geographical, historical, and topographical maps as well as aeronautical charts. All maps are less than $15.

NATIONAL PARKS

National parks protect some of America and Canada's most precious wildlife and spectacular scenery. Alaska's crowning Denali, Oregon's stone-still Crater Lake, and Alberta's Banff and Jasper are treasures that will remain intact for generations. The parks also make room for recreational activities such as hiking, skiing, and snowshoe expeditions; most have backcountry camping and developed tent camping, others welcome RVs, and a few offer opulent living in grand lodges.

Entry fees vary from park to park. Pedestrian and cyclist entry fees tend to range from $2-7, while vehicles go from $4-10. Most national parks in the U.S. offer discounts such as the one-year **Golden Eagle Passport** (US$50), which allows the bearer and family free entry into all U.S. parks. Visitors ages 62 and over qualify for the **Golden Age Passport** (US$10), entitling them to free entry and a 50% discount on basic fees like camping. Ask for details at the entrance station of parks. The **Golden Access Passport** (free) offers free access to travelers with disabilities. Reservations are essential at the more popular parks in the Pacific Northwest; make them through **DESTINET** (800-365-2267 in U.S., 619-452-8787 outside the U.S.; fax 619-546-1709; http://www.destinet.com/nps/nps1.html). Visitors centers at parks offer excellent free pamphlets and information, and the **U.S. Government Printing Office** (see p. 4) publishes *National Parks: Lesser-Known Areas* (US$1.75).

Less trammeled than their southern counterparts, Canada's national parks are every bit as spectacular. Reservations are being offered for a limited number of campgrounds on a trial basis for 1998 with a CDN$5.50 fee. For information or reservations, call Parks Canada at 800-213-7275, or consult their useful web page (http://parkscanada.pch.gc.ca). A patchwork of regional passes are available at relevant parks; the best is the **Great Western Pass,** which covers admission to all the parks in the Western provinces for a year (CDN$35, seniors $27, ages 6-16 $18, families $70).

U.S. Forest Service/National Park Service, Outdoor Recreation Information Center, 222 Yale Ave. N., Seattle, WA 98174 (206-470-4060). For the National Parks Main Headquarters in Washington, D.C., call (202) 208-4747.

Parks Canada, 220 4th Ave. SE., #552, Calgary, AB T2G 4X3 (800-748-7275 or 403-292-4401; email natlparks-ab@pch.gc.ca).

Alaska Public Lands Information Center, 605 W. 4th Ave. Suite 105, Anchorage, AK 99501 (907-271-2737; fax 907-271-2744).

STATE AND PROVINCIAL PARKS

In contrast to national parks, the primary function of **state and provincial parks** is recreation. Prices for camping at public sites are almost always better than those at private campgrounds. Don't let swarming visitors dissuade you from seeing the large parks—these places are huge, and even at their most crowded they offer many opportunities for quiet and solitude. Most campgrounds are strictly first-come, first-camped. Arrive early: many campgrounds, public and private, fill up by late morning. Some limit your stay and/or the number of people in a group.

U.S. NATIONAL FORESTS

If the national parks are too developed for your tastes, **national forests** provide a purist's alternative. While some have recreation facilities, most are equipped only for primitive camping—pit toilets and no running water are the norm. Entrance fees, when charged, are $10-20, but camping is generally free, or $3-4. **Reservations,** with a one-time $16.50 service fee, are available for most forests up to one year in advance, but are usually unnecessary except during high season at the more popular sites. For reservations, write or call the **National Recreation Reservation Center,** P.O. Box 900, Cumberland, MD 21501-0900 (800-280-2267; fax 301-722-9802). For general information, including maps and the free *Guide to Your National Forests,* contact the **U.S. Forest Service,** 201 14th St. SW., Auditors Building, Washington, D.C. 20250 (202-205-0957; fax 205-0885; http://www.fs.fed.us).

Backpackers can enjoy specially designated **wilderness areas,** which are even less accessible due to regulations barring all vehicles. **Wilderness permits,** required for backcountry hiking, can usually be obtained (generally free to enter, but occasionally a reservation fee) at the Forest Service field office in the area; check ahead.

The Forest Service also oversees more than 200 scenic and well-maintained wilderness **log cabins** for public use, scattered throughout the southern and central regions of Alaska. User permits are required along with a fee of $25 per party (of any size) per night. Reservations are usually necessary several months in advance. Most cabins have seven-day use limits (hike-in cabins have a three day limit May-Aug.) and are usually accessible only by air, boat, or hiking trail. For general information, contact the Forest Service's regional offices. The **U.S. Fish and Wildlife Service,** 1011 E. Tudor Rd., Anchorage 99503 (907-786-3487), maintains numerous campgrounds within the National Wildlife Refuges of the Alaska, including the **Kenai National Wildlife Refuge** (907-262-7021; 15 campgrounds with sites from $6-10; max. stay of either 3 or 14 days depending on the campground). Any remaining questions that you have can probably be answered by the **Alaska Public Lands Information Center** (907-271-2737), which also mails out maps, brochures, and other information.

The U.S. Department of the Interior's **Bureau of Land Management (BLM),** Public Affairs, Rm. 5600, 1849 C St. NW, Washington DC 20240 (202-209-3100 at Department of the Interior; 202-208-5717 fax at BLM), offers a wide variety of outdoor recreation opportunities—including camping, hiking, mountain biking, rock climbing, river rafting, and wildlife viewing—on the 270 million acres it oversees in ten western states and Alaska. These lands also contain hundreds of archaeological artifacts and historic sites like ghost towns. The BLM's many **campgrounds** include 20 sprinkled throughout Alaska, most of them free.

CAMPING AND HIKING EQUIPMENT

If you purchase **equipment** before you leave, you'll know exactly what you have and how much it weighs. Whether buying or renting, taking the time to find sturdy, light, and inexpensive equipment is a must. Peruse catalogues and talk to knowledgeable salespeople.

Sleeping bags: Most good **sleeping bags** are rated by "season," or the lowest outdoor temperature at which they will keep you warm ("summer" means 30-40°F, "three-season" means 20°F, and "four-season" or "winter" means below 0°F). Sleeping bags are made either of down (warmer and lighter, but more expensive, and miserable when wet) or of synthetic material (heavier, more durable, and warmer when wet). Prices vary, but might range from $65-100 for a summer synthetic to $250-550 for a good down winter bag.

Under your bag: If you're doing any serious camping, you'll need a **foam pad** ($15 and up) or **air mattress** ($25-50) to cushion your back and neck and insulate you from the ground. Another good alternative is the **Therm-A-Rest,** which is part foam and part air-mattress and inflates to full padding when you unroll it.

Over your head: The best **tents** are free-standing, with their own frames and suspension systems; they set up quickly and require no staking (except in high winds). Low-profile dome tents are best. When pitched, their internal space is almost entirely usable, which means little unnecessary bulk. Tent sizes can be somewhat misleading: 2 people *can* fit in a 2-person tent, but will find life more pleasant in a 4-person. If you're traveling by car, go for the bigger tent; if you're hiking, stick with a smaller tent that weighs no more than 3-4 lbs. Good 2-person tents start at $150, and 4-person tents at $400, but you can sometimes find last year's model for half the price. Be sure to seal the seams of your tent with waterproofer, and make sure it has a rain fly.

On your Back: If you intend to do a lot of hiking, you should have a **frame backpack.** Sturdy backpacks cost anywhere from $125-500. This is one area where it doesn't pay to economize—cheaper packs may be less comfortable, and the straps are more likely to fray or rip. For more information, see **The Backpack,** p. 18.

Boots: Be sure to wear hiking boots with good **ankle support** which are appropriate for the terrain you are hiking. Your boots should fit snugly and comfortably over one or two wool socks and a thin liner sock. Be sure that the boots are broken in—a bad blister will ruin your hiking for days.

Other necessities: Rain gear should come in 2 pieces, a top and pants, rather than a poncho. Ponchos turn into sails when the wind kicks up. **Synthetics,** like polypropylene tops, socks, and long underwear, along with a pile jacket, will keep you warm even when wet. When camping in autumn, winter, spring, or outer space, bring along a **"space blanket,"** which helps you to retain your body heat and doubles as a groundcloth ($5-15). Plastic **canteens** or water bottles keep water cooler than metal ones do, and are virtually shatter- and leak-proof. Large, collapsible **water sacks** will significantly improve your lot in primitive campgrounds and weigh practically nothing when empty, though they can get bulky. Bring **water-purification tablets** for when you can't boil water. Though most campgrounds provide campfire sites, you may want to bring a small **metal grate** or **grill** of your own. For those places that forbid fires or the gathering of firewood, you'll need a **camp stove**. The classic Coleman starts at about $30. A **first aid kit, Swiss army knife, insect repellent, calamine lotion,** and **waterproof matches** or a **lighter** are essential camping items. Other items include: a **battery-operated lantern,** a **plastic groundcloth,** a **nylon tarp,** a **waterproof backpack cover** (although you can also store your belongings in plastic bags inside your backpack), and a **"stuff sack"** or plastic bag to keep your sleeping bag dry.

The mail-order firms listed below offer lower prices than those you'll find in many stores, but shop around locally first in order to determine what items actually look like and weigh. Keep in mind that camping equipment is generally more expensive in Australia and the U.K. than in North America.

Campmor, P.O. Box 700, Saddle River, NJ 07458-0700 (800-CAMPMOR/526-4784, outside the U.S. 201-825-8300; email customer-service@campmor.com; http://www.campmor.com). A wide selection of name brand equipment at low prices. One-year guarantee for unused or defective merchandise.

Discount Camping, 880 Main North Rd., Pooraka, South Australia 5095, Australia (tel. (08) 8262 3399; fax 8260 6240). Specializes in tents, but has other equipment as well.

Eastern Mountain Sports (EMS), One Vose Farm Rd., Peterborough, NH 03458 (603-924-9591). Stores throughout the U.S. Though slightly higher-priced, they provide excellent service and guaranteed customer satisfaction on most items sold. They don't have a catalogue, and they generally don't take mail or phone orders; call the above number for the branch nearest you.

Recreational Equipment, Inc. (REI), 1700 45th St. E, Sumner, WA 98390 (800-426-4840; http://www.rei.com). Stocks a wide range of the latest in camping gear and holds great seasonal sales. Many items are guaranteed for life (excluding normal wear and tear).

L.L. Bean, Freeport, ME 04033-0001 (800-441-5713 in Canada or the U.S.; tel. (0800) 962 954 in the U.K.; 207-552-6878 elsewhere; fax 207-552-3080; http://www.llbean.com). This monolithic equipment and outdoor clothing supplier offers high quality gear. Call or write for their free catalogue. The customer is guaranteed 100 percent satisfaction on all purchases; if it doesn't meet your expectations, they'll replace or refund it. Open 24hr. per day, 365 days a year.

Mountain Designs, P.O. Box 1472, Fortitude Valley, Queensland 4006, Australia (tel. (07) 3252 8894; fax 3252 4569). A leading Australian manufacturer and mail order retailer of camping and climbing gear.

Sierra Designs, 1255 Powell St., Emeryville, CA 94608 (510-450-9555; fax 654-0705). Carries all seasons and types of especially small and lightweight tent models.

Sierra Trading Post, 5025 Campstool Rd., Cheyenne WY 82007-1802 (307-775-8000; fax 775-8088; http://www.sierra-trading.com). Mail-order savings on name brand outdoor clothing and equipment.

YHA Adventure Shop, 14 Southampton St., London, WC2E 7HA, U.K. (tel. (01718) 36 85 41). One of Britain's largest outdoor equipment suppliers.

WILDERNESS CONCERNS

Stay warm, stay dry, and **stay hydrated.** The vast majority of life-threatening wilderness problems stem from a failure to follow this advice. On any hike, however brief, you should pack enough equipment to keep you alive should disaster befall. This includes water, high energy food, rain gear, and appropriate clothing and equipment (see above). Never rely on **cotton** for warmth. This "death cloth" will be absolutely useless should it get wet (see **Packing,** p. 18).

Check **weather forecasts** and pay attention to the skies when hiking. A bright blue sky in Alaska or the Pacific Northwest can turn to rain or even snow before you can say "hypothermia." If on a day hike when the weather turns nasty, turn back. If on an overnight, start looking immediately for shelter. Whenever possible, let someone know when and where you are going hiking, either a friend, your hostel, a park ranger, or a local hiking organization. Do not attempt a hike beyond your ability—you may be endangering your life. A good guide to outdoor survival is *How to Stay Alive in the Woods,* by Bradford Angier (Macmillan, US$8). See **Health,** p. 13, for information about outdoor ailments such as giardia, rabies, and insects, as well as basic medical concerns and first-aid.

While protecting yourself from the elements, take a moment to also consider protecting the wilderness from you. For the sake of those who follow you, try to practice **"minimum impact"** camping techniques. Leave no trace of your presence when you leave a site. Don't cut vegetation or clear new campsites. A campstove is the safer (and more efficient) way to cook, but if you must, make small fires using only dead branches or brush. Make sure your campsite is at least 150 ft. from water supplies or bodies of water. If there are no toilet facilities, bury human waste (but not paper) at least four inches deep and above the high-water line 150 ft. or more from any water supplies and campsites. Always pack your trash in a plastic bag and carry it with you until you reach the next trash can.

BEAR IN MIND

The aggressiveness of **bears** varies from region to region, and popular theories on bear psychology are as common and as varied as cures for the hiccups. Rangers and other local authorities will always be your best resource for learning how to behave safely around bears in a particular region. Ask local rangers for information on bear behavior before entering any park or wilderness area, and obey any posted warnings. The one rule to follow in any area: no matter how tame a bear appears, don't be fooled—they're powerful and unpredictable animals who are simply not impressed or intimidated by humans. If you're close enough for a bear to be observing you, you're too close.

The best way to avoid a grizzly experience is not to come face to face with Ms. or Mr. Bear in the first place. Keep your camp clean—no trash or food lying around—and don't cook near where you sleep. Park rangers can tell you how to identify bear trails—don't camp on them. If you're near a beach, it's a good idea to eat in a tidal zone so that traces of food can be washed away at high tide. **Bear-bagging,** which amounts to hanging edibles and other good-smelling objects from a tree, out of reach of hungry paws, is trickier than it sounds (unless it sounds to you like bagging a bear). Ask a park ranger or a salesperson at a wilderness store to show you how. Avoid indulging in greasy foods, especially bacon and ham. **Grease** gets on everything, including your clothes and sleeping bag, and bears find it an alluring scent. Bears are also attracted to any **perfume,** as are bugs—do without cologne, scented soap, and hairspray while camping—and to **sex.** We won't tell you to do without *that,* but be warned.

Never feed a bear or tempt it with such delicacies as open trash cans. If you see a bear at a distance, calmly walk (don't run) in the other direction. If you stumble upon a sweet-looking bear cub, leave immediately lest its over-protective mother stumble upon you.

OUTDOOR SPORTS

Water Sports

The latticework of fast-flowing rivers in the Pacific Northwest is ideal for canoeing, kayaking, and whitewater rafting. Boating opportunities are suggested throughout the book. Travel agents and tourism bureaus can recommend others.

The **River Travel Center,** P.O. Box 6, Pt. Arena, CA 95468 (800-882-RAFT/7238; fax 707-882-2638), can place you in a whitewater raft, kayak, or sea kayak with one of over 100 outfitters. Trips range in length from one to 18 days and range in price from $80 (one day) to $2000 (extended). **Sierra Club Books** publishes a kayaking and whitewater rafting guide entitled *Wildwater* ($12). The club offers kayaking trips to the Pacific Northwest and Alaska every year. *Washington Whitewater* ($18.95) and *Canoe Routes: Northwest Oregon* ($12.95), published by The Mountaineers Books, might also be of interest.

Snow Sports

Tourism bureaus can help you locate the best sports outfitters and areas for winter hiking, camping, skiing, even snowshoeing and dog sledding. *Let's Go* suggests options throughout the book. For Oregon and Washington skiing guides and information (both downhill and cross-country), write the **Pacific Northwest Ski Areas Association,** P.O. Box 2325 Seattle, WA 98111-2325 (206-623-3777; fax 447-5897). The Sierra Club publishes *The Best Ski Touring in America* (US$10.95), which also includes British Columbia and Quebec.

Pay attention to cold weather safety concerns. Know the symptoms of hypothermia and frostbite, and bring along warm clothes and quick energy snacks like candy bars and trail mix (see **Hypothermia,** p. 14). Drinking alcohol in the cold can be dangerous: even though you *feel* warm, alcohol can slow your body's ability to adjust to the temperature, and thus make you more vulnerable to hypothermia.

Fishing

From arctic char to king salmon, the Pacific Northwest enjoys much of the best fishing in the world. Should you wish to take advantage of the region's well-stocked lakes and streams, contact the appropriate department of fisheries for brochures that summarize regulations and make sport fishing predictions. Some fishing seasons are extremely short, so be sure to ask when the expected prime angling dates occur. Licenses are available from many tackle shops, or you can purchase them directly from the state or provincial department of fisheries. Consult the appropriate departments of game to purchase licenses and receive regulations pamphlets.

Alaska: Department of Fish and Game: Licensing Section, P.O. Box 25525, Juneau, AK 99802-5525 (907-465-2376; fax 465-2440; open Mon.-Fri. 8:30am-5pm). Nonresident fishing license US$10 for 1 day, 1 day "salmon sticker" additional $10, $15 for 3 days, 3 day "salmon sticker" additional $15, $30 for 14 days, $50 for a year.

Alberta: Natural Resources Service, Licensing and Vendor Services, 9945 108th St., Edmonton, AB T5K 2G6 (403-427-6729; fax 422-9558; http: www.gov.ab.ca/dept/env.html). Nonresident fishing license CDN$18 for Canadians, CDN$36 for non-Canadians. CDN$24 limited 5-day fishing license for non-Canadians.

British Columbia: Fish and Wildlife Information, Ministry of Environment, 780 Blanshard St., Victoria, BC V8V 1X4 (604-387-9739). Non-Canadian angling license CDN$25 for 8 days, CDN$40 for 1 year, CDN$20 for steelhead tags.

Oregon: Department of Fish and Wildlife, 2501 SW 1st Ave., P.O. Box 59, Portland, OR 97207 (503-872-5275). Nonresident 1-year fishing license $40.50, plus tags for salmon ($10.50), sturgeon ($6), and halibut ($6). One-day license covers all tags ($6.75; also 2, 3, 7 day licenses).

Washington: Department of Fish and Wildlife, 600 Capitol Way, Olympia, WA 98501-1091 (360-902-2200). Nonresident game fishing license, good for 1 year,

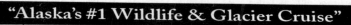

under age 14 $20, over 14 $48. Nonresident Personal Use Food Fish License $20. Nonresident Shellfish/Seaweed License $20.

Yukon Government, Department of Renewable Resources, Fish and Wildlife Branch, 10 Burns Rd., P.O. Box 2703, Whitehorse, YT Y1A 2C6 (403-667-5221). Non-Canadian license CDN$5 for 1 day, CDN$20 for 6 days, CDN$35 for 1 year.

Hunting

Regulations on hunting in Alaska and the Pacific Northwest are extensive. Certain animals may not be hunted, and others require special trapping licenses and permits. Since rules are often specific to a region, your best bet may be to start with an organization like the **Alaska Public Lands Information Center,** 605 W. 4th Ave. #105, Anchorage AK 99501 (907-271-2737; fax 271-2744). In Alaska, all nonresident hunters must have a license. Residents take precedence over nonresidents in the event of a game shortage. Since many regulations are not simple common-sense rules, and since (in the words of the State of Alaska) "ignorance is no excuse," would-be hunters should take a look at state hunting regulations before they pick up a gun.

ORGANIZED ADVENTURE

Organized adventure tours offer another way of exploring the wild. Activities include hiking, biking, skiing, canoeing, kayaking, rafting, climbing, photo safaris and archaeological digs, and go *everywhere.* Begin by consulting tourism bureaus, which can suggest parks, trails, and outfitters as well as answer more general questions. The **Specialty Travel Index,** 305 San Anselmo Ave., San Anselmo, CA 94960 (415-459-4900; fax 459-4974; http://www.specialtytravel.com) is a directory listing hundreds of tour operators worldwide. The **Sierra Club,** 85 Second St., 2nd Fl., San Francisco, CA 94105-3441 (415-977-5630; fax 977-5795; email national.outings@sierraclub.org; http://www.sierraclub.org/outings), plans many adventure outings, both through its San Francisco headquarters and its local branches throughout Canada and the U.S. **TrekAmerica,** P.O. Box 189, Rockaway, NJ 07886 (800-221-0596; fax 201-983-8551; http://www.trekamerica.com) organizes small group adventure camping tours throughout North and Central America. Trips run from seven days to nine weeks. **Footloose** (http://www.footloose.com) is an outfit run by TrekAmerica which plans more sedate adventures for a somewhat older clientele. **Alaska Wilderness Journeys,** P.O. Box 220204, Anchorage, AK 99522 (800-349-0064; fax 907-344-6877, email akwildj@alaska.net), organizes up to 10-day combination and trekking tours through Alaska as well as Africa, Australia, and the Russian Far East.

Keeping in Touch

MAIL

U.S. Mail Individual offices of the **U.S. Postal Service** are usually open Monday to Friday from 9am to 5pm and sometimes on Saturday until about noon; branches in many larger cities open earlier and close later. All are closed on national holidays. **Postcards** mailed within the U.S. cost 20¢; letters cost 32¢ for the first ounce and 23¢ for each additional ounce. To send mail to Canada from the U.S., it costs 40¢ to mail a postcard, 52¢ to mail a letter for the first ounce, 72¢ for two ounces, 95¢ for three ounces, and 19¢ for each additional ounce. It costs 35¢ to mail a postcard to Mexico; a letter is 46¢ for an ounce, 86¢ for 2 ounces, and 40¢ for each additional ounce up to 12 ounces. The U.S. Postal Service now requires that **overseas** letters be mailed directly from the post office and accompanied by a customs form. **Overseas rates** are: postcards 50¢, ½oz. 60¢, 1oz. $1, 40¢ per additional ounce. **Aerogrammes,** sheets that fold into envelopes and travel via air mail, are available at post offices for 50¢. (All prices in US$.) Domestic mail generally takes 3-5 days; overseas mail, 7-14 days. Write **"AIR MAIL"** on the front of the envelope for speediest delivery.

The U.S. is divided into postal zones, each with a five-digit **ZIP code** particular to a region, city, or part of a city. Some addresses have nine-digit ZIP codes, used primarily to speed up delivery for business mailings. Writing the ZIP code on letters is essential for delivery. The normal form of address is as follows:

Courtney Love
Hole (title and/or name or organization, optional)
123 4th Avenue, Apt.#456 (address, apartment #)
Olympia, WA 98501 (city, state, zip code)
USA (country, if mailing internationally)

Canadian Mail In **Canada** mailing a letter (or a postcard, which carries the same rate as a letter) to the U.S. costs 52¢ for the first 30 grams and 77¢ for 31-50 grams. To every other foreign country, a 20-gram letter costs 90¢, a 50-gram letter $1.37, and a 51- to 100-gram letter $2.25. The domestic rate is 45¢ for a 30-gram letter, and 71¢ for a letter between 31 and 50 grams. Aerogrammes cost 90¢. Letters take from seven to ten days to reach the U.S. and about two weeks to get to an overseas address by air. Canada Post's most reliable and pricey service is **Priority Courier,** which offers speedy delivery (usually next-day) to major American cities ($23.50 for a document). Delivery to overseas locations usually takes two days; to Europe $35.50 for a document; to the Pacific $40; International $69. Guaranteed next-day domestic delivery exists between any two Canadian cities and starts at $8.70 plus tax; cost varies depending on location. (All prices in CDN$.)

In Canada, **postal codes** are the equivalent of U.S. ZIP codes and contain letters as well as numbers (for example, L9H 3M6). The normal form of address is nearly identical to that in the U.S.; the only difference is that the apartment or suite number can *precede* the street address along with a dash. For example, 3-203 Colborne St. refers to Room or Apartment #3 at 203 Colborne St.

General Delivery and Other Services Depending on how neurotic your family is, consider making arrangements for them to get in touch with you. Mail can be sent **general delivery** to a city's main branch of the post office. Once a letter arrives it will be held for at least 10 days; it can be held for longer if such a request is clearly indicated by you or on the front of the envelope. Customers should bring a passport or other ID to pick up General Delivery mail. Family and friends can send letters to you labeled like this:

Norman Fell (underline last name for accurate filing)
c/o General Delivery
Main Post Office
Vancouver, BC V1L 2M6
CANADA (if mailing internationally)

American Express offices throughout the U.S. and Canada will act as a mail service for cardholders if you contact them in advance. Under this free **"Client Letter Service,"** they will hold mail for 30 days, forward upon request, and accept telegrams. The last name of the person to whom the mail is addressed should be capitalized and underlined. Some offices will offer these services to non-cardholders (especially those who have purchased AmEx Travelers' Cheques), but you must call ahead to make sure. A complete list is available free from AmEx (800-528-4800) in the booklet *Traveler's Companion* or online at http://www.americanexpress.com/shared/cgi-bin/tsoserve.cgi?travel/index.

If regular airmail is too slow, there are a few faster, more expensive, options. **Federal Express** (800-463-3339) is a reliable private courier service that guarantees overnight delivery anywhere in the continental U.S., at a price (a letter under ½ lb.sets you back US$13.26). The cheaper but more sluggish U.S. Postal Service **Express Mail** will deliver a ½ lb. parcel in two days for US$10.75 from any post office. Canada Post offers **Priority Courier** (next day delivery), **XPress Post**, and **SkyPak** for destinations in the U.S. and other countries. Rates vary by destination and weight.

TELEPHONES

Most of the information you will need about telephone usage—including area codes for Canada and the U.S., foreign country codes, and rates—is in the front of the local **white pages** telephone directory. The **yellow pages,** published at the end of the white pages or in a separate book, lists the numbers of businesses and other services alphabetically by the service or merchandise they provide. Federal, state, and local government listings are provided in the **blue pages** at the back of the directory. To obtain local phone numbers or area codes of other cities, call **directory assistance** at 411. Dialing "0" will get you the **operator,** who can assist you in reaching a phone number and provide you with general information. You can reach local directory assistance and the operator free from any pay phone. For long-distance directory, dial 1-(area code)-555-1212. All area codes are listed at the end of the **Practical Information** for a section.

You can place **international calls** from most telephones. To call direct, dial the international access code (from Canada and the U.S., the code is 011) followed by the country code, the area code, and the local number. Country codes and city codes may be listed with a zero in front (e.g., 033), but after dialing the international access code, drop successive zeros (e.g., 011 33). Calls between Canada and the U.S. are not considered international calls. Dial them as you would a domestic long distance call: 1-(area code)-number. Be aware, however, that many toll free numbers in the U.S. (those that begin with 800 or 888) do not work from Canada, or vice versa.

You may want to consider getting a **calling card** if you plan to make a lot of international calls. The calls (plus a small surcharge) are billed either collect or to a calling card. Some companies will be able to connect you to numbers only in your home country; others will be able to provide other worldwide connections. For more information, call **AT&T** about its **USADirect** and **World Connect** services (888-288-4685; from abroad call 810-262-6644 collect), **Sprint** (800-877-4646; from abroad, call 913-624-5335 collect), or **MCI WorldPhone** and **World Reach** (800-444-4141; from abroad dial the country's MCI access number). In Canada, contact Bell Canada **Canada Direct** (800-565-4708); in the U.K., British Telecom **BT Direct** (tel. (800) 34 51 44); in Ireland, Telecom Éireann **Ireland Direct** (tel. (800) 250 250); in Australia, Telstra **Australia Direct** (tel. 13 22 00); in New Zealand, **Telecom New Zealand** (tel. 123); and in South Africa, **Telkom South Africa** (tel. 09 03).

Phone rates tend to be highest in the morning, lower in the evening, and lowest on Sunday and late at night. Also, remember **time differences** when you call. See **Appendix,** p. 508, for time zones in Alaska and the Pacific Northwest.

EMAIL

With a minimum of computer knowledge and a little planning, **electronic mail** (now universally known as **email** instead of the much niftier short form "electro-mail") users can beam messages anywhere for no per-message charges. One option is to befriend college students as you go and ask if you can use their email accounts. If you're not the finagling type, **Traveltales** (http://traveltales.com) provides free, web-based email for travelers and maintains a list of cybercafes, travel links, and a travelers' chat room. Other free, web-based email providers include **Hotmail** (http://www.hotmail.com), **RocketMail** (http://www.rocketmail.com), and **USANET** (http://www.usa.net). Many free email providers are funded by advertising and some may require subscribers to fill out a questionnaire. Search through http://www.cyberiacafe.net/cyberia/guide/ccafe.htm to find a list of **cybercafes** around the world from which you can drink a cup of joe and email him too.

If you're already hooked up to the infobahn at home, you should be able to find access numbers anywhere in the Pacific Northwest. If you're not connected, and don't mind the occasional busy signal, one comparatively cheap, easy-to-use access provider is **America Online,** 8615 Westwood Center Drive, Vienna, VA 22070 (800-827-6364).

ALASKA

Alaska's beauty and intrigue are born of extremes: North America's highest mountains and broadest flatlands; windswept tundra and lush rainforests; underwater salmon runs and overland caribou herds; virgin spruce forests in the southeast and oil pumps at the top of the world. Harsh weather and a ruthless landscape left much of Alaska's land untouched until the 19th century, and even today the state remains largely undeveloped—America's last true wilderness.

To native Aleuts, who thrived for millennia on the rugged Aleutian islands, the spectacular and enormous expanses to the northeast were "Alyeska," or "the Great Land." To the Europeans and followers of "Manifest Destiny" who journeyed into the northwestern hinterlands, Alaska was the "Last Frontier." To summertime tourists, this region is the "Land of the Midnight Sun." Only to the ignorant is Alaska merely a "frozen wasteland." In summer, all but the northernmost reaches of the state explode in a riot of vegetation. The wilderness teems with caribou, bear, moose, Dall sheep, and wolves, and Alaska's waters churn with millions of spawning salmon, huge offshore halibut, and trophy-sized grayling and trout. With only one quarter of Alaska's land accessible by highway, hikers and campers find unparalleled opportunities for a truly solitary wilderness experience. But visitors needn't be hardcore backpackers/hikers/mountaineers to see much of the state's beauty—even many stunning glaciers can be reached by road.

The typical Alaskan, if the state's gallery of individualists and eccentrics does not render that term an oxymoron, bears a stubborn anarchist streak. Alaskans value their remote home not only for its beauty, but for the freedom to live life on their own terms. Travelers who don't step on any toes will find the people of Alaska to be extremely open, friendly, and down-to-earth. After surviving one winter—the traditional hazing process separating newcomers and Alaskans—some never want to leave.

Geography

Physically, Alaska truly is "The Great Land." The state contains 586,412 sq. mi.—over one-fifth of the land mass of the United States. The 33,000 mi. coastline stretches 11 times the distance from New York to San Francisco. Four major mountain ranges cross the state: the Wrangell Mountains, the Chugach Mountains, the Brooks Range, and the Denali-topped Alaska Range. Alaska is also home to Wrangell-St. Elias, the largest national park in America, which covers an area of 13 million acres, twice the size of Massachusetts. Nineteen Alaskan peaks reach over 14,000 ft., 94 lakes have a surface area of more than 10 sq. mi., and a handful of glacial icefields are each larger than the state of Rhode Island.

On the archipelago of the **Southeastern Panhandle,** the isolated state capital of Juneau rests among numerous fjord-scarred islands, verdant rainforests, and sub-arctic swamps known as *muskeg*. **Southcentral Alaska** is the home of Kodiak Island, the Kenai Peninsula, Prince William Sound, and the Kodiak brown bear. The 20,320-ft.-tall Denali (a.k.a. Mt. McKinley), the tallest mountain in North America, dominates the interminable flatlands of the **Interior,** the area north and east of Anchorage. **The Bush** encompasses the vast and empty areas north and west of the Interior, including the Brooks Range and the Arctic Circle, the Seward Peninsula, and all of western Alaska along the Bering Sea. The Alaska Peninsula and the storm-swept volcanic archipelago of the **Aleutian Islands** extends into the extreme southwestern reaches of the Bush, offering tenuous purchase to a handful of hardy humans.

Humanity has left its mark on "The Great Land": logging, overfishing, and oil drilling have stripped forests, emptied streams, and drawn a jagged pipeline across the belly of the tundra. But Alaskans are rarely permitted to forget Mother Nature's dominance. In 1964, the Good Friday quake, centered in Miner's Lake (located between

Whittier and Valdez), registered 9.2 on the Richter Scale and lasted eight terrible minutes. Its aftershocks continued for several days. Many coastal towns, including Kodiak and Whittier, were demolished by the tsunami that followed the earthquake; Valdez was completely destroyed and rebuilt on a new site.

Early and Native History

The first budget travelers in the Americas arrived over 20,000 years ago, migrating over the Bering Land Bridge from Siberia to Alaska, yellow-jacketed copies of *Let's Go* in hand. By 10,000 years ago, these people had spread across the entirety of two continents, the ancestors of all the indigenous peoples in North and South America. Today, four distinct native groups inhabit Alaska. The Southeast is home to the Tlingit (KLINK-it) and Haida (HIGH-dah) peoples, renowned for their exquisitely carved totem poles and the formidable wooden forts from which they almost staved off Russian invaders in the 19th century. The Interior and Southcentral regions harbor the once-nomadic Athabasca nation. The Aleutian Island chain is populated largely by the Aleuts, who were enslaved by the Russians for their skill as fur trappers. The Inuit (commonly given the misnomer of "Eskimos" or "raw meat-eaters") reside almost exclusively within the Arctic Circle and share a common language and heritage with Siberians across the Bering Strait.

Soft Gold

Under orders from Peter the Great to find a route from the Arctic to the Pacific, Russian seafarers led by Admiral Vitus Bering landed on Kayak Island off Prince William Sound in 1733. Bering's expedition brought the fur of seals and sea otters back to Russia, and began an intense competition with the British and Spanish for control of the lucrative trade in this "soft gold." The Russians based their colonization of the Alaskan wilderness in the southern coastal region, which retains an unmistakably Slavic imprint even today.

By the mid-1800s, the once-bountiful supply of furry animals was nearly exhausted, and the Aleut population had diminished as a result of forced labor. The Russians, deep in debt after the disastrous Crimean War, solicited bids for the "dead land," and found a buyer in the United States, ready to resume territorial expansion after the conclusion of the American Civil War.

Gold Gold

The U.S. bought Alaska for $7,200,000, or about 2¢ per acre, on October 18, 1867. Critics mocked the purchase, popularly called "Seward's Folly" after the Secretary of State who negotiated the deal under President Johnson. At this time, native Alaskans restated their claims to their ancestral lands. The issue went unresolved, and titles were held in abeyance for more than a century.

William Seward was vindicated 15 years after the purchase, when large deposits of gold were unearthed in the Panhandle's Gastineau Channel. Juneau, the northern Eldorado, was born. As gold-panning prospectors exhausted deposits on the Gastineau, they found other rivers such as the Yukon, the Charley, the Fortymile, and the Klondike, and hundreds of millions of dollars in gold made their way to the continental U.S.

Cold War

War came to Alaska in June 1942 when Japanese bombers attacked Unalaska and occupied two of the Aleutian Islands. The U.S. began a rapid buildup of military forces, and the Alaska Highway was hurriedly built to connect the territory with the rest of the U.S.—a mammoth undertaking that laid highway through 1,500 miles of wilderness in under nine months. After the defeat of the Japanese, Alaska's proximity to the Soviet Union kept attention focused on the north. The military remained a significant presence in the region, and Alaska became the 49th state in 1959.

Throughout the 60s, native Alaskans watched with growing frustration as the federal and state governments divvied up vast tracts of land. The discovery in 1968 of huge oil deposits beneath the shore of the Beaufort Sea in the Arctic Ocean brought

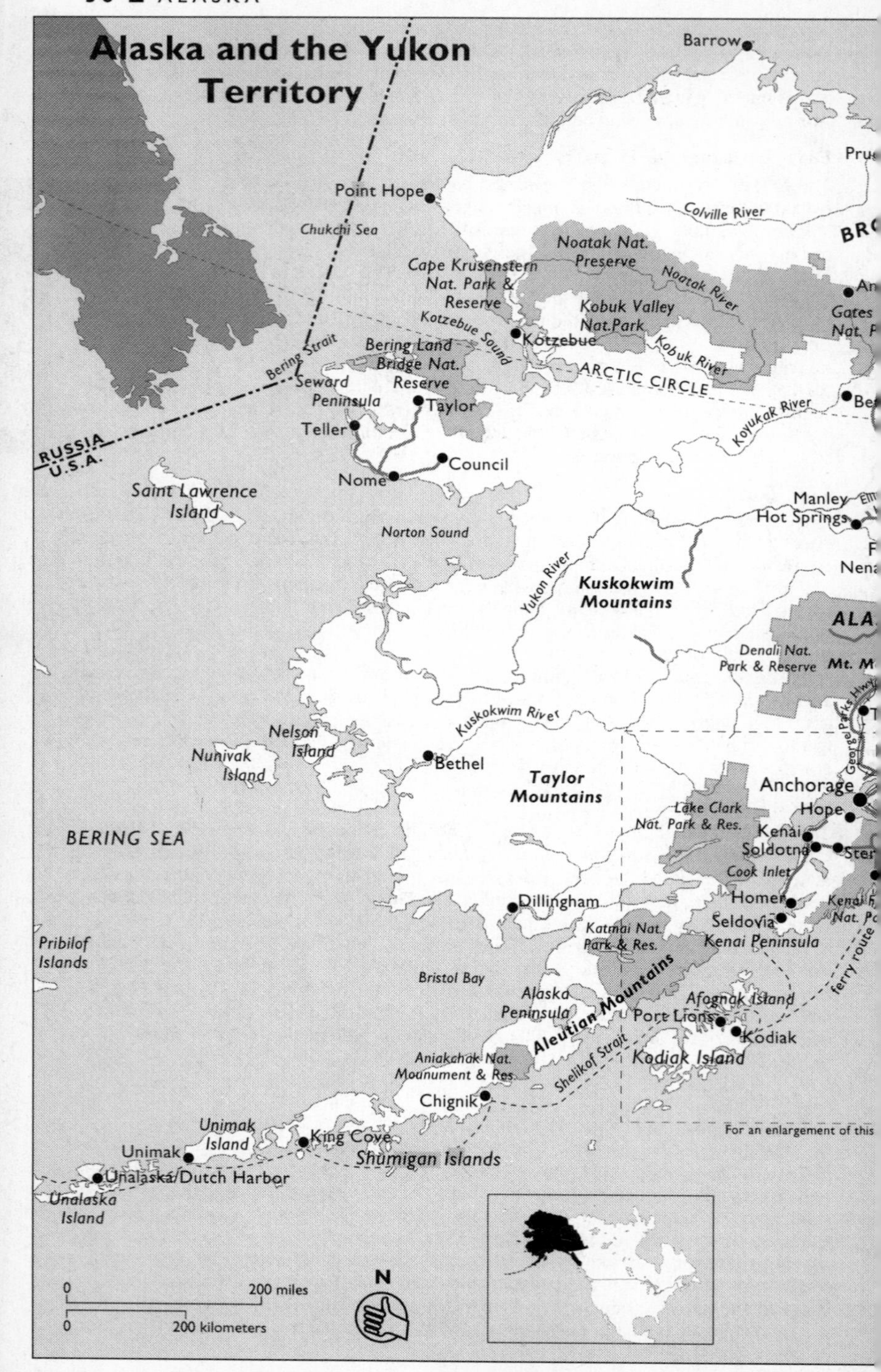
Alaska and the Yukon Territory
Barrow
Point Hope
Chukchi Sea
Colville River
Noatak Nat. Preserve
Noatak River
Cape Krusenstern Nat. Park & Reserve
Kobuk Valley Nat. Park
Kotzebue Sound
Kotzebue
Kobuk River
Bering Strait
Bering Land Bridge Nat. Reserve
ARCTIC CIRCLE
Seward Peninsula
Taylor
Teller
Koyukuk River
RUSSIA
U.S.A.
Council
Nome
Saint Lawrence Island
Manley Hot Springs
Norton Sound
Yukon River
Kuskokwim Mountains
Denali Nat. Park & Reserve
Kuskokwim River
Nelson Island
Nunivak Island
Bethel
Taylor Mountains
Anchorage
Hope
Lake Clark Nat. Park & Res.
Kenai
Soldotna
BERING SEA
Cook Inlet
Dillingham
Homer
Seldovia
Katmai Nat. Park & Res.
Kenai Peninsula
Pribilof Islands
Bristol Bay
Alaska Peninsula
Aleutian Mountains
Afognak Island
Port Lions
Kodiak
Shelikof Strait
Kodiak Island
Aniakchak Nat. Monument & Res.
Chignik
ferry route
For an enlargement of this
Unimak Island
King Cove
Unimak
Shumigan Islands
Unalaska/Dutch Harbor
Unalaska Island
0
200 miles
0
200 kilometers
N

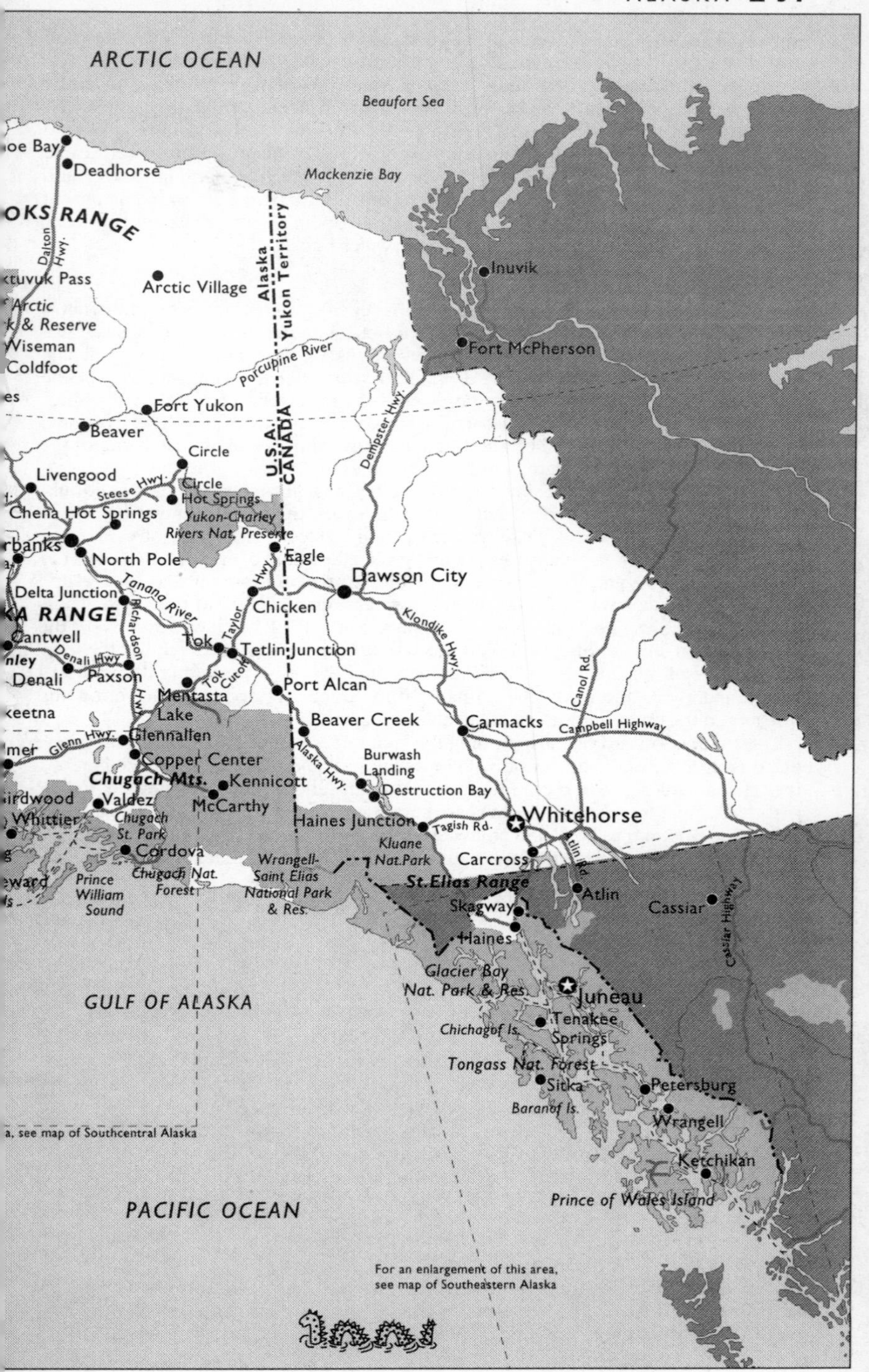
ARCTIC OCEAN
Beaufort Sea
Mackenzie Bay
Deadhorse
Dalton Hwy.
Arctic Village
Alaska
Yukon Territory
Inuvik
Wiseman
Coldfoot
Fort McPherson
Porcupine River
Fort Yukon
Beaver
U.S.A.
CANADA
Dempster Hwy.
Circle
Livengood
Steese Hwy.
Circle Hot Springs
Chena Hot Springs
Yukon-Charley Rivers Nat. Preserve
North Pole
Eagle
Dawson City
Delta Junction
Tanana River
Chicken
Taylor Hwy.
Klondike Hwy.
Richardson Hwy
Cantwell
Tok
Tetlin Junction
Denali Hwy.
Paxson
Denali
Tok Cutoff
Port Alcan
Mentasta Lake
Canol Rd.
Beaver Creek
Carmacks
Campbell Highway
Glenn Hwy.
Glennallen
Copper Center
Burwash Landing
Alaska Hwy.
Chugach Mts.
Kennicott
Destruction Bay
Valdez
McCarthy
Whittier
Chugach St. Park
Haines Junction
Tagish Rd.
Whitehorse
Cordova
Kluane Nat.Park
Carcross
Atlin Rd.
Prince William Sound
Chugach Nat. Forest
Wrangell-Saint Elias National Park & Res.
St.Elias Range
Atlin
Cassiar
Cassiar Highway
Skagway
Haines
Glacier Bay Nat. Park & Res.
Juneau
GULF OF ALASKA
Tenakee Springs
Chichagof Is.
Tongass Nat. Forest
Sitka
Petersburg
Baranof Is.
Wrangell
see map of Southcentral Alaska
Ketchikan
PACIFIC OCEAN
Prince of Wales Island
For an enlargement of this area,
see map of Southeastern Alaska

matters to a head. Natives increased the pressure for settlement of the claims that had been so long ignored and sought a share in the anticipated economic boom.

In December of 1971, the federal government finally made its peace with the native peoples, state and federal courts, and environmental groups by passing the Alaska Native Claims Settlement Act. Native Alaskans, who then numbered around 60,000, received a total of $1 billion and 40 million acres of land; unfortunately, these riches did not come without a price. "No trespassing" signs have shot up all over, and native corporations have been compelled to sell natural resources in exchange for the almighty dollar. Native-held land displays some of the state's ugliest logging scars, including the ragged moonscape of Prince of Wales Island.

Black Gold

In 1973, the Alyeska Pipeline Service Company received official permission to build a pipeline from Prudhoe Bay to Valdez—800 mi. through the heart of the Alaskan wilderness. This single pipeline has had a revolutionary effect on the state's political, social, and economic landscape. By 1981, four years after the Trans-Alaska pipeline was installed, $7,200,000 worth of crude oil—the exact price Seward had paid for the state more than 100 years before—flowed from the Arctic oil field every 4½ hours. State revenues from oil taxation have created a trust fund in the name of the people of Alaska and eliminated state sales and income tax.

In addition to jobs and wealth, the pipeline has brought pollution, drastic population growth, profligate spending, and, in some cases, tragedy. Twenty-five years to the day after the Good Friday earthquake of 1964 leveled the port city of Valdez, the Exxon oil tanker *Valdez* ran aground on Bligh Reef, spilling over 250,000 barrels (11 million gallons) of syrupy crude oil into the blue waters of Prince William Sound and onto shores as far away as Kodiak Island, several hundred miles to the south. Thousands of marine mammals and birds succumbed to the thick black tide that swept the Sound. By the summer of 1990, no oil was visible to the casual observer, but the long-term effects of the spill are uncertain at best; in addition to poisoning thousands of marine mammals and birds, the oil has disrupted feeding cycles in the sound and threatened the communities whose livelihoods come from the sea.

The tremendous uproar surrounding the spill underscored the present shift taking place within the Alaskan economy. Even as the pipeline's profits are divided among the oil companies, native corporations, and the state and federal governments, the oil rush has begun to subside. Alaskans are starting to realize that the vast expanses of unspoiled land, not to be found anywhere else in the U.S., are their most marketable commodity. Today, tourism is the state's second most important source of income. The astounding sum of Exxon's payment in the wake of the *Valdez* disaster—$3.4 billion in clean-up operations, plus $100 million in restitution to the state and federal governments and $25 million in criminal fines—attests to the growing political clout of the proponents of preservation and ecotourism.

Recent Events

For years, oil barons have been clamoring to perform exploratory drilling in and around the Arctic National Wildlife Refuge (ANWR), an enormous swath of land in the northwestern part of the state virtually untouched by anyone but a few Aleuts, several thousand caribou, and billions of mosquitoes. The oil companies claim that added federal and state revenue, as well as new jobs produced by a major oil strike, would be an economic boon to all Alaskans. Environmentalists, however, argue that the drilling would disrupt the pristine wilderness and the animals that depend on it. In 1997, a case on the legality of drilling the coastal plains surrounding ANWR went before the U.S. Supreme Court. The ultimate fate of Alaska's resources still hangs in the balance.

Further Reading

A rich literature exists for those who seek a deeper appreciation of the Great Land than reruns of *Northern Exposure*. John McPhee's *Coming Into the Country* sketches a fascinating overview of Alaskan issues and wilderness lifestyles. *Arctic*

Dreams, by Barry Lopez, employs science, natural history, poetry, and philosophy to paint a compelling portrait of the north. Jon Krakauer's *Into The Wild,* about the 1992 disappearance and death of Christopher McCandless in Denali National Park, makes compelling, if discouraging, reading. *Going to Extremes* by Joe McGinniss and *Alaska: The Sophisticated Wilderness* by Jon Gardey both acquaint the reader with Alaskan settlers seeking refuge from the lower 48. Finally, the venerable *Tundra Times,* founded in part by the legendary Inuit journalist Howard Rock, publishes out of Anchorage and provides the most up-to-date discussions of current Native American issues without glossing over internal diversity and factionalism.

For fictional Alaskana, dust off your grade school reader and rediscover Jack London's classic tales of gold rush adventure, *White Fang* and *The Call of the Wild.* James Michener's monster epic *Alaska* takes many liberties with historical fact, but does justice to the scope of the region and its dramatic past. Just don't drop it on your foot. And, of course, the lovable half-wits of Cicely, AK, continue to frolic in TV syndication on *Northern Exposure,* filmed for five years in Roslyn, WA, but allegedly based on the real life Talkeetna, AK.

PRACTICAL INFORMATION

Capital: Juneau.

Visitors Information

Alaska Division of Tourism, 33 Willoughby St., 9th Floor; P.O. Box 110801, Juneau 99811-0801 (465-2010; fax 465-2287). Open Mon.-Fri. 8am-5pm.

Alaska Public Lands Information Center and **National Park Service,** 605 W. 4th Ave. #105, Anchorage 99501 (271-2737), in the Old Federal Bldg. Help in crossing any and all wilderness areas. Extensive audio-visual displays and other resources. Branch offices in Fairbanks, Ketchikan, and Tok. Open daily 10am-5:30pm.

Alaska State Division of Parks, 3601 C St. #200, Anchorage 99510 (269-8400). Information on camping and other activities at all state parks. Open Mon.-Fri. 11am-5pm.

United States Forest Service, 101 Egan Dr., Juneau 99801 (586-8751). General information regarding national parks and reserves. Open daily 8am-5pm, winter Mon.-Fri. 9am-5pm.

Alaska Department of Fish and Game, 1255 West 8th St., P.O. Box 25526, Juneau 99802-5526 (465-4112/4100). Information on hunting and fishing regulations. Open Mon.-Fri. 8am-5pm.

Alaska State Employment Service, 10002 Glacier Highway #200, Juneau 99801 (465-4562). Information on jobs. Open Mon.-Fri. 8am-5pm.

Legislative Information Office, 716 W. 4th Ave. #200, Anchorage 99501-2133 (258-8111). For the scoop on Alaska's juicy political debates. Or call the **Alaska State Government General Information** service at 269-7460.

United States Customs Service: 202-927-5580. This Washington, DC office will connect you with the Canadian Customs and Excise office for information regarding the rules and regulations of traveling through Canada on your way to Alaska.

Pay phones: In many towns, phones will not return coins, even if the party you're calling doesn't answer. Dial, wait until the party picks up, and *then* deposit coins. They will understand the lag.

Population: 607,007. **State Motto:** "We're way bigger than Texas and have more oil!" ***Real* State Motto:** North to the Future. **State Bird:** Willow Ptarmigan. **State Flower:** Forget-Me-Not. **State Fish:** King Salmon. **State Tree:** Sitka Spruce. **State Holiday:** Alaska Day, Oct. 18.

Emergency: 911.

State Troopers: 269-5511; in Anchorage 269-5722; in Fairbanks 451-5100.

Time Zones: Alaska (most of the state; 4hr. behind Eastern Standard Time); Aleutian-Hawaii (Aleutian Islands; 5hr. behind Eastern Standard Time).

Postal Abbreviation: AK.

Sales Tax: None.

Drinking Age: 21.

Area Code: 907.

GETTING AROUND

Most of Alaska's major highways are known by their name, rather than their number. The **Dempster Highway,** for instance, is officially Highway 5, but no one refers to it as such. Driving to and through Alaska is not for the faint of car. See **Northcountry Driving,** p. 31, for advice on taking on the Alaskan road. Alaska's roads reward intrepid drivers with stunning views and access to true wilderness, but they barely scratch the surface of the massive state. The **Alaska Railroad** (see p. 27), constructed in the 1910s and 20s to service mining towns in the Interior, runs nearly 500 miles from Seward to Fairbanks and from Anchorage to Whittier and Valdez. The **Alaska Marine Highway** remains the most practical and enjoyable way to explore much of the Panhandle and the Kenai Peninsula. See p. 32 for info on the Marine Highway, and on the **AlaskaPass,** which combines access to Alaska's railroad, ferry, and bus systems. For Alaska's most remote destinations, air travel is an expensive necessity. Intrastate airlines and charter services, most of them based at the busy Anchorage airport, transport passengers and cargo to virtually every village in Alaska. Many are listed in the relevant **Practical Information** sections of this guide.

Southcentral Alaska

Southcentral Alaska stands on the threshold of Alaska's future, tenuously guarding its past. Anchorage, Prince William Sound, the Kenai Peninsula, and Kodiak Island are becoming more accessible as economic opportunities and an expanding network of well-maintained roads draw more and more escapees from the Lower 48. The cost of living is slowly declining as telecommunications burgeon, and Alaska's isolation, while in little danger of disappearing, is gradually eroding.

Anchorage is rapidly becoming the Strip Mall That Ate Alaska, and might reasonably be mistaken for suburban Los Angeles with some moose mixed in. Kodiak has gone the way of the dollar, as its industrial docks and pricey motels attest. In contrast, in much of the Kenai Peninsula and Prince William Sound, locals and newcomers alike enjoy a slow-paced lifestyle enriched by a cornucopia of cultural and artistic pursuits. Cordova's residents have staunchly refused to be joined by road to Anchorage, electing Green Party members into local government and entrenching their small-town lifestyle. Homer, though accessible by road, has maintained a distinct character and a remarkable population of artists, actors, and aging hippies. Valdez, the southern terminus of the Alaska Pipeline, spits black gold from the trans-Alaskan tube into cavernous tankers, trading the crude oil for a refined—and enormous—economy.

Massive and challenging peaks, rivers churning with fish, and a diverse cast of animal life is within a half-day's travel from Anchorage, and Herculean preservation efforts like the brand-new, $50 million Sea Life Center in Seward testify to Southcentral's foothold in the Great Outdoors. But the pristine and untouched expanses which, to many, define Alaska, are receding.

Anchorage

Even 80 years ago, cartographers wasted no ink on the modest tent city that is now Alaska's foremost metropolis. Almost half the state's population—about 250,000 people—lives in this overgrown strip mall unflatteringly nicknamed "Los Anchorage." The city achieved its comparatively monstrous size by serving as the headquarters of three economic "projects": the Alaska Railroad, WWII, and the Trans-Alaska Pipeline. Writer John McPhee has called it "condensed, instant Albuquerque." Anchorage sprawls for miles along highways and side streets; travelers search in vain for a downtown at the heart of the suburbs. Only the breathtaking wilderness that surrounds the pre-fab city redeems its obnoxious sprawl.

PRACTICAL INFORMATION AND ORIENTATION

Visitors Information: Log Cabin Visitor Information Center (274-3531; events hotline 276-3200), on W. 4th Ave. at F St. Crammed with visitors and volunteers. A new building behind the cabin is typically less crowded and has more brochures. Lots of maps, including the 50¢ **Bike Trails** guide. Open June-Aug. daily 7:30am-7pm; May and Sept. 8am-6pm; Oct.-April 9am-4pm. Smaller info outlets at the **airport** (266-2437) in the domestic terminal near the baggage claim (terminal open daily 9am-5pm); in the international terminal in the central atrium (terminal open during flight arrivals 10am-5pm); and the **Parkgate Building** in Eagle River (696-4636), 11723 Old Glenn Hwy. Call 276-3200 for a **recorded calendar** of weekly events. **Alaska Public Lands Information Center,** Old Federal Bldg., 605 W. 4th Ave., (271-2737), between F and G St. combines the **Park Service, Forest Service, Division of State Parks,** and the **Fish and Wildlife Service** under 1 roof. Popular **topographic maps,** a computerized **sportfishing map,** and live presentations on Alaska's outdoor attractions. Open daily 9am-5:30pm.

Fishing Information: Alaska Department of Fish and Game, 333 Raspberry Rd. (344-0541 or 349-4687 for recording). Open Mon.-Fri. 8am-5pm.

Employment: Alaska Employment Service; P.O. Box 107024, 3301 Eagle St. (269-4800). Take bus #3. Open Mon.-Fri. 8am-5pm.

Currency Exchange: Thomas Cook, 311 F St. (278-2822 or 800-CURRENCY/287-7362), next to the Hilton. Open summer Mon.-Fri. 8am-6pm, Sat. noon-4pm.

Airport: Anchorage International Airport, (266-2525). Serviced by 8 international and 15 domestic carriers, including **Delta** (800-221-1212), **Northwest Airlines** (800-225-2525), **United** (800-241-6522), and **Alaska Airlines** (800-426-0333). Smaller airlines like **Reno Air** (800-736-6247) have cheap deals. Nearly every airport in Alaska can be reached from Anchorage, either directly or through a connecting flight in Fairbanks. An entire section of the classified ads in the *Daily News* lists secondhand tickets. See also **Charter Flights and Ticket Consolidators,** p. 26.

Trains: Alaska Railroad, 411 W. 1st Ave., Anchorage 99510-7500 (265-2494, outside AK 800-544-0552). To: Denali ($100); Fairbanks ($150); and Seward ($50). No service to Seward in winter. A summertime "flagstop" also runs between Talkeetna and Hurricane, Thurs.-Sun. ($16). The train will make unscheduled stops anywhere along this route. Just wave it down with a white cloth and wait to be acknowledged with a whistle. For more info write to P.O. Box 107500, Anchorage. Ticket window open Mon.-Fri. 5:30am-5pm, Sat.-Sun. 5:30am-3pm.

Buses: Alaskon Express (800-544-2206). Daily to: Seward ($40); Valdez ($65); and Portage ($30). 3 per week to Haines ($185 plus overnight) and Skagway ($205). **Homer Stage Lines** (272-8644). To Homer daily except Sun. ($45). **Alaska Direct** (277-6652). To Whitehorse, YT (3 per week, $145).

Public Transportation: People Mover Bus (343-6543), in the Transit Center on 6th Ave. between G and H St. Buses leave from here to all points in the Anchorage area, 6am-10pm; restricted schedule on weekends. Cash fare $1, tokens 90¢, day pass $2.50 (purchase in the Transit Center). **Free fare zone** bordered by 5th Ave., Denali St., 6th Ave., and L St. Office open Mon.-Fri. 8am-5pm and has a 50¢ **map.** Service is only hourly to most spots, so plan ahead.

Ferries: Alaska Marine Highway, 333 W. 4th St. (272-7116), in the Post Office Mall. No terminal, but ferry tickets and reservations. Open Mon.-Fri. 9am-5:30pm.

Taxi: Yellow Cab, 272-2422. **Checker Cab,** 276-1234. **Alaska Cab,** 563-5353. About $13 from airport to downtown hostel. All 24hr.

Car Rentals: Affordable Car Rental, 4707 Spenard Rd. (243-3370), across from the Regal Alaskan Hotel. $36 per day plus 30¢ per mi. after 50; $50 per day for unlimited mileage. Must be 21 with major credit card. Free drop-off and pick-up from downtown or the airport. **Airport Car Rental,** 502 Northern Lights Blvd. (277-7662). $45 per day with unlimited mileage. Must be 21; $5 per day surcharge if under 25. Cash or credit card deposit required. Free shuttle to and from airport. Open Mon.-Fri. 8am-7pm, Sat. 8am-6pm, Sun. 8am-5pm.

Ride Board: At the **Anchorage Youth Hostel** (see **Accommodations,** below).

Bicycle Rental: Downtown Bicycle Rental (279-5293 or 279-8337), on 5th St. near C St. 7 blocks from the Coastal Trail. $11 per 4hr., $14 per 6hr., $18 per day. Lock, helmet, map, and gloves included. Credit card required. Open daily 9am-9pm.

Camping Equipment: Recreational Equipment, Inc. (REI), 1200 Northern Lights Blvd. (272-4565), near Spenard at Minnesota. High-quality packs, clothing, tents, stores, and dried foods. Open Mon.-Fri. 10am-9pm, Sat.-Sun. 10am-6pm. The **Army-Navy Store** (279-2401), on 4th Ave. across from the Post Office Mall. Good prices, but caters mostly to hunters and fishers. Open Mon.-Fri. 9am-8pm, Sat. 9am-6pm, Sun. 10am-5pm. For buying or selling **used equipment,** try **Play It Again Sports** (278-7529), at 27th and Spenard near REI. Rotating inventory of quality fishing and camping equipment at discount prices. Open Mon.-Fri. 10am-8pm, Sat. 10am-6pm, Sun. 11:30am-5:30pm.

Bookstore: Cook Inlet Books, 415 W. 5th Ave. (258-4544). Claims to offer the largest selection of Alaskana anywhere. Terrific collection of cheap classics. Open daily 8:30am-10pm. For a dog-eared copy of *White Fang,* try **C&M Used Books,** 215 E. 4th Ave. (278-9394). Open Mon.-Tues. and Thurs.-Fri. 10am-7pm, Wed. and Sat. 10am-6pm. **Title Wave,** 1068 W. Fireweed Lane (278-9283). A tsunami of used tomes. Open Mon.-Sat. 10:30am-6:30pm, Sun. noon-5pm.

Library: ZJ Loussac Library (261-2975), at 36th Ave. and Denali St. Take bus #2 or 60. The massive $40 million building devotes an entire wing to Alaskan material. Open Mon.-Thurs. 11am-9pm, Fri.-Sat. 10am-6pm; winter also Sun. noon-6pm.

Laundromat: K-Speed Wash, 600 E. 6th St. (279-0731). Wash $1.50, 7min. dry 25¢. Open Mon.-Sat. 7am-10pm.

Weather: 936-2525. **Motorists and Recreation Forecast:** 936-2626. **Road Conditions Report:** 273-6037. **Marine Weather Forecast:** 936-2727.

Crisis Line: 272-4048. 24hr. **Rape Crisis Line:** 276-7273 or 800-478-8999. 24hr.

Disabilities Access Line: Challenge Alaska, 563-2658.

Gay and Lesbian Helpline: 258-4777.

Hospital: Columbia Alaska Regional Hospital, 2801 DeBarr Rd. (264-1224).

STD Information: 343-4611. **HIV/AIDS Information: Alaska AIDS Assistance Association,** 276-4880 or 800-478-AIDS/2437.

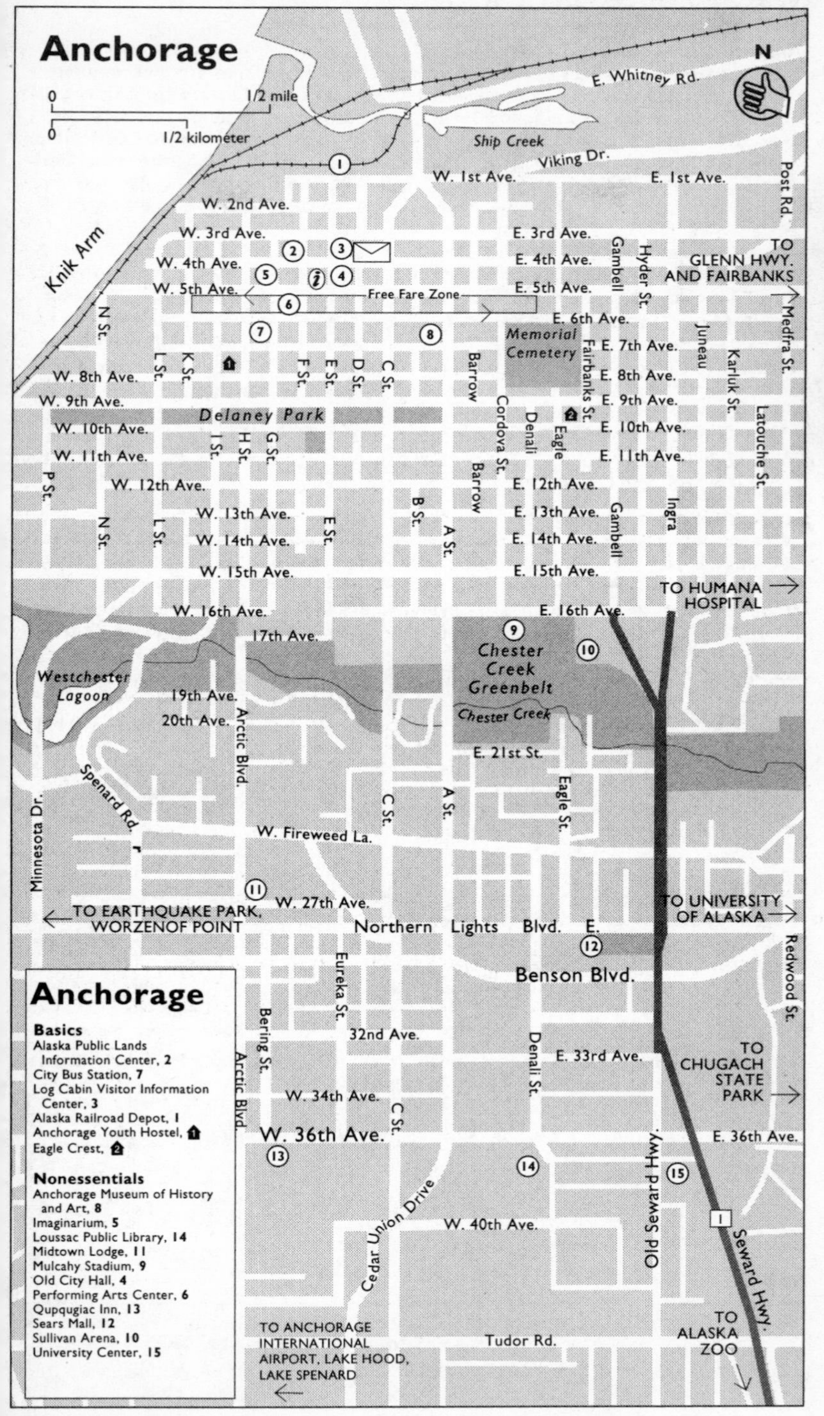
Anchorage
0 1/2 mile
0 1/2 kilometer
N
E. Whitney Rd.
Ship Creek
Viking Dr.
W. 1st Ave.
E. 1st Ave.
Post Rd.
Knik Arm
W. 2nd Ave.
W. 3rd Ave.
E. 3rd Ave.
W. 4th Ave.
E. 4th Ave.
W. 5th Ave.
E. 5th Ave.
Free Fare Zone
TO GLENN HWY. AND FAIRBANKS
E. 6th Ave.
Memorial Cemetery
E. 7th Ave.
E. 8th Ave.
E. 9th Ave.
E. 10th Ave.
E. 11th Ave.
W. 8th Ave.
W. 9th Ave.
Delaney Park
W. 10th Ave.
W. 11th Ave.
W. 12th Ave.
W. 13th Ave.
W. 14th Ave.
W. 15th Ave.
W. 16th Ave.
17th Ave.
E. 12th Ave.
E. 13th Ave.
E. 14th Ave.
E. 15th Ave.
E. 16th Ave.
TO HUMANA HOSPITAL
Chester Creek Greenbelt
Chester Creek
Westchester Lagoon
19th Ave.
20th Ave.
E. 21st St.
Spenard Rd.
Arctic Blvd.
W. Fireweed La.
Minnesota Dr.
W. 27th Ave.
TO EARTHQUAKE PARK, WORZENOF POINT
Northern Lights Blvd. E.
TO UNIVERSITY OF ALASKA
Benson Blvd.
Redwood St.
Eureka St.
Bering St.
32nd Ave.
E. 33rd Ave.
TO CHUGACH STATE PARK
W. 34th Ave.
W. 36th Ave.
E. 36th Ave.
Cedar Union Drive
W. 40th Ave.
Old Seward Hwy.
Seward Hwy.
TO ANCHORAGE INTERNATIONAL AIRPORT, LAKE HOOD, LAKE SPENARD
Tudor Rd.
TO ALASKA ZOO
N St.
L St.
K St.
F St.
E St.
D St.
C St.
B St.
A St.
I St.
H St.
G St.
P St.
Barrow
Cordova St.
Denali
Eagle
Fairbanks St.
Gambell
Hyder St.
Juneau
Karluk St.
Latouche St.
Medfra St.
Ingra
Eagle St.
Denali St.
Anchorage
Basics
Alaska Public Lands Information Center, 2
City Bus Station, 7
Log Cabin Visitor Information Center, 3
Alaska Railroad Depot, 1
Anchorage Youth Hostel, 1
Eagle Crest, 2
Nonessentials
Anchorage Museum of History and Art, 8
Imaginarium, 5
Loussac Public Library, 14
Midtown Lodge, 11
Mulcahy Stadium, 9
Old City Hall, 4
Performing Arts Center, 6
Qupqugiac Inn, 13
Sears Mall, 12
Sullivan Arena, 10
University Center, 15

ALASKA

Emergency: 911. **Police:** 786-8500.

Internet Access: Surf City Cafe: 415 L St. (279-7877). Charges 10¢ per min. Open Mon.-Fri. 7am-midnight, Sat.-Sun. 9am-midnight. **Loussac Library** (see above) has free internet access (30min. limit), but no swanky leather chairs.

Post Office (279-3062), W. 4th Ave. and C St. on the lower level in the mall. Open Mon.-Fri. 10am-6:30pm, Sat. 10am-4pm. Stamp machine in lobby open 24hr. **General Delivery ZIP Code:** 99510. The **state's central post office** (266-3259) is next to the airport. It does not handle general delivery mail, but is open 24hr.

Area Code: 907.

From its seat 114 mi. north of Seward on the Seward Highway, 304 mi. west of Valdez on the Glenn and Richardson Highway, and 358 mi. south of Fairbanks on the George Parks Highway, Anchorage serves as the transportation hub of Southcentral Alaska.

The city sprawls across some 50,000 acres of the **Anchorage Bowl,** framed by military bases to the north, the Chugach Mountains to the east, and the Knik and Turnagain Arms of the Pacific to the west and south. **Downtown** Anchorage is laid out in a grid. Numbered avenues run east-west, and addresses are designated east or west from **C Street.** North-south streets are lettered alphabetically west of **A Street,** and named alphabetically east of A Street. The rest of Anchorage spreads out along the major highways. The **University of Alaska** lies on 36th Ave., off Northern Lights Blvd.

ACCOMMODATIONS

Anchorage is blessed with a multitude of hostel and quasi-hostel accommodations. Hotels and B&Bs—especially downtown—are expensive. Even most so-called "budget" motels start at $75. Try **Alaska Private Lodgings** (258-1717) or **Stay With a Friend,** 704 W. 2nd St. Suite #2 (272-5909) for out of town B&B rooms (from $50).

Anchorage International Youth Hostel (HI-AYH), 700 H St. (276-3635), at 7th St., 1 block south of the city bus station on the edge of downtown. Somewhat subdued, but you can't beat the facilities: kitchens, TV, balconies, and laundry. Lockout noon-5pm. Curfew 1am; watchman can check you in until 2am. 5-night max. stay in summer. Pay by 11am or lose your spot. $15, nonmembers $18; photo ID required. Filled to the rafters in summer; write or call ahead for reservations.

Spenard Hostel, 2845 W. 42nd Pl. (248-5036). Take bus #7 from downtown or #6 from the airport out Spenard to Turnagain Blvd. 42nd Pl. is the 1st left from Turnagain. Not an ideal neighborhood, but a comfortable alternative to the gargantuan downtown facility. 3 kitchens, free local calls, bike rental to guests ($5). No curfew, no lockout. Chore requested. 6-day max. stay. Beds $15.

Qupqugiaq Inn, 640 W. 36th Ave. (563-5633), between Arctic Blvd. and C St. Take bus #9. Common lounge and kitchen, private rooms with locks. Rooms face the occasionally noisy street. No smoking or alcohol; common areas closed at 10pm. Singles from $27; doubles $30. No reservations; get there by 3pm to get a room.

Camping

Excellent camping opportunities await in nearby **Chugach State Park** (354-5014). Two of the best areas are **Eagle River** ($15) and **Eklutna** (EE-kloot-nah; $10), respectively 12½ mi. and 26½ mi. northeast of Anchorage along Glenn Hwy. The secluded wooded spots are popular with locals; show up early, especially on weekends.

Centennial Park, 5300 Glenn Hwy. (333-9711), north of town off Muldoon Rd. Take bus #3 or 75 from downtown. 90 sites for tents and RVs. Showers, dumpsters, fireplaces, pay phones, water. 7-day max. stay. Quiet hours 10pm-6am. Noon checkout. Sites $13, Alaskans or Golden Age $11. Open May-Sept.

FOOD

The largest city in Alaska presents travelers with the most affordable and varied culinary fare in the state. Natch. The **Great Harvest Bread Company,** 570 E. Benson Blvd. (274-3331), stocks great fresh bread. A loaf starts around $5, but slices are free (open Mon. 10am-6pm, Tues.-Fri. 7am-6pm, Sat. 7am-5pm). The 24-hour **Carr's** (277-2609), at 13th and Gambell St., has groceries a 1 mi. walk from the hostel. At night, take bus #11; this neighborhood is tough for the six months per year it's dark.

Twin Dragon, 612 E. 15th Ave. (276-7535), near Gambell. Take bus #11. Lures hungry travelers with promises of great Mongolian barbecue. (Are there really barbecues in Mongolia?) One of the town's finest dining delights. The all-you-can-eat buffet includes marinated meats and vegetables, hot off the giant grill. Lunch $6.50; dinner $10. Open Mon.-Sat. 11am-midnight, Sun. 1pm-midnight.

Moose Tooth, 3300 Old Seward (258-ALES/2537). Take bus #2 or #36. Named for one of Denali's high neighbors, Moose Tooth provides eats as hearty as the climbers who tackle the peak. Revel in fresh, tasty pizza, sip Moose Tooth's own beers, and enjoy the relaxed atmosphere. Caters to the healthy at heart—3 no-cheese pizzas for vegans. Try the "Popeye" (small spinach pizza, $8.75) and Raspberry Wheat beer ($3.25). Family atmosphere changes at night to a popular hang-out for the young and restless. Open daily 11am-midnight.

L'Aroma (562-9797), in New Sagaya's City Market. American, Mexican, Asian, and Italian dishes abound in this deli-style cafe. Pick up a burrito ($5) or tasty pizza ($6) and enjoy the outdoor patio, or brightly painted garage. When you've had your fill of lunch and Alaskan yuppies, hit the road with a scoop of Italian gelato ($1.25).

Kumagoro Restaurant, 533 4th Ave. (272-9905). The fish may be Alaskan, but the atmosphere is anything but: wooden thatched walls, hanging potted plants, and tasteful art give an ambiance appropriate to Japan. Skip the pricey dinners; daily lunch specials (served 11:30am-2pm) include dishes like halibut teriyaki with soup, rice, and vegetables ($7.25). Bar and restaurant open daily 11am-11pm. Sushi bar open 11am-2:30pm and 5-11pm.

Downtown Deli, 525 W. 4th Ave. (276-7116). A nod to the New York deli, this upbeat cafe offers meals never dreamed of in Manhattan. Democrats can sit on the outdoor patio and mull over the next two years while enjoying the reindeer stew Bill Clinton complimented ($10). Budget-minded Republicans may opt for one of the sandwiches ($6). Open daily 6am-10pm.

Blondie's Cafe (279-0698), at the corner of 4th and D St. Bizarre combination of neon-pink zebra carpeting and Iditarod memorabilia dresses looks like a reincarnation of the gold rush, but this time in drag. Outdoor seating, too. All-day breakfast includes 3 hotcakes for $7.50. Open daily 5am-11pm.

Muffin Man, 529 I St. (279-6836). Enjoy the fruits of a creative muffin mind. Raspberry ripple or apple crumble (75¢, jumbo $1.50). Bagels, oatmeal, and sandwiches, too. Open Mon.-Fri. 6am-3pm, Sat. 6am-2pm.

Thai Cuisine, 444 H St. (277-8424). This pleasant restaurant performs two noteworthy feats: it serves terrific Thai fare and avoids the hordes that mob many downtown restaurants. 18 vegetarian dishes. Open Mon-Sat. 11am-10pm, Sun. 4-10pm.

Cafes and Coffeehouses

Side Street Espresso, 428 G St. (258-9055). A gathering spot for the hip and the yup, with weekly political salons, frequent acoustic music, a decent book exchange, and bound copies of local writers' efforts. Sip a cappuccino ($2) or espresso ($1.50) beneath Anchorage artists' more abstract meanderings. Open Mon.-Fri. 7am-7pm, Sat. 7am-5pm, Sun. 8am-5pm.

Sorella's Coffee and Cafe, 335 E St. (274-0070). A far cry from the meat and potatoes restaurants of the old Bush days, Sorella's caters to liquid dieters with a variety of fruit and vegetable smoothies. The "Not-Short-On-Flavor" smoothie ($5.25) lives up to its billing as a jubilee of flavor and taste. Hungry travelers wanting more than a squished carrot can buy the hummus wrap for $4.50.

Firehouse Cafe (562-5555), on the corner of Spenard and Benson St. Flamingo-pink exterior. Converted warehouse that does little to hide its past. Wisecracking counter boys and an alternateen crowd joined by hippies on acoustic evenings. Recently expanded menu includes pasta and other "real food." Killer drinks. Tall latté ($2.25); mocha ($2.75). Open Mon.-Fri. 6am-11pm, Sat.-Sun. 8am-11pm.

SIGHTS AND ACTIVITIES

Watching over Anchorage from Cook Inlet is **Mt. Susitna,** known to locals as the "Sleeping Lady." Legend has it that it marks the resting spot of an Athabascan maid who dozed while awaiting her lover's return from war. When peace reigns in the world, the stories say, she will awake. Closer to town off Northern Lights Blvd., **Earthquake Park** recalls the 1964 Good Friday quake, the strongest ever recorded in North America, registering 9.2 on the Richter scale.

Walk, skate, or bike to the **Tony Knowles Coastal Trail,** an 11 mi. paved track that skirts Cook Inlet on one side and the backyards of Anchorage's upper-crust on the other. The heavily traveled trail is arguably one of the best urban bike paths in the country, weaving through lush forests with glimpses of Cook Inlet. In the winter it is groomed for cross-country skiing.

The **Anchorage Museum of History and Art,** 121 W. 7th Ave. (343-6173), at A St., is the best museum in town. It features permanent exhibits of Native Alaskan artifacts and art, as well as national and international art. The gallery gives tours daily at 10 and 11am, 1 and 2pm ($5, seniors $4.50, under 18 free). The **Alaska Aviation Heritage Museum,** 4721 Aircraft Dr. (248-5325), provides a fun look at Alaska's pioneer aviators. The collection includes 22 rare planes, dated 1928-1952, some salvaged from remote Bush areas, and a theater featuring tales of aerial adventure and derring-do. A free shuttle runs from the airport (open daily 9am-6pm; admission $5.75, seniors $4.50, youths $2.75, military personnel and AAA members $4.50).

Just in case you haven't glimpsed any of Alaska's animals in the wild, you're guaranteed to spot them at the **Alaska Zoo,** Mile 2 on O'Malley Rd. (346-3242). Take bus #91. **Binky the Polar Bear** mauled an Australian tourist here in 1994 and became a local hero (open daily 9am-6pm; $6, seniors $5, under 18 $4, under 12 $3). He has since passed away. (*Let's Go* does not recommend attempting to endear yourself to locals by maiming tourists. Unless they're *really* asking for it.)

Glacier tours are an excellent way to spend what might otherwise be hours of aimless wandering through the mean streets of Anchorage. **Philips' 26 Glacier Cruise,** 509 W. 4th Ave. (276-8023 or 800-544-0529), actually departs from Whittier, but most opt for a round-trip journey from Anchorage instead. The five-hour voyage travels 110 mi. through College and Harriman Fjords and brings you close to six tidewater glaciers (the other 20 are worshiped from afar). It's one of the best opportunities in the state to witness the amazing spectacle of huge chunks of ice plummeting into the ocean. The 26 Glacier Tour is far from cheap: $121 plus a round-trip to Whittier.

SHOPPING

Works from the Alaskan Bush are sold at the **Alaska Native Arts and Crafts Showroom,** 333 W. 4th Ave. (274-2932). Birch baskets, beadwork and other jewelry, and ivory carvings tempt all (open in summer Mon.-Fri. 10am-7pm, Sat. 10am-6pm, Sun. noon-5pm; in winter Mon.-Fri. 10am-6pm, Sat. 10am-5pm). More made-in-Alaska products, as well as made-in-Alaska produce and fish, are available at the outdoor **Saturday Market** (276-7207), at the Lower Bowl parking lot at the corner of 3rd and E St., held on Saturdays from May through early September.

For an unconventional shopping experience, head to a non-profit gift shop at the **Alaska Native Medical Center,** 4315 Diplomacy Drive (729-1122), off Tudor Rd. Many native Alaskans pay for medical services with their own arts and handicrafts, and the proceeds from these works go to scholarships and aid the native community. Walrus bone *ulus* (a type of knife), fur moccasins, parkas, and dolls highlight the selection (open Mon.-Fri. 10am-2pm). Bargain shoppers can head to the **Salvation Army Thrift Store,** 533 W. Northern Lights (561-5514). Wide range of cheap secondhand clothing (open Mon.-Sat. 9am-7pm). **Mammoth Music,** 2906 Spenard Rd. (258-3555), stocks a behemoth supply of new and used CDs (open Mon.-Fri. 9am-10pm, Sat. 10am-10pm, Sun. noon-6pm).

ENTERTAINMENT

Trek to the **Alaska Experience Theater,** 705 W. 6th Ave. (276-3730), to experience "Alaska the Greatland," a 40-minute presentation of scenery and wildlife projected on the inner surface of a hemispherical dome. The 70mm film will make your head spin ($7, children 5-12 $4; every hr. 9am-9pm). An earthquake exhibit at the theater costs $5 (children $4). The earth quakes for 35 minutes each hour between 8:50am and 8:30pm. Live entertainment can be found nearby at **Cyrano's Off Center Playhouse,** at 413 D St. (274-2599). Monthly events include music, poetry readings, and comedy. Plans are in the works for a small theater showing cult flicks.

If you're yearning for a touch of Arctic Broadway, the **4th Avenue Theatre,** 630 4th Ave. (257-5600), one block west of the Log Cabin Visitors Center (see **Practical Information,** above), has been faithfully restored to its original 40s decor. The neon-clad building now contains a small grocery and gift shop, and sponsors concerts and comedy. The **Capri Cinema,** 3425 E. Tudor Rd. (561-0064), runs a mix of art flicks and second-run mainstream works ($4). Take bus #75. On a rainy day, park yourself at the **Denali Theater,** 1230 W. 27th St. (275-3106), at Spenard St., where double-features in limbo between the big screen and the video store show for $1.01.

NIGHTLIFE

The brewpub revolution has finally hit Anchorage, and microbrews gush from taps like oil from the pipeline. **Railway Brewing Co.,** 421 W. 1st. (277-1996; http://www.railwaybrews.com), in the railroad depot, offers six tasty creations. The burger-and-brew special is $8 (open Mon.-Thurs. 11am-midnight, Fri.-Sat. 11am-2am, Sun. 10:30am-11pm). **Glacier Brewhouse,** 737 W. 5th Ave. (274-BREW/2739) takes the brewpub upscale. Nachos cost $8, pints $3 (open 11am-11pm daily). If local beer doesn't move you, head to **Humpy's** (276-BEER/2337), at F Ave. and 6th St., a rowdy roadhouse where you can get a draft beer from just about anywhere else ($3.75 and up). Halibut tacos are $7 (open Mon.-Sat. 11am-2am, Sun. noon-2am).

Anchorage's gay and lesbian hotspot is **The Wave,** 3103 Spenard St. (561-9283), a bright, upbeat dance bar with splashy, colorful decor and a loyal clientele, both gay and straight. Stop by on Wednesday for drag shows, or jump into country line dancing on Thursdays. The Granada, a kind of alcoholic Slurpee, may help you get up and get down ($4; open Wed. 8pm-2:30am, Thurs. 7pm-2:30am, Fri.-Sat. 8pm-3am).

In midtown, Alaskans party at the cavernous **Chilkoot Charlie's,** 2435 Spenard Rd. (272-1010), at Fireweed. Take bus #7. You'll pay extra for the elbow room. Charlie's

Does the Word "Mush" Mean Anything to You?

Charlie Darwin would have liked these odds: snow, wind, and frigid cold, separating the women from the girls. The infamous **Iditarod** begins in Anchorage in the first weekend in March. Dogs and mushers alike traverse the trail over two mountain ranges, along the mighty Yukon, and over the frozen Norton Sound to Nome. Alaskan state pride holds that the route is 1049 mi. in honor of Alaska's status as the 49th state (the distance is actually closer to 1100 mi.).

The race commemorates the 1925 rescue of Nome when sled dog mushers ferried 300,000 units of life-saving diptheria serum from Nenana (near Fairbanks) to Nome. The first Iditarod was a 27 mi. jaunt in 1967 organized by historian Dorothy G. Page. By 1973, the first full race was run in 20 days. Today, an average of 57 mushers race each year. The Iditarod record is held by Susan Butcher, who finished in less than 11 days and won the race in 1986, '87, '88, and '90.

The race has recently come under fire by animal-rights activists because of the hardships of sled dogs, some of whom inevitably die en route to Nome. Still, the city turns out in force for the ceremonial start (just outside Anchorage, the teams are unceremoniously loaded onto trucks and shuttled to the actual starting line). For more information contact the **Iditarod Trail Committee,** Dept. M, P.O. Box 870800, Wasilla, AK 99687 (376-5155; http://www.iditarod.com).

is open Mon.-Thurs. 10:30am-2:15am, Fri.-Sat. 11am-2:45am. Just down the road, **Mr. Whitekey's Fly-by-Night Club,** 3300 Spenard Rd. (279-SPAM/7726), serves "everything from the world's finest champagnes to a damn fine plate of **Spam.**" Try Spam nachos ($5.50) or coconut beer-battered Spam ($5). Nightly comedy and "musical off-color follies" play at 8pm ($5-17). Live music after the show on Fri. and Sat. Take bus #7 (open Tues.-Thurs. 4pm-2am, Fri. and Sat. 4pm-3am).

Blues Central, 825 Northern Lights Blvd. (272-1341), at the corner of Arctic St., answers Anchorage's cry for good live music. Take bus #9. This smoky, sophisticated bar sponsors live acts daily and free form Sunday jam sessions. Drafts start at $2.50 (open Mon.-Thurs. 11am-2:30am, Fri. 11am-3am, Sat. 5pm-3am, Sun. 5pm-2:30am).

OUTDOORS

The best thing about visiting Anchorage is that it's easy to leave. Within minutes, travelers can escape suburban sprawl and seek refuge in the 770 sq. mi. of **Chugach State Park,** which surrounds the city to the north, east, and south. The Public Lands office (see **Practical Information,** above) provides a wealth of info on hiking and canoeing in the park. **Eagle River Nature Center,** 12 mi. up Eagle River Rd. off the Glenn Hwy., is another great resource (open Tues.-Sun. 10am-5pm; $3 parking fee).

Chugach offers the avid dayhiker 25 established trails that leave from different points in Anchorage and along the Glenn Hwy. A 15-minute drive from the heart of the city, **Flattop Mountain** (4,500 ft.) provides an excellent view of the inlet, the mountains of the Aleutian Chains, and on a rare clear day, Denali. This most frequently climbed mountain in Alaska—it's an easy but occasionally slippery 2 mi. one-way hike—is crowded at the top. To reach the trailhead without a car, jump on bus #92 to the intersection of Hillside Rd. and Upper Huffman Rd. From there, walk ¾ mi. along Upper Huffman Rd., then right on Toilsome Hill Dr. for 2 mi. Less crowded hikes branch from the **Powerline Trail,** which begins at the same parking lot as Flattop Trail. The **Middle Fork Loop,** ¾ mi. off of Powerline, is a gentle 12 mi. through spruce woods and open tundra.

Twelve miles up Eagle River Road is the trailhead for the **Old Iditarod Trail,** also known as **Crow Creek Pass,** which begins the 26 mi. journey to Girdwood. The entire trip is a good two- to three-day venture, but the first part of the trail, past waterfalls, beaver dams and alpine lakes, makes an excellent dayhike. Five miles along the lush valley lies a tremendous view of water shooting down over the jagged walls of twin falls. Just off Glenn Highway at Mile 26 is the trailhead to **Thunderbird Falls.** The gorge and falls are a leisurely 1 mi. walk from the highway.

Chugach has several trails geared towards the **cyclist.** The **Lakeside Trail** extends 13 mi. one-way from the Eklutna Campground, off Mile 26 of the Glenn Highway. A relatively flat dirt road, the trail follows blue-green **Eklutna Lake** for 7 mi. before entering a steep river canyon. Although the lake is spectacular, the highlight comes when the trail terminates at the base of the Eklutna River. **Kayakers** and **canoeists** also relish the quiet waters of Eklutna Lake. **Lifetime Adventures** (746-4644), at the Eklutna Campground, rents bikes and kayaks. Bikes cost $12 per 4 hr., $20 per day; tandems are twice the price (which seems fair). Double kayaks start at $20 per half-day, $40 per day. Adrenaline junkies turn to **NOVA Riverrunners** (745-5753) for **whitewater rafting** down the Matanuska Valley. Get wet but stay in one piece on the 4½-hour Class III and IV trip ($75).

■ Near Anchorage

GLENN HIGHWAY: ANCHORAGE TO PALMER

The Glenn Highway runs from Anchorage through Glennallen, 189 mi. northeast of Anchorage, to Tok and the Richardson Highway. The first 37 mi. are also the beginning of the George Parks Highway to Denali and Fairbanks.

Leaving Anchorage on 5th Ave., the highway traces the western edge of Chugach State Park. At Mile 26, off the Eklutna exit, is **Eklutna Village Historical Park** (688-

6026), an Athabascan village dating back to 1650 that offers a glimpse into the mingling of Russian and Athabascan culture. The restored village is home the oldest building in greater Anchorage, **St. Nicholas Russian Church,** a small log structure built in 1830 and still used for local services. To see the church, you must take the 45-minute guided tour that leaves from the gift shop (tours $3.50; open mid-May to Sept. daily 10am-6pm).

From Eklutna, the Glenn Highway heads into the **Matanuska Valley.** Farmers who settled this area in the 30s watched in astonishment as the long summer daylight turned garden-scale vegetables into cabbages and potatoes big enough to feed a ship. The valley is still famous for its produce, legal and illegal: those in the know claim that **Matanuska Valley Thunderfuck** is some of the world's best marijuana. (*Let's Go* does not recommend getting thunderfucked.)

Palmer

Near the entrance to the Matanuska Valley is the turn-off for the George Parks Highway. The Glenn Highway soon rolls into the agricultural hamlet of Palmer, home every August to the **Alaska State Fair** (745-4827 or 800-850-FAIR/3247). Palmer's **Visitors Center,** 723 South Valley Way (745-2880), provides the standard info plus specimens of the region's freakishly big fruits and legumes—sorry, no Thunderfuck (open May to mid-Sept. daily 8am-6pm). Four blocks from the visitors center is the artsy alternative to Palmer's agriculture, **Vagabond Blues,** 642 S. Alaska (745-2233). Espresso, live music, and an "open wall" for upstart artists—what is a place this cool doing in Palmer?

A few miles off Parks Hwy., at Mile 50.1 of the Glenn Hwy., lies the **world's only domesticated musk-ox farm.** Introduced from Greenland in 1934, Palmer's domesticated oxen are prized for their fleece, called *qiviut,* the foundation of a cottage industry for Inuit weavers (admission $7, seniors and students $6, under 6 free; open daily 9am-7pm). The musk-oxen's cousins play their little reindeer games at the **Reindeer Farm** (745-4000), on the Bordenburg Butte Loop Rd., off the Old Glenn Hwy., 11 mi. from its southern junction with the Glenn. Hand-feed the affable beasts and pet their babies (open daily 10am-6pm; $5, seniors $4, ages 3-11 $3).

SEWARD HIGHWAY: ANCHORAGE TO PORTAGE

For heart-stopping scenery, just point your wheels south on the Seward Highway from Anchorage, and aim your gaze out the window. The highway runs south along the **Turnagain Arm** of the Cook Inlet, known for its dramatic tidal fluctuations. Miles of the arm are temporarily uncovered at low tide, only to be inundated by 10 ft. "bores," walls of water created as the 15 mph riptide races in. The bore tides generally reach Turnagain Arm two hours after the low tide in Anchorage; consult the *Daily News* for a tidal report. Be careful not to walk on the exposed sand at low tide. About 15 mi. down the arm, at the Seward Mile 117.4, is **Potter Marsh,** a wetlands bird and wildlife sanctuary and one of Alaska's best centers for wildlife photography.

At Mile 90 is the turnoff for the small community of **Girdwood.** Immediately to the left off the turnoff is the **Chugach National Forest Service Visitors Center** (783-3242; open Mon.-Fri. 8am-5pm; call for winter hours). The rangers at the visitors center can provide information on hikes within the protected lands that stretch from just south of Anchorage to Prince William Sound. The most spectacular short hike in the vicinity of Anchorage can be reached along **Crow Creek Road.** Climb the **Old Iditarod Trail** 3½mi. to the base of Raven Glacier on the Crow Pass; the trail continues 26mi. to Crow Creek in Chugach State Park (see p. 62).

Girdwood has a **clinic** (783-1355), and a **post office;** follow signs to the "new townsite" off Hightower (783-2922; open Mon.-Fri. 9am-5pm, Sat. 9am-noon; **ZIP code** 99587). **Eagle Mercantile Grocery** (783-3900) sports a fair selection of groceries along with deli sandwiches (open Sun.-Thurs. 7am-midnight, Fri. and Sat. 7am-1am; $3). **Max's** is the local bar of choice. Make your way past the band of dogs lying at the door and bar, and order a "photon tea" ($4; open daily 4pm-3am.)

Three miles from Mile 90, on the Alyeska Access Rd., lies the **Alyeska Ski Resort** (754-1111), boasting seven chair lifts and a 3934 ft. vertical drop. The resort is open November through April for skiing (full-day ticket around $32). Nearby cross-country and heli-skiing options abound. The **Girdwood-Alyeska Home Hostel (HI-AYH)** (783-2099) is a rustic wooden cabin run by the same folks who manage the Anchorage Hostel. To get there, turn left onto the Alyeska Access Rd., go 2 mi., take a right on Timberline Dr., and another right on Alpina. The hostel has 11 beds and a sauna but no hot showers ($10, nonmembers $13). Winter or summer, it's worth the detour into Alyeska just to visit the **Bake Shop** (783-2831), an outstanding restaurant below the resort. People from across the state sing the praises of its bottomless bowls of soup ($4) and sourdough ($3; open Mon.-Fri. and Sun. 7am-7pm, Sat. 7am-8pm.)

Several miles up pothole-ridden Crow Creek Rd. is the **Double Musky Inn** (783-2822), set back from the road in the trees ¼ mi. from the junction. The Musky deserves its reputation as one of the best restaurants in Alaska. If you can't swing a spicy Cajun-style dinner ($16-30), at least treat yourself to a drink or the double musky pie ($4; open Tues.-Thurs. 5-10pm, Fri.-Sun. 4-10pm).

PORTAGE

The town of Portage, little more than a train and bus stop, is 45 minutes from downtown Anchorage at Mile 80 of the Seward Hwy. The **Alaska Backpacker Shuttle** (344-8775 or 800-266-8625) runs buses between the train station and Anchorage for $20. Hitchers report that rides are easy to find.

The **Portage Highway,** beginning at Seward Mile 78.9, runs through magnificent **Portage Valley.** Four roadside glaciers sit staunchly along the Portage Valley periodically "calving" spectacular blue ice chunks into Portage Lake. One of the best ways to marvel at the region's glaciers is not on a pricey boat tour but on the Whittier-Valdez Ferry (see **Valdez,** p. 89). On the lakeside, the **Begich and Boggs Visitors Center** (783-2326) houses what are perhaps the most modern displays of any Alaskan information outlet. Unfortunately, Portage Glacier is no longer visible from the visitors center. It has receded about 2000 ft.—almost half a mile—since the center's construction (open daily 9am-6pm; winter Sat.-Sun. 10am-4pm). To reach the center, take the 5 mi. detour off Seward Hwy. south of Alyeska, along the well paved Portage Highway. The cheapest official tour may be the one given by **Gray Line** (277-5581), which conducts the seven-hour mother-of-all-tours of Portage Glacier ($55), leaving from Anchorage and including stops at the Visitor Center and Alyeska Ski Resort (daily tours at 9am and noon). Tours run from May to September.

Two state-run campgrounds near Portage—**Black Bear** (tents only; $9) and **Williwaw** ($10)— have excellent sites (water, toilets) with panoramic glacial views. Williwaw also has a short hiking trail and a viewing ledge overlooking salmon-spawning areas. Several short, worthwhile hikes leave from Portage Highway. The wheelchair accessible **Moraine Nature Trail** is a quick half-hour loop with fine views of the glacier and lush green valley. The 1½ mi. **Byron Glacier Trail** begins in an alder forest and continues past Byron Creek, with whitewater rapids stemming from the glacier. For information on the hikes and trails in the area, contact the Anchorage office of the **Chugach National Forest,** 3301 C St., Anchorage 99503 (271-2500).

KENAI PENINSULA

Hope

The only town on the southern side of Turnagain Arm, Hope is the twinkle of lights across the water from the Seward Highway. Without a major salmon run or ferry terminal, this minuscule former gold rush town of 250 remains untrampled.

The first gold discovered in Alaska was found here by Russians as early as 1849, but they kept it secret for fear of losing their claim. The first major American strike was made in 1889, and the town grew to 3000 people years before Anchorage even existed. The boom was short-lived, but many of its relics, and the view of the Turnagain Arm, remain. Much of the federal land around Hope is still open to recreational mining, but more people visit Hope for its pink salmon fishing and tranquil setting. Hope lies near the end of the scenic 18 mi. Hope Highway. This road joins the Seward Hwy. 71 mi. outside of Anchorage, just where it turns sharply south down the Kenai (KEEN-eye) Peninsula toward Seward.

Practical Information The Hope **information center** (782-3268) sits ¼ mi. out Palmer Creek Rd., just before the townsite (open mid-April to mid-Sept. daily 8am-8pm). The center provides information on mining and hiking near Hope; maps of the Resurrection Trail and other excellent hikes. The **post office** (782-3352) sits across from the museum on the way into town (open Mon.-Fri. 8:30am-4:30pm, Sat. 10am-2pm; **General Delivery ZIP Code:** 99605).

Accommodations, Camping, and Food **Porcupine Campground,** at the end of the Hope Hwy., is 1.3 mi. from town. Its waterside sites have a superb view of glimmering inlet water. Deep in the valley beyond Hope, amidst a jubilee of wild flowers, the **Coeur d'Alene Campground** is beautiful and free, and it's a good thing, because it's located 7 mi. up pothole-ridden Palmer Creek Rd. (pit toilets, no water). If you just can't stand camping (what are you doing in Alaska?), **Henry's One-Stop Grocery and Motel,** Mile 15.8 of the Hope Hwy. (782-3222), has motel rooms ($50), showers ($3), full RV hookups ($15), groceries, and laundry facilities (wash $1, dry 75¢; open daily 8:30am-7:30pm; winter Tues.-Sun. 10am-5pm). Henry also sells **fishing** licenses. In town, the **Seaview Motel** (782-3364) rents singles (shared baths) for $35. They also have tent and RV sites ($9, electrical hookups $14).

In late afternoon, the sun slants into the peaceful **Seaview Cafe** (782-3364); marvel at the small-town ambiance over a piece of pie, the Seaview's pride and joy ($3.25). **Tito's Discovery Cafe** (782-3274), located just before the townsite on Hope Hwy., cooks hearty, homemade omelettes in an even homier environment. The cheese omelette starts at $5.25, and sandwiches go for $5 (open Mon.-Thurs. 7:30am-7pm, Fri.-Sun. 7:30am-8pm).

Outdoors Hope is the starting point for one of the most popular and impressive hikes in Southcentral Alaska. The **Resurrection Pass Trail,** originally a 19th-century gold miner byway, leads 39 mi. through the Chugach National Forest from Hope to the Sterling Hwy. This four- to five-day hike traverses mountain passes and lake shores, and extends through aspen forests and alpine tundra. Many people take a week or more to enjoy the wildlife and varied scenery. To reach the Resurrection Pass trailhead, turn south onto Palmer Creek Rd. at Mile 16.2 of the Hope Hwy. and take the immediate right fork to reach Resurrection Creek Rd. The trail begins 4 mi. down the road. No fewer than seven Forest Service **cabins** punctuate this hike. They can be reserved for $9-25, and probably have been, long before you arrived in Alaska; call 800-280-2267 well in advance. The southern trailhead lies on the Sterling Hwy. near Cooper Landing, 106 mi. south of Anchorage and 53 mi. east of Soldotna.

Resurrection Creek is an excellent place to fish and is usually far less crowded than other streams as close to both the Turnagain Arm and the beaten path. The creek is home to dolly varden and every type of salmon except sockeye; fishers can catch supper anytime between June and September. Getting to the creek is easiest near the Old Hope Townsite or off Resurrection Creek Rd. about 5 mi. from the Hope Hwy. The Forest Service permits **recreational gold mining** along Six Mile Creek from Mile 1.5 to 5.5 on the Hope Hwy, beginning at the Resurrection trailhead footbridge off Resurrection Creek Rd.

Seward

Glacier-sculpted mountains slant to the edge of glimmering **Resurrection Bay,** making Seward yet another of Alaska's super-scenic coastal towns. The dramatic blend of land and sea affords outdoor opportunities almost as rich and diverse as the landscape itself; lush alpine trails in nearby **Chugach National Forest,** the impressive tidal glaciers and cascading waterfalls of nearby **Kenai Fjords National Park,** and the teeming fish in Resurrection Bay draw drooling hikers, kayakers, and anglers as well as major cruise lines.

So far, Seward's demure seaside demeanor has endured amid this onslaught; the strip malls that blight its peninsular neighbors, Soldotna and Kenai, have yet to make an appearance. But the unveiling of the $50-million **Sea Life Center** in May 1998 promises to wake Seward from its peaceful slumber. The first cold-water marine research center in the western hemisphere, the facility anticipates more visitors than even Denali National Park. Anchorage, 127 mi. north, is connected to Seward by the scenic **Seward Highway.**

PRACTICAL INFORMATION

Visitors Information: Chamber of Commerce (224-8051), at Mile 2 on the Seward Hwy. Encyclopedic knowledge of Seward. Computerized directory of accommodations and restaurants. Open Mon.-Fri. 8am-5pm, Sat.-Sun. 9am-6pm. Also operates a **railroad car,** at 3rd Ave. and Jefferson St., where you can pick up a self-guided walking tour and mark your home town on the world map. Another information center is located in the small boat harbor. Both are open daily 6am-5pm. **Kenai Fjords National Park Center** (224-3175, info line 224-2132), at the small-boat harbor. Info and **maps** on the spectacular park. Nature talks daily in summer at 5:30pm. Open daily 9am-6pm; in winter Mon.-Fri. 8am-5pm. **Seward Ranger Station, Chugach National Forest,** 334 4th Ave. (224-3374), at Jefferson St. Extensive trail info, maps, and detailed advice on trails close to town. Cabin reservations for the Seward Ranger District (see **Hope: Outdoors,** p.65). Open Mon.-Fri. 8am-5pm.

Employment Service: Seward Employment Center, P.O. Box 1009 (224-5276), 5th Ave. and Adams St., on the 2nd floor of the City Building. Open Mon.-Fri. 9am-noon and 1-4:30pm.

Airport: 2 mi. north of town on Seward Hwy. **Alaska Airlines** (800-426-0333) flies to Anchorage ($69). **Scenic Mountain Air** (288-3646) offers 1hr. flightseeing trips over the fjords ($99 per person, 2 person min.) and a fly-in, hike-out package leaving from Moose Pass at Seward Hwy. Mile 29 ($79 per person, 2 person min.).

Trains: Alaska Railroad (800-544-0552). Depot at the northern edge of town, across from the visitors center. Service to Anchorage nightly in summer ($50).

Buses: Seward Bus Lines, 1914 Seward Hwy. (224-3608). 1 bus per day to Anchorage at 9am ($30, $5 extra for service to the airport).

Ferries: Alaska Marine Highway (224-5485, reservations 800-642-0066). Ferry dock at 4th Ave. and Railway St. Served by the *Tustumena.* 1 per week in summer to: Kodiak ($54); Valdez ($58); and Homer ($96). No service during one week of every month. Call for schedule.

Trolley: Runs through the greater portion of Seward. Designated stops, but will stop if you flag it down ($1.50). Operates daily 10am-6pm. Group tours available.

Taxi: Independent Cab, 224-5000. **PJ's Taxi,** 224-5555. Both 24hr.

Car Rental: Hertz Car Rental (224-4378), in the boat harbor. $70 per day plus 30¢ per mi. over 100. Must be at least 25 with a credit card.

Road Closure Information: 800-478-7675.

Laundromat and Showers: Seward Laundry (224-5727), at 4th Ave. and C St. Wash $2, 5min. dry 25¢. Showers $3.75 per 15min. Open Mon.-Sat. 8am-8pm, Sun. noon-8pm; last wash 7:30pm. Showers also at the Harbormaster Bldg. (5min. $1).

Bookstore: Reader's Delight, 222 4th Ave. (224-2665). Mostly paperbacks, but has a collection of used books-on-tape so you can finally quit listening to that Steely Dan tape you found on your car floor. Open daily 10am-6pm.

Pharmacy: Seward Drug, 224 4th Ave. (224-8989). Open Mon.-Sat. 9am-6pm.

Fishing Supplies: The Fish House (224-3674), across from the Harbormaster. Rent rods ($10), buy tackle. $100 cash or credit card deposit required. Tips and instructions free. Fishing licenses available (see **Fishing,** p. 43). Open daily 6am-10pm.
Crisis Line: 224-3027. 24hr.
Hospital: Seward General (224-5205), 1st Ave. and Jefferson St.
Emergency: 911. **Police:** 224-3338.
Internet Access: In-home Video (224-3008), on 4th Ave. downtown. Email $3; Internet access $15 per hour. Open daily 10am-11pm.
Post Office: (224-3001), at 5th Ave. and Madison St. Open Mon.-Fri. 9:30am-4:30pm, Sat. 10am-2pm. **General Delivery ZIP Code:** 99664.
Area Code: 907.

ACCOMMODATIONS AND CAMPING

Seward offers a host of reasonable housing and camping options, though the tidal wave of visitors each summer often floods these resources. Book well in advance. The visitors center carries information on B&Bs.

Moby Dick Hostel (224-7072), at 3rd Ave. and Madison St. Making a splash in Seward, this newly opened hostel is the cheapest indoor option in town. Cramped quarters and thin beds may make you feel like you're stowed away in the hold. No monomaniacs allowed. $17.50; cash payment $16.50. Showers; full kitchen.

Ballaine House Lodging, 437 3rd Ave., Box 2051 (224-2362). Bright, clean, and well furnished, this charming B&B is conveniently located 2 blocks from downtown. Pleasant rooms, scrumptious breakfast. Generous owner divulges all sorts of info on Seward. Single with breakfast $55; double with breakfast $79. Available at lower rates without breakfast.

Kate's Roadhouse (224-5888). Several miles outside Seward, Kate proffers hostel accommodation in a clean, family-style environment, including a continental breakfast, bedding, well-stocked kitchen, shuttle service into town, two private cabins...and a pig. Startled travelers needn't worry; he lives affably enough in the TV room (though his snoring does get a bit loud at times). 7 beds in one room, $17; private room $59; cabins from $29.

Meg and Pete's Hostel (224-7137), on 3rd Ave. downtown. Meg and Pete offer roomy, clean, but bare-boned accommodations. Kitchen without dishes, common room with TV, laundry ($2), and cots. $20, breakfast included.

Exit Glacier Campground, 8½ mi. down Exit Glacier Rd., off Seward Hwy. Mile 3.7. All budget tenters should set up here: water, pit toilets, secluded sites, and a half-mile walk to Exit Glacier. Stroll to your walk-in tentsite and fall asleep to the far-off ring of the cash register at fee-charging campgrounds. Free.

Municipal Waterfront Campground, along Ballaine Rd. between Railway Ave. and D St. A scenic spot on which to plop, if you nab a grassy plot. Gravel lot hosts many RVs. Toilets are scattered throughout the campground; restrooms and showers at the Harbormaster Bldg. 2-week max. stay. Check-out 4pm. Sites $6; RV $8. Open May 15-Sept. 30.

Farther from Seward, at Mile 29 on Seward Hwy., the nearby town of **Moose Pass** has four campgrounds with excellent fishing: **Primrose** (Mile18; $9), **Ptarmigan Creek** (Mile 23; $9), **Trail River** (Mile 24; $9 single), and **Tenderfoot** (Mile 46; $9). All are run by the **Chugach National Forest;** for info, contact Alaska Public Lands Information, 605 W. 4th, Anchorage 99501 (271-2737). All have pit toilets and water.

FOOD

Although affordable, Seward's food is not its forte. Stock up on groceries at the **Eagle Quality Center,** 1907 Seward Hwy. (224-3698). It's a hike from downtown, but you can reward yourself after the trek with a $1.70 ice-cream cone at the in-store soda fountain (open 24hr.). At night, the younger crowd's bar-hopping usually begins at the **Yukon Bar** (224-3065), at 4th Ave. and Washington St., where travelers pin a dollar to the ceiling to leave a mark in Alaska and protect themselves against the ghastly possibility that they may someday return with an empty wallet. Pool tables and live rock from Thursday to Saturday keep 'em comin' (open daily noon-2am).

Resurrect Art Coffee House Gallery, 320 3rd Ave. (224-7161). Seward's most intriguing coffee shop has arisen in a converted Lutheran church. Food limited to plastic-wrapped muffins and sweets, but the lattés are so good, they're almost sinful ($2.25). Sip your Italian soda ($1.50) at the altar-turned-art display or in the balcony-turned-loft. Art books available for browsing; Luther's Small Catechism is missing. Occasional live music and poetry readings. Open daily 7:30am-10pm.

Peking, 338 4th Ave. (224-5444), at Jefferson St. Tasty lunch specials with rice and soup ($6.25-8), served 11:30am-3pm. The *Kung Pao* halibut is especially scrumptious ($8). Open Mon.-Thurs. 11:30am-10:30pm, Fri.-Sun. 11:30am-11pm.

Ray's (224-5606), located on the waterfront. Reward a hard day's fishing at this harborside haven. Although entrees are on the steep side (from $15), waterfront location and fresh, fresh, fresh seafood make Ray's a choice restaurant for a splurge. Locals land the cioppino ($21), but budget travelers can opt for a bowl of the best seafood chowder in Seward ($6). Reserve a waterside table and relish the view. Open daily 11am-11pm.

Miller's Daughter (224-6091), on waterfront across from the National Park center. This miller's daughter must be a baker's daughter, too. If not, she probably went to a top-flight culinary school and now makes fresh baked bread for the miller, his wife, his children, her boyfriend, his parents, her teachers...and hungry travelers like you. The Seward Sourdough ($4 a loaf) is especially spectacular. Open daily 7am-6pm.

Christo's Palace (224-5255), at 4th Ave. and Railway Ave. Cavernous pizza joint and bar. Wide variety of Italian and Mexican fare; $6 fetches a hearty burger. 16 in. pizza $13. Dinner served until 11pm, pizza until 1am. Open daily 10am-1am.

SIGHTS AND EVENTS

The **Alaska Sea Life Center** (224-3080 or 800-224-2525), at the end of downtown between 3rd and 4th Ave., opening in May 1998 after much state-wide fanfare and anticipation, has become Seward's (and one of Alaska's) most prized attractions even before its salty debut. Created in the wake of the Exxon *Valdez* spill to ensure understanding of marine life, the $50-million center gives visitors a heretofore impossible glimpse at Alaska's coastal and underwater goings-on. More than your average aquarium, the center's informative galleries provide a host of information on marine animals, and the huge outdoor habitats allow the eager to view the creatures in their natural habitat. Watch frisky sea otters play underwater, touch various shell-covered animals, and marvel at nature's splendor (open May-Sept. daily 9am-9:30pm, last tickets sold at 8pm; winter Wed.-Sun. 10am-5pm, last tickets sold at 3:30pm; $12.50, seniors $11.25, ages 4-16 $10).

The self-guided **walking tour** of Seward, detailed on the map available at the visitors center, passes many turn-of-the-century homes and businesses. A complete tour takes two to three hours. The **Resurrection Bay Historical Society Museum,** in the Senior Center building at 3rd Ave. and Jefferson St., exhibits traditional Alaskan artifacts, including a fine collection of woven baskets (open Memorial Day-Labor Day daily 10am-5pm; extended hours when cruise ships are in town; $2, ages 5-18 50¢). Those feeling a bit too sedentary can get all shaken up by the "Earthquake Movie" at the **Seward Community Library** (224-3646), 5th Ave. and Adams St. (mid-June to Sept. Mon.-Sat. 2pm). The movie shows actual footage of the 1964 Good Friday earthquake. With a supporting cast of fires and tsunamis, the quake destroyed much of Seward and Southcentral Alaska (library open Mon.-Fri. noon-8pm, Sat. noon-6pm; $3 donation requested, 12 and under free). The 40-year-old **Liberty Theater,** 304 Adams St. (224-5418), projects current films ($6, $4 for matinees). In the spring of 1994, the Liberty began to show films on their national release date. All of Seward was very, very proud.

The **Silver Salmon Derby** opens each year on the second Saturday in August and closes eight days later. In 1995 the city upped the prize for the elusive tagged fish to

$100,000. No one has caught the fish since 1980, when Japanese tourist Katsumi Takaku nabbed it from the city docks.

The other annual event that gets Seward hopping is the **Mountain Marathon** on the 4th of July. Alaska's oldest footrace, the run began when a sourdough challenged a neighbor to run up and down the 3022 ft. Mt. Marathon in less than an hour. The current record is 43 minutes for men and 50 minutes for women. The race has been joined by a parade while the governor of Alaska and hundreds of fellow competitors run, slide, fall, and bleed down the steep mountainsides to the shores of Resurrection Bay. Thousands of sadistic spectators set up lawn chairs in town and watch the painful spectacle with binoculars. The annual **Seward Silver Salmon 10K Run** takes off during the Labor Day weekend, and the **Exit Glacier 5K and 10K Run** happens in mid-May. While these races may sound tough, Seward's truest test of physical endurance comes in the third weekend of January when the three-day **Seward Polar Bear Jump** plunges participants into the frigid water of Resurrection Bay, resurrecting them from any type of winter in which they may have been hibernating.

OUTDOORS

Just around the corner from **Chugach National Park** and **Kenai Fjords National Park,** Seward's promoters call the town and its environs "Alaska's Playground." If glaciers and waterfalls are the traveler's jungle gym and monkey bars, the claim may well be true.

All sorts of **hiking trails** weave through the high alpine passes and lush valleys between Seward and its neighbor to the north, Portage. Although many of these routes take days, some are easily accessible for dayhikes. The Seward Ranger Station (see **Practical Information,** above) provides helpful information on trails in this area.

A coastal trail weaves through **Caines Head State Recreation Area,** at the mouth of Resurrection Bay. One and a half miles into the 7 mi. trail, there is a 3 mi. stretch negotiable only at low tide. Most hikers stay overnight before returning in order to catch another low tide. Consult the newspaper, the chamber of commerce, the Coast Guard, or any commercial fishing outfitter for tide information. The last 2½ mi. lead along sand, ending at South Beach, where camping is free. Nearby **Mt. Marathon** offers a view of the city and ocean. From 1st Ave. and Jefferson St., take Lowell St. to reach the trail, which begins with a steep ascent up a rocky stream bed. Once above vegetation, a network of trails continues up the rocky ledge to the left. Another route climbs through the scree to the right. The route provides better footing for the ascent, and the scree can be fun to run through on the way down. Unless you're training for the Mountain Marathon (see **Sights and Activities,** above), plan on a two-hour climb to the top and a 45-minute hop-and-slide back down. There is no definitive peak at the end of the trail, but the views over Resurrection Bay are worth it.

The **Lost Lake Trail** is a strenuous dayhike or overnight trip venturing 7 mi. one-way into the mountains. The trail starts at the end of a gravel road at Seward Hwy. Mile 5. Meandering above treeline for about half the trail, Lost Lake offers day hikers a wide-open view of surrounding glacially carved peaks. The trail is open to mountain bikers in the summer, and is popular with cross-country skiers in the winter. Marvel at the interplay of rich lakes and mountain passes on the **Primrose Trail,** which begins at Primrose Campground, 1½ mi. from Mile 17 on the Seward Hwy. Though the first 4 mi. of the 8 mi. trip offer few vistas from a dense spruce forest, persistent travelers can enjoy a view of the glimmering Porcupine Creek Falls which lies off a spur trail at Mile 3. The last two or three miles of the Primrose Trail extend beyond timberline. True to its name, the path is strewn with spectacular wildflowers.

Starting from Seward Hwy. Mile 34, the **Carter Lake Trail** gives grunting hikers a good survey of local terrain. The 6.6 mi. round-trip begins in hemlock forests, but after a steep incline flattens out into fields of wildflowers and low brush, with striking views of peaks and sapphire lakes. To transform this jaunt into a journey, continue on the **Crescent Creek Trail** for another 6.5 mi.

The true path to illumination, however, starts at Sterling Hwy. Mile 52. The **Resurrection Pass Trail** (see **Hope,** p. 64) is a favorite among mountain bikers and weekend hikers—expect to see an eighth of Anchorage's population on this trail on any given Saturday. The **Johnson Pass Trail** serves as another ideal route for a two- to three-day trip. The north trailhead starts at Seward Hwy. Mile 64; turn south on a gravel road ¼ mi. to the trailhead. The south trailhead lies at Seward Hwy. Mile 32.5. A road less traveled, Johnson Pass offers dramatic views of rich emerald meadows, alpine tundra, and spruce forests without the crowds that swarm Resurrection Pass. Johnson Pass Trail is an ideal way to view different Kenai Peninsula ecosystems as it passes through a spruce forest, sub-alpine regions of shrubs, and extends into alpine tundra. The intricate web of trails in this area enable creative hikers to combine some of these routes for longer, more rigorous hikes. Forest cabins are available to the public; check with Chugach National Forest (800-280-CAMP/2267) for locations and availability (see **Practical Information and Orientation,** above).

Salmon and halibut fill the bay, and grayling and dolly varden can be hooked right outside of town. Charters are available for both halibut and salmon throughout the summer; prices run from $95-145, with all gear provided. Call **The Fish House** (800-257-7760; see **Practical Information,** above), the largest charter-booking service in Seward. You can also fish for free from the shore or docks.

KENAI FJORDS NATIONAL PARK

One of Seward's greatest claims to fame is its role as gateway to Kenai Fjords National Park. The park's coastal mountain system is packed with wildlife and glaciers, but is largely inaccessible to novice kayakers unless they care to spend a considerable amount of money and is almost entirely inaccessible to hikers without mountaineering equipment.

The lay traveler does have a few opportunities to revel in the park's glory. The **Exit Glacier** lies 9 mi. west on the road that starts at Mile 3.7 of the Seward Hwy. From the Ranger Station at the end of the road, a leisurely ¾ mi. stroll leads to the impressive base of the glacier, where tremendous crevasses catch trickling water that melts into a roaring stream. The first ½ mi. of this trail is wheelchair accessible. Rangers lead one-hour nature walks four times daily as well as a geology talk Saturday at 2pm. The only significant, accessible hike within the park is the grueling 3000 ft. climb to the top of the Exit Glacier. A full day's scramble, the trail begins at the visitors center (see **Practical Information and Orientation,** above) and continues 4 mi. to the top of the trail. An impressive view, even by Alaskan standards, the summit overlooks **Harding Ice Field,** a glimmering wonderland that encompasses 700 sq. mi. and is the source of over 30 glaciers.

Boat cruises are the easiest and most popular way to see the park beyond Exit Glacier. The best and most expensive cruises access either **Aialik Bay,** for forested terrain and views of wildlife, or **Northwestern Lagoon,** which offers peeks at tidal glaciers and spectacular geological formations. Take either of these trips, and you are likely to see bald eagles, humpback whales, sea otters, Steller's sea lions, and Dall's porpoises frolicking near the bow of your boat. **Kenai Fjords Tours** (224-8068 or 888-4-PUFFIN/478-3346; http://www.kenaifjords.com) runs to the Lagoon ($139, children $59) and Aialik Bay ($99, children $49). **Major Marine Tours** (224-8030 or 800-764-7300; http://majormarine.com) offers another tour to Aialik. For $89 you get a ranger on board to explain wildlife and glacier facts, and an excellent salmon, halibut, and shellfish dinner for an extra $10. There are also a variety of tours within Resurrection Bay, including overnight trips, and it is best to shop around for the type of trip you want. The cheapest start at $54. Pick up a list of charters at the chamber of commerce (see **Practical Information,** above) or from shops along the boardwalk near the harbormaster's office.

For an even closer-to-water experience, **kayaking tours** probe into Resurrection Bay. **Kenai Fjords Kayaks** (224-0024 or 800-992-3960) leads full-day trips for $95 and half-day trips for $65. The best deal is the 2½ hour evening trip for $45. No experience is necessary for this flit over the filmy waters of the bay. **Sunny Cove Sea Kayaking Company** offers a joint trip with Kenai Fjords Tours. The trip includes the

Kenai Fjords Wildlife Cruise and a 3-hour wilderness paddle for $139. Arrangements can be made through Kenai Fjords Tours (see above).

Sterling Highway: To Kenai

The Sterling Highway begins 37 mi. north of Seward at **Tern Lake** and continues south along Cook Inlet to Homer. Shortly after its intersection with the Seward Hwy., it passes **Kenai Lake,** which stretches in a giant Z-shape through the Chugach Range. The Sterling continues along the Kenai River to the town of **Cooper Landing.**

Anglers rejoice: you have reached the Promised Land of salmon fishing, a land flowing with kings, silvers, reds, and pinks. During the summer runs, Cooper Landing and surrounding campgrounds take on a carnival-like atmosphere as eager fisherfolk line up on the banks of the Kenai River to try their luck. It is not unusual to see anglers standing shoulder to shoulder and filling their baskets with fish. Licenses are available at most grocery and fish stores. Guided fishing charters abound, but for hefty prices.

The Kenai offers several places to whitewater raft without risking life and limb. Some of these floats are as scenic as Class III river-rafting gets. Rafting and fishing tour companies generally supply lunch and gear on full-day trips, but anglers should buy their own licenses beforehand. Try **Alaska Wildland Adventures** (800-478-4100) in Cooper Landing for a variety of full- and half-day rafting or fishing trips ($42-185). The **Alaska River Company** (595-1226) offers hiking as well as rafting and fishing tours; the most economical trip, a three-hour raft trip through mild Class II waters costs $42. Fishing tours can extend well into the $100 range. Another much less pricey option is the ferry trip to the opposite bank of the Kenai River, which yields comparable views ($4, children 3-11 $2). The boat uses cables and current to carry it across at Mile 55 on the Sterling Hwy.

From Cooper Landing, the Sterling stretches 50 mi. to **Soldotna** and parallels the Kenai River until it enters the **Kenai National Wildlife Refuge.** This stretch of the Peninsula is prime moose territory (the 1,730,000 acres of land were designated the Kenai National Moose Refuge in 1941) and offers excellent canoeing and hiking opportunities. In 1980, the refuge grew to 1.97 million acres and was given its present-day name.

The **Fuller Lakes Trail,** a 6 mi. round-trip hike at Mile 56.9 of the Sterling Hwy., is one of the most strenuous established hikes in the region with an elevation gain of 1400 ft. After a challenging first mile of steady ascent through dense forests, the persevering hiker will be rewarded with striking views of the glimmering Lower Fuller Lakes and the lush Kenai Mountains. The **Kenai River Trails** provide a moderate alternative to the Fuller Lakes Trail. There are two trails departing from Skilah Lake Rd. To reach the trailheads, turn south on Skilah Lake Rd. at Sterling Hwy. Mile 58. The upper trail starts at Mile 2.2 of Skilah Lake Rd. A 5.6 mi. round-trip with a scant elevation gain of 260 ft., the trail provides impressive views of the turquoise waters off the Kenai coast. The lower trail begins at Mile 3 of Skilah Lake Rd. and affords similar views to those on the upper trail. Scamper through the open meadows teeming with wildflowers and linger to munch on blueberries in late summer. Plenty of bears in the area keep the moose company. The **Hidden Creek Trail** is a mild 3 mi. roundtrip hike beginning at Mile 5.4 of Skilah Lake Rd., 1 mi. west of Hidden Lake Campground. A quick afternoon hike, the trail leads through forests to Skilah Lake and the mouth of not-so-Hidden Creek. If the water level is low, it is possible to hike around the lake (a bold traveler might even submerge herself in its frigid waters for a refreshing swim).

The refuge also boasts some of the best canoeing systems in Alaska. The **Swan Lake Route** has three different passages suitable for two- to four-day paddles. Over 30 lakes dot the wooded lands, providing fishing and wildlife viewing opportunities. The more challenging **Swanson River System** connects 40 lakes through marshy wetlands, affording several two-day routes. Canoeists attempting this route should be experienced in backcountry skills. Both Swan Lake and Swanson River Route lie north of Sterling Hwy.

For more information on hikes and canoeing possibilities, contact **Kenai National Wildlife Refuge Visitor's Center,** P.O. Box 2139, Soldotna (262-7021), on Sterling Hwy. between Miles 95 and 96. Turn left on Funny River Rd., then right onto Ski Hill Rd. Pick up a free copy of *Refuge Reflections,* which gives detailed fishing, hiking, and canoeing tips. The center also features 20-minute nature talks (Mon.-Thurs. 11am) and hour-long nature walks (Fri.-Sun. 11am; center open Mon.-Fri. 8am-5pm, Sat.-Sun. 9am-6pm).

Soldotna spreads its strip mall tentacles for several miles along the northern stretch of the Sterling Hwy. An urban blemish on the face of the peninsula, Soldotna serves the convenient, though unglamorous, function of supplying travelers en route to Kenai's somewhere else with groceries and camping gear. **Wilderness Way** (262-3880), several miles east of Soldotna, packs an impressive amount of high-quality backpacking and canoeing gear into a relatively small store (open in summer daily 9am-8pm). The **Sports Den** (262-7491) has fishing supplies and canoes for $35 per day, $25 per day for three or more days (rents daily 8am-8pm). Boats are sometimes available alongside the highway; residents put their vessels in their front yards and hang "for rent" signs.

Soldotna's **Visitors Center** (262-1337) is located just over the Kenai River on the way to Homer (open daily 9am-7pm). Stop in, pick up a pamphlet on fishing and recreation possibilities in the area, and watch rugged anglers reel in fish from the river while standing on the harsh bike path next to the center. The center also hands out free canoe route maps and houses the wildlife refuge's manager, available to answer questions on recreation within the refuge. Call 262-9228 for **road conditions** and 911 in an **emergency.** Call 260-FIRE/3473 in case of a **fire.** The nearest **hospital** is **Central Peninsula General,** 250 Hospital Pl. (262-4404). The **post office** (262-4760), Binkley St., in downtown Soldotna, is open Monday through Friday 8:30am to 5pm. and Saturday 10am-2pm. The **General Delivery ZIP Code** is 99669. The **area code** is 907.

Camping is available pretty much anywhere along the Sterling Hwy. The sites are too numerous to name, and in the high season, almost all of these spots fill up. Grab a meal at **Sal's Klondike Diner,** 44619 Sterling Hwy. (262-2220), ½ mi. from the river and several hundred miles from the Klondike. A model train circles overhead, watching over the menu "loded" with gold rush trivia. Chicken fried steak with mashed potatoes, vegetable, roll, and salad is a favorite ($9; open 24hr.). After loading up on supplies, the next best thing to do in Soldotna is to leave.

Kenai

Perched on a bluff overlooking the Cook Inlet, Kenai has a magical view of the Aleutian-Alaska Range and its prominent volcanoes, Mt. Redoubt and Mt. Augustine. The fishing industry dominates the town, leaving its trademark fishy smell along Kenai's beaches. Alaska's residents swarm to the town to take advantage of dip-netting—the oh-so-rugged-and-complex sport in which a net is placed at the bottom of a stream until a fish swims in. Kenai is one of the peninsula's fastest-growing cities—a dubious honor. Its larger population has brought a refreshing variety of restaurants and services, but the hurried expansion spared few traces of the city's history and left a forgettable cityscape of RV parks and low-rises. Kenai lacks Seward's surroundings and Homer's hominess, making it an overgrown pit stop. However, the pristine **Captain Cook State Recreation Site** lies 30 mi. away, and the mouth of the Kenai River is a good place to catch salmon or watch beluga whales do the same.

PRACTICAL INFORMATION AND ORIENTATION

Visitors Center: Visitor and Cultural Center, 11471 Kenai Spur Hwy. (283-1991), just past the corner of Spur and Main St. A reservoir of information of Alaskan proportions. Usual array of pamphlets supplemented by a room of stuffed native wildlife, an area dedicated to traditional Alaskan artifacts, and a small theater with films on the area's development. Open Mon.-Fri. 9am-8pm, Sat.-Sun. 10am-7pm; winter Mon.-Fri. 9am-5pm, Sat.-Sun. 10am-4pm. **National Park Service,** 105 Trading Bay

Rd., P.O. Box 2643 (283-5855). Best source of info on **Lake Clark National Park and Preserve,** across Cook Inlet from Kenai. Open 8am-5pm.

Airport: 1 mi. north of downtown. Take Kenai Spur Rd. to Willow St.; follow signs for Airport Loop. **Alaska Airlines** (800-426-0333) has service to Anchorage (from $44). Reserve in advance for lowest rates.

Taxi: Alaska Cab, 283-6000. **Inlet Cab,** 283-4711. Both 24hr.

Car Rental: Hertz (283-7979), at the airport. $59 per day, 20¢ each mi. after 125. Must be 25 with credit card. Several other companies also at the airport.

Auto Repair: Alyeska Sales and Service, 200 Willow St. (283-4821). Open Mon.-Fri. 8am-6pm, Sat. 9am-5pm.

Buses: Seward Bus Line (563-0800). To Anchorage (1 per day, $30) and Homer (Mon. and Fri., $30).

Library: 163 Main St. Loop (283-4378). Open Mon.-Thurs. 8:30am-8pm, Fri.-Sat. 8:30am-5pm.

Laundromat and Showers: Wash-n-Dry (283-8473), at Lake St. and Kenai Spur Rd. Wash $1.75, 8min. dry 25¢. 20min. shower $4.20. Open daily 8am-10pm.

Pharmacy: Carr's (283-6300), at Kenai Spur Hwy. and Airport Way. Open Mon.-Fri. 9am-9pm, Sat. 9am-7pm, Sun. noon-5pm.

Job Service: 283-2900 or **Dial-a-Job,** 283-4606.

Crisis Line: 283-7257. 24hr.

Women's Resource Center: 325 S. Spruce St. (283-9479). Hotline and shelter. 24hr.

Hospital: Central Peninsula General Hospital, 250 Hospital Pl. (262-4404).

Emergency: 911. **Police:** 283-7879.

Post Office: 140 Bidarka (283-7771). Open Mon.-Fri. 8:45am-5:15pm, Sat. 9:30am-1pm. **General Delivery ZIP Code:** 99611.

Area Code: 907.

Kenai, on the western Kenai Peninsula, is about 158 mi. from Anchorage and 96 mi. north of Homer. Kenai can be reached via **Kalifornsky Beach Road,** which joins the Sterling Highway from Anchorage just south of Soldotna (but gets nowhere near California), or via **Kenai Spur Highway,** which runs north from Soldotna and west to Kenai. Kalifornsky mile markers measure distance from Kenai, while the Kenai Spur mile markers measure distance from Soldotna. Both roads provide access to the peninsula's lakes and peaks. On a clear day, you can see the 10,000 ft. volcano **Mt. Redoubt** across Cook Inlet.

ACCOMMODATIONS AND CAMPING

Adam Smith would be proud of tourists' and anglers' demands for housing in Kenai and the resulting bloom of B&Bs that keep costs reasonable. Most B&Bs start around $50 per night. Check with visitors center for listings. Besides the B&Bs, there is little other inexpensive lodging in Kenai. Backpackers used to stay in a free municipal campground that has since been moved to the park at Kenai Spur Hwy. and Marathon Rd. where campers must pay $8 for gravelly sites (water, pit toilets). Although camping down by the beach (take Spruce Dr. from the Kenai Spur Hwy.) is illegal, hard-core budget travelers are reportedly not harassed.

Beluga Lookout RV Park and Lodge, 929 Mission St. (283-5999 or 800-745-5999). Take Main St. toward the water and go right on Mission St. Prime location and unbeatable view, but no tent sites. Scan the sea for belugas from the viewing benches or the lounge. Full hookups $15-20; with bay view $25. Wash and dry $1.50; showers $2.

Katmai Hotel, 10800 Kenai Spur Hwy. (283-6101), 1 block from downtown. Small rooms with nice decor and cable. Singles $79; doubles $89.

FOOD

Carr's Quality Center (283-6300), in the Kenai Mall next to the K-Mart on Kenai Spur Rd. and Airport Way, is the city's largest grocery store. They have a bakery, fruit, natural foods section, pharmacy, and fast food (open 24hr.).

Veronica's (283-2725), at the end of Mission Rd. across from the Russian church. Situated in a renovated historic building and decorated with colorful hand-painted pictures, this seaside coffeehouse is almost as pretty as the inlet it overlooks. Espresso, pastries, and sandwiches are a classy respite from fishsticks. Tall latté $2.50, sandwiches around $6. Free sugar and creamer. Open Sun.-Thurs. 7am-6pm, Fri.-Sat. 8am-10pm.

Shannon's Kitchen Express, 115 S. Willow St. (283-5397), across from the Merit Inn. A great catch in Kenai's shallow culinary sea, Shannon's Kitchen cooks up healthy, light cuisine. Lunch sandwiches start at $5. Dinner entrees $9-15. Bowl of clam chowder with bread $3. Live music on Friday nights. Open daily 7am-6:30pm; dinner Wed.-Sat. 6-10pm.

New Peking, 145 S. Willow St. (283-4662), off Kenai Spur Rd. Savor the all-you-can-eat lunch buffet ($6) amid potted plants and a lush oriental setting. Dinner entrees, including vegetarian options and the famed Mongolian barbecue grill, from $9. Open Mon.-Fri. 11am-10pm, Sat.-Sun. noon-10pm.

Little Ski-Mo's Burger-n-Brew (283-4463 or 283-4409), on Kenai Spur Rd. across from the visitors center. Staggering array of burgers in a dimly lit lodge-like interior, complete with fireplace. Try the Twin Cities ($6.50), with egg, bacon, cheddar, and sprouts. Burger and fries $5. Open Mon.-Sat. 11am-10pm, Sun. 11am-9pm.

Thai Lotus, 106 S. Willow St. (283-7250). A little pricey, but you'll forget about the nondescript decor once you taste Top of the World Chicken Cashew Nut ($10.50) or devour one of many lunch specials ($6.50-8.50). All-you-can-eat lunch buffet $7. Open Mon.-Sat. 11am-9pm.

SIGHTS AND ACTIVITIES

The **Holy Assumption Russian Orthodox Church,** on Mission off Overland St., offers a look at Kenai's Russian heritage and an excellent view of the inlet. Originally built in 1846 and rebuilt in 1896, this National Historic Landmark contains 200-year-old icons (open in summer Mon.-Fri. 11am-4pm; public services held Sat. 6-7pm and Sun. 10am-noon; tours upon request).

The most breathtaking sight in Kenai is **Cook Inlet,** framed by smooth sand, two mountain ranges, and volcanic **Mt. Augustine** and **Mt. Redoubt.** Take in the magic of the inlet and its beluga whales, salmon runs, and eagles as you stroll the beach at the end of Spruce Dr. The best time to see whales is two hours before or after high tide. If you coordinate your visit with the arrival of the fishing boats, you may see a free-loading seal or sea lion as well.

Better yet, travel the 30 mi. out to **Captain Cook State Recreation Area** at the northern end of the Kenai Spur Rd. The premier views of the inlet and the Alaska-Aleutian Range beyond make for a lovely picnic on a bluff or a boulder-strewn beach or a night of solitary tenting (camping $10; water and pit toilets). Although there are no hiking trails, Captain Cook has swimming opportunities at Stormy Lake and serves as one jumping-off-point for the Swanson River Canoe Trail (see **Sterling Hwy. to Kenai,** p. 71). Bald eagle sightings are especially common here, and a small caribou herd, often spotted trotting along Kenai Spur Hwy. or Bridge Access Rd., roams the flatlands between Kenai and Soldotna.

Fishing dominates Kenai's recreational activities. In fact, that's really all there is to do in Kenai. Check at the chamber of commerce for charter information (prices are comparable to those in Soldotna). The majority of fishing takes place in the **Kenai River.** Anglers can do their stuff on any public land along the river. Inexperienced fisherfolk should ask at fishing shops for recommended locations so they do not damage the banks of the river and jeopardize the fish habitat. The best place to look for fish is in the slower eddies where they rest. You can fish for free at the mouth of the Kenai River if you have a license and rod (park at the end of Spruce Dr. and hike to the mouth). **Swanson River** and **Stormy Lake,** in the Captain Cook recreation area, offer chances at rainbow trout, silver salmon, and arctic char. Contact the State Division of Parks for regulations.

Outside Kenai, hiking and canoeing opportunities abound on the peninsula. The closest hikes lie along Sterling Hwy. between Cooper Landing and Soldotna (see

Sterling Hwy. to Kenai, p. 71). **Nikiski,** 12½ mi. north of Kenai at Mile 23.4 of the Spur Rd., is home to an alien spacecraft cleverly disguised as a **geodesic-domed pool** (776-8472), located behind the Nikiski school. Near the pool, a hockey rink, ski/running trail, and picnic area await playful Earthlings (open Tues.-Fri. noon-5pm and 6-9pm, Sat.-Sun. 1-5pm and 6-9pm; $3, seniors $2, waterslides $6).

Sterling Highway: Kenai to Homer

From Kenai, the Sterling Highway winds through short, shoreline forest on a bluff overlooking the Cook Inlet. Across the inlet looms the Alaska-Aleutian Range, with fantastic views of **Mt. Redoubt** and **Mt. Iliamna,** both volcanoes that rise over 10,000 ft. and have erupted in the last 50 years. The highway winds into the town of **Ninilchik,** another hamlet with spectacular fishing, fantastic scenery, a strong Russian heritage, and an excellent clamming beach, but very few resources. In the last year, not only has the visitors center closed, but the building in which it was located has been moved. The **Village Cache Store** at the end of Village Rd. (turn off at Sterling Hwy. Mile 135.1) has information on the area (open Mon.-Sat. 8am-9pm). The nearby parking lot is a good stopping point for minor expeditions into the neighborhood. Besides the unmatched views of the volcanoes and the Aleutian-Alaska Range, local attractions include the old **Russian fishing village** on Village Rd., and the **Holy Transfiguration of Our Lord Orthodox Church,** built in 1901. Both overlook Cook Inlet, and the church, towering above on a bluff, offers an unparalleled view of the overgrown seismic molehills offshore. The church interior is closed to the public, but services are held twice a month on Sundays. To get there, hike up the trail beginning behind the Cache Store. The church and cemetery are still in use, but the Russian village is abandoned and dilapidated.

Have a sleepover in Ninilchik just to stay at the **Eagle Watch Hostel (HI-AYH)** (567-3905), 3 mi. east of town on Oil Well Rd., which starts at the gas station. Though the building is spacious and clean, the hostel's highlight is outdoors. The house overlooks a verdant valley with a meandering stream, and the wildlife viewing from the deck is almost as good as in Denali—eagles soar by nightly and bears and moose make occasional showings. A full kitchen, showers, friendly hosts, a tree swing, and the playful dog, Nadia make this one of the best hostels in Alaska. The hostel is closed between 10am and 5pm, with an 11pm curfew ($10, nonmembers $13; linen $2, no sleeping bags; cash and traveler's checks only). Hostel guests can head farther down Oil Well Rd. and take the first left onto a gravel road to view a weird metal contraption that cages in salmon swimming upstream. Marvel at their reproductive drive as you watch them flounder and jump, trying to get through the cage.

For campers, the obvious choice is to stay at one of the **state campgrounds** near Ninilchik, each complete with water and toilets (sites $10). Superb sites in the **Ninilchik State Recreation Area,** some overlooking the inlet from a bluff, are less than 1 mi. north of town (sites $10). The nearby, beach-level **Deep Creek Recreation Area** is one of the most popular places to camp on the peninsula. Locals claim it has the world's best saltwater king salmon fishing; dolly varden and steelhead trout bite anglers' hooks here, too ($8; day-use parking $5; boat launching available). **Clamming** on the beaches bordering the village is Ninilchik's main low-tide attraction. You can rent a shovel and pail ($5-10) at the Cache Store. **Hylen's Camper Park** (567-3393), at Mile 135.4 of Sterling Hwy., has showers ($2 for 10min).

Buy groceries and fishing supplies at the **General Store** (567-3378), on Sterling Hwy. (open daily 6am-midnight). On the east side of the highway, a long, low restaurant and bar sit back on a gravel plot. The **Inlet View Cafe** (567-3330), at Sterling Hwy. Mile 135.4, offers a sterling view of the Cook Inlet and hearty sandwiches named for the mountains across the water ($6.25). The Iliamna pasta is a tasty choice for vegetarians ($9; open daily 5:30am-midnight). The bar is a laid-back local hangout (open daily 10am-5am).

The Sterling Highway continues from Ninilchik along the western edge of the peninsula until it turns east toward **Homer.**

Homer

In a state where the unique is commonplace and gorgeous is the norm, Homer's eclectic culture and idyllic setting stand out nonetheless. Fisherfolk and aging counterculturalists rule the roost, but Homer is also home to many artists, several Russian Orthodox colonies, a fabulous public radio station, and the newest pop star to send stones rolling and flashbulbs clicking, Jewel. These diverse cultural elements mix against a spectacular backdrop. One end of town rises up on bluffs above Kachemak Bay, providing wide views of the blue mountains and pale glaciers across the water. Below the bluffs, Homer supports its own theater group, scores of galleries stocked with the work of local artists, and one of the best small newspapers in Alaska. Moderate temperatures and a mere two feet of annual rainfall have earned Homer the nickname, Alaska's "banana belt."

The town extends into the bay along an improbable 4½ mi. tendril of sand and gravel known as the **Spit.** The ruggedly beautiful island and wilds of **Kachemak State Park** lie across the Kachemak Bay, where the southern end of the **Kenai Mountains** reaches the sea. Also on the south side of the bay are the artist/fishing colony of **Halibut Cove,** the scantly populated **Yukon Island,** the **Gull Island** bird rookery, and the Russian-founded hamlet of **Seldovia** (see p. 81).

PRACTICAL INFORMATION AND ORIENTATION

Visitors Information: Homer Chamber of Commerce and Visitor Information Center, P.O. Box 541, 135 Sterling Hwy. (235-7740), near Main St. All the necessary info and pamphlets. Staff help find a room in the area. Open June-Labor Day daily 9am-8pm; Labor Day-May Mon.-Fri. 9am-5pm.

Park Information: Alaska Maritime National Wildlife Refuge Visitor Center, 509 Sterling Highway (235-6961), next to the Best Western Bidarka Inn. Wildlife exhibits, marine photography, and helpful advice on backcountry adventures in Kachemak Bay. Also leads bird walks on the Spit twice a week. Open summers daily 9am-6pm. **Southern District Ranger Station,** Kachemak Bay State Park, P.O. Box 321 (235-7024), 4 mi. outside town on the Sterling Hwy.

Fishing Licenses: $15 for 3 days, available at local sporting goods stores and charter offices, or contact the **Alaska Department of Fish and Game,** 3298 Douglas St. (235-8191), near Owen Marine. Open Mon.-Fri. 8am-5pm.

Bank: First National Bank (235-5150), on Homer Bypass at Heath St. 24hr. **ATM.** Open Mon.-Thurs. 10am-5pm, Fri. 10am-6pm. **National Bank of Alaska,** 203 W. Pioneer Ave. (235-8151) and 4014 Lake St. (235-2444). Both open weekdays and limited hr. on Sat.

Employment: Alaska State Employment Service, 601 E. Pioneer Ave. #123 (235-7791). Open Mon.-Fri. 8am-noon and 1-4:30pm.

Airport: Competing airlines have terminals on opposite sides of the runway. **Southcentral Air** (283-3926 or 800-478-2550), on Kachemak Dr. off Homer Spit Rd. 4-6 flights to Anchorage per day (round-trip $131), plus daily flights to Seldovia and Kenai. **Era Aviation** (800-866-8394) is in the airport; follow signs from Ocean Dr. just before it becomes the Spit Rd. To Anchorage (round-trip $141) and Kenai (2 per day). **Homer Air** (235-8591) has service to Seldovia (round-trip $55).

Buses: Homer Stage Line, 424 Homer Spit Rd. (235-7009). Make reservations through **Central Charters** (235-7847). To: Soldotna (1 every other day, $25); Anchorage (1 every other day, $45); and Seward. $5 extra for drop-off at Anchorage Airport. Runs Memorial Day-Labor Day.

Ferries: Alaska Marine Highway, P.O. Box 166 (235-8449 or 800-382-9229). Office and terminal just before the end of the Spit. To: Seldovia ($18); Kodiak ($48); Seward ($96); Cordova ($138); and once a month to Dutch Harbor Aleutian Islands ($242). Open Mon.-Fri. 8:30am-4pm and when ferry is in.

Taxi: Chux Taxi (235-2489). To downtown from the airport ($4) or ferry ($8). **Day Breeze Shuttle** (399-1168). Runs between the spit and town twice daily ($3), cruises up and down the spit the rest of the day ($1).

Share-A-Ride: KBBI Public Radio, AM 890 (235-7721; email: kbbi@alaska.net; http://www.alska.net/~kbbi). Serves as an on-air bulletin board several times daily, broadcasting requests for those both seeking and offering rides. Entertaining listening even if you're not in the ride market.

Car Rental: Polar Car Rental, 4555 Sterling Hwy. Suite B (235-5998). $50 per day plus 30¢ per mi. after 100. $5 extra for unlimited mileage (open daily 8am-9pm; winter 8am-5pm).

Auto Repair: Sunny's Repair, 152 E. Pioneer Ave. (235-8800).

Bike Rental: Homer Saw and Cycle, 1532 Ocean Dr. (235-8406). Top-of-the-line Trek mountain bikes, $15 per ½ day, $25 per day. Open Mon.-Fri. 9am-5pm, Sat. 11am-4pm. Also rents through **Trips** (235-0708), on the spit. **Chain Reaction** (235-0750), in the Lakeside Mall. $16 per ½ day, $24 per day.

Camping Gear: Kachemak Gear Shed, 41955 Kachemak Dr. (235-8612; open Mon.-Fri. 8am-8pm, Sat.-Sun. 10am-6pm).

Bookstore: The Bookstore, 436 Sterling Hwy. (235-7496), next to the Eagle Quality Center. Open Mon.-Sat. 10am-7pm, Sun. noon-5pm.

Library: Homer Public Library, 141 Pioneer Ave. (235-3180), near Main St. Free Internet access. Open Mon.,Wed., and Fri.-Sat. 10am-6pm, Tues. and Thurs. 10am-8pm.

Laundromat and Showers: Homer Cleaning Center, 3684 Main St. (235-5152), downtown. Wash $1, 8min. dry 25¢. Last load 1hr. before closing. Shower $2.50 for unlimited time, towel included. Open Mon.-Sat. 8am-10pm, Sun. 9am-9pm.

Women's Crisis Line: 235-8101. 24hr.

Hospital: South Peninsula Hospital, 4300 Bartlett (235-8101), off Pioneer St.

Emergency: 911. **Police:** 235-3150.

Internet Access: one computer at the Homer Public Library (see above).

Post Office: 3261 Wadell Rd. (235-6125), off Homer Bypass. Open Mon.-Fri. 8:30am-5pm, Sat. 10am-1pm. **General Delivery ZIP Code:** 99603.

Area Code: 907.

Surrounded by 400 million tons of coal, Homer rests on **Kachemak ("Smoky") Bay,** named after the mysteriously burning deposits that greeted the first settlers. Homer is on the southwestern Kenai Peninsula, on the north shore of the bay. **The Sterling Highway** links Homer with Anchorage (226 mi. away) and the rest of the Kenai Peninsula. The heart of Homer lies in a triangle defined by the shoreside Homer Bypass, downtown drag Pioneer Avenue, and cross-cutting Lake Street. Homer Bypass becomes Sterling Highway west of town, while east of town it becomes Ocean Drive and veers right to follow the spit as Homer Spit Road. Biking is a great way to get around this rather spread-out town, but be forewarned—there are lots of hills.

ACCOMMODATIONS AND CAMPING

There are plenty of cheap accommodations in town, making Homer a home away from home for budget travelers. Contact the **Homer B&B Network** for lodgings starting at $50 per night (800-764-3211), or check with the visitors center.

Sunspin Guest House, 358 E. Lee Dr. (235-6677 or 800-391-6677). From Pioneer Ave., take Kachemak Way toward the bluff to Lee Dr. on left. Convenient location, but little personality. High-class bunkroom (real beds, clean sheets, and a continental breakfast) is worth the $25; private rooms $50 and up.

Driftwood Inn, 135 W. Bunnell (235-8019 or 800-478-8019 in AK), a short walk from downtown. Take the Homer Bypass, turn toward the ocean on Main St., then right on Bunnell. Spotless, ultra-modern rooms in a rustic building. Laundry and luggage storage for guests. Free local calls, coffee, and tea. Homey guest lounge and a great view. Singles $54; doubles $64.

Seaside Farm, 58335 East End Rd. (235-7850), 4½ mi. out of town. An amazingly beautiful but inconvenient ($12 cab ride from the airport) location. Mossy, the friendly, crunchy matron, runs a commune of sorts here. Hostel facilities, while bearable, are not nearly as appealing as the view across the bay. Camping out in the clover field is the better bet. Enjoy a roofed, outdoor common area and seaside strolls. Lodging in exchange for farm work available. Bunks $15 with shower. Tent sites $6, showers an additional $3. Private cabins with kitchenettes: single $30; double $55; discount available for backpackers.

Road Runner B&B, 4657 Sabrina Rd. (235-6581 or 235-3678), 2 mi. out of town off East End Rd. A steal, considering the price-to-service ratio. Spacious, comfortable rooms, a full fridge, and free rides to town, the Spit, and the airport. Singles $28, with bath $44; doubles $39, with bath $60. Full breakfast or lunch $5.

Karen Hornaday Park, 491 E. Pioneer St. (235-3170), with office at Public Works Dept., City Hall. From Pioneer, go uphill on Bartlett St. to Fairview, left to Campground Rd., then right to the park. Each site looks like a personal grassy driveway, bordered by purple lupine and cow parsley. A classy camping crowd. Water, pit toilets, and nice view of the bay. Sites $7.

Spit Municipal Camping, 3735 Homer Spit Rd. (235-2617), across from the fishing hole. The city controls 2 areas for RVs, 1 for tents and RVs. The once-beautiful spot is now a giant gravel parking lot. Extremely popular and crowded nonetheless. Terrific views, if no one camps in front of you. Water, flush toilets. Tents $3. RVs $7, with hookup $17.

Kachemak Bay State Park, 7 water mi. across from the Spit. Gorgeous, secluded and free, but it will cost nearly $50 per person to get there. Most locals vehemently maintain that it's well worth the expense. Spend a couple days and enjoy the hiking trails. For further info, stop by or call the Southern District Ranger Station (see **Practical Information,** above). A public use cabin is also available ($50).

FOOD

Homer has one of the best collections of restaurants in the state and a darn snazzy selection of grocery stores. The huge, 24-hour **Eagle Quality Center,** 436 Sterling Hwy. (235-2408), has a stunning array of options. **John's Corner Market** (235-5494), on Lake St. at Pioneer Ave. sells fantastic produce (open Mon.-Sat. 10am-7pm). Wheat germ, spirolina, and local crunch are available at **Smoky Bay Natural Foods,** 248 W. Pioneer Ave. (235-7252; open Mon.-Fri. 8:30am-8pm, Sat. 9am-7pm, Sun. 10am-6pm).

On the Spit, you can usually hook or snag a salmon from the **Fishing Hole.** Buy fresh seafood directly from fisherfolk or at a retail outlet. **Katch Seafoods,** 765 Fish Dock Rd. (235-7953 or 800-368-7400), offers salmon and halibut for $3 per lb. **The Coal Point Trading Co.,** 4306 Homer Spit Rd. (235-3877 or 800-235-3877), will sell it to you raw or will vacuum-pack and deep-freeze your catch for 70¢ per lb. (open 6am-after 11pm). Wash away fish breath with locally brewed Broken Birch Bitter from the **Homer Brewing Company,** 1562 Homer Spit Rd. (235-FOAM/3626; open Mon.-Sat. 11am-8pm, Sun. noon-6pm). Mmmm...Homer likes beer.

Downtown

Red Pepper Kitchen, 475 Pioneer (235-8362). So popular with the locals, it's hard to find a seat after 9:30am. Deluxe burritos with homemade beans $4.50, Mediterranean pizza slice $3.50. Don't miss the locally made Snap Dragon Ginger Brew ($2). Open daily until 10pm.

Two Sisters Bakery, 106 W. Bunnell (235-2280). Take Main St. toward the water. Mild-mannered bakery/cafe by day transforms into a world culinary tour at night. 4 evenings per week, the sisters concoct masterpieces from one of over 10 countries. Pricey ($10-14), but perhaps the only Turkish and Moroccan food in Alaska. Certainly the only *good* Turkish and Moroccan food in Alaska. Fri. and Sat. always feature Indian and Thai. Lunch treats include focaccia sandwiches ($4.50) and salmon chowder ($3). Open Mon.-Sat. 7am-3pm, Sun. 9am-2pm; world tour served Wed.-Sat. 6-10pm.

Cafe Cups, 162 Pioneer Ave. (235-8330). A gathering place for artists and young travelers. The best of a big-city cafe successfully hybridized with Homer's offbeat charm. Try the tasty, unusual sandwiches ($7-8.25 with salad), and espresso milkshake ($4.50). Outdoor seating underneath the mammoth, multi-colored cups (it is, after all, the Cafe Cups). Open daily 7am-10pm.

Young's Oriental Restaurant, 565 E. Pioneer Ave. (235-4002). The 20 ft. buffet sends Young's shooting ahead in the race for all-you-can-eat Asian lunch buffet champion ($6.29, dinner $7.95). Open daily 11am-11pm.

The Spit

Fishwife's Gallery, 4460 Homer Spit Rd. (235-9951). The country kitchen on the Spit seems something of an anomaly. Halibut chowder $3.50; veggie pizza $3.50. A hot pastrami sandwich, prepared with love by an honest-to-goodness fishwife goes for $6. Open Mon.-Sat. 9am-9pm.

Little Taste of Russia, next to the Fishwife's Gallery. Big taste of Russia. Little price. *Blini* $2.25. *Borscht* $2. Typical Russian service: take-out only. Open daily 10am-7pm.

Kaeto's Crepe Escape (235-7443; http://www.xyz.net/~bikerdoc). Third boardwalk on the right of the Spit. No matter your caste, escape with a crepe and some change. Breakfast crepe $4. Homer's delight—zucchini, halibut, and other relishes on a whole wheat crepe $7.50. Open daily dawn-dusk (in summer roughly 5am-10pm); wheelchair accessible.

Alaska's Italian Bistro, 4241 Homer Spit Rd. (235-6153). Magnificent ocean views in a tastefully unaffected space. Dinners aren't cheap, but lunch beckons with a *tapas* bar of clams casino ($8.50) or oysters bistro ($10.50). Open Mon.-Sat. noon-10pm, Sun. 1-10pm.

SIGHTS AND EVENTS

The **Pratt Museum,** 3779 Bartlett St. (235-8635; email pratt@alaska.net), is the best museum on the peninsula. Recently remodeled, the Pratt houses a gallery of local art and historical exhibits of Kenai artifacts. Displays range from homesteader cabins to artifacts of the Inuit and Denali peoples, and include some great exhibits on marine mammals. View the skeleton of the Bering Sea beaked whale or witness the feeding frenzy in the salt water aquarium (fish frenzied Tues. and Fri. 4-5pm; open daily 10am-7pm, Oct.-Dec. and Feb.-April Tues.-Sun. noon-5pm; $4, seniors and students with ID $3, under 18 $2; wheelchair accessible).

Homer's residents take art seriously (even the supermarket has a gallery), and serious art it is. **Ptarmigan Arts,** 471 Pioneer Ave. (235-5345), displays the work of over 40 Alaskan artists and craftspeople (open Mon.-Sat. 10am-7pm, Sun. 10am-5pm). The **Bunnell Street Gallery,** 106 W. Bunnell (235-2662), features innovative contemporary art ranging from paintings to edible art (open summer daily 10am-6pm; winter 11am-5pm). The visitors center offers a complete list of area galleries. The town's hyperactive theater group performs at **Pier One Theater,** P.O. Box 894 (235-7333; www.alaska.net/~wmbell), one of the first buildings on the Spit. Catch plays there on the mainstage throughout the summer (shows Thurs. and Sun. at 7:15pm, Fri.-Sat. at 8:15pm; $11, seniors $10, children $7, Thurs. all seats $8). A series of other performances take place Sunday through Thursday, many featuring Homer's most famous son (only outdone by the even-more-famous daughter), Tom Bodett, of National Public Radio and Motel 6 ("We'll leave the light on for ya") fame. Check the *Homer News* for schedules. The **Homer Family Theater** (235-6728), at Main St. and Pioneer Ave., features current blockbusters and feel-good movies ($6). Mmmm...edible art.

The sun never sets on Homer summers (figuratively and almost literally). Nightlife ranges from beachcombing in the midnight sun to hanging at the tourist trap and sometimes local joint, **Salty Dawg Saloon** (235-9990), under the log lighthouse toward the end of the spit (open 11am-whenever, as the sign says). Notice three generations of Let's Go business cards tacked to the wall behind the right end of the bar amidst other cards, napkins, and bills that give the big Dawg the feel of a 3-D, quasi-historical message board (or the *Sgt. Pepper* album cover). **Alice's Champagne Palace,** 196 Pioneer Ave. (235-7650), is a wooden barn with diverse live music. Many young locals drop in as the midnight sun creeps along the horizon (Tues.-Sat. from 2pm into the morning).

Since Homer is often billed "the halibut capital of the world," it should come as no surprise that the **Homer Jackpot Halibut Derby** generates a whole lot of hoopla. The competition runs from May 1-Labor Day and offers a grand prize in the neighborhood of $30,000. Each year, several would-be winners are left crying at the scales after they land prize-winning fish with no ticket. Tickets are available in local charter offices on the Spit ($7). For those who prefer feathers to fins, the **Homer Shorebird Festival** (May 8-11 in 1998; info 235-PEEP/7337) offers birding tours, educational workshops, an arts fair, and 8-10,000 migrating birds. Last year, the event drew over 2000 registered participants and guerilla ornithologists. On the second Sunday in August, KBBI stages the fabulous **Concert on the Lawn** on the town commons, featuring blues, rock, and bluegrass from 11am-8pm. The annual **Winter Carnival,** held during the first week in February, features sled dog races and snow machine competitions.

OUTDOORS

Nearly everyone who comes to Homer spends some time on the **Homer Spit.** Don't feel obligated to follow the crowds; this 5 mi. strip of sand is one of the most heinous tourist traps in the state. While there is no denying that the Spit offers some great views, the utter lack of greenery and the concentration of vehicles makes the area a virtual parking lot. To actually get your own patch of sand, head to **Bishop's Beach** (take Main St. toward the water, and follow the signs to the left on Bunnell Ave.).

About the only good justification for visiting the Spit is to leave it via one of the many boats (or eat at one of its restaurants). The vast majority of them are halibut charters. On a particularly good day, as many as 90 set off in search of big, ugly fish. Choosing a charter, like fishing itself, is something of a crap shoot. Although most charter companies are reputable businesses, there are a few that strip their customers more cleanly than a filleted halibut. Many of the boats are booked through **Central Charters** (235-7847; email central@ptialaska.net; http://www.ptialaska.net/~central), located near the middle of the spit. Full-day trips start at $150. All tackle and bait are included, and there is a refund policy for foul weather. A fishing license (3 days $15) earns you a daily one-fish limit. Check with the tourist office for a list of companies; not every reliable business will necessarily be a member, but those that are should be reputable.

If you don't have enough cash to chase after the big sea monsters, head to the **fishing hole** near the start of the Spit, where anyone who can hold a rod can probably catch a salmon. A vigorous stocking program plants fry, which return years later to spawn in this tidal lagoon. The lagoon is unsuitable for spawning, and anglers manage to hook or snag most of the fish that return. Pick up poles and tackle at **Sportsman's Supplies** (the white building near the fishing hole). Daily rental is $10.

For those only interested in catching great views, bikes are the best bet. If you're feeling brave, bike up the killer **East Hill Rd.** (predictably, to the east of town off East End Rd.) for a panorama of the Kenai Mountains. The road levels out to quiet, flat gravel and fields of fireweed and other wildflowers. By foot, you can either take to the beach or check out the 6 mi. **Homestead Trail** just to the west of town. The trail has three different access points; check the *Homer Tourist Guide* for details and information on how to identify the arctic star flowers, marsh violets, green rein orchids, and other wildflowers that bloom along the trail. Or take a horse. Mark, at **Trail's End Horse Adventures** (235-6393) will rent you one for $20 per hour, $65 for four hours, or $110 per day.

■ Near Homer

KACHEMAK BAY

Locals are vocal in their praise of **Kachemak Bay State Park**—most maintain that a visit to Homer is not complete without a trip across the bay. One of the largest coastal parks in the country, the area contains roughly 375,000 acres of beaches, tide pools, mountains, and glaciers, and includes one of the northernmost temperate rainforests in the world. Stop by the **Southern District Ranger Station** (see **Practical Information**) for information on the park's myriad hiking and camping opportunities. **Saint Augustine's Charters** offers regularly scheduled water-taxi service to the park (daily 9am and 4pm; round-trip $45). Personalized service is also available. Call **Inlet Charters** (235-6126 or 800-770-6126) for reservations. **Mako's Water Taxi** (399-4133;

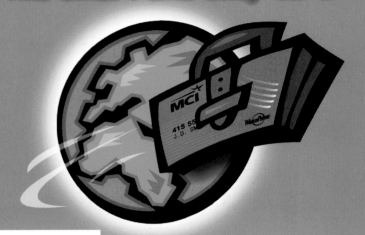

http://akms.com/makotaxi) and **Rainbow Tours** (235-7272) offer similar services for about the same price, but price varies depending on number of passengers and your specific destination. If you're just looking for an excuse to cruise and don't care to land anywhere, Rainbow offers a 1½ hour cruise to **Gull Island,** where you'll see murres, cormorants, guillemots, other birds with unpronounceable names, a few puffins, and about sixteen bijillion gulls. Tours depart the spit at 9am and 4:30pm and cost $15 (under 12 $10, seniors $12.50). To cruise the bay in style, go for a sailing tour on the 30s-era **St. Augustine's Fire,** a gorgeous wooden sailing yacht. Two hours in the lap of nautical luxury costs $35 per person. Call **Inlet Charters** for a booking (see above). For a self-powered water adventure, consider a full-day kayak trip with **True North Kayak Adventures,** P.O. 2319 (book through **Trips,** 235-0708). The tour, although expensive, comes with a great lunch and lots of sea otters ($125, including round-trip water taxi).

HALIBUT COVE

Yet another great way to spend an expensive afternoon in the Homer area is with **Danny J. Tours** (235-7847), visiting the colorful artist/fishing colony of Halibut Cove and its few dozen residents. An early trip leaves the spit daily at noon and makes a short visit to Gull Island before dropping passengers off at the village for two and a half hours (round-trip $35, seniors $28, children $17.50). The evening run (5pm departure, 10pm return) costs only $18 for adults, and while a reservation at the Saltry restaurant (see below) is required, the meal pays for itself. Once landed, head to the **Saltry** (296-2223), the cove's only restaurant, for a meal of raw and cooked fish. Try the halibut salad ($8), or the *nori maki* ($10; open 1-5pm and 6-9pm). Walk the raised boardwalk to the **Halibut Cove Art Gallery** and view a collection of works by residents. Explore octopus-ink paintings at **Diana Tillion's Cove Gallery.** Diana extracts ink herself with a hypodermic needle from stranded octopi, eats the octopi, then paints with their body fluids. Farther down the path, past the resident dock, the six-foot-tall portrait of Alex Duff Combs' head welcomes visitors to his gallery. World-traveled and universally acclaimed, Combs' pottery and painting now rest in a house filled with everything from faded buoys to peacock feathers. Several hiking trails surround the town, winding away from art into animalia. The most convenient is the 1 mi. **Saddle Trail,** which departs from behind the Saltry and rambles along a ridge, past intriguing rock formations, to an overlook of the cove.

Seldovia

Virtually untouched by the tourist mania rampant on the rest of the Kenai peninsula, this isolated hamlet combines marine charm with rolling terrain and funky ambience a la Homer. The Russians named Seldovia for its herring, and the fish have lived up to their reputation for centuries, buoying the town's economy. Unique geological surroundings keep them company and lure less scaly visitors—Seldovia overlooks four active volcanoes: **Augustine, Iliamna, Redoubt,** and **Spur.**

Practical Information **Synergy Artworks,** (234-9901), on Main St. across from the boat harbor, houses the **Chamber of Commerce** and rooms stacked to the rafters with visitors information, including a free and detailed **map** (open Memorial Day-Labor Day daily 11am-5pm; in winter Sat.-Sun. 11am-4pm). The **airport** is less than 1 mi. out of town on Airport Ave. Seldovia is served by **Homer Air** (235-8591; to Homer $29, round-trip $55), **Southcentral** (800-478-2550), and **Great Northern Airlines** (800-243-1968), which flies directly to Anchorage (one-way, $33). The **ferry** *M/V Tustumena* chugs from Homer to Seldovia twice a week (Tues. 12:30pm and Sun. 3am; $18, round-trip $36). Ferry loyalists can either stay four hours (while the Tustumena refuels) or a few days (until the next ferry) in Seldovia. Three tour boats cruise daily to Homer. None of the tour commentary is worth paying for, but if the planes aren't flying, it's your only way out. **Rainbow Tours** (235-72725) offers the least expensive service (one-way $25, round-trip $40; seniors $36, youth $25), and **Jakolof Bay Express** provides an eco-friendly and just plain friendly Ferry/Bus service for $45. Call **Trips** (235-0708) for reservations. Bring money to Seldovia—there are no banks and few stores accept credit cards.

Once in town, **Southshore Cab** (234-8000) will shuttle you about (open 8am-2am), or you can shuttle yourself on a **bicycle** rented from **Rocky Raven's** (234-7810) for $4 per hour or $15 per day (open daily 10am-6pm). **The Buzz** (234-7479), on the harbor side of Stamper's Market on Main St., rents slightly more expensive bikes ($20 per day, $25 per 24hr.) and fishing tackle ($15 per day; $25 deposit; open daily 6am-6pm). Stock up on books for the long ferry ride at the **library,** on Seldovia St. near Main St. (open Tues. 2-4:30pm and 7:30-9:30pm, Thurs. 3:30-6pm and 7:30-9:30pm, Sat. 11:30am-4:30pm) or at **Lost Horizons Books,** 235 Main St. (234-7839; email lsthoriz@alaska.net; open Memorial Day-Labor Day, Mon.-Sat. 10am-5pm, Sun. 11am-5pm). For kayak rental, call **Kayak'atak** (234-7425; http://www.alaska.net/~kayaks; singles $45 per day, doubles $70 per day). The **Seldovia Medical Clinic** is at 234-7825 (open Mon., Wed., Fri. 9am-4pm); in an **emergency** call 911. The **police** can be reached at 234-7640. The **fire hall** is at 234-7812. The **post office** (234-7831) is at Main and Seldovia St. (open Mon.-Fri. 9am-5pm). The **general delivery ZIP Code** is 99663; the **area code** is 907.

Accommodations, Camping, and Food The **Dancing Eagles Lodge** (234-7627), at the end of Main St. by the boardwalk, offers rustic cabins, a private extension of the town's boardwalk, and a terrific view of the bay. Rooms start at $45 per person per night. Wheelchair-accessible, less attractively situated cabins overlook the airport at **Seldovia Seaport Cottages,** 313 Shoreline Dr., Box 118 (234-7483). Pleasant interiors frame kitchenettes and double or twin beds (singles or doubles $60, each additional person $10). The chamber of commerce (234-9901) keeps a list of Seldovia's B&Bs, most of which cost $60-85. RV camping ($8; no hookups) and more secluded tent sites ($5) are available at **Wilderness Park,** approximately half a mile past the marked turnout for **Outside Beach** on Anderson Way. Register at the City Hall on Main St. **Seldovia Market** (234-7633), on Main St., stocks a modest supply of groceries, hardware, tackle, liquor, and pharmaceuticals (open Mon.-Sat. 9am-8pm, Sun. noon-5pm). Frozen dairy treats, hot showers, and laundry services mingle in a bizarre but happy matrimony at the **Harbor Laundromat** (234-7420), also on Main St. (10min. shower $4, towel and soap included; wash $2-4, 5min. dry 25¢). Enjoy a delicious cone ($1.75) or a smacktastic milkshake ($3.50) as you towel off or fold your clothes (open Mon.-Sat. 10am-9pm, Sun. 11am-7pm; in winter weekends only; last shower 8:30pm).

The Buzz (234-7479) serves coffee and espresso and provides good rainy-afternoon loitering space with great food—perhaps a $6.25 calzone or a $4.75 slice of quiche. The cappuccino ($2) and raspberry rhubarb tart ($2.75) are delectable (open daily 6am-6pm; in winter 8am-4pm; credit cards accepted). **Pumi's Oriental Barbecue** (234-7558), next to the harbormaster's office, cooks up verdant-green broccoli and garlic sauce and golden dragon, both for $6, including egg roll and rice (open Mon.-Sat. 10am-9pm; wheelchair accessible).

Sights and Entertainment Stop by the small **museum,** 328 Main St. (234-7898), sponsored by the Seldovia Native Association (open Mon.-Fri. 8am-5pm). The adjacent **Berry Kitchen/Museum Gift Shop,** 328 Main St. (234-7898), in the Seldovia Native Association Building, whips up a mean blueberry jam (open daily 10am-2pm). The native houseboat grounded at Anderson Way also houses a small museum, with a collection that includes a meteorite older than earth and an antique broad axe (open Tues.-Sun. noon-4:30pm; free; call 234-7496 for tours). The **St. Nicholas Orthodox Church,** built in 1891, peers out over the town from a hilltop. It's a beautiful place to poke around. Tours are given by Fred and Tinette Paulson (234-8000), who provide commentary at anytime (donation requested).

The **Otterbahn Hiking Trail,** starting at the Susan B. English School, near Winifred Ave., and winding 1 mi. to Outside Beach, takes trekkers to a small lighthouse perched above cliffs that plunge into the bay. On a clear day, the view of the volcanoes is magnificent. There is also a 6 mi. hike up the bay on the dirt extension of Rocky St.; consult the map of Seldovia (available at the visitors center, see above) on how to get there. For indoor kicks, the **Linwood Bar** in town (234-9906; open 10am-2am) or the bar in the **Seldovia Lodge** hit the spot (234-7673; open 4pm-2am; wheelchair accessible).

Seldovia triples in size on **Independence Day** (July 4). An old-fashioned celebration draws hundreds of visitors (a mob, in Seldovan terms) from all over the peninsula and includes parades, log-rolling, the 5K "Salmon Shuffle," a horseshoe tournament, greased pole climbing, and a pancake feed at the fire hall.

KODIAK ISLAND

Kodiak Island is the Cinderella of the Gulf of Alaska—a beautiful victim of astonishingly hard luck. In this century, Kodiak has been rocked by earthquakes, engulfed by tsunamis, doused in the oil of the Exxon *Valdez*, and blanketed in nearly two feet of volcanic ash. Rain falls 180 days each year on the island, which shelters the **Kodiak National Wildlife Refuge,** home to about 3000 Kodiak brown bears, the largest carnivorous land mammals in the world. The refuge's 800 mi. of coastline encircle the island's sharp inland peaks, pushing Kodiak's human population onto its eastern shore. The rich waters around Kodiak Island have made its fishing fleet the state's most productive, drawing tidal waves of young people each summer to work its canneries. Islanders take their seafood seriously, and until recently, tourism has been only an afterthought.

Kodiak

Kodiak was the first capital of Russian Alaska before Alexander Baranof moved the Russian-American Company to Sitka. The glittering ladies of St. Petersburg dressed to the hilt back in the early days of colonial Kodiak, thanks to Russian enslavement of the indigenous Alutiiq people, who were forced to hunt local otters to near-extinction.

Unlike the sea otters, nearby **Novarupta Volcano** is anything but extinct. It erupted in 1912 with a force 10 times greater than the 1980 eruption of Mount St. Helens, spewing so much ash that residents could not see a lantern held at arm's length for two days. In 1964, the biggest earthquake ever recorded in North America (9.2 on the Richter Scale) shook the area, causing $24 million in damage and creating a tsunami that destroyed much of downtown Kodiak. When the swamped fishing port was rehabilitated by the Army Corps of Engineers, one 200 ft. vessel, *The Star of Kodiak,* was cemented into the ferry dock and converted into a cannery.

Local color is hard to find—if it exists at all. Unless you fancy waiting for the next natural disaster to liven things up, come to Kodiak for the outdoors or not at all. Keep in mind that the gorgeous shorelines to the north are virtually inaccessible without a car, and that no one on the island rents to travelers under 25.

PRACTICAL INFORMATION AND ORIENTATION

Visitors Information: Kodiak Island Convention and Visitors Bureau, 100 Marine Way, (486-4782; fax 486-6545; http://www.kodiak.org), in front of the ferry dock. Hunting and fishing info, charter and accommodations arrangements, and an inconveniently enormous **map.** Open daily 8am-5pm, and for most ferry arrivals; in winter Mon.-Fri. 8am-noon and 1-5pm. **Fish and Wildlife Service and Wildlife Refuge Visitor Center,** 1390 Buskin River Rd. (487-2600), just outside Buskin State Recreation Site, 4 mi. southwest of town on Rezanof Rd. Wildlife displays, stuffed brown bears, films on the island's wildlife, and info on Kodiak National Wildlife Refuge and its cabins. Open Mon.-Fri. 8am-4:30pm. **State Department of Parks,** SR Box 3800;

1200 Abercrombie Dr. (486-6339), at Fort Abercrombie. Info on local state parks and campgrounds. Open Mon.-Sat. 8am-5pm.

Fishing Information: Alaska Department of Fish and Game, Box 686, 211 Mission Rd. (486-1880, 24hr. recorded info 486-4559). Info on regulations and seasons. **Licenses** available at all local sporting goods stores. Open Mon.-Fri. 8am-4:30pm.

Employment: Alaska State Employment Service, 305 Center St. (486-3105), in Kodiak Plaza. Open Mon.-Fri. 8am-noon and 1-4:30pm. First stop for fish canners.

Banks: National Bank of Alaska, 202 Marine Way (486-3126). Open Mon.-Thurs. 10am-5pm, Fri. 10am-6pm, Sat. 10am-2pm. **First National Bank,** 202 Marine Way (486-3251). Open Mon.-Fri. 10am-5pm., Sat. noon-4pm. **Key Bank** (486-6104), in the Mall off of Marine Way. Open Mon.-Fri. 10am-5pm, Sat. 10am-2pm.

Airport: 5 mi. southwest of town on Rezanof Dr. Served by **Era Aviation** (800-866-8394). To Anchorage (5-7 per day, round-trip $216). **Pen Air** (487-4014). To: Karluk (round-trip $150); Port Lions (round-trip $60); and Larsen Bay (round-trip $120). Office open daily 5am-10pm.

Ferries: Alaska Marine Highway (800-562-6731; fax 486-6166), terminal next to the visitors center. The *Tustumena* docks in Kodiak May-Sept. 1-3 times weekly; less frequently in winter. To: Homer ($48); Seward ($54); Valdez ($98); and Cordova ($98). 5-day run to Dutch Harbor (Aleutian Islands) once every month ($202). Terminal open Mon.-Fri. 8am-5pm, Sat. 8am-4pm, and when ferries are in.

Car Rental: Budget, 516 Marine Way (486-8500), at the airport (487-2220), or downtown. From $51, base prices are higher than its partner, **Rent-a-Heap** ($29 per day, 29¢ per mile), but unlimited free milage may make Budget a better deal. Must be 25 with credit card. Downtown open Mon.-Sun. 9am-7pm. Airport open daily 6:30am-10pm.

Car Repair: R.C. Enterprises, 2017 Mill Bay Rd. (486-8476). Open Mon.-Fri. 9am-6pm. Sat. 10am-2pm.

Taxis: A&B Taxi (486-4343) and **AAA Ace Mecca Taxi** (486-3211). $3 plus $2 per mi. $13 to the airport. 24hr. **Airporter** (486-7583) offers a $5 shuttle to the airport from downtown. Call ahead.

Camping and Fishing Equipment: Mack's Sports Shop, 117 Lower Mill Bay (486-4276), at the end of Center Ave. Open Mon.-Sat. 7am-7pm, Sun. 9am-6pm. **Cy's Sporting Goods,** 202 Shelikof St. (486-3900), near the harbor. Open Mon.-Fri. 8am-8pm, Sat. 8am-7pm, Sun. 9am-5pm.

Bookstore: Shire Bookstore, 104 Center Ave. (486-5001). Extensive mystery and romance sections, and a coffee bar. Open Mon.-Sat. 9:30am-7pm, Fri. 9:30am-9pm. Sun. 1-5pm.

Library: 319 Lower Mill Bay Rd. (486-8686). Open Mon.-Fri. 10am-9pm, Sat. 10am-5pm, Sun. 1-5pm. Periodicals section is an ideal escape from rainy streets.

Public Radio: KMXT 100.1 FM.

Laundromat and Showers: Ernie's, 218 Shelikof (486-4119), across from the harbor. Wash $3, 4min. dry 25¢. 20min. shower $4. Open daily 8am-8pm. Last wash 6:30pm; last shower 7:30pm.

Weather: Local forecasts, 487-4313. **Marine forecasts,** 487-4949.

Pharmacy: Wodlinger Drug and Photo, 312 Marine Way (486-4035), across from the harbormaster. Pharmacy open Mon.-Fri. 10am-6pm. Store open Mon.-Sat. 9:30am-6:30pm, Sun. noon-4pm.

Hospital: Kodiak Island Hospital, 1915 E. Rezanof Dr. (486-3281).

Crisis Line: 486-3625. **Women's Crisis Line:** 422 Hillside Dr. (486-6171). **AIDS Helpline:** 800-478-2437.

Emergency: 911. **Police:** 217 Lower Mill Bay Rd. (486-8000). **Fire:** 219 Lower Mill Bay Rd. (486-8040).

Post Office: 419 Lower Mill Bay Rd. (486-4721). Open Mon.-Fri. 9am-5:30pm. **Downtown Contract Station,** in the AC Grocery, is open Mon.-Sat. 10am-6pm. **General Delivery ZIP Code:** 99615.

Area Code: 907.

The city of Kodiak is on the eastern tip of Kodiak Island, roughly 250 mi. south of Anchorage. One hundred miles of paved and rutted gravel roads follow the scenic coastlines north and south of the city. Chiniak Road, which heads south for 42 mi., is an especially worthwhile trip. In town, the main drag is Center Street, which starts at the ferry terminal and heads inland, ending at the intersection with Rezanof Drive to the left, and Lower Mill Bay Road to the right.

ACCOMMODATIONS AND CAMPING

Kodiak has no hostel and no true budget accommodations. The available alternatives present a dilemma: you can get a cheap motel room in a convenient location or a room in a B&B with a few more bells and whistles that is far, far away from the ferry and airport. Many B&B owners frown on renting to unmarried couples. Finding a room becomes almost impossible when, as often happens, the airport shuts down due to bad weather. Watch for Kodiak's brutal 11% hotel tax.

Backpackers can head for **Gibson Cove,** 2 mi. west of Kodiak on Rezanof Dr. Built by the city for transient cannery workers, Gibson Cove looks, feels, and smells like a gravel parking lot soaked in fish innards. In fact, it *is* a gravel parking lot soaked in fish innards, but at $2 per night with free hot showers, no one quibbles. Better scenery and more breathable air can be found slightly farther away at two pleasant state-run facilities.

Lakeview Terrace B&B, 2426 Spruce Cape Rd., P.O. Box 3107 (486-5135). Take Mission St. 2½ mi. northeast of town until it becomes Spruce Cape Rd. Large, spotless rooms with comfortable queen beds, cable, private sinks, semi-private bath, and breakfast. Born-again hostess offers free Bibles to guests upon departure. Singles $45. Doubles $55.

Russian Heritage Inn, 119 Yukon (486-5657; fax 486-4634), off Lower Mill Bay Rd. near Mark's Sports Shop. Nothing Russian besides the little blue domes on the doors. Congenial owner offers recently remodeled rooms. About half have fridges. Big cable TVs. Laundry: $1.50 wash, same to dry. One tiny room rents for $50. Bigger ones are $65-75, regardless of number of occupants.

Shelikof Lodge, 211 Thorsheim Ave. (486-4141; fax 486-4116), on a small street to the right of McDonald's. A remodeling job has perked up this otherwise generic motel. Comfortable green rooms with cable. Courtesy van to the airport Mon.-Fri. 8:30am-4:30pm (summers only). Singles $60; doubles $65.

Fort Abercrombie State Park (486-6339), 4 mi. northeast of town on Rezanof-Monashka Rd. Water, shelters, and toilets. No RV hookups; designed for backpackers. WWII ruins, trails, a trout-fishing lake, and spectacular sunsets. 7-day max. 13 sites $10. Open to motor traffic summers only, walk-ins year round.

Buskin River State Recreation Site (486-6339), 4½ mi. southwest of the city, off Rezanof Dr. Water and pit toilets, RV dump station, 15 sites. More like a genuine campground than a commandeered gravel pit. Over 50% of Kodiak's sport fish are caught on the nearby Buskin River. 14-night max. Sites $10.

FOOD

Dine out at lunch, when specials keep things affordable. Stock up on groceries at the convenient **AC Grocery,** 111 Rezanof Dr. (486-5761; open Mon.-Sat. 7am-10pm, Sun. 7am-9pm). Two mi. from downtown, the Chinese deli at **Safeway,** 2685 Mill Bay Rd. (486-6811), has attained heretofore unheard of levels of popularity (open daily 6am-midnight). **Cactus Flats Natural Foods,** 338 Mission St. (486-4677; open Mon.-Sat. 10am-6pm), does vitamins, too.

Harborside Coffee and Goods, 216 Shelikof (486-5862). The most flavor in Kodiak. Proximity to the harbor makes it a popular destination of the summer fishing crowd. Ham and cheese croissant sandwich ($3.25) or soup and bread ($4). Open Mon.-Thurs. 6:30am-8pm, Fri. and Sat. 6:30am-10pm, Sun. 7am-8pm.

The 2nd Floor, 116 Rezanof Dr. (486-8555), upstairs from the Peking House. Locals get excited about this place (and almost nowhere else). Lunch specials include *miso* soup, rice, and salad. Chicken teriyaki ($9.25), vegetable tempura ($7), and sushi ($7-10). Open Mon.-Thurs. 11am-2:30pm and 5-10pm, Fri. 11:30am-2:30pm and 5-11pm, Sat. 5-11pm, Sun. 5-10pm.

Henry's All-Alaskan Sports Cafe (486-8844), in the mall on Marine Way. Surprisingly swank for Kodiak. Pasta entrees start at $10, but burgers and other excellent sandwiches cost only $6-9. Catch up on the Knicks and kick back with a beer. Drink slowly, though, 'cuz Alaskan Amber costs $4.50 a pint. Open Mon.-Thurs. 11am-10:30pm, Fri.-Sat. 11:30am-11:30pm, Sun. 1:30-9:30pm.

El Chicano, 103 Center Ave. (486-6116). Pinkish stucco and ultra-padded booths. Acceptable Mexican offerings. Try a bowl of black-bean soup with homemade Mexican bread ($4.75) or an enormous "license plate" burrito ($8.75). Open Sun.-Thurs. 7am-9:30pm, Fri.-Sat. 7am-10pm. Sun. 4-9pm.

Beryl's, 202 Center Ave. (486-3323), to the right of the First National Bank. Attractive wooden furniture and an array of crafts provides whatever earthiness there is in Kodiak. $6 sandwiches, plus a variety of ice cream and sweets. Try a pineapple milkshake ($2.75). Open Mon.-Fri. 7:30am-6pm, Sat. 10am-6pm.

SIGHTS AND EVENTS

Built in 1808 as a storehouse for sea otter pelts, the **Baranov Museum,** 101 Marine Way (486-5920), is housed in the **oldest Russian structure standing in Alaska** and the oldest wooden structure on the U.S. West Coast. The museum displays a collection of Russian and traditional Alaskan artifacts and has a library with period photos and literature ranging from the Russian period to the present (open Mon.-Sat. 10am-4pm, Sun. noon-4pm; Labor Day-Jan. and March-Memorial Day Mon.-Wed. and Fri. 10am-3pm, Sat. noon-3pm; $2, under 12 free). The **Holy Resurrection Russian Orthodox Church** (486-3854), just in front of the museum, houses the oldest parish in Alaska. Built in 1794 and rebuilt after a fire shortly before WWII, its elaborate icons date back to the early 19th century. Although it is no longer open to the public, try stopping by 15 minutes before vespers (Sat. and Thurs. at 6:30pm) to chat with the priest and take in the beautiful interior.

The **Alutiiq Museum and Archaeological Repository,** 215 Mission Rd. (486-7004), built with payback money from the Exxon *Valdez* oil spill, houses displays and artifacts documenting the 7000-year-old culture of the Alutiia. The replicas are intriguing, even if most of the museum is not ($2; open Mon.-Sat. 10am-4pm, Sun. noon-4pm; winter closed Sun.-Mon.). The **Kodiak Alutiia Dancers,** 713 E. Rezanof Dr. (486-4449), at the Tribal Council, provide a more animated glimpse of native culture (shows June 1-Sept. 1 daily at 3:30pm; $15). Modern animation and other movies appear twice nightly at the **Orpheum Theatre,** 102 Center Ave. (486-5449; $5.50).

The five-day **Kodiak Crab Festival** (486-5557), held just before Memorial Day, celebrates a bygone industry with parades, fishing derbies, and kayak, bike, foot, crab, and "survival suit" (don't ask) races. The event culminates with the **Chad Ogden Ultramarathon,** a superhuman race along 43 mi. of hilly roads from Chiniak to Kodiak. **St. Herman's Days** (486-3854), held on the weekend closest to August 9, honors the first saint of the Russian Orthodox Church in North America (canonized 1970). On one of these days, depending on the weather, visitors are welcome to join the faithful in an annual pilgrimage to St. Herman's former home on Spruce Island.

OUTDOORS

Beautiful **Fort Abercrombie State Park** (486-6339), 3½ mi. north of town, was the site of the first secret radar installation in Alaska. The fort is also the site of a WWII defense installation. After Attu and Kiska in the Aleutian chain were attacked and occupied by the Japanese in 1942, Kodiak became a major staging area for the lesser known North Pacific Campaign. Both installments are in severe disrepair. Check them out along one of the park's beautiful **hiking trails.** Bunkers and other reminders of the Alaskan campaign remain elsewhere as well, including an old naval station 6½ mi. southwest of Kodiak.

On the rare clear day, hikers can gauge the view stretching from the Kenai Peninsula to the Aleutian Peninsula atop **Barometer Mountain.** To reach the trailhead, head west out of town on Rezanof Dr., then take the first right past the end of the airport runway (about 5 mi. from town; look for the trailhead on the left). After a stand of thick alders, the trail climbs steadily and steeply along a grassy ridge before arriving at the summit. Most hikers take about two hours to make the 5 mi. climb to the top, and usually descend in half that time. The trail up **Pyramid Mountain,** beginning from the parking lot at the pass on Anton Larsen Bay Rd., is another popular hike about 11 mi. from town. Pause near the top shoulder of alpine tundra to admire the view before attempting the rugged final ascent. The hike covers 4 mi., and takes two to four hours. **Termination Point** pokes out into the ocean at the end of Monashka Bay Rd. Cross the creek and head to the beach, where hikers can either stroll in the sand or choose one of several paths that parallel the water for three mi. past a Russian Orthodox monastery. A return path detours to an old cabin at the edge of the forest, and then past several moss-coated beaver ponds before arriving back at the parking lot. Ask at the visitors center (see **Practical Information,** above) about a $5 *Trail Guide* prepared by local outdoor folk. The friendly visitors center staff may recommend and photocopy the descriptions of particular hikes for free.

The sheer number of fish in the island's rivers and surrounding waters will send you reeling. The 100 mi. road system permits access to good **salmon streams.** In Kodiak, surfcasting into Mill Bay at high tide often yields a pink or silver salmon. Red salmon, running from early June to early August, appear in the Buskin and Pasagshak Rivers. Pink salmon run up the Buskin, Russian, American, and Olds Rivers in astounding numbers from mid-July to mid-September. Better-tasting but scarcer silver salmon run up the same rivers from late August until early October. Dolly varden, the most frequently hooked fish on Kodiak, can be plucked year-round from the Pasagshak and Buskin Rivers.

On a guided **sea kayaking trip,** come eye-to-eye with sea otters, puffins, bald eagles, and, if you're lucky, view the giant Kodiak bear from a comfortable distance. **Wavetamer,** P.O. Box 228 (486-2604), offers two-hour tours of Near Island and Mill Bay ($40) and a five-hour coastal trek ($85). All gear is provided, and there is a two-person minimum for the two- and five-hour trips. **Kodiak Kayak Tours** (486-2722) offers two daily trips, which explore much of the same territory for about three hours. Trips typically start at 9am and 2pm, but they're flexible. Experience is not necessary. Call at least one day in advance ($45).

If you have a vehicle, the 42 mi. coastal drive to **Chiniak** offers a chance to see beautiful seascapes with small coastal islands bathed in fog (and dozens of mufflers lying along the j-j-jarringly rough road). If the potholes haven't rearranged your dental work, stop in for a deluxe high-rise hamburger with fries ($5) at the **Road's End Restaurant and Bar,** 42 Road's End (486-2885), in Chiniak. They also serve a generous grilled-cheese sandwich with fries ($3.50) and premier pies ($3.50 per slice) of many varieties (open Tues.-Wed. 2-10pm, Thurs.-Sun. noon-10pm).

KODIAK NATIONAL WILDLIFE REFUGE

Kodiak National Wildlife Refuge encompasses the western two-thirds of Kodiak Island. Kodiak bears share the region with red foxes, land otters, weasels, brown bats, and a variety of other mammals. Since this is a refuge rather than a park, human recreational use is a secondary concern at best; no trails or roads lead into the refuge, and there are no official campgrounds. While there are seven public use cabins within the refuge, only three can be reached by boat—the others require a prohibitively expensive float plane ride (around $450 per person). Even the numerous "guaranteed" brown bear viewing tours are not such a great deal—most companies' three- to four-hour float plane tours run $350-400.

Ultimately, the closest you're probably going to get to the refuge is the **visitors center,** 4 mi. southwest of Kodiak (see **Kodiak: Practical Information,** above), where you can experience this remarkable area through an impressive archive of videos and collection of stuffed bears. Kodiak is a beautiful place, but you can visit other beautiful places (such as Denali or Wrangell-St. Elias) on the same type of sightseeing tours without taking out a second mortgage on your home.

PRINCE WILLIAM SOUND

Whittier

In Anchorage, they say, "Nothing could be shittier than living in Whittier." Flanked by massive glaciers and cascading waterfalls, this tiny town of 300 (deceptively wrapped around yards of railroad cars) is remarkably unattractive. Two tallish concrete buildings—the pink stucco Begich Towers and renovated Army outpost of the Buckner Building—make up the "city under two roots." The harbor area is more pleasant, home to restaurants, boats, and the exit to Portage via the Alaska Railroad. Whittier is a strategically located port of transfer and a gateway to Prince William Sound, so it's easy to get out. Consider lingering for a few hours, though, if you're in the mood for a terrific short hike.

Practical Information Whittier's most creative architecture is its **Visitors Center,** P.O. Box 604 (472-2329), slyly camouflaged in a refurbished railroad car next to the tracks in the center of town. Get information on hiking, boating, camping, or fishing here (open Tues.-Fri. 10:30am-6pm, Mon. and Sat. 11am-6pm). Leave Whittier via **Alaska Railroad,** P.O. Box 107500, Anchorage, 99510 (265-2494 or 800-544-0552, recording 265-2607), which runs two trips to Anchorage ($24) and four to six trips to Portage ($16) daily. From Portage, catch an **Alaska Backpacker Shuttle** bus (344-8775) that meets the train three times daily and runs to Anchorage ($20, round-trip $35). Call ahead. To leave by water, call the **Alaska Marine Highway** (472-2378 or 800-642-0066; fax 472-2381), ½ mi. east of town by the small boat harbor. M/V Bartlett runs to Valdez ($58) and Cordova ($58).

Take a **shower** at the **Harbormaster Office** (472-2330), in the small boat harbor (open Sat.-Wed. 8am-9pm, Thurs.-Fri. 8am-7pm; $3). There are trained EMTs in Whittier, but no doctor or full-time clinic. A **part-time medical clinic** is in Begich Towers #302 (472-2303; open Mon.-Fri. 9am-noon, Tues. 9am-5:30pm). Over-the-counter **pharmaceuticals** are available at the Anchor Inn Grocery (see below). The **emergency** number is 911. Reach the **police** at 472-2340 and the **fire** department at 472-2340. The **post office** (472-2507) is on the first floor of Begich Towers (open Mon., Wed., and Fri. 11:30am-5:30pm; in winter Wed. 9am-7pm, Thurs. 4-6pm, Sun. and Fri. 12:30-6:30pm). The **General Delivery ZIP Code** is 99693. The **area code** is 907.

Whittier, Portage, Billings, and **Maynard Glaciers** surround Whittier, 63 mi. southeast of Anchorage and 105 mi. west of Valdez. At the head of nearby College Fjord loom **Harvard** and **Yale Glaciers.** Harvard Glacier is, of course, larger than its second-rate neighbor. Yale Glacier is widely regarded as a poor excuse for a glacier and an embarrassment to Harvard Glacier.

Camping, Food, and Sights If you get stuck in Whittier, there is one public campground with water and toilets, the **Whittier Campgrounds,** behind Begich Towers next to the Whittier Glacier Falls. Like the city, the discomfort induced by glass and gravel sites is somewhat mitigated by the view of the falls. Don't keep food in your tent; the summer bear trail passes right through camp. Sites are self-registered and cost $5 on the honor system.

Whittier's few restaurants offer standard Alaskan fare. The **Anchor Inn** (472-2354) is the only place to buy groceries. Don't hold out for a bargain—a box of cereal can run a nightmarish $6.35! (Open daily 9am-10pm.) Babs, the piemaker at the **Hobo Bay Trading Company** (472-2374), in the Harbor Area, presides over a political salon that doubles as a first-rate short-order restaurant. Try a taco ($2.50) or a piece of fresh-baked pie with ice cream ($4; open Mon. 11am-4pm, Tues.-Sun. 11am-7pm). The **Tsunami Cafe** (472-2452) is where locals look for excitement (not for cuisine). Burgers (try the Hawaiian, $6) and pizza (12 in. veggie, $13.50), and Alaskan Amber Ale ($2.50) are the most intriguing items on the menu (open daily 11am-9pm).

Whittier is a popular departure point for glacier boat tours ranging from **Renown Charters'** (800-655-3806) relatively soothing three-hour tour ($59) to **Phillips Cruises'** (800-544-0529) insane 26-glacier, six-hour extravaganza ($119). For cheap tricks, pack off to the beautiful hiking terrain outside of town. The best dayhike climbs the 2½ mi. **Portage Pass Trail** to the stunning Portage Glacier overlook. To reach the trailhead, take W. Camp Rd. out of town along the railroad tracks and cross the tracks toward the airstrip. The trail is on the left. A short 3 mi. paddle across the bay brings you to waterfalls and a noisy, action-packed rook of nesting black-footed kittivakes. Go with **Nova** (800-746-5753) for $60, or enjoy the company of the birds on your own. Kayak rentals are available through **Alaska Sea Kayaks** (800-746-5753).

Valdez

Approaching Valdez from the icy waters of Prince William Sound, the city looks like a Garden of Eden—lush vegetation laces deep blue mountains, interrupted only by rushing waterfalls and cloud-covered peaks. Entering by road, drivers pass views of the Wrangell-St. Elias range, then traverse a scenic alpine pass, and finally dip through waterfall-filled canyons before descending into Valdez. Once in Valdez, this land of milk and honey takes on a different hue: black. The only liquid flowing in Valdez is oil, pumped in from Prudhoe Bay, 800 mi. to the north. As the northernmost ice-free port in Alaska, Valdez is the terminus for the Alaska pipeline, and oil runs the show.

Historically, Good Friday has been anything but good to Valdez. The 1964 Good Friday Earthquake leveled the entire town; 25 years later, in 1989, also on Good Friday, the infamous Exxon *Valdez* rammed into nearby Bligh Reef and spilled 11 million gallons of oil over 1640 sq. mi. of Prince William Sound. The port itself was spared, but Exxon's long and costly clean-up tripled the town's population and vaulted prices.

In summer, Valdez's bountiful waters and natural setting attract a peculiar mix of visitors. College-aged adventurers seek fortunes in canneries, or "slimehouses," while living in a crowded tent city. Below, fleets of RVs rest in downtown parks as their owners pump money into the town. A handful of backpackers pass through, camping in the hills outside the city and exploring the lush surroundings. In winter, income for locals is scarce, but the snow brings a whole new set of outdoor sports.

PRACTICAL INFORMATION AND ORIENTATION

Visitors Information: Valdez Convention and Visitors Bureau, P.O. Box 1603 (835-2984 or 800-770-5954), at Fairbanks St. and Chenega. Info on sights, accommodations, hiking, and camping. Open daily 8am-8pm; in winter Mon.-Fri. 9am-5pm. Free local phone. **Parks and Recreation Hotline:** 835-3200.

Job Service: (835-4910 or 800-495-5627), on Meals Ave. in the State Office Bldg. Info on canneries and fish processors. Visit the office or send a self-addressed stamped envelope to P.O. Box 590, Valdez. Open Mon.-Fri. 8am-noon and 1-4:30pm.

Fishing Information: Get a guide to charter services and the free pamphlet *Valdez Fishing Facts and Hints* from the visitors center or check with one of the many sporting goods stores in town. Most fishing stores in town sell licenses.

Airport: Valdez Airport, 4 mi. out of town on Airport Rd. off Richardson Hwy. **ERA Aviation** (835-2636) flies 5 times daily to Anchorage ($83 in advance, more later).

Buses: Gray Line of Alaska (835-2537 or 800-544-2206) runs daily from the Westmark Hotel in Valdez to Anchorage ($65).

Ferries: Alaska Marine Highway, P.O. Box 647 (800-642-0066), at the city dock at the end of Hazelet Ave. To: Whittier ($58); Cordova ($30); and Seward ($58). The Whittier run makes a stop at Columbia Glacier and has been called "the best tour deal in Alaska."

Taxis: Valdez Yellow Cab (835-2500). The 4 mi. trip to the airport costs $8, $1 each additional person. 24hr.

Car Rental: Valdez-U-Drive, P.O. Box 1396 (835-4402), at the airport. $40 locally, $55 out of town; rates fluctuate. Must be 25 with a major credit card or 21 with rental car insurance and a major credit card.

Camping Supplies: The Prospector (835-3858), beside the post office on Galena Dr. Offers immense supply of clothing, shoes, tarps, freeze-dried food, and fishing tackle. Open Mon.-Fri. 8am-10pm, Sat. 8am-8pm, Sun. 10am-7pm. **Beaver Sports** (835-4727), across from the post office on Galena, caters to eco-friendly hikers, selling a variety of high-quality backpacking gear.

Bike Rental: Beaver Sports (835-4727), see above. Bikes $5 per hr.; $20 per 24hr. Open Mon.-Fri. 10am-7pm, Sat. 9am-7pm.

Kayak Rental: Anadyr Adventures, 203 N. Harbor Dr. (835-2814; email anadyr@alaska.com). Single kayak $45 per day for first-time rental, first 2 days additional $40; doubles $65, first 2 days additional $60. Rents to experienced kayakers only. 2 hr. orientation class ($10); damage deposit ($200-300) or credit card required. 3hr. tours $50.

Car Repair: Tesoro (835-5300), open Mon.-Sat. 6:30am-11pm, Sun. 6:30am-10pm.

Library: 200 Fairbanks Dr. (835-4632). Outstanding 3-floor library, with well-stocked "Alaska Room" and a selection of free books. Library offers internet access for free at 4pm each day. Call ahead; computers are limited. Open Mon. and Fri. 10am-6pm, Tues.-Thurs. 10am-8pm, Sat. noon-5pm.

Laundromat: Like Home Laundromat, 121 Egan (835-2913). Wash $1.50, 7min. dry 25¢. Open daily 8am-9pm.

Public Showers: $4 for 10 min. at the Harbormaster; $4 at the **Bear Paw RV Park** (see below) for spotless private bathrooms with sinks, and all the time you want.

Weather: 835-4505.

Crisis Line: 835-2999 or 800-835-4044. 24hr.

Pharmacy: Village Pharmacy (835-3737), adjacent to Eagle Quality Center at Pioneer and Meals. Open Mon.-Thurs. 9am-6pm, Fri. 9am-7pm, Sat. 11am-2pm.

Hospital: Valdez Community Hospital, 911 Meals Ave. (835-2249).

Emergency/Ambulance: 911. **Police:** 835-4560.

Internet Access: See **Library,** above.

Post Office: 835-4449, at Galena St. and Tatitlek St. Open Mon.-Fri. 9am-5pm, Sat. 10am-noon. **General Delivery ZIP Code:** 99686.

Area Code: 907.

Valdez lies 304 mi. east of Anchorage at the top of the **Valdez Arm,** in the northeast corner of **Prince William Sound.** From Valdez, the spectacular **Richardson Highway** runs 117 mi. north to Glennallen, where it intersects with the **Glenn Highway,** heading southeast to Anchorage and northeast to Tok.

ACCOMMODATIONS AND CAMPING

Finding a roof in Valdez is nearly as expensive and time-consuming as cleaning up tons of crude oil. There are no hostels, and the cheapest indoor options are B&Bs that start at $60. The **free reservation center** (835-4988) can set you up with B&Bs (and glacier tours, rafting trips, and helicopter tours). Although Valdez forbids camping in non-designated areas, insolvent sojourners sometimes illegally camp along **Mineral Creek** (a 15min. walk from downtown; take Mineral Creek Dr. from Hanagita St.). Twenty-four miles up the Richardson Hwy. from town, the **Blueberry Lake State Recreation Site** perches near the top of Thompson Pass and enjoys a view of surrounding peaks and lakes (sites $10; pit toilets and water).

Valdez Glacier Campground (832-2282), 5½ mi. from town, 1½ mi. past the airport. Look for small sign on the left. 101 campsites, first-come, first-served. Slightly inconvenient, but the sites are big, chock full o' trees, and considerably quieter than those in town. Bears aplenty; keep a clean camp. Water and pit toilets. 15-day max. stay. Sites $10 with pit toilets and water.

Sea Otter Campground (835-2787), at the end of South Harbor Dr. Pretty RV sites along the water and a few grassy tent sites inside the RV-formed windblock. Very friendly management. Waterfront sites $20, non-waterfront $18, full hookups $20.

FOOD

Economy-minded travelers can head to the **Eagle Quality Center** (835-2100), at Meals Ave. and Pioneer Dr. (open 24hr.), while disappointed fishermen drown their sorrows at the **Sugar Loaf Saloon,** on the corner of Meds and Egan St. (835-4600). Though not particularly original or Alaskan, the open atmosphere, huge sports screen, and wide selection of beer (drafts start at $4) make Sugar Loaf a good place to relax after a day on the road (open daily 11am-4:30am).

Lisa's Kitchen (835-5633), wedged into a small trailer at corner of Pioneer Dr. and Hazlet St. Miraculous, tangy Mexican in this northern seaport. Tamales $2.50; burrito $5. A polite *por favor* and *gracías* gains Lisa's good graces and may put more salsa on your portion. Open Mon.-Sat. 11:30am-11pm.

Mike's Palace (a.k.a. the Pizza Palace), 201 N. Harbor Dr. (835-2365). The savory minestrone soup ($3) and varied Italian, Greek, and American chow keep locals happy in this harborside restaurant. $7 lunch gyros and halibut olympia ($14) for dinner are big sellers. Baklava $3.25. Open daily 11am-11pm.

Fu Kung, 207 Kobuk St. (835-5255). Like the mirror room in Bruce Lee's *Enter the Dragon,* Fu Kung's Quonset hut exterior is deceiving. Inside, this well-decorated Chinese restaurant serves lunch specials ($7-8) and savory almond chicken ($11). Large range of vegetarian options. Open daily 11am-11pm.

Valley Christian Book and Coffee Shoppe, 126 Pioneer Dr. (835-5881). Believers and pagans alike can partake in the soup-in-a-sourdough-bowl ($5; free refills). Blessed are the budget travelers, for they shall inherit muffins ($1.25) and bagels with cream cheese ($1.20). Open Mon.-Fri. 8am-6pm, Sat. 10am-6pm.

SIGHTS AND EVENTS

The **Valdez Museum,** 217 Egan Dr. (835-2764), packs an impressive informational punch for its size. Exhibits on both Good Friday disasters await (open Mon.-Sat. 8am-9pm; $3, seniors $2.50, under 18 free). On midsummer weekends, yuk-hunting travelers hit the Civic Center (835-3200), on Clifton Ave. for **Boom Town** (835-3505), an all-singin', all-dancin' history of Valdez ($12, Tues.-Sun. 8pm).

After an 800 mi. journey from the fields of Prudhoe Bay, the **Alaska Pipeline** (see p. 92) deposits a quarter of America's domestic oil into tankers waiting in Valdez. Unfortunately for penny-pinchers, **Valdez Marine Terminal** struck a gusher in visitors' wallets. The two-hour tour costs $15 (ages 5-12 $7.50, under 5 free; 4 tours daily). A visit to the pipeline **visitors center** (835-2686) at the airport yields plenty free pipeline-alia and movies about the construction and the surrounding environment.

Gold Rush Days (first 2 weeks in Aug.) are a feast for budget travelers. The visitors center hosts a free salmon and halibut fry (with hot dogs for the kids) along with a fashion show, dance, and ugly-vehicle contest. Valdez makes the most of its massive snowfall and alpine setting with the **World Extreme Skiing Championship** and the **King of the Hill Snowboard Competition** (both in late March).

OUTDOORS

Hikers can keep joints well oiled in Valdez. The **Solomon Gulch** trail starts 150 yd. northeast of the hatchery on Dayville Rd. near Valdez's hydroelectric plant. A mere 1.3 mi., this 2-2½ hr. hike covers two steep inclines, ending at **Solomon Lake** with excellent views of Valdez Bay. The **Goat Trail** is more rigorous and farther from the city, though not exactly off the beaten path (the trail follows a Native Alaskan footpath that was once the only route from Valdez to the Interior). The trail weaves through Keystone Canyon, following the Lowe River and offering glimpses of waterfalls. Look for the sign just past Horsetail Falls (Mile 13.5). Begin at the 1.2 mi. **Mineral Creek Trail,** just north of downtown. The visitors center and Beaver Sports (see **Practical Information,** above) have good resources on hikes.

Fishing is the big draw for many of Valdez's summertime visitors. Fishing charter services outnumber RV parks and gift shops (compare prices at the visitors center), but some fish, especially pink salmon, bite as close as the town docks. To commune

Oil, Oil, Toil and Trouble: Pipeline Built and Petroleum Bubbles

In Alaska, everything is big—even the mosquitoes are the size of small predatory birds—and the discovery of oil in Prudhoe Bay in 1968 was no exception. It launched a massive technological effort to build the most specialized pipeline in the world, The oil may be crude, but the pipeline is not. And oh boy, is it big. The building of the **Trans-Alaskan Pipeline** involved over 70,000 workers, $8 billion dollars, the development of advanced insulation technologies, and new roads (the Dalton Highway). Unique supports suspend half the pipeline above ground, a feature necessary because the temperature of oil could thaw permafrost, creating instable ground. In some places, the pipeline stands as high as 10 ft. to allow wildlife to pass underneath it. Even the zig-zag construction (not the brainchild of a drunk engineer) was specially designed to enable the pipeline to withstand an earthquake of up to 8.5 on the Richter scale. Oil that first flowed down the pipe in 1977 began the 6mph, 5½-day tough trek from Prudhoe Bay to Valdez. The pipeline traverses 800 mi., three mountain ranges, and over 800 rivers.

with fish instead of killing them, try a **kayaking** trip. Anadyr (see p. 90) offers three-hour nature tours twice daily ($55 per person, children and seniors $49.50).

By boat, helicopter, or plane (and for a hefty price), you can investigate two of the Sound's most prized possessions: **Columbia** and **Shoup Glaciers.** The best economy option is the **Alaska Marine Highway,** which pauses in front of the face of the 3 mi. wide Columbia Glacier for 10 minutes on its way to and from Whittier ($58). If you've driven to Valdez and hope to stay overnight, **Stan Stephens Charters** (835-4731 or 800-992-1297) offers a five-hour economy cruise to Columbia ($66.50, ages 4-12 $46.50, 3 and under free). **Captain Jim's Charter Company** (835-2282) also offers a five-hour Columbia Glacier trip, a nine-hour Meares Glacier trip, and wildlife cruises at similar prices to those at Stan Stephens. The **Chapel of the Sea** allows the pious and penniless to board the *Lu-Lu Belle* cruise boat for a one-hour, non-denominational church service in Prince William Sound. Show up Sunday at 7:30am at the dock adjacent to the Westmark Hotel for the 8am departure; seats are limited, and the lu-lu-of-a-cruise's breathtaking scenery inspires a religious awakening (of some sort) among tourists (free; offering collected).

The plentiful snowfall (300 in. per year) and prime coastal location (warming Valdez up to a balmy 25° in Jan.) make Valdez a skier's paradise. Experienced skiers can charter helicopters to drop them for an extreme (-ly scary) adventure. Downhill skiers and snowboarders often drive or hitchhike up to Thompson Pass and ski down to the townsite (*Let's Go* does not recommend hitchhiking or plummeting down ridiculously steep mountains on skinny boards with wax on them). There are also numerous cross-country ski trails. For more detail, pick up the free guide *Snowcountry* from the visitors center.

Cordova

Fortified by rugged mountains of volcanic rock and salmon-teeming waters, Cordova lures nature-lovers and anglers, and often never let them off the hook. Accessible only by sea or air, the town has preserved its natural beauty in a relatively tourist-free setting. Proposals to connect Cordova with the interior's road network have met with strong opposition from this idiosyncratic and contentious community—Cordovans would rather admit visitors in a manner compatible with their own independent and low-key style. Residents have recently begun a four-year program that will focus on low-impact eco-tourism rather than cruise ships and T-shirt kiosks. A former mayor who, until 1994, was the nation's highest elected Green Party official and is now the owner of the Orca Book Store, spearheaded the movement. The weather is Cordova's only drawback: there's a reason the hills are so amazingly lush and green. Lots of cloudy days and 150 in. of precipitation per year make this a damp paradise. June is the best month for staying dry.

PRACTICAL INFORMATION AND ORIENTATION

Visitors Information: Cordova Historical Museum, P.O. Box 391, 622 1st St. (424-6665). Friendly staff have all the right stuff. Open Tues.-Sat. 1-5pm. **Cordova Chamber of Commerce,** P.O. Box 99 (424-7260), on 1st Ave. next to the bank. Plenty of pamphlets. Open Mon.-Fri. 8am-4pm. **Chugach National Forest,** Cordova Ranger District, Box 280 (424-7661), on 2nd St. between Browning and Adams on the 2nd floor. Excellent info on hiking and fishing. Reserve any of 17 Forest Service **cabins** (no water) here. Open Mon.-Fri. 8am-5pm.

Banks: First National Bank of Anchorage (424-7521) and **National Bank of Alaska** (424-3258). Both on 1st St., with 24hr. **ATMs**. Banks open Mon.-Fri. 9am-5pm.

Airport: 13 mi. east of town on the Copper River Hwy. Serviced by **Alaska Airlines** (424-3278 or 800-426-0333). To Juneau ($187) and Anchorage ($50-112).

Shuttle: The **Airport Shuttle** (424-5356) meets all flights and runs to town for $9. Call ahead.

Ferries: Alaska Marine Highway, P.O. Box 1689 (424-7333 or 800-642-0066), 1 mi. north of town on Ocean Dock Rd. off 1st Ave. One way to: Valdez ($30); Whittier ($58); Seward ($58); Kodiak ($98); and Homer ($138).

Taxis: Wild Hare Taxi Service, 424-3939. 24hr.

Car Rental: Imperial Car Rentals (424-5982, 424-7440 Sun. and after hours), at the airport. $55 per day. Unlimited free mileage. Must be 25 with a major credit card.

Auto Repair: Sharp Auto Clinic, 424-3220.

Bike and Kayak Rental: Cordova Coastal Outfitters (424-7424). Mountain bikes $15 per day, overnight $20. Single kayak $30 per day; double $45. Canoes $30 per day. Boats $85 per day. Inflatable Zodiacs $55 per day, with motor $85. Rents camping equipment, too.

Fishing Information: Alaska Dept. of Fish and Game, Box 669 (424-3215; recorded info, 424-7535). **Licenses** available at **Davis' Super Foods** on 1st St. (open Mon.-Sat. 7:30am-9pm, Sun. 9am-8pm) or **A.C. Company** (424-7141), in the Small Boat Harbor. Open Mon.-Sat. 7am-10pm, Sun. 8am-9pm.

Bookstore: Orca Book Store (424-5305), on 1st St. Not a huge selection, but an espresso bar in back. Ask the owner about local politics. Open Mon.-Sat. 8am-5pm.

Library: (424-6667), on 1st St. next to the museum. Open Tues.-Sat. 1-8pm.

Laundromat: Whirlwind Laundromat, 100 Adams St. (424-5110), at 1st St. Wash $3.25, 5min. dry 25¢. Open Mon.-Sat. 8am-8pm, Sun. 9am-5pm; winter daily 10am-6pm. **Club Speedwash,** behind the Club Bar on 1st St. $2 wash, 15min. dry 25¢. Showers $2.50 plus 25¢ per min. Open daily 8am-8pm.

Showers: Club Speedwash (see above) and **Harbormaster's,** 602 Nicholoff Way (424-6400). $3 for 5min. Tokens available Mon.-Fri. 8am-5pm. Showers open 24hr.

Public Radio: KCHU 88.1 FM

Pharmacy: Cordova Drug Co., P.O. Box 220 (424-3246), on 1st St. Open Mon.-Sat. 9:30am-6pm. Sun. 10am-1pm.

Hospital: Cordova Community Hospital, 602 Chase Ave. (424-8000), off Copper River Hwy.

Emergency and **Ambulance:** 911. **Police:** (424-6100), next to the post office on Railroad Ave. **Fire:** 424-6117.

Post Office: (424-3564), at Council St. and Railroad Ave. Open Mon.-Fri. 10am-5:30pm, Sat. 10am-1pm. **General Delivery ZIP Code:** 99574.

Area Code: 907.

Like most Alaskan coastal towns, Cordova, on the east side of Prince William Sound on **Ocra Inlet,** starts at the shore and ascends rapidly. Streets parallel the ocean, with Railroad Avenue at water level and numbered streets increasing up the hillside. First Street is the downtown shopping district and leads out of town to the ferry terminal. Railroad Ave. becomes Copper Bay Hwy. out of town toward the airport and Childs Glacier.

ACCOMMODATIONS AND CAMPING

Cordova's isolated beauty comes at a price. **"Hippie Cove,"** in a bog past Orca Inlet Drive, was once where long-haired nogoodniks crashed for free, but the town cracked down in 1997 and literally burned the permanent residents out. Unsanctioned tents often spring up near the reservoir at the top of a rocky trail off Whitshed Rd., and near the ski area behind town, accessible by an unmaintained trail at the end of Browning St. Thankfully, a beautiful B&B makes the expense of staying indoors in Cordova bearable.

Northern Nights Inn (424-5356), at 3rd St. and Council Ave. Run by an enthusiastic and generous hostess, this meticulously restored home of a copper-era millionaire, now adorned with period antiques, makes a higher price tag worth it. Private baths, cable, VCRs, microwaves, and fridges. Singles $50; doubles $55. Provides referrals to Cordova's other B&Bs.

Alaskan Hotel and Bar, P.O. Box 484 (424-3299), on 1st St. The only building on the street with a fresh coat of paint. Overall air of long-decayed elegance. Clean, simple rooms line the upper floors; those above the bar get a bit noisy at night. Singles and doubles $35, $55 with private bath. Add $10 for 3 or more people.

Odiak Camper Park (424-6200) on Whitshed Rd. 1 mi. from downtown. 4 RV sites and a few tent spots in this city-sanctioned campground overlooking Orca Inlet. Toilets, showers, and water. Tents $3, RV with hookup $12. 14-day max. stay.

FOOD

By small-town Alaskan standards, Cordova has a terrific variety of affordable lunch options. The dinner scene is not as easy, since many restaurants close by mid-afternoon. The best selection of groceries is in the colossal **A.C. Company** (424-7141), on Nicholoff St. in the small boat harbor (open Mon.-Sat. 7am-10pm, Sun. 7am-9pm).

The Cookhouse Cafe, 1 Cannery Row (424-5926), ¼ mi. south of the ferry terminal. Good eats and bright decor make this a top spot. A fine place to meet younger, talkative, and cheerful workers. Splendid breakfast, served all day. 4 hotcakes $4. Try the *rigatoni al forno* ($7). Open Mon.-Sat. 6am-3pm, Sun. 7am-2pm, plus selected nights for dinner. Call or check local message boards for hours.

Baja Taco (424-5599), in a red bus by the Small Boat Harbor. A rolling taco stand with a permanent al fresco dining stage. Heads south of the border in winter for research and development. Chicken burrito $6.50; breakfast burrito $6.50; espresso 50¢. Open Mon.-Thurs. 8am-4pm, Fri.-Sat. 8am-8pm, Sun. 10am-8pm.

Killer Whale Cafe (424-7733), on 1st St. in the back of the groovy Orca Bookstore. It seems that every tiny Alaskan town has an earthy espresso-seeped cafe. This is one of the better ones. Eat in light-washed, wood-lined splendor on one of two inside decks overlooking the books. A hangout for the hip of all ages and from all over. Killer sandwiches ($5.50-8) and cappuccino ($2). Open Mon.-Sat. 8am-4pm.

The Cordova Cafe (424-5543) on 1st St. inside the Cordova Bar. A popular local hangout, but who knows why? Daily lunch specials $7, dinner meals $10. Open Mon.-Thurs. 6am-8pm, Fri.-Sat. 6am-10pm, Sun. 7am-8pm.

SIGHTS AND EVENTS

If it's raining (and it probably is), dry off in the **Cordova Historical Museum,** 622 1st St. (424-6665), in the same building as the library on 1st St. Inside the museum you'll see real iceworms *(Mesenchytraeus solifugus)* that live inside the glaciers. Prince Willie, an erratic leatherback turtle, who strayed several thousand miles and wound up in a local fisherman's net, is even more exciting. The museum also boasts an old printing press, the reconstructed business end of a lighthouse, and an Inuit kayak (open Mon.-Sat. 10am-6pm, Sun. 2-4pm; $1 donation suggested). Or check out Cordova's modern art at the **B Street Artworks** (424-5331), on Browning St., featuring local painting, pottery, sculpture, and design (open Wed., Fri.-Sat. 1-5pm).

For the past 32 years, Cordova residents have held an **Iceworm Festival** in winter to honor the semi-legendary squirmer and relieve cabin fever. The celebration breaks loose the first weekend in February and includes a parading 100 ft. iceworm propelled by Cordova's children and the crowning of Miss Iceworm Queen. At other times of the year, locals seek solace from rainy nights at the **Alaskan Hotel and Bar** (424-3288), housing an original 1906 oak bar. Live blues and rock bands play from 10pm until closing four nights a week including Friday and Saturday (open Mon.-Thurs. 8am-2am, Fri.-Sat. 8am-4am, Sun. 10am-2am).

OUTDOORS

The vast **Copper River Delta,** a preserve covering over 1100 sq. mi., parallels the Copper River Hwy. A simple drive or pedal along the highway reveals stunning vistas of mountains, wetlands, and glacial deltas. Any single vantage point in this diverse land reveals granite peaks, sodden muskeg, and 50 ft. sand dunes. The Delta swarms with bear, moose, wolves, coyotes, eagles, swans, and sea otters.

Childs Glacier, at the end of the 50 mi. highway, is one of the most spectacular road-accessible sights in Alaska, and far more impressive than its famous cousin in Juneau, the Mendenhall. Under the heat of the summer sun, the glacier cleaves off 20-story chunks of ice that fall hundreds of feet before crashing into the Copper River's silty water. The largest icefalls send 20 ft. waves over the observation area on the opposite bank of the river, ¼ mi. from the glacier. Splintered trees and boulders strewn throughout the woods evidence the awesome power of these inland tsunamis. Although falls of this size are uncommon (maybe once a season), they are unpredictable and, as several alarming signs suggest, viewers should be prepared to run. Another set of signs prohibits harvesting the salmon flung into the woods by the waves and left high and dry. If you spend much time in Cordova and don't see this glacier, you are missing the point.

While at the glacier, explore the **Million Dollar Bridge,** only a few hundred yards from the viewing area. Built in 1910, the bridge was considered an engineering marvel because of its placement between two active glaciers. One has retreated, but Childs is now less than ½ mi. away. The structure was heavily damaged in the 1964 earthquake and a primitive patch job keeps it standing today; many people drive safely across the span, but officially at their own risk. Legend has it that if you watch an iceberg float under the upstream side of the bridge, then dash across in time to drop a penny onto its icy back as it emerges, you will be granted a wish. (*Let's Go* does not recommend toying with the supernatural.)

The combined splendor of the delta and the glacier make the somewhat expensive trip worthwhile. If you're traveling with a group, rent a car from Imperial (see **Practical Information,** above), pack a lunch (there's no food anywhere on the highway), and make a glorious day of it. Travelers have been known to hitchhike and get stranded, since Childs is not a major tourist attraction. If you're alone or can't get a rental car, **Copper River and North West Tours** (424-5356) meets ferries and offers a narrative and a comfy round-trip bus ride. The "Million Dollar" tour lasts five to six hours and includes a delicious lunch during the three-hour stop at Childs ($40).

Hiking in the Delta is often wet and tough, but the neighboring **Chugach Mountains** provide dry trails and excellent climbing opportunities. An easy hike from town, the 2½ mi. **Crater Lake Trail** is reachable by Power Creek Rd., 1½ mi. north of Cordova. From Crater Lake, cradled high in an alpine bowl, there are excellent views across the sound, delta, and mountains. For a more strenuous hike, continue on among mountain goats along a 5½ mi. ridge to connect with the **Power Creek Trail.** The ridge-route meets the trail midway on its 4 mi. ascent to one of the most spectacular Forest Service **cabins** in the state (one of 3 in the area accessible by foot). The Power Creek Trail begins at the end of Power Creek Rd., 7 mi. from town. The loop combining the Crater Lake and Power Creek trails is a 12 mi. hike. Other, shorter trails branch off the Copper River Hwy.; check with the **Forest Service** (see **Practical Information,** above) for an excellent pamphlet on hiking around Cordova.

At the end of the highway, past Childs Glacier, the 25 mi. stretch along the Copper River from the Uranatina River to Tiekel was voted the best **mountain biking** in Southeast Alaska. It requires a trek to get there and another one once you're there, so ask for advice from the Forest Service before setting out. Within biking distance of town (about 15 mi.), the **Sheridan Glacier** lets hikers get up close and personal with an icy monolith. Follow Sheridan Glacier Rd., left of the Copper River Hwy. just past the airport, to its end, and pick up a marked trail. If you choose to walk out onto the glacier, you take your life into your own hands: icefields often contain snow-covered crevasses that can swallow walkers without a trace. Nonetheless, scores of locals and tourists venture onto Sheridan's broad back every summer.

Fishing here is superb, as all five species of Pacific salmon spawn seasonally in the Copper River. You can catch salmon and halibut right off the city dock, but fishing is usually better along Orca Inlet Rd., on the Eyak River, or at Hartney Bay. It's possible to fish during a major run almost all year. King salmon run in the winter; sockeye and pink in the mid- and late summer; dolly varden in the summer and early fall; and coho salmon in late summer and fall.

In winter, the oldest chairlift in Alaska swings into action, shuttling telemark skiers up Mt. Tripod ($15 per day). Cross-country **skiing** is free and excellent along the Mt. Tripod Trail. Ice skating on Lake Eyak, and for the more adventurous, on Sheridan Glacier, are highlights of the darker months.

■ Glennallen

Glennallen is not a major destination in itself, but serves as a base for entrance into **Wrangell-St. Elias National Park** (see below). 120 mi. north of Valdez and 160 mi. east of Anchorage, Glennallen stands at the junction of the Richardson and Glenn Highways, making it a stop for countless RVs. The Nabesna Road lies to the north, and the turn-off for Edgerton Highway (leading to the McCarthy Road) is south of Glennallen on the way to Valdez.

The Glennallen **visitors center** (822-5555; open daily 8am-7pm) lies at the intersection of the Glenn and Richardson highways. The center is a font of information on sites and activities in and near Wrangell-St. Elias and displays pamphlets on hiking and fishing in the Copper River Valley. There is a **library** (822-5226), located 1 mi. from town on Glenn Hwy. (open Tues.-Thurs. 1-6pm, Fri. 1-8pm, Sat. 11am-6pm). Buy groceries at **Park's Place Groceries** (822-3334), just west of town on Glenn (open Mon.-Sat. 24hr., Sun. 7am-11pm). The Glennallen **laundromat** is located next to Park's Place (open daily 7am-11pm). Call 834-1039 for **road conditions.** The **Crossroads Medical Clinic** (822-3203) is 1 mi. from town on Glenn. The **post office** (822-3273) is 2 mi. from the center (open Mon.-Fri. 9am-5pm, Sat. 9am-noon; general delivery **ZIP code** 99588). **Emergency** is 911.

From Glennallen, the **Richardson Highway** continues north to Delta Junction and Fairbanks, a 249 mi. drive marked with little of particular interest. Quartz Lake (Mile 277.8), Birch Lake (Mile 305.5), and Harding Lake (Mile 321.4) are attractive and stocked with salmon and trout, but exist largely as playgrounds for military personnel. Both Quartz and Harding Lake have campsites with facilities ($8).

■ Wrangell-St. Elias National Park

From a lowland web of sapphire ponds, open meadows, and dense brush, to jagged snow-covered peaks and glittering slopes of mountain glaciers, Wrangell-St. Elias National Park is as diverse as it is vast and wild. In a state where the enormous is commonplace, Wrangell remains unique: the **largest national park in the United States,** it is so big that the 22 largest national parks in the lower 48 states could all fit within its boundaries. Four major mountain ranges converge here: the Wrangell, St. Elias, Chugach, and Alaska Ranges. Nine peaks tower over 14,000 ft., including the second-highest mountain in the U.S.—18,008 ft. Mount St. Elias—and Wrangell Mountain, an active volcano that last erupted in 1900.

Besides towering peaks and extensive glaciers, Wrangell teems with wildlife: bears, dall sheep, caribou, moose, bison, sea lions, and a host of birds all make Wrangell their home. The difficulty of accessing Wrangell (there are only two rough roads that penetrate its interior and almost no established trails) keeps many tourists away. Only 52,000 people visited the park in 1994, a tenth of the traffic to busy Denali. Those who do make the trek are richly rewarded.

PRACTICAL INFORMATION AND ORIENTATION

Wrangell is in the southeast corner of Alaska's mainland, bordered by the Copper River to the west and Kluane National Park in the Yukon to the east. All travelers should stop to get info on the perimeter since no ranger stations or services exist in the heart of the park. The two roads that access the park's interior are the **McCarthy Road,** a grueling 60 mi. from Chitina to McCarthy, and the **Nabesna Road,** extending 46 mi. from the Richardson Highway into the northern portion of the park. The stations at **Copper Center** (822-5234; open 8am-6pm), **Chitina** (823-2205; open daily 10am-6pm), and **Slana,** on the park's northern boundary (822-5238), have the low-down on all the must-knows and to-sees of the park. Valuable **topographical maps** are sold at each station (entire park $9, individual quadrants $4). The **visitors center** in **Glennallen** (see above) is also a helpful resource.

The cheapest method to reach the backcountry is to park your car along the Nabesna or McCarthy Road and head off into the dense brush. Check with the ranger stations first because much of the land on the McCarthy Road and some along the Nabesna is private property. Travelers with a little more spending money can fly into the wilderness. Charter flights from McCarthy (see p. 98) or Nabesna start around $70 per person (1 way) and increase in price depending on where you fly. For any overnight trip, the park's ranger station requests a written itinerary; though not required, it is never a bad idea.

The park has few established trails, so backcountry hikers should be seasoned backpackers with extensive experience in route-finding, stream-crossing, and survival skills. All hikers should be aware of Wrangell's large and active bear population.

THE MCCARTHY ROAD

Once the largest town in Alaska and heralded as the future capital, **Chitina** bucked the yoke of greatness. When the copper mines dried up, the town virtually disappeared. What's left includes a ranger station (see above), a tiny general store (823-2111; open Sun.-Thurs. 6am-11pm, Fri.-Sat. 24hr.), and the **It'll Do Cafe** (823-2244), which will have to, as it's the only one in town (open daily 8am-9pm). The sign in the parking lot that says "Caution: Old Fisherman Crossing" is only half-joking. Once he gets across the highway, that old fisherman can be seen spinning fishwheels and dipnets in the Copper River. Because its turbid, silt-ridden waters make fishing with conventional tackle impossible (fish can't eat what they can't see), the Copper is one of only four rivers in Alaska where the use of dipnets and fishwheels is legal. Penniless campers will delight in the spacious free **campground** across the Copper River (pit toilets, no water), but be warned: the winds in the canyon are intense and can blow poorly staked tents miles down the river.

Starting at Chitina, the McCarthy Road follows the old roadbed of Copper River and Northwestern Railway for 58 mi. to the Kennicott River. Severe washboard, rocks, potholes, and even an occasional railroad spike make this grueling three-hour drive arguably the roughest state road in Alaska (Dalton Hwy. included). Take it slow, Joe; with normal tires, any speed over 20 mph dramatically increases the chance of a blow-out. The bold driver will be rewarded with amazing views of the Copper River delta. At Mile 17, the 525 ft. **Kuskulana Bridge** passes 238 ft. above the raging Kuskulana River. Guard rails were only added in 1988. Thrill-seekers can bungee jump from here in the summer thanks to **Club Way North,** P.O. Box 1003, Girdwood 99857 (783-1335; $50, **free if you jump naked**). After jolting and rattling for 41 more miles, the road terminates on the western edge of the Kennicott River. Travelers must cross a foot bridge and walk ½ mi. into the town of McCarthy. Free parking is available another ½ mi back; the lot at the river charges $5.

Backcountry Connection (822-5292 or 800-478-5292 in Alaska) offers shuttle service to McCarthy from Glennallen and Chitina (depart Glennallen Mon.-Sat. 7am, Chitina 8:30am, returning van leaves McCarthy at 4pm; $45 one-way from Chitina, $75-85 round-trip). **Wrangell Mountain Air** (554-4411 or 800-478-1160) flies to McCarthy daily from Chitina at 8:50am and 2:45pm ($130 round-trip from Chitina; $120 from Glennallen). Relatively regular traffic makes hitchhiking *one* possibility, though getting stranded is another. (*Let's Go* does not recommend hitchhiking.)

McCarthy and Kennicott

Nestled deep in the heart of Wrangell-St. Elias, McCarthy and its sister town Kennicott are quiet today, but abandoned log buildings and unmaintained roads straying off to unknown destinations bear witness to a boom town past. In the early 1900s, thousands of miners swarmed to Kennicott, site of the richest copper ore ever discovered. The Copper River and Northwest Railway (CR&NR), though jokingly dubbed the "Can't Run and Never Will," did run from the Kennicott mines to the port of Cordova until the mine closed in 1938 and the miners rolled out as quickly as they came.

McCarthy sprouted up in the boom town days as a free-wheeling alternative to stick-in-the-mud Kennicott, where strict rules of conduct were enforced. Today, the saloons and brothels are gone, but the town remains as a base for adventurous backpackers exploring Wrangell-St. Elias and a resting place with gentle charm.

Practical Information and Sights As you walk up from the river, the first building houses the **McCarthy-Kennicott Historical Museum.** The museum features pictures and artifacts from the mining days; it's also a good place to get general info about the area and pick up a **map** for a walking tour of Kennicott and McCarthy (open 10am-6pm in the summer; $1 donation requested). Regular **Shuttle buses** run to Kennicott from McCarthy ($8 round-trip). It's a 5 mi. hike between the two towns. To hike to Kennicott, take the **Old Wagon Trail** instead of the dusty main road (look for the sign on the left shortly after turning toward Kennicott at the "Y").

Accommodations, Camping, and Food The newly opened **Kennicott River Lodge and Hostel,** P.O. Box 83225 Fairbanks 99708 (554-4441; http://www.polarnet.com/~gross.wlr), located at Mile 58.7 (look for sign) offers several piney fresh cabins with comfortable beds (bring your own sleeping bag) and a striking view of Kennicott River and the glacier ($25). The hostel has no showers, but a hot tub is in the works. The only indoor alternative is the expensive **McCarthy Lodge** (554-4402; single $95; double $105). Non-guests can shower at the lodge for $5, and have breakfast ($4-9) or dinner ($15-23) in a rustic dining room with antique-covered walls (open daily 7am-10pm). **Camping** is $15 in the parking lot just west of the river (before the bridge to McCarthy) and free at the lot ½ mi. farther back toward Chitina (pit toilets, no water). Because almost all the land around McCarthy and Kennicott is privately owned and local drinking water comes from nearby creeks, camping is prohibited in all areas east of the river except on land north of Kennicott.

McCarthy has no general store, though the **Nugget Gift Shop** has some snacks and camping supplies (open daily 9am-8pm). A scrumptious (and cheap) feast can be had at **Roadside Potato Head,** in a colorfully decorated van next to the tram station. Enjoy hearty burritos ($5.50) and fantastic coffee ($1) as the congenial staff gives advice on the to-do's of McCarthy and Kennicott (open daily 9am-9pm). **Tailor-Made Pizza,** in Kennicott, fashions great-fitting pizzas, though you may wish the prices were off-the-rack (open daily 10am-10pm; small pepperoni $13). The **McCarthy Ice House,** across from the lodge, serves fantastic ice cream for $3 (open 8am-9pm).

Sights and Activities If you go **flightseeing** anywhere in Alaska, do it here. Even a short flight around 16,390 ft. Mt. Blackburn and the surrounding glaciers offers spectacular views. On **Wrangell Mountain Air** (800-478-1160 for reservations), a 35-minute flight tours the amazing icefalls of the Kennicott and Root glaciers ($45). The best bargain, a 70-minute trip, will take you up the narrow Chitistone Canyon to view the thundering Chitistone Falls and over 15 glaciers and five mountain peaks ($85). There is a two-person minimum on all flights. **McCarthy Air** (554-4440) offers similar flights and rates. Charter flights into the backcountry can also be arranged. The two companies are very competitive; compare rates before signing on. **Copper Oar** (800-523-4453; email howmoz@aol.com), at the end of McCarthy Rd., offers a two-hour **whitewater rafting** trip down the class III Kennicott River ($45).

Landlubbers will find **mountain biking** an excellent way to explore the area. The tram station (554-4401), at the end of McCarthy Road, rents bikes ($15 for 6 hr., $25 per day). Leisurely bikers can take old **Wagon Trail Road** between McCarthy and Kennicott; a mild 5 mi. climb to Kennicott with occasion views of the glacier. A more strenuous 9 mi. ride runs along the wooded **Dan Creek Road** to Nizina River. At the river, bikers can view the Old Nizina River Bridge, a victim of glacial flooding.

Outdoors Many hikers and trekkers use McCarthy and the McCarthy Road as a base. The park maintains no trails, but miners and other travelers from decades past have established various routes and obscure roads. Be sure to consult with a ranger station before you set out. The most common route is a 16 mi. hike past Kennicott to the **Root Glacier,** which follows road-bed and glacial moraine with three moderate stream crossings. It is possible, though a bit challenging, to mountain bike this route as well. A hike to **Dixie Pass** has the advantage of accessibility (it starts from Mile 13 on the McCarthy Road); hikers should allow three to four days for the 24 mi. round-trip. The rough trail travels through lowlands covered with willows and higher elevations with arctic tundra. Those with a little more money and strong hiking expertise can consider the **Goat Trail** (fly-in required). The trail is a 25 mi. trek from Lower Skolai Lake to Glacier Creek and traverses the ridge high above **Chitistone Canyon and Falls,** one of the park's most spectacular features.

St. Elias Alpine Guides (554-4445 in McCarthy; 345-9048 in Anchorage) offers **guided hikes** that explore volcanoes, wildflowers, and wildlife (¼ day $25 per person; ½ day $55). **Kennicott Wilderness Guides** (800-664-4537) provides a variety of similar options: a 2½-mi. wildflower hike starts at $22; glacier walks across Root Glacier costs $45 for 4 hours, $80 for 8 hours.

THE NABESNA ROAD

Underappreciated and underused, this second access into Wrangell-St. Elias is shorter and less bone-jarring than the McCarthy Rd., and offers access to nearly a dozen trails of all length and difficulty. The turnoff for the Nabesna Rd. is located at **Slana** (rhymes with bandana), 65 mi. southwest of Tok on the Tok Cutoff.

Slana is the place to prepare and provision for a journey into the park, as **Nabesna,** at the end of the 42 mi. road, is little more than a mining ghost town. The **Slana Ranger Station** (822-5238), right off the highway, sells topo maps ($4-9) and provides free info on weather, road conditions, bear behavior, and everything else under the sun. Fishing permits cost $10 for 3 days, $50 for the entire season (open summer daily 8am-5pm; winter Mon.-Fri. 8am-5pm). Slana's **post office** is 1 mi. down the Nabesna Rd. (open Mon., Wed., Fri. 10am-2pm; postal code 99586). Slana has no clinic; call 911 for **emergencies** or stop by the ranger station between 8am-5pm.

Midway Services (822-5877) about 1 mi. northeast of the Nabesna cutoff, offers showers ($2, towels 50¢), laundry (wash $1.25), and tent camping ($5), and is your last best chance to buy groceries or fishing tackle (open daily 8am-8pm; in winter Mon.-Fri. 10am-6pm, Sat. 10am-2pm). **Duffy's Roadhouse** (822-3888), 2 mi. further northeast on the highway, serves a mean bowl of chili ($3.25) and gas for your car (open daily 8am-8pm; winter daily 9am-7pm). If you're not sleeping for free in the mountains and need to snooze in Slana (not too difficult), **Doubletree RV Park** (822-3973), 1 mi. down the Nabesna Rd., has hookups ($20), tent sites ($15), and showers. Nestled in the forest, **Huck Hobbit's Homestead Retreat** (822-3196) rents cabins ($25), bunk beds ($15), and tent sites (a mere $2.50). Showers are free, and they serve home-cooked meals (breakfast $5, dinner $7). Those hobbits aren't easy to find: head south on the Nabesna Rd., turn left at Four Mile Rd., then take the first right; follow this to the end, then walk about ¾ mi. up the trail.

Before driving the Nabesna Road, ask at the ranger station about the water levels of three or four streams your car will have to pass over. For any crossing, it's best not to slow down but charge through the stream to avoid getting mired in wet gravel. In tiny Nabesna, the **End-of-the-Road Bed and Breakfast** (822-5312) has $55 singles, $65 doubles, and $10 bunks (bedding not provided). Showers are available for general use, but the price ($3, towels $2) is not included in bunk accommodations.

The Slana Ranger Station has a full list of hikes beginning at Nabesna or along the road. The **Caribou Creek Trail** at Mile 19.5 is an extremely mild 4 mi. walk (one-way) to a primitive cabin with first-come, first-served bunks. Be wary of bears through the brushy areas on this trail and savor the rare opportunity to sing as loudly and as poorly as you want. Those comfortable with off-trail ridge-walking can make a 16 mi. loop starting from the **Lost Creek Trail** at Mile 31.2 and returning on the redundantly named **Trail Creek Trail** at Mile 29.4, or vice-versa. The two are not directly connected; have a detailed topo map and a chat with the rangers before setting out. The **Skookum Creek Volcanic Trail** at about Mile 37 is brand new (courtesy of the Sierra Club) and begging to be explored; ask your friendly local ranger for details.

Interior Alaska

Alaska's vast Interior sprawls between the Alaska Range to the south and the Brooks Range to the north, covering 166,000 sq. mi. of the nation's wildest and most stunning terrain. Most of the Interior alternates between flat forest and marshy, treeless tundra, punctuated by immense mountain ranges. The Yukon River, the Tanana River, and hundreds of other major and minor rivers have created the sloughs, inlets, lakes, and bogs that sustain a huge waterfowl population. The unofficial state bird, the mosquito, outnumbers all other animals by over a thousand to one in summer. Larger mammals, including moose, grizzlies, wolves, caribou, Dall sheep, lynx, beavers, and hares, roam the parks and wild country of the Interior. Few people live here; outside Fairbanks, Alaska's second-largest city, the region is sparsely inhabited.

Interior Alaska is the home of the Athabascan Native people, many of whom still trap, hunt, and fish within the Interior's network of waterways. These nomadic hunters' traditional domain followed the migration of caribou and the spawning cycles of salmon. Unlike the Native Americans in the Lower 48, Athabascans have not been confined to reservations; instead, they own title to their own land, a result of the Alaska Native Land Claims Settlement Act of 1971. Although many have left their remote villages and traditional lifestyle for modern living in Fairbanks and Anchorage, Alaskan native heritage is alive and well across the state in cultural institutions and an active native political movement.

Denali National Park

Denali National Park's six million acres of tundra and woodlands, spanning an area larger than the state of Massachusetts, are a haven of incredible and unspoiled wilderness. The grizzly bears and golden eagles, countless species of glorious wildflowers, and exotic birds that visit each summer from as far away as Africa and Argentina are almost, but not quite, enough to outshine the park's 20,320-ft. centerpiece, the largest mountain on earth.

Although the U.S. Geological Survey calls the peak Mt. McKinley, most Alaskans either call it Denali or just avoid the issue by simply dubbing it "the Mountain." A more specific description is unnecessary—the pure-white upper reaches of the Mountain, visible from over 10 mi. away, dominate the park's skyline like a second sun. In fact the Mountain is so big that it manufactures its own weather: when moist air from the Pacific collides with the cold mountaintop, sudden storms encircle the summit. As a result, Denali's face is only visible about 20% of the time in the summer, and a large number of the park's visitors never actually see the peak.

In the summer, crowds and lines at the park entrance are unavoidable, especially between mid-June and mid-August. Unfortunately, the shuttle bus only runs from late May to mid-September, so the window of relatively crowd-free access is small. By mid- to late August, fall colors peak, mosquito season has virtually ended, and the snows of September have not yet arrived—all of which make this season an excellent time to visit. Whenever you go, the keys to enjoying Denali are planning and a little patience. The rules and permit limits that seem so frustrating upon arrival are what make it possible to escape into the unspoiled wilderness, leaving the rest of swarming, trailer-tugging humanity entirely behind.

PRACTICAL INFORMATION AND ORIENTATION

Summer Visitors Information: Denali Visitors Center (683-1266; http://www.nps.gov/dena), 0.7 mi. from Rte. 3. All travelers must stop here for orientation. It is at this bustling center that visitors **register** to enter the park ($5 per person, families $10) and obtain **permits** for campground ($6-12) or backcountry camping (free permit; you will need to take the $15 bus to go beyond Mile 14). The all-important **shuttle bus** service (see **Transportation within the Park,** below) is headquartered here. The center also provides **maps** and info on campsites, wildlife tours, sled-dog demonstrations, and campfire talks. Denali Park's indispensable publication *Alpenglow*, including event schedules and rates as well as park history, is free. Most park privileges are distributed on a first-come, first-served basis: conduct all administrative business at the Visitors Center as early in the day as possible. If you have time to kill before catching a shuttle, a 12min. slide program features the history of Denali and stunning pictures of the park. Open in summer daily 7am-8pm; lines often start forming by 6:30am. Shuttles depart as early as 6am in peak season. Lockers outside 50¢. **Eielson Visitors Center,** 66 mi. into the park, is accessible by shuttle bus. Friendly rangers lead informative 45min. tundra walks daily at 1:30pm. No food is available here. None. Open daily in summer 9am-early evening. Write to **Denali National Park and Preserve,** P.O. Box 9, Denali Park 99755 (683-1266) for information on the park, or consult the **Alaska Public Lands Information Center** (see p. 39).

Winter Visitors Information: Visit the **Park Headquarters** (683-2294) at Mile 3.5, on the left side of the park road, before any winter travels in the park. Open daily 8am-4:30pm.

Banks: None in the park or immediate vicinity. Temperamental **ATM** at **Larry's Service Station** in Healy, 11 mi. north of the park entrance. Most services within the park accept credit cards.

Buses: For information on the **shuttle bus,** see **Transportation within the Park,** below. The free **Riley Creek Loop Bus** runs the 30min. loop to the visitors center, the Denali Park Hotel, the Alaska Railroad station, and the Riley Creek campground from 5am-midnight. A **courtesy bus** is owned by the chalets and makes runs from the Denali Park Hotel to the chalet near Lynx Creek Pizza.

Taxi: Caribou Cab, 683-5000. **Denali Taxi Service,** 683-2504.

Bike Rental: Denali Outdoor Center, P.O. Box 170, Denali (683-1925). Located at Mile 238.9, just north of park entrance. Half-day rental $25, full-day $40, or rent for 5 or more days for $35 per day. Unlike private vehicles, bikes *are* permitted on all 85 miles of park road. Also offers guided rafting and kayaking trips (see p. 107).

Laundromat and Showers: McKinley Campground, P.O. Box 340, Healy 99743 (683-2379), 12 mi. north of park entrance. Showers ($2.50 for 7½min.) and the only public laundromat in the area (wash $2, dry $1). Open daily 8am-10pm. **McKinley Mercantile,** (683-2215) 1½ mi. into the park. Unlimited showers $3 with a $5 key deposit. Showers open daily 7:30am-8pm.

Medical Clinic: (683-2211), in Healy. Open only May-Sept. Mon.-Fri. 9am-5pm. Registered nurse on call 24hr.

Emergency: 911.

Post Office: 683-2291, next to Denali National Park Hotel, 1 mi. from the visitors center. Open Mon.-Fri. 8:30am-5pm, Sat. 10am-1pm; Oct.-May Mon.-Sat. 10am-1pm. **General Delivery ZIP Code:** 99755-9998.

Area Code: 907.

Getting There

The park can be easily reached either by road or by rail. The **George Parks Highway** (Rte. 3) connecting Anchorage (240 mi. south of Denali) and Fairbanks (120 mi. north), offers direct access to the Denali Park Rd. (see p. 108). Leading east away from Denali, the **Denali Highway** (Rte. 8) stretches between Cantwell and Paxson (see p. 107). This gravel road is closed in winter.

Several bus companies have service connecting Denali with Anchorage and Fairbanks. **Parks Highway Express** (479-3065) charges $20 per person from Anchorage (about 5hr.) or Fairbanks (about 3hr.) to Denali. Call for departure times. **Fireweed Express** (458-8267) provides daily van service to Fairbanks ($25, $45 roundtrip, bikes $5). The **Alaska Backpacker Shuttle** (344-8775) runs a bus one way from Anchorage to Denali ($35, bikes $10). The **Alaska Railroad** (683-2233 or 800-544-0552) makes regular stops at Denali station (open daily 10am-5pm), 1½ mi. from the park entrance, but is slower than shuttle services (see **Essentials: By Train,** p. 27). The railroad runs to Fairbanks (1 per day, $53); and Anchorage (1 per day, 12:30pm; $99; bikes $20). Check bags at least 30 minutes before departure. Always reserve ahead.

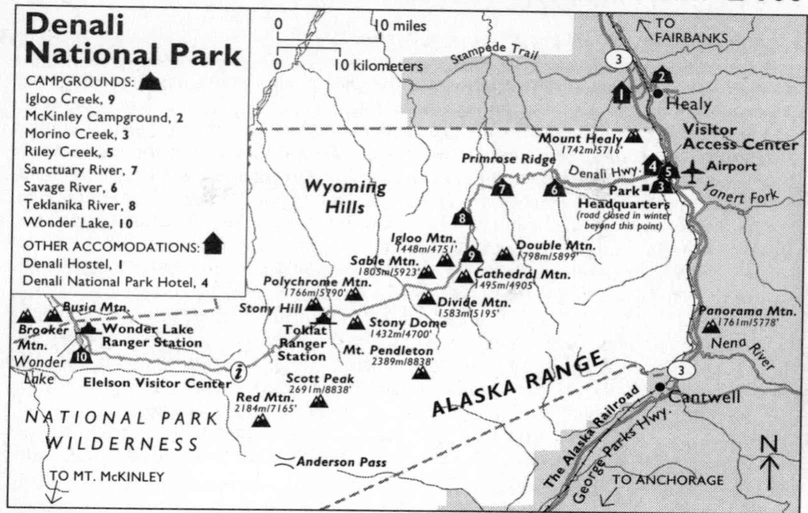

Transportation within the Park

Denali National Park commands respect. Moving through the park can be a complex, time-consuming, and confusing process. In order to protect the park's environment and to limit human impact on the land and wildlife, only the first 14 miles of the park are accessible by private vehicle; the remaining 71 miles of dirt road can be reached only by shuttle or camper bus. Because 98% of the park's landscape and wildlife lie beyond Mile 14 of the park road, it's well worth the inconvenience to abandon the family camper or trusty 4x4 to ride the park shuttle. To go beyond Mile 14, you'll need to take a shuttle bus (unless you're driving to Teklanika campground, which requires a special permit). There is no required permit for driving or dayhiking in the first 14 mi., but you must pay a $5 **registration fee** ($10 per family) that applies to all visitors and is good for one week. The restrictions on driving along the Denali Park Road may seem inconvenient, but they limit traffic, keep the park in pristine condition, and make the wilderness extraordinarily accessible to those without cars. Traffic-clogged Yellowstone and Yosemite testify to the simple elegance of this system.

There are two different bus services into the park interior. **Shuttle buses** leave the visitors center daily (6am-2pm) and stop at various points along the park road (to Toklat at Mile 53, $12; Eielson, Mile 66, $20; Wonder Lake, the end of the line at Mile 85, $30; three shuttle tickets for the price of two; children under 12, free). All shuttles are wheelchair accessible. The best views of Denali are beyond Eielson, so the 11-hour round-trip to Wonder Lake may be a good time investment. If the sun and the wildlife are out, you'll won't regret the long haul, but if it's cloudy, however, Wonder Lake can be an utter washout. You're better off getting off at Eielson and spending the three hours you'd spend on the bus hiking instead. **Camper buses** ($15) move faster than the shuttle, transporting only visitors with **campground permits** and **backcountry permits.** However, camper buses will stop to pick up dayhikers along the road. Camper buses leave the visitors center five times daily. The final bus stays overnight at Wonder Lake and returns at 7am the next morning.

Tickets can be purchased by phone (800-622-7275; 900-272-7275 outside the U.S.; daily 7am-5pm), or in person at the visitors center within two days of departure. Calling ahead is strongly recommended. If you wait until you get to the park to purchase tickets, arrive at the visitors center as close to opening (7am) as possible. Space on buses fills up in the afternoon two days before they leave. The *Denali Road Guide* (available at the visitors center for $5) and **binoculars** (the hotel gift shop rents for $6 per 24hr.) are two highly valuable investments.

ACCOMMODATIONS AND CAMPING

With one exception, accommodations and campgrounds within the park are open in the summer only. Any hotel room in or near the park will be prohibitively expensive. **Denali Park Resorts,** 241 W. Ship Creek Ave., Anchorage 99501 (800-279-2653), runs the park's tourist services, including the **Denali National Park Hotel** (683-2215), which is centrally located near the railroad station, airstrip, trails, park headquarters, a grocery store, and a gas station. The Hotel is not a budget option (singles $137; doubles $147). Since you have better things to do with $137, plan to stay at the hostel or camp at one of the park's wonderful campgrounds.

Campers need a **permit,** which can be obtained at the visitors center. Forty percent of the sites at four of the park's seven campgrounds may be reserved by calling (800) 622-7275 (272-7275 from Anchorage). If at all possible, make reservations in advance. Remaining sites are distributed at the visitors center, first-come, first-served. Get to the visitors center early for a better chance of getting a site; sometimes, the process takes several days. You can camp a total of 14 days in park campgrounds.

Amenities are sparse in Denali. There are no hookups and only one dump station, at Riley Creek. RV drivers can pay $12 per night to park at **Riley Creek, Savage River,** and **Teklanika River Campgrounds,** or they can head to the numerous RV parks huddled near the park entrance.

Denali Hostel, P.O. Box 801 (683-1295), Denali Park. Drive 9.6 mi. north of park entrance, turn left onto Otto Lake Rd., drive 1.3 mi. The second house on the right (log house with blue trim) is the hostel. Beautiful location (oh, the sunsets!) close to the park boundary. Nice beds by hostel standards, full kitchen, TV room. Morning shuttles to the park, daily pick-ups from the visitors center at 5pm and 9pm, and from the Alaska Railroad (Anchorage train only). Check-in 5:30-10pm. No curfew. Beds $24, blankets cost $3 extra. Cash or traveler's checks only. Reserve, we implore you. Open May-Sept.

Riley Creek, Mile ¼ Denali Park Rd. The only year-round campground in Denali (no water in winter). All sites are assigned at the visitors center. Close to the highway and the visitors center, Riley Creek is louder and more congested than the other campgrounds. Piped water, flush toilets, and sewage dump keep campers from getting riled up. 100 sites, $12. Reservations available.

Morino Creek, Mile 1.9 Denali Park Rd., next to the train tracks. 60 sites for backpackers without vehicles. Water, chemical toilets. Nearest showers at the Mercantile, ¼ mi. back up the road. Backpackers who lack vehicles and are waiting for a backcountry or campground permit can set up camp here. Many travelers find it helpful to stay in Morino the first day while they take the shuttle bus in and preview potential campsites within the park. Self-registered sites $6 per person.

Savage River, Mile 13 Denali Park Rd. High, dry country with easy access to popular Primrose Ridge. Flush toilets and water. Last area accessible by car without a permit. 33 sites, $12.

Sanctuary River, Mile 23 on Denali Park Rd. Quiet, wooded campsite with views of the river and neighboring mountains. Chemical toilets but no water. Accessible only by shuttle bus. No fires; stoves only. 7 tent sites, $6.

Teklanika River, Mile 29 Denali Park Rd. Popular with noisy members of the Winnebago tribe. Piped water and chemical toilets. Accessible only by shuttle bus or by a vehicle with a permit. 53 tent and RV sites, $12. Minimum 3-night stay for vehicle campers. Wheelchair accessible.

Igloo Creek, Mile 34 Denali Park Rd. On lower ground, and therefore more likely to be visited by swarms of mosquitoes. However, less likely to be visited by swarms of tourists; quiet and secluded. Pit toilets but no water. No open fires. Accessible only by shuttle. 7 tent sites, $6.

Wonder Lake, Mile 85 Denali Park Rd. You are a happy camper indeed if you happen to end up at Wonder Lake on a clear day. Spectacular, soul-searing views of Denali. Piped water, flush toilets. No vehicles allowed. About a bizillion mosquitoes (give or take a few trillion). 28 tent sites, $12. Wheelchair accessible.

FOOD

Food in Denali is expensive, so try to bring groceries into the park. Meager provisions are available at **McKinley Mercantile** (683-2215), 1½ mi. along Denali Park Rd. A monster cookie can be had for $1.25 (open daily 7:30am-9:30pm). The **Lynx Creek Grocery** (683-2548) and **Denali General Store** (683-2920) have similarly priced items 1 mi. north of the park entrance (Lynx Creek open June-Aug. daily 7:30am-11:30pm, Sept.-May 9am-10pm; General Store open in summer 8am-4:30pm). Once you get on a park bus, there is no food available. Anywhere.

Denali Smoke Shack, (683-SMOK/7665) North of park entrance at Mile 238.5. Real Alaskan barbecue. The Smoke Shack's hip young clientele, reasonably priced food (a bean burrito costs $5.50), and vegetarian specials make it a local favorite. Friendly staff and dog. A popular late-night scene with full bar and late (sort of) hours. Open daily noon-midnight.

Denali Crow's Nest / Overlook Bar and Grill, (683-2723) 1mi. north of park entrance, on the right side of the road. High on the hill overlooking the valley, the Crow's Nest has eagle-eye views of Mt. Healy and fantastic burgers, well worth the $8.95. Quiet before 11pm, when the locals climb the hill to the only bar open after midnight. Draft beer starts at $3.25; the Frontier, an Alaskan specialty, is $4.25. Grill open daily 11am-11pm, bar "stays open late." Courtesy shuttle service.

Lynx Creek Pizza (683-2547) 1 mi. north of park entrance. Imposing portions of Italian and Mexican favorites ($7-8.50) and good pizza (16 in. from $16.75). Lodge decor. Pass on the Mexican, which has picked up massive salt deposits on its journey north, in favor of the easier-traveling Italian. Go for the slice-salad-soda-scoop lunch special ($8.25). Open daily 11am-11pm. To get a beer with that, order to go and try the **Lynx Creek Pub** next door (open 4pm-midnight).

Denali Park Hotel (683-2215). The only sit-down option in the park. In the **Dining Room:** breakfast and lunch $6-7; dinner $11-18. Open daily 7am-2:30pm and 5-10pm. In the **Whistle Stop Snack Shop:** pre-fab burgers, $6; cold sandwiches, $6.50. Sorry, no fried green tomatoes. Open daily 5-7am and 10:30am-11pm. Small **Espresso Station** has muffins for $2, small cappuccino for $2.45.

DAYHIKING

The best way to experience Denali is to get off the bus and explore the land—feel the sun shining on your face, the wind whipping through your hair, the mosquitoes feasting on your blood.

You can **dayhike** anywhere in the park by riding the shuttle bus to a suitable embarking-point and asking the driver to let you off. Don't feel obligated to get off at one of the designated rest stops (about every 1-1½hr. along the routes). The drivers are usually happy to drop you off anywhere that isn't restricted. Once you have wandered to your heart's content, head back to the road and flag down a shuttle bus heading in your direction. The first couple of buses that pass may be full, but it's rare to wait more than a half hour or so to find a ride. Many of the buses stop running fairly early, so be sure to check with your driver regarding when the last buses will be passing your area.

Denali's backcountry operations are guided by the conviction that independent wandering provides more rewards than structured trekking. With this in mind, and in an effort to disperse hikers as widely as possible, rangers will not recommend specific routes, although many will suggest areas that meet hikers' desires. One popular destination is **Primrose Ridge,** beginning at Mile 16 on the right side of the road. The area is plastered with wild flowers (particularly primrose, believe it or not!) and spectacular views of the Alaska Range and the carpeted emerald valley below. A rigorous ascent up the tundra of **Dome Mountain,** at Mile 60, will reward hikers with close views of the Alaska Range, and on a clear day, Mt. McKinley. The area surrounding **Wonder Lake** is marshy and dense with willows, but offers what may be the best view of the Mountain in the park.

McKinley or Not McKinley—That is the Question

History has not been generous to William McKinley, the 25th president of the United States. Washington, D.C. has no McKinley Memorial. Nobody has celebrated McKinley's birthday since he last marked the occasion himself in 1901. Teddy Roosevelt, McKinley's vice-president and successor, is immortalized on South Dakota's Mt. Rushmore. McKinley doesn't even appear on a dime.

In Alaska, however, an attempt that would dwarf puny Mt. Rushmore was once made to memorialize McKinley. In 1896, a Princeton-educated prospector named the highest mountain in North America "Mt. McKinley." With a little pressure on Congress, the name was made official. Of course, the mountain had a name long before any Ivy-league Republicans laid eyes on it. The Athabascans, the native tribe of Alaska's interior, referred to the 20,320-ft. mountain as Denali: "the Great One" or "the High One." Most Alaskans and many visitors not hailing from Princeton still use this name.

The mountain certainly deserves its ancient title. 18,000 ft. from base to summit, Denali boasts the greatest total altitude of any mountain in the world. Mt. Everest—originally called Sagamartha—is higher, but rises only 11,000 ft. from its base on the Plateau of Tibet. Denali is literally the largest mountain on earth. In 1980, an official effort to rename the mountain Denali failed, but as a compromise, the park in which it stands was designated Denali National Park. Today, almost everyone ignores the U.S. Geological Survey and uses the original Athabascan name. The upshot of all this is that you can comfortably call Denali—or Mt. McKinley—anything you want. To avoid controversy altogether, call it only "the Mountain," or just point. Everyone will know what you're talking about.

When trapped in visitors center limbo waiting for a hot date with the shuttle bus, don't despair. **Horseshoe Lake Walk** is an easy-to-moderate 3 mi. walk providing beautiful views of the mountains surrounding, you guessed it, Horseshoe Lake. The **Rock Creek Trail** runs 2.3 mi. from the hotel to near Park Headquarters where the sled-dog demonstrations are held. Although conveniently located, its close proximity to the road makes it noisy for a hike. The more challenging **Mt. Healy Overlook Trail** climbs steeply for 2½ mi. to an impressive view of the valley. If you're feeling particularly ambitious you can continue up the ridge to the 5700 ft. summit.

If you're seeking a more structured hiking experience, the park rangers will oblige. **Discovery hikes** ("disco hikes" to those in the know) are guided three- to five-hour hikes, which leave in the afternoon from the visitors center. A ranger will lead you through a "cross-country scramble" or a moose trail excursion, providing a comprehensive introduction to local wildlife, flowers, and geological formations. The treks are free (you will have to pay for a ticket on the shuttle bus), but require advance sign-up. More sedate 45-minute **tundra walks** leave from Eielson Visitors Center daily at 1:30pm. Many other talks and naturalist programs are posted at the visitors center.

EXPLORING THE BACKCOUNTRY

Like boxing without gloves, like black coffee without a drop of sweetener, Denali's backcountry is The Real Thing. There are no trails in the backcountry. The intrepid are free to explore the wilderness on their own terms, with only grit, savvy, and ultra high-tech Gore-Tex® gear to help out. Dayhiking is unlimited and requires no permit wherever there are no wildlife restrictions, but only 2 to 12 backpackers can camp at one time in each of the park's 43 units. Overnight stays in the backcountry require a free permit, available one day in advance at the backcountry desk at the visitors center. The **quota board** there reports which units are still available. Type-A hikers line up outside as early as 6:30am in order to get permits for prime units. Talk to rangers or research your choices with the handy *Backcountry Description Guides.* Also peruse *The Backcountry Companion,* available in the visitors center bookstore.

The park covers a variety of terrain. Park literature is teeming with a special lingo that describes the diverse landscape: **Taiga** is low-lying, forested country. **River bars** are level, rocky areas by rivers; these offer very good footing for hikers, but be prepared to get wet fording the rivers. **Low tundra** means brushy, wet areas above the treeline; the soggy terrain is not easily navigable and makes for difficult, exasperating hiking in insect-infested conditions. **Alpine tundra** or **dry tundra** is high, dry ground above the treeline. The higher elevation means fewer mosquitoes. Generally, the southern reaches of the park contain dry tundra and river bars, opening wide vistas of Denali. The North is more brushy, but contains high points with incredible views of the Mountain. Some of the most enjoyable hiking and wildlife-viewing is in the middle of the park, near the **Toklat River** and **Polychrome Pass.**

The rangers will usually leave 2 or 3 zones open to unlimited backcountry camping, but these areas tend to be thick with mosquitoes and set back from the road behind other units. Some units are temporarily closed after a fresh wildlife kill or a "bear encounter." **Sable Pass,** a bastion for bears, is closed to hikers and campers.

No matter where you camp, keep within the zone for which you signed up. Pitch your tent completely out of sight of the road. To keep from getting lost, pick up **topographic maps** ($8) at the visitors center. Before you leave the visitors center, rangers will give you a short introduction to bear management, and you should also spend some time with the center's **"backcountry simulator,"** which allows virtual hikers to react to a variety of potentially dangerous wilderness situations. Most zones require that you carry a **bear-resistant food container,** available free at the backcountry desk. These are bulky; be sure to leave extra space in your backpack.

BIKES, RAFTS, KAYAKS, PLANES, AND DOG SLEDS

Unlike private vehicles, **bicycles** are permitted on the entire length of the Denali road, making them a perfect way to escape the shuttle-bus blues. Park at Savage Creek and ride into the heart of Denali. Most of the road is unpaved, so thick tires are best. Off-road biking is not permitted anywhere in the park. **Denali Outdoor Center** (683-1925), just north of the park entrance, rents bikes by the day, half-day, or week (see **Practical Information,** p. 102).

Several **rafting** companies run the rapids of Denali's Nenana River. **Denali Outdoor Center** boasts the most experienced guides on the river, and provides drysuits—something you'll rapidly come to appreciate if you take a spill into the 36°F (2°C) water. A two-hour canyon run costs $40 per person in an oar boat, $50 if you want to help paddle. DOC also runs guided **kayak** tours ($70, no experience necessary). **McKinley Raft Tours** (683-2392) and **Denali Raft Adventures** (683-2234) offer rafting trips for $45, but with mustang suits or raingear instead of drysuits.

Flightseeing tours are a wonderful way to see the Mountain, especially on a clear day, but the park is ironically not the best place to do this. **Denali Air** (683-2261) will take you up for one hour for $150, but the town of Talkeetna, south of the park, has companies that offer more trips at lower rates (see p. 110).

Cross-country skiing and **dog sledding** allow the brave to see the park during winter. Despite 20-hour nights and temperatures below -40°, many consider winter the most beautiful time of year. (At least that's what they say.) If you plan to travel Denali in the winter, you *must* visit the Park Headquarters and inform them of your route.

Denali Highway

The breathtaking Denali Highway runs east to west from Paxson (80 mi. south of Delta Junction on the Richardson Hwy.) to Cantwell (27 mi. south of the Denali park entrance), skirting the foothills of the Alaska Range amid countless lakes and streams teeming with grayling, trout, and Arctic char. Fortunately for solitary sorts, the Denali Hwy.'s 112 mi. of gravel scare away most tour buses and RVs. This makes it a scenic road-less-traveled to Denali, and the pristine free campgrounds and unique geological formations along the way make the road a worthwhile destination in itself. Bullet-riddled road signs attest to the popularity of hunting in this area, but mountain bikers, hikers, fishermen, birders, and archeologists also frequent the region. Glaciers and permafrost have been up to geological mischief, creating bizarre mounds, ridges, and basins all along the highway. For explanations of these features and general highway information, pick up the Bureau of Land Management's *Denali Highway Points of Interest* pamphlet, available at most local roadhouses, visitor centers, and pit stops.

The Denali Highway is closed from October to mid-May. Except for the 21 mi. west of Paxson, it is entirely gravel. Rocks and potholes vigorously assert their presence along some stretches, wreaking havoc on windshields and suspension systems but the road is for the most part well maintained. The Tangle Lakes area serves as a base for mountain bikers, ATVers, and birders. Pick up the BLM's free *Trail Map and Guide to the Tangle Lakes National Register District* at the Tangle River Inn for detailed trail information. The area is ecologically fragile and contains 400 local archeological sites. For more information on the area, write the **Bureau of Land Management** at Box 147, Glenallen, AK 99588 (822-3217). At Mile 21 (heading west), the **Tangle Lakes Campground** (toilets, no water) and, ¼ mi. farther on, the **Tangle River Campground** (toilets, water pump), are both scenic and free. Both campgrounds provide easy access to the **Delta River Canoe Route** (a 35 mi. canoe route with one difficult stretch of class III rapids) and the **Upper Tangle Lakes Canoe Route** (an easier paddle beginning at Tangle River and ending at Dickey Lake, 9 mi. to the south). Topographic **maps** are necessary for both routes. If you crave the great indoors, the **Tangle River Inn,** Mile 20 (822-7304, 895-4022 in winter), right across the highway from the boat launch, has bunkhouse beds for $25 (shared bath, common room with pool table, TV, VCR) and rooms for $45, all of which are in heavy demand; book ahead. The folks at the Inn also rent canoes ($3 per hr., $24 per day). Birders and flora fans should continue to the **Tangle River Lodge** (688-9173) at Mile 22, where the owners have the lowdown on the area's wildlife and canoe routes.

On a clear day, spectacular mountain scenery lines the rest of the highway, interrupted by an occasional roadhouse or cafe. At Mile 80, the highway crosses the beautiful Susitna River. At Mile 95, pull into an unmarked turn-off and jog an easy 600 yd. up the hill for a prime view of Mt. Deborah and the valley below. The turnoff at Mile 130, 5 mi. east of Cantwell, blesses drivers with an excellent view of Denali on rare clear days.

George Parks Highway

The George Parks Highway links Anchorage and Fairbanks, Alaska's two largest cities. Called simply "The Parks" by locals, the highway passes through some of Alaska's finest, most mountainous country. All 358 miles of the two-lane highway are paved and, except for a few frostheaves, in excellent condition. **Denali National Park** (see p. 101) and the hub **Talkeetna** are located a few driving hours north of Anchorage on this route, and for that reason most tourists who use a car in Alaska will drive the Parks Highway. Between moose sightings and spectacular mountain views, the two- to three-hour drive from Anchorage to Talkeetna will pass quickly.

From **Wasilla** (see p. 64), the highway runs north past a number of scenic state campgrounds and state recreation areas. The parks offer unlimited canoeing opportunities, though many of the lakes are also open to noisy jet skis and motorboats. The highway then passes the town of **Willow** (look back, you missed it) which boasts the distinction of having been passed up for the site of a new Alaskan capital. A state referendum defeated the crucial bill that would have funded the move.

Talkeetna

Talkeetna (tah-KEET-nah) is a Tanaina word meaning "rivers of plenty," and an apt name for this eclectic settlement located at the confluence of the Talkeetna, Susitna, and Chulitna Rivers. A cluster of narrow dirt roads lined with log cabins and clapboard stores, Talkeetna is home to an off-beat population of miners, climbers, bush pilots, and general oddballs. The wayward traveler may meet an amputee craftsman whose wheelchair is pulled by a huskie, a woman who boasts of having skinned and cleaned 27 moose in a single winter, or a young man who scaled Denali at age 12. In 1923, President Warren G. Harding died after stopping in Talkeetna to hammer in the golden spike completing the railroad between Anchorage and Fairbanks. (The First Lady, on hearing of her husband's death, is reported to have questioned, "How can they tell?") There was no evidence of foul play, but the rumor that President Harding had been poisoned at the Fairview Inn has become a perverse point of local pride.

Because of its proximity to **Denali National Park** (only 60 air mi. to the north), Talkeetna is a popular flight departure point for climbers of the mountain. Every year between May and July, mountaineers from around the globe converge on Talkeetna, creating an international village in an unlikely place. From the town, climbers fly to a base camp on the Kahiltna Glacier at 7200 ft.; from there it's all uphill. Denali is one of the world's most demanding climbs: of the over 1000 mountaineers who attempt the summit every year, fewer than half are successful. In the spring and summer of 1992, a record 13 climbers lost their lives on the Mountain's unforgiving slopes.

Practical Information **Visitors Information** (733-1686) for Talkeetna, including pamphlets about local air charters and walking tours, is located at Main St. and Talkeetna Spur (open mid-May-Labor Day daily 10am-5:30pm). If it's closed, **Talkeetna Gifts and Collectibles** (733-2710) next door has most of the same information, plus a wide selection of knick-knacks made by local artisans (open daily 8am-7pm; in winter 10am-5:30pm). To get to the bran' spankin' new **Talkeetna Ranger Station** (733-2231), follow Main St. to its terminus and turn left. The station sits on the left side of the street. Although the building is primarily used by climbers, it's also a tranquil place to plan a trip to Denali National Park (open daily April-Sept. 8am-6pm). There are **no banks** in town, but locals are in a joyful tizzy over the recent installation of an **ATM** ($1.50 surcharge) at the **Three Rivers Tesoro Gas Station** (733-2443), on Main St. The station also hosts a **laundromat** (wash and dry $3.50) and **showers** ($2; open Mon.-Sat. 8am-9pm, Sun. 9am-7pm).

Talkeetna sits 113 mi. north of Anchorage, 280 mi. south of Fairbanks, and 14 mi. off the Parks Hwy. on Talkeetna Spur Rd. (Mile 98.5). The **Alaska Railroad Station,** P.O. Box 107500, Anchorage 99510 (733-2268 or 265-2615), is a platform ½ mi. south of town behind the Latitude 62° motel. There is one train per day to Denali (peak season $57; non-peak $53), Anchorage (peak season $49; non-peak $45), and Fairbanks (peak season $108; non-peak $104). Call (800) 544-0552 for ticket information. A far cheaper and equally pleasant transportation option is the **Parks Highway Express** shuttle bus (479-3065) which stops in Anchorage ($20), Denali ($25), and Fairbanks ($39). The **Talkeetna Shuttle Service** (733-1725 or 800-288-6008; fax 733-2222; email tshuttle@alaska.net) provides daily service from Anchorage to Talkeetna ($40). The **Alaska Backpacker Shuttle** (334-8775 or 800-COM-TOAK/266-8625; fax 522-7382; email abst@juno.com) offers similar services with trips to Anchorage ($40) and Denali ($35).

The **library** (733-2359) is 1 mi. from town on Talkeetna Spur Rd. (open Tues. noon-8pm, Wed. and Fri. 11am-6pm, Thurs. 10am-6pm, Sat. 10am-5pm). The **Sunshine Community Health Clinic** (733-2273) is 8 mi. farther on the same street. The **emergency number** is 911. Reach the **fire** department at 733-2443. The **post office** (733-2275) is in town on the Spur (open Mon.-Fri. 9am-5pm, Sat. 10am-2pm; **General Delivery ZIP Code:** 99676).

Accommodations and Camping The **K2 Bunkhouse,** a hostel geared to climbers, sits just beyond Main St. Take a right after the McKinley Deli (see **Food,** below), then an immediate left down the dirt trail. The bunkhouse is on the right. K2 offers a clean, cheerful lodge-style ambience along with its full kitchen, brimming with tales of Denali, 18 bunks in a co-ed dorm, hot showers, and toilets (!). To register, drop by the **K2 Aviation** office, Box 545-B (733-2291; fax 733-1221), ½ mi. south of town on the Spur (bunks $15; laundry $1.25 wash, $1.25 dry). Reservations are essential during the climbing season (mid-May to mid-July). A good alternative to the Bunkhouse is the **Talkeetna Roadhouse** (733-1351) at Main and C St. This comfortable, homey establishment offers cheap, bunk-style accommodations for $21, as well as private rooms, both with access to shared baths (singles $47.25; doubles $63). Make reservations well in advance for stays during the climbing season. The **Fairview Inn,** P.O. Box 645 (733-2423), the alleged site of Harding's undoing, offers a good deal for private rooms (singles $42, doubles with shared bath $52).

The **Talkeetna Boat Launch and Camping** offers a quiet night. To launch off in search of the campground, turn right off of Spur Rd. at the airport, then turn left and follow the signs. The area is wooded and clean and has 60 campsites, water, outhouses, and easy river access. Several paths beginning at the railroad tracks across from the waiting booth make a convenient shortcut to town (campsites $12; parking $6). Registration is required at the park office. Camping is convenient, if a bit crazy, at the **River Park Campground** at the end of Main St. The town hopes to install flush toilets soon and plans to start charging a fee. While beautiful, the area is a popular late-night hangout for local teens and may not be particularly serene.

Food A sparse selection of groceries populates the shelves at **Nagley's Store** (733-FOOD/733-3663), on Main St. A latté, ice cream cone, or hot dog will only set you back 99¢ (open daily 8am-10pm, in winter 8am-8pm). For a sit-down meal, go straight to the **Roadhouse Café** (see **Accommodations,** above), where a hot sandwich and soup will rack up a $6 tab. The cafe bakes a blueberry muffin with a history, made from geriatric sourdough starter that dates back to 1902, as well as its own bread, muffins, cookies, and cinnamon rolls (open Sun.-Wed. 6am-4pm, Thurs.-Sat. 6am-10pm). Talkeetna's spot for pizza, sandwiches, and espresso is the **McKinley Deli** (733-1234), at Main and C St. The $7.50 spaghetti dinner with bread and salad is a tasty deal. If you're really lucky, they might be grilling fresh halibut and salmon on the barbecue outside (open daily 6am-11pm). For a speedy meal, try **Spankey's,** located across from the visitors office (see **Practical Information,** above). A cheeseburger goes for $3.50 and a milk shake costs $2.50.

Sights, Events, and Entertainment The **Talkeetna Historical Society Museum** (733-2487), off Main St., between C and D St., has displays on Alaskan transportation and a keen-lookin' model of the Mountain (not actual size). Admission is $1. If it's raining, check out the light-hearted **Museum of Northern Adventure** (733-3999), on the Talkeetna Spur next to Talkeetna Gifts and Collectibles ($2.50, seniors $2, under 12 $1.50; open in summer daily 11am-7pm, but somewhat flexible). If the weather is nice, get out there and have some Northern Adventures of your own.

The second weekend in July brings Talkeetna's increasingly famous **Moose Dropping Festival.** Animal-rights advocates need not be alarmed: "moose dropping" in this context is a noun, not a verb. Thousands come for the opportunity to kiss a moose, purchase moose-dropping earrings or moose droppings-on-a-stick, and compete in the moose-dropping toss, certain to be an experimental sport in the 2000 Sydney Olympics (surely, we jest). January brings the **Wilderness Women Contest,** which includes events like fish-gutting and tree-chopping, and the associated **Bachelor's Ball.** A local theatrical group called **Denali Drama** is in the process of converting a hangar into a playhouse and has big plans for a premier season in 1998.

Outdoors Even if you can't climb the Mountain, you can look at it. The Denali **overlook,** 1 mi. down the Talkeetna Spur, boasts one of the state's best car-accessible views of Denali. If the clouds cooperate, you will be treated to a view of nearly 4 mi. of rock and ice climbing straight to the sky. This perspective pales in comparison, however, to the views accessible by plane. **Flightseeing tours** sometimes cost less than a fortune, and to see the Mountain from such a distance—not to mention the countless other sheer peaks and marine glaciers along the way—is an incomparable experience. Talkeetna's air services are actually closer to the Mountain than services at the park entrance, so they can get to Mt. McKinley more cheaply and faster. **Doug Geeting Aviation,** P.O. Box 42 (800-770-2366; fax 733-1000) and **Hudson Air Service,** P.O. Box 648 (733-2321 or 800-478-2321; fax 733-2333; email hasi@custom-cpu.com) offer one-hour tours of the Mountain starting at $55 and $75, respectively. An hour is plenty of time to be overwhelmed by the view, but for another $30-45, you can extend the trip by half an hour and fly all the way around the summit, taking in all 14,000 feet of **Wickersham Wall,** the longest uninterrupted slope in the world. Most services also offer **glacier landings** near the base of the peak for anywhere from $15-45 extra. Be wary of companies offering landings far into July, though, as snow conditions then can be unsafe. **K2 Aviation** (see **Accommodations,** above), **McKinley Air Service** (733-1765 or 800-564-1765; fax 733-1965; email mckair@alaska.net; http://www.alaska.net/~mckair), and **Talkeetna Air Taxi** (733-2218 or 800-533-2219; email flytat@alaska.net; http://www.alaska.net/~flytat) offer similar services for comparable prices. If you come to Talkeetna intent on flightseeing, plan on staying for a couple of days. The clouds frequently fail to cooperate.

Fishing opportunities and river tours abound in the waterways around town. **Talkeetna River Guides,** P.O. Box 563 (733-2677 or 800-353-2677; email trg@alaska.net; http://www.alaska.net/~trg/trg_dir), offers a two-hour float trip with views of Denali and frequent wildlife sightings for $39 per person, $15 for children under 15. River Guides also offers fishing tours for a bundle (½-day $129, full-day $175). **Mahay's Riverboat Service,** P.O. Box 705 (733-2223), also offers access to the wet 'n' wild wilderness. Their two-hour jet boat trips are significantly louder and a little less expensive ($34.50, kids $17.25). They also have a one-hour "sunset cruise" up the Susitna River ($19.50, kids $9.75). An alternative is to rent a canoe from **Alaska Camp and Canoe** (733-CAMP/733-2267) on Railroad Ave.

For **mountain biking,** turn to **Cowley Guide Services** (733-1279; fax 733-1278). Rentals for a ½-day are $10, $18 for a full day. Guided trail tours go for $20 a person.

■ George Parks Highway: Talkeetna to Fairbanks

From Talkeetna, the Parks Highway begins a gradual ascent into the Alaska Range and offers some of the finest views of Mt. McKinley available from the ground. The **South Denali Viewpoint,** near the entrance to Denali National Park, offers a particularly spectacular profile of the 20,320 ft. peak and keeps rubberneckers from running off the road. The turn-off to the viewpoint is just a few mi. from the Ruth Glacier, but it may not be worth taking unless the frequent clouds have dissipated, usually between 10pm and 4am. **Denali State Park** (907-745-3975) offers a few pleasant campgrounds, plenty of hiking trails, and more solitude than the ever-popular national park. Two campgrounds are accessible from the highway: **Troublesome Creek Campground** (Mile 137.2) charges $6 per vehicle, and sites at the **Byers Lake Campground** (Mile 147) cost $12. Both campgrounds have toilets and drinking water.

Lest travelers on the Parks have not wearied of "excellent views" of Mt. McKinley, the **Denali Viewpoint** is yet *another* pretty place to take a picture of the peak, and is only a 10-minute drive north of the state park. From here, the road winds northward through the Alaska Range, passing over a few surprisingly steep creek canyons and through **Broad Pass,** the scenic high point of the road. The Parks soon passes the turn-off for the Denali Hwy., a rocky road through the basins that drain the Alaska Range (see p. 107). It is about a 20-minute drive from the turn-off to the park.

Leaving Denali, the highway winds north along the **Nenana River** for about 70 mi. to the town of the same name. Fifty-three miles south of Fairbanks, **Nenana** plays host to the **Nenana Ice Pool.** Bored out of their skulls during the long winter, residents of Alaska and the Yukon bet on the precise minute when the river will thaw in the spring. The pot has recently amassed $300,000. Call 832-5446 or write P.O. Box 272, Nenana 99760, to place a $2 bet. If waiting for the ice to break doesn't hold your interest, check out the free **Alaska State Railroad Museum** (832-5580), in the Train Depot at the end of A St., for exhibits on the construction of the Alaska Railroad.

The only major town between Denali and Fairbanks, Nenana is a natural spot to camp or have lunch. A fine place to eat is **The Little Cabin** (832-5277), on 1st Ave., where $2.50 buys coffee and a piece of pie and $5.50 buys a submarine sandwich. Hunt down an inexpensive dinner at the **Depot Cafe and Bar,** located just before the

Depot on the left. The "Iditarod" sandwich is $5.25 (open 8am-around midnight). Campers should head to **Nenana Valley RV Park** for large grassy sites, laundry services (wash $2, dry $1), nice bathrooms, bicycle rentals ($1 per hr.) and free showers (tents $10, RVs $14, hookups $17). The **Finnish Alaskan Bed and Breakfast,** at Mile 302 (832-5628), costs a pretty penny, but offers pretty rooms to match (singles or doubles with shared bath $50).

Fairbanks

Had E.T. Barnette not run aground with his load of goods near the junction of the Tanana and Chena Rivers and decided on the spur of the moment to set up a trading post, and had Felix Pedro, an Italian immigrant-turned-prospector, not unearthed a golden fortune nearby, Fairbanks might never have been born. But they did, it was, and today, Fairbanks stands unchallenged as North American civilization's northernmost hub (witness such landmarks as the "world's northernmost Woolworth's," "northernmost Southern barbecue," and "world's northernmost Denny's"). From here adventuresome travelers can drive, fly, or float to the Arctic Circle and into the tundra. Most do not make the long and arduous trip to Fairbanks merely to visit this outpost. Fairbanks is a means, not an end. That said, the endless strip malls and omnipresent tourism industry can't hide the rough-and-ready flavor of this frontier town. Men noticeably outnumber women, the streets are filled with 4WD steeds, and any road leads out of town into utter wilderness in minutes. Through frigid winters and swarms of vicious hybrid mosquitoes, Fairbanks residents persevere and enjoy everything from moose hunting to Shakespeare in the Park.

PRACTICAL INFORMATION AND ORIENTATION

Visitors Information: Convention and Visitors Bureau Log Cabin, 550 1st Ave. (456-5774 or 800-327-5774), at Cushman, distributes a free *Visitor's Guide* listing tourist offices, services, events, activities, and shops. Free local calls. Open daily 8am-8pm; Labor Day-Memorial Day Mon.-Fri. 8am-5pm. **Fairbanks Information Hotline** (456-INFO/4636) has a 24hr. recording for upcoming events. **Alaska Public Lands Information Center (APLIC),** 250 Cushman St. #1A, Fairbanks 99707 (456-0527), has info on Alaskan parks and public lands and welcomes requests for advice on hiking. Visit this office if you are considering a trip to either **Gates of the Arctic National Park** or the **Arctic National Wildlife Refuge** (see p. 169); the staff gives thorough, indispensable advice on how to navigate these immense expanses of wilderness. Open daily 9am-6pm; in winter Tues.-Sun. 10am-6pm.

Airport: Located 5mi. from downtown on Airport Way. Served by: **Delta** (800-221-1212) to the lower 48; **Alaska Air** (452-1661) to Anchorage ($111) and Juneau ($313); **Frontier Flyer Services** (474-0014) to smaller Bush towns such as Bettles ($248). Fares change at the drop of a hat, and cheaper fares are often possible with advance purchase. A number of other carriers also serve Fairbanks including **Northwest, United,** and **Reno Air.**

Trains: Alaska Railroad, 280 N. Cushman St. (456-4155), next to the *Daily News-Miner* building. An excellent way to see the wilderness. From mid-May to mid-Sept., 1 train daily to Anchorage ($149) and Denali National Park ($53). In winter, a train leaves for Anchorage once a week ($78). Ages 2-11 ½-price. Depot open daily 7:30am-3pm.

Buses: Parks Highway Express (479-3065) runs daily to Denali ($25, round-trip $45) and Anchorage ($40, round-trip $75). **Alaskon Express** (800-544-2206) runs to Haines (4 per week, $180). **Alaska Direct** (800-770-6652) runs 3 buses per week to Denali ($25) and Anchorage ($65). **Fireweed Express** (458-8267) runs daily van service to Denali ($25, round-trip $45), with pick up at Billie's Backpackers Hostel (see **Accommodations,** below); call for times and reservations.

Public Transportation: the **Municipal Commuter Area Service (MACS)** (459-1011), at 6th and Cushman St. 2 routes (red and blue) through downtown Fairbanks and the surrounding area. Fare $1.50; seniors, students, and disabled 75¢;

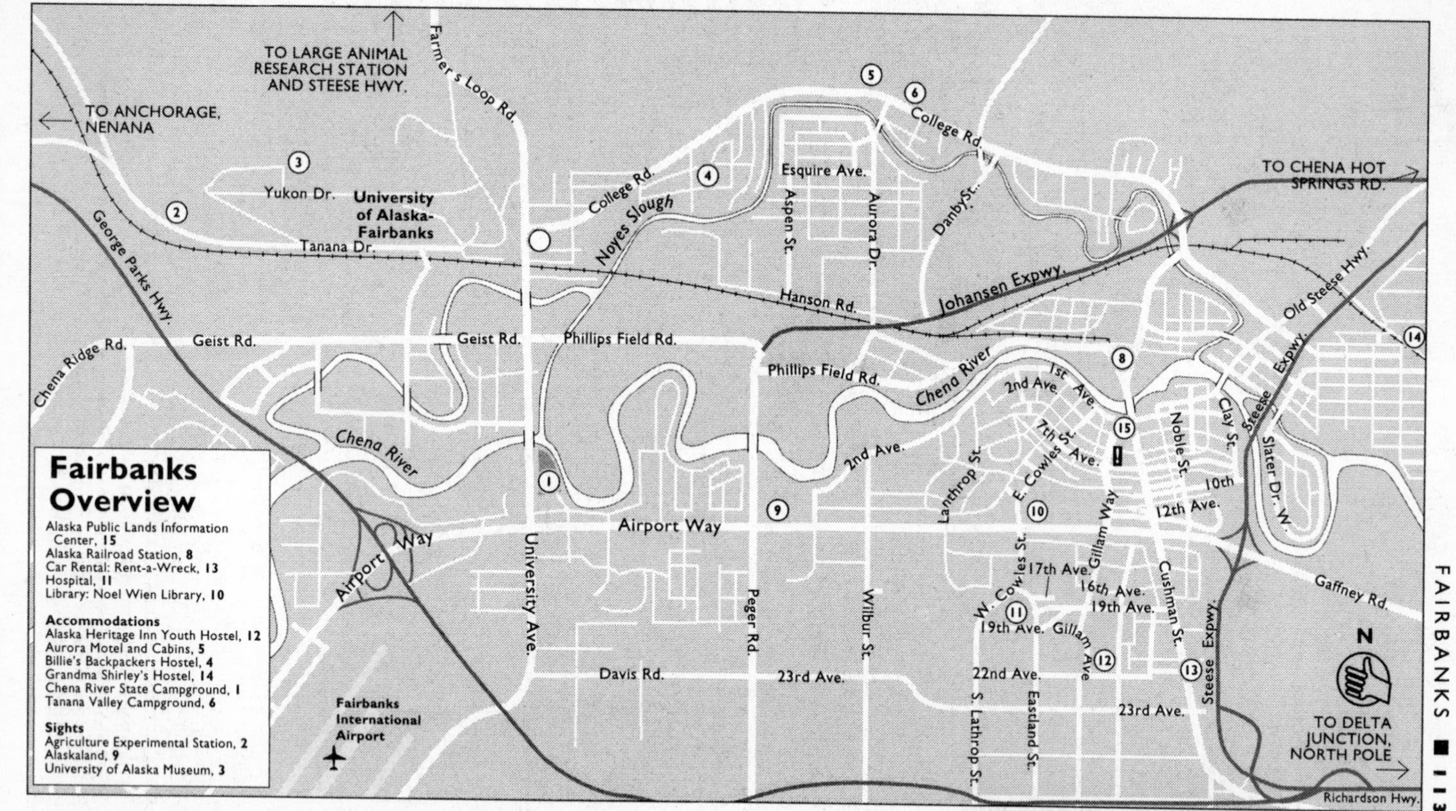
TO LARGE ANIMAL RESEARCH STATION AND STEESE HWY.
TO ANCHORAGE, NENANA
TO CHENA HOT SPRINGS RD.
TO DELTA JUNCTION, NORTH POLE
N
University of Alaska-Fairbanks
Fairbanks International Airport
Chena River
Noyes Slough
Farmer's Loop Rd.
College Rd.
Esquire Ave.
Aspen St.
Aurora Dr.
Danby St.
Yukon Dr.
Tanana Dr.
Hanson Rd.
Johansen Expwy.
Old Steese Hwy.
Steese Expwy.
George Parks Hwy.
Chena Ridge Rd.
Geist Rd.
Phillips Field Rd.
1st Ave.
2nd Ave.
7th Ave.
E. Cowles St.
W. Cowles St.
Lanthrop St.
Noble St.
Clay St.
Slater Dr. W.
10th
12th Ave.
Airport Way
University Ave.
Peger Rd.
Wilbur St.
Gillam Way
Gillam Ave
17th Ave.
16th Ave.
19th Ave.
22nd Ave.
23rd Ave.
Davis Rd.
S. Lathrop St.
Eastland St.
Cushman St.
Gaffney Rd.
Richardson Hwy.
Fairbanks Overview
Alaska Public Lands Information Center, 15
Alaska Railroad Station, 8
Car Rental: Rent-a-Wreck, 13
Hospital, 11
Library: Noel Wien Library, 10
Accommodations
Alaska Heritage Inn Youth Hostel, 12
Aurora Motel and Cabins, 5
Billie's Backpackers Hostel, 4
Grandma Shirley's Hostel, 14
Chena River State Campground, 1
Tanana Valley Campground, 6
Sights
Agriculture Experimental Station, 2
Alaskaland, 9
University of Alaska Museum, 3

under 5 free. Day pass $3. Transfers good within 1hr. of stamped time. Pick up a schedule at the Convention and Visitors Bureau (see above).

Taxi: King Cab, 452-5464. **Fairbanks Taxi,** 452-3535. **Yellow Cab,** 452-2121. **Diamond Taxi,** 455-7777. All 24hr.

Car Rental: Nearly all national companies offer packages with free mileage; however, they will *not* allow you to drive on dirt roads. Many smaller companies, on the other hand, charge hefty fees for extra mileage. **Rent-a-Wreck,** 2105 Cushman St. (452-1606). $40 per day, 30¢ per mi. after 150mi.; must be 21 with credit card. Local use only. **U-Save Auto Rental,** 3245 College Rd. (479-7060). $43 per day, 26¢ per mi. after 100mi.; must be 21 and credit card "preferred." $250 deposit; under 25 $500 deposit.

Road Conditions: 456-7623 or 800-478-7675.

Bike, Canoe, and In-line Skate Rental: Beaver Sports, 3480 College Rd. (479-2494), across from College Corner Mall. Mountain bikes $16 for 6hr., $20 overnight, $94 weekly. $250 deposit required (cash or credit). Canoes $24 per day, $17 per day for 3-6 days, $12 per day for 7-10 days; paddles and life jackets included. $500 per boat deposit required. Skates $13 per day; $125 deposit required. Open Mon.-Sat. 10am-7pm, Sun. 1-5pm.

Camping Equipment: Rocket Surplus, 1401 Cushman St. (456-7078). Open Mon.-Sat. 9am-6pm. **Apocalypse Design, Inc.,** 101 College Rd. (451-7555), at Illinois. Speedy repairs on zippers and straps. Open Mon.-Fri. 9am-6pm, Sat. 10am-4pm. (Also see **Beaver Sports** above.)

Laundromat and Showers: B & C (479-2696), at University and College, in Campus Mall. $2 wash, 8min. dry 25¢. Showers $2.50, towels 50¢. Open Mon.-Sat. 7am-10:30pm, Sun. 8am-10:30pm. **B & L** (452-1355), at 3rd and Steese. Wash and dry each $1.50. Showers $2.50 for 20min. Open daily 8am-11pm.

Bookstore: Gulliver's New and Used Books, 3525 College Rd. (474-9574), in College Corner Mall. Open Mon.-Fri. 9am-8pm, Sat. 9am-6pm, Sun. noon-6pm. Also in the **Shopper's Forum,** 1255 Airport Way (456-3657). Open Mon.-Fri. 10am-9pm, Sat. 10am-6pm, Sun. noon-6pm.

Library: Noel Wien Library, 1215 Cowles St. (459-1020). Open Mon.-Wed. 10am-9pm, Thurs.-Fri. 10am-6pm, Sat. 10am-5pm.

Weather: 452-3553.

Crisis Line: 452-HELP/4357; also provides contact with gay and lesbian groups. **Rape Crisis:** 452-7273 or 800-478-7273. **Poison Control Center:** 456-7182.

Pharmacy: Payless Drugstore, 38 College Rd. (456-2151), in the Bentley Mall. Open Mon.-Fri. 9am-9pm, Sat.-Sun. 10am-6pm.

Hospital: Fairbanks Memorial, 1650 Cowles St. (452-8181), off Airport Hwy.

Emergency: 911. **Alaska State Troopers:** 451-5333.

Internet Access: Noel Wien Library (see above). **Cafe Latté,** 519 6th Ave. (455-4898). $4 per hr., 30min. free with coffee or food.

Post Office: 315 Barnette St. (452-3203). Open Mon.-Fri. 9am-6pm, Sat. 10am-2pm. **General Delivery ZIP Code:** 99707.

Area Code: 907.

Fairbanks lies 358 mi. north of Anchorage via the **George Parks Hwy.,** and 480 mi. south of Prudhoe Bay along the gravelly **Dalton Hwy.** Delta Junction is 97 mi. southeast of Fairbanks on the **Richardson (Alaska) Hwy.** Fairbanks itself is a confusing city to navigate as it is difficult to identify "downtown" in its maze of urban sprawl. Nearly every tourist destination lies on one of four thoroughfares, however: **Airport Way, College Road, Cushman Boulevard,** or **University Way.** The city center lies in the vicinity of South Cushman, north of Airport Way. Fairbanks also features an extensive **bike trail** system. None of the urban trails are particularly scenic, but it's a lot quicker than walking. Pick up a guide to local bike trails and pamphlets mapping out self-guided walking and driving tours at the visitors center.

ACCOMMODATIONS AND CAMPING

Grandma Shirley's Hostel, 510 Dunbar St. (451-9816). From the Steese Expressway, turn right onto Trainor Gate Rd., then left at E St., and finally right on Dunbar St.

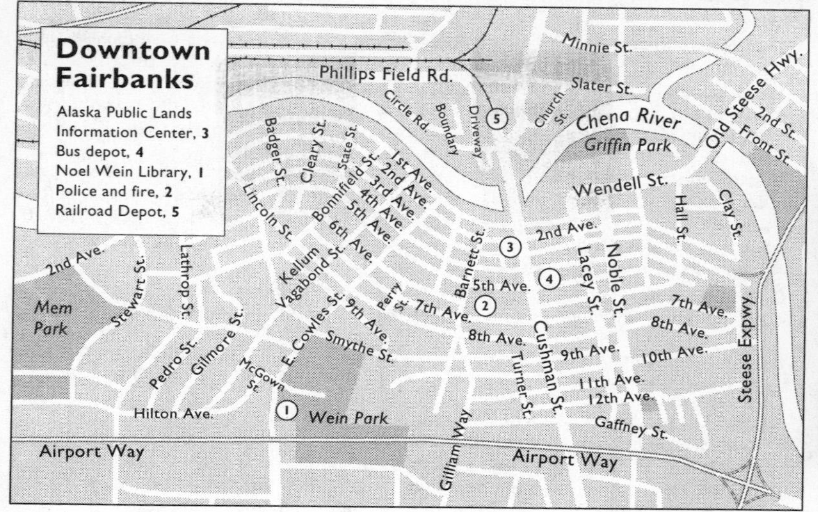

Grandma beats out all other contenders to earn the title of Fairbanks überhostel. (The painted bear on the bathroom door put her over the top.) Bedding, a spectacular kitchen, showers, a TV room, a big backyard, and free use of three old, but road-worthy bikes. Men and women share a room with 9 beds. $15.

Billie's Backpackers Hostel, 2895 Mack Blvd. (479-2034). Take Westwood Way 1 block off College to Mack Rd. Look for the house on the corner with the "Billie's B&B" sign. Conveniently located near College Rd., Billie's maintains 3 rooms with 4 beds each. Hot showers and kitchen. $15, plus $5 for a full breakfast or dinner.

Alaska Heritage Inn Youth Hostel (AAIH), 1018 22nd Ave. (451-6587). Take Cushman to 22nd Ave., then go west; the hostel is a large grey building on the right. Prepare to cozy up to European neighbors, as the rooms are tight in this cosmopolitan hostel. Common room with TV, picnic area, and 15 beds. $14, nonmembers $15 plus an 8% bed tax.

North Woods Lodge, P.O. Box 83615 (479-5300 or 800-478-5305) on E. Chena Hill Dr. Take Roland Rd. west off Chena Pump Rd., then turn right on Chena Hills Rd. Lodge is ¼mi. up the road on the right. Travelers with vehicles will appreciate the quiet of North Woods, a rustic campground and hotel hybrid. Wooden cabins are back-to-the-basics with electricity, but no water. Small kitchen facilities; shared showers (one is outdoors). Cabins $40, double cabin $45. Tent sites $12, 2 people $15. Beware mosquitoes!

Chena River State Campground, off Airport Way on University Ave. With 2 or more people, this place is worth the $15 per night fee. Well-landscaped, clean, and situated on a particularly quiet stretch of the Chena River. 56 sites. Self register.

Tanana Valley Campground, 1800 College Rd. (456-7956), by the fairgrounds on College Rd. near Aurora Ave. Somewhat noisy, but surprisingly grassy and secluded given its in-town location. 18 spots with power hookup available. Free showers, laundromat ($2 wash and dry). Sites $12. Tentsites for travelers with no vehicle $6.

FOOD

For an artery-blocking good time, look no further than Airport Way or College Rd., where the northernmost franchises of almost every fast-food chain in existence lure burger lovers to their doom. Groceries are available 24 hours at **Carr's**, 526 Gaffney (452-1121), and at **Safeway,** 3627 Airport Way (479-4231), or 30 College Rd. (451-6870). If you're really stocking up, **Sam's Club,** 48 College Rd. (451-4800), lets nonmembers buy in bulk for an additional 5% of the low total price (open Mon.-Sat. 9am-8pm, Sun. 10am-7pm). The **Farmers Market,** at the fairgrounds at Aurora and College, is the place for fresh produce (open Wed. 11am-4pm, Sat. 9am-4pm).

The Whole Earth, 1157 Deborah St. (479-2052), behind College Corner Mall. This health food store and restaurant could well have been a joint venture by Rachel Carson and Jane Fonda. Southwestern art and perhaps the only cactuses in Alaska accompany organic coffee and a variety of good-for-you foods: the giant No Bull Burger is $4.25; Anna's Hummus Sandwich is $3.75. Open Mon.-Sat. 8am-8pm, Sun. noon-6pm. Hot food served 11am-7pm.

Gambardella Pasta Bella, 706 2nd Ave. (456-3417) at Barnette. Fresh flowers, an airy air, and excellent food make this classy family-run restaurant worth its heftier prices. The lunch menu offers subs for $7; a *bellisima* pasta dinner starts at $10. Stare down the "Mother of all Lasagnas" for $15. Open Mon.-Sat. 11am-10pm, Sun. 4-9pm. Reservations recommended in summer.

Pikes Landing, 4438 Airport Way (479-6500). Although fine (read: "more expensive") dining is available inside, the deck of Pikes Landing or the screened-in patio is a better place to eat and soak up some midnight sun. Dinner starts around $7; halibut fish-and-chips (a local favorite) goes for $9.75. In June and July, diners can strut their golf skill, attempting to put a ball over the river and sink it in a hole on the far bank ($1 per ball, goes to charity). Deck open 2:30-11pm.

Alaska Espresso and Chowder House, 3226 Airport Way (474-0409), across from Sears. Sampling the tasty clam chowder, it's difficult to believe that New England is 4000 mi. away. The house offers more than seafood: deli sandwiches ($3 half, $5 whole) and an impressive assortment of ice cream ($1.50) keep hungry youngsters clammed up. Open Mon.-Fri. 7am-8pm, Sat. 9am-6pm, Sun. 10am-5pm.

The Pumphouse Restaurant and Saloon, Mile 1.3 Chena Pump Rd. (479-8452). The food is expensive, but if a night on the town is what you're after, head to the Pumphouse—the place is so popular that 1 of the city's bus lines goes out of its way to drop passengers here. The decor celebrates the glamorous world of mining. Lunch buffet for $10. Dinner entrees average $18. Open daily 11:30am-11pm.

Thai House, 528 5th Ave. (452-6123). The planet's northernmost Thai restaurant never advertises, but is jam-packed. Lunch entrees $6-8, dinner starts at $8. Try the *Pad Thai* noodles ($7), but don't say "spicy" unless you *mean* it. Open Mon.-Sat. 11am-4pm and 5-10pm.

Souvlaki, 112 N. Turner (452-5393), across the bridge from the visitors center. You can almost get your fill on the heavenly aroma alone. Succulent stuffed grape leaves (3 for $1.25). Mmm, mmm, falafel ($4.75). Take-out. Open Mon.-Fri. 10am-9pm, Sat. 10am-6pm; in winter Mon.-Sat. 10am-6pm.

Little Saigon, 1753 College Rd. (452-4399). Just east of Aurora Dr. The few locals who have discovered it can't stop raving about this small Vietnamese restaurant. Service is slow (the owner makes everything fresh herself), but you'll be glad you waited after tasting the *Goi Chon* spring rolls ($3 for 3 big rolls) or the *Bún Thit Nuong* (a hearty serving of pork with vermicelli, $4.25). Open daily 11am-10pm.

Bakeries and Coffeehouses

Wolf Run Dessert & Coffee House, 3360 Wolf Run (458-0636), near University and Geist. Travelers with a sweet tooth will love this rustic coffeehouse with scrumptious desserts, plush chairs, and a stone hearth fireplace. Outdoor seating makes it that much better. Warm your cockles with blueberry or peanut butter pies ($4.25). Open Tues.-Thurs. 11am-10pm, Fri.-Sat. 11am-midnight, Sun. noon-8pm.

Bab's Bakery, 402 5th Ave. (457-1213). In the heart of downtown, Bab's Bakery bestows bunches of bagels on blissfully breakfasting travelers (70¢ each). Relaxed atmosphere and fresh baked goods make it an ideal breakfast stop. Grab Bab's bagel sandwich ($3.50) or a latté ($2.25). Open Tues.-Fri. 6:30am-6pm, Sat. 8am-6pm; winter Tues.-Fri. 6:30am-3pm, Sat. 8am-3pm.

Into the Woods, 3560 College Rd. (479-7701). Greenwich Village meets the Yukon in this log cabin coffeehouse. Relax in a large wicker chair and listen to a live guitarist, or take a book to a dome tent outside. Sip a tall latté ($2) while perusing *Outhouses of Alaska.* Open summers Mon.-Thurs. 8am-midnight, Fri. 8am-3pm, Sat. 10am-3am, Sun. 10am-6pm.

SIGHTS

One of Fairbanks's proudest institutions and main attractions is the **University of Alaska-Fairbanks (UAF),** at the top of a hill overlooking the flat cityscape. Both bus routes stop at the **Wood Campus Center** (474-7034), located on Yukon Dr. across from the fire station, which has pool tables, flyers advertising campus goings-on, and enough video games to entertain all the little brothers of the world. The **Student Activities Office** (474-6027), located in the Wood Center, has the skinny on movies, music, and campus activities during the school year (open Mon.-Fri. 8am-5pm). The **University of Alaska Museum** (474-7505), a 10-minute walk up Yukon Dr. from the Wood Center, features exhibits ranging from displays on the *aurora borealis,* to tales of the Russian involvement in Alaska, to indigenous crafts; an extremely rare 36,000 year-old bison recovered from the permafrost is perhaps the most impressive display. (Museum open daily 9am-7pm; May and Sept. 9am-5pm; Oct.-April noon-5pm; $5, seniors $4.50, 13-18 $3, families $12.50.) Weekdays at 10am, the university offers free tours of the campus beginning in front of the museum (2hr.; weather permitting).

The search for a good picnic spot ends at the **Georgeson Botanical Gardens** (474-1944), on Tanana Dr. west of the museum. Tiptoe through the tulips (the best viewing time is July or Aug.) and enjoy the view of Fairbanks overlook and the Alaska Range. Be sure to sit upwind of the bovine and porcine populations housed by the university's **Agriculture Experimental Station.** The **Large Animal Research Station** (474-7207) is also worth a visit for a rare chance to see baby musk ox and other arctic animals up close. Take Farmer's Loop to Ballaine Rd. and turn left on Van Kovich; the farm is 1 mi. up on the right (tours Tues. and Sat. at 11am and 1:30pm, Thurs. at 1:30pm; $6, seniors $5, students $2). If you miss the tour, grab some binoculars and view the musk ox, reindeer, and caribou from the viewing stand on Yankovitch Rd.

Alaskaland, P.O. Box 71267 (459-1095), on Airport Way, is a small-scale, would-be Arctic Disneyland, but rides are limited to a train and merry-go-round. Overrun by kids, Alaskaland is a tourist trap of woolly mammoth proportions. But there's no general admission charge, and the gates are open from 11am to 9pm, making for great night picnics. (The park's rides and museums charge nominal fees.) Featuring winners from the International Ice Sculpting Competition, the **Fairbanks Ice Museum** (451-8222), near the visitors center on 2nd Ave., demonstrates what a Fairbanks winter can do to the average under-stimulated sculptor ($6, seniors $5, 13-18 $3).

Well worth the 9 mi. trip north along the Steese Hwy., **Gold Dredge #8** charges $19 for a day of panning and a guided tour. Not only is it possible to earn the cost of admission back in gold, but fossilized fragments of mammoths, mastodons, and Keith Richards abound. An extra $8 buys the "Miner's Buffet Lunch" (open daily mid-May-mid-Sept. 9am-6pm; 5 tours daily).

There are many **trails** throughout Fairbanks for the hiker, biker, or cross-country skier. Ideal for a leisurely stroll, **Creamer's Nature Path,** starting at 1300 College Rd., offers 2 mi. of trail through open pastures (home to various migratory birds) encircled by birch and spruce groves. The **Skailand Trails,** weaving through the hilly woods behind the university campus, are 3-12 mi., visiting several ponds and offering glimpses of the Alaska Range. **Maps** are available at the Wood Center.

EVENTS

A lively time to visit the city is in mid-July when citizens don gold rush duds and whoop it up for **Golden Days,** a celebration of the Felix Pedro discovery that sparked the Fairbanks gold rush. Watch out for the traveling jail; without a silly-looking pin commemorating the event (sold at most businesses), an unknowing tourist may be taken prisoner and forced to pay a steep price to spring free. The budget traveler might want to stay on board the paddywagon; it's a free ride and goes all over town. For details, contact the Visitors Bureau (see **Practical Information,** above). Be warned that Fairbanks teems with tourists during Golden Days. Make hotel reservations several months in advance.

The summer solstice inspires some wild activity in Fairbanks. The **Yukon 800 Marathon Riverboat Race** sends high-horsepower competitors in low-slung powerboats on an 800-mi. quest up the Tanana and Yukon Rivers to the town of Galena and back. A few days before the solstice, the 10km **Midnight Sun Run** happens on a well-lit Saturday night, beginning at 10pm. The Fairbanks Goldpanners play their annual **Midnight Sun Baseball Game** on the solstice itself. The game begins as the sun dips at 10:30pm, features a short pause near midnight for the celebration of the midnight sun, and ends as the sun rises. The Goldpanners play more than 30 home games throughout the summer and have won five minor league national championships since 1970. Barry Bonds and Dave Winfield have played here. Games are played at **Growden Memorial Park** (451-0095), near Alaskaland (tickets $5).

For a sports spectacular with native flavor, see the **World Eskimo-Indian Olympics,** P.O. Box 2433 (452-6646), in late July. Inuit and other native peoples from all over Alaska compete in traditional tests of strength and endurance. Watch participants engage in the **ear pull,** in which sinew is wrapped around the ears of contestants, who then pull to see who can endure the most pain. Ears have been pulled off in this event. Mike Tyson, eat your heart out. (Nightly pass $10, seniors and children $8; season passes $20, seniors and children $15.)

The **Tanana Valley Fair** (452-3750), in early August, is a traditional country fair with rides, lots of food, and "biggest cabbage" and "cutest baby" competitions. Suggestions for replacing them with "biggest baby" and "cutest cabbage" have so far been ignored. The fairground is at the intersection of College and Aurora ($7, seniors $3, ages 6-17 $5). Each September, Fairbanks hosts the **Equinox Marathon,** the second most rigorous in the nation. Hearty competitors run 26.2 mi. up Ester Dome, sometimes in blizzard conditions, gaining 4500 ft. in elevation.

In winter, February's **Yukon Quest Dog Sled Race** runs between Fairbanks and Whitehorse, starting in Fairbanks in even years, and in Whitehorse in odd. The Quest is far more rigorous than the famous Iditarod: fewer dogs, fewer stops, and less compassion for the human condition. For information, contact the Yukon Quest Business Office, 558 2nd Ave. (452-7954), in the co-op.

ENTERTAINMENT AND NIGHTLIFE

Howling Dog Saloon (457-8780), 11½ mi. down Steese Hwy., at the intersection of the Old and New Steese Hwy. Look for a colorful wooden structure in the middle of nowhere encircled by pick-up trucks. Carouse with UAF students, military personnel, and just about everyone else at the legendary Howling Dog. The summer crowd is especially diverse, described by management as "rough, tough, and good-lookin'." Rough and tough volleyball, pool, and horseshoe games go on until 4am or so. Live rock-and-roll Wed.-Sat. Open May-Oct. daily 9pm-5am.

Senator's Saloon, Mile 1.3 Chena Pump Rd. (479-8452), in the Pumphouse Restaurant. Where yuppies and oysters meet. If the portrait of Ronald Reagan affects your appetite, take drinks out to the deck and watch river boats whiz by. Those with stronger stomachs can try the "oyster shooter," a live oyster in a shot glass, topped with cocktail sauce and lemon. Happy hour Sun.-Thurs. 4-6pm and 10-11pm. Open Sun.-Thurs. 11:30am-1am, Fri.-Sat. 11:30am-2am.

Blue Loon Saloon, 2999 Parks Hwy. (457-5666), 5 mi. out of town. A free shuttle runs Fri.-Sat. after 9pm between the Marlin (under the same management), Blue Loon, and the UAF Wood Center. Live bands play 4 nights a week, drawing a mixed crowd of hippies, college students, and military types. The building, huge even by bloated Fairbanks standards, looks like an enormous quonset hut. Open Tues.-Sat. 4pm-4am; $3 cover.

The Marlin, 3412 College Rd. (479-4646). Fairbanks's only jazz bar. Live music Tues.-Sat.; open mike Tues.; blues Wed.; jazz Thurs. Sit under the portrait of your favorite musician and enjoy the vibes. Open Sun.-Thurs. 4pm-2am, Fri.-Sat. 4pm-3:30am.

Malamute Saloon (479-2500), located 7 mi. south of Fairbanks on the Parks Hwy. Follow signs to the one-time gold camp of Ester. This gold rush legacy still draws as big a crowd as in the olden golden days, but today rowdy tourists have replaced burly miners. Every evening at 9pm (7 and 9pm in July), the saloon gives a vaudeville show with songs, dance numbers, and Robert Service. Tickets $12, children $6; dinner buffet (5-9pm) $15. Reservations required; complimentary bus service.

■ Near Fairbanks

A short drive in any direction plunges travelers into bona fide Alaskan wilderness. In the vicinity of Fairbanks, you can soak your feet in hot spring lakes, look for wildlife in a river basin, or hike up a ridge for a view of the Brooks or Alaska Range, both over 200 mi. away. Maps and detailed info on hikes are available at the APLIC office in Fairbanks (see p. 112). **Fishing** enthusiasts can find numerous places in and around Fairbanks to reel in a keeper. Along the **Chena River,** graylings are common, as are king salmon in early July. The **Chatanika River,** which runs along the Steese Hwy. between Miles 29-39 teems with shellfish, burbot, and northern pike. Would-be Bob Izumis should stop by the visitors center (see p. 112) for licenses and information.

CHENA RIVER AND HOT SPRINGS

The **Chena River Recreation Area** (451-2695) spills across both sides of Chena Hot Springs Rd. (which branches off the Steese Hwy. at Mile 5) from Miles 26 through 51. Encompassing almost 400 sq. mi. of wilderness, the area offers outstanding fishing, hiking, canoeing, and camping. Tent sites convenient to Chena Hot Springs Rd. are available at quiet, secluded **Rosehip Campground** (Mile 27) and **Tors Trail Campground** (Mile 39). Both cost $8 and offer pit toilets and water.

The **Granite Tors Trail,** across the road from Tors Trail Campground, begins in boreal forest at river level and climbs past the treeline to a peak topped by giant granite pillars, or "Tors," and blessed with fantastic views of Chena Dome to the north and Flat Top Mountain to the west. Rangers recommend taking the east trail (left) to do the 15 mi. loop clockwise. In July and August, blueberries abound along the first stretch of the trail. The **Angel Rocks Trail** (look for signs near Mile 49) follows the Chena River before turning up to the top of Angel Rocks, prominent granite slabs that offer views of the river valley and the Alaska Range. A steep ascent, this 3½ mi. loop through exquisite wilderness is a wonderful afternoon hike, but be sure to bring bug juice. It's mosquito country. The **Chena Dome Trail,** open to mountain bikers, is the most spectacular trail in the park, a 29 mi. adventure that follows the high, rocky rim of the Angel Creek Valley.

The North Pole

The town of North Pole, AK, celebrates Christmas 365 days a year. Santa officially came to town in 1953, when the sleepy little village of Moose Crossing changed its name as a gimmick to woo toy manufacturers. Town planners hoped that corporations would rush to display "made in the North Pole" on their products, but somehow they resisted this lure. This hasn't stopped the North Pole's 1700 residents, most of them military personnel stationed at nearby Fort Wainwright, from transforming their town into a shrine to the jolly fat man. St. Nicholas Drive runs into Santa Claus Lane. Holiday cheer is mandatory. Bus stops, lampposts, and shopping malls all reflect the Christmas theme. The U.S. Postal Service redirected Santa's mail to the newly christened "North Pole," and now Santa receives 20,000 letters each year—so many letters, in fact, that the merry old elf has recruited North Pole schoolchildren to help answer his mail.

When he's not finding out who's been naughty or nice, Santa moonlights as a North Pole entrepreneur. Eat Mexican at Santa's Tortilla Factory, do your duds at Santa's Suds, or go on a ride at Santaland Caravan Park. Best of all, anyone can get a personalized letter from the old geezer himself. Just send $5, the recipient's name, age, sex, full mailing address, brothers' and sisters' names (or pets), favorite hobby, and anything special you would like Santa to write. His official address is 325 S. Santa Claus Lane, North Pole, AK 99705.

Fifty-seven miles northeast of Fairbanks, the **Chena Hot Springs Resort** (369-4111, Fairbanks office 452-7867) steams away, luring travelers and Fairbanks residents. In the winter, scores of Japanese tourists shiver their way to the resort for its prime Northern Lights viewing. In the summer, lower 48ers and Europeans are more frequent guests. Rooms are dear (in summer, singles $85; doubles $95), but tent and RV campsites are available by the river ($10, with electricity $12) and non-guests may use the hot pool, too. (Pool open daily 9am-midnight; $8, ages 5-12 $6; after 7pm $6, ages 5-12 and seniors $4.) The resort's restaurant serves excellent but pricey food, including quesadillas, exotic salads, and espresso. Lunch starts around $8 and dinner entrees are $15-21 (open daily 7-11:30am, noon-4pm, and 5-10pm). Handsome hiking/biking trails and fine fishing (once the water level has dropped from the spring snow melt) are also nearby. The resort rents bikes for $7 per hour, $25 per day.

STEESE HIGHWAY

The **Steese Highway** heads northeast out of Fairbanks, 162 mi. to the town of **Circle** on the **Yukon River.** Just outside Fairbanks, the Steese meets Chena Hot Springs Rd., where a right turn brings you toward Chena River Recreation Area and the Chena Hot Springs. The **Elliot Highway** comes hard on the heels of the Chena Rd.; make a right turn at the intersection to stay on the Steese. For the next 20 mi., the highway winds through boreal forest, past two ski resorts, and into a region of stunted spruce and fir trees known as **taiga.** At Mile 16.5 is the **Felix Pedro Monument,** a plaque honoring Pedro's discovery of gold in the creek across the highway.

The **Upper Chatanika River Campground,** at Mile 39, provides secluded, woodsy campsites ($8). **Cripple Creek Campground,** at Mile 60, offers good fishing and recreational goldpanning (sites $6, walk-in $3). Both campgrounds have access to the **Chatanika River Canoe Trail,** which parallels the Steese for nearly 30 mi. The easygoing stream is clear and class II; its only treacherous obstacles are low water and overhanging trees. The road begins to climb consistently at about Mile 70, and heads towards the highway's nicest scenery. The **White Mountain Recreation Area** and the **Steese National Conservation Area** lie side-by-side to the north.

At Mile 86 is the trailhead for the **Pinnell Mountain Trail,** the most spectacular—and popular—hike in the vicinity of Fairbanks. The 27 mi. trail is entirely above treeline, passing through alpine tundra flora. With proper timing you can bask in the midnight sun (June 18-24), witness an explosion of wildflowers (early July), or watch the migration of caribou in the valleys below (Aug.-Sept.). Allow three days for the entire trip. Two cabins are well spaced along the trail for both nights, but as the trail has no water it is important to bring 3-4 days' worth per person. The trail ends up on the highway at Mile 107; most hikers hitch back to their cars. (*Let's Go* does not recommend hitchhiking.) Even if you don't have time to schlep 27 mi., a scramble up either end of the trailhead is worthwhile.

For white-water enthusiasts, **Birch Creek,** with several entry points between Mile 94.5 and 147, offers a 127-mi. course including several class III rapids. At Mile 108, the highway passes over **Eagle Summit.** The panoramic view of countless peaks and fragile tundra is well worth a stop.

Central (Mile 127), a small, pit-stop town of about 400 summer residents, is anything but central. Few travelers make it this far. The **Circle District Museum** displays beautiful native beadwork, samples of local gold, and a pipe organ that was carried over the Chilkoot Trial and floated down the river to Circle (open Memorial Day-Labor Day daily noon-5pm; $1, children 50¢). The **Central Motor Inn** (520-5228) serves nondescript meals (sandwiches $6, dinner from $8) and offers laundry and shower facilities (showers $3, wash and dry $2 each). **Gas** is available here and at **Crabb's Grocery,** just down the street.

From Central, the road gets considerably worse and winds its way down towards the **Yukon River Flats Basin.** Unless you are planning to float the mighty **Yukon River** or urinate into its great waters—an unsavory activity favored by some tourists—there is little reason to drive the highway's final 34 mi. to **Circle**. For those who do make the trek, the **Yukon Trading Post** (773-1217) sells groceries at gold rush-era prices and runs a cafe that isn't much cheaper (open daily 9am-8pm). Camping on the river is free (pit toilets), and water is available at the **Washeteria** (5min. showers $2, wash $3, dry $3). There is a **post office** (773-1220) at Mile 161 on the Steese (open Mon., Wed. and Fri. 10am-3pm, Tues.-Thurs. 10am-2:30pm; **ZIP Code:** 99733).

Alaska Highway: Tok to Delta Junction

Like many other pit-stop towns plunked down on the Alaska Hwy., Tok (TOKE) has the ambiance of a strip mall. Because this strip mall is conveniently situated 12 mi. from the Alcan's intersection with the **Taylor Highway** at **Tetlin Junction,** and the **Tok Cutoff** (Rte. 1, or the Glenn Hwy.) turns southwest from Tok itself towards **Wrangell-St. Elias National Park** (see p. 96). Tok is a good place to stock-up and view the yonder Alaska Range. A cavernous **visitors center** (883-5775; http://www.TokAlaskaInfo.com), near the west end of town, is the largest single-story log building in Alaska (open mid-May to mid-Sept. daily 8am-8pm). The visitors center and the **Public Lands Information Center** (883-5666 or 5667), in the same building, offer everything a traveler needs to plan a vacation in Alaska, including a "trip planning" room and free coffee. Across the highway is the headquarters for the **Tetlin National Wildlife Refuge** (883-5312), which offers info on the waterfowl preserve (open Mon.-Fri. 8am-4pm). There is a **laundromat** and **showers** at the Northstar RV Park (see below; wash $1.25, 8min. dry 25¢, shower $3.50). In an **emergency,** dial 911. The **Public Health Clinic** (883-4101) is across from the visitors center (open Mon.-Fri. 8:30am-5pm; call ahead), in the same building as the **police station.** The **post office** (883-5880) is near the intersection of the Tok Cutoff and the Alaska Hwy. (open Mon.-Fri. 8:30am-5pm, Sat. 11am-4pm; no window services; mail must be prestamped). Call (800) 472-0391 for a **weather** message. **ZIP Code:** 99780.

On the Alcan, Fairbanks is 208 mi. northwest, and Whitehorse, YT is 387 mi. (619 km) southeast. Hitchers struggle to catch a ride out of town. If you're stuck, **Alaska Direct** (800-770-6652) runs buses leaving from the front of Northstar RV Park (at 3pm Wed., Fri., and Sun.) to Fairbanks ($40); Anchorage ($65); and Whitehorse, YT ($80).

The **Tok Youth Hostel (HI-AYH)** (883-3745) is 2 mi. west of town in the woods. Going west, take Pringle Dr. on the left and follow for ¾ mi. The hostel is an authentic M.A.S.H. tent from WWII with limited conveniences (drinking water; not running water; solar showers) but unlimited character ($10; open May-Sept.). In town, the **Golden Bear Motel & RV Park** (883-2561), 100 yd. up the Tok Cutoff on the right, offers secluded tent sites for $10 plus $2 per person after 2, including firewood, showers, and use of a lounge with VCR. A gas fill-up at **Saveway** (883-5389), next to the Golden Bear, earns free RV parking (no hook-ups) or a tent site with no facilities (except bathroom in 24hr. store). You can also get a free RV or tent-site (no hook-up or facilities except bathroom) at the **Gateway Salmon Bake** (883-5555), on the Alcan on the east end of town, when you chow on the all-you-can-eat dinner (open Mon.-Sat. 11am-9pm, Sun. 4-9pm; king salmon $16.50, chicken $11). The **Snowshoe Motel** (883-4511), at Mile 1314 across from the visitors center, has singles for $52, doubles for $68, and free breakfast and cable. For those addicted to serene government campgrounds, the **Tok River State Recreation Area Campground,** 4 mi. east of town, offers woodsy riverside sites for $10.

Tok has plenty of expensive, forgettable food. The atypical (for Tok) **Loose Moose Espresso Cafe** (883-JAVA/5282) offers a fresh alternative with a largely vegetarian repertoire. A quiche with salad runs $4.75, and a sourdough waffle is $3.75 (open June-Sept. daily 7am-9pm; May daily 7am-2pm). For large portions, the **Northstar Restaurant** (883-4503) next to the Northstar RV Park, has an 8 oz. rib-eye dinner ($11) and hefty hoagies with soup ($5.75; open daily 6am-9pm). At **Frontier Foods** (883-5195), across from the visitors center, shoppers rejoice in reasonably priced bulk items and fresh fruit (open daily 7am-11pm; winter 7am-10pm).

DELTA JUNCTION

Delta Junction, what's your function? Aptly named "the crossroads of Alaska," the Junction lies at the intersection of two major highways. The Alcan leads southeast 108 mi. to Tok, while the Richardson Hwy. runs 100 mi. northwest to Fairbanks and 266 mi. south to Valdez. The huge post in front of the visitor center declares Delta Junction the terminus of the Alaska Hwy. (though Fairbanks argues otherwise). For $1, you can buy a macho certificate stating that you've successfully reached its end.

The **visitors center** (895-5063) stands at the intersection of the two highways (open mid-May to mid-Sept. daily 8am-7:30pm). **Hendrick's Auto Parts and Garage** is at Mile 269 on the Richardson Highway (open Mon.-Sat. 9am-6pm and Sun. 9am-5pm). In an **emergency,** call 911. A **health clinic** is at 895-5100. The **post office** (895-4601) is just north on the east side of the highway (open Mon.-Fri. 9:30am-5pm, Sat. 10:30am-noon; **General Delivery ZIP Code:** 99737).

Tenters should head to **Delta State Recreation Site,** ½ mi. north from the visitors center, for roomy, protected sites with drinking water and pit toilets ($8). No one has ever accused Delta Junction cuisine of being distinctive or unpredictable, but two restaurants near the visitors center give a fair deal. At **Pizza Bella Restaurant** (895-4841 or 895-4524), across from the visitors center, hearty subs on fresh toasted rolls provide the highest nourishment-to-dollar ratio ($5 half; $7 whole). Locals favor the *bellisima* pizza (7 in. pizza starts at $13; open daily 10am-11pm). **Buffalo Center Drive-in** (895-4055) fills Delta Junction's meat quota, serving all sorts of burgers (around $6; open Mon.-Sat. 10am-10pm, Sun. 11am-8pm). Gung-ho grocery-grabbers should hit the **IGA Food Cache** (895-4653), just north toward Fairbanks (open Mon.-Sat. 7am-10pm, Sun. 8am-8pm).

Towards Fairbanks, 10 mi. north of town, is **Big Delta Historic Park,** home of **Rika's Roadhouse** (895-4201), a restored homestead complete with a barnyard and farm animals (free walking tour on request). Well-groomed lawns and a spectacular view of the river and pipeline make Rika's an ideal spot for lunch or stretch break. Travelers wanting to catch a glimpse of mighty bison (cousin of your lunch) head to the **buffalo ranch,** 7 mi. toward Tok on the Alcan. Turn left on Clearwater Rd.; after 4 mi., turn left after the fire station and drive up to the fence for a view of the herd.

A Case of the Runs

France hosts the Tour de France, Boston the Boston Marathon...and Delta Junction the **Great Alaskan Outhouse Race.** The most exciting event at the Deltana Fair, held in early August, the race pits locals in a contest to see which team can push or pull an occupied outhouse through the 1½ mi. course the fastest. Contestants hand-build the outhouses for the speediest, lightest commode possible. In the race, four competitors struggle with the ungainly box while one lucky team-member sits on the "throne." Begun in 1987, the race has included as many as five teams. Winners receive the coveted "Golden Throne Award," a painted toilet with the team names engraved on the lid. The "Silver Plunger" goes to the second place finishers, and the third place prize is the "Copper Snake."

Taylor Highway

Driving the Taylor Highway is not for the high strung. This 160 mi. dirt-and-gravel road, open only from April to October, leads through some of the hairiest turns and carries the dustiest summertime RV caravans in the north. Beginning at **Tetlin Junction,** 12 mi. east of **Tok** (see p. 121), the highway is initially tolerable, with wide, smooth lanes. At Mile 96, the highway intersects with the **Top-of-the-World Highway,** which careens 79 mi. east to Dawson City, YT (see p. 268). The Taylor continues north 64 mi. through worsening roads, until hitting the tiny town of **Eagle** (see below). If cutting off towards Dawson City, be prepared to cross the border, open only from May through September 8am-8pm Alaska time. No scheduled bus service follows the Taylor (although there is service between Eagle and Dawson City; see p.

268). Some car-less travelers hitchhike, but sparse RV traffic makes this difficult; most hitchers have a good book and start early in the morning. (*Let's Go* does not recommend hitchhiking.) The border patrol can be hard on hitchhikers, and the station is on a high mountain pass in the middle of nowhere. Make sure to have proof of funds (see **Customs,** p. 7). Only the wooden and phoneless **Bound'ry Cafe,** a tad west of the border, will feed you if you get stuck. There is expensive **gas** and repair only at **Chicken** (Mile 66; see below); it's a good idea to start with a full tank.

From **Mile 0,** the Taylor Hwy. gradually and painlessly climbs to over 3500 ft. as it rolls toward 5541 ft. Mt. Fairplay. Unfortunately, this is the last fair play Taylor travelers will encounter. A sign just past the summit (Mile 35) explains the history of the Taylor. Stretch your legs here (handicapped toilet available). At Mile 49, the Bureau of Land Management operates the **West Fork Campground,** with 32 sites, pit toilets, and water ($6, self registration).

The megalopolis of **Chicken,** rumored to have received the name after local miners couldn't spell their first choice, "Ptarmigan," lies at Mile 66. Each summer, Chicken's population burgeons from its winter level of 16 to upwards of 100 from the influx of gold miners, and the **Chicken Creek Saloon** throws the wildest pre-solstice, solstice, and 4th of July parties in the region (open 8am-"whenever"). Forty-five-minute walking tours of old ghost-town Chicken leave daily at 1pm from the parking lot in front of the saloon and are the only way to see the original mining cabins ($5). Next to the Saloon, the **Chicken Creek Cafe** will flip you two weighty flapjacks ($4.75) or a weiner with potato salad ($6; open daily 8am-6pm). If passing through in the evening, check out the nightly Salmon Bake (open in summer daily 4-8pm, $15). Tenters and RVs can set up on the lot next to the cafe for free, although the site is less than ideal for tents. The **Chicken Mercantile Emporium** pushes plastic souvenirs aplenty and sells **gas** for a whopping $1.89 per gallon (open summer daily 7:30am-9 or 10pm; Visa, MC, AmEx accepted). Cheaper gas ($1.79) and (hallelujah!) tire repair ($17.50) is at the **Goldpanner,** on the Taylor south of the "downtown" turn-off (open May-Oct. daily 8am-8pm; Visa, MC accepted).

The **Jack Wade Dredge,** a huge machine used for placer mining, lies rusting away right next to the highway at Mile 86. The dredge has deteriorated considerably, and its safety is dubious, but that doesn't stop passersby from wandering around its eerie skeleton. From this point until Eagle, tourists and locals practice under-the-table roadside mining, although a good portion of the area is owned by larger operations. At Jack Wade Junction the road forks north for Eagle and east for Dawson via the Top-of-the-World. For the last 64 mi. from the Eagle junction, the road tightropes and snakes along mountainsides and canyons of **40 Mile River,** another popular, though difficult, spot for rafters (see **Eagle,** below, for canoe outfitters). Occasional pull-outs provide respite for small, RV-dodging vehicles.

Eagle

Many of Eagle's 240 residents say there's no place they'd rather live than this unpretentious wilderness town. Connected to the "outside" world only by the **Taylor Hwy.** during the summer, Eagle is no tourist mecca. But eager Eagle-ites have quick grins and plenty a close-to-home tale about a pioneer great-grandmothers to share with travelers passing through. Log and tin remain the standard architectural media, and escaped urbanites continue to make the Yukon paddle to Eagle and beyond, beginning from this beautiful bend in the Yukon River (see **Floating from Eagle to Circle,** below). Gold mining in Eagle is alive but only somewhat well. Eagle's heyday was in 1899, when the Secretary of War established a military base here to keep the towns's booming gold rush population in check. In 1901, Eagle became the interior's first incorporated city. The military went south after mining fizzled, but unlike other forts along the Yukon, **Fort Egbert's** buildings and paraphernalia remain untouched by marauding miners. Sponging up the town's living history makes a day's stop in Eagle a worthwhile sabbatical.

Practical Information Bo Fay, the proprietor of **Telegraph Hill Services** (947-2261), on the Taylor Hwy., is an unofficial visitors center that knows and loves Eagle, and will readily provide coffee, conversation, a map of the town, gas, and car repairs (open summer daily 8am-6pm, winter Mon.-Sat. 10am-5pm; accepts checks but no credit cards). The real **Visitors Center** (547-2233) is hidden at the end of 1st St.; take a left towards the river (open summers daily 8am-5pm). The center works in conjunction with the **Yukon-Charley Rivers National Preserve Headquarters** (same phone) next door, which has the lowdown on canoe trips to Circle and beyond (see below). The **Village Store and Hardware** (547-2270), on 1st St. towards the boat landing, is the only place in Eagle to buy gas with a credit card (open summer Mon.-Sat. 9am-6pm, Sun. 9am-5pm; winter Mon.-Sat. 9am-5pm). In any **emergency** call the Village Protective Safety Officer at 547-2285. The **post office** (547-2211) is on 2nd St. at Jefferson (open Mon.-Fri. 8:30am-4:30pm). The **ZIP Code** is 99738.

The Taylor Hwy. closes from mid-October to mid-May, making Eagle accessible by air or dog sled only. **Tatonduk** (547-2285) flies to and from Fairbanks twice daily (to Fairbanks, $44; to Eagle, $77). Ask at the **Eagle Trading Co.** (see below) for details.

Camping, Accommodations, and Food Campers will rejoice upon finding the **Eagle BLM Campground,** a 1 mi. hike from town past Fort Egbert, or the first left after Telegraph Hill Services. Ask Bo—he knows (sites $6; no water; pit toilets). Several short hiking trails start at the campground. The unremarkable looking **Yukon Adventure Bed and Breakfast** (547-2221), sits about ½ mi. east of town. Facing away from the river, turn left on 1st Ave., and follow signs for the boat launch. Adventure sets a new standard for rural B&Bs. Have a mental adventure on the sun deck, or watch a film from the wide selection of videos (in doubles). There are only three rooms, so call in advance (singles $50; doubles $60). The **Eagle Trading Co.** (547-2220), on Front St., has it all: gas, groceries, hot, high-pressure showers ($4), laundromat ($4 per load), RV hookups ($15), and rooms for rent (singles $50; doubles $60; open summer daily 9am-8pm; winter 10am-6pm; no credit cards). The adjacent **Riverside Cafe** (547-2250) serves standard fare at reasonable backcountry prices (burgers with fries or salad $5, pancakes $3.50; cash only; open daily 7am-8pm).

Sights No visit to Eagle is complete without the three-hour **walking tour** offered daily in the summer by the **Eagle Historical Society and Museums.** The tour leaves at 9am from the **Courthouse Museum** at 1st and Berry St., and includes the courthouse, customs house, and Fort Egbert ($5, children under 12 free; call 547-2297 or 547-2325 for info or to arrange a different tour time). Well-preserved relics of frontier life, from birchbark canoes to prospectors' ice skates, decorate the tour. The guides harken to a time when permafrost ice cream was Eagle's desert of choice, and king salmon was so plentiful that Eagle dogs ate it daily.

Amundsen Park, on 1st St. at Amundsen, honors the Norwegian explorer of the same name who hiked several hundred miles across northern Canada into Eagle when his ship was frozen in the ice floes of the Arctic Ocean in the winter of 1905. Amundsen used Eagle's new telegraph to cable his government for money, then mushed back to his ship and successfully completed the first northward journey from the Atlantic to the Pacific.

Floating from Eagle to Circle 1,979 mi. long, the Yukon River is the fourth longest river in North America and has the fifth largest flow volume of any river on earth. No other American river is as undeveloped, and floating the entire river has become a cult experience. The trip takes four months and ends 1200 mi. from Eagle near Nome at the Bering Sea. Don't despair if four months is too daunting. The 154 miles between Eagle and Circle (see p. 120) take only four to six days, depending on how many hours you plan to paddle or camp on the river. The trip passes through the **Yukon-Charley Rivers National Preserve** and some of Alaska's wildest country, but remains wide and relatively calm the whole way. Rumor has it that any decent boat or even Huck Finn-style raft can make the trip. Campers do their best to avoid numerous bears and countless mosquitoes by pitching tents on the gravel bars along the river. For detailed info, visit the Visitors Center (see above) or write to the National Preserve at P.O. Box 167, Eagle, AK 99738. **Eagle Canoe Rentals** (547-2203) will set you afloat for a five-day trip to Circle for $165 (paddles, life jackets, and canoe return included) or bargain with Bill Elmore, owner of **Eagle Commercial** (547-2355), just behind the Riverside Cafe on First St., for guided trips (open summer Mon.-Sat. 10am-5pm). Bill also sells maps and the handy guide *Yukon River* by Mike Rourke (Rivers North Publications, $22).

Southeastern Alaska

Southeastern Alaska (a.k.a. "the Panhandle" or just "Southeast") spans from the basins of Misty Fiords National Monument, past Juneau, to the town of Skagway at the foot of the Chilkoot Trail—a full 500 miles. The waterways that lace the Panhandle are collectively known as the Inside Passage, and make up an enormous saltwater soup, spiced with islands, inlets, fjords, and the ferries that flit among them. This region, hemmed in by glorious mountains, is distinguished by a cold-temperate rainforest climate, over 60 major glaciers, and a neverending stack of sourdough pancakes.

Some communities of the Interior and Southcentral Alaska have experienced what Alaskans consider urban sprawl, but towns along the Panhandle cling to narrow pockets of coast that provide little or no room for growth. A profound absence of roads in steep coastal mountains has helped these towns maintain their diminutive size and demonstrative personalities. While Skagway remembers 100 years of gold rushes and railroads, Ketchikan looks forward to a growing sea-based economy. Signs of the Russian occupation linger in Sitka, while Juneau, the capital of Alaska, has emerged as a cosmopolitan commercial center.

The Alaska Marine Highway system provides the cheapest, most exciting way to explore the Inside Passage. In order to avoid the pricey accommodations in towns without hostels, plan nighttime ferry trips and sleep on deck, where only the swarms of bald eagles soaring above outnumber the hordes of mummy-bagged travellers.

SOUTHERN PANHANDLE

Ketchikan

Ketchikan is the first stop in Alaska for northbound cruise ships and ferries laden with flocks of tourists and would-be cannery workers. Despite crowds and notoriously bad weather (the town averages nearly 14 ft. of rainfall a year) Ketchikan is a major destination for many travelers. Its location is the key: the city provides access to Prince of Wales Island, Metlakatla, and most notably, Misty Fiords National Monument. Access to "Misty," as locals affectionately call it, does not come cheap. Although the monument is only 20 mi. from Ketchikan at its nearest point, transportation to the soaring cliffs and crashing waterfalls of this spectacular patch of the world costs at least $125.

Over 3 mi. long and several hundred yd. wide, Ketchikan stretches along the coast in typical Panhandle fashion. The city is Alaska's fourth largest (pop. 15,000), and is split between a tourist-oriented historic district and long chains of unremarkable, weather-beaten stores and homes. Refugee artists from the lower 48 and indigenous carvers make their livings within the confines of the historic district and nearby Saxman Village, while loggers and fisherfolk romp about the rest of the community.

PRACTICAL INFORMATION AND ORIENTATION

Visitors Information: Ketchikan Visitors Bureau, 131 Front St. (225-6166 or 800-770-3300), on the cruise ship docks downtown. Info on Ketchikan proper, maps, and access to local charter and touring companies. Open May-Sept. daily 7am-5pm; limited winter hours. **Southeastern Alaska Visitors Center (SEAVC)** (228-6214), on the waterfront next to the Federal building, provides info on public lands around Ketchikan, including Tongass and Misty Fiords. Inquiries or reservations can be made for free; access to a regional ecology exhibit costs $3. Open May-Sept. daily 8:30am-4:30pm; Oct.-April Tues.-Sat. 8:30am-4:30pm.

Banks: National Bank of Alaska, 306 Olain St., at Dock St. 24hr. **ATM.** (Bank open Mon.-Thurs. 9:30am-5pm, Fri. 9:30am-6pm). **First Bank,** 331 Dock St. (228-4218). Open Mon.-Fri. 9:30am-5:30pm.

Southeastern Alaska
TO WHITEHORSE
TO KLUANE
CANADA
U.S.A.
Alaska Hwy.
Klondike Hwy.
Haines Hwy.
Atlin
Skagway
Haines
Atlin Prov. Park
Glacier Bay Nat. Park & Preserve
Lynn Canal
Alaska Ferry Routes
Glacier Bay
Gustavus
Cross Sound
Alaska Ferry Routes
Pelican
Icy Strait
Juneau
Gastineau Channel
Hoonah
Chichagof Is.
Tenakee Springs
Douglas Is.
Chatham Strait
Admiralty Is.
Angoon
Stephens Passage
Alaska Ferry Routes
Sitka
Baranof Is.
Kake
Kuiu Is.
Kupreanof Is.
Petersburg
Mitkof Is.
Wrangell
Zaremba Is.
Wrangell Is.
Etolin Is.
Sumner Strait
Alaska Ferry Routes
Clarence Strait
Klawock
Thorne Bay
Craig
Hollis
Hydaburg
Prince of Wales Island
Ketchikan
Gravina Is.
Annette Is.
Metlakatla
Behm Canal
Revillagigedo Is.
Misty Fiords Nat. Monument
Portland Inlet
Stewart
37A
BRITISH COLUMBIA
ALASKA
Dease Lake
Telegraph Creek
Mt. Edziza Prov. Park
Stikine River
Cassiar Hwy.
37
ALEXANDER ARCHIPELAGO
PACIFIC OCEAN
Dundas Is.
Dixon Entrance
Alaska Ferry Routes
Yellowhead Hwy.
16
Chatham Sound
Prince Rupert
Porcher Is.
Grenville Channel
Graham Is.
Masset
Port Clements
16
Yellowhead Hwy.
Tlell
BC Ferry Route
Banks Is.
Pitt Is.
Queen Charlotte City
Skidegate
TO BELLINGHAM
Sandspit
Queen Charlotte Islands
Moresby Is.
Hecate Strait
Gwaii Haanas South Moresby Nat. Park Reserve
N
0
50 miles
0
50 kilometers

Airport: Across from Ketchikan on Gravina Island. A small ferry runs from the airport to just north of the state ferry dock (every 15min., in winter every 30min. $2.50). **Alaska Airporter** (225-1111) and **Ketchikan Airporter** (225-5429) carry people and bags between the airport and the ferry terminal. **Alaska Airlines** (225-2145 or 800-426-0333), in the mall on Tongass Ave., provides flight info from Ketchikan. Daily flights to Juneau, $134. Open Mon.-Fri. 9:30am-5pm.

Ferries: Alaska Marine Highway (225-6181), at the far end of town on N. Tongass Hwy. Ferries to: Wrangell ($24), Petersburg ($38), Sitka ($54), Juneau ($74), Haines ($88), and Skagway ($92). Wheelchair accessible. Turn right from the terminal to reach the city center. Buses to town until 6:45pm; after that, split the $8 cab fare with a pal.

Public Transportation: Local bus fare $1, seniors and children 75¢. Buses run Mon.-Sat. 6:40am-7pm, every 30min. The main bus route runs a loop with turnaround points at the airport parking lot near the ferry terminal at one end and Dock and Main St. downtown at the other. Stops about every 3 blocks.

Taxi: Sourdough Cab, 225-5544. **Alaska Cab,** 225-2133. **Yellow Taxi,** 225-5555. Call ahead; all run 24hr.

Air Taxis and Tours: Island Wings (225-2444, 247-7432 or 888-854-2444), **Taquan** (225-8800 or 247-6300; email taquan.ptialaska.net; html://www.AlaskaOne.com/Tequan Air), **ProMech** (225-3845 or 800-860-3845).

Car Rental: Alaska Rent-A-Car (225-2232) at the airport, or 2828 Tongass Ave. (225-5000 or 800-662-0007). Free local pick-up and delivery. Call for latest prices. Must be 21 or older to rent. Open Mon.-Sat. 8am-5pm, Sun. 8am-3pm.

Bike Rental: Southeast Exposure (225-8829), across from the tunnel. $6 per hr., $22 per day. Open 8am-5pm. **The Pedalers** (225-0440), around the corner from the visitors center, on the boardwalk. $6 per hr., $25 per day.

Kayak Rental: Southeast Sea Kayaks, PO Box 7281 (225-1258 or 800-287-1607; email bbkayak@ktn.net). Call or visit office in the Visitors Center. Singles $40 per day, more than 6 days $30 per day. Doubles $50, more than 6 days $40 per day. $200 damage deposit. Trip planning service available. **Southeast Exposure,** 507 Stedman St. (225-8829). Required 1½hr. orientation class, $30. Singles $35 per day, 6 or more days $30 per day. Doubles $50 per day, 6 or more days $45 per day. $200 damage deposit. Office empty on good kayaking days. Open daily 8am-5pm.

Camping Equipment Rentals: Alaska Wilderness Outfitting, 3857 Fairview (225-REEL/7335).

Bookstore: Parnassus, 5 Creek St. (225-7690). A special-subject book shop with an eclectic selection of used and new books. Talk to owner Lillian for the scoop on new publications, controversial politics, and local personalities. Open daily 8:30am-6pm; winter closed Mon.

Library: Ketchikan Public Library, 629 Dock St. (225 3331), south of Creek St. Open Mon.-Wed. 10am-8pm, Thurs.-Sat. 10am-6pm, Sun 1-5pm.

Showers: Seamen's Center (247-3680), on Mission St. next to St. John's. A warm, dry lounge to clean up and watch television in. Frequented by Ketchikan's down-and-out, but welcomes backpackers and other travelers. Showers $1.50, laundry 75¢. Open daily 1-8pm; Sept.-May Wed. and Sat.-Sun.4-8pm. Volunteers help cook or clean for 2hr. any evening. **The Mat,** 989 Stedman (225-0628), about ¾mi. from downtown, offers TV and a play area as well as showers.

Pool and Recreation Center: Kayhi Pool, 2160 4th Ave. (225-2010). **Valley Park Pool,** 410 Sihocubar Rd. (225-8755). Call for hours.

Public Radio Station: KRBD 105.9, 123 Stedman St. (225-9655; email rainbird@ktn.net).

Weather: 874-3232.

Laundromat: Highliner Laundromat, 2703 Tongass (225-5308). Wash 25¢, 7min. dry 25¢. Showers $2 for 10min. Open 6am-9:30pm.

Senior Citizens Help: 225-8080.

Pharmacy: Downtown Drugstore, 300 Front St. (225-3144). Open Mon.-Fri. 8am-6:30pm, Sat. 8am-6pm, Sun. 10am-4pm.

Hospital: Ketchikan General Hospital, 3100 Tongass Ave. (275-5171). **Clinic:** 3612 Tongass (225-5144). Open Mon.-Fri. 7:30am-6:30pm.

Fire Dept.: (225-9616), on Main St. near Dock St. **Police Station:** (225-6631), at Main St. and Grant St., across from the hostel.

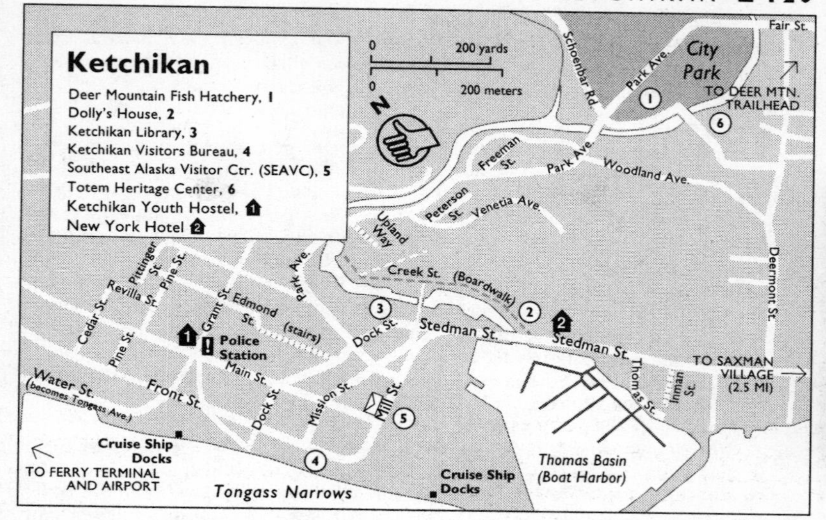

Post Office: (225-9601), next to the ferry terminal. Open Mon.-Fri. 8:30am-5pm. Substation at corner of Race and Tongass (225-4153). Open Mon.-Fri. 9am-6pm, Sat. 9am-5pm. Another **substation** (225-2349) is in the Trading Post, at Main and Mission St. Open Mon.-Sat. 9am-5:30pm. **General Delivery ZIP Code:** 99901.

Area Code: 907.

Ketchikan rests on Revillagigedo Island, 235 mi. southeast of Juneau, 90 mi. northwest of Prince Rupert, BC, and 600 mi. northwest of Seattle, WA. Upon reaching Ketchikan from Canada, you should **roll back your watch** by an hour. If you're flying in, a shuttle ferry ($2.50) will bring you to the main island, dropping you near the ferry terminal. Catch a bus ($1) or walk the 2 mi. downtown from the ferry terminal to avoid a hefty cab fare.

ACCOMMODATIONS

As the locations of the cruise ship and the ferry docks reflect (right downtown and 2 mi. north, respectively), Ketchikan caters to the travel elite. Excepting the hostel, rooms are expensive. The **Ketchikan Reservation Service** (800-987-5337; fax 247-5337) provides info on B&Bs (singles starting at $60).

Ketchikan Youth Hostel (HI-AYH), P.O. Box 8515 (225-3319), at Main and Grant St. below the First Methodist Church. Discouraged job-seekers and bargain-hunting seniors keep the social scene skimpy in this busy hostel. No beds, but foam mats on the floor pass muster if you have a sleeping bag. Clean kitchen, common area, 2 showers, tea, and coffee. Strict lockout 9am-6pm. Lights out at 11pm, on at 7am. Curfew 10:30pm. Call ahead if you plan to arrive on a late ferry. 4-night max. stay, subject to availability. Overflow sleeps in the church sanctuary. Baggage storage during lockout. Open June 1-Aug. $8, nonmembers $11. Reservations advisable.

Miller Street House, P.O. Box 7281, 1430 Miller St. (225-1258 or 800-287-1607; email bbkayak@ktn.net). Call for directions. Owners Kim Kiry and Greg Thomas fill their 2 spacious rooms with cheer and the comforting smell from their extra-large bread machine. Just outside downtown in a historic house overlooking the ocean. An essential stop for transplanted Aussies or anyone else looking for a good time. Call for directions. Single $65; doubles $75.

Innside Passage B&B, 114 Elliot St. (247-3700), on the stairway just above Tongass Ave., about ½mi. from downtown, next to Panhandle Rigging Loft. Dark wood jacuzzi (with complimentary bubble bath) adds an exotic flourish to this simple, clean accommodation. Rooms overlooking the water make for an excellent eagle watching perch. Reservations strongly recommended; mail in a check in advance (no credit cards). Singles $60; doubles $70.

CAMPING

Travelers who plan ahead can escape the lofty price for lodgings in Ketchikan by camping, although the city's infamous rain can make tenting it a soggy, drippy chore. Check out **The Outfitter,** 3232 Tongass (225-6888; open Mon.-Fri. 8am-7pm, Sat. 8am-6pm, Sun. 8am-4pm), or **Plaza Sports,** in the Plaza Mall (225-1587; open Mon.-Sat. 8am-8pm, Sun. 8am-5pm), for supplies before setting out. Campgrounds usually have stay-limits of a week or two, but cannery workers tent up in the public forests for up to a month. There is no public transportation from the town to the campgrounds, so plan on hiking, biking, or paying an exorbitant cab fare. SEAVC (228-6214; see **Practical Information,** p. 126) provides information for all the campgrounds listed, as well as info about cabins with stoves ($25) in remote locations of the **Tongass National Forest.** To reserve, call 800-280-CAMP/2267, TTD 800-879-4496. Spaces fill rapidly in the summer.

A number of leafy, well-maintained campgrounds serve as a haven for counter-culture visitors to K-town. **Signal Creek and Three C's Campgrounds,** (800-280-CAMP/2267 for reservations) sit across the street from each other on Ward Lake Rd. (drive north on Tongass Ave. and turn right at the sign for Ward Lake, approximately 5 mi. from the ferry terminal). The camps share 28 spaces, water, and pit toilets. There is a one-week maximum stay and an $8 fee collected May-September. RVs should head one mile farther on Ward Lake Rd. to **Last Chance Campground** (also 800-280-CAMP/2267 for reservations), where larger sites recently redesigned by a landscape architect go for $10 and are fully wheelchair accessible. Anyone can camp for up to 30 days in Tongass National Forest. Sites are not maintained, but any clearing is free. After 30 days, campers may not return for six months.

FOOD

If there were a cure for the dread Northwest 1000-Island Disease (an affliction that leaves neither frankfurter nor falafel without a heart-stopping gob of mayo), Ketchikan would be first on the list for treatment. The restaurant scene here follows a typical Panhandle pattern: one or two worthwhile, semi-creative establishments mingled with a heap of mediocre "standard fare" joints aimed at travelers just stepping off cruise ships. Stock up on groceries at **Ketchikan Market,** 3816 Tongass Ave. (225-1279; open daily 24hr.). The supermarket most convenient to downtown is **Tatsuda's,** 633 Stedman, at Deermount St. (225-4125; open daily 7am-11pm). The freshest seafood swims in Ketchikan Creek; anglers frequently hook King salmon from the docks by Stedman St. in the summer. If you get lucky, **Silver Lining Seafoods,** 1705 Tongass Ave. (225-9865), will custom smoke your catch for $2.50 per lb. (open Mon.-Fri. 9am-6pm, Sat. 10am-5pm, Sun. 11am-4pm).

5 Star Café, 5 Creek St. (247-7827). Not a dollop of killer mayo to be found in this oasis of health. The communal silverware drawer compliments the homey style of the black bean burrito with Basmati rice ($6.75) and soup-of-the-day ($3) or banana *streusel* muffin ($1). Stenciled-on salmon swim up the wall, pointing the way to the upstairs "Cotto," a gallery showcasing local artists. Open Mon.-Sat. 7:30am-5:30pm, Sun. 9am-5pm.

The Pizza Mill, 808 Water St. (225-6646), through the tunnel, 2 blocks north of downtown. Serves "pizza with an attitude," if they do say so themselves. Red-checked table cloths, garlic on the walls—the quintessential local pizza place. Personal pan pizza with 2 toppings ($5.50). Disenfranchised youths can split a 12in., trendy, veggie-sporting "Generation X" with a hungry friend ($16). Open Mon.-Wed. 11am-11pm, Thurs.-Sat. 11am-3am, Sun. 11am-11pm.

Burger Queen, 522 Water St. (225-6060), 1 block past the tunnel. Request "no mayo," and the regal veggie burgers, chicken troika sandwiches, and guacamole cheddar burgers will please even the pickiest palate. Everything in 3 sizes ($2-$8). Open 10:30am-9pm, Oct.-Feb. 11am-7pm, March-April 11am-8pm.

Jimbo's Café, 307 Mill St. (225-8499), across from the cruise ship docks. Where the inebriated stagger after the bars have closed. During more sober hours, tourists slip into the semi-circular lunch counter in search of local color. Colorful locals willingly oblige. Try a 1 lb. Alaskan burger for $9. Stack of 3 pancakes $3.75. Phone for free local calls. Open daily 6am till "very, very late."

SIGHTS AND ENTERTAINMENT

Each summer day, up to 6000 wealthy travelers tumble down crispest gangplanks into downtown Ketchikan, heavy purses and small children in tow. With little time to spend exploring, they are immediately sucked into the capitalist trap of horse-drawn carriages and chartered fishing boats, leaving more of Ketchikan for your romping pleasure. The official walking tour makes no distinction among good, bad, and ugly; checking out Ketchikan's high points solo makes for a more memorable stay.

Ketchikan's primary cultural attraction is, not surprisingly, the **Saxman Native Village,** the largest totem park in Alaska. Two and a half miles southwest of Ketchikan on Tongass Hwy. ($8 by cab or a short ride on the Tongass Hwy. bike path), the park was founded at the turn of the century to preserve indigenous culture. The village has a traditional house, dancers, and an open studio where artisans create new totems. The poles on display are a melange of recent and historic carving, some dating back as far as 150 years (open weekdays 9am-5pm, weekends when a cruise ship is in).

The **Totem Heritage Center,** 601 Deermount St. (225-5900), on the hill above downtown, houses 33 well-preserved totem poles from Tlingit, Haida, and Tsimshian villages. It is the largest collection of authentic, pre-commercial totem poles in the U.S., but only a few are on display (open daily May-Sept. 8am-5pm; $3, under 13 free). A $5 combination ticket also provides admission to the **Deer Mountain Fish Hatchery** (225-9533), across the creek. A self-guided tour explains artificial sex, salmon style. Unfortunately, visitors can only peer at the frothy action from a small, central deck. Best to seek your jollies elsewhere (open daily May-Sept. 8am-4:30pm). The **Ketchikan Library,** overlooking a waterfall and rapids, is quite a place to while away a rainy day. Text-starved sophisticates catch up here on *The Nation, The New Yorker,*

Totem 101

Totem poles. They're everywhere in the Northwest—poking out from tourist-happy McDonald's, planted in local cemeteries, decorating cheap motels, or even lurking in primeval forests. A voyage through the Panhandle weaves among hundreds of the red and black carvings. A totem here, a totem there, ho, hum. By the eighth or ninth, you'll find yourself ready to use these glorified sticks for firewood. But hold those matches! Totems are a bit more than dry timber; in fact, these artistic monuments are a sort of secret decoder ring for Native American legend. The tribes of many Northwest indigenous peoples have long used these intricate carvings both to honor each other and relay over a thousand years of their history and culture. Each figure vertically stacked up the totem has a specific significance, depending on the artist's tribe. These symbols represent local Haida and Tlingit myths.

Raven: The creator of the tribes, Raven is identifiable by a long, straight beak. Able to change form on command, he is the hero of many myths.

Eagle: Eagle is the second-most important character in the cast of local myths and signifies peace and friendship. His pointy beak distinguishes him from Raven.

Beaver: His flat tail and two front chompers make Beaver stand out from the rest. He's often associated with the eagle.

Bear and Wolf: These guys look remarkably similar—sharp teeth and a high forehead. Both caused a lot of trouble (and still do) by having relationships with humans, or so the legend goes.

Killer Whale: With razor teeth and a large fin, the whale stands for strength.

and the Sunday *New York Times* (open Mon.-Wed. 10am-8pm, Thurs.-Sat. 10am-6pm, Sun. 1-5pm). The **Tongass Historical Museum,** which shares the library building, features seasonal (and slightly dull) exhibits on the city of Ketchikan (open daily 8am-5pm; Oct.-May 14 Wed. Fri. 1-5 pm., Sat.-Sun. 1-4pm; $2 in the summer, but free Oct.-May).

The colorful stretch of houses perched on stilts along **Creek Street** combats the doldrums of the unremarkably "historic" Ketchikan downtown. This festive area was once a thriving red-light district where, as tour guides quip, both sailors and salmon went upstream to spawn. Women in black fishnets and red-tasseled silk still beckon passers-by into **Dolly's House,** 24 Creek St. (225-6329), a brothel-turned-museum. Antiques nestle in secret hideaways where Dolly kept money, bootleg liquor, and customers during police raids (hours vary with cruise ship arrivals; typically open until 2:30 or 4:30pm; call ahead; $4).

The town is chock full of establishments where Ketchikanians drink like proverbial fish. Downtown is lined with tourist-oriented pubs, while every third building on Water St. houses a bar. Fisher-types crowd into **The Potlach** (225-4855), on Thomas St., at the docks off Stedman St., just south of downtown. Uprooted railroad car seats proffer a place to sip a beer and gander at the blackboard-bearing messages from one boat's crew to another's (open daily 9am-midnight or 2am, depending on the crowd). Younger, more diverse imbibers gathers first at the **First City Saloon** (225-1494), on Water St. toward the ferry terminal. First City serves Guiness, St. Pauli Girl, and a variety of microbrews (domestics, $2-3). Local bands play Thurs.-Sun. Drink first. Open daily 9am-2am, with a meat-and-potatoes kitchen from 11am-2am. If you can get there (and find it too), **Hole in the Wall Marina,** 7500 S. Tongass (247-2296), is high on local flavor. Fish off the dock, then drink a pint or two while your catch cooks. More varieties of beer (18) than chairs (4; open when you get there).

But like Mom always said, you don't have to drink to have a good time. Ketchikan's **First City Players** present a variety of plays to sell-out crowds Thursday through Saturday at 8pm. On Fridays in July and August, check out the bawdy *Fish Pirate's Daughter,* a super-melodrama about Prohibition-era Ketchikan. Shows ($12, Sunday rush tickets $8) are performed at the **Main Street Theatre,** 338 Main St. (225-4792). The annual **Timber Carnival,** a spirited display of speed-chopping, axe-throwing virtuosity and virility, coincides with Ketchikan's boisterous 4th of July celebration. On the second Saturday in August, the **Blueberry Festival** stuffs town streets with crafts, food, and live music, as well as a fiercely contested **slug race.**

OUTDOORS

Although Ketchikan offers boundless hiking and kayaking opportunities within the nearby Misty Fiords National Monument (see p. 134), hikers need only flirt with the city limits to find a trailhead. From Ketchikan, a good dayhike is 3001 ft. **Deer Mountain.** Walk up the hill past the city park on Fair St.; the marked trailhead branches off to the left just behind the dump. The ascent is steep but manageable, and on the rare clear day, the walk yields sparkling views of the town and sea beyond. While most hikers stop at the 2½ mi. point, a longer route leads over the summit and past an A-frame overnight shelter that can be reserved at the SEAVC (see p. 126). The trail runs above treeline along a steep ridge, where snow and ice sometimes linger into the summer. At the peak, clear skies open upon a mountain-and-lake vista that extends as far as Misty Fiords. **Blue Lake,** an alpine pond stocked with trout, shimmers in the middle of the ridge walk.

At the summit of the 3237 ft. John Mountain, the **John Mountain Trail** descends from the ridge, passing the **Stivis Lakes** on its way down to the **Beaver Falls Fish Hatchery** and the South Tongass Highway, 13 mi. from Ketchikan. This section of the hike is poorly marked and may test hikers' ability to read topographic maps. The entire hike, manageable in a full day for experienced hikers, is 10 mi. long and requires a pick-up at the end. A less strenuous and equally accessible outing is the trek along a boardwalk built over muskeg up to **Perseverance Lake.** The **Persever-**

ance Trail, beginning 10 mi. north of the city just before the Three C's campground, climbs 600 ft. over 2.3 mi. to an excellent lake for trout fishing.

Fishing begins with a license purchase at the Outfitter or Plaza Sports (see above, p. 128). Licenses cost $10 per day, $15 for 3 days, $30 for 2 weeks, and $50 for the season. By renting a boat and equipment from **Mountain Point Charter and Boat Rental,** 5660 S. Tongass Hwy. (225-1793 or 800-634-6878; fax 225-7994), anglers can fish beyond the docks without forking over high charter prices.

If all you want is plain ol' water, **Ward Lake,** at the Signal Creek campground on Ward Lake Rd., offers (cold) swimming, a sandy beach, and sheltered picnic tables, as well as a 1.3 mi. trail around the grassy pond that is perfect for first-time mountain bikers. More experienced bikers can explore the surrounding logging roads. To escape water (often in the form of Gore-Tex piercing rain), defy weather and gravity at Kave Sport's indoor climbing gym, 615 Stedman Ave. (225-KAVE/5283; email kavesp@hotmail.com). Over 2300 sq. ft. of climbing wall challenge beginners and expert climbers alike (open Mon.-Thurs. 10am-10pm, Fri. 10am-midnight, Sat. 10am-10pm, Sun. noon-6pm; $6 per hr., $12 per day; equipment rentals $9).

■ Near Ketchikan

METLAKATLA

Metlakatla, where even the local dogs are too relaxed to open their eyes for passers by, offers a refreshing alternative to hyper-hyped Ketchikan. Perched only 15 mi. southwest of Ketchikan on Annette Island, the town, whose name means "salt water channel passage" in Tsimshian (sim-SHEE-an), lies entirely within the Tsimshian Reservation. The community was founded in 1887, when Anglican lay-minister William Duncan led 800 Tsimshian to the island from British Columbia after having difficulties with Canadian religious authorities. Ever since, this village of 400 has basked in the quiet of its permanent vacation from the mainland, but locals are hopeful that a new tour package from Ketchikan will attract visitors and their money.

Although staying for more than a day requires a permit (available at the **Municipal Office Building** (886-4441) on Upper Multon St. (open Mon.-Fri. 8:30am-3pm), little else on the island takes much effort. Metlakatla is an easy, happy, low-priced place to escape the Ketchikan crowds. It's almost worth the trip solely for the bird's-eye view of incredible scenery on the float plane trip over.

Pro-Mech Air (225-3845 in Ketchikan, 886-3845 in Metlakatla, or 800-860-3845) offers safety-conscious float plane service ($19, round-trip $30; 4 flights per day; trip takes 15min.; no credit cards). **Taquan Air** (886-6868) offers comparable service for a slightly higher price. The **Alaska Marine Highway** (800-624-0066) makes six trips a week to the island, including two on Saturdays. Scheduling can be inconvenient. The trip takes about 75 minutes and costs $14. From the ferry terminal, it's a short walk Totten (turn right upon arrival and follow the signs).

Travelers toting tents in Metlakatla are in for a treat—although there are no official campgrounds on the reservation, it is acceptable to pitch a tent for free off Western Ave. past the cemetery. Rumor has it that the **Annette Inn** (886-5360) on Tait St., offers large rooms, private baths, and cable TV, but the owners are often hard to locate (single $60; double $95). Food options are predictably limited. The hungry snacker should head to **Leask's Mini Mart** (886-3000) at the south end of Upper Milton St. for egg rolls ($2.25) or hefty cinnamon rolls ($1.75; open daily 8am-10pm). To support the island grocery monopoly, a larger (but, alas, roll-less) **Leask's Market** sits at the other side of town on Western Ave. (open Mon.-Fri. 10am-6pm, Sat. 10am-5:30pm, Sun. noon-5pm). The friendly owners of the **Pizza Place** (886-5360), downstairs from the Annette Inn, serve up diminutive pizzas from $8 and righteous subs for $6.50 (open Mon.-Fri. 11am-7pm, Sat. noon-7pm).

Walking down the rocky beach that parallels Western Ave., past the cemetery to **Pioneer Park** is perhaps the most enjoyable way to spend a languorous Metlakatla afternoon. Newly remodeled, the park has a boardwalk, picnic tables, and a rope-swing over the water. For some upward mobility, a trail up **Yellow Hill** offers splendid views of the island's west side and takes about 30 minutes. The trail starts about 1½ mi. south of town on Airport Rd.; look for the boardwalk on the right. The route leading to **Purple Lake,** where many a tasty trout has met its untimely end, is a bit longer, but yields even more view per precious mile. Reach the trailhead by taking Airport Rd. south for 2.7 mi., then continuing another 1.8 mi. on Purple Mountain Rd. Bat some eyelash and ask the pilot of your charter plane of choice to take you to the trailhead. This steep 3 mi. trail leads up a rocky mountainside that gushes waterfalls.

The official tour of Metlakatla costs $89. Alternatively, the $17 salmon or halibut **barbeque** and a **tribal dance performance** give a taste of reservation culture and leave you full to boot. You can book the plane flight and take the walking tour yourself. Stop by the Long House down Western Ave. from Leasks Market or call 247-8737 or 800-643-4898 to find out if the show is on for the day.

If you're not a fish fan and have a hankering for local culture, the **Duncan Museum** (886-7363) is free. The museum, once the home of founding father William Duncan, features a collection of his personal effects and old photographs of the village. Look for the bright yellow cottage at the south end of town (open Mon.-Fri. 1-4pm) or peek at the exhibit in the front room of the longhouse (open Mon.-Fri. 1-4:30pm).

MISTY FIORDS NATIONAL MONUMENT

The jagged peaks, plunging valleys, and drippy, dense vegetation of **Misty Fiords National Monument,** 20 mi. east of Ketchikan, make biologists dreamy and outdoor enthusiasts salivate. Only accessible by kayak, power boat, or float plane, the 2.3 million-acre park offers superlative camping, kayaking, hiking, and wildlife viewing. Walls of sheer granite, scoured and scraped by retreating glaciers, rise up to 3000 ft., encasing saltwater bays. More than 12 ft. of annual rainfall and a flood of runoff from large icefields near the Canadian border feed the streams and waterfalls that empty into two long fjords, **Behm Canal** (117 mi. long) and **Portland Canal** (72 mi. long), on either side of the monument. **Camping** is permitted throughout the park, and the Forest Service maintains four first-come, first-serve shelters (free) and 14 cabins ($25). You can write directly to the **Misty Fiords Ranger Station** (225-2148) at 3031 Tongass Ave., Ketchikan, but it's always a good idea to ask ahead at SEAVC (see p. 126).

Although seasoned kayakers with the know-how to navigate the harsh currents between Ketchikan and Behm Canal often paddle straight into the park, kayaking neophytes should contact **Alaska Cruises,** 220 Front, Box 7814 (225-6044). They will pack you and your boat along on one of their four weekly sightseeing tours, drop you off, and pick you up anywhere along their route for $225, $175 at the entrance or head of Rudyard Bay. **Southeast Sea Kayaks** (225-1258; email bbkayak@ktn.net) at the Visitors Bureau, will arrange transportation for you and your kayak for $175-$200 per person. For $12, they will plan a trip for you, book a cabin, and give you topographical maps for kayaking, fishing, and other activities within the monument. If you take the DIY route, visit the trip-planning center at SEAVC for detailed maps and helpful suggestions. **Walker Cove, Punchbowl Cove,** and **Rudyard Bay,** off Behm Canal, are several choice destinations for paddlers. However, these waters are frigid and large stretches of coast have no good shelter or dry fire wood.

A slew of charter operations visit the monument, all for monumental prices; plan on spending at least $125 for a visit. Alaska Cruises offers an 11-hour **boat tour** with three meals ($145). **Combination boat and flight tours** last six hours ($185). Island Wings (225-2444 or 247-7432) has the cheapest flightseeing trips ($125), but these airy jaunts still cost more than $1 per airborn minute. Call the Ketchikan Visitors Bureau (see **Ketchikan: Practical Information,** p. 126) for more information.

Prince of Wales Island

Prince of Wales Island sits less than 30 mi. west of Ketchikan. The island hovers beneath a thick rainforest broken only by mountain peaks, patches of muskeg, and large clear-cut. Tongass National Forest and Native American tribal groups manage most of the island, which is criss-crossed with roads built to facilitate logging. The industry has left some scars, but even so, a great deal of Prince of Wales Island remains swathed in virgin forest.

Prince of Wales is a prime destination for hunters and sport fishers. Canoers, kayakers, and scuba-divers also flock here for some of the best scenery in the region, and numerous, expensive charter companies happily await them. Accommodations and transportation companies follow suit: although it's cheap enough to *get* here, it's prohibitively expensive to *stay* here. Car rentals cost an arm and a leg, and even taking a car on the ferry from Ketchikan puts the frugal out $41. Navigating the island by car is difficult, and thumbing it is usually fruitless and time-consuming. **Float planes** are an option—try Promech (800-860-3845 or 826-3845), or Taquan Air (826-8800), but the best strategy is to befriend a native on the ferry and let him or her take you home This option will get you to at least one town on the island with little hassle and cost. Then try to get back....

CRAIG

Craig, on the west coast of Prince of Wales, is home to most of the island's tourist resources: charter services, the district ranger station, a number of very nice hotels you probably can't afford (sigh), and one outstanding restaurant. Outside of these niceties, there's little reason to linger. The surrounding area is heavily clear-cut and there are no convenient hiking trails.

Even so, the **Craig Chamber of Commerce** (826-3870) on Easy St., will cheerfully oblige requests for info (open Mon.-Sat. 9:30am-5pm; wheelchair accessible). For the skinny on caves, camping, and the 19 wilderness cabins on Prince of Wales Island, drop by the **Forest Service Office** (826-3271) at 9th Ave. and Main St. (open Mon.-Fri. 7am-5pm). **National Bank of Alaska** is on Craig Klawock St. by the post office (open Mon.-Thurs. 10am-5pm, Fri. 10am-6pm). A bookstore, **The Voyager,** is located on Cold Storage Rd. in the Southwind Plaza (open Mon.-Sat. 7am-7pm, Sun. noon-5pm). **JT Brown,** next to Ruth Ann's, helps out fishing types with licenses and tackle (open Mon.-Sat. 8am-7pm). The **Seaview Family Medical Center** (826-3257) is on 3rd St. (open Mon.-Fri. 8am-5pm, Sat. 9am-3pm). For **emergencies** (police, fire, ambulance), dial 911. The **police station** (826-3330) is across from the library on 3rd St. Send love letters home from the **Craig Post Office** (826-3298) on Craig-Klawock St. next to Thompson House (open Mon.-Fri. 8am-5pm, Sat. noon-2pm) The **General Delivery ZIP Code** is 99921. The **area code** is 907.

Anyone in Craig will sing songs of praise for **Ruth Ann's** (826-3376; open daily 6am-10pm), on Front St., which offers affordable and creative breakfast or lunch options ($6-8). Ruth Ann must make a bundle on dinners, when prices skyrocket (entrees start at $18). **Thompson House Groceries** (826-3394) on Craig-Klawock St., is the best bet for dinner food. A salad bar and a deli complement a good selection of groceries (open Mon.-Sat. 7:30am-8pm, Sun. 9am-7pm). Take it easy at **Healthy Generations** (826-4200) on Easy St., which has a large selection of bulk organic food and some killer salsa and nachos ($6.25; open Mon.-Fri. 10am-6pm, Sat. 10am-6pm).

Although most of Prince of Wales Island falls within the free-camping zone of Tongass National Forest, Craig is surrounded by private tribal lands where camping is prohibited. The **TLC Laundromat and Rooms** (826-2966), on Cold Storage Rd. behind the supermarket, offers affordable *and* legal slumber space (singles $40; doubles $50). The laundromat ($1.25 wash, 25¢ dry; open daily 7am-9pm) also has showers ($2 for 5min.).

Craig lies about 30 mi. west of Hollis where the ferry docks. **Jackson Cab** will drive to Craig for around $23 (755-2557) and **Wilderness Rent-a-Car** (826-2205 or 755-2205) rents at wild rates ($59 per day, 30¢ per mi. over 25) to those lucky, credit card-owning over-21-year-olds (open Mon.-Thurs., Sat. 8am-6pm, Fri. 8am-7pm, Sun. 10am-3pm). Locals report that between Hollis and Craig, hitchhikers rarely wait long for rides. Light traffic on logging roads makes for significant waits elsewhere. (*Let's Go* does not recommend hitchhiking.)

THORNE BAY

A narrow, dusty logging road cuts a 38 mi. swath northeast across the island from **Klawock,** 4.3 mi. north of Craig, to Thorne Bay, an unpretentious town recently created by the incorporation of a logging camp. The area boasts attractive waters for kayaking, and its tributary rivers win the praise of anglers. Unlike Craig, Thorne Bay lies within **Tongass National Forest,** where campers may pitch tents for up to one month, limiting themselves to two weeks on any site. Call or stop by the **Forest Service Station** (828-3304) for more information (open Mon.-Fri., 8am-5pm). Locals recommend the **Eagles Nest Campground,** 12 mi. north of Thorne Bay; a steal-of-a camp unit ($5) includes access to a bathroom, water, cooking grates, a canoe launch, picnic tables, and RV parking. For lovers of cover, **Marilyn Black's B&B,** in a double-wide trailer on 1009 Sandy Beach Rd. (828-3456), offers $50 singles and continental breakfasts, but is no place for adamant non-smokers. **Brenda's Beehive B&B** (828-3945), on Bayview Ct., offers two comfortable beds ($65). The **Thorne Bay Market,** where a gallon of milk goes for a precious $4, lies in a cove beyond the docks (open Mon.-Sat. 9am-7pm, Sun. noon-6pm). **Some Place to Go** (828-8888), an outdoor hamburger stand on the road out of town, is, well, a place to go. And eat. The stand serves a tasty cheeseburger for $3 (open 10am-7pm).

SIGHTS AND OUTDOORS

The most distinctive of the Island's attractions is **El Capitan Cave,** North America's deepest cavern. The cave bores into the limestone bedrock of Prince of Wales and is adorned with striking marble outcroppings. Recently, speleologists (not to be confused with amateur "spelunkers") uncovered the remains of a 12,000-year-old grizzly bear deep within the cave. In less exciting news, the Forest Service has installed a gate 150 ft. inside the cave to reduce damage to El Capitan's delicate interior. Free two-hour tours start behind the gate (May-Sept., Wed.-Sun. at noon, 1pm, and 3pm) and require a hard-hat and flashlight. Off-season tours are available with 14-day advance notice. Make reservations at the **Thorne Bay Ranger District** (828-3304). The cave is about a three-hour drive from either Craig or Thorne Bay.

The **Craig Dive Center** (826-3481 or 800-380-DIVE/3483), at 1st and Main in Craig, rents canoes and windsurfing equipment ($25 per day). Owners Ann and Craig also offer a two-tank boat dive for groups of four ($125 per person). Owner Craig lives in Craig. Weird. **Island Adventures** (826-2710) rents kayaks for $20 per day. **Log Cabin** (755-2205 or 800-544-2205) in Klawock rents canoes for $20 per day. The Forest Service can provide maps for a number of established **canoe trails** and reserve you a spot at one of the **wilderness cabins** that line these watery routes ($25 per night).

■ Wrangell

Wrangell is the only place in Alaska to have been ruled by four different nations. The Russian-American Company ousted a Tlingit village near the mouth of the Stikine River in 1834 to build a fort. In 1840, the British-owned Hudson Bay Company took out a lease on the Russian fort. When the United States purchased Alaska from Russia in 1867, Britain forked over control of the fort to the Americans. As the only gateway to Canada's interior between Prince Rupert and Skagway, the Stikine River became a crucial transportation corridor during the three gold rushes of the next forty years. As miners traveled to and from the goldfields, they tramped through the little town that became Wrangell. Explorer and ecologist John Muir was duly unimpressed with the result: "It was a lawless draggle of wooden huts and houses, built in crooked lines, wrangling around the boggy shores of the island."

Now an orderly, prosperous lumber and fishing town with a picturesque harbor, Wrangell's attractions are convenient enough to allow a brief visit during a ferry layover and plentiful enough to merit a night's stay. Locals take their day of rest very seriously: grocery stores, the museum, and the tourist office are all closed on Sunday.

PRACTICAL INFORMATION

Visitors Center: Chamber of Commerce (874-3901 or 800-367-9745; email wrangell@wrangell.org; http://www.wrangell.org) on Front St. at the side of the Stikine Inn. Friendly, knowledgeable staff. Open Tues.-Fri. 9am-4pm. **Forest Service,** 525 Bennett St., ¾mi. east of town (874-2323). Open Mon.-Fri. 8am-5pm. Reserve cabins here. **Alaska Department of Fish and Game** (874-3822), in the green Kadin Building on Front St. Info on fishing and hunting regulations.

Bank: National Bank of Alaska (874-3341), on Front St. Home of Wrangell's sole **ATM.** Bank open Mon.-Fri. 9:30am-5:30pm.

Airport: Alaska Air (874-3309, recorded info 874-3308). 1 flight daily to Petersburg and Juneau and 1 to Ketchikan ($90) and Seattle, WA.

Ferries: Alaska Marine Highway (874-2021, recorded schedule 874-3711) at Stikine Ave. and McCormack St. Frequent service to: Sitka ($38); Juneau ($56); and Ketchikan ($24). Open 1½hr. before arrivals. Luggage lockers 25¢.

Taxi: Porky's Cab Co., 874-3603; **Star Cab,** 874-3622. Both 24hr.

Car Rental: Practical Rent-A-Car (874-3975; fax 874-3911), on Airport Rd. near the airport. Compact car $42 per day, van $46, unlimited mileage.

Auto Repair: Wrangell Auto Body (874-3857), at Mile 2¼ of Zimovia Hwy.

Air Charters: Sunrise Aviation, P.O. Box 432 (874-2319). **Ketchikan Air Service,** P.O. Box 874 (874-2369). **Temsco Helicopters,** P.O. Box 5057 (874-2010).

Public Library: (874-3535), on 2nd St. Open Mon. and Fri. 10am-noon and 1-5pm, Tues.-Thurs. 1-5pm and 7-9pm, Sat. 9am-5pm.

Public Radio: KSTK 101.7 FM

Laundromat: Thunderbird Laundromat, 233 Front St. (874-3322). Wash $2, dry 25¢. Open daily 6am-7pm.

Swimming Pool: (874-2444), indoors at Wrangell High School on Church St. Hours vary; closed Sun. Pool, weight room, gym $1.50, under 18 $1. Racquetball: 2 players $6.

Showers: in **Hungry Beaver Pizza,** on Shakes St. Unusual but clean. $3.

Pharmacy: Wrangell Drug, 202 Front St. (874-3422). Open Mon.-Sat. 9am-6pm, Sun. 11am-6pm.

Hospital: (874-3356), at Bennett St. and 2nd Ave.

Emergency: 911. **Police:** 874-3304. **Fire:** 874-3223. Both are in the Public Safety Building on Zimovia Hwy.

Post Office: (874-3714), at the north end of Front St. The town rejected home delivery in 1983 in favor of the P.O. box-checking ritual. Open Mon.-Fri. 8:30am-5pm, Sat. 11am-1pm. **ZIP Code:** 99929.

Area Code: 907.

ACCOMMODATIONS AND CAMPING

Wrangell Hostel, 220 Church St. (874-3534), 5 blocks from the ferry terminal. Just look for the groovy neon cross. A surprisingly underutilized resource—you may end up having the entire place to yourself. Showers, kitchen, and spacious common room with a piano. Daytime luggage storage. 10pm curfew unless you're on a late ferry; call ahead. Reception daily in summer 5pm-9am. 20 foam mats on the floor $10, blanket and pillows $1.

Harbor House B&B, 645 Shakes Ave. (874-3084 or 800-488-5107), across from the Hungry Beaver. Ahoy! 3 rooms decked out with nautical antiques and a prime harborside location. Shared bath and small kitchen. Ride around town on complimentary "vintage" bikes. Continental breakfast included. Singles $55; doubles $70.

Rooney's Roost B&B, 206 McKinnon St. (874-2026 or 874-3622), at 2nd St. Other B&Bs come and go, but Rooney's has come home to roost for good. Well-kept rooms have nice (if bland) views. Singles $55; doubles $60. July-Aug. reserve several weeks in advance.

City Park, 1½mi. south of town on Zimovia Hwy. (2nd St. changes names several times before becoming Zimovia Hwy. south of town; trust us), immediately beyond the cemetery and baseball field. Picnic tables, shelters, drinking water, and toilets of dubious comfort, but a beautiful view of the water. The price is right, too (free). 24hr. max. stay. Open Memorial Day-Labor Day.

Alaskan Water RV Park, 241 Berger St. (874-2378 or 800-FISH-INC/347-4462; fax 874-3133) off Zimovia Hwy. ½ mi. from town. 6 RV hookups. Clean and convenient, but gravelly and little privacy. Open mid-March to mid-Oct.

FOOD

If you're not in the mood for pizzas or burgers, pick up some tasty deli sandwiches at **Benjamin's Groceries** (874-2341), on Outer Dr. (open Mon.-Sat. 8am-8pm) and picnic at **Kik Setti Totem Park,** around the corner at Front St. and Episcopal.

J&W's, 120 Front St. (874-2120). Good, messy burgers from $3.60, fried mini-burritos for $1.65. More creative alternatives include salmon and shrimp burgers ($5) and 13 flavors of shakes ($2.65). Open Mon.-Sat. 11am-7pm, Sun. noon-7pm.

Hungry Beaver Pizza/Marine Bar (874-3005), on Shakes St. near the island. Where guzzlers and high school grease-lovers mix. One-person pizzas from $5.50. Waterfront bar is low key and a last refuge for late-night eaters. Capricious bar menu. Kitchen open daily 4-10pm. Bar open daily 10am-2:30am. Showers (?!?) $3.

SIGHTS AND OUTDOORS

If the ferry schedule only permits you 45 minutes in Wrangell, a walk out to **Shakes Island** might be the best use of time. Follow Front St. to Shakes St., where a short bridge leads to the island in the middle of Wrangell's snug harbor. Outdoor totems guard the **Shakes Tribal House** (874-2023), a meticulous replica of the communal home of high-caste Tlingits. A Civilian Conservation Corps work team built the house during the Depression without the aid of a sawmill or a single nail. Inside, finely carved totems stand below large timbers scarred by the original adze marks. (Open in summer whenever a ferry docks for more than 1hr., or by appointment with a donation of $10 or more; regular donation $1.50.)

Stone carvings by the region's first inhabitants litter **Petroglyph Beach,** ¾ mi. north of the ferry terminal on Evergreen Ave. Although some are simple circles and spirals, others illustrate complex facial patterns, thought to represent spirits or totem animals. Archaeologists are uncertain about the age of these petroglyphs, but local Tlingit tradition maintains that the petroglyphs were in place before the Tlingit reached the harbor. The **Wrangell Museum** (874-3770) temporarily dwells in the basement of the community center on Church St. Besides interesting (if predictable) collections of Native American artifacts, the museum houses a communications and aviation room and an exhibit on the region's natural history (open May-Sept. Mon.-Fri. 10am-5pm, Oct-April Tues.-Fri. 10-11:30am and 12:30-4pm; $2, under 16 free).

Hikers can follow in John Muir's footsteps and scramble up nearby **Mt. Dewey** to an observation point with a commanding view of town and the Stikine River flats. Walking down 2nd St. toward the center of town, McKinnon St. is on the left. Follow McKinnon St. to a left on 3rd St. and look for a white sign marking the trailhead. The trail is primitive and not regularly maintained. Three miles beyond City Park on Zimovia Hwy., the **Rainbow Falls Trail** runs 0.7 mi to the top of a 40 ft. waterfall. The **Institute Creek Trail,** which breaks off from the Rainbow Fall Trail just before the top of the falls, is much more rewarding. The result of a Herculean trail-building effort, the route follows a boardwalk for 2.7 mi, paralleling a series of impressive waterfalls (50min. from trailhead) before breaking into several muskeg openings on a ridgetop. A three-sided Forest Service shelter (available for overnight stays on a first-come first-served basis) sits on the ridge at the end of the trail. Both taxi services in town will take you to the trailhead for $7-8 if you don't want to walk. The **Wrangell Ranger District,** Box 51 (874-2323), has more info on the trails, campsites, and cabins in the Wrangell area (open Mon.-Fri. 8am-4:30pm).

The Stikine River is the fastest navigable river in the Northwest. The bold and daring can rent kayaks (single $40; double $50) from **Alaska Vistas** (874-2429 or 874-3006; email info@alakavistas.com; http://www.alaskavistas.com). Less adventuresome souls can join a charter boat expedition up the Stikine and over to Garnet Ledge. There are six Forest Service cabins throughout the Stikine delta and two bathing huts at **Chief Shakes Hot Springs,** a few mi. up river. The **Anan Bear Observatory** is also accessible by boat—watch rapacious bears feast on the pink salmon that climb the falls to spawn. Call **Stickeen** *(sic)* **Wilderness Adventures,** Box 934, 107 Front St. (874-2085 or 800-874-2085; fax 874-2285) for info; they will schedule departures around your ferry schedule (open Mon.-Fri. 9am-5pm). A daytrip to the Anan Observatory or up the Stikine River runs $145 per person. For a listing of charter boat services (Wrangell has over 24), contact the chamber of commerce (see **Practical Information,** above). The chamber also provides information on scuba-diving tours, whale-watching, and fishing and hunting trips.

Petersburg

In 1897, Norwegian immigrant Peter Buschmann saw opportunity in the natural harbor, abundant fish, and convenient glacier ice around Petersburg and built a cannery here. Now P-Burg claims the world's largest halibut fleet and a strong Scandinavian legacy. Fishing is the mainstay of the local economy and Petersburg draws hordes of summer workers. Its isolation lends the island community an uncommon cohesiveness: a few years ago when a cannery found itself understaffed with a heap of salmon to process, the management went through the phone book calling for extra hands. Retirees, housewives, and adults just home from work all rallied to help. Unfortunately, Petersburg's strong sense of community has made it somewhat cool towards strangers. The polite townsfolk evince no hostility, but make little effort to accommodate budget travelers. There are no hostels or storage facilities for packs.

PRACTICAL INFORMATION AND ORIENTATION

Visitor Information Center: P.O. Box 649 (772-3646; http://www.petersburg.org), at 1st and Fram St. Home of a replica of the world-record 126½lb. king salmon. Reserve Forest Service cabins here. Pick up the free *Viking Visitors Guide,* featuring Sven, the friendly Viking! Open Mon.-Fri. 9am-5pm, Sat. 10am-4pm, Sun. noon-4pm; winter Mon.-Fri. 10am-noon and 1-3pm. **Forest Service,** P.O. Box 1328 (722-3871), above the post office. Info on hiking and fishing. Reserve cabins here, too. Open Mon.-Fri. 8am-5pm.

Bank: National Bank of Alaska, 201 Nordic Drive. Open Mon.-Thurs. 9am-5pm, Fri. 9am-5:30pm. 24hr. **ATM.**

Flights: Alaska Airlines, 1506 Haugen Dr. (772-4255), 1 mi. from the Federal Bldg. To Juneau ($114) and Seattle ($346, $181 with 2-week advance purchase). Next door, **Haines Air** (772-4200) often beats Alaska's prices with 3 daily flights to Juneau. For **flightseeing,** call **Temsco Air** (772-4780) or **Pacific Wing** (772-4258).

Ferries: Alaska Marine Highway, Mile 0.9 Mitkof Hwy. (772-3855), 1 mi. from the center of town. To: Ketchikan ($38); Sitka ($26); Wrangell ($18); and Juneau ($44). Open 1½hr. before ferry arrivals.

Employment: Petersburg Employment Service (772-3791), at Haugen Dr. and 1st St. Fish-steeped staff provide info on all 3 canneries. Call to request the lyrically succinct pamphlet *Alaska Job Facts and Seafood Processing Jobs in Alaska.* Open Mon.-Fri. 9-11am and noon-8pm, Sat. 9-11am and noon-3pm.

Taxi: City Cab, 772-3003. Rates start at $4. Open 24hr.

Car Rental: Allstar (772-4281 or 800-722-5006), at the Scandia House Hotel. $45 per day with unlimited mileage. Must be 21 with a credit card. Also rents 18 ft. boats ($150 per day, $125 for guests of the hotel).

Auto Repair: Mike's Autobody, 772-3052.

Bike Rental: Northern Bikes (772-3978), next to the Scandia House. Seize the deal: $3 per hr., $20 per day. Try out a tandem at $5 per hr. Open Mon.-Fri. 10am-5pm, Sat. 10:30am-5pm.

Laundromat: Glacier Laundry (772-4400), at Nordic and Dolphin. Wash $2, 5min. dry 25¢. Open daily 6am-10pm. Also at **Twin Creek RV Park** (see below).

Showers: Glacier Laundry ($2, towels $1), **Tent City** (see below), and **Twin Creek RV Park** (see below).

Bookstore: Sing Lee Alley Books, 11 Sing Lee Alley (772-4440). Classics and popular/mid-brow contemporary. Open Mon.-Sat. 10am-5pm.
Library: (772-4425), at Haugen and Nordic Dr. above the Fire Hall. Free internet access. Open Mon.-Thurs. noon-9pm, Fri.-Sat. 1-5pm.
Public Radio: KFSK 100.9 FM.
Alcohol and Drug Help: Changing Tides (772-3552).
Pharmacy: Rexall Drug, 215 Nordic Dr., downtown. Open Mon. and Fri. 9am-9pm, Tues.-Thurs. and Sat. 9am-6pm, Sun. noon-6pm.
Hospital: Petersburg Medical Center (772-4291) at Fram and N. 1st St.
Emergency: 911. **Police:** 16 S. Nordic Dr. (772-3838). **State Troopers:** 772-3100.
Internet Access: Free at the **library** (see above).
Post Office: (772-3121), at Haugen and Nordic Dr. Open Mon.-Fri. 9am-5:30pm, Sat. 11am-2pm. Lobby with stamp machine open Mon.-Fri. 7am-8pm, Sat. 8am-6pm. **General Delivery ZIP Code:** 99833.
Area Code: 907.

If you're looking for Nordic Drive, Main Street, or Mitkof Highway, you're probably on it. The main drag goes by all three aliases. The ferry drops you off 1 mi. south of downtown, but it's a painless walk. Cabs to the center run about $4, $6 out to Tent City.

ACCOMMODATIONS AND CAMPING

The only two places within city limits for backpackers are often packed with summer cannery workers. Camping solo is impossible because wet, untentable muskeg covers the entire area; the next nearest campground to Petersburg is 22 mi. away. However, an 8 mi. journey gets one to the Tongass National Forest and its free, month-long camping may be worth it. Many cannery workers camp illegally in the woods beyond the muskeg. Contact the visitors center (see **Practical Information,** above) for comprehensive B&B listings, though prices can be appalling compared to nearby **Sitka.**

Harbor House B&B, 404 Noseeum St., Box 1255 (772-3971). From ferry terminal, take a right onto Marian St. and keep your eyes peeled for Noseeum. Noseeum? Keep looking. Fine Scandinavian-styled rooms with a health-conscious breakfast. A half-mile from town and half-way through your budget. Singles $55, doubles $70.

Nordic House B&B, 806 Nordic Dr., Box 573 (772-3620; fax 772-3673; email nordicbb@alaska.net), ¼ mi. north of the ferry terminal. 3 lovely rooms, a common kitchen and bath, and a sitting space with a fine view cheer Norwegians pining for the fjords. Continental breakfast. Singles start at $65. Doubles start at $75. Make reservations for July and Aug.

Narrows Inn, Box 1048 (772-4284), at Mile 1 of Mitkof Hwy. Generic motel with generic rooms right across the street from the ferry. Overpriced, but still the cheapest bed in town. Private baths and cable. Kitchenettes in many rooms. 25 units. Singles from $55; doubles from $65. Call early for summer reservations.

Twin Creek RV Park, Box 90B (772-3244), Mile 7 of Mitkof Hwy. The only home for a large RV in Petersburg. Steps away from foliage, fishing, and hiking. Hookups, showers, laundry, fishing tackle.

Ohmer Creek Campground, Mile 22 of Mitkof Hwy. Maintained by the Forest Service. A long haul from town proper is rewarded by 10 sites for tents or small RVs amidst the lupine, columbine and wild iris of the woods. 14-day max. stay. Gravel trail leads to choice fish-watching venues. Water, pit toilets. Free.

Tent City (772-9864), on Haugen Dr. past the airport, 2 mi. from the ferry. Established by the city and administered by Parks and Recreation in a sort of cannery workers' apartheid, this ramshackle collection of tarps and wooden platforms rests atop muskeg swamp. Camp manager Charlie Freeman has added several amenities (pay phone, griddle, hotplate, refrigerator, and a shelter) and a dose of order to what used to be largely self-governed. The new no-alcohol policy has mellowed things a bit, but Tent City is generally not the friendliest or safest place in the world. Several sites are set aside for tourists and short-term visitors. Water, toilet, 4

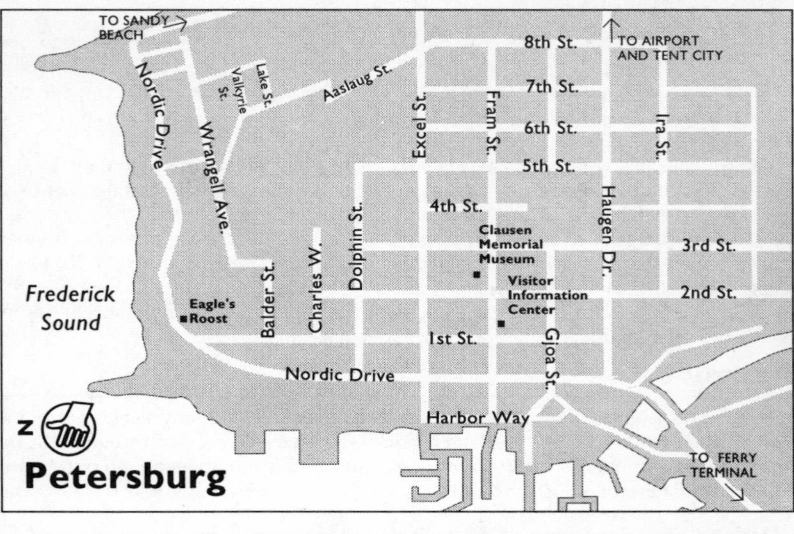

showers (50¢), and pit fires with wood. Quiet hours 10pm-noon. Open May-Sept. $5, $30 per week, and $125 per month. As the name suggests, tents only.

FOOD

Although swimming in fish, Petersburg still charges a bundle for seafood. **The Trading Union** (772-3881), on Nordic Dr. downtown, offers a selection of both sea- and land-dwelling groceries (open Mon.-Fri. 8am-7pm, Sat. 8am-5:30 pm, Sun. 9am-5pm).

Helse-Health Foods and Deli (772-3444), on Sing Lee Alley off Nordic Dr. With flowers, little wooden stools, and plenty of reggae, this place offers refuge from typical Alaskan *bourgeois cuisine.* Soup and bread $5, "Cheese Breeze" (avocado, shrimp, mushrooms, and havarti) $6.75. Lots of juices. Open Mon.-Fri. 7:30am-5pm, Sat. 10am-4pm; winter Mon.-Fri. 7:30am-3pm, Sat. 10am-3pm.

Alaskaté (772-JAVA/5282), on Excel St. above Costal Cold Storage. Globetrotting gourmets import panini to Petersburg. Overdosing on Norse culture? The Fellini—mozzarella and gorgonzola cheeses, artichoke hearts and sun-dried tomatoes—should fix you right up (half $5.45, whole $7.75). Open Mon.-Sat. 7:30am-5pm, Sun. 9am-3pm; winter Tues.-Sat. 7:30am-5pm.

El Rincon (772-2255), sets up camp each summer inside Kito's Kave on Sing Lee Alley. Authentic and dirt-cheap tacos ($1.25) and burritos ($2.50) are best when consumed ex-cavum. Open daily in summer 11am-10pm; migrates south with cannery workers in winter.

Homestead Cafe (772-3900), on Nordic Dr. at Excel St., across from the general store. Run by fishermen's wives who understand large appetites, and frequented by fishermen who know how to eat. The good ol' boys of Petersburg play dice on the tables and chat at the counter. Just you try to finish their stack of pancakes ($3.50). We dare you. Prodigious plate of biscuits and gravy $5.50. Open Mon.-Sat. 24hr. Lunch starts at 11am.

SIGHTS AND ENTERTAINMENT

This is one of the best places on the Panhandle to see a fishing town at work, as long as the fish are biting. Patti Norheim leads groups of four or more on three-hour tours (watch out, Gilligan) through the shrimp cannery next to the harbormaster's office, through the rest of the city and a hatchery, and finally back to her home for cocktails. Find out about the **"Patti Wagon"** ($25) at 772-4837. The **Clausen Memorial**

Museum, 203 Fram St. (772-3598), at 2nd Ave., displays native artifacts and an inspiring history of fishing techniques (open Mon.-Sat. 9:30am-4:30pm, Sun. 12:30-4:30pm; winter Wed. 9:30am-4:30pm, Sun 12:30-4:30pm; $2, under 12 free). Outside the museum is the bizarre **Fisk Fountain,** a hulking metal monolith featuring an abstract array of fish.

On the third full weekend in May, Petersburg joins its international brethren in joyous celebration of Norwegian independence (1905) from Sweden. During the **Little Norway Festival,** mock Vikings dance, sing, parade, hunt their own furs, wear horns, sail in long boats, and violently "board" a plane at the local airport in traditional Viking style. Memorial Day weekend brings the **Salmon Derby.** This search for a specially tagged fish, and the accompanying $10,000 prize, has been sadly unsuccessful in recent years. Hold your nose and stay away from open spaces on the **4th of July** in Petersburg: celebrations feature a **competitive herring toss.**

OUTDOORS

The island's fishing sites yield salmon, halibut, crab, shrimp, dolly varden, and cutthroat trout, while the land teems with black bears, deer, moose, and waterfowl. For more info, or to obtain Alaska state sportfishing and hunting licenses, contact the **Alaska Department of Fish and Game** (see p. 43). Contented amateurs will discover that **jigging** for herring from the docks is alarmingly fun.

While the Petersburg area offers a multitude of hiking opportunities, only a couple of trails are readily accessible by foot. The 4 mi. **Raven's Roost Trail** leads to a Forest Service cabin by the same name ($25 per night; call 772-3871 well in advance for reservations). Another popular walk follows what locals call the **Loop.** From Nordic Dr., walk past the Eagle's Roost Picnic Area and Sandy Beach Park (indigenous petroglyphs are visible on the beach at low tide), onto the Frederick Pt. Boardwalk, and back on Haugen Dr. (about 1½hr.). Pick up the *Petersburg Map* at the ferry terminal or visitors center (see **Practical Information,** above) for a complete illustration of the trails and logging roads on Mitkof Island.

The planked **Petersburg Creek Trail,** ½ mi. across the Wrangell Narrows on neighboring Kupreanof Island, runs 11½ mi. up to Petersburg Lake through a wilderness area to another Forest Service cabin. If the tide is high enough, you can go up the creek a few miles by boat to make a 6½ mi. hike to the lake. Many charter operators in town ferry people across the narrows and rent skiffs, but this can cost more than $100. Ask at the harbormaster's office about boats making the crossing with space for an extra passenger. A small number of people also live across the narrows and make the afternoon commute home. (*Let's Go* does not recommend skiffhitching.)

Several area outfitters offer reasonably priced outdoor adventures. Scott Roberge at **Tongass Kayak Adventures,** 106 N. Nordic Dr., P.O. Box 707 (772-4600), offers guided sea kayak tours up Petersburg Creek. (5hr. tours daily June-Aug., $55 per person, children under 12 $30; includes gear.) Or do it yourself: kayak rentals are $40 per day for a single, $50 for a double, with a three-day minimum.

Sitka

The turquoise water of the Pacific washes up college students, leather-faced fishers, pain-spattered artists, and an occasional Californian intellectual refugee onto the shores of a community that has regained its native name and long since strayed from its Russian roots. Assimilation, however, was not always this easy. In 1802, the native Tlingit, resentful of a three-year Russian occupation, burned and razed the settlement, massacring nearly every inhabitant. Two years later, the Russians returned and bombarded the Tlingit fort. After a bloody 10-day battle, the Tlingit ran out of ammunition and withdrew under cover of darkness. "New Archangel" then became a cultural and economic center, the capital of Russian America. Today, the influx of urbane exurbanites adds fresh flavor to a long-diverse ethnocultural mix

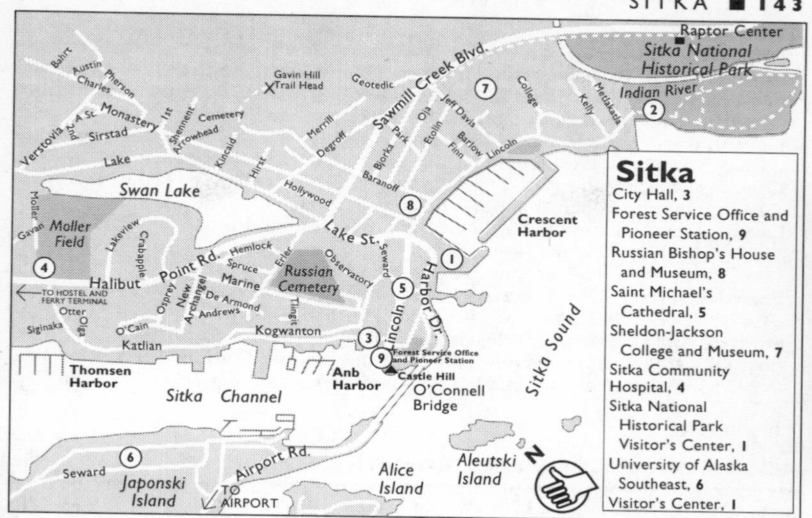

PRACTICAL INFORMATION AND ORIENTATION

Visitors Information: Sitka Convention & Visitors Bureau, P.O. Box 1226 (747-5940; email scub@ptialaska.net; http://www.ptialaska.net/~scub). The bureau's most convenient booth is in the Centennial Bldg. at 330 Harbor Dr. Few brochures, but a helpful volunteer staff. Open when cruise ships are in and when the Centennial Bldg. hosts events (most of the time in summer). **Forest Service: Sitka Ranger District, Tongass National Forest,** 201 Katlian, #109 (747-6671). Pick up *Sitka Trails* or other pamphlets about cabins ($25 per night). Open Mon.-Fri. 8am-5pm.

Banks: Two banks are located on Lincoln St. behind the church: **Nations Bank of Alaska** (747-3226), open Mon.-Thurs. 9:30am-5:30pm, Fri. 9:30am-6pm, and **First National,** open Mon.-Fri. 9am-5pm.

Flights: Alaska Airlines (966-2266 or 800-426-0333; http:\\www.alaskaair.com). Service to Juneau ($96) and Ketchikan ($124). Also flies to Seattle, Anchorage, Wrangell, and Petersburg.

Ferries: Alaska Marine Highway, 7 Halibut Rd. (747-8737 or 800-642-0066), 7 mi. from town. To: Ketchikan ($54); Petersburg ($26); and Juneau ($26). Open 2hr. before arrival until departure.

Shuttle: Sitka Tours (747-8443) offers affordable rides to both the ferry terminal and airport, as well as tours around town. Call ahead (7am-5pm) for a pick-up. $3 one-way. Most sights are concentrated along the waterfront, all within walking distance of each other, but **Tribal Tours** does offer a **Visitor Transit System** (747-7290) which drives travelers to and from all the major attractions ($5 per day).

Luggage Storage: The **fire station,** on Halibut Point Rd. near downtown, stores backpacks for free, as does the **Centennial Bldg.** The ferry terminal has 25¢ lockers. 24hr. max.

Taxis: Sitka Taxi, 747-5001. $12.50 from Sitka to the ferry, $6 to the airport, 50¢ per additional person. 24hr.

Car Rental: Advantage Car Rental (747-7557), at the airport. From $31 per day with unlimited mileage. Must be 21 with credit card.

Bike Rental: J&B Bike Rental, 203 Lincoln St. (747-8279), in **Southeast Diving & Sports.** Clunky old 5-speeds $5 per hr., $15 per day, $25 overnight. Open Mon.-Sat. 10am-5pm, Sun. 11am-5pm.

Kayak Rental: Baidarka Boats (747-8996; email 72037.3607@compuserve.com; http://www.execpc.com/~bboats), on Lincoln St. above Old Harbor Books. Single $25 per ½-day, $30 per day; double $35 per ½-day, $45 per day. Rates less with longer rentals. Required 1hr. instructional class for novices ($25). Open daily 10am-6pm; in winter closed Sun.

Bookstore: Old Harbor Books, 201 Lincoln (747-8808). Info on local arts events., marine charts, and **topo maps.** Free copies of the *New York Review of Books,* the *New York Times Book Review,* and the *Bloomsbury Review*. Ecopolitical diatribes available on request. Open Mon.-Fri. 9am-6pm, Sat.-Sun. 9am-5pm.

Library: Kettleson Memorial Library, 320 Harbor Dr. (747-8708). Open Mon.-Thurs. 10am-9pm, Fri. 1-6pm, Sat.-Sun. 1-5pm. Wheelchair accessible.

Camping Equipment: Mac's, 213 Harbor Dr. (747-6970). Well stocked with gear for fish and humans. Open Mon.-Sat. 8am-6pm, Sun. 9am-5pm.

Laundromats and Shower Facilities: Duds 'n Suds Laundromat, 906 Halibut Point Rd. (747-5050), near the hostel. Wash $1.75, 10min. dry 50¢. Shower $2 for 10 min. Open Mon.-Fri. 7am-8pm, Sat.-Sun. 8am-8pm.

Pharmacy: Harry Race Pharmacy, 106 Lincoln St. (747-8666), near Castle Hill. Also has 1hr. photo. Open Mon.-Sat. 9am-6pm, Sun. 9am-1pm.

Hospital: Sitka Community Hospital, 222 Tongass Dr. (747-3241).

Post Office: For all general delivery, go to the **Pioneer Station,** 201 Katlian Ave. (747-5525), inside the Westmark Hotel Annex, open Mon.-Sat. 8:30am-5:30pm. **ZIP Code:** 99835.

Area Code: 907.

ACCOMMODATIONS AND CAMPING

In an effort to lure backpackers, the park service has renovated Sitka's two campgrounds. Unfortunately, they are far away; the youth hostel is probably still a budget traveler's best bet. Sitka also has 20 **B&Bs,** from $40 per night. The visitors bureau lists their rates and numbers.

Sitka Youth Hostel (HI-AYH), 303 Kimshan St., Box 2645 (747-8356), in the United Methodist Church at Edgecumbe St. and Kimshan. Find the McDonald's 1 mi. out of town on Halibut Point Rd., then walk 25 yd. up Peterson St. to Kimsham. 20 cots, kitchen facilities, VCR, and several videos. Sleeping bags required. Free showers and local calls. Lockout 9am-6pm, but enforcement is lax. Will store packs during the day. Curfew 11pm. 3-day max. stay. $7, nonmembers $10. Open June-Aug.

Sitka Hotel, 118 Lincoln St. (747-3288; fax 747-8499; email: mail@sitkahotel.com; http://www.sitkahotel.com), downtown. A safe bet for those without hostel-level energy. Tastefully decorated rooms with shared baths. Single $55; double $65. Fills quickly. Private baths $10 extra; kitchens $10 extra. Free local calls, cable, laundry facilities. Reserve 2 weeks in advance and request a view.

Abner's B&B, 200 Seward St. (747-8779). Clean, pleasant room in a modest house listed on the National Register of Historic Places. Inviting living room and an extensive book and video collection. One block from the heart of downtown. Full breakfast. Friendly, liberal hosts. Single $43; double $55.

Starrigavan Creek Campground, at the end of Halibut Point Rd., 1 mi. from the ferry, 8 mi. from town. 30 secluded sites for tents and RVs under a canopy of trees. Water, pit toilets, picnic shelter, proximity to a scenic estuary trail. 14-day max. stay. No vehicle access 10pm-7am. Sites $8. Wheelchair accessible.

Sawmill Creek Campground, 8½ mi. south of town. Take Halibut Point Rd. to Sawmill Creek Rd. junction in Sitka. Follow Sawmill Creek Rd. to the pulp mill, then take the left spur for 1.4 mi. Unmaintained 11-unit campground. Trees, stream, solitude, picnic tables, fireplaces, and pit toilets. Decent fishing in nearby Blue Lake. Quiet hours 10pm-6am. 14-day max. stay. Free.

FOOD

Function clearly outweighs aesthetics in the Sitka cuisine scene. Even posh restaurants rely on the waterfront to spice up their culinary creations. Find standard fare at **Lakeside Grocery,** 705 Halibut Point Rd. (747-3317; open daily 6am-midnight). Pick up fresh seafood along the docks or at **Seafood Producers Coop,** 507 Katlian Ave. (747-5811), where halibut and salmon run $2-3 per lb. (open daily, 9am-5pm). Granola ($2.50 per lb.) hides at **Evergreen Natural Foods,** 101 American Way (747-6944; open Mon.-Fri. 9am-6pm, Sat. 10am-5pm, Sun. 11am-4pm; winter closed Sun.).

Channel Club, 2906 Halibut Point Rd. (747-9916), 3 mi. from downtown. Call from town or the hostel for a courtesy van. The restaurant every Sitkan recommends (they ignore the unremarkable decor and concentrate on the food). Over 30 salads ($12), each a culinary delight. Open Sun.-Thurs. 5-10pm, Fri.-Sat. 5-11pm.

The Backdoor, 104 Barracks St. (747-8856), behind Old Harbour Books. An amiable coffee shop and popular hostelers' hangout with attractive local art, unpredictable poetry readings, and occasional live accordion music (!). 12oz. Buzzsaw (coffee with espresso) $2.25, big-ass cookies $1, scones $1. Open Mon.-Sat. 7am-5pm and frequently after hours.

The Bayview Restaurant, 407 Lincoln St. (747-5440), upstairs in the Bayview Trading Company. Yet another great view. Food is well-prepared, but portions are more modest than prices. Chow on *pirogies* (Russian dumplings) with salad and borscht, $8. More than 25 variations on the hamburger theme. Open Mon.-Sat. 6:30am-8pm, Sun. 7am-3pm; winter Mon.-Sat. 7am-7:30pm, Sun. 7am-3pm.

Lane 7 Snack Bar, 331 Lincoln St. (747-6310), near the bowling alley. The cheapest in town! Revel in the budget glory of $4 burgers and $2 curly fries. Lots of formica. Open daily 7am-11pm; winter Mon.-Sat. 10:30am-11pm, Sun. 10:30am-10pm.

SIGHTS, EVENTS, AND ENTERTAINMENT

Sitka is one of the few cities in Southeast with indoor attractions that are more than just an excuse to get out of the rain. The onion-domed **St. Michael's Cathedral,** built in 1848 by Bishop Innocent, is a reminder of Sitka's Slavic heritage. Haunting icons gleam next to neo-Baroque paintings from a movement supported by Catherine the Great. Services are open to the public and conducted in English, Tlingit, and Old Slavonic (hours vary with cruise ship schedules, generally open Mon.-Sat. 11am-3pm., Sun. noon-3pm; $1 donation). Two blocks down Lincoln St., the meticulously refurbished **Russian Bishop's House** is one of four remaining Russian colonial buildings in America. For $3, see the magnificent chapel upstairs, dedicated to the Annunciation of the Virgin Mary and adorned with gold and silver icons (open 9am-1pm and 2-5pm, tours every 30min.; downstairs free; call 747-6281 for tour reservations). At the east end of Lincoln St., **Castle Hill,** at one time the site of Baranov's Castle, the seat of Russian administration in Alaska, provides an easily accessible view of the cathedral and the Sound (open daily 6am-10pm).

The **Sheldon-Jackson Museum** (747-8981), on the tidy Sheldon-Jackson College campus at the east end of Lincoln St., is one of Alaska's best museums for Native artifacts and history. The collections date back to the 1880s and represent Athabascan, Aleut, Inuit, and Northwest Coast artistic styles. Pull-out drawers hold Inuit children's toys and the raven helmet worn by Chief Katlean, the Tlingit hero of the 1804 battle. Give yourself a good hour here (open daily 8am-5pm; winter Thurs.-Sat 10am-4pm; $3, free with student ID)..

The Alaskan Flamingo

"And don't miss the flamingos in the trees!" Naturalists aboard the Alaska Marine Highway ferry into Sitka never fail to rouse green, groggy ocean-goers, prompting a starboard-ward stampede to witness this biological freak show. Pink flamingos in the subarctic forest! Alas, the hubbub isn't over a true scientific rarity—it's just **Porky Bickar**'s way of saying hello to the thousands of ferry-goers who frequent Sitka each year. This life-long resident and funnyman is famous for all sorts of random acts of silliness, like the time he hired a stripper for Sitka's 4th of July parade. Perhaps his finest moment was the "eruption" of Mt. Edgecombe. The volcano, 10,000 years dormant, lies 10 mi. west of Sitka on Kruzof island. One fine April morning 20 years ago, the forest service received panicked reports of smoke spewing from Edgecombe's crater. Fire-fighters rushed to the scene to prepare for a mass evacuation. They found no molten lava, only some burning tires, arranged to spell "April Fool's." Porky was fined.

The manicured trails of the **Sitka National Historic Park,** a.k.a. "Totem Park" (747-6281), lie a few minutes' walk down Lincoln St., ½ mi. east of St. Michael's. The trails pass 15 masterfully replicated totems placed along the shoreline among old-growth trees. At one end of the 1 mi. loop stands the site of the **Tlingit Fort,** where hammer-wielding chief Katlean almost held off the Russians in the battle for Sitka. The park **visitors center** offers a film on the fight and the opportunity to watch traditional artists at work in the **Southeast Alaskan Native American Cultural Center** (747-8061), where woodcarvers, silversmiths, costume-makers and weavers demonstrate their crafts in intimate quarters (open daily 8am-5pm).

Recovering bald eagles and owls perch dutifully for snapshots at the **Alaska Raptor Rehabilitation Center** (747-8662), on Sawmill Creek Rd. There are guided tours for $10, but visitors can get in for free with a donation of frozen mice or other appropriate raptor food. No joke (open daily 8am-5pm and with cruise ships).

The June **Sitka Summer Music Festival** draws world-renowned chamber musicians to play at one of Alaska's most popular musical events. The concerts, held in the Centennial Building on Tuesday, Friday, and some Saturday evenings, are often crowded; reservations are a good idea. Rehearsals, however, are free and rarely crowded (all shows $14, under 18 $7). Order tickets by calling 277-4852 or 747-6774; write to P.O. Box 3333. Contact the visitors bureau for more information.

OUTDOORS

The Sitka area offers excellent **hiking** opportunities. Rain gear and a copy of *Sitka Trails* (pick up at the forest service info booth or office) prove invaluable on almost any hike. **Gavan Hill** provides relatively easy access to sensational views of the Sound. The trailhead is near downtown, at the end of Baranof St. While steep, the majority of the 2500 ft. ascent is a boardwalk trail and the three- to four-hour climb is pleasant. The ridge along the top leads to **Harbor Mountain.** A road also winds almost all the way to the top of the peak, so you can avoid backtracking by arranging a ride back down in advance. The Harbor Mountain trailhead is about 10 mi. from downtown on Harbor Mountain Rd. Bring lots of water, since little is available along either trail.

Play Indiana Jones as you bushwhack through the overgrown **Mount Verstovia Trail,** which provides challenging access to incredible panoramas. The shoulder of Mt. Verstovia is about 2½ mi. along the route, although you can continue on farther to the peak. This route is hard work and not particularly safe (do not take it alone), but it is a rewarding challenge. The trailhead is about 2 mi. east of town right next to Rookie's Sports Bar and Grill on Sawmill Creek Hwy. The sign has long since been overgrown by trees; just look for a little bridge to the left of the building. A great rainy day hike is the gentle and intimate **Indian River Trail,** a 5½ mi. riverside trek to the base of Indian River Falls. Follow the gravel road for about ¾ mi. until you reach a blue pump house. From there, the trail branches into the old growth forest and meanders through muskeg and tall trees alongside the clear pools of the Indian River. The rocky **Three Sisters Mountains** occasionally come into view, as do spawning salmon in early fall. The trail gains 250 ft. in elevation; plan on a four to five-hour round-trip.

The forest service also maintains a number of **remote trails** in the Sitka region, most accessible only by boat or floatplane, and many leading to **wilderness cabins** ($25 per night). The most striking is the **Mt. Edgecombe Trail,** a full-day, 7 mi. one-way clamber to the crater of Sitka's dormant volcano, whose broken cone dominates the view across the sound from Sitka (see p. 145). The trailhead lies behind Fred's Creek Cabin, a half-hour skiff journey from Sitka, and a shelter for exhausted hikers sits another 3 mi. up the trail. The end of the hike offers stunning views of the Sitka region and a close look at the red volcanic ash that coats the ground.

In addition to kayak and bicycle rental services, over 30 **charter operators** vie to separate you from Sitka and your money. **Fly North Adventures,** PO Box 1555 (714-3469; email flynorth@aol.com), charges $75 per person for a half-day of a wildlife-watching, picture snapping journey. **Coastal Helicopters** (747-5557) offers flightseeing tours of the volcano for $135 per person. **Sitka Secrets,** 500 Lincoln St. #641 (747-5089), offers a comparable full-day service for $170 per person.

NORTHERN PANHANDLE

Tenakee Springs

Children push groceries in wheelbarrows while fishermen loll outside the mercantile on Tenakee's one street—a dirt path that accommodates only vehicles that travel under 10 mph. Residents thrive on the slow pace, cultivating gardens and friendships in this close-knit community of 100. Nevertheless, locals are quick to welcome visitors, even those heavy in pack and light in wallet. In a town that provides no sewer or sanitation services, it's only natural that beer flows more freely than water. No place is better than Tenakee for cleansing travelers of their tourist wearies.

Practical Information **Bring cash.** There are **no banks** on Chicagof Island and no one accepts credit cards. Residents value their isolation and are adamantly opposed to forest service proposals to construct a road link with neighboring **Hoonah.** The state ferry *LeConte* makes a short stopover in Tenakee on its route between Juneau and Sitka. An hour is all you'll need to survey the town, but a day's stay is worth it if the ferry schedule allows. The one-way fare to Tenakee from either Sitka or Juneau is $22. Both **Loken Aviation** (736-2306 or 800-478-3360) and **Wings of Alaska** (736-2247) fly from Juneau six or seven days a week ($60-65). Confirm your flight by dialing the **weather forecast** (800-472-0391).

To get to the **library** (736-2248), which is located in the same building as the **city office** (736-2207), take a left from the ferry, continue about ¼ mi., and enter the big wooden building on your right (open Tues. and Thurs. 11am-3pm, Sat. noon-3pm). Check out the decent selection of "trade 'em" paperbacks. The **post office** (736-2236; open Mon.-Fri. 7:30am-noon and 12:30-4:30pm, Sat. 7:30-11:30am), is right off the dock (**General Delivery ZIP Code:** 99841). The **area code** is 907.

The Hot Spring Tenakee's namesake, a natural sulfuric hot spring that feeds the public bath house at the end of the ferry dock, is the town's epicenter. You won't find this small, unglamorous blue bathhouse on any postcards, but miners and fishers have been soaking out aches and worries in these therapeutic 106°F (41°C) waters for more than a century, and the Tlingit maintained a winter settlement at the spring long before European arrival. Since few homes have showers, this is where most of modern Tenakee's retirees and urban refugees take daily baths.

If you're ambitious, you can get in a good soaking during a layover—assuming that members of your gender happen to be bathing. Men and women have separate bathing hours (men 2-6pm and 10pm-9am, women 9am-2pm and 6-10pm), largely because bathers are required to be nude. They are also required to be clean before entering; bring your soap. The bath is free, but donations are welcome at Snyder Mercantile across the street.

Accommodations, Camping, and Food There are exactly two places to stay in town, and one of them has a price tag in the thousands. The only affordable option is to rent one of six available cabins from **Snyder Mercantile** (736-2205). The smaller, more basic cabins sleep one to two people comfortably (from $40). A larger cabin sleeps four to five (from $45). Both have outhouses and cooking facilities; bring your own towels and bedding. A $65 cabin sleeps seven, with carpet, fireplaces, and (a rare find in Tenakee) a flush toilet. Reservations are essential in summer. The more adventurous can brave the bears (Chichagof Island has about one bear per sq. mi.; only Admiralty Island has a denser population) and head for the woods. Walking from the ferry dock to town, a right turn on the dirt path points you east. After about ¾ mi., the path leads to a wooded area with several free, primitive **campsites.** Another ¾ mi. along the trail, the free **Indian River Campground** provides tent sites, a shelter, and a picnic table beside the Indian River, a spot favored by bears in summer.

Other than the salmonberries along the main path, food in Tenakee can be difficult to find. **Snyder Mercantile** stocks a limited supply of groceries including vegetables and fruit flown in weekly (open Mon.-Sat. 9am-noon and 1-5pm, Sun. 9am-2pm). **The Bakery** (736-2262) in the Shamrock cooks up fresh bread ($3) and sinful cinnamon rolls ($2.50) daily, as well as a diverse lunch menu. Spinach calzones are $2.50 and a fisherman-sized plate of biscuits and gravy goes for $5.25. The **Blue Moon Cafe,** unassuming as it may appear, is a Tenakee institution. If Rosie is there, and if she feels like cooking, try the french fries ($3.75). Ham and eggs are $7.50, a chicken dinner, $9. Arrange in advance for anything other than a cheeseburger or cans of Rainier Beer ($1.50); Rosie needs time to thaw her ingredients.

Sights and Outdoors Tenakee's only street extends several mi. in either direction and is closed off to motor vehicles after a short distance. To the west, the street leads along the water past a communal saw mill and small homesteads. Tread carefully around private land here; not everyone loves wanderers. Several mi. from town, the path turns out onto the shore of the inlet, where silver salmon leap from the water in midsummer and smooth rocks make good footing for an extended beach walk. Avoid shore walks in town where outhouses and garbage detract from the beach's appeal. To the east, the wide beach makes for better walking than the faint path that parallels the shore through the woods. Bears have realized this too—use caution, and bring your camera.

Fifteen minutes from shore by kayak brings you to a small reef where dozens of sea otters will scrutinize you from land before performing their water show. Again, bring that camera. An excellent **paddling** adventure begins in Hoonah and follows the long inlet of Port Frederick back to its end. From there, a 100 yd. portage leads to the upper region of Tenakee Inlet. Paddlers can explore the unbroken shores and hidden coves of the inlet on their way out to Tenakee Springs. The 40 mi. trip could also be made in the reverse direction, but the hot springs are probably best savored at the end. **Mother Truckers** (736-2323) rents bicycles ($20) and kayaks. (Open daily 8am-5pm; single: half-day $40, full day $65; double: half-day $50, full day $75.) Or rent a kayak in Juneau and bring it over on the ferry for $9.

For **chartered expeditions** to fish, view wildlife, and learn about the intricacies of the inlet from someone who has been on the water around Tenakee all his life, contact **Jason Carter** (736-2311). Jason runs half-day and full-day trips and transports kayaks, all for reasonable prices.

Juneau

In October 1880, in a move he probably regretted later, Tlingit Chief Kowee led Joe Juneau and Richard Harris to the gleaming "mother lode" in the hills up from Gold Creek. The next summer brought boatloads of prospectors to dig in the mines. Harris's irritating habit of staking multiple claims extended to his desire for the town's name, but angry miners vetoed "Harrisburg." ("Koweeville" was not considered.)

Juneau today is unique among the nation's fifty state capitals. Victorian mansions crowd against log cabins, and teenage hipsters rile state politicians. Monolithic Mt. Juneau looms large over both statespeople and skateboarders. Accessible only by water and air, Juneau has happily avoided the urban sprawl that plagues Anchorage. The tourist industry, however, has had no problem establishing its presence: Juneau is the second busiest cruise ship port in the U.S. (after Miami).

PRACTICAL INFORMATION AND ORIENTATION

Visitors Information: Davis Log Cabin Visitors Center, 134 3rd St., Juneau 99801 (586-2201 or 586-2284; fax 586-6304), at Seward St. Excellent source for pamphlets on walking tours, sights, and natural wonders. Open Mon.-Fri. 8:30am-5pm, Sat.-Sun. 9am-5pm; Oct.-May Mon.-Fri. 8:30am-5pm. **National Forest and National Park Services,** 101 Egan Dr. (586-8751; fax 586-7928), at Willoughby, in Centennial Hall. Helpful staff provide info on hiking and fishing in the Juneau area, as well

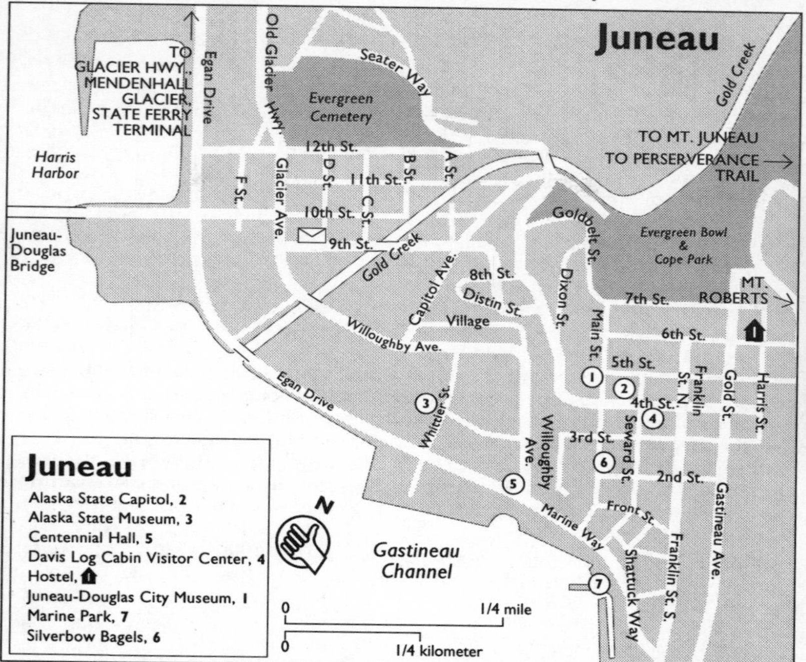

as info on, and reservations for, Forest Service cabins in Tongass National Forest. Pick up a copy of the valuable *Juneau Trails* booklet ($4) listing many 5-12 mi. hikes. Open daily in summer 8am-5pm; winter Mon.-Fri. 8am-5pm.

Fishing Licenses: Alaska Dept. of Fish and Game (465-4112; licensing 465-2376). **Fishing Information Hotline** (465-4116). Weather, licenses, and fish locations.

Bank: National Bank of Alaska, 123 Seward St. Open Mon.-Thurs. 9:30am-5pm, Fri. 9:30am-6pm. There are other options, but this bank accepts most **ATM** cards.

Currency Exchange: Thomas Cook, 127 N. Franklin (586-5688). Open Mon.-Fri. 9am-5:30pm, Sat. 10am-4pm, Sun. 10am-2pm.

Airport: Juneau International Airport, 9 mi. north of Juneau on Glacier Hwy. Served by Alaska Airlines, Delta Airlines, and local charters. **Alaska Airlines** (789-0600 or 800-426-0333), on S. Franklin St. at 2nd St., in the Baranov Hotel. To: Anchorage ($99-222); Sitka ($96); Ketchikan ($124); and Gustavus ($65). Open Mon.-Fri. 8:30am-5pm. Check at the visitors center for schedules and routes of all airlines. **Island Waterways** provides transportation to downtown if you don't feel like dealing with the bus ($7, $12 round-trip).

Buses: Capital Transit (789-6901). From downtown to Douglas, the airport, and Mendenhall Glacier. Mon.-Sat. 7am-10:30pm, Sun. 9am-5:30pm. Hourly express service downtown, Mon.-Fri. 8:30am-5pm. The closest stop to the ferry is at Auke Bay, 1½ mi. from the terminal. Fare $1.25; exact change required. **Schedules** available at municipal building, library, Davis Log Cabin, and on buses. **MGT Ferry Express** (789-5460). Meets all ferries and runs to downtown hotels or airport ($5). Call between 6-8pm a day in advance to reserve a ride from any major hotel to the airport or ferry (whether you're staying at a hotel or not). Rides $5. From the hostel, the Baranov is the closest hotel. Also offers a 2½ hr. guided tour of Mendenhall Glacier ($12.50). Tour times vary; call ahead.

Ferries: Alaska Marine Highway, 1591 Glacier Ave., P.O. Box 25535, Juneau 99802-5535 (465-3941 or 800-642-0066; fax 277-4829). Ferries dock at the Auke Bay terminal 14 mi. from the city on the Glacier Hwy. To: Bellingham, WA ($226); Ketchikan ($74); Sitka ($26); and Haines ($20). Lockers (25¢ for 48hr.) are limited.

Taxis: Capital Cab (586-2772) and **Taku Taxi** (586-2121). Both run a 1hr. charter to Mendenhall Glacier for about $45, to the ferry about $25. Exact services differ slightly; both let you split charter cost.

Car Rental: Rent-A-Wreck, 9099 Glacier Hwy. (789-4111), next to the airport. $30 per day plus 15¢ per mi. after 100. Must be at least 21 with a credit card or piles of cash. Open Mon.-Fri. 8am-6pm, Sat.-Sun. 9am-5pm.

Auto Repair: Sam's Auto Body, 8575 Airport Rd. (789-4114).

Bike Rental: Mountain Gears, 126 Front St. (586-2575), opposite McDonald's. Mountain bikes $6 per hr., $25 for 24hr. Prices include helmet and lock. Open Mon.-Fri. 10am-6pm, Sat. 10am-5pm. Call for advice on area trails or to find out about informal group rides. **Cycle Alaska** (364-3377) will deliver a bike to your door. $30 for 8hr. Open 9am-4pm.

Kayak Rental: Juneau Outdoor Center (586-8220), on Douglas Island. Will deliver kayaks anywhere in Juneau. Single $35 per day; double $45. Experience required, but instruction happily provided.

Camping Equipment: Foggy Mountain Shop, 134 N. Franklin St. (586-6780), at 2nd St. High quality, high prices. Open Mon.-Sat. 9am-6pm. Less expensive equipment at **Outdoor Headquarters,** 9131 Glacier Hwy. (800-478-0770 or 789-9785), near the airport. Open Mon.-Fri. 9am-8pm, Sat. 8am-6pm, Sun. 11am-5pm.

Luggage Storage: At the hostel (free if you're staying there, otherwise $1 per bag). Lockers at the ferry terminal (see above). Also try the counter at the **Alaskan Hotel** (see below). In theory they charge $1.56 (includes tax) per bag, but they'll often store for free. 24hr. access.

Bookstore: Hearthside Books, 254 Front St. (800-478-1000 or 586-1726). Dedicated to pleasing intellectuals of the southeast year-round. Hours vary but usually open daily 9am-5pm. **The Observatory,** 235 2nd St. (586-9676). A used and rare bookstore with many **maps** and prints. Open Mon.-Fri. 10am-5:30pm, Sat. noon-5:30pm; winter Mon.-Sat. noon-5:30pm.

Library: (586-5249), over the parking garage at Admiral Way and S. Franklin St. Great views and a gorgeous stained-glass window. Open Mon.-Thurs. 11am-9pm, Fri.-Sun. noon-5pm. The **State Library** and the **Alaska Historical Library** hold large collections of early Alaskan photographs. Both are on the 8th floor of the State Office Building and are open Mon.-Fri. 9am-5pm.

Laundromat: Dungeon Laundrette (586-2805), at 4th and Franklin St. Wash $1.50, dry $1.50. Open daily 8am-8pm. Also at the **hostel** (see below).

Showers: The Alaskan Hotel (see below). $3.12 including shower tax.

Events Hotline: 586-5866. **Weather:** 586-3997.

Pharmacy: Juneau Drug Co., 202 Front St. (586-1233). Open Mon.-Fri. 8am-9pm, Sat.-Sun. 9am-6pm.

Suicide Prevention Hotline: 586-4357.

HIV/AIDS Information and Counseling: AIDS Helpline (800-478-2437). **Alaskans Living With HIV** (463-5688), on N. Franklin St. Upstairs from Heritage Coffee. Provides conversation and information. Friendly gay staffers will also provide advice on being gay in Juneau. Open Mon.-Fri. 8am-4pm.

Gay/Lesbian Information: Southeast Alaska Gay and Lesbian Alliance (586-GAYS/4297). 24hr. hotline.

Hospital: Bartlett Memorial (586-2611), 3½ mi. north off Glacier Hwy.

Emergency and Ambulance: 911. **Police:** 210 Admiral Way (586-2780), near Marine Park. Visitors can pick up a permit here to allow 48hr. **parking** in a 1hr. zone. Open for permits Mon.-Fri. 8am-4:30pm.

Post Office: Main Office, 709 W. 9th St. (586-7987). Open Mon. 8:30-5pm, Tues.-Fri. 9am-5pm, Sat. 6am-3pm for parcel pick-up only. A **Substation** (586-2214), for outgoing mail, is located at 221 S. Seward St. Open Mon.-Fri. 9:30am-5pm, Sat. 9:30am-2pm. **ZIP Code:** 99801.

Area Code: 907.

Juneau sits on the Gastineau Channel opposite Douglas Island, 650 mi. southeast of Anchorage and 900 mi. northwest of Seattle. Franklin St. is the main street downtown. **Glacier Highway** connects downtown, the airport, the residential area of the Mendenhall Valley, and the ferry terminal.

ACCOMMODATIONS AND CAMPING

The few establishments that have affordable options have them in limited quantities, so phone ahead. One of the best sources for rooming advice is the **Alaska Bed and Breakfast Association,** P.O. Box 2800 (586-2959; http://www.wetpage.com/bbaaip), which can help you find a room downtown (from $65). While the Forest Service offers two beautiful campgrounds, neither is easily accessible without a car.

Juneau International Hostel (HI-AYH), 614 Harris St. (586-9559), at 6th St. atop a steep hill. A beautiful facility in a prime location with an astoundingly rigid management. Sweep the floor or be swept out the door. Kitchen available 7-8:30am and 5-10:30pm. Common area with comfy couches. Coin-op laundry (wash $1.25, dry 75¢); small charges for sheets, towels, soap, and detergent. Strict lockout from 9am-5pm and non-negotiable 11pm curfew. 3-day max. stay if they're full. All 48 beds $7, nonmembers $7. Fills fast, but you can make reservations with a $10 deposit mailed in advance. No phone reservations.

Alaskan Hotel, 167 Franklin St. (586-1000 or 800-327-9347 from the lower 48), right downtown. A handsome hotel built of dark wood, meticulously restored to original 1913 decor. Bar features live tunes and dancing. Rent your own hot tub with a radio (noon-4pm $10.40 per hr., 4pm-2am $20.80 per hr.). Free luggage storage for guests. Laundry ($1 wash, $1 dry). Kitchenettes and TVs available. Singles $55, with bath $70; doubles $65, with bath $80. Rates lower in winter.

Inn at the Waterfront, 455 S. Franklin (586-2050), over the Summit Restaurant. The classy looking restaurant downstairs belies the Inn's origins as a gold rush brothel. 14 clean, comfortable rooms. A few have shared baths (single $51; double $60). Ask for these specifically, or you'll get a room with several more stars and zeros attached. Continental breakfast included.

Mendenhall Lake Campground, on Montana Creek Rd. Take Glacier Hwy. north 9 mi. to Mendenhall Loop Rd.; continue 3½ mi. and take the right fork. If asked, bus drivers will let you off within walking distance (2 mi.) of camp (7am-10:30pm only). About 6 mi. from ferry terminal. 60 newly renovated sites have stunning views of the glacier and convenient trails to take you even closer. Fireplaces, water, pit toilet, picnic tables, free firewood. 14-day max. stay. Sites $8, seniors $4. Reserve for an extra $7.50 by calling 800-280-CAMP/2267.

Auke Village Campground (586-8800), on Glacier Hwy. 15 mi. from Juneau. 1½ mi. west of ferry terminal near a scenic beach. 12 sites to enclose your tent or RV in verdant seclusion. Fireplaces, water, flush toilets, picnic tables. No reservations. 14-day max. stay. Sites $8, seniors $4.

FOOD

Juneau accommodates seekers of anything from fresh salmon to filet-o'-fish sandwiches. The **Juneau A&P Market,** 631 Willoughby Ave. (586-3101; fax 586-6775), near the Federal Building, is one of the best grocery stores in the region, with an extensive salad bar ($3.29 per lb.), and jumbo deli sandwiches ($4.50; open daily 24hr.). Find costlier health food at **Rainbow Foods** (586-6476), at 2nd and Seward St. (open Mon.-Fri. 10am-7pm, Sat. 10am-6pm, Sun. noon-6pm). The corner of Front and Seward St. is home to Juneau's fast food hangouts.

Armadillo Tex-Mex Cafe, 431 S. Franklin St. (586-1880). Authentic Southwest paintings and a few kitschy plastic armadillos make this always packed cafe one of the few Tex-Mex places not decorated by Plastic Sombreros "R" Us. Hunker down to a heaping plateful of T. Terry's nachos ($8). The *chalupa,* a corn tostada heaped with chicken, beans, guacamole, and cheese, goes for $8. Two enchiladas $6. Excellent free chips and salsa. Open Mon.-Sat. 11am-10pm, Sun. 4-10pm.

Channel Bowl Cafe (586-6139), on Willoughby Ave. across from A&P. A spirited, sometimes manic stopping place with blaring blues. Try pancakes with berries, pecans, and real maple syrup ($5.50) or "cheeburg" ($6). Breakfast served "as long as we're vertical." Open daily 6:30am-1:30pm.

Fiddlehead Restaurant and Bakery, 429 W. Willoughby Ave. (586-3150), ½ block from the State Museum. Fern-ishings for affluent sprout-lovers. Seafood, exquisite desserts, and fresh Alaskan sourdough. Wholesome sandwiches with soup or salad $7-10. Open Mon.-Fri. 6:30am-10pm, Sat.-Sun. 7am-10pm; winter open until 9pm. The **Fireweed Room** upstairs serves more expensive fare with evening jazz ($5 cover) in summer. Open Mon.-Fri. 11:30am-1pm and 5:30-9pm, Sat.-Sun. 5:30-9pm.

Thane Ore House Salmon Bake, 4400 Thane Rd. (586-3442). A few mi. out of town, but "Mr. Ore" will pick you up at your hotel. All-you-can-eat salmon, halibut, ribs, and fixings ($18.50). Open May-Sept. daily 11:30am-9pm.

Cafes and Coffeehouses

Silverbow Bagels, 120 2nd St. (586-YUMM/9866). In 1997, Jill and Ken serendipitously discovered a mythic silver bagel atop the Perserverence Trail and were inspired to meet the needs of expatriate bagel connoisseurs. Scarf 75¢ bagels at 6am or quaff $1 Blue Willow tea at 5pm. Sandwiches ($1-7) and magazines in between.

Heritage Coffee Co., 174 S. Franklin St. (586-1087). A popular place to escape for an hour or two from Juneau's often wet and tourist-ridden streets. Easygoing staff assembles large sandwiches ($6.25) and pours fine coffee (espresso $1; cappuccino $1.75). Open Mon.-Fri. 6:30am-6:30pm, Sat.-Sun. 7am-5pm.

Valentine's Coffee House and Bakery, 111 Seward St. (463-5144). Mom's kitchen, with calico tablecloths and wooden chairs. Fresh baked calzones ($5.95), burritos ($6.25), and all sorts of breads.

SIGHTS

The excellent **Alaska State Museum,** 395 Whittier St. (465-2901), leads you through the history, ecology, and culture of Alaska's four major indigenous groups: Tlingit, Athabascan, Aleut, and Inuit. The museum houses the famous "First White Man" totem pole, a carved likeness of Abraham Lincoln, and traveling displays of photography and painting. ($3, seniors and children free; open Mon.-Fri. 9am-6pm, Sat.-Sun. 10am-6pm; Sept. 18-May 17 Tues.-Sat. 10am-4pm.)

The hexagonal, onion-domed 1894 **St. Nicholas Russian Orthodox Church** on 5th St. between N. Franklin and Gold St. holds rows of icons and a glorious altar. Services, held Saturday at 6pm and Sunday at 10am, are conducted in English, Old Slavonic, and Tlingit. Tours are open to the public ($1 donation requested; open summers daily 9am-5pm). The **State Office Building** (the S.O.B.) on Willoughby St. has an 8th-floor **observation platform** overlooking Douglas Island and the channel. A large atrium on the same floor contains a totem pole and a pipe organ fired up for a free **concert** every Friday afternoon. The **House of Wickersham,** 213 7th St. (586-9001), was home to one of Alaska's founding fathers, Judge James Wickersham. As a U.S. District Court judge, Wickersham steamed and sledded around Alaska to oversee a region extending from Fort Yukon to the Aleutian Islands when he wasn't busy founding the Alaska Railroad, establishing the University of Alaska, or pushing for statehood ($2; open May 15-Oct. 1 daily 9am-4pm).

If you're visiting town between mid-July and September, trek to **Gastineau Salmon Hatchery,** 2697 Channel Dr. (463-5113 or 463-4810). When the salmon are running, thousands pack into the parking lot; the salmon crammed into the spawning ladder are pretty impressive too. The spectacle is free, but admission to the small aquarium inside is $2.75 (children $1; open Mon.-Fri. 10am-6pm, Sat.-Sun. noon-5pm).

While you're in the neighborhood, head farther to the **Alaska Brewing Co.,** 5429 Shaune Dr. (780-5866) for a free tour (must be 21 or accompanied by a parent or guardian). Given the price of beer in Alaska, it's hard to turn down the free samples of its award-winning brews. To reach the brewery, take the hourly city bus to Lemon Creek, turn onto Anka Rd. from the Glacier Hwy., and right on Shaune Dr. (Tours available every 30min. Mon.-Sat. 11am-4:30pm; Oct.-April Thurs.-Sat. 11am-4:30pm.)

ENTERTAINMENT

The doors swing and the cash registers ring at the **Red Dog Saloon,** 278 S. Franklin (463-9954). Juneau's most popular tourist trap hosts live music on weekends. In the winter, locals return to their customary stools between walls lined with bear pelts and money ("tourist pelts"). Beer will set you back $3.50-4.50 in pelts. (Open Sun.-Thurs. 10am-midnight, Fri.-Sat. 10am-1am; off season Sun.-Thurs. noon-midnight, Fri.-Sat. noon-1am.) The **Alaskan Hotel,** 167 Franklin St., hosts frequent live Cajun and blues and manages to retain its local crowd year-round despite the shocking cost of beer (bar open daily noon-midnight). The gay-friendly **Penthouse** (463-4141), on the 4th floor of the Senate Building, features a dance floor and flocks of hard-partying youngsters. (Must be 21; $2 cover on the weekends; open Sun.-Thurs. 9pm-1am, Fri.-Sat. 9pm-3am.) **The Hanger on the Wharf,** on Marine Way is another youth-magnet, with a huge selection of micro-brews and views of the Channel. (Open Mon. 4-11pm, Tues.-Wed. 11:30am-11pm, Thurs.-Sun. 11:30am-1am.)

Catch the latest blockbusters at the **20th Century Theater** downtown at 222 Front St. or **The Glacier Cinema** in Mendenhall Valley at 9091 Cinema Dr. Both theaters have two nightly shows and weekend matinees. Check a paper or call 463-FLIX/3549 for information. The **Naa Kahidi** dancers perform nightly at the Marine Park on the waterfront. Find a coupon in the visitors office and get $5 off the $16 price. Call 587-3871 for a recording of performance times.

OUTDOORS

Juneau's trail system is the most extensive in the southeast, and undoubtedly one of the most spectacular in the state. If you're looking for the best view of Juneau and are willing to sweat for it, go to the end of 6th St. and head up the trail to the summit of **Mt. Roberts** (3576 ft.). It's a steep, 4 mi. climb, but worth it. Higher elevations reveal panoramic views up the Gastineau Channel and west toward the Pacific, as well as a look at nearby Mt. Juneau. The recent addition of a **tramway** means that you'll have to deal with many who didn't sweat for the view. The trams run every half hour from a terminal on the cruise ship dock (463-3412; $16.90).

Please, Just One Cruise...

Everywhere you go in Alaska, you will find tour companies plying to part you from your money. Don't pass up the 8½-hour tour of **Tracy Arm,** a mini-fjord near Juneau, simply because you don't wish to subsidize another crackpot tour operation. The $99 you spend on a tour is one of the best investments you can make in Alaska. If you can come up with the funds to get to the region, you owe it to yourself to take the trip. Fondly known as **"the poor man's Glacier Bay,"** Tracy Arm offers much of the same spectacular beauty and wildlife at well under half the cost. On a typical day, you can count on seeing humpback and killer whales (about 75% of the time), hundreds of seals, and bald eagles. The trip passes by the **Sawyer Glaciers,** which frequently calve large chunks of ice into the sea. If you don't catch them in the act, you can still admire the massive icebergs glowing blue in the water.

The biggest tour company is **Auk Nu Tours,** 76 Egan Dr. (800-820-2628). The tour is cheap ($99), but the huge boats and resulting impersonality might detract from the joy of an included free lunch. **Bird's Eye Charters** (790-2510), whose small boats take only 16 passengers, is on the opposite end of the spectrum. $140 procures you breakfast, lunch, snacks, and all the personal attention money can buy. A happy medium lies near **Adventure Bound,** 245 Marine Way. (463-2509 or 800-228-3875). Friendly owner Steve personally pilots a midsized boat with a maximum of 28 passengers. There's no free food, but snacks and simple sandwiches are available (probably best just to bring your own). The list price is $99 ($49 for those under 18; $20-off coupon in the Juneau visitors guide). Ahoy!

With an afternoon to devote to hiking, bus or bike to the **West Glacier Trail,** which begins off Montana Creek Rd. by the Mendenhall Lake Campground. The five to six hour walk yields stunning views of the glacier from the first step to the final outlook. The 3½ mi. trail (1-way) parallels the river of ice, through lush western hemlock forest and up a rocky cairn-marked scramble to the summit of 4226-ft. Mt. McGinnis.

A number of excellent trails start at the end of Basin Rd. The **Perseverance Trail,** which leads to the ruins of the Silverbowl Basin Mine and booming waterfalls, is one of the most popular. The **Granite Creek Trail** branches off the Perseverance Trail and follows its namesake to a beautiful basin 3.3 mi. from the trailhead. The summit of Mt. Juneau lies 3 mi. farther along the ridge and, predictably, offers terrific views. The shorter, steeper **Mt. Juneau Trail,** which departs from Perseverance Trail about 1 mi. from the trailhead, offers similar panoramas. For more details on area hikes, drop by the visitors center or any local bookstore to pick up *Juneau Trails,* published by the Alaska Natural History Association ($4). Rangers provide free copies of maps from this book at the Centennial Building (see **Practical Information,** above). If the trails don't have steps (or even if they do) consider renting a bike to see more in less time. Because all trails are well-maintained, beginner (but granted, adventurous) mountain bikers may experience breathtaking vistas while pedaling over dirt, gravel, and the occasional rock or root. Check with **Mountain Gears** (see **Practical Information**) for their difficulty rankings and suggestions. Biking off-road is sometimes prohibited. Whatever your mode of transport, be sure to keep the bears in mind.

In winter, the **Eaglecrest Ski Area,** 155 S. Seward St., Juneau 99801 (586-5284 or 586-5330), on Douglas Island, offers decent alpine skiing. ($24 per day, ages 12-17 $17, under 12 $12; ski rental $20, children $14). The Eaglecrest ski bus departs from the Baranov Hotel at 8:30am and returns from the slopes at 5pm on winter weekends and holidays (round-trip $6). In the summer, the Eaglecrest **"Alpine Summer" trail** is a good way to soak in the mountain scenery of virtually untouched Douglas Island.

The best excuse to spend $100 in town is on an incredible boat tour of **Tracy Arm** (see p. 153). If you've rented a kayak and want to go beyond Gastineau Channel, **Kayak Express,** 4107 Blackberry St. (780-4591; http://www.adventuresports.com/asap/kayak/express) will drop you off and pick you up at Gustavus, Hoonah, or Port Adolphus for $220 (1-way $110), or at Oliver's Inlet, Port Couverden, St. James Bay, or Funter Bay for $150 (1-way $75). **Alaska Discovery,** 5449 Shuane Dr. (780-6226 or 800-586-1911), provides both equipment and guides for its daily kayak trips through the inside passage north of Juneau ($125 per person; transport from downtown $18). If you prefer the skies, **Temsco Helicopters,** Juneau Airport (789-9501; fax 789-7989), offers a one-hour flight to the Mendenhall Glacier, or a 1½ hour glacier landing ($142 per person).

Glacier Bay National Park

Glacier Bay was once referred to by explorer Jean François de Galaup de la Perouse as "perhaps the most extraordinary place in the world." The little-known Frenchman was right. Crystal monoliths broken off from glaciers float peacefully in fjords, while humpback whales manoeuver the maze of the icy blue depths. Glacier Bay National Park encloses nine tidewater glaciers, backed by the Fairweather Mountains, the highest coastal range in the world (Norway, eat your heart out). Charter flights, tours, and cruise ships all probe Glacier Bay, offering close encounters with glaciers, rookeries, whales, and seals. The Bay itself is divided into two inlets. The westward Tarr Inlet advances as far as the Grand Pacific and Margerie Glaciers, while the eastward Muir ends at the Muir and Riggs Glaciers.

Glacier Bay provides a rare opportunity to see geological and ecological processes radically compressed. A mere two centuries ago, the **Grand Pacific Glacier** covered the entire region under a sheet of ancient ice. Severe earthquakes separated the glacier from its terminal moraine—the silt and debris that insulates advancing ice from the relatively warm surrounding seawater—and the glacier retreated 45 mi. in 150 years (approaching light speed in glacial time). As a result, the uncovered ground is virgin territory, colonized by pioneering vegetation, which visitors can observe progressing gradually up the bay.

Any visit to the park begins at the **Visitor Information Station** (697-2627), at the tour boat dock in Bartlett Cove, 10 mi. north of Gustavus, where a mandatory orientation to the backcountry is given and permits and bear canisters are distributed (open daily 7am-9pm). Additional maps and wildlife info are available at the information center on the second floor of the **Glacier Bay Lodge** (697-2230 or 800-451-5952; open Mon.-Fri. 11:30am-2pm and 4-9pm).

Wilderness camping and hiking are permitted throughout the park. Tour-boat skippers drop passengers off at one of four points designated by the Park Service; arrange beforehand to be picked up later. Drop-off and pick-up, and an unavoidable but spectacular tour, cost $178 on the *Spirit of Adventure* (see below). Visitors should contact the **Glacier Bay National Park,** P.O. Box 140, Gustavus 99826 (697-2230), for assistance with planning a backcountry trip. Glacier Bay is rapidly becoming the destination of choice for extended kayak trips in the region. Kayak rental is available at **Glacier Bay Sea Kayaks,** P.O. Box 26, Gustavus 99826 (697-2257; double kayaks $50 per day 1-3 days, $40 per day 5-9 days, $35 per day for 10 days or more). **Sea Otter Kayaks** (967-3007; email seaotter@he.net; http://www.he.net/~seaotter) also rents to paddlers at the same rates.

Seeing the most stunning segment of the park, the **West Arm,** means taking a boat tour (and may mean finding a buddy with a thick billfold). The *Spirit of Adventure* is owned by the Glacier Bay Lodge (800-622-2042), next to Bartlett Cove, and offers six **sightseeing packages** to the glaciers, ranging in price and niceties from a half-day whale-watching trip ($78) to a package including flights to and from Juneau, a night at the B&B, and an eight-hour glacier tour ($379). **Puffin Travel** (see **Gustavus,** below) also operates a booking service for sightseeing, fishing, photography tours, and other accommodations.

■ Gustavus

The gateway to Glacier Bay, Gustavus is rarely noticed by glacier-greedy backpackers and ecotourists who don't even stop to eat. Friendly locals are quick to share experiences and reveal secrets of the surrounding land, however, and their enthusiasm for the outdoors is infectious. The second graders of Gustavus Elementary (and authors of the aptly titled pamphlet *Gustavus, the way to Glacier Bay*) advise this: "In Gustavus there is no bank, no hospital, no toystore, no McDonalds, no other fast food places, and no zoo." Be prepared. Should a metaphorical elephant land on your toe, or other injuries arise, visit the **Gustavus Clinic** (697-3008), or, in an **emergency,** dial 911. The **post office** sits on the main road near the airport. The **ZIP code** is 99826.

Gustavus is accessible only by boat or plane. The cheapest way to get there (provided that a ferry/plane fare truce is not reached soon) is via **Alaska Airlines** (800-426-0333; $39 one-way from Juneau). The smaller, more expensive local airlines including **Air Excursions** (697-2375), **Haines Air** (766-2646), **Wings of Alaska** (766-2030), and **LAB** (766-2222 or 800-426-0333). They depart frequently from Juneau and Haines. Another option is the two-hour ferry ride from Auke Bay on **Auk Nu Tours** (800-820-BOAT/2628; $45, $85 round-trip). Bartlett Cove, the entrance to Glacier Bay National Park, is 10 mi. out of town. A bus from the Glacier Bay Lodge (see above) meets every Haines Airways and Alaskan Airlines flight, and rolls on to Bartlett Cove ($10). If you've brought a bike, kayak or more than two people, the cheaper option is **TLC Taxi** (697-2239), which charges $15 plus $7 per additional person, $5 per bike, and $10 per kayak.

Gustavus's second graders might have added that their town offers little in the way of budget accommodations. Some locals rent cabins ($85 per night), which sleep two to four. The **Bear's Den** (697-2440) maintains two hand-painted, artsy cabins, as does the **Puffin Lodge** (697-2260). Puffin lacks the paint job, but offers complimentary breakfasts, bikes, and a shuttle service. Once at Bartlett Cove, backpackers can stay in the free **campground,** which has 25 sites and is rarely full. Glimpses of orcas and humpback whales are common from the beachfront sites. Those without a tent can collapse in comfortable dorm beds at the Glacier Bay Lodge ($28). Showers ($1 per 5min.) and laundry ($2 wash, $1.25 dry) are available to all.

The most affordable food in Gustavus comes from **Bear Track Mercantile** (697-2358; open daily 9am-7pm). If days of peanut butter cause a craving for *haute cuisine,* head to the **Bear's Nest Cafe** (697-2440) to feast on soup, salad, and lasagna for $15; emu, the local red meat, is an extra $3 (open daily 11am-1pm and 4:30-9pm).

The **Fireweed Gallery** (697-2325) displays local painting, sculpture, and handicrafts in an earthy setting (open Mon.-Fri. 1-5pm and by appointment). Besides the Fireweed, everything to see and do in Gustavus is outside. The boat dock offers astonishing purple-gold sunsets and 360° of mountain views. Logging roads that criss-cross the land beg for bike exploration, and there are several short trails around Bartlett Cove. The most substantial is the 3 mi. **Park River Trail,** featuring frequent bear sightings. After having paid to reach Glacier Bay, however, you will likely crave the wild slopes and remote coves beyond Bartlett. Indulge and enjoy—it's worth it.

Haines

Clear blue water, snow-covered coastal peaks, glaciers and sunny days lend magic to the breathtaking trails winding through Haines' wonderland. In late fall or early winter, when warm upwellings in the Chilkat River encourage an out-of-season salmon run, as many as 4000 bald eagles—more than double the town's human population—flock to the peninsula's "Council Grounds" for a feast. Haines heartily welcomes the few travelers who stop by en route to Skagway with a flourishing outdoor recreation industry and a spirited community.

PRACTICAL INFORMATION AND ORIENTATION

Visitors Information: Haines Convention and Visitors Bureau (766-2234 or 800-458-3579; fax 766-3155; email hainesak@wwa.com; http://www.haines.ak.us), 2nd Ave. near Willard St. Worth stopping by just for a chat with the enthusiastic director. Info on accommodations, nearby hikes, and surrounding parks. Pick up the free pamphlet *Haines is for Hikers.* Free tea and coffee. Open Mon.-Fri. 8am-8pm, Sat. 9am-6pm, Sun. 10am-7pm; winter Mon.-Fri. 8am-5pm. **State Park Information Office,** 259 Main St., P.O. Box 430 (766-2292), above Helen's Shop between 2nd. and 3rd Ave. Rangers tell all about area hiking, dangers of bears, and the Chilkat Bald Eagle Preserve. Open Tues.-Sat. 8am-4:30pm, but call ahead: rangers are often out on patrol.

Bank: First National Bank of Anchorage, on Main St. Only bank in town. 24hr. **ATM.** Open Mon.-Thurs. 10am-4pm, Fri. 10am-5pm.

Air Service: Haines Air (766-2646) and **LAB Flying Service** (766-2222 or 800-426-0543), both on Main St., offer comparable rates on flights to Juneau ($110-120 round-trip), Skagway, and Glacier Bay, as well as special deals one-way from Juneau to Glacier Bay to Haines.

Buses: Alaska Direct (800-770-6652). Provides non-stop service to Anchorage ($150) and Fairbanks ($125), departing Haines at 6am Sun., Wed., and Fri. **Alaskon Express.** Make reservations through **Ft. Seward Tours** (766-2000), in the lobby of the Hotel Halsingland. Buses travel north on Tues., Thurs., and Sun., with an overnight stop in Beaver Creek, YT, near the Alaskan border. To: Anchorage ($185); Fairbanks ($180); and Whitehorse, YT ($86). Open daily 9am-8pm.

Ferries: Alaska Marine Highway (766-2111). Terminal on Lutak Rd., 4 mi. from downtown. Hitchers report they can usually get to town; others take a cab. Daily to Juneau ($20) and Skagway ($14).

Taxi: The New Other Guy's Taxi (766-3257). $6 from ferry to downtown. Long-term parking for ferry passengers $5 per day, $25 per week. 24hr.

Car Rental: Eagle's Nest Car Rental (766-2891 or 800-354-6009), at Eagle's Nest Motel. Must be 21 with a major credit card. $45 per day plus 35¢ for every mi. over 100. **Avis** (766-2733), at Hotel Hälsingland. Grudgingly offers an 8hr. deal for $40, unlimited mileage. Must be 25 with a credit card. Don't be late, or pay the regular $57 per day. Call ahead to reserve.

Car Repair: Charlie's Repair, 225 2nd Ave. (766-2494). Open Mon.-Fri. 8am-5pm.

Bike Rental: Sockeye Cycle (766-2869), on Portage St. in Ft. Seward. $6 per hr., $20 per ½-day, $30 per 8hr. Helmets and locks included. Open Mon.-Sat. 9am-6pm, Sun. 1-5pm. Also offers guided daytrips on and off road, led by the man who began the Kluane-Chilkat Bike Relay (see **Sights and Entertainment,** p. 159).

Kayak Rental: Tanani Bay Kayak and Canoe Rentals (766-2804), near the corner of Union and Front St. Single kayaks and canoes $18 per day; double kayaks $26 per day. **Deishu Expeditions** (766-2427 or 800-552-9257; email paddle@seakayaks.com; http://www.seakayaks.com), on Portage St. near the cruise ship dock. Single $35 per day; double $55 per day. Open daily 9am-6pm; call to arrange pick up or drop off at other times.

Bookstore: The Babbling Book (776-3356), on Main St. near Howser's Supermarket. Good collection of Alaskana, current and non-fiction. Open Mon.-Sat. 10am-6pm, Sun. noon-6pm.

Library: (766-2545), on 3rd Ave. Open Mon. and Wed. 10am-9pm, Tues. and Thurs. 10am-4:30pm and 7-9pm, Fri. 10am-4:30pm, Sat. 1-4pm, Sun. 2-4pm.

Camping Equipment and Fishing Licenses: Alaska Sport Shop (766-244). Focus on fish. Open Mon.-Sat. 8:30am-6pm. Sun. 10am-4pm; winter Mon.-Sat. 10am-6pm.

Laundromat and Showers: Port Chilkoot Camper Park (766-2000), across from the Halsingland Hotel. Wash $2, 7min. dry 25¢. Showers $1.50. Open daily 7am-9pm. **Susie Q's** (766-2953), on Main St. near Front St. Wash $2, dry 50¢. Showers $2. Open daily 8am-8pm; in winter 8am-6pm.

Health Center: 766-2521.

Emergency: 911. **Police:** 766-2121. **Fire:** 766-2115.

Post Office: On Haines Hwy., between 2nd Ave. and Front St. Open Mon.-Fri. 9am-5:30pm, Sat. 1-3pm. **General Delivery ZIP Code:** 99827.

Area Code: 907.

Most of the Haines business district lies in a rectangle outlined by Main Street and the Haines Highway and their perpendiculars, 2nd and 3rd Avenues. Haines, a 10-minute walk to Fort Seward, lies on a thin peninsula between the **Chilkat and Chilkoot Inlets,** just southwest of Skagway on the Chilkoot Inlet. Below this peninsula, the two inlets merge into **Lynn Canal.** There are U.S. (767-5511) and Canadian (767-5540) **customs offices** at Mile 42 of the Haines Hwy. (open daily 7am-11pm). Travelers must have at least $200 cash (although the requirement varies based on destination), a credit card, and valid proof of citizenship to cross into Canada, and rental cars are not always allowed across (see **Customs,** p. 7).

ACCOMMODATIONS AND CAMPING

Since the weather in Haines is better than almost anywhere else in Southeast Alaska, there are few reasons not to camp. In addition to the private campgrounds listed below, there are several state campgrounds (with water and toilets) around Haines. **Chilkat State Park,** 7 mi. south on Mud Bay Rd. by the sea, has guided nature walks and good king salmon and halibut fishing (32 sites; $6). **Chilkoot Lake,** 10 mi. north of town on Lutak Rd., provides views and sockeye salmon (32 sites; $10). **Mosquito Lake,** 27 mi. north on Haines Hwy., earns its name in late summer (13 sites; $6).

Bear Creek Camp and International Hostel, Box 1158 (766-2259), on Small Tracts Rd. 2 mi. outside of town. From downtown, follow 3rd Ave. out Mud Bay Rd. to Small Tracts. Location is convenient to nothing; call ahead for ferry terminal pickup. A ring of basic cabins, each with its own unique odor. Spartan furnishings—a roof and a "bed" (foam pads on bunks). No coed social space besides the kitchen. No curfew. $14, family cabins $38, tentsites $8.

Hotel Hälsingland, Box 1589 MD (766-2000, 800-542-6363, or 800-478-2525 in YT and BC). Play soldier in old Ft. Seward officers' quarters. Several small economy rooms with sinks and shared bath ($39; doubles $49). Call ahead for cheap rooms—a bath doubles the price.

Fort Seward Lodge, Box 307 (766-2009 or 800-478-7772). Another historic Fort Seward building, a 10min. walk from Haines. A bit dark, but clean and attractive with hand-finished furniture. 10 rooms at reasonable rates. Singles with shared bath $45; doubles from $55. Private bath $15 more. Oct.-April $10 off.

Portage Cove, ¾ mi. from town on Beach Rd. Accepts only backpackers and cyclists. 9 grassy sites ($6) overlooking the water. Little privacy, but other campers are congenial. Pit toilets and a food-hanging site. 7-day max stay.

Port Chilkoot Camper Park, Box 41589 (766-2000 or 800-542-6363), across from Hotel Hälsingland. A few trees provide protection from the road, but little natural setting. Gravelly but well maintained. Convenient to downtown. Laundromat and showers ($1.50). Summer only. 60 sites. Tents $8; RVs with full hookup $19.

Salmon Run RV Campground (766-3240), at Lutak Inlet, ½ mi. from the ferry terminal, away from town. Half of the sites overlook the beach. Wooded, with streams on grounds. Restrooms. Sites $10. Open year-round.

FOOD

Overstuffed burritos are beginning to replace steak and potatoes on Haines menus as new establishments strive to please outsiders' delicate palates. Groceries are expensive; stock up in Juneau. Of the two markets in town, most locals prefer **Howser's Supermarket** (766-2040), on Main St. (open daily 8am-9pm). For fresh seafood, head to **Bell's Seafood** (766-2950), on 2nd Ave., under the "Old City Jail and Firehouse" sign. Try salmon ($7 per lb.), or prawns ($13 per lb.; open Sun.-Tues. and Thurs.-Sat. 9am-6pm, Wed. 9am-10pm).

Chilkat Restaurant and Bakery (766-2920), on 5th Ave., near Main. Family-style, with healthy portions. Sugary baked goods available for takeout. All-you-can-eat soup-and-salad bar ($9). Basic sandwiches $5, "creative" ones $8. Popular Mexican night on Fridays. Open Mon.-Sat. 7am-9pm, Sun. 9am-9pm. Wheelchair accessible.

Mountain Market (766-3340), on Haines Hwy. at 3rd Ave. Granolas feed at the Mountain Market, Haines' health food grocery store and cafe. Sandwiches overflowing with sprouts and avocado from $5.50, with daily soup add 75¢. Standard espresso schtick. Open daily 6am-6pm.

Bamboo Room (776-2800), on 2nd Ave. near Main St. No bamboo in sight. This unpretentious diner is a favorite breakfast spot, crowded until 3pm with fisherfolk downing buckwheat hotcakes and coffee ($4.25). Lunch specials $6, dinner specials $9-10. Open daily 6am-10pm.

Port Chilkoot Potlatch (766-2000 or 800-542-6363), at the Tribal House in Ft. Seward. Not the cheapest salmon bake in the region, but mmmmmm. All-you-can-eat BBQ salmon and ribs, plus salad bar and cheesecake ($21.75). One free beer or wine. You must mingle with cruise ship crowds, but it's probably worth it. Open daily in summer, 5-8:30pm. Reservations recommended.

Bear-ritos (766-2117), on Main St. across from the museum. Lots of open space, but none in your stomach after a pinto bean burrito ($4.50) or chicken chimichangas ($6.25). North of the border burgers, too. Open daily 11am-10pm.

Wild Strawberry, 138 2nd Ave. (766-3608), off Haines Hwy. Sandwiches ($6), and, if Jim's been lucky on the water, barbecued halibut and king salmon ($9-10). Dine upstairs, downstairs, or outside. Caffeine addicts sated at the coffee bar. Open Mon.-Fri. 7am-9pm, Sat. 9am-9pm, Sun. noon-9pm.

SIGHTS AND ENTERTAINMENT

Fort William Seward, on the west side of town, was established in 1901 to assert American presence during a border dispute with Canada. With little to do other than shovel snow and watch for fires, the colonial-style post quickly became known as a gentle assignment. Boredom was the soldiers' only enemy: "Even among men with the most modern arms, time is the hardest thing to kill," lamented one observer in a 1907 newspaper. After WWII, the fort shut down, and five veterans bought the entire 400-acre compound to make a commune. Their utopian venture never succeeded, but most of these settlers became free-enterprising members of the community. Today, Ft. Seward lies at the center of Haines's tourist activity, showing off a replicated **Totem Village** (766-2160), complete with a tribal house.

The **Chilkat Dancers** perform traditional Tlingit dances with interpretive narration at the **Chilkat Center for the Arts.** Performances are usually at 8pm, but revolve around cruise ship and ferry schedules. Call the Hotel Hälsingland (766-2000) for tickets ($10, under 18 $5, under 5 free). The village is also home to **Sea Wolf Studio-Gallery** (766-2540), where you can watch artist Tresham Gregg carve Tlingit masks (open Mon.-Fri. 9am until the last ship leaves). The **Alaska Indian Arts Center** (766-2160) is at the far side of the fairgrounds. Watch artisans in their workshops and marvel at the craft of totem pole carving (open Mon.-Fri. 9am-noon and 1-5pm).

The **American Bald Eagle Association Center,** P.O. Box 49 (766-3094), at the intersection of Haines Hwy. and 2nd Ave., offers an indoor look at Haines' wildlife and screens a film of the November bald eagle occupation (free; open Mon.-Sat. 9am-6pm, Sun. 1-6pm, and to accommodate cruise ships).

Wildlife of a different sort hits Haines in early July (July 4-5 in 1998), when the **Haines Rodeo** brings the **Hats, Boots, and Buns Cowboy Beauty Contest,** line dancing, multiple barbecues, and of course, rodeo riding galore. Call the visitors center (see **Practical Information,** above) for details. Haines becomes Party Central in May with a **Craft Beer and Home-brew Festival** (May 15-17 in 1998), a **Bald Eagle Run** and **Harley Davidson Rodeo** (May 22-24), and an Alaskan version of **Mardi Gras** (May 13-15). If wheels are your thing, but Hogs aren't, team up for the **International Kluane to Chilkoot Bike Relay** (June 20 in 1998). The 153 mi. course covers the Haines Hwy. from Haines Junction, YT to Haines, AK, with checkpoints every 20 mi. to relieve saddle soreness. Call **Sockeye Cycle** (see **Practical Information,** above) for more info.

OUTDOORS

The **Haines Highway** winds 40 mi. from Haines through the **Chilkat Range** north through the Yukon, with views guaranteed to blow you through the back of your Winnebago. **Chilkat Bald Eagle Preserve** (766-2202 or 800-246-6268), a 19 mi. drive or bike up the highway, protects the feeding grounds where thousands of eagles gather in November—the world's largest annual concentration. A handful of eagles make the preserve their year-round home.

Three main **trails** head into the wilderness around Haines. The **Mt. Riley Trail** starts in several places and ends on a 1760 ft. summit with a panoramic view of the Lynn Canal, the Chilkoot and Chilkat inlets, and everything else within 30 mi. The primary trailhead is marked by a large sign 3½ mi. from town, 1½ mi. down Mud Bay Rd. past the hostel. This route is steep for most of its 2 mi. **Mount Ripinsky,** the 3920 ft. mountain looming over the north end of town, provides a challenging hike over two summits connected by an alpine ridge for more ambitious view-seekers. On a clear day, the view from the ridge extends all the way to Juneau; on partly cloudy days, the summit is often shrouded, but the shorter Mt. Riley continues to provide excellent views. To reach Mt. Ripinsky's trailhead, follow 2nd Ave. north to Lutak Rd., branch off Lutak onto Young St. at the hill, then turn right along a pipeline for 1 mi. After cresting the 3610 ft. **North Summit,** the trail dips down along the ridge and may be difficult to follow in poor weather. At the end of the ridge, it climbs again to the 3920 ft. peak, and descends steeply to its end at Mile 7 of the Haines Hwy. This strenuous 10 mi. hike makes for a long day of walking or a relaxed overnight trip. The more relaxing **Seduction Point Trail** offers 6¾ mi. of birds, beaches, ocean bluffs, berry picking, wildflowers, and seductive views of the Davidson Glacier. Take Mud Bay Rd. out of Haines 7 mi. to Chilkat State Park. Try to time the last part of the hike along David's Cove to coincide with low tide.

Skagway

In August 1896, a Tlingit man named Skookum Jim was washing a pan in a tributary of the Klondike River when he discovered strips of gold so thick they looked "like cheese in a sandwich." By the next October, Skagway was a thriving town of 20,000, large even for today's Alaskan standards. From Skagway, the stampeders drove their pack horses mercilessly along the rocky but relatively gradual White Pass Trail, then floated north on the Yukon River to their diggings. Over 3000 horses perished along this route in the winter of 1897-98, earning it the name **Dead Horse Trail.** The shorter **Chilkoot Trail,** starting in the nearby ghost town of **Dyea,** climbs too steeply for pack animals, but was just as popular (see p. 263). When the Nome gold rush began in 1900, Skagway dwindled, surviving only as a port and the terminus of a railway over White Pass.

The railroad still runs today, but carries tourists rather than miners and supplies. Although Skagway's population is only 700, gargantuan Inside Passage cruise ships and ferries deposit as many as 7000 passengers per day. Strangely, *everyone* stays on Broadway Street, the town's renovated historic district, leaving the surrounding trails and streets (except the Chilkoot), relatively uncrowded. While July and August may not be the best time for serenity, Skagway's sky-meets-sea location and open-hearted hostel make any visit worthwhile.

PRACTICAL INFORMATION AND ORIENTATION

Visitors Information: Klondike Gold Rush National Historical Park Visitor Center (983-2921), at 2nd and Broadway. 45min. free walking tours 4 times daily; self-guided tour brochures available upon request. Open May and Sept. daily 8am-6pm, Jun.-Aug. 8am-7pm. The **Trail Center** (983-3655), across the street on Broadway, is a joint-run U.S./Canada Parks headquarter for info and maps on the Chilkoot Trail and local hikes. Sells overnight permit for the Canada side of the trail (US$35), keeps itinerary records, and sells a few trail guides. Open late May to mid-Sept. daily 7am-7pm. **Skagway Convention and Visitors Bureau** (983-2854; http://www.skagway.org), on 5th Ave. off Broadway. A plethora of brochures and accommodations info. Open May-Sept. daily 8am-5pm, Oct.-Apr. Mon.-Fri. 8am-noon and 1-5pm. **Forest Service** (983-3088), on 2nd St. near Spring St. Hours vary widely and are posted. To reserve a cabin, call the Juneau office (586-8751).

Bank: National Bank of Alaska (983-2264), at Broadway and 6th Ave. 24hr. **ATM**. ATM also available on Broadway near 2nd Ave. Open Mon.-Fri. 9:30am-5pm.

City Tax: 4% on all merchandise, food, and services, and 8% on accommodations.

Air Service: Skagway Air Service, (983-2218), on Broadway between 5th and 6th Ave. 3 flights per day to Haines ($35), 9 to Juneau ($75). Also several flights to Gustavus ($85) and tours of Glacier Bay ($120). Open daily 7am-10pm.

Trains: White Pass and Yukon Route, P.O. Box 435 (983-2217 or 800-343-7373), 1 block off Broadway on 2nd Ave. towards the tracks. 3hr. round-trip excursion to White Pass Summit on one of the steepest and most scenic railroad grades in North America. Trains run May 16-Sept. 22, leaving daily at 8:30am and 1pm ($78, under 13 $38). Accesses remote hiking trails along the route (see **Outdoors,** below). Combined train and bus service to Whitehorse, YT daily at 12:40pm ($95 one-way, under 13 $48). All trains wheelchair accessible.

Buses: Alaska Direct (983-2311 or 800-770-6652) runs vans from the ferry terminal, visitors center, and hostel by appointment to Whitehorse ($35, $50 round-trip) daily, with connections on Wed., Fri., and Sun. to Fairbanks ($120) and Anchorage ($145). Requires an overnight stay in Whitehorse. **Alaskon Express** (983-2241 or 800-544-2206), in the Westmark Inn, on 3rd Ave. between Broadway and Spring. Buses Sun., Tues., and Thurs. to Anchorage and Fairbanks ($205). Trips include an expensive overnight stop near the Alaska border in Beaver Creek, YT. One per day in summer to Whitehorse, YT ($56, at 7:30am).

Ferries: Alaska Marine Highway (983-2941). Ferries daily to Haines ($14) and Juneau ($26). Beware dockside ticket office's erratic hours. **Water Taxi** (983-2093 or 888-766-3395 in AK and Canada). 2 per day to Haines ($18, round-trip $29). Buy tickets via phone or in person at 470 Broadway (open daily 9am-5pm).

Taxi: Frontier Excursions (983-2512), at 7th Ave. and Broadway. To the Chilkoot trailhead in Dyea ($10); pick up at "log cabin" near trail's terminus ($20). **Skagway Hostel Shuttle** (983-2131) also runs to the trailhead ($10). Call for reservations.

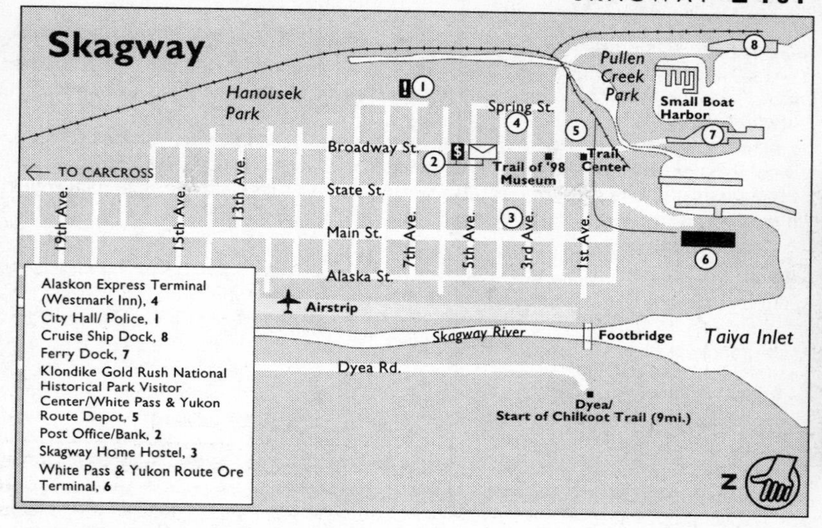

Car Rental: Sourdough Van & Car Rentals (983-2523 or 800-478-2529; email rental@pialaska.net), at 6th Ave. and Broadway. The cheapest. Starts at $30 per day, plus 5¢ per mi. over 100.

Auto Repair: Hoover's (983-2454), on 4th and Main St. Open Mon.-Sat. 7am-7pm, Sun. 8am-6pm.

Bike Rental: Sockeye Cycle (983-2851; http://www.haines.ak.us/sockeye), on 5th Ave. off Broadway St. From $6 per hr., $30 per day, including helmet and lock. Guided tours available. Open May-Sept. daily 9am-6pm. **Rent-a-Bike** (983-2643 or 2687), on 4th Ave. at State St. $5 per hr. or $25 per day. Open daily 9:30am-5pm.

Outdoor Equipment: Skagway Hardware (983-2233), on Broadway St. at 4th Ave. Sells fishing permits ($50 per season), limited outdoor gear, and fix-its. Open Mon.-Sat. 10am-6pm, Sun. 10am-4pm. The **Sports Emporium** (983-2480), on 4th Ave. between Broadway and State sells more high-tech gear. Open May-late Sept. daily 9am-7pm; call for winter hours.

Library: (983-2665), at 8th Ave. and State St. Open Mon.-Fri. 1-9pm, Sat. 1-6pm.

Laundromat: Services Unlimited Laundromat (983-2595), at 2nd Ave. and State St. Wash $2, 5min. dry 25¢. Open daily 8am-8pm, last load 6:30pm. **Garden City RV Park** (983-2378), at State St. and 5th Ave., also has a laundromat.

Showers: Garden City RV Park (see above), 75¢ for 5min. Quarter-fed public showers also at the wharf.

Hospital: Skagway Medical Service (983-2255), on 11th Ave. between State and Broadway.

Police: (983-2232), on 7th Ave. in City Hall.

Internet Access: in the Skagway **library,** see above.

Post Office: (983-2320), at Broadway and 6th, next to the bank. Open Mon.-Fri. 8:30am-5pm. Be prepared for long lines in the summer. Lobby open 24hr. **General Delivery ZIP Code:** 99840.

Area Code: 907.

At the northernmost tip of the Inside Passage, Skagway is the terminus of the Alaska Marine Hwy. From here, wheeled travelers connect to the interior Alaska Highway by taking the **Klondike Highway** (Rte. 98 in AK; Hwy. 2 in YT) 113 mi. to Whitehorse, YT. This stretch of road is haunting and foggy, snaking gently alongside lichen-covered crags interspersed with waterfalls. Both Canadian and U.S. customs are passable 24 hours a day, although the U.S. office is not staffed between midnight and 6am. If crossing into Canada, have enough cash on hand (at least $150), a credit card, and proof of ID (see **Customs,** p. 7). There are no services between Skagway and Carcross, 66 mi. away. **Haines** is 15 mi. away by water, 360 mi. by land. Hitchers say they do better spending $14 on the ferry to Haines, then thumbing the more heavily traveled Haines Highway to Kluane and interior Alaska. (*Let's Go* does not recommend hitchhiking.)

The ferry drops passengers off at the southern end of downtown. Skagway's main drag, **Broadway,** runs inland from the docks. Broadway is paralleled by Spring St. to the right as you leave the docks, and State and Main St. to the left. Numbered avenues intersect these streets, then numbers increasing towards the hills.

ACCOMMODATIONS AND CAMPING

The hostel is reason enough to visit Skagway. If you're not a hosteler, it's wise to make reservations at least one month in advance at all hotels. Penniless tenters are out of luck, as Skagway has no free tenting and maintains strict regulations.

Skagway Home Hostel, P.O. Box 231 (983-2131), on 3rd Ave. near Main St., ½ mi. from the ferry. This living definition of "Home Sweet Home" invites travelers into a generous, idiosyncratic family. Kitchen and facilities shared by owners and guests alike. Up to 10 may sign up for dinner before 4:30pm ($5; free if you cook). No lockout; curfew 11pm; showers, kitchen, bike use and plenty of Chilkoot trail advice. $3 wash, dry, and detergent. 21 beds and 1 private room. Chore required. Will store packs. Sheets and towels $1. Check-in 5:30-9pm. Cash or travelers checks only.

Golden North Hotel, P.O. Box 431 (983-2295), at 3rd Ave. and Broadway St. The classiest affordable hotel in the Southeast and the oldest hotel in the state still in business (since 1898). Each room in a unique period style with canopy beds and antique furniture. Singles or doubles $55 with shared bath; private bath $75.

Skagway Inn Bed and Breakfast (983-2289 or 800-4788-2290 from AK), on Broadway at 7th Ave. Built as a brothel in 1897. Now respectably refurbished, each room retains the name of one of the brothel's illustrious women. Tons of original or restored antique furniture. Pick-up and delivery to ferry and airport. Transport to Chilkoot Trail with 1-day notice. Shared baths. Rooms start at $55.

Pullen Creek RV Park (983-2768), on 2nd Ave. by the harbor. Small, quiet, with an unobstructed view of the mountains. Bathrooms, coin showers. Hookup $20; cozy nook for tents $10. No open fires.

Dyea Camping Area, 9 mi. northwest of Skagway on Dyea Rd., near the start of the Chilkoot Trail. 22 spacious, woodsy sites. Pit toilets, fire rings, no drinking water or showers. 2-week max. stay. Not recommended for RVs. Free.

Miner's Inn (983-3303, 983-3305 during day, or 800-764-7670), at Broadway St. and 6th Ave., cheapest indoor accommodations in town, but rooms lack pizazz and size. Shared bath. Singles $45; doubles $60. Complimentary simple breakfast.

FOOD

Eating in Skagway can be a bummer for the budget traveler. Groceries and film are beyond expensive, so stock up before coming. If you need to shop in Skagway, try the **Fairway Supermarket** (983-2220), at 4th Ave. and State St. (open Mon.-Sat. 8am-9pm, Sun. 9am-6pm, winter Mon.-Sat. 9am-6pm, Sun. 10am-4pm). Health-conscious backpackers love **You Say Tomato** (983-2785), on State St. and 9th Ave., for its dry, natural meals sold by the pound (open Mon.-Sat. 10am-8pm, Sun. noon-6pm).

Stowaway Cafe (983-DINE/3463), on 2nd Ave. by the small boat harbor. Though pricey, the Stowaway is ten steps above the Broadway mayhem. Fresh seafood gumbo $16, lunch veggie curry $7.50, unlimited bread (made in heaven). Worth the splurge. Open May-Sept. daily 11am-10pm. Reservations suggested.

Corner Cafe (983-2155), at 4th Ave. and State St. Where the locals head for basic grub. Open-air seating helps you avoid the smoke. Listen to that fryer sizzle! Stack of sourdough pancakes $4. Burgers ($4.50-7). Open May-Sept. daily 6am-9pm.

Mabel G. Smith's, 342 5th Ave. (983-2609). The caffeine addict's nook, yet to be discovered by the Broadway "Love Boat" stampede. Yummy muffins and cookies from $1.25. Open May-Sept. daily 6am-6pm; call for winter hours.

Bonanza Bar and Grill (983-6214), on Broadway between 3rd and 4th Ave. As American as they come, with basic sports grill fare to chow on as you catch the game on TV. Pizza, sandwiches (from $8), but no wealth of entrees ($10). Pitchers from $10 and good music for the young at heart. Open May-Sept. daily 10am-midnight.

SIGHTS AND EVENTS

Most of Broadway Street is preserved in pristine 1898 form as the **Klondike Gold Rush National Historical Park.** The Park Service leases a restored vintage saloon and many other period buildings to local businesses. Check out the worthwhile hourly film at the park's visitors center (see **Practical Information,** above). Polish up on your gold rush trivia at the **Trail of '98 Museum** (983-2420), housed in the 1899 **Arctic Brotherhood Hall,** on Broadway between 2nd and 3rd. Testament to the state's dearth of interesting architecture, the hall's driftwood-coated facade is Alaska's most photographed building. Among the museum's treasures are the world's only duck-neck robe and the bloodstained tie that local con-man Soapy Smith (supposedly) wore on the day of his death. For slightly more lively history, head next door to the **Red Onion Saloon** (983-2222), Skagway's first bordello. A century ago, the bartender marked each lady's availability by placing dolls on a rack downstairs in the appropriate position: upright or prostrate. Now the Red Onion is a popular bar with an enviable collection of bed pans adorning one wall. Come for live afternoon jazz (courtesy of cruise ship musicians) or for the open jam Thursday nights, when the locals come out to play (open daily 10am-12:30am; no cover). For a little less ambiance but a whole lot of taste, the **Skagway Brewing Company,** in the Golden North Hotel (see **Accommodations,** above) serves up stout straight from its own in-house microbrewery. The *oosic* stout is named after the bone of a male walrus's private parts. Dark beer lovers will rejoice anyway (open May-Sept. 11am-midnight).

Skagway's history is almost overshadowed by its shiny, packaged souvenir and jewelry shops. One of the few true artist-run galleries is **Inside Passage Arts** (983-2585), at Broadway and 4th St., which sells work by local indigenous craftspeople. Stop in, if only to gander (open daily 9am-6pm). **Corrington Alaskan Ivory** (983-2580), at 5th Ave. and Broadway St., contains a copious display of expensive carved bone and fossilized ivory in their showroom and free museum (open daily 9am-6pm).

If Skagway's Champs Elysées (Broadway) gets to be too much, the **Gold Rush Cemetery** on the inland edge of town is the perfect getaway. Take Main St. and head

The Cleanest Con Man in the North

Skagway's most notorious ne'er-do-well, Jefferson Randolph "Soapy" Smith, got his name from his favorite con, the "soap game." He would sit on a street corner selling bars of soap for an outrageous $5. Eventually, Soapy would wrap some $50 and $100 bills around a few of the slow-selling bars. A crowd gathered, and some impetuous spenders would step forward to buy bars. As luck would have it, those first two or three invariably held very large bills and triggered a buying frenzy. Most purchasers ended up with only a very precious bar of soap. The two or three lucky fellows (a.k.a. accomplices) would meet up with Soapy later and return the planted bills for a handsome payoff. Ultimately, **Soapy Smith** wasn't such a bad sort: he donated money to the community for a new church, started an "adopt a dog" program, and rarely robbed locals. In appreciation of his peculiar brand of philanthropy, the town named him Grand Marshall of the 4th of July parade in 1898. A few days later, Soapy met his untimely end in a shootout. Skagway's lovable anti-hero was buried outside the limits of the town cemetery, while his terminator was given a choice plot and a tombstone inscribed, "He gave his life for the honor of Skagway." Today, Soapy's spirit is celebrated each July at a debaucherous evening gathering called "Soapy's Wake."

for the parking lot before the bridge and the sign directing you to a dirt road; the cemetery is about 1½ miles from downtown. The graveyard retains an eerie serenity rare in other gold rush historical monuments. Soapy fans will have to worship his grave slightly beyond the cemetery boundaries. A short trail from the cemetery leads to lower Reid Falls, which cascades 300 ft. down the mountainside.

Those wanting to catch the "true story" of Soapy and his exploits without reading another pamphlet can head to the **Skagway Days of '98** show in the Eagles Hall (983-2545), 6th and Broadway. For over seven decades, the vaudeville show has featured song and dance, play-money gambling, and audience-actor interaction ($14, children $7). Matinees are a little cheaper ($12, kids $6), but evening shows tend to be better (daily in summer; gambling 7:30pm, show 8:30pm).

OUTDOORS

Backpacking buffs in Skagway won't pass up the Chilkoot Trail. Before you go, pick up the complete *Hiker's Guide to the Chilkoot Trail,* a publication of the Alaska Natural Historical Association ($2 at the Trail Center, see **Practical Information,** above). Even if not camping out in Canada ($35 permit), hikers still need to register at the trail center ($10). Call (800) 661-4086 or (867) 667-3910 between 8am and 4:30pm PST. Only 50 people per day are allowed on the Chilkoot during the summer. Park officials patrol the trail, and rangers are also usually at the trailhead in Dyea. If you're planning to continue into British Columbia, call **Canadian customs** (867-667-3943; 8:30am-4:30pm PST) and have a credit card, valid photo ID, and birth certificate or passport before you cross the border. According to rangers, these requirements are enforced only on a whim, but are most likely to trip up the scruffy and potentially indigent.

Although the Chilkoot Trail is the marquee name in Skagway hiking, shorter local hikes have inspiring views and fewer people around to block them. The **Dewey Lake Trail System** provides some of the best and closest hiking, ranging from a 20-minute stroll to a strenuous climb up to two alpine lakes at 3700 ft. To reach the trail system, walk east toward the mountains along 2nd. Ave. Follow the dirt path just before the railroad tracks to the left, and look for signs pointing out the trail on the right. **Lower Dewey Lake,** a long, narrow pond surrounded by woods, lies less than a mile up the trail. Here one trail branches to the lake (about 2 mi.), and another branches left toward **Icy Lake** and **Upper Reid Falls** (about 1½ mi.). Both of these walks are gentle with little change in elevation. A third trail to **Upper Dewey Lake** branches off the Icy Lake trail near the northern end of Lower Dewey Lake. The first section of the 2¼-mi. trail is brutal, but the climb mellows out somewhat and switchbacks its way to the lake. Upper Dewey rests in a stunning amphitheater of serrated peaks. A small **cabin,** newly renovated with bunks and cooking utensils, with cramped space for four and a permanent smoky odor. It is available on a first-come, first-served basis. The best **tenting sites** are along the opposite shore. You need a permit for overnight camping anywhere in the forest surrounding Skagway; get one free at the **Skagway Police Station,** at 7th Ave. and Broadway. **AB Mountain,** named for the pattern created by the melting snow on its side each spring, dominates the skyline on the west side of town. The **Skyline Trail** leads up this mountain. Both the directions to the trailhead and the challenging trail itself are confusing, so pick up a **Skagway Trail Map** at the Trail Center. From town, it's about 5 mi. to the panoramic 3500 ft. summit. Many other hikes start from trailheads in or near Skagway. Contact the Trail Center to find out about them, then head for the hills.

The Bush

Known as the Country or the Bush, this vast expanse of arctic tundra and jagged coastline overwhelms the tiny settlements and narrow landing strips that hint at human presence. The Bush towns of Nome, Barrow, and Prudhoe Bay are places few Alaskans have ever seen. Polar bears ride ice floes and hundreds of thousands of caribou roam freely across the tundra. Native Alaskan settlements are few and far between, accessible only by plane, boat, or snow machines. Cannery workers and oil drillers swarm to remote settlements for big money, knowing it's theirs to save because there's nowhere to spend it.

Each area of the Bush has distinctive features. The Southwest includes the flat, soggy, buggy terrain of the Yukon-Kushkowin delta, the mountainous Alaska Peninsula, and the Aleutian Islands, a volcanic archipelago with some of the worst weather on earth. Western Alaska includes the Seward Peninsula, a treeless, hilly expanse of tundra. Nome lies at the tip of a peninsula on the coast of the storm-lashed Bering Sea. The Brooks Range, Alaska's arctic crown, stretches from the northwest to the Canadian border, while the flat, endless expanses of tundra on the North Slope spread northward from the Brooks to the Arctic Ocean, where oil companies employ thousands of Alaskans. The town of Barrow on the Arctic Ocean is the world's largest Inuit village and the northernmost point of the United States. Anyone who hopes to travel in the bush must have a strong sense of adventure and self-reliance, or tons of money and trust in tour guides; most towns won't expend energy entertaining guests. Revel in the isolation and prepare to rough it.

Be prepared to spend, too. Because all supplies (even gas) must be flown in from Fairbanks, transportation in the Bush is expensive. Alaska Airlines (800-426-0333) services Nome, Kotzebue, Barrow, and Prudhoe Bay. Smaller companies like Larry's Flying Service (474-9169) and Frontier Flying Services (474-0014) fly to even more remote spots like Anaktuvuk Pass ($294 round-trip from Fairbanks), Bettles ($248 round-trip), and Fort Yukon. Once in the Bush, tour outfitters abound, ready and willing to take the adventuresome into the wilds to fish, hunt, hike, kayak, or canoe (for a steep price, of course).

ARCTIC ALASKA

Dalton Highway

The Dalton Highway parallels the Alaska Pipeline from Fairbanks to the Arctic Circle, then reaches all the way to Deadhorse and the gates of Prudhoe Bay, the second northernmost settlement in Alaska. Before considering the drive, check your wallet to see if a tour is possible. They aren't cheap—the **Northern Alaska Tour Company** (474-8600) offers a day-trip to the Arctic Circle boundary ($99), and a three-day trip to Prudhoe Bay ($549)—but they are the best way to view the area while preserving both car and sanity; a single flat tire halfway up the Dalton Hwy. could be a far worse drain to a traveler's resources.

The entire highway was opened to the public on January 1, 1995. Truckers driving 36-wheel rigs spitting rocks and dust dominate; a tiny number of RVs, a handful of 4WD vehicles, and an occasional crazy motorcyclist constitute the tourist traffic. It is passable, however, in a standard passenger car. Some hitchers proceed on the logic that no one will leave someone stranded in the middle of nowhere, but truckers, the vast majority of the traffic, almost never stop for hitchers. Simply put, it is not a smart choice to make the drive in your own vehicle, and the visitors center in Fairbanks discourages ignorant yokels from making the attempt. Rocks, boulders, ditches, and mud—often so deep that you are lucky to reach the other side—interrupt the sharp gravel road. Your suspension will be wrecked, and if you drive more than 50 mph, you may end up with at least one flat tire and no services in sight. The drive, for those who dare, is breathtaking. The key to surviving the Dalton is good preparation and a healthy dose of patience. The visitors center in Fairbanks recommends bringing two spare tires. Bring at least one, plus extra gas, tools, clothing, food supplies, and drinking water. You do not want to pay to be towed back to Fairbanks, since it costs around $7 *per mile.* The journey takes about four days round-trip.

FROM FAIRBANKS TO THE ARCTIC CIRCLE

A drive up the Dalton Hwy. begins with an 83 mi. jaunt from Fairbanks along the **Elliot Hwy.** to Mile 0 of the Dalton. Enjoy the pavement as you head out of Fairbanks; it's the last you'll see for almost 900 mi. At Mile 49.5, sojourners pining for a glimpse of homestead life might stop at the **Wildwood General Store.** The owners and their 23 children (!) keep the store open "whenever someone's around." The Dalton crosses the **Yukon River** at Mile 56 (139 mi. from Fairbanks). On the north side of the river is one of the highway's two (count 'em, two) service stations. **Yukon Ventures** (655-9001) sells unleaded gas and rents rooms ($50 per person). The gas station and a small cafe are open daily 7am-9pm.

The road next winds through its first alpine region as it gains elevation and passes **Finger Rock** (to the east at Mile 97.5) and **Caribou Mountain** (to the west). The rest area just past Finger Rock is an ideal place to calm pothole-jarred nerves and enjoy the view of the **Brooks Range.** Next comes the **Arctic Circle** (Mile 115), the southernmost point at which the sun does not set on the longest day of the year. A recently constructed pulloff has several picnic tables and presents the visitor with four interpreted displays on the Arctic seasons (summer, winter, winter, and winter). The enormous "Arctic Circle" sign is a great photo opportunity, and the spot is good for free camping. If you're satisfied with reaching the Arctic Circle, camp here and retreat to Fairbanks come morning; the road only gets worse.

FROM THE ARCTIC CIRCLE TO DEADHORSE

Continuing north over 1500 ft. **Gobblers Knob,** the Dalton rattles along past Prospect Camp and Pump Station No. 5, over the Jim River and the South Fork of the Koyukuk River, to the town of **Coldfoot,** which has the last services available before Prudhoe Bay (240 mi. away). Coldfoot, "the northernmost truck stop in North America," was originally a mining town that, at its peak, boasted "one gambling hall, two road houses, seven saloons, and ten prostitutes." Its name originated in 1898, when a group of timid prospectors got "cold feet" about wintering above the Arctic Circle and headed south again. "Downtown" is a huge and muddy parking lot. Just north of Coldfoot is the **Coldfoot Visitor Center** (678-5209), an excellent source of info for travelers planning on intense trekking or paddling in the Brooks Range (open daily 1-10pm; nightly slide presentations 8:30pm). On the perimeter of the downtown field, the **Coldfoot Cafe** (678-5201) serves good, hot, and (surprise!) expensive food (open 24hr.). The **general store** has some supplies (open daily noon-9pm). The **Arctic Acres Inn** (678-5224) maintains several RV sites (electrical hookups $20), but there is free camping out of town; ask at the visitors center in Fairbanks about public land around Coldfoot. A **shower** at the hotel costs $3 and a load of **laundry** costs $4. Eight miles north of Coldfoot, the BLM-administered **Marion Creek Campground** has sites in muskeg forest with water and pit toilets ($6). The **post office** (678-5204) is next to the general store (open Mon., Wed., and Fri. 1:30-6pm). **ZIP Code:** 99701.

Twelve miles north of Coldfoot at Mile 188.6 is the junction for the village of **Wiseman,** truly the last frontier and worth the short side trip. Three miles off the beaten path, this town was immortalized by Robert Marshall in his 1933 book, *Arctic Village.* Perhaps the wildest frontier town accessible by road in Alaska, Wiseman is home to many of the movie *White Fang*'s canine stars (including W.F. himself).

From Wiseman, the highway continues into the heart of the Brooks Range. Keep your eyes open for moose, Dall sheep, bear, caribou, and hawks. At Mile 235, **the last**

Old Pilots and Bold Pilots, But No Old Bold Pilots

Most Alaskans say that Bush pilots are one or the other, but never both. The state has the highest per capita ownership of small planes, the greatest number of pilots, the greatest number of float planes, and one of the nation's most heavily used airports (in Anchorage). In much of the Interior, small planes aren't simply the best way to get there; they're the only way to get there. Some of the state's most colorful lore is based in aviation—for example, the story of the third governor of Alaska who broke both ankles crash landing his small plane rather than endangering the children playing in the landing field. Tales of unusual cargo are as common as tales of unusual landings: bush pilots have been know to transport canoes, beer, furniture, and even moose to the farthest reaches of the state.

tree found along the highway—a surprisingly tall and majestic spruce—marks the beginning of the steep and awe-inspiring ascent toward **Atigun Pass** (4752 ft.). The highway cuts steeply into the mountainside as it approaches the pass and offers spectacular views of the Dietrich River Valley. Be prepared for snow on the pass year-round. Check out the glacial **cirque** (an amphitheater-shaped depression) on the mountainside east of the highway. Once the mountains are breached, the long descent toward the **Arctic Ocean** begins.

In the final stretch of the highway, the mountains gradually flatten into a broad expanse of monotonous tundra. The tundra is perpetually brown except for a short month-long summer in July and August. Walking on the tundra is not as easy as it looks. It is filled with bumps and lumps of moss called tussocks, and is underlaid by tremendous amounts of water unable to escape through the frozen ground. Try a tundra walk and you're guaranteed a wet, soggy, difficult hike, though you may be rewarded by seeing wildlife not found below the Brooks range, such as **musk oxen, arctic fox, snow owls,** and **tundra swans.** Even under perpetual sunlight, the temperature is noticeably cool, typically about 43°F (5°C) in summer.

Approximately 10 mi. from the highway's end, a layer of coastal fog enshrouds the land, blocking the sun and forcing a temperature plummet. **Deadhorse** suddenly appears on the horizon, and 3 mi. beyond is **Prudhoe Bay** (see below). And then you're there. At the **Arctic Ocean.** The northernmost point accessible by road in North America. Fun, wasn't it? Now you just have to get back.

DEADHORSE AND PRUDHOE BAY

The camp of **Deadhorse,** on the southern perimeter of **Lake Colleen,** owes its name to the gravel company who brought the first road-building materials north, and whose motto was: "We'll haul anything, even a dead horse." Deadhorse's airport is served by **Alaska Airlines** (800-225-2752). A one-way flight from Fairbanks costs $279. In an emergency, call the ARCO operator at 659-5900, as there are no "public" emergency services.

Prudhoe Bay, owned by oil companies and accessible only by guided tour, is not a normal community. Everything exists for and because of oil. Every building and structure contributes in some manner to oil production. No permanent residents, extremely limited tourist facilities—the Atlantic Richfield Co. (ARCO) runs a visitor center (659-5748)—and no "town proper" can be found in Prudhoe Bay. **Arctic Caribou Inn** (659-2368) offers excellent four-hour tours for $60. You'll stand next to Mile 0 of the pipeline, check out the interior of the workers' bunkhouses (surprisingly nice), and dip your fingers into the icy waters of the Arctic Ocean, among other things. There is also a "shuttle" tour to the ocean that costs $20 and lasts one hour. This abbreviated version is mostly a driving tour of the fields, but still affords you the chance to leap into the Arctic Ocean. Shuttle tours are only given at 8 and 10am, so arrive in the morning if you want to take one.

Keep in mind that Prudhoe Bay is a "dry" community. No alcohol or firearms are allowed. The **post office** (659-2669) is located in the general store (open daily 1-3:30pm and 6:30-9pm). The **ZIP Code** is 99734. The **area code** is 907.

Brooks Range

Defining Alaska's north coast, the magnificent Brooks Range describes a great semi-circle from the Bering Strait in the west, through the Noatak National Preserve and **Gates of the Arctic National Park,** to the **Arctic National Wildlife Refuge (ANWR)** and the Canadian border in the east. The range covers gargantuan expanses of remote territory and remains the last stretch of truly untouched wilderness in the U.S.

Accessing the Brooks Range and the parks which protect it is both difficult and expensive. It is possible to hike into the Brooks Range from the Dalton Hwy. near Wiseman, but to get to the best parts of the range, or even to get more than 10 mi. from the highway, most people fly into the park. Talk to park officials before planning a trip into the Brooks (the headquarters for both ANWR and the Gates are located in Fairbanks; see p. 112). The **Coldfoot Visitors Center** (see p. 166) can give specific info on where to hike into the range from the Dalton Hwy.

ANAKTUVUK PASS

Many travelers heading into Gates of the Arctic National Park fly to Anaktuvuk Pass. Literally translated, "Anaktuvuk" means "caribou crap," an appropriate name given the swarms of caribou that migrate every year through the only break in the 1000 mi. Brooks Range. Though Anaktuvuk is within the park and protected by U.S. law, it is private land owned by the **Nunamiut** (NOON-ah-myoot). North America's last true nomads, this inland Inuit people only began to make permanent settlements in the last 50 years. Surrounded by **Gates of the Arctic National Park** and nestled in a mirage-like mountain pass in the tundra of the Arctic Divide, the Nunamiut struggle to maintain their lifestyle amid the pressures and developments of the 20th century.

Until recently, the Nunamiut have been wary of opening up their land to tourist use. They manage it, as well as hunt and trap aboard motorcycles and ATVs. They are careful not to overrun the land, though the trail of ATV tracks around town is initially startling to visitors. Travelers are quite welcome, but residents politely and steadfastly request the following: if you come, do not litter or interrupt the activities of the Nunamiut; use low impact camping techniques (see **Camping and the Outdoors: Wilderness Concerns,** p. 42), and absolutely never take pictures of the local people without permission. There are other requests about wilderness travel as well, but these are best learned by speaking to a ranger.

Larry's Flying Service (474-9169), one of the most well-respected Bush airlines, offers flights to Anaktuvuk Pass from Fairbanks (Tues. and Fri. $246 round-trip), as do several others. If you can stop your stomach from staging a coup, the flight over the tops of the awe-inspiring Brooks Range is worth the money. Wilderness so pristine and beautiful is found few places on earth. If stuck in town, visitors should head to the **Simon Panaek Museum** (661-3413), which has extensive displays on traditional Nunamiut culture. The **Hans van der Laan Brooks Range Library** also houses a huge collection of material on the people and land of Alaska's Far North (both open June-Aug. Mon.-Fri. 8:30am-5pm; free).

Anaktuvuk has no rooms for rent, but visitors can camp anywhere just outside of town. The hills on the other side of the John River offer good camping spots. The **Nunamiut Corporation Store** (661-3327) sells groceries at prices as steep as the mountains (open Mon.-Thurs. 10am-6pm, Fri. 10am-7pm, Sat. noon-6pm). The **Nunamiut Corporation Camp Kitchen** (661-3123), a hole-in-the-wall restaurant on the south end of town, has breakfast ($7) and burgers ($7.50; open daily 6-9am, 11am-1pm, and 3-7pm). The **Washeteria** (661-9713), next to the enormous blue-roofed school, has **showers** (free!) and **laundry** facilities (wash $1, 10min. dry 50¢; open Mon.-Tues. 8:30am-5pm, Wed.-Fri. 8:30am-9:30pm, Sat. 1-9:30pm, Sun. 10am-6pm). **Emergency numbers** include: **police,** 911; **medical/fire,** 611; **public safety officer,** 661-3911; **health clinic,** 661-3914. The **post office** (661-3615) is next to the airstrip (open Mon.-Fri. 8:30-11:30am, 12:30-5:30pm). The **ZIP Code** is 99721.

GATES OF THE ARCTIC NATIONAL PARK AND THE ARCTIC NATIONAL WILDLIFE REFUGE

The Gates of the Arctic National Park and Preserve exists for nature, not for people. Established in 1980, the park protects over 8.4 million acres of wilderness in the central Brooks Range. Central to the park's creation were mandates insisting that the area remain undeveloped. Travelers to Gates will be acutely aware that the park exists to protect the environment, not to maximize human pleasure; there are no trails or facilities in the park, and transportation there is difficult and expensive. Nevertheless, the park's remote setting and untouched interior make it attractive to the most adventuresome of outdoor types. Six National Wild and Scenic Rivers run through the park and provide excellent floating opportunities. Heavy glaciation has carved huge U-shaped valleys throughout the park that aid hiking and route-finding.

Covering a huge swath of northeast Alaska, the **Arctic National Wildlife Refuge (ANWR)** encompasses more than 31,100 incredibly remote sq. mi., an area larger than Maine. The calving ground of the porcupine caribou herd and the Brooks Range's highest mountains are here. Oil companies are close to winning their battle to move in for exploration, and this may soon alter the area forever.

The park and refuge are most accessible to the decidedly wealthy and the powerfully determined. Budget backpackers sometimes hitch up the Dalton Hwy. and hike in from several access points along the road, a long and uncertain journey. (*Let's Go* does not recommend...aw, you know the rest.) Those with a bit more money fly commercially into Anaktuvuk Pass and head out from there. Those with still more cash to spare can charter a plane and immerse themselves in true isolation. The town of **Bettles** lies south of the mountains on the Middle Fork of the Koyukuk River and is the jumping-off point for those chartering a plane. Several companies offer charter service. Ask around for the best deal, and expect to pay several hundred dollars an hour for a plane.

The public lands office advises that only travelers with extensive backpacking knowledge, experience in Alaska parks, and wilderness survival skills should enter Gates. If you have any doubts about your preparedness, simply *do not go.* This is the most extreme and isolated wilderness still in existence, and only a healthy respect for Mother Nature will get you through it. For more info, contact **Park Headquarters,** 201 1st Ave. (456-0281), in Fairbanks. The Park Service operates a **Gates of the Arctic Field Station** (692-5494) in Bettles for those seeking information (open daily 8am-5pm). In Bettles, **Sourdough Outfitters** (692-5252) offers guided and unguided adventures in the Brooks Range. Canoes and other kinds of equipment are available for rent, and guides are extremely knowledgeable about the park. Stop by for tips before venturing out. The **post office** (692-5236) is at the northern end of town (open Mon. 8am-5pm, Tues., Thurs., and Fri. 8am-3pm, Wed. 8am-4pm, and Sat. 1-4pm). The **ZIP Code** is 99726.

Ask around about good places to pitch a tent, or stay in the **Bettles Lodge** (692-51111 or 800-770-5111). The lodge has a bunkhouse ($15, sleeping bag required), which is a better deal than the regular rooms (singles $85, doubles $115). The lodge's restaurant has good cheeseburgers ($6.25; open daily 8-10am, 11:30-2pm and 6-8pm). At the lodge, a **shower** costs $3.50 (towel $1) and **laundry** costs $8 per load. The **Bettles Trading Post** (692-5252) sells expensive groceries (open Mon.-Sat. 9am-6pm, Sun. 1-4pm).

Barrow

Huddled on flat brown tundra next to the icy waters of the Chukchi Sea, Barrow endures some of the harshest conditions in the world: temperatures below -60°F and months of perpetual twilight. Barrow is the northernmost point on the North American mainland, almost 330 mi. north of the Arctic Circle. Even more remarkable than the pluck it takes for locals to withstand Mother Nature's aggressions is how long Barrow natives have been doing so. As early as 2000 BC the native Inūpiat roamed the area; by 1200 AD, Barrow had become the site of their permanent establishment.

Today, the Inūpiat vein still runs strong in Barrow—60% of the 4000-person population is Inūpiat. As in ancient times, bowhead whaling remains an economic mainstay, with extensive hunts in the fall and spring. Here, the native Inūpiat tongue is spoken as much as English, and ancient customs co-exist with more modern innovations. Fresh seal meat or a bear hide hang drying beside $30,000 cars—all across the street from the local espresso shop. This unique blend gives Barrow a distinct flavor (and smell!) and helps attract the smattering of tourists who visit each year. After dipping their toes in the chilly arctic water and taking several pictures of native dancing, however, most travelers content themselves with the fact they've been to the "top of the world," then head south, leaving the persistent town to fend for itself in a world of permafrost, blubber, and pervasive grey.

PRACTICAL INFORMATION AND ORIENTATION

Visitors Center: The Barrow visitors center recently closed, leaving the **Top-of-the-World Hotel,** at the corner of Stevenson and Agvik St. (see **Accommodations,** below), as the best source of local information. Pick up a walking map of town. Lobby open 24hr.

Airport: Located downtown, a couple blocks from the water on Ogrook St. The only way to get to Barrow is to fly. **Alaska Airlines** (800-426-0333), flies a couple of times daily from Anchorage (from $512).

Tours: A packaged tour is the cheapest way to see Barrow. Several companies offer 1-day and overnight packages that include guided tours and cost less than an independent ticket and hotel accommodation. **Alaska Airlines Vacations** offers 2 tours in conjunction with Top-of-the-World Hotel and Tundra Tours. Trips run mid-May through mid-Sept. The daytrip from Fairbanks costs $395. The overnight package includes overnight accommodation at Top-of-the-World Hotel ($438 per person; from Anchorage $85 more each way). **Gray Line** (277-5581) also offers similar services. 1-day package with 4hr. flightseeing tour from Anchorage, $582. Overnight package $690 per person.

Buses: Across from airport. Buses swing around town every 20min. To be picked up, flag it down anywhere along its route. 50¢; seniors free.

Taxis: City Cab (852-5050); **Arctic Cab** (852-2227); **Polar Cab** (852-3030). All 24hr. Rides around Barrow cost $5-6 with $1 every extra person.

Car Rental: UIC Car Rental (852-2700). $75 per day; $20 extra if uninsured. Must be 25; credit cards accepted. **Top-of-the-World** (852-3900) rents for $85 per day with unlimited mileage (a non-issue given the amount of road). Must be 21 to rent; cash and checks only. Open 24hr.

Library: Tuzzy Library (852-4042), on Stevenson St. 3 doors down from Polar Coffee Shop. Open Mon.-Thurs. noon-9pm, Fri.-Sat. noon-5pm.

Hospital: (852-4611), at the end of Agvik St. by the Middle Lagoon.

Crisis Line: 852-0267.

Public Safety: 852-6111.

Emergency: 911.

Post Office: 601 Cunningham St. (852-6800). Open 10am-5:30pm Mon.-Fri., 9am-1pm Sat. **General Delivery ZIP Code:** 99723.

Area Code: 907.

As with all true Bush communities, Barrow is only accessible by plane, and at quite a price. Buy a ticket far in advance; the earlier the reservation, the lower the price. Barrow itself is infinitely walkable.

ACCOMMODATIONS AND CAMPING

Accommodations in Barrow are outrageously expensive; if you're planning to stay the night, be prepared to pay an arm and a leg. Harsh weather makes camping a purgatory, but diehard tenters can ask permission to camp on the beach outside the Top-of-the-World Hotel.

Top-of-the-World Hotel, P.O. Box 109 (800-882-8478, in AK 800-478-8520). The most prominent hotel in town. Full-service accommodations. Clean and bright rooms equipped with cable and refrigerators brighten up the tundra-enveloped view just outside the window. Many rooms overlook the icy waters of the Arctic. Singles $159; doubles $179.

Airport Inn, P.O. Box 933 (852-2525). Friendly and informative staff. Cheerful but plain 70s decor suggests a Motel 6 a loooong way from the Interstate. The prices do not. Singles $115; doubles $125. Kitchenettes available for no extra charge.

FOOD

Although costly, Barrow's food options are surprisingly good. Economy minded travelers hunting groceries can mush to **Alaska Commercial** (852-6711), one block from Top-of-the-World Hotel on Agvik St. (open Mon.-Sat. 8am-11pm, Sun. 10am-9pm).

Arctic Pizza (852-4222 or 852-4223), on corner of Ogrook and Apayauk St. A local favorite, this spacious oceanside restaurant offers a variety of seafood, Italian, and Mexican chow. Ignore the name and order Shrimp a la Arctic, Halibut a la Arctic, or Scallops a la Arctic (around $16). Hamburgers (a la New Jersey) $5.50. Open Mon.-Thurs. 11:30am-10:45pm, Fri.-Sat. 11:30am-11:45pm, Sun. 4-10:45pm.

Polar Haven Coffee Company (852-BEAN/2326), across from Top-of-the-World Hotel. A town with 85 straight days of darkness had better have some damn good coffee. Thanks to Polar Haven, Barrow does. Steaming hot lattés (tall $3) and cocoa ($1.75) in a country-style cafe. Bright decor and a selection of art books. Tasty sandwiches ($6.75) sold 11:30am-2pm. Open Mon.-Fri. 7am-7pm, Sat.-Sun. 8am-7pm.

Pepe's North of the Border Restaurant (852-8200). Prices are high at the world's northernmost Mexican restaurant. A la carte burritos are $4.25, but entrees run around $13. The food is decent but the ambience is far from authentic. About 4000 mi. to be precise. Open Mon.-Sat. 6am-10pm, Sun. 8am-10pm.

Teriyaki House (852-2276), around the corner from the airport. The Bering Land Bridge is gone, but the Asian influence holds on in this modest downtown restaurant. A host of Chinese and Japanese options. Top-of-the-World sushi starts at $6. Lunch specials like *Kung Pao* chicken with fried rice, egg roll, and soup ($8.50) offered 11:30am-2pm.

SIGHTS AND ACTIVITIES

The most obvious sight in Barrow is **Point Barrow,** the northernmost tip of the continent. The tip is not accessible by car, so purists must walk the 2 mi. stretch or rent a Hummer to access the lonely point. Follow Stevenson St. north.

Those nostalgic for the days of Mutual Assured Destruction (or *Dr. Strangelove* fans) might appreciate a trip across town to the **DEW Line,** the Distant Early Warning system designed to detect Soviet missiles flying over the north pole. The radar post, which resembles a giant golf ball, remains a reminder of Cold War fear.

Across the street from Arctic Pizza at Apayauk and Ogrook St. are the **Mounds,** the site of Barrow's original Inūpiat settlement. Today, the ancient sod buildings lie below the grassy knoll and there is little to see, but in 1982 five bodies, 650 years old, were discovered here. The two women and three children, well preserved by permafrost, were dubbed the **Frozen Family**. In 1994, an even older body was discovered—a girl, still dressed in a hooded parka, dating back to around 1200 AD.

The jaws of a giant bowhead whale sprout up from the ground on Eben Hopson St. Next to the whale bone arch is **Brower's Store,** the original whaling station for Barrow and the oldest wooden structure in the Arctic. In the spring of 1998, Barrow is planning the opening of a new **cultural center,** which will house Barrow's **museum** (852-2611 for info), stocked with native artifacts from whaling instruments to caribou-skin masks.

An important ritual of Inūpiat culture, the **Nalukatag,** or "blanket toss festival," celebrates the end of a successful whaling season every June. Children are tossed high into the frigid air on hide blankets. In early August, bold travelers can one-up the Polar Bear Club with a short plunge into the icy arctic water. The ceremonial swim takes place in early August, on the first fall day the sun sets.

NORTHWEST ALASKA

Nome

The Klondike's counterpart in Alaska, Nome owes its existence to the "three lucky Swedes" who discovered gold on nearby Anvil Creek in 1898 and its name, it is said, to the poor penmanship of a British sailor. Baffled as to what to call this barren, weather-beaten camp on the edge of the sea, he scribbled "Name?" on his map. Cartographers back in England took his "a" for an "o," and Nome was born. Despite arctic temperatures and Bering Sea storms, Nome is home to a population of 4000, half of which is native Alaskan. Built almost entirely on permafrost, Nome's buildings are elevated on pilings to prevent the ground from thawing beneath them, and most have extremely ramshackle exteriors. Those who can afford to get here will find untamed wilderness surprisingly accessible by road, refreshingly non-commercialized relics of mining history, and some famously wild saloons.

PRACTICAL INFORMATION

Visitors Center: P.O. Box 240 (443-5535; http://www.alaska.net/~nome), on Front St. Don't miss the uproariously funny video *No Place Like Nome.* Open in summer daily 9am-9pm; off-season 9am-6:30pm. **National Park Service** (443-2522), on Front St. in the Sitnasuak Native Corp. Building. Information on the Bering Land Bridge National Park and Preserve plus local hiking and driving tips. Open Mon.-Fri. 8am-noon and 1-5pm, Sat. 10am-noon and 1-6pm.

Bank: National Bank of Alaska, 250 Front St. (443-2223). Open Mon.-Thurs. 10am-5pm, Fri. 10am-6pm.

Airport: about 2 mi. west of town. **Alaska Airlines** (800-426-0333) flies from Fairbanks (round-trip $460) and Anchorage (round-trip $360). **Alaska Airlines Vacations** (800-468-2248) offers circuit tours from Anchorage to Nome to Kotzebue (north of Nome). **Frontier Flying Services** (in Fairbanks 474-0014) flies from Fairbanks (round-trip $506, seniors and children $436), as does **Yute Air** (888-359-9883).

Taxis: Checker Cab, 443-5211. **Nome Cab,** 443-3030. $3 per person for places in town, $5 to the airport. Both 24hr.

Car Rental: Stampede (443-3838). 2WD pickup $65 per day; 4WD pickup, Bronco, or van $75 per day, unlimited mileage (credit card or $100 cash deposit required). **Alaska** (443-2939). 2WD pickup $75 per day; 4WD $85 per day. Also provides auto repair services. Open Mon.-Fri. 7am-9pm, Sat. 7am-6pm. All renters must be 21. **Gas** sells for around $2.14 per gallon.

Books: McGee's Books and Things (443-5001) has the biggest selection around, which isn't saying much. Open Mon.-Sat. 9am-7pm.

Library: Kegoayah Kozga Library (443-5133), above the museum on Front St. Open summers Mon.-Fri. noon-8pm, Sat.-Sun. noon-6pm.

Laundromat: Nome Washeteria (443-5335), at Seppala and C St. The only laundromat in town. Wash $4, dry $4. Open Mon.-Sat. 11am-8pm.

Shower: Rec Center (443-5431), at the northern edge of town on 6th Ave. Free with $4 admission. Also rents cross-country skis and ice skates in winter.

Radio: KICY 100.3 FM, 850 AM and **KNOM** 780 AM.

Weather: 443-2321. Or check the box outside the visitors center.

Hospital/Pharmacy: Norton Sound Hospital (443-3311), at the end of Bering St.

Emergency: 911. **Police:** 443-5262.

Post Office: 240 E. Front St. (443-2401). Open Mon.-Fri. 9am-5pm. **ZIP Code:** 99762.

Area Code: 907.

ACCOMMODATIONS

Beds in Nome are costly, but free camping is permitted on Nome's flat, sandy beaches, about a one mi. walk east on Front St., past the sea wall. Gold miners dot the beaches; enjoy the company. If you have a car, head for **Salmon Lake,** at Mile 38 of the Taylor Hwy. (see **Outdoors,** below).

Ocean View Manor B&B, 490 Front St. (443-2133), on the beach about 1 block from the bank. Offers a deck-side view across Norton Sound and the Bering Sea. TV, phones, refrigerators. Prices include continental breakfast and kitchen privileges. Singles $40-55, with private bath $60; doubles $50-60, with private bath $65.

Betty's Igloo, P.O. Box 1784 (443-2419), at the eastern edge of town on 1st Ave. and K St. Clean and comfortable with kitchen facilities, a spacious common room, and friendly hosts. Shared bath. Children not allowed. Breakfast included. Singles $55, doubles $70. Reservations strongly recommended.

Weeks Apartments, 697 3rd. Ave. (443-3194), at G St. A mother lode of amenities: TV, maid service, kitchen, private bath, and private washer and dryer. Prices and hours are confusing—everything is negotiable. Singles $50-60; doubles $70-80. Call ahead.

FOOD

Don't be alarmed by the dilapidated exteriors of Nome's restaurants—almost all the buildings in town look like that. Stock up on groceries and supplies at **Hanson's Trading Company** (443-5454), on Bering St. (open Mon.-Sat. 7:30am-10pm, Sun. 10am-7pm). The rowdy bars in town, grouped together on Front St., are always packed with locals.

Fat Freddie's (443-5899), next to the visitors center. Popular tour destination because it's a clean, well-lighted place that overlooks the ocean. Admire the blue expanses of the Bering Sea while you chow down on the soup and all-you-can-eat salad bar for $8. Breakfast omelettes for $7. Open daily 6am-10pm.

Pizza Napoli (443-5300), at the corner of Front St. and Lanes Way. Join the local crowd for burgers (from $6) or pizza (from $10). Booths offer privacy and dim lighting—this might be the best place in Nome to make a romantic move. Open daily 11am-11pm.

Twin Dragon (443-5552), at the corner of Front St. and Steadman. Avoid the tackiness and grease that plague lesser Chinese joints. Unbelievably fresh vegetables—how'd they do that? The bright, well-decorated interior makes the Almond Chicken or Sweet and Sour Pork (both $12) taste all the better. Look for lunch specials. Open Mon.-Fri. 11am-11pm, Sat. noon-11pm, Sun. 3-11pm.

The Glue Pot (443-5474), on Front St., diagonally from the visitors center. Not for those seeking a refined atmosphere. But the hamburgers ($4) or breakfast specials ($8.75-10) will fill you up. Then play some pinball or pawn your necklace (the Glue Pot brokers gold and jewelry on the side). Nome's only after-bar hangout. Open Mon.-Sat. 11am-3:30am, Sun. 1pm-2am.

EVENTS

Isolation from the rest of the world makes people do strange things. And you can't get much more isolated that Nome. The **Bering Sea Ice Golf Classic** is held in March on the frozen Bering Sea. Contestants use bright orange balls and face a number of unique hazards: ice crevasses, bottomless snow holes, and frosted greens. Course rules dictate: "If you hit a polar bear (Endangered Species List) with your golf ball, you will have three strokes added to your score. If you recover said ball, we will subtract five strokes." The **Midnight Sun Festival** marks the summer solstice (June 21) with a parade, a barbecue, and a simulation bank robbery. Go figure. On Labor Day, the **Great Bathtub Race** sends wheeled bathtubs, filled with water, soap, and bather, hurtling down Front St. The biggest event of the year, however, is the **Iditarod** (800-545-MUSH; http://www.iditarod.com). The world's foremost **dogsled race** begins in Anchorage (see p. 61) and finishes here in mid-March beneath the log "banner" visible year-round next to City Hall. Thousands of spectators journey in, and it is not uncommon for local accommodations to be booked nearly a year in advance.

OUTDOORS

Branching out into the surrounding wilderness, Nome's three highways are a godsend for the adventurous traveler. Though entirely gravel, all are generally well-maintained and navigable in a rental car. According to the visitors center, hitching a ride up the Taylor or Council Highway is fairly easy on weekends, when many Nome residents head that way. (*Let's Go* does not recommend hitchhiking.) There are excellent **fishing** rivers along the highways, including the **Nome** and **Pilgrim Rivers,** both accessible via the Taylor Hwy. Bring mosquito repellent or you will curse the day you ever heard of Nome.

The **Taylor Highway** (also known as the Kougarok Road) heads north from Nome for 85 mi., then peters out without reaching any destination of note. Along the way is **Salmon Lake,** near Mile 38. Popular with locals, the lake offers excellent fishing and primitive campsites. At Mile 53.6, an unmarked 7 mi. road leads to the **Pilgrim Hot Springs** area. The Catholic Church ran an orphanage here from 1917 to 1941, and, surprisingly, many of the buildings are intact and undisturbed. This is private land, but if you hunt down the curator and ask nicely, he is likely to let you soak in the natural hot springs or wander around the abandoned church, which still contains original statues, paintings, and stained glass. If you don't check in first, you may be hunted down, when he releases the hounds. The **Kigluaik Mountains** are accessible via this highway and offer some good hiking and wildflower viewing.

The **Council Highway** travels 73 mi. from Nome to **Council,** a ghost town and summer home for Nome residents (appealingly below the treeline). En route, the highway goes around Cape Nome, passing beaches, fishing camps, and the fascinating **"Last Train to Nowhere"** at Mile 33, a failed railroad immortalized by the engine and cars that sit slowly rusting on the tundra. The **Nome-Teller Highway** winds west from Nome for 72 mi. to the tiny Native village of **Teller,** home to Libby Riddles, the first woman to win the Iditarod.

Nome is also one of two departure points to the **Bering Land Bridge National Park and Preserve.** Allegedly the least visited park in the United States, the park encompasses the northern third of the Seward Peninsula, and contains lakes, lava fields, and ancient indigenous ruins. Stone tools, thousands of years old, still rest untouched in the valley surrounded by granite spires. The most popular destination (relatively speaking) is the **Serpentine Hot Springs,** just inside the southern border of the park approximately 30mi. from the end of the Taylor Hwy. The temperature of the water is 140-170°F, and a primitive bathhouse is open year-round. The park maintains a rustic sleeping cabin that cannot be reserved, but sleeps 20, and all are welcome. Contact the Park Service Office (443-2522) for info on the cabin, and air charters to get you there (see **Practical Information,** above).

Nome's outskirts are home to the remnants of over 40 abandoned gold **dredges,** as well as a handful that still operate. The closest non-operating dredge, Swansberg Dredge, is about 1½ mi. from downtown on Front St., on the way to the Taylor Hwy.

ALEUTIAN ISLANDS

This is no place to go on a budget. At the fiery boundary between two tectonic plates, the string of snow-capped volcanoes that make up the Alaska Peninsula and the Aleutian Islands stretches more than 1000 mi. into the stormy North Pacific. The Aleutians are one of the most remote locations on earth; the westernmost islands are within a few hundred miles of Kamchatka, Russia. The lava-scarred cones on these green but treeless isles are abused by some of the world's worst weather. Vicious storms packing winds of over 100mph can blow in any time.

In the 19th century, Russia used these islands as stepping stones into Alaska. In June 1942, the Japanese tried to divert American forces from the southern Pacific by occupying the outer islands, Attu and Kiska, and bombarding the town of Unalaska. A year later, the U.S. military stormed Attu, touching off a bloody, if obscure, battle that left thousands of American and Japanese soldiers dead on the wind-swept tundra.

The Peninsula and the islands are home to Aleut villages, small military installations, and larger towns dedicated to serious deep-sea fishing. In the summer, a few hundred tourists come here, despite the cost and time involved, to explore the natural beauty of this volcanic wilderness and join the millions of migratory seabirds that stop here. Several species of birds found here nest nowhere else.

GETTING THERE

The only two methods of getting to the Aleutian Islands are both prohibitively expensive. A one-way flight from Anchorage to **Dutch Harbor,** the largest town on the Aleutians, costs around $450 and lasts about two to three hours. A round-trip ferry on the **Alaska Marine Highway** from Kodiak costs about $400 and takes five to six days. The ferry is the better choice, as the whole point of traveling to the Peninsula and the Aleutians is not merely the destination (there is really nothing there) but to enjoy the unique panoramas and wildlife. The ship is hardly a cruiseliner, and it's probably a good idea to try it out on a day trip before committing yourself for five days. If you are serious about a ferry voyage to the Aleutians, consider purchasing the **AlaskaPass,** which might make the trip more affordable (see p. 32). The Alaska Marine Highway makes this trip only seven times per year between April and September, and it is best to go in July, when the weather is mildest. Make reservations at least two weeks in advance; boats often fill in summer. The *M/V Tustamena* serves the Aleutian chain from Kodiak. It features a dining room with limited hours and decent food (bringing some of your own from Kodiak is a very good idea), showers, and a lounge where an on-board naturalist regularly gives slide shows on the plants and wildlife seen from the ship. Cabinless passengers can sleep above decks. The solarium is (cough) right next to the (ack) exhaust tower. If you want to splurge for the trip, spend the extra $470 for a four-person cabin (about $23.50 per person per night).

Most people on the trip will be senior citizens taking advantage of the $200 they save on discount tickets, with a scattering of families, students, fisherfolk, and maniacal birdwatcher types who run around with binoculars the size of small children screaming, "It's a Whiskered Auklet!" The ferry stops briefly at several small towns, ranging from quaint fishing villages to prefabricated cannery quarters, before reaching Dutch Harbor, the most interesting town in the Aleutians. Unfortunately, it only stops here for about five hours before turning around and heading back, so you're not left with much time to explore. Stock up on Dramamine or another seasickness remedy before you leave. You'll be weathering five to 15 ft. seas; they don't call the *Tustamena* the "Vomit Comet" for nothing.

Location, Location, Location

And you thought that all of the action during World War II was in Europe and the South Pacific. The Aleutian Islands, due to their extreme westerly location, were the site of many (or at least several) tussles between the Japanese and the U.S. Beyond providing a fertile ground for military confrontation away from the tender eyes of American citizens, the Aleutian chain was also a convenient spot after the war for unsavory practices like nuclear testing. Take, for example, the idyllic Amchitka Island. The U.S. military built a base on Amchitka during the war, and then from 1965 to 1973 conducted underground nuclear testing under the auspices of the Atomic Energy Commission. In the late 80s, the Navy took advantage of Amchitka's location (closer to Russia than it is to any city in the U.S.) to build a radar station there. The military installation folded by the end of the Cold War, and now there's little in the way of action on Amchitka. It seems that proximity to the enemy is really only an advantage when there's an enemy to be near. With all quiet on the (far) Western front, strategic defense points are of little use.

Unalaska and Dutch Harbor

Isolated in the Pacific Ocean, at the western limit of the extensive Alaska Marine Hwy. ferry service, Dutch Harbor and Unalaska are about as remote a community of 4300 as you'll find in North America. In 1942, the Japanese began their ill-fated Aleutian campaign with a bombing raid on Unalaska, a heavily fortified stronghold.

Unalaska (un-uh-LAS-ka) and Dutch Harbor are at the head of stunning Unalaska Bay, on Unalaska and Amaknak Islands respectively. For years, the name Dutch Harbor only referred to the port harbor itself, but recently a town, complete with its own zip code, has sprouted 1 mi. from the old town of Unalaska.

Unalaska is hardly a haven for the budget traveler. Remoteness and unusually high incomes (over $130 million in seafood passes through this port every year) keep prices high. Take heart: the view of treeless, snow-capped mountains soaring thousands of feet from Unalaska Bay's chilly blue waters is always free.

Practical Information and Orientation For general information, go to the **Unalaska Convention and Visitors Bureau,** P.O. Box 545 (581-2612), in the Grand Aleutian Hotel (open Mon.-Fri. 8am-5:30pm and occasionally on weekends). **Alaska Marine Highway** (800-642-0066) ferries dock at the City Dock about 1½ mi. from Dutch Harbor and 2½ mi. from Unalaska. The *M/V Tustamena* arrives about once every three to four weeks in the summer (one-way to Kodiak, $202). The **airport,** located about ¼ mi. from City Dock on the main road into town, is served by **Pen Air** (581-1383), which is owned by **Alaska Airlines** (266-7700), and offers flights to Anchorage (one-way $452). **Taxi** service is available from five companies (locals are as baffled by that number as you are), including **Harbor Express** (581-1381) and **Alaska Taxi** (581-2129), both on call (24hr.; call ahead). **Aleutian Adventure Sports** (581-4489) rents mountain bikes, kayaks, and other outdoor equipment. The **clinic** in town is **Iliuliuk Family and Health Services** (581-1202), in a big green building around the corner from the police station (open Mon.-Fri. 8:30am-6pm, Sat. 9am-5pm; after-hours call 581-1233). In an **emergency,** dial 911. The **post office** in **Unalaska** (581-1232) is open Monday to Friday 9am-5pm and Saturday 1-5pm. The **ZIP Code** for Unalaska is 99685 and for Dutch Harbor 99692. The **area code** is 907. Unalaska lies about 300 mi. from the tip of the Alaska Peninsula. It is in the same time zone as the rest of Alaska. Dutch Harbor and Unalaska are connected by a short bridge.

Accommodations and Camping Once again: it ain't cheap. The visitors bureau (see **Practical Information,** above) keeps a list of accommodations including several guest houses. Most land in the area, with the notable exception of Summer Bay, is owned by native corporations, and a fee must be paid to camp there. Contact the **Ounalashka Corporation** (581-1276) for details. Camp for free at **Summer Bay.** From the City Dock or the airport, hike 2½ mi. through Dutch Harbor and Unalaska. Follow Summer Bay Rd. along the shore for another 2 mi. to Summer Bay. A bridge, some sand dunes, and a few picnic tables and barbecues mark the spot, though there are no other facilities. Set your tent in a sheltered location, or the vicious wind gusts will introduce your possessions to Iliuliuk Bay. **The Bunkhouse,** P.O. Box 920185, Dutch Harbor, 99692 (581-4357), offers respectable rooms with shared baths, a lounge with TV, fridge and microwave, and laundry facilities (singles $40, weekly $200; doubles $50; weekly $300).

Food The big money here is in seafood—you'll find no Big Macs. Two enormous grocery stores, with enough square footage to comfortably house most of the town's residents, compete for town-wide supremacy. **Eagle Quality Center** (581-4041), on Airport Beach Rd. in Dutch Harbor, has a good selection, plus a tempting salad bar and hot deli items (open daily 7am-midnight). **Ziggy's** (581-2800), next door to the Eagle, is a favorite local hang-out. A full stack of sourdough pancakes costs $5, sandwiches and burgers are $6 to 8, and Mexican dinners go for $9 to 16 (open daily 6am-

11pm). **Stormy's Restaurant** (581-1565), in Unalaska, serves macho pizzas from $13 (open daily noon-midnight).

Sights If you have the good fortune to have your ferry layover in Unalaska on a sunny day, you would be utterly foolish not to hike to the top of **Mt. Ballyhoo,** just behind the airport. The summit affords one of the most mind-bogglingly beautiful, amazingly awe-inspiring sights in the entire universe. (Superlative overkill is not possible here.) Amazing gold, red, and black rock formations jut out of the sheer cliff that plummets 1634 ft. to the translucent green water of the ocean below. While the winners of an annual race make the roundtrip to the summit in 26 minutes, a slightly more sane pace will get you to the top in 45 minutes to an hour. You can wander along the ridge for another 20 to 30 minutes past the summit, and still easily make it back to catch the ferry.

If the weather is lousy, or the thought of climbing 1600 ft. makes you cringe, then get a cab (see **Practical Information**) to drive you the 3 mi. to the **Unalaska Cemetery and Memorial Park** on the eastern edge of Unalaska. These two sights include a description of the Japanese air attacks of June 1942. You can still see the bow of the *USS Northwestern,* sunk during the attack, slowly rusting in the bay.

Heading back toward Unalaska on Beach Front Rd., you will soon reach the impressive **Holy Ascension Orthodox Church,** built 1824-27 and expanded in 1894, the oldest standing Russian-built church in the U.S. The once dilapidated church has recently been restored to its former splendor. This area was once the thriving (if misguided) center of Orthodox missionary activity in Alaska. Right after you cross the "bridge-to-the-other-side" on the way back to the ferry, you will come to **Bunker Hill,** which was heavily fortified during WWII. A quick 420ft. climb gets you to a large concrete bunker and a great view of the surrounding bays and mountains.

Those planning to stay longer than three to four hours should ask locals or the visitors bureau about the numerous trails and military artifacts strewn across the local countryside. Check with Aleutian Adventure Sports for info on kayaking and other outdoor activities (see above). If you happen to be in Unalaska on any night except Sunday, join commercial fishermen fresh from the open sea at the **Elbow Room Bar** (581-1470), between 2nd and 3rd on Broadway. Once voted the second rowdiest bar in the world, the place has calmed down considerably.

WESTERN CANADA

Western Canada's vast expanses of wilderness contain a broad spectrum of ecological wonders and some of the most idyllic urban areas in the Pacific Northwest. British Columbia is home to spongy arctic tundra in the north, lush coastal forests in the west, and a high, arid plateau in the east. Alberta's endless prairies and the vast sweep of the Yukon, where caribou still outnumber people five-to-one, seem a world away from the big-city bustle of Vancouver, North America's busiest port. Six thousand miles from its former colonial rulers in Britain and France, Western Canada has always taken pride in its spirit of self-reliance.

Early and Native History

Western Canada's natives are among the most important and least recognized participants in its history. Thousands of years before the European arrival, coastal nations like the Haida, Salish, and Kwakiutl had developed sophisticated societies from southeast Alaska to Oregon. Blessed with an abundance of salmon and cedar, coastal peoples established fixed villages where they constructed giant lodge houses and elaborate totem poles. Further inland, the nomadic people of the plains followed bison migration patterns throughout the long, harsh winter. These people served as indispensable guides and translators during the fur boom, but many were crippled by the onslaught of white settlers that followed the discovery of gold.

Today, Canada's First Nations have begun to reclaim their lands and autonomy, and the native peoples of the Pacific Northwest often lead the campaign. Haida watchmen now oversee the spectacular lands of Gwai Haanas in the Queen Charlotte Islands. In 1996, after three years of talks between government officials and the Nisga'a band in northern British Columbia, representatives reached an agreement granting the Nisga'a greater control over their resources and the right to limited self-government. Constitutional negotiations are underway to secure self-determination on a much larger scale: an Inuit homeland in Canada's vast north.

China Needs Pelts

For white settlers, Western Canada's earliest claim to fame rested on the backs of small furry animals. The English explorer James Cook landed on Nootka Sound in 1778, where his sailors traded some rusty nails for a few ragged sea otter pelts from the native Nuuchahnulth. The furs fetched a fat ransom in China during Cook's return trip, and soon the Pacific fur frenzy was on. The fur trade of the late 1700s was among the most lucrative and highly developed industries of its time. The English Hudson's Bay Company engaged in cutthroat competition with the Montreal-based Northwest Company. These warring fortune-hunters were linked by the trading language of the native Chinook, who served as mercenary go-betweens. For decades, the fur companies searched in vain for the Northwest Passage, a navigable sea route from the Atlantic to the Pacific. (No such passage exists south of the Arctic Ocean, a route not completed until 1905.) In 1821, the Hudson's Bay Company absorbed its competitor and ruled the Northwest as a virtual fiefdom for decades to come.

Gold in Them Thar Hills

Miners found small deposits of gold near Vancouver in 1856, and prospectors swarmed up the coast from Northern California. Alarmed by the influx of unruly Americans, the governor of Vancouver Island enlarged his jurisdiction to establish British control over the mineral-rich mainland. In 1871, the coastal colony of British Columbia joined the Confederation of Canada, created by the British North America Act on July 1, 1867. The coming of the Canadian Pacific Railroad and the Northwest Mounted Police—the Mounties—brought prosperity and some semblance of order to the frontier region, and the population boomed. In 1896, prospectors struck the mother lode near Dawson, in the Yukon, and the remote territory became host to a mythic gold rush stampede. Again, government followed the sweet smell of revenue: the Yukon became a Canadian territory in 1898. Alberta, whose fertile agricultural plains would later yield valuable oil, became a Canadian province in 1905.

Recent Events

Western Canadians have long been frustrated with a remote federal government seemingly driven by the concerns of the central Canadian provinces, Ontario and Quebec. Two events in the summer of 1997 revealed the depth of such regional sentiments. In June, a federal election returned Prime Minister Jean Chrétien and his Liberal Party to power, but the Liberal majority was based almost entirely in central Canada. The west was won by the Reform Party, a young protest party born in rural Alberta and known for its tough stance against special status for French-speaking Quebec. The starkly regional election returns, and Reform's new status as Official Opposition, hardly bode well for national cooperation in the years to come.

In July 1997, a fleet of tiny Canadian fishing boats blockaded an Alaska Marine Highway ferry in the harbor of Prince Rupert to protest U.S. overfishing of British Columbia salmon. The illegal blockade held over 300 tourists "hostage" for several days—though they were free to leave the ferry, and those that stayed received free food and lodging—was directed as much against Ottawa's failure to take a hard line against American overfishing as it was against Washington, D.C.

The Arts

In the centuries before European settlement, the Kwakiutl tribe of the present-day Canadian coast enacted "world-renewal" ceremonies with such harrowing and theatrical effects as tunnels, trapdoors, ventriloquism, and bloody sleight-of-hand beheadings. Such traditions are continued today by *The X Files,* filmed in and around Vancouver with similarly harrowing theatrical effects.

Vancouver native Bryan Adams has charged that "CanCon" laws, requiring TV and radio stations to program a minimum amount of Canadian content, breed mediocrity in Canadian music and art. Beyond Adams' syrupy ballads, however, there is little evidence to support this complaint. Western Canada in particular is home to a thriving popular music scene. Major acts from the region include the Crash Test Dummies, 54-40, Chixdiggit (proclaimed "the cutest band in Canada" by *Sassy* magazine), Spirit of the West, Lilith Fair diva Sarah McLachlan, and, perhaps the world's first "hockey-punk" band, the *Slapshot*-inspired Hanson Brothers.

Further Reading

The 90s owe two of their most pervasive buzzwords to young Vancouver authors. William Gibson coined the term "cyberspace" and spawned a genre of science fiction with novels like *Neuromancer* and *Mona Lisa Overdrive,* while Douglas Coupland bestowed an unshakable label on his age group with the seminal *Generation X.*

Outside of Vancouver, the literature of Western Canada is often heavily influenced by native cultures and the physical beauty of the land. Canadian poet Robert Service and American novelist Jack London kept the Yukon mystique alive long after the decline of Dawson. *Notes from the Century Before: A Journal of British Columbia,* by Edward Hoagland, are just that. Popular historian Pierre Burton has written a number of gripping retellings of the region's dramatic past, including *Klondike, The Arctic Grail* and *The Last Spike.* W.P. Kinsella is known south of the border for tales of baseball like *Shoeless Joe* and *Field of Dreams,* but his *Fencepost Chronicles* and *Dance Me Outside,* set in Alberta, give a touching, funny portrait of modern native life. Jean Craighead George's *Julie of the Wolves* is perfect for younger readers. Finally, the cartoon adventures of Dudley Do-Right are an astonishingly accurate portrayal of frontier life among the heroic Northwest Mounted Police.

Southern British Columbia

British Columbia attracts so many visitors that tourism has become the province's second-largest industry after logging. Despite excellent skiing, most tourists arrive in the summer and flock to the beautiful cities of Vancouver and Victoria and to the pristine lakes and beaches of the warm Okanagan Valley. Heading north, thick forests, low mountains, and occasional patches of high desert are interrupted only by supply and transit centers such as Prince George and Prince Rupert. Still farther north, even these outposts of civilization defer to thick spruce and fir forests, intermittently logged or blackened by lightning fires. This chapter covers only the southern part of the province; for coverage of northern British Columbia, including the Cariboo Highway, Yellowhead Highway 16, the Queen Charlotte Islands, the Cassiar and Alaska Highways, and the Yukon Territory, see the following chapter.

British Columbia's parks are popular with hikers, mountaineers, cyclists, rafters, and skiers. On Vancouver Island, the coastal rainforests of Strathcona and Pacific Rim National Parks are unlike any other and largely untrammeled. In the southeastern part of the province, Glacier, Yoho, and Kootenay Parks allow visitors to escape into some of Canada's most amazing outdoor country. Here, you can enjoy environs just as spectacular as Alberta's Jasper and Banff without the tourist mobs.

PRACTICAL INFORMATION

Capital: Victoria.
Visitors Information: Tourism British Columbia, 6-1166 Alberni St. Suite 601 Vancouver, BC V63 3Z3 (604-387-1642 or 800-888-8835 in Canada; 800-663-6000 in the U.S.; http://www.tbc.gov.bc.ca/tourism/tourismhome.html)
Park Information: Parks Canada, 220 4th Ave. SE #552, Calgary, AB T2G 4X3 (800-748-7275 or 403-292-4401; email natlparks-ab@pch.gc.ca). **BC Parks,** 1610 Mt. Seymour Rd., North Vancouver, V7G 1L3 (666-0176).
Population: 3,855,000 **Provincial Motto:** *Splendor sine Occasu* (Splendor Undiminished). **Provincial Bird:** Stellar Jay. **Provincial Flower:** Pacific Dogwood. **Provincial Tree:** Douglas Fir. **Provincial Holiday:** British Columbia Day, 1st Mon. in Aug.
Emergency: 911 in most areas; some rural areas may not have 911 service.
Time Zone: Mostly Pacific (1hr. behind Mountain, 2 behind Central, 3 behind Eastern). Small eastern part is Mountain (1hr. behind Central, 2 behind Eastern).
Postal Abbreviation: BC.
Provincial Sales Tax: 7%.
Drinking Age: 19.
Traffic Laws: Mandatory seatbelt law.
Area Code: 604 in and around Vancouver, 250 in the rest of the province.

GETTING AROUND

British Columbia is Canada's westernmost province, covering over 890,000 sq. km, bordering four U.S. states (Washington, Idaho, Montana, and Alaska) and three Canadian jurisdictions (Alberta, the Yukon Territory, and the Northwest Territories). Vancouver, on the mainland, can be reached by interstate highway from Seattle; Victoria, on Vancouver Island to the southwest of Vancouver, requires a ferry trip (for ferry information, see p. 32) from Anacortes, Port Angeles, Seattle, or the **Tsawwassen and Horseshoe Bay Terminals** near Vancouver. However you travel, get used to thinking of distances in terms of kilometers in three digits.

The **Coquihalla Highway** (Hwy. 5) was completed in 1986 to carry tourists comfortably from Hope to Jasper National Park. The $10 toll buys a faster, more direct route to the east. The **Trans-Canada Highway** (Hwy. 1) is slower and more scenic. It connects Vancouver and Kamloops, continuing east to Banff National Park. Much of British Columbia is served by **Greyhound** (662-3222 in Vancouver; 800-231-2222 from the U.S.)

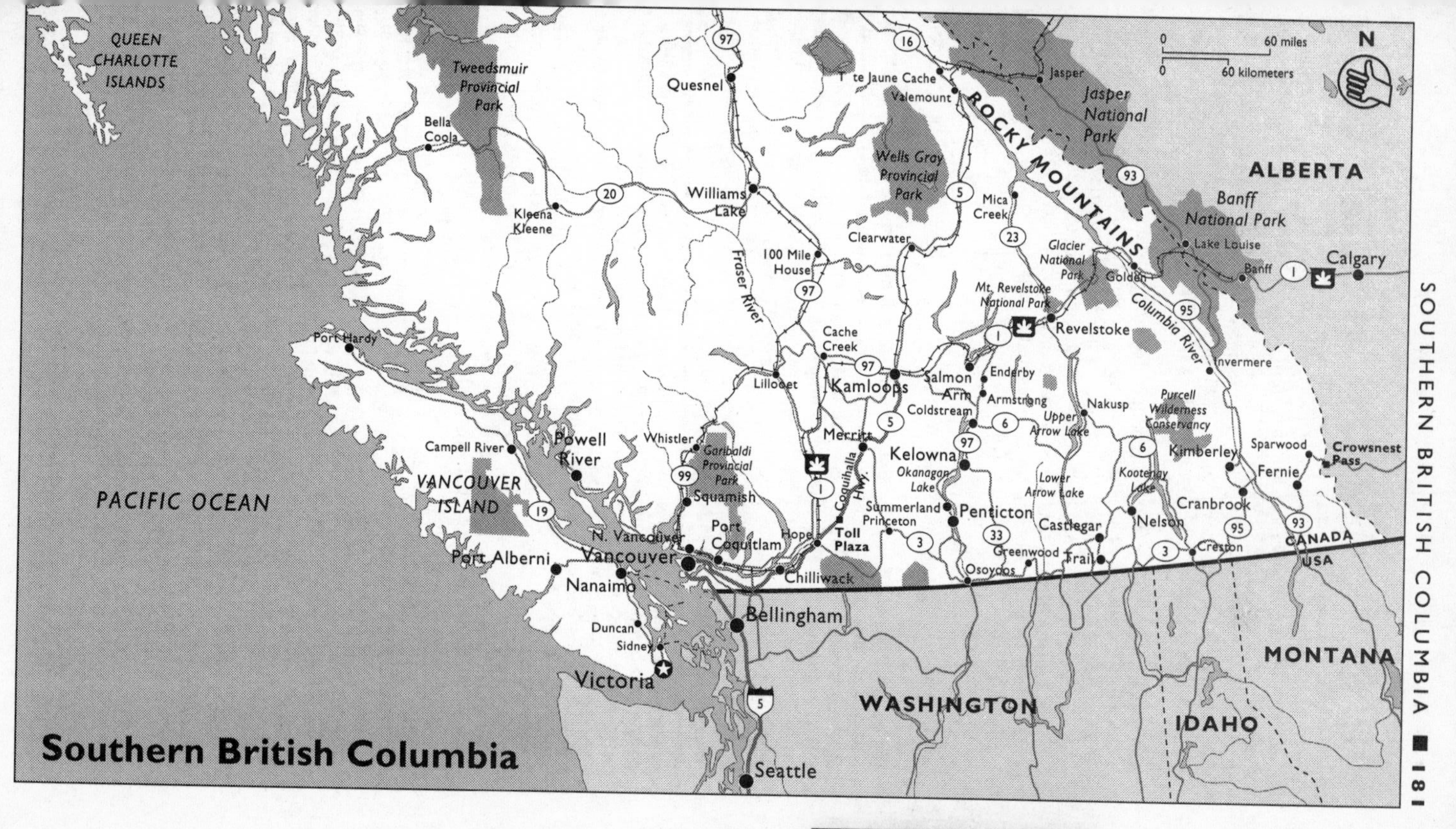
Southern British Columbia
N
0 60 miles
0 60 kilometers
QUEEN CHARLOTTE ISLANDS
Tweedsmuir Provincial Park
Bella Coola
Kleena Kleene
Quesnel
Williams Lake
100 Mile House
Fraser River
Te Jaune Cache
Valemount
Wells Gray Provincial Park
Clearwater
Mica Creek
Jasper
Jasper National Park
ROCKY MOUNTAINS
ALBERTA
Banff National Park
Lake Louise
Banff
Calgary
Glacier National Park
Golden
Mt. Revelstoke National Park
Revelstoke
Columbia River
Invermere
Cache Creek
Lillooet
Kamloops
Salmon Arm
Enderby
Armstrong
Coldstream
Nakusp
Upper Arrow Lake
Purcell Wilderness Conservancy
Kimberley
Sparwood
Crowsnest Pass
Fernie
Cranbrook
Kootenay Lake
Nelson
Lower Arrow Lake
Castlegar
Trail
Creston
Greenwood
Osoyoos
Merritt
Coquihalla Hwy.
Kelowna
Okanagan Lake
Summerland
Penticton
Princeton
Toll Plaza
Hope
Chilliwack
Whistler
Garibaldi Provincial Park
Squamish
Port Coquitlam
N. Vancouver
Vancouver
Port Hardy
Campell River
Powell River
VANCOUVER ISLAND
Port Alberni
Nanaimo
Duncan
Sidney
Victoria
Bellingham
Seattle
PACIFIC OCEAN
WASHINGTON
IDAHO
MONTANA
CANADA
USA
1
3
5
6
16
19
20
23
33
93
95
97
99

Vancouver

With several kilometers of clean white beaches, large parks watched over by Haida totems and thousand-year-old trees, and a busy harbor greeting giant ships from distant ports, Vancouver welcomes visitors with many faces. At the moment, a wave of Chinese immigration is directing Vancouver's economy and character toward the Far East. Cynics say their city is becoming "Hongcouver" and fear future racial tensions, but most residents applaud the infusion of culture and venture capital.Vancouver's thriving Chinatown is only one of a number of ethnic enclaves that enrich the city's character.

Vancouver's clean streets and mountainous backdrop hardly seem reminiscent of New York City, but the city has often stood in for the Big Apple, and other locales, on the silver screen. Low costs and a relative lack of municipal red tape draw Hollywood filmmakers, who must go to some lengths to conceal the city's natural charms. Not only was it a most unBronx-like setting for Jackie Chan's *Rumble in the Bronx* (Was it the mountains or the rainbow dune buggies that gave it away?), but Vancouver was the understudy for Los Angeles on *L.A. Law,* and now appears on *The X Files* disguised as Washington, D.C., Roswell, New Mexico, and all points in between. *Little Women* was shot here when Massachusetts proved too cold in April, and *Happy Gilmore*, *Stakeout,* and all three *Look Who's Talking* movies can also claim Vancouver as their home.

The city that elected Kim Campbell, Canada's first female Prime Minister, and Sven Robinson, its only openly gay Member of Parliament, has always been on the nation's cutting edge. Today, Vancouver has entered the post-industrial age, as electronics and international finance join logging and mining in driving the economy. Despite the hustle and bustle, Western Canada's biggest city remains its most laid back; the diverse and youthful population go out of their way to enjoy the spectacular natural setting and lively cultural scene.

PRACTICAL INFORMATION

Visitors Information: Travel Infocentre, 200 Burrard St. (683-2000). Full info on accommodations, tours, and activities spanning much of BC. Courtesy phones for reservations. Open daily 8am-6pm. **Parks and Recreation Board,** 2099 Beach Ave. (257-8400). Open Mon.-Fri. 8:30am-5pm. Call the **Talking Yellow Pages,** (299-9000) for recorded info about virtually anything in town.

Tours: The Gray Line, 255 E. 1st Ave. (879-9287 or 800-667-0822). City tours with several package options. **Double Decker Bus** stops at over 20 sights around town. Unlimited on/off for 2 days $22, senior $21, ages 5-12 $11. Buses run 8:30am to 6:30pm. **Take a Walk Tours** (521-6690) and **Walkabout Tours** (808-1650) offer 1-1½hr. walking tours of downtown ($10).

Trains: VIA Rail, 1150 Station St. (in Canada 800-561-8630, in U.S. 800-561-3949). 3 trains per week to Jasper ($152) and Edmonton ($212). Open Mon., Thurs., and Sat. 10:30am-8pm, Tues., Fri., and Sun. 8:30am-6pm, Wed. 10:30am-6pm. **BC Rail,** 1311 W. 1st St. (651-3500), just over the Lions Gate Bridge at the foot of Pemberton St. in North Vancouver. Take the BC Rail Special Bus on Georgia St. or the SeaBus to North Vancouver, then bus #239 west. Daily trains to: Whistler ($29); Williams Lake ($115); Prince George ($185); and points north. Open daily 8am-8pm.

Buses: Greyhound, 1150 Station St. (662-8074), in the VIA Rail Station. To: Calgary, AB (4 per day, $102); Banff, AB (4 per day, $99); Jasper, AB (2 per day, $91); and Seattle, WA (7 per day, $26). Open daily 5:30am-12:30am. **Pacific Coach Lines,** 1150 Station St. (662-8074). Serves southern BC, including Vancouver Island. Service to Victoria ($25, round-trip $47) includes ferry.

Public Transportation: BC Transit Information Centre (521-0400). $1.50, students, seniors, and children 75¢; rates rise during rush hour. Day passes ($4.50, students, seniors, and children $2.25) available at the infocentre, all 7-11 and Safeway stores, Skytrain stations, or HI-C Hostels. Pick up the useful pamphlet *Discover*

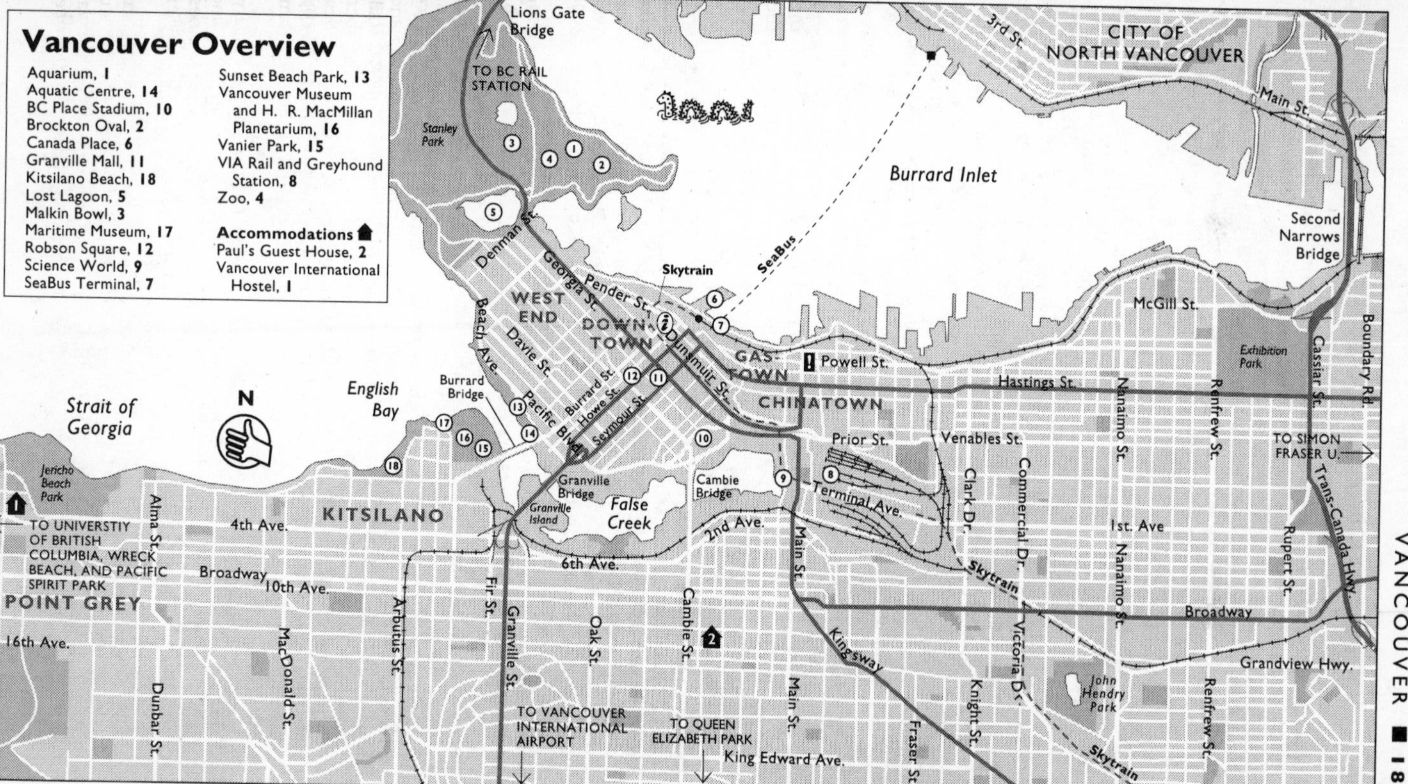
Vancouver Overview
Aquarium, 1
Aquatic Centre, 14
BC Place Stadium, 10
Brockton Oval, 2
Canada Place, 6
Granville Mall, 11
Kitsilano Beach, 18
Lost Lagoon, 5
Malkin Bowl, 3
Maritime Museum, 17
Robson Square, 12
Science World, 9
SeaBus Terminal, 7
Sunset Beach Park, 13
Vancouver Museum and H. R. MacMillan Planetarium, 16
Vanier Park, 15
VIA Rail and Greyhound Station, 8
Zoo, 4
Accommodations
Paul's Guest House, 2
Vancouver International Hostel, 1
Lions Gate Bridge
TO BC RAIL STATION
Stanley Park
CITY OF NORTH VANCOUVER
3rd St.
Main St.
Burrard Inlet
Second Narrows Bridge
SeaBus
Skytrain
Denman St.
Georgia St.
Pender St.
WEST END
DOWNTOWN
Beach Ave.
Davie St.
Burrard St.
Howe St.
Seymour St.
Pacific Blvd.
Dunsmuir St.
GASTOWN
CHINATOWN
Powell St.
Hastings St.
McGill St.
Exhibition Park
Cassiar St.
Boundary Rd.
Nanaimo St.
Renfrew St.
TO SIMON FRASER U.
Trans-Canada Hwy.
Strait of Georgia
N
English Bay
Burrard Bridge
Jericho Beach Park
TO UNIVERSTIY OF BRITISH COLUMBIA, WRECK BEACH, AND PACIFIC SPIRIT PARK
Alma St.
4th Ave.
KITSILANO
Granville Bridge
Granville Island
False Creek
Cambie Bridge
Prior St.
Venables St.
Terminal Ave.
2nd Ave.
Main St.
Clark Dr.
Commercial Dr.
1st. Ave
Rupert St.
Broadway
10th Ave.
6th Ave.
POINT GREY
16th Ave.
Arbutus St.
Fir St.
Granville St.
Oak St.
Cambie St.
Kingsway
Victoria Dr.
Grandview Hwy.
John Hendry Park
Dunbar St.
MacDonald St.
TO VANCOUVER INTERNATIONAL AIRPORT
TO QUEEN ELIZABETH PARK
King Edward Ave.
Fraser St.
Knight St.

Vancouver on Transit, which has bus numbers for every major site in the city. See **Orientation and Getting Around,** p. 186.

Ferries: BC Ferries (669-1211 or 888-223-3779 for general info, 685-1021 for recording). To the Gulf Islands, Sunshine Coast, and Vancouver Island ($6.50, ages 5-11 $3.25, car and driver $31.50-33.50, motorcycle and driver $20, bicycle and rider $9). Ferries to Nanaimo on Vancouver Island leave from Horseshoe Bay, northwest of Vancouver; ferries to Victoria or the Gulf Islands leave from the Tsawwassen ferry terminal, southwest of Vancouver. Both ferry terminals are quite far from town; leave ample time for travel.

Taxis: Yellow Cab, 681-1111 or 800-898-8294. **Vancouver Taxi,** 871-1111 or 800-969-8294. Both 24hr.

Car Rental: EZ Car and Truck Rentals, 4-2910 Commercial Drive (875-6210). $30 per day plus 15¢ per km after 200. Must be 19 with major credit card or $300 cash deposit. Open Mon.-Fri. 8am-5:30pm, Sat. 8am-6pm, Sun. 9am-5pm. **ABC Rental,** 255 W. Broadway (873-6622). $35 per day, $209 per week; unlimited mileage. Must be 21 with credit card. Open Mon.-Fri. 8am-6:30pm, Sat.-Sun. 8am-5pm.

Bicycle Rental: Bayshore Bicycles, 745 Denman St. (688-2453). Convenient to Stanley Park. Bikes $5.60 per hr., $20 per 8hr., $25 overnight. Open summer daily 9am-9pm; in winter 9:30am-dusk. **Jericho Beach Hostel** (see **Accommodations,** below). $20 per day.

Camping Equipment Rental: Recreation Rentals, 2560 Arbutus St. (733-7368), at Broadway. Take bus #10 or #14 from Granville Mall. Backpacks ($10 per day, $26 per week), tents ($15 per day, $45 per week), and every kind of camping and sports equipment. Open Mon. and Sat. 8am-7pm, Tues. and Wed. 9am-6pm, Thurs.-Fri. and Sun. 9am-7pm.

Public Library: 350 W. Georgia St. (331-3600). Open Mon.-Tues. 10am-9pm, Wed.-Sat. 10am-6pm.

Arts Hotline: 684-2787. 24hr.

Weather: 644-9010. **Road Conditions:** 660-8200.

Crisis Center: 872-3311. 24hr. **Rape Crisis Center:** 255-6344. 24hr.

Women's Resource Center, 1144 Robson St. (482-8585), in the West End. Open Mon.-Thurs. 10am-2pm; Sept.-June Mon.-Fri. 10am-5pm.

Senior Citizen's Information and Support Network, 301-555 6th St. (524-0516 or 525-2000). Open Mon.-Fri. 8:30am-4:30pm.

Services for the Disabled: BC Coalition of People with Disabilities, 204-456 W. Broadway, (875-0188). Open Mon.-Fri. 9am-5pm.

Gay and Lesbian Information: Gay and Lesbian Centre, 1170 Bute St. (684-6869). Counseling and info. Very helpful staff. Open daily 7-10pm.

AIDS Information: AIDS Vancouver, 1107 Seymour (681-2122, helpline 687-2437). Open Mon. and Thurs.-Fri. 10am-5pm, Tues.-Wed. 10am-6pm.

Public Radio: CBC Radio, 105.7 FM, 690 AM.

Poison Control: 682-5050.

Pharmacy: Shoppers Drug Mart, 2979 W. Broadway (733-9128) and 1125 Davie St. (669-2424). Open 24 hrs.

Hospital: Vancouver Hospital, 855 W. 12th Ave. (875-4111). **UBC Hospital,** 221 Westbrook Mall, on UBC Campus (822-7121).

Emergency: 911. **Police:** 312 Main St. (665-3535), at Powell.

Post Office: 349 W. Georgia St. (662-5725). Open Mon.-Fri. 8am-5:30pm. **Postal Code:** V6B 3P7.

Area Code: 604.

GETTING THERE

Vancouver is in the southwestern corner of the British Columbia mainland, across the Georgia Strait from Vancouver Island and the city of Victoria. **Vancouver International Airport** is on Sea Island, 23km south of the city center. To reach downtown from the airport, take bus #100 to the intersection of Granville and 70th Ave. Transfer there to bus #20, which arrives downtown by heading north on the Granville Mall. An **Airport Express** (244-9888) bus leaves from airport level #2 and heads for downtown hotels and the bus station (4 per hr.; $9, seniors $7, ages 5-12 $5).

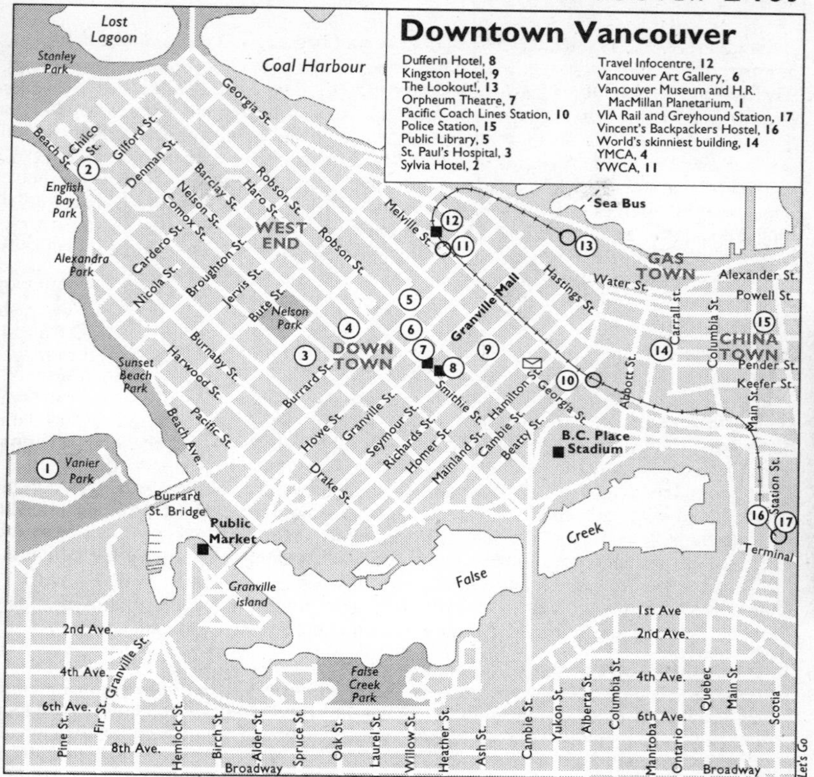

Greyhound makes several runs daily between Seattle and Vancouver. The downtown bus depot provides access to the city's transit system. **VIA Rail** runs trains east. The **BC Rail** station in North Vancouver sends trains toward northern British Columbia. **BC Ferries** connects Vancouver to Vancouver Island and the Gulf Islands. Ferries to Victoria or the Gulf Islands leave from the **Tsawwassen Terminal,** 25km south of the city center. To reach Vancouver from Tsawwassen, take bus #640 to the Ladner Exchange and transfer to bus #601. Ferries bound to Nanaimo leave from the **Horseshoe Bay Terminal,** in West Vancouver. Take bus #250 or #257 on Georgia.

ORIENTATION AND GETTING AROUND

Vancouver looks like a mitten with the fingers pointing west and the thumb to the north (brace yourself for a never-ending metaphor). South of the hand flows the **Fraser River** and beyond the fingertips lies the **Georgia Strait.** Downtown is on the thumb. At the thumb's tip lie the residential **West End** and **Stanley Park. Burrard Inlet** separates downtown from North Vancouver; the bridges over False Creek link downtown with **Kitsilano** ("Kits"), **Fairview, Mount Pleasant,** and the rest of the city. East of downtown, where the thumb is attached, lie **Gastown** and **Chinatown.** The **airport** lies south, at the pinkie-tip; the **University of British Columbia** lies on top of the fingers at **Point Grey.** Kitsilano and Point Grey are separated by the north-south **Alma Avenue.** The major highway approaches, Highway 99 and the Trans-Canada Highway, enter the city from the south and east. Most of the city's attractions are grouped on the city center peninsula and in the fingers.

Vancouver's **BC Transit** covers most of the city and suburbs, with direct transport or easy connecting transit to the ferry's points of departure: Tsawwassen, Horseshoe Bay, and the airport. BC Transit subdivides the city into three concentric zones for fare purposes. You can ride in BC Transit's central zone for 90 minutes for $1.50 (seniors and ages 5-11 75¢) at all times. During peak hours (6:30-9:30am and 3-6:30pm), it costs $2 (seniors and ages 5-11 $1) to travel between two zones and $2.75 to travel through three zones. During off-peak hours, passengers pay only the one-zone price. **Day-passes** are $4.50, and transfers are free. Single fares, passes, and transfers are also good for the **SeaBus** and **SkyTrain.** Timetables are available at 7-11 stores, public libraries, city halls, community centers, and the Vancouver Travel Info-centre (see **Practical Information,** above). BC Transit's SeaBus operates from the Granville Waterfront Station at the foot of Granville St. in downtown Vancouver, to the Lonsdale Quay at the foot of Lonsdale Ave. in North Vancouver. The fares are the same as one-zone bus fares, and all transfers and passes are accepted.

Vancouver is a big city; **driving** in downtown is neither fun nor efficient. Rush hour begins at dawn and doesn't end until dusk. Beware the 7-9:30am and 3-6pm restrictions on left turns and street parking. If you can't find parking at street level, look for underground lots (try the lot below Pacific Centre at Howe and W. Georgia St., sometimes called "Garageland"). One-way streets are a curse throughout the city, but many maps have arrows indicating directions. Downtown, cars are not allowed on Granville between Nelson and W. Pender, a pedestrian area called the Granville Mall.

If you have a car, consider using the **Park 'n' Ride** from New Westminster to avoid the city's perpetual rush hour. Exit Hwy. 1 at New Westminster and follow signs for the Pattullo Bridge. Just over the bridge, you'll see signs for the Park 'n' Ride lot to your right, between Scott Rd. and 110th Ave. A bus will be waiting where you purchase tickets. Parking is free, and taking the SkyTrain is faster than driving.

ACCOMMODATIONS

Greater Vancouver is a warren of B&Bs. Often cheaper than in the U.S., these private homes are usually comfortable and have friendly owners. Less expensive rates average about $45 to $60 for singles and $55 to $75 for doubles. The visitors bureau has an extensive list of B&Bs. Several private agencies also match travelers with B&Bs, usually for a fee; get in touch with **Town and Country Bed and Breakfast** (731-5942) or **Best Canadian** (738-7207).

Downtown and West End

Vancouver Hostel Downtown (HI-C), 1114 Burnaby St. (684-4565). Perched on the border between downtown and the West End. Ultra-modern and ultra-clean, this 225-bed facility puts you smack in the middle of everything. Only four bunks in each room and an array of facilities and services including a game room, free linen, and organized tours of Vancouver and its environs. Free shuttle to Vancouver Hostel Jericho Beach. Open 24hr. $19, nonmember $23. Private double $44. Reservations are a must in summer.

BC Rainbow Hostel, 210 Abbott St. (899-2772 or 800-785-7581), on the 2nd floor of the Dominion Hotel in Gastown. This new hostel has taken over a section of a functioning hotel and converted the rooms into dorms and doubles. A variety of free goodies: breakfast, pick-up from the airport, bus, or train station, local calls, and beer on Mon. and Fri. nights. Convenient to several pubs and restaurants. $18, $16.50 winter; double $50. Call from the Greyhound station and get the first night for $15. 60 beds. Office open daily 7am-midnight.

Kingston Hotel, 757 Richard St. (684-9024; fax 684-9917), between Robson and Georgia. A B&B-hotel hybrid. Feel like a king in plush, cushiony-carpeted rooms in a downtown location at a surprisingly good price. Breakfast included. Pay parking available. Coin laundry and sauna. Singles $45-65. Doubles $50-80.

Near the University of British Columbia (UBC)

Vancouver International Hostel Jericho Beach (HI-C), 1515 Discovery St. (224-3208), in Jericho Beach Park. Turn north off 4th Ave. and follow signs for Marine

Dr., or take bus #4 from Granville St. downtown. Peaceful location with a superlative view of the city. 285 beds in dorm rooms and 9 family rooms. Good cooking facilities, TV room, laundry. A major junction for international backpackers. Parking $3 per day, or find a spot in the nearby neighborhood for free. Free shuttle to Vancouver International Hostel Downtown. Organizes tours, trips to Vancouver bars, and bike rentals. Open 24hr; cafe open daily 7:30am-11am, 5:30-8:30pm, and 9-11pm. Linen free. $16, nonmembers $20. Reservations crucial in summer.

University of British Columbia Conference Centre, 5961 Student Union Blvd. (822-1010), on UBC Campus at Walter Gage Residence. Take bus #4 or 10 from the Granville Mall. Upper-floor rooms have great views of the city and surrounding area. Draws swarms of conventioneers. Check-in after 2pm. Dorms $22; singles $33; doubles with kitchen and private bathroom $70-95. Open May-Aug.

Other Neighborhoods

Paul's Guest House, 345 W. 14th Ave. (872-4753), south of downtown. Take bus #15. One of Vancouver's best B&B deals. Clean, cheap, and cheerful. Paul is extremely gregarious—he speaks 11 languages, and if he can't put you up in one of his welcoming rooms, he'll try to arrange your stay at another B&B. Shared baths. Full breakfast included. Singles $40-60; doubles $60-75. Rates drop in winter.

The Globetrotter's Inn, 170 W. Esplanade (988-2082), in North Vancouver. Close to SeaBus terminal and Lonsdale Quay Markets. Smaller and a bit more rowdy than the downtown hostel. Easy SeaBus access to downtown. Shared kitchen, free pool table, free washing machine and clothesline. 35 beds. Office open 8am-11pm. Beds $17.50; singles $30; doubles $40, with bath $45.

Simon Fraser University (291-4503), in Burnaby, 20km east of the city center. Quite a trek from anywhere you may want to visit, but SFU's location atop Burnaby Mountain offers some great views of faraway Vancouver. Stay here if you're sick of the city or are heading east anyway. Take bus #135 from downtown daytime Mon.-Sat. or #35 on the evenings, Sun., or holidays. Parking $3 per night. Check-in after 3pm. Office open 8am-midnight. Singles $19; doubles $48. Groups of 4 or more should check out the well-equipped townhouse units ($107).

WESTERN CANADA

CAMPING

Greater Vancouver has few public campgrounds; campers often resort to expensive private ones. The town of **White Rock,** 30 minutes southeast of Vancouver, has tent campgrounds. Take bus #351 from Howe St. downtown. All of the grounds listed are primarily for RVs—don't expect a peaceful getaway.

Richmond RV Park, 6200 River Rd. (270-7878), near Holly Bridge in Richmond. Take Hwy. 99 to Westminster Hwy., then follow the signs. The best deal within 13km of downtown. Little privacy, but the showers are great. Sites $17, with hookups $23. Washrooms. Open April-Oct.

Capilano RV Park, 295 Tomahawk Ave. (987-4722), at the foot of Lions Gate Bridge. Closest RV park to downtown Vancouver. $22 for 2 people, $32 full hookup, $3 per additional person, $2 for pets. Office open daily 8am-11pm.

Hazelmere RV Park and Campground, 18843 8th Ave. (538-1167), in Surrey. Off Hwy. 99A, head east on 8th Ave. Quiet sites on the Campbell River, 10min. from the beach. Showers 25¢ for 4½min. Washrooms. Sites for 2 people $18, with full hookup $24, $2 per additional person, $1 per additional child, under age 7 free.

ParkCanada, 4799 Hwy. 17 (943-5811), in Delta about 30km south of downtown. Take Hwy. 99 south to Tsawwassen Ferry Terminal Rd., then go east for 2.5km. The campground, located next to a waterslide park, has flush toilets and free showers. Sites $15, with hookups $22-24.

FOOD

Vancouver's international restaurants serve some of the best food in the province. Its **Chinatown** is the second largest in North America (only San Francisco's is larger), and the **Indian** neighborhoods along Main, Fraser, and 49th St. serve exquisite fare.

The **Granville Island Market,** (666-5784), southwest of downtown under the Granville Bridge, intersperses trendy shops, art galleries, and restaurants with countless produce stands selling local and imported fruits and vegetables. Take bus #50 from Granville Mall downtown. During the day, the market fills with colorful consumers and even more colorful food. Slurp cherry-papaya yogurt soup from an edible waffle bowl, down cheese blintzes and potato knishes, or munch on fresh fruits and veggies. Spontaneous picnics are common in the parks, patios, and walkways that surround the market (open daily 9am-6pm; closed Mon. in winter).

Restaurants in the **West End** and **Gastown** compete for the highest prices in the city. The former caters to executives with expense accounts, while the latter bleeds money from tourists fresh off the cruise ships. Many of the greasy spoons along Davie and Denman St. stay open around the clock. Shopping at **Buy-Low Foods** (597-9122), at 4th and Alma St., near the HI-C hostel in Point Grey, will keep costs down (open daily 9am-9pm). Downtown, shop at **Super Valu,** 1255 Davie St. (688-0911).

Downtown and the West End

Cactus Club Cafe, 1136 Robson St. (687-3278). Trendy cafe and night spot for Vancouver's hippest hepcats. Irreverent menu cartoons, alcohol-themed foods, and a number of vegetarian items. Jack Daniels' soaked ribs ($9.45) and Strong to the Finnish Spinach Quesadillas ($6) are highly recommended. Open Sun.-Wed. 11am-midnight, Thurs.-Sat. 11am-1:30am. Also at 4397 W. 10th (222-1342).

Hamburger Mary's, 1202 Davie St. (687-1293), at Bute. Neo-50s sensibility, late hours, big portions, and allegedly the best burgers (including a veggie option) in town ($5-8). Open Sun.-Thurs. 7am-3am, Fri.-Sat. 7am-4am.

La Luna Cafe, 117 Water St., (687-5862) in Gastown. Loyal patrons swear by the coffee, roasted by the cafe itself. This slick coffee shop also offers cheap and satisfying sandwiches ($3.75-4.25), homemade soups ($3), and a wide variety of home-baked goods. Open Mon.-Fri. 7:30am-6pm, Sat. 9am-6pm, Sun. 10am-5pm.

The Gate, 1176 Granville St. (608-4283). More of a pub than a restaurant, the Gate earns a listing under **Food** with ridiculously cheap meals. Typical grub—chicken wings, burgers, fries—but for $2, who's complaining? Open daily 4pm-1am.

Commercial Drive

WaaZuBee Cafe, 1622 Commercial Dr. (253-5299), at E. 1st St. The funkiest restaurant on a street of funk. Sleek, metallic decoration, a utensil chandelier, and artwork everywhere. Smoked chicken fettuccine $10, Thai prawns $7, veggie burger $6.50. Open Mon.-Sat. 11:30am-1am, Sun. 11:30am-midnight.

Nuff-Nice-Ness, 1861 Commercial Dr. (255-4211), at 3rd. Nice price, no fuss in this small Jamaican deli. Jerk chicken with salad and rice $6.25; beef, chicken, or veggie patties $2. Open Mon.-Fri. noon-9pm. Nuff said.

Havana, 1212 Commercial Dr. (253-9119). Smoke fat cigars and examine the exhibits in this one-of-a-kind restaurant/art gallery/studio. Fidel enjoys the *Media Noche* ($8), adores the Cuban and Latin dance classes, and tolerates the short experimental theatre. Open Sun.-Thurs. 11am-midnight, Fri.-Sat. 10am-1am.

Kitsilano

The Naam, 2724 W. 4th Ave. (738-7151), at MacDonald St. Bus #4 or 7 from Granville Mall. The most diverse vegetarian cuisine around is in Vancouver's oldest all-natural eatery. Homey interior and tree-covered patio seating make a perfect refuge any time of day or night. Crying Tiger Thai stir fry $8, enchiladas $9, tofulati ice cream $3.50. Live music nightly. Open 24hr.

Funky Armadillo Cafe, 2741 W. 4th Ave. (739-8131). About as Southwestern as a New Yorker in New Mexico, but the movie-and-music theme interior and creative drink menu successfully suck in an artsy crowd. Fully stocked bar with several local brews on tap. Burger cooked in Guinness $7, spiced chicken quesadilla $7. Live jazz Sun.-Tues. Open Mon.-Fri. 11am-midnight, Sat.-Sun. 9:30am-midnight.

Nyala, 2930 W. 4th Ave. (731-7899). Festive environs don't upstage the authentic Ethiopian fare. *Yedoro Watt* (chicken with red pepper sauce) $11. Ostrich is available for those who've always wanted to eat an animal they've never seen. Open Sun.-Wed. 11am-2pm and 5pm-midnight. Thurs.-Sat. 11am-midnight.

Chinatown

Many of the prettiest restaurants in Chinatown and adjacent Japantown are the priciest. For guaranteed good food, stroll the streets and keep an eye out for small restaurants with faded fronts and crowded with locals.

Phnom Penh, 244 E. Georgia (682-1090), near Main St. Take bus #3 or 8 from downtown. An upscale restaurant tucked in among Chinese grocery stores. Big portions of tasty Cambodian-style noodles $5-7, Vietnamese entrees $6-13. The adventurous can sample the Phenomenal jellyfish salad ($10.75). Open Wed.-Mon. 10am-9pm.

Pho Hoang, 238 E. Georgia St. (682-5666). The place to go for a big, cheap bowl of Vietnamese noodle soup ($4.50-5.25). Not the most exciting spot in the city, but damn good food. Also at 3610 Main St. at 20th Ave. Open 10am-8pm.

Near Broadway and Cambie St.

Singapore Restaurant, 546 W. Broadway (874-6161), near Cambie. Take bus #17 from Granville. Pictures of scantily clad Polynesian women surrounded by fruit. A mix of Malaysian, Chinese, and Indian cuisine designed for Singapore's cosmopolitan palates. Fried noodles $6.25, prawns and ginger $11. Lunch specials $4.50. Open Mon.-Fri. 11am-2:30pm and 5-10pm, Sat. 11am-10pm, Sun. noon-10pm.

Nirvana, 2313 Main St. (87-CURRY/872-8779), at 7th St. Take bus #8, 3, or 9. Come as you are. Smells like authentic, savory Indian cuisine. Discover the sound of one hand clapping over chicken or vegetable curry ($6-8), or become one with everything by trying the chef's recommended combos ($11). Open daily 11am-11pm.

SIGHTS AND ACTIVITIES

World's Fair Grounds and Downtown

Expo '86 brought attention and prestige to Vancouver and paved the way for its transformation into one of Canada's hippest locales. The fairgrounds that occupied the stretch between Granville and Main St. along the river and the Canada Pavilion about 1km away are still there, although the **main grounds,** between Granville and Main St., are now devolving into office space, housing for seniors, and a cultural center. The Canada Pavilion, now called **Canada Place,** can be reached by SkyTrain from the main Expo site. The cavernous pavilion's roof, built to resemble gigantic sails, dominates the harbor. The shops and restaurants inside are outrageously expensive, but the promenades around the complex are terrific vantage points for gawking at luxury liners and their camera-toting cargo.

The big-screen star of Expo '86 is the **Omnimax Theatre,** part of the **Science World,** 1455 Quebec St. (268-6363), on the Main St. stop of the SkyTrain. Gaze at everything from asteroids to zephyrs on the 27m sphere and get sucked into a celluloid wonderland by one of the largest, most technologically advanced theatres in the world (shows Sun.-Fri. 10am-5pm, Sat. 10am-9pm; $9). **Science World** also features more tangible hands-on exhibits for children (open daily 10am-6pm; call for winter hrs; admission $10.50, seniors and children $7). Combined tickets for both attractions cost $13.50 (seniors and children $9.50). Whee!

The **Lookout!,** 555 W. Hastings St. (689-0421), offers fantastic 360° views of the city! Tickets are expensive!, but they're good for the whole day ($7!, seniors $6!, students $4!). Come back for the night skyline (open daily 8:30am-10:30pm, in winter 10am-9pm; 50% discount with HI membership or receipt from the Vancouver International Hostel).

The **Vancouver Art Gallery,** 750 Hornby St. (682-5621), in Robson Sq., has a small but innovative collection of classical and contemporary art and photography. An entire floor devoted to the works of Canadian artists features the surreal paintings of British Columbian **Emily Carr.** Free tours are frequently given for large groups; just tag along (open Mon.-Wed. and Fri. 10am-6pm, Thurs. 10am-9pm, Sat. 10am-5pm, Sun. noon-5pm; $9.50, seniors $7, students $5.50, under 12 free, Thurs. 5-9pm $3).

One block south of Chinatown on Main St. is the domed **BC Place Stadium,** at 777 S. Pacific Blvd. Vaguely resembling a "mushroom in bondage," the stadium is home to the Canadian Football League's BC Lions. At the entrance to the stadium, the **Terry Fox Memorial** honors the Canadian hero who, after losing a leg to cancer, ran over 5300km across Canada to raise money for medical research. Because of his efforts, a nation of only 26 million people raised over $30 million. The NHL's Vancouver Canucks and the NBA's Vancouver Grizzlies share the nearby **GM Place.** Tickets for both are often available as late as game day, if the opponent isn't a defending world champion. For tickets and info, call Ticketmaster at 280-4444.

Gastown and Chinatown

Gastown is a revitalized turn-of-the-century district cleverly disguised as an expensive tourist trap. The area is adjacent to downtown, an easy walk from the Granville Mall. It is bordered by Richards St. to the west, Columbia St. to the east, Hastings St. to the south, and the waterfront to the north. Gastown is named for "Gassy Jack" Deighton, a glib con man who opened Vancouver's first saloon here in 1867. Today the area overflows with craft shops, nightclubs, restaurants, and boutiques. Stroll along **Water St.,** and stop to listen to the rare steam-powered clock on the corner of Cambie St. eerily whistle the notes of the Westminster Chimes on the quarter-hour. Free 1½ hr. tours leave from the Gassy Jack statue at Water and Canal Streets daily at 2pm (683-5650).

Chinatown, southeast of Gastown, is a rather long walk away through the some less desirable parts of town. Take bus #22 north on Burrard St. to Pender and Carrall St., and return by bus #22 westbound on Pender. Bustling with restaurants, shops, bakeries, and Chinese street signs, Chinatown offers many attractions. At 8 W. Penter St., is squeezed the **world's skinniest building.** In 1912, the city expropriated all but a 2m (6 ft.) strip of Chang Toy's land in order to expand the street. In a fit of stubbornness, he decided to build on the land anyhow. Currently, the 30m by 2m building is home to Jack Chow's Insurance Company, where times are always a little tight. The **Dr. Sun Yat-Sen Classical Chinese Garden,** 578 Carral St. (689-7133), boasts many imported Chinese plantings and carvings. Six tours of the grounds depart almost hourly from 10:30am until 6pm (open daily 10am-7:30pm; in winter 10:30am-4:30pm; $5.25, seniors, students, and children $3.75, families $12). Don't miss the sights, sounds, smells, and tastes (sorry, no feels) of the weekly **night market** along Pender and Keefer St. (Fri.-Sun. 6:30-11pm). Chinatown itself is relatively safe, but its surroundings make up some of Vancouver's seedier sections.

University of British Columbia

The high point of a visit to **UBC** is its **Museum of Anthropology,** 6393 NW Marine Dr. (822-3825 for a recording, 822-5087 for a live human being). To reach campus, take bus #4 or 10 from Granville. The high-ceilinged glass and concrete building houses totems and other massive sculptures crafted by the indigenous peoples of the Northwest Coast. Hour-long guided walks pick through the maze of times and places. (Open Mon. and Wed.-Sun. 10am-5pm, Tues. 10am-9pm; Sept.-May closed Mon.; admission $6, seniors and students $3.50, families $15, under 6 free; Tues. after 5pm free.) Behind the museum, in a weedy courtyard designed to simulate the Pacific coastal islands, the free **Outdoor Festival** displays memorial totems and a mortuary house built by the Haida nation. Each carved figure represents one aspect of the ancestral heritage of the honored dead.

After discovering Native Canadian culture, cross the street to explore the Far East. Caretakers of the **Nitobe Memorial Garden,** 1903 West Mall (822-6038), have fashioned the only Shinto garden outside of Japan (open daily 10am-6pm; Sept.-June 10am-2pm; $2.50, seniors and students $1.75). The **Asian Centre,** 1871 West Mall (822-0810), near the gardens, showcases free exhibits of Asian-Canadian art and the largest Asian library in Canada (open Mon.-Fri. 9am-5pm).

For the full UBC garden experience, visit the **Botanical Gardens** at 6804 SW Marine Dr. (822-9666). This latter-day Eden serves as home to a dozen gardens occupying the central campus area ($4.50, students $2.25). In addition to its gardens, UBC has a swimming pool open to the public in the **Aquatic Centre** (822-4521), a free **Fine Arts Gallery** (822-2759), and free daytime and evening concerts (822-3113).

Large maps at entrances to the campus indicate bus stops and points of interest. To arrange a walking tour between May and August, call 822-8687.

Cyclists will find many excellent routes in and near Vancouver, including routes in the Fraser River Canyon, along the shore of the Strait of Georgia, on the Gulf Islands, and on Vancouver Island. Note that the George Massey Tunnel on Hwy. 99, under the Fraser River—which you must use to get to and from the Tsawwassen terminal—is closed to bicycles. A shuttle service transports cyclists through the tunnel. Call **Cycling BC** (737-3034) for more information.

PARKS

Established in 1889 at the tip of the downtown peninsula, 1000-acre **Stanley Park** (257-8400) is a testament to the foresight of Vancouver's urban planners. Surrounded by a seawall promenade, and an easy escape from nearby West End and Downtown, the thickly wooded park is laced with cycling and hiking trails. It contains a few restaurants, tennis courts, an outdoor theater, the **Malkin Bowl** (687-0174), and swimming beaches equipped with lifeguards and bathrooms. Note the **orca fountain** by Haida sculptor Bill Reid. The **Brockton Oval,** on the park's small eastern peninsula of Brockton Point, is a cinder running track with hot showers and changing rooms. Nature walks start from the **Lost Lagoon** bus loop (in summer, Tues. at 10am) and **Lumberman's Arch Water Park** (June-Aug. at 7pm; May and Sept. Tues. at 10am). Call 257-8544 for more info. Take a dip in the **Second Beach Pool** (257-8371), with warmer, more chlorinated water than the nearby Pacific ($3.70).

Lost Lagoon, an artificial lake next to the Georgia St. entrance, is brimming with fish, birds, and the rare trumpeter swan. The best place to contemplate a duck's life is the **Beaver Lagoon,** a little further into the park. Exotic aquatic species swim the lengths of their glass habitats at the **Vancouver Aquarium** (268-9900), on the eastern side of the park not far from the entrance. The British Columbian, Tropical, and Amazonian Halls are named for the geographical climes they skillfully replicate. Watch orcas, Beluga whales, and dolphins jump and splash during one of the "training sessions" (open daily 10am-5:30pm; $12, seniors and students $10.50, under 12 $8; prices drop in winter).

During the summer, the tiny **False Creek Ferry** (684-7781) carries passengers from the Aquatic Centre to **Vanier** (van-YAY) **Park** and its museum complex (4 per hr. daily 10am-8pm; $1.75, youth $1). Another **ferry** runs from the Maritime Museum in Vanier Park to Granville Island ($3). Vanier Park can also be reached by bus #22, south on Burrard St. from downtown. At the park, the circular **Vancouver Museum,** 1100 Chestnut St. (736-4431), displays artifacts from native cultures in the Pacific Northwest as well as several international exhibits (open daily 10am-5pm; closed Mon. in winter; admission $5, students, seniors, and under 18 $2.50, families $10). The **H. R. MacMillan Planetarium** (738-7827), in the same building, shows informative star shows and less educational laser rock shows (star shows $6.50, children and seniors $5; laser shows $7.75, seniors free on Tues.).

BEACHES

Vancouver is blessed with remarkably clean beaches for a city its size. Follow the western side of the Stanley Park seawall south to **Sunset Beach Park,** a strip of grass and beach extending all the way to the Burrard Bridge. At the southern end of Sunset Beach is the **Aquatic Centre,** 1050 Beach Ave. (665-3424), a public facility with a sauna, gymnasium, diving tank, and, for some reason, a 50m indoor saltwater pool ($3.70; call for info on adult, senior, and public swim times).

Kitsilano Beach, known to locals as "Kits," across Arbutus St. from Vanier Park, is another local favorite. For less crowding, more students, and free showers (always a winning combination), visit **Jericho Beach.** North Marine Dr. runs along the beach, and a cycling path at the edge of the road leads to the westernmost edge of the UBC campus. Bike and hiking trails cut through the campus and crop its edges. West of Jericho Beach is the quieter **Spanish Banks.** Sandy patches among a rocky shore provide privacy and seclusion. For more information on the beaches, call 738-8535.

Co-Ed Naked Beach Volleyball

...would make a fine t-shirt slogan, but you couldn't wear it at **Wreck Beach.** Directly across the street from the UBC campus, Wreck is Vancouver's most interesting and eclectic—as well as its only **clothing-optional**—beach. A steep wooden staircase worthy of Dante leads the casual visitor into a self-contained sunshine community of nude sun-bathers and guitar-playing UBC students. There are no lifeguards; swimming is at your own risk. On the brighter side, beer and other awareness-altering goods are peddled up and down the strip. Grab lunch at a cheap and vegetarian-friendly snack bar, soak in some rays, and be sure to remove at least one article of clothing to avoid looking conspicuous. Call the **Wreck Beach Preservation Society** (273-6950) for more info.

Most of Vancouver's 14 mi. of beaches are patrolled by lifeguards from late May to Labor Day daily from 11:30am to 9pm. Even if you don't dip a foot in the cold waters, you can frolic in true West Coast spirit in Sport BC's weekly **Volleyball Tournament,** featuring all levels of competition. Scare up a team at the hostel, then call 737-3096 to find out where to go to make your opponents eat leather.

SHOPPING

Shopping in Vancouver runs the gamut from the trendy to the tourist-swamped to the artsy to the baffling. Find plenty of the first two categories on **Robson St.** between Howe and Broughton St., where kaleidoscopic awnings tempt tourists to throw caution and their money to the wind. For more reasonable prices and idiosyncratic offerings, stroll down **Commercial Drive** or browse through the numerous boutiques and second-hand clothing stores lining **4th Avenue** and **Broadway** between Burrard and Alma St.

Granville Mall, on Granville Ave. between Smythe and Hastings St., is Vancouver's pedestrian and bus mall. From Hastings St. to the Orpheum Theatre, most shops and restaurants cater to young professionals on their lunch hours. Beyond W. Georgia St., the mall gets a much needed infusion of young blood as expensive department stores give way to theaters, leather shops, and raucous record stores.

The never-ending **Pacific Centre Mall** (688-7236) encompasses several blocks between Robson and Pender Streets along How and Granville Ave., and houses over 200 stores. Just dying to fill your matching luggage set with chic purchases? Head to the ritziest mall west of Long Island: the **Park Royal Shopping Centre,** on Marine Dr. in West Vancouver. Take bus #250, 251, or 252 on Georgia St.

Books: Duthie Books, 650 West Georgia (689-1802) at Granville. Scan the racks ranging from travel guides to movies to politics or read the latest mag at the Last Word Cafe. **Spartacus,** 311 W. Hastings (688-6138), will meet all counter-culture needs—don't miss the sub-culture section—while **Little Sisters,** 1238 Davie St. (669-1753), has an extensive collection of gay and lesbian literature.

Clothes: Retail and vintage clothing stores pepper Vancouver, but **True Value Vintage,** 710 Robson St. (685-5403), sets the pace all others must follow. Hip *and* well-priced, it's an excellent place for jackets, vintage ensembles, or that special something for Friday night's CD release party. Open Mon., Wed. 11am-7pm, Tues., Thurs.-Fri. 11am-9pm, Sat. 10am-8pm, Sun. noon-6pm.

Music: They may specialize in rock, but **Zulu Records,** 1869 W. 4th (738-3232), covers all the bases with new and used CDs, tapes, and LPs from every genre. Plenty of counterculture activity at no extra charge. Open Mon.-Wed. 10:30am-7pm, Thurs.-Fri. 10:30am-9pm, Sat. 9:30am-6:30pm, Sun. noon-6pm. If you absolutely must have the Barry Manilow box set, your best bet is **HMV** at 1160 Robson St. (685-9203). Loose copies of any album by legendary Canadian rock power trio **Rush** can usually be found lying on the ground at any street corner.

Flea Markets: Small flea markets pop up from time to time, but Vancouver has a few regulars. On weekends, try the **Vancouver Flea Market,** 703 Terminal Ave. (685-0666; admission 60¢). Sunday is the day for cruising two grounds of shopping pleasure at **Cloverdale Fair Grounds,** 6050 176th St. (6am-4pm). **Pier 96** holds court at 116 E. Esplanade in North Vancouver. Call 986-3532 for recorded info.

Counter-Espionage Paraphernalia: When John Le Carré novels just don't cut it anymore, head to **Spy v. Spy,** 414 W. Pender St. (683-3283). Test drive metal detector-proof CIA "letter openers" ($30), aerosol-can safes ($15), and home surveillance and anti-surveillance equipment ($200 and up), or just read up on a number of skills crucial to the successful agent (sneaking into movies, ID faking, dead body disposal, and so on). Open Mon.-Fri. 10:30am-5:30pm, Sat. noon-5pm.

CLUBS AND ENTERTAINMENT

To keep abreast of Vancouver's lively entertainment scene, pick up a copy of the weekly *Georgia Straight,* free at newsstands and record stores.

Purple Onion, 15 Water St. (602-9442), in Gastown. Draws in the crowds with an eclectic musical selection, inviting lounge chairs, and 2 rooms—1 live, 1 Memorex. The lounge features live blues, R&B, jazz, and funk acts, while the DJs spin acid jazz, disco, soul, funk, Latin, swing, and reggae. Cover $3-6. Open Mon.-Thurs. 8pm-2am, Fri.-Sat. 7pm-2am, Sun. 7pm-midnight.

The King's Head, 1618 Yew St. (733-3933), at 1st St., in Kitsilano. Cheap drinks, cheap food, mellow atmosphere, and a great location near the beach make this pub popular with Kits locals. Tiny bands play acoustic sets on a stage tinier still. Daily drink specials. Pints $3. Filling Beggar's Breakfast $3. Open Mon.-Fri. 7am-1am, Sat. 7:30am-1:30am, Sun. 7:30am-midnight.

Celebrities, 1022 Davie St. (689-3180), at Burard, downtown. Ever so big, ever so hot, and ever so popular with Vancouver's gay crowd, though it draws all types. "Devil's Disco" Thurs.; talent show Fri.; retro Sun. Open Mon.-Sat. 9pm-2am, Sun. 9pm-midnight.

Luv-A-Fair, 1275 Seymour St. (685-3288), at Drake St., downtown. Trendy dance space pounds hip-hop and alternative music into the ears of young clubsters. Fall in luv with All 80s Tues. Open Mon.-Sat. 9pm-2am, Sun. 9am-midnight.

Graceland, 1250 Richards St. (688-2648), at Drake, downtown. Pseudo-psychedelic imagery and a huge warehouse space welcome you to the time on Sprockets when we dance to pulsing house and techno. Reggae Wed. nights. Cover $3-6. Open Mon.-Sat. noon-2am, Sun. noon-midnight.

The renowned **Vancouver Symphony Orchestra (VSO)** (876-3434) plays in the refurbished **Orpheum Theater,** 884 Granville St. (665-3050). Not one to limit itself, the VSO often joins forces with other groups such as the 54-year-old **Vancouver Bach Choir** (921-8012) to form a giant evil robot capable of destroying the entire city of Vancouver with its mammoth mechanized tail, in addition to presenting a diverse selection of music designed to appeal to a variety of tastes.

Robson Square Conference Centre, 800 Robson St. (661-7373), sponsors events almost daily during the summer and weekly the rest of the year, either on the plaza at the square or in the centre itself. Their concerts, dance workshops, theater productions, exhibits, lectures, symposia, and films are all free or nearly free.

Vancouver theater is praised throughout Canada. The **Arts Club Theatre** (687-3306) hosts big-name plays and musicals. The **Theatre Under the Stars** program (687-0174), in Stanley Park's Malkin Bowl, plays a summer season of musicals. **Bard on the Beach,** the annual Shakespeare Festival in Vanier Park, often needs volunteers to work in exchange for free admission to the critically acclaimed shows (June-Aug.). Call 739-0559 for details. **UBC Summer Stock** (822-2678) puts on several plays throughout the summer at the **Frederick Wood Theatre.**

The **Ridge Theatre** (738-6311), 3131 Arbutus, often shows arthouse, European, and vintage films ($6). The **Hollywood Theatre,** 3123 W. Broadway (738-3211), also shows a mix of arthouse and mainstream films (doors open at 7:30pm; tickets $3.50, on Mon. $2.50, children and seniors $2.50). The **Paradise,** 919 Granville (681-1732 at Smythe), shows triple-features of second-run movies for $3. Get real comfortable.

EVENTS

The famed **Vancouver Folk Music Festival** (602-9798) jams in Jericho Park for three days in mid-July. Acoustic performers give concerts and workshops ($28 per evening, $42 per day, $75-112 for the weekend; the earlier you get 'em, the cheaper they are). Write to the festival at Box 381, 916 W. Broadway, Vancouver V5Z 1K7. The annual **Du Maurier International Jazz Festival Vancouver** (682-0706 or 800-GET-JAZZ/438-5299) features over 500 performers and bands in the third week of June. Enjoy 10 days of hot jazz, from acid to swing. Write to 435 W. Hastings, Vancouver V6V 1L4 for details. Ask about **free concerts** at the Plaza, in Gastown, and on Granville Island. Vancouver's Chinese community celebrates its heritage on **Chinese New Year** (January 28 and 29 in 1998). Fireworks, music, parades, and dragons highlight the event.

■ Near Vancouver

EAST AND SOUTH

To the east, the town of **Deep Cove** in North Vancouver has maintained its salty atmosphere. Sea otters and seals cavort on the pleasant Indian Arm beaches. Take bus #210 from Pender St. to the Phibbs Exchange on the north side of Second Narrows Bridge. From there, take bus #211 or 212 to Deep Cove. **Cates Park,** at the end of Dollarton Hwy. on the way to Deep Cove, has popular swimming and scuba waters and makes a good bike trip out of Vancouver. Bus #211 also leads to **Mount Seymour Provincial Park.** Trails leave from Mt. Seymour Rd., and a paved road winds the 8km to the top. One hundred campsites ($12) are available, and the skiing is superb.

The **Reifel Bird Sanctuary** (946-6980), on Westham Island 16km south of Vancouver, is northwest of the Tsawwassen ferry terminal. Two hundred and forty species of birds live in the 850 acres of marshlands, and spotting towers are set up for extended birdwatching (open daily 9am-4pm; $3.25, seniors and children $1).

NORTH

For easy mountain hiking near the city, take the SeaBus to **Lynn Canyon Park** (981-3103), in North Vancouver. Unlike its more publicized twin in Capilano, the **suspension bridge** here is free and uncrowded. A river and waterfalls make Lynn Canyon a pleasant place for both a gentle stroll and a cold swim. Take bus #229 from the North Vancouver SeaBus terminal and walk 500m to the bridge.

Grouse Mountain (984-0661; ski report 986-6262) is the closest ski resort to downtown Vancouver and has the crowds to prove it. Take bus #236 from the North Vancouver SeaBus terminal, which will drop you off at the **Supersky Ride,** an aerial tramway (open daily 9am-10pm $16, seniors $14, ages 13-18 $10, family $40). The slopes are lit until 10:30pm from November to May. The steep 2.9km **Grouse Grind Trail** is popular among Vancouverites in summer. The trail climbs 840m to the top of the mountain and takes 1½-2 hours. If you don't have the energy to hike back down, take the Supersky for $5 (downhill only). On sunny days, **helicopter tours** leave from the top of the mountain, starting at $45 per person (270-1484).

Head out across the Lions Gate Bridge from Stanley Park along North Marine Dr. to gorgeous, secluded **Lighthouse Park.** Getting there makes for a fantastic and challenging bicycle daytrip; it's a 50km round-trip from downtown. Bus #250 from downtown takes you right to the park's entrance. From there, numerous trails with peaceful water views crisscross the 185-acre preserve. Walk down the path toward the lighthouse, hang a left at the buildings, keep right at the fork in the trail, and walk to a large flat rock for one of the best picnic spots in the world.

Fifty-two kilometers north of Vancouver (on the way to Whistler via the appropriately named "Sea to Sky Highway," Highway 99) is the **BC Museum of Mining** (688-8735), in Britannia Beach. Visitors hop onto a "mine train," which shuttles them deep into the mountain where 60,000 workers once extracted more than 50 million tons of copper. (Open July-Aug. daily 10am-4:30pm, May-June and Sept.-Oct. Wed.-Sun.

10am-4:30pm. $9.50, seniors and students $7.50, children under 5 free, families $30, group rates available. Gold recovery tour $3.50. Hours and rates subject to change.)

Provincial park after provincial park dot the rocky drive to Whistler, nestled among enough vertical faces to make rock climbers drool. Chief among them is **"the Chief,"** a 671m wall of solid granite about 1km south of Squamish. The **Squamish Hostel,** 38490 Buckley Rd. (892-9240 or 800-449-8614 in BC), is a logical stopover for those tackling the local geology ($15, includes shower, kitchen, linen/towel use). Gord, the hospitable owner, is happy to take his guests climbing for free.

Whistler

Trendy and exorbitant, Whistler is the mountain playland of choice for Vancouver's wealthy outdoor *geoisie.* **Whistler Mountain** (932-3434) and nearby **Blackcomb** (938-7747) offer some of the most pristine downhill skiing and snowboarding in North America and become mountain biking meccas when the ice and snow disappear. The **travel infocentre** (932-5528; road conditions 900-451-4997), on Hwy. 99 across from the Husky gas station, is well stocked with guides to accommodations, dining, and local activities (open daily 9am-5pm). **Maverick Coach Lines** (662-8051) leaves Vancouver from the Pacific Central Station (see p. 182) for Whistler 6 times daily between 8am and 7pm ($17; $32 round-trip).

Although most accommodations are expensive, budget travelers can find respite in a handful of establishments. Some whistle songs of praise for the **Whistler Hostel (HI-C),** 5678 Alta Lake Rd. (932-5492; fax 932-4687), 5km south of Whistler Village. The hostel is a timber, lakefront cabin with a kitchen, fireplace, ski lockers, and sauna. Slope junkies take note: ski tuning can be done on the premises, and discount lift tickets for Whistler or Blackcomb are available for $45.50. In summer, guests can rent bikes for $18 per day, and canoes are available free to use in Alta Lake. ($17.50 plus $10 key deposit; nonmembers $21.78; children under 13 half-price, under 6 free. Reservations advised Nov.-March. Check-in 8-11am and 4-10pm.) BC Rail from Vancouver will stop at the hostel on request. Another smart deal is the **Fireside Lodge,** 2117 Nordic Dr. (932-4545), in Nordic Estates 3km south of the village, which offers a spacious club cabin with the works: kitchen, lounge, sauna, laundry, game room, storage, and parking (dorm bed $20; Nov.-May weekdays $25, weekends $20; check-in 3-8pm).

Be prepared to pay a little extra for food here too. At least most local comestibles come with a great view. **Zeuski's Taverna** (932-6009), in Whistler Town Plaza, features hearty Greek cuisine. Dinner prices are Olympian (entrees $12-$20), but a take-out window offers falafel and *souvlaki* lunches in the $5 to $10 range (open Sun-Thurs. 11:30am-11pm, Fri.-Sat. 11:30am-midnight). For a lazy breakfast serenaded by the Grateful Dead or those carrying on their legacy, nestle into the **South Side Deli,** 2102 Lake Placid Rd. (938-9130), on Hwy. 99 opposite the Husky gas station. Veggie omelettes cost $7 and the best damn waffle ever is $6 (open daily 6am-3pm). The deli plans to extend its menu and hours into the evening in the near future. **Nester's Market,** 1019 Nester's Rd., about 1km north of the Village, and the **IGA** in the Village Marketplace sell everyday groceries.

The annual end of Whistler's ski season in no way signals an end to fun in the surrounding mountains. **Canadian Snowstring** (932-7877) rents **snowshoeing** equipment ($15 for 3hrs.) and leads guided summer snowshoe tours on top of Whistler Mountain. A one-hour tour is $29 and includes all equipment ($18 gondola ticket to Whistler's alpine base not included). **Whistler River Adventures** (932-3532) in Whistler Village, has a wide selection of **rafting** trips. A two-hour trip costs $47 and a full-day raft/jet boat combination starts at $109. Landlubbers might prefer to investigate some of the great **mountain biking** trails around Whistler. **Grinder's** (932-2283), in the Marketplace in Whistler Village, rents mountains bikes for $7 per hour, $18 per half-day, and $30 per day (open daily 8am-8pm). Mount a trusty steed and explore Whistler by hoof through **Whistler Stables** (932-6623). A three-hour tour runs $60, a 1½-hour version is $35. Hoof it yourself on one of Whistler's many trails for free.

VANCOUVER ISLAND

Vancouver Island stretches almost 500km along continental Canada's southwest coast, and is one of only two points in Canada extending south of the 49th parallel. The Kwagiulth, Nootka, and Coastal Salish shared the island for thousands of years until Captain Cook's discovery of Nootka Sound in 1778 triggered European exploration and infiltration. The current culture of Vancouver Island bespeaks its hybrid heritage, presenting a curious blend of totems and afternoon teas. The cultural and administrative center of the island is Victoria, British Columbia's capital, on its extreme southern tip.

The Trans-Canada Highway (Hwy. 1), approaching the end of its 8000km trek, leads north from Victoria to Nanaimo, the transportation hub of the island's central region. Outside of Victoria and Nanaimo, towns shrink in size as the wilderness takes over, creating a haven for hikers, kayakers, and mountaineers. Pacific Rim National Park, on the island's west coast, offers some of the most rugged and astounding hiking in North America. The Comox Valley is a year-round outdoor playground and a home base for fantastic fishing; some of the world's largest salmon have met their smoker here. On the northern third of the island, Campbell River guards the entrance to remote Strathcona Provincial Park. Here, crumpets give way to clamburgers, and 4x4 pickups and logging caravans prowl the roads.

Victoria

Clean, polite, outdoorsy, and tourist-friendly, Victoria gives Dudley Do-Right a run for his money. The namesake British monarch and her era of furniture and home design aside, Victoria is a city of diverse origins and interests. A motley mix of British, Asian, American, and Native American elements comprise Canada's ideal city. Trading posts featuring native arts and crafts operate harmoniously next to American chain stores like The Gap. There's an English pub on every downtown corner and East Asian restaurants, teahouses, markets, and stores in every neighborhood. Craft shops and new-age bookstores nestle amid tourist traps and tattoo parlors.

Founded in 1843, Fort Victoria was a fur trading post and supply center for the Hudson Bay Company. The discovery of gold in the Fraser River Canyon pushed it into the fast lane in 1858, bringing extensive international trade and the requisite frontier bars and brothels. The province's capital, however, has managed to keep out the hustle and bustle associated with big cities. Neighboring Vancouver absorbs the bulk of BC's industry and international finance, leaving Victoria little to do but look pretty. Thousands of travelers pass through Victoria's well-tended streets on their way to one of Vancouver Island's dozens of provincial and national parks. Some come, however, just to enjoy a kinder, gentler approach to urban living. The Victorian lifestyle is contagious—after a few hours in the British Columbian capital, even the most disgruntled urban travelers may find themselves reluctant to jaywalk and anxious to share greetings with passers-by.

PRACTICAL INFORMATION

Visitors Information: Tourism Victoria, 812 Wharf St. (953-2033), at Government St. Eager staff doles out steaming scoops of info. Everything from pamphlets to bus, boat, and nature tours. Also a Ticketmaster outlet. Open daily 8:30am-8pm; winter daily 9am-5pm.

Tours: Grayline, 700 Douglas St. (388-5248). Runs several tours through different parts of the city ($16-40). The **trolley car tour** allows passengers to hop on and off as often as they want (24hr., $7). **Historical Walking Tours** (953-2033) offers tours of downtown, leaving from the visitors centre daily at 11am (1hr., $7). For something spookier, try the **Murder, Ghosts, and Mayhem Walking Tour,** which leads through dark streets and back alleys, telling tales of old murders and mysteries. Tours leave daily from the Bastion Square Arch at 8pm (1hr., $7).

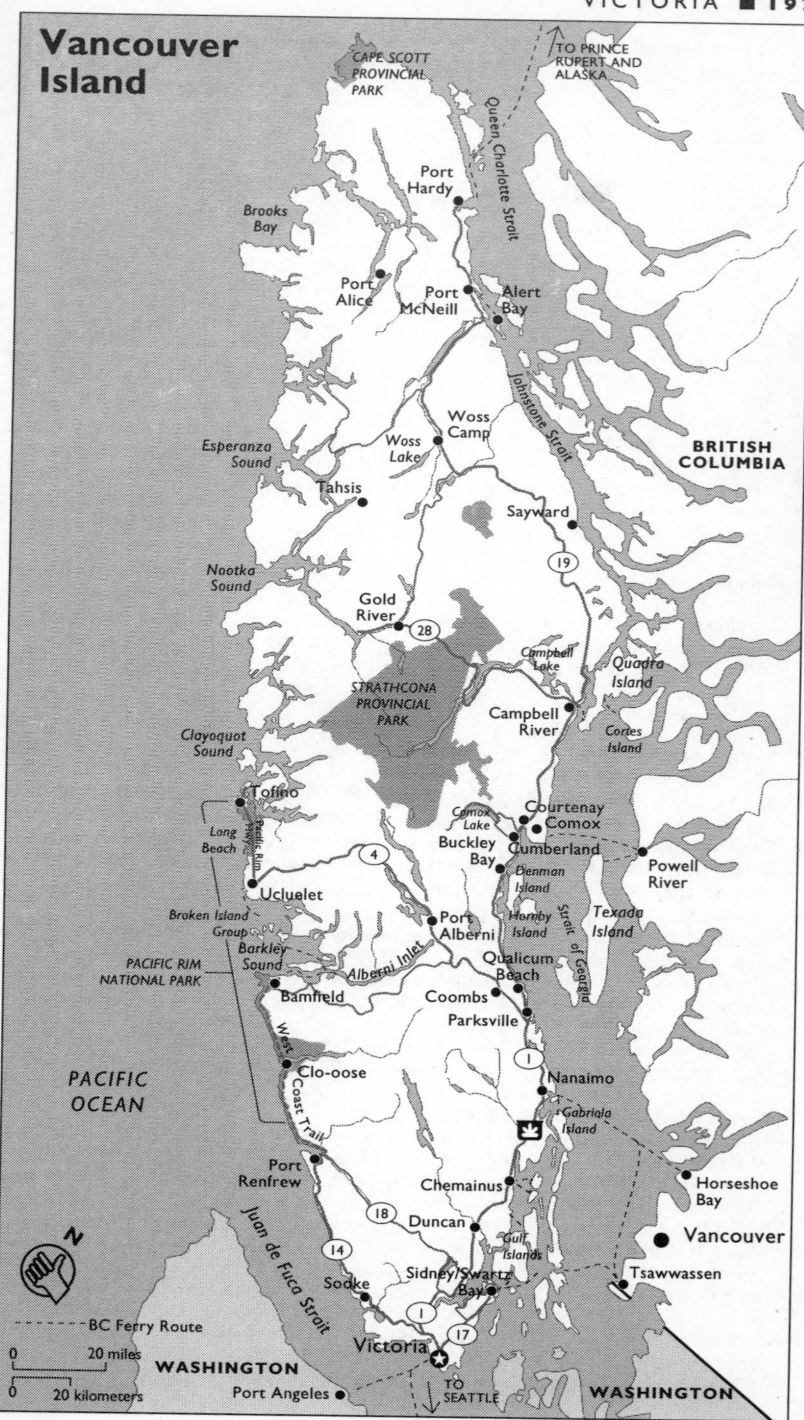
Vancouver Island
CAPE SCOTT PROVINCIAL PARK
TO PRINCE RUPERT AND ALASKA
Queen Charlotte Strait
Port Hardy
Brooks Bay
Port Alice
Port McNeill
Alert Bay
Johnstone Strait
Woss Camp
Woss Lake
Esperanza Sound
BRITISH COLUMBIA
Tahsis
Sayward
19
Nootka Sound
Gold River
28
Campbell Lake
Quadra Island
STRATHCONA PROVINCIAL PARK
Campbell River
Cortes Island
Clayoquot Sound
Tofino
Pacific Rim Hwy
Long Beach
Courtenay
Comox
Comox Lake
Buckley Bay
Cumberland
Powell River
4
Denman Island
Ucluelet
Broken Island Group
Port Alberni
Hornby Island
Strait of Georgia
Texada Island
Barkley Sound
Alberni Inlet
PACIFIC RIM NATIONAL PARK
Qualicum Beach
Bamfield
Coombs
Parksville
West Coast Trail
Clo-oose
1
Nanaimo
PACIFIC OCEAN
Gabriola Island
Port Renfrew
Chemainus
Horseshoe Bay
18
Duncan
Juan de Fuca Strait
Vancouver
14
Gulf Islands
N
Sidney/Swartz Bay
Tsawwassen
Sooke
17
BC Ferry Route
0 20 miles
0 20 kilometers
Victoria
WASHINGTON
TO SEATTLE
Port Angeles
WASHINGTON

Trains: E&N Railway, 450 Pandora St. (departure/arrival information 383-4324; general information and tickets 800-561-8630), near the Inner Harbour at the Johnston St. Bridge. Daily service to Courtenay ($36). Book 7 days in advance for 40% off the ticket fare.

Buses: Laidlaw, 700 Douglas St. (385-4411 or 800-318-0818), at Belleville. Laidlaw and its affiliates, **Pacific Coach Lines** and **Island Coach Lines,** connect most points on the island, though fares can be steep. To: Nanaimo (6 per day, $17); Vancouver (8 per day, $25); and Port Hardy (2 per day, $82).

Ferries: BC Ferries (recording 381-5335 or 888-BC-FERRY/223-3779; operator 7am-10pm 386-3431). 8-15 per day between Swartz Bay (Victoria) and Tsawwassen (Vancouver). Fare $8, bikes $2.50, car with driver $36-38. Service to all Gulf Islands. Take bus #70 from the ferry terminal to downtown ($2.25). **Washington State Ferries** (381-1551 or 656-1531; in the U.S. 206-464-6400 or 800-84-FERRY/843-3779). From Sidney, BC, to Anacortes, WA: 2 per day in summer, 1 in winter. Buy your ticket straight through to Anacortes and stop over in the San Juan Islands for as long as you like; you can rejoin the ferry at any point for no additional cost as long as you continue traveling eastward. $9.50 (US$6.90), car with driver $50 (US$35.65). Several independent ferries also run between the islands and the mainland. **Victoria Clipper,** 254 Belleville St. (382-8100 or 800-888-2535). Direct service from Victoria to Seattle ($58-66, child $29-33, senior $52-60). Passengers only. 4 per day May-Sept., 1 per day Oct.-April. **Black Ball Transport,** 430 Belleville St. (386-2202). Connects Victoria with Port Angeles, WA. Mid-May to mid-Oct. 4 per day; Oct.-Nov. and mid-March to mid-May, 2 per day; Dec. to mid-March, 1 per day. US$6.75, car and driver US$27.25, ages 5-11 US$4.50.

Public Transportation: BC Transit (382-6161). City bus service with major connections downtown at the corner of Douglas and Yates St. Single-zone travel $1.75; multi-zone (north to Sidney and the Butchart Gardens) $2.50; seniors $1.10; under 5 free. Day passes ($5.50, seniors $4) and free **transit maps** at 7-11, Money Mart, Shoppers Drug stores, and Tourism Victoria (see above). **Disabilities Services for Local Transit** (727-7811). Open Mon.-Fri. 8am-5pm.

Car Rental: Island Auto Rentals, 837 Yates St. (384-4881). $20 per day, plus $12 insurance and 12¢ per km after 100. Must be 19 with a major credit card. **Rent-a Wreck,** 2634 Douglas St. (384-5343 or 800-809-0788). $27 per day plus 12¢ per km. Must be 21 with major credit card.

Auto Club: BC Automobile Association, 1075 Pandora Ave. (389-6700). Full range of services for CAA and AAA members. Open Mon.-Sat. 9am-5pm.

Taxi: Victoria Taxi, 383-7111. **Westwind,** 474-4747. 24hr.

Bike Rental: Harbour Rental, 843 Douglas St. (384-2133). Mountain bikes $6 per hr., $18 per day. Lock and helmet included. Open daily 9am-5pm. Also rents scooters for $10-12 per hr., $35-40 per day.

Camping Supplies and Rentals: Jeune Brothers, 570 Johnson St. (386-8778; fax 380-1533). 3-person tent $42 for 2 days, $75 for a week. 10% HI discount. Open Mon.-Thurs. 10am-6pm, Fri. 10am-9pm, Sat. 10am-5:30pm, Sun. noon-5pm.

Library: 735 Broughton St. (382-7241), at Courtney St. Open Mon., Wed., and Fri.-Sat., 9am-6pm; Tues. and Thurs. 9am-9pm.

Crisis Line: 386-6323. 24hr. **Rape Crisis:** 383-3232. 24hr.

Gay and Lesbian Information: (598-4900). Volunteer staff Mon.-Fri. 6:30-10pm. Recording at all other times.

Poison Control: 682-5050 or 800-567-8911. 24hr.

Pharmacy: London Drugs, 911 Yates St. (381-1113), at Vancouver St., in the Wilson Centre. Open Mon.-Sat. 9am-10pm, Sun. 10am-8pm.

Emergency: 911. **Police:** 625 Fisgard St. (non-emergency 384-4111), at Government St.

Post Office: 905 Gordon St. (381-6114). Open Mon.-Fri. 9am-5:30pm, Sat. 9:30am-5pm. Pick up general delivery mail at 621 Discovery St. (963-1350). **General Delivery Postal Code:** V8W 1L0.

Area Code: 604.

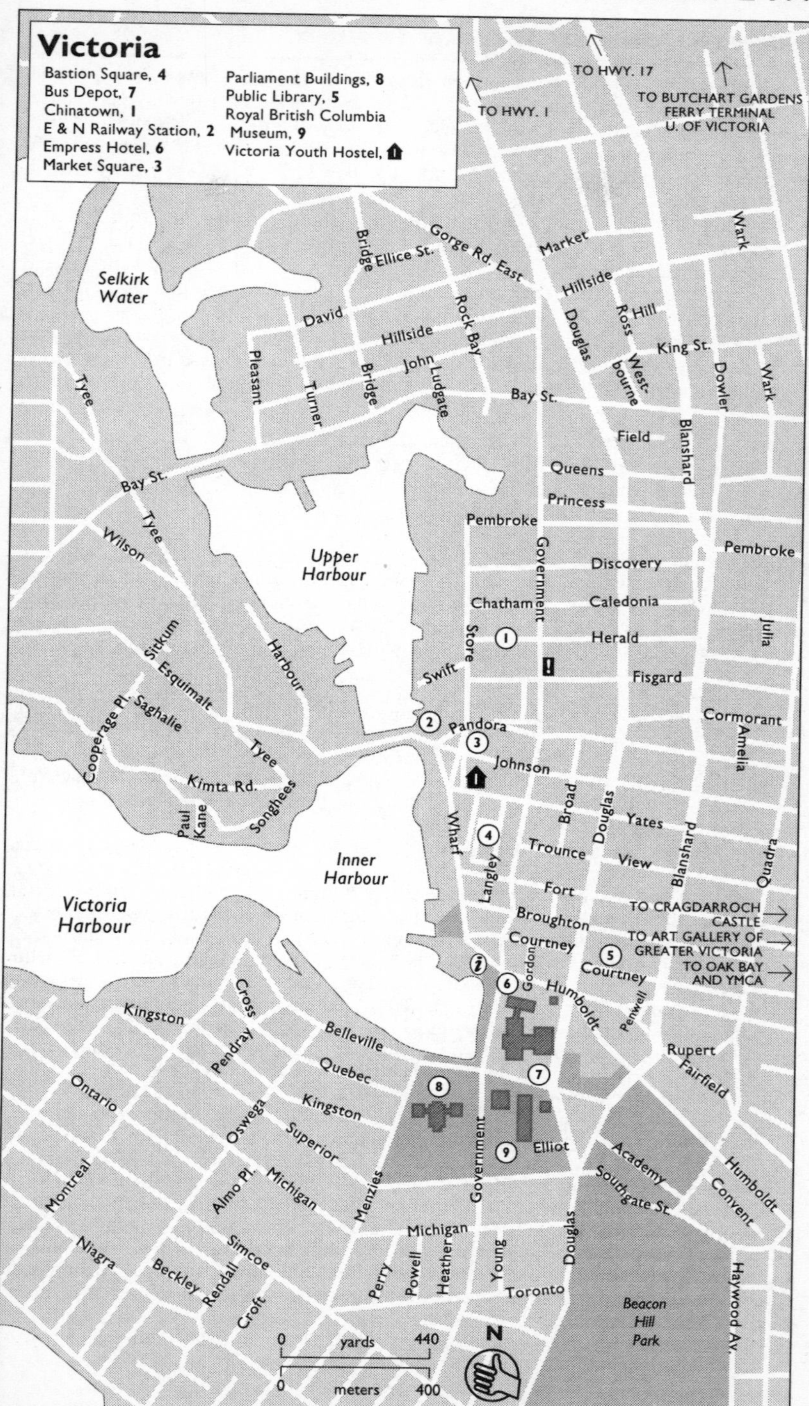
Victoria
Bastion Square, 4
Bus Depot, 7
Chinatown, 1
E & N Railway Station, 2
Empress Hotel, 6
Market Square, 3
Parliament Buildings, 8
Public Library, 5
Royal British Columbia Museum, 9
Victoria Youth Hostel
TO HWY. 1
TO HWY. 17
TO BUTCHART GARDENS
FERRY TERMINAL
U. OF VICTORIA
Selkirk Water
Upper Harbour
Inner Harbour
Victoria Harbour
TO CRAGDARROCH CASTLE
TO ART GALLERY OF GREATER VICTORIA
TO OAK BAY AND YMCA
Beacon Hill Park
yards
meters
0
440
400
N

ORIENTATION AND GETTING AROUND

While the commercial Seattle and Port Angeles **ferries** dock downtown, the WSF ferry from the San Juan Islands docks at **Sidney,** 28km north on **Highway 17,** and the Vancouver/Gulf Islands ferry docks at **Swartz Bay,** 32km north. **Highway 1,** the **Trans-Canada Highway,** leads north and turns into Highway 19 at Nanaimo, stretching north to the rest of Vancouver Island; **Highway 14** leads west to **Port Renfrew** and **Pacific Rim National Park.**

While driving in Victoria is relatively easy, **parking** downtown is difficult and expensive. Meters charge $1 for 48 minutes while most lots cost $1-1.50 for an hour; offenders are ticketed with zeal. Cross the Johnson St. Bridge and take the second right onto Tyee St. for free street parking, a mere 10-minute walk from downtown. Parking in most residential neighborhoods is also free.

Victoria enfolds the Inner Harbour; **Government Street** and **Douglas Street** are the main north-south thoroughfares, running through all of downtown. Residential neighborhoods, wealthier in the east, form a semicircle around the Inner Harbour.

ACCOMMODATIONS

A capitol city, Victoria has capital budget accommodations scene, but a less-than-perfect selection of campgrounds. A number of flavorful hostels and B&B-hostel hybrids make a night inside in Victoria an altogether pleasant experience.

Victoria Youth Hostel (HI-C), 516 Yates St. (385-4511), at Wharf St. downtown. 108 beds in the big, modern, and spotless Victoria Heritage Building. Staff and volunteer concierges offer a wealth of info, including valuable tips on where to park. Extensive kitchen and laundry facilities, ping pong, video games. Laundry $1.75. Linen rental $1.50. Family rooms available. Desk open from 7am-midnight; curfew 2:30am. $15, nonmembers $19.

Selkirk Guest House, 934 Selkirk Ave. (389-1213), in West Victoria. Take bus #14 along Craigflower to Tillicum; Selkirk is one block north. Become a part of the family in the Jacksons' (very) lived-in home. Cushy dorms with flowery sheets, free canoes (row into downtown), and a hot tub right on the water. Lynn, the House Mom, a.k.a. Sparkle the Clown, knows loads of magic tricks—guests can watch Spike the Wonder Dog jump through her arms. Dorms $18, linen and towels free. Private rooms $50.

Renouf House Bunk & Breakfast, 2010 Stanley Ave. (595-4774; fax 598-1515). Take bus #10 or walk down Johnson to Fernwood St. Stanley Ave. is one block west of Fernwood and two blocks north of Johnson. Built in 1910 and full of antique furniture and dark wooden staircases. Large continental breakfast features homemade granola and breads. Owners run kayaking tours of the islands, and give guests useful city guidebooks. Kitchen and laundry. Bunk $18.25. Single room $33.25, with private bath $55; double $45, with private bath $65.

The Cat's Meow, 1316 Grant St. (595-8878). Take bus #10 to Fernwood and Grant. A mini-hostel with 12 quiet and comfy beds. The hostel's namesake, Rufus, is cute and cuddly, and his "mother" Daphne is a font of info about the area. No kitchen, but breakfast is included in the $17.50 bed rate. Private double, $43.

Victoria Backpackers Hostel, 1418 Fernwood Rd. (386-4471). Take bus #10 to Fernwood and Douglas. 36 beds with coed and female-only rooms. It's as if your elderly aunt turned her house—the one with the huge, well-kept garden and Johnson-era furniture—into a hostel. Kitchen and lounge. Free parking. Laundry $2 per load. Linen $1. Bunks $13 first night, $12 after; private doubles $35. Dinner served every evening, $3.

University of Victoria (721-8395), 20min. northeast of the Inner Harbour by bus #4 or 14. From Hwy. 17, take MacKenzie to Sinclair. Housing office is in Lot 5. Private dorms with shared baths. Coin-op laundry. Cute wild rabbits living under the buildings. Registration after 3pm, reservations advised. Singles $38; doubles $50. Cafeteria breakfast included. Open May-Aug.

CAMPING

The few campgrounds on the perimeter of Victoria cater largely to wealthy RV drivers. Many fill up in July and August; reservations are a good idea.

Goldstream Provincial Park, 2930 Trans-Canada Hwy. (391-2300; reservations 800-689-9025), 20km northwest of Victoria. Great short hiking trails and swimming in this forested riverside area. In Nov., the river is crowded with spawning salmon. Flush toilets and firewood available. 150 gorgeous, gravelly sites ($15.50). The nearby **Freeman King Visitor Centre** gives the history of the area from the Ice Age to the welfare state. Open daily 9:30am-4:30pm; weekends only in winter.

Thetis Lake Campground, 1938 Trans-Canada Hwy. (478-3845), 10km north of the city center. Sites are peaceful and removed. Thetis Lake is popular among locals for great cliff diving (cliff diving is not recommended by *Let's Go* or your mother). Laundry, metered showers. Sites $19 for 2 people, 50¢ per additional person.

Fort Victoria Camping, 340 Island Hwy. (479-8112; fax 479-5806), 7km northwest of downtown. Take bus #14 or, from Victoria, turn left onto Helmcken Rd. from the Trans-Canada Hwy., then turn right on Island Hwy. Both RV and tent sites available, though a "tent site" is just a patch of grass next to a gravel driveway. Free hot showers. Laundry. Sites $21 for 2 people, hookups $24, with cable TV $26.

FOOD

The variety and high quality of food in Victoria undermines the city's attempts to pass itself off as the North American equivalent of Jolly Old England. The abundance of coffee shops crawling with in-house baked pastries bespeaks Victoria's proximity to Seattle. A stroll along **Government** and **Wharf Streets** offers countless restaurants, but *caveat emptor*—some raise their prices for the summer tourists and are dutifully avoided by locals. **Chinatown,** extending from Fisgard and Government St. to the northwest, contains the expected range of Chinese cuisine. In **Fernwood Village,** three blocks north of Johnson St. and accessible by bus #10, creative restaurants are scattered among craft shops, a respite from the tourist-swarmed downtown. If you feel like cooking, head down to **Fisherman's Wharf** at the corner of Harbour and Government St. to buy the day's catch as it flops off the boats. For large-scale grocery shopping, try **Thrifty Foods,** 475 Simcoe (544-1234), six blocks south of the Parliament buildings (open daily 8am-10pm).

John's Place, 723 Pandora St. (389-0711), between Douglas and Blanshard St. Only the Place's portions can outdo its enormous reputation among locals. Complete with jukebox and Marilyn pinups, John's offers Canadian fare with a Thai twist and a little Mediterranean thrown in. Savory fresh herb bread and butter. Try John's favorite *panang goong* (sauteed tiger prawns in curry sauce $11.50). Open Mon.-Thurs. 7am-10pm, Fri.-Sat. 7am-11pm, Sun. 8am-3pm and 5-10pm.

Milky Way, 128-560 Johnson St. (360-1113), at the corner of Johnston and Wharf St. Breakfast, lunch, and dinner specials ($3-10) for a multi-course meal make this one of the better bargains in town; the star-studded decor makes it one of the more entertaining. Live music weekend nights. The $3 breakfast special is available until 4pm. Open daily 7am-11pm.

Pluto's, 1150 Cooke St. (385-4747). Judy Jetson meets the 50s in a wacky converted gas station. Blessed by the budget fairy, Pluto's lies far from the bustle of downtown. Burgers ($7-8), burritos ($10), and bloated desserts ($4-4.50). Eat in the garage or out by the pumps. (Sorry, no gasoline.) Open Mon.-Thurs. 8am-11pm, Fri.-Sat. 8am-midnight, Sun. 8am-10pm.

Wah Lai Yuen, 560 Fisgard St. (381-5355), in Chinatown. (As in all Chinatowns, the smaller, less glitzy restaurants are the cheapest and the best.) This restaurant and bakery offers ridiculously cheap wonton noodle soup ($3.50-$4.50), curry chicken dishes ($4.75), and hot, fresh pastries (40¢-$1.50).

El Rancho Restaurant, 1600 Bay St. (595-7422). Take bus #2 to Bay St. Or, take Johnson to Quadra, turn left, then right on Bay. One of the only places in Victoria where "South of the Border" doesn't mean Washington State. El Rancho specializes in "Latino" food—a mix of Mexican, Spanish, Tex-Mex, and Californian cooking. Free parking. Steak, chicken, seafood, and vegetarian fajitas $12. Sunday is chef's creation night: a 3-course meal is $17. Early bird specials on weekends. Open Sun.-Thurs. 5:30-10pm, Fri.-Sat. 5:30-11pm.

The Sally Cafe, 714 Cormorant St. (381-1431). Great for lighter fare and heavier conversation, the Sally Cafe is so vegetarian friendly that even the menus are green. Curried chicken and apricots $6, sandwiches from $4.75. Open Mon.-Fri. 7am-5pm, Sat. 8am-5pm.

The Blethering Place, 2250 Oak Bay Ave. (598-1413), at Monterey St. Take bus #2 or drive west on Fort St. and turn right on Oak Bay. The sun never set on the British Empire in upscale, upright Oak Bay. Despite the Anglophilia, live music is diverse, ranging from Celtic folk songs to flamenco. High Tea (the Victorian way) with appropriate pastries baked on the premises is $12. Ploughman's Lunch ($8) is a cheesier, meatier alternative. Dinners from $9. Open daily 8am-10pm.

Benny's Bagels, 132-560 Johnson St. (384-3441), on the Wharf St. side of Market Sq. Creative bagel sandwiches are a meal in themselves. Whole-grain, environmentally-safe, round food hurts no one (65¢). Brie melt $4.25. Open Mon.-Thurs. 7am-7pm, Fri.-Sat. 7am-11pm, Sun. 10am-5pm.

Zombies Pizza, 1219 Wharf St. (389-2226). Cheerfully morbid decor and $2 slices make this a good, quick stop. Open super late for post-pub-closing munchies and the restless dead. Open Mon.-Sat. 11am-3am, Sun. 11am-1am.

SIGHTS AND ACTIVITIES

If you don't mind becoming one with the flocks of tourists hurling themselves lemming-like toward the shores of Victoria, wander along the **Inner Harbour** and watch the boats come in as the sun sets behind the neighboring islands. A trip through the fantastically thorough **Royal British Columbia Museum,** 675 Belleville St. (387-3014 recording; 387-3701 operator) will remind you of why you came to Canada in the first place. Excellent, intense, and extensive exhibits on the biological, geological, and cultural history of the province from protozoans to the present. The First Nations exhibit features a totem pole room and a transplanted native house ($7, seniors $3.21, youth $2.14, under 5 free; open daily 9am-5pm). **Thunderbird Park** and its many totems loom large behind the museum. Tours available after July 1. **The Art Gallery of Greater Victoria,** 1040 Moss St. (384-4101), houses a rotating collection of 10,000 pieces from contemporary Canada, traditional and contemporary Asia, North America, and Europe, as well as one of the only **Shinto shrines** outside of Japan (open Mon.-Wed. and Fri.-Sat. 10am-5pm, Thurs. 10am-9pm, Sun. 1-5pm; $4, seniors and students $2, under 12 free; free on Mon.). The tourist office has pamphlets aplenty on Victoria's historic houses and parks.

Across the street from the museum stand the imposing **Parliament Buildings,** 501 Belleville St. (387-3046), home of the Provincial government since 1898. The 10-story dome and Brunelleschi-esque vestibule are gilded with almost 50oz. of gold. Be sure to see the building at night, when 3330 lights line the facade. Free tours leave from the main steps daily 9am to 5pm (open Mon.-Fri. 8:30am-5pm, on weekends open for tours only). Swing by the public gallery and witness the members of Parliament yapping on about matters of great import while the House is in session.

Just north of Fort St. on Wharf is **Bastion Square,** the original site of Fort Victoria, the Hudson Bay Company's original trading post in the area. The fort no longer stands, but Bastion Square is home to the **Maritime Museum,** 28 Bastion Sq. (385-4222), which exhibits ship models, nautical instruments, and a 13m native canoe that shoved off from Victoria in 1901 on a daring but unsuccessful trip around the world (open daily 9:30am-4:30pm; $6, seniors and students $5, ages 6-11 $3; tickets good for 3 days).

Since the end of the legal opium trade, **Chinatown,** beyond the "Gate of Harmonious Interest" on Fisgard St. at Government St., has diminished substantially, but its many restaurants and inexpensive shops make it a worthwhile destination. **Market Square,** the bulk of which lies on Johnson St. four blocks south of Fisgard, is a collection of countless stores, restaurants, and wooden walkways home to a popular public fair on summer Sundays.

Beacon Hill Park, off Douglas St. south of the Inner Harbour, is a flowering oasis just blocks from downtown that pleases walkers, bikers, and the picnic-inclined. More adventurous mountain bikers can tackle the **Galloping Goose,** a 60km trail beginning in downtown Victoria and continuing to the west coast of the island through cities, rainforests, and canyons. The trail is open to cyclists, pedestrians, and horses. Horses on bicycles strongly discouraged.

By sea, Victoria is a hub for a number of the sailing, kayaking, and whale-watching tours available on Vancouver Island. For an active aquatic experience, **Oak Bay Marine Group** (598-3369), at the Oak Bay Marina, rents deep sea fishing charters for $6 per hour, minimum 4 hours. Group rates, like the hungry seals sunning themselves along the Marina, are always plentiful. After a few days of hiking, biking, and museum visiting, unwind with a tour of the **Vancouver Island Brewery** at 2330 Government St. (361-0007). Free tours start at 1 and 3pm Friday and Saturday and include free samples. The free tour is educational as well as alcoholic.

ENTERTAINMENT

Those crazy Canooks may be on the metric system, but their beer is still sold by the pint. English pubs and watering holes are abundant throughout town, many of which look exactly like one another after a few Guinness. **Harpo's Cabaret,** 15 Bastion Sq. (385-5333), at Wharf St. brings in an eclectic array of bands ranging from blues and jazz to neo-hippie rock acts. Two blocks away, **Steamer's Public House,** 570 Yates St. (381-4340), ships in local acts and world beat grooves. The free weekly *Monday Magazine* (inexplicably released every Wednesday) is available at hostels, hotels, and most restaurants downtown and provides an exhaustive listing of who's playing where. For even more up-to-the-minute information, check the telephone poles and light posts downtown—posted fliers are often the best source for what's going down.

Nightlife in Victoria doesn't really start jumping until Thursdays, but once the weekend comes, the whole city seems ready to party. Most clubs offer weekday drink specials to draw crowds—cheap beer nights have the highest success rates.

Drawing Room, 751 View St. (920-7797). A happening club considerate enough to offer a lounge, with easy chairs, pool tables, and a wall-to-wall carpet for dancers fleeing the frenzied techno/alternative/house music next door. Fresh fruit bar for mixed drinks and vitamins. Cover $3, weekends $4. Open Tues.-Thurs. 8pm-2am, Fri.-Sat. 9pm-2am.

Rumors, 1325 Government St. (385-0566). Gay and lesbian clientele enjoy one of Victoria's more inviting dance floors. Drag shows every other Sun., male strippers Thurs. Every 3rd Fri. is women's night. Open Mon.-Sat. 9pm-2am, Sun. 9pm-midnight.

Sticky Wicket, 919 Douglas St. (383-7137). Seven bars and a club all in one building, next door to the Strathcona Hotel. **The Roof Top Bar** (on the roof!) even has its own beach volleyball court available for rent. The club, **The Forge,** specializes in 70s and 80s rock with a wattage that could vaporize tungsten. The Forge charges a $4 cover on weekends, but the pubs are cover-free and serve food until 1am. Open Mon.-Sat. 11:30am-2am, Sun. 11:30am-midnight.

Scandals, 770 Yates St. (389-0666). Laser beams shoot across the floor with reckless abandon in this second home for Victoria's swinging under-25 set. Mostly alternative music with Tues. and Wed. retro nights, Sun. disco night. Cover $2-3. Open Mon.-Sat. 9pm-2am, Sun. 9pm-midnight.

The **Victoria Symphony Society,** 846 Broughton St. (385-6575), performs regularly under conductor Peter McCoppin. The highlight of its year is the Symphony Splash, a free concert on the first Sunday in August played on a barge in the Inner Harbour that concludes with fireworks and usually draws 40-50,000 international listeners. For the last week and a half of June, Victoria oozes jazz during **JazzFest,** as over a dozen performers play venues throughout the city (388-4423).

On Tuesdays, first-run movies at the **Cineplex Odeon,** 780 Yates St. (383-0513)—and virtually every other first-run theater in Canada—are half-price ($5). For more offbeat and foreign films, head to the University of Victoria's **Cinecenta** (721-8365) in the student union (bus #4 and 14). **Phoenix Theaters** (721-8000), at UVIC, has productions in June, as well as term-time live theater performances. From mid-July to mid-August, Victoria goes Elizabethan on your ass when the **Annual Shakespeare Festival** (360-0234) lands in the Inner Harbour.

■ Near Victoria

SOOKE

West of Victoria on Hwy. 14 lies the town of Sooke, named for the T'sou-ke people and host to the logging events and festivities of **All Sooke Day** on the third Saturday in July. The **Sooke Region Museum,** 2070 Phillips Rd. (642-6351), just off Hwy. 14, houses a **travel infocentre,** and delivers an excellent history of the area (open July-Aug. daily 9am-5:30pm, Sept.-June Tues.-Sun. 9am-5pm; free). To get to Phillips Rd. from the city, take bus #50 to the Western Exchange and transfer to #61. Also on Phillips Rd., past the museum, is the **Sooke River Flats Campsite** (642-6076), with a phone, showers, toilets, and running water (gates locked 11pm-7am; sites $12). Turn right at Sooke's only stop light to find **Camp Barnard,** 3130 Young Lake Rd. (642-5924), a former Boy Scout camp with cabins that sleep eight ($20-32) and tent sites ($12) as well as fire pits, hot showers, and swimming (reservations required).

Sooke is a haven for wealthier Victorians, making cheap indoor accommodations scarce. Try the **Blackfish B&B,** 2440 Blackfish Rd. (642-6864), 7 mi. west of the stop light (singles $35; doubles $50-60). Large groups should ask about the great **bungalow** down on the pebble beach with free laundry and a full kitchen (sleeps 9; $125).

North of Sooke lie some of the best beachcombing opportunities on the southern island. Highway 14 continues along the coast, stringing together two provincial parks: **Juan de Fuca,** home to **China Beach** and **Loss Creek** (both day use), and **French Beach** (391-2300) with tent sites (May-Oct. $9.50). Camping is free at the popular **Jordan River Recreation Area** ten minutes past French Beach.

GULF ISLANDS

Just off the southeastern coast of Vancouver Island lie the quiet waters and stunning scenery of British Columbia's **Gulf Island Archipelago.** Five islands are accessible by BC Ferries (call 386-3431). The three principle islands in the chain are Salt Spring, Mayne, and Pender. For information on the five main islands, call the **Tourist Information Centre** in Salt Spring (537-5252) or Victoria (953-2033). On Salt Spring, the **HI-C hostel** at 640 Cusheon Lake Rd. (537-4149) has its own hiking trails ($14, nonmembers $17). **Maxine's Boardwalk Cafe,** 2-104 Fulford Ganges Rd. (537-5747), on Salt Spring, sports a reasonably priced breakfast and lunch menu with colorful daily specials and a waterfront view. Salt Spring offers the largest population and widest number of activities of the five islands. Options range from climbing **Mt. Maxwell** for a panoramic view of BC and Washington to playing golf at **Blackburn Meadows,** 269 Blackburn Rd. (537-1707), a farm converted into an organic golf course next to an Audobon sanctuary (9 holes $12, club rental $10). Or just play with the mounties at the **Royal Canadian Mounted Police** outpost on the outskirts of Ganges. (*Let's Go* does not recommend taunting or sassing national police forces.)

■ Nanaimo

Primarily a stopover point for travelers en route to the rainforests of north and west Vancouver Island, Nanaimo appears along the highway as little more than a strip of motels, gas stations, and greasy spoons. Those who linger discover Nanaimo's mysterious ability to convert "just-passing-throughs" into "let's-stay-a-few-days." Could it have something to do with the town's beach, 25 parks, and several more provincial parks nearby? Nanaimo isn't telling.

PRACTICAL INFORMATION AND ORIENTATION

Visitors Information: Travel Infocentre, 2290 Bowen Rd. (756-0106), west of downtown. Head south on Bowen Rd. from Terminal Ave., or north on Northfield Rd. from the Nanaimo Pkwy. Open daily 8am-7pm, winter 9am-5pm.

Trains: VIA Rail, 321 Selby St. (800-561-8630). 2 trains per day to Victoria ($20; with 7-day advance purchase $13). Student and senior discounts.

Buses: Laidlaw (753-4371), at Comox and Terminal behind Tally Ho Island Inn. To: Victoria (6 per day, $17); Port Hardy (2 per day, $65); Tofino and Ucluelet (2 per day, $29).

Ferries: BC Ferries (753-1261 or 800-223-3779). Terminal at the northern end of Stewart Ave. 8 per day to Vancouver ($6.50, car and driver $31.50) with connections to Bowen Island and Langdale. Take the ferry **shuttle** from Gordon St. Exchange downtown. Ferries also leave from the Maffeo-Sutton Park in downtown to Newcastle Island (753-1431; $4.50).

Car Rental: Rent-A-Wreck, 111 Terminal Ave. S. (753-6461). From $30 per day first plus 16¢ per km after 100. Must be 21 with a major credit card. Open Mon.-Fri. 8am-6pm, Sat. 9am-4pm, Sun. 10am-4pm. **Budget,** 33 Terminal Ave. S. (754-7368). $60 per day with unlimited mileage ($50 with coupon from hostel). Must be 21. Free pickup in most parts of town.

Public Transit: (390-4531), Gordon St. Exchange, at Front St. and Gordon St. Fares $1.30, seniors $1.05. Buses run Mon.-Sat. 7am-11pm, Sun. 10am-6pm.

Laundromat: 702 Nicol St. (753-9922), at Robins in **Payless Gas Station.** 24hr.

Crisis Line: 754-4447. 24hr.

Gay and Lesbian Information: Gayline, 754-2585. Call Mon.-Fri. 6-9pm.

Pharmacy: London Drugs, 650 S. Terminal Ave. (753-5566), in Harbour Park Mall. Open Mon.-Sat. 9am-10pm, Sun. 10am-8pm.

Hospital: 1200 Dufferin Crescent (754-2141).

Emergency: 911. **Police:** 303 Pridaux St. (754-2345), at Fitzwilliam. **Fire:** 666 Fitzwilliam St. (753-7311/7344), at Milton.

Post Office: 650 S. Terminal Ave. (741-1829), in Harbour Park Mall. Open Mon.-Fri. 8:30am-5pm. **Postal Code:** V9R 5E2.

Area Code: 250.

Nanaimo lies on the east coast of Vancouver Island, 111km north of Victoria on **Highway 1,** the **Trans-Canada Highway,** and 391km south of **Port Hardy** via **Highway 19,** the **Island Highway.** Highway 1 transforms into Highway 19 in Nanaimo but only after three successive name changes: Nicol St., Terminal Ave. S., and finally Terminal Ave. N. The **ferry** terminal is 2km north of downtown on Stewart Ave. The brand-new **Nanaimo Parkway** circumvents the town to the south.

ACCOMMODATIONS AND CAMPING

Nicol St. Hostel, 65 Nicol St. (753-1188). A quick walk from the ferry, bus station, or downtown. 25 beds stuffed into dorms, private rooms, and hallways. Tent sites in the back yard. Free paint to add to the mural next door. $15, double $30. Tent sites $8. Groups of 3 or more should ask for the private suite. Free parking.

Thompson's Hostel, 1660 Cedar Rd. (722-2251), off the Cedar Hwy. about 5km south of downtown. Indoor accommodations are considerably nicer than the building's exterior. Camping, too, right on the Nanaimo River with refrigerator and gas stove at the sites. 12 indoor beds, free pool, darts, ping-pong, and a piano. Free parking and linen. No curfew. Laundry $3. Beds $13, sites $6.

Big 7 Motel, 736 Nicol St. (754-2328). Pink and baby blue decor circa 1986 suggests an episode of *Nanaimo Vice.* As compensation, all rooms have cable and HBO. Desk open 24hr. Singles $39, in winter $32; doubles $51, in winter $41.

Living Forest Campground, 6 Maki Rd. (755-1755), 3km southwest of downtown. Large, spacious campground with several sites on steep, short cliffs overlooking the ocean. Closest campground to town and the most natural, with large cedars throughout. Sites $15, oceanfront $17.

Westwood Lake, 380 Westwood Rd. (753-3922), west of town off Jingle Pot Rd. Take bus #5. Only 200m from a busy swimming hole. Follow giant concrete footprints to the office. Full facilities. 66 sites $16, hookups $19.

Brannen Lake Campsite, 4220 Biggs Rd. (756-0404), 6km north of the ferry terminal. Take Biggs Rd. just off the intersection of the Nanaimo Pkwy. and Mostar Rd., scoot past the Nanaimo Correction Centre, and look for the signs. Site is on an operating beef ranch, but don't worry, the cows live in a separate area. Clean bathrooms with hot showers ($1). Free hayrides. Sites $14, with hookup $16.

FOOD

Nanaimo supports a multitude of budget eateries. Cafes and restaurants speckle the downtown area while the highway hosts an endless party of little dives, many open late or 24 hours. Those wanting greaseless spoons can seek refuge in the massive **Thrifty Foods** (754-0655), in the Harbour Park Mall (open daily 8am-10pm). Nanaimo is known in Canada for the **Nanaimo Bar,** a chocolate confection that suggests a brownie with attitude. Visiting Nanaimo without trying one is like scoring a home run and forgetting to touch third.

Filthy McNasty's, 14 Commercial St. (753-7011). An eclectic oasis of multi-media wall art, gourmet food, and tantalizing desserts. Simple Salmon (was a pizza; $8). Chicken parmigiana sandwich $7.50. Live jazz Fri. and Sat. nights. Open Mon.-Wed. 9am-11pm, Thurs.-Sat. 9am-midnight, Sun. 10am-4pm.

Gina's Mexican Cafe, 47 Skinner St. (753-5411), up the hill off Front St. A self-proclaimed "Tacky but Friendly Place," Gina's lives up to its billing with wild bright colors and dishes that have won "countless gringo awards." There's a party every night. Combo plates $9, nachos starting at $5.75. Open Mon.-Thurs. 11am-9pm, Fri. 11am-10pm, Sat. noon-10pm, Sun. 2-8:30pm.

The Scotch Bakery, 87 Commercial St. (753-3521). Nanaimo Bar seekers come here for a fix (80¢). Don't ignore the apple fritters (85¢), giant pretzel pizzas (95¢), or sausage rolls ($1.29). Open Mon.-Sat. 8am-4:30pm.

SIGHTS

The **Nanaimo District Museum,** 100 Cameron Rd. (753-1821), pays special tribute to Nanaimo's Chinese presence. It also features a semi-interactive exhibit on the native Snunēmuxw (SNOO-ne-moo, sort of) and a full-scale walk-through model of a coal mine (open Mon.-Fri. 9am-6pm, Sat.-Sun. 10am-6pm; winter Tues.-Sat. 9am-5pm; $2, students and seniors $1.75, under 12 75¢). Just up the street from the museum is the **Bastion,** a fur-trading fort built by the Hudson's Bay Company (open in summer Wed.-Mon. 10am-4:30pm).

Three kilometers south of town on Hwy. 1, the **Petroglyph Provincial Park** protects the carvings of hundreds of generations of Salish shamans. A menagerie of animals and mythical creatures decorates the soft sandstone. Rubbings can be made off concrete replicas at the base of the trail leading to the petroglyphs.

Get away from civilization by taking the quick ferry to **Newcastle Island Provincial Park.** Only accessible by boat, this automobile-free 756-acre park is filled with hiking trails, picnic spots, and campsites ($9.50). The **Shoreline Trail,** which weaves along the shore (duh.) provides great vantage points of Departure Bay. Ferries every hour leave from Swy-A-Lana Lagoon, near downtown ($4.25 round-trip).

If you've been doubting the theory of gravity, go to the **Bungy Zone** (753-5867), 35 Nanaimo River Rd. The Zone stretches a dimension of sight, sound, and giant rubber bands. Thrill-seekers from all over the continent make a pilgrimage here to bungee jump 42m (140 ft.) into a narrow gorge. The short but exhilarating trip costs $95 (group rates; 2 for 1 if you rent a car from Budget; HI discount; seniors free). Bungee variations—swinging, "zipline," rapelling—available, too. To reach the Zone, take

Brother (XII), Can You Spare a Dime?

The new age-ism common on Vancouver Island started early in Nanaimo when a man calling himself **Brother XII** heralded the coming of the Age of Aquarius in the 1920s. He developed his own theology and attracted a large cult following among wealthy islanders. Brother XII (just XII to his friends) and his followers left Nanaimo in 1927 to form Utopia at Cedar-by-Sea on the nearby DeCourcy Island. Stories began to leak from Utopia of Brother XII's greed, his nasty habit of forcing the elderly to commit suicide once they'd left their money to him and, of course, his network of sex slaves. He was put on trial in 1932 and fled to Europe where he died in 1934. When he disappeared, Brother XII supposedly left $1.4 million in gold buried somewhere around Cedar-by-Sea. In 1982, the Nanimo paper ran a story of an unemployed 35-year-old steam fitter who found the gold but only after facing death III times at the hands of Brother XII's lingering magic. (The article turned out to be an April Fool's joke.) These days, most residents steer clear of magic, and Nanaimo's mystical side has toned itself down. While the area once sported a witch-run coffee shop and is rumored to have a pagan church, the most popular cult these days is nature worship.

Hwy. 1 south to Nanaimo River Rd. and follow the signs. A free shuttle runs to and from Nanaimo and Victoria.

Departure Bay washes onto a pleasant beach in the north end of town off Stewart Ave. **North Island Water Sports,** 2755 Departure Bay Rd. (758-2488), rents kayaks ($30 per day, $70 for a double; long term rates available) and scramblers (like kayaks, but you sit on top of them; $8 per hr., $20 per 3hr.). The three-day **Marine Festival** is held during late July. Highlights include the **Silly Boat Race** and the **Bathtub Race.** Bathers from all over the continent race porcelain tubs with monster outboards from Nanaimo to Vancouver across the 55km Georgia Strait. They hand out prizes to everyone who makes it across, and ceremoniously present the "Silver Plunger" trophy to the first tub that sinks. The organizer of this bizarre but beloved event is the **Royal Nanaimo Bathtub Society,** 51A Commercial St., Nanaimo V9R 5G3 (753-7223).

■ Near Nanaimo

PORT ALBERNI

Port Alberni is the only pit stop on Hwy. 4 en route to Pacific Rim National Park, and sits about 40km west of Hwy. 19 and 34km from Nanaimo. The town bills itself the "Salmon Capital of the World" and hosts an annual **Salmon Festival** each Labor Day weekend. Brochures and advice on the general area are at the **Port Alberni Infocentre** (724-6535), on the highway (open daily 8am-8pm; in winter closes at 5pm). **Naesgaard's** (723-3622), a farmer's market just west of town, overflows with farm-fresh fruit, flowers, and vegetables (open Mon.-Sat. 9am-8:30pm, Sun. 10am-8:30pm; in winter Mon.-Sat. 9am-6pm, Sun. 10am-6pm). **Sproat Lake Provincial Park,** 13km west of Port Alberni off Hwy. 4, offers space to explore mysterious petroglyphs, boat, swim, fish, and camp (sites $14.50, summer $12; showers, flush toilets). Sleep to the sounds of waterfalls at the less crowded, more out-of-the-way **Stamp Falls Provincial Park** (sites $9.50; no showers). For more info on the two parks, call 954-4600; for reservations, call (800) 689-9025. Three ferries per week run by **Alberni Marine Transportation** (723-8313 or 800-663-7192) leave from Port Alberni to Bamfield ($19).

CHEMAINUS

About 37km south of Nanaimo on Hwy. 1 lies the town of Chemainus. When the closing of the town's sawmill threatened economic disaster in 1980, an ambitious revitalization program, centered on a series of more than 30 striking murals, helped bring in the tourists and turn things around. The murals depicting the town's history now rival Madonna in self-promotion.

Contact the **Travel Infocentre,** 9758 Chemainus Rd. (246-3944), for info on all things Chemainus. Locals have picked up on the tourism industry and virtually every home on the main drag hosts a B&B. The **Chemainus Hostel,** 9694 Chemainus Rd. (246-2809), is not only a good place to find a bed, a kitchen, and laundry facilities, but provides info on activities around the island. The **Horseshoe Bay Inn,** 9576 Chemainus Rd. (416-6411), has loud rooms above the pub ($35), and quieter rooms with private bath ($70).

HORNBY ISLAND

In the 1960s, large numbers of draft-dodgers fled the U.S. to settle peacefully on quiet Hornby Island, halfway between Nanaimo and Campbell River. Today, hippie-holdovers mingle on the island with the descendants of 19th century pioneers. At the hub of all Hornby's excitement sits the **Co-op** (335-1121) at the end of Central Rd. by Tribune Bay, home to **tourist information,** the **post office** (**postal code:** V0R 1Z0), a well-stocked grocery store, and a deli (open daily 9am-7pm). The **area code** is 250.

Laidlaw (753-4371) has a flag stop at **Buckley Bay,** on Hwy. 19, where the ferry docks. **BC Ferries** (888-223-3779, Hornby Island terminal 335-2733) sails nine times daily ($7 round-trip). It's a 10-minute ride from Buckley Bay to **Denman;** passengers must disembark and make the 11km trek across the island for another 10-minute ride to Hornby. Once on Hornby, there are only two roads to worry about: **Shingle Spit Rd.** (try saying *that* 10 times fast) and **Central Rd.** The island has no public transit and is difficult to cover without a bike or car. Some foot-travelers ask friendly faces for lifts at Denman or on the ferry. (*Let's Go* does not recommend hitchhiking.)

With light traffic and smooth roads, Hornby Island is easily explored on two wheels. You can rent bikes ($7 per hr., $25 per day, $30 overnight) from **Hornby Island Off-Road Bike Shop** (335-0444), at the Co-op (see above; open daily 10am-5pm). The calm, protected waters of the island provide superb ocean kayaking. **Hornby Ocean Kayaks** (335-2726) transports kayaks to the calmest of seven beaches and provides guided tours, lessons, and rentals (tours $30, full day $65; rentals $24 per 4 hr., $40 per day). Low tide on Hornby uncovers over 300m of the finest sand near Vancouver Island. **Tribune Bay,** at the base of Central Rd., is the more accessible of the two beaches. The alternative, **Whaling Station Bay,** is about 5km farther north. On the way there from Tribune Bay, Helliwell Rd. passes stunning **Helliwell Provincial Park,** where well-groomed trails lead through old-growth forest to bluffs overlooking the ocean. Cormorants dive straight into the ocean to surface moments later with trophy-quality fish, while bald eagles cruise on the sea breezes.

If you plan on spending more than a day here, bring a tent and food. The B&Bs dotting the island can be rather expensive during the summer. The **Hornby Island Resort** (335-0136), right at the ferry docks, is a pub/restaurant/laundromat/hotel/campground. The pub fare is standard but reasonably priced and the restaurant has breakfast plates from $6, sandwiches $4-5, and burgers $6-7 (open daily 9:30am-9pm). Campsites cost $17 per night (hookup $18; Jan.-March $10). Private hotel rooms start at $65. **Bradsdadsland Country Camp,** 1980 Shingle Spit Rd. (335-0757), offers standard tent sites ($19 for 2 people, $1.50 per additional person or pet; Brad's Dad stays free).

Pacific Rim National Park

The three regions of Pacific Rim National Park vary so greatly in landscape and seascape that only a national government could have combined them under the same jurisdiction. The park, a thin strip of land on Vancouver Island's remote Pacific coast, can be reached in three ways. To reach the south end of the park, the **West Coast Trail** at **Port Renfrew,** take Hwy. 14 to its end. Highway 14 runs west from Highway 1 not far from Victoria. The middle section—the **Broken Group Islands** in **Barkley Sound** and **Bamfield**—is far more difficult to reach. The Broken Islands can only be reached by water, and the trip to Bamfield requires a 100km drive over bone-jarring logging roads either from Highway 18 or through Port Alberni. Highway 18 connects to Hwy. 1 at **Duncan** (City of Totems!) about 60km north of Victoria. For access to **Long Beach,** at the Park's northern reaches, take the spectacular drive across Vancouver Island on Hwy. 4 to the Pacific Rim Hwy. This stretch connects **Ucluelet** (yoo-CLOO-let) to **Tofino** (toe-FEE-no). Highway 4 branches west of Highway 1 about 35km north of Nanaimo and leads through **Port Alberni** on the way to the Pacific coast.

Each spring, around 22,000 **gray whales** stream past the park. Orcas, sea lions, black-tailed deer, bald eagles, and black bears also frequent the area. The park is part of the second largest temperate rainforest in North America, and it is wise to be prepared for frequent downpours.

WEST COAST TRAIL: PORT RENFREW & BAMFIELD

Port Renfrew is the most easily accessible of the three gateways into the **West Coast Trail,** a.k.a. the Katmandu of North American backpacking. The trail covers the southern third of the Pacific Rim National Park between Port Renfrew and Bamfield, weaving through 77km of forests and waterfalls, scaling steep wooden ladders and rocky slopes, and tracing the treacherous shoreline that has been the graveyard of many ships. Only **experienced hikers** should attempt this slick trail, and never alone. Gray whales, sea otters, and black bears along the route may provide company, but they can't help you in an accident. The trail is regulated by a strict quota system and reservations are necessary to hike it. For information on the legendary trek, call BC Parks at 800-663-6000 or write to Box 280, Ucluelet V0R 3A0. Hikers end up paying about $100 in fees, including a reservation fee, a trail use fee, and a ferry crossing fee. The trail is open from May 1 to Sept. 30, but you can (and probably should) make reservations by March 1.

Both Port Renfrew and Bamfield are somewhat isolated. Trucks and boats are the best vehicles to get you where you're going. A long winding drive down Hwy. 14 lands you in Port Renfrew, while hours of logging roads and the Pacific are the only two ways into Bamfield. Because Bamfield lies on two sides of an inlet, water transit is necessary to cross town. The **Kingfisher Marina** (728-3228) operates a water taxi service just for such occasions.

If you only want to spend an afternoon roughing it, visit Port Renfrew's **Botanical Beach Provincial Park.** Nature enthusiasts will delight in the many varieties of intertidal life, as well as sandstone, shale, quartz, and basalt formations. Botanical Beach offers a hiking trail of its own, connecting Port Renfrew to the nearby **Juan de Fuca Provincial Park** and **China Beach.**

Seek out **maps** and information on the area and registration information for the West Coast Trail at the **Trail Information Center** (647-5434) in Port Renfrew (open May-Sept. daily 9am-5pm). or Pachena Bay, 5km from Bamfield (728-3234). **West Coast Trail Express** (477-8700) runs one bus per day from Victoria to Bamfield, from Nanaimo to Bamfield, and from Nanaimo to Port Renfrew (each $50; reservations required; no service from Victoria to Port Renfrew). The **Pacheenaht Band Bus Service** (647-5521) provides transportation from Port Renfrew to Bamfield ($40) and points between. The local hospital is the **Bamfield Red Cross Outpost Hospital** (728-3312). The **post office** is in Bamfield, across the inlet near the Bamfield Inn, next to the General Store (open Mon.-Fri. 8:30am-5pm). The **postal code** is V9P 2G2. The **area code** is 250.

Accommodations in town are limited, making camping in the park your best bet. Campgrounds pop up in both towns and some locals rent tent sites on their property. Near Port Renfrew, the **Pacheenaht Campground** offers campsites ($8) and RV sites ($13). The **Seabeam Fishing Resort and Hostel** (728-3286) in Bamfield sports the area's cheapest indoor accommodations ($15, nonmembers $20) complete with full kitchen and laundry facilities. Head to **Camp Ross** (337-5935) at the West Coast Trailhead for an amazing shoreside location (free; outhouses, pay phone, 3-day max.). To wash the trail dust off in Port Renfrew, most hikers and campers use the public **shower** ($1) and **laundry** ($2), available at the **Port Renfrew Hotel** (647-5541).

Almost all the restaurants in both towns are inexpensive, but campers and hikers might prefer the convenience of shopping at Port Renfrew's **General Store** (647-5587) and Bamfield's **Kamshee Store** (728-3411). Both are open daily 9am-9pm, in winter 9am-7pm. Dinner out is likely to disappoint.

LONG BEACH: UCLUELET AND TOFINO

At the northern end of the Pacific Rim National Park lie Ucluelet and Tofino. Thirty kilometers apart at opposite ends of the Pacific Rim Hwy. and on either side of the park, the two towns also stand at either end of the cultural spectrum. Ucluelet retains its fishing-village attitude until it floods with Long Beach travelers every July and August. The commercialized Tofino, by contrast, is Canada's best answer to California (it even has its own surfing subculture). Both towns provide ample access to Pacific Rim's many trails and to the surrounding waters.

Find **Parks Canada Visitor Information** 3km north of the Port Alberni junction on the Pacific Rim Hwy. (726-4212; open mid-April to mid-Oct. daily 9:30am-5pm); in **Tofino** at 351 Campbell St. (725-3414; open daily 9:30am-8pm; March-June and Sept.-Oct. Sat.-Sun. 9am-5pm; Nov.-Feb. phone 9am-6pm); and in **Ucluelet** at 227 Main St. (726-4641; open daily 10am-5pm; Sept.-June Mon.-Fri. 10am-3pm).

Laidlaw (385-4411 in Victoria, 724-1266 in Port Alberni, 725-3101 in Tofino, 726-4334 in Ucluelet) connects Victoria and Nanaimo with Tofino and Ucluelet through Port Alberni. Four buses leave daily (Victoria to Tofino $45, to Ucluelet $42). **Alberni Marine Transportation, Inc.,** P.O. Box 188, Port Alberni V9Y 7M7 (723-8313 or 800-663-7192), operates the freighter *Lady Rose* year-round from Port Alberni to Bamfield ($19, round-trip $38), Ucluelet ($22, round-trip $44), and Gibraltar Island in the Broken Group Islands ($20, round-trip $40).

The laundromat in Ucluelet is **Koin Laundrette** in Davison's Shopping Plaza on Peninsula St. (open 9am-9pm). In Tofino try the **Tofino Laundromat** at 448 Campbell (open 24hr.). The **hospital** is at 261 Neill St., Tofino (725-3212). Reach the **police** at 725-3242 in Tofino and 726-7773 in Ucluelet. The **post office,** 161 1st St., (725-3734) is at 1st and Campbell in Tofino (open Mon.-Thurs. 10am-3pm, Fri. 10am-5pm). The **area code** is 250.

Even in the off-season, a bed in Tofino can be pricey, and once summer rolls around camping gets expensive too. Reservations can make or break a July-August visit, as those without can easily find themselves shut out of the handful of reasonably priced accommodations and forced into a motel room, all of which start at $75 for a single. The **Tofino Hostel,** 241 Campbell (725-2288), has beds for $20 and a private double for $45, as well as a clean kitchen, laundry facilities, and a back yard deck. **Stephanie's,** a B&B at 420 Gibson St. (725-4230), has three rooms ($45-60 in July and Aug.; off-season $35-50). Kids are a fixture at Stephanie's, so if you don't want to hang with the under-10 set, look elsewhere. In Ucluelet, the **Ucluelet Lodge** (726-4234), on Main St., provides inexpensive rooms and a bar downstairs (singles and doubles $29 with shared bath, $40 with private bath). **Agapé,** 246 Lee St. (726-7073), 4km before Ucluelet, is a treasure at $40-45 for a single, $50-65 for a double, including a gourmet hot breakfast.

While there are a number of private campgrounds between the park and Tofino, they average at least $20 to camp and almost $30 for a hookup. It costs $5 per day to remain in the park; annual passes are also available ($70). These fill quickly in the summer; if you can't find a spot, try the golf course—they often have sites when no one else does. The **Park Superintendent** can be contacted year-round for advance information at Box 280, Ucluelet V0R 3A0 (726-7721). Locals can often provide tips on free camping in the area. The only campground in the park itself is **Green Point Campground** (726-4245), 10km north of the park information center. Green Point has 94 sites equipped with hot water, flush toilets, fire rings, and (in July and Aug.) swarms of campers and mosquitoes ($22; reservations required, call 800-689-6025). **Ucluelet Campground** (726-4355), off Pacific Rim Hwy., offers sites with showers and toilets ($17, full hookup $20, 4min. showers $1; open March-Oct.).

Shop for groceries at Tofino's **Co-op,** 140 1st St. (725-3226; open Mon.-Sat. 9:30am-8pm, Sun. 11am-5pm). For the late night bowler in all of us, **Smiley's Family Restaurant,** 1992 Peninsula Rd. (726-4213) is open from 7am-midnight and has a bowling alley ($3 per game), a pool table, and an arcade to help you burn off the calories from their fish 'n' chips ($5.50) and homemade pies. Grab a sandwich at the small, friendly **Munch Box,** 131 1st St. (725-2778), in Tofino. A decent-sized sub sandwich will only sink you $3.70, and an even larger, $5.70 (open daily 9am-9pm). More than just a restaurant and bakery offering some of the finest eats in Western Canada, the **Common Loaf Bake Shop,** 180 1st St. (725-3915), is also Tofino's social center. A slice of gourmet pizza goes for $3.75. The colorful **Alleyway Cafe,** 305 Campbell (725-3105), is hard to find (hint: it's in an alley), but offers veggie burgers ($6.25), salmon quesadillas ($7), and burritos ($4.85) to those who make it.

Orcas and **gray whales** migrate past the park and the neighboring **Clayoquot Sound** every spring. The grays stay in the area all summer at the feeding grounds in the Sound. Ask some of the local boaters for a ride; some will take you out for $50-60 if they have time. Or go with the professionals at **Jamie's Whaling Station,** 606 Campbell St. (725-3919 or 800-667-9913), just east of 4th St. Look for the big wood whale. Smooth rides in large boats are available (3hr. $70), but the daring venture out in **Zodiacs,** hard-bottomed inflatable rafts with huge outboards that ride the swells at 30 knots (2hr. $50).

A trip to the west side of the island is not complete without **hiking** on one of the park's magnificent **trails.** Pick up a *Hiker's Guide* at the visitors center for a list of eight hikes ranging from 100m to 5km in length along the Long Beach stretch. The 1km **Rain Forest Trail,** off the Pacific Rim Highway brings hikers through gigantic trees and fallen logs of old-growth rainforest. When the unending rain finally overwhelms you, seek refuge in the art galleries in Ucluelet and Tofino. Ucluelet's **Du Quah Gallery,** 1971 Peninsula Rd. (726-7223), is more modest than Tofino's **Eagle Aerie Gallery,** 350 Campbell St. (725-3235), which houses paintings behind its striking and unusual carved wooden doors (open daily 9am-9pm; free).

Comox Valley

With fine hiking, fishing, and skiing, and the southern regions of Strathcona Provincial Park just a llama's trot away, the tourist season never ends in the self-proclaimed "recreation capital of Canada." Sheltering the towns of Courtenay, Comox, and Cumberland, the Comox Valley boasts the highest concentration of artists in Canada, along with many museums and galleries. The discovery of the 80-million-year-old "Courtenay Elasmosaur" in 1989 has transformed the valley into a minor mecca of paleontology as well. Outdoor adventure abounds.

Practical Information The **tourist office** in Courtenay is at 2040 Cliffe Ave. (334-3234; open 8am-8pm). **Laidlaw** (334-2475) connects the area to points north and south along Hwy. 19. The bus stop is in Courtenay on Moray Ave. behind the Driftwood Mall. The **Comox Valley Transit System** (339-5453) has a cavalry of coaches that connect the three towns. Buses ($1.25, seniors $1) run from 6:40am to 10:20pm. **BC Ferries** (800-BC-FERRY/223-3779) connects Comox with Powell River on the mainland. The **King Koin Laundrette** is at 467 4th St. (open daily 7:30am-10pm). Some useful numbers in the Comox Valley: **emergency,** 911; **weather,** 339-5044; **police,** 338-1321; **hospital,** 339-2242. The **post office** is in Courtenay at 219 4th St. (334-4341), across from the museum (open Mon.-Fri.8:30am-5pm; **postal code** V9N 7G3). The **area code** is 250.

Accommodations, Camping, and Food Pricey motels line the highway south of Courtenay. B&Bs are common, and offer a homey stay for better prices. The **Comox Lake Hostel,** 4787 Lake Trail Rd. (338-1914), about 10km from town, trades a bed for $15, a tent site for $8, and linen for a smile. To get there, drive west from Courtenay on Lake Trail Rd. until you think you've gone too far. Then keep on going.

Within hiking distance of the Strathcona Provincial Park, the hostel is a popular back-packing base camp (free pick up and drop off in town with prior reservation). Close to both Courtenay and Comox, the **Estuary House,** 2810 Comox Rd. (890-0130), has three spacious rooms with private baths. If you call ahead, get dibs on the enormous front room with private deck and plush bathtub (singles $35; doubles $45). The **Mountain View Bed and Breakfast,** 605 Ellcee Pl. (338-0157), in Courtenay, offers spotless bathrooms, a TV lounge, and a balcony view of the Comox glacier (singles from $30; doubles from $45; reservations recommended). For a spectacular view of the Georgia Strait and the Coastal Mountains, lodge at the **Bed and Breakfast By the Sea,** 650 Hutton Rd., Comox (339-0492). A sundeck, the beach, and a home-cooked breakfast make for a pleasant stay (single $40; double $50). Campers can try **Kin Beach** (339-6365), on Astra Rd. in Comox, where $7.50 rents one of 16 sites, a beach 100m away, and tennis courts. **Miracle Beach** (337-5720), on Miracle Beach Dr., 25km north of Courtenay in Black Creek, has more facilities than Kin Beach, but is harder to reach and often full ($14.50; showers, flush toilets).

The many **farmer's markets** in the area tend to be more appealing than nearby restaurants. The most comprehensive and conspicuous market is **Farquharson Farms,** 1300 Comox Rd. (338-8194), in Courtenay. Not satisfied with fresh fruit and vegetables alone, Farquharson also sells gardening supplies and patio furniture for those determined to settle the nearby beaches (open daily 9am-6pm). The **Bar None Cafe,** 244 4th St. (334-3112), off Cliffe Ave. in Courtenay, stocks exceptional all-vegetarian fare. Choose your own rice and pasta dishes, salads, and fresh salsas, and pay $1.85 per 100g. Espresso and juice bar, too (open Mon.-Sat. 8am-7pm, Sun. brunch 10:30am-5:30pm). The **Old House Restaurant,** 1760 Riverside Ln. (338-5406), features luxurious, lodge-style architecture and a menu big enough for sushi (from $5), pizza ($3.75 per slice), organic coffee, and fresh muffins (open Tues.-Thurs. 8am-7pm, Fri. 8am-8pm, Sat. 9am-5pm). **Safeway** (open Mon.-Sat. 8am-9pm, Sun. 9am-9pm) is on 8th St. in Courtenay.

Sights and Activities The **Comox Valley Art Gallery,** 367 4th St. (338-6211), in Courtenay, a focal point for the local arts community, houses craft galleries (open Tues.-Sat. 10am-5pm). The valley boasts several studios and galleries; contact the tourist office for more information. The **Courtenay District Museum,** 360 Cliffe Ave. (334-3611), holds permanent exhibits on pioneer life, native culture and art, industry, and geology. A paleontology annex, next to the museum, stores the bevy of dinosaur bones uncovered in the area (open daily 10am-4:30pm; in winter Tues.-Sat. 10am-4:30pm; free). **Horne Lake Caves Provincial Park,** south of Courtenay on Horne Lakes Rd., opens its caves to the public. Several guided tour programs are offered ranging from half-hour explanations to five- and six-hour rappelling and climbing journeys ($69-99). Call 757-8687 for recording, 248-7829 for reservations.

Strathcona Provincial Park

Elk, deer, marmots, and wolves all inhabit the over 2000 sq. km. of Strathcona, one of the best-preserved and most beautiful wilderness areas on Vancouver Island. The park's two visitors centers are on **Buttle Lake,** on Hwy. 28 between Gold River and Campbell River, and **Mt. Washington/Forbidden Plateau**, outside Courtenay off Hwy. 19. The two official campgrounds, sharing 161 campsites between them, are Buttle Lake and Ralph River, both on the shores of Buttle Lake and accessible by Hwy. 28 and secondary roads (follow the highway signs). **Buttle Lake,** closer to Campbell River, has comfortable sites, a playground, and sandy beaches on the lake ($12). Less crowded **Ralph River** provides convenient access to the park's best hiking trails ($9.50). From Ralph River, the difficult 12km **Phillips Ridge** hike takes about seven or eight hours round-trip, passing two waterfalls in a 790m climb and ending atop a wildflower-strewn mountain by an alpine lake. Those with less than a day or eight hours of endurance can hit the **Karst Creek Trail,** a mellow 2km hike passing limestone sinkholes and waterfalls, or the **Myra Falls Trail,** a 1km hike from the south end of Butte Lake to the cascades.

Visitors who wish to explore Strathcona's **backcountry areas** must camp 1km from main roads. To minimize environmental impact, camp at least 30m away from water sources as well. Backcountry campers are rewarded by lakes, waterfalls, ancient cedar and fir forests, and wildflower meadows. Campfires are discouraged in the park. Those entering the undeveloped areas of the park should notify the park service of their intended departure and return times, and should be well-equipped (**maps** and **rain gear** are essential). The **Forbidden Plateau** and **Mt. Washington,** just outside the park boundaries, hit their high-seasons in the winter with a heavy influx of skiers. For information on the park, contact BC Parks, District Manager, Box 1479, Parksville, BC V9P 2H4 (604-248-3931).

Campbell River

A large rock covered with aquatic-themed graffiti welcomes you to Campbell River, another of BC's many self-proclaimed "Salmon Capitals of the World." It also sports incredible fishing and scuba diving "second only to the Red Sea," according to *National Geographic.* The abundance of gas stations illustrates Campbell River's role as the transportation hub of the Northern Island, providing easy access to Strathcona, Port Hardy and its Alaskan ferry, and Quadra, Cortes and Discovery Islands.

Practical Information The **Travel Infocentre,** 1235 Island Hwy. (287-4636), in the Tyee Mall, has a helpful staff and *beaucoup de* brochures (open daily 8am-6pm; in winter Mon.-Fri. 9am-5pm). **Laidlaw** (287-7151), at 13th and Cedar, sends 5 buses per day to Nanaimo ($22). **BC Ferries** runs from Campbell River to Quadra Island (15 per day; $3.50, cars $9.50, ages 5-11 $1.75, under 5 free). Find the cheapest rental cars ($25 per day plus 15¢ per km after 100) at **Rent-a-Wreck,** 1811 Island Hwy. (287-4677), in the Esso station (open Mon.-Tues. and Sat.-Sun 8am-5pm, Wed.-Fri. 8am-9pm). Clean your clothes at the **laundromat** in the Tyee Mall (open daily 8am-10pm). Useful numbers are: **emergency,** 911; **crisis hotline,** 287-7743; **hospital,** 375 2nd Ave. (287-7111); **poison control,** (800) 567-8911; **police,** 286-6221.

Accommodations, Camping, and Food Finding inexpensive lodging in Campbell River is like swimming upstream in spawning season. The most affordable places are the campgrounds; among the best is **Elk Falls Provincial Park,** on Hwy. 28, which offers spacious sites among large firs ($9.50; flush toilets, no showers). If Elk Falls is full, continue on to the campsites at **Strathcona Provincial Park** (see above). The **Lighthouse Bed and Breakfast** offers clean rooms, a full morning meal, and an exceptional view of the harbor for $45 (doubles $55).

Picadilly Fish and Chips (286-6447), in the double decker bus at 798 Island Hwy., serves up better-than-British fish 'n' chips. An oyster or salmon burger and "chips" costs $5.25. Discover *poutine,* a sloppy Canadian concoction of fries, cheese curds and gravy, for $3 (open daily 11:30am-7pm). Shop for yourself at **Super Valu** (287-4410) in the Tyee Mall (open daily 8:30am-9:30pm).

Sights and Activities If you dig **salmon,** this is the place. Sockeye, coho, pink, chum, and chinook are hauled in by the boatload from the waters of the Campbell River. The savvy can reap deep-sea prizes from **Discovery Pier** in Campbell Harbour (fishing charge $1; rod rentals $2.50 per hr., $6 per ½-day). The pier has 200m of boardwalk plants and an artificial underwater reef built to attract astigmatic fish. Get a **fishing licence** (separate salt water and fresh water permits required) at the infocentre or any sports outfitter in town. A "salmon sticker" costs extra (see p. 179 for what happens when people don't buy their stickers).

Scuba-gear rentals can be pricey and require proper certification, but **Beaver Aquatics,** 760 Island Hwy. (287-7652), offers a nifty $25 **snorkeling** package including suit, mask, snorkel, and fins (open Mon.-Sat. 9am-5pm, Sun. 10am-2pm). See how the Canadian government keeps nature in balance with a tour of the **Quinsam River Salmon Hatchery,** 4217 Argonaut Rd. (287-9564). The hatchery provides a sheltered area for young fishies to develop, blissfully unaware of the rods and reels ahead. Nature trails and picnic tables dot the hatchery grounds (open daily 8am-4pm).

Alert Bay

The cultural legacy of the Kwakiutl, one of the many coastal native nations, sets the fishing village of Alert Bay apart from its aquatourist siblings. One of the richest repositories of native culture on Vancouver Island, Alert Bay boasts a 173 ft. totem pole—the second largest in the world (Victoria, BC slapped a few extra feet onto its old one to claim the prize)—that tells the story of the Kwakiutl. The pole towers over the **U'Mista Cultural Center** (974-5403), 2km north of the ferry terminal (see p. 214). Alert Bay lies in the Johnstone Straight, where the protected waters and plentiful fish provide an excellent summer home to orcas, or "killer whales."

Practical Information Find **travel information** in **Port McNeil** by the ferry dock (956-3131; open Mon.-Thurs. 9am-5pm, Fri. 9am-8pm). In Alert Bay, there's info galore at 116 Fir St. (974-5213; open daily 9am-6pm). **BC Ferries** (956-4533) operates a ferry from Port McNeill to Sointula and Alert Bay (daily 8:45am-10:05pm; round-trip $4.50, car and driver $16.25) and **Laidlaw** runs one bus from Port McNeil to Victoria per day ($76). Some useful numbers are: **emergency,** 911; **St. George's Hospital,** 182 Fir St. (974-5585); **police,** 974-5544. The **area code** is 250.

Sights and Accommodations Alert Bay's star attractions are the pods of orcas which frequent the straits nearby. Expensive sighting charters are everywhere ($60 for 3-4hr.). Lucky visitors might glimpse the orcas while on the ferry or even from the shores of town. Head approximately 25km south of Port McNeill to Telegraph Cove and hike to the shore or rent kayaks for the day for a cheaper, less-touristy view. **Jinnouchi Kayaks** (949-7707), in Port Hardy, will drop off and pick up kayaks in the cove. If you can't find the whales, look up for some great views of bald eagles.

At the fabulous **Pacific Hostelry (HI-C),** 349 Fir St. (604-974-2026), play the piano and watch for whales from a roomy wooden living room with a view of the strait ($17, nonmembers $19). Call ahead for reservations, and to be certain the hostel is still open; it may be closing for the 1998 season. Restaurants are limited and most are expensive; you may want to stock up at the **Blueline Supermarket,** 257 Fir St. (974-5521; open Mon.-Fri. 9am-9pm, Sat. 9am-6pm, Sun. 10am-5pm).

The U'Mista Cultural Centre

The traditional gift-giving ceremony of the **potlatch,** held by many Northwest Coast natives, was outlawed by Canada's government in 1884. In 1921, police officers stumbled upon a ceremony held on Village Island, and 20 men and women were briefly sent to prison for participation in the event. The ceremonial gear from the potlatch was confiscated and sent to museums and private collections (including that of the officer responsible for the raid and the Superintendent General of Indian Affairs). It was not until the late 60s that a serious effort was made to repatriate the lost objects. The Board of Trustees of the National Museum agreed to return a portion of the confiscated artifacts on the stipulation that museums be built in Cape Mudge and Alert Bay to house the collections. The **U'Mista Cultural Centre** (974-5403; open Mon.-Fri. 9am-5pm, Sat.-Sun. noon-5pm; closed Sat.-Sun. in winter) now holds one of the richest repositories of native culture on Vancouver Island. The centre takes its name from the traditional term for the return of a loved one taken captive by raiding parties. The return of the Kwakiutl's treasures is, therefore, a form of *u'mista.*

Port Hardy

Port Hardy was content to be a quiet logging and fishing community until BC Ferries made it the southern terminus for ferries carrying passengers from Prince Rupert and Alaska. Virtually overnight, the unassuming town etched a name for itself as a major transportation port, complete with a chainsaw-carved welcome sign. A mild coastal town, Port Hardy remains an excellent (as well as the only) place for ferry passengers to spend the night.

Practical Information Pick up a restaurant guide and tour **maps** at the **Travel Infocentre,** 7250 Market St. (949-7622). Take Hardy Bay Rd. off Hwy. 19 to Market St. (open Mon.-Sat. 8am-9pm, Sun. 9am-9pm; winter Mon.-Fri. 9am-5pm). **Laidlaw** (949-7532), on Market St. across from the Travel Infocentre, connects Port Hardy to Victoria through Nanaimo (1 per day, and whenever the ferry arrives; $81 from Victoria, $70 from Nanaimo). The **BC Ferry** terminal (800-BC-FERRY/223-3779) is 3km south at Bear Cove. Service between Prince Rupert and Port Hardy runs every other day; (1-way $102, with car $312). **North Island Taxi** can be reached at 949-8800. **North Star Cycle and Sports** (949-7221), at Market and Granville St., rents bikes for $15 per half-day or $25 per day. **Jim's Hardy Sports,** 7125 Market St. (949-8382), will tackle other equipment needs (open Mon.-Fri. 9am-6pm, Sat.-Sun 10am-5pm). Clean those stinkin' socks in the machines at **Payless Gas Co.** (949-2366), on Granville St. (open 24hr.; wash $1.75, 10min. dry 25¢). Some helpful phone numbers in Port Hardy are: **emergency,** 911; **crisis line,** 949-6033; **police,** 7355 Columbia Ave. (949-6335); **hospital,** 949-6161. Port Hardy's **postal code** is V0N 2P0. The **area code** is 250.

WESTERN CANADA

Accommodations and Camping Like any port town, the demand for hotel and motel rooms is quite high, and prices are even higher. Among the less expensive bed and breakfasts are the **Traveler's Friend B&B,** 6750 Bayview Dr. (949-7126; singles $40; doubles $50) and **Hamilton's B&B,** 9415 Mayors Way (949-6638; singles $45; doubles $55). The infocentre operates a free reservation service. For a quiet, wooded setting, pitch your tent at **Quatse River Campground,** 5050 Byng Rd. (949-2395). Toilets come in a choice of flush and pit (*Let's Go* recommends the flush); showers and laundromat available (sites $14, full hookups $18, seniors discount $1). The campground shares its grounds with a **fish hatchery** (949-9022); tours are available October through June. **Wildwoods Campsite** (949-6753), on the road from the ferry within walking distance of the terminal, has comfortable sites strewn with pine needles. Sites maintain reasonable privacy despite their close quarters. Expect a line for the hot showers in the morning (sites $11, with hookup $16, hiker/biker $5).

Food For a wide selection of groceries and bulk foods, go up Granville St. from Market St. to **Overwaitea Foods,** 950 Granville St. (949-6455; open daily 9am-9pm). It's not what you'd expect from the name, but **Giant Foods,** 8645 Granville St. (949-5758), is still big enough for most grocery needs (open 6am-10pm). Budget meals are hard to find unless you're willing to settle for burgers and fries. Some of the best can be found at **I.V.'s Quarterdeck Pub,** 6555 Hardy Bay Rd. (949-6922), which has burgers for $6, and a surprisingly large vegetarian selection, for a pub, (open daily 11am-midnight). **Sam's Place,** on Trustee Rd. near the junction of Hwy. 19 and Granville St., serves similar burgers ($4.50-6), and pizza ($8-11.50; open Mon.-Sat. 11am-11pm).

Cape Scott Provincial Park

Sixty kilometer of logging roads (watch for trucks) lead through wild and wet Cape Scott to parking lots near trailheads. Most begin from the lot on **San Josef Road,** near the entrance to the park, although Cape Scott will soon have a 100km trail connecting Port Hardy to the depths of the park.

Several trails run through the park; many are less crowded than those in nearby Strathcona. Get to the point on the 23.6km trail to the northwestern tip of the island,

Cape Scott. For a shorter hike, follow the mellow 2.5km trail to **San Josef Bay** and mingle with everyone else. Cape Scott has eight strategically placed campgrounds. Fresh water is available at popular **San Josef Bay** and **Nels Bight.** Good **topographic maps** help enterprising trekkers (available from **Maps BC,** Ministry of Environment, Parliament Bldgs., Victoria BC V8V 1XS). For more detailed information on the park, pick up the Cape Scott Provincial Park pamphlet at one of the travel infocenters elsewhere in the region, since none are available anywhere near the park, or write to BC Parks, District Manager, Box 1479, Parksville, BC V9P 2H4 (604-954-4600). And while the scenery may vary, the constant rain will not. Bring rain gear.

SOUTHEASTERN BRITISH COLUMBIA

Fraser River Canyon

The Fraser River courses down from the Rockies and hurls itself through 1300km of plateaus and steep canyons on its journey to the Pacific. Visitors today may not appreciate the audacity of Simon Fraser's 1808 expedition down the river from Mt. Robson to Vancouver—the easier route from Cache Creek to Hope on the Trans-Canada Hwy. (Hwy. 1) makes his trailblazing seem like a distant dream. The river's 200km of rapids are not as thrilling as the infocentre would have travelers believe, but the sheer size of the towering, pine-carpeted canyon walls makes it a striking scene.

Hope

The biggest thing happening in **Hope** is the intersection of several highways. **Highway 1,** the Trans-Canada Hwy., leads west into Vancouver and bends north at Hope, running to Yale and Cache Creek where it joins **Highway 97,** the Cariboo Hwy., and heads to northern British Columbia. **Highway 7** runs west to Vancouver's suburbs along the north bank of the Fraser River. **Highway 3,** the Crowsnest Trail, winds east through breathtaking country close to the U.S. border, to Osoyoos near Penticton, through Kootenay Country to Nelson, Crowsnest Pass, and into Alberta. Finally, **Highway 5,** the Coquihalla Hwy., is a new toll road ($10) running north to Kamloops with good access to the Okanagan country.

The staff at the **Travel Infocentre,** 919 Water Ave. (869-2021), take perverse pride in the way Sylvester Stallone laid waste to their town in the original Rambo blockbuster, *First Blood,* but are knowledgeable on other subjects as well (open daily 8am-8pm; Sept.-June 9am-5pm). Besides providing the riveting "Rambo Walking Tour," the infocentre also has info on the Fraser River Canyon. Buses arrive at the **Greyhound** station, 833 3rd Ave. (869-5522), and make connections further east in Chiliwack for destinations throughout Western Canada. Many ramblers try hitching north on Hwy. 1 where rides are reputedly easy to find. Rent a car at **Gardner Chev-Olds,** 945 Water St. (869-9511), next to the infocentre (open Mon.-Sat. 9am-6pm; $35 per day, $240 per week; 13¢ per km after 100). The Hope **police station,** 670 Hope-Princeton Hwy. (869-7750), is just off Hwy. 3. The **post office** is at 777 Fraser St. (open Mon.-Fri. 8:30am-5pm).

If stuck here for a night, trek a block north from the bus station to Wallace St. and hang a left. The **Hope Motor Hotel,** 272 Wallace St. (869-5641), rents singles ($49) and doubles ($59). Campgrounds abound in the Fraser Valley; ask the infocentre for enlightenment. In town, head for the giant firs and cedars of the **Coquihalla Campsite,** 800 Kawkawa Lake Rd. (869-7119), on the east side of Hope along the banks of the Coquihalla River (122 sites; $16, river site $19, hook-up $20).

Shop for groceries to the hippest elevator music in Canada at **Buy and Save Foods,** 489 Wallace St. (869-5318; open daily 8am-8pm). The **Suzie Q Family Restaurant,** 2591 Wallace St. (869-5515), a block north of the Greyhound station, has both cheap Western *and* Japanese cuisine (open daily 7am-10pm).

OUTDOORS

For a better look at the Fraser River, try one of the moderately difficult **hikes** that start from trailheads near Hope. The short, lush **Rotary Trail** starts at Wardle St. and runs to the confluence of the Fraser and Coquihalla Rivers. The two-hour climb to the summit of **Thacker Mountain** is more challenging. To reach this trailhead, cross the Coquihalla River Bridge, take a left on Union Bar Rd., then head left again on Thacker Mountain Rd. The parking lot at the end marks the beginning of a 5km gravel path to the peak, which provides clear views of Hope and the Fraser River. Pause for a pleasant diversion at **Kawkawa Creek** off Union Bar Rd., recently "enhanced" to aid the mid- and late-summer salmon spawnings. The boardwalk along the creek leads to a swimming hole and popular picnicking spot.

The **Coquihalla Canyon Recreation Area** is a five- to ten-minute drive out of Hope along Kawkawa Lake Rd. Here the **Othello Quintet Tunnels,** blasted through solid granite, provide mute evidence of the impressive engineering that led to the opening of the Kettle Valley Railway in 1916. Turn right on Othello Rd. off Kawkawa Lake Rd., and right again on Tunnel Rd. Allow half an hour to walk through the tunnels.

For an even closer view of the river, head 36km north on Hwy. 1 to the small town of **Yale** (don't let your feelings about this town's grungy namesake school keep you away). Take the first right after the stoplight, then follow the gravel road about 1km; you'll find a close-up view of the majestic **Lady Franklin Rock,** which splits the Fraser into two sets of heavy rapids. If you're interested in getting *on* the river, **Fraser River Raft Expeditions** (800-363-RAFT/7238), just south of town, can pave the way. Although the $95 fee for a full-day trip might seem as steep as the canyon walls, those who can pull together the funds shouldn't miss the heart-pounding, body-drenching thrills. Trips leave almost daily; call ahead to reserve.

When Simon Fraser made his pioneering trek down the river, he likened one particularly tumultuous stretch of rapids to the "Gates of Hell." Yale lies just beyond **Hell's Gate** on the Fraser. The foaming waters, 25km north of Yale on Hwy. 1, make Fraser's journey seem miraculous. When melting snow floods the river in spring, the 60m-deep water rushes through the narrow gorge with incredible force. A cluster of gift shops and eateries are now embedded in the precipitous cliffs where Fraser once advised "no human beings should venture." The gondolas of **Hell's Gate Airtram,** 43111 Hwy. 1 (867-9277), will "fly" you 150m across the canyon in four minutes ($9, seniors $8, ages 6-14 $6, families $24). Acrophobes and diehard budgeteers will save their money and hike down the nearby trail to the river.

■ Kamloops

Halfway between Vancouver and Banff, Kamloops anchors the junction of the heavily-traveled Yellowhead and Trans-Canada Highways. The **Visitors Infocentre** (374-3377 or 800-662-1994) is just west of town on the Trans-Canada Hwy. (open daily 9am-7pm; Sept.-May 9am-5pm). **Greyhound,** 725 Notre Dame Ave. (374-1212), makes regular stops in Kamloops en route to: Jasper (3 per day, $45), Vancouver, (8 per day, $49), and Calgary (5 per day, $75). **VIA Rail** (800-561-8630) also stops at North Station, off Hwy. 5 (3 per week to Vancouver, $73; to Edmonton, $162). To get around town, use the **Kamloops Transit System** (376-1216; fare $1.25), or rent bikes at **Java Cycle,** 297 1st Ave. (314-5282), just across from the hostel ($35 per day). Do your laundry at **McCleaners,** 437 Seymour St. (372-9655). In an **emergency,** call 911. The **police** (828-3000) are at 560 Battle St. The **post office** is at 301 Seymour St. (374-2444; open Mon.-Fri. 8:30am-5pm; **postal code:** V2C 5K2). The **area code** is 250. Kamloops lies 356km east of Vancouver, 492km west of Banff.

The **Kamloops Old Courthouse Hostel (HI-C),** 7 W. Seymour St. (828-7991), is, yes, an old courthouse (and an excellent hostel). The gargantuan common room still sports a jury box, judge's bench, and witness stand; the judge's chambers have become a private double (check-in 8am-1pm and 5-10pm; 68 beds; $15, nonmembers $19.50). Testify. For a less pedantic experience, pitch a tent at **Paul Lake Provincial Park,** 17km east of Hwy. 5 on Paul Lake Road (90 sites, $9.50).

Good Kamloops food hangs out on **Victoria St. Benny's Bagels,** 330 Victoria St. (372-2435), unloads fresh bagels, bagel sandwiches, and bagel-related treats on hungry travelers (open Mon.-Fri. 7am-10pm, Sat. 9am-10pm, Sun. 10am-8pm). Satisfy a sweet tooth at the **Sweet Pastry House,** 359 Victoria (372-2625), or stuff yourself silly on an all-you-can-eat lunch ($8.50) at **China Village,** 165 Victoria St. (372-2822).

Every summer night at **Riverside Park** on the banks of the Thompson River, Kamloops boogies down to live music. The park itself is a popular picnic place. See the river up close on a two-hour cruise aboard the **Wanda Sue Paddle Boat,** 1140 River St. (374-7447; 2-3 cruises per day; $11.50). Come face to face with nature sharp in tooth and claw at the **Kamloops Wildlife Park** (573-3242), west of town on the Trans-Canada Hwy. (open daily 8am-6pm; winter 8am-4:30pm; $6.50). Learn the secrets of everyone's favorite herb (well...) on the **Canadian Imperial Ginseng Tour,** 1274 McGill Rd. (851-2880), or explore the remains of a 2000-year-old Shuswap village at the **Secrepemic Museum and Heritage Park,** 355 Yellowhead Hwy. (828-9801; open summer Mon.-Fri. 8:30am-8pm, Sat.-Sun. 10am-6pm; $6).

Salmon Arm

With strong roots in agriculture and logging, Salmon Arm is yet another rural, honky-tonk town. But unlike many of its uncouth brethren, it is surrounded with an extraordinary setting. Lake Shuswap is sublime, and the gentle mountains that cradle the town are a poster-perfect backdrop, especially when the leaves turn in autumn.

Practical Information The **Travel Infocentre,** 751 Marine Park Dr., Box 999 (832-6247), has brochures for you and your grandmother. Follow the **"?"** signs from the Trans-Canada Hwy. (Hwy. 1) across the train tracks (open daily 9am-6pm; Labor Day-May Mon.-Fri. 9am-5pm). The **Salmon Arm Transit System** (832-0191) has regular service (Mon.-Sat.) and door-to-door service (Mon.-Fri.; regular route $1.25, door-to-door $1.50; call for booking). Wash grubby duds at the **B-Line Laundromat,** 456 Trans-Canada Hwy. (832-5500), in Smitty's Shopping Center (open daily 6am-11pm; wash $1.50, 12min. dry $1). For an **ambulance,** call 833-0188; the **hospital** is at 601 10th St. NE (832-2182), and the **police** hang out at 501 2nd Ave. NE (832-6044). The **post office** is at 370 Hudson St. NE (832-3093; open Mon.-Fri. 8:30am-5pm; **General Delivery Postal Code:** V1E 4M6). The **area code** is 250.

Accommodations, Camping, and Food B&Bs are the way of Salmon Arm. For a lake view, swimming pool, sauna, and warm British hospitality (sorry, no bangers), quack on over to **Ducks Galore,** 1961 16th St. NE (832-8906), near Lakeshore Dr. The welcoming owners are collectors of wooden and ceramic ducks, vaguely akin to the many wild ducks in the nature area nearby (singles $35; doubles $50-65). To be spoiled silly, stay at the **Cindosa Bed and Breakfast,** 930 30th St. SE (832-3342), where the Moores will pamper with comfy beds and home-cooked breakfasts. They'll pick you up at the bus station, or take bus #2. Ask Mrs. Moore to show you the "bootsaver" (singles $45; doubles $55). If you're mobile, it's worth the trek out to the **Squilax General Store Hostel** (675-2977), 50km west of Salmon Arm on the Trans-Canada Hwy., for a unique experience—sleep on board three Canadian National Railway cabooses, specially procured and outfitted for hosteling with showers, phone, and laundry. The proprietor, Blair, is a wellspring of info about the area. The sign on the front of the store is home to the remnants of an enormous bat colony (23 beds; $12.50, nonmembers $17). Squilax is an unofficial flag stop for **Greyhound.** While there, try the native **Bannock Bread,** sold at roadside booths.

Campsites in Salmon Arm, especially those on Shuswap Lake, are often crowded and cramped. **Pierre's Point** (832-9588), on 50th Ave. NW, just off Hwy. 1, gives a tiny bit more breathing space than its competitors, though it's still quite crowded (200 sites, 40 on the Shuswap shore; $18, electric hookup $20). For a quieter time, leave the town boundaries for a nearby **provincial park** (ask at the infocentre).

This Horse Talks

The beloved life companion of Salmon Armer Phyllis Olson, **Shag-ra the Horse** has earned fame and fortune through appearances on *America's Funniest Home Videos* and David Letterman's Stupid Pet Tricks. He opens cabinets, he answers phones, he stirs pots, and, most importantly, he sings. Well, sort of. A cross between Milli Vanilli and Mr. Ed, Shag-ra is the newest lip-synching sensation. In the face of skepticism and an unappetizing tooth discoloration, Shag-ra perseveres undaunted. For more information, ask the staff at the visitors centre.

Despite its name, Salmon Arm's culinary establishments showcase neither fish nor limbs. The best deal by far awaits at **Real Canadian Wholesale Club,** 360 Trans-Canada Hwy. (804-0258). Even the non-bulk items are considerably cheaper than any supermarket (open Mon.-Fri. 8am-9pm, Sat. 8am-6pm, Sun. 10am-6pm). For smaller items, walk next door to **Safeway,** 360 Trans-Canada Hwy. (832-8086; open daily 8am-10pm). Head west on Hwy. 1 to the **Pedro Gonzales Fruit Stand,** 3390 Trans-Canada Hwy. W (832-4919), for mounds of cherries, plums, and veggies (open summer daily 8am-9pm; fall and spring 9am-5pm). **Choices,** 40 Lakeshore Drive (832-7555), is the best choice (and the cheapest!) for a sit-down meal of homemade bread sandwiches ($4) and piping hot soups.

Sights Learn what curds and whey really are at **Gort's Gouda Cheese Factory,** 1470 50th St. SW (832-4274). The free tours only last a few minutes, shuttling visitors to the tasty cheese samples all the faster (tours Mon. and Fri. mornings; call to arrange tours at other times). Even if there's no tour, stock up on bargain cheeses and watch the cheesemaking process through viewing windows.

The Salmon Arm area, not to be outdone by its Rocky Mountain neighbors, teems with wildlife. **McGuire Park,** on Hwy. 1 next to the hospital, is the spot to view Canadian geese, muskrats, turtles, and ducks. Catch kokanee or rainbow trout in **Lake Shuswap** (day permits $10, 8 days $25; available at the Government Agent's office next to the infocentre), or get in with the fish by swimming or whitewater rafting on nearby **Adams River.** For a hike out to **Margaret Falls,** just west of town, follow the signs off Hwy. 1 for **Heral Park.** A 10km detour and a short hike bring you to the striking falls. Closer to town, take a walk along the **natural preserve** along the banks of Lake Shuswap to catch a glimpse of the rare Western Grebe.

Though a bit distant (45min. drive), the **Caravan Farm Theatre** (546-8533 or 838-6751) presents top-notch performances during the summer (call for show times). The Farm, 8km northwest of Armstrong, overflows with remnant hippie charm, organic produce, and musical instruments dangling from the trees ($6-12 depending on the show; tickets available at the Squilax General Store Hostel; see above).

Every four years in October, the Salmon Arm area sees two runs: the famous **salmon run** on the Adams River, 46km west of Salmon Arm, where more than a million sockeyes desperately thrash their way up from the Pacific Ocean to spawn, and the less-famous **tourist run,** in which thousands of bystanders cram into tiny Roderick Haig-Brown Provincial Park to catch a glimpse of the colorful fish.

Okanagan Valley

Known throughout Canada for its bountiful fruit harvests, the Okanagan Valley lures visitors with summer blossoms, plentiful sun, and tranquil lakes. The Okanagan Connector links Vancouver to the valley in a short four-hour drive, making the valley a popular vacation destination among sun-starved coastal British Columbians. In the north, the quiet valley is rudely interrupted by an explosion of bloated shopping centers and strip malls along Hwy. 97. Beyond the development, however, lies a series of parks and beaches where many a wanderer catches many a ray.

Kelowna

Kelowna is a city of unexpected juxtapositions. Settled in the heart of the Okanagan Valley, it has always been a center of agriculture. Alongside acres of orchards, however, development and urbanization is rapidly encroaching. Farmers, ranchers, and fruit pickers walk beside a younger generation of beach-goers, and VW vans weave among giant logging trucks on the highway.

PRACTICAL INFORMATION

Visitors Information: Kelowna Travel Infocentre, 544 Harvey Ave. (861-1515). Open Mon.-Fri. 8am-7pm, Sat.-Sun. 9am-7pm.
Buses: Greyhound, 2366 Leckie Rd. (860-3855). To: Vancouver ($49); Calgary ($73); and Penticton ($11).
Public Transportation: Kelowna Regional Transit System (860-8121). Goes virtually anywhere in town. Fare for 1-zone travel $1.25, seniors and students $1. Day passes available. Buses run Mon.-Sat. 6am-10pm.
Taxi: Kelowna Cabs (762-2222 or 762-4444). 24hr. Wheelchair accessible.
Car Rental: Rent-A-Wreck, 2702 N. Hwy. 97 (763-6632). $25 per day plus 12¢ per km after 100. Must be 21. Open Mon.-Sat. 8am-5pm, Sun. 9am-4pm.
Bike Rental: Samesun Hostel (see **Accommodations,** below). $20 per day. **Sports Rent,** 3000 Pandosy St. (861-5699). $22 per day. Open daily 9am-6pm.
Pharmacy: Canada Safeway, 697 Bernard St. (860-0332). Open daily 8am-10pm.
Library: Kelowna Public Library, 1380 Ellis St. (762-2800). Open Tues.-Thurs. 10am-9pm, Mon. and Fri.-Sat. 10am-5:30pm.
Laundromat: Capri Coin Laundromat, 150-1835 Gordon Dr. (860-6871). Wash $1.25, 8min. dry 25¢. Open daily 7:30am-11pm.
Hospital: Kelowna General Hospital, 2268 Pandosy St. (862-4000).
Emergency: 911. **Police:** 350 Doyle Ave. (762-3300).
Post Office: 530 Gaston Ave. (763-4095, general info 800-267-1177). Open Mon.-Fri. 8:30am-5pm. **General Delivery Postal Code:** V1Y 7N2.
Area Code: 250.

Kelowna lies 400km east of Vancouver, 602km west of Calgary, and 68km north of Penticton on the eastern shore of Okanagan Lake.

ACCOMMODATIONS AND CAMPING

In summer, Kelowna dries out thousands of soggy Vancouverites. Whether you're headed for a hostel, campground, or motel, always call ahead for reservations.

Samesun International Hostel, 730 Bernard Ave. (263-9800). Take the #10 bus from the terminal. Just a few blocks from the beach and cafes along Bernard Ave., Samesun's peace-for-all, save-the-world motif may be a calculated attempt to stay hip. $15, $40 for 3 nights. Nonmembers add 10%.
By the Bridge Bed and Breakfast, 1942 McDougall St. (860-7518), at the east end of Okanagan Lake Bridge. A tidy home minutes from the lake, BBB&B offers rooms with private baths, breakfast, and free bicycle use. Single $45-55; double $50-60; triple $65-75; quad $70-80.
Bear Creek Provincial Park (494-6500, reservations 800-689-9025), 9km north of Hwy. 97 on Westside Rd. With lakeside sites, its own beach, and views of Kelowna across the water, Bear Creek books solid in the summer. 122 sites; $15.50.
Lodged Inn Hostel, 2407 35th Ave., Vernon (549-3742 or 888-737-4927). If Kelowna beds are pulled out from under you, head north to nearby Vernon and this funky hostel. Epic pick-up games of ultimate frisbee on Mon. and Wed. 10 beds; $15.

FOOD

One of Canada's richest agricultural areas, Kelowna abounds with fresh produce. Shop for groceries at **Safeway,** 697 Bernard Ave. (860-0332), or cut out the middle man at the many **produce stands** outside town along Benvoulin Road and KLO Road. In town, **Bernard Avenue** is lined with restaurants and cafes, including:

The Bohemian Bagel, 363 Bernard Ave. (862-3517). This local favorite sells fresh, doughy bagels, home-made bread, and creative salads. Guatemalan-print tablecloths and ever-so-funky wall art complete *le scene.* Bagels 75¢, sandwiches $5. Open Mon.-Fri. 7:30am-5:30pm, Sat. 9am-3:30pm.

The Lunch Box, 509 Bernard Ave. (862-8621). The patio is always full at this no-frills sandwich shop that also serves hearty breakfasts. Build-your-own sandwich $4.50, salad $4. Lunch box not included. Open Mon.-Fri. 8am-8pm, Sat. 9am-4pm.

The Kitchen Cowboy, 353 Bernard Ave. (868-8288). Eclectic menu and "southwestern" decor rope in a trendy clientele. The Kitchen Cowboy is the place for young bucks to see and be seen. Burgers $7, grilled chicken and sundried tomato pizza $6.75. Open Mon.-Thurs. 8:30am-10pm, Fri.-Sat. 9:30am-11pm, Sun. 10am-4pm.

SIGHTS

Kelowna's main attraction is 93,000,000 mi. away—the **sun** that shines down on its parks and beaches for an average of 2000 hours per year. **City Park,** on the west end of downtown, is the principal point from which to view this gigantic ball of flaming gas, but **Boyce Gyro Park,** on Lakeshore Rd. south of the Okanagan Bridge, is also popular with a younger, hormone-laden crowd. Eight kilometers southeast of town, the old tracks of the **Kettle Valley Railbed** have been replaced by 12km of hiking and biking trails. A complete circuit passes over more than 18 trestles and through two long tunnels. The Kelowna Infocentre (see **Practical Information,** above) knows all.

Fuji apples from the valley sell for as much as $15 each in Asia. See how they grow at **Kelowna Land and Orchard (KLO),** 2930 Dunster Rd. (763-1091), Kelowna's oldest and largest family-owned farm. A 45-minute hayride and tour costs $5 (age 12-16 $2, under 12 free). (*Let's Go* does not recommend smuggling this fruit to Asia.)

The **wines** of the Okanagan Valley have made something of a name for themselves in recent years. **Mission Hill,** 1730 Mission Hill Rd. (768-7611), on the west bank of Okanagan Lake, is the most respected local winery. With a spectacular view of the lake from the front door, this large winery attracts connoisseurs with its award-winning 1992 Chardonnay. Free tours provide a glimpse of the complicated vintning process (open daily 10am-7pm; hourly tours 11am-5pm; call for winter hours).

Kelowna parties at the annual **Okanagan Wine Festival** in early October (call 861-6654 for info) and the **Kelowna Regatta** (861-4754) in late July. The Regatta has mellowed a bit since 1988, when Mounties had to break up the rowdy crowds with tear gas, but the boat races still pack 'em in.

■ Penticton

Close your eyes and imagine Florida. Replace the ocean with a large lake, convert palm trees into Douglas fir, add mountains and hockey fans with snow tires. Okay, now open your eyes. Voila: you're in Penticton. Indigenous peoples named the region between Okanagan and Skaha Lakes *Pen-tak-tin,* "a place to stay forever," but their eternal paradise was long ago transformed by heated pools and luxury hotels into one of Western Canada's biggest vacation towns. Hot weather, sandy beaches, and proximity to Vancouver and Seattle have ushered in the Tourist Age, and it may strain your budget to spend a weekend here, let alone eternity.

PRACTICAL INFORMATION AND ORIENTATION

Visitors Information: Penticton Wine and Information Centre, 888 Westminster Ave. W. (493-4055 or 800-663-5052), at Power St. Open daily 9am-6pm in summer. A smaller **Information Centre** (what, no wine?) is on Hwy. 97, 7km south of downtown. Open daily 10am-5pm in summer.

Buses: Greyhound, 307 Ellis (493-4101). To Vancouver (5 per day, $48) and Kelowna (3 per day, $11).

Public Transportation: Penticton Transit System, 301 E. Warren Ave. (492-5602). Bus service $1.35, seniors and students $1.10. Day pass $3.25, students $2.75. Many routes converge at Wade and Martin St. Buses run Mon.-Fri. 6:30am-10pm, Sat. 8:30am-6:30pm, Sun. 9:40am-5:40pm. Office open Mon.-Fri. 8am-5pm.
Taxi: Courtesy Taxi (492-7778).
Car Rental: Budget, 106-2504 Skaha Lake Rd. (493-0212). $49 per day, 18¢ per km after 100. Must be 21 with major credit card. Open Mon.-Fri. 7:30am-9:30pm, Sat.-Sun. 8:30am-9:30pm.
Bike Rental: Sun Country Cycle, 533 Main St. (493-0686). $25 per day, helmet included. Open Mon.-Sat. 9am-5:30pm. **Fan Cycles,** at Lakeshore Dr. and Riverside Dr., rents nifty pedal cars: 2-seaters $10 per hr., 4-seaters $20 per hr. Inline skates $6 per hr. Open summers daily 9:30am-9:30pm.
Laundry: Plaza Laundromat, 417-1301 Main St. (493-8710), in the Plaza Shopping Mall. Wash $1.50, 6min. dry 25¢. TV on premises. Open daily 8am-10pm.
Crisis Line: 493-6622. **Women's Shelter:** 493-7233. **Weather:** 492-6991.
Hospital: Penticton Regional, 550 Carmi Ave. (492-4000).
Emergency: 911. **Police:** 1103 Main St. (492-4300).
Internet Access: Pacific Brimm Coffee, 110-2210 Main St. (490-8720).
Post Office: 56 W. Industrial Ave. (492-5769). Open Mon.-Fri. 8:30am-5pm. **General Delivery Postal Code:** V2A 5M0.
Area Code: 250.

Penticton lies 395km east of Vancouver at the junction of **Highway 3** and **Highway 97** at the southern extreme of the Okanagan Valley. Lake Okanagan borders the north end of town, while smaller Skaha Lake lies to the south. Main Street bisects the city from north to south, turning into Skaha Lake Road as it approaches the lake.

ACCOMMODATIONS AND CAMPING

Penticton is a resort city year-round; cheap beds are few and far between. A campground on the shores of one of the lakes will be worth its hefty price tag. Make reservations during summer.

Penticton Hostel (HI-C), 464 Ellis St. (492-3992). One of Penticton's best bets. Near the Greyhound stop and 10min. from the beach. Comfortable lounge and patio, kitchen, laundry facilities, gas grill. Fills in July and Aug. Accommodates 52. $14.50, nonmembers $18.50, under 10 ½-price. Linen $1.50. Private rooms available.

Riordan House, 689 Winnipeg (493-5997). Much more elegant than the neon-bedecked concrete-box motels on Lakeshore Dr., and costs not a penny more. The Victorian-style mansion has 4 enormous, impeccably decorated rooms with plush carpeting, TV, and VCR. Mr. Ortiz makes a knockout breakfast (included in the room fee) of luscious local fruits and fresh scones. One single, a converted library with plants everywhere, $45; doubles $55-75.

South Beach Gardens, 3815 Skaha Lake Rd. (492-0628). Across from the beach, east of the Channel Parkway. 275 sites sprawled across 18 acres. More privacy than most campgrounds nearby. Sites $17, serviced sites $18-22.

Okanagan Mountain Provincial Park (494-0321). 50km north of Penticton on Hwy. 97. 168 sites packed between the highway and the lake in 2 separate units. Stay in the north park, where sites are roomier. Good beach swimming. No reservations; always full in summer. Cruise for sites early (8-10am). Sites $15.50.

FOOD

Stockpile in preparation for nuclear winter at **Super Valu Foods,** 450 Martin St., just west of Main (492-4315; open Mon.-Thurs. 9am-7pm, Fri. 9am-9pm, Sun 9am-6pm).

Whole Food Market (493-2855), in Creekside Plaza on Main St. A true supermarket of health food, with organic produce, bulk grains and pastas, and herbs. Best of all, the deli counter in the back slaps together fantastic sandwiches for $3-5. Open Mon.-Thurs. and Sat. 8am-6pm, Fri. 8am-8pm, Sun. 10am-5pm.

Judy's Deli, 129 W. Nanaimo (492-7029). Take-out only. Sit atop a bench in front of the radio station next door. Beach-goers stop for hearty homemade soups ($1.65-2) and butter-smeared sandwiches ($2.80-3.30). Browse about the herbs and homeopathic medicines. Open Mon.-Sat. 9am-5:30pm.

Hog's Breath Coffee Co., 202 Main St. (493-7800). A mellow cafe with energetic management and good food. All-day breakfast $3.75. Sandwiches (what else?) $4-6. Open daily 6am-10pm, roughly speaking.

SIGHTS AND EVENTS

Visitors with cars should explore Hwy. 97 and Hwy. 3A south of Penticton; eat fruit at a family stand, sample wines at a local vineyard, or fish in a pristine lake. The Penticton tourist trade revolves around **Okanagan Lake.** Long, hot summers and the sport facilities on the lake make Okanagan a popular hangout for the young. **California Connection** (490-7844), on the beach next to the Coast Lakeside Hotel, rents jet skis ($40 per 30min.), paddleboats ($10 per hr.), windsurfers ($12 per hr.) and sailboats ($18 per hr). Windsurfing and sailing lessons are available, too ($32-42).

To sample the local culture, take a trip to the **Art Gallery of the South Okanagan,** 199 Front St. (493-2928). This beachfront gallery exhibits local and Canadian artists (open Tues.-Fri. 10am-5pm, Sat.-Sun. 1-5pm; $2, free on Tues.). Looking suspiciously like an East African wildlife preserve, the **Okanagan Game Farm** (497-5405), on Hwy. 97 south of Penticton, covers 560 acres and protects 130 animal species from the crazy (human) lakeside wildlife. Zebras, rhinos, gnus, aoudads, and ankoli frolic free of fences and bars. Cars can drive through the park, and animal checklists keep kiddies entertained (open daily 8am-dusk; $10, ages 5-15 $7). The **Skaha Bluffs,** southeast of town on Valley View Rd., have developed into a popular **rock climbing** venue, offering pitches of varying difficulty. For info about area climbing, stop in at **Ray's Sports Den,** 215 Main St. (493-1216; open Mon.-Fri. 9:30am-6pm, Sat. 9:30am-5pm, Sun. 10am-4pm), or ask likely-looking locals.

Travelers in dire straits may consider signing on to **pick fruit** at one of the many orchards stretching south from Penticton to the U.S. border along Hwy. 97. Pickers usually camp free in the orchards, and are paid a per-quart wage; the faster you move, the more you're paid. Daily earnings of more than $40 are common for harvesting these grapes of wrath. Cherries are picked in June, pears in September, and assorted others in between. Contact the Kelowna Friendship Centre at 763-4905, or cruise Hwy. 97 and Hwy. 3A until you see a "Pickers Wanted" sign.

The mists and mellow fruitfulness of fall mark the ripening of the wine season. There are several wineries within easy driving distance of Penticton. **Hillside Cellars Winery** (493-4424), at the junction of Vancouver and Naramata Rd. northeast of Penticton, has a winery shop offering tastings and tours (open April 1-Oct. 31 daily 10am-6pm; Nov.-March by appointment only). North of Summerland, **Sumac Ridge Estate Winery** (494-0451) also offers tours daily at 10am, 2, and 4pm in the summer (open daily 9am-6pm; Nov.-April Mon.-Fri. 9am-5pm, Sat.-Sun. 11am-5pm). The **Okanagan Wine Festival** (490-8866) in early October is fun for those fond of squishing thick pulp between their toes. For more info, contact the **Penticton Wine and Information Centre** (see **Practical Information,** above).

The hills running throughout the Okanagan Valley are pretty to look at *and* pretty fun to play in, too. Heavy winter snowfalls make for excellent skiing and Penticton smoothly transforms from summer beach resort to winter mountain playland. **Apex Mountain Resort** (800-387-APEX/2739) sports a mix of downhill, cross-country, and night skiing within easy reach of town.

Revelstoke

In the 19th century, Revelstoke was a town straight out of a Zane Grey western, complete with dust-encrusted megalomaniacs maiming one another amid the gold-laden Selkirk Mountains. Located on the Columbia River and the Canadian Pacific Railway, the town was born as a stopover for boats and trains. Although still a stopover for travelers to the Rockies, Revelstoke's small-town feel and extensive outdoor activities make it a destination of its own.

PRACTICAL INFORMATION AND ORIENTATION

Visitors Information: Travel Information Centre (837-3522), at the junction of Hwy. 1 and Hwy. 23 N. Open July-Aug. daily 9am-7pm; May-June daily 9am-5pm. **Chamber of Commerce,** 204 Campbell Ave. (837-5345). Open Mon.-Fri. 8:30am-noon and 1-4:30pm. **Canadian Parks Service** (837-7500), at Boyle Ave. and 3rd St. Open Mon.-Fri. 8:30am-noon and 1-4:30pm.

Buses: Greyhound, 1899 Fraser Dr. (837-5874), 1 block south of Hwy. 1. To: Calgary ($51); Vancouver ($67); and Salmon Arm ($15). Open Mon.-Sat. 8am-7pm, Sun. 11am-1pm and 3-7pm.

Taxi: Johnnie's, 790 Lundell St. (837-3000). **R Taxi,** 857-4000. Both 24hr.

Car Rental: Tilden Car Rental, 301 W. 1st St. (837-2158). $56 per day, 15¢ per km after 100. Must be 21 with a credit card. Open Mon.-Sat. 8am-6pm.

Bicycle Rental: Spoketacular Sports, 2220 MacKenzie (837-2220). $5 per hr., $25 per day. Open Mon.-Sat. 9am-5pm.

Ambulance: 837-5885. **Police:** 320 Wilson St. (837-5255).

Internet Access: Perchè No Cafe (see **Food,** below).

Post Office: 307 W. 3rd St. (837-3228). Open Mon.-Fri. 8:30am-5pm. **Postal Code:** V0E 2S0.

Area Code: 250.

WESTERN CANADA

Revelstoke is situated on the Trans-Canada Hwy., 410km west of Calgary and 575km east of Vancouver. The town can be easily covered on foot or by bicycle. The 263 sq. km **Mount Revelstoke National Park** lies just out of town.

ACCOMMODATIONS AND CAMPING

Two relatively new hotels expand options for travelers and backpackers, striking a balance with the massive summer influx of RVs.

Revelstoke Traveler's Hostel and Guest House, 400 2nd St. W (837-4050), with office across the street at 403 2nd St. W. This downtown hostel has 40 beds in a maze of 25 rooms, all in a pristine, recently renovated historic house. Several kitchens and bathrooms allow for plenty of privacy, and (do the math) none of the bare-but-clean rooms have more than 3 beds. Free pick-up from the bus station. Guests get free internet access at the nearby Perchè No Cafe (see **Food,** below). Open 24hr. No curfew. Beds $14; private singles $19; doubles $28; family rooms available. Pitch a tent for $7, the cheapest in the area.

Daniel's Guest House, 313 First St. East (837-5530). Although Daniel's perches on the edge of town, Revelstoke is so small that it still only takes 5min. to walk. A private home-turned-hostel, Daniel's spotless hardwood floors and couch-filled common room make the place a home away from home. Free pick-up from the bus station. 18 beds. $14; doubles $28. Open 7-11am and 4-8pm.

Williamson's Lake Campground, 1818 Williamson Lake Rd. (837-5512 or 800-676-CAMP/2267), 1.5km southeast of downtown on Airport Way. Farther from the highway than its competitors, Williamson's Lake provides a nice change from the large signs and huge Smokey-the-Bear statues that litter the Trans-Canada. The lake itself is a popular (and rightly so) swimming hole for the locals. 44 sites, 28 unserviced ($13.25), 16 full hookups ($17.25). Closed winter.

FOOD

Food prices are on the rise in Revelstoke, but there are still good deals to be found. Cook for yourself courtesy of **Cooper's Supermarket,** 555 Victoria St. (837-4372; open Sun. 9am-6pm, Mon.-Thurs. and Sat. 8am-8pm, Fri. 8am-9pm).

Chalet Deli, 555 Victoria St. (837-5552), across the parking lot from Cooper's. The best place for lunch-grabbing. Try a personal pizza with your choice of sauce ($2.75) or settle for a meaty sandwich on fresh bread from the adjacent deli ($4). Open Mon.-Sat. 5am-6pm, Sun. 11am-5pm.

Perchè No Cafe 217 Mackenzie Ave. (837-6575). Owned by the same folks as the hostel, this used bookstore/cafe knows how to cut a deal. Huge sandwiches $3.50. For hostel guests, an extra $5.75 buys a Belgian waffle piled with fresh strawberries and whipped cream, escorted by fresh squeezed juice and all the coffee you can guzzle. Internet access. Open Mon.-Sat. 9am-9pm.

Frontier Restaurant, 122 N. Highway 23 (873-5119), at the junction of Hwy. 1 and 23N. Offers the "Ranchhand," a ½lb. cheeseburger with the works ($7.60) and saloon-inspired decor. Open daily 5am-midnight.

Alphaus, 600 W. 2nd St. (837-6380), at Garden Ave. Meat galore. Authentic German specialties $8-12.50. Open Tues.-Sat. 8:30am-8pm.

SIGHTS

Mt. Revelstoke National Park (837-7500), adjacent to town, provides a quick nature fix. A favorite of mountain bikers and hikers, the small but well-used park produces some astounding scenery. Two special **boardwalks** off Hwy. 1 on the east side of the park allow exploration of the local brush. The "skunk cabbage" trail (1.2km) leads through "acres of stinking perfection": skunk cabbage plants tower at heights of over 1.5m. Some of the majestic cedars on the "giant cedars trail" (500m) are over 1000 years old. There are two backcountry campgrounds in the park ($6 for backcountry camping permit); visit the Parks Canada office (see **Practical Information,** above) or the Rogers Pass information center (see **Glacier National Park,** p. 226). Drive the 24km of the **Meadows in the Sky Parkway** (Summit Rd.) and hike 1km up to some of the most accessible alpine meadows in western Canada. The Parkway branches off Hwy. 1 1.5km east of town. Brochures about the **Revelstoke Dam** (837-6515 or 837-6211), 5km north of Hwy. 1 on Hwy. 23, plaster the town. The dam visitors center illustrates the water-blocker's mechanical marvels with a free tour via "talking wand." Ride the elevator to the top of the dam for an impressive view (free; open daily in summer 8am-8pm; mid-May to mid-June and mid-Sept. to mid-Oct. 9am-5pm; wheelchair accessible).

The **Revelstoke Railway Museum,** 719 W. Track St. (837-6060), off Victoria Rd., is a shrine to the Iron Horse and features old photos and story-board exhibits outlining the construction of the first Canadian transcontinental line, as well as an actual steam locomotive. Upstairs, an observation deck peers down at the heavy traffic on the main C.P.R. line outside. (Open daily 9am-8pm; spring and fall Mon.-Fri. 9am-5pm; $5, seniors $3, ages 7-17 $2, under 7 free.)

The **Canyon Hot Springs** (837-2420), between Mt. Revelstoke National Park and Glacier National Park on Hwy. 1, sports two spring-fed pools that simmer at 40°C (104°F) and 26°C (80°F; single swim $5, day pass $7.50; open summer daily 9am-10pm, spring and fall daily 9am-9pm). The springs also provide campgrounds for spa-lovers who can't extract themselves from the warm elixirs ($7, full hook-ups $21).

Revelstoke has some curious variations on **downhill skiing** to spice up its winter season. Several companies offer heli-skiing, ski tours on nearby glaciers, and guided ski trips. For the less wealthy, **Mt. Mackenzie,** P.O. Box 1000, only 5km outside of town, maintains 21 trails on a 2000 ft. vertical drop. **Cross-country** skiers find more than enough snow and trails in the nearby national parks, and the area is becoming increasingly popular for **snowmobilers,** with several deep powder trails. The big game guides at **Monashee Outfitting,** 825 Olhausen (837-3538), are willing and able to organize hiking, fishing, horse rides, canoeing, cross-country skiing, and anything else your little heart desires.

Glacier National Park

Canada's most appropriately named national park is home to over 400 of the giant, slow-moving ice cubes. The jagged peaks and steep, narrow valleys of the Columbia Range prevent development in the 1350 sq. km park, even along the highway corridor. One would literally have to move mountains to build here.

The Trans-Canada Hwy. cuts a thin ribbon through the center of the park, blessing motorists with views of high-in-the-sky glaciers. More than 140km of rough trails lead from the highway, inviting rugged mountaineers to penetrate the near-impenetrable. For details on the park, talk to the Parks Canada staff or buy a copy of *Footloose in the Columbias* ($1.50) at the **Rogers Pass Information Centre** (814-5232), on the highway in Glacier. **Park passes** are required for those who linger ($4 per day, $35 per year). For more info about Glacier, write to the Superintendent, P.O. Box 350, Revelstoke V0E 2S0, or call 873–7500. Glacier lies 350km west of Calgary and 723km east of Vancouver. **Greyhound** (837-5874) makes four trips daily from Revelstoke ($9.20). In an emergency, call the **Park Warden Office** (837-6274; open daily 7am-5pm; winter hrs. vary; 24hr. during avalanche control periods). The **area code** is 250.

Try to visit the park in late July or early August, when brilliant explosions of mountain wildflowers offset the deep green of the forests. Glacier receives measurable precipitation every other day in summer, but the clouds of mist that encircle the peaks and blanket the valleys only add to the park's astonishing beauty. Unless you're directly descended from Sir Edmund Hilary or Tenzing Sherpa, avoid exploring the park in winter, as near-daily snowfalls and the constant threat of avalanches often restrict travel to the Trans-Canada Hwy.

There are two campgrounds in Glacier: **Illecillewaet** (ill-uh-SILL-uh-watt) and **Loop Brook.** Both offer flush toilets, kitchen shelters with cook stoves, and firewood (sites $13; open mid-June to Sept.). **Backcountry campers** need a backcountry pass ($6) from the Administration Office in Revelstoke (837-7500; see p. 224) or from the Parks Canada booth at the Rogers Pass Information Centre. Adventurers must pitch their tents at least 5km from the pavement. Food choices in the park are limited and unappealing; drop by a supermarket in Golden or Revelstoke beforehand.

Eight popular **hiking trails** begin at the Illecillewaet campground, 3.4km west of Rogers Pass. The easy 1km **Meeting of the Waters** trail leads to the impressive confluence of the Illecillewaet and Asulkan Rivers. The 4.2km **Avalanche Crest** trail offers spectacular views of Rogers Pass, the Hermit Range, and the Illecillewaet River Valley; the treeless slopes below the crest testify to the destructive power of winter snowslides. From early July to late August, the park staff run daily **interpretive hikes** beginning at 9am (contact the centre for info). Come prepared for the four- to six-hour tour with a picnic lunch, rain jacket, and a sturdy pair of walking shoes. Regulations prohibit biking on the trails in Glacier. The park's glacial meltwaters—a startling milky aqua color created by sediment suspended in the current—do not support many fish; determined anglers can try their luck with the cutthroat in the Illecillewaet River (get a permit, $6 for 7 days, at the Rogers Pass information centre).

Northwestern Canada

Northern British Columbia, the Queen Charlotte Islands, and the Yukon Territory remain among the most remote and sparsely inhabited regions of North America. Averaging one person per 15 sq. km, the land's loneliness and sheer physical beauty are overwhelming. Native peoples have lived here for thousands of years, adapting their lifestyle and culture to the patterns of animal migration and the uncompromising climate. White settlers began migrating West in the early 19th century, attracted by the wealth of natural resources. The first were fur traders looking for faster new routes through the area. Several major gold rushes, beginning in the Fraser Valley in 1858, brought stampeders who settled permanently. Since then, the lumber and mining industries have brought many more eager to extract the wealth of the land.

Despite the tell-tale signs of the logging and mining industries, Northwestern Canada remains a bountiful, beautiful, and almost entirely unspoiled region. Sadly, many Alaska-bound travelers mimic those gold-crazed prospectors and blow through British Columbia and the Yukon without appreciating their far less crowded attractions. Muttering "Must...get...to...Alaska," these new stampeders drive on without exploring the prime fishing of the Lakes Region, the untouched hiking terrain of Mt. Edziza Provincial Park, and the colorful history of Dawson City. Travel infocentres give abundant and indispensable council on where to go and what to find in these remote havens. Northwestern Canada is one of the last North American bastions of immense forests, stark mountains, yawning canyons, roaring rivers, clear lakes, abundant wildlife, *and* freedom from summer crowds.

A word to the wise: it can be very cold in Northwestern Canada, even in the summer and especially at night. If you plan on spending more than a couple of nights outdoors, you will need at least an excellent tent, an ensolite pad, and a warm sleeping bag for extra warmth. A wool hat and long underwear, and perhaps an extra blanket, won't hurt either. It can easily snow during the summer anywhere north of Prince George (for more information, see **Camping and the Outdoors,** p. 38).

NORTHERN BRITISH COLUMBIA

Cariboo Highway (97)

The **Cariboo Highway** is the portion of Hwy. 97 that runs north-south for approximately 450km between Cache Creek and Prince George, following the route of the historic Cariboo Wagon Road. From there, Hwy. 97 continues north to Dawson Creek (402km) and the start of the **Alaska Highway** (see p. 255). Due to the region's mighty cattle industry, you'll see many more cows along the highway than you will "cariboo." Still, the scenery is impressive, with dozens of small lakes nestled among patchy forest and rocky hills. A visit to one of the 12 provincial parks in the area is well worth a brief departure from the highway. Two of the nicest, both close to the Cariboo, are **Green Lake,** actually a series of glacial kettle lakes, and **Pinnacle** (see p. 228) where an eight-minute walk leads to an unexpected view of a steep sandstone canyon carved into the surrounding plateau. Nearly all of the provincial parks, even those farther from the highway, merit a visit from road-trippers with extra time.

Many small towns along Hwy. 97, born as gold-rush era road houses, are slowly becoming more than just pit stops en route to Prince George. **Cache Creek,** at the junction of the Cariboo Hwy. and the Trans-Canada Highway (Hwy. 1), does not have much sight-seeing to offer tourists, but weary travelers can stay at the **Cache Creek Kampground,** 3km north of town on Hwy. 97. The kampground offers a pool and a spa free to kampers, plus koin showers and laundry (sites $14; full hookups $19). Visitors can take a half-hour nature walk on one of the nearby trails, or perfect their putting with 18 holes of minigolf right on the premises. Hard-core budgeters might opt instead for the more secluded **Brookside Campsite** (457-6633), located 1km west of town toward Kamloops on Hwy. 1 East, which offers free showers, laundry ($1.25 each wash and dry), and costs $11 for a tent sites or $17 for a full hookup.

100 Mile House, 115km north of Cache Creek, offers services and groceries, and proudly displays the **world's largest pair of cross-country skis,** a fitting tribute to the cross-country skiers who flock to the area every winter. The **Travel Infocentre** (395-5353), located at the Chamber of Commerce next to the towering skis, is another helpful stop (open May-Sept. daily 9am-6pm; winter Mon.-Fri. 9am-5pm). **100 Mile House Campground,** ½km off the highway on Horse Lake Rd., is tranquil, woodsy, and cheap ($10; toilets, water, firewood).

The highway's biggest pit stops are the towns of **Williams Lake,** 90km past 100 Mile House, and **Quesnel** (kwuh-NEL), halfway between Williams Lake and Prince George. The **Travel Infocentre** (392-5025) in Williams Lake is on the highway and has the scoop on activities and events in the area (open May-Sept. daily 9am-5pm, Oct.-April Mon.-Fri. 9am-4pm). You can secure a roof over your head at the **Valleyview Motel** (392-4655), on Hwy. 97 near the south end of town (single $44, in winter $38; double $48, in winter $42). If you're looking for a swim, try the **Slumber Lodger** (392-7116 or 800-577-2244), located at 27 7th Ave. downtown. Rooms are $49 for a single, $55 for a double, and swimming, cable, and local calls are free. As with most of the motels in Williams Lake, kids under 12 stay free. For campers who can tolerate another 13km of driving, **Wildwood Campsite** (989-4711) provides sites for tents ($13) or RVs ($16), free showers, and cheap laundry ($1). **Whispering Willows Campground** (989-0359) beckons northward, another 6km past Wildwood. Free showers and firewood come with a $10 site; RVers also pay $10 but miss out on the free wood. And yes, the willows do whisper.

WESTERN CANADA

Williams Lake is home to the province's most active cattle marketing industry. The town celebrates its cowboy heritage over Canada Day weekend with the four-day **Williams Lake Stampede.** The festivities include a rodeo, mountain race, and "wild cow milking." Beware the jump in motel prices during Stampede weekend.

As you leave Williams Lake to the north or west, make sure to have enough gas for 80km of lonely road. Immense, wild **Tweedsmuir** and **Ts'il?Os** (SIGH-loss) **Provincial Parks** can be reached on Hwy. 20 west from Williams Lake. Tweedsmuir, British Columbia's largest Provincial Park, protects the Atnarko River, Hunlen Falls, Monarch Glacier, and the colorfully streaked shield volcanoes of the Rainbow Mountains. Rugged Ts'il?Os, 160 km west of Williams Lake, is home to Canada's first grizzly bear refuge and the glacier-fed, trout- and salmon-rich Lake Chilko. Currently, highways to each park are only half-paved but easily navigable, except in foul weather. For general park information call (250) 398-4414 in Williams Lake; for campground reservations, call **BC Parks** at (800) 689-9025. About 50km north of Williams Lake on Hwy. 97 the free **Marguerite Ferry** shuttles off-road enthusiasts across a narrow stretch of the rambling Fraser River; the gravel road on the other side parallels Hwy. 97 all the way to Quesnel. Ask the ferry captain for directions. Even more scenic is the gravel road from Williams lake to the ferry, but be sure to ask at the infocentre for directions beforehand—it's very easy to get lost.

In Quesnel, the **Travel Infocentre,** 703 Carson Ave. (992-8716), is just off Hwy. 97 in Le Bourdais Park (open daily 8:30-6pm; Sep.-Jun. Mon.-Fri. 8:30-4:30). Stretch your weary car-cramped limbs on the **River Walk,** a paved trail along the river dotted with tidbits of information about Quesnel's history. It's only a 10-minute drive to **Pinnacle Provincial Park** (cross the river on Marsh Rd., then turn right on Baker Drive), where a short walk leads to "hoodoo" rock formations and impressive views. The **Wheel Inn** (992-8975), on Carson and Front Streets, directly across from the foot bridge that spans the Fraser River, offers basic accommodations (singles and doubles, $40). **Roberts Roost Campground,** 3121 Gook Rd. (747-2015), is 8km south of town. Open from April to October, this landscaped, lakeside campground has coin showers, laundry, fishing, and rowboat and canoe rentals ($5.25 per hour). Tent sites are $15, hook-ups $20. **10 Mile Lake Provincial Park,** 11 km north of town on Hwy. 97, offers

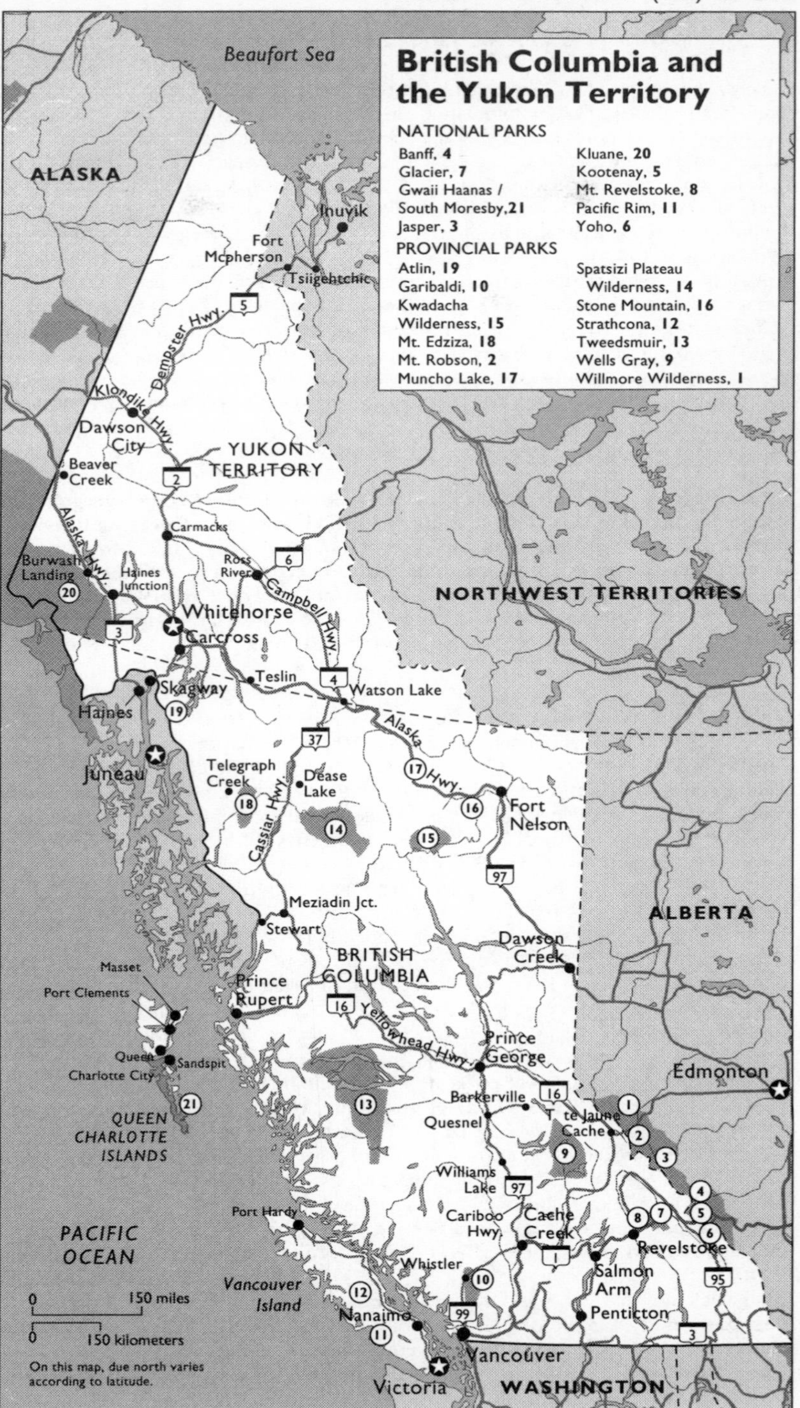
British Columbia and the Yukon Territory
NATIONAL PARKS
Banff, 4
Glacier, 7
Gwaii Haanas / South Moresby, 21
Jasper, 3
Kluane, 20
Kootenay, 5
Mt. Revelstoke, 8
Pacific Rim, 11
Yoho, 6
PROVINCIAL PARKS
Atlin, 19
Garibaldi, 10
Kwadacha Wilderness, 15
Mt. Edziza, 18
Mt. Robson, 2
Muncho Lake, 17
Spatsizi Plateau Wilderness, 14
Stone Mountain, 16
Strathcona, 12
Tweedsmuir, 13
Wells Gray, 9
Willmore Wilderness, 1
Beaufort Sea
ALASKA
Inuvik
Fort Mcpherson
Tsiigehtchic
Dempster Hwy.
Klondike Hwy.
Dawson City
YUKON TERRITORY
Beaver Creek
Alaska Hwy.
Carmacks
Burwash Landing
Haines Junction
Ross River
Campbell Hwy.
Whitehorse
Carcross
Teslin
Watson Lake
Skagway
Haines
Juneau
NORTHWEST TERRITORIES
Telegraph Creek
Dease Lake
Cassiar Hwy.
Alaska Hwy.
Fort Nelson
Meziadin Jct.
Stewart
ALBERTA
BRITISH COLUMBIA
Dawson Creek
Masset
Port Clements
Prince Rupert
Yellowhead Hwy.
Prince George
Queen Charlotte City
Sandspit
QUEEN CHARLOTTE ISLANDS
Edmonton
Barkerville
Quesnel
Tete Jaune Cache
Williams Lake
Cariboo Hwy.
Cache Creek
Port Hardy
Revelstoke
PACIFIC OCEAN
Whistler
Salmon Arm
Vancouver Island
Nanaimo
Penticton
Vancouver
Victoria
WASHINGTON
0 150 miles
0 150 kilometers
On this map, due north varies according to latitude.

more secluded camping, with coin showers, toilets, firewood and a network of trails (tent site $12).

For hikers beyond hard-core and off the deep end, the **Alexander Mackenzie Heritage Trail** might just be the ultimate hiking challenge. The over-250km trail begins from Hwy. 97 just north of Quesnel and stretches across western British Columbia to **Bella Coola** on the Pacific, tracing the final leg of Mackenzie's 1793 journey across Canada to the western coast (allow 14-21 days for the trip). Mackenzie reached the Pacific before Lewis and Clark, although the Americans continue to hog all the glory. For history and trail guides on the Mackenzie Trail, visit the **Quesnel Public Library** at 593 Barlow St. (992-7912).

Anyone traveling north to Prince George on Hwy. 97 will live a better life for having stopped at **Cinema Second Hand General Store** (998-4774), 83km south of Prince George on Hwy. 97. Cash-strapped road warriors will find everything they need here (except an actual cinema), plus a wide variety of things they could never possibly need, such as old-fashioned snowshoes and disco LPs (open daily 9am-9pm). The store also offers **free camping,** handily equipped with a pit toilet. Ah, luxury.

Prince George

At the confluence of the **Nechako** and **Fraser** Rivers, Prince George's magnificent riverbanks are slowly succumbing to the pulp and lumber mills that infest the valley floor. Even with more than 100 parks, several museums, and 76,000 friendly residents, Prince George is fighting an uphill battle to become more of a destination and less of a stopover. Recent additions to the town include a civic center, a national university, and the Cougars, a Western League Hockey Team. In the summer, bands of young, hip treeplanters flock to Prince George on their days off, providing some rowdiness and local color.

Practical Information Useful maps of Prince George are available free at either of the two **Travel Infocentres** in town (800-668-7646 for general information). The first is at 1198 Victoria St. (562-3700), at 15th Ave. (open daily 8:30am-5pm); the second (563-5493) is at the junction of Hwy. 16 and 97 (open May-Sept. daily noon-7pm). Just look for the giant "Mr. P.G." logger—you can't miss him. **BC Rail** (561-4033), at the end of Terminal Blvd., 2km south off Hwy. 97, runs the scenic "Cariboo Prospector" train to Vancouver (3 per week, $185 with meals included; station open Mon., Thurs., Sat. 6am-9pm; Sun., Wed., Fri. 7am-9:30pm). **VIA Rail,** 1300 1st Ave. (564-5233 or 800-561-8630), serves Prince Rupert. (3 per week, with seven day advance purchase $50, student $42, child $25; otherwise $83, student $75, child $42; station open Mon., Thurs., Sat. 6am-9:30pm; Sun., Wed., Fri. 5:30am-9:30pm.) **Greyhound,** 1566 12th Ave. (564-5454), across from the Victoria St. infocentre, offers service to Edmonton (1 per day, $87), Vancouver (3 per day, $85), Prince Rupert (2 per day, $82), Dawson Creek (2 per day, $49), and other points. Coin lockers are available. (Call ahead to unravel the station's bizarre hours.)

Prince George's **public library** is at 887 Dominion (563-9251; open Mon.-Thurs. 10am-9pm, Fri.-Sat. 10am-5:30pm). Northcountry trekkers and outdoor gurus will want to stop at **Centre City Surplus,** 1222 Fourth Ave. (564-2400 or 800-661-3773), for any last minute items at extremely competitive prices (open Mon.-Thurs., Sat. 9am-6pm, Fri. 9am-9pm, Sun. 11am-4pm). You can do your laundry at that nameless place at 231 George St. for $1.25 each wash and dry (open Mon.-Sat. 7:30am-7pm, Sun. 9am-5pm). Ed Delorme's **Auto Service and Repair Center** is at 620 George St. (563-2002). In an **emergency,** call 911. **Prince George Regional Hospital** is at 2000 15th Ave. (565-2000, emergency 565-2444). The **police** have set up camp at 999 Brunswick St. (562-3300), and the **crisis center** is at 1306 7th Ave. (563-1214). The **post office** is at 1323 5th Ave. (561-2568; open Mon.-Fri. 8:30am-5pm). The **Postal Code** is V2L 4R8. The **area code** is 250 unless otherwise noted.

Accommodations and Camping If you're only stopping in Prince George to get a good night's sleep and stock up on provisions, a good bet is the **Queensway Court Motel,** 1616 Queensway (562-5068) at 17th Ave., close to downtown. Singles are $36, doubles $41, and the well-kept rooms come with fridges, cable TV, and free local calls. A pricey **laundromat** next door is filled with dirt-encrusted treeplanters spending their days off spinning their long johns. During the summer, the **College of New Caledonia,** 3330 22nd Ave. (604-561-5832 or 800-371-8111), off Hwy. 97 near downtown, offers clean and quiet dorm rooms with fridge, microwave, sink, desk, and shared bathrooms for $20 (linen $5 extra). Wheelchair accessible rooms and monthly rates can be arranged (office open Mon.-Fri. 10am-noon, 2-4pm, and 6-8pm; Sat.-Sun. noon-2pm and 6-8pm). Ambitious campers can head for the **Log House Restaurant and Kampground,** (963-9515), located on the shores of Tabor Lake. To get there, head out of town on 16E, turn right on "Old Cariboo Hwy.," and then left on Giscome Rd. This German-owned steakhouse and RV park is popular among European vacationers, but that doesn't excuse their spelling of "kampground." Sites $14, full hookups $20, cabins with no amenities $40. Rowboat, canoe, and pedalboat rentals are $5, $8, and $8 per hr. respectively. Hunting and fishing trips via seaplane can be arranged.

Food Cruelty or coincidence? The oddly named **Overwaitea's,** 1666 Spruce St. (564-4525), is a grocery store a short walk from the downtown infocenter (open daily 8am-10pm). Any number of interchangeable pizza/pasta joints can be found on or near **George St.** For something a little different, the cool, calm, and collected **1085 Cafe,** 1085 Vancouver St. (960-2272), offers fresh soup and salad-type lunch fare in the $4 range, and live entertainment most Friday nights. After lunch, head to the hip, traveler-happy **Javva Mugga Mocha Cafe,** 304 George St. (562-3338), for a $2 muffin or espresso. The cafe also sells a random selection of used books. **Jade Garden Restaurant,** 1533 3rd Ave. (562-6110), just off Victoria St., has an all-you-can-eat lunch smorgasbord for $6.25 and a dinner smorg $9.25. Entrees are $7-10.

Sights and Events Fishing is excellent near Prince George, with more than 1500 stocked lakes within a 150km radius. The closest is **Tabor Lake,** where the rainbow trout all but jump into your boat in spring and early summer. Tabor is 13km east on Hwy. 16; take a right onto "Old Cariboo Hwy." and a left onto Giscome Rd. For a complete listing of lakes and licensing information, contact the infocentres.

For a bird's eye view of this industrial city, scramble up to **Connaught Hill Park,** where you'll find picnic tables and ample frisbee-throwing space. To reach the park, scale the yellow metal staircase across from the visitors center or take Connaught Dr. off Queensway. **Forests for the World,** a wildlife preserve on nearby Cranbrook Hill, is only a 15-minute drive from town and one of the prettiest parts of Prince George. To get there, take Hwy. 97 north, turn left on 15th Ave., right on Foothills Blvd., and left onto Cranbrook Hill Rd., and finally left on Kueng Rd.

Centre City Surplus (see **Practical Information,** p. 230) sells guides to hiking in the Prince George area, and the infocentre has its own helpful tips. **Fort George Park,** on the banks of the Fraser River off 20th Ave., offers expanses of lawn, picnic tables, and barbecue pits, plus a perfect starting point for the 11km **Heritage River Trail,** which wanders through the city and along the Fraser and Nechako Rivers. Also lurking inside the park is **Fort George Regional Museum** (562-1612), which houses frontier artifacts, including several primitive chain saws (open daily 10am-5pm; call for winter hours; $4.25, children $3.25, families $8). **McMillan Creek Regional Park** is right across the Nechako off Hwy. 97 north, and features a deep ravine and a view of the city from the Nechako cutbanks. **Cottonwood Island Nature Park,** off of River Rd., has plenty of leisurely riverside walking trails along the banks of the Nechako River, and **Esker's Provincial Park,** off Hwy. 97 on Ness Lake Rd., 40km north of downtown, has trails accessible to the disabled. Call (604) 565-6340 for details.

Mardi Gras, which lasts for 10 days in late February, features events such as snow gold, dog-pull contests, and jousting with padded poles. You'll swear you're in New

Orleans. For information call 564-3737. **Sandblast** sends a group of daring skiers down the steep, sandy, snowless Nechako Cutbanks on the third Sunday in August.

■ Yellowhead Highway (16): Mt. Robson to Prince George (319km)

In British Columbia, Hwy. 16's scenic drama heightens as it winds west. Eighty km west of Jasper stands **Mt. Robson.** At 3954m, it is the highest peak in the Canadian Rockies. Only the robust can conquer Robson: it took five unsuccessful attempts until climbers reached her summit in 1913. Wimps (i.e. normal people) can appreciate Robson's beauty from the parking lot beside the **park headquarters** (566-4325; open daily 8am-8pm; May and Sept. daily 8am-5pm; closed Oct.-April). Visitors can choose from five nearby hiking trails ranging from 8½km dayhikes to 70km treks (hiking permit $3 per person per night). Stationary types can hang out in the campground at **Mt. Robson Provincial Park** ($14.50 with flush toilets and hot showers) or **Lucerne Campground** ($9.50, no toilets, no showers). Call (800) 689-9025 for trail information and campsite reservations.

Just west of Mt. Robson is **Tête Jaune Cache** where Hwy. 16 intersects Hwy. 5 leading south to Kamloops (339km) and the Okanagan country. Highway 5 is the fastest route from Jasper to Vancouver. Between the Rockies and Cariboo Mountains, 63km west of Tête Jaune Cache, lies the hamlet of **McBride.** Travelers not driving wood-burning vehicles are advised to fill up in McBride, since 205km of timber separate it from Prince George, the next significant town to the west. Huddled masses unwilling to negotiate the steep, winding grades to Prince George find refuge (including flush toilets, showers, and laundry) at the **Beaver View Campsite** (569-2513) in McBride, 1km east of McBride on Hwy. 16 (sites $13; partial hookup $15-$17). Stop at scenic **Purden Lake Provincial Park** (565-6340), 48km east of Prince George, for fishing or camping (sites $12 with flush toilets).

The woodchips littering Hwy. 16 from McBride to Prince George are proof of the heavy local logging activity. This region produces over six million cubic meters of lumber annually. Visitors tempted to chain themselves to trees or condemn the practices of the timber industry are invited to read the brochure *Don't Believe Everything That Greenpeace Tells You,* available at tourist information counters. Here, as in much of the rural Northwest, terms like "deforestation" and "clear-cutting" are ways of describing how people make a living; loggers don't often take kindly to ecological reprimands from abroad.

■ Yellowhead Highway (16): Prince George to Prince Rupert

West of Prince George, steep grades and towering timbers gradually give way to the gently rolling pastures and tiny towns of British Columbia's interior Lakes District. If late-night roadtrip munchies kick in, stop at the 24hr. **PetroCan** in **Fort Fraser** (690-7542), where the "restaurant" fries a mean plate of hash browns for $2.25. Inhale second-hand smoke and experience the ebb and flow of life in a small, northern BC town. Thanks to a wayward (must-have-been-drunk) surveyor, Highway 16 takes a turn at the town of **Burns Lake,** where almost every building is adorned with the likeness of a trout. The **infocentre,** on the highway, is the best place to stop for fishing info (692-3773; open daily 9am-7pm; in winter Mon.-Fri. 9am-5pm).

Eighty kilometers west of Burns Lake is **Houston** and its Texas-scale contribution to the rampant superlativism of the late 20th century: the **world's largest flyrod** (20m long and over 365kg). Houston's **infocentre** (845-7640; open Mon.-Fri. 8am-6pm, Sat.-Sun. 9am-5pm; in winter Mon.-Fri. 9am-5pm) offers a guide explaining how to "realize your fishing fantasies"—indulge these fantasies at one of more than 25 area lakes and streams. Sixty-four kilometers northwest of Houston, **Smithers** offers skiing on the slopes of Hudson Bay Mountain. The town of **New Hazelton** is 125 km past Smithers, and 44km farther west is the **junction** with the **Cassiar Highway (Hwy. 37)** leading north 733km to the Yukon Territory and the Alaska Highway (see p. 249). For the remaining 97km to **Terrace,** Hwy. 16 winds along the base of the Hazelton Mountains and follows the thundering Skeena River. There is **no gas** available along the 144km stretch of Hwy. 16 between Terrace and coastal Prince Rupert.

Terrace

In 1944, an extended spell of bad weather and a highly disproportionate male-to-female ratio caused 3000 Canadian Army troops stationed in Terrace to mutiny. For three weeks, disgruntled enlisted men ruled Terrace, and officers took refuge in Prince Rupert, 144km to the west. In the years since the mutiny, Terrace has calmed down considerably. Today, fishing has replaced armed rebellion as the most popular means of easing boredom here along the banks of the Skeena River.

Practical Information The **Visitors Center** is at 4511 Keith St. (635-2063; http://www.terrace.bc.ca; open daily 8am-8pm; winter Mon.-Fri. 8am-4:30pm), off Hwy. 16. **Greyhound,** 4620 Keith St. (635-3680), runs two westbound and two eastbound buses daily. **VIA Rail** (800-561-8630) sends 3 trains per week to Prince Rupert ($21) and Prince George ($68). Terrace's **banks** huddle together near the Safeway, downtown. **Greig Avenue Auto,** (638-8373), on Greig between Kenney and Munroe St., makes repairs (open Tues.-Sat. 9am-6pm). Do your duds at **Richard's Cleaners,** 3223 Emerson St. (635-5119; open Mon.-Sat. 7:30am-9pm, Sun. 10am-9pm), or suds yourself at the **public showers** at the **Terrace Aquatic Center,** 3220 Kalum Ave. (615-3030), with pool, hot tub, and gym facilities ($4, seniors $2.10, children $1.60). **Mills Memorial Hospital** is at 4720 Haugland Ave. (635-2111). The **police** are at 3205 Eby St. (635-4911). Phone 638-1102 for an **ambulance.** The **public library** at 4610 Park Ave. has **Internet access,** and books, too (open Tues.-Fri. 10am-9pm, Sat. 10am-5pm). **Chalky's Billiards** (638-1162), across from the Safeway, has **Internet access** for $7 per hour (open Mon.-Thurs. and Sun. noon-midnight, Fri.-Sat. noon-2am). Mail post cards from the **post office** at 3232 Emerson St. (635-2241; open Mon.-Fri. 8:30am-5pm). The **postal code** is V8G 4A1. The **area code** is 250.

Accommodations, Camping, and Food **AAA Terrace Bed and Breakfast,** 3802 deJong Crescent (635-0079 or 888-635-0079), boasts spic-and-span rooms from $45. Take Sparks or Eby St. north from Lakelse to McConnell and left to deJong. The **Alpine House,** 4326 Lakelse (635-7216 or 800-663-3123), is also clean and happily removed from the noisy downtown (singles $50; doubles $55; single or double with kitchenette $65). Campers can head to **Ferry Island Municipal Campground** (615-3000), just east of Terrace on Hwy. 16. The island's prime fishing spot is a short walk from the wooded campsite, and lined with eager anglers who got there first. The community pool is half-price if you stay at Ferry Island (sites $9.50, hookups $12). **Kleanza Creek Provincial Park** is the site of an abandoned gold mine 19km east of the city on Hwy. 16. Sites are a little cramped, but the tall trees and riverside picnic area compensate (sites $9.50).

Terrace offers a handful of welcome breaks from the dreariness of highway diner cuisine. **Anka's** (635-1510), on Tetrault St. right before the overpass heading west, serves up a scrumptious vegan burger with soup or salad for $6 (open Mon.-Fri. 10am-8pm, Sat. 9am-8pm). **Don Diego's,** 3212 Kalum St. (635-2307), is a small, laid-back joint that serves Mexican, Greek, and whatever's in season. Corn and yam enchiladas go for $6.50, and dinners run between $9-19. Try the house iced tea ($1; open Mon.-Sat. 11:30am-9pm; Sun. 4:30-9pm). **Safeway,** 4655 Lakelse Ave., is the cheapest place to buy not-yet-cooked food (open Mon.-Fri. 9am-9pm, Sat.-Sun. 9am-6pm).

Sights **Heritage Park Museum** (635-4546), at Kalum and Kerby St., houses countless artifacts from the pioneer era, including a working pump organ and an elaborate wreath made from human hair—perfect for pursuers of the grisly side of kitsch (open May-June Tues.-Sat. 10am-6pm, July-Aug. Wed.-Sun. 10am-6pm; $4, children $2, family $8). The **Northern Light Studio and Gardens,** 4820 Halliwell Ave. (638-1403), a few blocks from Heritage Park, feature a Japanese garden with BC jade and artistry (open Mon.-Sat. 9:30am-5:30pm; free). **Gruchy's Beach** is 8km south of Terrace on Hwy. 37. It's a 1½km hike from the parking lot and is big, sandy, and begging to be picnicked upon. For more solitude and a little adventure (and some danger), check out the cliff-jumping at **Humphrey Falls.** The cliffs are a local secret—mum's the word at the infocentre. Take Hwy. 37 south towards Kitimat and turn off at a gravel road on the left after approximately 35km. Drive or walk to the water. The **Tseax Lava Beds,** Canada's youngest lava flow and British Columbia's newest provincial park, lie 100km north of Terrace. To reach this 54 sq. km swath of moonscape, follow Kalum Lake Dr. through the scenic valleys of the Tseax and Nass Rivers.

Amble, sashay, skip, run, or walk along Terrace's 11 well-maintained **trails.** Hikers with some time can check out the **Redsand Lake Demonstration Forest,** 26km north on West Kalum Forest Road. The Forest Service is developing a network of trails around beautiful Redsand Lake and through a variety of forested areas. Grab an interpretive pamphlet at the infocentre. Anglers can strap on their hip-waders and try their **fishing** luck on the east shore of **Ferry Island,** or ask for hot tips at the **Misty River Tackle Shop,** 5008 Agar Ave. (638-1369; open Sun.-Thurs. 6:30am-11pm, Fri.-Sat. 6:30am-11:30pm; in winter daily 7am-10pm).

Prince Rupert

In 1910, railway magnate Charles Hays made a covert deal with British Columbia's provincial government that ended in his purchase of 10,000 acres of choice land at the western terminus of the Grand Trunk Pacific Railway. When the shady operation was exposed two years later, Hays was already under water—not drowned in his dire financial straits or the area's constant rain, but in the wreckage of the *Titanic*'s tragic maiden voyage. A nationwide contest to name the town that was the sole fruit of Hay's illegal labors settled on the shockingly bland "Prince Rupert"—the name of a 17th-century British-Canadian business magnate—foreshadowing Prince Rupert's present-day penchant for the drab. Besides Cow Bay, a quasi-historic artisan community born out of attempts to increase tourism, the town has little more to offer visitors than a few small museums and a handful of totem poles. The weather is notoriously rainy (earning Prince Rupert the euphemistic nickname "The City of Rainbows"), and the closest hiking trails are several kilometers outside of town.

PRACTICAL INFORMATION AND ORIENTATION

Visitors Information: Traveler's Information Centre (624-5637 or 800-667-1994), at 1st Ave. and McBride St. Stacks of pamphlets, free maps, and a less-than-riveting self-guided tour. More impressive is the small **Museum of Northern British Columbia** that shares the same building and helpful staff. Open May 15-Labor Day Mon.-Sat. 9am-8pm, Sun. 9am-5pm; winter Mon.-Fri. 10am-5pm.

Banks: Plenty of choices, but the only one with a 24hr. **ATM** is **CIBC,** on 3rd Ave. at 4th St. **Northern Savings Credit Union,** on 3rd Ave. at 1st St., is open Mon.-Thurs. 9:30am-5pm, Fri. 9:30am-6pm, Sat. 9am-3pm. **Express Travel** (627-1266), on 3rd Ave. across from Shoppers Drug Mart, handles traveler's checks. Open Mon.-Fri. 9am-5:30pm, Sat. 10:30am-4pm.

Airport: Prince Rupert Airport, on Digby Island. The ferry and bus connection to downtown costs $11 and takes about 45min. Swimming is not an option. **Air BC,** 112 6th St. (624-4554), flies to Vancouver ($402, standby $141). **Canadian Airlines** (624-9181 or 800-665-1177), on the ground floor of the mall on 2nd Ave. W., offers the same service ($436, standby $158). Wheelchair accessible. Standby flights are sometimes cheaper than the bus or train.

Trains: VIA Rail (984-5246 or 800-561-8630 from BC; 800-663-8238 outside of BC), toward the water on Bill Murray Way. Trains to Prince George (3 per week; with 7-day advance purchase $50, students $42). **BC Rail** continues to Vancouver from Prince George ($177, students $159), but an overnight stay is required (see **Essentials: By Train,** p. 27). Wheelchair accessible.

Buses: Greyhound, 822 3rd Ave. (624-5090), near 8th St. 2 buses daily to Prince George ($81), Vancouver ($165). Station open Mon.-Fri. 8:30am-12:30pm and 4-8:45pm, Sat.-Sun. 9-11:15am and 6-8:45 pm. Lockers available.

Public Transportation: Prince Rupert Bus Service (624-3343). Provides local service downtown Mon.-Sat. ($1, seniors 60¢; day pass $2.50, seniors $2). Stops are marked by white and red signs. The #52 bus runs from 2nd Ave. and 3rd St. to within a 5-min. walk of the ferry terminal, about every 30min. 7am-10pm.

Ferries: Alaska Marine Highway (627-1744 or 800-642-0066; fax 627-1744; http://www.state.ak.us), at the end of Hwy. 16 (Park Ave.). Runs ferries north from Prince Rupert along the Alaskan panhandle, including Ketchikan (US$38, car US$75) and Juneau (US$104, car US$240). Next door is **BC Ferries** (624-9627 or 888-223-3779; fax 381-5452; http://bcferries.bc.ca/ferries). Serves the Queen Charlotte Islands (6 per week; in peak season, $23, car $87) and Port Hardy (every other day, $102, car $210). Vehicle reservations required 3 weeks in advance. Ferry-goers may not leave cars parked on the streets of Prince Rupert. Some establishments charge a daily rate for storage; check with the ferry company or the information center (see above).

Shuttle: Seashore Charter Services (624-5645). Cheap and convenient. Call ahead and they'll take you from the mall on 2nd Ave. to the ferry terminal for $3. Look for their minibus at the terminal when you arrive.

Taxi: Skeena Taxi (624-2185). A ride from town to the ferry port costs from $6-8. Open 24hr.

Car Rental: Tilden Auto Rental (624-5318), in the mall at 2nd Ave. and 5th St. During the week $53 per day, on weekends $28 per day. 35¢ per km, must be over 21 with a credit card.

Bike Rental: Far West Sporting Goods (627-1766 or 624-2568), on 3rd Ave. near 1st St. $18 for 3hr., $25 for 24hr. High-quality bikes; includes lock and helmet. Good selection of camping gear to boot. Open Mon.-Thurs. and Sat. 9:30am-5:30pm; Fri. 9:30am-9pm.

Kayak Rental: Kalen Sports (624-3633), on the corner of 2nd Ave. and 3rd St. Rents kayaks for $30 per day. Open summer Mon.-Thurs. 9am-6pm, Fri. 9am-9pm, Sun. 9am-4pm. **Sea Kayaking Adventures** (624-8311; fax 624-8318; email ecotreks@citytel.net; http://www.citytel.net/ecotreks) offers guided 3hr. trips that leave from Cow Bay at 9am, 1pm, and 6pm ($40 per person).

Bookstore: Star of the West Books, 518 3rd. Ave. (624-9053). A fine collection of regional titles. Open Mon.-Fri. 9am-9pm, Sat. 9am-6pm; Jan.-April Mon.-Sat. 9am-6pm.

Public Library: 101 6th Ave. W. (627-1345; email chieflib@citytel.net), at McBride St. Internet access $2 per hr. Open Mon. and Wed. 1-9pm, Tues. and Thurs. 10am-9pm, and Fri.-Sat. 1-5pm; in winter also open Sun. 1-5pm.

Seniors' Center: (627-1900), off Fraser St. on Greenville Ct. Open daily 10:30am-4pm.

Laundromat: For mother loads, head to **Mommy's Laundromat,** on 6th St. between 2nd and 3rd Ave. She won't do the laundry for you, but her machines are cheap. Wash 75¢, dry 75¢ for 15min. Open daily 9am-9pm.

Swimming Pool: Jim Ciccone Civic Center (main office 624-6707; pool 627-7946). Pool (with waterslide and rope swing), ice skating rink, and climbing wall. 50¢ swims Mon. 3:30-5pm, Sat. noon-1pm. Call their 24hr. information line (624-9000) for current schedule and rates. Wheelchair accessible.

Showers: Both Pioneer Rooms and the Park Avenue Campgrounds open their showers to the public (see **Accommodations and Camping** below).

Local Radio: CFPR 860 AM. News and local events.

Crisis Hotline: 888-562-1214.

Emergency: 911. **Hospital:** 1305 Summit Ave. (624-2171). **Ambulance:** 800-461-9911. **Fire:** 627-1248. **Police:** 100 7th Ave. (624-2136).

Internet Access: At the **Public Library** ($2 per hr., see above) and **Cowpuccino's Coffee House** ($5 per hr.; see p. 237).

Post Office: (624-2136), on 2nd Ave. and 3rd. St. General delivery mail available at the main office (open Mon.-Fri. 8:30am-4:30pm), but only **substations** sell stamps and postal supplies. The most convenient substation is in the **Shoppers Drug Mart**

at 3rd Ave. and 2nd. St. (open Mon.-Tues. and Sat. 9am-6pm, Wed.-Fri. 9am-9pm, Sun. 11am-5pm). **Postal code:** V8J 3P3.

Area Code: 250.

The only major road into town is **Hwy. 16,** also known as **McBride St.** within the city limits. At the north end of downtown, Hwy. 16 makes a sharp left and becomes 2nd Ave. Downtown, avenues run north-south and increase in number from west to east; streets run east-west and increase in number from north to south. McBride St. is one block northeast of 1st St. At the south end of downtown, Hwy. 16 becomes Park Ave., continuing to the ferry docks.

From the ferry docks, the walk downtown takes 30 minutes, or 45 with a heavy pack. Hitching is feasible, but inconsistent. A safer bet is the Seashore Charter Services Shuttle (see above) or a cab to downtown.

ACCOMMODATIONS AND CAMPING

Nearly all of Prince Rupert's hotels nestle within the six-block area defined by 1st Ave., 3rd Ave., 6th St., and 9th St. Everything fills to the gills when the ferries dock, so call a day or two in advance. Unfortunately, most motels are pricey—a single costs at least $55.

Pioneer Rooms, 167 3rd Ave. E. (624-2334), one block east of McBride St. A new but supposedly "historic" facade enlivens the drab but well kept interior. Singles, blocked off by curtains, can get noisy ($20). Single with walls and a door $25; doubles $30. Laundry facilities ($5 wash and dry, including soap), microwave, and TV downstairs. Showers for non-guests $3.

Eagle Bluff Bed and Breakfast, 201 Cow Bay Rd. (627-4955 or 800-833-1550; email eaglebed@citytel.net), on the waterfront. No need to call a bluff at this straightforward and attractively furnished oceanside B&B. Private deck for sunset watching. $45 singles; $50 doubles, both with shared bath; $10 extra for private bath. Wheelchair accessible. No pets.

Rose's Bed and Breakfast, 943 1st Ave. W. (624-5539). Hostess Teresa Rose's doting attention and scrambled eggs will lure even the weariest traveler out of bed in the morning. Large white rooms, a shared lounge area, full kitchen, and a view of the harbor. Teresa speaks French. Singles $40; doubles $50. Open June-Sept.

Park Ave. Campground, 1750 Park Ave. (624-5861 or 800-667-1994). Less than 2km east of the ferry terminal via Hwy. 16. The sole campground in Prince Rupert. Some sites are forested, others have a view of the bay, all are well maintained. An RV metropolis. Sites $10.50; RV sites $18.50; showers $3.50 for non-guests. Laundry facilities. Reservations recommended. Accepts Visa and MasterCard.

FOOD

The best budget food options in Prince Rupert begin in the bulk food department at the colossal **Safeway** (624-2412) at 2nd St. and 2nd Ave. (open daily 9am-9pm). Most other food options are unexceptional and overpriced. Take locals' recommendations with a grain of salt—no place is fantastic.

Restaurants

Cow Bay Café, 201Cow Bay Rd. (627-1212), around the corner from Eagle Bluff B&B. Local patrons and an ever-changing menu. Such diverse delights as vegetarian *chilaquiles* ($11.50), ribs in guava BBQ sauce ($14.50), shrimp *quesadillas* ($9), and an extensive wine list. Put away your deflated wallet, gaze out at the harbor, and thank your lucky stars that you found this place. Open Tues. noon-2:30pm, Wed.-Sat. noon-2:30pm, and 6-9pm.

Galaxy Gardens, 844 3rd Ave. W. (624-3122). Just one in a surprisingly large Chinese restaurant crowd. Enjoy very good *chow meins* ($7.50) and Cantonese entrees ($11 and up). Open daily 11am-10pm.

Rodho's (624-9797), on 2nd Ave. near 6th St. Pleasing pasta platters ($7-8) or Greek entrees ($11-13) preface Rodho's less impressive plastic tablecloths. The "Hellenic art" (read: line drawing by children) on the walls testifies to local appreciation for this Italian and Greek dinner joint. Open daily 4pm-1am.

Cafes and Coffeehouses

It took a while for the gourmet coffee waves to wash this far north of Seattle, but the espresso tsunami has finally drenched Prince Rupert.

Cowpuccino's Coffee House, 25 Cow Bay Road (627-1395). The newest addition to the Cow Bay coffee community, Cowpuccino's takes its name seriously. Chew on rich desserts (Sex in a Pan, $4) or assorted coffees (tall coffee-of-the-day, $1.25) while sitting on a varnished cable reel surrounded by black and white spotted hitching posts. Explore greener pastures online with the cafe's internet connection, $5 per hr. Open Mon.-Sat. 6:30am-11:30pm, Sun. 6:30am-10pm. In winter, Mon.-Sat. 7:30am-10pm, Sun. 9am-9pm.

Lambada's Cappucino & Espresso, 101 3rd Ave. (624-6464). New York ambiance and a mixed clientele of backpackers, local fishermen, and barely-urban professionals. The Lambada, a quadruple shot of flavored mocha ($4.50), will make them all dance. Open Mon.-Thurs. 7am-5:30pm, Fri. 7am-9pm, Sat. 8am-5:30pm.

The Loft, 34 Cow Bay Road (624-6442), upstairs. Spin a bowl at the pottery studio that shares the building, and while it's firing, warm yourself with Ginseng Peppermint, Mango Ceylon, or Tea of Inquiry teas ($1.50 for one, $2.50 for two). Open Mon.-Fri. 11am-9pm.

ENTERTAINMENT

Well, there's always the movies. The cinema at 2nd Ave. and 6th St. shows three features twice a night ($8, children and seniors $4.50). While drinking establishments abound, kickin' back with a beer may prove alarmingly expensive. Two clubs compete for "dockers"—the tourists who come off the ferry—but those in search of big-city entertainment may wish they'd stayed on the boat.

The Commercial Inn, 901 1st Ave. (624-6142), on the Waterfront. Local color in the form of tipsy fishermen and other down-to-earth folks. Quiet during the week, but commercialism kicks in on the weekends when the live bands break out their guitars. Comfortable, spacious setting with free billiards. Occasionally rowdy. $2.75 beer on tap. Sell your soul or your first-born and splurge on a premium bottle ($4.75). Open Sun.-Thurs. 11am-1am, Fri.-Sat. noon-2:30am.

Breaker's Pub, 117 George Hills Way in Cow Bay (624-5990). The "no rollerblades" sign on the door is a good indication of the kind of crowd this place attracts. Pool tables, nice view, vintage 80s tunes, and expensive beers ($4 for a pint on draft). Bar open Mon.-Thurs. 11:30am-midnight, Fri-Sat. 11:30am-1am, Sun. noon-midnight; kitchen closes earlier.

Bogey's (624-6711), on 3rd Ave. near Rodho's. You guessed it: lots of *Casablanca* posters, but Rick would be alarmed by the black lighting that bathes the interior and sets the big white stars on the carpet aglow. An enthusiastic and notably older crowd of drinkers and dancers. Drinks around $4. Open daily 9am-2am.

SIGHTS AND OUTDOORS

Some of the best sights in Prince Rupert aren't in Prince Rupert. Locals boast of the **North Pacific Cannery** (628-3538) in Port Edward, 30 minutes by car from Prince Rupert, claiming the cannery presents "a true-to-life glimpse" into the canning industry. (*Let's Go* wonders if perhaps Prince Rupert natives really just want to reclaim their home town from the hordes by sending tourists out of town.) Follow the main highway out of Prince Rupert, take the Port Edward turn-off, and keep following the narrow, winding road for another 15-20 minutes. No actual packaging of fish has gone on at the cannery since the late 80s; it is now strictly a museum with hourly tours for the public. Recent attention has revitalized the surrounding village and improved museum itself. (Open May 1-Sept. 30 daily 10am-7pm; Oct. 1-April 30 Wed.-Sun. 10am-4pm; admission $5, ages 6-15 $3, under 6 free.)

Few visitors realize that Prince Rupert Harbor has the highest concentration of archaeological sites in North America. Three-hour **archaeological boat tours** leave from the **Traveler's Information Centre** daily (see **Practical Information,** p. 234). A local expert will escort you to several sites, including the modern village of **Metlakatla,** in addition to pointing out many more from the boat. (Tours depart June 19-30 daily 12:30pm, July-early-Sept. daily 1pm; $20, children $12, under 5 free.)

A number of attractive small parks line the hills above Prince Rupert and are a nice place for leg-stretching between ferry-trip legs. Tiny **Service Park,** off Fulton St., offers panoramic views of downtown and the harbor beyond. Get an even broader view from a trail leading up the side of **Mt. Oldfield,** to the east of town. The trailhead is at Oliver Lake Park, about 6km from downtown on Hwy. 16—consider renting a bike to get there if you don't have a car. The **Butze Rapids** and **Tall Trees** trails depart from the same location. Guided nature walks ($5) leave from the parking lot (May-Oct. every hour 10am-4pm). Ambitious cyclists can bike 16km down the road to **Diana Lake Park,** which features a picnic area set against an enticing lake.

The best time to visit Prince Rupert may be during **Seafest,** an annual four-day celebration held in mid-June. Surrounding towns celebrate, well, the sea, with parades, bathtub races, and beer contests. The **Islandman Triathalon** (1000m swim, 35km bike, 8km run) is also part of the Seafestivities (and was won in 1997 by an intrepid *Let's Go* researcher). The Traveler's Information Center has the lowdown.

QUEEN CHARLOTTE ISLANDS

Travel brochures bill the Charlottes as "the Canadian Galápagos," or "the Grand Canyon of the North," but these islands have a character all their own. Floating in the Pacific Ocean about 130km west of Prince Rupert, the islands form an archipelago made up of two principal islands, **Graham** and **Moresby,** and 148 surrounding islets. Graham, the northern island, is home to all but one of the islands' peaceful communities, a particularly potent (and illegal) strain of hallucinogenic mushroom, the world's largest black bears, and, until recently, the world's only known Golden Spruce. Hot springs steam from mountainous Moresby Island and its smaller neighbors to the south. The massive wooden totem poles of the islands' first inhabitants decay on the shores of the Pacific Ocean in Canada's newest national park.

The timber industry is the islands' main employer, narrowly edging out the Canadian government. In the 1980s the islands attracted global attention when environmentalists from around the globe joined the native **Haida Nation** and other locals in demonstrations to stop logging on parts of Moresby Island. In 1981, UNESCO declared parts of Moresby Island a World Heritage Site, and in 1988, the Canadian government established the **Gwaii Haanas** (Gwy-HAH-nus) **/ South Moresby National Park Reserve.**

The park, which is only accessible by boat or plane, covers the southern third of the Queen Charlottes and protects them from logging and development. The Haida Nation, noted for its elaborate totem poles and jewelry, maintains over 500 archaeological and historical sites, including dugout canoes, burial caves, and rock shelters. The protests and the creation of the national park reserve sparked a significant amount of media attention, and tourist activity in the area rose dramatically. This free publicity was relatively short-lived, however, and the islands today are once again quiet, uncrowded, and mystical. The lack of public transportation and the exorbitant cost of car rentals deter the faint of heart, but residents are rumored to be generous in picking up hitchhikers.

The BC Ferry from Prince Rupert docks at **Skidegate Landing,** between **Queen Charlotte,** 4km west of the landing, and the village of **Skidegate,** 2km to the northeast. Most visitors stay and eat in Queen Charlotte, the largest town in the islands, but all of the island communities have at least some tourist facilities. Many of the best accommodations and attractions lie farther to the north off Hwy. 16 in **Tlell, Port Clements,** and especially **Masset.** To the south sits **Moresby Island** and the town of **Sandspit.** From Skidegate Landing, 12 daily ferries make the 20-minute crossing between the islands. Locals refer to Queen Charlotte City as "Charlotte," Port Clements as "Port," and Tlell as "Tuh-LEL."

Queen Charlotte City

Queen Charlotte City's central location and size make it the starting point for drivers exploring the two major islands. "Size" is relative, however; this community of just over 1,000 people is not the city its name claims it is. Charlotte grew around a sawmill, and logging is still its foremost industry, though fishing and the government also supply a significant number of jobs. The location is pleasant, but there's little to do here besides enjoy views of the waterfront. Many businesses, including most grocery stores, are closed on Sundays and Mondays. Try to visit on a Tuesday.

PRACTICAL INFORMATION

Visitors Information: Visitor Reception Centre (559-8316; fax 559-8952), Wharf St. on the east end of town. Beautiful new facility provides information both on Gwaii Haanas National Park and the islands as a whole. Ornate 3-D map of the islands and a creative natural history presentation. A copy of the *Guide to the Queen Charlotte Islands* is $3.95; detailed maps of the towns are worth the price. Open May-Sept. daily 10am-7pm.

Banks: Northern Savings Credit Union (559-4407), Wharf St. One of two banking locations on the island (also a branch in Masset). The **ATM** on 3rd Ave. next to the City Centre Store is a lifesaver since many businesses don't take credit cards. Bank open Tues.-Thurs. 10am-5pm, Fri. 10am-6pm, Sat. 10am-3pm.

Parks Canada: Gwaii Haanas Park Information (559-8818), on 2nd Ave. off 2nd St. Try the Visitor Reception Centre for information during the summer. Register here during the rest of the year. Open Mon.-Fri. 8am-4:30pm.

Ministry of Forests: (559-6200 or 559-8324), on 3rd Ave. at the far west end of town. Information on free campsites maintained by the Forest Service on Graham and Moresby Islands. Open Mon.-Fri. 8:30am-noon and 1-4:30pm.

Fishing Licenses: Obtain a saltwater license at **Meegan's Store,** 3126 Wharf St. (559-4428), or at the **Sea Raven Hotel,** 3301 3rd Ave. (559-4423). Freshwater licenses are available only from the **Government Agent** (559-4452 or 800-663-7674). Prices vary depending on how long the license lasts.

Ferries: BC Ferry, terminal in Skidegate Landing (559-4485 or 800-663-7600), 4.5km east of Queen Charlotte City. To Prince Rupert (July-Aug. 6 per week, Sept. 5 per week, Oct.-June 4 per week; $22.25, car $84.75, bike $6). If you have a car, reserve at least 3 weeks in advance. Car fares do not include driver. Ferries also run between Skidegate Landing on Graham Island and Alliford Bay on Moresby Island (12 trips per day; $3 roundtrip, car $8.50, off-season car $7.50). See **Essentials: By Ferry,** p. 32.

Taxi: Eagle Cabs, 209 3rd Ave. (559-4461). $7-10 from Charlotte to the ferry terminal. Open daily 8am-2pm.

Car Rental: Rustic Rentals (559-4641), west of downtown at Charlotte Island Tire. Another office at 3922 3rd Ave. (559-8865), by the ferry at Jo's Bed and Breakfast (see **Accomodations and Camping,** p. 240). Will rent to 18-yr.-olds with a credit card. Reliable if unimpressive collection of used cars. $39 per day plus 15¢ per km over 50. Office open Mon. 8am-6pm, Tues.-Fri. 8am-7pm, Sat. 9am-5:30pm, but available 24hr. Will pick up at the ferry terminal in Skidegate.

Auto Repair: Twin Services (559-8700) offers 24-hr. towing and a garage. Open Mon.-Fri. 8:30am-8:30pm, Sat. 8:30am-7pm, Sun. 9am-7pm.

Bike Rental: Moonglow 3611 Hwy. 33 (559-8831), just east of town. High quality mountain bikes in many sizes. $5 per hr. or $25 per day, includes helmets, water bottles, and detailed maps of local logging roads and campsites. Open daily 9am-6pm.

Books: Bill Ellis Books (559-4681), on 3rd Ave. at the far west end of Charlotte. A remarkable collection of works by and about the Haida and other Native American peoples. Open Mon.-Fri. 8:15am-4pm. **Bradley Books** (559-0041), on 7th St. off 3rd Ave., may be a better bet for fiction and current magazines. Open Tues.-Sat. noon-6pm.

Laundromat: 121 3rd Ave. (559-4444), in the City Center mall. Wash $1.50, dry 25¢. Open daily 9am-9pm.

Showers: Ask at **Jo's Bed and Breakfast** (see **Accomodations and Camping,** p. 240).

Pharmacy: (559-4310), downstairs in the hospital building. Open Mon.-Tues. and Thurs.-Fri. 10:30am-12:30pm and 1:30-5:15pm, Wed. 1:30-5:15pm.

Hospital: (559-4300), on 3rd Ave. at the east end of town.

Women's Center: Queen Charlotte Islands Women Society (559-4743).

Emergency: Police (RCMP): 3211 Wharf St. (559-4421). **Ambulance:** 800-461-9911. **Fire:** 559-4488.

Local Radio: WCBC 102.9 FM.

Post Office: (559-8349), in the City Centre mall on 3rd Ave. Open Mon.-Fri. 8:30am-5:30pm, Sat. noon-4pm. **Postal code:** V0T 1S0.

Area Code: 250.

ACCOMMODATIONS AND CAMPING

The small hotels of Queen Charlotte City are pristine, cozy, charming, and expensive. During the summer, make reservations or arrive early in the day to secure a room. The cheaper options are limited in number and highly in demand.

Jo's Bed and Breakfast, 4813 Ferry Loop Rd. (559-8865). Follow the road from the ferry terminal up the hill to the white house with blue trim. Convenient to the ferry, but a significant distance from anything else. Some rooms are skylit and feature cinematic ocean views. Others enjoy a communal kitchen and lounge, as well as communal noise. Supple beds with fluffy comforters make getting up in the morning a challenge, but Jo's generous continental breakfasts are persuasive. Free local calls and a shed for baggage storage. Singles $30; doubles $40; campsite on lawn $5 including use of bathroom and shower. Cash only. Reservations a good idea.

Dorothy and Mike's Guest House, 3125 2nd Ave. (559-8439), up the hill opposite Meegan's Store. A standing hammock chair, stained pine interiors, a library, and a loving breakfast to warm even the soggiest traveler. Centrally located. Singles $35; doubles $45. Call ahead, won't you?

The Premier Creek Lodging, 3101 3rd Ave. (888-322-3388 or 559-8415; fax 559-8198). Built in 1910, this low-key hotel has been renovated with a veranda and balconies. Rooms in the back hall are old (88yr!) and small, but cost only an equally dated $30 (with shared bath). Newer rooms with balconies start at $65 and can serve as doubles at no extra charge. Cheaper rooms go quickly, so reserve early.

Gracie's Place, 3113 3rd Ave., Box 447 (888-244-4262 or 559-4262). Pay a smidgen more for a significant upgrade in atmosphere. Gracie adorns her rooms with antique furniture and down quilts. Say good night, Gracie. Singles $50; doubles a deal at $60; kitchen units $20 extra.

Haydn Turner Park Campsite, at the west end of 4th Ave. A 25-min. walk from the town center. Sites include free firewood from the towering spruces that dwarf tents (and campers). A few spots at the end overlook the water. Toilets and water (boil before drinking). Tents $5, RVs $7.

FOOD

Most locals save eating out for trips to the mainland and will direct visitors to the grocery store for *haute cuisine à la Charlotte*. Buy basic grub at **City Center Stores Ltd.** (559-4444), in the City Center mall (open Tues.-Fri. 9:30am-9pm, Mon. and Sat. 9:30am-6pm). On nights and Sundays try **Sam and Shirley's,** on 7th St. at the west end of town (open daily 7:30am-10:30pm).

Howler's Bistro (860-2559), above the Howler's Pub on 3rd Ave. Howler's sneaks a bit of art onto the palates of unsuspecting hungry diners. Each dish is served with creative garnishes and festive flair. Try the chicken burrito ($8.95) or a veggie burger ($6.95), but leave room for one of five varieties of cheesecake ($4.95) for dessert. Open Wed.-Sun. 11am-11pm.

Oceana Restaurant (559-8683; fax 559-8699), 3rd Ave. 1 block from Wharf St. By far the better of the town's two Chinese restaurants, and rumored to be the best in B.C. A bit pricey, but worth it for *Ma Poo* tofu ($11) or a fried rice plus sweet and sour pork combo platter ($12). Ice cream shop next door for those craving fortune cookie *à la mode*. Open Mon.-Sat. 11:30am-3pm and 5-10pm.

Hummingbird Café, 3301 3rd Ave. (559-8583). Upscale for Charlotte, the Hummingbird offers an airy, sun-washed dining area, stellar ocean view, and entrees ranging from a $5.25 burger to an $8 plate of spaghetti. Sizable, sustaining salads for vegetarians and the health-conscious. Does not serve hummingbird. Open daily 7am-2pm and 5-8:30pm; in winter 11:30am-2:30pm and 5-8:30pm.

Isabel Creek Store, 3219 Wharf St. (559-8623), next to Margaret's Café. Organic fruits and vegetables, juices, and some nitty-gritty home-baked breads. A break from fried food, and a good place to drop by before a backpacking trip. Open Mon.-Sat. 10am-5:30pm and, they guarantee "during power outages."

Hanging by a Fibre (559-4463; fax 559-8430), on Wharf St. underneath the Pub. Home of all things fibrous and a place to interweave with local hipsters and the occasional artist. Store and gallery specializing in paper-art and basketry. Cappuccino $2.50, café latte $3.25, regular coffee $1.50, muffins and cookies 50¢. Open Sat.-Wed. 9am-7pm, Thurs.-Fri. 9am-9pm. Wheelchair accessible.

SIGHTS AND OUTDOORS

Skidegate Mission, known as "the Village," is a cluster of small, worn houses on Rooney Bay, 2km east of the ferry landing along the northern branch of Hwy. 16. The Haida village of Skidegate is a community of 470, a nexus of Haida art and culture, and a continuation of centuries of Haida life. Residents are resigned to tourists, yet hopeful that visitors will exhibit discretion and respect concerning local culture and practices. Visit the **Skidegate Band Council Office** (559-4496), in a Haida longhouse built in 1979 according to ancient design specifications. Many a bald eagle has perched upon the totem pole out front. Ask the receptionist for permission to view the artwork and old photographs inside (office open Mon.-Fri. 8am-4:30pm). Halfway between Skidegate Landing and Skidegate Mission is the **Queen Charlotte Islands Museum** (559-4643), housing totem poles from remote village sites, an extensive collection of stuffed birds, and contemporary Haida prints and carvings. The shed next door protects the 50-foot cedar canoe carved for Vancouver's Expo '86 by renowned Haida artist Bill Reid. Take it out for a paddle ($200 per day) or just admire its artistry on dry land. (Museum admission $2.50, children free; open May-Sept. Mon.-Fri.10am-5pm, Sat.-Sun. 1-5pm.)

Unlike most mountains allegedly in the shape of something, **Sleeping Beauty Mountain** actually resembles the prettily snoozing royalty. Ask a local to point out her distinct facial features. The challenging climb up the Beauty starts about 12km west of town off a logging road (follow the signs after 3rd Ave. turns to gravel) and takes a witchy three hours to ascend. The peak blesses climbers with stunning views in every direction. A natural attraction requiring significantly less effort is **Balance Rock,** which teeters on a roadside beach 1km north of Skidegate. A group of brawny loggers once failed in an attempt to dislodge the mighty boulder, so the stone is unlikely to topple from its precarious perch. The scenic and virtually traffic-free roads throughout the islands beckon seductively to cyclists. Navigating the tangle of local logging roads and trails is easy with *Trails on the Queen Charlottes,* by Fern Henderson ($5), sold at all the tourist centers and bookstores on the island. Locals swear by "Fern's book" as the outdoor bible of the Queen Charlottes.

■ Yellowhead Highway(16): Tlell and Port Clements

Two tiny towns dot the quiet highway between Charlotte and Masset. **Tlell,** 40km north of Queen Charlotte City, masquerades as a trail of houses and farms spread thinly along a 7km stretch of Hwy. 16. The "town" enjoys some of Graham Island's best beach vistas and a population of urban refugees who earn Tlell a reputation as the Charlottes' "hippie" zone. The rocky beaches of the south give way to sand here, and the Tlell River offers excellent fishing and water warm enough for swimming.

Port Clements, 20km north of its inverse, Tlell, is a gritty logging community. Although blessed with an enticing harbor and a few nearby curiosities, "Port," as the town is fondly known, has little to hold the footloose traveler. An intricate network of logging roads stretches inland from the port; these bumpy byways are open to public use and provide access to the heavily forested interior. Port Clements faces west onto Masset Inlet, and harbors some of the best sunsets in the Charlottes.

Practical Information Both communities boast a **post office** (and in Tlell and Port Clements, that's something to boast about). The post office in Tlell (557-4551; open Mon.-Sat. 2:30-5:30pm; **Postal code:** V0T 1Y0) is on Hwy. 16, 2km south of Wiggins Rd. Port Clements' lies between Hemlock and Spruce Ave. (open Mon.-Fri. 8:30am-12:30pm and 1:30-5:30pm, Sat. 1:30-5:30pm; **Postal code:** V0T 1R0). Port also offers a **Village Office** (557-4295), on Cedar Ave. between Tingley and Pard St., which provides information and free **maps** of the logging roads (open Mon.-Fri. 1-5pm). You can browse for more information at the **Port Clements Islands Regional Library** (557-4402) at Tingley St. and Cedar Ave. (open Wed. 3-5pm and 7-9pm, Fri. 2-6pm) or Tlell's **bookstore** (557-4241) in the Sitka Studio at the end of Richardson Rd. (open daily 10am-6pm). There is a **health clinic** in Port on Park St. (557-4478) next to the elementary school, with variable hours. Call **Island Taxi** in Port at 557-4230 (24hr.). In an **emergency,** call 557-4355 (**fire**) or 800-461-9911 (**ambulance**). The **area code** for both towns is 250.

Accommodations and Camping Sink into the lap of luxury at **Hltunwa Kaitza Bed and Breakfast** (557-4664), nestled against the dunes just north of Richardson Ranch on the ocean side of the road, just seconds from the beach. This may be the islands' nicest B&B and is certainly its most distinctive. The hostess, Cacilia, oversees a flock of friends and relations who are likely to drop by for tea in the evening. The common living space is adorned with driftwood furniture, and hanging chairs descend from giant spruce beams. Rooms are skylit, immaculate, and comfortable. (Singles $30, mat on the floor $15, laundry free.) Those seeking a more traditional motel experience can opt for the **Golden Spruce Motel,** 2 Grouse St. (557-4325), in a location in Port Clements that could use some sprucing up. Singles start at $42, doubles at $52, kitchenettes $8 extra, breakfast $4 for guests. Near Tlell, travelers can pitch a tent or park an RV at **Misty Meadows Campground,** just south of the Tlell River Bridge. Leafy trees line a short path to the beach. Pit toilets, picnic tables, and water grace 30 sites ($9.50, 14 day max. stay; call **Naikoon Provincial Park Headquarters** at 557-4390).

Food The only restaurant along the highway is the **Yakoun River Inn** (557-4440) on Bayview Dr. in Port Clements. This classically rural establishment features a country music jukebox and serves up some damn good burgers starting at $5.75. Enjoy the autographed $2 bill collection adorning the walls, and think of how many pints of beer it could buy (not many at $4.50 a pint). Just don't try to hustle the locals at a game of pool (open Mon.-Sat. noon-2am, Sun. noon-midnight). Very near the opposite end of the Tlell dining spectrum is **Dress for Les** (557-2023), 1km south of Richardson Ranch on Richardson Rd. off Wiggins Rd. **D**rink **R**ich **E**spresso, **S**odas, **S**undaes, **F**ashion **O**utrageous **R**etro, **L**arge **A**nd (?) **S**mall. (**W.H.A.T.E.V.E.R.**). Coffee sacks stapled to the ceiling, red shoe collection on the bathroom door, pink coffee bar nestled among racks of vintage clothing (cappucino $2.90, mocha $3.75;

The (Third-to-Last) Golden Spruce

For years, oddity-seekers of the world drove, biked, hiked, and ran to Port Clements, where the world's only **Golden Spruce** basked in a singular glory. Due to a rare genetic mutation, the 300-year-old tree contained only a fraction of the chlorophyll present in an ordinary Sitka Spruce, causing its needles to be bleached by sunlight. The striking 50m behemoth glowed a fiery yellow in the sun, beaming its way into Haida creation myths and horticulturists' dreams.

In January 1997, however, a disgruntled ex-forestry worker arrived at the site with an axe and a mission. To protest the logging industry's destruction of British Columbia's forests, he chopped down the tree. His actions won him no prize for logic, but certainly drew some province-wide attention.

While islanders reacted with astonishment at their beloved tree's untimely demise, the University of British Columbia revealed another shocker: there were not one but *three* Golden Spruces—two, created from clippings of the original taken in 1977, were growing peacefully in the botanical gardens of the UBC Victoria campus. UBC authorities donated the golden saplings to the Haida Nation, which is currently deciding the future of the tiny trees.

And their future is looking good. Concurrent with the fall of the Golden Spruce, an albino raven was born on the island, an event that locals took as a sign predicting a continuation of the Spruce's 300-year history. This harbinger of success is not such a good sign for the tree's murderer, however. Should the perpetrator return to Canada (he is now on the run in Mexico), he is sure to face a stiff penalty for his botanical terrorism.

open Tues.-Sun. 10am-5pm). **Riverworks Farm & Store** (557-4363), on Hwy. 16, 2km south of Wiggins Rd. next to the post office, peddles island-grown produce and eggs (open daily 10am-5:30pm). More traditional groceries lurk in the **Bayview Market** (557-4331), on Bayview Dr. (open Tues.-Sat. 10am-6pm). Given the mediocre selection, you'd be better off shopping in Charlotte or Masset. Or stop by **Golden Spruce Farms** (557-4583), 1km south of town on Bayview Dr. An astonishing variety of fresh vegetables (considering it's nearly impossible to grow potatoes here) are plucked from the garden in back.

Sights and Outdoors One of the most popular trails around Tlell leads to the **Pezuta shipwreck,** the hulking remains of a 246-foot lumber barge that ran aground during a gale in 1928. The two-hour hike to the site leaves from the Tlell River picnic area off Hwy. 16, just north of the river. The trail wanders through equal parts of lush forest, sand dunes, and agate-strewn beaches.

Diehard beachcombers should consider continuing on past the wreck and embarking on a multi-day expedition along **East Coast Beach.** The highway cuts inland just north of Tlell, so only backpackers have access to over 90km of incredibly pristine beach. A number of wooden shelters punctuate the beach, but a tent or tarp comes in handy nonetheless. Allow between four and six days to reach the road access at the north end of the route 25km east of Masset. Adventurers are required to register at **Naikoon Provincial Park Headquarters** (557-4390) before setting out.

Drive 5½km south of town to a roadside pullover; from there it's a 10-minute walk to the banks of the **Yakoun River.** Eight km south of the pullover, a trail leads to an unfinished **Haida canoe.** This would-be boat was uncovered by loggers and remains in its original site. Nearby stumps are full of test holes where the early builders sampled other trees for their canoe potential. **MacMillan Bloedel** (557-4212) sponsors daytrips into the woods along the river (Tues. and Thurs. 9am-2pm). Meet at the **Port Clements Museum,** 45 Bayview Drive in Port Clements.

The best place to spend **Canada Day** (July 1) is in Port, when the Port Clementsians celebrate Canada's birthday in what is allegedly "a big way."

Masset

Sitting at Mile Zero of the Yellowhead Highway, Masset's low-rise businesses and dilapidated houses present visitors an initially underwhelming facade. But some surprisingly eccentric establishments and truly eccentric eccentrics mingle within this rather drab collection of tired buildings (keep an eye out for the bearded old man paddling around in his handmade canoe). The majority of travelers who make their way to Masset come for the spectacular scenery surrounding the town. The rainforested region of Tow Hill and the expansive beachfront of the Blow Hole to the east of town in Naikoon Provincial Park more than justify the northern trek.

PRACTICAL INFORMATION AND ORIENTATION

Visitors Information: Tourist Information Centre, Old Beach Rd. (626-3300), at Hwy. 16. Plenty of local history and trail maps for choice birdwatching. Open daily July-Aug. 9am-8pm. **Naikoon Provincial Park Headquarters** (557-4390).

Bank: Northern Savings Credit Union (626-5231), on Main St. north of Collison. The only bank and **ATM** on the islands outside of Queen Charlotte City. Open Tues.-Thurs. 10am-3pm, Fri. noon-5pm, Sat. 10am-3pm.

Car Rental: Tilden Rentals, 1504 Old Beach Rd. (626-3318), at the Singing Surf Inn. New cars from $40 per day, plus 25¢ per km. Must be 25. Open Mon.-Sat. 7am-10pm, Sun. 8am-10pm. Better to rent in Queen Charlotte City or Sandspit than to have to hitch to get to your rental car in Masset.

Car Repair: Collision Motors (626-3756). These guys knew how to get business when they opened their shop on Collison Ave. Open Mon.-Fri. 8am-6pm.

Taxi: Jerry's Taxi (626-5017).

Laundromat: Raven & Eagle Gifts & Cleaners, 2132 Collison Ave. (626-3511), at Orr St. Wash $1.50, 35-min. dry for $1.25. Open Mon. 10am-4pm, Tues.-Sat. 10am-5pm.

Public Library: (626-3663), at Collison Ave. and McLeod St. Open Tues. and Sat. 2-6pm, Thurs. 2-5pm and 6-8pm.

Public Radio: Haida Nation Station 96.1 FM.

Emergency: Ambulance: 800-461-9911; **Fire:** 626-5511; **Police:** (626-3991), on Collison Ave. at Orr St.

Post Office: (626-5155), on Main St. north of Collison. Open Mon.-Fri. 8:30am-5:30pm, Sat. 8:30am-12:30pm. **Postal code:** V0T 1M0.

Area Code: 250.

ACCOMMODATIONS AND CAMPING

A friendly budget god has smiled on Masset and created cheap accommodations and campsites surrounded by centuries-old trees and expansive waterways. There is free **beach camping** on North Beach, 1km past Tow Hill (about 30km east) in the provincial park. Watch for signs indicating the end of Indian Reserve property.

Copper Beech House, 1590 Delkatla Rd. (626-5441), at Collison. Dine off china from Beijing, share a bath with carved wooden frogs from Mexico, and sleep under quilted comforters from Finland: this B&B is more like a private museum than a night's lodging. Owner David Phillips knows a lot about a lot of things, and is more than willing to share. Singles $50; doubles $75; lofts in the shed in the garden, $15. Longer-term visitors can arrange to exchange 4hr. per day of work for free room and board.

Harbourview Lodging, 1618 Delkatla Rd. (626-5109 or 800-661-3314; email lholland@island.net), just north of Collison. An ornately carved wooden door and a lime green plaid carpet have been waging an aesthetic war with each other for over 30 years. Everything in the clashing interior is in good shape. Downstairs singles have TVs, and share a bath and dry sauna. Two big upstairs rooms, each with living room, kitchen, free laundry facilities, and private deck. Fresh muffins in the morning. Singles $40; doubles $45. Call for reservations in summer.

Naikoon Park Motel (626-5187), on Tow Hill Rd. about 8km east of town. A difficult but not impossible place to reach for travelers thumbing it. Laid-back owners have polished up the place with an extremely bright paint job. Singles $37; kitchen units for 2-3 are $55. Beach is right across the road and free.

Masset-Haida Lions RV Site and Campground (626-3788), on Tow Hill Rd., next to the wildlife sanctuary. Functional but unexceptional. After coming this far, it would be worth it to press on to Agate Beach. On-site office open daily 7-10pm. 22 gravelly sites, toilets, pay showers. Sites $8, with electricity $10.

Agate Beach Campground, 26km east of town in Naikoon Provincial Park, at the base of Tow Hill. After driving for 2 hours through creeping vines and moss-swathed trees, the fairyland clearing looks nearly too good to be true. Gorgeous campsites right on the beach unfold with water as far as you can see. Stay a while: 32 sites with an area reserved for tenters. Picnic shelter, firewood, water, flush toilets. Free clamming (see **Food**, below, for instructions). Sites May-Sept. $9.50 for up to 4; in winter free. For more information call Park Headquarters (557-4390).

FOOD

Free and potentially toxic (!) razor clams on Agate and North Beach. Call the **red-tide hotline** (666-3169) before gathering the ingredients for a cup of chowder that could bite back. Stop by the **Department of Fisheries and Oceans** on Christie St. to pick up a free permit and tips on how to harvest your favorite bivalve. Lemons and other seafood garnishes sold at **Delmos Co-op** (626-3933) on Main St., south of Collison Ave. (open Mon.-Sat. 10am-6pm).

Sugar Mama's, above the rec center. Slip under Indian batiks, perch on a purple velvet-covered bar stool, and be transfixed by the chocolate ginseng smoothie ($4) and the revolving red disco ball above (free to look). This cultural collision produces multitextured Indian *samosa* ($8), picante rice and beans ($3), and thick soup and corn bread ($3.50). Plenty of veggie options. Open Wed.-Sat. 11am-8pm, Sun. 11am-4:20pm. Winter schedule may vary.

Café Gallery, 2062 Collison (626-3672). Lots of private dining spaces in a restaurant hung with local artists' work. An escape from the weary, dreary streets of Masset. The owners happily *Deutsch sprechen* with homesick Germans and serve up a stomach-soothing chicken burger with ham and cheese ($8.95). Open Mon.-Sat. 8:30am-9pm.

The Villager Cafe, 1690 Orr St. (626-3694), near the courthouse. The local choice for Chinese food. Almond chicken *chow mein* or shrimp *chop suey* (both $10). Open Tues.-Sun. 11:30am-9pm.

SIGHTS AND ACTIVITIES

Tow Hill, an incredible outcrop of volcanic basalt columns about 34km east of town, rises out of nowhere at the far end of Agate Beach and presides over Masset as the area's reigning attraction. An easy boardwalk trail leads up the back of the hill to a fabulous overlook. On a clear day, miles of virgin beach and even the most southern reaches of Alaska spread out below. Sunsets are stupendous. Footpaths lead away from the observation deck toward even more breathtaking vistas and a view of the rocky shoreline that snakes around the rocks over 100m below. On the way back down, take a detour to the **Blow Hole,** a small cave that erupts with 10-15-foot-high sprays of water when the tide comes in. Over the centuries, the sea has carved innumerable pools and mini-canyons out of the rocky cliffs. Coordinating a visit with mid-tide, when the hole is active, yields quite a show.

Two less-traveled trails depart from the Tow Hill Viewpoint parking lot: an 11km beach walk to **Rose Spit** at the northeast corner of the island and a 10km hike on the **Cape Fife** trail, with access to the East Coast Beach and the multi-day backpacking route of Tlell (see **Tlell and Port Clements,** p. 242). A lean-to at the end of the Cape Fife trail allows trail-hardy backpackers to link the two routes, exploring the entire island in a two- to three-day trek. Across the Hiellen River, **North Beach** is the site of the Haida creation myth in which Raven discovered a giant clam full of tiny men.

Closer to town, red-breasted sapsuckers, orange-crowned warblers, glaucous-winged gulls, great blue herons, and binocular-toting tourists converge on the **Delkatla Wildlife Sanctuary,** off Tow Hill Rd. in Masset. The best paths for observing the 113 local airborne species begin at the junction of Trumpeter Dr. and Cemetery Rd. Continue on Cemetery Rd. past the sanctuary to reach **Oceanview Cemetery,** set in a lush green forest right on the beach, and a lively place, all things considered.

With over 600 residents, **Old Massett,** 2km west of town, is the largest Haida village on the Charlottes. Unfortunately, outside of a few modern totem poles, there's not much to look at. Hold out for the **Queen Charlotte Islands Museum** in **Skidegate** (see p. 241). You can apply for permits to visit abandoned Haida villages on Graham Island at the **Masset Band Council Office** (626-3337), in the large cedar-and-glass building at the east end of town (open Mon.-Fri. 8:30am-noon and 1-4:30pm).

Sandspit

The only permanent community on Moresby Island, Sandspit lies about 13km east of the ferry dock at Alliford Bay on a thin strip of land. With neatly trimmed houses and yards, endless ocean views, and bald eagles in seaside trees, the town is the Charlottes' most attractive residential area. Homes line Beach Road and Copper Bay Road, which run perpendicular to the beach. While Sandspit has limited culinary options, reasonably priced accommodations are plentiful and tend to fill up less quickly than those on Graham Island. The town serves as one of the major launch points for kayak and boat trips to **Gwaii Hannas/South Moresby National Park Reserve** (see p. 248) and also provides access to logging roads that venture into the isolated interior.

Practical Information The **Parks Canada** office is in the airport at the north end of town (627-5362; open daily May 1-16 8am-noon; May 17-Sept. 8am-5pm). Register here or at their office in Queen Charlotte City before venturing into the park. Further information can be obtained from the **TimberWest Information Centre** (637-5436), on Beach Rd. (open Mon.-Fri. 9am-5pm). The friendly staff provides local information as well as access to free, primitive **campsites** in several locations on the island. This stop is essential for anyone planning to travel local logging roads, which are open to the public when free of gargantuan trucks.

There's not much traffic on the road between Alliford Bay and Sandspit; those hitching to catch a late ferry often have a hard time finding a ride and recommend getting an early start. Bringing a bike over on the ferry costs nothing extra, and the trip to town is an idyllic, easy, one-hour ride between deciduous forest and open ocean. **B.C. Ferries** (888-BC-FERRY (223-3779)) runs between Skidegate Landing on Graham Island and Alliford Bay on Moresby Island (12 trips per day between 7am and 10:30pm; $3 roundtrip, car $9). **Budget Rent-A-Car,** 383 Beach Rd. (637-5688), rents cars at luxury prices ($47 per day plus 30¢ per km; must be 21 with a credit card). Another Budget office is at the **airport.**

The **library,** 383 Alliford Bay (637-2247), sits at the north end of town (open Tues. 2:30-6:30pm, Thurs. 3-5pm and 7-9pm). The **health clinic** (637-5403) is on Copper Bay Rd. in the school building. (Open Mon.-Fri. 10am-noon; after hours, call the **Queen Charlotte City Hospital** at 559-8466.) In an **emergency** call 911. **Ambulance,** 559-4506 or 800-461-9911; **fire,** 637-2222; **police,** 559-4421 in Queen Charlotte City. The **post office** (637-2244) is at Beach and Blaine Shaw Rd. (open Mon.-Fri. 9am-5pm, Sat. 11am-2pm). The **postal code** is V0T 1T0. The **area code** is 250.

Accommodations, Camping, and Food Rooms in town are more affordable and less crowded than on most on the islands. The **Seaport Bed and Breakfast** (637-5678), just up the road toward Spit Point, offers island hospitality with guest pick-up at the airport, plush couches, cable TV, and a breakfast of fresh eggs and home-baked goods. The new studio space is bright and beautifully decorated, overshadowing its predecessors, the less impressive original rooms. Reservations are essential in summer (singles $30; doubles $40). If Seaport is short rooms, go a block away from town to **Bayside Bed and Breakfast** (637-2433), operated by the same family. The accomodations are similar to the Seaport, right down to the Aztec-patterned comforters on the beds (and to the prices: singles $30; doubles $40). Plunk down at the **Moresby Island Guest House** (637-5300), on Beach Rd. next to the post office, in one of eight rooms with shared washrooms, kitchen, and coin-operated laundry facilities. In the morning, ingredients are provided for you to make your own breakfast. Kitchen use after breakfast costs $10. (Singles $30; doubles start at $55; overflow cots $15.) Trail-weary explorers can spend an extra $10 on the outdoor hot tub at the **Gwaii Hanaas Bed and Breakfast,** 368 Cristina Pl. (637-5312), off Copper Bay Rd. Enjoy spacious rooms stuffed with the hostess' own ceramic creations. Hot breakfasts and a communal lounge (singles $40; doubles $60).

The **Sandspit Inn** (637-5334), across from the airport, recently opened a restaurant. Dinner, served from 4:30-9pm, is a bit expensive, but the lunch specials available until 4pm are more reasonable. Bacon fettucini with garlic bread is $7.95. Ramble on to **Dick's Wok Inn,** 388 Copper Bay Rd. (637-2275), where a heaping plate of fried rice costs $9 and up (open daily 5-10pm). Locals give Dick mixed reviews, but aside from burgers at one of the bars, he's the only other game in town for sit-down meals. Try the mango pudding with soft ice-cream ($3) for a cross-cultural treat. Dick also offers a limited selection of very expensive groceries. A more affordable option is the **Bun Wagon,** 396 Copper Bay Rd. (635-5722). Customers sit at roadside picnic tables and enjoy delicious $2.50 dogs or big burgers with fries from $5.50 (open Mon.-Wed. 11am-2pm and 4-7pm, Fri.-Sun. 11am-7pm). The **Supervalu Supermarket,** 383 Alliford Bay (637-2249), resides in the mini-mall near the spit (open Mon.-Tues. and Thurs.-Sat. 9:30am-6pm, Wed. 9:30am-7:30pm).

Sights and Outdoors Spectacular sunrises and sunsets await those who wander to the end of the spit. Anglers can cast for silver salmon in the surf. Well-maintained dirt logging roads lead south and west of town into some smashingly scenic areas. Several trails depart from the road between the ferry docks and the spit. The **Haans Creek Loop** begins 40m west of the Haans Creek Bridge and passes by several giant cedars with ancient Haida markings. The round-trip hike takes less than two hours, but can be continued on the **Skyline Loop,** which runs another 90 minutes or so along the shore. Rocky shores line the ocean north of **Copper Bay,** a haven for bald eagles and balding shell collectors (10km south), while **Grey Bay** (20km south) offers a virtually uninterrupted expanse of sand. Twenty free, primitive **campsites** line the beach, but the area is popular with locals so arrive early on weekends. A few km down the road from the campsites, a 4.5km **trail** follows the shore south to **Cumshewa Head.** Check with the TimberWest Information Centre (see **Practical Information,** above) to find out when the roads are open to the public. The roads are perfect for mountain biking, but the closest rental place is in Charlotte. Bikes are allowed on the ferry.

In the summer, TimberWest leads an informative and free 4½-hour **logging tour** to see the trees (and stumps). Get a view of an active logging site and the rare chance for a frank discussion of logging practices. While some may wince at the process of reducing glorious spruce trees to 2x4s, a great deal of environmental forethought goes into this modern logging. At the very least, the tour is a great way to venture into the backcountry if you're without transportation. Tours leave from the office on Beach Rd. at noon on Wednesday and Friday. In June or July, ask for information on **Logger Sports Day,** a festival featuring pole climbing, caber tossing, axe throwing, and other vigorous lumber-related activities.

Gwaii Haanas/South Moresby National Park Reserve

Arguably the most tranquil region of Canada's West Coast, Gwaii Haanas was born in a whirlwind of controversy. The territory was provincially-owned Crown Land until the late 80s, and was disrupted only by sporadic logging and nosy tourists' occasional visits to deserted Haida villages. In the mid-80s, a dispute over logging on one of the area's islands embroiled the timber industry, the Haida nation, environmentalists, and the government of British Columbia. The federal government interceded in 1988, purchasing the southern third of the Queen Charlotte Islands and declaring the region a Park Reserve. The Canadian Parks Ministry now administers and patrols the islands, while Haida representatives, known as **watchmen,** inhabit key locations, guide visitors, and collect fees for visits to Haida sites.

Only a few thousand visitors each summer make the long ocean journey south from Moresby Camp (no roads penetrate the reserve). Those who do enjoy a wonderland of remarkable beauty and diverse plant and animal life. Old-growth forest stands tall in **Hlk'Yaak** (Windy Bay). Chains of lakes and waterfalls span the breadth of southern Moresby Island. At **Gandla K'in** (Hotsprings Island), several seaside pools steam at a year-round 100°F (37°C). The **San Christoval Mountains** thrust up semi-alpine peaks, which bear snow well into summer. The waters of **Juan Perez Sound** teem with jellyfish and enormous orange and purple starfish.

The artifacts of several eras and cultures also rest in Gwaii Haanas. Deserted logging camps from the 1930s display bizarre, steam-driven logging devices, ancient, decaying trucks, and highways built entirely of wood. Clan totem poles slowly decay at **Skedans** and **Ninstints,** Haida villages deserted after late-19th-century epidemics of smallpox and tuberculosis. These settlements are being permitted to "return to the land" in keeping with Haida tradition. In 1982, Ninstints was declared a UNESCO World Heritage Site.

A journey into Gwaii Haanas begins with registration at the **Parks Canada** offices in Sandspit (at the airport) or in Queen Charlotte City, (559-8818) downtown on 2nd Ave. or with the **Haida Gwaii Watchmen** (559-8225) at Second Beach, 1km north of Skidegate Landing. Write to: Superintendent, Gwaii Haanas National Park Reserve, Box 37, Queen Charlotte, B.C. V0T 1S0; or to Haida Gwaii Watchmen, P.O. Box 609, Skidegate, Haida Gwaii V0T 1S0. Be sure to ask about appropriate camping locations. The Haida forbid camping in their traditional sites and require a $25 fee (good for a full year) for day visits.

Camp Moresby, near Gray Bay (see **Sandspit,** p. 246) is a logical place to enter the park. Check with **TimberWest** (637-5436) in Sandspit on Beach Rd. before traveling these sometimes hazardous logging roads. Two companies dominate the market for kayak rentals and charter trips into the Park Reserve. **Moresby Explorers** (637-2215 or 800-806-7633), run by the energetic and competent Doug Gould, offers $110 chartered day trips, $140 chartered overnight trips to Doug's floating cabin off Juan Perez Sound, and $250 week-long kayak rentals that include transportation to the cabin and back. While the charters are fun and hit many high points, kayak rental is a more affordable option for those who already have experience in a kayak. If you're short on cash, give Doug a call to see what he has planned—prices can be flexible if you are. Doug's business sits on Beach Rd. in Sandspit, just south of Copper Bay Rd. **Queen Charlotte Adventures** (800-668-4288 or 559-8990; fax 559-8983), run by Mary Kellie and Barb Rowsell, sits outside Queen Charlotte City on the road to Skidegate, and offers sea kayak rentals ($70 per day, $310 per week), marine transport ($120 from Queen Charlotte to Juan Perez Sound), and guided kayak, powerboat, and sailboat tours. Keep in mind that it may take several days to reach more remote regions of the reserve by kayak. **South Moresby Air Charters** (559-4222; fax 559-8589; email smoresby@island.net) runs flights over many of the heritage sites. For two hours and $326, a three- to four-person aircraft deposits culture seekers on the beach of Skedans for a guided 1½-hour tour—not a bad deal for four people short on time. Flights to Hot Springs and Ninstints are also available.

ALASKA APPROACHES

Cassiar Highway (37)

A growing number of adventurous travelers prefer **Highway 37,** the **Cassiar Highway,** to the Alaska Highway, which has become the institution for RV drivers. Any waiter or hotel owner along the Cassiar's 718km will readily list its advantages—less distance, better scenery, and fewer crowds. However, the Cassiar is remote and less well-maintained, and a substantial portion of it after Meziadin Junction is on-again, off-again seal coat dirt and gravel, which is *very* slippery when wet. Many large, commercial trucks roar up and down the Cassiar. Built in 1972, the highway slices through charred forests and snow-capped ebony peaks, and passes scores of alpine lakes on its way from Highway 16 in British Columbia to the Alcan in the Yukon. Three evenly spaced provincial parks offer scenic camping right off the highway, and the Cassiar's services, while sparse, are numerous enough to keep cars filled. *North to Adventure,* free at most BC infocentres, offers a partial list of facilities and campgrounds on the route. Hitchhiking is less popular here than on the Alaska Highway.

WESTERN CANADA

HIGHWAY 16 TO MEZIADIN JUNCTION

Just north of the junction of Hwy. 37 and Hwy. 16 stand the totem poles of **Gitwengak,** which relate the history of the Native fort that stood on nearby **Battle Hill** until 1800. The **Kitwanga Loop Road,** 4km north, leads through Kitwanga (gas, repair, and food available) to the National Historic Park where Battle Hill is located. The hill served as a stronghold and base for the mighty warrior **Nekt.** It was once equipped with a tunnel system and spiked logs that would roll down on intruders; fortunately for unarmed travelers, these have since given way to stairs and interpretive panels. The totem poles of **Kitwancool,** or "place of reduced number," lie another 17km to the north. The village was originally called **Gitenyow,** "the place of many people"; after extended warfare, however, the indigenous people changed its name.

Meziadin Lake Provincial Park (meh-zee-AD-in) lies 155km north of the 16-37 junction, with free firewood and plenty of fishing on Meziadin Lake ($9.50; water, firewood, and pit toilets). Meziadin Lake is one of three lakes in BC where Salmon spawn. Grab gas and shoot the bull with truckers at **Meziadin Junction** (636-1390; gas station open summers daily 6:30am-10:30pm; winter depending on traffic). The junction also has minor tire repair, an unspectacular but cheap cafe (open summer daily 7am-8pm), and a tiny general store (636-2836) that rents motor boats for $100 per day (open daily 7am-11pm, winter 9am-9pm). **Whitehorse,** YT lies 953km to the north. Sixty-two km west, along Hwy. 37A, are **Stewart,** BC and **Hyder,** AK. The road to Stewart and Hyder is also known as the "Glacier Highway" because immense ice-tongues creep down so close to the road, you can feel their frigid air on your skin. There are no services on this road.

Stewart, BC and Hyder, AK

"It's the prettiest place on earth," is the Hyderites' unofficial motto. Hyder, AK and its sister city, Stewart, BC, 1½ mi. away, lie at the headwaters of the Portland Canal on the eastern border of Misty Fiords National Monument. Mountains hulk over both towns, keeping national differences in perspective. The megalopolis of Stewart, pop. 450, is nearly seven times the size of Hyder and provides most "amenities," while Hyder sports the "night life" and blast-from-the-past dirt roads. With the local mining and timber industries facing an uncertain future, these tiny towns are teaming up to recruit tourists with attractions like the world's largest glacier accessible by road. The drive to the two towns via Highway 37A, leading 60km west from Meziadin Junction, is itself a destination as it winds its well-paved way under azure hanging glaciers. Many visitors also choose to navigate the Portland fjord via the bi-weekly ferry *Aurora* from Ketchikan, AK.

Although Hyder is technically in Alaska, its currency is Canadian (except at the U.S. Post Office), its clocks tick to PST, its area code is 250, and its children are taught in Stewart. From July 1-14, the two communities erupt in a kinship extravaganza of bacchanalian proportions, and visitors are heartily welcome to bond in local bars.

Practical Information A left turn from the ferry terminal takes you to Hyder; a right turn, to Stewart. Highway 37 melds into Stewart's Conway Street, which intersects 5th Avenue towards the water. Hyder's **information center** is open Monday-Saturday 10am-2pm from June to September. For info on local fishing or hiking, visit the **Forest Service** (636-2367) in the Hyder Community Association Building (bear right at the Sealaska Inn downtown; open June-Sept. Mon.-Fri. 8am-2pm). The principal activity in Hyder is sidling up to the bar in the historic **Glacier Inn** (636-9092) and asking to be "Hyderized." Nearly $30,000 in signed bills line the tavern walls, where early miners would tack up cash to insure against returning to town too broke to buy a drink (open 10am-sometime late; in winter 2pm-whenever). In Stewart, the **information centre** (636-9224; email stewhydcofc@hotmail.com) is open daily from 9am to 7pm. A recently renovated **museum** (636-2568) on Columbia St. offers, among other things, an exhibit on the Great Avalanche of '65 and a disturbing collection of photos documenting the 1981 filming in Stewart of John Carpenter's *The Thing* (open July-Aug. daily 10am-8pm; $3, children $1.50, under 6 free).

The **Canadian Imperial Bank of Commerce** (636-2235) has a 24hr. **ATM** in Stewart on 5th Ave. by the post office (bank open Mon. and Wed. noon-3pm, Fri. noon-5pm). The **PetroCan** (636-2307), in Stewart at 5th Ave. and Conway, does auto repairs (open Mon.-Fri. 7am-7pm, Sat.-Sun. 8am-7pm), although gas at Hyder's no-name **pump station** (636-9143) is cheaper because there is no tax (open summer daily 8am-8pm). Dust-painted journeyers can grab a **shower** ($3) and do **laundry** (wash $1.50, dry $1.75) next to the Sealaska Inn in Hyder (open 24hr.) or in Stewart at Brightwell and 16th St. (wash $1.50, 4min. dry 25¢; open daily 7am-11pm). The **health centre** in Stewart can be reached at 636-2614. **Rexall,** on 5th Ave. and Brightwell St., has a **pharmacy** (open Mon.-Sat. 9am-5:30pm and 7-9pm, Sun. noon-4pm).

Hyder's **library** (636-9148), in the Community Association Building, has **Internet access** (open Mon.-Fri. 1-3pm). The **Hyder post office** (636-2662) is at the beginning of Salmon River Rd. Unlike most of Hyder, it accepts only U.S. currency (**ZIP code:** 99923; open Mon.-Fri. 9am-1pm and 2-5pm, Sat. 10:30am-12:30pm). **Stewart's post office** (636-2553) is at Brightwell St. and 5th Ave. (open Mon.-Fri. 8:30am-5pm, Sat. 9-noon; **postal code:** V0T 1W0). The **police** (636-2233) are at 8th Ave. and Conway St. in Stewart. The **ambulance** is (800) 461-9911. The **area code** is 250. Both Hyder and Alaska are on Pacific Time.

Many visitors never stay overnight in Hyder because if they're traveling by **ferry,** spending one night means spending two weeks. The *Aurora's* biweekly round-trip from Ketchikan to Stewart/Hyder (US$58) includes a three-hour layover that gives pedestrians just enough time to see both towns. **Seaport Limousines** (636-2622) in Stewart cruises to Terrace (daily Mon.-Fri.).**Taguan Air's** mail plane (636-9150) also makes regular trips; call to arrange a seat.

Camping, Accommodations, and Food Both towns have campgrounds. Stewart's **Rainey Creek Campground** (636-2537) is orderly, quiet, and woodsy, with tent sites ($10 for 2 people, $3 per additional person), sites with electricity ($15), and impeccably clean showers ($1). Hyder's **Camp Runamuck** is split into a tent-site location ($8, each additional person $4) and a gravelly RV park (hookups $18-22). The office for Runamuck is in the **Sealaska Inn** (636-2486), which has cubicle-like but comfy "sleeping rooms" ($28) and singles or doubles (from $48). Bed-bound dozers may have no choice but to party vicariously to the tune of lounge music from down-

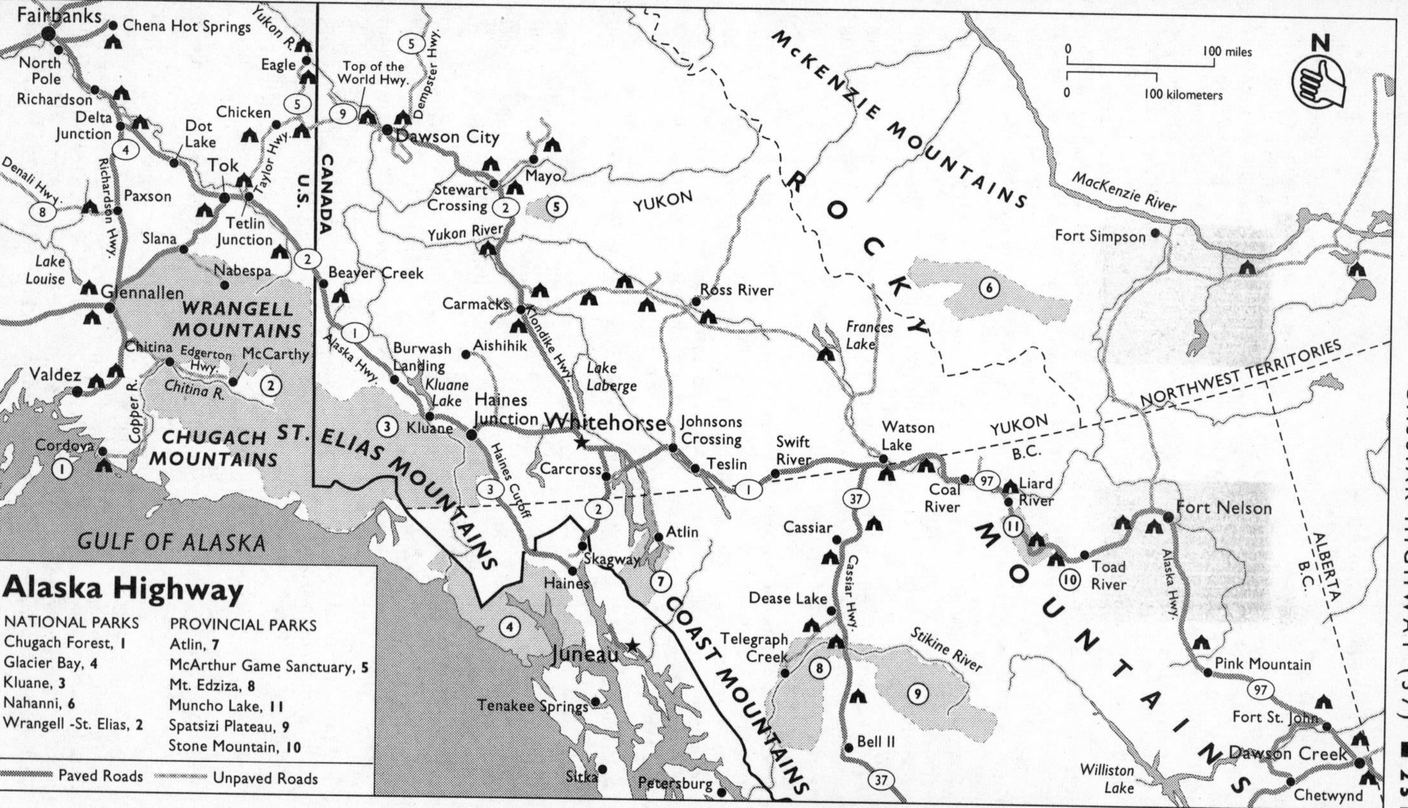

WESTERN CANADA

stairs. The **King Edward Hotel** (636-2244), on 5th Ave. and Columbia St. in Stewart, provides less lively accommodations starting at $55.

Cut-Rate Foods (636-2377) on 5th Ave. in Stewart, fulfills its calling with scores of cheap, generic products (open Mon.-Sat. 9am-8pm, Sun. 11am-6pm; winter Mon.-Sat. 10am-7pm, Sun. noon-5pm; no credit cards). The **Bitter Creek Cafe** (636-2166), on 5th Ave., displays historic photos and generates a wicked good artichoke-salad creation ($7; open May-Oct. daily 8am-9pm). Across the street, the **Dog House** (636-2308) serves a fruity smoothie for $3, but not kibbles or bits (open May-Sept. daily 8am-9pm). Hyder's **Border Cafe** (636-2379) has a "naked burger" with fries for $3.50, and a plate of huge hotcakes for $5.50 (open Tues. and Thurs.-Fri. 8:30am-7pm, Wed. 8:30am-6pm, Sat. 8:30am-4pm).

Sights **Fish Creek,** 5 mi. from Hyder on Salmon River Rd., is an excellent place to view bears, if you don't mind company. Each year during the salmon spawning season (late July), bears emerge from the bushes *en masse* to feed on bloated, dying salmon while tourists set up camp on the riverbank as if the feeding frenzy were a Dead show. Come early in the morning for an unimpeded view. The only maintained trail on the Hyder side of the action is the **Titan Trail,** a moderately challenging 5 mi. (8.3km) hike (one-way) up from the valley. It gains over 4000 ft. (1200m) of elevation and becomes rocky and difficult towards the end of the climb. Heading away from Hyder, the trailhead is on the right about 2 mi. (3.2km) past Fish Creek.

Salmon Glacier, 20 mi. from Hyder on the Salmon River Rd., is the fifth largest glacier in the world, but the largest accessible by road. Beginning at Mile 19, the road creeps along a ridge almost directly above the glacier for several miles, providing eagle-eye views. The rocks above the road make for good hiking, and at night the sun sets behind the immense glacier, creating a golden photo opportunity. At this point, the road is so poor that you might not want to drive it; **Grand View Express** in Hyder (636-9174) offers a no-frills shuttle ride to the glacier (round-trip US$20; call for reservations). Those taking their own car can check road conditions at the Forest Service (see above). **Bear Glacier,** 30 mi. east of Stewart in British Columbia, sits in plain view of Hwy. 37A and is also a noteworthy stop.

CASSIAR HIGHWAY (37): MEZIADIN JUNCTION TO THE ALASKA HIGHWAY

Ninety five kilometers North of Meziadin Junction is **Bell II Crossing,** a less-than-lush oasis of civilization in the Cassiar wilderness. Bell II houses a somewhat overpriced and underwhelming **restaurant** (638-9020; open daily 8am-8pm) and a **gas station** (open daily 8am-10pm). Minor car and tire repair is available. RV parking (no hookups) is $9.50, and showers for the mud-blanketed are $5.

After about 65km, new growth (and what is rumored by locals to be the largest huckleberry patch in BC) infiltrate the immense Iskut burn area. Fifty-three kilometers beyond the burn area is **Kinaskan Lake Provincial Park,** where a campground includes water, pit toilets, firewood, and a boat launch into the spectacular lake where trout thrive (lakeside campsites $9.50). At the far end of the lake is the head of a 24km hiking trail to Mowdade Lake in **Mount Edziza Provincial Park** (see p. 253). There is **gas** at **Tatogga Lake Resort,** another 25 km north (open daily 7am-10pm). A stone's throw farther is the **Ealue Lake** (EE-lu-eh) turn-off, which leads 12km to a recreation site (free camping) and 22km to a trailhead pointing deep into the virgin backcountry of the **Spatsizi Plateau Wilderness** (see p. 253).

Approaching the small native village of **Iskut** (350km north of Meziadin Junction), the traveler has a melee of resort options, earning Iskut the esteemed title of "resort capital of northwest BC" Even the most discriminating hostel connoisseurs heartily approve of the **Red Goat Lodge** (234-3261), just 3km south of Iskut. The **hostel (HI-C)** in the basement of this regal lodge boasts a full kitchen, spacious common room, wood stove, coin showers and laundry ($15, nonmembers $18). At the equally impressive **B&B** upstairs, singles are $65, doubles $85. Tent sites cost $10. **Canoe** rental starts at $10 for an evening on **Eddontenajon Lake** (ed-un-TEN-a-jon). Rentals for trips on the Stikine and Spatsizi Rivers start at $30 per day. Anglers can take a motor boat out to fetch rainbow trout ($65 per day).

At Iskut, travelers can fill the tank and grab some groceries at the sizeable **Kluachon Centre** (234-3241; open daily 8am-10pm; winter 9am-6pm), which doubles as the **post office** (open Mon., Wed., and Fri. 9am-4pm, Tues. 1-4pm; **postal code** V0J 1K0). If your car can stick it out a little longer, only 84km separate you from Dease Lake.

Dease Lake

Long known by the local indigenous Tahltan as "Tatl'ah" (Head of the Lake"), Dease Lake became a Hudson Bay Company outpost in the late 1800s. The town had its share of early gold rush glory in 1864 and 1873, but now serves as a simple service centre for Northwestern BC and as a base for backpackers exploring the vast and rugged **Mount Edziza** or **Spatsizi Wildernesses** nearby.

The **Dease Lake Tourist Information Office** is in the Northern Lights College (771-3900; open June-Sept. Mon.-Fri. 9am-6pm). For info on local trails or campsites, **BC Parks** (771-4591) and the **Forest Service** (771-8100) share the building next door. The **Shell station** (771-5600) has showers ($4) and a laundromat (wash $3, 5min. dry 25¢; open daily 7am-11pm). For repairs, **Chico's** (771-5656, emergency 771-3155) is on Boulder Ave. The **Stikine Health Center** (771-4272 or 771-4444) is at the north end of town (walk-in Mon.-Fri. 8:30am-4:30pm). Reach the **police** at 771-4111 or the **ambulance** at 771-3333. The **post office** is in the Shell station (771-5013; open Mon.-Fri. 8:30am-1pm, 2-5pm). The **postal code** is V0C 1L0.

The closest free forest service campsite to town is scenic **Allen Lake.** Luckily for tipsy tenters, the lake is a short stumble from the Tanzilla Bar (from Boulder St., go left on 1st Ave. and follow to its end; no water, pit toilets). Be sure not to drive your car to the campground's parking lot. The extremely steep gravel driveway is likely to hold it hostage until a tow truck can winch it out. For a complete listing of area campgrounds, get a Forest Service map at the tourist information centre or from the Forest Service (see above). The brand-spankin' raw-pine smellin' new **Arctic Divide Inn** (771-3119) is right on the Cassiar and has squeaky clean rooms with private bath, phones, and TV (singles and doubles $59; complementary coffee and muffins). There are two restaurants in Dease Lake. **Northway Country Kitchen** (771-4114), locally "the restaurant," offers decent food in a clean, spacious setting. Tickle your palate with "pirogies & smokies," cheese-filled dumplings accompanied by four sizable sausages ($8.50), or chomp on a garden burger with salad ($6.50; open daily 7am-10pm). The other place is called **The Other Place** (771-3667), and has a smaller, cheaper, meatier selection. A clubhouse sandwich and fries goes for $7.50 (open daily 6am-8pm; winter 7am-7pm; cash only). Groceries are available at the **Goodacres Store,** next to Shell (open Mon.-Sat. 7am-9pm, Sun. 9am-7pm).

Spatsizi Plateau Wilderness and Mount Edziza Provincial Park

Long a major hunting ground for the Tahltan people, Spatsizi Plateau became a provincial park and wildlife reserve in 1975. Supporting one of the largest populations of **Woodland Caribou** in British Columbia, Spatsizi is home to an extensive range of wildlife and varied eco-regions. **Ealue Lake Road,** near the **Tatogga Lake Junction,** 25km north of Kinaskan Lake Provincial Park, offers the only vehicle access into Spatsizi Wilderness Plateau. To reach the trailheads, follow the so-called "road" for 22 km until it joins with the BC Rail grade, a tertiary road of variable quality described by BC Parks as "rough, but driveable for most vehicles." Because of its isolation, BC Parks strongly recommends that only experienced hikers explore Spatsizi. There are also two popular multiple-day canoe routes through the Spatsizi area along the Spatsizi and Stikine Rivers.

Four million years ago, 2787m Mt. Edziza erupted violently, leaving behind a charred, craggy, obsidian landscape. Today the 230,000 hectare Provincial Park surrounding the mountain is dotted with deliciously named cinder cones such as "Coffee" and "Cocoa." Like Spatsizi, however, the park invites only the erudite outdoors explorer due to its extremely variable weather (summer snow) and lack of trail system, facilities, and staff. There is no vehicular access into this remote region. Most visitors access Mt. Edziza by plane, bypassing the grueling week-long trek into the park along the **Klastine River,** or find a boat from **Kinaskan Lake Provincial Park** to do the 7 day (or more) **Mowdade Trail.** For a donation, a comprehensive **trail guide** is available at the Stikine Riversong (see below). All hikers, regardless of previous wilderness experience, should make their itineraries and whereabouts known before venturing into the park. For more info, contact **British Columbia Parks Area Supervisor,** Box 118, Dease Lake, BC V0C 1L0 (604-771-4591).

Telegraph Creek

Lying 119km from Dease Lake on Telegraph Creek Rd., Telegraph Creek is the only remaining settlement along the Stikine River (stuh-KEEN). The highest navigable point on the Stikine, the town was an important rendezvous point for the coastal Tlingit and interior Tahltan people. Today, Telegraph Creek has about 400 residents, most of them Tahltan. There are no doctors in Telegraph Creek. There is a **health clinic** with two nurses on duty (235-3211; follow signs for Glenora). The **police** can be reached at 235-3111. For **tire repair,** contact Henry Vance (235-3300). For light mechanical repair, ask around for Bob Jornsen. The **post office** is on the right coming into town from Dease Lake, and the **postal code** is V0J 2W0 (open Mon and Wed 9:30-11:30am, Tues. and Thurs. 1-4pm, Fri 9:30-11:30am and 1-4pm).

The biggest attraction here for the thrill-seeking tourist is 112km **Telegraph Creek Road.** The gravel road is well maintained, and offers magnificent views of the Stikine Grand Canyon. It is no place, however, to lug a clumsy RV or give a failed brake system a second chance. After a blah start, the second half of the road features 20% grades and hairpin turns along the steep, perilous obsidian outbanks of the Taya, Tahltan, and Stikine River canyons. Travelers should allow 2½ hours to drive each way, with ample time to de-frazzle in between. The rest stop, 88km from Telegraph Creek, offers a gorgeous view of the Canyon and a chance to speak words of encouragement to your beleaguered transmission.

The "modern" village of Telegraph Creek revolves around the historic **Stikine RiverSong** (235-3196). Originally the Hudson Bay Company building near the neighboring town of **Glenora,** 12 mi. from Telegraph Creek, the RiverSong was disassembled in 1902 and moved to Telegraph Creek. Today, the jack-of-all-trades RiverSong acts as Telegraph Creek's sole hotel, general store, and cafe. They also sell gas, fishing licenses, and tees that tell the world "I wrote my will before driving the Telegraph Creek Road" The staff is extremely helpful and can answer almost any question about the history of the area. Wash off 119km of road dust with a shower ($4; open Mon-Sat 11am-7pm, Sun noon-7pm; winter closed Sun.). Hotel rooms at the RiverSong are clean, with cedar finishing and a common kitchen (single $46; double $50). Three free recreation sites along the road to and at Glenora provide primitive camping for the penniless.

Dease Lake to the Alaska Hwy.

This stretch of highway follows the old Cassiar Gold Route, and tailings and still-used dredges can be seen along its length. Eighty-five kilometers north of Dease Lake is **Moose Meadow Resort,** a roomy lakeside campground with access to canoe routes. Campsites are $11 per night (2 free showers). Lakeside log cabins for two are $30, $5 each additional person. Canoe rentals on the lake are $6 per hour (2 hr. min.), $27 per day. **Boya Lake Provincial Park** is 152km north of Dease Lake, 2km east of the Cassiar Hwy. Campsites ($9.50, pit toilets, firewood, water) are on a turquoise lake with a boat launch and swimming dock. The shallow lake is warm by northcountry standards, but the water is still numblingly "refreshing." **Jade City,** between Moose Meadows and Boya Lake is the last reliable service with gas for 122km (open daily 7am-10pm; winter 8am-8pm)

At the end of this 718km odyssey, dirty, hungry, and weary travelers can grab showers, souvenirs, grub, groceries, gas, and minor repairs at the **PetroCan Station** (536-2794), at the junction of the Cassiar Hwy. and the Alaska Hwy. The PetroCan doubles as the office for the RV park and motel next door ($11, full hookup $16; singles and doubles $30; shared bath; no TV or phone). **Showers** are $3, or free with accommodations. They also operate a 24-hour **laundromat** (wash $1.50, 14min. dry 50¢). Travelers can grab a bite of chili ($6) or a kamoboko crab melt ($8) at the **Junction 37 Cafe** (536-2795), next to PetroCan (open daily May-Oct. 6am-10pm). Strangely, the saloon in the next lot (536-2796) has slightly cheaper gas (open 10am-midnight). **Whitehorse** lies another 435km west.

Alaska Highway

They sweat and froze, laughed and cried, bled and labored until finally the unachievable was achieved. In a dozen American accents they had cussed and kissed me into being from Dawson Creek to Fairbanks. In less than nine months, the miraculous highway was born.

—Shirley Ravelli

Built during World War II, the Alaska Highway (also known as the "Alcan") maps out an astonishing 2647km route between Dawson Creek, BC, and Fairbanks, AK. After the Japanese attack on Pearl Harbor in December 1941, worried U.S. War Department officials planned an overland route, out of range of carrier-based aircraft, to supply U.S. Army bases in Alaska. The U.S. Army Corps of Engineers completed the daunting task in just 34 weeks; the one-lane dirt trail curved around swamps and hills (landfill would come later). In recent years, the U.S. Army has been replaced by an annual army of over 250,000 tourists, the vast majority of them RV-borne senior citizens from the U.S. Travelers making the trip in July, the busiest month, will face crowded campgrounds and mammoth RV caravans. They'll also be passed by the speediest semis the roads have ever known.

In general, there's a trade-off between the excitement you'll find on the "Alcan" and the speed with which you will reach Alaska. If you're willing to take the time, there are countless hiking, fishing, and wildlife viewing opportunities off the highway. If your priority is to beat the quickest path to the Alaska border, however, the **Cassiar Highway** (see p. 249) may be a better route for you.

A good beginning to any history of the highway and surrounding area is the one-hour **video** "Alaska Highway: 1942-1992" shown at the Dawson Creek Tourist Infocentre (see below). Before setting out on your epic Northwestern journey, pick up a copy of the free pamphlet *Driving the Alaska Highway,* often available at visitors bureaus, or contact the Department of Health and Social Services, P.O. Box 110601, Juneau, AK 99811-0601 (907-465-3030). The pamphlet includes a listing of emergency medical services and emergency phone numbers throughout Alaska, the Yukon, and British Columbia, plus tips on preparation and driving. Although the Alcan was "cussed and kissed" into being in a mere nine months, in many ways it is still a work in progress. For daily road conditions of the Alcan call (250) 774-7447 in BC, (867) 667-8215 in the Yukon. Mileposts along the highway were put up in the 1940s and are still used as mailing addresses and reference points, although the highway has been reconstructed and rerouted so many times that they no longer reflect mileage accurately. Kilometer posts were installed in the mid-1970s and recalibrated in 1990; the distances they report are more accurate.

Dawson Creek

Dawson Creek, BC (not to be confused with Dawson City, YT) is 590km northwest of Edmonton and is the Alaska Highway's official starting point (Mile 0). First settled in 1890, Dawson Creek was a frontier village of only a few hundred people until its location at the northern terminus of the railroad made it a natural base for the massive undertaking of building a 2600km highway in nine months. The town quite literally boomed during construction. On February 13, 1943, sixty cases of dynamite exploded in the center of town, leveling the entire business district except the COOP building, which still provides a home to Bing's Furniture downtown. You can see the building across the street from the Mile 0 post. The town of about 10,000 has quieted down considerably since the heyday of construction, but Dawson Creek residents still take their hometown's historical role as the birthplace of the Alcan seriously.

Practical Information and Orientation The **Tourist Infocentre,** 900 Alaska Ave. (782-9595), in the old train station just off Hwy. 97, has daily reports on the Alcan's condition and is also home to a small museum (open May 15-Labor Day daily 8am-7pm, off season Tues.-Sat. 10am-noon and 1-4pm). **Greyhound,** 1201 Alaska Ave. (782-3131 or 800-661-8747), can bus you to Whitehorse, YT (1 per day except Sun., Oct.-May 3 per week; $160), Prince George (2 per day, $48), and Edmonton (2 per day, $66). The station is open Mon.-Fri. 6am-6pm and 8-8:30pm, Sat. 6am-noon, 2-5pm, and 8-8:30pm, Sun. 6-10:30am, 3-4:30pm, 8-8:30pm. The **King Koin Laundromat,** 1220 103rd Ave. (782-2395), has showers for $2.75 (no time limit!), laundry (wash $2, 5min. dry 25¢), and a fax machine (open daily 8am-9pm). **Action Automotive,** 1041 Alaska Ave. (782-3516), is just one of many garages along Alaska Ave. The nearest **hospital** is Dawson Creek and District Hospital, at 11100 13th St. (782-8501). In an **emergency,** call for an **ambulance** (782-2211) or contact the **police** (782-5211) at Alaska Ave. and 102nd Ave. The **post office** (782-9429) sits at 104th Ave. and 10th St. The **postal code** is V1G 4J8, and the **area code** is 250.

There are two ways to reach Dawson Creek from the south. Drive northwest from Edmonton along **Hwy. 43,** through Whitecourt to Valleyview. Turn left on **Hwy. 34** to Grande Prairie, Alberta. From there, continue northwest on **Hwy. 2** to Dawson Creek, for a total journey of 590km. Or start in Prince George and drive 402km north on the John Hart section of **Hwy. 97.** Either drive takes most of a day.

Accommodations and Camping Travelers willing to trade a few amenities for bargain prices, good location, and an off-beat aura should head straight for the historic **Alaska Hotel** (782-7998), on 10th St., 1½ blocks from the infocenter, upstairs from the Alaska Cafe & Pub (see **Food,** below). For a $25 single or a $30 double, you can bed down in a comfortable room decorated with pictures of Marilyn and Elvis (prices decrease $5 in winter). Toilets and showers are shared and rooms have no TVs or phones. The **Voyageur Motor Inn,** 801 111th Ave. (782-1020), offers motoring voyagers phones, cable TV, and refrigerators in some rooms (singles $30; doubles $35). Peaceful and grassy, the **Mile 0 Campground** (782-2590), 1 km west of Mile 0 on the Alaska Hwy. by the Pioneer Village, has showers and coin laundry (sites $10, hook-ups $16). Campers can also head for the convenient but crowded **Alahart RV Park,** 1725 Alaska Ave. (782-4702), which has free showers, a dump station, and coin laundry (sites $8, full hook-up $16).

Food If foraging on your bug-splattered windshield fails to satisfy you, a great place for a meal in Dawson Creek is the **Alaska Cafe & Pub** (782-7040), "55 paces south of the Mile 0 Post" on 10th St., which serves excellent burgers and fries for $7. Proclaiming itself one of Canada's top 500 restaurants, the Alaska Cafe offers live music (mostly country) nightly, and homesick travelers can croon away their sorrows at Monday night karaoke (open daily 11am-11pm). Health-conscious travelers sick of fast food and Cheeze-Its can pick up a loaf for the road at the **Organic Farms Bakery,** 1425 97th Ave. (782-6533), a short drive west on the Alaska Hwy. from the infocenter. Breads are baked fresh from organically grown local grain and start at $1.25 for a loaf of whole wheat; croissants and pastries are also available. The piping-hot hospitality is free (open Wed.-Fri. 10am-5:30pm, Sat. 9:30am-4pm). Inside Pioneer Village (see **Sights,** below) the **Mile One Cafe** (782-1456) serves up frontier-style food in a pioneer schoolhouse. Lunch specials are $4.50 and "old school" sweet treats are $1-2 (open daily 10am-5pm). **Chevy's Diner,** 330 Alaska Ave. (782-CHEV/782-2438), will satisfy those hungry for a bit of 50s Americana. "The King's" Chili Con Carne is $5 (open daily 6am-10pm). Take some back to the Alaska Hotel (see above) and dine under a portrait of the chili's namesake. Stock up on bulk and retail groceries before heading north at the **Price Connection,** 11600 8th St. (782-8844). Great prices, if you need 12 lbs. of nutmeg (open Mon.-Sat. 9am-6pm, Sun. 11am-5pm).

Sights Travelers driving through Dawson Creek can't miss the **Mile 0 Cairn** and **Mile 0 Post,** both commemorating the birth of the Alcan, and both within a stone's throw of the infocentre. The **Art Gallery** (782-2601) in the old grain elevator next to the infocenter hosts a moving photo essay depicting the World War II Alcan creation saga. **Pioneer Village** (782-7144), 1km west of Mile 0, is an excellent re-creation of Dawson Creek life from the 20s to the 40s ($1 suggested donation; open May-Aug. daily 9am-6pm). Bird lovers can head 10km out of town to the highland marshes of **McQueen's Slough.** Take Hwy. 49 east from the infocentre, and turn right on Rd. 3. Watch for a binocular sign on the right. Finally, the **Community Forest,** 10 km south of town at Bear Mountain, has a network of **cross-country ski trails** and white aspens to shame Ansel Adams.

ALASKA HIGHWAY: DAWSON CREEK, BC TO WHITEHORSE, YT

The Alaska Highway between Dawson Creek and **Fort St. John** (76km up the Alcan) offers little more than cows and rolling hills—but a couple of roadside quirks do break the driving monotony. 20km south of Fort St. John, gold-grubbers converge upon the **World Invitational Gold Panning Championships,** at Peace River Park in early August, to pan for prizes and fame. Travelers who miss the invitational trudge on to **The Honey Place** (785-4808), just south of Fort St. John, to gaze in wonder at the **world's largest glass beehive** (open Mon.-Sat. 9am-5:30pm). Fort St. John itself, is hardly as a-buzz with excitement. The **Travel Infocentre,** 9923 96th Ave. (785-3033), at 100th St. in the museum complex, illustrates how little the town has to offer (open Mon.-Sat. 8am-8pm; Sep.-June Mon.-Fri. 8am-5pm, Sat. 11am-4pm). The **Ministry of Environment and Parks,** 10003 110th Avenue (787-3407), has a division in Fort St. John and can provide info on **hiking** opportunities on the Alcan (open Mon.-Fri. 8:30am-4:30pm). The **Motel Blue Belle** (785-2613), across from the Totem Mall at the south end of town, provides singles ($38) and doubles ($40) stocked with cable and kitchenettes. **Centennial RV Park,** behind the museum complex by the oil rig on 100th St., is packed with showers, laundry, horseshoes, a playground, and a lobby with a squishy sofa. Outside the lobby, Centennial has all the ambience of a parking lot (sites $10, with electricity and water $16; phone the infocentre for reservations). **Charlie Lake Provincial Park,** 14km north on the Alaska Hwy., is great for those with no desire to hook up; tent it in a grassy, secluded site near a picnic area ($9.50). Hiking trails wind 1km down to the lake.

To ease a grumbling stomach, rumble into **Busters,** 9720 100th St. (785-0770), for one of Fort St. John's few departures from fast food funk. An all-you-can-eat salad bar ($6) and the weekday luncheon buffet (noon-2pm; $9) fill your tank (open Mon.-Fri. 11am-10pm, Sat. 4-10pm, Sun. 10am-10pm). **Polly's** (787-1616), at the Northwoods Inn, across from McDonald's on the Alcan, is popular among discriminating truck drivers. A "gourmet" dog or burger with fries is $5, and the lunch smorgasbord (Sun.-Fri.) is $8.50 (open daily 6am-10pm).

Gas up in Fort St. John before heading north—the 109km stretch from Sikanni to Prophet River is entirely gas-less. **Fort Nelson,** 480 (of the highway's least exciting) km north of Dawson Creek, is the highway's next sizeable pit stop. The **Infocentre** (774-6400) hides itself in the Recreation Centre/Curling Rink on the northern edge of town and hands out a small brochure describing the doldrums that are Fort Nelson (open May-Sept. daily 8am-8pm). The **Fort Nelson Heritage Museum** (774-3536), is an exception from the drab. Across the highway from the infocentre, the museum features an impressive, if unsettling, collection of taxidermy of all the game species in the area (including a white cow moose) as well as doodads from the era of highway construction. An unlikely collection of **vintage cars** and a **trapper's cabin** top it all off (open in summer daily 8:30am-7:30pm; $2.50, children $1.25.) If you aren't expecting any calls, rest up at the **Mini-Price Inn,** 5036 51st Ave. W. (774-2136), hidden a block off the highway (no room phones; singles $37; doubles $42). The **Westend Campground** (774-2340) across from the infocentre, is a veritable Disneyland on the Alcan. Hot showers (3min. 25¢), a laundromat (wash $2, 30min. dry $1), a free car wash, free firewood, and mini-golf keep kids busy (sites $12, full hookups $18).

Small "towns," usually composed of one gas pump, one motel ($50-$60), and one cafe, pock the remainder of the highway every 80 to 160km on the way to Carcross, Whitehorse, and the Alaska border. Fortunately for the glassy-eyed driver, highway scenery improves dramatically after Fort Nelson. About 150km north, the stark naked and appropriately named **Stone Mountain** appears. Next door, **Summit Lake** keeps the metropolis of **Summit** company. (Gas pump? Check. Motel? Check. Cafe? Check.) This is the highest point (1295m) on the Alaska Hwy. The **Stone Mountain Campground,** right on the lake, makes an superb starting point for hiking the mountain (sites $9.50). A trail from the site climbs 6km to the alpine **Flower Springs Lake.**

40km farther along the road lies **Toad River,** a booming town of 60. The **Toad River Cafe** (232-5401), right on the highway, is a worthwhile stop just to peek up at the more than 4600 hats hanging from the ceiling. Donate your own if you want. Tasty burgers from $5 (open daily 6am-10pm, in winter 7am-9pm). 50km past Toad River, **Muncho Lake Provincial Park** delights even the weariest drivers. Glacial silt refracts sunlight to turn Muncho Lake ("big lake" in aboriginal Tagish) into an azure mirror, 7 mi. long. **Strawberry Flats Provincial Campground,** right on the lakeshore, is the pot of gold at the end of the driving rainbow (sites $9.50, with outhouse, firewood, water). If your head grows heavy and your sight grows dim and you have to stop for the night, **Muncho Lake Lodge** (604-776-3456), 10 km north of Strawberry Flats, can put you up in a plain single for $40 ($5 per additional person) or in the campground (has showers, $10 site, $12 hook-up).

After wiling its way along the Lake, the highway reaches the **Liard River Hot Springs,** near the 800km mark. These two naturally hot pools are a phenomenal place to soothe a driver's *derrierre*. For privacy and deeper water, skip the "alpha" pool and head up to "beta." The park service manages campsites ($12) and a free day use area here. Arrive early—the campsites are often full by noon.

Near the BC-Yukon border, the road winds through tracts of fire-scorched forest where gray arboreal skeletons mix with new growth and stretch in all directions. At night, this area offers prime viewing of the *aurora borealis* (beginning in late Aug. with peak viewing in the winter months). The Alcan winds across the BC-Yukon border several times before it passes through Whitehorse. Just after its second crossing into the Yukon, the highway runs through the small town of **Watson Lake** and the famed **"Sign Post Forest"** at Mile 635. The "forest" came to be 1942 when a homesick Army engineer erected a sign indicating the mileage to his hometown of Danville, IL. Today, over 32,000 travelers have followed suit. The **Visitor Reception Centre** (867-536-7469) is hidden in the woods (open May-Sept. daily 8am-8pm). Watson Lake also lures Alcan tourists with the **Northern Lights Centre** (867-536-7827; http://www.yukon.net/northernlights), located on the bay, which teaches about the science and legend behind them purty lights in the sky ($6, seniors and students $5, children $3). Wash your clothes while waiting for your car to be repaired at **Chevron** (536-2545), which has a licensed mechanic, tire shop, and coin **laundry** (wash $1.25, 8min. dry 25¢; open daily 7am-7pm).

Kilometer 1043 (a.k.a. Mile 626) marks the Alcan's junction with the **Cassiar Highway** (see p. 249) leading south to **Yellowhead Highway 16** (see p. 232). Outside the inconspicuous indigenous community of **Teslin,** about 260km west of Watson Lake, the **Dawson Peaks Resort** (390-2310) welcomes travelers with campsites ($8), hookups ($17), and amenity-free cabins ($26). Grab a slice of rhubarb pie while mellowing to mood music in the restaurant. Seven kilometers west, Teslin tells its story at the well-known **George Johnston Museum** (390-2550), on the Alcan at the west end of town. Born in Alaska in 1889, George Johnston was a Tlingit who made a living running a trap line and a general store while playing with photography on the side. Johnston's hobby left a legacy of stunning photographs that document Tlingit life in

Teslin Lake from 1910 to 1940 (open May 9am-6pm, June-Labor Day 9am-7pm; $2.50, seniors and students $2, children $1, families $7.)

YUKON TERRITORY

Whitehorse

Named for the once-perilous **Whitehorse Rapids,** whose crashing whitecaps were said to resemble a herd of galloping white mares, Whitehorse is a modern crossroads in an ageless frontier. With 23,000 residents, Whitehorse prides itself on being Canada's largest city "north of 60" (degrees latitude). The mountains, rivers, and lakes in all directions are a powerful reminder that "south of 60" is far, far away. While Yukon officials boast of their capital's rapid urban development, locals and thousands of wandering nature-worshippers understand that Whitehorse's real wealth lies in the gaping bush beyond the city limits and in the casual northern spirit in every Whitehorse "hello." Although the rapids have now been tamed by a monolithic industrial dam, far more remains that has yet to be cemented, chromed, captured, or caged.

PRACTICAL INFORMATION AND ORIENTATION

Visitors Information: Whitehorse Visitor Reception Centre (667-3084), in the conspicuous Tourism and Business Center at 100 Hansen St. on 2nd Ave. Open mid-May to mid-Sept. daily 8am-8pm. **Yukon Conservation Society,** 302 Hawkins St. (668-5678), offers maps and info on area hiking. Open Mon.-Fri. 10am-5pm.

Flights: Canadian Airlines (668-4466, for reservations 668-3535) flies to: Calgary, AB ($664); Edmonton, AB ($664); and Vancouver, BC ($545). All 3 per day except Thurs. and Sun. Student standby (under 24 with student ID) around $200; call for details. **Canada 3000** and **Royal Air** offer reduced fares to Vancouver on certain days ($348 and $420, respectively). Summer only; must be booked by an agent. Try **Uniglobe,** 2076 2nd Ave. (668-7464 or 800-661-0531; open Mon.-Fri. 8:30am-5pm).

Buses: Greyhound, 2191 2nd Ave. (667-2223). To: Vancouver, BC ($285); Edmonton, AB ($222); and Dawson Creek, BC ($157). Cheaper with 7-day advance purchase. Buses run late June-Sept. Mon.-Sat.; winter Tues., Thurs., and Sat.; no Greyhound service to AK. Desk open Mon.-Fri. 8am-5:30pm, Sat. 8am-1pm, Sun. 4-8am. **Alaska Direct,** 102 Wood St. (668-4833 or 800-770-6652) in the Regina Hotel. To: Anchorage (3 per week, US$145); Haines (3 per week, US$50); Fairbanks (3 per week, US$120); and Skagway (4 per week, US$35). In winter, 1 bus per week to above destinations. Open Mon.-Fri. 8am-5pm. **Norline** (668-3355), in the Greyhound depot. To Dawson City (3 per week, in winter 2 per week, $73).

Local Transportation: Whitehorse Transit (668-8381 for 24hr. info line). Limited service downtown and to local areas. Buses arrive and depart downtown next to Canadian Tire on Ogilvie St. Runs Mon.-Thurs. 6:15am-7:15pm, Fri. 6:15am-10pm, Sat. 8am-7pm; $1.25, seniors and handicapped 60¢, children and students $1.

Taxi: Yellow Cab, 668-4811. 24hr.

Car Rental: Norcan Leasing, Ltd. (668-2137 or 800-661-0445; 800-764-1234 from AK), on the Alcan at Mile 917.4. Cars from $40 per day. 15¢ per additional km after 100. Must be 21 with credit card or pay cash deposit of twice the rental price.

Auto Repair: Petro Canada, 4211 4th Ave. (667-4003 or 667-4366) Full service. Oil and lube $45. Open Mon.-Fri. 8am-5pm.

Bike Rental: Element Sports, 4198 4th Ave. (393-3993) at Ogilvie. Mountain bikes $25 per day, $10 per ½ day. Credit card required. Open Mon.-Sat. 10am-6pm.

Camping Equipment: The Sportslodge, 305 Main St. (668-6848) in the Hougen Centre. Basic outdoor gear, cheaper than most specialty stores. Open Mon-Wed. and Sat. 9am-6pm, Thurs.-Fri. 9am-9pm, Sun. 11am-4pm).

Library: 2071 2nd Ave. (667-5239) at Hanson. Internet access available. Open Mon.-Fri. 10am-9pm, Sat. 10am-6pm, Sun. 1-9pm.

Laundromat: Norgetown, 4213 4th Ave. (667-6113), next to McDonald's at Ray St. Wash $1.90; dry 50¢ per 7½min. Open daily 8am-10pm.

Public Showers: At the **Whitehorse Swimming Pool,** 4051 4th Ave. (668-7665) next to the High Country Inn. Pool and shower use $5, seniors $2, students and children $3.50. Call for swim times.

Pharmacy: Shoppers Drug Mart, 311 Main St. (667-2485). Open Mon.-Fri. 9am-9pm, Sat. 9am-6pm, Sun. 10am-6pm.

Hospital: (667-8700), on Hospital Rd., just off Wickstrom Rd. across the river from downtown.

Emergency: 911. **Police:** 4100 4th and Elliot. Desk open Mon.-Fri. 7am-5:30pm.

Internet Access: see **Library,** above.

Post Office: General services, 211 Main St. (668-5847) in basement of Shoppers Drug Mart. Open Mon.-Fri. 8am-6pm, Sat. 9am-5pm. Also in Qwanlin Mall at 4th Ave. and Ogilvie (667-2858) in Coffee, Tea and Spice. Open Mon.-Thurs. 9:30am-6pm, Fri. 9:30am-9pm, Sat. 9:30am-6pm. **General delivery** is at 3rd and Wood, in the Yukon News Bldg. Open Mon.-Fri. 8am-6pm. **General Delivery Postal Code** for last names beginning with the letters A-L is Y1A 3S7; for M-Z it's Y1A 3S8.

Area Code: 867.

To reach Whitehorse by car, take the downtown exit off the Alcan. The **airport** is off the Alaska Hwy., just west of downtown, and the **bus station** is on the northeastern edge of town, a short walk from the compact downtown. Locals suggest avoiding the riverbank if alone at night.

ACCOMMODATIONS AND CAMPING

Camping in Whitehorse is limited, and hotels are exorbitantly pricey. Cash-strapped tenters amenable to a 15-minute drive might head for the shores of **Long Lake,** where many a young wanderer has camped for free. (Though illegal, camping in non-designated areas is reportedly tolerated for one night. If, however, the police don't feel particularly tolerant—which is entirely within their rights—the fine is $500 and confiscation of camping equipment.) To get there, cross the bridge off 2nd Ave. in the southeast corner of town, turn left on Hospital Rd., turn left on Wickstrom Rd., then follow the winding road until it ends at the lake.

Roadhouse Inn, 2163 2nd Ave. (667-2594), at the north end of town near the Greyhound depot. Run-of-the-mill. Shared rooms, hall showers with bathtub, laundry (wash and dry $1.75 each), free local calls. $5 key deposit; $19.50 per person; private rooms $50, each additional person $5. Lobby open 7am-2:30am.

202 Motor Inn (668-4567), at Jarvis and 2nd Ave. in the north end of town. Standard motel rooms. Singles $50; doubles $55.

Robert Service Campground (668-3721), 1km from town on South Access Rd. along the Yukon River. A convenient stop for tenting folk, but no RV sites. Home-away-from home to crowds of college students who summer in Whitehorse and don't shave, Robert Service has free firewood and pits, a playground, drinking water, toilets, metered showers ($1 per 5min.), and a knack for rhyming verse. Open late May to early Sept. 68 sites, $11. Gates open 7am-11pm.

High-Country RV Park (667-7445), at the intersection of the Alaska Hwy. and South Access Rd., perched above town next to Yukon Gardens. Free showers, 2 coin-op laundromats, and for those on first dates, mini-golf. Rest your rig for $18 for 2 people ($20 for pull-through), $3 each additional person; tents $12.

FOOD

Get extra groceries at **Extra Foods** (667-6251), in the Quanlin Mall at 4th and Ogilvie (open Mon.-Wed. 8:30am-7pm, Thurs.-Fri. 8:30am-9pm, Sat. 8:30am-6pm, Sun. 10am-6pm) Pick up some roughage to assuage greasy highway stomach at **The Fruit Stand** (393-3994) at 2nd and Black St. (open Mon.-Sat. 10:30am-7pm, Sun. noon-5pm).

Blackstone Cafe (667-6598), on the corner of 3rd and Wood St. Attracts Whitehorse's crunchy clan. Sit on the patio with a veggie paté sandwich ($5) or a pie-like *torta rustica* ($6.50). A myriad of coffees come regular or organic (espresso $1.10). Open Mon.-Fri. 7am-midnight, Sat. 8am-midnight, Sun. 10am-6pm.

Klondike Rib and Salmon Barbeque, 2116 2nd Ave. (667-7554). Sample northern salmon here without breaking the bank. Salmon salad on sourdough comes with coleslaw for $7. Prices shoot up for other seafood selections. The 100-year-old Klondike-era building's ambience is a relief from the tedium of hotel lounges and McBLTs. Open May-Sept. Mon.-Fri. 11am-10pm, Sat.-Sun. 5-10pm.

No Pop Sandwich Shop, 312 Steele (668-3227), at 4th Ave. This alcove is popular with Whitehorse's suits. Enjoy a Tel Aviv (ground beef, alfalfa, cream cheese) or veggie sandwich ($4.25). No pop, but skim milk ($1.75) or specialty drinks (about $6). Leave large baggage elsewhere, lest it leave room for one less customer. Open Mon.-Thurs. 7:30am-9pm, Fri. 7:30am-9:30pm, Sat.-Sun. 9:30am-9pm.

Annie Mae's Neighborhood Pub, 2163 2nd Ave. (668-7263), next to the Roadhouse Inn. Yuppies from the No Pop flee from this meat-and-potatoes haven for the local truck crowd. Live country music, genuine character, and genuine cholesterol at genuinely low prices (chicken empanadas $5, all day, all-you-can-eat spaghetti $5, lotsa brews $3.50 a pint). Open daily 9am-11pm. Must be 19 to enter.

SIGHTS AND ACTIVITIES

There are more trails than people around Whitehorse. Well, almost. And as one local put it, the bush is so open and expansive that seasoned hikers "will just wander"—paying proper heed to bear population, of course. The aggressively outdoorsy often trek to the distant bush of Kluane National Park (see p. 265) or beyond, but there are plenty of accessible dayhiking opportunities around town. *Whitehorse Area Hikes and Bikes* ($18.95) sold by the **Yukon Conservation Society** (see p. 259) or at **Mac's Fireweed Books,** 203 Main St. (668-2434), is a helpful companion for woods-exploration. **Grey Mountain,** partly accessible by gravel road, is a somewhat rigorous day-hike. Take the Lewes Blvd. bridge by the S.S. Klondike across the river and continue, then take a left on Alsek. Turn left again at the sign that says "Grey Mt. Cemetery" and follow this gravel road until it ends. Joggers, bikers, and cross-country skiers love the **Miles Canyon** trail network that parallels the Yukon River. To get there, take Lewes Blvd. to Nisutlin Dr. and turn right; just before the fish ladder turn left onto the gravel Chadburn Lake Rd. and follow for 4km until you hit the parking area. The conservation society arranges free hikes (July and Aug. Mon.-Fri). and offers guided nature walks during the spring (office open Mon.-Fri. 10am-5pm, winters 10am-2pm).

During summer, the Yukon River begs to be played upon. The **MV Schwatka** (668-4716), on Miles Canyon Rd. off South Access Rd., floats those who fork over $17 (kids 6-11 $8.50, under 6 free) through Miles Canyon (2 hr. cruises daily June-early Sep.). **Up North Boat and Canoe Rentals,** 86 Wickstrom Rd. (667-7905), across the river from downtown, lets you paddle 25km to Jakkimi River ($20 per person; cost includes pick-up and return to Whitehorse; trip takes about 4hr.). An 8-day journey on the Teslin River costs $200, but there are cheaper options. Call for details. If still-water canoeing is too tame, **Tatshenshini Expediting** (633-2742) will give you the white water ride of your life for $100 (one day; group rates available).

Visitors hungry for local history can feed their heads at the **MacBride Museum** (667-2709), at 1st Ave. and Wood St. The sod-roofed log cabin in the museum courtyard was built in 1899 by Sam McGee, whose demise has been immortalized by the Yukon Bard, Robert Service: "The Northern Lights have seen queer sights, but the queerest they ever did see, was that night on the marge of Lake Labarge I cremated Sam McGee" (open June-Aug. daily 10am-6pm, call for winter hours; $4, seniors and students $3.50, children $2, 6 and under free). Beginning in late May, the **Yukon Historical and Museum Association,** 3126 3rd Ave. (667-4707), sponsors **Heritage Walking Tours.** The 45-minute strolls leave hourly from Donnenworth House, in Lepage Park next to the infocentre (daily 9am-4pm, some evening tours Mon.-Fri.; $2). If you're walking by 3rd Ave. and Lambert St., look up: those three-story **log skyscrapers** were built singlehandedly in the 70s by a local septuagenarian.

When the sun goes down (or at least dips closer to the horizon), **Town & Mountain Hotel** (668-7644) attracts tourists and locals alike, offering live music and fairly inexpensive drinks (open daily noon-2am). The restored *S.S. Klondike* (667-4511), on South Access Rd., is a dry-docked 1929 sternwheeler heralding the days when the Yukon River was the city's sole means of transportation. Pick up a ticket from the info booth at the entrance to the parking lot for a video and guided tour (open daily June-Aug. 9am-7pm, May and Sept. 9am-6pm; $3.50, children $2, families $8).

■ Carcross

Carcross, short for "Caribou Crossing," perches on the narrows between Bennet and Nares Lakes, entirely surrounded by snow-capped peaks and pristine waterways. The native Tagish people hunted caribou at the crossing until the early 1900s, when the herds had dwindled so much that only their name remained. Carcross also served as a link in the treacherous Chilkoot gold route from Skagway to the Yukon River and as a supply depot for the construction of the Alaska Hwy. Since then, mining and tourism have buoyed Carcross' population of 400. On the Klondike Hwy. (Hwy. 2), Carcross is 74km south of Whitehorse and 106km north of Skagway, AK (see p. 159).

The **Carcross Visitor Reception Centre** (821-4431), inside the depot, is open mid-May to mid-September (daily 8am-8pm). **Atlin Express** (604-651-7617) runs buses from Carcross to Atlin, BC ($21, seniors $18, children 5-11 $10.50, under 5 free) and Whitehorse ($26, seniors $20, children 5-11 $13, under 5 free). The two-story red building across from the back of the Caribou Hotel houses the **health station** (821-4444). The **ambulance** is at 821-3333, and the **police** can be reached at 821-5555 (if no answer call 667-5555). Suds your duds at **Montana Services** (821-7308) at the Chevron on Hwy. 2 just north of town (wash $2.25, 4min. dry 25¢; open daily 7am-11pm, winter 8am-8pm). **Public showers** are also available here for $3. The **post office** is the white building with red trim on Bennett Ave. (open Mon., Wed., Fri. 8am-noon and 1-4pm, Tues. and Thurs. 10-11:45am; **postal code:** Y0B 1B0). Tune in to **visitors info** on 96.1 FM. The **area code** is 867.

The **Caribou Hotel** (821-4501), across from the infocentre, is the only hotel in Carcross and the oldest operating hotel in the Yukon. If you don't mind its age, its permanent residents, and a little lounge noise from below, $38 will get you a single or double with a comfy bed (no phones, TVs, or room keys; shared bath). The Yukon Government maintains 14 secluded campsites ($8) with drinking water, firewood, and pit toilets by the airstrip, across Hwy. 2 from the Chevron. North of town 7km on Hwy. 2, **Spirit Lake Wilderness Resort** (821-4337) has woodsy lakeside sites ($9.50, hookups $12.50, cabins $50), but it's a bit of a haul for the camper without a car.

Don't look for gourmet food in Carcross. The **Caribou Hotel cafe** has standard soups and sandwiches in the $5-7 range (open daily 7am-9pm), and the **Spirit Lake resort** serves slightly fancier grub: enjoy a lunch of Dutch pancakes there for $7 (open daily 9am-around 7pm, depending on the spirits' whims).

Hiking in the Carcross area is excellent. If you can, find a copy of *Whitehorse Area Hikes and Bikes* at the Carcross infocentre or in a Whitehorse bookstore before visiting. The most popular hike in the area is the **Chilkoot Trail** (see below), a moderately difficult three-day adventure to the far end of Lake Bennet. The lake's 2 mi. sandy beach is understandably popular with locals in July and August. South of town, a rough mining road probes partway up Montana Mountain past lichen, snow, and boulders; leave a day for the trip. To get there, follow Hwy. 2 south, take the first right after crossing the bridge, then the first left, then follow until the road becomes impassable; from there, it's all on foot up to an astounding view of the Yukon.)

Visitors to the territory should come to Carcross just to check out **The Barracks** (821-3624), across the railroad tracks from the Reception Center. This 1920s building peddles Yukon-made crafts, clothing, and souvenirs (open daily 9am-6pm). If you're lucky, you'll be serenaded by the old player piano or thrown into the store's gold rush-era jail cell. **Frontierland** (667-1055), 1km north of the **Carcross "Desert"** (the exposed, sandy bottom of a glacial lake), houses a dramatic collection of dead wild-

The Chilkoot Trail

The winter of 1898 saw nine out of every 10 Klondike-bound stampeders slog 33 mi. through Skagway and Dyea on their way to Lake Bennett with at least 1000 lb. of provisions strapped to them and their horses. A vaguely touching and wholly naive Canadian law forced each miner headed north bring this staggering amount of supplies. (Libertarians of the world, look smug.) As one hiker put, "It's hard enough to do the trail with just yourself to look after. Imagine looking after yourself, plus a half a ton of mining supplies and beef jerky. And a horse."

The four-day hike (three days for seasoned mountaineers) over the precipitous Chilkoot Pass is littered with wagon wheels, horse bones, and plaques placed by the U.S. and Canadian National Park Services, but the rugged trail prods hikers along with dramatic changes of climate, terrain, and vegetation, trudging along above the treeline before descending into the forests of northern British Columbia. Today, the best approach to the Chilkoot today is to take a bus from Carcross to Skagway, then arrange to have a boat pick you up at the far end of Lake Bennet (3 buses per day to Skagway in the summer, $20-$30; boat service $50; call 821-3209). 4000 hikers ascend the demanding trail each summer. Most of them make it back alive.

life, including the **largest bear ever mounted** (open mid-May to mid-Sept. daily 8am-6pm; admission for museum and neighboring park $6, children $4; gallery or park alone $3.50 and $2.50).

Atlin, BC

Atlin (Tlingit for "Big Lake") gives meaning to the phrase "the good life." The town's 400 residents live humbly on the eastern shore of the 145km long, clear-as-glass Atlin Lake (or "Big Lake Lake," BC's largest), which blesses the town with a deceptive ocean-side aura. Often referred to as the "Little Switzerland of the North," Atlin is also engulfed by the massive mountains of Atlin Provincial Park. The huge park embraces a sizable chunk of the lake, as well as creeping ice fields, 80 islands, and untrodden wilderness. Fishing in the area is understandably some of BC's best.

Like many northern towns, Atlin owes its existence to the Klondike Gold Rush and was first settled in 1898. Nearly 10,000 money-hungry prospectors lived in Atlin at the turn of the century. Since then, the town has mellowed considerably, and locals maintain the mellowness by making little effort to draw visitors. Many pioneer-era buildings remain in mint condition, but are now quiet private residences rather than flamboyant tourist attractions like their Dawson City and Skagway cousins. For seekers of a peaceful few days, Atlin is a gem.

PRACTICAL INFORMATION AND ORIENTATION

The **Atlin Museum** (651-7522), on Trainor and 3rd St., doubles as the **Tourist Infocentre** and offers info on the town's history and resources (open mid-May to mid-Sept. daily 10am-6pm; museum $2.50, seniors $2, children $1). The BC **Provincial Government Building** (651-7595), across the street, sells fishing permits and area maps, and also houses a minuscule **Bank of Montreal** booth (open Mon.-Fri. 8:30am-noon and 1-4:30pm; bank closes at 3pm). Dusty roadsters rejoice in a shower and clean clothes at the **Caribou Laundromat,** on Discovery Ave., perhaps the world's homiest laundry, with a Harlequin Romance reading rack on site (open 24hr.; wash $2.25, dry $1, 5min. shower $2). Speaking of gas, the **Chevron** (651-7746), at Discovery and Third St., is the only station (open daily 7:30am-7:30pm; winter 8am-6pm). Chevron does minor car-care (oil change, tire repair), but seriously suffering cars should putter over to **Peace County Maintenance** (651-7527), at Trainor and 3rd St. (open Mon.-Fri. 6am-4:30pm; call in the winter). **Emergency** numbers include: **police,** 651-7511; **fire,** 651-7666; and **ambulance,** 651-7000. The non-emergency number for the Red Cross **clinic,** on 3rd and Pearl St., is 651-7677 (open Mon.-Fri.

9am-5pm). The **post office** (651-7513) is moving; ask at the infocentre for current location. The **postal code** is V0W 1A0. The **area code** is 250.

Although Atlin is in BC, the only way to drive there is via the Yukon Territory and the rocky Atlin Road (Hwy. 1), which branches off the Alcan at Jakes Corner, just south of Whitehorse and the turnoff to Carcross. There is no gas on Atlin Rd. between town and the Alcan junction (100km). **Atlin Express** (651-7617 in Atlin, 867-668-445 in Whitehorse) buses leave daily at 6:15am for Jakes Corner ($12), Carcross ($21), and Whitehorse, YT from the Atlin Inn on Lake St. **Summit Air Charters Ltd.** (651-7600 in Atlin or 800-661-1944), on 5th St., flies regularly to Juneau, AK for $185 round-trip. In Atlin, everything is within walking distance.

ACCOMMODATIONS AND FOOD

Atlin has a proliferation of homey, tucked-away B&Bs, a plethora of nearby camping on Warm Bay Rd., and a profound lack of over-sized, over-stuffed hotels. For convenience and comfort, try the **Fireweed Inn** (651-7729), at 2nd and Rant St. Its hosts are accommodating, and breakfast is "whatever you want" (single $60; double $70; shared bathrooms). **Tundra Bed and Breakfast** (651-7551), a five minute drive south from town; go 3km on Warm Bay Rd., then left on Pine Dr., and left again onto Spruce Dr. The B&B features handsome, friendly huskies and a German-speaking hostess. The log cabin rooms are intimate, sprucy-clean, and the most affordable in the area (single $40; double $50; cash or check only). **Glacier View Cabins** (651-7691), about 15 minutes down Warm Bay Rd., are more on the rustic side. The log huts come with propane lighting and stove, showerhouse, and an awe-inspiring view of Llewellyn Glacier ($65 single or double).

Campers love the spread-out and woodsy **Pine Creek Campground,** 2.5km south of town on Warm Bay Rd., for its pit toilets, fire barrel, and the delicious fresh-water spring 1km further south on the left ($5, payable at any Atlin business or the museum). Four extremely isolated, primitive, and free campsites with pit toilets are even further on Warm Bay Rd. **Palmer Lake** (19km) and **Warm Bay** (22km) are both lakeside sites. Easy to miss **Warm Springs** (23km, on the left) is a large grassy area with a lukewarm pool. The nearby meadow streams are warm as a bath and lined with watercress. **Grotto**, near the road's end (26km) is thickly forested and has 2 sites right on the road, with trails meandering back towards more enveloped sites.

The **Atlin Inn Restaurant** (651-7546), on Lake St., serves sandwiches and fries, with dinner entrees from $9. If you're over 19, the patio makes the food a tad more exciting (open daily 7am-9pm, less in winter). The **Pine Tree Restaurant** (651-7709), next to Chevron on Discovery Ave., is no more gastronomically stimulating, but has super-friendly service (open May-Sept. daily 7am-9pm; entrees from $5). The patio-esque **Taku BBQ,** on Mill St. at the south end of 1st St., is an exception from the greasy norm, offering fresh salmon dinners ($12.50; open 11:30am-2pm and 4-8:30pm, depending on salmon availability; closed Mon.). Contemplative readers and coffee junkies bask in spiritual music and unhurried service at the **Thimbleweed Tea Room,** in the Courthouse on 2nd St. between Trainor and Pearl Ave., which serves espresso for $1.50 and muffins for $1.25 (open Tues.-Sat. 10am-5pm; winter 11:30am-5pm). For groceries, the **Atlin Trading Post** (651-7574), at Discovery Ave. and 2nd St., has the largest selection (open Mon.-Tues. and Sat.-Sun. 9am-6pm, Wed.-Fri. 9am-8pm; winter daily 9am-6pm).

SIGHTS AND OUTDOORS

Besides the museum (see **Practical Information,** above), the **M.V. Tarahne** is the only other sizeable man-made tourist attraction. Now docked across from the Atlin Inn, the Tarahne was the first gas-powered, propeller driven boat in the north (tours Mon.-Fri. 5:30pm, Sat. 10am, Sun. 4pm; $4, seniors $3, children free). Visitors are also invited on board every Sunday for an elaborate brunch (651-7709 for reservations; $17, children $9, under 5 free, seniors 10% off). Lively locals head to the spacious lounge in the Atlin Inn come evening, where they groove to live music every second weekend (open daily noon-2am, winter 3pm-midnight).

Atlin's true wealth lies in its backyard. Because it remains unincorporated and largely unvisited, established trails are scarce. Lake activity, however, is a different story. Half-a-dozen canoe and kayak outfitters wait to take visitors out onto the water. Specializing in kayaks, **Cloudberry Adventures Ltd.** (651-7767) offers everything from guided trips ($49 per ½-day) to sea kayak lessons ($39 for 2 hr.) and kayak rental (single $35 per day; double $65 per day). Anglers will find themselves in heaven; BC's largest lake boasts plenty of lake trout, pike, whitefish, and grayling.

Old area mining operations took their fill of gold and have left behind a network of endless gravel roads perfect for the mountain biker. For those without their own two wheels, **Sidka Tours** (651-7691) rents bikes for $35 per day. The **Blue Canyon mining road** is rumored to be infinitely long. To get there, take Discovery Rd. east. After roughly 5km, there will be a pull-out on the right that overlooks rolling and tumbling Pine Creek, followed by a fork in the road. Bear right here onto Spruce Creek Rd. and follow for 4km, at which point the road makes a distinct curve to the right at a junction with a significantly smaller road continuing straight ahead. The road straight ahead is the one you want. The most established area trail, unsuitable for biking but perfect for a dayhike, is the 5km (one-way) **Monarch Trail,** which begins 3.7km south on Warm Bay Rd. This relatively strenuous hike begins below tree line, but soon gives way to bald rock face and tundra, which provides a panoramic view of nearby Atlin Lake. Monarch Mountian summits at 1,439m and takes about 2-3 hr. round-trip. After descending, throbbing, overheated feet can cool off on the Lake beach, reachable via a 50m trail beginning across from the Monarch trailhead.

Atlin Provincial Park is enormous, untouched, and mostly untouchable. The park remains so pristine largely because of its inaccessibility. Reachable only by plane or boat, venturing into Atlin Park demands considerable outdoor skill, especially because it has no personnel, services, or maintained trails. One third of the park is blanketed with icefields and glaciers sweeping down from the Juneau icefield. Call **Apex Air** (see **Practical Information,** above) about float plane drop-offs, or **Atlin Wilderness Adventures** (651-7621) about boat runs ($50 per hr., $350 per day per boat). For more info on the park, write or call **BC Parks,** Sheena District Office, Bag 5000, Smithers, BC V0J 2N0 (604-847-7320).

Kluane National Park

When the Southern Tutchone (tuh-SHOW-nee) named this area Kluane (kloo-AH-nee), meaning "place of many fish," they understated the truth. Kluane National Park is also a place of many sheep, glaciers, and untouched mountains. With adjacent Wrangell-St. Elias National Park in Alaska and Tatshenshini/Alsek Provincial Park in B.C., Kluane makes up one of the world's largest wilderness areas. It not only boasts Canada's highest peak, **Mt. Logan** (5959m or 19,545 ft.), but is home to the most massive non-polar ice fields in the world. The abundance of ice-blanketed mountains makes Kluane's interior a haven for the best expeditioners, but also renders two-thirds of the park inaccessible (except by plane) to more humble trekkers. Fortunately, the northeastern park border along the Alaska Hwy. has plenty of room for backpacking, canoeing, rafting, biking, and dayhiking. Many routes follow original Southern Tutchone and Tlingit trails or old mining roads left over from Kluane's brief and disappointing stint with the gold rush from 1904-1905.

Practical Information Find out everything you ever wanted to know about Kluane at the **Kluane National Park Visitor Reception Centre** (634-7207, winter 7209), on Logan St. in **Haines Junction** (Km 1635 on the Alcan). The Park Service staff provides wilderness permits ($5 per night, $50 per season), fishing permits ($5 per day, $35 per season), topo maps ($10), and trail and weather info. A helpful overview of Kluane's trails and routes costs $1 (open May-Sept. daily 8am-8pm; park staff available 9am-7pm; winter park staff hours 8:30am-4:30pm.) The **Sheep Mountain**

Visitor Centre (call operator and request Destruction Bay channel 2M3124), at Alaska Hwy. Km 1707, registers hikers headed for the Sheep Mountain area in the north of the park (open June to mid-Sept. daily 9am-6pm). Sheep Mountain's outdoor telescopes magnify sheep grazing on rocky slopes and turquoise Kluane Lake. **Triple S Garage** (634-2915), 1km north of town on the Alcan, has oil and lubes (about $58), tire and general repair, and 24-hour towing (open daily May-Sept. daily 7am-noon). The **library** (634-2215), on Haines Rd. next door to Madley's has **internet access** and air-conditioning (open Tues.-Fri. 1-5pm, Sat. 2-5pm). An erratically on-the-air (mid-May to mid-Sept.) **visitor radio station** is 96.1 FM. There is a **laundromat** and **showers** in the **Gateway Motel** (634-2371) at the junction of the Alaska Hwy. and Haines Rd. (open to the public 8am-10pm; wash $2, 6min. dry 25¢, shower $3). **Emergency numbers** for Haines Junction include: **police,** 634-5555 (if no answer, call 867-667-5555); **ambulance/clinic,** 634-4444; and **fire,** 634-2256. Both the **bank** (634-2820; open Mon.-Thurs. 12:30-4:30pm, Fri. noon-5pm; in winter Mon.-Thurs. 1-4pm, Fri. 12:30-4:30pm; no ATM) and the **post office** (634-3802; open Mon., Wed., Fri. 9-10am and 1-5pm, Tues. and Thurs. 9am-noon and 1-5pm) are in Madley's General Store on Haines Rd. and Bates St. The **postal code** is Y0B1L0. The **area code** is 867.

Kluane's 22,015 sq. km are bounded by the Kluane Game Sanctuary and the Alaska Highway to the north, and the Haines Highway (Hwy. 3) to the east. Haines Junction is at the eastern park boundary, 158km west of Whitehorse, and serves as the gateway and headquarters of the park. **Alaska Direct** (800-770-6652, 668-4833 in Whitehorse) runs from Haines Junction to Anchorage (US$125), Fairbanks (US$100), Whitehorse (US$20), and Skagway (US$35) on Sunday, Wednesday, and Friday.

Camping, Accommodations, and Food Haines Junction offers the standard array of clean-but-forgettable highway motels and RV parks; B&Bs and area campgrounds are the budget traveler's best bets. **Kathleen Lake Campground,** off Haines Rd., 27km south of Haines Junction, is close to hiking and fishing and has water, flush toilets, fire pits, firewood, and "campfire talks" (sites $10; open June-Oct.; handicapped access). The Yukon government runs four campgrounds in the Kluane Park region, all with water and pit toilets (sites $8). The closest by far to Haines Junction is aqua-streaked (and popular) **Pine Lake,** on the Alcan, 7km east of town, featuring a sandy beach complete with a firepit for late night bonfires. **Lake Creek** and **Congdon Creek** are on the Alcan at Km 1854 and 1723, respectively. The **Dezadeash Lake** campground is about 50km south of Haines Junction on Haines Rd. Seekers of an indoor bed with modern facilities and downtown access should march straight to **Laughing Moose Bed and Breakfast,** 120 Alsek Crescent (634-2335), four blocks from the junction, with a sparkling-clean kitchen, spacious common room with TV and VCR, and a view of the Auriol Mountains (single $55; double $65; shared bath). **Aspen Bed and Breakfast** (634-2816), just 2km east of town on the Alcan, has rustic, intimate cabins with propane heat and light (single $45; double $55; shared bath). For a bed without the flair, the **Stardust Motel** (634-2591), 1km north of town on the Alcan, offers spacious rooms with TV and antiseptic tubs, but no phone (single $45; double $55).

Haines Junction restaurants offer (yawn) standard highway cuisine. For groceries (hardware, tackle, slingshots, etc.), head to **Madley's General Store** (634-2200; open daily 8am-9pm; Oct.-April Mon.-Sat. 9am-6pm), at Haines Rd. and Bates St. At the **Village Bakery and Deli** (634-2867), on Logan St. across from the visitors center, you can sate a sweet tooth with a $1.50 cinnamon bun or have more substantial soup ($3.50). Check out the periodic live music (open May-Sept. daily 9am-9pm).

Outdoors in the Park Kluane makes its few trails quite accessible. Pictures of what seem to be a misshapen dog head are actually beavers (go figure) and indicate a trail head or park boundary. The visitors center has free general info. **Topo maps** cost $10, and detailed route descriptions are free, but guidebooks are pricey. There are also outdoor options outside of the park that the park staff won't disclose; a friendly local can be a great asset.

The **Dezadeash River Loop** (DEZ-dee-ash) trailhead is right downtown at the day-use area across from Madley's on Haines Rd. This flat, forested 5km stroll may disappoint those craving a vertical challenge, but it makes a nice jog. As always, have a noise-maker or belt out tunes to warn bears you're coming. The 15km **Auriol Trail** is another mellow option and has a primitive campground halfway through its loop. The trail begins 7km south of Haines Junction on Haines Rd. and cuts through boreal forest, leading to a subalpine bench just in front of the Auriol Range. The Auriol turns into a favorite cross-country ski route in the winter. The 5km (one-way) **King's Throne Route** is a challenging but rewarding dayhike with a 1220m elevation gain and a panoramic view. It begins at the Kathleen Lake day-use area at the campground (see **Accommodations,** above). The Sheep Mountain area also offers a handful of options, ranging from a ½km interpretive walk to a strenuous 25km loop. "**Routes,**" as opposed to "trails," are not maintained and do not have marked paths. Generally, they are more challenging and require backcountry navigation skills. If you register for an overnight trip, the park may recommend or even mandate use of **bear-resistant food canisters,** which they provide for free with a $150 refundable deposit (cash or credit). Registration for overnighters is mandatory (see **Practical Information,** above). Risks are the reality in Kluane country.

For **mountain bikers,** the **Alsek River Valley Trail** follows a bumpy old mining road 14km to Sugden Creek. The rocky road has no fluffy marshmallows and crosses several streams before gently climbing to a ridge with a stellar view of the Auriol Mountains. Be prepared for a battered rump the next day.

Two booking companies in Haines Junction can set the adrenaline junkie up with an outfitter free of charge. The **Kluane Park Adventure Centre** (634-2313), on the Alcan just east of downtown, specializes in rafting. For $100, travelers can ride the class III and IV rapids on the Tatshenshini River from Copper Mine, BC to Dalton Post, YT; the center also offers a three-hour scenic interpretive float trip on the Dezadeash River illustrating the park's ecology, fauna, and geology ($25) and books trail rides and flightseeing tours (open late May-early Sept. daily 8am-8pm). If a plain ol' canoe or bike will do it, **Paddlewheel** (634-2683), down the road from the Village Bakery, has reasonable rates (bikes $20 per day or $50 for three days; canoes $20 or $25 per day depending on size; call for hours).

Anglers can easily put the park's "place of many fish" reputation to the test. **Kathleen Lake** (see above) is home to lake and rainbow trout, arctic grayling, and Kokanee salmon. Grayling abound in **Jarvis Creek,** halfway between Haines Junction and Sheep Mountain. Visitors can get a **National Parks fishing permit** at the visitors center in Haines Junction or at Madley's General Store (see **Practical Information,** above). Those interested in fishing outside the park can purchase territorial licenses at Madley's and Kluane RV Park.

■ Alaska Highway: Kluane National Park to the Alaska Border

Heading northwest from Kluane National Park on the Alaska Highway, a smattering of petite pit stops pile up before the Alaska Border, where the **time jumps back an hour. Destruction Bay,** at Km 1743 (Historic Milepost 1083) has nothing but a **gas station** and a **health clinic** (841-4444; open Mon.-Fri. 9am-5pm; nurse on call 24hr.).

Burwash Landing, 16km uproad, is next in the Alcan's string o' little things, and offers modest thrills at the **Kluane Museum of Natural History** (841-5561), home to the Yukon's **largest wildlife display** and an informative collection of Southern Tutchone artifacts (open daily 9am-9pm; $3, seniors $2.75, children 6-12 $1.50). The **post office** (862-7013) is in the back of Community Hall (open Mon. 9am-noon and 1-5pm, Wed. 1-5pm, Fri. 1-5pm; **postal code:** Y0B 1A0). The **bank** (862-7409) is also housed in the Community Hall (open Tues. 10am-noon, Thurs. noon-3pm; in winter Tues. 10:30am-noon, Thurs. 1-3pm). Heading farther north, find the **visitor's center** (862-7321; open mid-May to mid-Sept. daily 8am-8pm). The **health center,** located by the Community Hall, can be reached at 862-4444. In an **emergency,** call the police at

862-5555 (or 1-867-667-5555 if no answer). The repair shop in town is **Far West Services** (862-7220; open Mon.-Sat. 8am-5:30pm).

Immense **Kluane Lake** offers some stellar camping options. Kluane First Nation's **Dalan Campground** has roomy, secluded sites on the lake with wood, water, and pit toilets ($10). Or camp for free on the grassy lawn at **Burwash Landing Resort** (867-841-4441; showers $3; RV hookups $15). The resort sits on a lakeside plot and has a restaurant with a view of the blue, where single-sized pizzas are $4.50 and served straight from the oven (open daily 7am-11pm). Those wanting a roof will have to dole out $60 for a single, $65 for a double, or $80 for a party of four. **Kluane Wilderness Village** at Km 1798 (Historical Mile 1118), though it flaunts a fancy name, is actually only a **gas station** (841-4141; open 24hr.) with tenting ($9) and hookups ($18).

The most booming of all these roadside wonders, **Beaver Creek** (176km north of Burwash Landing), has the last Canadian services before the border. The Alcan north of Beaver Creek is under sporadic repair; it's no wonder—it was the last section built by the southbound crew before the "final linkup" of the Alcan in 1942. The local *modus operandi* is to hit the lounge at **Beaver Creek Motor Inn** (862-7600; open until 2am), then nurse a hangover over breakfast at **Ida's Hotel and Cafe** (862-7223). Ida's grills up eggs and toast ($4.50) or pancakes ($4); for lunch, $6.50 fetches a mushroom burger and fries (open daily 24hr.). Travelers can **camp** for free in Ida's blah backyard area (no water), or head to **Westmark RV** (862-7501) for sites with showers (tent $10; hook-up $19; laundry, wash $1, 7min. dry 25¢).

Dawson City

Gold! Gold! Gold! Of all the insanity ever inspired by the lust for the dust, the creation of **Dawson City** must be one of the most insane. For 12 glorious, crazy months, from July 1898 to July 1899, Dawson City was the largest Canadian city west of Toronto and known as "the Queen of the North." Perched on the doorstep of the Arctic Circle and 1000 mi. from any other settlement, its 30,000 residents, with names like Swiftwater Bill, Skookum Jim, Arizona Charlie Meadows, and Evaporated Kid, made their fortunes. Each had lugged 1000 lb. of provisions over the treacherous Chilkoot Trail to the Yukon (see p. 263), and each was determined to become filthy, stinkin' rich.

After a year of frenzied claim-staking and legend-making, however, most of the once-eager Sourdoughs (Northwestern-speak for a prospector or, now, anyone who survives an arctic winter) followed the Yukon River to Nome, and the city fizzled almost as quickly as it had exploded. It wasn't until the early 60s that the Klondike Visitor's Association and the Canadian government set out to restore Dawson City and transform it into the lively RV and college student destination that it is today.

PRACTICAL INFORMATION AND ORIENTATION

Visitors Information: Visitor Reception Centre (993-5566), at Front and King St. Historic movies and extensive info. Sells tours of Dawson City's obvious attractions. Open mid-May to mid-Sept. daily 8am-8pm. For info by mail, write to **Klondike Visitors Association,** P.O. Box 389C, Dawson City, YT Y0B 1G0. The **Northwest Territories Visitors Centre** (993-6167) is across the street. Advice on driving the Dempster Hwy. (see p. 272). Open daily late May to early Sept. 9am-8pm. **Tourist radio (96.1 FM)** broadcasts weather, road conditions, and events.

Banks: The **Canadian Imperial Bank of Commerce,** at 2nd and Queen, is the only bank and **ATM** in town. Open Mon.-Thurs. 10am-3pm, Fri. 10am-5pm.

Buses: Norline Coaches Ltd. (993-6010), at the Gas Shack Chevron Station on 5th Ave. and Princess St. To Whitehorse, (3 per week, 2 in winter), $73. **Gold City Tours** (993-6424), on Front St. across from the Keno steamship, runs buses up the Dempster Hwy. Tues. and Thurs. at 8am. Roundtrip to Inuvik $240 with advance purchase and Sat. night stay. Office open May-Sept. daily 9am-6pm.

River Travel: Yukon Queen River Cruises (993-5599), on Front St. next to the Keno. Departs daily at 8:30am for Eagle, AK along the Yukon River. One-way

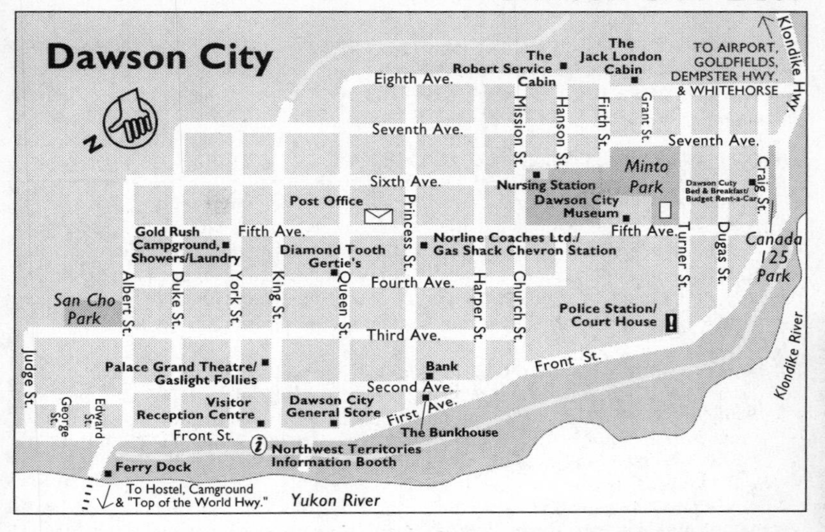

standby US$81; round-trip US$133; will return canoes from Eagle for US$50. Office open Mon.-Sat. 9am-5:30pm, Sun. noon-5:30pm. Call for times and reservations.

Car Rental: Budget, 451 Craig St. (993-5644), in the Dawson City B&B (see **Accommodations,** below), rents for $46 per day plus 19¢ for each km after 100km. Rates subject to change. Free pick up and delivery within Dawson City. Must be 21.

Auto Repair: Chevron (993-5057) at Princess and 5th. Open daily 7am-10pm, winter Mon.-Sat. 8am-6pm, Sun. noon-6pm.

Canoe and Bike Rental: At the hostel (see **Accommodations,** below). Bikes $20 per day, canoes $20 per day. Non-hostelers must present passport as deposit.

Library: 993-5571, at 5th Ave. and Princess St. in the school. Open summers Mon.-Thurs. 10am-9pm, Fri.-Sat. 10am-5pm; in winter Tues.-Wed. and Fri. 9am-7pm, Thurs. 1-8pm, Sat. noon-5pm.

Laundromat and Showers: Gold Rush Campground (see **Accomodations,** below). Wash $2.50, dry $1.50, 4min.showers $1. Open 9am-9pm.

Medical Emergency: Ambulance, 993-4444; **fire,** 993-2222. A **nursing station** (993-5744) is at 6th Ave. and Church. Open Mon.-Fri. 8:30am-5pm.

Crisis Line: Dawson Women's Shelter (993-5086 or 993-5239, pager 159). 24hrs.

Police: (993-5555; if no answer 1-667-5555), at Front St. and Turner St. in the southern part of town.

Internet Access: At the library (see above) and at **Black Sand and Gold Coffee and Tea House** (993-6141), at 2nd Ave. and Princess St.

Post Office: (993-5342), at 5th Ave. and Princess St. Open Mon.-Fri. 8:30am-5:30pm, Sat. 9am-noon. Must register for general delivery service; photo ID required. The **Historical Post Office,** at 3rd and King St., is closer to downtown. Open Mon.-Fri. noon-6pm. **Postal Code:** Y0B 1G0.

Area Code: 867.

Pannin' fer Gold I: Theory

Panning for gold is a bit like shampooing: lather, rinse, repeat. You'll need a 12- or 18-in. pan, easily found at local stores, and an unclaimed stretch of beach or river. Scoop up some likely-looking sand and gravel. Look for tree roots, turns in the river, and upstream ends of gravel bars, where heavy gold may settle. Swirl water, sand, and gravel in a tilted gold pan, slowly washing materials over the edge. Be patient, dreaming of how you'll spend your riches. Eventually you'll be down to black sand, and—hopefully—gold. Gold is shinier than brassy-looking pyrite (Fool's Gold), and it doesn't break down upon touch, like mica, another common glittery substance. Later, we'll practice this technique.

To reach Dawson City, take the Klondike Hwy. 533km north from Whitehorse, or follow the **Top-of-the-World Hwy.** about 100km east from the Alaska border (see **Taylor Hwy.,** p. 122). If you take the Klondike, fill up in Whitehorse, as there is limited gas along the way (approximately every 100km).

ACCOMMODATIONS AND CAMPING

The hostel and the campground on the west side of town, across the Yukon River, are by far the cheapest options in the trap that is Dawson City tourism. The **ferry** to float you and your wheels across is free and runs 24 hours. Hop on at Front St. and Albert, on the north end of town. The "tent city" in the woods next to the hostel is a happy home to many of the town's summer college crowd, despite the $100 per person fee the government recently began charging these temporary forest dwellers.

Dawson City River Hostel (HI-C) (993-6823). Across the Yukon River from downtown; take the 1st left off the ferry. The best bargain in town. Bunks in new log cabins, a wood-heated "prospector's bath," outdoor kitchen facilities, a cozy lounge with a wood stove and mini-library, and a beautiful hilltop view of the river and city beyond. Members $13, nonmembers $16; tent sites for up to 2 people $10, each additional person $7. Open May-Sept.

Yukon River Campground. Take the 1st right off the ferry. Roomy, secluded sites are a haven for nature-lovers. Peer at the peregrine falcons nesting across the river. Water and pit toilets. RVs welcome, but no hookups. Sites $8.

The Bunkhouse (993-6164), Front and Princess St. New, pristine, and conveniently located. Wood-planked rooms and tiny shared bathrooms. Singles $45, with bath $75; doubles $50, with bath $80; quads with bath $105. 10% senior discount.

Gold Rush Campground (993-5247), at 5th and York St. A monopoly on downtown RV sites; often packed. Trailer-tailored sites are a bummer for tenters. Laundromat (wash $2.50, dry $1.50), shower (4min. $1), and dump station. Sites $11.50, electric hookups $16, full hookups $20. Reception open 24hr.

Dawson City Bed and Breakfast, 451 Craig St. (993-5649) on the south end of town. More like home than your own. If you're in the mood to splurge, this is worth it. Shared bath. Singles $69; doubles $79. 5% discount for seniors or AAA members. Winter rates 10% less. Make reservations at least a week in advance.

FOOD

On Thanksgiving Day in 1898, a turkey in Dawson City cost over $100. Prices today are more reasonable, and there are a few good places to eat in town. Snag a bag of groceries at the **Dawson City General Store.**

Klondike Kate's (993-6527), at 3rd and King St. in one of Dawson's oldest buildings. Kate's breakfast special (served until 11am) should satisfy even the hungriest Sourdough (2 eggs, bacon or sausage, home fries, and toast for $4). At lunch, kick back on the shady patio with a gyros or veggie wrap ($5). Open mid-May to mid-Sept. daily 7am-11pm.

River West Food and Health (993-6339), on Front and Queen St. The all-natural place for all-natural travelers. Muffins, snacks, organic coffees ($1.25-3.50), and possibly the only hummus pitas in the Yukon ($6). Open Mon.-Sat. 8am-8pm, Sun. 10am-6pm, in winter Mon.-Sat. 9am-6pm, Sun. noon-6pm.

Midnight Sun Hotel Restaurant (993-5495), 3rd and Queen. Chinese entrees, created by chefs invited from Vancouver for the summer, start at $10. Chew on chow from the Fri. lunch smorgasbord ($10) or the Sun. dinner smorg ($14) into the wee hours of the midnight sun. Open Sun.-Thurs. 6am-1am, Fri.-Sat. 6am-3am.

The Jack London Grill (993-5346), in the Downtown Hotel at 2nd and Queen. Those a bit too road-worn for the posh dining room can sip for a bit in the accompanying saloon (must be 19). Lunch sandwiches start at $6. Gourmet dinners start at $11 for pasta primavera or veggie stir fry. Open Sun.-Thurs. 6am-10pm, Fri.-Sat. 6am-11pm; winters Sun-Thurs. 7am-9pm, Fri.-Sat. 7am-10pm

The Boardwalk Cafe (993-6728) on Front St. opposite the Keno steamship. Basic grub at the best price. Bagel and coffee a mere $2, veggie burger $5. Open May-Sept. daily 10am-10pm.

SIGHTS AND ENTERTAINMENT

The prospector's stampede to Dawson City died down in the early 1900s, but today's Dawson is a boomtown for museums and tours that provide enough information about gold mining and frontier life to break the bank. The visitors centre sells a package **Prospector's Pass** ($15) that's only worth it if you want to see everything.

The goldfields of **Bonanza** and **Eldorado Creeks** yielded some of the richest lodes discovered in the Klondike. Nearly 16km of maintained gravel road follows Bonanza Creek to the former site of **Grand Forks,** chewed up when the dredges came through. Along the way are **Gold Dredge #4,** a monster of a machine used to thoroughly mine Bonanza Creek after the rush was over, and **Discovery Claim,** the site of the first discovery of gold by George Carmack on August 16, 1896. The Park Service also maintains **Bear Creek,** 13km south of town on the Klondike Hwy. Mining here suddenly halted in 1966, leaving behind a ghost town of tools and machinery. Tours of Bear Creek or the Dredge are $5 each.

To dig up your own fortune, **Goldbottom Mining Tours and Gold Panning,** (993-5023), 30 km south of town, offers a tour of an operating mine and an hour of panning for $12 (open summers daily 11am-7pm). Anyone can pan for free at the confluence of the Bonanza and Eldorado Creeks; you need your own pan, available at local hardware stores. Panning anywhere else along the creeks could lead to a very unpleasant encounter with the owner/miner of the claim you're jumping.

Learn about frontier literary geniuses at the **Jack London Cabin,** on 8th Ave. and 5th, where admission is free and the great Californian author's life and times in the Yukon are recounted during readings (daily noon and 2:15pm). The cabin is worth a visit just to see the photos of a struggling young London (open daily 10am-6pm). Be sure to catch the animated **Robert Service readings** given at his nearby cabin. Authentic performances of witty ballads by the Yukon Bard, including "The Cremation of Sam McGee" and "The Shooting of Dan McGrew," are given in front of the cabin on 8th Ave. at Hanson where he penned them (shows daily at 10am and 3pm; cabin open 9am-noon and 1-5pm; $6, under 8 $3; cabin viewing only $2). Another popular performance with a different flavor is the **Gaslight Follies** (993-6217), a high-kicking vaudeville revue held in the **Palace Grand Theatre** on King St. between 2nd and 3rd St. (Wed.-Mon. 8pm; box office open daily 4-8pm; $15, children $6).

Diamond Tooth Gertie's, at 4th and Queen, was Canada's first legal casino and proves that Dawson is no movie set: for a $4.75 cover (or $11.50 season pass) gamblers can game away the night with roulette, blackjack, or even "Texas hold 'em" against local legends like Johnny Caribou and No Sleep Filippe. Or take in one of three nightly floor shows at 8:30pm, 10:30pm, and 12:30am (19 plus only; open nightly 7pm-2am). For down-and-dirty, late-night blackjack, the **Sun Tavern and Lounge** (993-5495) at 3rd Ave. and Queen St. is where "everyone eventually ends up." Once Dawson's roughest bar, the Sun has calmed down, but it's still no place to sip fruity drinks (open daily noon-2am). A macho pint of brew is $3.75.

Pleasure Island Restaurant and **Yukon River Cruises** (993-5482), on Front St. between King and Queen, wrap several elements of Yukon culture into a single package: the 2½-hour cruise on the *Yukon Lou* includes an all-you-can-eat salmon barbecue on Pleasure Island and a chance to meet the owner's sled-dog team ($40; children $20; departures at 4, 5:30, and 6:45 pm). The *Yukon Lou* also makes a daily 1½-hour cruise at 1pm ($20, children $12.50).

Pannin' fer Gold II: Practice

Swish. Swish. Swish swish. Swish. "Nope." Swish swish swish. Swish. "Nope." Swish. Swish swish swish. Swish. Swish. "GO-ALD! It's gold, gold, I tells ya!"

WESTERN CANADA

No, Ma'am, That's Not an Olive in Your Martini...

When some people run across amputated body parts, they take them to a hospital for surgical reattachment and a new career in the X-rated film industry. But for Capt. Dick Stevenson, the discovery of a **pickled human toe** in a cabin in the Yukon meant one thing: a damn fine cocktail. The drink became famous and spawned the **Sourtoe Cocktail Club,** an institution with a history as peculiar as its name. Aspiring initiates buy a drink of their choice and pay a small fee ($5) to Bill "Stillwater Willie" Boone (Dick's replacement as keeper of the sourtoe), who drops the chemically preserved (er, pickled) toe in the drink. Then it's bottoms up, and the moment the toe touches your lips, you've become one of the club's 12,000-plus proud members. "You can drink it fast, you can drink it slow—but the lips have gotta touch the toe." Listening to Stillwater Willie explain the club's sordid history and philosophize about life in the Yukon is itself worth the $5, but the fee includes a certificate, membership card, and pin. The toe gets around: inquire at the **Yukon River Cruises** (993-5482), on Front St. between King and Queen, for initiation times and location.

Like every town cradled in the Yukon, Dawson is a jungle-gym for the outdoor journeyer. The Dawson City River Hostel (see **Accomodations,** above) sells topographical maps of the region ($12), and can arrange a four-day canoe trip to Eagle, AK for US$110, and a ten-day trip to Circle, AK for US$270. A trip up the **Midnight Dome** (ask at the visitors centre for directions) is a tradition on the summer solstice (June 21), when the sun barely dips below the horizon for 20 minutes around 12:30am.

During the last weekend of July, the **Dawson City Music Festival** is a jammin' good time with artists hailing from all over Canada. Labor Day visitors will not want to pass up their chance to behold the **Great International Outhouse Race.** This bizarre athletic (?) event is a true measure of stamina as teams of contenders for the coveted trophy pull **occupied outhouses** on wheels through the streets of Dawson.

Dempster Highway

The 741km Dempster Highway is named after Inspector W.J.D. Dempster, one of the most courageous officers to wear the Mountie redcoat. It is the sole access road to Canada's isolated Mackenzie River Delta communities of Fort McPherson, Tsiigehtchic (SIG-uh-chik, formerly known as Arctic Red River), and Inuvik (ih-NOO-vik). Highway construction began in the 50s when "arctic gold" (gas and oil) was discovered near the Arctic Circle (66°33') at Eagle Plains, and ended in the 70s when large-scale oil exploration came to the Canada's northern shores on the Beaufort Sea. The Inuvialuit and Gwich'in peoples made homes here a millenia before the arrival of fuel-seeking pioneers, of course, and arctic communities remain largely indigenous.

Like no other highway in North America, the Dempster confronts its drivers with real, naked wilderness, unmolested by logging scars or advertisements. Driving the Dempster can be a religious experience: those who brave it cross the Arctic Circle, pass more animals than cars, and stare into the geologic beginnings of the continent (then have the right to write "I did it!" in the 6 inches of dust coating their car). Despite the thrill of it all, the Dempster is not to be taken lightly. While reasonably navigable, it is still very much an obedient subject of Queen Wilderness and should be approached with careful planning. Services are limited, weather is erratic, and the dirt and gravel roads give cars a thorough beating.

Practical Information The **Arctic Hotline** (800-661-0788) and **Road and Ferry Report** (800-661-0752, in Inuvik 777-2678) provide necessary and up-to-date road info. The **NWT Infocentre** in Dawson City has a free brochure on the highway. **Maxmillans** (993-5486), at Front and Queen St. in Dawson City, sells the ever-useful road guides *Along the Dempster* ($13) and *Western Arctic Travel* ($8; open Mon.-Sat. 9am-8pm, Sun. 10am-6pm, winter Mon.-Sat. 10am-5pm).

The highway begins 41km east of Dawson at the **Klondike River Lodge** on the Klondike Highway (Hwy. 2). A full tank of gas, dependable tires, a spare or two, and emergency supplies (a jerry can of gas, food, clothes, and a first aid kit) are necessary Dempster companions. The Klondike Lodge has full services, though Dawson City is just as good for preparations. To maintain health and sanity along the Dempster, bring a surefire bug repellant.

On the Road The first, spectacular 150km of the Demptser pass through the haunting crags of the **Ogilvie Mountains,** narrowly missed by glaciation during the last ice age. The road then descends back into forest and eventually endless blankets of velvet tundra as it approaches the **Arctic Circle,** the sourthernmost point at which the sun does not set on the longest day of the year. Although there are some man-made services along the way, most of joy of the journey lies in the driving, watching, and gazing itself. Accomodations are sparse. There are **government campgrounds** at Tombstone (Km 72), Engineer Creek (Km 192), Rock River (Km 447), Nitainlii (Km 547), Caribou Creek (Km 692) and Chuk (Km 737). Dry sites cost $8, and hookups are only available near the end of the line at Chuk.

There are few trails along the Dempster, but the land's expanse begs exploration. Off-trail hiking is the way of this wild and demands the most vigilant take-none-leave-none ethic. Distances are deceptively long, and flat, arid looking tundra often hides a sponge swampy, lumpy **muskeg** (thawed permafrosted land). There are a handful of more established paths, if "tundra-whacking" doesn't appeal.

At Km 58 on the highway, the **Grizzly Valley** hike leads through spruce forest which eventually yields to an alpine lookout and ridge. Take the small road behind the gravel pit at the garbage dump; eventually it gives way to a foot path. Allow six hours roundtrip. The **Interpretive Centre** at **Tombstone Campground** (Km 72) has a staff wiser than the Dalai Lama, and loans out a mile-by-mile taped travelogue of the Dempster's natural history and wildlife. Copies are limited and must be returned on the way home, but it's well worth it to get the lowdown on Dall sheep, golden eagles, glacial "pogues," and the migrating **Porcupine Caribou Herd,** which numbers 150,000 and is the largest in North America.

For a full-day adventure with 3300 ft. of ascent, the **Mt. Distincta** hike at Km 154 ("Windy Pass") treks over craggy rocks and boulders to one of the area's highest peaks at 5900 ft. From the highway, walk southeast across a narrow ribbon of tundra to the base of the ridge. Follow the ridge south 6km, past a radio tower, then up a slope to the west. This is the true summit. From here, hike north 6km and then descend back to the highway, 5km west of your car. Sturdy boots are a must for these rocky slopes. **Sapper Hill,** with its distinctness yellow-grey ridge, is one of the best half-day hikes along the highway. It begins just after **Engineer Creek,** (Km 194), and takes about 4 hours. As you climb toward the top, avoid walking along the fishbone crest of the ridge—the chunky limestone near the summit can be tricky to navigate.

Halfway to Inuvik, 364km from Dawson City, gas, food, supplies, and accommodations are available at the well-kept **Eagle Plains Hotel** (993-2453). You may or may not see eagles here, but you will witness monopoly pricing in action. Brace yourself (singles $90, each additional person $10). Rocky, parking lot-style camping is available ($10, $15 with electricity), with coin showers and laundry. Car juice is costs about 82¢ per liter, but what are you going to do? The next pump is 197km away. The hum-drum looking restaurant is startlingly reasonable and good: a burger with crispy, thick fries is $6.

Don't forget to set your watch ahead an hour when crossing the Yukon-Northwest Territories border at Km 471. **Ferries** (free) cross the Peel and Arctic Red Rivers 550km and 600km north of Dawson City about 15 times per day in summer (mid-June to mid-Oct.). In winter, you can drive across the thick ice. **No crossing** is possible during fall freeze-in or spring thaw. Call 800-661-0752 for current ice status.

INUVIK

Inuvik, at the end of the Dempster rainbow, is a fully serviced town of 3200 residents. The **Western Arctic Visitors Centre** (777-4727) is on Mackenzie Rd. downtown. Indoor accomodations in Inuvik are a budgeter's Hades, but those on the cheaper end are **Robertson's Bed and Breakfast,** 41 Mackenzie Rd. (777-3111) at Union St. (singles $70; doubles $80) and **Polar Bed and Breakfast** (777-4620), just down the street (singles $75; doubles $85). Cheer up: there's camping downtown at **Happy Valley Campground** on Happy Valley Rd. off of Union St. If you're feeling restless in the midnight sun, ask about **The Zoo,** Inuvik's rowdy arctic hotspot.

Still not far enough north? **Inuvik Air Charter** (777-4242) will fly up to seven passengers to isolated, glacier-bound **Tuktoyaktuk** ("Tuk" to its friends) for $686. Bring or make six friends and the 4-hour roundtrip (with 2hr. on the ground in Tuk) becomes a bargain... almost. As with *everything* in Inuvik, call in advance.

Alberta

With its gaping prairie, oil-fired economy, and conservative politics, Alberta is the Texas of Canada. Petrodollars have given birth to gleaming, modern cities on the plains. In 1988, the Winter Olympics temporarily transformed Calgary into an international mecca, and the city hasn't stopped collecting tourist interest off the legacy yet. Calgary is also the annual stomping grounds for the Stampede, the world's largest rodeo and meetingplace for the most skilled cowboys in the West. Alberta's capital, Edmonton, is slightly larger than Calgary, its hockey rival to the south, and serves as the trusty transportation hub for the stunning national and provincial parks that line the Alberta-British Columbia border.

For adventurous outdoor enthusiasts, Alberta is a year-round playground. Hikers, mountaineers, and ice climbers will find a recreational paradise in the Canadian Rockies in Banff and Jasper National Parks and Kananaskis Country. Canoeing centers adjoin the lakes of northern Alberta and the Milk River in the south. The province boasts thousands of prime fishing holes, internationally renowned fossil fields, and centers of indigenous Canadian culture. Oh, Alberta!

PRACTICAL INFORMATION

Capital: Edmonton.

Visitors Information: Alberta Tourism, Commerce 10155 102 St., 3rd floor, Edmonton T5J 4L6 (427-4321 or 800-661-8888). **Parks Canada,** 220 4th Ave. SE, #552, Calgary T2G 4X3 (292-4401. Has information on Waterton Lakes, Jasper, and Banff National Parks, and Wood Buffalo provincial park. **Alberta Wilderness Association,** P.O. Box 6398, Station D, Calgary T2P 2E1 (283-2025; fax 270-2743). Distributes info for off-highway adventurers.

Population: 2,790,000 **Motto:** *Fortis et Liber* (Strong and Free). **Bird:** Great Horned Owl. **Flower:** Wild Rose. **Tree:** Lodgepole Pine.

Emergency: 911 in most areas; some rural areas may not have 911 service.

Time Zone: Mountain (2hr. behind Eastern).

Postal Abbreviation: AB.

Provincial Sales Tax: None.

Drinking Age: 18.

Traffic Laws: Mandatory seatbelt law.

Area Code: 403.

GETTING AROUND

Alberta's extensive highway system makes travel between major destinations easy. **Highway 2** runs north-south between Calgary and Edmonton. The east-west **Yellowhead Highway** (Hwy. 16) connects Edmonton with Jasper and continues on across British Columbia. The north-south **Icefields Parkway** (Hwy. 93) runs from Jasper through Banff. The **Trans-Canada Highway** (Hwy. 1) completes the loop, connecting Banff with Calgary, 120km (75 mi.) to the east. **Buses** (Greyhound, Brewster, and Red Arrow) travel all of these routes. VIA Rail runs **trains** from Edmonton to Jasper. Alberta's major **airports** are in Calgary and Edmonton.

Edmonton

When western Alberta's glitz and glamour were distributed, Edmonton was last in line. Banff and Jasper won the spectacular scenery, Calgary got the Stampede, and Edmonton became the proud parent of...the provincial capital. But with a plethora of museums and a river valley beckoning to hikers and bikers, the city is rising in rank among Albertan travel destinations. The ever-competitive Oilers have made the trek to Edmonton a minor pilgrimage for hockey fans, while a perpetual stream of music, art, and performance festivals draws summer crowds. Add to the potion the largest mall in the world and Edmonton transforms into a pleasant urban oasis near the almost overpowering splendor of the neighboring Rockies.

PRACTICAL INFORMATION AND ORIENTATION

Visitors Information: Edmonton Tourism, Shaw Conference Center, 9797 Jasper Ave. (496-8400 or 800-463-4667), on the Pedway Level. Info, maps, and directions. Open Mon.-Fri. 8:30am-4:30pm. Also at **Gateway Park** (496-8400 or 800-463-4667), on Hwy. 2 south of the city. Open daily 8am-9pm; winter Mon.-Fri. 8:30am-4:30pm, Sat.-Sun. 9am-5pm. For info on greater Alberta, head to **Alberta Tourism,** Commerce Place, 10155 102 St., Edmonton T5J 4L6, 3rd floor (427-4321 or 800-661-8888). Open Mon.-Fri. 8:15am-4:30pm; by phone Mon.-Fri. 9am-4:30pm.

Budget Travel: The Travel Shop, 10926 88 Ave. (travel 439-3096, retail 439-3089). Regional office for **Alberta Hostels.** A travel agency with sundry hiking and travel gear, serving youth and student travelers. Will make international hostel reservations for $5. Open Mon.-Wed. and Sat. 10am-6pm, Thurs.-Fri. 10am-8pm, Sun. noon-5pm. Visa, MC.

Buses: Greyhound, 10324 103 St. (420-2412). To: Calgary (nearly every hr. 8am-8pm, plus a milk run at midnight, $35), Jasper (4 per day, $49), Vancouver (3 per day, $116), Yellowknife (1 per day Sun.-Thurs.; winter 3 per week, $184). A 7-($212), 15- ($277), 30- ($373), or 60-day Canada Pass ($480) will give more mileage per dear Canadian dollar. Open daily 5:30am-midnight. Locker storage $2 per 24hr. **Red Arrow,** 10010 104 St. (800-232-1958), at the Howard Johnson Hotel. To: Calgary (5 per day, $35), Fort McMurray (2 per day, $43). 10% discount with hosteling card. Open Mon.-Fri. 7:30am-8pm, Sat. 8am-8pm. All major credit cards accepted; charge on! The Edmonton International Youth Hostel also sells tickets.

Trains: VIA Rail, 10004 104 Ave. (422-6032 or 800-835-3037 for recorded info, 800-561-8630 for reservations), in the CN Tower, recognizable by the huge red letters on the front of the building. To Jasper and Vancouver. No train service to Calgary.

Public Transportation: Edmonton Transit (496-1611 for schedule info, 496-1600 for Buslink, the general info number; http://www.gov.edmonton.ab.ca/). Buses and light rail transit **(LRT)** run frequently throughout the city. LRT is free in the downtown area Mon.-Fri. 9am-3pm and Sat. 9am-6pm (between Grandin Station at 110 St. and 98 Ave. and Churchill Station at 99 St. and 102 Ave.). Fare outside the free zone $1.60, over 65 and under 15 $1. No bikes on LRT during peak hours (Mon.-Fri. 7:30-8:30am, 4-5pm). No bikes on buses. For info, stop by the **Downtown Information Centre,** 100A St. and Jasper Ave. (open Mon.-Fri. 9:30am-2pm and 3-5pm) or the Churchill LRT station info booth (open Mon.-Fri. 8:30am-4:30pm).

Taxis: Yellow Cab, 462-3456. **Alberta Co-op Taxi,** 425-8310. Both 24hr.

Car Rental: Budget, 10016 106 St. (448-2000 or 800-661-7027). Cars start at $27.95 per day, 12¢ per km after 200km. Must be 21; $12 per day surcharge if under 25. **Tilden,** 10133 100A St. (422-6097). Cars start at $19.95 per day, $29.95 per day on weekends, 12¢ per km after 200km. Must be 21. Open Mon.-Fri. 7am-7pm, Sat. 8am-4pm, Sun. 9am-5pm. All major credit cards accepted.

Bike Rental: The **Edmonton Hostel** (see **Accommodations,** below) rents bikes for $15 per day, $7.50 per ½day. **Redbike,** 10918 88 Ave. (435-2674), next to the Travel Shop, rents mountain bikes for $10 per hr., $20 ½day, $30 full day, $40 weekend, $100 per week.

Library: Edmonton Public Library, 7 Sir Winston Churchill Sq. Open Mon.-Fri. 9am-9pm, Sat. 9am-6pm, Sun. 1-5pm.

Gay and Lesbian Resources: Gay/Lesbian Community Centre, 10612 124th St. #103 (488-3234). Community listings and on-site peer counseling. Open Mon.-Fri. 7-10pm. Call 988-4188 for events, 489-9661 for the gay youth line. **Womenspace** (425-0511), is the Edmonton lesbian group. Call for recording of local events.

Square Dancing Resources: Edmonton and District Square Dance Association, 496-9136.

Weather Information: 468-4940.

Rape Crisis: Sexual Assault Centre, 423-4121. 24hr. **Distress Line,** 482-HELP/4357. 24hr.

Pharmacy: Shoppers Drug Mart, 11408 Jasper Ave. (482-1011). Open daily 24hr.

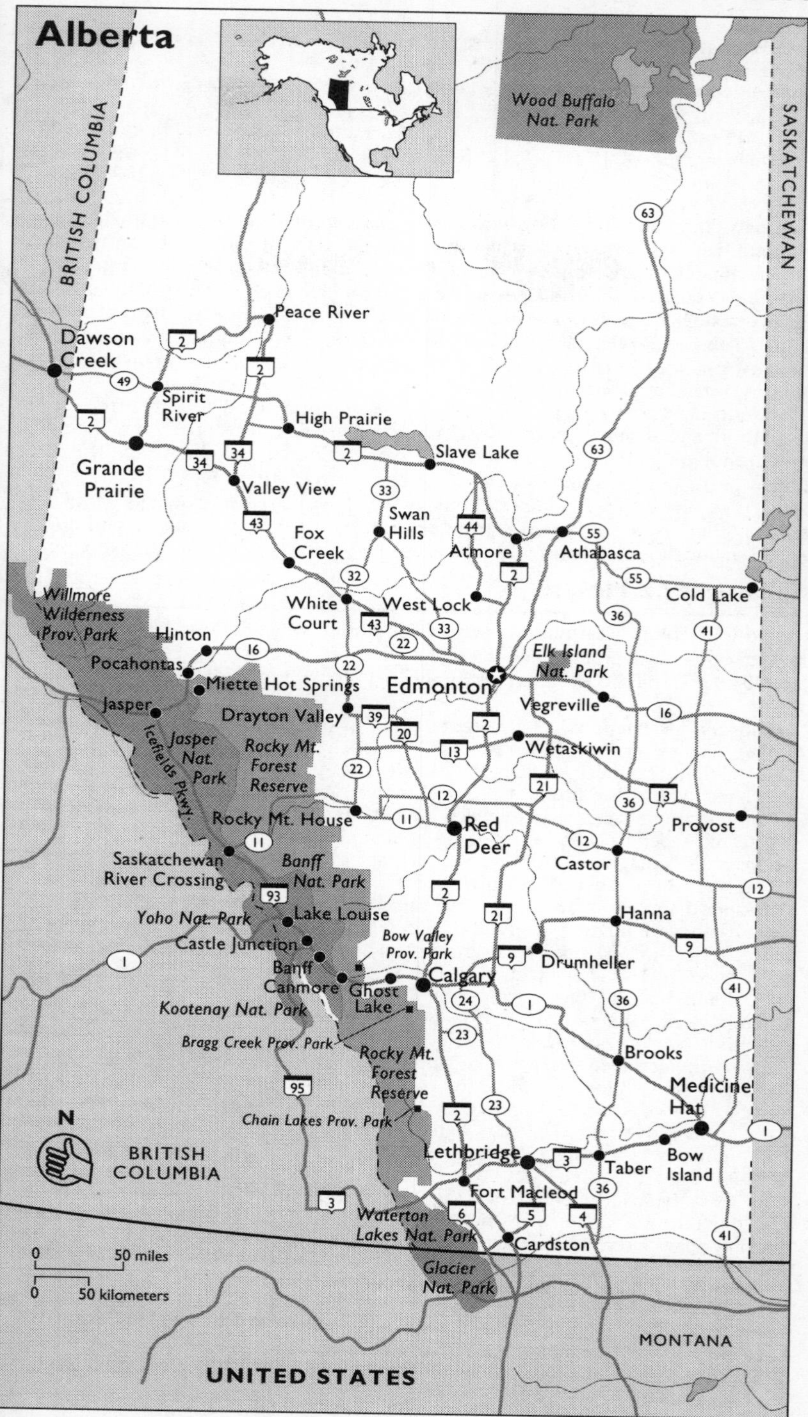
Alberta
Wood Buffalo Nat. Park
BRITISH COLUMBIA
SASKATCHEWAN
Peace River
Dawson Creek
Spirit River
High Prairie
Grande Prairie
Slave Lake
Valley View
Swan Hills
Fox Creek
Atmore
Athabasca
Cold Lake
White Court
West Lock
Willmore Wilderness Prov. Park
Hinton
Pocahontas
Elk Island Nat. Park
Miette Hot Springs
Edmonton
Jasper
Vegreville
Drayton Valley
Wetaskiwin
Jasper Nat. Park
Rocky Mt. Forest Reserve
Icefields Pkwy.
Rocky Mt. House
Red Deer
Provost
Saskatchewan River Crossing
Banff Nat. Park
Castor
Yoho Nat. Park
Lake Louise
Hanna
Castle Junction
Bow Valley Prov. Park
Banff
Canmore
Ghost Lake
Calgary
Drumheller
Kootenay Nat. Park
Bragg Creek Prov. Park
Rocky Mt. Forest Reserve
Brooks
Medicine Hat
Chain Lakes Prov. Park
N
BRITISH COLUMBIA
Lethbridge
Taber
Bow Island
Fort Macleod
Waterton Lakes Nat. Park
Cardston
0 50 miles
0 50 kilometers
Glacier Nat. Park
MONTANA
UNITED STATES

Hospital: Royal Alexandra Hospital, 10240 Kingsway Ave. (477-4111).
Emergency: 911. **Police:** 423-4567.
Internet Access: Dow Computer lab, 11211 142 St. (451-3344) at the Edmonton Space and Science Centre (see **Sights,** p. 280).
Post Office: 9808 103A Ave. (944-3265), adjacent to the CN Tower. Open Mon.-Fri. 8am-5:45pm. **Postal Code:** T5J 2G8.
Area Code: 403.

Although Edmonton is the northernmost major city in Canada, it's actually in the southern half of Alberta. The city lies 294km (184 mi.) north of Calgary, an easy but tedious three-hour drive on Hwy. 2. Jasper lies 362km (226 mi.) to the west, a four-hour drive on Hwy. 16. The **Greyhound** and **VIA Rail** stations are downtown. The **airport** sits 29km south of town, a prohibitively expensive cab fare away. The **Sky Shuttle Airport Service** (465-8545 or 888-438-2342) runs a shuttle downtown or to the university for $11 ($18 round-trip). Cheapskates are known to hop on an airport shuttle bus taking travelers to downtown hotels.

Edmonton's street system operates on a simple numerical system. Streets run north-south and avenues run east-west. Almost all streets and avenues are numbered. Street numbers increase to the west, and avenues increase to the north. The first three digits of an address indicate the nearest cross street: 10141 88 Ave. is on 88 Ave. near 101 St. City centre is quite off-center at 105 St. and 101 Ave. The only wrenches in these otherwise smooth works are subset streets (101A St., etc.) and streets known by both names and numbers (Whyte Ave., for instance, is the same as 82 Ave.).

ACCOMMODATIONS

The hostel is the liveliest place to stay in Edmonton, while St. Joseph's College and the University of Alberta provide the budgeteer a bit more privacy. For **B&B** listings, call **Alberta Gem B&B Reservation Agency,** 11216 48 Ave. (434-6098).

Edmonton International Youth Hostel (HI-C), 10422 91 St. (429-0140), off Jasper Ave. Take bus #1, 2, 111, or 120, or plan on a lengthy pedestrian journey from the bus station. The small building, low shower pressure, and squeaky beds make this a rather rustic urban hostel. Call ahead for availability, especially in summer. A/C, common room, snack bar, showers, kitchen, and laundry facilities. Family rooms available. Open daily 8am-midnight. $13, nonmembers $17.

St. Joseph's College (492-7681), on 89 Ave. at 114 St. near the University of Alberta. Take the LRT and get off at University. The rooms here are smaller, quieter, and cheaper than those at the university nearby. Available in summer only. Call ahead; dorms often fill up for concerts and conferences. Library facilities, TV lounge, pool table. Check-in desk open Mon.-Fri. 8:30am-4pm. Full board plan available. Singles $21, weekly $130; single with full board $34, or pay for meals separately: breakfast $3.25, lunch $4.50, dinner $6.50.

University of Alberta (492-4281), on 87 Ave. between 116 and 117 St. on the ground floor of Lister Hall. Generic rooms decorated by the same person who apparently designed every college dorm in Canada (if consistency were a virtue, this mystery designer would be the patron saint of architecture). Weight, steam, and game rooms, dry cleaning, convenience store, and restaurant/bar downstairs. Rooms available late April-Aug.; make reservations. Check-in after 3pm. Singles $27; doubles $36; suites $30-40. Weekly: singles, $162; doubles $218.

YMCA, 10030 102A Ave. (421-9622), close to bus and rail stations. Clean, modern facility in the heart of downtown. Free use of gym and pool facilities included with accommodation fee. Secure 4th-floor rooms (key-only access) available to women and couples. Dorm bunk beds $15 per night, $13 with student ID. 3-night max. stay in dorm. Singles for men $27, women $30; doubles $42-$45. Student rates $85 per week, $235 per month. Accepts Visa, MC.

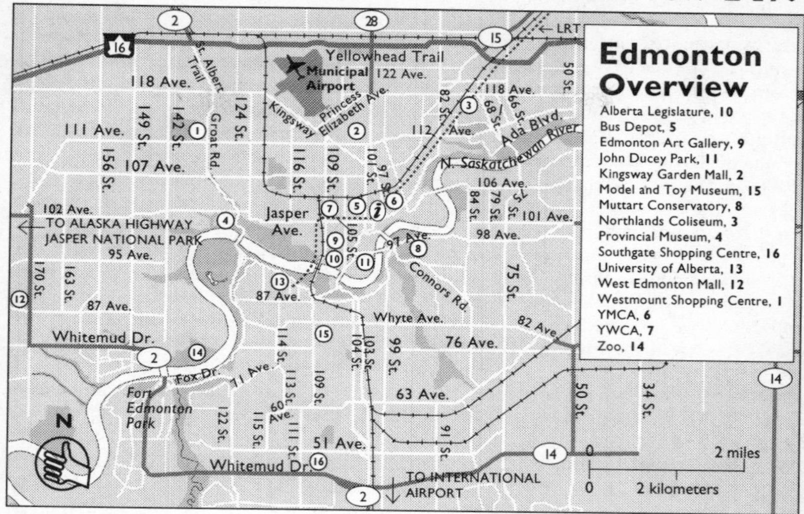

FOOD

Little evidence can be found to support the theory that citizens of the self-labeled "City of Champions" kick off their day with a big bowl of Wheaties. Instead, Edmonton locals swarm into the coffee shops and cafes that have infested the **Old Strathcona** area along Whyte (82) Ave. between 102 and 105 St.

Chianti's, 10501 Whyte (82) Ave. (439-9829). This old Strathcona post office seems to have adopted an Italian postmark, it's so authentic. Chianti's name attests to its lengthy wine lit. Daily specials, large portions, and expanse of pasta, veal, and seafood dishes will ship diners off satisfied (pastas $7-8, $6 Mon.-Tues.; veal $10-11). Open Mon.-Thurs. 11am-11pm, Fri.-Sat. 11am-midnight, Sun. 4-11pm.

Grounds for Coffee and Antiques, 10247 97 St. (429-1920), behind the Edmonton Art Gallery. Is it a coffee shop or is it an antique store? The answer is yes. This precious mom-and-pop shop features coffee and satisfying veggie dishes alongside old furniture and older trinkets. The Mid-Eastern Combo ($3.95) is a favorite among the local clientele. Open Mon.-Fri. 8:30am-5pm, Sat. 10am-5pm.

Dadeo's, 10548A 82 Ave. (433-0930). Good ol' cajun and Louisiana-style food. Try the gumbo ($3.95-$4.95) or a variety of poor boy sandwiches ($6.95-$9.95), particularly appropriate for poor, traveling boys and girls. *Let's Go* recommends the shrimp poor boy. Mmm. Mon.-Thurs. 11:30am-midnight, Fri.-Sat. 11:30am-2am.

Kids in the Hall Bistro, City Hall, 1 Sir Winston Churchill Square (413-8060). This bustin'-out lunchroom in City Hall is truly one-of-a-kind. Every employee, from waiter to chef, is a young person hired as part of a cooperative community service project. Various entrees ($5-$10) and sandwiches ($5-$7). Open daily 7am-5pm.

The Silk Hat, 10251 Jasper Ave. (428-1551), beside the Paramount theater. As old as the hills, but has character. Everything from the big-haired waitstaff to the Rock-Olas (those are jukeboxes to you and me) in every booth says "time warp." The prices are decades behind, too. Two eggs with 2 monstrous pancakes ($2.50). Hamburger Deluxe with fries or potato salad ($4.95). Wacky tea leaf readings 2-7pm. Open Mon.-Fri. 7am-7pm, Sat. 8:30am-7pm, Sun. and holidays 10am-7pm.

SIGHTS

After worshiping at West Edmonton's temple of commercialism, take a breather from the modern world at the refreshing **Fort Edmonton Park** (496-8787) on Whitemud Dr. at Fox Dr. Buses #2, 4, 30, 31, 35, 106, and 315 stop near the park. At the far end of the park sits the fort, a 19th-century "office building" for Alberta's first capitalists, the fur traders of the Hudson's Bay Company. Between the fort and the park entrance are three streets—1885 St., 1905 St., and 1920 St.—bedecked with period buildings from apothecaries to blacksmith shops, all gussied-up to match the streets' respective eras. Costumed schoolmarms and general store owners mingle with visitors, valiantly attempting to bring Edmonton's history to life. (Park open Victoria Day-Labor Day, Mon.-Fri. 10am-4pm, Sat.-Sun. 10am-6pm; $6.75, seniors and ages 13-17 $5Pet the salamanders and hike through birch groves at the **John Janzen Nature Centre** next door to the fort (open Mon.-Fri. 9am-6pm, Sat.-Sun. 11am-6pm, spring Mon.-Fri. 9am-4pm, Sat.-Sun. 11am-6pm, winter Mon.-Fri. 9am-4pm, Sat.-Sun. 1-4pm; free). From the fauna of the Nature Centre, turn to the flora of the **Muttart Conservatory,** 9626 96A St. (496-8755). Buses #1, 83, 88, 106, and 307 whisk you to Muttart. Plant species from around the world vegetate here in the climate-controlled comfort of four ultra-modern glass and steel pyramids. Palm trees and banana plants tower over orchids and hibiscus in the humid Tropical Pavilion ($4.25, seniors and youths $3.25, children $2; open Sun.-Wed. 11am-9pm, Thurs.-Sat. 11am-6pm).

Stargazers and movie lovers alike gather at the **Edmonton Space and Science Centre,** 11211 142 St. (451-3344). The oddly shaped building caters to elementary school students and graduates of all ages. The laser light shows in the largest planetarium dome in Canada challenges media limits, featuring a booming 23,000 watts of audio power. Or catch a flick at the IMAX theater, where short movies turn into real life on a 180° screen. A day pass includes planetarium shows and exhibits and one IMAX film or laser music show ($7, seniors and youths $6, children 3-12 $5; AAA, HI discounts). Check your **email** at the Dow Computer lab (see **Practical Information,** p. 278) or gaze at real stars for free at the **observatory** next to the Science Centre (open daily 1-5pm and 8pm-midnight).

To escape the hubbub of the city hub, hike or bike through the longest stretch of urban parkland in North America, Edmonton's **River Valley.** The valley boasts over 50km of paved multi-use trails (call 496-7275 for info).

Continue your *experience provinçiale* at the **Provincial Museum of Alberta,** 12845 102 Ave. (453-9100), which displays an impressive collection of Albertan animals, vegetables, and minerals. Take bus #1, 2, or 100. A boon to local taxidermists, the habitat exhibit is a better way to get up close and personal with Alberta's larger, more dangerous animals than surprising them in a forest or colliding with them on Hwy. 16. The museum's **Bug Room** is alive with a variety of insect species, some rodent-sized (yum!). (Open Victoria Day-Labor Day Sun.-Wed. 9am-9pm, Thurs.-Sat. 9am-5pm, winter Tues.-Sun.; 9am-5pm $6.50, seniors $5.50, youth $3.)

Edmonton sports a number of tiny museums (telephone history, anyone?), but most fun is the **Old Strathcona Model and Toy Museum,** McKenzie Historic House,

Capitalism's Mothership

A blow against Mother Nature in the battle for tourists, the **West Edmonton Mall** (444-5200) envelops the general area between 170 St. and 87 Ave (take bus #1, 2, 100, or 111). When the largest assembly of retail stores in the galaxy first landed, its massive sprawl of boutiques and eateries seized 30% of Edmonton's retail business, choking the life out of the downtown shopping district. No ordinary collection of stores, the World's Biggest Mall boasts a water park, an amusement park, and dozens of pathetically caged exotic animals, as well as over 800 stores, 110 eating establishments, twice as many submarines as the Canadian Navy, a full-scale replica of Columbus's *Santa Maria,* a 14-story roller coaster, an indoor bungee jumping facility, a casino, and a luxury hotel. You can spend your whole vacation without leaving the Über-Mall's climate-controlled embrace (don't forget the golf course and ice skating rink). To tour Western Alberta without passing through its hallowed halls is almost as insulting as claiming that Canadians drink watery beer. One note of caution: remember where you park. The world's largest mall also has the world's largest parking lot. (Mall open 365 days per year Mon.-Fri. 10am-9pm, Sat. 10am-6pm, Sun. noon-5pm).

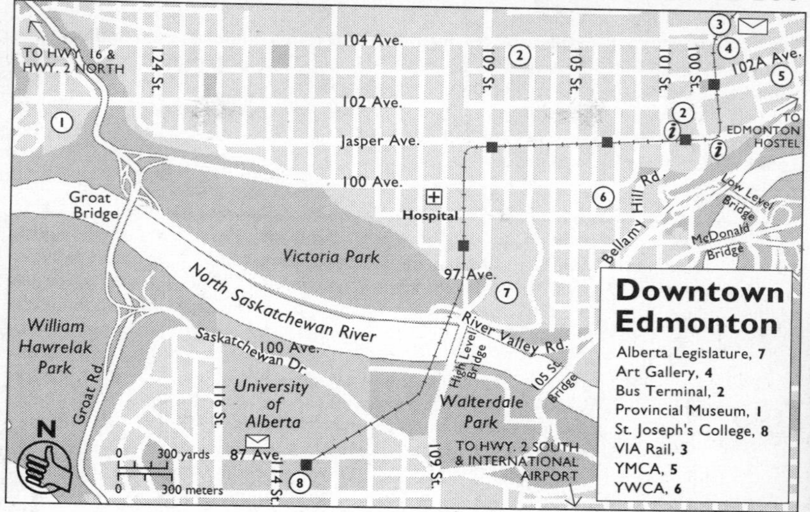

8603 104th St. (433-4512). Take bus #1, 4, 84, 86, or 106 to study over 700 models of monuments including the Taj Mahal, the Titanic, and Sir John A. MacDonald (open Mon.-Tues. 1-5pm, Wed.-Fri. noon-8pm, Sat. 10am-6pm, Sun. 1-5pm; free).

The small **Edmonton Art Gallery,** 2 Sir Winston Churchill Sq. (422-6223), showcases Canadian and Albertan art (open Mon.-Wed. 10:30am-5pm, Thurs.-Fri. 10:30am-8pm, Sat.-Sun. and holidays 11am-5pm; $3, students and seniors $1.50, Thurs. after 4pm free).

NIGHTLIFE AND ENTERTAINMENT

Edmonton nightlife is nearly dead early in the week, with rigor mortis settling in by Wednesday. Come Thursday, though, dead can dance. And drink. Many of the happening clubs are lined up along **Whyte (82) Ave.** in Old Strathcona.

The Billiard Club, 10505 82 Ave. (432-0335), 2nd floor, above Chianti's Restaurant. A busy bar filled with young up-and-comings and some older, already-theres. Ten pool tables plus a mellow back room and outdoor patio for self-contained socializers equals a good time. Open daily 11:30am-3am.

Blues on Whyte, 10329 82 Ave. (439-3981). If blues is what you want, blues is what you'll get. You asked for it. Live blues and R&B bands every night of the week, plus a kickin' Saturday afternoon jam. Don't let the joint's reputation as a biker bar make you blue. Brighten up and boogie down. 8oz. glasses of beer for just $1. Open daily 10am-3am.

Sherlock Holmes, 10341 82 Ave. (453-9676). Also at 10012 101A Ave. (426-7784). Homesick Brits hold support groups over sing-alongs, cigars, and staple English Ales on tap. The 82 Ave. location is young and sharp; downtown is popular with an older crowd. Open daily 11:30am-2am.

Cook County Saloon, 8010 103 St. (432-2665). Bring your hat and your best shitkickers to Edmonton's liveliest country bar. Live music keeps 'em stomping nightly; Thursday-night dance lessons ensure that no one gets hurt in the process. Open Wed.-Sat. 7pm-2am.

Rebar, 10551 82 Ave. (433-3600). Music ranges from alternative to dance. No worries—Rebar hosts the requisite 80s night. Come on, Eileen. Cheap drinks on weekends gather some crowds. Open daily 8pm-2:30am.

Led by Wayne Gretzky, the NHL's **Edmonton Oilers** skated off with five Stanley Cups between 1984 and 1990. The Great One now scores his goals for the New York Rangers, but true to form, Canadians oil up their vocal cords and cheer as loud for their team as they did for their hero. Hockey fans can catch the Oilers from October to May in the **Edmonton Coliseum** (451-8000 for tickets).

For a more cerebral evening, buy tickets to the **Princess Theatre,** 10337 Whyte (82) Ave. (434-6600; $7, seniors and children $3.25). Check the free magazine *See* for theater, film, and music listings.

EVENTS

Edmonton proclaims itself "Canada's Festival City" with celebrations of some kind going on year-round. The **International Jazz City Festival** (432-7166; June 26-July 5, 1998) packs 10 days with club dates and free performances by top international and Canadian jazz musicians. This musical extravaganza coincides with a visual arts celebration called **The Works** (426-2122). At the **International Street Performers Festival** (425-5162; July 10-19, 1998), musical and acting talent combust and burst into a fireball of artistic activity, warming up downtown's Winston Churchill Square. **Klondike Days** (426-4055 or 471-7210; July 16-25, 1998) are Edmonton's answer to the Stampede. In August, Edmonton hosts its **Folk Music Festival** (429-1889; Aug. 6-9, 1998), considered one of the best in North America (*Let's Go* is not sure who does the considering, however). The four-day celebration of blues, bluegrass, and world music takes over Gallagher Park. Only a week later, all the world's a stage on Whyte (82) Ave. for the **Fringe Theater Festival** (448-9000; Aug. 14-23, 1998). When top alternative music and theater pours forth from area parks, theaters, and streets. This celebration is the high point in Edmonton's festival schedule, so many travelers make their way to city simply to find the Fringe.

Whoop it up at one of many hilariously entertaining **small-town rodeos** in the Edmonton area. On any summer weekend there may be several; the $6-10 admission fee is negligible given the quality of competition. Where else can one watch leather-clad contestants grip bleating, bucking sheep or narrowly escape being impaled by enraged bulls? Spain? Well, okay. But these Albertan rodeos are just as fun. Contact **Alberta Tourism Info** (800-661-8888) for a list of cities and towns that hold rodeos.

Yellowhead Highway (16)

The **Yellowhead Highway** stretches 3185km (1911 mi.) across western Canada from Winnipeg, Manitoba to the Pacific Coast and Queen Charlotte Islands. The highway is named after Pierre Bostonais, the Iroquois trapper and guide who led the European traders of the Hudson Bay Company across the Rockies and into the British Columbia interior in 1826. A smidgen of Anglo ancestry lent a light tinge to Bostonais' hair, and the French voyageurs dubbed him *Tete Jaune*—Yellow Head. Lauded as the "less stress, more scenery" route through Alberta and British Columbia, Highway 16 is uncongested and user-friendly, with an increasing number of photo opportunities as the highway moves west. (For Hwy. 16 in British Columbia, see p. 242.) Drivers should pick up a free copy of *Yellowhead It,* a map showing the entire route with distances between major points and a complete listing of campgrounds along the way. The travel guidebook *Yellowhead,* also free, is more substantial, giving a province-by-province, city-by-city account of Hwy. 16's major (and not so major) tourist attractions. For **road conditions** along Hwy. 16, phone 800-222-6501. The **Yellow Emergency Shelter** offers confidential counseling and free accommodations and meals to women and children travelers in distress (800-661-0937; 24hr.).

Within Alberta, the Yellowhead's two lanes, smooth surface, and 110 km per hr. (66 mph) speed limit makes for easy driving. An hour west of Edmonton, amid undulations of farmlands, the town of **Fallis** cowers under a massive radio tower that testifies to the appropriateness of the town's appellation. (*Let's Go* will not comment on the name Uren, Saskatchewan.) Highway 16 briefly acknowledges the sleepy town of **Edson** 189km (118 mi.) west of Edmonton. Except for some good fishing in the surrounding lakes and rivers, the town has little to offer budget travelers.

Farther west, the many "Cold Beer" signs in downtown **Hinton** may distract those lacking the stamina to complete the remaining 70km (44 mi.) to Jasper. Plenty of pike, rainbow and cutthroat trout, dolly varden, and yellow perch lurk in nearby lakes and rivers for hook-happy anglers. Fishing permits are available at local hardware and fishing stores. Consult the *Alberta Guide to Sportfishing* for a detailed listing of stocked lakes, licensing fees, and regulations. The guide and other tourist information is available at the **Tourist Information Centre,** 308 Gregg Ave. (865-2777), downtown (open daily 9am-9pm, winter 10am-5:30pm).

Just west of Hinton, Hwy. 16 begins its long downhill meander toward the floor of the **Athabaskan River Valley** and into **Jasper National Park.** Jasper's scenic splendor drops even the most seasoned mountaineers' jaws. Mesmerized drivers are cautioned to pay close attention to **wildlife warnings** in the park. Jasper's animal inhabitants, including elk, bighorn sheep, and the occasional bear, invariably ignore the man-made paradigm of the highway and choose to graze in roadside ditches. In 1993, 138 large animals (and a fair number of fenders to boot!) were killed in collisions with vehicles. *Reduce your driving speed in the park, especially at night.*

CANADIAN ROCKIES

Jasper National Park

Northward expansion of the Canadian railway system led to the discovery and creation of Jasper National Park—a pot of gold at the end of an industrial rainbow. Established in 1907, Jasper is the largest of the four Canadian Rocky Mountain Parks. Its herculean peaks and plummeting valleys dwarf the battalion of motor homes and charter buses that parades through the region.

Before the Icefields Parkway was built, few travelers dared venture north from Banff into the untamed wilderness of Jasper. Those bushwhackers who braved this bit of the Rockies returned with stunning reports, and the subsequent completion of the Parkway in 1940 paved the way for the masses to appreciate Jasper's astounding beauty. Because 40% of the park is above the treeline, most visitors stay in the protected vicinity of Jasper Townsite. Every summer, with the arrival of the mosquito-bitten tourist brigades, the town's winter population of 5,000 balloons to over 20,000. In the face of this annual bloat, Jasper's permanent residents have struggled to keep their home looking and feeling like a genuine small town. They have mostly succeeded, and have even managed to keep the imitation totem pole at the VIA Rail station turned away from the town in a gesture of good taste. Jasper needs little touristification; the park's heavenly peaks and sweeping vistas do all the work.

PRACTICAL INFORMATION AND ORIENTATION

Visitors Information: Park Information Centre, 500 Connaught Dr. (852-6176). Trail maps and info on all aspects of the park. Open daily 8am-7pm; early Sept.-late Oct. and late Dec.-mid-June 9am-5pm. For further info, write to **Park Headquarters,** Superintendent, Jasper National Park, 632 Patricia St., Box 10, Jasper T0E 1E0 (852-6220).

Trains: VIA Rail (852-4102 or 800-561-8630), with station on Connaught Dr. 3 per week to: Vancouver ($152), Edmonton ($89), and Winnipeg ($242). Seniors and students discount 10%, children 50%. Coin-operated lockers $1 for 24hr.

Buses: Greyhound (852-3926), in the VIA station. To: Edmonton (4 per day; $45), Kamloops ($49), and Vancouver ($91). **Brewster Transportation Tours** (852-3332), in the VIA station. Daily to Banff ($49) and Calgary ($68).

Taxi: Heritage Taxi, 611 Patricia (852-5558) and **Jasper Taxi** (852-3146) both offer a flat rate of $10 between town and Whistler's Hostel, $15-16 to the Maligne Canyon Hostel.

Car Rental: Hertz, 702 Connaught Dr. (852-3888), at Esso West station. $49 per day, 25¢ per km after 100km. Must be 21 with credit card. **Tilden** (852-4972), in the train and bus station. $58 per day with 100 free km. Must be 21 with credit card. $500 insurance deductible for drivers under 25.
Auto Repair: Petro Canada, 300 Connaught Dr. (852-3366). **Shell Canada,** 638 Connaught Dr. (852-3022).
Bicycle Rental: Freewheel Cycle, 618 Patricia Ave. (852-3898). Mountain bikes $6 per hr., $18 per day, $24 overnight. Open in summer daily 9am-8pm; spring and fall daily 9am-6pm. **Jasper International Hostel** (see **Accommodations,** below) rents mountain bikes for $16 per day, $10 per ½day.
Laundry and Showers: Coin Clean, 607 Patricia St. (852-3852). Wash $1.50, 5min. dry 25¢. Showers $2 for 10min. Open daily 8am-9:30pm.
Pharmacy: Whistler Drugs, 100 Miette Ave. (852-4411). Open daily 9am-10pm; early Sept. to mid-June 9am-9pm.
Weather: 852-3185
Road Conditions: 762-1450.
Women's Shelter: 800-661-0937.
AIDS Services: AIDS Society Jasper, 852-5274.
Hospital: 518 Robson St. (852-3344).
Police: 600 Pyramid Lake Rd. (852-4848). **RCMP Emergency:** 852-4848. **Ambulance and Fire:** 852-3100.
Post Office: 502 Patricia St. (852-3041), across from the townsite green. Open Mon.-Fri. 9am-5pm. **Postal Code:** T0E 1E0.
Area Code: 403.

All of the above addresses are in **Jasper Townsite,** near the center of the park. **Highway 16** transports travelers through the northern reaches of the park, while the **Icefields Parkway** (Hwy. 93) connects with Banff National Park in the south. Buses run daily to the townsite from Edmonton, Calgary, Vancouver, and Banff. Trains arrive from Edmonton and Vancouver. Many bike shops rent one-way between Jasper and Banff. Hitching is both easy and popular along the Icefields Pkwy. (*Let's Go* would never even think of recommending hitchhiking.)

ACCOMMODATIONS

Hotels in Jasper Townsite are expensive. The modern Jasper International Hostel just outside of Jasper Townsite anchors a chain of **hostels** that stretches from Jasper to Calgary. The so-called "rustic hostels" farther into the park offer few amenities, but lie oh-so-close to some of Jasper's best outdoor activities. HI-C runs a **shuttle service** connecting all the Rocky Mountain hostels and Calgary with rates from $7 to $59 depending on the distance. For reservations in and info on the Rocky Mountain hostels, call Jasper International Hostel. If you can't get a reservation by phone, you can try for a wait-list bed (available at 6pm). For couples, a **bed and breakfast** may prove more economical than a hostel (doubles in summer $40-75, in winter $30-$55). Most are located in town near the bus and train stations. Ask for the *Private Homes Accommodations List* at the park information centre or the bus depot.

Jasper International Hostel (HI-C) (852-3215), on Sky Tram Rd., 5km south of the townsite off Hwy. 93. Also known as **Whistler's Hostel** just to confuse you. The only hostel in Jasper with running water (read: showers) and electricity, this hostel is often chock-full of gregarious backpackers and cyclists. A "leave-your-hiking-boots-outside" rule keeps the hardwood floors and spiffy dorm rooms spic and span. Play with the marmots who frequent the volleyball court, or chill out with Mika, Western Canada's mellowest dog. Midnight curfew. Accommodates 82 in 2 dorms and 3 private rooms. $15, nonmembers $20.

Maligne Canyon Hostel (HI-C), 11km east of the townsite on Maligne Canyon Rd. Small, recently renovated cabins on the bank of the Maligne River with access to the Skyline Trail. Don't malign this hostel for its gas heat and lack of electricity and running water—Volker, the hostel manager, is on a first name basis with several local bears and is happy to entertain with stories about his large furry friends.

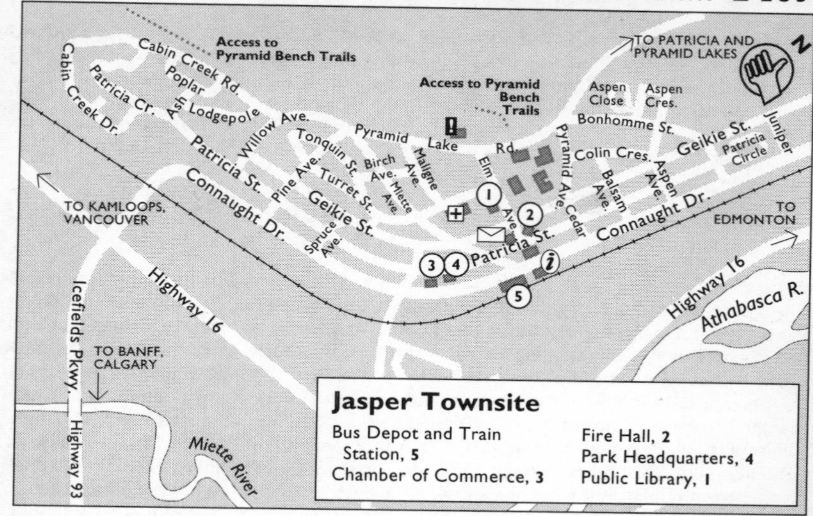

Accommodates 24. $10, nonmembers $15 (winter $9, $14). Fills up quickly; book in advance.

Mt. Edith Cavell Hostel (HI-C), on Edith Cavell Rd., off Hwy. 93A. 32 beds in small but cozy quarters, heated by wood-burning stoves. Propane light, pump water (boil or treat before drinking), and easy access to (surprise, surprise) Mt. Edith Cavell. The road is closed in winter, but the hostel welcomes anyone willing to pick up the keys at the Jasper International Hostel (see above) and ski 13km *uphill* from Hwy. 93A. $10, nonmembers $15 ($9 and $10 in winter).

Athabasca Falls Hostel (HI-C) (852-5959), on Hwy. 93, 32km south of Jasper Townsite. The dining room has electricity, but the only running water around is at Athabasca Falls, a 500m stroll away. Propane heating and lighting. Accommodates 40. $9, nonmembers $14.

Beauty Creek Hostel (HI-C) (852-3215) on Hwy. 93, 87km south of Jasper Townsite. On the banks of the glacier-fed Sunwapta River and close to the Columbia Icefields, the creek has natural beauty to spare. Hike the 3.2km Stanley Falls trail or borrow the canoe for a paddle down the river. 24 beds. $10, nonmembers $15 ($9 and $14 in winter, call Jasper International Hostel for the key). Reservations advised; bicycle touring groups often fill this hostel.

CAMPING

The campsites below are listed from north to south. Most are primitive sites offering few facilities but outdoor paradise nearby. They are first-come, first-served, so get there early or sleep in the trees. For detailed information, call the park information center at 852-6176. To build a fire, add $3 to campsite fees.

Pocahontas, on Hwy. 16, at the northern edge of the park, 46km northeast of the Townsite. The Disney film was named after this very campground. Or not. Closest campground to Miette Hot Springs (see p. 287). Flush toilets, hot running water. Hookups available. Wheelchair access. 140 sites, $13. Open mid-May to early Oct.

Snaring River, 16km north of the townsite on Hwy. 16. Kitchen shelters, dry toilets, splendid views, and even better sounds snare passers-by. Surrender to the nature's soundtrack as the river does its impression of a new age "babbling brook" relaxation tape. 56 sites with 10 walk-in tent sites, $10. Open mid-May to early Sept.

Whistlers, on Whistlers Rd., 3km south of the townsite off Hwy. 93. The closest campground to Jasper Townsite and the only one with full hook-ups: the Mother Jasper campground. The occupants of 781 neighboring sites will keep anyone with wilderness-phobia safe and sound. Showers $1. Wheelchair access, public phone. Tent sites $15, full hookups $22. Open early May to mid-Oct.

Wapiti, on Hwy. 93, 2km south of Whistlers. With 40 electrical hook-ups, Wapiti has become an unofficial RV headquarters. Plentiful brush offers tent campers protection from their land whale-driving neighbors. 366 sites; ask for one close to the Athabasca River. Hot showers $1. Public phone. Sites $15, with electricity $18. Open May 19-23 and early June to early Sept.

Wabasso, on Hwy. 93A, about 17km south of Jasper Townsite. Flush toilets, showers, trailer sewage disposal. Wheelchair access. 238 sites, $13. Open May 19-23, late June to early Sept.

There are five campgrounds along the Icefields Parkway with fairly comparable facilities (kitchen shelters, dry toilets) for a truly comparable price ($10 during late May to early Oct.). Location is the main distinction among them. **Mount Kerkeslin**, 35km south of Jasper Townsite, has 42 sites on the banks of the Athabaska River. **Honeymoon Lake,** about 52km south of town, sports its own swimming area and proximity to Sunwapta Falls (its own swim-here-and-risk-death area). **Jonas Creek,** 77km south of the townsite, is the smallest with only 13 sites along the Sunwapta River. The highlight of the Parkway campgrounds is **Columbia Icefield,** on Hwy. 93, 109km south of the townsite, which lies enough to the Athabasca Glacier to intercept an icy breeze and even a rare summer night's snowfall. A difficult and steep access road makes it RV free, but crowded nonetheless. Two km down the highway, find **Wilcox Creek,** on Hwy. 93, at the southern park boundary (46 sites).

FOOD

Eating inexpensively in Jasper is easy—if you only eat appetizers. **Super A Foods,** 601 Patricia St. (852-3200), satisfies basic grocery needs at a central location (open Mon.-Sat. 8am-11pm, Sun. 9am-10pm). The bakery at **Robinson's IGA Foodliner,** 218 Connaught Dr. (852-3195) makes the extra 10-minute walk worth it (open daily 8am-10pm). **Nutter's,** 622 Patricia St. (852-5844), offers a selection of canned goods, deli meats, and bulk snacks, plus a deli/sub sandwich bar (open daily 9am-11pm).

Jasper Pizza Place, 402 Connaught Dr. (852-3225). A bustling pie shop specializing in wood-oven pizzas (can feed two for $7-$12), cheap burgers, and sandwiches ($2.50-$5.95). With a handful of pool tables and a healthy (but not for livers) supply of liquor, the restaurant turns bar-ish towards the end of the evening. Free delivery (to Jasper International Hostel, for instance) on orders over $5. Open daily 11am-midnight. 10% HI discount.

Miss Italia, 610 Patricia St. (852-4002), 2nd floor. The menu is miss-able; head straight for the blackboard in front, which reveals the hearty—and cheaper—daily specials ($5-$6). 2 eggs, 2 slices bacon, 2 sausages, and 2 pancakes for breakfast ($5). Not 2 shabby. If that's not enough, come back on Wed. from 4-11pm for all-you-can-eat pasta, with soup and salad, for $8. Open daily 7:30am-12:30am.

Scoops and Loops, 504 Patricia St. (852-4333). That this is no ordinary ice cream parlor. Scoops dishes out tasty sandwiches ($3.50-$4.50), pastries ($1.50), sushi ($3-6), *udon* noodles ($8), and oh yes, ice cream, too. No Fruit Loops. Open Mon.-Sat. 10am-11pm, Sun. 11am-10pm.

Mountain Foods and Café, 606 Connaught Dr. (852-4050). In an attempt to live up to its name, Mountain Foods has hung pictures of rock climbers and an actual mountain bike on its walls. Come for breakfast or lunch; extensive selection of sandwiches, salads, and home-cooked goodies. Grilled foccacia sandwich $6. Wraps and burgers, $6. Breakfast $4-6. Open daily 7am-10pm.

EXPLORING THE BACKCOUNTRY

To truly enjoy the Canadian Rockies, stray from the beaten path. Whether on bike, boat, or foot, those who venture farther into the park—if only for a day—will escape crowds and better understand the experiences of early explorers and fur-traders.

An extensive network of trails weaves through Jasper, with many paths originating at the townsite itself. The trails cover three different ecological zones. The **montane zone** blankets the valley bottoms with lodgepole pine, Douglas fir, white spruce, and aspen, and hosts elk, bighorn sheep, and coyotes. Sub-alpine fir and Engelmann spruce share the middle part of the canopy, called the **sub-alpine zone,** with porcupines and marmots. Fragile plants and wildflowers struggle against mountain goats and pikas in the uppermost **alpine zone.** To avoid trampling endangered plant species, hikers should not stray from trails in the alpine area. Kick off any foray into the wilderness with a visit to the information center in the townsite (see p. 283). Experts there distribute free copies of *Day Hikes in Jasper National Park* and can give directions to appropriate hiking and mountain-biking trails. Overnight or multi-day hikers should snatch up a copy of *The Canadian Rockies Trail Guide,* by Brian Patton and Bart Robinson, also available at the information center. Before hitting the trail, ask about road and trail closures as well as water levels (some rivers are impossible to cross at certain times of the year). The **Icefield Centre,** on Hwy. 93 at the southern entrance to the park (see **Icefields Pkwy.,** p. 288), provides similar services.

DAYHIKING, CAVING, AND OTHER ADVENTURES

For those seeking higher altitudes without burning out lungs and quadriceps, the **Jasper Tramway** (852-3093), on Whistler's Road 2km from town, offers a panoramic view of the park as it rises 2km up the side of Whistler's Mountain. The gondola draws packs, which subsequently pack the parking lot ($15, children under 14 $8.50, under 5 free; open April-Aug. 8:30am-10pm, Sept.-Oct. 9:30am-4:30pm). To save pennies, burn calories, and feel studly, hike the steep 7km **Whistler's Trail,** which begins near the Jasper International Hostel. Bring sunglasses and a warm jacket; weather conditions change rapidly at the 2466m summit.

Maligne Lake, the longest (22km) and deepest (97km) lake in Jasper National Park, is the second largest glacier-fed lake in the world and sits just 48km southeast of the townsite at the end of Maligne Lake Rd. You can enjoy every conceivable water sport in Maligne's vivid turquoise waters. (*Let's Go* does not recommend enjoying every conceivable water sport.) **Maligne Tours,** 626 Connaught Dr. (852-3370), offers sea (sit-on-top) kayaking ($15 per hr., 2hr. min.), guided fishing trips, canoeing ($10 per hr.), **horseback riding** ($55 for 3 hr.), guided hiking ($10 per hr.), white water rafting ($55 for 2hr.), and—whew!—1½hr. scenic cruises ($31, seniors $27.50, children $15.50). Several trails permeate the area. Free maps are available at the Maligne Tours office or at the lake. The **Opal Hills Trail** (8.2km loop) winds through subalpine meadows and brings hikers 460m up to views of the lake. Farther north in the valley and 30km east of the townsite, the Maligne River flows into **Medicine Lake,** but, mysteriously, no river flows out. The water escapes underground through tunnels in the porous limestone, re-emerging 16km downstream in the **Maligne Canyon,** 11km east of the Townsite on Maligne Canyon Rd. (This is the longest known underground river in North America. Sneaky, eh?) Shuttle available (852-3370; $8 to Maligne Canyon, $12 to Maligne Lake, one-way; wheelchair accessible).

Named after an English nurse executed by the Germans for providing aid to the Allies during World War I, **Mt. Edith Cavell** is the ending point of Angel Glacier. The switchback road climbs 14.5km to a view of the mountains north face, where the road spits out 2 trails. Take the 1.6km loop **Path of the Glacier** to the top or the hike through **Cavell Meadows.** To find Edith, drive 30km south of the townsite on Mt. Edith Cavell Rd. The road is open from June to October. Several lakes in the region supply a bounty of swimming holes. Locals are known to leap off the cliffs into **Horseshoe Lake.** (*Let's Go* does not recommend jumping off cliffs).

Toast your toes in warmer water at **Miette Hot Springs** (866-3939), north of the townsite off Hwy. 16 along the clearly marked, 15km Miette Hotsprings Rd. The Hot Springs building contains lockers and 3 pools (one is wheelchair accessible; none are especially mesmerizing). Spring water is pumped from the smelly source and journeys through a series of pipes to arrive, miraculously scentless and chlorinated, at the pools. Unfortunately, the 40°C (104°F) water is off-limits in winter ($4, children

$3.50; day passes $7.25, children $6.50; suit rental $1.25, towels $1, lockers 25¢; open May 15-June 20 daily 10:30am-9pm; June 21-Sept. 2 daily 8:30am-10:30pm; Sept. 3-Oct. 14 10:30am-9pm).

Sekani Mountain Tours (852-5337) offers several whitewater rafting trips for $40-80 with discounts to HI members. **Whitewater Rafting (Jasper) Ltd.** (852-7238) offers similar trips from $40; a two-hour trip down the Maligne River costs $48. Register by phone or stop at the Esso station in the townsite. **Rocky Mountain River Guides,** 600 Patricia St. (852-3777), in On-Line Sport and Tackle, offers a three-hour trip ($55) and a calmer Mile 5 ride ($35). **Boat rental** is available at **Pyramid Lake** (852-4900; canoes $10 for 1hr., $7 each additional hr., $25 per day; $20 and a valid ID required for deposit) and **Maligne Lake** (see above).

Fish aren't stocked in National Park waters, but diligent anglers won't go home empty-handed if they can find a previously undiscovered spot. The key to finding a secluded **fishing** hole at Jasper is to hike somewhere inaccessible by car. Rent equipment and get tips on good spots at **Currie's,** in **The Sports Shop,** 414 Connaught Dr. (852-3654; rod, reel, and line $10; one-day boat rental $25, $18 if rented after 2pm, $12 after 6 pm). Permits cost $6 per week, $13 per year, and are available at fishing shops and the Parks Canada information centre.

With so much vertical variance, climbers clamber to get to Jasper. The **Jasper Climbing School,** 806 Connaught Dr. (852-3964), offers an introductory three-hour rappelling class ($25) for those who want to bounce down the imposing cliffs that surround Jasper. Learning how to climb up is more expensive. **Caving** is a little-talked-about and extremely dangerous pursuit, and is not permitted in the national parks without a permit; one should try it only with an experienced guide. Ben Gadd (852-4012), author of *Handbook of the Canadian Rockies,* leads tours to the **Cadomin Caves** and charges $25 per person for groups of 10-20 people. Because these caves are outside the National Park, a permit is not required.

Winter may keep the hot springs off-limits, but hot dogs can warm up on the ski slopes of **Marmot Basin** (852-3816), near Jasper Townsite. A full-day lift ticket costs $39, youths $33, juniors $17, seniors $28. Ski rental is available at **Totem's Ski Shop,** 408 Connaught Dr. (852-3078). A full rental package (skis, boots, and poles) runs $9 per day. Maligne Lake offers cross-country ski trails from late November through May.

■ Icefields Parkway

Begun in the 1930s as a Depression-era relief-work project, the Icefields Parkway (Hwy. 93) is arguably one of the most beautiful highways in North America. With dozens of ominous peaks and glacial lakes skirting the roadside, drivers may struggle to keep their eyes on the 230km road that connects Jasper Townsite in Jasper National Park in the north with Lake Louise in Banff National Park in the south.

Starting Out Parks Canada manages the parkway as a scenic route, so all users must obtain a **Park Pass,** available at entrance gates and park information centres, ($5per day, $35 per yr., includes all Canadian national parks.) Before setting your wheels on the road, pick up a free map of the *Icefields Parkway,* available at park information centres in Jasper and Banff or at the **Icefield Centre** (852-6560), 103km south of Jasper Townsite (open mid-June to Aug. daily 9am-6pm; mid-May to mid-June and Sept. 9am-5pm). Although the centre is closed in winter, the parkway is closed only for plowing after heavy snowfalls.

Thanks to the extensive campground and hostel networks that line the parkway, trips down the entire length of Jasper and Banff national parks are convenient and affordable (see **Accommodations and Camping** under each park). Most sightseers cruise along the parkway in motorized vehicles; an intrepid few choose to cycle. Weather conditions change quite rapidly—cyclists should be prepared for anything. Bicycles can be rented in Banff or Jasper for a one-way trip. Whether on four wheels or two, set aside some time for the parkway, its challenging hikes, and endless vistas.

On the Parkway Pull over at the head of one of 18 **trails** into the wilderness, or stop at one of 22 **scenic points** to take in spectacular views. At **Bow Summit,** one of the parkway's highest points, at 2135m (700 ft.) above sea level, a 10-minute walk leads to a magnificent view of fluorescent aqua **Peyto Lake,** especially vivid towards the end of June. The Icefield Centre, at the boundary between Banff and Jasper, lies in the shadow of the looming **Athabasca Glacier.** This great white whale of an ice flow is the most prominent of the eight major glaciers that flow from the 325 sq. km **Columbia Icefield,** the largest accumulation of ice and snow south of the Arctic Circle. Summer crowds have snowball fights on the vast icefields that flood the sides of the road. **Brewster Transportation and Tours** (762-2241) carries visitors right onto the Athabasca Glacier in monster buses called "Snocoaches" for a 75-minute trip (tours given May-Sept. daily 9am-5pm; Oct. daily 10am-4pm; $22.50, ages 6-15 $5). If you have a bone-chilling curiosity to know the geological history of the mighty Athabasca, sign up for a guided **interpretive hike** (offered mid-June to mid-Sept.). A three-hour hike called "Ice Cubed" costs $28 (ages 7-17 $12); the five-hour "Icewalk Deluxe" is $32 (ages 7-17 $14). The Icefield Centre has info, or write **Athabasca Glacier Icewalks,** attn.: Peter Lemieux, 371042 Ave. Red Deer, AB Canada, T4N 2Z4. Shoulder past the crowds for a warmer alternative: a 13-minute explanatory film inside the centre. For a quick off-road jaunt, try the **Parker Ridge Trail.** The 2.4km hike (one-way) guides trekkers away from the parkway, past the treeline, and over Parker Ridge. At the end, an astounding view of the **Saskatchewan Glacier** flatters those who make the climb. The trailhead is located 1km south of the **Hilda Creek Hostel,** 8.5km south of the Icefields (see **Banff: Accommodations,** p. 291).

■ Lake Louise

The highest community in Canada at 1530m (5018 ft.), Lake Louise and its surrounding glaciers often serve North American filmmakers' need for "Swiss" scenery. Unlike movie crews, most day-tripping visitors spend only enough time at the lake to take a few snapshots. Few stay as long as explorer Tom Wilson, who wrote of Lake Louise in the 1880s, "I never in all my explorations...saw such a matchless scene."

The **Lake Louise Visitor Centre** (522-3833), at Samson Mall, is stuffed with friendly staffers. The brand-new $4.4 million complex is also a museum, with exhibits and a short film on the formation of the Rockies (open daily 8am-8pm, June and Sept. daily 8am-6pm, Oct.-May daily 9am-5pm). Once at the lake, the hardest task is escaping fellow gawkers at the posh Chateau Lake Louise. Renting a canoe from the **Chateau Lake Louise Boat House** (522-3511) can help (open daily 11am-7pm; $24 per hr.). Several hiking trails begin at the water; the 3.6km **Lake Agnes Trail** and the 5.5km **Plain of Six Glaciers Trail** provide especially welcome escape from swarms of lakeside shutterbugs. The **Lake Louise Hostel** (see **Banff: Accommodations,** p. 291) is one of the best deals in Western Canada by far—$18.50 will get you a night in a hostel that's more like a resort. For satisfying grub, make trails to **Laggan's Deli** in Samson Mall (see **Banff: Food,** p. 293).

Nearby **Lake Moraine** has plenty of fans who say it packs more of a scenic punch than its sister Louise. The lake lies in the awesome **Valley of the Ten Peaks,** which cradles glacier-encrusted **Mount Temple.** Join the multitudes on the **Rockpile Trail** for an eye-popping view of the lake and valley, or explore the lake by canoe—rent at Moraine Lake Lodge (522-3733; $22 per hr.). If you don't get a chance to visit Lake Moraine, just get your hands on an old $20 bill; the Valley of Ten Peaks is pictured on the reverse. **Timberline Tours** (522-3743), located off Lake Louise Dr. near Deer Lodge, offers guided horseback rides through the area. A 1½-hour tour costs $28. **Brester Lake Louise Stables,** affiliated with Chateau Lake Louise (522-3511, ext. 1210 or 762-5454 in Banff), gives hourly rides ($20), rides to the Lake Louise Lakehead ($30), and half-day rides ($45-$50). For an even higher vantage point, the **Lake Louise Sightseeing Lift** (522-3555), across the Trans-Canada Hwy. from Lake Louise, runs up Mt. Whitehorn, providing yet another chance to gape at the landscape (runs early June 9am-6pm, June 16-Oct. 9am-9pm, early Sept. 9am-6pm; $9.50, seniors and students $8.50, youth 6-15 $6.50, 5 and under free). An early morning ride yields a $10.50 breakfast (includes lift ticket) at the peak-top cafe. In winter, the sightseeing lift becomes one of 11 ski lifts of the **Lake Louise Ski Area** (522-3555), which boasts 85 trails for skiers and snowboarders.

Banff National Park

With 6,641 sq. km (2,564 sq. mi.) of peaks, forests, glaciers, and alpine valleys, Banff is Canada's best-loved and best-known natural preserve. Originally called Rocky Mountains National Park, it soon took the name Banff, after Banffshire, Scotland, the birthplace of two financiers of the Canadian Pacific Railway. These officers convinced Canada's first Prime Minister Sir John A. MacDonald of Banff's potential for "large pecuniary advantage," telling him, "since we can't export the scenery, we shall have to import the tourists." Their plan worked with a vengeance. Streets littered with gift shops, clothing outfitters, and equipment rental stores cannot mar Banff's priceless beauty. Japanese tour buses and transient 20-somethings come equipped with mountain bikes, climbing gear, skis, and snowboards, but a trusty pair of hiking boots remains the park's most popular outdoor equipment.

PRACTICAL INFORMATION AND ORIENTATION

Visitors Information: Banff Visitors Centre, 224 Banff Ave. (762-1550). Includes **Banff/Lake Louise Tourism Bureau** (762-8421) and **Canadian Parks Service** (762-1550). Open daily 8am-8pm, Oct.-May 9am-5pm. **Lake Louise Information Centre** (522-3833). Open daily 8am-8pm, June and Sept. 8am-6pm, Oct.-May 9am-5pm. Both centres dispense detailed maps and brochures, and provide info on hiking and biking, restaurants, activities, and accommodations.

Tours: Brewster Transportation, 100 Gopher St. (762-6767), near the train depot. Monopoly on tours of the area; runs to: Jasper (1 per day, $49); Lake Louise (3 per day, $10); and Calgary (4 per day, $34). Depot open daily 7:30am-10pm.

American Express: Brewster Travel, 317 Banff Ave., upstairs in the Cascade Mall. Box 1140, Banff T0L 0C0 (762-3207). Holds mail free of charge for card members. Open Mon.-Fri. 8am-6pm, Sat. 9:30am-5pm.

Buses: Greyhound, 100 Gopher St. (800-661-8747). 4 per day to: Lake Louise ($10); Calgary ($18); and Vancouver ($99). HI discount.

Public Transportation: The **"Happy Bus"** runs 2 routes, 1 from the Banff Springs Hotel to the trailer court on Tunnel Mountain Rd., the other from the Tunnel Mountain Campground through downtown to the Banff Park Museum ($1, children 50¢). Exact change required to keep the happy bus happy. Runs summer 6:45am-midnight; call for winter hours.

Taxis: Banff Taxi, 726-4444. 24hr. **Taxi Taxi,** 762-3111.

Car Rental: Banff Used Car Rentals (762-3352), in the Shell Station at the junction of Wolf and Lynx. $36 per day, 10¢ per km after 100km. Must be 21 with a major credit card. **Budget,** 204 Wolf St. (762-4565). $46 per day, 18¢ per km after 100km. Must be 21 with major credit card.

Bike Rental: Bactrax Rentals, 337 Banff Ave. (762-8177), in the Ptarmigan Inn. Mountain bikes $7 per hr., $25 per day. Open daily 8am-8pm. Performance Ski and Sport (see below) rents bikes one-way to Jasper. Call for prices. HI discount.

Equipment Rental: Performance Ski and Sport, 208 Bear St. (762-8222). Rents everything from tents ($12 per day) to canoes ($10 per hr.) to fishing gear ($10-20 per day). 10% discount for HI members. Also sells gear. Open daily 9am-8pm.

Laundry: Cascade Coin Laundry, 317 Banff Ave. (762-0165), downstairs in the Cascade Mall. Wash $2, 6min. dry 25¢. Open daily 8am-11pm. **Lake Louise Laundromat** (522-2143), Samson Mall. $2 wash, 7min. dry 25¢. Showers $4. Open daily 9am-9pm.

Weather: 762-2088.

Road Conditions: 762-1450.

Pharmacy: Harmony Drug, 111 Banff Ave. (762-5711). Open daily 9am-9pm.

Hospital: Mineral Springs, 316 Lynx St. (762-2222), near Wolf St.

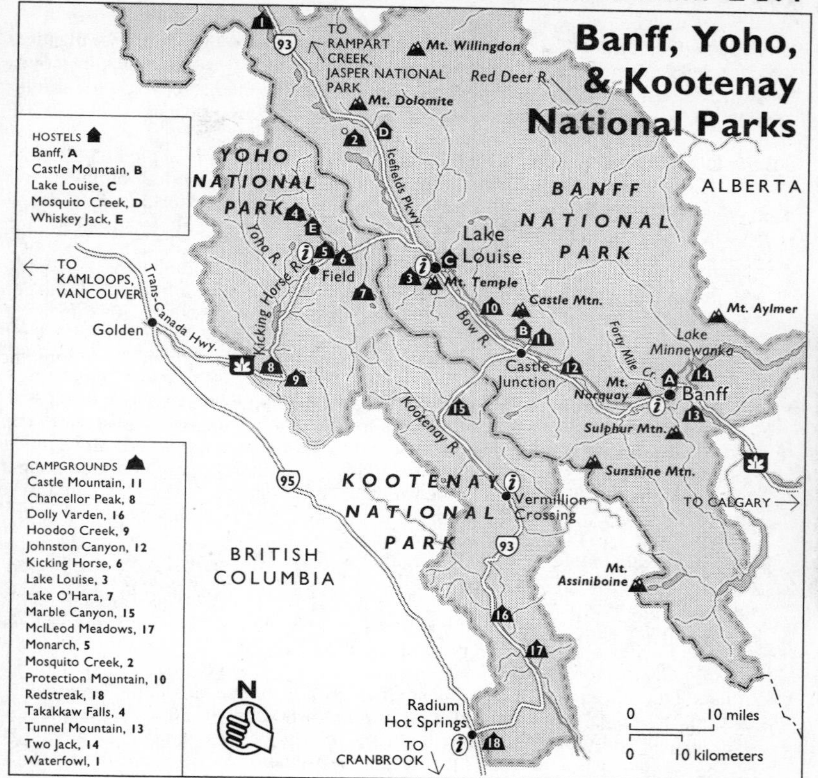

Emergency: Banff Warden Office (762-4506), **Lake Louise Warden Office** (522-3866). Open 24hr. **Police:** (762-2226; non-emergency 762-2228), on Railway St. by the train depot. **Lake Louise Police:** 522-3811.

Post Office: 204 Buffalo St. (762-2586). Open Mon.-Fri. 9am-5:30pm. **Postal Code:** T0L 0C0.

Area Code: 403.

Banff National Park hugs the Alberta-British Columbia border, 129km west of Calgary. The **Trans-Canada Highway** (Hwy. 1) runs east-west through the park, connecting it to **Yoho National Park** on the west side. **Icefields Parkway** (Hwy. 93) connects Banff with **Jasper National Park** to the north and **Kootenay National Park** to the southwest. Greyhound links the park to major points in Alberta and British Columbia. Civilization in the park centers around the towns of Banff and Lake Louise, 58km northwest of Banff on Hwy. 1. The **Bow Valley Parkway** (Hwy. 1A) parallels Hwy. 1 from Lake Louise to 8km west of Banff.

ACCOMMODATIONS

Finding a cheap place to stay in Banff is easy...if you reserve ahead. Residents of the townsite offer rooms in their own homes, often at reasonable rates, especially in the off-season. Check the list in the back of the *Banff and Lake Louise Official Visitors Guide,* available free at the Banff Information Centre. Mammoth modern hostels at Banff and Lake Louise anchor a chain of hostels spanning from Calgary to Jasper. The "rustic hostels" provide a more intense wilderness experience, and are often a stone's throw away from the best hiking and cross-country skiing in the park. HI-C runs a shuttle service connecting all the Rocky Mountain hostels and Calgary with rates from $9 to $59, depending on the trip length. Wait-list beds become available at 6pm for hostelers who can't get reservations, and six stand-by beds are saved for shuttle arrivals. For reservations at any rustic hostel, call Banff International at 762-4122.

Banff International Hostel (BIH) (HI-C), Box 1358, Banff T0L 0C0 (762-4122), 3km from Banff Townsite on Tunnel Mountain Rd., nestled amid condominiums and lodges. According to HI, it's one of the top 10 hostels in the world (number 6, to be precise). This heaven of a hostel has the look and feel of a ski lodge—2 lounge areas, 1 with a large fireplace, a game room with a pool table, and a hectic kitchen area. Each of the 4-8 beds per room (in bunks) has its own reading light, and many rooms have desks. Take the Happy Bus from downtown, or join the many other hostelers hoofing it. Cafe, laundry facilities, spacious hot showers with the gift of great water pressure. Accommodates 154. Private rooms available. Linen $1.50. Ski and snowboard storage area and workshop. Open 24hr., no curfew. $18, nonmembers $22. Wheelchair accessible.

Lake Louise International Hostel (HI-C) (522-2200), ½km west of Samson Mall in Lake Louise Townsite, on Village Rd. Not to be outdone by neighboring Banff, the Lake Louise hostel is ranked 3rd in the world by HI. And rightly so. More like a hotel than a hostel, this budget resort boasts a reference library, common rooms with open, beamed ceilings, a stone fireplace, 2 (yes 2) full kitchens, a sauna, ski/bike workshops, and a fully licensed cafe. Large rooms with 2, 4, and 6 beds. Accommodates 155. $19.50, nonmembers $23.55.

Castle Mountain Hostel (HI-C) (762-4122), on Hwy. 1A, 1½km east of the junction of Hwy. 1 and Hwy. 93 between Banff and Lake Louise. A quieter alternative for those seeking refuge from the hubbub of the Banff and Lake Louise Hostels. With running water and electricity, the hostel's 36 beds fill quickly. Relaxed common area has a general store and firepit. $11, nonmembers $15.

Mosquito Creek Hostel (HI-C), 103km south of the Icefield Centre and 26km north of Lake Louise. Across babbling Mosquito Creek from the Mosquito Creek campground, the hostel has a view of tents and motorhomes. Proximity to Wapta Icefield and its wood-burning sauna make up for the not-so-scenic company. Full-service kitchen, gas, and heat. 2 private rooms available. $11, nonmembers $15.

Rampart Creek Hostel (HI-C), 34km south of the Icefield Centre. Oh-so-close to several world-famous ice climbs (including Weeping Wall, 17km north), this hostel is a favorite for winter mountaineers. Accommodates 30 in rustic cabins. Sauna, full service kitchen, wood-heated bathtub. $10, nonmembers $14.

Hilda Creek Hostel (HI-C), 8½km south of the Icefield Centre. Perfectly perched at the base of Mt. Athabasca. Some of the Icefield's best hiking and skiing lie just beyond on Parker Ridge. Sauna, full-service kitchen. Manager sells groceries. Propane heat and light. 21 beds. $10, nonmembers $15.

CAMPING

As with the hostels, a chain of campgrounds connect Banff to Jasper, and large, fully hooked-up grounds serve as anchors. To avoid a stampede of RVs, try one of the primitive sites farther from Banff and Jasper Townsites. These campgrounds don't take reservations, so show up early. Proximity to sights in the park defines each campground; choose accordingly. The camps below are listed from south to north.

Tunnel Mountain Village, 4km from Banff Townsite on Tunnel Mountain Rd. With 3 separate grounds and over 1000 sites, it takes a village to out-size this campground. The trailer ground has 322 sites (full hookups, $22). Village 2 has 188 sites (power only, $19). Village 1 houses a whopping 622 sites ($16, no hookups or flush toilets). All have showers. Village 2 is open all year; all others closed in winter.

Two Jack, 13km northeast of Banff, across the Trans-Canada Hwy. Two Jack has 2 separate grounds—the main grounds ($13) have no showers, while the Lakeside grounds ($16) provide showers and proximity to Two Jack Lake. A good place to fry up some (two?) flapjacks. Open mid-May through Aug.

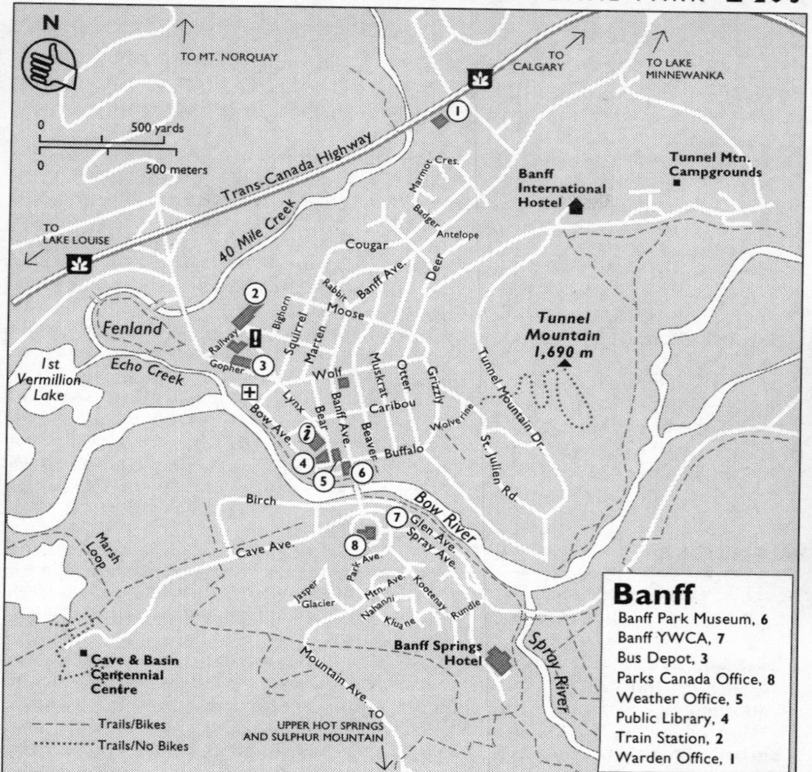

Johnston Canyon, 26km northwest of Banff on Hwy. 140. 140 sites with access to several trails. Located on the Bow Valley Pkwy. (Hwy.1A), the scenic route connecting Banff and Lake Louise. Showers. Open mid-May to mid-Sept.

Castle Mountain, midway between Banff and Lake Louise along Hwy. 1A. 44 sites close to relatively uncrowded hiking. Unserviced (no flush toilets, no showers). $13. Open late June-Aug.

Protection Mountain, 11km west of Castle Junction on Hwy. 1A. 89 spacious and wooded sites in one of Banff's most primitive campgrounds. Pit toilets, no showers. $13. Open late June-Aug.

Lake Louise, 1½km southeast of Samson Mall on Fairview Rd. Not actually on the lake, but plenty hiking and fishing awaits nearby. 189 trailer sites (open year-round; electricity only, $18). 220 tent sites (open mid-May through Sept.; $14).

Mosquito Creek, 103km south of the Icefield Centre and 26km north of Lake Louise. 32 sites with immediate hiking access. Dry toilets. $10. Open year-round.

Waterfowl, 57km north of Hwy. 1 on Hwy. 93. 116 sites near the Waterfowl lakes. Flush toilets but no water. $13. Open mid-June to mid-Sept.

Rampart Creek, 147km north of Banff, 40km south of the Icefield Centre. 50 sites across the highway from the Rampart Creek hostel. No showers or flush toilets. $10. Open mid-June through Aug.

FOOD

Restaurants in Banff generally serve expensive, mediocre food. Luckily, the Banff and Lake Louise International Hostels serve affordable meals for $3-8. For a safe bet on groceries, shop at **Safeway** (762-5378), at Marten and Elk St., just off Banff Ave. (open daily 8am-11pm; winter 9am-9pm). Some local bars offer reasonable daily specials.

Jump Start, 206 Buffalo St. (762-0332). This small, home-cookin' coffee shop and sandwich place makes a big bang for the buck. All varieties of coffee, soups ($3.75), sandwiches ($5), and a rib-sticking shepherd's pie ($5.50). Open Mon.-Fri. 7am-7pm.

Aardvark's, 304A Caribou St. (762-5500). This small pizza place does big business after the bars close. Skinny on seating, but thick slices of toppings-loaded pizza make this a phat place to eat. Slices $2.75. Small $6-8, large $12-19. Buffalo wings $5 for 10. HI discount. Open daily 11am-4am.

Laggan's Deli (522-3574), in Samson Mall at Lake Louise. Savor a thick sandwich on whole-wheat bread ($3.75) with a Greek salad ($1.75), or take home a freshly baked loaf ($2) for later. Excellent cappuccino ($2.50). Always crowded; there's nowhere better in Lake Louise Village. Open daily 6am-8pm.

Magpie & Stump, 203 Caribou St. (762-4067), at Bear St. Named after a London pub, Magpie & Stump fills up the famished with large portions of spicy Mexican food. A dark, all-wood interior and constant mariachi music packs 'em in latenight with a happy hour from 10pm-2am. Try the loco-gringo salad ($7), quesadillas ($6-7), or any of the meal-sized nachos ($5-7). 15 flavors of margaritas ($3.55). Veggie dishes galore. Open daily noon-2am.

Btfsplk's Diner, 221 Banff Ave. (762-5529). A clssc dnr, wth blck nd wht tl flr nd rd ptnt lthr. Meal-size Caesar salads ($7.25) and BBQ burgers ($7). Yummy desserts. Open daily 8am-10pm.

NIGHTLIFE

Bartenders maintain that Banff's true wildlife is in its bars. Check the paper to find out which nightspots are having "locals night," when bar-hoppers flock to cheap drinks.

Rose and Crown, 202 Banff Ave. (762-2121), upstairs. Even on busy nights, the Rose's enormity gives guzzlers elbow room. Throw back a few in the couch-adorned "living room" while cooing to nearly nightly live music. Happy hour (Mon.-Fri. 4:30-7:30pm) heralds $3-3.50 drafts. Open daily 11am-2am.

Barbary Coast, 119 Banff Ave. (762-4616), upstairs. Sports paraphernalia bedecks this snazzy bar. The kitchen itself is an excellent restaurant (pasta dishes are quite good). Look for lunch specials ($6-7). Nightly live blues and rock. Mon. is pizza night ($7 for a 10in.); happy hour 4:30-7:30pm. No cover. Open daily 11am-2am.

Outa Bounds, 137 Banff Ave. (762-8434), lower level. This is the place for those lookin' to knock some boots or cut some rug. Descend down dark, black-lit stairs to a raging room decked out with 2 bars, 3 pool tables ($1.25), a dance floor, and plenty of in-bounds seating. Arrive early on weekends and special nights (locals Wed., ladies' night Thurs.) to avoid lines. Open daily 8pm-2:30am.

SIGHTS AND EVENTS

The palatial **Banff Springs Hotel** (762-2211), on Spray Ave., overlooks town. Ride the guest elevator up to the 8th floor to see what those who can afford to stay here see. You can enjoy a Centennial Ale (the hotel's own brew), a basket of bread, and a view-of-views for $4.55 at the **Rundle Lounge** on the mezzanine level. In summer, the hotel offers guided tours of the grounds (daily 5pm; $5). The hotel also offers horseback riding (daily 9am-5pm; $26 for 1hr., $55 for 3hr.; for reservations call 762-2848).

A tour of Banff's small museums could fill a full snowy day. The **Whyte Museum of the Canadian Rockies,** 111 Bear St. (762-2291), offers a gander at the history of (surprise) the Canadian Rockies. Exhibits in the museum's **Heritage Gallery** explain how Banff grew: very rapidly, unchecked, and catering to the whims of wealthy guests (open mid-May to mid-Sept. daily 10am-6pm; $3, seniors and students $2, children free). The **Banff Park Museum** (762-1558), on Banff Ave. near the bridge, is a taxidermist's dream. Clippings in the reading room recount in loving detail violent encounters between elk and automobiles (open June-Aug. daily 10am-6pm, tours at 11am and 3pm; Sept.-May 10am-5pm, tours 3pm; $2.25, seniors $1.75, children $1.25).

In summer, the **Banff Festival of the Arts** takes over. The culture train trucks through during June, July, and August with a series of performances in tow; stop by the infocentre for a schedule (762-6300; prices vary from free-$27).

OUTDOORS

A visitor sticking to paved byways will only see 3% of Banff National Park. That's not enough. To truly make the park's acquaintance, hike or bike through the other 97% on more than 1600km of trails. Grab a copy of *Banff and Vicinity Drives and Walks* at infocentres. For more privacy, tread to the **backcountry,** away from the islands of civilization. Pick up the *Backcountry Visitors Guide* and a **permit** for overnight camping ($6 per person per day, up to $30 per person, or $42 per year) at the information centres (see **Practical Information,** above).

Two easy trails lie within walking distance of Banff. **Fenland** (closed for elk calving in late spring and early summer) winds 2km through an area shared by beaver, muskrat, and waterfowl. Follow Mt. Norquay Rd. out of Banff and look for signs across the tracks on the left side of the road. The summit of **Tunnel Mountain** provides a spectacular view of the Bow Valley and Mt. Rundle. Follow Wolf St. east from Banff Ave. and turn right on St. Julien Rd. to reach the head of the steep 2.3km trail.

About 25km out of Banff toward Lake Louise along the Bow Valley Pkwy. (Hwy. 1A), **Johnston Canyon** is a popular half-day hike. A catwalk along the edge of the canyon runs 1km to the canyon's lower falls, then another 2.7km to the upper falls. The trail then continues for another, more rugged, 3.1km to seven blue-green cold water springs known as the **Inkpots.** The trail beyond the inkpots is blissfully untraveled.

Many routes in the Banff area make for stunning drives. **Tunnel Mountain Drive** begins at Banff Ave. and Buffalo St. and proceeds 9km past Bow Falls and up the side of Tunnel Mountain. Several markers along the way point out views of the Banff Springs Hotel, Sulphur Mountain, and Mt. Rundle. Turn right onto Tunnel Mountain Rd. to see the **hoodoos,** long, finger-like limestone projections once part of the cliff wall and thought by indigenous Canadians to encase sentinel spirits.

Bicycling is permitted on public roads and highways and on certain trails in the park. Spectacular scenery and proximity to a number of hostels and campgrounds make the Bow Valley Parkway (Hwy. 1A) and the Icefields Parkway (Hwy. 93) perfect for extended cycling trips. **Mountain biking** is extremely popular. Every other store downtown seems to rent bicycles; head to **Bactrax** or **Performance Ski and Sport** (see **Practical Information,** above) for HI discounts. Parks Canada publishes *Mountain Biking-Banff* (free at bike rental shops and info centres), which describes trails where bikes are permitted.

You Are in Bear Country

Bear sightings are common in the Canadian Rockies, but one black bear took it upon himself to give the many residents of Banff an uncommon reminder of whose park it really is. Affectionately known as **Bear 16,** this furry beauty moved into town, disrupting everyday activity by grazing on front lawns and lying in the road, unwittingly blocking traffic. Bear 16 crossed the line when the scent from a bakery lured him too close to human territory. At the behest of scared bakers, park staff removed Bear 16 from the park, had him castrated, and plunked him down in the Calgary Zoo.

While most travelers to the park are eager to see its wildlife, few want as intimate a contact as Bear 16 offered. As a defense, many hikers carry **bear bells,** ranging from jinglers to mighty sleigh bells. While such devices offer psychological security, park officials suggest that the safest bet is to talk or sing loudly while hiking, especially near running water. One Banff official recommends regular yodelling as a way of warning nearby animals of your presence. In actuality, the number of bear attacks ranks low among the total number of attacks by park wildlife—dozens of visitors are bitten each year by pesky rodents pursuing hikers' food. Humans, however, are by far the most dangerous of Banff predators—road accidents are the most common cause of death within the park.

Banff might not exist if not for the **Cave and Basin Hot Springs,** once rumored to have miraculous healing properties. The **Cave and Basin National Historic Site** (762-1557), a refurbished resort built circa 1914, is now a museum that screens documentaries and stages exhibits. Follow the **Discovery Trail** from the museum to see the original spring discovered over 100 years ago by three Canadian Pacific Railway workers. The site is southwest of the city on Cave Ave. (open daily summer 9am-6pm, winter 9:30am-5pm; $2.25, seniors $1.75, children $1.25; tours meet at 11am). For an actual dip in hot spring water, follow the rotten-egg smell to the **Upper Hot Springs pool** (762-1515), a 40°C (104°F) sulphurous cauldron up the hill on Mountain Ave. A soak in the pool is relaxing, but soaks wallets, too (open daily 9am-11pm; call for winter hours; $7, seniors and children $6; towels $1, lockers 25¢). Take the moderate 5.3km (2hr.) hike along the well-trodden trail to the peak of **Sulphur Mountain,** where a spectacular view awaits, and the **Sulfur Mountain Gondola** charges nothing for the trip downhill. The gondola runs trips to the top, too—for a price (runs daily; $12, ages 5-11 $6, under 5 free). The **Summit Restaurant** (762-5438), perched atop Sulfur Mountain, serves an $8 breakfast buffet.

Brewster Tours (762-6767) offers an array of guided bus tours within the park. Without a car, these tours may be the only way to see some of the main attractions, such as the Great Divide, the Athabasca Glacier, and the spiral railroad tunnel. The regular Brewster bus from Banff to Jasper ($49) charges only $30 more to see the sights in between (one-way 9½hr., $79; round-trip 2 days, $109; tour of the Columbia Icefields, $22.50 extra; tickets available at the bus depot).

For those who'd rather look up at the mountains than down from them, the nearby lakes provide a serene vantage point. **Fishing** is legal virtually anywhere there's water, but live bait and lead weights are not. Get a fishing **permit** at the information centre (7-day permit $6, annual permit valid in all Canadian National Parks $13). The 7km trail to **Borgeau Lake** offers hiking and fishing with some privacy—and a particularly feisty breed of brook trout. Or, closer to the road, try **Herbert Lake,** off the Icefields Pkwy., or **Lake Minnewanka,** on Lake Minnewanka Rd., northeast of Banff, rumored to be the home of a half-human, half-fish Indian spirit. Lake Minnewanka Rd. also passes **Johnson Lake,** where sunlight warms the shallow water to a swimmable temperature. Several companies offer **whitewater rafting** trips along the **Kicking Horse River. Western Canadian Whitewater** (762-8256) gives full-day trips ($65, students with ID $45). **Hydra River Guides** (762-4544 or 800-644-8888) also offers daytrips ($65, $60 for HI members).

All this fun doesn't stop when the snow starts. Wintery Banff offers more than curling: snow sports range from dogsledding to ice climbing to ice fishing. The most obvious and popular activity is **skiing.** Those 1600km of summer hiking trails also provide exceptional cross-country skiing while **Sunshine Mountain** (762-6500), **Mount Norquay** (762-4421), and **Lake Louise** (522-3555) divide the downhill crowd. **Performance Ski and Sports,** 208 Bear St. (762-8222), rents downhill skis ($17 per day, 3 days $45), cross-country skis ($12, $31), snowboards ($28, $74), telemarking skis and boots ($18, $47), and snowshoes ($10, $26).

Kootenay National Park

Kootenay National Park hangs off the continental divide on the southeast edge of British Columbia. Almost all visitors trek through Kootenay to get to or from Banff National Park on the majestic Banff-Windermere Highway (Hwy. 93). The highway, running the length of Kootenay, is a magnificent drive, but it barely scratches the park's surface. Kootenay's best feature is what it doesn't have: people. Stately conifers, alpine meadows, and pristine peaks and rivers hide in Banff's shadow, eagerly awaiting the enlightened traveler who will spend some time in Kootenay discovering the solitude and beauty of the Canadian Rockies.

Practical Information The **Kootenay National Park Information Centre** (347-9505), on the park's western boundary at the Radium Hot Spring Pool Complex, hands out free maps, as well as a $1 backcountry hiking guide (free with purchase of a backcountry permit; open daily 9am-7pm; call for off-season hours). The **Park Administration Office** (347-9615), on the access road to Redstreak Campground (see **Accommodations, Camping, and Food,** below), gives out the same guide for free (open Mon.-Fri. 8am-noon and 1-4pm). **Greyhound** buses stop at the **Esso** station, 7507 W. Main St. (347-9726; open daily 7am-11pm), at the junction of Hwy. 93 and Hwy. 95 in Radium Hot Springs, just outside the park. Daily service runs the length of the Banff Windermere Hwy. to Banff ($19) and Calgary ($34). For an **ambulance,** call 342-2055. The nearest hospital is **Windermere District Hospital** (342-9201), in Invermere. For after-hour **emergencies,** call (403) 762-4506. Call the **police** in Invermere at 342-9292, and in Radium Hot Springs at 347-9393. The **post office** (347-9460) is on Radium St. in Radium Hot Springs (open Mon.-Fri. 8:30am-5pm; **Postal Code:** V0A 1M0). The **area code** is 250.

Kootenay lies southwest of Banff and Yoho National Parks. Highway 93 runs through the park from the Trans-Canada Hwy. in Banff to Radium Hot Springs, at the southwest edge of the park where it joins Hwy. 95 to run 143km south to Cranbrook.

Accommodations, Camping, and Food The park's flagship campground is **Redstreak,** with 242 sites, flush toilets, showers, firewood, playgrounds, and swarms of RVs. Look elsewhere for seclusion, although walk-in sites off Loop "D" offer some escape from company. From BC, take the access road that departs Hwy. 95 near the south end of Radium Hot Springs. The campground no longer takes reservations, so arrive early to secure a spot among the crowds (open mid-May to mid-Sept.; $16, full hookup $21). **McLeod Meadows,** 27km north of the West Gate entrance on Hwy. 93, offers more solitude, 98 wooded sites, plenty of elbow room, and few RVs ($13; open mid-May to mid-Sept.). **Marble Canyon,** 86km north of the West Gate entrance, also provides more privacy than its big brother down the road (61 sites, $13; open mid-June through Aug.). In winter, snag one of seven free sites at the **Dolly Varden** picnic area, 36km north of the West Gate entrance and frolic with free firewood, water, toilets, and a kitchen shelter. Free camping outside the park is plentiful in the nearby Invermere Forest district; ask the staff at the info centre for details. Seek refuge from the outdoors at the **Columbia Motel,** 4886 St. Joseph St. (347-9557), which offers clean rooms and some of the lowest rates in town ($45-50, $5 extra for rooms with kitchen).

There is no affordable food in the park; the town of Radium (insert radioactive food joke here) supports a few uninspiring eateries conveniently located within feet of each other on Main St. The restaurant at the **Husky** station, at the junction of Hwy. 93 and Hwy. 95 (347-9811), offers the greasiest, but most cost-efficient food in town (measured in calories per dollar) short of a 5 lb. bag of sugar (open daily 7am-10:30pm). If you decide to go with the sugar, get it at **Radium Foods,** 7546 Main St. E (347-9600; open Mon.-Sat. 9am-8pm, Sun. 10am-7pm).

Outdoors Kootenay National Park's main attraction is **Radium Hot Springs** (347-9485), the complex of pools responsible for the congested traffic and towel-toting tourists just inside the West Gate entrance to the park. The complex contains two pools—a hot pool for soaking (40°C/104°F) and a cooler swimming pool (27°C/81°F). Check out the scene from the deck above for free before making an investment (open daily 9am-10:30pm, winter noon-9pm; $5, seniors and children $4.50, winter 50¢ less; lockers 25¢, towel rental $1, suit rental $1.25).

The 95km **Banff-Windermere Highway** (Hwy. 93) forms the backbone of scoliosis-afflicted Kootenay. Stretching from Radium Hot Springs to Banff, the highway follows the **Kootenay** and **Vermilion Rivers,** with views of glacier-enclosed peaks, dense stands of virgin forest, and glacial-green rivers. The wild landscape of the Kootenay River valley remains stunning and unblemished but for this ribbon of road.

For most visitors, the park experience ends with the drive up Hwy. 93, where a handful of short trails lead right off the highway. One of these runs along **Marble Canyon,** about 15km from the Banff border. The 750m trail traverses a remarkably deep, narrow gorge cut by Tokumm Creek. Don't miss this unique geologic feature or the voluminous falls at the end of the trail. Another tourist-heavy trail is the 1.6km, 30-minute **Paint Pots Trail,** leaving Hwy. 93 3.2km south of Marble Canyon. This wheelchair-accessible trail leads to sunset-red springs rich in iron oxide. Local native Canadians quarried ochre from this oxide to make tipi and body paints. Bounce on the suspension bridge over the Vermilion River, and enjoy a picture-perfect view.

Beyond the self-guided trails, Kootenay's myriad of **hiking** trails are blissfully uncrowded. An easy dayhike, the **Stanley Glacier Trail** starts 2.5km north of Marble Canyon and leads 4.8km into a glacier-carved valley, ending 1.6km from the foot of Stanley Glacier, which gouged out the valley. For the more adventurous day-hiker, the awe-inspiring loop-hike over **Kindersley Pass** is an experience not soon forgotten. The 16.5km hike climbs more than 1000m and can tire even the most sure-footed, but the rewards are well worth it: views of the Columbia River Valley to the west and the crest of the Rockies to the east. The two trailheads at either end of the route, **Sinclair Creek** and **Kindersley Pass,** are less than 1km apart on Hwy. 93, about 15km inside the West Gate entrance.

Many longer backpacking routes cross the **backcountry.** One popular route is the four-day jaunt along the **Rockwall Trail** from Floe Lake to Helmet Falls. Backcountry campers should stop in at the information centre or Park Administration Office to pick up a hiking guide, which has useful maps, trail descriptions, and profiles. No permit is needed for dayhiking, but overnight backcountry camping requires a **Wilderness Pass** ($6 per person per night, $35 per season), also available from information centres. Two fire roads, and the entire length of Hwy. 93, are open for **mountain biking.** The **Hector Gorge Trail** and **Dolly Varden Trail** make a pleasant loop. As for **fishing,** rock flour from glaciers in the rivers makes for generally poor luck.

Yoho National Park

A Cree expression for awe and wonder, "Yoho" is the perfect name for this smaller, uncrowded park. Although a bit plainer than its neighbors, it does sport some of the niftiest names in the Rockies, like Kicking Horse Pass, titled when Captain John Hector, tired, hungry, and struggling to find a mountain pass for the Canada Pacific Railroad, was kicked in the chest by his horse. Then there's Takakkaw Falls. 'Nuff said. Besides funny-sounding names, Yoho is home to all sorts of scientific wonders: the largest waterfall in the Rockies, the Continental Divide, and the Burgess Shale, which made its way into paleontology textbooks in the early 20th century when it spewed evidence of the complexity of pre-Cambrian life. Even without a slide rule, this quiet park and its inconspicuous village, Field, wins its visitors over with natural splendor.

Practical Information The **Visitor Information Centre** (343-6783) is in the metropolis of **Field** on Hwy. 1 (open daily 9am-7pm; call for winter hours). Ironically, this town founded by the railroad company is no longer accessible by rail, and while Greyhound does stop in Field, it is not a destination in itself. Those without cars can try calling the bus company or hitching the well-traveled Trans-Canada Hwy. In case of emergency, call the **Warden Office** at 343-6324 or the **RCMP** (in nearby Golden) at 344-2221, although the scarcity of phones in the park makes it more efficient to just drive to Lake Louise for help. The **post office** is in Field, at 312 Stephen Ave. (343-6365; open Mon.-Fri. 8:30am-4:30pm). The **area code** is 250, but Yoho is still in Mountain Time. Yoho lies on Hwy. 1 (the Trans-Canada Hwy.), adjacent to Banff National Park. Lake Louise is 27km east of Field.

Accommodations, Camping and Food With one of the best locations of all Rocky Mountain hostels, the **Whiskey Jack Hostel,** 13km off the Trans-Canada on Yoho Valley Rd. just before Takakkaw Falls, is the best indoor place to stay while guzzling up Yoho's sights. Whiskey Jack offers indoor plumbing, propane light, easy access to Yoho's best trails, and all the splendor of the Takakkaw Falls right from the

A Mountie always Gets His Man

Think of the Canadian Rocky Mountains, and most also think of the Royal Canadian Mounted Police (RCMP). Known as one of the best police forces in the world, the Mounties have a reputation for honesty, integrity, and boldness. Originally named the Northwest Mounted Police, the force began in 1873 when 293 men from all parts of the world were brought together to regulate the whisky trade in Canada's west and combat the influx of Sioux Indians from Montana. Some say that once upon a time, 4 Mounties challenged an entire 10,000 person tribe to leave Canada. When the chief refused to take down his teepee, the sergeant, in front of the entire tribe, proceeded to take it down himself. Amazed at his courage, the tribe moved out.

Today, the RCMP are Canada's national police force, fully equipped with all the latest bad-guy fighting technology. Most Mounties have dismounted, but Mounties on horseback can still be seen around the towns of Banff and Jasper in their famous stetsons and scarlet tunics. They are proud of their heritage—so proud, in fact, that a Mountie was stationed in Hollywood, CA to ensure that actors portraying the Mounties in the movies had the correct uniform and haircut. To find out more about the RCMP, browse through the books in **Sgt. Preston's Outpost,** 208 Caribou St., Banff (762-5335).

front porch. Olga, the manager, plays a wicked game of Scrabble ($12, nonmembers $16; open June-Sept.) There is no phone, so make highly recommended reservations by calling the Banff International Hostel at (403) 762-4122 (see p. 292).

All frontcountry **camping** is first-come, first-served, but the abundance of backcountry camping keeps overcrowding to a minimum. The five official campgrounds offer a combined 320 sites, all easily accessible from the highway. Practice roadside voodoo at the biggest, **Hoodoo Creek,** on the west end of the park. Hoodoo has 106 sites, kitchen shelters, running hot water, a nearby river, and a playground ($14; open June-Aug.). It lies just across the Trans-Canada Hwy. from **Chancellor Peak,** which has 58 sites, pump water, and pit toilets ($12; open early May-Sept.). Wheelchair-accessible **Kicking Horse** on Yoho Valley Rd., off the highway, is much more popular than the genuine item (it has hot showers; kicking horses don't). 86 sites run $17. Scenery hounds will love the views from **Takakkaw Falls** campground on Yoho Valley Rd. It may have only pump water and pit toilets, but it also has a gimmick—no cars are allowed, requiring residents to park in the falls parking lot and haul their gear 650m to the sites (35 sites, $12; open late June-late Sept.). Close by, **Monarch,** at the beginning of Yoho Valley Rd., has 36 regular sites and 8 walk-ins ($12; open late June-early Sept.). The six **backcountry campgrounds** offer 48 total sites and an intense wilderness experience. Before heading up a trail, stop at the visitors centre for a permit and a map (see **Practical Information,** above). Backcountry campers should also ask at the information centre about the availability of backcountry **Alpine Huts.**

Food options in Field are incredibly diverse given the town's population, but laughably limited when compared with any other town on earth. The most convenient pit stop is the **Siding General Store** (343-6462), on Stephen Ave. Basic foodstuffs line the walls, beer fills the cooler, and the friendly owners push yummy food over their counter (sandwiches $4, breakfast around $4; open daily 7am-9pm).

Outdoors **The Great Divide** is both the boundary between Alberta and British Columbia and the breaking-away point for the Atlantic and Pacific watersheds. Here a stream forks with one arm flowing about 1500km to the Pacific Ocean, and the other flowing 2500km to the Atlantic. More obscure to unknowing passers by is the **Burgess Shale,** where the world's finest Cambrian-aged fossils were discovered in 1909. The Shale features imprints of the bizarre-looking, soft-bodied organisms that inhabited the world's murky waters following the heyday of the tiny amoeba. Bigger, clumsier organisms known as humans have forced the Canadian government to protect the Shale from excessive tourism. As a result, it is accessible only via guided day hikes led by the **Yoho-Burgess Shale Foundation** (800-343-3006). The hike to the **Mt. Stephen Fossil Beds** ($27) is a short but steep 6km loop, while the 20km round-trip trek to **Walcott's Quarry** ($43) brings you face to face with 515-million-year-old fossils. For other backcountry trails, pick up the *Backcountry Guide to Yoho National Park* at the information centre ($1). Take the 10.6km **Iceline Trail,** which starts at the hostel, for valley views and an up-close introduction to the **Emerald Glacier.**

Yoho's most splendid lake is also its least accessible. **Lake O'Hara,** in the northeast end of the park, can only be reached by a 13km pedestrian trail or on a park-operated bus. The bus requires reservations (call 343-6433), a $12 round-trip ticket, and a park permit. High peaks, cirque and rock basin lakes, and rock lichens appreciate the restriction on tourism and reward those who do venture to O'Hara with a cornucopia of mountain life. In contrast, Yoho's most splendid waterfall is ridiculously easy to access. The **Takakkaw Falls** are visible for a good portion of the drive up Yoho Valley Rd., and roadside vistas are often more spectacular than the view from the parking lot on Yoho Valley Rd., 14km off the Trans-Canada.

Calgary

Mounties founded Calgary in the 1870s to control the flow of illegal whisky, but a different sort of flow made the city great: oil. As the host of the 1988 Winter Olympics, Calgary's dot on the map grew larger as jobs, tourism, and flocks of Canadians from the East descended on Calgary. Already Alberta's largest city, Calgary continues to grow. No matter how big its britches, though, Calgary pays a yearly tribute to its original tourist attraction, the "Greatest Outdoor Show on Earth," the Calgary Stampede, when the city dons cowboy duds and lets out a collective "Yahoo!" every July for 10 days of world-class rodeo, country music, "Western Art," and pancake breakfasts.

PRACTICAL INFORMATION AND ORIENTATION

Visitors Information: For drop-in info, go to the **Visitor Service Center** near the Calgary Tower at 131 9th Ave. SW (750-2397). Open daily 8:30-5pm. For the cost of a local call, the **Talking Yellow Pages** (521-5222, ext. 8950) provides a wide range of info from local events to the latest in vomit-stain removal (no joke).

American Express: Canada Trust Tower, main floor, 421 7th Ave. SW (261-5085).

Buses: Brewster Tours (221-8242). Runs buses from the airport or downtown to: Banff (3 per day, $34); Lake Louise (3 per day, $39); and Jasper (1 per day, $68). **Greyhound,** 877 Greyhound Way SW (265-9111 or 800-661-TRIP/8747). Service to: Edmonton (10 per day, $35); Banff (5 per day, $8); and Drumheller (2 per day, $20). Students and seniors 10% discount, HI discount. Free shuttle from C-Train at 7th Ave. and 10th St. to bus depot (every hr. on the ½hr., 6:30am-7:30pm). **Red Arrow:** 101-205 9 Ave. S.E. (531-0350). To Edmonton (5 per day, $35) and Fort McMurray (via Edmonton; 2 per day, $79). 10% HI discount.

Public Transportation: Calgary Transit, 240 7th Ave. SW. Bus and "C-Train" schedules, passes, and maps. Office open Mon.-Fri. 8:30am-5pm. C-Trains are free in the downtown zone. Bus fare and C-Trains outside downtown $1.50, ages 6-14 90¢, under 6 free. Exact change required. Day pass $4.50, children $2.50. Book of 10 tickets $12.50, children $8.50. **Information line** (262-1000). Open Mon.-Fri. 6am-11pm, Sat.-Sun. 8:30am-9:30pm.

Taxi: Checker Cab, 299-9999. **Yellow Cab,** 974-1111. Both 24hr.

Car Rental: Rent-A-Wreck, 4201 MacLeod Trail SE (228-1660). From $35 per day, 200km free, 12¢ each additional km. Must be 21 with credit card. Open daily 8am-7pm.

Bike Rental: Budget Car Rental, 140 6th Ave. SE (226-1550). $12 per day. Must be 18 with credit card. **Sports Rent,** 9250 Macleod Trail (292-0066). $20 per day. HI discount.

Laundromat: Beacon Speed Wash & Dry, 1818 Centre St. N (230-9828). Open daily 8am-11pm.

Weather: Environment Canada, 299-7878. Calgary and Banff weather.

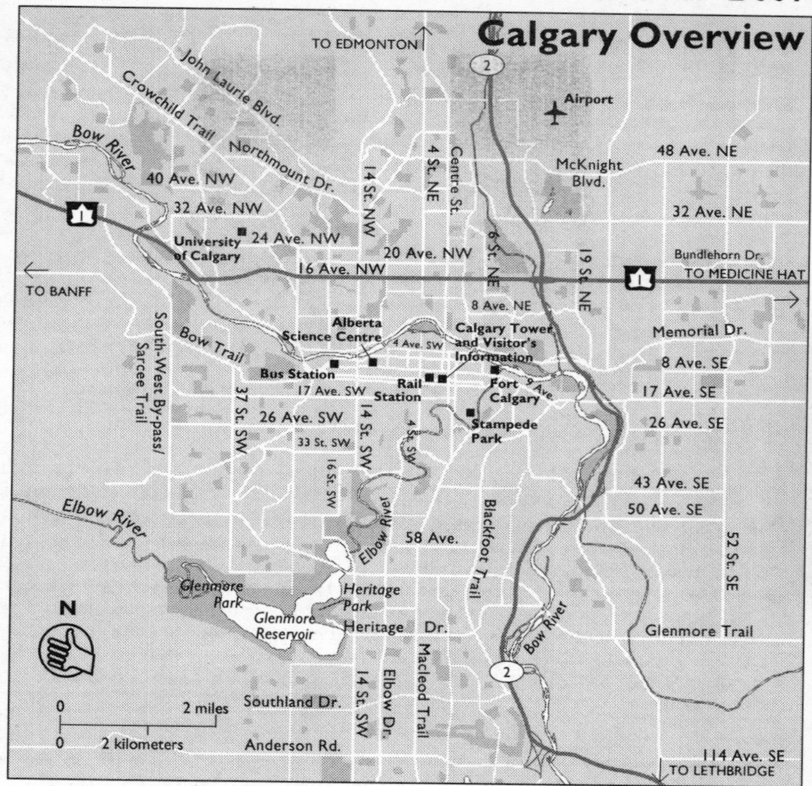

Library: Calgary Public Library, 616 Macleod Trail SE (262-2600). Open Mon.-Thurs. 10am-9pm, Fri.-Sat. 10am-5pm, Sun. 1:30pm-5pm.

Calgary Gay Community Support Services: Call 234-9752 for a recording of events; call 234-8973 daily 7-10pm for peer counseling and info.

Women's Resource Centre: 325 10th St. NW (283-5994), 1 block west of the Sunnyside C-Train stop. Info and referrals. Open Mon.-Fri. 9:30am-4:30pm.

Crisis Line: 266-1605. 24hr. **Poison Centre:** 270-1414. 24hr.

Pharmacy: Shopper's Drug Mart, 6455 Macleod Trail S (253-2424), in the Chinook Center. Open 24hr.

Hospital: Calgary General, 841 Centre Ave. E (268-9111).

Emergency: 911.

Police: 133 6th Ave. SE (266-1234).

Post Office: 207 9th Ave. SW (974-2078). Open Mon.-Fri. 8am-5:45pm. **Postal Code:** T2P 268.

Area Code: 403.

Calgary is 120km east of Banff along the **Trans-Canada Highway** (Hwy. 1). Planes fly into **Calgary International Airport,** about 6km northwest of the city centre. **Cab** fare from the airport to the city is about $20. Bus #57 provides sporadic service from the airport to downtown (call for schedule). A solid bet is the **Airporter Bus** (531-3907), which offers frequent service to major hotels in downtown Calgary ($8.50); if you ask nicely, they may drop you off at an unscheduled stop.

Calgary is divided into quadrants: **Centre Street** is the east-west divider; the **Bow River** divides the north and south sections. Avenues run east-west, streets run north-south, and numbers count up from the divides. Pay careful attention to the quadrant distinctions (NE, NW, SE, SW) at the end of each address. The cross streets can be derived by disregarding the last two digits of the 1st number: 206 7th Ave. is at 2nd Street, 310 10th St. is at 3rd Ave.

ACCOMMODATIONS

Lodging costs skyrocket when packs of tourists stampede into the city's hotels during the enormous July festival. Call far in advance. Contact the **B&B Association of Calgary** (543-3900) for information and availability on B&Bs. Prices for singles start around $35, doubles around $50.

Calgary International Hostel (HI-C), 520 7th Ave. SE (269-8239). Convenient, several blocks east of downtown. Walk east along 7th Ave. from the 3rd St. SE C-Train station; it's on the left just past 4th St. SE. This urban hostel has it all: clean, large kitchen, meeting rooms, laundry, and a big backyard with barbecue facilities. City volunteers act as "guest relations" personnel, touting a useful Rolodex overflowing with handy phone numbers. Gives free tours of downtown (2 per week). 114 beds. Open 24hrs. $15, nonmembers $19. Linen $1.50. Wheelchair accessible.

University of Calgary, in the NW quadrant. Booking for all rooms coordinated through **Kananaskis Hall,** 3330 24th Ave. (220-3203), a 12min. walk from the University C-Train stop (open 24hr.). The university is out of the way, but easily accessible via bus #9 or the C-Train. Sleep in the very beds of Olympians; U of C was the Olympic Village home to the 1988 competitors. Singles $31; doubles $39. More lavish suites with private bathrooms about $35. Student with ID: singles $21; doubles $32. Reservations recommended. Popular with conventioneers and often booked solid. Rooms available May-Aug. only.

Regis Plaza Hotel, 124 7th Ave. SE (262-4641). Despite its less-than-attractive streetside appearance, the Plaza has clean rooms smack in the middle of downtown. The old, stubborn elevator tugs guests to the 100 rooms of this behemoth. Great for groups, the roomy floors are ideal for cramming in extra sleeping bags. For ascetic types, "inside" rooms with no TV, bath, or windows cost $32.50; doubles from $64, Weekly rates $75-150. Front desk open 24hr.

FOOD

Downtown's comestibles are concentrated in the **Stephen Avenue Mall,** 8th Ave. S between 1st St. SE and 3rd St. SW. Good, reasonably-priced food is also readily available in the **"+15" Skyway System.** Designed to provide indoor passageways during bitter winter days, this futuristic mall-in-the-sky connects the second floors of dozens of buildings throughout downtown Calgary. The trendy, costlier chow-houses in the popular **Kensington District,** along Kensington Rd. and 10th and 11th St. NW, also hide some budget eateries. Take the C-Train to Sunnyside or use the Louise Bridge (9th St. SW and 10th St. NW). Shop for groceries at **Co-op Grocery,** 123 11th Ave. SE (299-4257; open Mon.-Fri. 9am-9pm, Sat. 9am-6pm, Sun. 10am-6pm). Even more restaurants, as well as fresh fruits, vegetables, baked goods, and flowers, grace the plaza-style, upscale **Claire Market** (264-6450), on 3rd St. SW near Prince's Island Park.

Satay House, 206 Centre St. S (290-1927). Large portions of authentic Vietnamese cuisine for laughably little. Chinatown is the best downtown bargain, and Satay House is one of the best bargains in Chinatown. Several varieties of *Pho* (beef noodle soup) $3.50-$4.50. The house special offers a taste of everything for only $5.50. Open Mon.-Fri. 11am-10pm, Sat.-Sun. 10am-10pm.

Island Experience, 314A 10th St. NW (270-4550). Tropical decor matched with hard-to-find Caribbean treats borrowed from India make this Kensington nirvana a complete island experience. The *Roti* and *Paratha* are over-stuffing meals; meat and vegetable patties are lighter ($2.25). Chutneys $1. For a taste of the mainland, request Mexican tacos ($1), not listed on the menu. Open Mon.-Wed. 11:30am-8pm, Thurs. 11:30am-9pm, Fri. 11:30am-10pm, Sat.-Sun. noon-8pm.

Take Ten Cafe, 304 10th St. NE (270-7010). A local favorite, Take Ten attracts customers not by being the coolest place in Kensington, but by offering dirt-cheap, good-quality food. All burgers under $4; lunch specials, usually a burger and fries,

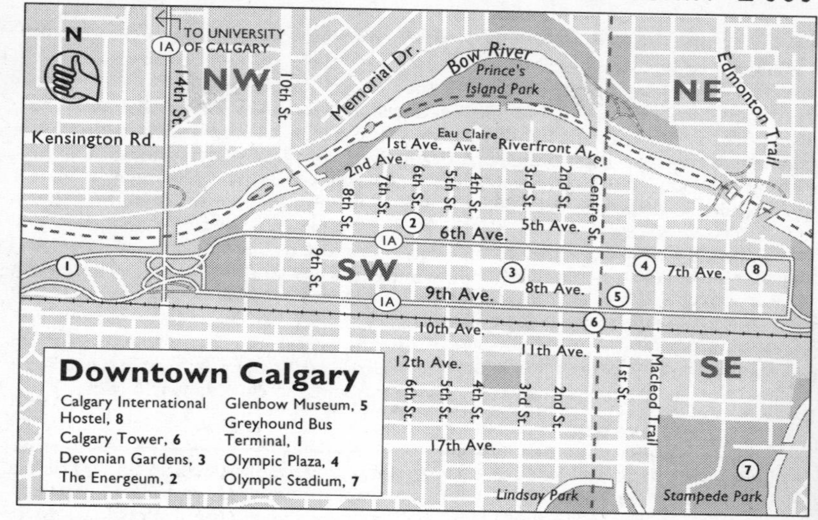

under $5. The Asian owners also offer a variety of Chinese food ($5.50). Open Mon.-Sat. 9am-6pm, Sun. 9am-3pm.

4th Street Rose, 2116 4th St. SW (228-5377). This California-cool restaurant serves a variety of dishes, but the best (and cheapest) is the "pro-size" Caesar salad ($4.50). If the weather's nice, ask for a table on the patio. Open Mon.-Thurs. 11am-midnight, Fri.-Sat. 11am-1am, Sun. 10am-midnight.

Heartland Country Store, 920 2nd Ave. NW (270-4541). This really is a country store. Hidden in a quiet neighborhood just outside of Kensington, Heartland serves hearty meals good for hearts (and $1 cookies). Sandwiches $2.50-4.25; varying hot meals depending on what's cookin' ($6-7). Lots of veggie dishes. Browse through collectibles in the adjacent antique shop. Open daily 7am-11pm.

SIGHTS

A decade later, Calgary still clings to its two weeks of Olympic fame. Visit the **Canada Olympic Park** (247-5452), 10 minutes west of downtown on Hwy. 1, to learn about gravity at the site of the quick, slick bobsled and luge tracks, as well as four looming ski jumps (open daily 8am-9pm). The **Olympic Hall of Fame** (247-5452), also at Olympic Park, honors Olympic achievements with displays, films, and lets visitors "experience" the Olympics with bobsled and ski-jumping simulators (open daily 9am-9pm; $3.75, seniors and students $3, children under 6 free). During the summer, the Park opens its hills to mountain bikers. Take the lift up the hill, then cruise down—no work necessary. Keep an eye on the sky for ski-jumpers who practice at the facility year-round. (Open daily May-Sept. 10am-9pm; hill pass $5.50; bike rental $6 per hr., full day $24.) The **Olympic Oval** (220-7890) is the most impressive of the remaining arenas from the Winter Olympics. An enormous indoor speed-skating track on the University of Calgary campus; the oval remains a major international training facility with the fastest ice in the world. Speed skaters work out in the early morning and late afternoon; sit in the bleachers and observe the ice-action for free. Or try to haul some ice yourself during the public skate hours (summer 8-9:30pm; $4, children $2; hockey skate rental $3.50; speed skates $3.75).

The **Olympic Plaza,** on 7th Ave. SE just east of Centre St., now hosts special events, including free concerts during the **Calgary Jazz Festival** in June. The **Glenbow Museum,** 130 9th Ave. SE (268-4100), packs everything from rocks and minerals, to native Canadian life, to Asian art, into one of Calgary's premier museums. (Open daily 9am-5pm, winter closed Mon.; $8, seniors and students $6, under 6 free; HI discount.) Footbridges stretch from either side of the Bow River to **Prince's Island Park.** On many summer evenings at 7pm, Mount Royal College puts on free Shakespeare in the park (call 240-6908 or Calgary Parks and Recreation at 268-3888).

Calgary's other island park, **St. George's Island,** is accessible by the river walkway to the east and houses the ark-like **Calgary Zoo** (232-9372). For those who might have missed out on the wildlife in nearby Banff and Jasper, the Canadian Wilds exhibit re-creates the sights, sounds, and, yes, smells of Canada's wilderness. A pamphlet available at the zoo entrance lists animal feeding times; visitors are invited to watch big animals eat little animals. The squeamish may be content to stroll through the **botanical gardens** or the **children's zoo.** (Gates open daily 9am-6pm, winter daily 9am-4pm; grounds open until 8:30pm, winter until 5:30pm; $9.50, seniors and children $4.75; winter $8, seniors and children $4; AAA and HI discounts.)

(To be sung to the tune of *The Beverly Hillbillies*:) Well this here's a story about the **Energeum,** a place about oil kinda like a museum. Play a game about drillin', watch a movie in the theater. And learn how Alberta puts th' power in your heater. The Energeum, that is, 640 5th Ave. SW (297-4293; open Mon.-Fri. 11am-4:30pm; free).

ENTERTAINMENT

Nightclubs in Alberta became legal in 1990, and Calgary is making up for lost time. With year-round city-wide events, Calgary is crawling with bars and nightclubs that cater to the waves of fun-hungry visitors. Live music ranges from national acts to a dude with a guitar. For an easy-to-find good time, rock down to **"Electric Avenue,"** the stretch of 11th Ave. SW between 5th and 6th St., and pound back local brew with oodles of young Calgarians. Beware of Electric Avenue during hockey playoff time: streets close and lines for bars and clubs wind around the block. Try others nearby, along 17th Ave. SW and 1st St. SW. Last call in Calgary is 2am, and is strictly observed.

Republik, 219 17th Ave. SW (244-1884; events line 228-6163). Grungeoids slam and grind with their Gap-clad brethren in Calgary's loudest nuclear bunker and biggest party zone. On the harder side of alternative, this is a favorite stage for up-and-coming bands (live music on Wed. and Fri. nights). The mosh pit likes its victims raw. Daily drink specials. Cover $2-7. Open Tues.-Sat. 7pm-2am.

Bottlescrew Bill's Pub (263-7900), 10th Ave. SW and 1st St. Take refuge from the boisterous Electric Ave. (and the Electric Slide) in this "Old English Pub." The source of "Buzzard Breath Ale," Bill's beckons beer-lovers with the widest suds selection in Alberta (over 200 to choose from, $3.30-15). Happy hour Mon.-Fri. 4-7pm, all day Sun. Watch the world pass by on the patio, grab some sun, and load up on free nachos Mon.-Fri. 4-6pm. Open daily 11am-2am.

The King Edward Hotel, 438 9th Ave. SE (262-1680). Anyone who knows blues knows the King Eddie Hotel. A well-known stop for North American blues bands, the hotel brings in phenomenal notemakers, including Clarence "Gatemouth" Brown, Matt "Guitar" Murphy, and Buddy "No Nickname" Guy. Nightly live music, cover $3-6. Open daily 11am-2am. Jam sessions Sat. 2:30-7pm and Sun. 7pm-1am.

Ranchman's Steak House, 9615 Macleod Trail SE (253-1100). This is the real thing. Herds of carousing cattle-ropers camp out at Ranchman's, showing off their Wranglers and the latest in country line-dancing. For those not content with watching, Ranchman's offers free line-dancing lessons on weekdays. $6-10 cover Thurs.-Sat. and Stampede week. Open Mon.-Sat. 10pm-2am.

THE STAMPEDE

The more cosmopolitan Calgary becomes, the more firmly it clings to its frontier origins. Drawing millions from across Canada and the world every summer, the Stampede is worth a special visit. It takes place July 3-12 in 1998. Make the short trip to **Stampede Park,** just southeast of downtown, for steer wrestling, saddle bronc, bareback, and bull riding, pig racing, wild cow milking, and the famous chuckwagon races, involving four horses per wagon and nerves of steel. Visit a re-created Wild

West town, ride the wild, thrashing roller coaster at the **Stampede Midway,** or try the gaming tables in the **Frontier Casino.**

Parking is ample and reasonably priced, but the crowd is more than reasonably sized. Instead of driving, take the C-Train from downtown to the Stampede stop. For info and ticket mail-order forms, write **Calgary Exhibition and Stampede,** Box 1060, Station M, Calgary T2P 2L8, or call (800) 661-1260 (261-0101 in Calgary). Tickets cost $7-43. Same-day rush tickets are $8 (youth $7, seniors and children $4). Plan now. The entire city, including campgrounds, gets booked for the occasion.

Kananaskis Country

Between Calgary and Banff lie 4000 sq. km of provincial parks and so-called "multi-use recreational areas," collectively known as the **Kananaskis Country Provincial Area.** Although summer use by travelers to the Canadian Rockies is heavy, the sheer size of Kananaskis and the wide nature of its attractions keep it unspoiled.

Greyhound buses stop at the **Rusticana Grocery,** 801 8th St. (678-4465), in Canmore. Three buses daily pass through bound for Calgary ($15) and Banff ($6). The Alberta hostels run a hostel-to-hostel shuttle connecting Calgary to Banff, including a stop in K-Country ($19). Call Banff International Hostel for reservations (762-4122).

No fewer than 3000 **campsites** are accessible via K-Country roads. When hiking or biking in areas with established backcountry campgrounds, visitors must use the areas provided. However, if none is established, open camping is permitted; just set up camp further than 50m from the trail. Backcountry camping permits are not required. Frontcountry campsites in Kananaskis cost between $5.50 and $24 per night. The **Ribbon Creek Hostel,** near the Nakiska Ski Area, 24km south of the Trans-Canada Hwy. on Hwy. 40, accommodates 47 people. The hostel's comfortable common room has a fireplace and snuggle-friendly couches ($12, nonmembers $17). For reservations, call the Banff International Hostel at 762-4122.

Kananaskis offers an overwhelming number of outdoor sports from skiing to windsurfing. Eager staff members at the park infocentres help design itineraries for weeks of outdoor entertainment; expect showers of maps and elaborate brochures describing your activity of choice. The main visitor center is on **Barrier Lake,** 6km south of Hwy. 1 on Hwy. 40 (673-3985; open Sat.-Thurs. 8:30am-6pm, Fri. 8:30am-7pm, winter Wed.-Sun. 9am-4pm). The country is divided into eight sections. The three most popular are the **Bow Valley Provincial Park** (673-3663), with an administration office just off Hwy. 1 (open Mon.-Fri. 8:15am-4:30pm), the **Elbow River Valley** (949-4261), on Hwy. 66 near Bragg Creek, and the **Peter Lougheed Provincial Park** (591-6344), just off Hwy. 40. In an emergency, call the **Canmore Police** (678-5516).

With over 1000km of trails, K-Country can provide anything from a one-hour quick fix to a full-blown Rocky Mountain High. Those with limited time or endurance can explore the 1.9km **Canadian Mt. Everest Expedition Trail** in Peter Lougheed Provincial Park, which provides a majestic view of both Upper and Lower Kananaskis Lakes (but no view of Mt. Everest). The **Ribbon Creek Trail** passes 8.1km of waterfalls and canyons to arrive at an uncrowded backcountry campground at Ribbon Falls. More serious hikers find Gillean Dafferns's *Kananaskis Country Trail Guide* (published by Rocky Mountain Books) the definitive source on lengthier trails. Browse through or purchase a copy at any of the information centres. The **Canmore Nordic Centre** (678-2400), the 1988 Olympic Nordic skiing venue, offers world-class cross-country skiing in the winter and 60km of mountain bike trails in summer.

WASHINGTON AND OREGON

In the 1840s, Senator Stephen Douglas ran his cane down a map of the Oregon Territory tracing the spine of the Cascade Range. He argued, quite sensibly, that the mountains would make the perfect natural border between two new states. Sense, of course, has little to do with politics, and it was the Columbia River, running perpendicular to the Cascades, that became the border between Washington and Oregon. But even today the range, not the river, serves as the region's most important geographic—and cultural—divide: to the west of the Cascades lie the microchip, coffee, and music meccas of Portland and Seattle, and to the east lie vast tracks of farmland and an arid plateau.

The world has "discovered" the Pacific Northwest in the 90s, and Portland and Seattle are two of the most popular and fastest growing cities in the U.S. Some residents fear the laid-back way of life and tremendous natural beauty that made them so popular in the first place will be casualties of their own success. Emmet Watson's "Lesser Seattle" movement has gone so far as to publish negative (and often misleading) statistics concerning the city in an attempt to dissuade outsiders (in particular, Californians) from moving there. Watson's crusade notwithstanding, residents of the Pacific Northwest are quick to welcome visitors to their beautiful home. Travelers need only keep in mind a few regional quirks: the typical driver does not like to honk, and pedestrians do not jaywalk in major cities. In Seattle and Portland, learn to blend in with the locals by ignoring the weather and leaving your umbrella behind. Finally, residents of the Beaver State wince to hear their home called or-i-GAHN, but will welcome you with open arms to OR-i-gun.

Early and Native History

Natives of the Pacific Northwest discovered the influence of the Cascades long before Senator Douglas. Plateau natives like the Palouse and Spokane were on the move nine months of every year, hunting migratory herds across the flat, dry region east of the Cascades. Their semi-nomadic lifestyle kept tribal ties in flux, necessitating an egalitarian social system and consensual government. Even wider nomadism was encouraged by the arrival of wild horses around 1730. Coast dwellers, by contrast, enjoyed a life of abundant resources and relative ease: salmon was a staple that supported a dense population, old-growth forest provided an endless supply of timber for building, and plentiful rainfall guaranteed an array of edible plants. An affluent and complex society thrived and practiced the custom of the potlatch, in which chiefs give away their possessions in a display of wealth and generosity that affirms their privileged status within a group.

The Fateful Expedition of Lewis and Clark

U.S. President Thomas Jefferson, eager to attain "geographical knowledge of our own continent" and strengthen American claims to the areas recently purchased from Napoleon, commissioned Meriwether Lewis and William Clark to explore the Northwest in 1803. These two proto-*Let's Go*-ers and their men were accompanied by the indomitable Sacajawea, a Shoshone translator. The calming presence of her infant child helped Sacajawea convince those the native people they encountered that Lewis and Clark's was a peaceful party. This was lucky, since Lewis' attempt to impress the Shoshone with his limited command of their language involved rushing an armed warrior, waving madly, and yelling "I am your enemy!"

The expedition traveled 4000 mi. each way from St. Louis to the mouth of the Columbia River and back, accumulating flora, fauna, and stronger claims to a region the U.S. still ostensibly shared with Britain. London, for its part, sent Alexander Mackenzie to cross the Rockies and Captains James Cook and George Vancouver to map the coast and waterways. Vancouver charted the island that now bears his name, but inexplicably failed to notice the Columbia River, an oversight soon remedied by the American Robert Gray. In 1818 Britain and the U.S. hammered out an agreement that divided their claims as far west as the Rockies at the 49th parallel, but left the Oregon question unresolved.

54-40 Or Fight! (Or Not)

The arrival of Europeans in the Northwest was devastating to the native population. The deliberate machinations of white settlers, as well as the unfamiliar diseases they inadvertently carried—measles, small pox, and influenza—wiped out as many as 90% of the natives by the late 1800s. Missionary fervor became an additional means of controlling and dispossessing Indians, and in some cases, brought tensions to a head. Crusaders such as Marcus and Narcissa Whitman rushed west to Walla Walla to "save" the natives. When an epidemic of measles broke out in the Cayuse tribe, natives blamed the missionaries. Marcus met his grisly end at the tomahawk of Chief Tilokaikt, and Narcissa and 10 others were killed shortly thereafter. The incident marked one of the first significant outbreaks of violence between Indians and whites in the Northwest. The indignation aroused by the incident was a crucial motivating factor in Oregon's transformation into an American territory. Those natives who survived the ensuing white invasion were herded, nation by nation, onto reservations on some of the worst land in the region.

Britain voiced strong opposition to U.S. control of the Northwest, prompting James K. Polk to win the presidency in 1846 with a Manifest Destiny platform and the slogan, "54-40 or Fight," a claim to the all the land south of the 54th parallel. Polk found the fight he wanted in Mexico rather than the Pacific Northwest, and proved content to settle for the 49th parallel as the dividing line between British and American territory. The southern half of the Oregon Territory became the state of Oregon in 1859, and the more thinly populated territory to the north joined it 30 years later, reluctantly giving up the name "Columbia" (reserved for that pesky congressional district back east) for "Washington."

Birds, Bees, and Bill Gates

With the pesky Brits long gone, present-day Oregon and Washington have found other problems to contend with. Oregonians have struggled with the birds and the bees in arenas as disparate as sexual harassment (witness the 1995 scandal surrounding Senator Bob Packwood) and gay rights legislation. Birds alone have also proven problematic, as the logging industry and environmentalists continue to butt heads over the endangered spotted owl. The Supreme Court, much to the chagrin of many timber industry groups, has upheld the Federal Government's broad (and, many would argue, anti-industry) interpretation of the 1973 Endangered Species Act. With the two states' once-lucrative timber and fishing industries on the downturn, many Oregonians and Washingtonians are looking to cities like Seattle for new economic leads. Computer software companies based in the Northwest are booming, and wealthy Pacific Rim nations are strengthening their ties to the West. Some wonder if a slicker Northwest has forgotten its rural history as it acquires a taste for coffee.

The Arts

The arts thrive in the soggy climate of the Pacific Coast. Long before European arrival, the relative leisure of the coastal way of life allowed indigenous peoples to devote time and energy to elaborate and sophisticated works of art like masks, lodges, totems, dances, and songs.

Today, Portland and Seattle funnel a 1% tax on capital improvements into the acquisition and creation of public art. The Northwest offers imported artistic treasures, such as the Oregon Shakespeare Festival in Ashland, which has an annual audience of nearly half a million. Orchestral music aficionados flock to the Bach Festival in Eugene, OR, where Helmut Rilling waves his exquisite Baroque baton. Seattle has a repertory theater community second in size only to Chicago and New York, and its opera has earned an international reputation for its productions of Wagner.

In popular culture, the region has made its mark with some of the smartest, sharpest talents of recent years. Filmmakers Gus Van Sant—*My Own Private Idaho*, *Drugstore Cowboy*—and Cameron Crowe—*Singles, Say Anything, Fast Times at Ridgemont High*—are natives of the Northwest. David Lynch grew up in Spokane and produced the Oregon-based television series *Twin Peaks* in Snoqualmie (see p. 333). Oregon and Washington have each produced at least one cartoonist of twisted but undeniable genius: Portland's Matt Groening, creator of *The Simpsons* and *Life in Hell,* and Washington State alumnus Gary Larson, of *The Far Side* fame.

The region is widely remembered for the Seattle rock scene, which exploded in the early 90s with the astounding success of grunge rockers like Soundgarden, Pearl Jam, and Nirvana. Grunge has had its day, and the record executives that once prowled the city, signing contracts with everything in plaid, have moved on. Rock in the region, however, is by no means defunct. An active, youthful population supports a range of excellent music, and a vibrant nightlife not only in Portland and Seattle, but also in Eugene (second home of the Grateful Dead) and Olympia, and even smaller cities like Spokane and Bend. Seattle's Bumbershoot, a blow-out festival every summer of folk, street, classical, and rock (see p. 332) is a great way to sample the music of the Pacific Northwest.

Further Reading

The *Journals of Lewis and Clark,* by Meriwether Lewis and William Clark, tell the tale of the Northwest's most famous budget travelers; 1996's *Undaunted Courage*, by Stephen Ambrose, and *Sacajawea,* by Flora Warren Seymour, revisit that history and myth. Jack Kerouac's *Dharma Bums* and Robert Pirsig's *Zen and the Art of Motorcycle Maintenance* are more recent road-tripping classics, even if Pirsig takes the fun out of Crater Lake. Raymond Carver's *Where I'm Calling From* describes the people of the region in blunt and brutal prose. Sherman Alexie depicts the Spokane Indians in his 1995 *Reservation Blues.* Ken Kesey is often associated with California, but his outstanding novels *One Flew Over the Cuckoo's Nest* and *Sometimes a Great Notion* are firmly set in the rain-drenched Oregon woods.

Other books from and about the Pacific Northwest include *Snow Falling on Cedars,* a mystery novel by David Guterson set amid Japanese-American tensions in post-WWII Puget Sound; *The Lathe of Heaven* by science fiction author Ursula K. LeGuin; *Another Roadside Attraction* and *Even Cowgirls Get the Blues* by Tom Robbins; *The Lost Sun* by poet and former University of Washington instructor Theodore Roethke; and *Paul Bunyan* by James Stevens. The fearless Ramona, from the series of the same name by Beverly Cleary, has inspired many a middle child.

Washington

Washington is a state with a split personality, no thanks to the Cascade mountains. On the state's western shores, wet Pacific storms feed one of the world's only temperate rainforests in Olympic National Park, and stubborn low clouds linger over Seattle, hiding the Emerald City from its towering alpine neighbors, Mt. Rainier and Mt. Olympus. The daunting clouds blanket a burgeoning land rich in greenery, urban culture, and software programmers. Visitors to Puget Sound enjoy both island isolation in the San Juans and cosmopolitan entertainment in the concert halls and art galleries of the mainland. Over the hill, the eastern half of the state spreads out into fertile farmlands and grassy deserts. Fruit bowls runneth over in agricultural centers around Yakima, Spokane, and Pullman.

"Dry-siders" complain of unwanted domination by Puget Sound-controlled political interests, despite Spokane's role as a major trade center. To them, a "wet-sider" might be a long-haired urban liberal pontificating endlessly about the environmental destruction that comes by making a living from the land. However, the animosity goes both ways. To "wet-siders"—the great majority of the state's population—the term "dry-siders" conjures images of rednecks tearing around in pickup trucks through wheat farms and ranches, kicking up clouds of dust. While these stereotypes are entertaining, they do no justice to a population as varied as Washington's.

PRACTICAL INFORMATION

Capital: Olympia.

Visitor Information: Washington State Tourism, Department of Community, Trade, and Economic Development, P.O. Box 42500, Olympia 98504-2500 (consultation 360-586-2088 or 800-638-8474, info requests 800-544-1800). Open Mon.-Fri. 9am-4pm. **Olympia State Capitol Visitors Center,** P.O. Box 41020 (360-586-3460). Open Mon.-Fri. 8am-5pm. **Washington State Parks and Recreation Commission,** 7150 Cleanwater Ln., Olympia 98504 (info 360-902-8500 or 800-233-0321, reservations 800-452-5687). Write to P.O. Box 42650. **Forest Service and National Park Service Outdoor Recreation Information Center,** 222 Yale Ave. N., Seattle (206-470-4060), in the new REI flagship store. Open Tues.-Fri. 10:30am-7pm, Sat. 9am-9pm, Sun. 9:30am-6pm.

Fishing and Hunting: Department of Fish and Wildlife, 600 Capitol Way N., Olympia 98501-1091 (360-902-2200). Send away for complete guides to fishing and hunting regulations and licensing fees. Open Mon.-Fri. 8am-5pm. **Recreational fishing hotline,** 360-902-2500. **Shellfish Hotline,** 360-796-3215.

Population: 5,533,000. **State Motto:** *"Alki,"* a Salishan word meaning "by and by." **Nickname:** Evergreen State. **State Song:** "Washington, My Home." **State Flower:** Western Rhododendron. **State Rock:** Petrified Wood. **State Bird:** Willow Goldfinch. **State Fish:** Steelhead Trout. **State Tree:** Western Hemlock.

Emergency: 911.

Time Zone: Pacific (3hr. behind Eastern).

Postal Abbreviation: WA

Sales Tax: 8.1%.

Drinking Age: 21.

Traffic Laws: Mandatory seatbelt law.

Area Codes: 206 in Seattle and immediate vicinity, 425 northeast of Seattle from Snoqualmie Pass to Everett, 253 in eastern Puget Sound from Roy to Tacoma, 360 in the rest of western Washington, and 509 in eastern Washington.

GETTING AROUND

Taking **buses** remains the cheapest way to travel long distances in Washington. **Greyhound** (800-231-2222) serves the two main transportation centers, Spokane and Seattle, as well as towns in between. Local buses cover most of the remaining cities, although a few areas (such as the northwestern Olympic Peninsula) have no bus service. The **Amtrak** (800-USA-RAIL/872-7245) train line from Los Angeles to Vancouver makes many stops in western Washington; another line extends from Seattle to Spokane and on to Chicago. Amtrak serves most large cities along these two routes.

"No hitchhiking permitted" signs are posted on all highways. **Hitchhiking** in the San Juans, Whidbey Island, and Vashon Island is locally accepted though not legal. Opportunities for thumbing decrease as one goes east. *Let's Go* does not recommend hitchhiking as a safe means of transportation. Women traveling alone should *never* hitchhike.

ACCOMMODATIONS AND CAMPING

With the exception of those in Seattle, Washington's **hostels** are generally uncrowded, even in summer. Cheap **motels** exist in the downtown areas of most large cities, but are not always in the most safe or savory locations.

State park **campgrounds** usually have less expensive, more secluded sites than private campgrounds and provide better access to trails, rivers, and lakes. Drivers will also find state park campgrounds more accessible than Department of Natural Resources (DNR) and National Forest campgrounds. Some parks allow self-registration, while others have rangers register campers at their sites in the evening. Expect long, slow lines if the campground requires office registration. Gates to state park campgrounds generally open at dawn and close at dusk. Pets must be leashed and accompanied by owners at all times. Be aware that many state parks accept reservations; campgrounds fill up weeks in advance, especially during July and August. Reservations can be made up to 11 months in advance, but they must be made at least two days in advance. Most state park campsites cost $10 per night, $15 per night for RV hookups; some popular parks may have slightly higher prices in the summer. There is a $6 fee to make a reservation.

Campers may enjoy the solitude of the many National Forest and DNR sites. National Forest campsites cost up to $15 and are often free. Call (800) 365-2267 to reserve campsites in National Parks. National Park campgrounds accessible by road are generally in great settings. Olympic National Park has some free campgrounds accessible by car, but campgrounds accessible by trail are usually free.

Seattle

Seattle's serendipitous mix of mountain views, clean streets, espresso stands, and rainy weather is the magic formula of the 1990s, attracting migrants from across the U.S. It seems that everyone living here was born elsewhere. As newcomers come in droves, armed with college degrees and California license plates, hoping for job offers from Microsoft (in nearby Redmond) and a different lifestyle, Seattle blesses them with a magnificent setting and a vibrant artistic community. As a result, Seattle is one of the youngest, most vibrant cities in the nation. A nearly epidemic fascination with coffee has also made it one of the most caffeinated.

Seattle sits on an isthmus with mountain ranges to the east and west. Every hilltop in Seattle offers an impressive view of Mt. Olympus, Mt. Baker, and Mt. Rainier. To the west, the waters of Puget Sound glint off downtown skyscrapers and nearly spotless streets. Although a daytrip in any direction leads travelers into wild and scenic country, the city itself, built on nine hills (Rome, you ask?) that define distinct neighborhoods, begs for exploration. While exploring, plan to get wet. Two hundred days a year are shrouded in cloud cover but when the skies clear, Seattleites rejoice that "the mountain is out" and head for the country. Whatever you do in Seattle, don't be dismayed by the drizzle and bag the umbrella. After all, you don't want to be tagged as an outsider.

The city's artistic landscape is as varied and exciting as its physical landscape. Opera performances always sell out, and *The New York Times* has complained that there is more good theater in Seattle than on Broadway. When Nirvana introduced the world to their discordant sensibility, the term "grunge" and Seattle became (tem-

Washington

National Forests

Colville, **14**
Gifford Pinchot, **7**
Mount Baker, **9**
Mt. Baker-Snoqualmie, **11**
Okanogan, **13**
Olympic, **3**
Umatilla, **17**
Wenatchee, **12**

Indian Reservations

Colville, **15**
Makah, **1**
Quinault, **2**
Spokane, **16**
Yakima, **8**

CANADA
U.S.A.
Vancouver Island
Strait of Georgia
Strait of Juan De Fuca
Victoria
San Juan Islands
Bellingham
Anacortes
Sedro Wooley
Mt. Vernon
Oak Harbor
Port Townsend
Port Angeles
Forks
Queets
OLYMPIC NATIONAL PARK
Everett
Seattle
Bellevue
Bremerton
Shelton
Tacoma
Olympia
Aberdeen
Montesano
South Bend
Long Beach
Cathlamet
Astoria
Chehalis
Morton
Elbe
Kelso
Vancouver
Portland
MOUNT RAINIER NATIONAL PARK
MOUNT ST. HELENS VOLCANIC MONUMENT
NORTH CASCADES NATIONAL PARK
Pasayten Wilderness
Winthrop
Twisp
Stehekin
Lake Chelan
Tonasket
Brewster
Chelan
Leavenworth
Wenatchee
Ellensburg
Yakima
Toppenish
Goldendale
Columbia River
Republic
Grand Coulee
Ephrata
Moses Lake
Othello
Ritzville
Wilbur
Davenport
Sprague
Washtucna
Richland
Prosser
Pasco
Walla Walla
Dayton
Pendleton
Colville
Chewelah
Newport
Spokane
Coeur d'Alene
Colfax
Pullman
Moscow
Pomeroy
Lewiston
IDAHO
OREGON
MEXICO
WA.
N
0 — 60 miles
0 — 60 kilometers

porarily) inseparable, and the same city that produced Jimi Hendrix again revitalized American rock and roll. An army of good bands remain in their wake, keeping "the Seattle scene" alive, *sans* national spotlight, as a mecca for come-as-you-are entertainment. But many Seattle success stories have happier endings than those of Hendrix and Cobain. The city is home to entrepreneurs like Bill Gates of Microsoft and Howard Shultz of Starbucks, who built empires out of software and coffee beans.

PRACTICAL INFORMATION

Visitors Information: Seattle-King County Visitors Bureau (461-5840), at 8th and Pike St., on the 1st floor of the **convention center.** Maps, brochures, newspapers, and transit and ferry schedules. Helpful staff. Open May-Oct. Mon.-Fri. 8:30am-5pm, Sat.-Sun. 10am-4pm; Nov.-April Mon.-Fri. 8:30am-5pm.

Parks Information: Seattle Parks and Recreation Department, 100 Dexter St. (684-4075). Open Tues.-Fri. 10:30am-7pm, Sat. 9am-7pm, Sun. 9:30am-6pm. **National Park Service, Pacific Northwest Region,** in **REI** at 222 Yale Ave. (470-4060). Answers questions about camping, hiking and general frolicking in area parks, gives info on discounts and passes, and sells a map of the National Park System ($1.20). Open Mon.-Fri. 8am-4:30pm.

Currency Exchange: Thomas Cook Foreign Exchange, 906 3rd Ave. (623-6203). Open Mon.-Fri. 9am-5pm. Also behind the Delta Airlines ticket counter and at other locations in **Sea-Tac Airport,** as well as on the 1st floor of the Westlake Shopping Center (on Pine at Westlake Ave. N.).

Airport: Seattle-Tacoma International (Sea-Tac) (431-4444), on Federal Way south of Seattle proper. Take the Metro #174 or 194 from downtown Seattle.

Trains: Amtrak (800-USA-RAIL/872-7245, 382-4125 for arrival/departure times), King St. Station, at 3rd and Jackson St., 1 block east of Pioneer Square next to the King Dome. To: Portland (3 per day, $26); Tacoma (3 per day, $9); Spokane (1 per day, $67); San Francisco (1 per day, $161); and Vancouver, BC (1 per day, $29). Check for cheaper winter rates and bus connections to smaller destinations. Ticket office open daily 6:30am-8pm, station open 6am-10:30pm.

Buses: Greyhound (628-5526 or 800-231-2222), at 8th Ave. and Stewart St. To: Sea-Tac Airport (2 per day, $5); Spokane (5 per day, $22); Vancouver, BC (8 per day, $25); Portland (9 per day, $20); and Tacoma (6 per day, $4). Try to avoid late buses, as the station can get seedy after dark. Ticket office open daily 6:15am-9pm and 12:15-2am. **Green Tortoise Bus Service** (800-227-4766). Buses leave from 9th Ave. and Stewart St. on Thurs. and Sun. at 8am. The cushion seats on this bus-turned-lounge fold down into beds at night, and the bus makes frequent stops for barbecue dinners and saunas. A slow, friendly, liberal alternative to Greyhound. To: Portland, OR ($15); Eugene, OR ($25); Berkeley, CA ($49); San Francisco, CA ($59); and Los Angeles, CA (Thurs. only, $71). Reserve 5 days in advance.

Public Transportation: Metro Transit, Customer Assistance Office, 821 2nd Ave. (553-3000 or 800-542-7876, 24hr.), in the Exchange Building downtown. Open Mon.-Fri. 8am-5pm. Fares are based on a 2-zone system. Zone 1 includes everything within the city limits ($1.10 during peak hours, 85¢ off-peak). Zone 2 includes everything else ($1.60 peak, $1.10 off-peak). Ages 5-18 always 75¢. Peak hours in both zones are Mon.-Fri. 6-9am and 3-6pm. Exact fare required. Transfers valid for 2hr. Weekend all-day passes $1.70. Ride free daily 5am-7pm in the downtown **ride free area,** bordered by S. Jackson St. on the south, 6th Ave. and I-5 on the east, Battery St. on the north, and the waterfront on the west. Always get a transfer; it can be used on any bus, including a return trip on the same bus within 2hr. All buses have free, easy-to-use **bike racks** and most are wheelchair accessible. See **Getting Around,** below, for more info.

Ferries: Washington State Ferries, Colman Dock, Pier 52, downtown (800-84-FERRY/843-3779; see p. 33). Service from downtown to: Bainbridge Island, Bremerton on the Kitsap Peninsula, and Vashon Island. Service from Fauntleroy in West Seattle to Southworth on the Kitsap Peninsula and Vashon Island. Ferries leave daily and frequently 5am-2am. The **Victoria Line** (800-668-1167; 625-1880 for reservations) leaves Pier 48 daily at 1pm. This is the only auto ferry service avail-

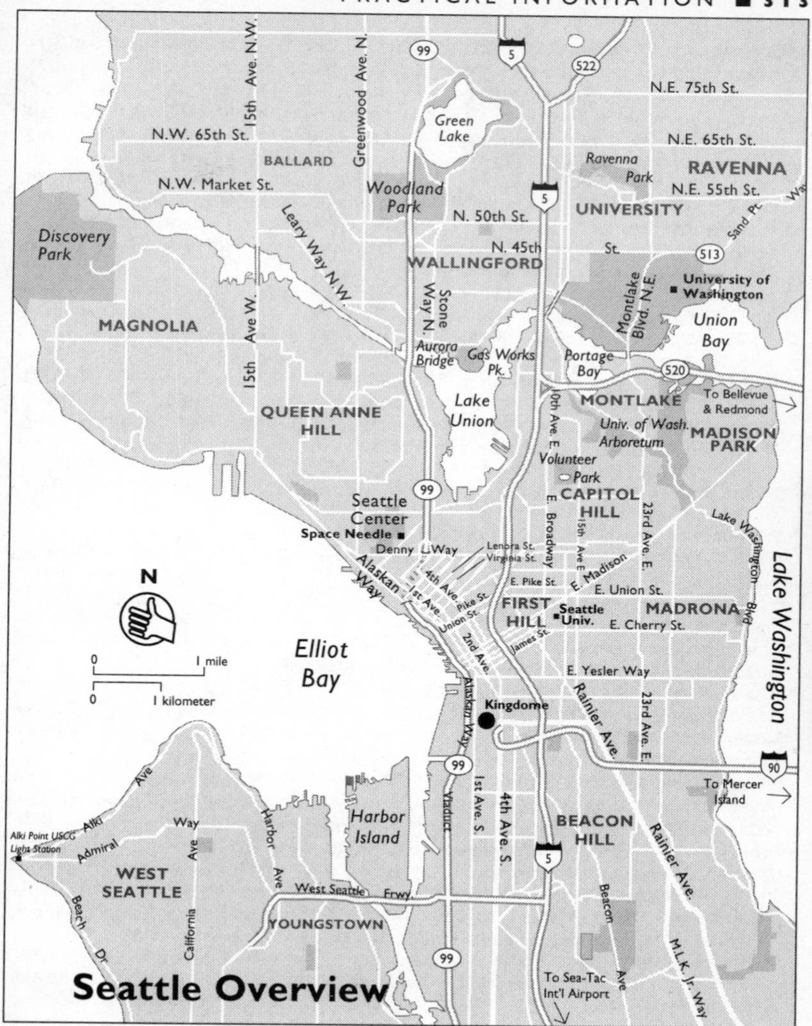

able from Seattle to Victoria. One-way: passengers $29, car and driver $49. Under 12 ½ price.

Car Rental: A-19.95-Rent-A-Car, 804 N. 145th St. (365-1995). $20 per day ($25 if under 21 with verifiable insurance); 10¢ per mi. after 100. Free delivery. Credit card required. Even cheaper, **Auto Driveaway** (235-0880) hires people to drive their cars to various locations across the U.S. (open Mon.-Fri. 9am-5pm).

Ride Board: 1st floor of the Husky Union Building (the HUB), behind Suzallo Library on the University of Washington main campus. Matches cars and riders for any destination. Also check the board at the downtown AYH.

Bicycle Rentals: The Bicycle Center, 4529 Sand Point Way (523-8300). $3 per hr. (2hr. min.), $15 per day. Credit card or license deposit required. Open Mon.-Fri. 10am-8pm, Sat.-Sun. 10am-5pm. **Gregg's Greenlake Cycle, Inc.,** 7007 Woodlawn Ave. NE (523-1822). Pricey, but close to Green Lake and Burke-Gilman bike trails ($15-20 per day, $25 24hr.). Photo ID and cash or credit card deposit required. Also rents in-line skates. Open Mon.-Fri. 9:30am-9pm, Sat.-Sun. 9:30am-6pm.

Camping and Outdoor Gear: REI, 222 Yale Ave (223-1944), near Capitol Hill. The mothership of camping supply stores. Open Mon.-Sat. 10am-9pm, Sun. 11-6pm.

Seattle Public Library: 1000 4th Ave. (386-4636, TDD 386-4697). A visitor's library card lasts 3 months ($8 with temp. local address). Free 90min. Internet access with library card. Open Mon.-Thurs. 9am-9pm, Fri.-Sat. 9am-6pm; Sept.-May Sun. 1-5pm.

Ticket Agencies: Ticketmaster (628-0888, or 292-ARTS/2778) for plays, the symphony, and other fine arts events, in every Tower Records store. **Ticket/Ticket,** 401 Broadway E. (324-2744), on the 2nd floor of the Broadway Market. ½ price day-of-show tickets to local theater, music, concerts, and dance performances. Cash only. Must purchase tickets in person. Open Tues.-Sun. 10am-7pm. Also in the Pike Place Market; open Tues.-Sun. noon-6pm.

Laundromat: Sit and Spin, 2219 4th St. (441-9484). Both a laundromat and a local hot spot (see **Clubs and Taverns,** p. 331). Wash $1.25, 10min. dry 25¢. Open Sun.-Thurs. 9am-11pm, Fri.-Sat. 9am-2am. **Downtown-St. Regis,** 116 Stewart St., attached to the St. Regis Hotel. Wash $1.25, dry 75¢. Open 24hr.

Crisis Clinic: 461-3222. 24hr. **Seattle Rape Relief:** 1905 S. Jackson St., #102 (632-7273). Crisis counseling, advocacy, and prevention training. 24hr.

University of Washington Women's Information Center: (685-1090), Cunningham Hall, in the main campus. Community resource and referral for women's groups throughout the Seattle area. Open Mon.-Fri. 9am-5pm.

Senior Information and Assistance: 1601 2nd Ave. #800 (448-3110). Open Mon.-Fri. 9am-5pm.

Travelers' Aid: 909 4th Ave. #630 (461-3888), at Marion on the 6th floor of the YMCA. Free services for stranded travelers who have lost their wallets or their marbles. Open Mon.-Fri. 9am-4pm.

International District Emergency Center: 623-3321. Medics with multilingual assistance available. 24hr.

Poison Information: 800-732-6985. 24hr.

AIDS Information: AIDS Prevention Project, 296-4999.

Alcohol/Drug Help Line: 722-3700. 24hr.

Gay Counseling: 1820 E. Pine (323-0220). Open Mon.-Fri. noon-9pm. **Lesbian Resource Center:** 1808 Bellview Ave. #204 (322-3953). Support groups, drop-in center, lending library, and workshops. Open Mon.-Fri. 9am-7pm.

Health Care: Aradia Women's Health Center, 1300 Spring St. (323-9388). Staff will refer elsewhere when overbooked. Open Mon.-Fri. 10am-6pm. **Chec Medical Center,** 1151 Denny Way (682-7418). Walk-in.

Emergency: 911. **Police Department:** 610 3rd Ave. (583-2111).

Internet Access: Speak Easy, 2304 2nd Ave. (728-9770). File under alt.cool.alternative.cybercafe. Open Mon.-Thurs. 9am-midnight, Fri. 9am-2am, Sun. 10am-2am. **Capitol Hill Net,** 219 Broadway #22 (860-6858). $6 per hr. Free surfing time if you mention *Let's Go.* Open daily 9am-midnight. Also see **library,** above.

Post Office: (800-275-8777), at Union St. and 3rd Ave. downtown. Open Mon.-Fri. 8am-5:30pm. **General Delivery ZIP Code:** 98101.

Area Code: 206.

GETTING THERE AND GETTING AROUND

Seattle is a long, skinny city, stretched north to south on an isthmus between **Puget Sound** to the west and **Lake Washington** to the east and linked by locks and canals.

The city is easily accessible by car via **I-5,** which runs north-south through the city, east of downtown, and by **I-90** from the east, which ends at I-5 southeast of downtown. From I-5, get to **downtown** (including **Pioneer Square, Pike Place Market,** and the **waterfront**) by taking any of the exits from James St. to Stewart St. Take the Mercer St./Fairview Ave. exit to the **Seattle Center.** The Denny Way exit leads to **Capitol Hill,** and, farther north, the 45th St. exit will take you to the **University District.** The less crowded **Route 99,** also called **Aurora Ave.** or the Aurora Hwy., runs parallel to I-5 and skirts the western side of downtown, with great views from the **Alaskan Way Viaduct.** Route 99 is often the better choice when driving downtown, to Queen Anne, Green Lake, Fremont, or the northwestern part of the city.

Once in Seattle, navigating can seem daunting, but even the most road-weary can learn their way around the Emerald City like so many munchkins. Downtown, avenues run northwest to southeast, and streets run southwest to northeast. Outside downtown, everything is simplified: with few exceptions, avenues run north-south and streets east-west. The city is split into **quadrants:** 1000 1st Ave. NW is a long walk from 1000 1st Ave. SE.

When driving in Seattle, do as the natives do: yield to pedestrians. Not only do locals drive slowly, calmly, and politely, but police ticket frequently. Even jaywalking pedestrians rack up $50 fines for crossing against the light. Downtown driving can be nightmarish. Parking is expensive, hills are steep, and one-way streets are ubiquitous. Parking is cheap, plentiful, and well-lit at the **Seattle Center,** near the Space Needle. Park there and take the **monorail** to the convenient **Westlake Center** downtown and walk or take a bus within the ride free zone, which covers most of downtown Seattle (see Public Transportation, above, in **Practical Information**). The Metro covers King County east to North Bend and Carnation, south to Enumclaw, and north to Snohomish County, where Metro bus #6 hooks up with **Community Transit.** This line runs to Everett, Stanwood, and well into the Cascades. Metro bus #174 connects to Tacoma's Pierce County System in Federal Way.

Seattle is an extremely bicycle-friendly city. All buses have free, easy-to-use **bike racks,** which hold two bikes. (Bike shops around town have sample racks for novices to practice on.) Between 6am and 7pm, bikes may only be loaded or unloaded at stops along the borders of the ride free zone. Check out Metro's *Bike & Ride* pamphlet, available at the visitors center and the hostel. For a bicycle map of Seattle, call the **City of Seattle Bicycle Program** (684-7583).

PUBLICATIONS

The city's major newspaper, the *Seattle Times* (464-2111), lists upcoming events in its Thursday "Tempo" section. The *Seattle Weekly* offers a free, left-of-center, advertisement-stuffed alternative to the dominant daily, complete with a weekend event listing section every Wednesday. *The Stranger* has its finger on the real pulse of the music and pop culture scene and mysteriously materializes every Thursday at the door of any Seattle music store, coffee shop, or thrift store. This is the best place to start for the low-down on Seattle nightlife or to read some entertaining personals (they say truth is stranger than fiction). *The Rocket* is another source of information on the music scene. *Arts Focus,* a free magazine available at most bookstores, carries information on the performing arts, while *Seattle Arts,* published by the Seattle Arts Commission, is especially good for events in the visual arts. Both are published monthly. The established weekly *Seattle Gay News* has an excellent map and listings of gay-owned and patronized business in Seattle and sells like hot-cakes on Fridays at newsstands (50¢). The *International Examiner* provides a free weekly news update of the Asian-American community and covers restaurants and upcoming community events.

ACCOMMODATIONS

Seattle's hostel scene is pumping, friendly, and clean. The **Seattle International Hostel** is the best option for the budget traveler staying downtown, though not the least expensive. Hostelers tired of the urban high-rise scene should head for the **Vashon Island Hostel** (sometimes called "Seattle B"; see p. 335). **Pacific Bed and Breakfast,** 701 NW 60th St., Seattle 98107 (784-0539), can set you up with a single room in a B&B in the $45-70 range (open Mon.-Fri. 9am-5pm).

Downtown

Seattle International Hostel (HI-AYH), 84 Union St. (622-5443; http://www.adhost.com/hi-seattle/itd/itd.html), at Western Ave. right by the waterfront. Take bus #174, 184, or 194 from the airport (#194 from the north end of the baggage terminal is fastest), get off at Union St. and walk west. Free breakfast buffet, free linens, and a diverse, international crowd make up for the expanses of formica

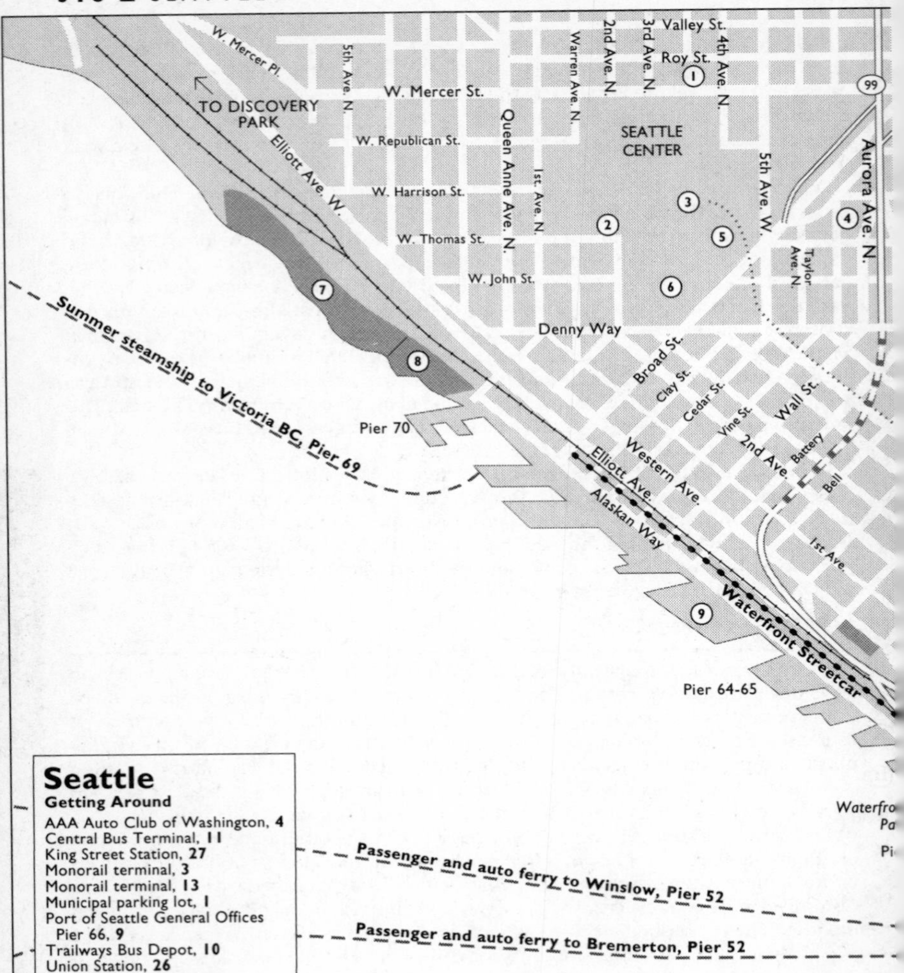

Seattle

Getting Around

AAA Auto Club of Washington, **4**
Central Bus Terminal, **11**
King Street Station, **27**
Monorail terminal, **3**
Monorail terminal, **13**
Municipal parking lot, **1**
Port of Seattle General Offices Pier 66, **9**
Trailways Bus Depot, **10**
Union Station, **26**
Washington State Ferry Terminal, **23**

Things to See

Broadway Playfield, **12**
Coliseum, **2**
Elliott Bay Park, **7**
Freeway Park, **14**
Kingdome Stadium, **28**
Myrtle Edwards Park, **8**
Pacific Science Center, **6**
Seattle Public Aquarium, **22**
Smith Tower, **24**
Space Needle, **5**
State Convention and Trade Center, **15**
Seattle Art Museum, **21**

Your Tax Dollars at Work

Harborview Medical Center, **18**
Post Office, **20**
Post Office, **25**
Public Library, **19**
Swedish Hospital Medical Ctr., **17**
Virginia Mason Hospital, **16**

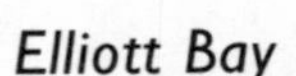

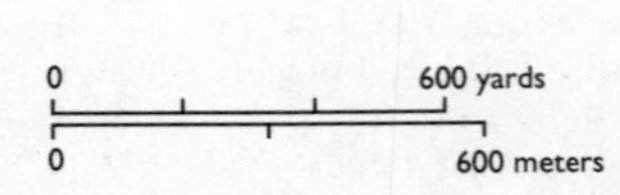

LAKE UNION
TO VOLUNTEER PARK
E. Roy St.
Republican St.
Harrison St.
Pontius Ave. N.
Dexter Ave. N.
8th Ave. N.
9th Ave. N.
Westlake Ave. N.
Terry Ave. N.
Boren Ave. N.
Fairview Ave. N.
Eastlake Ave. E.
Melrose Ave. E.
Bellevue Ave. E.
Summit Ave. E.
Belmont Ave. E.
Boylston Ave. E.
Harvard Ave. E.
Broadway East
12th Ave. E.
E. Harrison St.
E. Thomas St.
John St.
E. John St.
Denny Park
Denny Way
E. Olive Way
E. Denny Way
9th Ave.
Blanchard
7th Ave.
Virginia St.
Stewart St.
Howell St.
E. Howell St.
E. Olive St.
E. Pine St.
E. Pike St.
E. Union St.
Bellevue Ave.
Monorail
Lenora St.
5th Ave.
4th Ave.
Olive Way
Pine St.
8th Ave.
Hubble St.
Boren Ave.
Minor Ave.
Seneca St.
E. Madison St.
E. Spring St.
E. Marion St.
12th Ave.
Terry Ave.
9th Ave.
Pike St.
PIKE PLACE MARKET
Union St.
University St.
6th Ave.
7th Ave.
Madison St.
Marion St.
Columbia St.
Cherry St.
James St.
Broadway
E. Columbia St.
E. Cherry St.
E. Jefferson St.
E. Terrace
Alder St.
E. Spruce St.
E. Fir St.
E. Yesler Way
Western Ave.
Post Ave.
Spring St.
Marion St.
Alaskan Way S.
Pier 54
56
1st Ave.
2nd Ave.
3rd Ave.
4th Ave.
5th Ave.
Jefferson St.
Terry Ave.
Alder St.
PIONEER SQUARE
Yesler Way
S. Washington St.
6th Av. S.
S. Main St.
Pier 48
S. Jackson St.
Pier 46
S. King St.
S. Weller St.
8th Ave. S.
12th Ave. S.
S. Lane St.
S. Dearborn St.
E. Marginal Way S.
Alaskan Freeway
1st. Ave. S.
4th Ave. S.
Corwin Pl. S.
Golf Dr. S.
S. Royal Brougham Way
5
99

in this enormous hostel. The five-star common room overlooks the water, just off a palatial lounge and library/TV room. 8 people per dorm-like room. Amenities range from laundry facilities ($1 wash, 75¢ dry) to a ride board in the lobby. Offers discount tickets for Aquarium, Omnidome, and passenger ferry tickets. 7-day max. stay in summer. Front desk open 7am-2am. Checkout 11am. 24hr. living room; no curfew. $16, nonmembers $19. Often full in summer; make reservations.

Commodore Hotel, 2013 2nd Ave. (448-8868), at Virginia. Take bus #174 or 194 from airport. Get off at 4th Ave. and Virginia. Many rooms have pleasant decor and walnut furniture (with a few broken baseboards). Not the best area of downtown, but the Commodore is a great deal and 24hr. security keeps out the riff-raff. Singles $34, with bath $49; 2 beds and bath $64. 2 hostel-style rooms offer a bare-bones bunk room and shared bath for $12. Weekly single $134.

Moore Motel, 1926 2nd Ave. (448-4851 or 448-4852), at Virginia. 1 block east from Pike Place Market. Next to the historic Moore Theater. Big rooms include 2 beds, TV, a slightly moldy bathroom, and carpets in slight disrepair. A 24hr. diner off the lobby and cavernous halls with gargantuan heavy wooden doors makes the Moore seem like it hasn't changed since the 20s (as does the paint job). Singles $34, with bath $39; doubles $45. Discounts for HI members when the hostel is full.

Queen Anne

Green Tortoise Backpacker's Hostel, 1525 2nd Ave. (340-1222; fax 623-3207), between Pike and Pine St. Great location, great rooms, great hostel. 150 beds in 48 rooms plus 10 private rooms. Free breakfast. Shuttles to airport, Amtrak, and Vancouver. Beds $16, private rooms $40. No curfew.

Green Tortoise Garden Apartments, 715 2nd Ave. N (282-1222; fax 282-9075), on the south slope of Queen Anne Hill, 3 blocks east from the Space Needle and the Seattle Center. Long-term accommodations for travelers staying over 30 days. Back yard, kitchens, garden, laundry, free breakfast. Beds $200 per month, private rooms $500 per month.

Capitol Hill

Vincent's Backpackers Guest House, 527 Malden Ave. E (323-7849), between 14th and 15th Ave. Take bus #10 from downtown. A more subdued, long-term hostel. Many a fisherman calls Vincent's home while anchored in Seattle. The house is clean, but parking and living space is limited. Cable. Office open 9am-midnight, door locked at 2am. Beds $12. Private room $20-40.

University District

The College Inn, 4000 University Way NE (633-4441), at NE 40th St. For a place to crash near the UW campus and its youthful environs, this is a sure bet. Singles are tiny and rooms have no TVs or private baths, but the turn-of-the-century bureaus and brass fixtures make a charming substitute. The TV is nestled in the 4th-floor attic along with the kitchen, where a complementary breakfast materializes every morning and guests loll on couches in front of the fireplace. Singles from $42; doubles $55-75. Rates often rise in summer. Credit card required.

Other Neighborhoods

For inexpensive motels a bit farther from downtown, drive north on Hwy. 99 (Aurora Ave.) or take bus #6 to the neighborhood of Fremont. Chain motels like the **Nites Inn,** 11746 Huron Ave. N (365-3216), line the highway north of the Aurora bridge, and many cater to the budget traveler (rooms start at $30). Look for AAA approval to ensure a secure night.

FOOD

Though Seattleites appear to subsist on espresso and steamed milk, they have to eat sometimes. When they do, they seek out healthy cuisine—especially seafood. The best fish, produce, and baked goods can be purchased from various vendors in **Pike Place Market.** Seattle's cheapest food is available in the University district, where food from around the world can be had for under $5. Or visit one of Seattle's active **food cooperatives,** at 6518 Fremont Ave. N. (in Green Lake) or at 6504 20th NE (in the Ravenna District north of the university). Capitol Hill, the U District, and Fremont all close off main thoroughfares on summer Saturdays for their **farmer's markets.**

Pike Place Market and Downtown

Farmers have been selling their produce here since 1907, when angry citizens demanded the elimination of the middle-merchant and local farmers responded by selling produce from wagons by the waterfront. Not even the Great Depression slowed business at the market, which thrived until two disastrous events in the 40s: an enormous fire burned the building in 1941, and almost all of the market's 300 Japanese-American merchants were interned by the American government during WWII. But the early 80s prompted a Pike Place renaissance, and now thousands of tourists mob the market every day of the year. In the **Main Arcade,** which parallels the waterfront on the west side of Pike St., lunatic fish-mongers bellow at befuddled customers, competing for audiences and the contents of tourists' wallets by hurling fish from shelves to scales. The market's restaurants offer an escape from the crowded aisles, often with stellar views of the sound.

The best time to visit the market for shopping is between 7 and 9am, when the fish are still flopping and the fruit is freshest, though late in the day it's possible to score big discounts on produce. An information booth in front of the bike rack by the Main Arcade (at 1st Ave. and Pike St.) can give directions, maps, and answer questions (booth staffed Tues.-Sun. noon-6pm, with occasional coverage from 10am-noon; market open Mon.-Sat. 6:30am-6pm, Sun. 6:30am-5pm). Restaurants farther south of Pike's Place cater mostly to suits on lunch breaks. Find sandwich shops galore in the downtown grid.

Soundview Cafe (623-5700), on the mezzanine level in the Pike Place Main Arcade, down Flower Row. This wholesome self-serve sandwich-and-salad bar offers fresh

I'll Have a Double Decaf Espresso—with a Twist of Lemon.

Visiting Seattle without drinking the coffee would be like traveling to France without tasting the wine. Espresso stands line streets and infiltrate office buildings, and "*Let's Go* for coffee sometime" is a favorite local pick-up line.

It all started in the early 70s, when Starbucks started roasting its coffee on the spot in Pike Place Market. Soon, Stewart Brothers Coffee, now "Seattle's Best Coffee," presented Starbucks with a rival, and the race was on for the best cuppa joe. Today, hundreds of bean-brands compete for the local market, and Seattle coffee drinkers often claim undying allegiance to one or another. Follow this basic guide to the lingo when ordering espresso drinks:

Short: 8oz.; **Tall:** 12oz.; **Grande (or Large):** 16oz.
Single: one shot of espresso; **Double:** two—add shots (usually about 60¢) until you feel you've reached your caffeine saturation point.
Espresso: the foundation of all espresso drinks—a small amount of coffee brewed by forcing steam through finely ground, dark-roasted coffee (pronounced es-PRESS-oh, not *ex*-PRESS-oh).
Cappuccino (or "Capp"): espresso topped by the foam from steamed milk. Order "wet" for more liquid milk and big bubbles, or "dry" for stiff foam.
Latté: espresso with steamed milk and a little foam. More liquid than a "capp."
Americano: espresso with hot water—an alternative to classic drip coffee.
Macciato: a cup of coffee with a dollop of foam and a bit of espresso swirled onto the foam.

With skim (nonfat) milk, any of these drinks is called **skinny.** If all you want is a plain ol' coffee, say "drip coffee"; otherwise, cafe workers will return your request for "coffee" with a blank stare.

food, a spectacular view of Elliott Bay, and occasional poetry readings. Fill a $5 salad bar bowl with tabouli, pasta, salad, or fruit. Or bring a brown-bag lunch: the cafe offers a moment of solace from marketplace madness. Solid breakfasts too. Open daily 7am-5pm, Sun. 9am-3pm.

Piroshki, Piroshki, 1908 Pike Pl. (441-6068). For an ample, high-fat, and heavenly hands-on meal, try this Russian specialty. *Piroshki* are made of a croissant-like dough, baked around anything from sausage and mushrooms ($2.85) to apples doused in cinnamon ($3.50). Watch the *piroshki* process in progress as you wait for your order. Open daily 8am-7pm.

Delcambre's Ragin' Cajun, 1523 1st Ave. (624-2598), near Pike Place. Good food, tremendous portions. Have a spicy dish of red beans and rice with *andouille* (a kind of sausage) for $7, the same dish the nearly-famous deaf chef served to President Clinton 3 years ago. Lunch $5-7. Open Tues.-Sat. 11am-3pm and 5:30-9pm.

Three Girls Bakery, 1514 Pike Pl. (622-1045), at Post. Order to-go or sit in the tiny cafe. The rows of pastries will make you drool, as will the smell of fresh bread. Large portions. 7 kinds of rye $1.50-2.75 each. Sandwiches around $4. Open daily 6am-6pm.

Emmett Watson's Oyster Bar, 1916 Pike Pl. (448-7721). Watson is the local columnist and California-basher who founded the "Lesser Seattle" movement, attempting to keep away tourists and new residents with the candid motto, "Keep the Bastards Out." You haven't really experienced a vitamin E high until you've tried the Oyster Bar Special ($5.75). Lots of tourists try it, too—so much for idealism. Open Mon.-Sat. 11:30am-9pm, Sun. 10am-6pm. Closes 2hr. earlier in winter. No credit cards.

Mama's, 2234 2nd Ave. (728-MAMA/6262). Greasy cheap Mexican food (tacos $2.50) served in superfunk diner. You *will* eat in the Elvis Room. King-sized portions, too. Open Mon.-Fri. 11am-10pm, Sat.-Sun. 11am-1am.

Capitol Hill

With bronze dance-step diagrams paved into the sidewalks and artsy, neon storefronts above, Capitol Hill offers an escape from tourist traps to the espresso houses, imaginative shops, and elegant clubs of **Broadway Avenue.** At night, Broadway comes alive and Seattleites lollygag in droves to see and be seen. Here, even the yuppies have noserings, and drag queens frequent grocery stores. The eclectic array of restaurants line the avenue, provide a perfect perch for people-watching, and make some of the best food in the city. **15th Street,** also on the hill, is more sedate. Bus #7 runs along Broadway; #10 runs through Capitol Hill along 15th St. Unless you're taking out, avoid the metered parking on Broadway and head east for the free angled spots behind the reservoir at Broadway Field, on 11th Ave.

The Gravity Bar, 415 Broadway E. (325-7186), in the Broadway Market. Neo-healthy, organic food and crazy fruit and veggie juices. Stainless steel everything, and conical tables the Jetsons would die for fill this tiny room. Among the infamous fruit and vegetable drinks are Moonjuice (a melon/lime concoction, $3.50) and Mr. Rogers on Amino Acid ($5). Watch urban surfer employees cram grass into a meat grinder to prepare shots of the trendy health elixir, **wheatgrass juice.** This green sludge is not satisfying unless the threat of oxidation terrifies you. Daily psychic readings. Open Sun.-Thurs. 9am-10pm, Fri.-Sat. 10am-11pm.

HaNa, 219 Broadway Ave. E. (328-1187). Cramped quarters in this Japanese joint testify to the popularity of its sushi. Assorted sushi plate $8.25, large tempura lunch $6. Open Mon.-Sat. 11am-10:30pm, Sun. 4:30-10pm.

Dick's, 115 Broadway Ave. E. (323-1300). A Broadway institution, made famous in Sir Mix-A-Lot's rap "Broadway." This pink, 50s-style, drive-in burger chain also has locations in Wallingford, Queen Anne, and Lake City. Try Dick's Deluxe Burger ($1.60). Soft serve kiddie cones cost 50¢. Open daily 10:30am-2am.

Kokeb Restaurant, 926 12th Ave. (322-0485), behind Seattle University at the far south end of Capitol Hill near the First Hill neighborhood. This Ethiopian eatery was the first in the Northwest and serves hot and spicy meat or vegetable stews on spongy *injera* bread. Entrees $7-11. Open Mon.-Fri. 11am-11pm, Sat.-Sun. 5-11pm.

Bimbo's Bitchin' Burrito Kitchen, 506 E. Pine (328-9978). The name explains it all, except for the super sizes. Bimbo's basic burrito $3.50.

International District

Along King and Jackson St., between 5th and 8th Ave. directly east of the Kingdome, Seattle's International District is packed with great eateries. Fierce competition keeps prices low and quality high. Any choice here will probably be a good one, as three out of any four restaurants in the district have been named (at one time or another) the best in town by a *Seattle Times* reviewer. Locals often call these few blocks "Chinatown," but every kind of Asian food can be found here, too. Don't shy away from a shabby exterior; the quality of the facade is often inversely proportional to the quality of the food. **Uwajimaya,** 519 6th Ave. S. (624-6248), is the largest East Asian retail store in the Pacific Northwest. Take bus #7. A huge selection of Japanese staples, fresh seafood (often still swimming), a wide variety of dried foods (great for camping), a sushi bar, and a bakery make this a Seattle institution. It also sells toys, books, furniture, clothes, and jewelry (open daily 9am-8pm).

Tai Tung, 655 S. King St. (622-7372). A Chinese diner. The busiest hours at Tai Tung are 1-3am, when the munchies take hold of university students who shuffle all the way from the U district for the Chinese version of fried chicken. It's roasted, not fried, but still greasy. Waiters here rise to the occasion; they're likely to learn your name by the 2nd night you visit and are never tongue-tied. 10-page, constantly-changing menu plastered to the walls. Entrees $7-8. Open Sun.-Thurs. 10am-11:30pm, Fri.-Sat. 10am-1:30am.

Ho Ho Seafood Restaurant, 653 S. Weller St. (382-9671). Fields of pink formica and friendly service. Watch the demise of your dinner as staff pluck live seafood from tanks. Generous portions of great seafood. Dinner $7-9, lunch $3-5. Open Sun.-Thurs. 11am-1am, Fri.-Sat. 11am-3am.

House of Hong Restaurant, 409 8th Ave. S. (622-7997), at Jackson on the border of the International district. More upscale than most. The most popular *dim sum* in town ($2 per dish; served daily 11am-5pm). Open Mon.-Thurs. 11am-10pm, Fri. 11am-midnight, Sat. 10:30am-midnight, Sun. 10:30am-10pm. Call ahead.

Viet My Restaurant, 129 Prefontaine Pl. S. (382-9923), near 4th and Washington St. Consistently delicious Vietnamese food at great prices. Try *bo la lot* (beef in rice pancakes, $3.50) or shrimp curry ($4.25). Avoid the lunch rush. Open Mon.-Sat. 11am-3pm and 5pm-9pm.

Pioneer Square and the Waterfront

Budget eaters beware Pioneer Square: the Waterfront lures tourists with wharf-side fare that's better suited to the seagulls. The best option is a picnic in Waterfall Garden, on the corner of S. Main St. and 2nd Ave. S.

Mae Phim Thai Restaurant, 94 Columbia St. (624-2979), a few blocks north of Pioneer Sq. between 1st Ave. and Alaskan Way. Local business buffs who pack this tiny, unassuming restaurant at lunch attest to the glory of good, inexpensive take-out. Wait less than 5min. for an enormous meal of *pad thai,* then stroll one block west to the waterfront to enjoy your find. All dishes $4.55.

Ivar's Fish Bar, Pier 54 (624-6852), on the waterfront. One of a string of fast food seafood restaurants founded by and named for the late Seattle celebrity and shipping magnate Ivar Haglund. Try Fish 'n' chips ($4.30), or the definitive Seattle clam chowder ($1.40). Dine with the gulls and pigeons in covered booths outside and avoid the adjoining "Ivar's Acres of Clams" restaurant, replete with expensive food and Winnebago-haulers. Open daily 11am-11pm.

University District

The immense **University of Washington** (colloquially known as "U-Dub"), north of downtown between Union Bay and Portage Bay, supports a colorful array of funky shops, infinite international restaurants, and a slew of coffeehouses. The best restaurants, cinemas, and cafes are within a few blocks of **University Way.** Due to its large student population, this district offers more mileage per food dollar than anywhere in the city. Be prepared for puzzled looks when asking for "University Way"; it's known around here as **"Th' Ave."** To reach the university, drive north or take any one of buses #70-74 from downtown, or bus #7 from Capitol Hill.

Flowers, 4247 University Way NE (633-1903). This local landmark from the 20s spent its youth as a flower shop. Now a dark-wood bar and mirrored ceiling make a tasteful frame for an all-you-can-eat Mediterranean buffet ($5.50). Includes vegan options. Open Mon.-Sat. 11am-2am (kitchen closes at 10pm), Sun. 11am-11pm.

Pizzeria Pagliacci, 4529 University Way NE (632-0421), also on Capitol Hill. Voted Seattle's best pizza every year since 1986. At $1.56 a slice, it's also one of the city's best deals. Watch frat boys gobble pizzas whole and decipher Italian Hollywood movie posters while you eat. Open Sun.-Thurs. 11am-11pm, Fri.-Sat. 11am-1am.

Tandoor Restaurant, 5024 University Way NE (523-7477). Their all-you-can-eat lunch buffet ($5) is a great deal. Dinner is more expensive. Grab a cushion on a back-room bench. Open Mon.-Sat. 11am-2:30pm and 4:30-10pm, Sun. 11am-3pm.

CAFES AND COFFEEHOUSES

Though Seattle boasts a vibrant bar scene, the coffee bean is its first love. A traveler cannot walk a single block without passing an institution of caffeination. The Emerald City's obsession with Italian-style espresso drinks has driven even gas stations to start pumping out thick, dark, soupy java.

Capitol Hill

Vivace, 901 E. Denny Way (860-5869), off Broadway. Vivace's coffee is so delicious that other cafes advertise it. Prices in this sleek cafe reflect the coffee's excellence. Espresso $1.50. Open daily 6:30am-11pm.

The Globe Cafe, 1531 14th Ave. (324-8815). Seattle's next literary renaissance is brewing here. All vegan menu. Open Tues.-Sun. 7am-7:30pm.

Green Cat Cafe, 1514 E. Olive (726-8756), west of Broadway. A favorite with locals for a good reason. Sunny yellow walls and gilt-framed prints brighten up its already wonderful breakfast and lunch fare. Healthy diner food with a twist, and, of course, good coffee. Open Mon.-Fri. 7am-7pm, Sat. 7:30am-7pm, Sun. 9am-7pm.

Cafe Paradiso, 1005 E. Pike (322-6960). This proud-to-be-alternative cafe pumps in your RDA of caffeine and counterculture. Espresso bars on both floors. Angst-ridden artists exhibit their broodings on the public chalkboard upstairs. Wear black. Smoke. Free musical performances (Sat. 8:30pm). Open Mon.-Thurs. 6am-1am, Fri. 6am-2am, Sat. 8am-2am, Sun. 8am-1am.

Dilettante Chocolates, 416 Broadway Ave. E (329-6463). An escape from the coffeehouse, this "cocoa lounge" has an extensive tea menu, the best cocoa in Seattle, and a repertoire of "adult milk shakes" for the 21+ chocolate lover (under $3).

University District

Last Exit, 5211 University Way NE (528-0522). The Exit was established in 1967 and never quite outgrew the 60s. Aging hippies watch aspiring chessmasters battle it out in a large smoky room. The Exit claims to be Seattle's first-ever coffee bar. Dirt-cheap espresso (90¢) and coffee ($1). Open daily 9am-midnight.

Black Cat Cafe, 4113 Roosevelt Way NE (547-3887). Away from the fray, behind a dry cleaner. A sunny, non-smoking alternative to the Last Exit exists in a vegan world of its own, without additives or preservatives. This student-run co-op is so laid back, it's almost asleep on the deck chairs out front. Sandwiches and burritos $3-5. Open Tues.-Sat. 10:30am-8:30pm, Sun. 10:30am-3pm.

Ugly Mug, 1309 43rd St. (547-3219), off University Way. English majors and grad students, come to where turtlenecks are as black as coffee. Faculty and students get real sophisticated like, then munch on black forest ham sandwiches ($4.75) and sip the world's first Ovaltine lattés. Open Mon.-Fri. 8am-10pm, Sat. 9am-10pm.

SIGHTS AND ACTIVITIES

It takes only two frenetic days to get a closer look at most of Seattle's major sights, as most are within walking distance of one another or are within the Metro's ride free zone (see **Getting Around,** above). Rumor has it that Seattle taxpayers spend more

Pop Quiz, Hotshot

What would you call a 12oz. espresso with an extra shot, steamed milk (skim, of course), and foam?

on the arts per capita than any other Americans. The investment pays off in the form of numerous galleries, free art tours, and the renovated Seattle Art Museum. Beyond its cosmopolitan downtown, Seattle also boasts over 300 parks and recreation areas where you can take in the well-watered greenery. Don't pass up this opportunity: take a rowboat out on Lake Union, bicycle along Lake Washington, or hike through the wilds of Discovery Park. The best way to take in the skyline is from any one of the **ferries** that leave from the waterfront. The finest overview of Seattle, however, is a bit of a secret and an exclusively female privilege: the athletic club on the top floor of the **Columbia Tower** (the big black building at 201 5th Ave.) has floor-to-ceiling windows in the ladies' room that overlook the entire city. **Volunteer Park** in Capitol Hill (see below) has a (free) view from the east that captures the skyline and the Sound.

Downtown

The new **Seattle Art Museum,** 100 University Way (654-3100 for a recording, TDD 654-3137), near 1st Ave. and University Way, boasts a bombastic design by Philadelphian architect Robert Venturi. There's art *inside* the building, too. The museum has an entire floor dedicated to the art of Pacific Northwest Native Americans and houses an extensive collection of modern and contemporary Northwestern works. The African collection boasts a piece by Kane Kwei, the carpenter from Ghana who has found a niche in the art world with his theme coffins. Call for info on films and lectures (open Fri.-Wed. 10am-5pm, Thurs. 10am-9pm; free tours 12:30, 1, and 2pm; check for special tours at 7:15pm Thurs.; $6, students and seniors $4, under 12 free). One block north of the museum on 1st Ave. inside the Alcade Plaza Building is the free **Seattle Art Museum Gallery,** featuring contemporary works by local artists.

Westlake Park, with its Art Deco brick patterns and Wall of Water, is a good place to kick back and listen to steel drums. This small triangular park, on Pike St. between 4th and 5th Ave., is bordered by the gleaming new **Westlake Center,** where the monorail departs for the Seattle Center.

Bristling with excitement and only a short walk down Pike St. is the **Pike Place Market,** a public market frequented by tourists and natives in equal proportions. (See **Food: Pike Place Market,** above.) While downtown, trek a few blocks to **Freeway Park,** which straddles I-5 between Pike St. and Spring St., and marvel at a set of concrete waterfalls designed to mimic a natural gorge while simultaneously blocking freeway noise.

The Waterfront

The **Pike Place Hillclimb** descends from the south end of the Pike Place market down a set of staircases, past chic shops and ethnic restaurants, to Alaskan Way and the **waterfront.** (An elevator is also available.) The ever-popular **Seattle Aquarium** (386-4330) sits at the base of the Hillclimb at Pier 59, near Union St. Outdoor tanks recreate ecosystems of salt marshes and tide pools. The aquarium's star attraction, the underwater dome featuring fish of the Puget Sound and some playful harbor seals, fur seals, and otters, is worth the price. See the world's only aquarium salmon ladder and check out the $1 million exhibit on salmon opening in June 1998. Don't miss the daily 11:30am feeding (open daily 10am-5pm; limited hours on holidays; $7.50, seniors $6.75, ages 6-18 $5, ages 3-5 $2.45).

Next to the aquarium on Pier 59 is the **Omnidome** (622-1868). A unique theater experience, the Omnidome displays movies on a special rounded screen so that

Pop Quiz Answer

A tall, skinny, double latté.

patrons actually feel they are in the movie. The booming sound system may scare small children (films shown daily 9:30am-10pm; $7, seniors and students $6, ages 3-12 $5, second film $2; with admission to aquarium $12, seniors and ages 13-18 $9.25, ages 6-12 $8.50, under 12 $5.75).

Explore north or south along the waterfront by foot or by **streetcar.** The 20s cars were imported from Melbourne in 1982 because Seattle sold its originals to San Francisco, where they now enjoy fame as cable cars. (Streetcars run every 20-30min. Mon.-Sat. 7am-11pm, Sun. 8am-11pm; winter until 6pm. 85¢ for 90min. of unlimited travel. Metro passes are good on the streetcar; on Sun., children under 12 ride free if accompanied by a paying passenger.) Streetcars are fully wheelchair accessible and run from the Metro tunnel in Pioneer Square north to Pier 70 and Myrtle Edwards Park.

The Seattle Center

The 1962 World's Fair took place in Seattle, and the entertainment-oriented city rose to the occasion by building the Seattle Center, where visitors can find anything from carnival rides to ballet. For info regarding special events and permanent attractions at the Center, call 684-8582 for recorded information or 684-7200 for a speaking human. Take the **monorail** from the third floor of the Westlake Center; for 90¢ (ages 5-12 70¢, seniors 35¢) it ferries passengers to the Seattle Center every 15 minutes from 9am to midnight. The center is bordered by Denny Way, W. Mercer St., 1st Ave., and 5th Ave. and has eight gates, each with a model of the Center and a map of its facilities. Although Seattleites generally disdain the Center (leaving it to tourists and suburbanites), visitors just keep coming. The **Space Needle** (443-2111), sometimes known as "the world's tackiest monument," is a useful landmark for the disoriented and houses an observation tower and an expensive, 360° rotating restaurant. The Space Needle charges $8.50 (ages 5-12 $4) for a ride to its rotating top unless you have dinner reservations. (People have been known to make reservations with no intention of keeping them.) The **Pacific Science Center** (443-2001), within the park, houses a **laserium** (443-2850) and an **IMAX theater** (443-4629). Evening IMAX shows run Thursday through Sunday (tickets to IMAX *and* the museum $9.50, seniors and ages 6-13 $7.50, ages 2-5 $5.50). The evening laser shows quake to music by groups like Led Zeppelin and, of course, Nirvana (Tues. $3, Wed.-Sun. $6.75).

Pioneer Square and Environs

From the waterfront or downtown, it's just a few blocks to historic Pioneer Square, at Yesler Way and 2nd Ave. The 19th-century warehouses and office buildings were restored in the 70s and now house chic shops and trendy pubs. Pioneer Square today retains much of its historical intrigue, as well as suffocating tourist crowds.

Originally Seattle stood 12 ft. below the present-day streets. The **underground tours** (682-1511 for info or 682-4646 for reservations) take you into the subterranean rooms and passageways, explaining the sordid and soggy birth of Seattle. Be prepared for lots of company, comedy, and toilet jokes. Ninety-minute tours leave every day hourly from Doc Maynard's Pub, 610 1st Ave. ($6.50, seniors $5.50, students $5, children $2.75; reservations recommended). The earliest Seattleites settled on the site of Pioneer Square. "Doc" Maynard, a notorious early resident, gave a plot of land here to one Henry Yesler on the condition that he build a steam-powered lumber mill. Logs were dragged down the steep grade of Yesler Way to feed the mill, earning that street the epithet **"Skid Row."** Years later, the center of activity moved north, precipitating the decline of Pioneer Square and giving the term "skid row" its present meaning as a neighborhood of poverty and despair.

Klondike Gold Rush National Historic Park, 117 S. Main St. (553-7220), is an interpretive center that depicts the lives of miners. A slide show describes the role of Seattle in the Klondike gold rush. Daily walking tours of Pioneer Square leave the park at 10am (free). To add some levity to this litany of shattered dreams, the park screens Charlie Chaplin's 1925 classic *The Gold Rush* on the first Sunday of every month at 3pm (free; open daily 9am-5pm).

The International District

Three blocks east of Pioneer Square, up Jackson on King St., is Seattle's International District. Though sometimes called "Chinatown" by Seattleites, this area is now home to immigrants from all over Asia and their descendants. Prominent members of Seattle's Asian community have recently made big political debuts.

Start your tour of the district by ducking into the **Wing Luke Memorial Museum,** 407 7th Ave. S (623-5124), to get a thorough description of life in an Asian-American community. This tiny museum houses a permanent exhibit on different Asian nationalities in Seattle and exhibits by local Asian artists. This was one of four museums to win the National Award for Museum Service in 1985 for its community emphasis (open Tues.-Fri. 11am-4:30pm, Sat.-Sun. noon-4pm; $2.50, seniors and students $1.50, ages 5-12 75¢; Thurs. free). Other landmarks of the International District include the **Tsutakawa sculpture** at the corner of S. Jackson and Maynard St. and the gigantic dragon mural and red-and-green pagoda in **Hing Hay Park** at S. King and Maynard St. The community gardens at Main and Maynard St. provide a peaceful and well-tended retreat from the downtown sidewalks, though you may feel like you're walking through someone's back yard while you tiptoe through the turnips. Park next to the gardens in free three-hour angled parking to avoid meters.

Capitol Hill

From their elevated position above the Emerald City, Capitol Hill residents scan the city with an artist's eye. Alternative lifestyles and mainstream capitalism converge seamlessly—crowds have recently attracted national chains like Ben & Jerry's and The Gap to join the spend-happy atmosphere along Broadway Ave. The district's leftist and gay communities set the tone for its nightspots (see **Entertainment,** below), while retail outlets include collectives and radical bookstores. Explore Broadway to window shop and experience the neighborhood, or walk a few blocks east and north for a stroll down 15th Ave., lined with well-maintained Victorian homes. Bus #10 runs along 15th Ave. and makes frequent stops; the #7 cruises Broadway.

Volunteer Park, between 11th and 17th Ave. at E. Ward St., north of the Broadway activity, lures Seattleites away from the city center. Bus #10 runs parkward up 15th Ave. To get to the park, it's better to take the #10 than the 7; it runs more frequently and stops closer to the fun stuff. Named for the "brave volunteers who gave their lives to liberate the oppressed people of Cuba and the Philippines" during the Spanish-American War, the park boasts lovely lawns, an outdoor running track, a playground, and fields of rhododendrons that bloom in the spring and early summer. The outdoor stage often hosts free performances on summer Sundays. Climb the medieval-looking water tower at the 14th Ave. entrance for a stunning 360° panorama of the city and the Olympic Range. The views beat those from the Space Needle, and they're free. On rainy days, hide out amid the orchids inside the glass **conservatory** (open daily 10am-4pm, summer 10am-7pm; free). Be careful at night; the park has an unsavory reputation after dark. While in the park, visit the newly renovated **Seattle Asian Art Museum** (654-3100). A tour through the world-renowned collection of Asian art reveals Ming vases and ancient kimonos at every turn (open Tues.-Sun. 10am-5pm, Thurs. 10am-9pm; suggested admission $6, seniors and students $4, under age 12 free).

Just north of Volunteer Park on 15th St. is **Lake View Cemetery,** where the graves of **Bruce** and **Brandon Lee** rest among the founders of Seattle. One of the most famous martial artists of the century, Bruce Lee moved to Seattle in his youth; Brandon, his son, made a name for himself in the same field. The Lees' graves are at the top of the cemetery next to the American flag.

The **University of Washington Arboretum** (543-8800), 10 blocks east of Volunteer Park, houses the Graham Visitors Center, with exhibits on local plant life (open daily 10am-4pm; in winter Mon.-Fri. 10am-4pm, Sat.-Sun. noon-4pm) and is at the southern end of the arboretum at Lake Washington Blvd. Across the street, the tranquil, perfectly pruned **Japanese Tea Garden** (684-4725) offers a stroll through 3½ acres of sculpted gardens encompassing fruit trees, a reflecting pool, and a traditional tea house (open March-Nov. daily 10am-around sunset; $2.50, seniors and ages 6-18 $1.50, disabled $1, under 6 free). Take bus #11 from downtown. The arboretum also shelters superb walking and running trails and boasts 4000 species of trees and shrubs and 43 species of flowers. Tours of the arboretum leave Sat. and Sun. at 1pm from the visitors center (arboretum open dawn-dusk).

University District

With 33,000 students, the **University of Washington** is the state's cultural and educational center of gravity. The "U District" swarms with students year-round, and Seattleites of all ages take advantage of the area's many bohemian bookstores, shops, taverns, and restaurants. To reach the district, take buses #71-74 from downtown, or #7, 43, or 48 from Capitol Hill. Stop by the friendly **visitors center,** 4014 University Way NE (543-9198), to pick up a campus **map,** a self-guided tour book, and information about the university (open Mon.-Fri. 8am-5pm).

On the campus, visit the **Thomas Burke Memorial Washington State Museum** (543-5590), at NE 45th St. and 17th Ave. NE in the northwest corner of the campus. The museum exhibits a superb collection on the Pacific Northwest's native nations, but it is slowly phasing out this collection to make room for its growing exhibit on Pacific Rim cultures. This is the only natural history museum in the area, so savor the chance to see the only dinosaur bones in the Northwest. In addition to Allosauri, the museum also displays two beautiful Tiffany windows, a rare find outside of New York (open daily 10am-5pm; suggested donation $3, seniors and students $2, ages 6-18 $1.50). Across the street, the astronomy department's old stone **observatory** (543-0126) is open to the public for viewings on clear nights. Looming gothic lecture halls, red brick, and rose gardens transform the campus into a bowery fit for hours of strolling. The red concrete basin in the center of campus, known as **Red Square,** collects hundreds of students during the school year. The newly remolded **Henry Art Gallery** (543-2280) is across from the visitors center and hosts superb exhibitions of modern art in a stark white setting (open Tues.-Fri. and Sat.-Sun. 11am-5pm, Wed.-Thurs. 11am-8pm; $5, students $3, free Thurs. after 5pm).

Students often cross town for drinks in **Queen Anne,** and the intervening neighborhood, **Fremont,** basks in the intermediate jovial atmosphere. Fremont residents pride themselves on their love of art and antiques and the liberal atmosphere of their self-declared "center of the world" under Hwy 99. The annual **Fremont Fair** and Solstice Parade in mid-June bring Fremont to a frenzy of music, frivolity, and craft booths. A statue entitled "Waiting for the Inner-City Urban" depicts several people waiting in bus-purgatory, and, in moments of inspiration and sympathy, is frequently dressed up by passers-by. The immense **troll** who sits beneath the Aurora Bridge (on 35th St.) grasping a Volkswagen Bug has a confounded expression on his broad cement face. Some say kicking the Bug's tire brings good luck. Fremont is also home to **Archie McPhee's,** 3510 Stone Way (545-8344), a shrine to pop culture and plastic absurdity. People of the punk and funk persuasion make pilgrimages from as far as the record stores of Greenwich Village in Manhattan just to handle the notorious **slug selection.** You can get to Archie's on the Aurora Hwy. (Rte. 99) or on bus #26. The store is east of the highway between 35th and 36th, two blocks north of Lake Union and Gasworks Park (see below; open Mon.-Sat. 9am-7pm, Sun. 10am-6pm).

WATERWAYS AND PARKS

Seattle's jewel-like waterways distinguish this metropolis from other cities. In summer, they are a playground for boaters, and a string of attractions festoon the waterways linking Lake Washington and Puget Sound. Houseboats and sailboats fill **Lake Union,** situated between Capitol Hill and the University District. Here, the **Center for Wooden Boats,** 1010 Valley St. (382-2628), maintains a moored flotilla of new and restored small craft for rent (open daily 11am-6pm; rowboats $8-12 per hr., sailboats $10-15 per hr.). **Gasworks Park,** a much-celebrated kite-flying spot at the north end of Lake Union, was recently converted after its retirement from the oil-refining business and hosts a furious fireworks show on July 4th. **Gasworks Kite Shop,** 1915 N. 34th St. (633-4780), is one block north of the park (open Mon.-Fri. 10am-6pm, Sat. 10am-5pm, Sun. noon-5pm). To reach the park, take bus #26 from downtown to N. 35th St. and Wallingford Ave. N. If inspiration to sail strikes while at the park, head to **Urban Surf,** across the street at 2100 N. Northlake Way (545-WIND/9463), for windsurfing boards ($35 per day) or in-line skates ($5 per hr.).

Directly north of Lake Union, athletes run, ride, and roll around **Green Lake.** Take bus #16 from downtown Seattle. The lake is also given high marks by windsurfers, but woe be it to those who lose their balance. Whoever named it Green Lake wasn't kidding; even a quick dunk results in a coating of green algae. On sunny afternoons, boat-renters, windsurfers, and scullers can make the lake feel like rush hour. Rent a bicycle from **Greg's Green Lake Cycle, Inc.** (see **Practical Information,** above), also on the east side across the street from Starbucks. Ask for directions to the **Burke-Gilman trail** for a longer ride.

Next to the lake is Woodland Park and the **Woodland Park Zoo,** 5500 Phinney Ave. N (684-4800), best reached from Rte. 99 or N. 50th St. Take bus #5 from downtown. The park itself is not well manicured, but the zoo habitats are wonderfully realistic. Tropical Asia, a new exhibition on orangutans, and Northern Trail, a display of Alaskan wildlife, entrance children. It's one of only three zoos in the U.S. to receive the Humane Society's highest standard of approval (open daily 9:30am-6pm, Oct. 15-March 15 9:30am-4pm; $8; seniors and ages 6-17 $7.25, students $5.50, ages 3-5 $4; parking $3, winter $1.50).

Farther west, at the **Hiram M. Chittenden Locks** (783-7059) along the Lake Washington Ship Canal on NW St., crowds gather to watch Seattle's boaters jockey for position. Take bus #43 from the U District or #17 from downtown. A circus atmosphere develops as boats traveling between Puget Sound and Lake Washington try to cross over (June-Sept. daily 7am-9pm). If listening to the cries of frustrated skippers ("Gilligan, you nitwit!") doesn't amuse you, climb over to the **fish ladder** to watch homesick salmon hurl themselves up 21 concrete steps. The busiest salmon runs occur from June to September. Free tours of the locks start at 1, 2, and 3pm on summer weekends (open daily 10am-7pm; Sept.-June Thurs.-Mon. 11am-5pm). **Discovery Park** (386-4236), at 36th Ave. W and Government Way W on a lonely point west of the Magnolia District and south of Golden Gardens Park (bus #24), comprises acres of minimally tended grassy fields and steep bluffs atop Puget Sound. Next door to the Chittenden Locks, the park is the largest in the Seattle area, with 534 bucolic acres. It provides a wonderful haven for birds forced over Puget Sound by the "bad-weather" Olympic Mountains. Possessing a wide range of habitats with easily distinguishable transitions, this park provides a fantastic introduction to the flora and fauna of the Pacific Northwest for those unable to make the trek to Olympic or Mt. Ranier National Parks. A **visitors center** looms large at the entrance (3801 W. Government Way), waiting to sell you a handy map (75¢). Shuttles ferry elderly and handicapped visitors to the beach (June-Sept. daily 8:30am-5pm). At the park's northern end is the **Indian Cultural Center** (285-4425), operated by the United Indians of All Tribes Foundation, which houses the **Sacred Circle Gallery,** a rotating exhibit of Native American artwork (open Mon.-Fri. 9am-5pm, Sat.-Sun. noon-5pm; free).

Seward Park is at the south end of a string of beaches and forest preserves along the west shore of Lake Washington (take bus #39). Home to Seattle's orthodox Jewish community, the area offers sweeping views of downtown and Lake Union. After a jaunt in the park, refresh yourself with a tour of the **Rainier Brewery Co.,** 3100 Airport Way S (622-2600), off I-5 at the West Seattle Bridge. Beer (root beer for those under 21), cheese, and crackers are free (30min. tours on the hr. Mon.-Sat. 1-6pm).

SPORTS AND RECREATION

The Seattle professional sports scene is truly odd. Uglier and less productive than the Boeing factory, the **Kingdome,** 201 S. King St. (622-4487 for tickets), down 1st Ave., ranks second only to Houston's Astrodome as an insult to baseball. Seattle is the only city in America where fans might prefer to watch their home team (the **Mariners**) on

TV rather than see them live, under poor, flat, purplish light, on artificial turf, amid unearthly echoes. In the fall of 1995, sections of the roof viciously attacked fans hoping to see Seattle make the World Series. Fans responded in kind, by voting to build a new stadium, now in the works. Tickets are cheap: $15 on the 3rd base line (628-0888; open Mon.-Sat. 8am-9pm, Sun. 8am-6pm). Sunday is seniors discount day. The **Seahawks,** more of an afterthought than an NFL team, also play football here.

On the other side of town (and at the other end of the aesthetic spectrum), the new and graceful Key Arena in the Seattle Center is packed to the brim whenever Seattle's pro basketball team, the **Supersonics** (281-5800) play. Two years ago, Seattleites danced in the streets as the Sonics ascended the NBA ranks, only to be defeated by the unstoppable Chicago Bulls. Undaunted by a recent NCAA post-season prohibition, the **University of Washington Huskies** football team has dominated the PAC-10. Call the Athletic Ticket Office (543-2200) for Huskies schedules and price information.

Cyclists should gear up for the 19 mi., 1600-competitor **Seattle to Portland Race.** Call the **bike hotline** (522-2453) for more information. The Seattle Parks Department also holds a monthly **Bicycle Sunday** from May to September, when Lake Washington Blvd. is open only to cyclists from 10am to 6pm. For more information, contact the Parks Department's Citywide Sports Office (684-7092).

Many **whitewater rafting** outfitters are based in the Seattle area. Though the rapids are hours away by car, over 50 companies compete for a growing market. Call outfitters and quote competitors' prices; they are often willing to undercut one another. Two trade organizations, **PRO (Professional Rafters Organization)** (323-5485) and the **Washington State Outfitters and Guides Association** (392-6107), provide advice and information. The **Northwest Outdoor Center,** 2100 Westlake Ave. (281-9694), on Lake Union, gives instructional programs in **whitewater** and **sea kayaking** (2-evening intro to sea kayaking, including equipment, $50). The center also leads three-day kayaking excursions through the San Juan Islands (open Mon.-Fri. 10am-8pm, Sat.-Sun. 9am-6pm).

Skiing near Seattle is every bit as good as the mountains make it look. **Alpental, Ski-Acres,** and **Snoqualmie** co-sponsor an information number (232-8182), which provides conditions and lift ticket rates for all three. **Crystal Mountain** (663-2265), the region's newest resort, can be reached by Rte. 410 south out of Seattle and offers ski rentals, lessons, and lift ticket packages.

Since the Klondike gold rush, Seattle has been in the business of outfitting wilderness expeditions. Besides Army-Navy surplus stores and campers' supply shops, the city is home to many world-class outfitters. **Recreational Equipment Inc. Coop (REI Coop),** 222 Yale Ave., is the largest of its kind in the world. This paragon of woodsy wisdom can be seen from I-5. Take the Stewart St. exit. The brand-new flagship store offers a 65 ft. indoor climbing pinnacle, interactive pathways to test mountaineering equipment, and lessons on Northwest foliage (open Mon.-Sat. 10am-9pm, Sun. 11am-6pm; rental area open 3hr. before store).

ENTERTAINMENT

With one of the world's most notorious underground music scenes and the third largest theater community in the U.S. (only New York's and Chicago's are bigger), performances of all kinds take place in any Seattle building with four walls, from bars to bakeries. In the summertime, risers seem to grow out of asphalt during street fairs and farmers' markets, and outdoor theater springs up in most parks. High cost shows regularly sell half-price tickets, while alternative theaters offer high-quality drama at low prices. During lunch hours in the summertime, the free **"Out to Lunch"** series (623-0340) brings everything from reggae to folk dancing to the parks, squares, and office buildings of downtown Seattle. Pick up a schedule at the visitors center (see **Practical Information**). The **Seattle Public Library** (386-4636) shows free films as part of the program and has a daily schedule of other free events, such as poetry readings and children's book-reading competitions.

Music and Dance

The **Seattle Opera** (call 389-7676, Mon.-Fri. 9am-5pm, or Ticketmaster at 292-2787) performs at the Opera House in the Seattle Center throughout the year. The program's popularity requires that you order tickets well in advance, although rush tickets are sometimes available (students and seniors receive ½ price tickets day of performance, $15-30). Write to the Seattle Opera at P.O. Box 9248, Seattle 98109. The **Seattle Symphony Orchestra** (443-4747), also in Seattle Center's Opera House, performs a regular subscription series (Sept.-June; rush tickets $6.50 and up) and a popular children's series. The symphony is moving in September 1998 to its home in the new **Fifth Avenue Theater.** The **Pacific Northwest Ballet** (441-9411) starts its season at the Opera House in September. The spectacular Maurice Sendak-designed version of the *Nutcracker* always draws crowds, especially since this is one of only two major ballet companies on the West Coast (San Francisco's is the other). The season continues through May with six productions (tickets $14 and up). The **University of Washington** offers its own program of student recitals and concerts by visiting artists. Call the Meany Hall box office (543-4880; open Mon.-Fri. 10:30am-4:30pm).

Theater

The city hosts an exciting array of first-run plays and alternative works, particularly by many talented amateur groups. **Rush tickets** are often available at nearly half price on the day of the show (with cash only) from **Ticket/Ticket** (324-2744). Watch for the popular, free, open-air Shakespeare in the summer put on by the **University of Washington School of Drama Theaters** (543-4880).

Seattle Repertory Theater, 155 W. Mercer St. (443-2222, open Mon. 10am-6pm, Tues.-Sat. 10am-8pm), at the wonderful **Bagley Wright Theater** in Seattle Center. Their winter season combines contemporary and classic productions (usually including Shakespeare); Gilbert and Sullivan move in over the summer (292-7676 for G&S info). *The Heidi Chronicles* and *Fences* got their start here and later appeared on Broadway. Tickets $10-38. 30min. before each show senior and student rates are available at ½ price with ID (none on Sat.).

A Contemporary Theater (ACT), 100 W. Roy St. (285-5110), at the base of Queen Anne Hill. A summer season of modern and off-beat premieres. Box office open Tues.-Thurs. noon-7:30pm, Fri.-Sat. noon-8pm, Sun. noon-7pm. Tickets $14-26.

Annex Theatre, 1916 4th Ave. (728-0933). Refreshing emphasis on company-generated material. Regular productions run 4 weeks. Shows usually Thurs.-Sat. at 8pm and Sun. at 7pm. Pay-what-you-can previews. Tickets $10-12.

The Empty Space Theatre, 3509 Fremont Ave. N (547-7500), 1½ blocks north of the Fremont bridge. Comedies in this small theater attract the attention of the entire city. Season runs from mid-Nov. to late June. ½ price rush tickets 10min. prior to curtain. Box office open daily 1-5pm. Tickets $14-24, preview tickets (first 4 performances of any show) $10.

Northwest Asian American Theater, 409 7th Ave. S (340-1049), in the International District. This excellent new theater offers theater by, for, and about Asian Americans. Tickets $12, students, seniors, and handicapped $9 (Thurs. $6).

Bathhouse Theater, 7312 W. Green Lake Dr. N (524-9108), right by the lake. This small company is known for transplanting Shakespeare to unexpected locales (e.g. a Wild West *Macbeth,* Kabuki *King Lear,* and *Midsummer Night's Dream* in the 50s). Tickets $13-22. Rush tickets ($7.50) available Tues.-Thurs. before the show. Open Tues.-Sun. noon-7pm.

Cinema

Seattle is a cinematic paradise. Most of the theaters that screen non-Hollywood films are on Capitol Hill and in the University District. Large, first-run theaters—including a mammoth 16 screen **Cineplex Odeon** (223-9600) at 7th Ave. and Pike—are everywhere. Most matinee shows cost $4; after 6pm, expect to pay $7. Seven Gables, a local company, has recently bought up the Egyptian, the Metro, the Neptune, and others. $20 buys admission to any five films at any of their theaters. Call 44-FILMS/443-4567 for local movie times and locations.

The Egyptian, 801 E. Pine St. (32-EGYPT/34978), at Harvard Ave. on Capitol Hill. This handsome Art Deco theater shows artsy films and is best known for hosting the **Seattle International Film Festival** in the last week of May and the first week of June. The festival includes a retrospective of one director's work with a personal appearance by the featured director. Festival series tickets are available at a discount. Regular tickets $6.75, seniors and children $4, matinee $4.

The Harvard Exit, 807 E. Roy St. (323-8986), on Capitol Hill. Quality classic and foreign films. Half the fun of seeing a movie here is the theater, a converted residence that has its very own ghost (or so legend has it) and an enormous antique projector. The lobby was once someone's living room. Arrive early for a game of chess, checkers, or backgammon. $6.75, seniors and children $4, matinee $4.

Seven Gables Theater, 911 NE 50th St. (632-8820), in the U District just off Roosevelt, a short walk west from University Way. Another cinema in an old house. Independent and classic films. $6.75, seniors and children $4, matinee $4.

Grand Illusion Cinema, 1403 NE 50th St. (523-3935), in the U District at University Way. A tiny theater attached to an espresso bar, showing films made on 30s-style budgets. One of the last independent theaters in Seattle. $6, seniors and children $3, matinees $4.

United Artists Cinema, 2131 6th Ave. (883-9591), at Blanchard. Known around Seattle as the "$2 theater." Tickets to fairly recent Hollywood flicks cost $2, except for "midnight madness" shows that cost $5 but come with popcorn or a drink.

Shopping

Seattle's younger set has created a wide demand for alternatives to massive retail chains, though a swiftly growing population has certainly lured "syndicated" stores to popular shopping areas as well. Downtown, trendy and fairly expensive clothing stores and boutiques line the avenues from 3rd to 6th, between Seneca St. in the south and the **Westlake Center** in the north. You'll find the enormous **Nordstrom's** at 1051 5th Ave. (628-2111). The Westlake Center itself is an indoor conglomerate of mall chain stores and pricey gift shops.

For handmade crafts and jewelry, shop at **Pike Place Market** (see **Food**), where baubles are almost as plentiful as cherries and zucchini. **The Ave** (University Way) in the U District caters to the college crowd and promises good deals. **Used music stores** occupy almost every other storefront in this area, and music-lovers glory in deals on all sorts of tunes. Capitol Hill also supports the used music market—**Orpheum,** 618 Broadway E (322-6370), has an inspiring collection of imports.

Thrift stores thrive in Seattle, especially on The Ave and between Pike and Pine Streets on Capitol Hill. Find astounding temples to trendiness and thriftiness like **Rex and Angels Red Light Lounge and Cereal Bar,** 4560 University Way NE (545-4044), or **Righteous Rags,** 506 E. Pine (329-7847).

Bookstores

University Book Store, 4326 University Way NE (634-3400). Largest college book store chain on the west coast, with 7 stores in the Seattle area. Open Mon.-Wed and Fri.-Sat. 9am-6pm, Thurs. 9am-9pm, Sun. noon-5pm.

Elliott Bay Books, 101 S. Main St. (624-6600), in Pioneer Sq. Vast collection with 150,000 titles. Sponsors a reading and lecture series. Coffeehouse in the basement. Open Mon.-Fri. 7am-10:30pm, Sat. 10am-10:30pm, Sun. 11am-5pm.

Red and Black Books, 432 15th Ave. E (322-7323). Features multicultural, gay, and feminist literature, and frequent readings. Open Mon.-Thurs. 10am-8pm, Fri.-Sat 10am-9pm, Sun. 11am-7pm.

Beyond the Closet, 1501 Belmont Ave. E (322-4609). Exclusively gay and lesbian material. Open Sun.-Thurs. 10am-10pm, Fri.-Sat. 10am-11pm.

NIGHTLIFE

Seattle has moved beyond beer to a new nightlife frontier: the cafe and bar. The popularity of espresso bars in Seattle might lead one to conclude that caffeine is more intoxicating than alcohol, but often an establishment that poses as a diner by day brings on a band, breaks out the disco ball, and pumps out the microbrews by night.

Many locals tell tourists that the best spot to go for guaranteed good beer, live music, and big crowds is **Pioneer Square,** where UW students from "frat row" dominate bar stools. These "real" Seattleites are lying to you: they take their beer bucks downtown, to Capitol Hill, or up Hwy. 99 to Fremont. Most of the bars around the Square participate in a **joint cover** ($8) that will let you wander from bar to bar and sample the bands you like. **Fenix Cafe and Fenix Underground** (343-7740) and **Central Tavern** (622-0209) rock constantly, while **Larry's** (624-7665) and **New Orleans** (622-2563) feature great jazz and blues nightly. **Kells** (728-1916), near Pike Place Market, is a popular Irish pub with nightly celtic tunes. **J and M Cafe** (624-1670) is in the center of Pioneer Square but has no music. All the Pioneer Square clubs shut down at 2am Friday and Saturday nights and around midnight during the week.

Pioneer Square

Colorbox, 113 1st Ave. (340-4101). One of the few places in Pioneer Square that real rockers respect. Live music most nights in a bar that looks quaint with the lights on and violently grungy with them off. Open nightly 8:30pm-2am.

OK Hotel, 212 Alaskan Way S. (621-7903; call 386-9934 for the coffeehouse). One cafe, one bar, one building. Just below Pioneer Square toward the waterfront. Lots of wood, lots of coffee. Live bands play everything from rock to reggae and draw equally diverse crowds. Bar art is "curated" monthly. Occasional cover charge up to $6. Cafe open Mon.-Wed. 11am-9pm, Thurs. 11am-10pm, Fri. 11am-11pm, Sat.-Sun. 8am-9pm. Bar open daily 4pm-2am.

Downtown

Sit and Spin, 2219 4th St. This ain't your Mama's laundromat. Though the washers and dryers work, the real focus of this late-night cafe is the social scene. Furniture hangs from the walls and board games keep patrons busy while they sit waiting for their clothes to dry or for bands with an alternative spin to play in the back room (Fri. and Sat. nights). The cafe sells everything from local microbrews on tap to veggie bistro food (cashew chicken tarragon, $4.75) to boxes of laundry detergent. Artists recording in the Bad Animal recording studio down the street (where R.E.M. once recorded) stop by every once in a while to play a game of checkers and bask in the plastic glow of 50s trailer park decor gone mad. Open Sun.-Thurs. 9am-midnight, Fri.-Sat. 9am-2am. Kitchen opens daily at 11am.

The Alibi Room, 85 Pike St. (623-3180), across from the Market Cinema in the Post Alley in Pike Place. Created by a local producer, The Alibi Room proclaims itself a local "indie filmmaker" hangout. Smoky sophisticates star as themselves. Racks of screenplays, live music after 8pm (21+ only), and chic decor get an Oscar for ambience. Open daily 11am-2am.

Crocodile Cafe, 2200 2nd Ave. (448-2114), at Blanchard. Another diner-turned-club. Eat organic eggs and toast during the day, and jam to popular local and national bands after dark. Only 21+ groovesters after 9pm. Cover $5-20. Open Tues.-Fri. 8am-midnight, Sat. 8am-2am, Sun. 9am-3pm for brunch.

Re-Bar, 1114 Howell (233-9873). A mixed gay and straight bar with a wide range of tunes and dancing on the wild side. Hip-hop on Fri., lots of acid jazz and fringe theater on weekends. Cover $4. Open daily 9:30pm-2am.

Art Bar, 1516 2nd Ave. (622-4344). Exactly what the name says: a bar that doubles as a gallery. Lots of jazz and a diverse clientele. Open Mon. and Wed.-Thurs. noon-1am, Tues. and Fri. noon-2am, Sat. 2pm-2am, Sun. 2pm-1am.

Capitol Hill

Kid Mohair, 1207 Pine St. (625-4444), south of Broadway on Capitol Hill. Dark wood and rich velvet in this cabaret-style gay club make for a glamorous scene. Dance to deejayed house music with sequin-bedecked drag queens for a $5 weekend cover. Open Mon.-Sat. 4pm-2am, Sun. 6pm-2am.

Garage, 1130 Broadway (322-2296). Automotive warehouse turned upscale pool hall, this place gets suave at night. 8 pool tables, $6. Open daily 3pm-2am.

Neighbours, 1509 Broadway (324-5358). A very gay dance club priding itself on techno slickness. $1 cover weeknights, $5 Fri.-Sat. Open Sun.-Thurs. 9pm-2am, Fri.-Sat. 9pm-4am.

Linda's, 707 Pine St. E (325-1220). Major post-gig scene for Seattle rockers. Stop by to be seen with the next Soundgarden (or the last). Open 11am-2am daily.

Fremont

Red Door Alehouse, 3401 Fremont Ave. N (547-7521), at N. 34th St. across from the Inner-Urban Statue. Throbbing with university students who attest to the good local ale selection and a mile-long beer menu. A hint: try the Pyramid Wheaton or Widmer Hefeweizen with a slice of lemon. Open daily 11am-2am. Kitchen closes at 11pm Sun.-Wed. and at midnight Thurs.-Sat.

The Dubliner, 3405 Fremont Ave. N (548-1508). Irish soul in Fremont! Irish jam session Wed. 9pm. Friendly local crowd. Open 11am-2am.

The Trolleyman Pub, 3400 Phinney Ave. N. (548-8000). Also in Fremont, west on N. 34th St. from the Red Door. In the back of the **Red Hook Ale Brewery,** which rolls the most popular kegs on campus. Early hours make it a mellow spot to listen to good acoustic music while lounging on one of the pub's couches and enjoying a fresh pint. Live blues on Sat. and jazz on Mon. Come back during the day for a $1 tour of the brewery and a generous sampling of all 4 beers currently on tap. Wear Birkenstocks. Brewery open in summer daily noon-5pm. Pub open Mon.-Thurs. 9am-11pm, Fri. 9am-midnight, Sat. 11am-midnight, Sun. noon-7pm.

EVENTS

Pick up a copy of the Seattle-King County visitors center's *Calendar of Events,* published every season, for event coupons and an exact listing of innumerable area happenings. The first Thursday evening of each month, the art community sponsors **First Thursday,** a free and well-attended gallery walk. Watch for **street fairs** in the University District during mid- to late May, the Pike Place Market over Memorial Day weekend, and the Fremont District in mid-June. The **International District** holds its annual two-day bash in mid-July, featuring arts and crafts booths, East Asian and Pacific food booths, and presentations by a range of groups from the Radical Women/Freedom Socialist Party to the Girl Scouts. For information, call **Chinatown Discovery, Inc.** at 236-0657 or 583-0460 or write P.O. Box 3406, Seattle 98114.

Puget Sound's **yachting** season begins in May. **Maritime Week,** during the third week of May, and the **Seattle Boats Afloat Show** (634-0911), in mid-August, give area boaters a chance to show off their craft. At the beginning of July, the Center for Wooden Boats sponsors the free **Wooden Boat Show** (382-2628) on Lake Union. Blue blazers and deck shoes are *de rigeur.* Size up the entrants (over 100 wooden boats), then watch a demonstration of boat-building skills. The year-end blow-out is the **Quick and Daring Boatbuilding Contest.** Hopefuls go overboard trying to build and sail wooden boats of their own design using a limited kit of tools and materials. Plenty of music, food, and alcohol make the sailing smooth.

The Northwest Folklife Festival, one of the most notable Seattle events, is held on Memorial Day weekend at the Seattle Center. Artists, musicians, and dancers congregate to celebrate the heritage of the area.

Bon Odori, the Japanese community's traditional festival, is celebrated in the 3rd week of July in the International District. Temples are opened to the public and dancing fills the streets.

The Bite of Seattle (232-2982) is a celebration of food, held in mid-July (1998: July 17-19) in the Seattle Center (free).

Bumbershoot (281-7788), a massive festival that caps off the summer, is held in the Seattle Center over Labor Day weekend. This fantastic 4-day arts festival attracts big-name rock bands, street musicians, and a young, exuberant crowd. $29 for 4 days, $16 for any 2 days, $9 in advance or $10 at the door for 1 day; seniors $1, children free; prices are subject to change.

The Seattle Seafair (728-0123) is the biggest, baddest festival of them all, spread over three weeks from mid-July to early August. All of the city's neighborhoods contribute with street fairs, parades large and small, balloon races, musical entertainment, and a seafood fest.

Near Seattle

Seattle may seem like a world of its own, but just a short drive or float away, the city's environs, particularly to the west, hold any number of outdoor activities, museums, and views worth a daytrip. Puget Sound harbors small islands, cedar forests, and the Vashon Island AYH Ranch Hostel, one of the best hostels in the state.

East

Cross **Lake Washington** on one of two floating bridges to arrive in a bikers' and picnickers' (and suburbanites') paradise. Range Rovers and outdoor shopping plazas litter the landscape. Companies like Microsoft, which has nearly subsumed the suburb of Redmond, buy up expanses of East Sound land, smother them in sod and office complexes, and call them "campuses." But rapid growth has had its benefits; in the suburb of **Bellevue,** the July **Bellevue Jazz Festival** (455-6885) attracts both local cats and national acts. This wealthy and beautiful suburb is home to Bill Gates, among others. Neither tours of Bill's house, nor of Microsoft, are available, but Mac lovers can hurl abuse from a **boat tour** of Lake Washington. Contact **Argosy Cruises** (623-1252) for info.

Farther south on Rte. 405 toward Renton, rock pilgrims find the grave of Seattle's *other* rock legend, **Jimi Hendrix.** Take bus #101 from downtown to the Renton Park 'N' Ride, then switch to #105 to Greenwood Cemetery. Drivers should take the Sunset Blvd. exit from Rte. 405, turn right onto Union, and right again on NE 4th.

Head even farther out for wilder country excursions. Take I-90 east to **Lake Sammamish State Park,** off Exit 15, for swimming and water-skiing facilities, volleyball courts, and playing fields. In the town of **Snoqualmie,** 29 mi. east of Seattle, the **Northwest Railroad Museum,** 109 King St. (746-4025), on Rte. 202 dividing the two lanes of the town's main street, houses a small collection of functional early steam and electric trains. One of its exhibits, the oldest running train in the state, runs 7 mi. to **North Bend,** offering views of **Snoqualmie Falls.** Trips run on the hour and last one hour (open May-Sept. Sat.-Sun. 10am-5pm; round-trip $6.30, seniors $5.25, children $4.20).

From North Bend, take bus #211 (#210 on Sun.) or Rte. 202 north to view the astounding **Snoqualmie Falls.** Formerly a sacred place for the native Salish people, the 270 ft. wall of water has generated electricity for Puget Power since 1898. Five generators buried under the falls work hard to provide energy for 1600 homes. The falls were featured in David Lynch's cult TV series *Twin Peaks,* and the small town of Snoqualmie has been host to hordes of "Peaks freaks" (mostly Japanese) ever since.

I-90 cruises along some of western Washington's prettiest hiking country. Exit 20, High Point Way, leads to a beautiful set of trails on **West Tiger Mountain.** Past North Bend, find the 4 mi. trail to **Mt. Si,** a 4000 ft. peak that offers stellar views of Seattle and the surrounding valley. To find the trail, take North Bend Way off Exit 28 to Mt. Si Rd. A short, wheelchair-accessible loop trail starts at the base of Mt. Si.

South

The Seattle area is surrounded by the vast factories of **Boeing,** Seattle's most prominent employer. South of Seattle at Boeing Field is the **Museum of Flight,** 9404 E. Marginal Way S (764-5720). Take I-5 south to Exit 158 and turn north onto E. Marginal Way S, or take bus #123. The cavernous museum displays flying machines, from canvas biplanes to chic fighter jets, all hanging from a three-story roof. A tribute to the Apollo space shuttle missions, which landed the first man on the moon, exhibits a life-sized replica of the command module. Tour Kennedy's old Air Force One, or fly in a nauseatingly realistic flight simulator ($7.50). When tales of space-age technology become repetitive, explore the red barn, where William E. Boeing founded the company in 1916. Photographs and artifacts trace the history of flight from its beginnings through the 30s, including an operating replica of the Wright Brothers' wind tunnel. (Tours with enthusiastic airforce veterans leave the entrance on the half-hour 10:30am-1:30pm. Museum open Fri.-Wed. 10am-5pm, Thurs. 10am-9pm; $8, seniors $7, ages 6-15 $4, under age 5 free. Wheelchair accessible.)

TACOMA

Though spending time in Tacoma rather than Seattle is somewhat like hanging out in Newark instead of New York, Tacoma has a few worthwhile attractions suitable for a daytrip. Tacoma is Washington's second largest city and lies on I-5 about 35 mi. south of Seattle and 35 mi. east of Olympia. Get the skinny on Tacoma at the **Pierce County Visitor Information Center,** 1001 Pacific Ave. #400 (627-2836 or 800-272-2662). Take the 705 exit from U.S. 5. (open Mon.-Fri. 9am-5pm). **Greyhound** (383-4621), at the corner of Pacific and 14th St. in downtown Tacoma, runs buses to and from Seattle (station open daily 7:30am-2am; several buses per day, $4). Some important numbers are: **emergency,** 911; **crisis line,** 759-6700; **rape crisis,** 474-7273; **safeplace,** 279-8333. The Tacoma **post office** is on 11th at A St. (open Mon.-Fri. 8am-5:30pm; **General Delivery ZIP Code:** 98402). The **area code** is 253.

Downtown Tacoma is home to the new **Washington State History Museum,** 1911 Pacific Ave. (888-BE-THERE/238-4373), and its interactive exhibits on Washington's history through the 1800s. A sprawling model train on the fifth floor is a highlight for children (open Mon-Wed. and Fri.-Sat. 9am-5pm, Thurs. 9am-8pm, Sun. 11am-5pm; $7, seniors $5, youth $4).

The main attraction in Tacoma remains **Point Defiance Park** (305-1000), one of the most attractive parks in the Puget Sound area (open daily dawn-30min. after dusk; free). To reach the park, take Hwy. 16 to the 6th Ave. exit, head east on 6th Ave., then go north on Pearl St. Point Defiance is Tacoma's **ferry** terminal. From here, a Washington State ferry runs regularly to Vashon Island (see p. 33). A 5 mi. loop passes by all the park's attractions and offers postcard views of Puget Sound and access to miles of woodland **trails.** In the spring, stop to smell the flowers; a rhododendron garden lies nestled in the woods along the loop, and intricate fuschia, rose, and Japanese gardens make an Eden out of the park's entrance. **Owen Beach** looks across at **Vashon Island** and is a good starting place for a ramble down the shore. The loop then brushes by the spot where in 1841 Captain Wilkes of the U.S. Navy proclaimed that if he had guns on this and the opposite shore (Gig Harbor) he could defy the world: hence, "Point Defiance."

The park's prize possession is the **Point Defiance Zoo and Aquarium** (591-5337). Penguins, polar bears, beluga whales, and sharks populate the tanks of the aquarium. Kids and their distressed chaperones occupy the paths between them. A number of natural habitats are re-created within the zoo's boundaries (open daily 10am-7pm; Labor Day-Memorial Day 10am-4pm; $7, seniors $6.55, ages 5-17 $5.30, ages 3-4 $2.50, under 3 free). The meticulously restored **Fort Nisqually** (591-5339), in the park, also merits a visit. The Canadian Hudson's Bay Company built the fort in 1832 to offset growing commercial competition from Americans. The museum holds a compact but captivating exhibit on the lives of children, laborers, natives, and Hawaiians who worked there during the Hudson Bay years. Volunteers wear 19th-century garb and delight visitors with their raccoon hats and funny accents (open June-Aug. daily 11am-6pm, Sept.-April Wed.-Sun. 1-4pm; $1.25, children 75¢). **Camp Six Logging Museum** (752-0047), also in the park, retrieves an entire 19th-century logging camp from the dustbin of history. The camp also offers a 1 mi. ride on an original steam-powered logging engine (open Wed., and Sat.-Sun. 10am-4pm; ride costs $2, seniors and children $1).

On your way out of the park, stop in at **Antique Sandwich Company,** 5102 N. Pearl St. (752-4069), near Point Defiance, for some great natural food and an open mic on Tuesday nights. The "poor boy" sandwich ($6) will fill you for a week; espresso shakes are $3.50. The pies draw a faithful local following who eat among rose bushes in the sandwich company's "Garden of Eatin'" (open Mon. and Wed.-Thurs. 7am-8pm, Tues. 7am-10pm, Fri. 7am-9pm, Sat. 7am-7pm, Sun. 8am-7pm).

■ West

VASHON ISLAND

Only a short ferry ride from Seattle and an even shorter hop from Tacoma, Vashon (VASH-on) Island has remained inexplicably invisible to most Seattleites. That's their loss and the traveler's gain. With its forested hills and expansive sea views, the artists' colony of Vashon feels much like the San Juan Islands without oppressive crowds of tourists. Vashon's natural beauty and the small-town lifestyle of its islanders are largely uncluttered by its proximity to the city. Most of the island is undeveloped and covered in Douglas fir, rolling cherry orchards, wildflower and strawberry fields. Almost any Vashon road eventually winds its way to a rocky beach.

Practical Information Vashon Island stretches between Seattle and Tacoma on its east side and between Southworth and Gig Harbor on its west side. Four different **Washington State Ferries** can get you there (see **Planning Your Ferry Trips,** p. 33). Ferries leave for the northern tip of Vashon Island from Fauntleroy in West Seattle, downtown Seattle, and from Southworth in the Kitsap Peninsula; ferries leave for the southern tip from Point Defiance in Tacoma. Hostels give discounts on ferry tickets. To get to the ferry terminal from Seattle, drive south on I-5 and take Exit 163A (West Seattle/Spokane St.) down Fauntleroy Way to the Fauntleroy Ferry Terminal, or turn at the Spokane St. bridge 1 mi. south of the main ferry terminal. From Tacoma, take Exit 132 off I-5 (Bremerton/Gig Harbor) to Rte. 16. Get on 6th Ave. and turn right onto Pearl. Follow signs to Point Defiance Park and the ferry. **Buses** #54, 118, and 119 pick up at 1st and Union and serve the island ferries from downtown Seattle (call 800-542-7876 for bus info), and #118 and 119 continue onto the island to the town of Vashon; buses also service the island, beginning their runs from the ferry landing. Both can be flagged down anywhere. Fares are the same as in the rest of the system. The island is all within one zone, but Seattle to Vashon is two zones.

The steep hills on Vashon are a hindrance to hikers and bikers, though bicycles remain the recreational vehicle of choice on the island. You can pick up a map of Vashon at the local **Thriftway** (463-2100; open daily 8am-9pm) on 9740 SW Bank Rd., or call the **Vashon-Maury Chamber of Commerce** ahead of time (463-6217). Many locals and visitors resort to hitchhiking, which is reputed to be easier here than on the mainland.

Feed your head at the **Vashon Library,** 17210 Vashon Hwy. (463-2069), which offers **Internet access.** Wash duds at **Joy's Village Cleaner and Laundry,** 17318 Vashon Hwy. (463-9933; open Mon.-Sat. 7am-8:30pm, Sun. 8am-8pm; wash and dry $1 each). Pick up some sunscreen at the **Vashon Pharmacy,** 17617 Vashon Hwy. (463-9118; open Mon.-Fri. 9am-7pm, Sat. 9am-6pm, Sun. 11am-1pm). In case of **emergency,** call 911. Reach the **police** at 463-3618 and the **coast guard** at 463-2951. Vashon's **post office** (463-9390) is on Bank Rd. (open Mon.-Fri. 9am-1pm and 2:30-4:30pm, Sat. 9-11:30am; **General Delivery ZIP code:** 98070). The **area code** is 206.

Accommodations and Food The **Vashon Island AYH Ranch Hostel (HI-AYH),** 12119 SW Cove Rd. (463-2592; http://www.vashonisland.com/ayhranchhostel), west of Vashon Hwy., sometimes called the **"Seattle B,"** is the island's only real budget accommodation and reason enough to trek to Vashon. It's easy to get to: jump on any bus at the ferry terminal, ride to **Thriftway Market,** and call from the free phone inside the store, marked with an HI-AYH label. Judy will come pick you up during reasonable hours. This is the hostel version of Disneyland's Frontierland—it looks like an old ghost town, replete with teepees, covered wagons that moonlight as queen beds, and a sheriff's office. A free pancake breakfast, free firewood, and a squadron of bikes for hostelers to borrow attract every sort of traveler, from road-weary backpackers to couples escaping Seattle. Theme rooms (like the "Throne Room," a bathroom graced by a portrait of the Queen) add to the fun. The hostel accommodates 14 in bunk rooms. Hearty hostelers can also bed down under the stars in the teepees or covered wagons. When all the beds are full, pitch a tent ($10, bicyclists $8, nonmembers $13; sheets or sleeping bag $1; open May-Oct.). Ask about the hostel's new B&B down the road (rooms $35-45).

Get creative in the hostel kitchen with supplies from the large and slightly offbeat **Thriftway** downtown. The deli sports good ol' artery-plugging fried chicken, and the bulk foods aisle is a health food nirvana. Options for cooking-phobes include the **Dog Day Cafe and Juice Bar,** 17530 Vashon Hwy. (463-6404), on the Vashon Landing, a restaurant that changes its menu daily and juices just about anything (open daily 9am-4pm). For take-out, stampede to **Tatanka** for bison, bison, and more bison: bison burgers ($4.75), bison burritos ($3.50), and bison chili ($3). The much touted "meat of the 90s," bison has 10% the fat of beef and requires half as much rangeland. Hostelers get drinks for half price (open Mon.-Sat. 11am-7pm, Sun. noon-7pm).

Sights and Events The island is wonderful for **biking,** but despite short distances, Vashon's hills will turn even a short jaunt into a workout. Sweaty exploration will be rewarded, however, with rapturous scenery. **Vashon Island Bicycles,** 7232 Vashon Hwy. (463-1225), rents mountain bikes ($9 per hr., $25 per day). **Point Robinson Park** is a gorgeous spot for a picnic (from Vashon Hwy., take Ellisburg Rd. to Dockton Rd. to Pt. Robinson Rd.); schedule a free tour of the 1885 **Coast Guard lighthouse** that faces off with Mt. Ranier (217-6123). On a calm day at **Tramp Harbor,** rent a sea kayak or rowboat for an hour from **Vashon Island Kayak Co.** (463-YAKS/9257; open Fri.-Sun. 10am-5pm). More than 500 acres of woods in the middle of the island are interlaced with mild hiking trails. Call the Vashon Park District for more information (463-9602, daily 9am-1pm).

Count on some culture no matter when you visit—one in ten residents of Vashon is a professional artist. **Blue Heron Arts Center,** 19704 Vashon Hwy. (463-5131), coordinates most activities, including free local gallery openings on the first Friday of every month (6-9pm).

BAINBRIDGE ISLAND

Ferries (see p. 312) depart from Colman Dock in downtown Seattle for **Bainbridge Island,** a rural island homesteaded by late-19th-century Swedish, late-20th-century Californian, and many intermediate Japanese immigrants. The ferry ride and a stroll through the town of Winslow make a relaxing escape from Seattle. **Fay-Bainbridge State Park** (842-3931), on the northeast tip of the island, has good fishing, 26 trailer sites, and 35 tent sites with pay showers and flush toilets (trailer sites $11, tent sites $8). Eat at the firecracker- and flower-festooned **Streamliner Diner,** 397 Winslow Way (842-8595), where natural foods and rich pies ($2.50) tempt (open Mon.-Fri. 7am-3pm, Sat.-Sun. 8am-2:30pm). Wash dinner down with a bottle of Ferry Boat White from the **Bainbridge Island Vineyards & Winery** (842-9463), where you can sample the local grapes or tour the fields where they are grown; turn right at the first white trellis on Rte. 305 as you leave the ferry. Bottles range from $7.80 to $23.50 (open Wed.-Sun. noon-5pm, tours Sun. 2pm).

WHIDBEY ISLAND

Clouds, wrung dry by the time they finally pass over Whidbey Island, release a scant 20 in. of rain each year over this slow-paced strip of land in Puget Sound. At the island's many forts (turned state parks), rocky beaches lead back to bluffs crawling with wild roses and blackberry brambles. Whidbey's points of interest are few and far between, and most of those who make the trek come in caravans of RVs to camp, but Whidbey's circle of beaches makes it beautiful nonetheless. The town of **Coupeville,** at the island's center, is a great place to start exploring its four major State Parks. Stay away from the towns of **Oak Harbor** and **Clinton**—they offer little more than K Marts and fast food.

Two **ferry** lines provide frequent service from the mainland to the island (see p. 33). One ferry connects **Mukilteo,** a tiny community just south of Everett, with **Clinton,** a town on the south end of Whidbey. The other connects **Port Townsend** on the Olympic peninsula with the terminal at **Keystone State Park,** at the "waist" of the island. You can drive onto the island on Rte. 20, which departs west from I-5 at Exit 230. Rte. 20 and Rte. 565 meet near Keystone and form the backbone of the island, linking all the significant towns and points of interest. **Island Transit** (678-7771 or 321-6688) provides free, hourly public transportation throughout the island, and gives information on connections to and from Seattle, but it has no service on Sundays and limited service on Saturdays.

If the ferry ride whetted your appetite, stop by **La Pax** (341-4787), a Mexican restaurant in Clinton, right off the dock (taco and rice $5). Next door, the **Whidbey Cybercafe** (341-5922) links the island with the rest of the universe (terminals $6 per hr., 30min. minimum).

Cyclists and drivers alike venture to **Ebey's Landing,** a Department of Interior protected beach with crystal views of the islands, the surrounding Olympic Mountains, and Port Townsend. On the way, climb to the top of Sherman Rd. off Rte. 20; next to the cemetery is a gentle view of the island's idyllic prairie and beaches. This is prime biking country, with easy slopes and rustic scenery. From Ebey's Landing, follow signs to **Ft. Casey State Park,** an archipelago of old fortresses. An interpretive center is at the Admiralty Point lighthouse (open April-Oct. Thurs.-Sun. 11am-5pm). The park's campground is a peninsula in itself ($10).

In Coupeville's **Knead and Feed,** 4 Front St. (678-5431), there is plenty of soup to be supped (or sipped, if that's your style). This small restaurant makes everything from scratch and has a serene view of the eastern waterfront. A lunch costs $3-7 (open Mon.-Fri. 10:30am-3pm, Sat.-Sun. 8:30am-4pm). For a caffeine fix, stop in at **Great Times Espresso,** just south on Front Street, and chat with LaVonda, who makes some of the best scones this side of the UK and has all the local lowdown.

At the north tip of the island, the **Deception Pass Bridge,** the nation's first suspension bridge, connects Whidbey Island to the Anacortes Islands, and has a secret cave at one end where 17th-century prisoners were held and forced to make wicker furniture (Oh, the humanity!). When the Skagit lived and fished around Deception Pass, the area was often raided by the Haida from the north. A bear **totem** of the Haidas now occupies the Fidalgo Bay side of **Deception Pass State Park,** 5175 N. Rte. 20 (675-2417), just south of the same-named bridge. The pass itself was named by veteran explorer Captain George Vancouver, who found the tangled geography of Puget Sound as confusing as most visitors do today. This is the most heavily used of Whidbey's four state parks, and its views are magnificent. A new **interpretive center** in the Bowman area, just north of the Works Progress Administration bridge on Rte. 20 E, describes the army that built many of the parks in the Northwest during the Depression. There are camping facilities, a saltwater boat launch, and a freshwater lake for swimming, fishing, and boating. A license, available at most hardware stores, is required for **fishing** in the lake; the season runs from mid-April to October. Thirty miles of trails link some of the best views of Puget Sound's shore line and lure ambitious mid-summer crowds into this magnificent old-growth forest. **Campers** will find 250 sites ($11 apiece). Four rustic hiker/biker sites ($5) have limited facilities but make a pleasant alternative to the bustling campground. The campground is often subjected to jet noise from A-6 Navy attack aircraft at Whidbey Island Naval Air Station. Reservations are such a very, very good idea (800-452-5687; reservation fee $6).

PUGET SOUND

According to Native American legend, Puget Sound was created when Ocean, wishing to keep his children Cloud and Rain close to home, gouged out a trough and molded the leftover dirt into the Cascade Range. Since then, Cloud and Rain have stayed close to Ocean, rarely venturing east of the mountain wall. Millions of Washingtonians live along Puget Sound in the Everett-Seattle-Tacoma-Olympia belt, but with a pristine rural setting, outdoor adventure is never far from urban sophistication.

Olympia

From the castle-like hilltop capitol of Olympia, a one-hour drive south of Seattle, the Washington State government keeps an eye on the college students and local fisherpeople who thrive in the Capitol Dome's shadow. The Evergreen State College campus lies just a few miles from the city center, and its super-liberal, highly pierced student body spills into town to mingle with preppy politicos. Many locals scorn these "Greeners," nostalgic for the long, lost era when Olympia was a small industrial city with a thriving fishing industry. But newcomers keep pouring into Olympia, drawn to its spotless exterior and alluring diversity, and acknowledging the success of the Evergreen State capital's continuing beautification and park-expansion projects.

PRACTICAL INFORMATION

Visitors Information: Olympia State Capitol Visitors Center, P.O. Box 41020 (586-3460), on Capitol Way between 12th and 14th Ave. Follow the signs on I-5. Friendly staff helps navigate the center's plethora of brochures and provides maps of both the capitol itself and the greater Olympia area. Open Mon.-Fri. 8am-5pm. **Olympia/Thurston Chamber,** 521 E. Legion Way (357-3362 or 800-753-8474). Less enthusiastically provides less enthusiastic information on local businesses, services, and festivals. Calling is best. Open Mon.-Fri. 9am-5pm. **Department of Natural Resources (DNR),** 1111 Washington St. (902-1000 or 800-527-3805). A maze of offices that provide information about outdoor activities on DNR land. The Maps Department, P.O. Box 47031 (902-1234), can provide any publication that includes a **DNR map,** including the *Guide to Camp and Picnic Sites,* which points out free DNR sites statewide. The **Fish and Game** office down the hall offers recreational fishing licenses and regulations (902-2200). Open Mon.-Fri. 8:30am-4:30pm. For information on and reservations for state parks and facilities, call the **Washington State Parks and Recreation Commission Information Center** (800-233-0321).

Trains: Amtrak, 6600 Yelm Hwy. (800-872-7245). To Seattle (3 per day, $15) and Portland (3 per day, $19).

Buses: Greyhound, 107 E. 7th Ave. (357-5541), at Capitol Way. To: Seattle (7 per day, $8), *but check out the Olympia Express below,* Portland (6 per day, $15), and Spokane (3 per day, $29). Open daily 7:30am-7:30pm. Taxi dispatch next door.

Public Transportation: Intercity Transit (IT) (786-1881 or 800-BUS-ME-IT/287-6348). For maps and schedules, visit the Customer Service Department at the Transit Center on State Ave. between Washington St. and Franklin St. Olympians boast about their easy, reliable, and flexible transit system. Use it to get almost anywhere in Thurston County, even with a bike. The IT is open for info Mon.-Fri. 7am-6pm, Sat. 8am-5pm. Fare 50¢, seniors and disabled 25¢. Day passes $1. The **Capitol Shuttle** is free. Buses run from the Capitol Campus to downtown or to the east side and west side (every 15min., 6:30am-6:15pm). For the standard fare, **Custom buses** continue on from where normal fixed routes stop Mon.-Sat. after 7pm; call 943-7777 for info (Mon.-Sat. 6:30pm-9:30pm, Sun. 8:15am-5:30pm). Supplementary transport is provided for seniors and the disabled by Dial-A-Lift (754-9393 or 800-244-6846) with appropriate certification, available through the IT Business Office (786-8585). **Olympia Express** (Intercity Transit) runs between Olympia and Tacoma Mon.-Fri. 5:50am-6pm; fare $1.50. Transferring to a Seattle bus in Tacoma costs an additional $1. The full trip to Seattle takes 2hr.

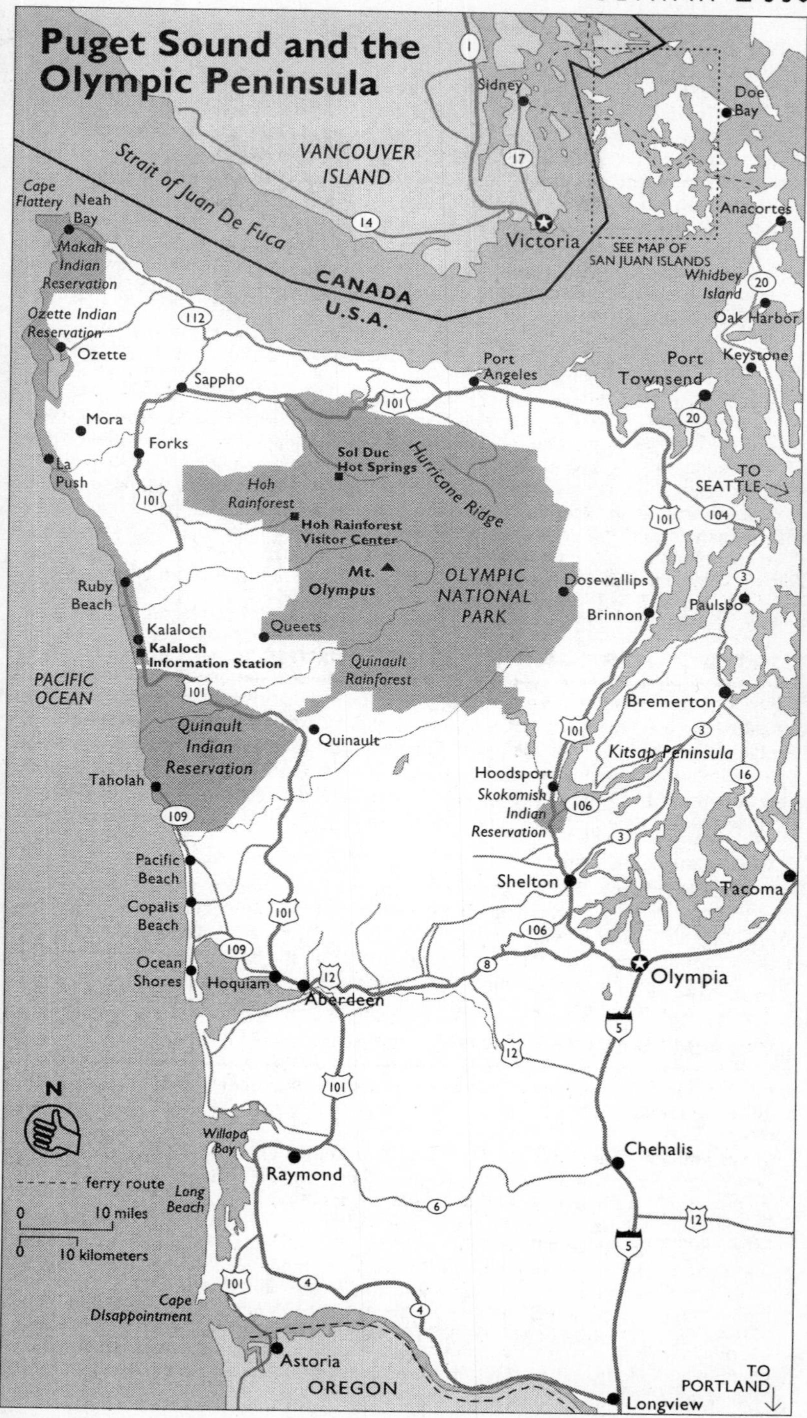
Puget Sound and the Olympic Peninsula
VANCOUVER ISLAND
Strait of Juan De Fuca
CANADA
U.S.A.
Sidney
Victoria
Doe Bay
Anacortes
SEE MAP OF SAN JUAN ISLANDS
Whidbey Island
Oak Harbor
Keystone
Port Townsend
Port Angeles
Cape Flattery
Neah Bay
Makah Indian Reservation
Ozette Indian Reservation
Ozette
Sappho
Mora
Forks
La Push
Sol Duc Hot Springs
Hurricane Ridge
Hoh Rainforest
Hoh Rainforest Visitor Center
TO SEATTLE
Mt. Olympus
OLYMPIC NATIONAL PARK
Dosewallips
Brinnon
Paulsbo
Ruby Beach
Kalaloch
Kalaloch Information Station
Queets
Quinault Rainforest
PACIFIC OCEAN
Quinault Indian Reservation
Quinault
Bremerton
Kitsap Peninsula
Hoodsport
Skokomish Indian Reservation
Taholah
Pacific Beach
Copalis Beach
Ocean Shores
Shelton
Tacoma
Hoquiam
Aberdeen
Olympia
N
Willapa Bay
Raymond
Chehalis
ferry route
Long Beach
0 10 miles
0 10 kilometers
Cape Disappointment
Astoria
OREGON
TO PORTLAND
Longview

Taxi: Red Top Taxi, 357-3700. **Capitol City Taxi,** 357-4949. **DC Cab,** 786-5226; handicap accessible. All 24hr.

Car Rental: U-Save Auto Rental, 3015 Pacific Ave. (786-8445). $21-$30 per day plus 20¢ for each mi. over 150. Must be at least 21 with credit card.

AAA Office: 2415 Capitol Mall Dr. (357-5561 or 800-562-2582). Open Mon.-Fri. 8:30-5:30, Sat. phones open only.

Auto Repair: Rotters, 2225 Carriage St. (357-5561), off Exit 104 from U.S. 101. Open Mon.-Fri. 7am-5pm. AAA approved.

Climbing and Skate Rental: Park Place Pro Shop, 215 7th Ave. SW (705-1585). Rents in-line skates ($4 per hr., $12 per day), kayaks ($5 per hr, $25 per day), canoes ($5 per hr., $25 per day), and double kayaks ($10 per hr., $45 per day). This warehouse-turned-shop also houses a climbing gym ($8 per day) and offers local climbing trips. Open Mon.-Sat. 10am-9pm, Sun. 10am-6pm.

Olympia Timberland Library, 313 8th Ave. SE (352-0595), at Franklin St. Sign up for a free hour on the Internet. Open Mon.-Thurs. 10am-9pm, Fri.-Sat. 10am-5pm; winter Sun. 1-5pm.

Laundromat: The Wash Tub, 2103 Harrison Ave. NW (943-9714). Wash $1.10, 8 min. dry 25¢. Open Mon.-Sat. 7am-10pm, Sun. 8am-11pm. **Eastside Tavern,** 410 E. 4th Ave. (357-9185). A laundromat behind the bar for all your sudsy needs. Pints $1.75. Open Mon.-Fri. noon-2am, Sat.-Sun. 3pm-2am.

Crisis Clinic: 352-2211 or 800-627-2211. 24hr. hotline for info and referral.

Women's Shelter: Safeplace, 754-6300 or 800-562-6025. 24hr.

Emergency: 911. **Police:** 753-8300. **Fire:** 753-8348.

Internet Access: at the Olympia Timberland Library (see above).

Post Office: 900 Jefferson SE (357-2286). Open Mon.-Fri. 7:30am-6pm, Sat. 9am-4pm. **General Delivery ZIP Code:** 98501.

Area Code: 360.

GETTING THERE AND GETTING AROUND

Olympia, located where I-5 meets U.S. 101, is an easy stopping point for those heading north to the Olympic Peninsula and Seattle or south to the Cascade peaks and Portland. Exit 105 off I-5 leads to the Capitol Campus and downtown Olympia. The west side of the downtown area borders freshwater Capitol Lake and salty West Bay, also known as Budd Bay. A bridge on 4th Ave. divides the two and leads to the city's northwest section, where fast food chains and plastic-happy shopping plazas sprawl.

Parking and Biking

Parking is Olympia is free for three hours per day in downtown "blue zones," and metered lots abound. Navigating Olympia on bike or foot is less confusing than groping around its zillions of one-way streets in a car. Olympians love to cycle, and bike racks adorn every public bus. A program called **The Bicycle Library** paints donated bikes pink and plants them around the city for public use—just take one where you find it and leave it where you're finished. A turned seat means the bike is occupied.

ACCOMMODATIONS AND CAMPING

Because motels in Olympia cater to lobbyists and lawyers rather than budget tourists, they are generally pricey. Camping is the cheapest option.

Grays Harbor Hostel, 6 Ginny Ln. (482-3119; email ghhostel@techline.com), just off Rte. 8 in Elma, WA. Take the fairground exit off Rte. 8 and make the first right. If you reach the fairgrounds, you've gone too far. A whopping 25 mi. west of Olympia, this hostel is a destination unto itself and the perfect place to start a trip down the coast. Legends of the hosteling industry Jay and Linda Klemp run the establishment as if it were their home (actually, it is), or a ranch, or a resort. Access to a hot tub, 24hr. common room, and a 3-hole golf course. Beds $10; single rooms available. Bikers can camp on the lawn for $6. Ask Jay about local bike rides or for a lesson in Jay and the Art of Motorcycle Maintenance.

Motel 6, 400 W. Lee St. (754-7320; fax 705-0655), in Tumwater. Take Exit 102 off I-5 and follow signs. A left off Lee St. onto Capitol Way takes you to downtown Olympia in less than 5min. Reliably clean rooms. Cable TV, swimming pool, and weak coffee in the office. Singles $40; doubles $46. Each additional person $3. Under 17 free with parent. AARP discount.

The Golden Gavel Motor Hotel, 909 Capitol Way (352-8533). Only a few blocks from the Capitol Campus. Immaculate, spacious rooms are sirens for businesspeople traveling without the corporate Visa. Cable TV, morning coffee, phones. Singles $43; doubles $49. AAA and senior discounts.

Millersylvania State Park, 12245 Tilly Rd. S. (753-1519), 10 mi. south of Olympia. Take Exit 99 off I-5 South, or Exit 95 off I-5 North, then follow signs on Rte. 121. 168 smallish, family- and RV-filled campsites nestled among firs. 6 mi. of needle-carpeted trails and **Deep Lake** (which has 2 unguarded swimming areas) add to the fun. Pay showers 25¢ for 6min., flush toilets, and facilities for the disabled. Hiker-biker sites $5.50, standard sites $11, 48 RV hookups $16. Call 800-452-5687 for reservations (recommended on summer weekends and holidays). 10-day max. stay.

Capital Forest Multiple Use Area, 15 mi. southwest of Olympia, Exit 95 off I-5. Administered by the DNR. 50 campsites spread among 6 separate campgrounds. Camping is free and requires no notification or permit. Pick up a forest **map** at the state DNR office (see **Practical Information,** above) or the Central Region DNR office (748-2383) in nearby Chehalis. The area is unsupervised, so lone women may be better off paying at Millersylvania. In summer, grab a space early in the day; "free" is a magical word. Pit toilets. No showers.

FOOD

Old-school diners, vegi-intensive eateries, and Asian quickstops line bohemian 4th Ave. east of Columbia. The upstairs "waterfront" tables at the **Bayview Deli & Bakery,** 516 W. 45h Ave. (352-4901), offer the best view in town and a pricey supermarket right below. If a 2am urge for carrot sticks hits, try the 24 hr. **Albertson's Supermarket,** 705 Prosper Rd. (705-3589), Exit 102 off I-5. The **Olympia Farmer's Market,** 401 N. Capital Way (352-9096), piles up an inspiring collection of in-season fruits and berries in a grandiose new building. Plenty a fantastic cheap lunch is found here—the grilled salmon burger ($3.75) is a local treat (open March-April Sat.-Sun. 10am-3pm, May-Sept. Thurs.-Sun. 10am-3pm, Oct. Fri.-Sun. 10am-3pm).

The Spar Café & Bar, 114 E. 4th Ave. (357-6444). An ancient logger-haunt that moonlights as a sweet-smelling pipe and cigar shop. Polished wood and a long counter send some patrons back to the age of Bogart (some are that old anyway). Mellow bar in back, with live jazz Sat. nights 9pm-1am (no cover). Sandwiches and burgers run in the $5-7 range. Restaurant open Mon.-Sat. 6am-9pm, Sun. 7am-8pm; bar open daily 11am-2am.

Jo Mama's Restaurant, 120 N. Pear St. (943-9849), at State St. in an old house. An all-wood, candle-lit atmosphere turns pizza-eaters into mafia dons as they churgle steaming pies. Steep prices (10 in. veggie pizza for 2, $14.75), but the convivial staff, menus in Braille, and porch swing to play on compensate. Open Mon.-Thurs. 11am-10pm, Fri. 11am-11pm, Sat. 4-11pm, Sun. 4-10pm. Wheelchair accessible.

Santosh, 116 4th Ave. (943-3442). Northern Indian cuisine with an all-you-can-eat lunch buffet for $6, served Mon.-Fri. 11am-3:30pm. Hindu statues and paintings to bewilder and delight. Open for politician-priced dinners too (entrees around $11). Mon.-Fri. 11am-9:30pm, Sat.-Sun. 11am-10pm.

The Dancing Goat (754-8187), on the corner of 4th Ave. and N. Washington St. A corner cafe with a corner on the thirtysomething lunch market. At night, aspiring writers sip tea in quiet desperation. A rack of alternative publications and carafes of locally roasted Batdorf and Bronson coffee please the Greeners. Lunches vary according to chef's whims ($5); 88¢ for a cuppa joe and 1 refill. Open Mon.-Wed. 7am-10pm, Thurs.-Sat. 7am-11pm.

Saigon Rendezvous, 117 W. 5th Ave. (352-1989). The most established of Olympia's budding Asian eateries. Vietnamese and Chinese cuisines rendezvous to spawn a menu that's sexy to vegetarians. Most lunches under $5.50, dinners around $7. Open Mon.-Fri. 10:30am-10:30pm, Sat. 10am-10pm, Sun. 11:30am-9pm.

Otto's Bagels and Deli, 111 N. Washington St. (352-8640). Where Olympia's friendly youth get their bagel fix and compare angst. Flyers on the walls direct visitors to nightly poetry readings or indie rock shows. Bagels 50¢; sandwiches $3.95. Open Mon.-Sat. 6am-7pm, Sun. 7am-5pm.

SIGHTS AND ACTIVITIES

Olympia's crowning glory is the State Capitol Campus, the complex of state government buildings, meticulously manicured gardens, and veterans' monuments where (Madonna fans, take note!) part of the movie *Body of Evidence* was filmed in 1991. Take a free tour of the **Legislative Building** (586-8677) to sneak a peek at the priming of the public sphere. Only tour guides can usher oglers into the legislative chambers, January through February on even years, and January through April on odd years. The newly repainted and decorated interior boasts a six-ton Tiffany chandelier and six two-ton bronze doors depicting the history of Washington. Unfortunately, the building's spectacular **dome,** the fifth tallest stone dome in the world, is indefinitely closed to the public. Although the panoramic view of Olympia is no longer available, the rest of the magnificent building is worth traversing. Tours leave from just inside the front steps daily on the hour 10am-3pm (building open Mon-Fri. 8am-5:30pm, Sat.-Sun. 10am-4pm). The mansionesque **State Capitol Museum,** 211 W. 21st Ave. (753-2580), houses historical and political exhibits (open Tues.-Fri. 10am-4pm, Sat.-Sun. noon-4pm; admission $2, children $1, families $5). Several different free tours of buildings on the capitol campus leave hourly on weekdays. Call 586-TOUR/8687 for more info and accommodations for the disabled.

Every lunch hour, droves of state employees tumble out of the capitol in spandex and sneakers and head for the various parks surrounding **Capitol Lake.** Trails begin in **Capitol Lake Park** at the west end of 7th Ave. and empty into the newly constructed **Heritage Park** with its $620,000 computerized, interactive fountain, where politicians and children playing in their Underoos frolic. Ah, the peaceable kingdom. Boats jam the Port in **Percival Landing Park** (743-8379), a reminder of Olympia's oyster-filled past. The 4th Ave. bridge is a perfect place to spot spawning salmon as the leaping lox-to-be cross the lake from late August through October. The **Yashiro Japanese Garden** (753-8380), at the intersection of Plum and Union, right next to City Hall, hoards hundreds of colorful plants behind high walls, making it Olympia's very own secret garden (open 10am-dusk for picnickers and ponderers).

NIGHTLIFE AND ENTERTAINMENT

Olympia's ferocious nightlife seems to have outgrown its daylife. Old men playing pool and pinball rumble with college students slamming super cheap pints ($1.75) at **Eastside Club and Tavern,** 410 E. 4th St. (357-9985). Kurt Cobain was once ejected from the Eastside for rowdiness, but that's probably true of a lot of bars in the Northwest. If you crave fries with your ale, **Proffitt's Cafe** smuggles food in through a hole in Eastside's wall. Those brave enough to explore Olympia's startlingly clean alleys in search of a scene will find **Thekla,** 155 E. 5th Ave. (352-1855), under the neon arrow off N. Washington St. between 4th Ave. and Capitol. This gay-friendly dance joint spins nightly entertainment, from karaoke to d.j.'d hip-hop, for a small cover. Only those 21 or older can enter (Thurs.-Sat. $2-4, Sun.-Wed. free).

Record labels like **K Records** and **Kill Rock Stars,** with their flagship feminist band Bikini Kill, have made Olympia a crucial pitstop on the indie rock circuit. Respected thespian Courtney Love and her band Hole also hail from Olympia. Local groovesters mosh and mingle at **The Backstage at Capitol Theater,** 206 E. 5th Ave. (754-5378). Three to five bands play on most weekend nights, usually for a $5 cover. Ask in record shops about shows or look for posters and flyers. If the prospect of hearing the next Hole pre-stardom doesn't thrill you, take in a free jazz, ensemble, or symphony concert at **Sylvester Park** (Fri. at noon; call 953-2375).

Capitol Lakefair is a not-to-be-missed bonanza the third week in July, with an overwhelming array of food, carnival rides, and booths staffed by non-profit organizations. Contact the Chamber of Commerce for more info (see **Practical Information,** above), and watch out for increased motel rates.

■ Near Olympia

Olympia Beer (754-5177) is actually brewed less than a mile south of the capital city on Capital Way in **Tumwater.** The brewery for good ol' Oly is now owned by locally nefarious Pabst, which now produces several different beers on the premises, including Hamm's and Olde English "800" (known as "8-Ball" to beer connoisseurs). You can tour the facility and, if you're 21, chug a few suds on the house (open Tues.-Sat. 9am-4:30pm; tours at 9:30am, 11:30am, 1:30pm, 3:30pm; free). Olympia Beer, visible from I-5, can be reached from exit 103 in Tumwater and provides parking for nearby **Tumwater Falls Park**. This tree, trail, and fish ladder-laden park, built by the brewery, is perfect for salmon-watching, picnicking, or a midday run.

Ten miles south of the city is **Wolfhaven,** 3111 Offut Lake Rd. (264-4695 or 800-448-9653). Take Exit 99 off I-5, turn east, and follow the brown signs. The haven now preserves 40 wolves that have been reclaimed from zoos or illegal owners. Take a guided tour of the grounds (open May-Sep. 10am-4pm, Oct.-April 10am-3pm; $5, ages 5-12 $2.50) and if you've lost that howlin' feelin', join the Howl-In (May-Sept. Fri.-Sat. 7-9:30pm; $6, children $4). Groups roast marshmallows and tell stories around a campfire to the accompaniment of the howling residents (open May-Sept. daily 10am-5pm; Oct.-April Wed.-Sun. 10am-4pm). The **Nisqually National Wildlife Refuge** (753-9467), off I-5 between Olympia and Tacoma at Exit 114, offers a safe haven to 500 species of plants and animals as well as miles of open trail for the I-5-weary traveler to stop and meander. The notorious northern spotted owls, bald eagles, and a plethora of shorebirds nest in the reserve. The trails are open daily during daylight hours, but are closed to cyclists (office open Mon.-Fri. 7:30am-4pm; $2).

Kitsap Peninsula

The Kitsap Peninsula fills in Puget Sound between the Olympic Peninsula and Seattle. With natural deep-water inlets, it was long-destined to house a major naval base and a fleet of nuclear-powered Trident submarines. A residue of rich maritime history coats the entire area, but even without top secret clearance, travelers can enjoy the area's forested and hilly terrain. The peninsula's backyards and campgrounds are a cycler's paradise and the tiny **coastal hamlets** outside of Bremerton beckon tourists.

Bremerton is the hub of the Kitsap Peninsula. Once there, you'll swear you've stepped into a Tom Clancy novel; every third person has a Navy security pass swinging from his or her neck. The Navy Yard skyline rivals that of a small city, and when the **USS Nimitz** is home, the local barber works overtime providing crew cuts for all. For the Navy or military history buff, Bremerton is quite a find. For others, the city contains few sights other than dingy apartment buildings. However, it is a good base for exploring the peninsula and Hood Canal, which separates the Kitsap and Olympic peninsulas. **Kingston,** at the northern tip of the Kistsap peninsula, about 20 mi. from Bremerton on Rte. 3 and Rte. 104, is linked by ferry to **Edmonds** on the mainland. **Southworth,** about 10 mi. east of Bremerton on Rte. 16 and Rte. 160, is connected to West Seattle and Vashon Island by ferry. Rte. 3 and Rte. 104 lead north to the Olympic Peninsula across the **Hood Canal Bridge.** Rte. 16 leads south to Tacoma.

Practical Information **The Bremerton Area Chamber of Commerce,** 120 Washington St. (479-3579; http://www.bremertonwa.com), resides just up the hill from the ferry terminal in Bremerton and will help you navigate the area *sans* sonar. A booth at the ferry dock is open on weekends when the office is not. The chamber puts out a flotilla of pamphlets on Bremerton and nearby towns, and the lively staff valiantly attempts to dress up the city's fundamental drabness. If you're sounding out the area on bicycle, pick up the indispensable *Kitsap and Olympic Peninsula Bike Map* here (open Mon.-Fri. 9am-5pm).

Frequent **ferry service** to the Kitsap Peninsula arrives at three points. (For schedules and information, see **By Ferry,** p. 32.) From Bremerton, ferries run to downtown Seattle; from Southworth, to Fauntleroy in West Seattle and Vashon Island; and from Kingston to Edmonds on the mainland.

Once there, **Kitsap Transit,** 234 Wycoff St. (373-BUSS/2877), about 1½ blocks from the Bremerton Information Bureau, runs several bus lines. Call ahead for times, pick up schedules at the Winslow, Bremerton, or Kingston ferry terminals, or visit the customer service office at the ferry dock. (Mon.-Fri. 6am-7pm, Sat.-Sun. 8am-4pm, open most holidays; before 8am and 4pm-7pm 75¢, off-peak times 50¢, seniors off-peak 25¢.) Buses serve most small communities on the peninsula and Bainbridge Island, and generally run until 8pm. A bike will get you almost anywhere, but towns are spread out, so prepare for a strenuous, if pleasant, ride. Kitsap Transit accommodates **bikes** on almost all buses.

The **post office** (373-1456) is stationed at 602 Pacific Ave. (open Mon.-Fri. 9am-5pm). The **General Delivery ZIP Code** is 98337.

Camping and Food If you're intent on dropping anchor for the night here, your best bet is to camp, though a day trip from Seattle or Vashon Island may be more rewarding. Those traveling by foot will find **Illahee State Park** (478-6460 or 800-452-5687 for reservations) convenient, but a bit cramped and close to Bremerton road noise. To get there, hop on bus #29 at the ferry terminal in Bremerton and take it to the corner of Perry St. and Sylvan Rd. From there, walk ¼ mi. up the hill on Sylvan until you reach the entrance. By car, drive north on Hwy. 303 from Bremerton to Sylvan Rd., turn right, and follow signs. The park has 25 campsites with water, restrooms, and hot showers (sites $10 with a vehicle, primitive sites without vehicle $5). Another port of call is **Scenic Beach State Park** (830-5079), near the village of Seabeck on the west coast of the peninsula. The park has 50 campsites with water and bathrooms (sites $10, walk-in sites $5). From Silverdale, take Anderson Hill Rd. or Newberry Hill Rd. west to Seabeck Hwy., then follow the highway 7 mi. south to the Scenic Beach turn-off. Cyclists should be prepared for steep hills along this route. Winter hours are limited; call for reservations.

Culinary choices in Bremerton are few, since most workers and locals eat spinach on Uncle Sam's tab on base in the shipyard. Get webbed in **Charlotte's Cafe,** 246 E. 4th St. (479-8133), a family-run deli with daily changing menus. All sandwiches under $3.50, and breads are baked in back; w-c accessible (open Mon.-Fri. 6am-3pm). **Emperor's Palace Chinese Restaurant,** 221 Wash. Ave. (377-8866), serves predictable but tasty Mandarin and Szechuan dishes in a dark, vinyl-upholstered dining room. Any one of the eight lunch platters is $4.50 and a two-person family dinner starts at $9.95 (open Sun.-Thurs. 11am-10pm, Fri-Sat. 11am-11pm).

Sights and Events Navy buffs, start salivating. Next to the Chamber of Commerce (see **Practical Information,** above) nests the dustily endearing **Bremerton Naval Museum** (479-7447). Friendly volunteers explain the room full of patriotic gore with exhibits of World War II photos and transparent models of destroyers and aircraft carriers measuring up to 10ft. (open Mon.-Sat. 10am-5pm, Sun. 1-5pm; free, but donations requested). Behind the museum, explore the destroyer **USS Turner Joy** (792-2457), before a stroll along the **Bremerton Boardwalk,** which extends along the water beyond the boat. The Turner Joy fired the first, not-so-Joy-ful American shots of the Vietnam War during the notorious Gulf of Tonkin incident. To get a combat-close view of the shipyard, join the **Navy Ship Tour** (792-2457), which departs from the Turner Joy and scoots along mothballed submarines, aircraft carriers, and the famous WWII battleship Missouri. The surrender document ending WWII was signed on the decks of this mammoth vessel. (Turner Joy tour $5, seniors $4. Shipyard tour $8.50, seniors $7.50, children $5.50. Combined package available.) To find out when the U.S.S. Nimitz and other active Navy vessels are in town, call the shipyard public relations office at 476-1111. At the ferry dock, catch the **foot ferry** from the Bremerton terminal across the Sinclair Inlet to **Port Orchard** for an expansive view of the shipyards. The ferry leaves every hour on the ¼hr. (fare is 70¢, free on weekends May-Oct.). The recently opened, somewhat bare **Kitsap Historical Museum,** 280 4th St. (479-6226), provides a minor reprieve for those uninterested in naval lore. Instead, the museum is simply about war—it houses exhibits on WWII history and the shipyard's illustrious past (open daily 10am-5pm; closed Tues. in winter; free, but donations encouraged). If naval paraphernalia still floats your boat, take Hwy. 303 north from Bremerton or the **Kitsap Fast Ferry** (396-4148), which runs in the summer for passengers only to the **Keyport Naval Station,** home of the **Naval Undersea Museum,** 610 Donell St. (396-4148). Navigate among artifacts salvaged from the seas, including a Kaiten torpedo used by Japanese sailors (open June-Sept. daily 10am-4pm; Oct.-May Mon. and Wed.-Sun. 10am-4pm).

Across Liberty Bay "fjord" from Keyport, Norwegian immigrants have erected a tourist-luring shrine out of the town of **Poulsbo,** where various Scandinavian festivals take place year-round on streets with names like King Olav V St. Contact the **Greater Poulsbo Chamber of Commerce** at 779-4848. Stop by the "world famous" Sluy's Poulsbo Bakery, 18924 Front St. for sweet Scandinavian breads and exotic Norwegian delicacies like *is krem* and *kaffe*.

North of Poulsbo, the **Historic Port Madison Indian Reservation** provides ample opportunity to learn about the history of Seattle-area Native Americans. Ask nicely, and the driver of bus #90 will let you off at the Longhouse Convenience Store. Follow the road 1 mi. to the **Suquamish Museum** (598-3311, ext. 422), where tribal artifacts mingle with contemporary portrayals of Suquamish life. Drivers should follow Rte. 305 towards Bainbridge Island and turn off at Sandy Hook Rd. The museum is on the north side of the **Agate Pass Bridge** on Rte. 305. Run by the **Port Madison Reservation,** this small museum is devoted entirely to the history and culture of the native Puget Sound Suquamish people. Striking photographs and quotations from respected elders piece together the lives of those who inhabited the peninsula before, during, and after the "great invasion" (open daily 10am-5pm; Oct.-April Fri.-Sun. 11am-4pm; $2.50, seniors $2, under 12 $1). Around here, lore about **Chief Sealth** abounds. (The Suquamish people believed that the chief's real name was secret and not to be pronounced; the word "Seattle" is only a European approximation.) The legendary chief's grave is within driving distance of the town of Suquamish. His memorial, constructed of cedar war canoes, is in the middle of a nearby Catholic cemetery. Pick up a map of the area at the museum.

Bellingham

Strategically located between Seattle and Vancouver, Bellingham is a hub of Northwest transportation. The city is the southern terminus of the **Alaska Marine Highway** (see p. 32), so most travelers who stay the night are either starting or completing a nautical journey to or from Alaska. The Lummi, Nooksack, and Semiahmoo tribes of the region maintain strong ties to their fishing pasts, while commercial fishing, coal mining, and a giant paper mill support the city's economy. Students at **Western Washington University** attract budget-oriented businesses, and a recent influx of young people has converted this former lumber town into a lively community with parks to ramble in and a boom town atmosphere.

PRACTICAL INFORMATION AND ORIENTATION

Visitors Information: 904 Potter St. (671-3990). Take Exit 253 (Lakeway) from I-5. Extremely helpful staff and a flood of Whatcom County trivia. Pick up a map of Bellingham's miles of footpaths. Open daily 8:30am-5:30pm.

Trains: Amtrak, 401 Harris Ave. (734-8851 or 800-USA-RAIL/872-7245), in the Greyhound/Amtrak station next to the ferry terminals. 1 per day to Seattle ($23) and Vancouver, BC ($18).

Buses: Greyhound, 401 Harris Ave. (733-5251 or 800-231-2222), next to the ferry terminals. To: Seattle (7 per day, $13); Vancouver, BC (4 per day, $13); and Mt. Vernon (6 per day, $7). Open Mon.-Fri. 7:30am-5:30pm.

Ferries: Alaska Marine Highway Ferry, 355 Harris Ave. (676-8445 or 800-642-0066). Ferry terminal is in Fairhaven, just south of Bellingham. Take Exit 250 off I-5 and take Hwy. 11 west. 1 per week to Ketchikan, AK ($168) and beyond. **Lummi Island Ferry** (676-6692), at Gooseberry Pt. Take I-5 north to Slater Rd. (Exit 260), then take a left on Haxton Way. Frequent trips to Lummi (1-2 per hr.) each day. The first leaves the island at 6:10am, 7am on weekends; the last departs the mainland at 12:10am. Round-trip fare $1 per person, $3 per car. Private shuttles also run ferries to the nearby San Juan Islands (see p. 351).

Public Transportation: Whatcom County Transit (676-7433). All buses originate at the terminal in the Railroad Ave. Mall between Holly and Magnolia St., where **maps** and schedules are available. 35¢, under 5 and over 90 free; no free transfers. Buses run every 15-30min. Mon.-Fri. 6:10am-7:30pm, reduced service 7:30-11pm and Sat.-Sun. 9am-6pm.

Taxi: City Cab, 734-TAXI/8294 or 800-281-5430. 24hr.

Car Rental: U-Save Auto Rental, 1100 Iowa St. (671-3688). $20 per day plus 15¢ per mi. after 100. Must be 21 with credit card or $250 deposit. Open Mon.-Fri. 9am-5:30pm, Sat. 9am-4pm.

Ride Board: Viking Union, at WWU. Usually more riders available than rides, but lucky folks may be able to catch one to Seattle or eastern Washington.

Laundromat: Bellingham Cleaning Center, 1010 Lakeway Dr. (734-3755). Wash $1.25, 10min. dry 25¢. Open daily 6am-10pm.

Public Library: 210 Central St. (676-6860), at Commercial St. across from City Hall. A fountain and pristine lawn in back make for a great lazy afternoon picnic site; inside, the library offers free **Internet access.** Open Mon.-Thurs. 10am-9pm, Fri.-Sat. 10am-6pm, Sun. 1-5pm.

Outdoor Supplies: The Great Adventure, 201 E. Chestnut St. (671-4615). Rents kayaks (from $30 per day), camping, climbing, and backpacking gear, and skis at reasonable rates. Deposit required. Open Mon.-Thurs. 10am-6pm, Fri. 10am-7pm, Sat. 9am-6pm, Sun. 11am-5pm.

Senior Services: 315 Halleck St. (city 733-4033, county 398-1995). Take bus 10B to the corner of Ohio and Cornwall St. Open daily 8:30am-4pm.

Crisis Line: Bellingham, 734-7271. **Whatcom County,** 384-1485. Both 24hr.

Pharmacy: Payless Drug, 1400 Cornwall St. (733-0580). Open Mon.-Fri. 8am-7pm, Sat. 9am-6pm. Pharmacy opens 30min. after store.

Hospital: St. Joseph's General, 2901 Squalicum Pkwy. (734-5400). Open 24hr.

Internet Access: free in the public library (see above).

Post Office: 315 Prospect (676-8303). Open Mon.-Fri. 8am-5:30pm, Sat. 9:30am-2pm. **General Delivery ZIP Code:** 98225.

Area Code: 360.

Bellingham lies along I-5, 90 mi. north of Seattle and 57 mi. south of Vancouver, and is the only major city between the two. The downtown shopping and business area centers on Holly St. and Cornwall Ave., next to the Georgia Pacific pulp mill, accessible by Exits 252 and 253 off I-5. Western Washington University sits atop a hill to the south. One hundred and thirty acres of city parks encircle Bellingham. The town of **Fairhaven,** where the ferries, bus, and trains stop, lies directly south of Bellingham, and Whatcom County Transit provides service throughout the area.

ACCOMMODATIONS AND CAMPING

For both atmosphere and price, the hostel is the best bet. For help with other accommodations, try the **Bed & Breakfast Guild of Whatcom Co.** (676-4560). Many B&Bs offer rooms in the $60 neighborhood.

Fairhaven Rose Garden Hostel (HI-AYH), 107 Chuckanut Dr. (671-1750), next to Fairhaven Park, about ¾ mi. from the ferry terminal. Take Exit 250 from I-5, and go west on Fairhaven Parkway to 12th St.; bear left onto Chuckanut Dr. From down-

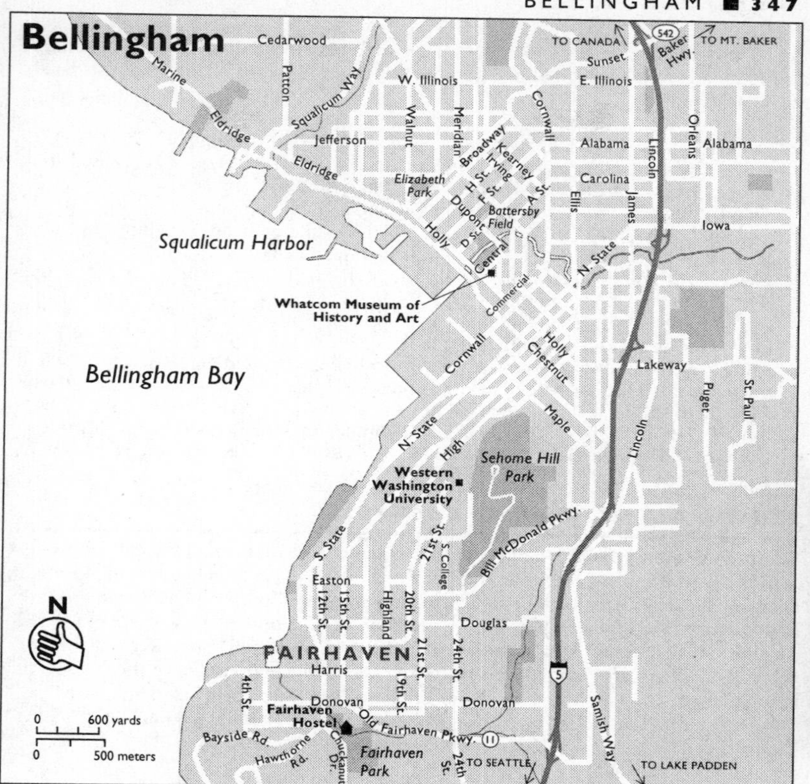

town Bellingham, take bus # 1A or 1B. We never promised you a rose garden; delinquent local deer have done their best to mow Fairhaven's roses down. A clean and tiny hostel with 10 beds. Sleeping quarters, bathrooms, and showers are in the basement; the excess moisture sometimes gives the place a mildewy smell. No curfew, but living room closes at 10pm. Check-in 5-10pm, check-out 9:30am. Beds $12. Make-your-own, all-you-can-eat pancakes $1; linen $2. Call ahead, especially if you plan to stay on Wed. or Thurs. night, when Alaska-bound travelers fill the hostel. Reservations mandatory July-Aug. Open Feb.-Nov.

Travelers Lodge, 202 E. Holly St. (734-1900). Take Exit 253 off I-5. Roll out of the lodge's big beds and clean rooms right into downtown Bellingham. Cable and coffee makers in the rooms make up for Bellingham's slight *eau de paper plant* and occasional 2am noise. Free local calls. Singles $35; doubles $42.

Mac's Motel, 1215 E. Maple St. (734-7570), at Samish Way. Take Exit 252 from I-5. Large clean rooms, pleasant management, and exterior paint like an ice-cream sundae. Rooms (single or double occupancy) $32. Open daily 7am-10pm.

Larrabee State Park (676-2093), on Chuckanut Dr., 7 mi. south of Bellingham. 87 sites tucked in among the trees on Samish Bay, a half-hidden flatland outside the city. Ditch the crowds in 1 of 8 walk-in tent sites. Check out the nearby tide pools or hike to alpine lakes. Sites $11; walk-ins $7. Hookups $16. Open daily 6:30am-dusk.

FOOD

The **Community Food Co-op,** 1220 N. Forest St. (734-8158), at Maple St., has all the essentials and a health food sit-down deli in the back. Watch a grinder turn peanuts into peanut butter and buy it by the pound (open daily 8am-9pm). If you're in town on a Saturday, head to the **Bellingham Farmer's Market** (647-2060), at Chestnut St. and Railroad Ave., for fruit and vegetable stands and homemade donuts (April-Oct. Sat. 10am-3pm).

Casa Que Pasa, 1415 Railroad Ave. (738-TACO/8226). Bellingham's best burritos are a great deal. Humongous burritos made with fresh vegetables purchased from local growers start at $2.10. Vegan and vegetarian options aplenty. Open Mon.-Thurs. and Sat. 11am-11pm, Fri. 11am-midnight, Sun. 11am-9pm.

The Old Town Cafe, 316 West Holly St. (671-4431). Scrumpdiddlyumptious breakfasts made with ingredients from the local farmer's market. Play a few songs on the piano in the adjoining art gallery and earn yourself a free drink to go with your buttermilk hotcakes ($3) or french toast ($4.25). Vegan and vegetarian friendly. Nothing on the menu over $6. Open Mon.-Sat. 6:30am-3pm, Sun. 8am-2pm.

Tony's Coffees and Tea Shop, 1101 Harris Ave. (733-6319), in Fairhaven Village, just a few blocks away from the ferry terminal. Dining garden complete with old railway car serves coffee, ice cream, bagels, and the infamous, high-voltage **Toxic Milkshake,** made with coffee and espresso grounds ($3.50). 6 pancakes $3. Open Mon.-Fri. 6:30am-9pm, Sat.-Sun. 7:30am-9pm. Same cinnamon rolls for ½ price at the **Great Harvest Bakery** (671-0873), in Sehome Village Mall on Samish Way. Bakery open Tues.-Sat. 9:30am-6pm.

SIGHTS, ACTIVITIES AND EVENTS

Western Washington University (WWU) generates continuous cultural and artistic activity, as well as 7 mi. of hiking trails with views of Bellingham Bay and the San Juan Islands. Twenty-two outdoor sculptures commissioned by local and nationally known artists stud the campus; a free brochure and headphones, available at the visitors information center, guide the wandering art critic around campus from piece to piece. The **Western Visitors Center** (650-3424) is at the entrance to the college on South College Dr. (open summer Mon.-Fri. 7am-5pm, during the academic year 7am-7pm). Friendly staff will give you the scoop on campus cultural events like the **Summer Stock Theater** (650-3876). Several buses from downtown—# 7, 11, 16, 26, 27, and 28—stop at WWU.

The **Whatcom Museum of History and Art,** 121 Prospect St. (676-6981), occupies four buildings along Prospect St., most notably the looming old city hall. Find rotating exhibits on local topics ranging from native art to gardening history. Climb to the third floor of the old city hall to watch the clocktower innards at work (open Tues.-Sun. noon-5pm; free; fully wheelchair accessible). The reserved and renovated **Mount Baker Theatre,** 104 N. Commercial St. (734-6080), is the locus of performing arts in the area. Everything and anything from drama troupes to symphony orchestras to the Peking Acrobats perform in this 10-year-old movie and vaudeville palace (box office open Mon.-Fri. 10am-5:30pm). The **Bellingham Music Festival** (676-5997) brings symphony, chamber, folk, and jazz music to the Bellingham's ears. A series of concerts featuring musicians from around the world goes on in early August for about two weeks. Concerts ($18-21) are performed in the Mount Baker Theatre and the WWU concert hall. Call or write to the festival at 1300 N. State St. #202 for information and ticket reservations.

In the second week of June, lumberjacks converge here from throughout the region to compete in axe-throwing, log-rolling, and speed-climbing at the **Deming Logging Show** (676-1089). To reach the Showgrounds, take Mt. Baker Hwy. 12 mi. east to Cedarville Rd. and turn left. Signs lead to the grounds (tickets $5, ages 3-12 $3). Mid-May sees the mother of all races, the **Ski to Sea Race.** This relay race starts at Mt. Baker and ends at the Bellingham Bay with participants skiing, running, canoeing, biking, and sea kayaking to the finish line. Call 734-1330 or write to P.O. Box 958, Bellingham 98227 for information.

OUTDOORS

Hike up **Chuckanut Mountain** through a quiet forest for a view of the islands that fill the bay. On clear days, Mt. Rainier is visible from the top. The 2½ mi. uphill hike leaves from Old Samish Hwy. about 1 mi. south of the city limits. A beach at **Lake Padden Park,** 4882 Samish Way, delights those who find Puget Sound a little chilly; the water here is the warmest in the Sound. Take bus #44 1 mi. south of downtown. The park also has miles of tennis courts, playing fields, hiking trails, a boat launch (no motors allowed), and fishing off the pier (open daily 6am-10pm).

Whatcom Falls Park, 1401 Electric Ave., due east of town, has hiking trails, picnic facilities, and tennis courts, and is home to thousands of future fishsticks in the Bellingham Hatchery. The **Upper Whatcom Falls Trail** leads 1½ mi. to the falls themselves, used by locals as a waterslide. Take bus #40 or 41 (park open daily 6am-dusk). The fishing is good in **Lake Samish** and **Silver Lake,** north of the town of **Maple Falls** on the Mt. Baker Hwy. The lake trout season opens on the third Sunday in April. Fishing licenses are available from the **Department of Fisheries** (902-2464), sporting goods stores, and some hardware stores ($5-48, depending on residency and what you're aiming to catch).

Popular with Bellingham residents, the **Interurban Trail** runs 5.9 mi. from Fairhaven Park to Larrabee State Park along the relatively flat route of the old Interurban Electric Railway. Occasional breaks in the trees permit a glimpse of the San Juan Islands; watch for divided paths and unmarked street crossings. Several trails branch off the main line and lead up into the Chuckanut Mountains or down to the coast. Pick up a map from the visitors center (see **Practical Information,** above). Along the Interurban Trail you may stumble on the 1 mi. trail to **Teddy Bear Cove.** The cove is also accessible from Chuckanut Drive, 2 mi. south of Fairhaven. This clothing-optional beach offers revealing views of the local wildlife.

Big Rock Garden Park, 2900 Sylvan St. (676-6801), is a 2.7-acre Japanese tea garden, and a hidden treasure in the residential area of Bellingham. Take Alabama St. east, then go left on Sylvan for several blocks. The park frequently hosts outdoor musical performances; call ahead for a schedule (park open March-Nov. Wed.-Sun. 11am-5pm).

■ Near Bellingham

MT. BAKER

Crowning the Mt. Baker-Snoqualmie National Forest, Mt. Baker contains excellent downhill and cross-country skiing, and some of the best snowboarding in the state. During the summer, hikers and mountaineers find its trails and ascents challenging and exhilarating. To reach the volcano, take Exit 255 off I-5, just north of Bellingham, to Rte. 542, better known as the **Mt. Baker Highway.** Fifty-six miles of roadway traverse the foothills, affording spectacular views of Baker and the other peaks in the range. The highway ends at Artist Point (elevation 5140 ft.), with spectacular views of the surrounding wilderness (the road is closed at Mt. Baker Ski Area in winter).

The popular **Lake Anne Trail** leads 4¾ mi. to the lake of the same name, and continues to the Lower Curtis Glacier. Road junkies can ponder Robert Frost on the short but picturesque **Fire and Ice Trail,** a ½ mi. loop beginning on Hwy. 542. For trail maps, backcountry permits or further area info, stop by the **Glacier Public Service Center** (599-2714; open daily 8:30am-4:30pm) or write to **North Cascades National Park,** Mt. Baker Ranger District, 2105 State Rte. 20, Sedro Woolley, WA 98284.

The volcano packs soft powder for longer than any other nearby area; the ski slopes usually stay open from early November through May (lift tickets $29, seniors and under 15 $21.50). Call the Mt. Baker Ski Area Office (734-6771) in Bellingham for more information. On your way to the slopes, stop by **Carol's Coffee Cup,** 5415 Mt. Baker Hwy. (592-5441), for pre-ski carbo-loading with the biggest cinnamon rolls on earth ($1.10).

Silver Lake Park, 9006 Silver Lake Rd. (599-2776), is 28 mi. east of Bellingham on the Mt. Baker Hwy. and 3 mi. north of Maple Falls on Silver Lake Road. The park tends 73 campsites near the lake with facilities for swimming, hiking, and fishing (tent sites $12, hookups $14). Closer to the mountain are the **Douglas Fir Campground,** at Mile

36 off Hwy. 542, with 30 sites, and the **Silver Fir Campground,** at Mile 47 off Hwy. 542, with 21 sites (both have water, no hookups; both $10). On the way to Mt. Baker, turn right at Mile 16 onto Mosquito Lake Rd., pull over at the first bridge, and look for **bald eagles** hunting for fish along Kendall Creek.

BLAINE

A border town 20 mi. north of Bellingham, Blaine is the busiest port of entry between Canada and the U.S. Those who get turned away from the **Canadian border** for insufficient identification or funds (if you're headed for Alaska you need CDN$500 per car and $50 per extra passenger to prove financial solvency) often stay in Blaine, plotting revenge against the Great White North. The **Blaine Visitors Center,** 215 Marine Dr. (332-4544 or 800-624-3555), at Exit 276 off I-5, is a warehouse of information on Blaine as well as American and Canadian points of interest (open daily 9am-5pm, winter Mon.-Sat. 9am-5pm).

The main attraction in Blaine is the **Peace Arch State Park** (332-8221). Directly over the Canada-U.S. border, the Peace Arch contains pieces of wood from early U.S. and Canadian ships of discovery, and commemorates the Treaty of Ghent, which ended the War of 1812 and inaugurated the long era of peace between Canada and the U.S. Summertime happenings include "hands across the border" events packed with kids, balloons, and Rotarians. To reach the park, take Exit 276 off I-5, then turn north onto 2nd St. (open April-Sept. 6:30am-dusk; Oct.-March 8am-dusk; toilets, kitchen facilities).

The spit of land encompassing **Semiahmoo Park,** 5 mi. southwest of Blaine, was first inhabited by the coastal Salish people who harvested shellfish when the tide was low. Clam digging is still a popular activity. Buckets and shovels may be rented from the park; a license is required ($3-31, depending on residency and type of activity). Take Drayton Harbor Rd. around to the southwestern side of Drayton Harbor (open mid-Feb. to Dec., Wed.-Sun. 1-5pm). A wooden passenger ferry, the **Plover,** putts across the Drayton Harbor from Blaine to the Inn at Semiahmoo (Fri.-Sat. noon-dusk, Sun. 10am-6pm; free, but donations appreciated).

The **Birch Bay Hostel (HI-AYH),** 7467 Gemini St. (371-2180; email bbhostel@az.com), Bldg. #630 on the former Blaine Air Force Base, has lots of small, clean rooms with more privacy than most hostels; some have magnificent views of the marshes. All enjoy full kitchen facilities and a large, homey living room. Off I-5, take either the Birch Bay-Lynden Rd. exit or the Grandview Rd. exit and head west to Blaine Rd. ($10, nonmembers $13; open April-Sept.). The **Westview Motel,** 1300 Peace Portal Dr. (332-5501), offers clean rooms with nice views of the bay (singles $29; doubles $33; with kitchens $40).

Birch Bay State Park, 5105 Helwig Rd. (371-2800, reservations 800-452-5687), 10 mi. south of Blaine, operates 167 campsites near the water. The Semiahmoo used this area and the marshland at the southern end of the park to harvest shellfish and hunt waterfowl; today, 300 species of birds live in the park's **Terrell Creek Estuary.** The park is also a good area for crabbing, scuba diving, water-skiing, and swimming. To get there, take the Birch Bay-Lynden exit off I-5 and turn south onto Blaine Rd. When you run out of road, turn east onto Bay Rd. Turn south on Jackson Rd. and take it to Helwig Rd. The way is well-marked from the freeway (sites $11, hookups $16; open year-round; reservations ($6) recommended during summer).

Satisfy your sweet tooth at the **C Shop,** 4825 Alderson Rd. (371-2070), just down the street from the hostel in Birch Bay. This bakery and candy shop offers over 100 desserts, including fudge, caramel apples, sundaes, and "peanut butter yummms," along with inexpensive made-to-order sandwiches and homemade pizza (open mid-May to mid-June, Sat.-Sun. 1-10pm; mid-June through summer daily 1-10pm). The best seafood in town, fresh daily, is at the **Harbor Cafe,** 295 Marine Dr. (332-5176), halfway down the pier. The $9 fish 'n' chips, salad bar or chowder included, is hard to resist (open Sun.-Thurs. 6am-10pm, Fri.-Sat. 6am-11pm).

SAN JUAN ISLANDS

If you're in pursuit of the picturesque Northwest, you'll find it in the lush San Juan Islands, home to great horned owls, puffins, sea otters, sea lions, and more deer, raccoons, and rabbits than they can support. Pods of orcas ("killer whales") patrol the waters, keeping a protective eye on these glacier-carved islands. Today, pods of tourists mimic the whales, circling the islands in everything from yachts to kayaks in pursuit of cetacean encounters.

Although the population of San Juan, the chain's main island, has doubled in the last five years, there are still fewer than 3000 permanent residents. The populations of the other islands are far lower, and endless parks and coastline offer ample opportunity to commune with cedars and tidepools in relative seclusion. Over 1.5 million visitors come ashore the San Juans each year, usually in July and August; to avoid the rush but still enjoy good weather, try the islands in late spring or early fall. Some residents frown on the transplants from Seattle and California—including rocker Steve Miller and the Oakley sunglasses king—who are buying up huge chunks of the islands at exorbitant prices, but well-behaved tourists and their dollars are always welcome. The San Juans, with hundreds of tiny islands to weave among, are a sea kayaker's dream; many locals consider their cars an alternative to their kayaks.

Two excellent guides to the area are *The San Juan Islands Afoot and Afloat* by Marge Mueller ($15) and *Emily's Guide,* a series of detailed descriptions of each island ($4, $11 for a set of three), available at bookstores and outfitting stores. *The San Juans Beckon,* published annually by the local *Island Sounder,* includes maps and info on island recreation. The *San Juanderer* also has useful info, including tide charts and ferry schedules. Both are free on ferries or at visitors centers.

GETTING THERE AND GETTING AROUND

Washington State Ferries (see p. 32) serve the islands daily from **Anacortes** on the mainland. To reach Anacortes, take I-5 north from Seattle to Mt. Vernon. From there, Rte. 20 heads west to Anacortes. The way to the ferry is well-marked. The **Bellingham Airporter** (800-235-5247) makes eight trips from Sea-Tac to Anacortes on weekdays and six trips on weekends ($27 one way, $49 round-trip). Of the 172 islands in the San Juan archipelago, only **Lopez, Shaw, Orcas,** and **San Juan** are accessible by ferry (9 times daily from Anacortes). Not every ferry services all the islands; be sure to check the schedule. Ferries run from approximately 6am to midnight. The ferry system revises its schedule seasonally and there are no reservations. Puget Sound visitors centers have schedules aplenty.

You can purchase **ferry tickets** in Anacortes. Foot passengers travel in either direction among the islands free of charge. **No charge is levied on eastbound traffic;** pay for a vehicle only on **westbound** trips to or between the islands. **An important money-saving tip:** to see more islands and save on ferry fares, travel directly to the westernmost island on your itinerary, then make your way eastward to the mainland island by island. The San Juan ferries are packed in summer, so arrive early. On peak travel days, show up with your vehicle at least one hour prior to departure. The ferry authorities accept only cash or in-state checks as payment.

Short distances and good roads make the San Juans excellent for biking. **Island Transit** provides bus service on San Juan and Orcas Islands (800-887-8387 or 376-8887). Hitchhiking is reputed to be easy on the islands. (*Let's Go* does not recommend hitchhiking.)

San Juan Island

The biggest and most popular of the islands, San Juan Island was discovered by the tourist world in the early 80s. San Juan is the last stop on the ferry route and is home to **Friday Harbor,** the largest town in the archipelago. It is also the easiest to explore, since the ferry docks right in town, roads are fairly flat for bicyclists, and a shuttle bus runs throughout the island. **Lime Kiln State Park** is the only designated **whale-watching** park in the world. But popularity has its price: Seattle weekenders flood the island throughout the summer, bringing fleets of undesirable traffic.

PRACTICAL INFORMATION AND ORIENTATION

Visitors Information: Chamber of Commerce (468-3663), in a booth on East St. up from Cannery Landing. Open sporadically daily dawn-dusk. **San Juan Transit** (see below), located upstairs in the cannery landing next to the ferry dock, also distributes scores of San Juan-oriented brochures and maps. **National Park Service Information Center** (378-2240), on the corner of 1st and Spring St., answers questions about San Juan National Historical Park. Open Mon.-Fri. 8:30am-5pm, off-season 8:30am-4pm.

Bus: San Juan Transit (376-8887 or 800-887-8387) circles the island every 35-55min. Many convenient stops, but the driver will make additional stops upon request. Point to point $4. Day pass $10. 2-day pass (also good on Orcas Island) $17. If you plan to see San Juan Island only, it may be cheaper to leave your car in Anacortes and use the shuttle once you get to the islands.

Ferries: Washington State Ferries, (378-4777 or 800-84-FERRY/843-3779; http://www.wsdot.wa.gov/ferries), in Friday Harbor. Waiting room opens 30min. before scheduled departures.

Taxi: San Juan Taxi, 378-3550. 24hr.

Bike Rental: Island Bicycles, 380 Argyle St. (378-4941), in Friday Harbor. 7-speeds $15 per day, 12-speeds $20 per day, mountain bikes $25 per day. Locks and helmets included. Also rents child strollers ($5) and trailers ($15). Provides **maps** of the island and suggests bike routes. Credit card required. Open daily 9am-6pm; May-Sept. Wed.-Sat. more limited hours.

Moped Rental: Susie's Mopeds (378-5244 or 800-532-0087), 1 block above the landing. Mopeds $15 per hr., $45 per day, fuel included. Credit card required. Open March-Oct. daily 9am-6pm. Also available at Roche Harbor July 4-Labor Day.

Kayak Tours: San Juan Safaris (378-2155, ext. 258 or 800-451-8910, ext. 258), leaves from Roche Harbor on the north tip of the island, at the end of Roche Harbor Rd. A 3hr. trip will set you back $35, but the scenery may be worth it.

Camping Supplies: Kings Marine, 110 Spring St. (378-4593). Open daily 8am-7pm.

Laundromat: Sail In Laundromat, behind tourist booth on East St. Wash $2.25, 11min. dry 25¢. Open daily 7:30am-9pm.

Senior Services: At the **Gray Top Inn** (378-2677). Open Mon.-Fri. 9am-4pm.

Red Tide Hotline: 800-562-5632 for info on safe shellfish-harvesting.

Pharmacy: Friday Harbor Drug, 210 Spring St. (378-4421). Open Mon.-Sat. 9am-7pm, Sun. 10am-4pm.

Medical Services: Inter-Island Medical Center, 550 Spring St. (378-2141). Open Mon.-Fri. 8:30am-5pm, Sat. 10am-noon.

Emergency: 911. **Sheriff:** 135 Rhone St. (non-emergency 378-4151), at Reed St.

Post Office: (378-4511), at Blair and Reed St. Open Mon.-Fri. 8:30am-4:30pm. **General Delivery ZIP Code:** 98250.

Area Code: 360.

With bicycle, car, and boat rentals all within a few blocks of the ferry terminal, Friday Harbor is a convenient base for exploring the island. Miles of road access all corners of the island, but are poorly marked. It's smart to plot your course carefully on one of the free **maps** available at the information centers in town (see above), or stop at one of the island's real estate offices or gas stations.

ACCOMMODATIONS AND CAMPING

San Juan's campgrounds have become wildly popular; call ahead for a reservation or show up early in the afternoon to secure a spot. Outside of camping, cheap accommodations in the San Juans are an endangered species. There's not a bargain to be found in the busy season. If you plan to stay overnight and camping is not your style, try one of the many B&Bs: although expensive, they are often beautiful. The **Bed and Breakfast Association** (378-3030) can help.

San Juan County Park, 380 Westside Rd. (378-2992), 10 mi. west of Friday Harbor on Smallpox and Andrews Bays. If you're lucky enough to snag one of the 20 sites in this quiet waterside campground, you might catch views of whales from your tent. You're guaranteed a great sunset at the very least. Cold water, flush toilets, but no showers or RV hookups. Park open daily 7am-10pm. Office open daily 9am-7pm. Vehicle sites $15. Hiker/biker sites $5. Reservations highly recommended.

Lakedale Campgrounds, 2627 Roche Harbor Rd. (378-2350 or 800-617-CAMP/2267; http://www.lakedale.com), 4 mi. from Friday Harbor. The mothership of campgrounds. Very attractive sites surrounded by 50 acres of lakes, hosting almost every imaginable water sport. Rents almost every variety of water vessel to match. Lakes are stocked with trout, and fishing within the campground requires no permit. Sites for 1-2 people with vehicle $16 (July-Aug. $19), each additional person $3.50 (July-Aug. $4.50). Day use $1.50. Hiker/biker sites $5 (July-Aug. $5.50). 6-person cabins start at $150. Showers $1. Reservations suggested, but management boasts that they've never turned a camper away. Open March 15-Oct. 15.

Pedal Inn, 1300 False Bay Dr. (378-3049). A campground designed for bikers and hikers. Very rustic, a bit ramshackle, quiet, and cheap. Hot water is only on during evening hours, but the self-described "mean old manager" Jim will negotiate. Sites $4.50. Any "accessories" like cars or vans cost $4.50 more. Open June-Sept.

FOOD

Stock up on groceries at **King's Market,** 160 Spring St. (378-4505; open Mon.-Sat. 7:30am-10pm, Sun. 8am-10pm). Most island restaurants serve vegetarian food.

Katrina's, 135 2nd St. (378-7290), between Key Bank and Friday Harbor Drug. The tiny kitchen cooks up a different menu every day, but invariably serves organic salads, freshly baked bread, and gigantic cookies ($1.25). What you might cook in your own kitchen if you could cook that well. Open Mon.-Sat. noon-5pm.

La Cieba, 420 Argyle St. Former Mexican/Southwestern restaurant now operates out of a convenience store. Cheap but fresh and hearty burritos ($5), along with pizza, deli, and candy bars. Open daily 7am-8pm.

San Juan Bakery and Donut Shop, 225 Spring St. (378-2271). Cheap eats. Bottomless coffee ($1), inexpensive breakfasts, lunch sandwiches, and a tour of the local rumor mill. Grilled cheese, bacon, and chips $3.75. They will pack up a lunch if you call ahead. Open Mon.-Sat. 5am-4pm, Sun. 6am-3pm.

SIGHTS AND ACTIVITIES

Friday Harbor is crowded when the tourists are out in full force, and a bit more appealing in spring and fall. The **Whale Museum,** 62 1st St. (378-4710), exhibits skeletons, sculptures, and info on new whale research. The museum even operates a toll-free **whale hotline** (800-562-8832) to report sightings and strandings (open daily 10am-5pm; Oct.-May 11am-4pm; $4, seniors $3.50, ages 5-18 $1, under 5 free). The **San Juan Historical Museum,** 405 Price St. (378-3949), in the old King House across from the St. Francis Catholic Church, explodes with exhibits, furnishings, and photographs from the late 1800s. A free pamphlet maps out a walking tour of Friday Harbor (open Wed.-Sat. 1-4:30pm; Labor Day-May Thurs.-Fri. 1-4pm).

A drive around the 35 mi. perimeter of the island takes about two hours, and the route is perfect for cyclists. The **West Side Rd.** traverses gorgeous scenery and provides the best chance for sighting **orcas** offshore. Three resident pods frolic in the nearby waters and there are several orca sightings per day in peak seasons.

To begin a tour of the island, head south and west out of Friday Harbor on Mullis Rd. Bikers may want to take this "tour" in the opposite direction, as climbs heading counterclockwise around the island are much more gradual. Mulles Rd. merges with Cattle Point Rd. and takes you straight into **American Camp** (378-2902), on the south side of the island (open daily 8am-dusk). The camp dates to the **Pig War** of 1859; a visitors center explains the history of that epic conflict (open daily 8:30am-5pm; guided walks Wed.-Fri. at 11:30am and 2:30pm, Sat.-Sun. at 11:30am). A self-guided trail leads from the shelter through the buildings and past the site of a British sheep farm. Every Saturday afternoon, volunteers in period costume reenact daily Pig War life (June-Sept. 12:30-3:30pm; free). If the sky is clear, make the ½ mi. jaunt farther down the road to **Cattle Point** for views of the distant Olympic Mountains (and hundreds of less distant rabbits), or stop by South Beach, a stretch of shoreline that dazzles beach walkers and whale lookey-loos.

Returning north on Cattle Point Rd., the gravel False Bay Rd. to the west will guide you to **False Bay,** home to nesting **bald eagles** and a great spot for watching them. During the spring and summer, walk along the northwestern shore (to your right as you face the water) at low tide to see the nesting eagles. Continuing to the western part of the island, farther north on False Bay Rd., you'll run into **Bailer Hill Rd.,** which turns into West Side Rd. when it reaches Haro Straight. **Lime Kiln Point State Park,** along West Side Rd., is known as the best **whale-watching** spot in the area, as the crowds of cliff-crawling visitors to the park can attest. Killer whales prowling for salmon frequent this stretch of coastline more than any other on the islands. Sometimes orcas will even perform acrobatics, to the delight of *Free Willy* watchers on shore. Before you head out, gauge your chances of actually seeing **orcas** by inquiring at the Whale Museum for day-to-day information on whale sightings. Those truly determined to see some blubber can shell out for a cruise; most operations charge

I Regret that I Have But One Life to Give for My Country.

Back in 1859, when Washington was officially part of "Oregon Country" and the San Juan Islands lay in a territorial no man's land between British Vancouver Island and the United States to the south, one brave swine gave his life for truth, justice, and the American Way. Twenty-five Americans lived and farmed on San Juan Island at a time when the British Hudson Bay Company claimed the island for Mother England. When Lyman Cutter caught a Hudson Bay pig making a royal mess of his potato patch, he understandably shot him dead. The Brits threatened to arrest him, and the Americans looked to Uncle Sam for protection. Three months, five British warships, and 14 American cannons later, war between the two nations seemed inevitable. Though the squabble cooled off, the **"Pig War"** lasted 12 years. Both countries occupied the island until 1872, when Kaiser Wilhelm of Germany was invited to settle the dispute and granted the U.S. the island. In the end, only the pig lost his life. But as we all know, everlasting fame is better than a life of wallowing in the mud any day.

about $40 (children $30) for a three- to four-hour boat ride. For info, pick up one of the many brochures at the chamber of commerce or the National Park Service Information Center (see **Practical Information,** above).

The Pig War also casts its comic pallor over **British Camp,** the second half of the **San Juan National Historical Park.** The camp lies on West Valley Rd. on the sheltered **Garrison Bay.** Take Mitchell Bay Rd. east from West Side Rd. Ascend the steep ½ mi. trail to "Mount" Young, the tallest hill on the island and a perfect place to take snapshots of Victoria and the Olympic Mountains (park open year-round; buildings open Memorial Day-Labor Day daily 8am-4:30pm).

Stop by the information kiosk in front of the **Hotel de Haro,** the **first hotel in Washington,** at the **Roche Harbor Resort,** Roche Harbor Rd. (378-2155), on the northern side of the island. The $1 brochure *A Walking Tour of Historic Roche Harbor* leads you through this old mining camp. Don't miss the bizarre gothic mausoleum—especially eerie at sunset—and the masonic symbolism that bedecks it. To get there, follow signs to Roche Harbor, then park on the lot behind the airfield. Signs guide visitors to the mausoleum foot path.

The annual **San Juan Island Dixieland Jazz Festival** brings swing bands to Friday Harbor in late July. A $45 badge ($40 if purchased before July 1) gets you into all performances, but you'll have just as much fun for free if you join the crowds of revelers outside the clubs. Single performance tickets range from $15 to $25. For more information, contact the San Juan Island Goodtime Classic Jazz Association, P.O. Box 1666, Friday Harbor 98250 (378-5509).

Orcas Island

Mount Constitution overlooks much of Puget Sound from its 2409 ft. summit atop Orcas Island. A small population of retirees, artists, and farmers dwell here in understated homes surrounded by green shrubs and the red bark of madrona trees. With a commune-like hostel and the largest state park in Washington, Orcas has the best budget tourist facilities of all the islands. Unfortunately, much of the beach is occupied by private resorts and is closed to the public.

PRACTICAL INFORMATION AND ORIENTATION

Visitors Information: There is no visitors center, but the **Chamber of Commerce** (376-2273) returns phone calls. Your best bet is to pick up info about Orcas Island on San Juan Island or visit **Nature's Art** (376-4343), an embroidery shop on Horseshoe Hwy. in Eastsound that doubles as an informal information center.

Ferries: Washington State Ferry, 376-4389 or 376-2134. 24hr.

Taxi: Orcas Island Taxi, 376-TAXI/8294.

Transportation: San Juan Transit, 376-8887. Service about every 90min. to most parts of the island. From the ferry to Eastsound $4.
Bike Rental: Wildlife Cycle (376-4708), at A St. and North Beach Rd., in Eastsound. 21-speeds $5 per hr., $25 per day. Open Mon.-Sat. 10:30am-5pm.
Moped Rental: Key Moped Rentals (376-2474), just north of the fire station on Prune Alley in Eastsound. $12 per hr., $45 per day. Driver's license and $10 deposit required. Helmets, gas, and **maps** included. No pregnant women. Open May-Sept. daily 10am-6:30pm.
Library: 376-4985, at Rose and Pine in Eastsound. Open Tues.-Thurs. 10am-7pm, Fri.-Sat. 11am-4pm, Sun. 10am-3pm.
Senior Services Center: 376-2677, across from the museum on North Beach Rd. in Eastsound. Open Mon.-Fri. 9am-4pm.
Pharmacy: Ray's (376-2230, after-hours emergencies 376-3693), in Templin Center. Open Mon.-Sat. 9am-6pm, Sun. 10am-6pm.
Emergency: 911.
Internet Access: At the library in Eastsound (see above).
Post Office: (376-4121), on A St. in Eastsound Market Place. Open Mon.-Fri. 9am-4:30pm. **General Delivery ZIP Code:** 98245.
Area Code: 360.

Orcas is shaped like a horseshoe, which makes getting around a chore. The ferry lands on the southwest tip. Travel 9 mi. northeast to the top of the horseshoe to reach **Eastsound,** the island's main town. Olga and Doe Bay are an additional 8 and 11 mi. from Eastsound, respectively, down the eastern side of the horseshoe. Stop in one of the four shops at the ferry landing to get a free **map.** Renting some wheels is not a bad idea, as the island is a bit spread out.

ACCOMMODATIONS AND CAMPING

It's a good idea to avoid B&Bs on Orcas, which charge upwards of $60 per day; stay at the Doe Bay Resort or try a campground. Reservations help in summer.

Doe Bay Village Resort, Star Rte. 86, Olga 98279 or P.O. Box 437 (376-2291), off Horseshoe Hwy. on Pt. Lawrence Rd., 5 mi. out of Moran State Park. This fun resort includes kitchen facilities, a health food store and cafe, and extensive grounds for romping. There's even a treehouse. The crowning attraction is the steam sauna and mineral bath ($3 per day, nonlodgers $6; bathing suits optional, coed). Be prepared to sacrifice tidiness for free-frolicking atmosphere. Hostel beds $16, $14 for hostel-card carriers. Camping $16. Cottages from $41. Reservations recommended. Office open 8am-9:30pm. Guided kayak trips twice daily, $39 for 3hr; call 376-4755.
Moran State Park, Star Rte. 22, Eastsound 98245 (376-2326). Follow Horseshoe Hwy. straight into the park. The grandiose white arches tell you and hundreds of others that you're there. All the best of San Juan fun: swimming, fishing, and miles of hiking. 4 campgrounds with 151 sites. About 12 sites open year-round, as are the restrooms. Rowboats and paddleboats $10-13 for the 1st hr., $7 per hr. thereafter. Standard sites with hot showers $11. Hiker/biker sites $5. Reservations strongly recommended May-Labor Day.
Obstruction Pass. Accessible only by boat or on foot. Turn off Horseshoe Hwy. just pass Olga and hang a right to head south on Obstruction Pass Rd. Soon you'll come to a dirt road marked "Obstruction Pass Trailhead." If you reach the bay, you've gone too far. The sites are a ½ mi. hike from the end of the road. Pit toilets, no water. A rocky but well maintained trail leads to a beach overhang, and, with patience, to a beach. Be careful where you light campfires—there are bald eagle nests in the trees above the campground. 9 sites. Free.

FOOD

All essentials can be found at **Island Market** (376-6000), on Langdell St. (open Mon.-Sat. 8am-9pm, Sun. 10am-8pm). Make a bee-line for **Orcas Homegrown Market** (376-2009), on Northbeach Rd., for all your natural needs. Large selection of groceries, medicines, and mysterious vegan cheeses. Try their deli for lunch, particularly the $5 vegetarian special (open daily 8am-11pm, winter 8am-9pm). For loads of fresh local produce, try the **Farmer's Market** in front of the museum (Sat. 10am-3pm).

Garden Cafe, 10 Northbeach Rd. (376-5177), behind the Starfire gallery. Fresh, tasty Asian cuisine. The only seating is outside, but on a clear day, the peaceful garden and a plate of the cafe's *Panang* (a vegetable dish with coconut curry, $4.50) is a refreshing retreat from the bakery/cafe standard. Open Wed.-Sat. 11am-6pm.

Chimayo (376-MEXI/6394), in the Our House Building on Northbeach Rd. A Southwestern theme and comfy booths. Delve into a burrito-built-for-two ($2.75-3.50). Open Mon.-Tues. and Thurs.-Sun. 11am-7pm.

Comet Cafe (376-4220), in Eastsound Sq. Two sisters run a bright, happy-go-lucky cafe. One bakes sweets, the other makes delicious sandwiches and roasts. Roast beef with Vermont cheese, $5.95. Open daily 8am-5pm.

SIGHTS AND ACTIVITIES

Trippers on Orcas Island don't need to travel with a destination in mind; half the fun lies in simply tramping about. The trail to **Obstruction Pass Beach** is the best of the few ways to clamber down to the rocky shores. Take advantage of the climbs on the hilliest of the San Juans for inspiring views of the Sound and the rest of the archipelago. Between meandering and meditations, stop by the island's numerous **galleries.**

Moran State Park (see above) is unquestionably Orcas' star outdoor attraction. Over 21 mi. of hiking trails cover the park, ranging in difficulty from a one-hour jaunt around Mountain Lake to a day-long constitutional up the south face of **Mt. Constitution,** the highest peak on the islands. Pick up a copy of the trail guide from the **registration station** (376-2326). From the summit of Constitution, you can see the Olympic and Cascade Ranges, Vancouver Island, and Mt. Rainier. The stone tower at the top was built as a fire lookout in 1936 by the Civilian Conservation Corps. It is possible to drive to the top—though rental mopeds are not powerful enough to reach the summit—but the best way to go is on foot. The most scenic route runs to Mountain Lake and then up the peak from there, a moderately taxing route (1½hr.). To shorten the hike, park your car at any one of the tree-lined lots along the road to the summit and proceed from there. The **Orcas Tortas** (800-967-1892) offers a slow ride on a green bus from Eastsound to the peak ($16). For an abbreviated jaunt, drive up Mt. Constitution and hike part-way down to Cascade Falls, which is spectacular in the spring and early summer. Down below, you can swim in two freshwater lakes easily accessible from the highway or rent rowboats and paddleboats ($9 per hr.) from Moran State Park. Head from the lake to the lagoon for an oceanside picnic (park open daily 6:30am-dusk; Sept.-March 8am-dusk).

Continue along Horseshoe Highway to **Doe Bay Village Resorts** (376-2291), where you can soak in natural mineral waters, sweat in the sauna, and have prophetic visions as you jump into a cold bath (bathing suits are the exception; see **Accommodations and Camping,** above). The **Sea Kayak Tour** (376-4699) of the surrounding islands, run by Shearwater Adventures, is a fascinating, albeit expensive, "water-hike" of the north end of Puget Sound. See bald eagles, seals, and blue herons up close. The three-hour tours ($35) include 30 minutes of dry-land training and also leave from Deer Harbor and Rosario Beach. Kayaking without a guide is not recommended.

Lopez Island

Smaller than either Orcas or San Juan, "Slow-pez" lacks some of the tourist facilities of the larger islands. Lopez was settled largely by mutineers who thrived in the secluded woods of the island. Today, Lopez Islanders still shy away from the mainland and maintain an age-old, if freakish, tradition of waving at every single car they pass.

Lopez Island is ideal for those seeking solitary beach-walking, bicycling, or a true small-town experience. Free of imposing inclines and heavy traffic, the island is the most cycle-friendly of the chain. Lopez's idyllic hills and farmland resemble that of Vermont. **Lopez Village,** the largest "town," is 3½ mi. from the ferry dock off Fisherman Bay Rd. To get there, follow Ferry Rd. until it splits, then take a right. It's best to bring a bicycle unless you're up for the hike. To rent a bike or kayak, head to **Lopez Bicycle Works** (468-2847), south of the village next to the island's Marine Center. Even if you don't rent, the cheerful staff will give you a detailed **map** of island roads complete with mileage counts. (Open June-Aug. daily 10am-6pm; call for winter hours; bikes $5 per hr., $23 per day; single kayaks $15 per hr., $50 per day; double kayaks $75 per day; half-day guided tours $45, "sunset paddle" $30.)

Shark Reef and **Agate Beach County Parks** are two small parks on the south end of the island that offer a change from mainland campgrounds. Shark Reef has tranquil and well maintained hiking trails, and Agate's beaches are calm and deserted. The **Lopez Island Vineyards** (468-3644), on Fisherman's Bay Rd., are a must-see; for $1 you can sample all of their wines, and for $8-12 you can have a souvenir of your own (open June-Aug. Wed.-Sun. noon-5pm; Sept.-Dec. and March-May Fri.-Sat. noon-5pm).

If you decide to spend the night on Lopez, camping is your only hope for a good deal. **Spencer Spit State Park** (468-2251), on the northeast corner of the island about 3½ mi. from the ferry terminal, has six sites on the beach and 45 pleasant wooded sites up the hill, with flush toilets but no showers or hookups. Spencer Spit enjoys good clamming in the late spring unless there is red tide. Two eight-bunk lean-tos (called "Adirondacks") can be rented for $15 each; sites are $11. Call (800) 452-5687 for reservations for summer weekends ($6 reservation fee). Campers may enter until 10pm; the park is closed November 1 to February 2. **Odlin Park** (468-2496) is close to the ferry terminal, 1 mi. south along Ferry Rd., and offers 30 sites and cold running water, with a boat launch, volleyball net, baseball diamond, and pay phone on the grounds (sites $13 plus $2 for each additional person after 5; hiker/biker sites $10). Visit the "information booth" just west of the museum for free maps and clean pay showers.

Ferry transport has caused price inflation, so it's a good idea to bring a lunch to Lopez Island. **Village Market** has groceries (open Mon.-Thurs. 8am-7pm, Fri.-Sat. 8am-8pm, Sun. 9am-7pm). Sample fresh pastries, bread, and pizza at **Holly B's** (468-2133) in the village or buy day-olds at a discount (open Wed.-Sat. 8am-5pm, Sun.-Mon. 8am-4pm). For a taxi, call **Angie's Cab** (468-2227). **Laundry** facilities lurk along Fisherman's Bay Road at **Keep It Clean,** 100 yards south of the winery (wash $1.75, 5min. dry 25¢; open Mon.-Sat. 8am-8pm, Sun. 9am-5pm). The **seniors' helpline** is 468-2421 (open Mon.-Fri. 9am-4pm). In an **emergency,** call 911. The health clinic is **Lopez Clinic** (468-2245). You can find the **post office** (468-2282) in the Village on Weeks Rd. The **General Delivery ZIP Code** is 98261. The **area code** is 360.

WASHINGTON

■ Other Islands

Shaw Island is home to one store, 100 residents, wild turkeys, apple orchards, and a bevy of Franciscan nuns. The convent lies on the water next to the ferry dock, and for the last 15 years, these women have been running the store/post office/gas station/ferry dock. Stop in for a couple of hours if only to take a walk, chat with a nun, or buy a postcard at the "Little Portion" store. The island's 11 mi. of public roads are endearing to hikers and bikers. **Shaw Island County Park,** on the south side of the island, has eight campsites ($10) that fill quickly despite the lack of running water. There is also a shared hiker/biker camping site ($3), but space is limited. There are no other accommodations on the island. Pick up a map at the ferry-side store.

Washington State Parks operates over 15 **marine parks** on some of the smaller islands in the archipelago. These islands, accessible by private transportation only, have anywhere from one to 51 mainly primitive campsites. The park system publishes a pamphlet on its marine facilities, available at parks or supply stores on the larger islands. One of the most popular destinations is tiny **Sucia Island,** which boasts gorgeous scenery and a few flopping seals. Canoes and kayaks can easily navigate the archipelago when the water is calm, but when the wind whips up the surf, only larger boats (at least 16 ft.) go out to sea. **Navigational maps** are essential to avoid the reefs and nasty hidden rocks that surround the islands. The Department of Natural

Resources operates three island parks, each with three to six free campsites. Cypress Head on **Cypress Island** has wheelchair-accessible facilities.

OLYMPIC PENINSULA

Due west of Seattle and its busy Puget Sound neighbors, the Olympic Peninsula is a remarkably different world. A smattering of logging and fishing communities and Indian reservations lace the peninsula's coastline along U.S. 101, but most of the ponderous land mass remains remote—a backpacker's paradise. **Olympic National Park** dominates much of the peninsula and prevents the area's ferocious timber industry from threatening the glacier-capped mountains and temperate rainforests. However, locals outside the park make a tenuous living off the land (or sea) in the local logging and fishing industries, the peninsula's largest employers. To the west, the Pacific stretches to a distant horizon; to the north, the Strait of Juan de Fuca separates the Olympic Peninsula from Vancouver Island; and to the east, Hood Canal and the Kitsap Peninsula isolate this sparsely inhabited wilderness from the sprawl of Seattle.

GETTING THERE AND GETTING AROUND

Getting around the peninsula is best done by car. Distances are tremendous, and public transportation, while passable for traveling to and between the peninsula's small towns, does not serve the magnificent natural areas that are the peninsula's main attractions. Most bus travel on the peninsula itself is free or costs 75¢ and accommodates bicycles. Public transportation heading into Olympic National Park, however, is sparse; hiking U.S. 101 to a trailhead can add many a paved and exhaust-filled mile to an otherwise tranquil trip. For a listing of public transportation options on the peninsula, contact the **Rainforest Hostel,** 169312 U.S. 101, Forks 98331 (360-374-2270; see p. 370). The owners will be happy to help you navigate the peninsula's myriad transit routes. Direct transfers between Greyhound, Grays Harbor Transit, West Jefferson Transit, Clallam Transit, and Port Angeles-Seattle Bus Lines can get you from Seattle, around the peninsula, and back for $24 (on weekdays).

Bicycling on U.S. 101 is very dangerous. Long stretches have no shoulder and immense log trucks speed heedlessly along the winding, two-lane road. Secondary roads on the peninsula are often gravelly and poorly suited to cycling. Hitchhiking is poor on the Olympic Peninsula and illegal on most of U.S. 101.

Port Townsend

Unlike the salmon industry, Port Townsend's Victorian splendor has survived the progression of time and weather. In the 1880s, civic boosters speculated that their booming port would become the new state capital. Every ship *en route* to Puget Sound stopped here for customs inspection, and the town caroused in the spoils of its apparent never-ending wealth...until the railroads came. Perched on the isolating northeast tip of the Olympic Peninsula, the town plummeted into a century-long economic ice age. In the last twenty years, however, the entire business district has been restored and declared a national landmark, and the town takes advantage of its 19th-century aura to keep its economy afloat and its facades freshly painted. Countless cafes, galleries, and bookstores line P.T.'s drippy streets, cheering the homesick urbanites who move there to escape the rat race. Port Townsend is one of the few places on the peninsula where espresso stands outnumber live bait shops.

Practical Information and Orientation The town's **Chamber of Commerce,** 2437 E. Sims Way (385-2722; email ptchamber@olympus.net), lies about 10 blocks from the center of town on Rte. 20. Ask the helpful staff for a free **map** and visitors guide (open Mon.-Fri. 9am-5pm, Sat. 10am-4pm, Sun. 11am-4pm).

Jefferson County Transit (JCT), 1615 W. Sims Way (385-4777), operates Port Townsend's public transportation. Riders can easily reach Port Angeles, Poulsbo, Winslow, and Bremerton on JCT and connect with a neighboring transit system. Most buses do not run on Sunday (fares 50¢ and 25¢ per zone, seniors and disabled travelers 25¢ per zone, ages 6-18 25¢; day passes $1.50). A Port Townsend **shuttle bus** loops around the town itself, and other services extend west along the strait to Sequim (50¢, seniors and students 25¢, under 6 free; day passes $1.50). For a **taxi,** call **Peninsula Taxi** (385-1872; open 24hr.).

P.T. Cyclery, 100 Tyler St. (385-6470), rents mountain bikes ($7 per hr., $25 per day; open Mon.-Sat. 9am-6pm, Sun. by appointment). **Kayak P.T.,** 435 Water St. (385-6240), rents to kayakers with some experience (singles $25 for 4hr., doubles $45 for 4hr.; anyone over 84 rents free; tours $39 for a ½-day, $68 for a day). **Sport Townsend,** 1044 Water St. (379-9711), rents camping equipment (tents $12, sleeping bags $8, backpacks, pads, and stoves also available; open Mon.-Sat. 10am-6pm, Sun. 11am-4pm). Find the **Public Library** at 1220 Lawrence (385-3181), uptown (open Mon. 11am-5pm, Tues.-Thurs. 11am-9pm, Fri.-Sat. 11am-5pm).

There is a **Safeway pharmacy** at 442 Sims Way (385-2860; open Mon.-Fri. 8:30am-7:30pm, Sat. 8:30am-6pm, Sun. 10:30am-6pm). The **hospital** is Jefferson General, 834 Sheridan (385-2200 or 800-244-8917). The **Jefferson County Crisis Line** is 385-0321 (24hr.). **Poison control** is (800) 732-6985. For **Senior Assistance,** call 385-2552 (Mon.-Fri. 8:30am-4:30pm). **Emergency Medical Care** (385-4622) is on the corner of Sheridan and 9th St. at the west end of town. In an **emergency,** call 911. The **police,** at 607 Water St., can be reached at 385-2322. Port Townsend's **post office** is at 1322 Washington St. (385-1600; open Mon.-Fri. 9am-5pm). **General Delivery ZIP Code:** 98368. The **area code** is 360.

Port Townsend sits at the terminus of Rte. 20 on the northeast corner of the Olympic Peninsula. By land, it can be reached from **U.S. 101** on the peninsula, or from the **Kitsap Peninsula** across the Hood Canal Bridge. By water, take the **Washington State Ferry** ($7.10; see p. 33 for scheduling and ticket information) from Seattle to Winslow on Bainbridge Island, and catch one of the Kitsap County Transit buses that meets every ferry and runs to Poulsbo. At Poulsbo, transfer to a Jefferson County Transit bus to Port Townsend. The Washington State Ferry also crosses frequently to and from Keystone on Whidbey Island. Ferries dock at Water St., west of downtown.

Accommodations and Camping The **Olympic Hostel (HI-AYH)** (385-0655), in Fort Worden State Park 1½ mi. from downtown (follow the signs), is situated right in the fort in an old barrack with views of the ocean, plenty of space, and cushy hospital beds in impeccable bunk rooms. Check out the Commanding Officer's house and Marine Science Center (see **Sights,** below). Rooms for couples and kitchen facilities are available. Call ahead—a hostel this elegant fills up quickly (beds $11, nonmembers $14, cyclists $9-13; July-Sept. $12, nonmembers $15; check-in 5-10pm, check-out 9:30am; no curfew.) The **Fort Flagler Hostel (HI-AYH),** in Fort Flagler State Park (385-1288), overlooks the ocean on handsome **Marrowstone Island,** a 20 mi. stone's throw from Port Townsend. From P.T., drive south on Rte. 19, which connects to Rte. 116 East and leads directly into the park. Another hostel in an old military haunt, the rooms are bright, clean, and cheery, if a bit farther from local attractions. Miles of pastoral bike routes wind over Marrowstone, and the hostel is less crowded than most. A storage and repair shed is open to bicyclists and has tools and a bike stand. (Beds $11, nonmembers $13, cyclists $9-12; open by reservation only; check-in 5-10pm, lockout 10am-5pm.) Call ahead if you're arriving late, and hostel staff will attempt to accommodate.

Campers might try **Old Fort Townsend State Park** (385-4730), which has 40 cramped sites and no potable water in a pretty woods for $10 (hiker/biker sites $5). It is 5 mi. south of Port Townsend just off Rte. 20 (open mid-May to mid-Sept.). **Fort Worden State Park** (385-4730) has seaside sites for $15 ($16 April-Oct.). Or camp on the beach at **Fort Flagler State Park** (385-1259; 116 sites; tents $11, RVs $16, hiker/biker sites $5). Reserve at both by calling the parks directly.

WASHINGTON

Olympic National Park

HOSTELS
- Rainforest Hostel, 20
- The Spa, 2

CAMPGROUNDS
RANGER STATIONS
- Altaire, 7
- Bogachiel State Park, 14
- Boulder Creek Campground, 8
- Cottonwood, 19
- Deer Park, 4
- Dosewallips, 28
- Dungeness Recreation Area, 1
- Elwha, 6
- Fairholm, 10
- Heart O' the Hills, 3
- Hoh Oxbow, 18
- Hoh Rain Forest, 15
- Hurricane Ridge, 5
- Kalaloch, 21
- Lake Cushman State Park, 26
- Minnie Peterson, 16
- Mora, 13
- Ozette, 12
- Queets, 22
- Queets, 23
- Quinault, 24
- Quinault USFS, 25
- Salt Creek County Park, 9
- Soleduck, 11
- Staircase, 27
- Willoughby Creek, 17

TO CAPE FLATTERY & NEAH BAY
Sekiu
Clallam Bay
Strait of Juan de Fuca
N
0 5 miles
0 5 kilometers
OZETTE INDIAN RESERVATION
Wedding Rocks
Ozette
Ozette Lake
Dungeness National Wildlife Refuge
Old Town
Dungeness
Agnew
Sequim
Freshwater Bay
Ediz Hook
Port Angeles
Joyce
Lake Crescent
Pioneer Memorial Museum Vistor Center
Sappho
USFS/NPS Information Station
Fairholm
Storm King Information Station
Marymere Falls
OLYMPIC NAT'L FOREST
Soleduck River
Soleduck Falls
Mt. Angeles
Hurricane Ridge
Deer Park
Olympic Hot Springs
Elwha River
Obstruction Peak
Cake Rock, Hole-in-the-Wall
Rialto Beach
La Push
Forks
Beach 1
Second Beach
Third Beach
QUILEUTE INDIAN RESERVATION
Bogachiel River
PACIFIC OCEAN
Hoh Rain Forest Visitor Center
Mount Olympus
Hayden Pass
Mount Deception
Oil City
Hoh
Hoh River
HOH INDIAN RESERVATION
OLYMPIC NATIONAL PARK
Mount Anderson
Dosewallips River
TO U.S. 101 11 MI.
Ruby Beach
Beach 6
Beach 4
Beach 3
Clearwater River
Queets River
Duckabush River
North Shore Rd.
South Shore Rd.
North Fork Quinault River
East Fork Quinault River
Kalaloch Information Station
Kalaloch
Beach 2
Beach 1
OLYMPIC NAT'L FOREST
North Fork
Skokomish River
North Shore Rd.
South Shore Rd.
Quinault Lake
QUINAULT INDIAN RESERVATION
OLYMPIC NAT'L FOREST
Lake Cushman
TO U.S. 101 5 MI.

WASHINGTON

Food A burly **Safeway** at 442 Sims Way (385-2806), south of town along Rte. 20, serves any need. **Burrito Depot,** 609 Washington St. (385-5856), at Madison, offers quick, tasty Mexican food. Tango with the tasty veggie fajita ($4.25), or tank up on big burritos from $3 (open Mon.-Sat. 10:30am-8:30pm; wheelchair accessible). For ridiculously healthy and even more ridiculously entertaining food, try the **Coho Cafe and Juice Bar,** 1044 Lawrence St. (379-1030), at Polk St., uptown. A peppy paint job and local health nuts spice up the veggie roll-up ($4). Take this opportunity to de-oxidate with a wheat grass shot ($1) or substitute a sampling of tofu (open Tues.-Thurs. 7am-4pm, Fri.-Sat. 7am-8pm, Sun. 8am-4pm). The **Elevated Ice Cream Co.,** 627 Water St. (385-1156), serves delicious homemade ice cream and decent espresso (90¢) in a 1920s shop that is, ironically, on the ground floor. One scoop of ice cream or two mini-scoops of Italian ice costs $1.40 (open daily 9:30am-10pm; winter daily 11am-10pm). **Waterfront Pizza** (385-6629) on Water St., offers little historical ambience, but churns out a damn good pizza. Plain cheese slice $1.75, vegetarian slice $2.50 (open daily 11am-10pm).

Sights and Events Port Townsend is *full* of huge Queen Anne and Victorian mansions. No, really. Of the over 200 restored homes in the area, some have been converted into B&Bs and are open for tours. The **Ann Starret Mansion,** 744 Clay St. (385-3205), has nationally renowned Victorian architecture, frescoed ceilings, and a free-hanging, three-tiered spiral staircase. Though it's now a bed and breakfast, visitors can take tours daily from noon to 3pm ($2). Even the architecturally ignorant will stand slack-jawed under the staircase like Cinderella at the ball.

Go down the steps on Taylor St. to **Water Street,** the town's neo-quaint main artery. Hallowed halls from the 1890s muscle in between "historic" shops with faux facades. The **Jefferson County Museum** (385-1003), at Madison and Water St., showcases vestiges of the town's raucous past. A dazzling kayak parka made of seal intestines, jail cells in the basement (rumored to have held Jack London for a night), and an old-time pedal-powered dentist drill make up for the visitors sign-in rigmarole at the door (open Mon.-Sat. 11am-4pm, Sun. 1-4pm; suggested donation $2).

Point Hudson, where Admiralty Inlet and Port Townsend Bay meet, is the hub of the small shipbuilding area and forms the corner of Port Townsend. North of Point Hudson are several miles of beach, **Chetzemolka Park,** and the larger **Fort Worden State Park** (open daily 6:30am-dusk). **Fort Worden** (385-4730; see p. 360), a military post dating from the 1890s, guards the mouth of Puget Sound. The fort went into service again in 1981 as a set for the movie *An Officer and a Gentleman.* Military historians (or would-bes) should check out the **Commanding Officer's house** which, like every other building in Port Townsend, is stuffed to the rafters with Victorian furniture ($1; open April 1-Oct. 5 daily 10am-5pm). The **Coast Artillery Museum** (385-0373) offers a no-nonsense display on Fort Worden's uneventful military history. Out on the pier at Fort Worden is the **Marine Science Center** (385-5582). Get up close and personal with the local sea life that lives in several tanks ($2, children $1; open Tues.-Sun. noon-6pm; fall and spring Sat.-Sun. noon-4pm).

Port Townsend's music scene is surprisingly lively. Hang your hat at **Town Tavern** (385-1706) at the corner of Quinsy and Water St. This western-style saloon hosts live entertainment Thursday through Saturday. **Sirens,** 823 Water St. (379-0776), sponsors blues shows on its ducky deck-with-a-view. Make $10 carrying kegs upstairs to the bar on Friday evenings. Spend it emptying them.

From mid-June to early September, **Centrum** sponsors a series of festivals in Fort Worden Park including the **Port Townsend Blues Festival** at the end of June, the **Festival of American Fiddle Tunes** in early July, and **Jazz Port Townsend** later in the month. Ticket prices vary; combination tickets can be purchased for all of each festival. For a schedule, write the Centrum Foundation, P.O. Box 1158, Port Townsend 98368 (385-3102 or 800-733-3608, ext. 1). Other annual attractions include the **Wooden Boat Festival,** held the first weekend after Labor Day, and the **House Tour,** held the following weekend, when many mansions are open to visitors free of charge. For more information, contact the Chamber of Commerce.

Port Angeles

Ideally situated between Olympic National Park (ONP) and the chilly, blue waters of the Strait of Juan de Fuca, Port Angeles proudly presides over the "Gateway to the Olympics." Unfortunately, the town's mountainous neighbors win all the local glory, and the Port of the Angels maintains a character that hovers on the bland side of nebulous. An era of domination by paper and plywood mills has ended, and Port Angeles joins the legions of small towns hungering after the tourist dollar.

Practical Information The **Chamber of Commerce,** 121 E. Railroad (452-2363), next to the ferry terminal, one block from the intersection of Lincoln and Front St. boisterously hands out tourist info. The office allows free local calls (open daily 8am-9pm; winter Mon.-Fri. 10am-4pm, Sat.-Sun. noon-4pm; email pangeles@olypen.com). The all-important **Olympic National Park Visitors Center** (see p. 364) is located in Port Angeles at 3002 Angeles Rd. (452-0330).

A Greyhound subsidiary, **Olympic Bus Lines,** 612 Lincoln Ave. (800-550-3058; http://www.northolympic.com), serves Port Angeles. Buses run to Seattle (Mon.-Sat. 2 per day, once Sunday; $20, seniors $16). **The Coho Ferry,** 101 E. Railroad Ave. (457-4491), has service to Victoria ($6.75, with bicycle $10, with car $27.25, children $3.50). The **Clallam Transit System,** 830 W. Lauridsen Blvd. (800-858-3747 or 452-4511), serves the Port Angeles area and all of Clallam County, as far as Forks and Neah Bay (Mon.-Fri. 4:15am-11pm, Sat. 10am-6pm; fare within downtown $1, ages 6-19 35¢, disabled 25¢). **Car Rental** is available at **Evergreen Auto Rental,** 808 E. Front St. (452-8001; from $29 per day, weekly $170; 50 mi. free, 20¢ per mi. thereafter; must be 21 with proof of insurance). **Budget Rent-a-Car,** 111 E. Front St., has all-day parking across from the ferry for $7 and also rents cars. **Olympic Mountaineering, Inc.,** 140 W. Front St. (452-0240), rents every conceivable type of mountain equipment except sleeping bags. Two-person tents cost $20 per day; external frame packs are $13 per day, cross-country ski gear is $15 per day. The list goes on and on, and weekly rates are lower. Call about fairly inexpensive overnight (and longer) treks into the ONP wilds (open Mon.-Sat. 9am-6pm, Sun. 10am-5pm). **Pedal 'n' Paddle,** 120 E. Front St. (457-1240), rents mountain bikes (that's the pedal part: $8 per hr., $22 per day, helmets included) and offers kayak trips (that's the paddle: $50 for a half-day).

The local **laundromat** is the **Peabody Street Coin Laundry,** 212 Peabody St. (452-6493; wash $1.25, 8min. dry 25¢; open 24hr.). The **post office** sits at 424 E. 1st St. (452-9275), at Vine (open Mon.-Fri. 8:30am-5pm, Sat. 9am-noon). **General Delivery ZIP Code:** 98362. **Area code:** 360.

Accommodations and Camping A night indoors in Port Angeles is pricey and hardly angelic, especially in the summer (winter rates drop $5-15). Budget believers should check out **The Spa,** 511 E. First St. (452-3257); get off the bus at Bonnie's Bakery. Reserve a mat or futon ahead of time, and experience everything you dreamed of in a Pacific Northwest hostel. It's one big slumber party as everyone huddles down in the same room. Do each other's hair and talk about boys ($15 per night including breakfast in the garden tea room; 1hr. in downstairs steam room $10). The least expensive motel options line noisy U.S. 101. A few miles west of town, the **Fairmont Motel,** 1137 U.S. 101 W. (457-6113), has decent, if dark, cable-equipped rooms and a food mart next door (queen $37; winter rates lower). The **Royal Victorian Motel,** 521 First St. (452-2316), has newly remodeled rooms with microwaves and refrigerators. Managers provide limo service to and from the ferry dock (singles by the street $34; doubles $40-79; check-in between 2pm and 11pm; AAA approved).

Leave your heart at **Heart o' the Hills,** the closest campground (see p. 367); unless you come after hours, you'll need to pay the $10 park entrance fee (good for 7 days) plus the $11 camping fee. The camp has no hook-ups, but offers lush surroundings, handicap sites, and ranger-led programs on summer evenings (first-come, first-served; open year-round). Or try **Salt Creek County Park** (928-3441), a 20-minute mosey along Hwy. 112 from Port Angeles. Many of the 80 sites ($10) have waterfront views, and the nearby tidepools are a treasure trove of shells and sea stars. Pay showers; no hook-ups or reservations. The nearest super-cheap camping is at **Boulder Creek Campground,** at the end of Elwha River Rd., 8 mi. past Altaire. Park at the end of the road, and hike 2 mi. along a closed-off road. Check out the natural hot springs while you're there (see **Olympic National Park: Northern Park Rim,** p. 367). A $5 **backcountry permit** ($2 for each additional person; see p. 367), available at the trailhead, lets you pitch a tent at one of the 50 sites. Be sure to bring water and warm clothes.

Food Port Angeles is stuffed with seafood, only sometimes fresh. An excellent place to sample the local catch is **La Casita,** 203 E. Front St. (452-2289). This Mexican restaurant stuffs its seafood burrito ($7) with gobs of crab, shrimp, and fish, and has free all-you-can-eat tortilla chips to nibble on between $2 margaritas (open Mon.-Thurs. 11am-9pm, Fri. 11am-10pm, Sat. 11am-10pm, Sun. noon-9pm). **Bella Italia,** 117B E. First St. (457-5442), gets rave reviews from Port Angelinos. For $7, a hungry vegetarian can sit down to a hunk of veggie lasagna in a romantic, candle-lit booth. The bustling **First Street Haven,** 107 E. 1st St. (457-0352) serves up strawberry Belgian waffles ($5.50), or the "Prospector," a behemoth shrimp sandwich (open Mon.-Fri. 7am-4pm, Sat. 8am-4pm, Sun. 8am-2pm). They also have a selection of magazines for browsing that puts dentist's offices to shame. Picnickers can peruse the shelves of **Safeway,** 110 E. 3rd St. (457-0788) at Lincoln St. (open 24hr.).

Sights This "gateway" city has little more to offer than its gate. Before any trails or travails, stop by **Port Brook and News,** 104 E. 1st, which has a large **map** selection and can provide insider's advice on the best trails and campgrounds in the area. For those without a vehicle and disinclined to ride a bike uphill for 20 mi., **Olympic Van Tours** (452-3858) runs three-hour or all-day excursions to Hurricane Ridge for $13-28 (see p. 367). The **Olympic National Park Visitors Center,** 3002 Mt. Angeles Rd. (452-0330), at Race St., dispenses free **maps** (open daily 8:30am-6pm, off-season daily 9am-4pm). More accessible by foot is the **Arthur D. Feiro Marine Laboratory** (417-6254), offering a large classroom of touch-tanks and aquariums (open daily 7am-8pm; Oct.-June 14 Sat.-Sun. noon-4pm; $2, seniors and under 12 $1). The 6 mi. **Waterfront Trail,** a handicapped-accessible path that provides an overview of the city's portside activities, passes over the pier.

The **Fine Arts Center,** 1203 E. 8th St. (457-3532), in the vicinity of the National Parks Visitors Center, has great views of the water and small but inspiring exhibits by regional artists. And hey, it's free (open Thurs.-Sun. 11am-5pm). A **brewery** will be opening in the fall of 1997 at some mysterious Port Angeles location, promising to inject newfound vigor into the gateway's not-too-spicy nightlife.

Olympic National Park

Olympic National Park (ONP) is the centerpiece of the Olympic Peninsula and shelters one of the most diverse landscapes of any North American park. From its glacier-encrusted peaks, to its lush and dripping river-valley rainforests, to its jagged shores along the Pacific Coast, the park appeals to the wide range of tastes of an even wider range of visitors. Roads lead to many corners of Olympic National Park, but they really only scratch the surface of this outdoor wonderland. A dive into the backcountry exposes the park's many faces, and leaves the hordes of summer tourists behind. Despite ONP's dire financial straits (it is one of the poorest national parks) and subsequently rising fees, a little effort and planning can easily yield a day of salmon fishing on the Hoh River, an afternoon of shell hunting on miles of isolated beach, or a week of glacier-gazing from the tree line.

The Olympic Mountains are the park's trophy. The entire **Olympic Mountain Range** is packed into ONP's center, where conical peaks wring huge quantities of moisture from heavy Pacific air. Average precipitation in the park varies, but 12 ft. of rain and snow yearly is common; certain locations average over 17 ft., and above 3500 ft. it is not rare to encounter snow through late June. The mountains take so much of the clouds' water that some areas northeast of the park get less than 1½ ft. of precipitation per year, making them among the driest in Washington.

The **rainforests** lie on the west side of the park, along the coast, and in the **Hoh, Queets,** and **Quinault** river valleys, where moderate temperatures, loads of rain, and summer fogs support a fantastic Northwestern jungle dominated by Sitka spruce and western red cedar. The rest of the park is populated by Douglas fir and hemlock lowland forest, silver fir at higher elevations, and flower-filled mountain meadows that offer stunning views and are often accessible only by foot.

Sea stacks—boxy bluffs left standing offshore—and ancient Native American petroglyphs lend the beaches along the unspoiled Olympic coastline a sense of mystery. Wind-whipped forests and rocky headlands edge the long, driftwood-strewn beaches. During the winter, evidence of human presence vanishes, and the coast casts off a primeval air. Swaths of Olympic National Forest and private land separate these seaside expanses from the rest of the park.

The extensive patches of naked mountainside left by **logging,** particularly on the western side of the peninsula, may shock visitors. The National Park is protected from logging, and views of scarred hillsides disappear within its boundaries, but timber companies regularly harvest both private land and the surrounding National Forest. The State of Washington manages huge tracts along the Hoh and **Clearwater** Rivers, near the western shore. Until recently, private and state agencies clear-cut old-growth forests on the peninsula, a policy the western segment of U.S. 101 testifies to. At points, the highway weaves through bald patches of land, with roadside placards indicating the dates of harvest and replanting. Due to the spotted owl uproar and federal regulations banning logging on public land, the Forest Service stopped harvesting any ONP timber in the late 1980s, and private and state harvesting has also slowed. Environmentally conscious travelers should avoid the issue with locals. Those who earn a living from forest resources dislike lectures on how to manage them and will likely point out that the consumer of forest products is as responsible for clearcutting as the industries themselves.

PRACTICAL INFORMATION AND ORIENTATION

Visitors Information: Olympic Visitors Center, 3002 Mt. Angeles Rd., Port Angeles (452-0330), off Race St. This is the park's main information center and fields questions about the entire park, including camping, backcountry hiking, and fishing. Distributes the invaluable **map** of the park and locations of other park ranger stations. Also houses exhibits and a hands-on **Discovery Room** for children and adults (open daily 9am-4pm). **Park Headquarters,** 600 E. Park Ave., Port Angeles (452-4501, ext. 311), is just an administrative office but can answer phone questions. Open Mon.-Fri. 8am-4:30pm. **Olympic National Park Wilderness Center** (452-0300), just behind the visitors center, has a helpful staff, well-versed in backcountry procedures. Rangers will gladly sit down with backpackers to help design trips within the park. The Wilderness Center is the only place on the north side of the park to make reservations for the 4 ONP backcountry areas that require reservations (see p. 366). **State Parks Information:** 800-233-0321.

Entrance Fee: $10 per car and $3 per hiker or biker charged during the day at developed entrances, such as Hoh, Heart o' the Hills, Sol Duc, Staircase, and Elwha (all with paved roads and toilet facilities). The fee pays for 7 days' access to the park—keep that receipt!

Park Weather: 452-0329. 24hr.

Park Radio: 530 AM for road closures and general weather conditions, **610 AM** for general park rules and information.

Park Emergency: 452-4501. Daily 8am-5pm; at other times phone 911.

Area Code: 360.

Only a few hours from Seattle, Portland, and Victoria, the wilderness of **Olympic National Park** is most easily and safely reached by car. Existing roads are accessible from U.S. 101 and serve as trailheads for over 600 mi. of hiking. No roads cross the entire park. The perimeters of the park are well defined, but are surrounded by

National Forest, Washington Department of Natural Resources, and other public land. There are few outposts within the park—**Port Angeles** (see p. 363) on the Northern Park Rim, and **Forks** (see p. 369), on the east side of the park are the only (barely) sizeable towns where gas and food are always available. U.S. 101 encircles the park in the shape of an upside-down U, with Port Angeles at the top. From Port Angeles, many visitors drive down the western leg of the U and through the park in one (long) day. (For more information, see **Olympic Peninsula: Getting There and Getting Around,** p. 359.)

July, August, and September are best for visiting Olympic National Park, since much of the backcountry remains snowed-in until late June, and only summers are rain-free (which, of course, brings flocks of fellow sightseers; expect company). Coming from Seattle, the best place to begin an exploration of the park is the **Olympic Visitors Center** (see above), where cheerful rangers hand out park maps and give advice on all aspects of travel within the park. The Park Service runs **interpretive programs** such as guided forest walks, tidepool walks, and campfire programs out of its ranger stations (all free). For a schedule of events, pick up a copy of the park newspaper from ranger stations or the visitors center.

For a knock-down, drag-out tour of the different climates of the park, drive to **Hurricane Ridge,** then continue on U.S. 101 southward, detouring to the **Hoh Rain Forest Visitors Center** and then again southward on U.S. 101 to the pristine beaches near the **Klaloch Information Station.** While this sightseeing blitzkrieg gives a good overview of the park's potential, it in no way does it justice. There are innumerable trails to hike, beaches to comb, and photos to take along the way. One could easily spend weeks here. The map distributed at the park gates and most ranger stations and information centers gives an excellent overview of the entire park as well as most of the peninsula. Robert Steelquist's *Olympic National Park and the Olympic Peninsula: A Traveler's Companion* gives clear, accurate descriptions of the area, and Robert Wood's *Olympic Mountains Trail Guide* is the best book for those planning to tackle the backcountry ($14.75 at any area bookstore or information center).

Fishing within park boundaries does not require a permit, but, for salmon and steelhead, you must obtain a state game department punch card at local outfitting and hardware stores or at the Fish and Game Department in Olympia. Though fishing is good in any of the park's 15 major rivers, the **Elwha River,** coursing through the northeastern part of the park, is best for **trout.** The Hoh River, flowing west through the park, is excellent for **salmon.** Ask at an anglers' store for current information.

Refer to the more detailed listings below covering the park's different geographical regions for information on campsites, hikes, and specific events.

CAMPING ON THE PENINSULA

On the peninsula, campers can tent it within walking distance of one of the world's three temperate rainforests for the price of a sandwich. Although hotels litter the area, sleeping in one would defy the point of visiting. Camp, camp, camp! Olympic National Park, Olympic National Forest, and the State of Washington all maintain free campgrounds, and the **Washington Department of Natural Resources** (DNR) allows **free backcountry camping** off any state road on DNR land, as long as campers set up over 100 yd. from the road. The majority of DNR land is near the western shore along the Hoh and Clearwater Rivers, though they also manage smaller, individual campsites sprinkled about the peninsula. Visitors centers and ranger stations hand out a DNR guide to all its Washington sites as well as information on camping within the park and national forest. In summer, weekend competition for sites can be fierce. From late June to late September, most spaces are taken by 2pm, so start hunting early; in more popular areas and along the Hoh River, find a site before noon. See the various park regions, below, for specific campground listings.

Camping by Car

Free **National Park campgrounds** include **Ozette** (with drinking water) and **Queets** (no water). In addition, ONP has many standard campgrounds (sites $10). Fees in

National Forest Campgrounds range from $4 to 12; six campgrounds in the **Hood Canal Ranger District** are free. Reservations can only be made for three Forest Service campgrounds (Seal Rock, Falls View, and Klahowga) by calling (800) 280-CAMP/2267. Most other drive-up camping on the peninsula is first-come, first-served. Any ranger station can provide info on park and forest service campgrounds. Several **State Parks** are scattered along Hood Canal and the eastern rim of the peninsula (generally $10-16; occasionally $4-5), and are reservable by calling (800) 452-5687.

Backcountry Camping

Strap on your backpack, stock up on instant oatmeal, hike into the ONP backcountry, and die happy. Whether in the rainforest, along the coast, or in the high country, certain general guidelines and rules apply: backcountry camping anywhere in the park requires a $5 **backcountry permit,** available at any ranger station and most trailheads. The purpose of the permit is to provide the park with information on internal traffic as well as your location in case of an emergency. Park offices issue limited numbers of backcountry permits for four destinations within the park in response to their extreme popularity. These are **North Beach** by Lake Ozette (452-0300), the **Soleduck District** and **Grand Valley** (327-3534), and **Lake Constance** and **Flapjack Lakes,** both overseen by the Hood Canal Ranger Station in Hoodsport (877-5254).

Reservations are crucial, especially at Lake Ozette and the campgrounds to the west that are 100% reservable (the rest are 50% first-come, first-served); call a few days in advance. Backpackers should always prepare for a mix of weather conditions. Even in summer, the driest season, parts of the park are very wet. Always have a good waterproof jacket and waterproof hiking boots with plenty of traction; trails can become rivers of slippery mud. Layers of warm clothing and a wool hat are a good idea (see p. 40). *Never* drink any **untreated water** in the park. *Giardia lamblia,* a nasty bacteria, lives in all these waters and causes severe diarrhea and abdominal cramps (see **Common Ailments,** p. 14). You can boil your water or buy water purification tablets at the visitors center and most camping supply stores. **Black bears** and **raccoons,** eager to partake of hikers' granola and peanuts, are another hazard for backcountry campers. To prevent mishaps, ranger stations offer lessons on hanging food out of reach when they issue backcountry permits. Some stations have free rope, but don't count on it. Bring your own 50-100 ft. of thin, sturdy rope. A map and signs at the trailhead will disclose whether **open fires** are permitted in the backcountry area. For any backcountry trip, make sure to inquire in advance at a ranger station about trail closures. Winter weather has destroyed many a popular trail.

■ Northern Park Rim

The most developed section of Olympic National Park lies along the northern rim near Port Angeles, where day trips to glaciers, rainforests, and sunsets over the Pacific are all only a drive away. **Heart o' the Hills Campground** (452-2713), 5½ mi. from Port Angeles on Race Rd., is overflowing with vacationers poised to take **Hurricane Ridge** by storm the next day (102 sites; $10, plus the $10 entrance fee; see p. 363). The campground has no hookups or showers, but plenty of giant trees, fairly private sites, handicap access, and family-oriented evening campfire programs. The road up the ridge is an easy, but curvy drive for those short on time. Before July, an assault on the ridge usually involves a bit of snow-stepping. Clear days promise splendid views of Mt. Olympus and Vancouver Island, set against a foreground of snow and indigo lupine. RVs and German tourists crowd the ridge; the ideal time to go is sunrise. After the herds arrive, more seclusion can be found on the many short trails that originate here, including some designed for seniors and the disabled. Among the redundantly extraordinary views, try the uphill **High Ridge Trail,** which is a short walk from Sunset Point. Signs at the visitors center give updates on visibility at the summit, but call ahead of time (452-0330) before tackling the 40-minute drive. On weekends from late December to late March, the Park Service organizes free guided **snowshoe walks** atop the ridge. Call the visitors center (452-0330) for details.

For similarly stunning views without the company of Buicks and BMWs, drive up the spur to **Deer Park,** just east of Port Angeles, where trails are less crowded and vistas are just as plentiful. After hiking, gasp thin mountain air at the park's highest car-accessible camping (4500 ft.), **Deer Park Campground** ($6, summer only). Come early and bring water—the campground's 14 sites have none. Trailers and RVs are prohibited. Still looking for solitude? Head past Deer Park to the **Royal Basin Trail** and meander 6.2 mi. to the Royal Basin waterfall. In the opposite direction on U.S. 101, a short spur road to the south leads to two campgrounds along the waterfall-laced Elwha river: **Elwha Valley** (452-9191; 41 sites, $10), 5 mi. south off U.S. 101, and the nearby **Altaire** (452-9191; 30 sites, $10). Both have drinking water and flush toilets. Just past the Altaire campground, park at the Appleton Pass and **Olympic Hotspring** trailhead and hike 2½ mi. to the natural hotsprings. Intrepid dippers beware: the warm, bacteria-full water can jump-start infections. To stay on the safe side, follow the unmarked foot paths to more secluded, less used baths. The nearby backcountry camping area has 14 primitive sites (free with a backcountry permit).

Back on U.S. 101, **Fairholm Campground** (928-3380) sits 30 mi. west of Port Angeles, snuggled at the tip of **Lake Crescent.** Fairholm has handicap access and plenty of drinking water (87 sites, $10). **The Storm King Ranger Station** (928-3380; hours vary) runs evening interpretive programs at the campground. Hikers exploring the trails around this glacier-scarred lake gasp at views of old-growth forests and the brilliantly blue waters of one of the only natural lakes in Washington (most were created by dammed rivers, natural processes be damned!).

The **Marymere Falls Trail** (2 mi. roundtrip) through old-growth Douglas firs, western hemlock, and red cedar is great for travelers with kids or without time. It leaves from the ranger station and the first ¼ mi. is wheelchair accessible. A number of more difficult and equally more scenic trails begin here; check at the ranger station for conditions. Even farther west on U.S. 101, 13 mi. of paved road pierce into to the **Sol Duc Hot Springs Campground** (327-3534), which has 80 sites ($12) with handicapped-accessible restrooms near the popular **Sol Duc Hot Springs Resort** (327-3583), where retirees de-wrinkle in the hot springs and eat at the restaurant or snack bar inside the lodge. Chlorinated pools are wheelchair accessible. There are scheduled programs every evening except Friday (open daily 9am-9pm, winter Fri. and Sat. 9am-5pm, $6.50 per day, seniors $5.50). According to Native American legend, the source of the **Sol Duc Springs** and the **Olympic Springs** are two "lightning fish" who, after a long and indecisive battle, gave up the fight and crept into two caves, where they still weep hot tears of mortification (apparently, the Sol Duc fish wept chlorinated tears). The Sol Duc trailhead is also a starting point for those heading for the heights; stop by the **Eagle Ranger Station** (327-3534) for information and backcountry permits (open June-Aug. daily 8am-5pm). The **Sol Duc Trail** draws its share of traffic, but crowds thin dramatically above Sol Duc Falls.

CAPE FLATTERY AND NEAH BAY

Pursuers of trivia take heed: Cape Flattery is the most northwest point in the contiguous U.S. Not only that, but it's drop-dead gorgeous. In 1778, the area caught the attention of explorer James Cook, who named the tip Cape Flattery because it "flattered us with the hopes of finding a harbor." Unfortunately, flattery got them nowhere, as the nearest port is all the way across the peninsula at Port Angeles. Although the cape and Neah Bay are not in ONP, they are only accessible via the gateway town of Port Angeles, and they perch just north of the park on the western park rim. At the westernmost point on the Juan de Fuca Strait (*Let's Go* begs your pardon) is **Neah Bay,** the only town in the **Makah Reservation** and home to a museum displaying finds from a 15th century Makah village. Rte. 112 leads west from Port Angeles to Neah Bay; from the south, take the short road north from **Sappho.** Even the short road is not too neah to Neah Bay; the drive takes at least one hour from U.S. 101. The **Clallam Transit System** (452-4511 or 800-858-3747) reaches Neah Bay. Take bus #14 from Oak St. in Port Angeles to Sappho (75min.). Then take bus #16 to Neah Bay (60min.). Check schedules at the Port Angeles Greyhound Station to avoid long layovers (75¢, ages 6-19 60¢, seniors free). In case of **emergency,** call 911. The **area code** is 360.

Still teasing would-be explorers, **Cape Flattery** can be reached only through Neah Bay. Follow the road until it turns to dirt and continue on it for another 4 mi. until you reach a small, circular parking area. A trailhead leads toward Cape Flattery from the parking lot. The recent construction of the trail and cliffside viewing areas has rendered the previously ankle-breaking journey to the cape easily negotiable. You'll know you're close to the bombastic views of Tatoosh Island just off the coast and Vancouver Island across the strait when you hear the sound of the island's bullhorn. There is a camping and picnicking area within car's reach at Hobuck Beach, only a few miles south of Cape Flattery. Coming from Neah Bay, turn left just before the Cape Flattery resort, cross the bridge, then take the first right to the **Hobuck Beach Park** (645-6422), which has outhouses, running water, and camping space for $10 per night (no reservations), but is rumored to have experienced frequent theft. To the south, the Makah reservation's beaches are solitary and peaceful; respectful visitors are welcome to wander them.

Back in Neah Bay, the **Makah Cultural and Research Center** (645-2711), on Hwy. 112, houses artifacts from an archaeological site at Cape Alava, where a huge mudslide 500 years ago buried and perfectly preserved a small Makah settlement. One exhibit expertly reproduces a room from a longhouse, complete with animal skins, cooking fire, and the smell of smoked salmon. This Pompeii of the Northwest and, in fact, the entire museum, seem to have stepped out of the Smithsonian, they are so expertly constructed. The center also serves as the town's social and cultural center. the museum is just inside the reservation on the first left, right across from the Coast Guard station (open daily 10am-5pm; Sep.-May Wed.-Sun. 10am-5pm; $4, seniors and students $3). The Makah nation, whose recorded history goes back 2000 years, still lives, fishes, and produces artwork on this land, though now in a slightly startling state of poverty. During the weekend closest to August 26, Native Americans from around the region come to participate in canoe races, traditional dances, and bone games (a form of gambling) during the **Makah Days.** Visitors are welcome and the delicious salmon bake is a definite highlight. Contact the museum for information.

Neah Bay today caters to Bluto-like fishers, and it is not the place to spend the night. If stuck, try the oceanside **Cape Motel** (645-2250) on Bay View Ave. Old but clean, narrow rooms (singles $40; double bunk beds $49). A better option may be to camp 11 mi. east of Neah Bay at **Trettenks RV Park** (963-2688). Tent sites line the Juan de Fuca Strait. Ahh, and pleasant bathrooms, too ($14, each additional guest $2).

■ Western Park Rim

The western edge of the Olympic Peninsula traps visitors in its intricate web of park, national forest, and private lands, all laced with stellar views and hiking trails. One of three temperate rainforests in the world hugs the river valleys on the west side of the Olympic Mountains, just a short drive east from U.S. 101. Expansive timber lands line the highway, separating Olympic National Park's craggy coastline from the rest of the park. Where U.S. 101 hugs the shore, many a paved parking lot gives travelers easy access to sunsets and rocky beaches.

FORKS

Between the Northern Park Rim and Western Park Rim rainforests, the logging town of **Forks** on U.S. 101—the only town to speak of on the western side of the park—is the perfect place to stop, stock up, and learn about timber culture from plaid-shirted, suspendered locals. Actually, it's the *only* place to stop. Get your dose of country-western here—the only radio station plays nothing but Garth Brooks and Tammy Wynette. Forks lies a hefty two hours west of Port Angeles. Make sure to buy **gas** in Forks, since there are few stations farther south.

On the south end of town on U.S. 101, stop at the **Forks Visitors Center** (374-02531 or 800-44-FORKS/36757; open daily 9am-4pm). Route 14 of **Clallam Transit**

(452-4511 or 800-858-3747; see p. 359) serves Forks with trips to Port Angeles every day but Sunday (50¢, seniors free, ages 6-19 35¢, disabled 25¢). The **post office** is on the corner of Spartan Ave. and A St., one block east of U.S. 101 (open Mon.-Fri. 9am-5pm, Sat. 10am-noon). Call the **police** at 374-2223 and the **hospital** at 674-6271. For emergencies, call 911. **General delivery ZIP code:** 98331. **Area Code:** 360.

The closest non-camping budget accommodation to Forks is the **Rainforest Hostel,** 169312 U.S. 101 (374-2270). To get there, follow the hostel signs off U.S. 101, 4 mi. north of Ruby Beach; buses travel to the hostel from Quinalt (North Shore Brannon's Grocery, 8:40 pm). Owners Kay and Jim take any traveler into their home-turned-hostel, and daytime passers-by can stop in for a shower ($1.50). The house has a roaming cat and dog, but those with allergies can escape to two tiny trailers balanced on the lawn out back. The place is a font of information and provides shelter from surprise western-rim rain showers. Two family-size rooms, and, in summer, a heatless men's dorm with five double bunks (beds $10; 11pm curfew, 8am wakeup). With so many stunning campgrounds in the area, staying in Forks itself should be a last resort. If in need of a town motel, check out the **Town Motel,** 1080 S. Forks Ave. (374-6231 or 800-742-2429), which has well-kept rooms that break the ruffle-quota and a gardenful of dahlias (singles $34; doubles $46).

To experience Forks "cuisine," drop by the smoke-filled **Raindrop Café,** 111 E. A St. (374-6612), at S. Forks Ave., for a $6 gourmet burger. Play the "table topic" games while waiting for food (open Mon.-Sat. 6am-9pm, Sun. 6am-8pm; winter daily 5am-8pm). Grab groceries and a (bad) coffee at **Forks Thriftway** (374-6161), on U.S. 101 (open daily 8am-10pm; winter 8am-9pm).

THE RAINFOREST

In Olympic National Park's temperate rainforests, gigantic old-growth trees, ferns, and mosses blanket the valleys of the Hoh, Queets, and Quinault Rivers. Although fallen foliage and decaying trees blanket the rainforest floor, rangers keep the many walking and hiking trails clear, well-marked, and accessible. On any of these walks through the drippy wonderland, be prepared to be overwhelmed by green. The entrances to each of the three valleys are clearly marked from U.S. 101.

The **Hoh Rainforest Trail,** which begins at the **Hoh Rainforest Visitor Center** (see below) and parallels the Hoh River for 18 mi. to **Blue Glacier** on the shoulder of **Mount Olympus,** is the most heavily visited trail in the rainforest. Shy Roosevelt elk, the ever-persecuted northern spotted owl, and the gods and heroes of ancient Greece inhabit this area. The drive to the Hoh is alternately stunning and barren, depending on how many DNR trees have fallen to the axe (or chainsaw, or hydraulic splitter) in recent months. The first two campgrounds along the Hoh River Rd., which leaves U.S. 101 13 mi. south of Forks, are administered by the DNR, accept no reservations, and are free. Only the **Minnie Peterson** site has potable water. Fellow campers seem to ignore palatial DNR sites except in July and August; stay at one and drive to the Hoh trailhead to get a **map** and begin your rainforest exploration. You can obtain a separate **map** of the Hoh-Clearwater Multiple Use Area from the DNR main office, just off U.S. 101 on the north side of Forks.

The **Hoh Rainforest Visitors Center** (374-6925) provides posters and permits (open daily 9am-6:30pm; Sept.-June daily 9am-3:30pm). Once at the visitor's center (a good 45min. drive from U.S. 101), take the quick **Hall of Mosses Trail** (45min.) for a Cliff Notes version of rainforest vegetation or try the slightly longer, one-hour **Spruce Nature Trail.** The Spruce leads through lush forest and along the banks of the river with a smattering of educational panels to explain Mama Nature's bizarre quirks. A short handicapped-accessible trail circles the visitors center. Backcountry trails leading to Mount Olympus and Blue Glacier also begin here. Near the visitors center, the national park maintains 89 sometimes soggy sites ($10) with drinking water and flush toilets, but limited facilities for the handicapped.

Several other trailheads from U.S. 101 offer more solitude for the hiker and opportunities for in-depth exploration of the rainforest amid surrounding ridges and mountains. The **Queets River Trail** hugs its namesake east for 14 mi. from the free Queets

Campground. The road is unpaved and unsuitable for RVs or large trailers. High river waters early in the summer can thwart a trek. Hiking is best in August, but there's still a risk that water will cut off trail access. A shorter, 3 mi. loop is as much as most visitors see of Queets. Elk are often spotted in fields along the trail, which passes a broad range of rainforest, lowland river ecosystems, and the park's largest Douglas fir. A ranger station at the trailhead expounds.

The park and forest services and the Quinalt Reservation quibble for control of the land surrounding **Quinault Lake and River.** The Forest Service operates an information center at the **Quinault Ranger Station,** 353 South Shore Rd. (288-2525; open daily 9am-4:30pm; winter Mon.-Fri. 9am-4:30pm). From the Quinalt Ranger Station, it's 20 mi. to the North Fork trailhead, from which intrepid hikers can journey 44 mi. north across the entire park and finish at Whiskey Bend. Those with less time or energy have the day-hike options of trails leaving from the Quinault Ranger Station or the Graves Creek Ranger Station, located 8 miles up Shore Rd. For a quick roll through Washington's own Jurassic Park, try the 4 mi. **Quinault Lake Loop** or the ½ mi. **Maple Glade Trail.** Adventure-seekers flock to Three Lakes Point, an exquisite summit covered with snow until July.

Quinault Lake itself lures anglers, rowers, and canoers. Rental canoes and rowboats ($10 per hr.) are available at the **Lake Quinault Lodge** located next to the ranger station. Jim Carlson (288-2293) offers horseback rides around the lake and through the forest in summer ($35 for 2hrs.). Campers can drop their gear right at the lakeside in **Williby Campgrounds** (288-2213), located ¼ mi. before the ranger station.

THE BEACHES AND COAST

Fifty-seven miles of pristine coastline trace the park's western coast, separated from the rest of ONP by U.S. 101 and non-park timber land. Fields of driftwood, sculptured arches, and dripping caves frame flamboyant sunsets, and **sea stacks** (bits of coast stranded at sea after erosion swept away the surrounding land) jut from the waves. The entire coastline has an eerie, rugged look. Bald eagles soar on windy days as whales and seals speed through the Pacific.

Between the Hoh and Quinault Reservations, U.S. 101 hugs the coast, with parking lots just a short walk from the sand. This 15 mi. stretch of beach begins in the north with **Ruby Beach** near Mile 165 on U.S. 101, where sea otters and eagles hang out amid tide pools and sea stacks. Camping on this stretch of beach is not allowed; head north for beach camping. South of Ruby Beach at Mile 160 is Beach #6, a favorite whale-watching spot. Beach #4, 3 mi. south, has abundant tidepools, plastered with sea stars. South of Beaches #4 and #6 is **Kalaloch** (KLAY-lok) **Center** (962-2283), a crowded campground with 177 sites ($12) near the ocean, including a lodge, a general store, a gas station, and a ranger station. Gather at low tide for talks on the tidepools; consult the park newspaper or bulletin boards for specific times.

Parts of ONP's protected coastal wilderness are open for hiking and **backcountry camping.** Beach camping is only permitted south of the Kalaloch strip. Those who camp along this stretch of beach bask in the glory of easy, flat hiking, long evenings of reflected sunlight capped by resplendent sunsets, and an ever-changing seascape. Before hiking or camping along the coast, pick up a required **overnight permit,** a park **map,** a **tide table,** and the useful *Olympic Coastal Strip* brochure at a ranger station. Find the tide line from the previous tide and use the tide table to calculate how many feet the tide will change while you are there. Then set up camp well above where the next tide will be. The same common-sense approach applies to walking the coast: don't traverse beach that could sink under the waves while you're walking it. Several beach strands lie within land belonging to the Makah, Ozette, Quileute, Hoh, and Quinault native nations. A continuous 57 mi. coastal trek is impossible; reservation land is private and may not be crossed by hikers without permission.

Farther north, between the Hoh and Quileute reservations, a 17 mi. stretch of rocky headlands dominates the coastline. At the end of this strip, **Mora Beach** (374-5460), due west of Forks near the Quileute Reservation, has a drive-in campground (sites $10) and a ranger station. From **Rialto Beach** near Mora, 21 mi. of coast stretch north to a campground and roadhead at **Ozette Lake** (sites $10, by reservation only; call 452-0300). Rialto Beach itself hosts eccentric caves and sea stacks worth a gander. Ozette is a 20 mi. trek from Rte. 112.

Many day hikers and backpackers adore the 9 mi. loop that begins at Ozette Lake. The trail is a triangle with two 3 mi. legs along boardwalks through the rainforest. One heads toward the sea stacks at **Cape Alava,** the other to the picturesque beach at **Sand Point.** A 3 mi. hike down the coast passes ancient native petroglyphs as it connects the two legs. The entire area is relatively flat, but has plenty to sand to slog through. Overnighters must make permit reservations in advance; spaces fill quickly in summer. The **Ozette Ranger Station** (963-2725; open daily 8am-4:30pm) has further information. For permit reservations, call 452-0300.

■ Eastern Park Rim

What the western rim has in ocean and rainforest, the eastern rim matches in canals and grandiose views. Canyon walls here rise treacherously, their jagged edges leading to mountaintops that offer glimpses of the entire peninsula and Puget Sound. A good source for information about this region is the joint park/forest service **Hood Canal Ranger Station,** P.O. Box 68, Hoodsport 98548 (877-5254; open daily 8am-4:30pm; winters closed weekends). Hikers use campgrounds along the east side of the park as trailheads to the interior, parking their cars and hiking in. **Staircase Campground** (877-5569) is a major camping hub 16 mi. northwest of **Hoodsport** at the head of Lake Cushman (59 sites, $8 on top of the $10 park entrance fee; RV accessible) and the trailhead to a rugged river hike. To get there, turn west off U.S. 101 at Hoodsport, pass the Hood Canal Ranger Station on Rte. 119, take a left after 9 mi. and follow the signs. **Lake Cushman State Park** (877-5491; 800-452-5687 for reservations), on the way to Staircase, is a popular base camp for extended backpacking trips into the national forest and park. As well as fine swimming beaches, the park has showers (3min. for 25¢) and flush toilets (80 sites for $11, 30 with full hookup $16).

WASHINGTON

Super-tough hikers often tackle the steep 3 mi. trail up **Mt. Ellinor,** 5 mi. past Staircase on Rte. 119. Follow signs to Jefferson Pass and Upper/Lower Trailhead. Once on the mountain, hikers can choose the 3 mi. trip or opt for an equally steep but shorter journey to the summit. Look for signs to the Upper Trailhead along F.I. Road #2419-04. On a clear day at the summit, the Olympic range towers to the northwest, and Puget Sound, Seattle, Mt. Rainier, Mt. Adams, and the rim of Mt. St. Helens unfold to the southeast. Adventure-seekers who hit the mountain before July should bring snow clothes to "mach"—as in Mach 1, the speed to which sliders accelerate—down a ¼ mi. snow chute. Find free refuge from all this fun at the **Lilliwap Creek Campground.** Follow signs from Rte. 119 or inquire at the ranger's station.

Hoodsport, on U.S. 101, has a few small **grocery stores** where travelers fill up ice chests, since the next stores lie 50 mi. north in Sequim. Drop by the **Hoodsport Winery,** 23501 U.S. 101 N. (877-9894), south of town, for tasting and tours (open daily 9am-7pm). Next to the ranger station in Hoodsport is a **post office** (877-5552; open Mon.-Fri. 9am-5pm, Sat. 8:30am-11:30pm). **General Delivery ZIP Code:** 98548.

Fourteen miles north of Hoodsport off U.S. 101, **Lena Lake** entices hikers and birdwatchers alike. A 3.2 mi. hike ascends to the lake itself. Follow Forest Service Rd. 25 (known as the Hamma-Hamma Rte.) off U.S. 101 for 8 mi. to the trailhead. There are 29 rustic sites at **Lena Lake Campground.** This year, the Park Service is charging $3 for entrance into many areas, including the lake trail.

Dosewallips (doh-see-WALL-ups), on a road that leaves U.S. 101 27 mi. north of Hoodsport, has 32 less developed campsites ($10; not for RVs). A pretty (and pretty popular) several-day trail leads from Dosewallips across the park to **Hurricane Ridge** and a number of other oft-traversed backpacking trails. Those looking for a one-day hike should jump on the **West Forks Dosewallip Trail,** a 10½ mi. trek to the Mt. Anderson glacier. A recently constructed bridge makes this trail the shortest route to any glacier in the park. Thirty miles north of Hoodsport, the **Quilcene Ranger Station,** 295142 U.S. 101 S. (765-3368), can point trippers to the **Mt. Walker View**

Point, 5 mi. south of Quilcene on U.S. 101. A one-lane gravel road leads 4 mi. to the lookout, the highest viewpoint in the park accessible by car. The road is steep, has sheer drop-offs, and should not be attempted in foul weather or a temperamental car. Yet another view of Hood Canal, Puget Sound, Mt. Rainier, and Seattle awaits intrepid travelers on top. Picnic tables perch on the east side; feast there or feast your eyes on 7743 ft. **Mt. Constance** from the north side.

PACIFIC COAST

Willapa Bay

Willapa Bay, which divides the Long Beach peninsula from the Washington mainland, is a great place to go for wildlife viewing. U.S. 101 passes the bay as it winds along the border of the Olympic National Park and down the Pacific Coast into Oregon. On its way out of the park, the highway passes by Grays Harbor and through the industrial cities of **Aberdeen** and **Hoquiam** at the mouth of the Chehalis River. Unpleasant and grimy, these industrial cities have everything an American would expect in the way of malls, movie theaters, and motels. Aberdeen even sports a legendary native son, Kurt Cobain, who (rather understandably and legendarily) got the hell out as soon as he legendarily could. U.S. 101 continues amid Willapa Bay's sparkling sloughs and pastoral farmlands, and provides views that compensate for the protected bay's ban on swimming and sunning. From the north, stop at the headquarters of the **Willapa National Wildlife Refuge** (484-3482), just off U.S. 101 on the left, to visit the last unpolluted estuary in the U.S. and a sanctuary for seabirds and waterfowl. Check out the array of stuffed birds inside the office—they'll help you know what to look for in the refuge (open Mon.-Fri. 7:30am-4pm).

No trails are directly accessible from the headquarters, but rangers can give directions to several "units" scattered through the Willapa Bay region, including a unit at **Leadbetter Point** at the tip of the Long Beach Peninsula and one on **Long Island** in Willapa Bay, accessible only by boat. The refuge offers a rare opportunity to observe Canada geese, loons, grebes, cormorants, trumpeter swans, and other birds. Avian diversity descends upon the area during the fall and winter; simultaneously, the greatest number of birdwatchers descend on the Leadbetter Point unit, about 45 minutes from headquarters. Long Island is Willapa Bay's most impressive attraction. The island teems with deer, bear, elk, beaver, otter, and grouse. It also supports a 274-acre cedar grove, one of the Northwest's last **climax forests,** still growing new trees after 4000 years. The cedars average 160 ft. in height; some reach 11 ft. in diameter.

Long Island is home to five limited-use **campgrounds,** all inaccessible by car. Reaching the island is a problem; you'll have to find your own boat or bum a ride. Boats should be launched from the Wildlife Refuge Headquarters; the channel at this point is only about 100 yd. wide, though too muddy to swim. After reaching the island, hike 2½ mi. along the island's main road to reach the **Trail of Ancient Cedars.** The **office** at the Refuge furnishes advice on getting to the island and **maps** marked with campgrounds.

Long Beach Peninsula

Long Beach Peninsula, with 28 mi. of unbroken beach accessible by U.S. 101 and Rte. 103 (which runs the length of the peninsula), is an overwhelming frenzy of kites, souvenir shops, and beaches. Fishing, swimming, boating, and kite-flying fill the warmer months, allowing residents to recuperate from the pounding winter storms. You can beachcomb for **glass balls** from Japanese fishing nets; locals say they have the most luck on the Ocean Park section of the beach. Permits are required for gathering **driftwood** in state parks. Access to the "world's longest beach" is easy; almost any east-west road on the peninsula ends in a parking lot by the sand.

During clamming season (usually from Oct. to mid-March; call the **shellfish hotline** at 360-796-3215 to check with the **Washington Department of Fish and Wildlife** for season status), look for dimples or bubbles in the sand to find the notoriously fast-digging but succulent razor clams. If you're willing to shell out $20 for an annual non-resident license (available at **Short Stop,** across the street from the Visitors Bureau, see below) and spend a few days learning the ropes, you can harvest a seafood feast. (Be extra careful of the **red tide,** when vicious bacteria can barrel through your digestive tract via innocent bivalves. These bacteria are sometimes deadly; for status, call the **red tide hotline** at 800-562-5632.) Free tide tables are available at information centers and businesses.

Make Yogi Bear proud by **blackberry and blueberry picking** in late summer. Wild varieties are an arm's reach away along many roadsides (though they may also be coated in exhaust). The peninsula also harbors nearly 500 acres of cranberry bogs and is one of only four places in the U.S. where cranberries are grown. Most of the bogs are in Grayland along Cranberry Rd., parallel to Hwy. 105, and are harvested in October. Be careful not to pick on private property.

The **Long Beach Peninsula Visitors Bureau** (642-2400 or 800-451-2542), five minutes south of Long Beach on U.S. 101, has pamphlets galore on activities in Long Beach and the vicinity. **Pacific Transit** buses (in Raymond 642-9418, in Naselle 484-7136, farther north 875-9418) provide local transportation. For 85¢, you can take a bus as far north as Aberdeen; exact change required. Local buses run up and down the peninsula itself 15 times per day. Schedules are available in post offices and visitors centers (service daily 2-3 times per day; weekends local service only).

The city of Long Beach invites kite flyers from Thailand, China, Japan, and Australia to the **International Kite Festival** (642-2400) during the third week of August. Late July brings the **Sand-Sations Sand Sculpture Contest** to town. In 1989, a world record tumbled when participants built a 3 mi. long fortress of sand. Call the Long Beach Peninsula visitors bureau (see above) for more info. If you're stopping in the town of Long Beach, check out **Marsh's Free Museum** (642-2188) along S. Pacific Way. Mechanical fortune tellers and "Jake," the petrified alligator-man featured in the *National Enquirer* keep company with honky-tonk souvenirs galore. Open (ironically) whenever tourists bring money. Alanis, eat your heart out.

THE COLUMBIA RIVER ESTUARY

Several miles south of Long Beach on Washington's southern border, **Cape Disappointment** guards the **Columbia River Estuary.** In 1788, bitter British fur trader and well-known grouchy-gus Captain John Meares, frustrated by repeated failures to cross the treacherous Columbia River sandbar, named the water now known as Baker Bay **Deception Bay,** and the large promontory guarding the river mouth Cape Disappointment. Over the past 300 years, almost 2000 vessels have been wrecked, stranded, or sunk where the Columbia meets the ocean, a region aptly named "the graveyard of the Pacific."

Fort Columbia State Park (777-8221) lies on U.S. 101 northwest of the Astoria Megler Bridge, 1 mi. east of **Chinook** on the west side of the highway. The fort was built in 1896 and armed with huge guns to protect the mouth of the river from an enemy that never materialized (even more disappointment). The park's **interpretive center** recreates life at the fort and includes an exhibit on the indigenous Chinook people who once occupied this land. A wooded 1 mi. trail meanders past several historical sites (park open daily 6:30am-dusk; Oct. 16-March Wed.-Sun. 8am-dusk; center open Wed.-Sun. 10am-5pm). What was once the area's hospital is now the fantastic **Fort Columbia Youth Hostel,** P.O. Box 224, Chinook (777-8755; see p. 431).

Three miles southwest of the fishing town of **Ilwaco,** at the southern tip of the Peninsula, **Fort Canby State Park** (642-3078) offers camping and a megadose of Lewis and Clark. The Park was the dynamic duo's final destination and boasts two lighthouses and a well-pruned campground packed with RVs and alders. The sites fill up quickly in the summer months (180 tent sites $11, 27 sites with water and electric and 60 full hookup sites $16, 5 hiker/biker sites $5, 3 cabins and 3 yurts sleep 4 for

$35; hot pay showers; 2 handicapped-accessible sites; call 800-452-5687 to make reservations, $6 fee). Unregistered campers can enter until 10pm.

At the end of the main road, the spaceship-esque **Lewis and Clark Interpretive Center** hovers above the ruins of the fort. Inside, a winding display documents the Lewis and Clark expedition from its Missouri origins to the party's arrival at the mouth of the Columbia, and the explorers' painstakingly detailed journal entries speak for themselves (park open daily dawn-dusk; center open daily 10am-5pm). The **North Head Lighthouse,** built in 1898, is in the northwest corner of the park and is accessible by a paved path. A clear day allows both a dizzying view of the Pacific cliffs and $1 tours between 10am and 6pm (summers only). The **Cape Disappointment Lighthouse,** built in 1856—the oldest in the Northwest—is in the southeast corner of the park and can be reached by puffing ¼ mi. up a steep hill from the Coast Guard station parking lot or by clambering a ½ mi. along a narrow trail from the interpretive center (see above). For a magnificent beach-level view of the Cape Disappointment Lighthouse, drive through the campground area past **Waikiki Beach** on the **North Jetty.** Though not quite Honolulu, Waikiki Beach is ideal for swimming in summer, beachcombing after storms in winter, and year-round ship-watching.

The early 90s is an era Ilwaco would like to forget. The recent record-low salmon counts and 1993 Endangered Species Act closed the commercial salmon season for two years. But salmon populations are on the rise again, and gleeful local fishing companies are back on the water. Picking up a salmon steak from one of many fisheries along the Ilwaco waterfront is the budget way to sample the tasty fish, but many charter companies offer fishing trips for landlubbers who want to learn the art of angling first hand. **Pacific Salmon Charters,** P.O. Box 519, Ilwaco 98624 (642-3466), leads eight-hour fishing tours (providing coffee and tackle), starting at $59 (trips run daily at 6am). Wander farther down to **The Galley** (642-7131), which serves tasty clam chowder ($3.25), fish and chips ($7), and garden burgers with fries ($6.25; open May-Oct. Wed.-Mon. 11am-10pm).

Among the cheapest places to hit the hay on the Long Beach Peninsula is the **Sand-Lo-Motel,** 1910 Pacific Hwy., equipped with the perk of coffee makers in each room (642-2600; singles and doubles $42, rates drop in winter; call early for reservations). Keep in mind that the beautiful and inexpensive Fort Columbia Youth Hostel lies just 15 minutes down the road in **Fort Columbia State Park** (see **Astoria, OR,** p. 431). The friendly folks at **My Mom's Pie Kitchen** (642-2342), 4316 S. Pacific Hwy., make a meal that is an inexpensive and welcome respite from Long Beach's steak houses and greasy spoons. "My Mom's special," a half sandwich, soup or salad, and half a piece of pie costs $7.25 (open Wed.-Sun. 11am-4pm).

For the best meal around, point your car down Rte. 103 to historic **Oysterville,** and purchase a dozen oysters for $3.50. A tiny, whitewashed town, Oysterville's featured attraction is, not surprisingly, **Oysterville Sea Farms** (665-6585) which raises, cleans, packs, and dishes out the delicacy (oysters!). They'll even let you check out the baby oysters (open daily 10am-5pm, Oct.-May weekends 10am-5pm). Before leaving Oysterville, stop by the picture-pretty church for a free map of the town, or have a wedding if the rumor that oysters are an aphrodisiac proves true.

CASCADE RANGE

In 1859, an explorer making his way through the Cascade Range gushed: "Nowhere do the mountain masses and peaks present such strange, fantastic, dauntless, and startling outlines as here." Native people summed up their admiration more succinctly, dubbing the Cascades "Home of the Gods."

Intercepting the moist Pacific air, the Cascades divide Washington into the lush, wet green of the west and the low, dry plains of the east. The white-domed peaks of Mounts Baker, Vernon, Glacier, Rainier, Adams, and St. Helens are accessible by four major roads. **U.S. 12** through White Pass approaches Mt. Rainier National Park and provides access to Mt. St. Helens from the north; **I-90** sends four lanes past the ski resorts of Snoqualmie Pass; scenic **U.S. 2** leaves Everett for Stevens Pass and descends along the Wenatchee River, a favorite of whitewater rafters. **Rte. 20,** better known as the **North Cascades Hwy.,** is the most breathtaking of the trans-Cascade highways and one of the most amazing drives in North America. From spring to fall, it provides access to the wilderness of Cascades National Park. Route 20 and U.S. 2 are often traveled in sequence as the **Cascade Loop.**

Greyhound runs on I-90 and U.S. 2 to and from Seattle, while **Amtrak** parallels I-90. Rainstorms and evening traffic can slow hitchhiking; locals warn against thumbing across Rte. 20. The Cascades can only be explored properly with a car (some say a motorcycle is even better). The mountains are most accessible in the months of July, August, and September; many high mountain passes are snowed in during the rest of the year. The Cascade range is attractive primarily to serious backpackers; amateurs are usually deterred by the day's climb to most flat spots. The best source of general information on the Cascades is the joint **National Park/National Forest Information Service,** 915 2nd Ave., Seattle 98174 (206-220-7450).

Mount St. Helens

In a single cataclysmic blast on May 18, 1980, the summit of Washington's Mount St. Helens exploded into dust, creating a hole 2 mi. long and 1 mi. wide in what had been a perfect cone. The postcard-perfect peak that so many Washingtonians had camped, fished, and played upon suddenly ceased to exist. The force of the steam and ash-filled blast robbed the mountain of 1300 ft. in height and razed entire forests. Ash from the crater rocketed 15 mi. upward, blackening the sky for days and blanketing towns with black powder. Debris spewed from the volcano flooded Spirit Lake and choked rivers as far away as the Columbia. The explosion itself was three times the force of the atomic bomb dropped on Hiroshima.

The **Mount St. Helens National Volcanic Monument,** administered by the Forest Service, encompasses most of the "blast zone," the area around the volcano affected by the explosion. This ashen landscape, striking for its initially bleak expanses, is steadily recovering from the explosion that transformed 150 sq. mi. of prime forest into wasteland. The spectacle of disaster is now speckled with signs of life; saplings push their way up past denuded logs, and insects and small mammals are returning. Much of the monument is off-limits to the public because of ongoing delicate geological experiments and the fragile nature of the blossoming ecosystem. Like many other Cascade Peaks, the volcano still threatens to erupt, but probably won't do so again for several hundred years.

PRACTICAL INFORMATION

Visitors Information: A number of visitors centers and information stations line the highways surrounding the volcano, both inside and outside the monument. Plan the side from which you will approach the monument, and find the most convenient visitors center.

Mount St. Helens National Volcanic Monument Visitor Center (253-274-2100, 24hr. recorded info 253-274-2103). For most visitors, especially those coming from Seattle on I-5, this is the first stop. An excellent introduction to the mountain, with displays on eruption and regeneration and plenty of interactive exhibits for the gadget-lover or aspiring geologist. An infinitely patient staff helps visitors find camping spots and navigate maps. Check for road closures. The free 22min. film *The Eruption of Mount St. Helens,* with graphic footage of the eruption and its aftermath, is shown every hr. on the hr. daily mid-June to Aug. To reach the center (and the western side of the volcano), take Exit 49 off I-5 and follow signs along Rte. 504. The visitors center is 5 mi. east, across from Seaquest State Park. Open daily May-Sept. 9am-5pm; call for winter hrs.

Coldwater Ridge Visitors Center (274-2131; fax 274-2129), follow Rte. 504 38 mi. from Monument Visitor Center. This sprawling glass-and-copper building has a superb view of the collapsed cavity and trails leading to a boardwalk along **Coldwater Lake,** which was created by the eruption. Emphasis on the recoloni-

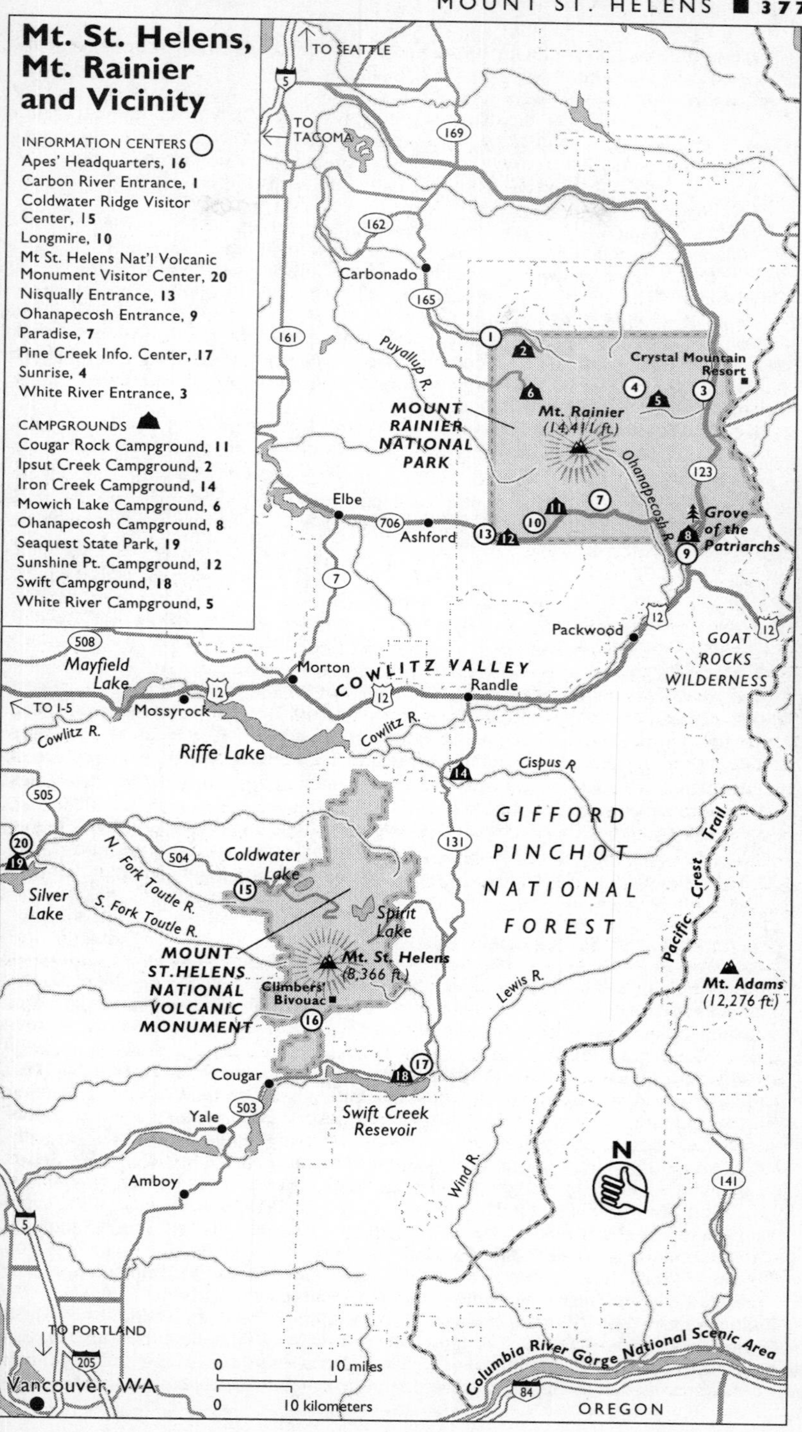
Mt. St. Helens, Mt. Rainier and Vicinity
INFORMATION CENTERS
Apes' Headquarters, 16
Carbon River Entrance, 1
Coldwater Ridge Visitor Center, 15
Longmire, 10
Mt St. Helens Nat'l Volcanic Monument Visitor Center, 20
Nisqually Entrance, 13
Ohanapecosh Entrance, 9
Paradise, 7
Pine Creek Info. Center, 17
Sunrise, 4
White River Entrance, 3
CAMPGROUNDS
Cougar Rock Campground, 11
Ipsut Creek Campground, 2
Iron Creek Campground, 14
Mowich Lake Campground, 6
Ohanapecosh Campground, 8
Seaquest State Park, 19
Sunshine Pt. Campground, 12
Swift Campground, 18
White River Campground, 5
TO SEATTLE
TO TACOMA
Carbonado
Puyallup R.
MOUNT RAINIER NATIONAL PARK
Mt. Rainier (14,411 ft.)
Crystal Mountain Resort
Ohanapecosh R.
Grove of the Patriarchs
Elbe
Ashford
Packwood
GOAT ROCKS WILDERNESS
Mayfield Lake
Morton
COWLITZ VALLEY
Randle
TO I-5
Mossyrock
Cowlitz R.
Riffe Lake
Cispus R
GIFFORD PINCHOT NATIONAL FOREST
Coldwater Lake
N. Fork Toutle R.
S. Fork Toutle R.
Silver Lake
Spirit Lake
MOUNT ST.HELENS NATIONAL VOLCANIC MONUMENT
Mt. St. Helens (8,366 ft.)
Climbers' Bivouac
Lewis R.
Pacific Crest Trail
Mt. Adams (12,276 ft.)
Cougar
Yale
Swift Creek Resevoir
Amboy
Wind R.
N
TO PORTLAND
Vancouver, WA
0 10 miles
0 10 kilometers
Columbia River Gorge National Scenic Area
OREGON

zation of living things. Picnic areas, interpretive talks, and a gift shop/snack bar. Open daily 10am-6pm; Sept.-April 9am-5pm.

Johnston Ridge Observatory, at the end of Rte. 504, overlooking the crater. Opened in May of 1997, the observatory offers the best view from the road of the steaming lava dome and blown-away crater. The center, which focuses on geological info, is named for David Johnson, a geologist who predicted the events of May 18, 1980, but stayed to study the eruption and was killed. Open mid-May to Sept. daily 9am-6pm.

Forest Learning Center (414-3439), outside the monument boundaries on Rte. 504, between the Mount St. Helens Visitor Center and the Coldwater Ridge Center. This massive propaganda machine houses impressive exhibits on the reclamation of the thousands of acres of Weyerhauser timber downed by the explosion. Open May-Oct. 10am-6pm.

Woods Creek Information Station, take Hwy. 12 on the north side of the volcano, go 6 mi. south of Randle on Rd. 25. A drive-through information center; get the scoop on the great outdoors without even getting out of your car. Pick up **maps** here. Open June-Sept. daily 9am-4pm.

Pine Creek Information Station, 17 mi. east of Cougar on Rd. 90, on the south side of the monument. Shows a film of the eruption of Mt. St. Helens to prepare visitors for an excursion. Open June-Sept. daily 9am-6pm.

Apes Headquarters, at Ape Cave on Rd. 8303, on the south side of the volcano, Answers all your lava tube questions. Open daily May 25-Sept. 30, 10am-5:30pm.

The Monument Headquarters (750-3900, 24hr. recorded info 750-3903), 3 mi. north of Amboy on Rte. 503. Not a visitors center, but call for specific, detailed info on road conditions, or for permits. They are in charge of **crater-climbing permits** (see below). Open Mon.-Fri. 7:30am-5pm.

Fee: In 1997, Mount St. Helen's began charging an $8 entrance fee at almost every visitors center, viewpoint, and cave (seniors, Golden Eagle Pass $4; children free). It is possible to stop at the viewpoints after 6pm without paying or to drive through the park without stopping at the main centers.

Publications: *The Volcano Review,* available free at all visitors centers and ranger stations, is the tourist's Bible for Mount St. Helens. Contains a **map** (you *will* get lost without it), copious info, and schedules concerning activities at the monument. For a more thorough tour of the area, buy a copy of the *Road Guide to Mount St. Helens* ($5) at a visitors center.

Forest Information: Gifford Pinchot National Forest Headquarters, 6926 E. 4th Plain Blvd., P.O. Box 8944, Vancouver, WA 98668 (425-750-5000). Info on camping and hiking info within the forest. Additional **ranger stations** at: **Randle** (497-1100), north of the mountain on U.S. 12 and east of the Wood Creek visitors center; **Packwood** (494-0600), east on U.S. 12; **Wind River** (509-427-3200), south of the mountain on Forest Service Rd. 30 and north of the town of Carson in the Columbia River Gorge; and **Mt. Adams** (509-395-3400), at Trout Lake, southeast of the mountain on Rte. 141 and above White Salmon in the Columbia River Gorge. All stations are open Mon.-Fri. 8am-5pm; some are open on weekends, but hours change season to season; call ahead.

Crater Climbing Permits: Between May 15 and Oct. 31, the Forest Service allows 100 people per day to hike to the crater rim. Reserve in person or write to **The Monument Headquarters,** 1hr. north of Portland off Rte. 503 at 42218 NE Yale Bridge Rd., Amboy 98601 (750-3900). 60 permits are available on reserve. The Forest Service begins accepting applications Feb. 1. Write early; weekends are usually booked before March, and weekdays often fill up as well. Climbers who procrastinate should head for **Jack's Restaurant and Country Store** (231-4276), Rte. 503, 5 mi. west of Cougar (I-5 Exit 21), where a lottery is held at 5:30pm every day to distribute the next day's 40 unreserved permits. All permits are free. Call the Monument Headquarters (750-3900) for more info.

Climbing Hotline: (247-5800). Info on snow, temperature, visibility, wind, and other vital factors that might affect climbing an ascent.

Radio Station: 530 AM. Road closures and station hrs.

Emergency: 911.

Area Code: 360.

GETTING THERE AND GETTING AROUND

In order to have a blast at the still-smoldering volcano, visitors must do a little planning. The main access routes—Route 504, Route 503, and U.S. 12—spiral around Mount St. Helens from different directions and do not connect. It would be impossible to explore all sides in a day. Vigorous winter rains often decimate access roads; check at a ranger station for **road closures** before heading out.

There are three ways to approach the monument. From the **west,** many Seattleites and interstate travelers take Exit 40 off I-5 and travel Rte. 504, otherwise known as the **Spirit Lake Memorial Highway.** The brand new 48 mi. road has wide shoulders and astounding views of the crater. For most, this is the quickest and easiest day trip to the mountain, and the **Mount St. Helens Visitors Center,** the **Coldwater Ridge Visitors Center,** and the **Johnston Ridge Observatory** (see above) line the way to the volcano. This drive also lures Winnebago battalions and summer crowds.

From the **north**, visitors take **U.S. 12** east from I-5. The towns of **Mossyrock, Morton,** and **Randle** line U.S. 12 and offer the closest major services. From U.S. 12, visitors drive south on Route 25 or Route 26, both of which lead to Route 99. The 16 mi. dead-end road travels into the most devastated parts of the monument and has a handful of lookouts. Route 25 offers access to the **Iron Creek Campground,** with good hiking and striking views of both the crater and the blow zone, where acres of blasted trees abut healthy forests.

Route 503 parallels the **south** side of the volcano until it connects with **Rd. 90.** Visitors climb up Rte. 83 to lava caves and the Climber's Bivouac, a launch pad for climbs up the mountain. From the southern approach, Mt. St. Helens tricks the viewer with the illusion of pre-eruption serenity. Though views from this side don't highlight recent destruction, green glens and remnants of age-old explosions make this the best side for hiking and camping.

CAMPING

Although the monument itself contains no campgrounds, a number are scattered throughout the surrounding national forest. Free dispersed camping is allowed within the monument, meaning that if you stumble upon a site on an old forest service road, you can camp out there, but finding a site is a matter of luck. The closest campsite to the scene of the explosion is the **Iron Creek Campground,** just south of the Woods Creek Information Center on Forest Service Rd. 25, near its junction with Rd. 76 (98 sites, $10). For reservations call 800-280-CAMP/2267. Only 15 sites can be reserved; the rest are first-come, first-camped. Water is available from 8-10am and 6-8pm. Farther south is spacious **Swift Campground,** on Forest Service Rd. 90, just west of the Pine Creek Information Station. Swift is run by Pacific Power & Light (503-464-5023; 93 sites, $12; free firewood; no reservations). Two other PP&L campgrounds lie west of Swift Campground on Yale Reservoir; both accept reservations and have toilets and showers. **Beaver Bay,** with 63 RV and tent sites ($12), sits 2 mi. east of **Cougar Campground,** which offers 45 sites ($15).

Seaquest State Park (274-8633), on Rte. 504, 5 mi. east of the town of Castle Rock at I-5 Exit 49 and across from the main Mount St. Helens Visitors Center, has 92 pleasant wooded sites ($10), four of which are primitive and reserved for hikers and bikers ($5). Full facilities include wheelchair-accessible sites and pay showers. No trails begin here, but this is one of the easiest campgrounds to reach on I-5 and the closest state park with showers and hookups. Reservations in summer are a must. Call **Reservations Northwest** (the state park reservation system) to make one (800-452-5687).

OUTDOORS

The drive east on Rte. 504 offers plentiful views of the crater and blast devastation, but little opportunity for rigorous hiking. The ½ mi. "Winds of Change" trail at Coldwater Lake has signposts aplenty to explain the eerie surrounding landscape. Another

10 mi. east, a hike along Johnson Ridge approaches the crater where geologist David Johnston died studying the volcano.

The first stop for visitors traveling south on Rd. 25 from Randle and U.S. 12 should be the **Woods Creek Information Station.** Viewpoints are listed on various handouts at the visitors center and include the **Quartz Creek Big Trees** and **Ryan Lake.** Continue south 9 mi. until you reach Rd. 99 going west. The newly paved, two-lane Rd. 99 passes through 17 mi. of curves, clouds of ash, and cliffs. Trailer owners should leave their "crafts" in the **Wakepish Sno-Park,** the designated trailer drop at the junction of Rd. 25 and 99. It takes nearly one hour to drive straight out and back on Rd. 99, but the many talks, walks, and views along the way make stopping longer worthwhile. Rd. 99 winds among the trees before opening onto the blast area. Make sure to check for road closures (listen to 530 AM) before heading to Rd. 25 or 99.

On the way west along Rd. 99, **Bear Meadow** provides the first interpretive stop, an excellent view of Mt. St. Helens, and the last restrooms before Rd. 99 ends at spectacular **Windy Ridge.** The monument begins just west of here, where Rd. 26 and 99 meet. Rangers lead 45-minute walks to emerald **Meta Lake;** meet at the old **miners' car** at the junction of Rd. 26 and 99 (June-Sept. daily at 12:30pm and 3pm). The trail around the lake is an easy ½ mi. stroll, and illustrates the regenerative abilities of lake ecosystems.

Farther west on Rd. 99, frequent roadside turnouts offer trailheads, information on the surroundings, and unbeatable photo-ops. The effects of the blast are inescapable: trees felled like matchsticks, pumice plains, stump-choked lakes. **Independence Pass Trail #227** is a difficult 3½ mi. hike with overlooks to Spirit Lake and superb views of the crater and dome that get only better as you go along. For a serious hike, continue along this trail to its intersection with the spectacular **Norway Pass Trail,** which runs directly through the blast zone and ends on Rte. 26. Considered the best hike in the park, the trail is 6 mi. long, takes about five and a half hours, and requires a vehicle at both ends. Farther west, 2 mi. **Harmony Trail #224** provides the only public access to Spirit Lake. Rangers lead a daily hike from the **Harmony Viewpoint** to Spirit Lake along this trail during the summer at 1:30pm. This trail is easy going down, but the return trip is tough.

Windy Ridge is worth the winding trip to the end of Rd. 99. From here, you can climb atop an ash hill for a magnificent view of the crater from 3½ mi. away. In summer, forest interpreters describe the eruption during talks held in the Windy Ridge Amphitheater (daily 11:30am-4:30pm every hr. on the ½hr.). The **Truman Trail** leaves from Windy Ridge and meanders 7 mi. through the "Pumice Plain," where hot pyroclastic flows sterilized the land, leaving absolutely no life. Because the area is under constant scrutiny by biologists, its important to stay on the trails at all times.

Caves and lava tubes take intrepid visitors inside "the Beast." The **Pine Creek Information Station** lies 25 mi. south of the Rd. 25-Rd. 99 junction. Take Rd. 90 12 mi. west and then continue 2 mi. north on Rd. 83 to **Ape Cave,** a broken 2½ mi. lava tube formed by an ancient eruption. To explore the cave, wear a jacket and sturdy shoes. Each expedition must begin by 4pm and take at least two flashlights or lanterns (rent for $3 each or bring your own). One-quarter mile before Ape Cave on Rd. 83 is the **Trail of Two Forests,** a lava-strewn path above the forest floor. Rangers lead walks daily in summer; the path is wheelchair accessible. Rd. 83 continues 9 mi. farther north, ending at **Lahar Viewpoint,** the site of terrible mudflows that followed the eruption. Nearby, **Lava Canyon Trail #184** offers three hikes with views of the **Muddy River Waterfall.**

Those with strong legs and a taste for conquest can scale the new, stunted version of the mountain to glimpse the lava dome from the crater's rim. Although not a technical climb, the route up the mountain is a steep pathway of ash strewn with boulders. Often, the scree (a layer of loose shale) is so thick that each step forward includes a half-step back. (The trip down is often accomplished on the triumphant climber's behind.) The view from the lip of the crater—of Mt. Rainier, Mt. Adams, Mt. Hood, Spirit Lake, and the lava dome directly below—is magnificent. Average hiking time is five hours to get up and three hours to get down. Bring sunglasses, sunscreen, sturdy climbing boots, foul-weather clothing, plenty of water, and gaiters to keep your boots from filling with ash. Free camping (no water) is available at the **Climber's Bivouac**, the trailhead area for the **Ptarmigan Trail #216A,** which starts the route up the mountain. The trail is located about 4 mi. up Rd. 83. For information on permits, see **Practical Information,** above.

Cowlitz Valley

The **Cowlitz River** begins at the tip of a Rainier glacier and cuts a long, deep divot west between Mt. Rainier and Mount St. Helens, before turning south to flow into the Columbia River. Although your views of St. Helens and Rainier will be obscured when you sink into the Cowlitz Valley, your loss is compensated by miles of lush farmland. There is not much to do in the valley besides travel between Mt. Ranier and Mt. St. Helens, but it does contain the nearest major services to the parks.

The river forms part of the watershed for both the **Mt. Adams** and **Goat Rocks Wilderness Areas,** to the west and northwest of Mt. St. Helens. The rugged Goat Rocks are named for their famous herds of mountain goats, and Mt. Adams seduces hundreds of climbers each year with its snow-capped summit (12,307 ft.). Both areas are excellent hiking country, accessible only by foot or horseback, and include sections of the **Pacific Crest Trail** among their extensive trail networks. This area is particularly attractive because it receives less traffic than neighboring wilderness areas. Two **ranger stations** are in the valley, in **Packwood,** 13068 U.S. 12 (494-0600), and **Randle,** 10024 U.S. 12 (497-1100). Contact the Forest Service at one of these locations for trail guides and other information.

The Cowlitz passes closest to Mount St. Helens near the town of **Morton.** This logging town is accessed by U.S. 12 from the east and west (I-15 Exit 68), Rte. 508 from the west (I-5 Exit 71), and Rte. 7 from the north. The **Cody Cafe** (496-5787), on Main St., serves a mountainous stack of pancakes ($2.25). Lunches run from $3 to $5 (open Mon.-Fri. 4am-9pm, Sat. 5am-9pm, Sun. 6am-2pm). If you're staying overnight in the area, head for the lime-green **Evergreen Motel** (496-5407), at Main and Front St. The rooms may be plain, but they're still cheap and clean (singles $27; doubles $40). **Roy's Motel** (456-5000), on 2nd St., has somewhat nicer rooms for $50. Morton's **post office** (496-5316) is also on 2nd St. (open Mon.-Fri. 8am-5pm; **General Delivery ZIP code:** 98356). The **area code** is 360.

The Cowlitz River, once wild and treacherous, has been tamed considerably by a Tacoma City Light hydroelectric project. The **Mayfield** and **Mossyrock Dams** back up water into the river gorge to create two lakes, **Mayfield** and **Riffe,** both popular recreation areas. **Ike Kinswa State Park** and **Mayfield Lake County Park,** on Mayfield Lake off U.S. 12, offer camping and excellent rainbow and silver trout **fishing** year-round. Ike Kinswa (983-3402) has over 100 sites with showers (sites $11, full hookups $16). Mayfield Lake (985-2364) offers 54 tent and RV sites ($11). Public boat launches provide access to Mayfield, the lower of the two lakes.

Mount Rainier National Park

At 14,411 ft., Mt. Rainier (ray-NEER) presides over the Cascade Range. The Klickitat native people called it *Tahoma,* "mountain of God," but Rainier is simply "the Mountain" to most Washington residents. Perpetually snow-capped, this active volcano draws visitors from around the globe. Because of its height, Rainier creates its own weather. It juts into warm, wet air, pulling down vast amounts of snow and rain. Clouds mask the mountain 200 days per year, frustrating visitors who come to see the summit. Seventy-six glaciers patch the slopes and combine with sharp ridges and steep gullies to make Rainier an inhospitable host for the thousands of determined climbers who attempt its summit each year.

Those who don't feel up to scaling the mountain can find outdoor enjoyment in the old-growth forests and alpine meadows of Mt. Rainier National Park. With over

305 mi. of trails through meadows of wildflowers, across rivers, and past bubbling hot springs, solitude is just a step away.

PRACTICAL INFORMATION AND ORIENTATION

Visitors Information: Each of the park's four **visitors centers** has displays and brochures on everything from hiking to natural history, postings on trail and road conditions, and rangers to point visitors in the right direction. The **free map,** distributed at park entrances, is invaluable. The best place to plan a backcountry trip is at the **Longmire Wilderness Center** (569-2211, ext. 3314), near the Nisqually entrance in the southwest corner of the park, or the **White River Ranger Station** (569-2211, ext. 2356), off Rte. 410 on the park's east side. Both distribute free **backcountry permits.** Both open Sun.-Thurs. 8am-4:30pm, Fri. 8am-7pm, Sat. 7am-7pm; closed in winter. All centers can be contacted by writing Superintendent, Mt. Rainier National Park, Ashford 98304, or by calling the park's central operator (569-2211). Obtain additional backpacking and camping info by writing or calling the **backcountry desk,** Mt. Rainier National Park, Tahoma Woods, Star Route, Ashford 98304 (569-2211, ext. 3317). **Park Administrative Headquarters,** Tahoma Woods, Star Route, Ashford 98304 (569-2211) are open Mon.-Fri. 8am-4:30pm. Not a visitors center, but good for phone inquiries. The park **web site** is at http://www.nps.gov/mora.

Entrance Fee: $5 per car, $3 per hiker. Gates are open 24hr.

Buses: Gray Line Bus Service, 720 S. Forest St., Seattle 98134 (206-624-5077). Excursions from Seattle to Rainier daily May-Oct. 13 (1-day round-trip $46, under 13 $17). Buses leave from the Sheraton Hotel in Seattle at 8:15am and return around 6pm, giving passengers about 1½hr. at Paradise and 3½hr. total at the mountain. The **Ranier Shuttle,** P.O. Box 374, Ashford, 98304 (569-2331), runs daily between Sea-Tac Airport (Seattle) and park lodges or Ashford area lodges; also between Ashford and Paradise (1-way $8).

Hiking Supplies: Rainier Mountaineering Inc. (RMI) (569-2227), in Paradise. Rents ice axes ($9), crampons ($9.25), boots ($17.25), packs ($17.25), and helmets ($6.25) by the day. Expert RMI guides also lead summit climbs, seminars, and special schools and programs. Open May-Oct. daily 9am-5pm. Winter office: 535 Dock St. #209, Tacoma 98402 (627-6242). Beginners must buy a 3-day package that includes a day of teaching and 2 days of climbing ($458).

Ski Supplies: White Pass Sports Hut (494-7321), on U.S. 12 in Packwood. Alpine package $11.50 per day, Nordic package $9. Also rents snowshoes and snowboards and sells camping equipment. Open daily 8am-6pm; winter Mon.-Thurs. 8am-6pm, Fri.-Sun. 7am-6pm.

Park Emergency: 911, or 569-2211, ext. 2334. 24hr.

Post Office: In the **National Park Inn,** Longmire, and in the **Paradise Inn,** in Paradise. Both open Mon.-Fri. 8:30am-noon and 1-5pm. **General Delivery ZIP Code:** Longmire 98397; Paradise 98398.

Area Code: 360.

To reach Mt. Rainier from the **west,** take I-5 to Tacoma, then go east on Rte. 512, south on Rte. 7, and east on Rte. 706. This scenic road meanders through the town of **Ashford** and into the park by the Nisqually entrance. **Rte. 706** is the only access road open year-round; snow usually closes all other park roads from November to May. Mt. Rainier is 65 mi. from Tacoma and 90 mi. from Seattle.

Buy **gas** and groceries before entering the park. Longmire does have a small store, but supplies are often limited and the distance from the Nisqually entrance to the first visitors center is considerable.

All major roads offer scenic views of the mountain and have roadside lookouts for camera-clicking and general gawking. The roads to **Paradise** and **Sunrise** are especially picturesque. **Stevens Canyon Road** connects the southeast corner of the national park with Paradise, Longmire, and the Nisqually entrance, unfolding spectacular vistas of Rainier and the rugged Tatoosh Range. **Hitchhiking** is technically illegal on National Park roads, though walking to a lookout point or parking lot and asking for a ride is not. However, many visitors say that hitchhiking is easy along the park's mountain roads. (*Let's Go* does not recommend hitchhiking.)

Be prepared for changing weather; pack warm clothes and cold-rated equipment (see **Wilderness Concerns,** p. 42). Before setting out, ask rangers for the two information sheets on **mountain-climbing** and **hiking** that contain helpful hints and a list of recommended equipment for the Rainier explorer. Party size is limited in many areas, and campers must carry all trash and waste out of the backcountry. Potable water is not available at most backcountry campsites. All stream and lake water should be treated for *giardia* with tablets, filters, or boiling before drinking (see **Health,** p. 14). Rangers can provide first aid. The nearest **medical facilities** are in **Morton** (40 mi. from Longmire) and **Enumclaw** (5 mi. from Sunrise).

The section of the **Mt. Baker-Snoqualmie National Forest** that adjoins Mt. Rainier is administered by **Wenatchee National Forest,** 301 Yakima St., Wenatchee 98807 (509-662-4314). The **Gifford Pinchot National Forest** is headquartered at 6926 E. Fourth Plain Blvd., P.O. Box 8944, Vancouver, WA 98668 (425-750-5000). The **Bronson Pinchot National Forest** does not exist. Closer **ranger stations** are at 10061 U.S. 12, Naches 98937 (509-965-8005), and Packwood Ranger Station, P.O. Box 559 Packwood 98361 (206-494-5515).

ACCOMMODATIONS

Longmire, Paradise, and Sunrise offer accommodations that are usually too costly for the budget traveler. For a roof, stay in Ashford or Packwood. Otherwise, camp and see the sky from a rooftop of the world.

Hotel Packwood, 102 Main St. (494-5431), in Packwood. A charming reminder of the Old West. Clean rooms with a mish-mash of antique furniture. Shared bathrooms. Singles $20-38; doubles (bunks) from $30-38.

Whittaker's Bunkhouse, 30205 SR 706 E., P.O. Box E, Ashford 98304 (569-2439). Spiffy bunk accommodations with firm mattresses and sparkling clean showers (but no kitchen) for $20. The rooms are co-ed; most of the clientele is male. Bring your own sleeping bag. The hotel also has traditional and more expensive rooms, as well as a homey espresso bar. Reservations strongly recommended.

Paradise Inn, (569-2275), in Paradise. This rustic inn, built in 1917 from Alaskan cedar, offers gorgeous views of the mountain, but they'll cost ya. Small, cheerful singles and doubles with shared bath from $68, each additional person $10. Open late May to early Oct. Reservations required in summer; call at least a month ahead.

FOOD

The general stores in the area sell only last-minute trifles like bug repellant and marshmallows, and items are charged an extra state park tax. Stock up before you go. **Blanton's Market** (494-6101), on Rte. 123 in Packwood, is the closest decent supermarket to the park and has an **ATM** in front (open daily 5am-10pm).

Sweet Peaks, 38104 Hwy. 706 (569-2720), on the way to the Nisqually Entrance. Stop off for a "killer cinnamon roll" ($1.50) or a loaf of fresh bread ($1-2). The bakery also sells an assortment of camping gear, fresh from the oven. Open daily in summer 7:30am-8pm; winter weekends and holidays 7:30am-8pm.

Wild Berry Restaurant (569-2628), in Ashford on Hwy. 706. An expensive local favorite. Fried foods are against their religion. The popular veggie lasagna goes for $8. Open daily 11am-9pm.

Ma & Pa Rucker's (494-2651), on Hwy. 12 in Packwood. Piping hot pizza (small $7, large $11) and typical roadhouse burgers. A scoop of peppermint candy ice cream is $1. Open Mon.-Thurs. 8am-9pm, Fri.-Sun. 7am-10pm.

CAMPING

Camping at auto-accessible campsites in the park between mid-June and late September is available on a first-come, first-served basis ($10-12). National Park campgrounds all have facilities for the handicapped, but no hookups or showers. There are five campgrounds within the park. Drive to: **Ohanapecosh** (205 sites) for a serene high canopy of old-growth trees; **Cougar Rock** (200 sites), near Longmire, for strictly maintained quiet hours (10pm-6am); **Isput Creek** (29 sites) for lush vegetation; and **White River** (117 sites), in the northeastern corner of the park, or **Sunshine Point** (18 sites), near the Nisqually entrance, for fine views. The grounds fill only on the busiest summer weekends. Sunshine Point is the only campground open year-round.

Backcountry camping requires a permit, available free at ranger stations or visitors centers. Be sure to ask about trail closures before you set off. Hikers with a valid permit can use any of the free, well-established trailside camps scattered in the park. Most camps have toilet facilities and a nearby water source, and some have shelters for groups of up to 12. Cross-country and alpine sites are high up the mountain on glaciers and snow fields. *Fires are prohibited in all areas,* except front-country campgrounds, and there are limits to the number of members in a party. **Glacier climbers** and **mountain climbers** intending to scale above 10,000 ft. must register in person at ranger stations to be granted permits.

The **national forests** outside Rainier Park provide developed sites ($5) and thousands of acres of freely campable countryside. When camping outside established sites, be sure to avoid eroded lakesides and riverbanks; flash floods and debris flows can catch unwary campers in their paths. Minimum-impact **campfire permits,** allowing hikers to burn small fires that don't sterilize the soil, are available at National Forest ranger stations (see **Practical Information,** above), but numbers are limited.

OUTDOORS

Mount Adams and Mount St. Helens, not visible from the road, can be seen clearly from such mountain trails as **Paradise** (1½ mi.), **Pinnacle Peak** (2½ mi.), **Eagle Peak** (7 mi.), and **Van Trump Park** (5½ mi.). The visitors centers have handouts for hiking in each of the park's sections, often including maps, travel time, and level of intensity for several hikes in one area.

A segment of the **Pacific Crest Trail,** which runs in its entirety from Mexico to the Canadian border, dodges in and out of the park's borders at the southeast corner of the park. The **Wonderland Trail** winds 93 mi. up, down, and all around the Mountain. Hikers must get permits to make the arduous but stunning trek, and must complete the hike in 10-14 days. Call the backcountry desk (see **Practical Information,** above) for details on both hikes.

A trip to the **summit** of Mt. Rainier requires substantial preparation and expense. The ascent is a vertical rise of more than 9000 ft. over a distance of nine or more miles, usually taking two days and an overnight stay at **Camp Muir** on the south side (10,000 ft.) or **Camp Schurman** on the east side (9500 ft.). Each camp has a ranger station, rescue cache, and some form of toilet. Permits for summit climbs cost $15. Only experienced climbers should attempt the summit on their own; novices can sign up for a summit climb with **Rainier Mountaineering, Inc. (RMI)** (see **Practical Information,** p. 382), which offers a one-day basic-climbing course followed by a two-day guided climb. You must bring your own camping gear and carry four meals to the camp. For more information, contact Park Headquarters or RMI.

Less ambitious, ranger-led **interpretive hikes** delve into everything from area history to local wildflowers. Each visitors center conducts hikes on its own schedule and most of the campgrounds have evening talks and campfire programs.

Longmire

Just inside the Nisqually entrance, Longmire is pretty and woodsy, but by no means the best that Rainier has to offer. Hit the visitors center for permits and maps, then head to higher altitudes.

Longmire's **museum,** near the visitors center, dutifully documents both Rainier's natural history and the history of human encounters with the mountain. Mostly it shows that Rainier's most impressive lessons lie out of doors (open summer daily

9am-5:30pm; off-season daily 9am-4:30pm; hrs. may vary). Check out the relief model of the Mountain in the visitors center before taking on the real thing.

The **Rampart Ridge Trail** (a 2½hr., 4½mi. loop) has excellent views of the Nisqually Valley, Mt. Rainier, and Tumtum Peak. The **Van Trump Park & Comet Falls Trail** (a steep 4hr., 5 mi. hike) passes Comet Falls and often a mountain goat or two. The trip to Comet Falls is only 1½ mi. and the spectacular view of the 320 ft. drop is well worth the traffic on the trail.

Longmire remains open during the winter as a center for snowshoeing, cross-country skiing, and other alpine activities. **Guest Services, Inc.** (569-2275) runs a **cross-country ski center** which rents skis ($15 per day, $9.75 for children) and gives skiing lessons on weekends.

Paradise

Paradise, the most heavily visited corner of Rainier, is perhaps the only place in the park where the sound of babbling brooks and waterfalls might be drowned out by screaming children. If you can manage to avoid the hustle and bustle and arrive on a clear, sunny weekday, the name Paradise will make perfect sense. Above timberline, the sparkling snowfields can blind visitors looking out over forest canyons thousands of feet below, even in mid-June. Last year, record snowfalls kept Paradise's trails snowed in through August.

The road from the Nisqually entrance to Paradise is open year-round, but the road east through Stevens Canyon closes from October to June. The **Paradise Visitors Center** offers audio-visual programs, an observation deck, and all the requisite kitsch. From January to mid-April, park naturalists lead **snowshoe hikes** to explore winter ecology around Paradise (Sat.-Sun. at 10:30am, 12:30, and 2:30pm; snowshoe rental $1). In summer months, look for postings in the visitors center for ranger-led hikes, talks and wildflower walks.

Paradise is the starting point for several trails heading through the meadows to the nearby Nisqually Glacier or up the mountain to the summit. Many trails allow close-up views of Mt. Rainier's glaciers, especially the two closest to Paradise, the **Paradise** and the **Nisqually** glaciers. The 5 mi. **Skyline Trail** is the longest of the loop trails out of Paradise. The marked trail starts at the Paradise Inn; it is probably the closest a casual hiker can come to climbing the mountain. The first leg of the trail is often hiked by climbing parties headed for Camp Muir (the base camp for most ascents to the summit). The trail turns off before reaching Camp Muir, rising to its highest elevation at **Panorama Point.** Although only halfway up the mountain, the point is within view of the glaciers, and the summit appears deceptively close.

The mildly strenuous 2½ mi. hike up to **Pinnacle Peak** begins just east of Paradise, across the road from Reflection Lake, and offers clear views of Mt. Rainier, Mt. Adams, Mount St. Helens, and Mt. Hood. One of the most striking aspects of hikes out of Paradise are the expanses of wildflower-strewn alpine meadows; they are some of the largest and most spectacular in the park.

Ohanapecosh and Carbon River

Though in opposite corners of the park, the Ohanapecosh and Carbon Rivers are in the same ranger district. Ohanapecosh's visitors center and campground snuggle under lush, old-growth cedars along a river valley in the park's southeast corner just a few miles north of Packwood. One of the oldest stands of trees in Washington, the **Grove of Patriarchs,** grows here. An easy 2 mi. walk leads to these 500 to 1000-year-old Douglas firs, cedars, and hemlocks. The visitors center leads walks to the Grove, **Silver Falls,** and **Ohanapecosh Hot Springs,** a trickle of warm water in an area returning to the wild after development as a therapeutic resort in the 1920s. The **Summerland** and **Indian Bar Trails** are excellent for serious hiking—this is where rangers go on their days off.

Carbon River Valley, in the northwest corner of the park, is one of the only rainforests in the continental U.S., and its trails are on every ranger-in-the-know's top 10 list for hiking. **Spray Park** and **Mystic Camp** are superlative free backcountry campsites.

Carbon River also has access to the **Wonderland Trail** (see **Sunrise,** below). Winter storms keep the road beyond the Carbon River entrance under constant distress. Because of floods in the spring of 1996, the road only reaches to the edge of the park. Check with rangers for updates and trip planning tips. Your time here will no doubt leave you hoping that Carbon River remains a secret.

Sunrise

On the second day, God created Sunrise. We're not kidding. Too far from the entrance for most tourists to bother, Sunrise is unruffled God's country. The winding road to the highest of the four visitors centers provides gorgeous views of the Pacific Ocean, Mt. Baker, and the heavily glaciated eastern side of Mt. Rainier. Trails vary greatly in difficulty; the visitors center has invaluable maps. Try the comfortably sloping **Mt. Burroughs Trail** (5 mi.) for unbeatable glacier views. Those ready for more leg stress should head to **Berkeley Park,** a 5 mi. round-trip trek into a wildflower-painted valley. Many continue on 3 mi. to **Grand Park,** a higher, even more scenic meadow.

■ U.S. 2: Everett to Leavenworth

Stretching between the Puget Shore and Leavenworth, the **Skyhomish** district begs urbanites to roam its river-plush, sub-alpine trails. Stop by the **Skyhomish Ranger Station** (360-677-2414), off U.S. 2, to chat about local hikes and campgrounds (open daily 8am-4:30pm). View-seekers, flower-lovers, and overnight campers will want to assault the 3.5 mi. **Tonga Ridge Trail,** located ½ mi. past the ranger station. Turn right off the highway onto Foss River Rd., then left on Tonga Ridge Rd. and continue 6 mi. to Spur #310. Bear right at the sign and continue 1 mi. to the trailhead. If in search of lakes, continue along Foss River Rd. 6 mi., then turn left at Rd. 6835 to get to **West Fork Foss Lake Trail.** Mountain bikers haul ass on the **Johnson Ridge Trail,** the only trail open to cyclists. Get directions at the ranger station. Families and train aficionados make a much slower mosey along the **Iron Goat Trail,** a recently completed route along the old train tracks. Hikes rumble through tunnels and wildflowers. To find the Iron Goat, turn left onto Rd. #67, the Old Cascade Hwy., past Mile 50. Proceed 1.4 mi. to Rd. 6710, then turn left and tumble into trailhead parking.

Leavenworth

"*Willkommen zu* Leavenworth" proclaims the carved wooden sign at the entrance to this resort town/theme park. After the logging industry exhausted Leavenworth's natural resources and the railroad switching station moved to nearby Wenatchee, this rural mountain town was forced to invent a tourist gimmick to survive. By the mid-60s, "Project Alpine" had painted a thick Bavarian veneer over Leavenworth. One can only wonder at the planners' *Weltanschauung.* Today, an estimated one million people annually visit this living Swiss Miss commercial, with massive influxes during the city's three annual festivals. Waiters in *Lederhosen* work in restaurants with comical, faux Anglo-German nomenclature; loudspeakers pump relentless yodeling into the streets. Even the local McDonald's steps to the inescapable oompah beat. Never mind that no one knows any German; this town is an experience in bizarre American tackiness. Renting a bike and heading for the nearby mountain splendor may be the best way to take a vacation from your vacation in Leavenworth.

PRACTICAL INFORMATION AND ORIENTATION

Visitors Information: Chamber of Commerce, 894 U.S. 2 (548-5807), in the Clocktower Bldg. Helpful staff, many of whom see absolutely nothing amusing in their town's *Töricht* gimmick. Open Mon.-Sat. 9am-6pm, Sun. 10am-4pm. **Ranger Station,** 600 Sherbourne (782-1413 or 548-4067), just off U.S. 2. The source for info on the mountains surrounding Leavenworth, especially the world-class rock climbing scene. Pick up a list of the 9 developed campgrounds within 20 mi. of Leavenworth. Open daily 7:45am-4:30pm; winter Mon.-Fri. 7:45am-4:30pm.

Buses: Greyhound (662-2183). Stops west of town on U.S. 2 at the Department of Transportation. 1 bus per day to Spokane ($25), and 3 to Seattle ($20).

Public Transportation: Link (662-1155 or 800-851-5465). Free bus service! Runs 20 buses per day Mon.-Sat. between Wenatchee and Leavenworth, with several stops around town. The main stop is at the Park 'n' Ride lot, next to the ranger station. Pick up a schedule at the chamber. All buses have bike racks.

Bike Rental: Der Sportsmann, 837 Front St. (548-5623). Mountain bikes $6 per hr., $20 per day, cross-country skis $12 per day. Also rents climbing shoes ($8) and snow shoes ($2). Hiking and biking **maps** available. Open summer daily 9am-7pm; off-season 10am-6pm.

Weather: 884-2982. **Cascade Snow Report:** 353-7440.

Senior Citizen Center: 423 Evans (548-6666), behind the chamber of commerce.

Pharmacy: Village Pharmacy, 821 Front St. (548-7731). Open Mon.-Fri. 8:30am-6:30pm, Sat. 9am-5:30pm, Sun. 11am-5pm.

Hospital: Cascade Medical Center, 817 Commercial St. (548-5815). Clinic open Mon.-Fri. 8am-7pm, Sat. 8am-5pm, Sun. 11am-5pm. Emergency room 24hr.

Emergency: 911.

Post Office: 960 U.S. 2 (548-7212). Open Mon.-Fri. 9am-5pm, Sat. 9-11am. **General Delivery ZIP Code:** 98826.

Area Code: 509.

Leavenworth is on the eastern slope of the Cascades, near Washington's geographic center. **U.S. 2** bisects Leavenworth in the main business district. The north-south route through the area is **U.S. 97,** intersecting U.S. 2 about 6 mi. southeast of town. Leavenworth is approximately 121 mi. east of Seattle and 190 mi. west of Spokane.

ACCOMMODATIONS AND CAMPING

Hotels start at $50 for singles, and most cost even more. **Camping** is plentiful, inexpensive, and spectacular in the surrounding national forest. If you seek solitude, avoid weekend stays after Memorial Day. Otherwise, come early, or you may not find a spot at any of *die Kampingplatzen.*

Wenatchee National Forest (782-1413). 10 mi. from town along **Icicle Creek Road,** a series of 7 Forest Service campgrounds squeeze between the creek and the road. The farther west the campground, the prettier the site—try the **Johnny Creek** campground for secluded forest sites or **Ida Creek** for proximity to the river. RVs and trailers may find the road difficult to maneuver. To get there, take the last left in town on U.S. 2 heading west. All have drinking water and pit toilets; the closest to town is $8, all others $7.

Tumwater (800-280-2267), 10 mi. west of Leavenworth on U.S. 2. A forest service campground with water, flush toilets, and wheelchair access. 84 sites, $8.

FOOD

Predictably, Leavenworth's food mimics German cuisine; surprisingly, it often succeeds. German *Wurst* booths are tucked between buildings everywhere, but those looking for much more than *die Frankfurters* should be prepared to pay at least $8-16 for a full dinner. If you're heading into the wilderness, shop at **Safeway,** 940 U.S. 2 (548-5435; open daily 7am-11pm).

The Leavenworth Brewery, 636 Front St. (548-4545). This microbrewery justifies Leavenworth's Disney-fication of Bavaria by serving up tasty local ales (16 oz. $3) and pub fare (potato stuffed with cheese, onions, and peppers $4). The brewery also sponsors Sat. night performances and the occasional "Tacky Polyester Prom Night." Open Sun.-Thurs. 11am-10pm, Fri.-Sat. 11am-midnight.

Leavenworth Pizza Company, 892 U.S. 2 (548-7766). Located next to the visitors center, this family-owned restaurant offers tasty pizzas and a mostly-locals atmosphere as a respite from *Schnitzel*-crazed tourists. 2-person pizza $7-9. Open Sun.-Thurs. 11am-9pm, Fri.-Sat. 11am-10pm.

Oberland Bakery and Cafe, 703 Front St. (548-7216). The "Europeans" painted on the wall keep you company as you nibble on your Bavarian almond pretzel. Generous subs $4.50. Lunch specials $5. Open daily 9am-5:30pm.

Los Comparos, 200 6th St. (548-3314). Not cheap, but, hey, it could be *Wurst.* Chunky Mexican food $7-11. Open daily noon-10pm.

OUTDOORS

Except for tourist-watching, the most compelling reason to come to Leavenworth is for the extensive hiking, mountain biking, and climbing opportunities in the **Wenatchee National Forest.** The heavily visited **Alpine Lakes Wilderness,** stretching south of town, is as beautiful as it is clogged with hikers. Be careful to stay on the trails; the region is home to many black bears and western rattlesnakes lacking *Gemütlichkeit.* The **ranger station** in Leavenworth (see **Practical Information,** above) hands out free descriptions of hikes near town, ranked by distance and difficulty. An informative guide to all the area's trails sells for $3. One pleasant dayhike is the moderately sloping 3½ mi. trail to **Eight Mile Lake,** a great spot for a picnic or overnight backpacking. Drive 9.4 mi. up Icicle Creek Rd., make a left onto Eight Mile Rd., then continue 3 mi. uphill to the trailhead. On a hot day, stay near water and hike the 3½ mi. **Icicle Gorge Trail,** which starts just east of the Chatter Creek Campground on Icicle Rd. and moseys along beside the cool creek river waters.

Although most trails in this area are unrestricted, permits are required to enter the popular **Stuart Lake, Colcheck Lake, Snow Lakes,** and **Enchantment Lakes** areas. If you're a dayhiker, the permits are free and "self-issuing," meaning you just have to fill out a form at the ranger station or the trailheads. Permits for **backcountry overnights,** however, cost $6-7 and must be reserved at least 21 days in advance. Dig out your Visa or Mastercard and call (800) 735-2900 (Mon.-Fri. 8am-5pm). More spur of the moment types can cross their fingers and visit the ranger station, where a number of free permits are distributed by **lottery** each morning at 7:45am.

The **Leavenworth Winter Sports Club,** P.O. Box 573, Leavenworth 98826 (548-5115), maintains the trail system in winter. Pick up a free copy of their *Cross-Country Ski Guide* at the ranger station. In a riding mood? Try the **Eagle Creek Ranch** (548-7798 or 800-222-7433), which offers horseback rides ($15 per hr.), hay rides ($12), and horse-drawn sleigh rides in winter. To get there, go north on Rte. 209, turn right on Eagle Creek Rd., and go 5½ mi.

On your way south to the U.S. 97 junction, stop in **Cashmere** at the **Aplets and Cotlets Factory,** 117 Mission St. (782-2191; follow the signs from U.S. 2), for free tours of the plant and ample samples of their gooey candies. You have to wear a hat during the tour, but they'll give you a goofy paper one if you don't bring your own. (Open Mon.-Fri. 8am-5:30pm, Sat.-Sun. 10am-5pm; in winter Mon.-Fri. 9am-5pm, Sat. 10am-4pm; closed on weekends Jan.-Feb.)

Lake Chelan

The serpentine body of Lake Chelan (sha-LAN) undulates over 50 mi. northwest from the Columbia River and U.S. 97 into the eastern Cascades. Perched amid bone-dry hills and apple orchards, the town has developed a pricey tourist industry geared to seniors and families with motor boats in tow. Up the lake, brown hills transform into vermilion mountains as the North Cascades flaunt their awesome beauty. The lake, at points 1500 ft. deep (the third deepest in the U.S.), extends far into Wenatchee National Forest and pokes its northwesternmost tip into the **Lake Chelan National Recreation Area,** a section of **North Cascades National Park.** While the town of Chelan has become an aquatic Disneyland, **Stehekin** (ste-HEE-kin), at the other end of the lake, offers solitude, space, and access to a vast wilderness.

Practical Information The **Chelan Ranger Station,** 428 W. Woodin Ave. (682-2576, National Park Service 682-2549), on the lakeshore just south of town, dishes the goods on the area's forests and recreation areas (open daily 7:45am-4:30pm; Oct.-May Mon.-Fri. 7:45am-4:30pm). If you'll be in Chelan for a while, stop by the **Chamber of Commerce,** 102 E. Johnson (682-3503 or 800-424-3526); it has plenty of info on Chelan and nearby Manson, but not much on the surrounding wilds (open Mon.-Fri. 9am-5pm, Sat. 10am-3pm; winter Mon.-Fri. 9am-5pm).

Link (800-851-5465), the local bus service, has hourly service to Wenatchee, a Greyhound stop. Rent a bike, inline skates, or even paragliding equipment at **Nature Gone Wild,** 109 S. Emerson (682-8680). Bikes go for $5 per hour or $20 per day; inline skates are $3 for the first hour, $2 for each hour thereafter (open Mon.-Fri. 9am-6pm, Sat. 8am-5pm). **Surf the 'Net** ($6 per hr.) or get your info the old fashioned way at **River Walk Books,** 113 Emerson St. (682-8901; open daily 9:30am-8pm). Chelan's pharmacy is **Green's Drugs,** 212 E. Woodin Ave. (682-2566; open Mon.-Sat. 9am-5:30pm, Sun. as posted). The **Lake Chelan Community Hospital,** 503 E. Highland St. (682-2531), is open 24 hours. Important phone numbers are: **emergency,** 911; 24hr. **crisis line,** 662-7105; and **police,** 207 N. Emerson St. (682-2588). Wash them clothes (wash $1.25; 10min. dry 25¢) at **Town Tub Laundry** on Woodin Ave. (open daily 8am-10pm). The **post office** is at 144 E. Johnson (682-2625; open Mon.-Fri. 8:30am-5pm; **General Delivery ZIP Code:** 98816). The **area code** is 509.

Accommodations, Camping, and Food Most Chelan motels and resorts are too busy exploiting sun-starved visitors from Puget Sound to bother being affordable. One exception is **Apple Inn,** 1002 E. Woodin (682-4044), an AAA-approved motel that boasts a small-time hot tub and pool. Eccentric rooms are clean and neat, though a bit small ($49-59; up to $20 cheaper in winter). Another budget find lies around the corner at **Mom's Montlake Motel,** 823 Wapato (682-5715), at Clifford, a mom-and-pop operation with clean, microwave-equipped rooms (starting at $48). Most campers head for **Lake Chelan State Park** (687-3710), a pleasant grassy campground 9 mi. up the south shore of the lake with a beach and swimming area, small store, and jet ski rentals. (144 sites; $11, hookups $16; reservations recommended April-Sept.) The brave reach **Ramona Park,** a free, primitive campground, by turning left onto Forest Rd. 5900 near the end of the South Shore Rd., left again onto Forest Rd. 8410 after 2½ mi., and continuing another ½ mi. Campers may also pitch tents for free anywhere they please in the National Forest. Fires must be kept in already established fire rings.

The cheapest eats in Chelan are at local fruit stands, the **Safeway,** 106 W. Manson Rd. (682-2615; open daily 6am-11pm), or **Bear Foods,** 125 E. Woodin Ave. (682-5535), which sells a wide variety of natural foods and everything from Ben and Jerry's ice cream to books on tofu (open Mon.-Sat. 9am-7pm, Sun. noon-5pm). For an enlightened lunch, hunt down **Dagwood's International Kitchen,** at 246 W. Manson Way (682-8630). This unpretentious joint serves $6 Thai shrimp pizzas (open daily 11am-"the after-dinner slow down"). For the coffee addict, **Flying Saucers,** 116 S. Emerson (682-5129), offers lattés and aura galora in a converted 50s diner.

■ Stehekin

For less than the price of a motel room in touristy Chelan, you can take a ferry over 50 mi. of sparkling turquoise waters to Stehekin, a tiny town at the mouth of a magnificent valley. Catch a shuttle bus a few miles up the valley, camp for free on the banks of a rushing, crystal green river, and spend days exploring some of the most beautiful country in the Cascades.

The **Lake Chelan Boat Company,** 1418 W. Woodin (682-2224), about 1 mi. west of town, runs the Lady of the Lake II, a 350-person ferry that makes one round-trip to Stehekin per day ($22). You can catch the ferry at Chelan (daytime parking free, overnight $5) at 8:30am and return at 6pm, or at **Fields Point,** 16 mi. up the South Shore Rd. near Twenty-Five Mile Creek State Park (parking $3 per day, $17 per week) at

9:45am and return at 4:45pm. The *Lady Express* is a smaller boat that makes a faster, non-stop trip to Stehekin for a higher price ($41 round-trip). Purchase tickets in advance on summer weekends; the ferries often fill with eager tourists and backpackers, and they will not accept credit cards on the day of travel. The scenery gets increasingly spectacular as the boat proceeds "uplake"; the views on the ride alone are worth the price. You may catch a glimpse of mountain goats or brown bears roaming the lakeside.

When the ferry arrives at Stehekin at 12:30pm, most people stay only until the boat's 2pm departure. If that's your plan, the **Rainbow Falls Tour** ($5), leaving as soon as the *Lady* arrives, is a good way to see the valley and its major sights: the one-room **Stehekin School;** the **Stehekin Pastry Company,** a bakery in a log cabin in the woods; and **Rainbow Falls,** a misty 312 ft. waterfall.

Camping and Food To truly appreciate the Stehekin area, let the rabble take the ferry back to Chelan and camp in the valley overnight. The Park Service maintains 12 primitive campgrounds along the **Stehekin Valley Road.** Get the free but required permit at the ranger station in Chelan (see p. 389) or at Stehekin's **Golden West Visitor Center** (856-6055, ext. 14), where exuberant rangers can help plan anything from a one-hour jaunt to a 10-day backcountry trip (open daily 8am-4:30pm). The closest campground is at **Purple Point,** right next to the ferry landing. Its six sites have water, free hot showers, and bathrooms. Solitude seekers can take the Stehekin Adventure Shuttle to Harlequin Campground, 5 mi. upriver. Harlequin has tables and fire pits, as well as riverside views, but no water.

If you want a meal in the valley, you have a few options. Three, to be exact. A delicious country dinner at the **Stehekin Valley Ranch** (682-4677) will set you back about $12. You'll need to make reservations (by phone or at **Discovery Bikes,** just north of the ferry dock) and catch a bus up to the ranch. The **Lodge Restaurant** (682-4494), at the landing, serves expensive burgers ($5-6) and dinners ($7-15). Bring **groceries** from Chelan; the store in Stehekin has only a small selection of fish bait and Fritos. Just a mile up the only road, the **Stehekin Pastry Company** lures hikers out of the hills to snack on Rubenesque sticky buns ($1.85; open daily 7am-5pm).

Outdoors Some short but scenic day hikes surround the landing. The mellow **Lakeshore Trail** starts behind the visitors center and follows the west shore of Lake Chelan for 17 mi. to Prince Creek. A more strenuous alternative begins with the ¾ mi. **Imus Creek Trail,** a self-guided interpretive trail starting behind the Golden West Visitor Center. After passing fast-flowing Purple Creek, take a right turn up the switchbacks of the steep **Purple Creek Trail.** The 5500 ft. climb is tough, but rewards effort with a magnificent view of the lake and surrounding glaciers. In the opposite direction, the moderately steep **Rainbow Loop Trail** offers more stellar valley views. The 5 mi. trail begins 3 mi. from Stehekin—**Stehekin Transportation Services** will shuttle you up there five times a day, but it's close enough to walk, and residents rarely hesitate to provide a ride. Pick up a **bike,** if the spirit moves you, at **Discovery Bikes** (884-4844; $8 per hr., $10 per ½ day, $15 per day), or at the Lodge ($3.50 per hr., $10 per day).

An unpaved road and many trails probe north from Stehekin into the **North Cascades National Park.** In summer, the **Cascades Stehekin Lodge** (682-4494) runs four shuttle buses daily from Stehekin to **High Bridge,** deeper into the park ($4). The National Park Service runs a second shuttle from High Bridge to **Bridge Creek,** which provides access to the **Pacific Crest Trail.** All walk-in campgrounds in the park are free and open May to October (drinking water is not provided). **Backcountry permits** are mandatory in the park throughout the year and are available at the visitors center or the Chelan Ranger Station (see p. 389) on a first-come, first-served basis.

Two **dayhikes** start from High Bridge. The mellow **Agnes Gorge Trail** begins 200 yd. beyond the bridge (2nd trail on the left), and travels a level 2½ mi. through forests and meadows with views of Agnes Mountain, ending where Agnes Creek takes a dramatic plunge into Agnes Gorge (oh, Agnes...). Behind the ranger cabin, the **McGre-**

gor Mountain Trail is a straight shot up the side of the mountain, climbing 6525 vertical ft. over a distance of 8 mi. The last ½ mi. is a scramble up ledges. This extremely difficult trail is often blocked by snow into July; check at the visitor center before starting out. The persevering hiker is rewarded with unsurpassed views of the high North Cascades peaks.

North Cascades (Rte. 20)

A favorite stomping ground for grizzlies, deer, mountain goats, black bears, and Jack Kerouac (*The Dharma Bums*), the North Cascades remain one of the most rugged expanses of land in the continental U.S. The dramatic peaks stretch north from Stevens Pass on U.S. 2 to the Canadian border and are preserved in pristine condition by several different government agencies. The centerpiece of the area is **North Cascades National Park,** which straddles the crest of the Cascades. The untamed wilderness and astonishingly steep peaks attract backpackers and mountain climbers from around the world. **Route 20** (open April-Nov., weather permitting), a road designed for unadulterated driving pleasure, is the primary means of access to the area and awards jaw-dropping views at every curve.

Much of the wilderness is inaccessible without at least a day's uphill hike. Few are willing to spend the energy, but those who do will be rewarded with untrammeled land, jagged peaks, and an Eden of wildlife and flora. Ira Springs's *100 Hikes in the North Cascades* is a good guide for recreational hikers, while Fred Beckley's *Cascade Alpine Guide* targets the more serious high-country traveler. Both are published by the Mountaineers Books (see p. 38).

Route 20 (Exit 230 on I-5) follows the Skagit River the small towns of Sedro Wooley, Concrete and Marblemount in the **Mount Baker/Snoqualmie National Forest.** The highway then enters North Cascades National Park via the **Ross Lake National Recreation Area,** one of the two designated recreation areas within the National Park. After passing through Newhalem, Diablo Lake, and Ross Lake, Route 20 leaves the National Park and enters the **Okanogan National Forest District,** crossing Washington Pass (5477 ft.), and descending to the Methow River and the dry Okanogan rangeland of Eastern Washington. The **Lake Chelan National Recreation Area** occupies the southern tip of the national park, bordered on the south by the **Wenatchee National Forest.** When making phone calls to the area, make note of the **area code**—it changes as quickly as the scenery.

SEDRO WOOLLEY TO MARBLEMOUNT

Though situated in the rich farmland of the lower Skagit Valley, Sedro Woolley is primarily a logging town. The volunteers at the **Visitors Information Center** (360-855-0974), in the train caboose at the intersection of Hwy. 20 and Ferry St., have far too much time on their hands and are extremely eager to help those who drop in (open daily 9am-5pm).

Sedro Woolley also houses the headquarters of North Cascades National Park and Mt. Baker/Snoqualmie National Forest at 2105 Rte. 20 (360-856-5700). Call 206-526-6677 for snow avalanche information. Backcountry campers must contact the **Wilderness Information Center,** (360-873-4500), in Marblemount, for a backcountry permit. The main attraction of this village is the annual **Sedro Woolley Loggerodeo,** which takes place in late June and early August. Axe-throwing, pole-climbing, and sawing competitions vie for center stage with rodeo events such as bronco-busting and calf-roping. Call 855-1129 or write the Loggerodeo at P.O. Box 712, Sedro Woolley 98284.

Route 9 leads north from Sedro Woolley, providing indirect access to **Mt. Baker** (see p. 349) through the forks at the Nooksack River and Rte. 542. Twenty-three miles east of Sedro Wooley, at Mile 82, is the turnoff for **Baker Lake Highway,** which dead-ends 25 mi. later at **Baker Lake.** Several campsites can be found along the road to Baker Lake. The best bargain is the crowded **Kulshan Campground,** which has 79 free sites, drinking water, and flush toilets. Among the others, **Horseshoe Cove** (34 sites; handicapped accessible) and **Panorama Point** (15 sites) have drinking water and toilets (call 800-280-CAMP/2267 for reservations ($8.25); sites $10, $6.50 for additional vehicles).

Don't blink while heading east or you may miss the town of **Concrete,** where rows of businesses made of (yes) concrete pay homage to the a now defunct local industry. *This Boy's Life,* starring Robert DeNiro and Leonardo DiCaprio was filmed in this picturesque locale. On the western boundary of the relatively small **Rockport State Park,** Sauk Mountain Road (a.k.a. Forest Service Rd. 1030) makes a stomach-scrambling climb up Sauk mountain. A view of Mt. Rainier, Puget Sound, and the San Juan Islands awaits the intrepid peak-bound driver (7 mi. up and a right turn at Rd. 1036). The **Sauk Mountain Trail** begins at the parking lot and winds 3½ mi. to back-country campsites near Sauk Lake. The road promises pot holes galore and a thorough dust bath; trailers, RVs, and the faint of heart should not attempt the ascent.

The park also has a trail that accommodates wheelchairs and 50 fully developed campsites ($10, with full hookup $15, each extra vehicle $5; 3-sided adirondack cabins with bunk beds for 8 are $15, no reservations). If Rockport is full, continue 1 mi. east to Skagit County's **Howard Miller Steelhead Park** (360-853-8808), on the Skagit River, where anglers come to catch the park's tasty namesake (steelhead, not Howard Miller; 49 sites; tents $12, hookups $16, 3-sided adirondack lean-tos $16). The surrounding **Mt. Baker/Snoqualmie National Forest** permits free camping closer to the high peaks, but **trail park passes** ($3 per day; available at Forest Service and local businesses) are required. These passes are not required when parking in the North Cascades National Park.

At **Marblemount,** consider stopping at **Good Food** (873-2771), a small family diner at the east edge of town along Rte. 20. This pithy eatery not only boasts riverside picnic tables and bikers to talk Harleys with, but also a great vegetarian sandwich ($3.60). Shakes ($2.25) are thick and tasty (open daily 9am-9pm). Stock up on drinking water at **Marblemount Mercantile Market** (873-4274), on Hwy. 20 (open 9am-9pm), and cruise 8 mi. east along Cascade River Rd. to **Marble Creek** (24 sites) or 16 mi. east to **Mineral Park** (5 sites). Both are free, but have no drinking water.

From Marblemount, it is 22 mi. along Cascade River Rd. to the trailhead for a 3½-mi. hike to the amazing **Cascade Pass. Stehekin,** at the northern tip of Lake Chelan, is reachable only by boat, plane, or foot (see p. 389). Call the **Golden West Visitors Center** (856-5700 ext. 14), in Stehekin, for detailed information on shuttle buses and trails, or stop by the **Marblemount Wilderness Information Center,** 728 Ranger Station Rd., Marblemount 98267 (873-4500, ext. 39), 1 mi. north of Marblemount on a well-marked road from the west end of town. This is also the place to go for a back-country permit and to plan longer backpacking excursions. Say what you will about their hats; the rangers are on the ball (open in summer Sun.-Thurs. 7am-6pm, Fri.-Sat. 7am-8pm; call for winter hours).

ROSS LAKE & NORTH CASCADES NATIONAL PARK

Newhalem is the first town on Rte. 20 after it crosses into the Ross Lake Recreation Area, a buffer zone between the highway and North Cascades National Park. At the tourist-friendly **North Cascades Visitors Center and Ranger Station** (206-386-4495), off Rte. 20, a cheesy informational video (are there any other kinds?) provides a peek at the diversity of flora and fauna in the Cascades (open daily 8am-6pm; in winter Sat.-Sun. 9am-4:30pm). Serious backpackers and climbers should bypass this kinder, gentler center and head directly to the hard-core Marblemount Wilderness Information Center (see above).

Seattle City Light (206-684-3030), in Diablo, operates a small museum and provides tours of the **Skagit Hydroelectric Project,** which generates 40% of Seattle's electricity. Tour highlights include a walk across Diablo Dam, a ride up the 560 ft. Incline Railway, and another thrilling informational video! (Visitors center open Thurs.-Mon. 9am-4pm; tours 10am, 1, and 3pm; $5.) The artificial and astoundingly blue expanse of **Ross Lake,** behind Ross Dam, snakes into the mountains as far as the

Canadian border. The lake is only accessible by trails and ringed by 15 campgrounds, some accessible by trail, others only by boat. The National Park's **Goodell Creek Campground,** just south of Newhalem, has 22 leafy sites suitable for tents and trailers with drinking water and pit toilets, and a launch site for **whitewater rafting** on the Skagit River (sites $7; water turned off after Oct. when sites are free). **Colonial Creek Campground,** 10 mi. to the east, is a fully developed, wheelchair-accessible campground with 164 sites, flush toilets, a dump station, and campfire programs some evenings (sites $10, no hookups). **Newhalem Creek Campground,** at Mile 120 near the visitors center, is a similarly developed facility with a less impressive forest of small pines, especially good for trailers and RVs (129 sites, $10). The **Skagit General Store** (386-4489), east of the visitors center, sells fishing licenses and basic groceries (open Mon.-Fri. 7:30am-5:30pm, Sat.-Sun. 8am-7pm).

Hiking abounds in the area. Among the most popular and accessible are the **Thunder Creek Trail,** which extends through old growth cedar and fir forests, and the **Fourth of July Pass Trail,** which begins approximately 2 mi. into the Thunder Creek Trail. The 3.2 mi. to the pass climb to 3500 ft., offering views better than fireworks.

EAST TO MAZAMA AND WINTHROP

This is the most beautiful segment of Route 20. Leaving the basin of Ross Lake, the road begins to climb, exposing the jagged, snowy peaks of the North Cascades. Thirty miles of astounding views east, the **Pacific Crest Trail** crosses Rte. 20 at **Rainy Pass** on one of the most scenic and difficult legs of its 2500 mi. Canada-to-Mexico route. Near Rainy Pass, groomed **scenic trails** 1 to 3 mi. long can be hiked in sneakers, provided the snow has melted (about mid-July). Just off Rte. 20, an overlook at **Washington Pass,** at Milepost 162, rewards a ½ mi. walk on a wheelchair-accessible paved trail with one of the state's most dramatic panoramas, an astonishing view of the red rocks exposed by Early Winters Creek in **Copper Basin.** The area has many well-marked trailheads off Rte. 20 that lead into the desolate wilderness. The popular 2½ mi. walk to **Blue Lake** begins just east of Washington Pass. An easier 2 mi. hike to **Cutthroat Lake** departs from an access road 4½ mi. east of Washington Pass. From the lake, the trail continues 4 mi. farther (and almost 2,000 ft. higher) to **Cutthroat Pass,** treating determined hikers to a breathtaking view of towering, rugged peaks.

The hair-raising 23 mi. road to **Hart's Pass** begins at **Mazama,** on Rd. 1163, 10 mi. east of Washington Pass. The gravel road snakes up to the highest pass crossed by any road in the state. Breathtaking views await the steel-nerved driver, both from the pass and from **Slate Peak,** the site of a lookout station 3 mi. beyond the pass. The road is closed to trailers and is only accessible when the snow has melted. Check at the Methow Valley Visitors Center in Winthrop to find out its status.

A Room with a View

While on Route 20 anywhere east of Mazama, look north to the highest mountain, and on top you'll see a small hut, the **Goat Peak Lookout,** home to local celebrity, **Lightnin' Bill** and his trusty dog **Lookout Turk.** Lightnin' Bill (nicknamed "Lightnin'" not because he's speedy but because he "loves to be up here during those lightnin' storms") inhabits one of the last manned (and dogged) **fire lookouts** in the state. What does he do for weeks at a time in a one room hut 7000 ft. in the sky? Bill writes poetry (ask him to read you some), enjoys the view, and chats with visitors that make the hike to his isolated home. To visit Bill and Turk, head east from Mazama on County Rd. #1163 onto the gravel Forest Rd. #52. Continue 2.7 mi. along the dusty road and turn left on Forest Road #5225. Drive 6.2 mi. and turn right on road #5225-200. Continue 2.4 mi. to the end of the road and the beginning of the trailhead. (Don't lose heart; the directions are far more complicated than the actual driving.) The trail to the fire lookout is short but steep, and passes through colorful alpine meadows. Bill will show you everything about his little home, from the lightning rod above to the glass ashtrays under the bedposts that insulate him from the electrical storms. Then he'll take your picture and you'll be recorded in his photo album forever.

WINTHROP TO TWISP

Farther east is the town of **Winthrop,** the child of an unholy marriage between the television series *Bonanza* and Long Island yuppies who would eagerly claim a rusty horseshoe as an antique. Find the **Winthrop Information Station,** 202 Riverside (996-2125), at the junction with Rte. 20, and the staff will laud the beauty of this "Old West" town (open early May-mid-Oct. daily 10am-5pm). The summer in Winthrop is bounded by **rodeos** on Memorial and Labor Day weekends. Late July brings the top-notch **Winthrop Rhythm and Blues Festival** (509-997-2541), where big name blues bands flock to belt their tunes, endorse radio stations, and play cowboy. Tickets for the three-day event cost $35, $45 at the door. Take a guided trail ride at the **Rocking Horse Ranch** (996-2768), 10 mi. west of Winthrop on Rte. 20 ($25 per 1½hr.). Or rent a bike ($15 for 4hr., $20 per day) at **Winthrop Mountain Sports,** 257 Riverside Ave. (996-2886; open Mon.-Fri. 9am-6pm, Sat. 9am-6:30pm, Sun. 9am-5:30pm).

The **Methow** (MET-how) **Valley Visitors Center,** Bldg. 49, Hwy. 20 (996-4000), hands out information on area camping, hiking and cross-country skiing (open daily 9am-5pm; in winter Thurs.-Mon. 8am-4:30pm). For more in-depth skiing and hiking trail information, call the **Methow Valley Sports Trail Association** (996-3287), which cares for 175km of trails in the area.

Between Winthrop and Twisp on East Country Rd. #9129, the **North Cascades Smokejumper Base** (997-2031) is a center for folks who get their kicks by parachuting into forest fires and putting them out. The courageous (and a little crazy) smokejumpers will give a thorough tour of the base and explain the procedures and equipment used to help them fight the fires and stay alive (open summers and early fall daily 10am-1pm and 2-5pm).

Flee Winthrop's prohibitively expensive hotels and restaurants to sleep in **Twisp,** the town that should have been a breakfast cereal. It was actually named for the Native American word for yellowjacket, "T-wapsp." Nine miles south of Winthrop on Rte. 20, this peaceful hamlet offers lower prices and far fewer tourists than its neighbor. The **Twisp Ranger Station,** 502 Glover St. (997-2131), employs a crunchy and helpful staff fortified with essential trail and campground guides (open Mon.-Fri. 7:45am-4:30pm). Stay at **The Sportsman Motel,** 1010 E. Rte. 20 (997-2911), a hidden jewel, where a barracks-like facade masks tastefully decorated rooms with kitchens (singles $33; doubles $38). The **Glover Street Cafe,** 104 N. Glover St. (997-1323), offers gourmet salads ($3.75) and sandwiches ($5.25 with soup or salad) that won't bust your budget (open Mon.-Fri. 8am-3pm). Grab desert at the **Cinnamon Twisp Bakery,** 116 N. Glover St. (997-5030; open Mon.-Fri. 7am-5pm, Sat. 7am-3pm).

From Twisp, Rte. 20 continues east to Okanogan and Rte. 153 runs south to **Lake Chelan.** There are many campgrounds and trails from 15 to 25 mi. up **Twisp River Road,** just off Rte. 20 in Twisp. Although the campsites are primitive, many are free. For camping closer to the highway, head to the **Riverbend RV Park,** 19951 Rte. 20 (997-3500 or 800-686-4498), 2 mi. west of Twisp. Despite an abundance of slow-moving beasts (RVs), Riverbend has plenty of comfy tent sites situated along the Methow River (office open 8am-10pm; sites $14, hookups $18, $2 per person after 2).

EASTERN WASHINGTON

In the rain shadow of the Cascades, the hills and valleys of the Columbia River Basin once fostered little more than sagebrush and tumbleweed. The 20th century brought the construction of 10 dams on the Columbia, making irrigation possible. Now, the basin yields bumper crops of fruit and high-quality wine. Sunshine defies the rainy Washington stereotype, ripening some of the world's best apples while bronzing flocks of visitors from Puget Sound. Agriculture gives the valleys a calm beauty, visible in patchwork expanses from the Cascade foothills, and the region's rivers, lakes, and streams are well known for fishing and water sports. In some areas, the hills dissolve into sand dunes, where the Army has established training grounds and the Park Service has designated wilderness reserves. **Spokane** is the largest city east of the Cascades. **U.S. 97** runs north-south along the eastern edge of the mountains, stringing together the fruit centers and mountain resorts of the Columbia River Basin. **I-90** snakes through the Cascades from Seattle to cut a route through Ellensburg, Moses Lake, and Spokane. **I-82** dips south from Ellensburg through Yakima and Richland to Hermiston, OR. **Greyhound** (509-624-5251) runs along both interstates. **Amtrak** (509-624-5144) runs its "Empire Builder" through Spokane and Richland to Portland, and through Ellensburg to Tacoma and Seattle.

Yakima

With 300 days of sunshine per year, volcanic soil, and a fresh groundwater supply, Yakima and the Yakima Valley have earned the title "fruit bowl of the nation" by producing more apples, mint, and hops than any other U.S. county. East of the Cascades, Yakima is a fruit stand paradise—pounds of in-season peaches often cost less here than single peaches do in other parts of the country—making it a perfect pit stop on the way to the mountains. Unfortunately, not everything in the fruit bowl is peachy. Yakima has an extremely high crime rate, and the city itself offers little besides accommodations for the mountain-bound or Vancouver-Portland travelers. Most attractions of the Yakima Valley are wineries and orchards outside the city proper.

Practical Information Yakima is on I-82, 145 mi. southeast of Seattle and 145 mi. northwest of Pendleton, OR. The Yakima Valley lies southeast of the city, along I-82. Pick up one of the local handouts from the friendly staffers at the **Yakima Valley Visitors and Convention Bureau,** 10 N. 8th St. (575-3010), at E. Yakima (open Mon.-Fri. 8am-5pm, Sat.-Sun 9am-5pm; Nov.-Jan. closed Sat.-Sun.). A lush path follows the Yakima River through the Yakima Greenway, a corridor of preserved land running from Robertson Landing (Exit 34 off I-82) to Harlan Landing in the town of **Selah Grove** (Exit 31 off I-82).

Numbered streets line up east of Front St., while numbered avenues are west. **Yakima Transit** (575-6175), centered at 4th and Chestnut St., runs buses on 10 convenient routes (50¢, seniors 25¢, ages 6-17 35¢; Mon.-Fri. 6:15am-7pm, Sat. 8:45am-6:30pm). **Greyhound,** 602 E. Yakima (457-5131; open Mon.-Fri. 8am-5pm), stops in Yakima on the way to Portland (5 per day, $27) and Seattle (4 per day, $22). There is no service from Yakima to Mt. Rainier. For a taxi, call **Diamond Cab** at 453-3113 (24hr.). It's worth renting a car to see the Cascades. Get a sweet deal at **Savemore Auto Rentals,** 615 S. 1st St. (575-5400; $18 per day plus 15¢ per mi. over 100; must be 21). For **senior information and assistance** call 574-1080 (Mon.-Fri. 8:30am-5pm)..

Washington Wine Country

At one time, wine connoisseurs would have turned up their *nez* at pedestrian Washington labels, but the state is now the second-largest producer of wine in the nation, and local vineyards have been garnering international acclaim. The majority of wineries are situated in the Yakima, Walla Walla, and Columbia Valleys. These areas, just east of the Cascades, benefit from a rain shield that keeps the land naturally dry (and thus easily controlled by irrigation) and a mineral-rich soil bequeathed by ancient volcanoes. Sunlight produces grape sugars, and cool nights protect acids. And, as almost every wine brochure in the land points out, this region is at *exactly* the same latitude as Burgundy.

Wineries proliferate in the small towns between Yakima and Richland. Call the Yakima Valley Wine Growers Association for info (800-258-7270). Almost all offer tours and tastings, and many boast spectacular scenery right off I-82 that you don't have to be tipsy to appreciate. Hours vary, but most are open Monday through Saturday 10am-5pm; call ahead for hours or make an appointment. A free guide available at visitor centers across the region lists active wineries in the area, and has maps and information on tours and tastings.

The **crisis line** is 575-4200 (24hr.). Seniors get a discount on all prescriptions at **Medicine Mart,** 306 E. Yakima Ave. (248-9061; open Mon.-Fri. 9am-6pm). Yakima has two **hospitals,** both open 24 hours: **Yakima Valley Memorial,** 2811 Tieton Dr. (575-8000), and **Providence Medical Center,** 110 S. 9th Ave. (575-5000). In an **emergency,** call 911. The **police** are at 200 S. 3rd St. (575-6200). Rinse your rags at **K's Coin Laundry,** at the corner of N. 6th and Fruitvale St. (452-5335; open daily 7am-9pm). The **post office** (454-2450) is at 205 W. Washington Ave. at 3rd Ave. (open Mon.-Fri. 8:30am-5pm; **General Delivery ZIP Code:** 98903). The **area code** is 509.

Accommodations The "fruit bowl" is overflowing with reasonably priced, run-of-the-mill motels. A good bet for clean and comfortable rooms is the **Red Apple Motel,** 416 N. 1st St. (248-7150), where the friendly management does its best to keep out the rotten ones (21+ only; A/C, cable, apple-shaped pool; singles $42, doubles $46, weekdays $36 and $42, respectively). **Motel 6,** 1104 N. 1st St. (454-0080), a 20-minute walk from downtown, is more reliable and professional than most of the budget motels along 1st St. The pool provides welcome relief from the scorching Yakima heat (singles $39; doubles $45).

Yakima's few **campgrounds** are overcrowded and noisy. The **Yakama Nation RV Park,** 280 Buster Rd. (865-2000 or 800-874-3087), in **Toppenish,** 20 mi. southeast of Yakima on U.S. 97, is the exception. Though primarily an RV park, there are teepees to sleep in and a pool set in a field on the reservation (sites $12, RV $18). If you're desperate to camp closer to town, **KOA,** 1500 Keys Rd. (248-5882), will gladly take $20 in return for a compact tent site with nice bathrooms. Cheaper, more pleasant campgrounds lie along the Naches River on U.S. 12, about 30 mi. west of town on the way to Mt. Rainier. Sites with drinking water are $5; those without are free.

WASHINGTON

Food A cluster of boxcars-turned-tourist-bait on W. Yakima Ave. house mid-cost, mid-quality restaurants. Stop by **Box Car Freddie's** for diner food (burger and fries $3.50) and to kibbitz with the owners (open daily 8am-1:30pm). **Ruben's Tortillería y Panaderia,** 1518 1st St. (454-5357) sells freshly baked Mexican pastries for around 35¢ apiece and packages of 10 tortillas for $1 (open daily 8am-10pm). For a hearty Italian dinner, call **Deli de Pasta,** 7 N. Front St. (453-0571), and make the often-necessary reservation. At lunch, "pick a pasta" and one of seven sauces for $7. At dinner, pay $8 for the same deal and splurge on *tiramisu* for dessert (open Mon.-Sat. 11:30am to when the customers leave). After dinner, cross the street for even more carbohydrates at **Grant's Brewery Pub,** 32 N. Front St. (575-2922), at the north end of the train station. Call to arrange a tour of the microbrewery, the oldest in the Northwest and still a great place to have a good time. A pint of Grant's Scottish Ale or Yakima cider costs $3; the small lunch menu varies, but usually includes fish and chips ($6.25). Live jazz, blues, and folk bands play on weekends (open Mon.-Thurs. 11:30am-11pm, Fri.-Sat. 11:30am-midnight, Sun. 11:30am-8pm). The *Yakima Valley Farm Products Guide,* distributed at the visitors bureau and at regional hotels and stores, lists local fruit sellers and u-pick farms. Fruit stands are common on the outskirts of town, particularly on 1st St. and near interstate interchanges. A good fruit stop for interstate travelers is the **Donald Fruit and Mercantile,** 4461 Yakima Valley Hwy. (877-3115), in **Wapato,** 11 mi. southeast of Yakima, at Exit 44 off I-82 (open May-Oct. Mon.-Sat. 9am-6pm, Sun. 10am-6pm). **Johnson Orchards,** 4906 Summitview Ave. (966-7479), is the u-pick farm closest to town, specializing in tree-ripened cherries (June-July) and apples (Aug.-Nov.).

Sights and Events Most sights in Yakima are actually a little bit out of Yakima. A jaunt can yield a wide range of **u-pick** produce, from cantaloupes to jalapeño peppers. Farms generally stay open in summer from 8am to 5pm, but check in the *Farm Products Guide* or call ahead to be sure. Wear gloves and sturdy shoes, and bring as many empty containers as you can. U-picks are good deals and fun, but you can save almost as much by buying directly from the farms. While exploring the fruitful possibilities, stop by **Washington's Fruit Place Visitor Center,** 105 S. 18th Ave. (576-

3090) to push buttons and pull levers on exhibits that explain and illustrate the area's crop productions. Your labors will be rewarded with free apple juice (open Mon.-Fri. 9am-5pm, Sat. 10am-5pm, Sun. noon-4pm).

Toppenish, 19 mi. southeast of Yakima, is the jumping-off town for the **Yakama Reservation** (the tribe recently changed the official spelling of its name). The **Yakama Nation Cultural Center** (865-2800), 22 mi. south on U.S. 97 in Toppenish, presents exhibits on the culture of the 14 tribes and bands that inhabit the Yakima Valley. The fabulous museum concentrates on the oral tradition of the Yakama Natives and houses a small bookstore as well ($4, students and seniors $2; open Mon.-Sat. 9am-6pm, Sun. 9am-5pm). The rest of the cultural center surrounds the museum includes a public library and a restaurant that serves (expensive) native dishes. On the way out, the town of Toppenish itself is worth a quick drive-through. Maintained as a wild-west throwback, the town has commissioned 42 exquisite historical murals on its buildings. Each painting details the valley's settler history. Take Rte. 22 off I-82 to get there. The **Toppenish Powwow Rodeo and Pioneer Fair** (865-3262) occurs during the first weekend of July on Division Ave. in Toppenish, and features games, dancing, live music, a rodeo, and fair food (fair $2, rodeo $10). The **Central Washington State Fair** is held in Yakima in late September. The nine-day event includes agricultural displays, rodeos, big-name entertainers, and horse racing (call 248-7160 for more info).

WASHINGTON

Spokane

Ah, 1974. Gerald Ford was in the White House, Elvis was in the white suit, and streaking was a national phenomenon. And for one brief moment, the eyes of the world turned to Spokane, site of the 1974 World's Fair. A city built on silver mining, grown fat and prosperous after decades as a central rail link for Northwestern agriculture, Spokane has regressed since 1974 to become a gateway rather than a destination. Today, enormous and oddly empty department stores linked by covered skyways mix with 50s-style burger joints for a comfortable, if predictable, suburban atmosphere. All this middle-Americana fused with bottom-of-the-barrel prices make Spokane a convenient, inexpensive stopover. But residents still talk about the fair as Spokane's moment in the sun. The magnificent remains of Expo '74 slumber in Riverfront Park as the city dreams about bygone days.

PRACTICAL INFORMATION AND ORIENTATION

Visitors Information: Spokane Area Convention and Visitors Bureau, 201 W. Main St. (747-3230 or 800-248-3230), Exit 281 off I-90. Overflowing with literature extolling every aspect of Spokane. Open Sat. 8am-4pm, Sun. 9am-2pm; in winter Mon.-Fri. 8:30am-5pm. The **Spokane River Rest Area Visitor Center** (226-3322), at the Idaho state line, Exit 299 off I-90, offers similar pamphlets and enthusiasm. Open daily May-Sept. 8:30am-4pm.

Airport: Spokane International (624-3218 for automated info), off I-90 8 mi. southwest of town. Most major carriers serve Seattle, Portland, and beyond.

Trains: Amtrak, W. 221 1st St. (624-5144, reservations 800-USA-RAIL/872-7245), at Bernard St. 1 per day to: Chicago, IL ($219); Seattle ($67); and Portland, OR ($67). Amtrak counter open Mon.-Fri. 10am-6pm and 10pm-6am, Sat.-Sun. 10am-10pm.

Buses: Greyhound, W. 221 1st St. (tickets 624-5251; info 624-5252), at Bernard St.,in the same building as Amtrak. To Seattle (5 per day, $25) and Portland (2 per day, $36). **Northwestern Trailways** (838-5262 or 800-366-3830) shares the terminal, serving other parts of WA, OR, ID, and MT. Ticket office open daily 7:30am-7:30pm and midnight-2:30am. Student and military discounts.

Local Transit: Spokane Transit System, W. 1229 Boone Ave. (328-RIDE/7433). Serves all of Spokane, including Eastern Washington University in Cheney. 75¢, seniors and travelers with disabilities 65¢. Operates until 12:15am downtown, 9:45pm in the valley along E. Sprague Ave. All buses have bike racks.

Taxi: Checker Cab, 624-4171. **Yellow Cab,** 624-4321. Both 24hr.

Car Rental: U-Save Auto Rental, W. 918 3rd St. (455-8018), at Monroe St. Cars from $36, unlimited mileage. Must be over 21 with a major credit card. Open Mon.-Fri. 7am-7pm, Sat. 8am-5pm, Sun. 10am-5pm.

Camping Equipment: White Elephant, N. 1730 Division St. (328-3100) and E. 12614 Sprague (924-3006). All imaginable equipment sandwiched between Barbies and shotguns. Open Mon.-Thurs. and Sat. 9am-6pm, Fri. 9am-9pm.

Public Library: W. 906 Main St. (626-5336). **Internet access** available. Open Mon.-Thurs. 10am-9pm, Fri.-Sat. 10am-6pm.

Laundromat: Ye Olde Wash House Laundry and Dry Cleaners, E. 4224 Sprague (534-9859). Washe ye olde clothes for 75¢, 12min. drye 25¢.

Gay & Lesbian Community Services: 489-2206.

Travelers Aid Service, E. 140 Broadway (456-7164), at Madison St., near the bus depot. Open Mon.-Fri. 7-11:30am and 1-5pm. If they can't help, try the **Salvation Army** (325-6813).

Crisis Hotline: 838-4428. 24hr.

Poison Information: 800-732-6985. 24hr.

Senior Center: W. 1124 Sinto (327-2861). Open Mon.-Fri. 8:30am-4:30pm, Sat. 9am-1:30pm. **Elderly Services Information and Assistance:** 458-7450.

Pharmacy: Hart and Dilatush, W. 501 Sprague (624-2111), at Stevens. Open Mon.-Fri. 8am-10pm, Sat.-Sun. noon-8pm.

Urgent Care Center: Rockwood Clinic, E. 400 5th Ave. (838-2531). Open 8am-8pm. Walk-in. **Hospital: Deaconess Medical Center,** W. 800 5th St. (emergency 458-7100; info 458-5800), at Lincoln St. 24hr. emergency room.

Emergency: 911. **Police:** W. 1100 Mallon (456-2233), at Monroe St.

Post Office: W. 904 Riverside (626-6860), at Lincoln. Open Mon.-Fri. 6am-5pm. **General Delivery ZIP Code:** 99210.

Area Code: 509.

Spokane lies 280 mi. east of Seattle on I-90. Avenues run east-west parallel to the river, streets north-south, and both alternate directions one-way. The city is divided north and south by **Sprague Avenue** and east and west by **Division Street.** Downtown is the quadrant north of Sprague and west of Division, wedged between I-90 and the Spokane River. I-90 Exits 279 through 282 access Spokane. As in many western cities, street addresses begin with the compass point first, list the number second, and the street name third (e.g., W. 1200 Division). All Spokane Transit System buses start and finish their routes at the bus station at the intersection of Riverside and Wall.

ACCOMMODATIONS AND CAMPING

Stay indoors here. Spokane is very good to budget travelers.

Brown Squirrel Hostel, 920 W. 7th Ave. (838-8102). Bus #34 drops hostelers off 2 blocks away at 54th and Monroe St. Tom Baker runs a tight, clean ship in an elegant Spanish-style apartment building. Subdued, suburban atmosphere welcomes quieter travelers. 12 beds in 2 bedrooms. $12, sheets $1. Office open 4-10pm. No curfew. Walk up to 7th and make a left. 2 clean, large dogs roam premises.

Rodeway Inn City Center, W. 827 1st Ave. (838-8271 or 800-4-CHOICE/24-6423), at Lincoln St. Elevated pool in the middle of the parking lot (*everyone* will see you in your bathing suit!), great location, and pristine rooms. Free continental breakfast, evening snack, and 24hr. coffee in the office. Indoor sauna and spa, A/C, cable, 10% AAA discount. Singles $44; doubles $54. Rates fall $10 in the off-season.

Select Inn, W. 1420 2nd St. (838-2026 or 800-641-1000). Decent motel with cable (HBO), A/C, and pool. Next to railroad tracks. Ask for newly renovated rooms. Singles $36; doubles $42. $4-6 each additional person. 10% AAA discount.

Riverside State Park (456-3964, reservations 800-452-5687), 6 mi. northwest of downtown on Rifle Club Rd., off Rte. 291 or Nine Mile Rd. Take Division St. north and turn left on Francis, then follow the signs. 101 standard sites in a sparse, dry Ponderosa forest next to the river. Showers. Wheelchair access. $11.

Yogi Bear's, (747-9415 or 800-494-7275), 5 mi. west of the city. Take I-90 to Exit 272. Follow the signs along Hallett Rd. east to Thomas-Mallon Rd., then 1 mi. south.

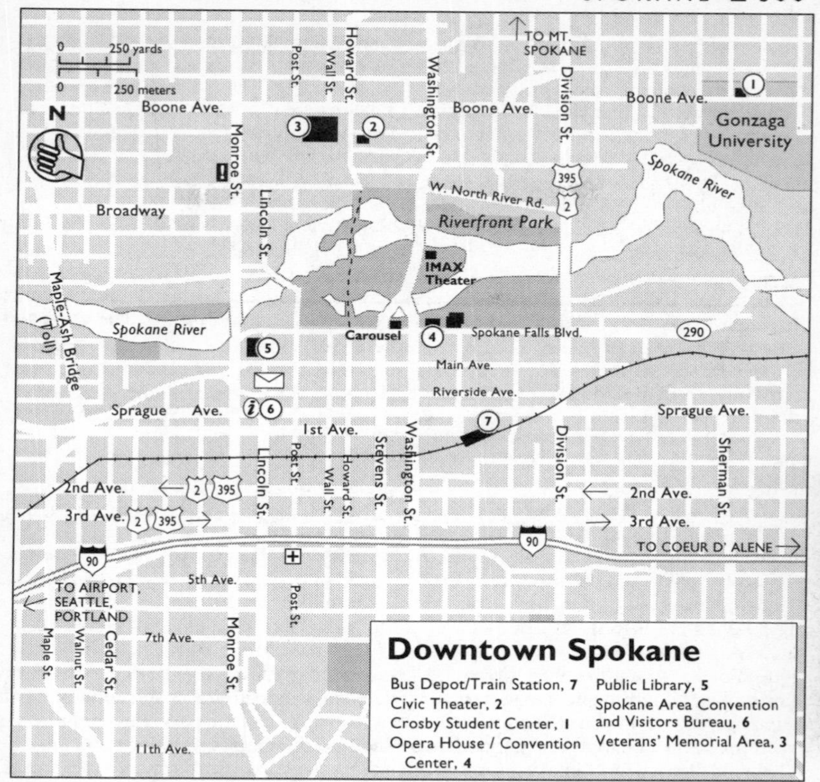

Friendly hosts run a campground so big (168 full hookups) it deserves its own ZIP code. Showers, laundry facilities, phone and cable hookups. RVs $23, tents $14, tents with electricity $15. 10% AAA discount.

FOOD

Spokane is a great place for produce. The **Spokane County Market** (482-2627), between 1st Ave. and Jefferson St., sells fresh fruit, vegetables, and baked goods (open May-Oct. Wed., Fri. and Sat. 9am-5pm, Sun. 10am-4pm). The **Green Bluff Growers Cooperative,** E. 9423 Green Bluff Rd., Colbert 99005, is an organization of 20-odd fruit and vegetable farms, marked with the big red apple sign off Day-Mountain Spokane Rd., 16 mi. northwest of town. Many farms have u-pick arrangements and are near free picnic areas. To tank up on caffeine downtown, dash into **Nordstroms** and up the escalator to the third floor, where the cafe serves 25¢ bottomless cups of coffee.

Dick's, E. 10 3rd Ave. (747-2481), at Division St. Look for the huge pink, er, panda sign near I-90 and "buy burgers by the bagful." This takeout burger phenomenon is a time warp: customers eat in their parked cars and pay prices straight out of the 50s (burgers 55¢, fries 49¢, sundaes 67¢, soft drinks 53-73¢). Since there's no breakfast menu, start off your day with a "Whammy" ($1.07), which has twice the meat and double the cheese. Dick's proves that Spokane isn't just an apple and potatoes town—it's also a *meat* and potatoes town. Always crowded, but battalions of workers move things along quickly. Open daily 9am-1am.

Europa Pizzaria, S. 125 Wall St. (455-4051). Located in the **Atrium**, a small brick building with a movie theatre and several stores. The aromatic scent of melting cheese has been known to lead movie-goers astray. Solid prices (6 in. pizza $3; sandwiches $5) in a classy joint. Plenty of vegetarian choices; dinners are more expensive. Open daily 11am-midnight.

The Il Moon Cafe at the Mars Hotel, W. 300 Sprague (747-MARS/6277). The lunar interior of this bizarre restaurant overshadows the gourmet food. Movie set experts crafted these large trees and gigantic rocks, complete with vegetation and a waterfall. There's even a casino downstairs, popular with a, um, "funky" crowd. Breakfast and dinner are pricey, but lunch is reasonable: salads, sandwiches, vegetarian and chicken dishes are $6-7. Or soak up the atmosphere over dessert and gourmet coffee ($1.25). 24hr. Lunch served Mon.-Sat. 11:30am-2:30pm.

SIGHTS

Spokane's best attractions concentrate on local history and culture. The **Cheney Cowles Memorial Museum,** W. 2316 1st Ave. (456-3931, ext. 101), houses displays on area history, from the Lewis and Clark expedition to Expo '74. Follow 2nd Ave. west out of town, turn right onto Poplar, and in two blocks you're there. Included in the price of admission is a tour of the **Campbell House**, a throwback to Spokane's "Age of Elegance." (Open Tues. and Thurs.-Sat. 10am-5pm and Wed. 10am-9pm, Sun. 1-5pm; $4, students and seniors $3, Wed. ½ price 10am-5pm, free 5-9pm.)

Riverfront Park, N. 507 Howard St. (625-6600 or 800-336-PARK/7275), just north of downtown, is Spokane's civic center and greatest asset. Developed for the 1974 World's Fair, the park's 100 acres are divided down the middle by the roaring rapids that culminate in Spokane Falls. In the park, the **IMAX Theater** (625-6686) holds a five-story movie screen and a projector the size of a Volkswagen Bug (open Sun.-Thurs. 11am-8pm; Fri-Sat. 11am-9pm; shows on the hr.; $5.25, seniors $4.75, under 18 $4.25; on Mon. $3). Another section of the park offers a full range of kiddie rides, including the exquisitely hand-carved **Looff Carousel** (open summers daily 11am-8pm, Fri.-Sat. 11am-10pm; $1 a whirl). A one-day pass ($10) covers both these attractions, plus the ferris wheel, park train, sky ride, and others. If that's not enough, you can rent in-line skates and bikes from **Quinn's** (456-6545), in the park, for $5 per hour with pads and a helmet. The park also offers ice-skating in the winter.

Manito Park, 4 W. 21st Ave. (625-6622), has four sections for both hard-core botanists and those just wishing to spend time in one of the most beautiful spots in Spokane. Check out the carp in the Nishinomiya Japanese Garden, overdose on roses on Rosehill (they bloom in late June), relax in the elegant Duncan Garden, or sniff the flowers in the David Graiser Conservatory. From downtown, go south on Stevens St. and turn left on 21st Ave. (open daily 8am-8pm; free).

The spectacular views and eastern Washington wine at the **Arbor Crest Estate,** N. 4705 Fruithill Rd. (927-9894), will make your head spin. After a self-guided tour that explores stunning vistas overlooking the valley below, sip excellent wine (both free). Take I-90 to Exit 287, travel north on Argonne over the Spokane River, turn right on Upriver Dr., proceed 1 mi., then bear left onto Fruithill Rd. Take a sharp left at the top of the hill. The chamber of commerce (see **Practical Information**) hands out various publications on area wineries. Stop by for a copy of the *Washington Winery Tour.*

Hard-core Bing Crosby devotees and other obsessive types will be drawn into the vortex of the **Crosby Student Center,** E. 502 Boone St. (campus switchboard 328-4220), at Gonzaga University. Here, in the tiny Crosbyana Room in the White Student Center, faithful fans exhibit the Bingmeister's relics and gold records. The Oscar is a replica. Amusing (open Mon.-Fri. 8:30am-4:30pm; free).

ENTERTAINMENT AND EVENTS

Spokane has the best of both worlds—minor league teams for travelers in search of small-town USA, and great nightclubs for those desperate for a big city fix. The *Pavement,* the *Spokane Spokesman-Review*'s Friday "Weekend" section, the *Spokane Chronicle*'s Friday "Empire" section, and the *Inlander* (a free local publication) give the lowdown on area happenings.

Spokane's **Indians** play single A baseball in the Seafirst Stadium at N. 602 Havana (535-2922) from June to August (tickets $3.50-6), while the **Chiefs** skate at the **Veteran's Memorial Arena** (better known as "the Arena"), 720 W. Mallon Ave. (Chiefs info and tickets 328-0450, other events 328-7000). The arena has enough seating for 12,500 whooping fans or concert goers, and hosts musical talents from James Taylor to Garth Brooks. To get to the Arena, follow signs on the Maple St. exit off I-5 (box office open Mon.-Fri. 10am-6pm). All city-sponsored events are ticketed by **Select-A-Seat** (recorded info 325-7469, tickets 325-7328; open Mon.-Fri. 8am-5pm).

Spokane also has its share of cultural institutions. **The Opera House,** W. 334 Spokane Falls Blvd. (353-6500), is home to the Spokane Symphony Orchestra and traveling Broadway shows, and special performances ranging from rock concerts like Sammy Hagar to chamber music to G. Gordon Liddy (open Mon.-Fri. 8am-5pm; sorry, combined Sammy Hagar/chamber music/G. Gordon Liddy show sold out). The **Civic Theater,** N. 1020 Howard St. (325-2507 or 800-248-3230), is opposite the Arena. Known for locally produced shows, the theater has a downstairs space for more experimental productions (tickets for musicals Fri.-Sat. $15, seniors and students $12; for plays Fri.-Sat. $12, seniors $10, students $7, discounted on Thurs. and Sun.). The **Spokane Interplayers Ensemble,** S. 174 Howard (455-7529), is a resident professional theater that performs a broad range of plays (Sept.-June, Tues.-Sat; tickets $12.50-16).

Spokane is also home to a treasure trove of budget movie theatres. The **Fox Theatre,** W. 1005 Sprague (624-0105), is the most convenient of several theatres with grand old 20s decor and major releases anywhere from one month to a year after mainstream release ($1). The box office opens at 5pm, noon in summer. The **Magic Lantern Theatre,** S. 123 Wall St. (838-4919), shows foreign, independent, and art films with the occasional major release. It is blessed with a lobby stuffed with cafe tables and Lautrec prints—the place to be on Friday nights ($5.50, seniors and students $4.50, and $3 for matinees and *Rocky Horror*, Fri.-Sat. at midnight).

Residents of Washington's dry-side capitol know good beer just as well as their soggy Seattle cousins. At the **Fort Spokane Brewery,** W. 401 Spokane Falls Blvd. (838-3809), try the house specialty, Border Run, or sample five microbrews for $4. The kitchen is open for lunch and dinner, serving burgers for under $5 (closes at 10pm). Happy hour (daily 4-7pm), features $2 microbrew pints. Live blues on Friday

Grand Coulee

Eighteen thousand years ago, the weather warmed and a little glacier blocking a lake in Montana slowly melted and gave way. The resulting flood swept across eastern Washington, gouging out layers of loess and basalt to expose the granite below. The washout, believed to have taken a little over a month, carved massive canyons called "coulees" out of a region now known as the **Channeled Scab Lands.** The largest of these coulees is appropriately named **Grand Coulee.**

From 1934 to 1942, 7000 workers toiled on the construction of the Grand Coulee Dam, a local cure for the economic woes of the Great Depression. Nearly a mile long, the behemoth is the **world's largest solid concrete structure** and irrigates the previously parched Columbia River Basin while generating more power than any other hydroelectric plant in the United States. The backed-up Columbia River formed both the massive Franklin D. Roosevelt Lake and Banks Lake, where "wet siders" from western Washington now flock for sunny lakeside recreation. Go with the flow and visit the rotund **Visitors Arrival Center** (633-9265), on Rte. 155 just north of Grand Coulee, filled to the brim with exhibits on the construction, operation, and legacy of the dam, all set to a Woody Guthrie soundtrack (open 8am-11pm). When night falls during the summer, find a seat for the spectacular and spectacularly cheesy laser show projected on the dam's tremendous face (late May-late July 10pm, Aug. 9:30pm, Sept. 8:30pm; free). Watch from the visitors centre or park your car at Crown Point Vista off Rte. 174 and tune your radio to 89.9 FM.

and Saturday and occasional big names on Thursday nights (open Mon.-Thurs. 11am-midnight, Fri.-Sat. 11am-2am, Sun. noon-midnight).

Outback Jack's, W. 321 Sprague Ave. (624-4549), is where Spokane puts on thrashing live music (Tues., Fri., Sat.), DJ dancing (Wed., Thurs., Sun.), and pool tournaments (Mon.). This self-proclaimed "Party Capital" has hosted such legends as Quiet Riot and is painted floor to ceiling an absosmurfely aggravating blue. Draft pints (Beware of Schlitz!) are $1.25 and up (open daily noon-2am). Come on, feel the noise. **Dempsey's Brass Rail,** W. 909 1st Ave. (747-5362), has a good dance floor and a lounge featuring big screen Nintendo games on the second floor. Dempsey's proclaims itself "the place to be gay." Draft pints are $1.50-3.25 (open daily 3pm-2am). **Ichabods,** 1827 Division St. (328-5720), is an "on the other side of the tracks" kind of joint. Locals and Seattle hipsters alike go for house Thursday through Saturday, techno on Tuesday, and open mic on Wednesday (open 11am-2am).

■ Near Spokane: Coeur d'Alene, ID

When French and English fur traders passed through northern Idaho in the late 1800s, they attempted to trade with uninterested local Native Americans. The trappers' French-speaking Iroquois guides dubbed the dismissive natives "people with pointed hearts," which the trappers shortened to "hearts of awls"—Coeur d'Alene (kur-duh-LANE). Today, locals call Coeur d'Alene "CDA." Gaggles of resort-bound golfers and lakeside loungers do little to mar the rustic beauty of this town 20 minutes from Spokane—no matter how many newcomers, the deep blue waters of Lake Coeur d'Alene offer a serene escape.

Practical Information Get info at the **North Idaho Visitors Center,** 200 Sherman St. (667-4990; open Sun.-Tues. 9am-5pm, Wed.-Sat. 9am-7pm). The **bus station** lies at 1527 Northwest Blvd. (664-3343), 1 mi. north of the lake (open daily 8am-8pm). **Greyhound** serves: Boise (1 per day, 11hr., $65); Spokane (3 per day, 45min., $9); Lewiston, ID (2 per day, 3hr., $30); and Missoula, MT (3 per day, 4hr., $31). **U-Save Auto Rental,** 501 Northwest Blvd. (664-1712), rents cars (open Mon.-Fri. 9am-4pm, Sat. 8am-3pm, Sun. 10am-4pm; $30 per day, 20¢ per mi. over 200). **Crisis Services** can be reached at 664-1443 (24hr.). Coeur d'Alene's **post office** is at 111 N. 7th St. (664-8126), 5 blocks east of the chamber of commerce (open Mon.-Fri. 8:30am-5pm); the **ZIP code** is 83814, and the **area code** is 208.

Accommodations, Camping Cheap lodgings are hard to find in this resort town. Try the motels on Sherman Ave., on the eastern outskirts of the city. **Budget Saver Motel,** 1519 Sherman Ave. (667-9505), offers roomy rooms with cable (singles $35; doubles $42-47; late Sept.-early June $30-40). **Star Motel,** 1516 E. Sherman Ave. (664-5035), fits phones and TVs with HBO in tiny, tidy cubicles (singles $40; doubles $45). For bed and breakfast info, call the **B&B Information Center** at 667-5081 or 800-773-0323. Some are fairly reasonable at about $60 a night.

Camping is the way to go for cheap lodging in Coeur d'Alene. There are five **campgrounds** within 20 mi. of town. **Robin Hood RV Park,** 703 Lincoln Way (664-2306, 800-280-CAMP/2267), lies within walking distance of downtown and just a few blocks from a swimmable beach (showers, laundry, hookups, no evil sheriffs; tent sites $15.50; RVs $17.50). There are a few first-come, first-served national forest campgrounds in the area: popular **Beauty Creek,** 10 mi. south from Robin Hood along the lake, boasts the trailhead to the much acclaimed Caribou Ridge Trail #79, and **Bell Bay,** on Lake Coeur d'Alene (off U.S. 95 south, then 14 mi. to Forest Service Rd. 545), has 26 sites and good fishing. All sites cost $9 and have access to potable water and pit toilets; the campgrounds are generally open May through September. Call the **Fernan Ranger District Office,** 2502 E. Sherman (769-3000), for details on these and other Forest Service campgrounds (open Mon.-Fri. 7:30am-4pm).

Food Coeur d'Alene has, inexplicably, oysters aplenty. For the best and most entertaining shellfish slurp, go to **Cricket's Restaurant and Oyster Bar** (765-1990), on Sherman Ave. (the one with the car on the roof), to sup on six oysters ($7.50) and watch the toy train chug by on raised tracks (open Mon.-Fri. 11am-10pm, Sat.-Sun. 11am-11pm). If you like your snacks without shells, "Wake up and Live" at the **Java Cafe,** 324 Sherman Ave. (667-0010). Sip gourmet coffee, eat confetti eggs for breakfast ($4), or gourmet pizza for lunch ($4-5; open daily 7am-10pm). On weekends, roll with your crew to the **Parkside Bistro,** bordering the city park on Mullan Ave., for crispy barbecue, burger, and fries—you know, the works (open daily 11am-1am).

Get a dose of Thai flavor and hilarious marketing at **Mad Mary's,** 1801 Sherman Ave. (667-3267), where Mary chops, dices, yells and generally makes herself heard. Let her light your fire with $7.50 spicy chicken livers or more traditional *pad thai* ($8.50-11.95). The portions are huge (open Tues.-Thurs. 11am-9pm, Fri. 11am-10pm, Sat.-Sun. noon-whenever). Or head north and turn right for **Tubs Coffee House,** 313 Coeur d'Alene Lake Dr., where locals munch on 7 in. pesto pizzas ($4) and sip perfect espresso drinks. The tubs in question are private, cedar-enclosed outdoor hot tubs ($15 per hr.; open daily 6am-10pm).

Sights and Activities The lake is Coeur d'Alene's *raison d'être.* Hike 2 mi. up **Tubbs Hill** to a scenic vantage point, or head for the **Coeur d'Alene Resort** and walk along the **world's longest floating boardwalk** (3300 ft.). You can tour the lake on a **Lake Coeur d'Alene Cruise** (765-4000) and see the world's only floating golf green. Oooooh. (Departs from the downtown dock May-Sept. 1:30, 3:30, and 5:30pm; 90min.; $10.75, seniors $9.75, kids $5.75.) Or hit the water on your own terms by renting a canoe or a pedal boat at the city dock ($7 per hr., $20 per ½ day, $35 first whole day, $15 per day thereafter). A 3 mi. bike/foot path follows the lake shore. **Four Seasons Outfitting,** 200 Sherman Ave. (765-2863), organizes horse rides (first 45min. $13, 3hr. $36) and a variety of other expensive outdoor activities.

Pullman

Pullman's two main attractions are the strange, undulating, green-and-yellow wheat and lentil-carpeted hills of southeast Washington's Palouse (puh-LOOZ) region and the enormous **Washington State University (WSU)** ("Wazoo," to its friends, fans, and student body), alma mater of cartoonist Gary Larson and cultural oasis in a desert of agriculture. With WSU Cougar banners on every street light—the 20,000-student university is home to PAC 10 football and basketball teams—the college *is* the town. Roll into the countryside to escape the all-consuming football fever.

PRACTICAL INFORMATION

Visitors Information: The **Pullman Chamber of Commerce,** N 415 Grand Ave. (334-3565 or 800-365-6948), doles out free **maps** of Pullman and the surrounding Palouse, and will tell you *all* about Pullman's favorite vegetable, the lentil. Open Mon.-Fri. 9am-5pm, Sat. 10am-2pm.

Buses: Northwestern Trailways, NW 1002 Nye (334-1412). To: Boise (1 per day; $39); Seattle (2 per day $35 and $39); and Spokane (2 per day; $13 and $22.75). Open Mon.-Fri. 6am-4:30pm.

Public Transportation: The two lines of **Pullman Transit,** NW 775 Guy St. (332-6535), run between the WSU campus and the downtown area. 35¢, seniors and under 18 20¢. Operates Mon.-Fri. 6:50am-5:50pm.

Taxi: Moscow-Pullman Cab, (208-883-4744). Taxis Sun.-Thurs. 7am-midnight, Fri.-Sat. 7am-2am.

Car Rental: U-Save Car Rental, S 1115 Grand Ave. (334-5195), rents cars for $32 per day, 20¢ per mi. after 100. Must be 21 with a major credit card. Open Mon.-Fri. 8am-5:30pm, Sat. 9am-4:30pm.

Laundromat: Betty's Brite and White, N 1235 Grand Ave. (332-3477).

Senior Services: Pullman Senior Center, SE 325 Paradise St. (332-1933), in City Hall. Open Mon.-Sat. 11am-4pm.
Hospital: Pullman Memorial Hospital, NE 1125 Washington Ave. (332-2541).
Pharmacy: Corner Drug Store, E 255 Main St. (334-1565), at Kamiaken.
Crisis Line: 332-1505. 24hr. **Rape Crisis: Rape Resource,** 332-4357. 24hr.
Emergency: 911. **Ambulance and Police:** 332-2521. The **police station** is behind City Hall.
Post Office: S 1135 Grand Ave. (334-3212). Open Mon.-Fri. 8:30am-5pm, Sat. 8:30-11:30am. **General Delivery ZIP Code:** 99163.
Area Code: 509.

Pullman lies at the junction of Routes 27 and 272. U.S. 195, running from Spokane south to Lewiston, ID, bypasses the city to the west. Spokane lies 70 mi. north. Pullman lies 8 mi. west of Moscow, ID, on Rte. 270.

ACCOMMODATIONS AND CAMPING

The steady stream of students through Pullman fosters a decent selection of moderately priced, no-frills motels. Rooms are easy to find, except on home football weekends (when rooms are booked one year in advance; fans have bequeathed motel rooms to their children in their wills) and during commencement (the first week of May).

Nendels Inn, 915 SE Main St. (332-2646), on the way to Moscow. Clean rooms 1 block from WSU. Singles $35; doubles $45-49.
The American Travel Inn Motel, S 515 Grand Ave. (334-3500), on U.S. 195. 35 spacious, spic-and-span rooms, with A/C, cable, laundry facilities, and a nice pool. Singles $40; doubles $45.
The Manor Lodge Motel, SE 455 Paradise (334-2511), at Main St. The pleasant innkeepers offer clean rooms with cable, refrigerators, and microwaves. The decor is Brady Bunch chic. Office open 7am-11pm; after hours ring night bell. Singles $37; doubles $42.
Kamiak Butte Park, 11 mi. north of Pullman on U.S. 27, offers 10 forested campsites with water, toilets, and a view of the Palouse for $5.

FOOD

WSU has spawned a thriving gaggle of cheap eats. Take your pick from hip cafes, a university-run dairy, and a classic drive-in.

Basilios, E 337 Main St. (334-7663). There has been no end to business in this fabulously frescoed joint since its doors opened in 1996. Order a plate of pesto and penne ($4.25) or just about any other Italian dish. Open Mon.-Thurs. 7am-10pm, Fri. 7am-11pm, Sat. 11am-11pm, Sun. 11am-10pm.
Ferdinand's (335-4014), on the WSU campus. From Stadium Way, turn toward the tennis courts onto South Fairway and follow it to the Food Quality Building. Makes everything with milk from WSU's dairy. Ferdinand's Cougar Gold cheese ($11 for a 30 oz. tin) may be Pullman's biggest attraction. One excellent ice cream cone ($1) and a large glass of milk will do your body good. Open Mon.-Fri. 9:30am-4:30pm.
Cougar Country Drive-In, N 760 Grand Ave. (332-7829), a 10min. walk from downtown. Motor to the drive-through or slide into one of the booths inside. This popular student hangout offers burgers wider than Whoppers with their own special sauce ($2.39). They've also got shakes as thick as mud ("dozens of flavors" $1.49). Open daily 10am-11pm.

SIGHTS AND ENTERTAINMENT

There are nearly as many bars in Pullman as there are lentils in the Palouse. Frat boys and athletes get tough at **Shakers,** NE 600 Colorado St. (332-2250) and the **Cougar Cottage,** N 1000 Colorado St. (332-6818), where regulars have their own mugs. By midnight, students stagger one block up the street to **The Zoo,** a collegiate dance joint. Off campus, **Rico's,** E 200 Main (332-6566; open Mon.-Sat. 11:30am-2am), and **Pete's Bar and Grill,** SE 1100 Johnson Ave. (334-4200; open Mon.-Sat. 11am-9pm, Sun. 4-9pm) are local favorites.

Near the end of August of each year, the **National Lentil Festival** explodes onto the Pullman scene with a parade, live music, a 5km fun run, and so much more. The centerpiece of the festival remains the lentil food fair, showcasing lentil pancakes and lentil ice cream. Nearly all the lentils grown in the U.S. come from the Palouse. The festival gained national recognition a few years back when it became the first engagement ever cancelled by Jerry Seinfeld. The festival remains a small-town tribute to a major player in the local economy. For more info, write National Lentil Festival, N 415 Grand Ave., Pullman 99163, or call the chamber of commerce at 334-3565 or 800-365-6948.

OUTDOORS

Pullman's gentle terrain and the broad, sweeping vistas of Washington's majestic Palouse region make the area ideal for exploration by bicycle or automobile. Professional photographers gather here annually to capture the purple-tinted prairies and wheat fields. In 1996, the Palouse made its film debut in a Nissan commercial and the Robin Williams film *Toys.* **Kamiak** and **Steptoe Buttes,** north of town off Rte. 27, both make enjoyable day trips. Pack a picnic lunch and head for the hills.

From this basin of baking summer temperatures, a glimpse of the **Blue Mountains,** 25 mi. south of Pullman, may spark a yearning for high, cool forests. A good approach is along Rte. 128 from the town of **Pomeroy,** a 40 mi. drive southwest of Pullman. Follow U.S. 195 south to Clarkston, and then proceed on U.S. 12 west. This area, including the vast, remote **Wenaha-Tucannon Wilderness,** is administered by the **Pomeroy Ranger District** of Umatilla National Forest, Rte. 1, Box 53-F, Pomeroy 99347 (843-1891; open Mon.-Fri. 7:45am-4:30pm). Information is also available at the **Walla Walla Ranger District** office at W 1415 Rose St., Walla Walla 98362 (522-6290; open Mon.-Fri. 7:45am-4:30pm). The Snake River is also accessible from Pullman. Ask at the visitors center for directions.

■ Near Pullman: Moscow, ID

Moscow (MOS-ko) is Pullman's conjoined twin, fused at the spinal column by Highway 8. Although there's not a lot of revolutionary excitement fermenting in town, Moscovites take pride in their sense of community and in the local branch of the University of Idaho. When asked what to do in Moscow (MOS-ko) for only two hours, one resident answers, "I'd just walk down Main Street." The helpful **Moscow Chamber of Commerce,** 411 S. Main St. (882-1800 or 800-380-1801), may have a few more ideas (open Mon.-Fri. 9am-5pm).

As one might expect, **The Beanery,** 602 S. Main St. (882-7646), serves great coffee. But it serves all three meals, too—get a full breakfast for $5, or a hefty Belgian waffle for $3, from 6:30am-11am. After 11am, it's sandwich time ($3.50-4); add $1.50 for soup or salad and coffee or Coke. Dinners are more expensive (open Mon.-Sat. 6:30am-7pm, Sun. 8am-3pm). This local hangout serves more than the "liberal, commie, hippy fringe" and sponsors live jazz every Thursday at lunch. **Mikey's Gyros,** 527 S. Main St. (882-0780), whips up Greek grub for under $4 (open Sun.-Thurs. 11am-8pm, Fri.-Sat. 11am-9pm; in summer closed Sun). **Casa d'Oro,** 415 S. Main St. (883-0536), is a cantina that somehow avoids cheesiness, even though piñatas and sombreros hang from the walls. Dinner entrees range from $7-9; locals come for the margaritas. For a good deal, split a two-burrito meal, or just order an appetizer (open Sun.-Thurs. 11am-10pm, Fri. and Sat. 11am-11pm).

Two events exemplify why Moscovites call their town the **Heart of the Arts. The Lionel Hampton Jazz Festival** sizzles during the third week in February. Concerts and workshops are given by some of the country's best jazz musicians, including Lou Rawls and, of course, Lionel Hampton. Call 885-7212 or (800) 345-7402 for more information. On the first weekend of May, the **Renaissance Fair** brings out the 16th-century Italian courtesan in everyone. Call the chamber of commerce for more info.

The Camas Winery, 110 S. Main (882-0214 or 800-616-0214), has free tastings and an informative display (open Tues.-Sat., noon-6pm, except during University of Idaho's spring break). **Mingles Bar and Grill,** 102 S. Main (882-2050), is cool, dark, and full of pool tables. Their extensive bar food collection (pizza, burgers, chili, and salads) is reasonably priced ($4.50-6). Domestic pitchers are $4.50 (restaurant open Mon.-Fri. 11am-2am, Sat.-Sun. 9:30am-midnight; bar open daily 11am-2am).

Oregon

Over one hundred years ago, entire families liquidated their possessions and sank life savings into covered wagons, corn meal, and oxen, high-tailing it to Oregon in search of prosperity and a new way of life. Today, Oregon remains as popular a destination as ever for backpackers, bicyclists, road warriors, fishers, beachcrawlers, and families alike. The coastal towns of Newport and Cannon Beach are enticing oases, and the caves and cliffs of Oregon's coastline are a siren call to tourists. But the coast is just part of the full Oregonian experience; other fabulous attractions lace the state's interior. Majestic Mt. Hood in the Cascade Range, volcanic cinder-cones near Crater Lake National Park, Ashland's Shakespeare festival, and North America's deepest gorge make an enormous outdoor playground out of Oregon. Both town and country are worth a closer look; Oregon's cities are as scenic and challenging as its wilderness. Portland is casual and idiosyncratic—its name was determined by a coin toss (one more turn of a coin and it would have been "Boston, Oregon")—while the college town of Eugene embraces hippies and Deadheads. Bend, a tiny interior city with a young, athletic population, competes for the title of liveliest town. From excellent microbrews to snow-capped peaks, a visit to Oregon is still worth crossing the Continental Divide.

PRACTICAL INFORMATION

Capital: Salem.

Visitors Information: Oregon Tourism Commission, 775 Summer St. NE, Salem 97310 (800-547-7842; fax 503-986-0001). **Oregon State Parks,** 1115 Commercial St. NE, Salem 97310-1001 (503-378-6305 or 800-551-6949; fax 378-6447). For **reservations** in most state parks, call 800-452-5687. **Department of Fish and Wildlife,** P.O. Box 59, Portland 97207 (503-229-5222 for a recording of fishing seasons and legal sites). For a complete list of licensing restrictions and fees, send away for *Sport Fishing Regulations, Ocean Salmon Sport Fishing Regulations, Game Bird Regulations,* or *Big Game Regulations.* Contact the **Oregon State Marine Board,** 435 Commercial St. NE, Salem 97310 (503-378-8587; fax 378-4597) for info on boating. **Statewide Road Conditions:** 541-889-3999.

Population: 3,230,735. **State Motto:** "She flies with her own wings." **Nickname:** Beaver State. **State Song:** "Oregon, My Oregon." **State Flower:** Oregon Grape. **State Animal:** Beaver. **State Fish:** Chinook Salmon. **State Rock:** Thunderegg. **State Gemstone:** Oregon Sunstone. **Land Area:** 97,060 sq. mi.

Emergency: 911.

Time Zone: Mostly Pacific (1hr. behind Mountain, 2hr. behind Central, 3hr. behind Eastern). A small southeastern section is Mountain (1hr. ahead of Pacific, 1hr. behind Central, 2hr. behind Eastern).

Postal Abbreviation: OR.

Sales Tax: None.

Drinking Age: 21.

Traffic Laws: Seatbelts required. Also, state law prohibits self-serve gas stations.

Area Codes: Portland and the Willamette Valley 503, everywhere else 541.

OREGON

Portland

Still the quietest, mellowest, and rainiest big city on the West Coast, Portland is steadily becoming more populated and more popular. Even so, downtown is a spotless pedestrian paradise. Like the famed poster depicting local tavern owner "Bud" Clark in a trenchcoat flashing a public sculpture (he was shortly thereafter elected mayor), Portland has nothing to hide. The city government keeps it that way, regulating building height to preserve views and writing zoning laws that require all new buildings to have street-level retail space. In fact, despite its substantial size, Portland sometimes feels like a pleasantly overgrown town.

Driven indoors for the better part of the year by the stubborn winter rain, Portlanders have developed a love of art, music, and good beer. It is these common pursuits that bring the community together in endless theaters and pubs. Funded by a one-percent tax on new construction, Portland has fostered a growing body of outdoor sculpture and a series of outdoor concerts. Local artists fill galleries and cafes with paint and plaster, much of which spills out onto muralled walls and street art. Improvisational theaters are in constant production, and Portland's performing arts put the edge on cutting edge. The city's venerable symphony orchestra, the oldest in the western United States, tops all this artistry off.

Knowing that good beverages are essential to the full enjoyment of any event, the city's first-rate flock of small breweries pump out barrels of the nation's finest ale. Beer in hand, Portlanders browse the stuffed interior of Powell's Books, the largest bookstore in the country. But that's only when it's raining. On rare sunny days, Portland's consummate hikers, bikers, and runners take advantage of their area's sylvan surroundings. The Willamette River and its wide park border downtown, and dense forests at the city's edge cloak miles of manicured hiking trails. With a bit of effort, Portlanders can journey to the edens of Mt. Hood in the east or the Pacific shore in the west—on any July day near Portland, they can ski in the morning, watch the sun drop into the sea from an empty beach, and return to town in time to catch live jazz.

PRACTICAL INFORMATION

Visitors Information: Portland/Oregon Visitors Association, 25 SW Salmon St. (222-2223 or 800-345-3214; http://www.pova.com), at Front St. in the Two World Trade Center complex. From I-5, follow the signs for City Center. Extensive info on Portland and its surroundings; worker bees explain the free *Portland Tour Map, Official Visitors Guide,* and *Portland Book,* which has maps, historical trivia, and comprehensive info on local attractions. Open Mon.-Fri. 9am-5pm, Sat. 10am-4pm, Sun. 10am-2pm; closed Sun. Sept.-April. **Portland Parks and Recreation,** 1120 SW 5th Ave. #1302 (823-2223). Open Mon.-Fri. 8am-5pm.

Airport: Portland International Airport, 7000 NE Airport Way (335-1234). For transportation to and from the airport, see **Getting There and Getting Around,** p. 410.

Train: Amtrak, 800 NW 6th Ave. (recording 273-4866; Union Station 273-4865; national reservation line 800-USA-RAIL/872-7245), at Hoyt St. in Union Station. To: Seattle (3 per day, $29); Eugene (2 per day, $21); and Spokane (1 per day, $67). Open daily 7:45am-9pm.

Buses: Greyhound, 550 NW 6th Ave. (243-2357 or 800-231-2222), at Glisan. To: Seattle (12 per day, $21.50); Eugene (11 per day, $143); Spokane (4 per day, $37); and Boise (4 per day, $329). Lockers $2 for 6hr. Ticket window open daily 5am-11:45pm. Station open daily 5am-1am. **Amtrak** (see above), 200 yd. from Greyhound, runs buses to Eugene (3 per day, $20) and a bus-train combo to Boise via Seattle ($51). **Green Tortoise** (800-867-8647) picks up at 616 SW College Ave. at 6th Ave. Confirm 2 days in advance. To Seattle (Tues. and Sat. 4pm, $15) and San Francisco (Sun. and Thurs. 12:30pm, $39).

Public Transportation: Tri-Met, Pioneer Courthouse Sq., 701 SW 6th Ave. (238-7433). Open Mon.-Fri. 7:30am-5:30pm. Several 24hr. recorded information numbers available: **Call-A-Bus** info system (231-3199); fare info (231-3198); updates, changes, and weather-related problems (231-3197); TDD information (238-5811); senior and disabled services (238-4952; open Mon.-Fri. 7:30am-5:30pm); lost and found (238-4855; open Mon.-Fri. 9am-5pm). Service generally 5am-midnight, reduced on weekends. Fare $1.05-1.35, ages 7-18 80¢, over 65 and disabled 50¢; free in Fareless Square downtown (see **Getting There and Getting Around,** p. 410). All-day pass $3.25. All buses have bike racks ($5 lifetime permit available at area bike stores). **MAX** (228-7246), based at the Customer Service Center is an efficient, light-rail train running between Gresham in the east and downtown. Same fares as Tri-Met. Runs 4:30am-11:30pm toward downtown and 5:30am-12:30am toward Gresham on weekdays (starts slightly later on weekends). More MAX lines toward Beaverton planned and under construction.

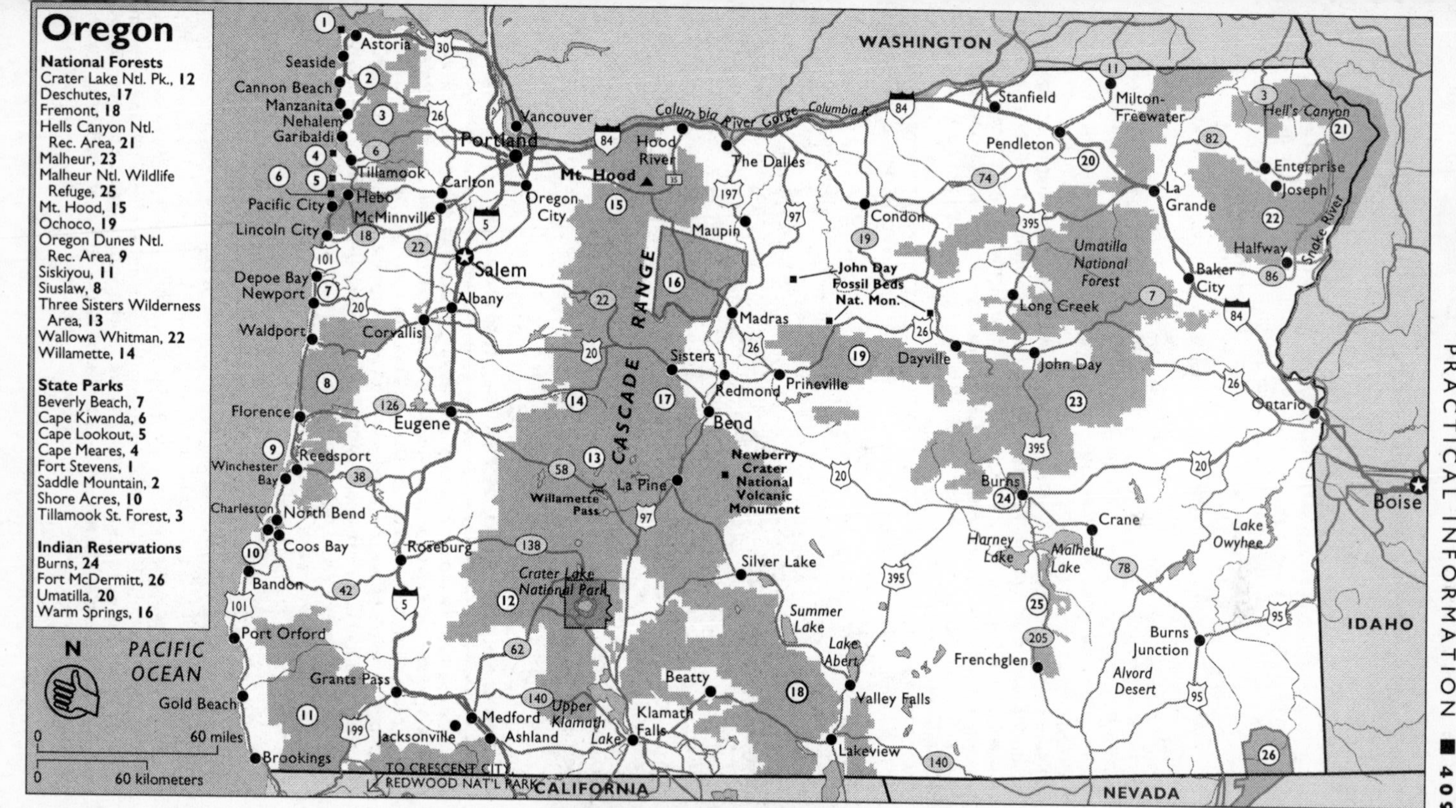
Oregon
National Forests
Crater Lake Ntl. Pk., 12
Deschutes, 17
Fremont, 18
Hells Canyon Ntl. Rec. Area, 21
Malheur, 23
Malheur Ntl. Wildlife Refuge, 25
Mt. Hood, 15
Ochoco, 19
Oregon Dunes Ntl. Rec. Area, 9
Siskiyou, 11
Siuslaw, 8
Three Sisters Wilderness Area, 13
Wallowa Whitman, 22
Willamette, 14
State Parks
Beverly Beach, 7
Cape Kiwanda, 6
Cape Lookout, 5
Cape Meares, 4
Fort Stevens, 1
Saddle Mountain, 2
Shore Acres, 10
Tillamook St. Forest, 3
Indian Reservations
Burns, 24
Fort McDermitt, 26
Umatilla, 20
Warm Springs, 16
N
PACIFIC OCEAN
0
60 miles
0
60 kilometers
WASHINGTON
IDAHO
NEVADA
CALIFORNIA
Astoria
Seaside
Cannon Beach
Manzanita
Nehalem
Garibaldi
Tillamook
Hebo
Pacific City
McMinnville
Lincoln City
Depoe Bay
Newport
Waldport
Florence
Reedsport
Winchester Bay
Charleston
North Bend
Coos Bay
Bandon
Port Orford
Gold Beach
Brookings
Grants Pass
Jacksonville
Medford
Ashland
Roseburg
Eugene
Corvallis
Albany
Salem
Carlton
Portland
Vancouver
Oregon City
Mt. Hood
Hood River
The Dalles
Columbia River Gorge
Columbia R.
Maupin
Madras
CASCADE RANGE
Sisters
Redmond
Prineville
Bend
La Pine
Willamette Pass
Newberry Crater National Volcanic Monument
Crater Lake National Park
Upper Klamath Lake
Klamath Falls
Beatty
Silver Lake
Summer Lake
Lake Abert
Valley Falls
Lakeview
TO CRESCENT CITY, REDWOOD NAT'L PARK
Condon
John Day Fossil Beds Nat. Mon.
Dayville
John Day
Long Creek
Umatilla National Forest
Stanfield
Pendleton
Milton-Freewater
La Grande
Baker City
Halfway
Enterprise
Joseph
Hell's Canyon
Snake River
Ontario
Boise
Burns
Harney Lake
Malheur Lake
Crane
Lake Owyhee
Frenchglen
Burns Junction
Alvord Desert

OREGON

Taxi: Broadway Cab, 227-1234. **Radio Cab,** 227-1212. Airport to downtown $22-25. Airport to Hostelling International Portland $20. Both 24hr.

Car Rental: Rent-a-Wreck, 1800 SE M.L. King Blvd. (233-2492 or 888-499-9111). From $15 per day, $105 weekly with 75 free mi. per day. Must be 25 or older with credit card. Open Mon.-Fri. 8am-6pm, Sat. 9am-2pm. **Dollar Rent-a-Car** (800-800-4000), at airport. From $32 per day, $135 weekly with unlimited free mileage. Must be over 25 with credit card or 21-25 with proof of insurance ($19 per day surcharge). Open 24hr. **Practical Rent-A-Car,** 1315 NE Sandy Blvd. (224-8110). Transport from airport. From $24 per day, 15¢ per mi. after 100 or $27 per day with unlimited mileage. Must be 21 or older with credit card, or under 21 with proof of full coverage insurance (daily surcharge). Open Mon.-Fri. 8am-5:30pm, Sat. 9am-4pm; winter Mon.-Fri. 8am-5:30pm, Sat. 9am-noon.

Car Club: AAA Automobile Club of Oregon, 600 SW Market St. (222-6777 or 800-AAA-HELP/222-4357). Open Mon.-Fri. 8am-5pm.

Library: 801 SW 10th Ave. (248-5123). Open Tues.-Wed. 12:30-8:30pm, Thurs.-Sat. 10am-5:30pm.

Tickets: Ticketmaster (224-4400), for OR and WA only. Also **Fastixx,** 224-8499.

Laundromat: Springtime Thrifty Cleaners and Laundry, 2942 SE Hawthorne Blvd. (232-4353), across from the hostel. Wash $1, 10min. dry 25¢. Open Mon.-Fri. 7:30am-10pm, Sat.-Sun. 8am-10pm. **City Laundry** (224-4204), at NW 14th and Glisan. Attendant always on duty. Same day wash and fold (95¢ per lb.). Wash $1, 10min. dry 25¢. Open daily 7am-10pm.

Swimming Pools: Aquatics Office (823-5130). Lists Portland's 10 public pools.

Ski Conditions: Timberline, 222-2211. **Ski Bowl,** 222-2695. **Mt. Hood Meadows,** 227-7669. **Weather/Road Conditions:** 541-889-3999.

Crisis and Suicide Hotline: 215-7082. 24hr.

Women's Services: West Women's Hotel Shelter, 2010 NW Kearney St. (224-7718). **Women's Crisis Line:** 235-5333. 24hr.

AIDS Hotline: 223-2437. Open Mon.-Fri. 10am-9pm, Sat.-Sun. noon-6pm.

Gay and Lesbian Information: Phoenix Rising, 620 SW 5th Ave. #710 (223-8299). Counseling and referral for gay, bisexual, transgendered, and transsexual people. Open Mon.-Sat. 9am-9pm.

Senior Services: Aging and Disabilities Helpline (248-3646). Open Mon.-Fri. 8am-5pm. **Oregon Retired Persons' Pharmacy,** 9800 SW Nimbus Ave., Beaverton (orders 800-456-2277, info 646-3500). Open Mon.-Fri. 8am-5:30pm, Sat. 9am-1pm.

Emergency: 911. **Police:** 1111 SW 2nd Ave. (230-2121 for non-emergency response, 823-4636 for info). **Fire:** 55 SW Ash St. (823-3700).

Post Office: 715 NW Hoyt St. (800-ASK-USPS/275-8777). **General Delivery ZIP Code:** 97208-9999. Open Mon.-Fri. 7am-6:30pm, Sat. 8:30am-5pm.

Area Code: 503.

GETTING THERE AND GETTING AROUND

Portland lies in the northwest corner of Oregon, where the Willamette (wi-LAM-it) River flows into the Columbia River. **I-5** connects Portland with San Francisco and Seattle; **I-84** follows the route of the Oregon Trail through the Columbia River Gorge, along the Oregon-Washington border, toward Boise. West of Portland, **U.S. 30** follows the Columbia downstream to Astoria, but **U.S. 26** is the fastest way to reach the coast. **I-405** runs just west of downtown to link I-5 with U.S. 30 and 26.

The cheapest way to reach downtown from the **Portland International Airport** is to take Tri-Met bus #12 (a 45min. ride, 4 per hour), which passes south through town on SW 5th Ave. ($1.05). **Raz Tranz** (246-3301) provides an airport shuttle that stops at most major hotels downtown (2 per hr.; fare $8.50, ages 6-12 $2).

Portland is divided into five districts. All street signs are labeled by their districts: N, NE, NW, SE, and SW. **Burnside Street** divides the city into north and south, while east and west are separated by the Willamette River. **Williams Avenue** cuts off a corner of the northeast sector, called simply "North." **Southwest Portland** is known as **downtown,** but also includes the southern end of historic **Old Town** and a slice of the wealthier **West Hills.** In the middle of downtown, between SW 5th and 6th Ave., lies the **transit mall,** home to the Tri-Met bus system and closed to all but pedestrians and

buses. Almost all downtown streets are one-way, with few legal left turns. Parking is plentiful but expensive: meters are 85¢ per hr., usually limited to one to three hours. The city's **Smart Park** decks are common and well marked (1st 3hr. 75¢ per hr., over 3hr. $3 per hr., after 6pm $1.50, weekends $3 per day). Tri-Met is the best choice when spending the day downtown. For walkers, jaywalking is risky: cars will stop for you, but so will police (and they will ticket jaywalkers); it's a bit like using an umbrella—everyone will know you're not from Portland.

Old Town, in **Northwest Portland,** encompasses most of the historic part of the city. The southernmost blocks of the quarter, around W. Burnside, are best not walked alone at night. Overlapping with Old Town and stretching north is the up-and-coming **Pearl District,** a quickly revitalizing industrial zone. Farther north and west, NW 21st and NW 23rd St., collectively known as **Nob Hill,** are hot spots for boutique shopping. **Southeast Portland** is host to residential areas of all classes, parks, factories, and local businesses. The wide green quads and brick halls of **Reed College** lie deep within Southeast Portland, but perhaps the best known part of Southeast is **Hawthorne Boulevard** with its rich collection of cafes, stores, theaters, and restaurants. **North** and **Northeast Portland** are chiefly residential, punctuated by a few small, quiet parks, though North Portland is also the site of the **University of Portland.** Drug traffickers base their operations in Northeast Portland; parts of the area are dangerous and there is little reason to go there.

The award-winning **Tri-Met bus system** boasts a logical organization, making it one of the most rider-friendly public transit systems in America. In the transit mall, 31 covered passenger shelters serve as stops and info centers. Southbound buses pick up passengers along SW 5th Ave.; northbound passengers board on SW 6th Ave. Bus routes fall into seven service areas, each with its own individual "Lucky Charm": orange deer, yellow rose, green leaf, brown beaver, blue snow, red salmon, and purple raindrop. Shelters and buses are color-coded for their region. A few buses with black numbers on white backgrounds cut through town north-south or east-west.

Most of downtown, from NW Hoyt St. in the north to I-405 in the west and south and the Willamette River in the east, is in **"Fareless Square,"** where buses and MAX are free. Monthly passes, bus maps, and schedules are available at the Tri-Met Customer Assistance Office in Pioneer Courthouse Square (for directions and fares outside this zone, see **Practical Information,** p. 408).

PUBLICATIONS

The city's major daily newspaper, the *Oregonian,* (nicknamed the *Boregonian* by locals), lists upcoming events in its Friday edition. Portland's favorite free cultural reader, *Willamette Week* (published on Wed.), is a reliable, if somewhat uninspiring, guide to local events. The free monthly magazine *Anodyne* has been rated one of the best new start-ups and offers left-of-center listings. For a look at music and culture even farther from the fray, turn to *PDXS* (biweekly, free). *The Rocket* is the most comprehensive music publication (bimonthly, free). Yuppies find their interests represented weekly in *Ourtown,* which also lists downtown goings-on. Biweekly *Just-Out* caters to gay, lesbian, bisexual, transsexual and transgendered interests throughout Oregon. *Willamette Week, PDXS,* and *The Rocket* all have complete club listings, and are available on street corners, in restaurants, and in hostels.

ACCOMMODATIONS AND CAMPING

Although downtown is studded with Marriott-esque hotels and the smaller motels are steadily raising prices, Portland still welcomes the budget traveler. The **Hostelling International Portland** is an old standby and offers quality affordable housing closest to downtown. Many other options lie farther from downtown, but it's nonetheless wise to make reservations early. Portland accommodations fill in a flash, especially during the Rose Festival and frequent conventions. Camping spots are distant, but nature abounds; there are no gravel RV-only sites around Portland.

Hostelling International—Portland (HI-AYH), 3031 SE Hawthorne Blvd. (236-3380), at 31st Ave. Take bus #14 (brown beaver). Interesting travelers come to Portland, and this is the place to meet them. Cheerful, clean, and crowded. Front porch, side yard, kitchen facilities, laundromat across the street. All-you-can-eat pancakes every morning (a paltry $1) and free pastries from a local bakery. Open daily 7:30-11am and 4-11pm. 34 beds. No curfew. $15, nonmembers $18. Fills early in summer (women's rooms go first), so reserve a spot (credit card required) or plan to arrive at 4pm to get one of 12-15 walk-in beds. HI Members only June-Sept.

McMenamins Edgefield Hostel, 2126 SW Halsey St., Troutdale (669-8610 or 800-669-8610), 20min. east of Portland. Take I-84 east to exit 16A, take a right, then a left at the first light onto Halsey St. The hostel is ¼ mi. down on right. McMenamins converted this farm into a crown jewel of a hostel that shares the estate with a winery (wine tasting!), brewery (beer tasting!), movie theater, and 2 restaurants (food tasting!). Dark wood bunks and vast rooms off muralled hallways. 2 single-sex dorm-style rooms, each with 12 beds. Shower facilities and two claw-footed tubs. Restaurants are pricey, but good. No curfew. 24hr. desk service. $18 plus tax.

Ben Stark Hotel and International Hostel, 1022 SW Stark St. (274-1223). This old building is charming but run-down. Ascend the imposing staircase to find 6 well-kept hostel rooms, 2 bathrooms, and a sunny, if "stark," common room down the hall. Laundry and lockers downstairs. Convenient location, but take note: there are some shady characters in this neighborhood, and the club across the street is noisy on weekends. Passport or hostel membership required. No curfew. 24hr. desk service. $15 per night, Nov.-May $12. Private rooms $36-45.

4th Avenue Motel, 1889 SW 4th Ave. (226-7646), at Hall St. Location, location, location. Unremarkable rooms with dim lighting, but just blocks from the center of downtown. A/C, phones, and HBO. Check-out 11am. From $60, $50 in winter.

Portland

Sights
City Hall, **12**
Civic Auditorium, **11**
Civic Stadium, **13**
Pacific Northwest College, **9**
Pioneer Courthouse Square, **6**
Portland Building, **10**
Portland/Oregon Visitors Association, (i)
Portland State University, **8**
Powell's Book Store, **3**
Rose Garden Arena, **14**
Skidmore Fountain, **4**

Essentials
Ben Stark Hostel, **7**
Bus Station, **1**
Library, **5**
Post Office, ✉
Union Station (Amtrak), **2**

Parks
Fareless Square
MAX

Portland State University is bounded by Route 405 to the west and south, Market St. to the north, and 6th Ave. to the east.

NW Kearney St.
NW Johnson St
NW Irving St
NW Hoyt St.
NW Glisan St.
NW Flanders St
NW Everett St.
Davis St.
NW Couch St.
NW Burnside St.
keny St. SW
NW 23st Ave
NW 21st Ave.
NW 19th Ave.
17th Ave.
14th Ave.
NW 10th Ave.
NW Park Ave.
Broadway Ave.
NW 6th Ave.
NW 5th Ave.
NW 4th Ave.
NW 3rd Ave.
NW 2nd Ave.
NW 1st Ave.
Front Ave.
Steel Bridge
Willamette River
Burnside Bridge
Morrison Bridge
Hawthorne Bridge
SW Front Av
SW 1st Ave
SW 2nd Av
3rd Ave
4th Ave
SW 6th Ave
Broadway
Park Ave.
9th Ave.
Transit Mall
SW Stark St
Washington St.
SW Alder St.
SW Morrison St.
SW Yamhill St.
SW Taylor St.
SW Salmon St.
SW Madison St.
Oak St.
Main St.
Jefferson St.
SW Columbia St.
SW Clay St.
SW Market St.
TO WASHINGTON PARK ZOO
TO DOWNTOWN INN 4TH AVE. MOTEL
TO ONDINE
TO LEWIS AND CLARK COLLEGE
0 1/2 mile
0 1/2 kilometer
NE Hassalo
Lloyd Blvd.
TO COLUMBIA RIVER GORGE
NE Everett St.
NE Burnside St.
TO AIRPORT
Sandy Blvd.
Stark St. SE
12th Ave. SE
SE 2nd Ave.
SE 3rd Ave.
SE Martin Luther King Jr. Blvd.
SE Grand Ave.
SE 7th Ave.
SE Morrison St.
SE Belmont St.
SE Yamhill St
SE Taylor St.
SE Salmon St.
SE Main St.
SE Madison St.
SE Hawthorne Blvd.
TO OREGON MUSEUM OF SCIENCE AND INDUSTRY
TO REED COLLEGE
TO PORTLAND HI-AYH

Motel 6, 3104 SE Powell Blvd. (238-0600; fax 238-7167). Take bus #9 (brown beaver) from 5th Ave. Everything you'd expect from a Motel 6. Clean rooms without the color-coordinated watercolors. Phones, HBO, and outdoor pool. $45, 2 people $51, $54 for 3, or $57 for 4. Always full; call in advance or show up at 6pm to catch a room that's been cancelled. Wheelchair access.

Sixth Avenue Motel, 2221 SW 6th Ave. (226-2979), at south end of town near the freeway. Smallish rooms with mauve rugs. Phones, color cable, and coffee. Singles $52; doubles $57. 9% senior discount.

Champoeg State Park, 8239 NE Champoeg Rd. (678-1251 or 800-452-5687). Take I-5 south 20 mi. to Exit 278, then follow the signs west for 6 more mi. Play along miles of paved bikeway or hike by the Willamette River. 48 shady RV sites ($19) have water and electricity. Tent sites ($16) do not afford much privacy. Famous for its outdoor concert series. 2-day advance reservation required.

Ainsworth State Park, 37 mi. east of Portland, at Exit 35 off I-84 on scenic Hwy. 30, in the Columbia Gorge. Close to the highway; convenient but noisy. Not a natural getaway, but the drive through the gorge is beautiful. Hot showers, flush toilets, hiking trails, full hookups. $18; non-camper showers $2. Open Apr.-Oct.

FOOD

Dining in Portland is never dull and rarely expensive. Portland has more restaurants per capita than any other American city. Family establishments and quirky cafes, scattered heavily across the NW and SE quadrants, offer great food at reasonable prices.

Northwest

If lunch or dinner time finds you prowling the trendy eateries on NW 21st and 23rd St., you are not alone. **Food Front,** a small cooperative grocery at 2375 NW Thurman St. (222-5658), has a superb deli selection amid a wonderland of natural foods, fruit, and baked goods (open daily 9am-10pm, winter daily 9am-9pm).

Garbonzo's, 922 NW 21st Ave. (227-4196), at Lovejoy. Seek refuge from mad boutique-seekers on the street at this delicious falafel bar. Cheap, healthy food served by conversational staff. The falafel pita ($3.75) is only a bit better than the hummus ($3), baba ghanoush ($3.50), or mouth-watering baklava ($1.25). Other locations at 3433 SE Hawthorne Blvd. and 6341 SW Capital Hwy. Open Sun.-Thurs. 11:30am-1:30am, Fri.-Sat. 11:30am-3am.

Accuardi's Old Town Pizza, 226 NW Davis St. (222-9999). Relax on a couch, at a table, or at a private booth in this former whorehouse. Reported ghost sightings by the staff have not affected their pizza-crafting abilities (small cheese $5.50). 26 toppings from A (artichokes) to Z (zucchini)! Open daily 11:30am-11:30pm.

Kornblatt's, 628 NW 23rd Ave. (242-0055). Take bus #15 (red salmon). The only one of its kind in Portland, this New York-style deli is an overdone sight for sore eastern eyes. "What! You're not eating? You look so thin!" Matzoh-ball soup ($4), knishes ($2.50), and latkes (2 for $3.75). Sandwiches are huge ($6). Or just stick to bagels (6 for $2.75). Open Sun.-Wed. 7am-9pm, Thurs.-Sat. 7am-10pm.

Southwest

The center of town and tourist activity, Southwest is sometimes expensive. Streetcars provide an array of portable food, but the best deals are indoors. A row of fast and cheap ethnic restaurants peddle eats between 10th and 11th Ave. on Morrison St.

Western Culinary Institute: Chef's Diner, Chef's Corner, and the **Restaurant,** 1239 and 1316 SW Jefferson (800-666-0312). The testing ground for the cooking school's creative adventures. Sit on stools while cheerful students in tall white hats serve, taste, and discuss sandwiches, or go for a sit down meal, proper. Five-course restaurant lunches ($8) are rivaled only by the spectacular seven-course dinners ($15). Call ahead. Diner open Tues.-Fri. 7am-noon; deli open Tues.-Fri. 8am-6pm; restaurant open Tues.-Fri. 11:30am-1pm and 6-8pm.

Chang's Mongolian Grill, 1 SW 3rd St. (243-1991), at Burnside. After an all-you-can-eat lunch ($6.25) or dinner ($9.50), you will be fit to conquer Asia. Select a meal from a buffet of fresh vegetables, meat, and fish, mix your own sauce, and watch your chef make a wild show of cooking it all on a domed grill the size of a Volkswagen Beetle. Rice, soup, and/or pancakes included. Open Mon.-Fri. 11:30am-2:30pm and 5-10pm, Sat.-Sun. noon-2:30pm, Sat. 5-10pm and Sun. 4:30-9:30pm.

Mayas Tacqueria, 1000 SW Morrison (226-1946). Have a veggie taco ($2.25) while examining colorful pseudo-Mayan art and listening to loud Latin tunes. Main dishes are reasonable: super burritos are $7 and combo plates cost $7-8. (Watch out for the $1.25 side of sour cream.) Open Sun.-Thurs. 11am-10pm, Fri.-Sat. 11am-11pm.

Rocco's Cafe, 949 SW Oak St. (223-9835), at W. Burnside Blvd. Gigantic slices of good, thick pizza ($2) in a funky 90s pizza joint. Take your pie to a psychedelic booth or walk across the street to Powell's Books (see **Sights and Activities**). Open Mon.-Thurs. 11am-11pm, Fri.-Sat. 11am-4am, Sun. noon-9pm.

Brasserie Montmartre, 626 SW Park Ave. (224-5552). This elegant restaurant has a subtle funny bone. Paper tablecloths, crayons, magicians, and nightly live jazz make good diversions for dull dates. The bistro menu is slightly less expensive. Thai chicken $7.75, seafood and steak $12-18, burgers $5.25. Open Mon.-Thurs. 11:30am-2am, Fri. 11:30am-3am, Sat. 10am-3am, Sun. 10am-2am.

Southeast and Northeast

Anchored by happening Hawthorne Blvd., Southeast is a great place to pass time or fill tummies, day or night. Eclectic eateries with exotic decor and economical menus hide in residential and industrial neighborhoods. Granola-seekers will glory in **People's Food Store Co-op,** 3029 SE 21st Ave. (232-9051), which runs a farmer's market on Wednesday afternoons in summer (open daily 9am-9pm), and the larger, more equipped **Nature's,** 3016 Division St. (233-7374; open daily 9am-10pm).

Cafe Lena, 2239 SE Hawthorne Blvd. (238-7087). Take bus #5 (brown beaver). Portland intelligentsia reverently frequent this cafe, known for its open-mic poetry (Tues. 9:30pm), and sumptuous homemade *challah.* Loads of local art. An eclectic menu features Thai, Italian, and American ($7-10). Try the bees knees with cheese ($5) or Venetian veneration submarino ($6.50). Spoken word or acoustic music every night. Breakfast served until 4pm. Open Wed.-Thurs. 7am-11pm, Fri. 7am-1am, Sat. 8am-1am, Sun. 8am-3pm for brunch.

Montage, 301 SE Morrison St. (234-1324). Take bus #15 (brown beaver) to the end of the Morrison Bridge and walk under it. An oasis of Louisiana style and cooking in an off-kilter atmosphere. Gumbo you wish your mama made ($5), unreal frogs legs (3 for $9), and alligator jambalaya ($14). Come just to hear the waiters yell for oyster shooters. Lunch Mon.-Fri. 11:30am-2pm, dinner 6pm-2am, Sat.-Sun. 6pm-4am.

Delta Cafe, 4607 SE Woodstock Blvd. (771-3101). Take bus #5 or #19 (brown beaver) from 5th Ave.; look left 2 or 3 blocks after you pass Reed College. Boasting dishes like fried okra, succotash (both $2), and green eggs 'n' ham ($6), the food is decidedly soul. Adamantly free-spirited decor with hanging beads. Worth the trek to Woodstock. Mon.-Fri. 4pm-11pm, Sat. 10am-11pm, Sun. 10am-10pm. Mon. and Wed.-Fri. 11am-2:30pm and 5-10pm, Sat.-Sun. 11am-10pm.

Cup & Saucer, 3566 SE Hawthorne Blvd. (236-6001). Take bus #14 (brown beaver). Friendly, frantic neighborhood restaurant famous for its pancakes ($3.75) and grilled veggie sandwich ($4.75). The world's biggest blocks of coffee cake, brownies, and rice krispy treats made there daily (50¢-$1.50). Open daily 7am-9pm.

Saigon Kitchen, 835 NE Broadway (281-3669). Take bus #9 (purple raindrop). Quite possibly the best Vietnamese restaurant in town, with no pretensions. The *chazio* rolls, deep fried and served with fresh herbs and sauce ($5.75), are a perennial favorite. Most entrees $7-9. Open Mon.-Sat. 11am-10pm, Sun. noon-10pm.

Nicholas' Restaurant, 318 SE Grand Ave. (235-5123), across from Miller Paint. Take bus #6 (red salmon) to the Andy and Bax stop. The unassuming facade means nothing. Nicholas serves tantalizing Lebanese and Mediterranean food at incredible prices. Try the Mezza ("I'll-try-a-little-bit-of-everything") platter ($7) or the Shatta pizza ($3). Mediterranean sandwiches $4-7. Open Mon.-Sat. 10am-9pm.

PaRaDoX Palace Cafe, 3439 SE Belmont St. (232-7508). Take bus #15 (brown beaver) to 34th St. Classic 50s greasy spoon decor, complete with obligatory turquoise vinyl seats, but the food is strictly 90s. One lonely hamburger cowers in a menu of vegetarian and vegan options like the veggie haystack ($3.50) or the tofu burrito ($5). Open Thurs.-Mon. 8am-9pm, Tues.-Wed. 8am-3pm.

Hawthorne Street Cafe, 3354 SE Hawthorne Blvd. (232-4982). Take bus #14 (brown beaver). In a converted Victorian house, this cafe has magnificently huge windows and light-strewn bistro tables. Lunch features enticing sandwiches like sundried tomato, avocado, sprouts and cheese ($5.50). Some come in just for the marionberry coffee cake ($3.25). For dinner try the honey-mustard chicken salad ($6). 20% discount for hostel guests. Open Mon.-Fri. 7:30am-2:30pm; dinner Wed.-Fri. 5-10pm, Sat.-Sun. 7:30am-10pm.

Thanh Thao Restaurant, 4005 SE Hawthorne Blvd. (238-6232). Take bus #14 (brown beaver). You'll come back to Portland just for a 2nd helping of this fabulous Thai cuisine. The long menu, ranging from cashew beef ($7) to eggplant in black bean sauce ($6.25), makes up for a lack of decor. Salad rolls ($3) are a successful mutation of spring rolls. Often a wait for dinner. Open Mon. and Wed.-Fri. 11am-2:30pm and 5-10pm, Sat.-Sun. 11am-10pm.

CAFES AND COFFEEHOUSES

Portland has no shortage of places for an old-fashioned cuppa joe. Requisite Starbucky chains grace most neighborhoods, but search out the local hidden treasures for atmosphere and a caffeinated place to spend a rainy afternoon.

Pied Cow Coffeehouse, 3244 SE Belmont St. (230-4866). Take bus #15 (brown beaver) to the front door. Sink into the velvety cushions, pet the fuzzy tiger-print walls, and admire the light fixtures inside the Victorian parlor. Espresso drinks ($1-2.75) and a wide selection of teas (pot for 2, $2.50). Open Tues.-Thurs. 10am-midnight, Fri.-Sat. 10am-1am. 10am-11midnight. Closed Jan.

Coffee Time, 712 NW 21st Ave. (497-1090). Sip a cup of chai tea ($1.85) while visiting the natural wonders of the world on the wall mural in the main room, then escape through hanging beads to the 3-sided enclave, sit by the faux fire in the middle mustard room, or push on into the muralled parlor with tapestries, chill music, and dim lighting. Lattés $2, time warp with extra caffeine $1. Open Mon.-Sat. 6:30am-midnight, Sun. 8am-midnight.

Giant Steps, 1208 NW Glisan St. (226-2547). This chic Pearl District coffeehouse sports art from 7 surrounding galleries and shots of wheatgrass juice ($1.25). Named after John Coltrane's classic album, Giant Steps plays great jazz (live jazz on first Thurs. 7-9:30pm). Open Mon.-Fri. 7am-7pm, Sat. 8am-5pm, Sun. 8am-3pm.

Torrefazione Italia, 838 NW 23rd Ave. (800-727-9692). *Willamette Week*'s "Best Coffee in Portland" headlines this crowded Nob Hill destination. When it's nice out, the giant windows slide open to let in fresh air and conversation from hipsters on the street. Espresso drinks $1-3. Get your drink here just to admire the pottery. Open Mon.-Thurs. 6am-10pm, Fri. 6am-11pm, Sat. 7am-11pm, Sun. 8am-9pm.

Rimsky-Korsakoffee House, 707 SE 12th Ave. (232-2640). Take bus #15 (brown beaver) to 12th St., then walk 2 blocks north. Big red Victorian house converted into a cozy salon. Bacchanalian frenzy of desserts. Ask for a "mystery table." Live classical music nightly. Open *flexibly* Sun.-Thurs. 7pm-midnight, Fri.-Sat. 7pm-1am.

The Roxy, 1121 SW Stark St. (223-9160). *The* most frequented 24hr. cafe. Crowded late-night after bars and clubs close as people come to drink an entire pot of joe ($1 per person), smoke, and pay homage to Quentin Tarantino. Sit on a leopard-print booth, play a song on the old-fashioned Wurlitzer jukebox, and eat a soylent green omelette ($5.65) or some chocolate suicide cake ($2). Open Tues.-Sun. 24hr.

SIGHTS AND ACTIVITIES

Shaded parks, magnificent gardens, bustling open-air markets, and innumerable museums and galleries beckon Portland's tourists and residents. For $1.05, bus #63 (orange deer or brown beaver) delivers its charges to at least 13 tourist attractions. Catch the best of Portland's dizzying arts scene on the first Thursday of each month, when the small galleries in the Southwest and Northwest and the **Portland Art Museum** (see below) all stay open until 9pm (galleries free admission, museum half-price). Contact the **Metropolitan Arts Commission,** 1120 SW 5th Ave. (823-5111), for info or grab the *Art Gallery Guide* at the visitors center.

Downtown

Portland's downtown centers around the **pedestrian and bus mall,** running north-south on 5th and 6th Ave. between W. Burnside Blvd. at the north end and SW Clay St. to the south. The **Pioneer Courthouse,** a downtown landmark, sits at 5th Ave. and Morrison St. This monument is still a federal courthouse and the centerpiece of **Pioneer Courthouse Square,** 701 SW 6th Ave. (223-1613), which opened in 1983 and has since earned the affectionate name "Portland's Living Room." Portlanders of every ilk hang out in this massive brick quadrangle, bounded Starbucks in one corner and the travel branch of Powell's in the other. With Tri-Met's Customer Service Office at its center and plenty of seating, the square is a shrine to the pedestrian. At the square's construction, area citizens purchased personalized bricks to support the construction of an amphitheater that hosts live jazz and folk music. During the summer, the **Peanut Butter and Jam Concerts** draw thousands of music lovers (Tues. and Thurs. noon-1pm).

The most controversial building in the downtown area is Michael Graves' postmodern **Portland Building,** 1120 SW 5th Ave., on the mall. The building's 1984 opening was attended by King Kong (full-sized and inflatable), perched upon the roof. Since then, this confection of pastel tile and concrete has been both vigorously praised and condemned as an overgrown jukebox. On a niche outside its second floor, *Portlandia* reaches down to crowds below. This immense bronze statue portrays the trident-bearing woman of the state seal, but to many, she looks like a man with breasts brandishing a large salad fork. The **Standard Insurance Center,** nearby at 900 SW 5th Ave., has also engendered controversy for *The Quest,* a white marble sculpture out front, more commonly known to locals as "Three Groins in the Fountain."

Anyone who doubts the corporatization of the world need only visit **Niketown,** 930 SW 6th Ave. (221-6453) at Salmon for a conversion. TVs in the floor and a life-size Michael Jordan sculpture have tourists wandering around this mock town glassy-eyed. Sports fans enjoy the various artifacts: jerseys and shoes worn by famous athletes, balls they've played with, and even an autographed Jordan Wheaties Box (open Mon.-Thurs. and Sat. 10am-7pm, Fri. 10am-8pm, Sun. 11:30am-6:30pm)

There is room for romping just west of the mall on the **South Park Blocks,** a series of cool, shaded parks down the middle of Park Ave., enclosed on the west side by **Portland State University (PSU).** Also on the west side of the park sits the **Portland Art Museum,** 1219 SW Park (226-2811; http://www.pam.org/pam), at Jefferson St., which houses Western painting and sculpture from the 1350s to the 1950s, as well as prints, photos, contemporary works, and a collection of international art. The excellent Pacific Northwest Native American exhibit displays masks, textiles, and sacred objects. The 1998 season boasts "Splendors of Ancient Egypt" (Mar. 8-Aug. 16) and a Monet exhibit (Sept. 20-Dec. 31; open Tues.-Sun. 10am-5pm; admission $6, seniors and students over 16 $4.50, under 16 $2.50; call for ticket info). The **Pacific Northwest College of Art** (226-4391) and the **Northwest Film Center** (221-1156) share space with the museum. The film center shows classics, documentaries, and off-beat flicks almost daily ($6, students $5).

Across the park, the **Oregon Historical Society Museum and Library,** 1200 SW Park Ave. (222-1741; www.ohs.org/ohsinfo.html), stores photographs, artifacts, and records of Oregon's last two centuries. Interactive exhibits on Oregon, Willamette County, and Portland (open Tues.-Sat. 10am-5pm, Sun. noon-5pm; $6, students $3; Thurs. seniors free; 2 for 1 AAA discount). If the kiddies get bored, take them to the **Portland Children's Museum,** 3037 SW 2nd Ave. (823-2227), at Wood St. (not in downtown; take bus #1, 12, 40, 41, 43, 45, or 55, all yellow rose), which schedules games, arts activities, and hands-on exhibits, including the ever-popular grocery store where plastic celery and bananas are the currency of fun. The recently reopened Water Room and its bubble machine are a blast (open daily 9am-5pm).

The part of downtown just south of the Burnside Bridge and along the river is considered the gateway to **Old Town.** In recent years, large-scale restoration of store fronts, new "old brick," polished iron and brass, and a bevy of new shops and restaurants have revitalized Old Town. A popular people-watching spot, the **Skidmore Fountain,** at SW 1st Ave. and SW Ankeny St., marks the entrance to the quarter. Had the city accepted resident brewmeister Henry Weinhard's offer to run draft beer through the fountain, it would have been a cordial watering hole indeed. The fountain also marks the end of **Waterfront Park.** This 20-block-swath of grass and flowers along the Willamette River provides locals with a place to picnic, fish, and stroll.

The eclectic and festive **Saturday Market,** 108 W. Burnside St. (222-6072), by the Skidmore Fountain between 1st and Front St., is overrun with street musicians, artists, craftspeople, chefs, and greengrocers, clogging the largest open-air crafts market in the country (March-Dec. Sat. 10am-5pm, Sun. 11am-4:30pm). The **New Market Village,** 120 SW Ankeny, is in a restored old port building. Inside, check out the living gallery courtyard, a veritable Noah's Ark of "chia" animals. Grass sprouts instead of fur and feathers on this life-size menagerie of lions, bears, birds, and more. Nineteen frolicsome **fountains** decorate the city. Cool your feet in **Ira's Fountain** (between 3rd and 4th ST. and Market and Clay St., in front of the Civic Auditorium) as 13,000 gallons cascade down cobblestoned terraces every minute. Pick up the free *Portland's Municipal Fountains* guide at the visitors center, and as you do, watch **Salmon St. Springs** (in Waterfront Park, at SW Salmon St.) rocket high into the air and change form as an underground computer manipulates the fountain's 185 jets.

Downtown's waterfront district is laced with a complex web of underground passages, known as the **"Shanghai" tunnels.** Urban lore has it that seamen would get their victims drunk, drag them down to the tunnels, and store them there till their ship sailed. Forced aboard and taken out to sea, these hapless Portlanders would provide a free crew. North of Burnside lies what was once a thriving **Chinatown,** but only its arched gateway remains today. The area has been recycled again as the **Pearl District.** Stretching north from Burnside to I-405 along the river, the old industrial zone is packed with galleries, loft apartments, and warehouse-turned-office buildings. Storefronts and cafes have made the area welcoming, but the boxy architecture, like the mild lawlessness of its curbless streets, has been preserved.

For a dose of fun that might go over youngsters' heads, pay a visit to the first and only **Church of Elvis,** 720 SW Ankeny St. (226-3671). Listen to synthetic oracles, witness satirical miracles, and, if you're lucky, experience a tour in the church's Art-o-Mobile. Although this church once was (and hopes to be very soon again) a 24-hour coin-operated funhouse, there are temporarily free guided tours. Hours are usually noon-5pm and often 8-11pm (the one-woman show needs time to renovate!), and is still well worth the visit.

Nicknamed "Munich on the Willamette," Portland is the uncontested **microbrewery** capital of the U. S., and Portlanders are proud of their beer. The visitors center hands out a list of 26 metro area breweries, most of which happily give tours. Henry Weinhard, a German brewmaster, started this tradition when he established the first brewery in the Northwest, outside of Fort Vancouver, in 1856. Today **"Henry's"** is an Oregon standard, outgrowing its status as a microbrew. Visit the **Blitz Weinhard Brewery,** 1133 W. Burnside (222-4351), for a 45-minute tour and samples (free; tours Tues.-Fri. noon, 1:30pm, and 3pm). Many of these beer factories are **Brew Pubs,** which offer food, and sometimes live music with their wares. Try the **Lucky Labrador Brew Pub,** 913 SE Hawthorne Blvd. (236-3555), where miser Monday pints are $2. (For others, see **Nightlife,** below.) For a more detailed explanation of why the water, hops, and grains of Oregon make it a "Beer Lover's Promised Land," visit the **Oregon Brewers Guild,** 510 NW 3rd Ave. (295-1862).

Northwest, North, and Northeast

Washington Park (see **Parks**, below), provides easy access by car or on foot to sprawling **Forest Hills Park,** the largest park completely within an American city. The 5000-acre park is laced with trails through lush forests, scenic overviews, and idyllic picnic areas. The **Pittock Mansion,** 3229 NW Pittock Dr. (823-3624), within Forest Park, was built by Henry L. Pittock, founder of the daily *Oregonian.* Take in a striking panorama of the city from the lawn of this 80-year-old, 16,000 sq. ft. testament to the French Renaissance. From downtown, take crosstown bus #20 (orange deer) to NW Barnes and W. Burnside St., then walk ½ mi. up Pittock Ave. Or follow the green and white mansion signs west on Burnside Blvd. for 2½ mi. (open daily noon-4pm; tours $4.50, seniors $4, ages 6-18 $2; closed the first 3 weeks of Jan.).

Downtown on the edge of the Northwest district is the gargantuan **Powell's City of Books,** 1005 W. Burnside St. (228-4651 or 800-878-7323; http://www.powells.com), a cavernous establishment with almost a million new and used volumes, more than any other bookstore in the U.S. If you like to dawdle in bookstores, bring a sleeping bag and rations. It's so huge, they even provide a map; you'll need it. Seven color-coded rooms house books on everything from Criminology to Cooking. The **Anne Hughes Coffee Room,** inside Powell's, serves bagels, cookies, and coffee for those who can't find their way out. Powell's also features frequent poetry and fiction readings (7:30pm in the purple room) and an extensive travel section on Portland and the Northwest (open Mon.-Sat. 9am-11pm, Sun. 9am-9pm).

The American Advertising Museum, 50 SW 2nd Ave. (226-0000) at the Skidmore stop on MAX, chronicles worldwide attempts to sell things. The gallery shows temporary exhibits; summer 1997 showcased 100 years of Coca-Cola (open Wed.-Sun. 11am-5pm; $3, seniors and under 12 $1.50).

Southeast

Southeast Portland is largely residential, with scattered pockets of activity. To the south, **Reed College,** 3203 SE Woodstock (771-1112; campus events 777-7522), a small liberal arts college founded in 1909, sponsors a number of cultural events. The ivy-draped grounds, encompassing a lake and a state wildlife refuge, make for an exceptionally attractive campus. Ironically, in 1968, this enclave of progressive politics became the first college to open its own nuclear reactor. Today, the students are much more committed to turning their compost heap than to generating nuclear energy. One-hour tours, geared mainly to prospective students, leave Eliot Hall #220, 3203 Woodstock Blvd. at SE 28th, twice daily (Mon.-Fri. 10am and 2pm).

Across the street from Reed is the **Crystal Springs Rhododendron Garden,** SE 28th Ave., at Woodstock (take bus #19), where 2500 rhododendrons of countless varieties surround a lake and border an 18-hole public golf course. Unwind among ducks, man-made waterfalls and 90-year-old rhodos. The flowers are in full bloom Mar.-June (gates open daily 6am-10pm; Oct.-March daily 8am-7pm; admission $2 March 1-Labor Day Thurs.-Mon. 10am-6pm).

The **Oregon Museum of Science and Industry (OMSI),** 1945 SE Water Ave. (797-4000), at SE Clay St., keeps children mesmerized with do-it-yourself science exhibits, including an earthquake-simulator chamber (open Fri.-Wed. 9:30am-7pm, Thurs. 9:30am-8pm; Labor Day-Memorial Day Fri.-Wed. 9:30am-5:30pm, Thurs. 9:30am-8pm; $6, seniors and children $4.50). The **OMNIMAX** theater (797-4640 for hours and shows), in OMSI, awes visitors (shows start on the hour, daily 11am-4pm and Wed.-Sat. 7-9pm; $5.50, seniors and ages 4-13 $4). The Murdock Sky Theater rocks with **laser light music shows** (797-4646) like "Lazed and Confused" and Pink Floyd's *The Wall* (daily matinees free with museum admission or $2.00; evening shows Wed.-Sun. $6.50). While at OMSI, visit the *U.S.S. Blueback* (797-4624), the Navy's last diesel submarine. This sub set a record by traversing the Pacific Ocean underwater. She never failed a single mission, and starred in the 1990 film *The Hunt for Red October.* The sub is now open for exploration (open daily 10am-6pm; 40min. tour $3.50).

Hawthorne Boulevard has a high concentration of quiet cafes, antique shops, used book stores, and theaters. It's a hip strip where prices aren't too high and parking can still be found on weekends. It ends at the bottom of **Mt. Tabor Park,** one of two city parks in the world on the site of an extinct volcano. To get there, take bus #15 (brown beaver) from downtown, or hunt it down at SE 60th Ave. and Salmon Ave. or SE 69th Ave. two blocks south of Belmont Ave. Shops have also sprouted on **Bel-**

Don't Expect to Play Frisbee in This Park

No one knew that a hole cut through the sidewalk at the corner of SW Taylor St. and SW Front St. in 1948 was destined for greatness. Indeed, it was expected to accommodate an inglorious lamp post. But the post was never installed, and the 24-inch circle of earth was left empty until Dick Fagan, a columnist for the *Oregon Journal*, noticed it. Fagan used his column, called "Mill Ends," to publicize the patch of dirt, pointing out that it would make a great, though microscopic, park. After years of lobbying, the park was officially added to the city's roster in 1976. At 452.16 sq. in., **Mill Ends Park** is recognized by the *Guinness Book of World Records* as the **world's smallest park.** Locals have enthusiastically adopted the park, planting flowers and hosting a hotly contested **snail race** on St. Patrick's Day. Imagine all the things you can do there: eat your lunch (alone), wave at passing cars, read Habermas, meditate, develop a national healthcare plan everyone will accept, or just stand (in the place where you are).

mont Ave. (a few avenues north), which some have touted as the new Hawthorne. **Oogla Plentium,** 3437 SE Belmont Ave. (234-7933) carries self-defined omniumgatherum resales like clothes, jewelry, books, and housewares, and is worth a visit.

Parks

Portland has more park area than any other U.S. city. **Forest Park,** the 5000-acre splotch of wilderness in the city's northwest, might have something to do with this. Less than 2 mi. west of downtown, the posh neighborhoods of **West Hills** form a manicured buffer zone between soul-soothing parks and the turmoil of the city below. In the middle of West Hills, mammoth **Washington Park** and its nearby attractions typify the blend of urbanity and natural bounty Portland has perfected. To get there, take the animated "zoo bus" (#63) on SW Main St. or drive up SW Broadway to Clay St., take U.S. 26 West, and get off at the zoo exit. The park's gates close at 9pm to keep out lawless riff raff; by day Washington Park is beautiful. **Hoyt Arboretum,** 4000 SW Fairview Blvd. (228-8733 or 823-3655), at the crest of the hill above the other gardens, features 200 acres of trees and trails, including the charming—and wheelchair accessible—**Bristlecone Pine Trail.** The 26 mi. **"Wildwood" Trail,** which winds through Washington and Forest Parks, connects the arboretum to the zoo in the south. **Maps** are available for .50¢ at the info stand near the arboretum parking lot (trails open daily 6am-10pm; Washington Park Visitors Center open Mon.-Fri. 9am-3pm, Sat.-Sun. 10am-2pm). The spectacular **Japanese Gardens,** 611 SW Kingston Ave. (223-4070), are reputed to be the most authentic outside Japan (open daily June-Aug. 9am-8pm; April-May and Sept. 10am-6pm; Oct.-March 10am-4pm; $5, seniors and students $2.50).

The **Washington Park Zoo,** 4001 SW Canyon Rd. (226-1561 or 226-7627), is renowned for successful elephant breeding and its scrupulous re-creation of natural habitats. Whimsical murals decorate the #63 "zoo bus," connecting the park to SW Main St. in the downtown mall. A steam engine pulls passengers on a mini railway out to Washington Park gardens and back, giving a better view of flowers and animals (30min. tour $2.75, seniors and ages 3-11 $2). The zoo features a number of "animal talks" on weekends and has a pet-the-animals **children's zoo.** If you're around in late June, July, or August, grab a picnic basket and head to the zoo's sculpture garden to catch live outdoor music at the **Rhythm and Zoo Concerts** (234-9694) on Wednesday and Thursday nights at 7pm. These concerts are free with zoo admission and range in international styles. The zoo also hosts **Zoobeat** concerts on selected summer weekend nights at 7pm (tickets $14; call zoo for more info).

ENTERTAINMENT

Once an uncouth and rowdy port town, Portland maintains its irreverent attitude. Nightclubs cater to everyone from the casual college student to the hard-core rocker. Upon request, the Portland Oregon Visitors Association hands over a thick packet outlining that month's events. Outdoor festivals are a way of life (see **Publications,** p. 412, for more sources of info).

Music

Although first-rate travelling shows never miss Portland, and many have bargain tickets available, some of the greatest shows are free and outdoors. For stellar local rock, visit the **Satyricon** and **La Luna** (see **Nightlife,** below).

Oregon Symphony Orchestra, 719 SW. Alder St. (228-1353 or 800-228-7343), in the Arlene Schnitzer Concert Hall. Plays a classical and pop series Sept.-June. Tickets $10-50. "Symphony Sunday" afternoon concerts $10-15. Half-price student tickets available 1hr. before showtime on Sat. and Sun. "Monday Madness" offers $5 student tickets available 1 week before showtime. One ticket per student ID.

Portland Civic Auditorium, 222 SW Clay St. (796-9293 for info; call Ticketmaster for tickets). Attracts the usual hard rockin' arena acts and a few jazz and opera stars. Ticket prices vary ($8-30).

Sack Lunch Concerts, 1422 SW 11th Ave. (222-2031), at Clay St. at the Old Church. Free concert every Wed. at noon. Sometimes organ, sometimes acoustic guitar—you never know what you'll find.

Chamber Music Northwest, 522 SW 5th Ave. #725 (294-6400). Performs summer concerts from late June-July at Reed College Commons. Classical music Mon.-Tues., and Thurs.-Sat. at 8pm. $12-27, ages 7-14 $5.

Peanut Butter and Jam Sessions (223-1613), at Pioneer Courthouse Square from noon-1pm every Tues. and Thurs. during the summer. A potpourri of rock, jazz, folk, and world music (with the crusts off). Always jammed.

Aladdin Theatre, 3017 SE Milwaukee Ave., (233-1994), just off SE Powell by the Ross Island Bridge. A popular gig for a wide range of talent from alternative to country. Atmosphere depends on the band.

Theater

Theater in Portland covers all tastes, ages, and budgets. The **Portland Center for the Performing Arts (PCPA)** (796-9293 for tickets) is the largest independent arts center in the U.S. Friends of the Performing Arts Center put on the **Brown Bag Lunch** series, giving free glances at professional productions (occasional weekdays at lunchtime; check the *Oregonian*). Tickets for most other productions can be charged by phone at Ticketmaster or Fastixx (see **Practical Information,** p. 410).

Portland Center Stage (248-6309), at the Intermediate Theater of PCPA, at SW Broadway and SW Main. 5-play series of classics and modern adaptations runs Oct.-April. Tickets: Fri.-Sat. $12.50-35, Sun. and Tues.-Thurs. $11-30.50. Half-price tickets sometimes available at the Intermediate Theater 1hr. before showtime.

Portland Repertory Theater, 25 SW Salmon St. (224-4491), in Two World Trade Center, Bridge level. 5 plays per year. Intimate 223-seat theater. Professional, with prices to match. Tickets start at $25, half-price tickets sold 30min. prior to curtain.

Oregon Ballet Theater, 1120 SW 10th Ave. (241-8316, 222-5538, or 888-922-5538). Performs at the Civic Auditorium at 3rd and Clay St. and at the Intermediate Theater at Main and Broadway. 5 creative ballet productions per season Oct.-June. The 1997-8 season includes an American choreographers' showcase and *The Nutcracker.* Tickets $5-85, student rush half-price 1hr. before curtain for some shows.

Artists Repertory Theater, 1516 SW Alder St. (241-1ART/1278). This theater puts on excellent low-budget and experimental productions. Tickets Fri.-Sat. $24, Wed., Thurs., and Sun. matinees $21.

Portland Civic Auditorium, 222 SW Clay St. (274-6560). Occasional big splashy opera, touring shows like Broadway musicals, and small rock concerts. Part of the PCPA. Tickets $25-55.

Cinema

Most of Portland's countless movie theaters have half-price days or matinees. With the help of the *Oregonian,* the $7.25 ticket price for a "major motion picture" can be the exception. McMenamins runs two **theater/pubs** (Bahgdad and Mission) where 21-and-over viewers sit in sofas or at tables and order food and brew during the show.

Bagdad Theater and Pub, 3702 SE Hawthorne Blvd. (230-0892). Take bus #14 (brown beaver). Built in 1921 for vaudeville, this magnificently renovated theater shows 2nd-run films set to the tune of an excellent beer menu ($3.15 a pint). Have a pricey pizza delivered to your seat. Doors open 5pm. All you can watch for $1.

Mission Theatre and Pub, 1624 NW Glisan (223-4031). Serves excellent home-brewed ales and delicious sandwiches and burgers ($4-6). Watch recent, out-of-first-run movies while lounging on couches, at tables, or perched in the old-style balcony. Showtimes 5:30, 8:05, and 10:30pm. Shows cost a whole buck.

Cinema 21, 616 NW 21st (223-4515), at Hoyt St. Mean, clean, and pistachio green. Mostly documentary, independent, and foreign films. Highly acclaimed student haunt; plenty of progressive literature in the lobby. Tickets $5.50; students $4.50; seniors, under 12, and first show on Sat. and Sun. $2.50.

Northwest Film Center, 1219 SW Park Ave. (221-1156), in the Berg Swann Auditorium at the Portland Art Museum. Documentary, foreign, classic, experimental, and independent films like "The Life and Times of Allen Ginsberg" and "North by Northwest." Films rotated every 3 months. Film and video festival in early Nov. Box office opens 30min. before each show. Tickets $6, seniors $5.50, students $5.

Clinton Street Theater, 2522 SE Clinton St. (238-8899). This multimedia theater hosts meetings, cabaret, and even Sunday night theater sports ($5). Do the time-warp again with the longest running *Rocky Horror Picture Show* in the States every Sat. at midnight ($4).

Act III Theatre, 820 SW. 9th Ave. (225-5555, ext. 4610). Hosts recent releases transferred from other theatres. Mucho artfare. Adults $3; children, seniors and matinees $2; Mon. $1.

Lloyd Cinema (225-5555, ext. 4600), across from the Lloyd Center mall. For a first-run movie, this 10-screen, ultra-modern neon wonderland does the trick.

Shopping

For some, shopping in the **Nob Hill** district is a religious experience. Fashionable boutiques run from Burnside to Thurman St., between NW 21st and NW 24th Ave., mostly on 23rd Ave. Or make the pilgrimage to NE Halsey and 15th Ave. to shop at the **Lloyd Center** mega mall (282-2511). Slide on over to the indoor **ice-skating rink** (288-6073; hours vary; $8.50, under 17 $7.50, skate rental included; open year round) and do your impression of Portland's own Tonya Harding. Parking can be a hassle on the weekends, but Lloyd Center is on the MAX line, and Nob Hill can be reached by bus #15 (red salmon) or the cross town bus #77.

Upscale shops can also be found up and down **Newberry St.,** where moneyed hipsters roam for rags. Those without a hefty wad should check out **Hawthorne** between 30th and 40th. For books, check out **Powell's** (see **Sights,** above). Portland is also home to a thriving thrift-store culture, especially near **Dot's Cafe** on Clinton St. (see **Nightlife,** below).

Sports

When Bill Walton led the **Trailblazers** (234-9291) to the 1979 NBA Championship, Portland went berserk—even the landing of an NBA team was a substantial accomplishment for this overgrown town. Residents even go bonkers when a former Trailblazer wins with another team, as they did when Clyde "The Glide" Drexler helped lead the Houston Rockets to the 1995 championship. The Trailblazers play in the sparkling new **Rose Garden Arena,** by the Steel Bridge in the northeast quadrant of the city, fully equipped with its own stop on the MAX line. The season lasts from November to May. From June-September, the city's indoor soccer team, **Portland Pride,** takes over the Rose Garden (call 684-5425 for schedule info and tickets). The **Winter Hawks** (238-6366) of the Western Hockey League play at the Rose Garden and next-door at the **Coliseum** in the winter, September through March. Take bus #9 (brown beaver) or MAX. **The Civic Stadium,** 1844 SW Morrison St., on the other side of town, is home to the **Portland Rockies** (223-2837), Colorado's AAA farm team, who played their inaugural season in 1995. Their season is June through September; reserved tickets cost $6.50, general admission $5.50, seniors and children 12 and under $4.50.

NIGHTLIFE

The best clubs in Portland are the hardest to find. Neighborhood taverns and pubs usually have the most character, the best music, and the smallest signs. Clubs in Northwest Portland are easily accessible from downtown. Park close or come with a friend since walking alone at night can be dangerous. Flyers advertising upcoming shows plaster Portland telephone poles, especially on SE Hawthorne and NW 23rd. Pubs are plentiful and half of them are owned by McMenamins. Mischievous minors be warned: the drinking age is strictly enforced in Portland. Between their liquor license or your business, bars know which choice to make.

Southwest

Crystal Ballroom, 1332 W. Burnside Blvd. (225-0047). Since its opening in Feb. 1997, this shimmering venue has hit Portland with a bang. The grand ballroom, with its immense paintings and gaudy chandeliers, begs boogiers to get down. Sometimes, lucky boogiers get bumped about by the bouncing floor! Take a break on a couch on the 2nd floor and gaze into their microbrewery at a surprising rendition of Lola, everyone's favorite cross-dresser. Micropints $3. Hosts only live music (of every sort); shows usually start at 9pm; doors open 1hr. before showtime. Tickets $3-20. Weekend shows often sell out, so call ahead.

Panorama, Brig, and **Boxx's,** 341 SW 10th St. (221-RAMA/7262), form a network of interconnected clubs along Stark St. between 10th and 11th. Shake it until you break it on Panorama's cavernous dance floor amid a thriving gay and straight crowd (open Fri.-Sat. 9pm-4am; $4 cover). The bpms are higher still in smaller Brig, where Fridays are disco night (open daily 9pm-2:30am). Push even farther into Boxx's, the video bar with routine karaoke (open daily noon-2:30am). Dance yourself silly into the wee hours.

Lotus Card Room and Cafe, 932 SW 3rd Ave. (227-6185), at SW Salmon St. Grooviest dance floor in the city has a movie screen with trippy projections, glowing cartoon paintings, and a cage. Packed with 20-somethings, the Lotus also has a room full of tables. Sun. disco ($3), Wed. new wave 80's ($2), Thurs. dance classics ($5), Fri. retro ($5), Sat. pop ($5); other nights before 10pm no cover. Happy hour (Mon.-Fri. 4-6:30pm) features pints ($2.50). Open daily 11am-2am.

Berbati's Pan, 231 SW Ankeny St. (248-4570). This ever-expanding nightspot started as a small Greek restaurant on 2nd Ave. Now the upscale dining room, 3-table pool room, 3 bars, dance hall, and late-night cafe wind all the way back to 3rd. The stage belongs to comedy on Mon., jazz on Tues., and acid jazz on Wed. Authentic Greek dishes run $3-7, or stick with a burger ($5). Club open Sun.-Thurs. 11:30am-2:30am, Fri.-Sat. 11:30am-4am.

Southeast

Biddy McGraw's, 3518 SE Hawthorne Blvd. (233-1178). Take bus #14 (brown beaver). You couldn't get more authentically Irish in Belfast. With live Irish tunes and raucous dancing, weekends are always boisterous. Good beer, engaging bartenders and cool clientele. 22 kegs of Guinness are consumed here a week. Do your part for $3.25 a pint. Micros $3, Henry's $2. Hours not set in stone, but should be open Mon. 11am-2am, Tues.-Sun. 11am-2:30am.

La Luna, 215 SE 9th Ave. (241-LUNA/5862), at Pine. Take bus #20 (purple raindrop), get off at 9th, walk 2 blocks south. One of Portland's larger, hipper venues. Hosts many of the more prominent bands that come to Portland. Music generally 4 times a week. Mon. night is queer night with dancing. The non-smoking cafe is open every show night to an anything-goes crowd. All ages admitted, except to the bars. Call ahead for concert listings. Pints $2-3.50. Cover $0-15.

Produce Row Cafe, 204 SE Oak St. (232-8355). Take bus #6 (red salmon) to SE Oak and SE Grand, then walk west along Oak toward the river. Though they remodelled 3 years ago, none of this 30-year-old enclave's character was lost. 27 beers on tap, over 200 bottled domestic and imported beers. Soak in the summer starlight and industrial ambience from the walled-off deck out back. Live music: Sat. rock ($2), Sun. mostly jazz ($2), Mon. jazz jam ($2), free Bluegrass Tues., free Irish music Wed. Domestic bottles $1.25, domestic pints $1.85. Open Mon.-Fri. 11am-1am, Sat. noon-1am, Sun. noon-midnight.

Dot's Cafe, 2521 SE Clinton St. (235-0203). Take bus #4 (brown beaver) to 26th, and walk 3 blocks south, or bus #10 (green leaf) and get out in front. The place burned down in 1993, but today, only Dot's business is aflame. Can be crowded and smoky. Dotted with alternative artifacts like the treasured Velvet Elvis pool table and costume jewelry. Caters to musicians and their bohemian brethren. Food, too ($4-6). Vegan Vavoom $4. Open daily 11am-2am.

Barley Mill Pub, 1629 SE Hawthorne Blvd. (231-1492). This smoky temple to Jerry Garcia has not been the same since his demise. Bring your bootlegs on Wed. nights and let the music live on. Full of fantastic murals and long bench tables that may land you next to a stranger. Upbeat, but mellow, like the man himself. McMenamins beer on tap (pints $2.85). Happy hour daily 4-6pm (pints $2.25). Open Mon.-Sat. 11am-1am, Sun. noon-midnight.

The Space Room Lounge, 4800 SE Hawthorne Blvd. (235-8303). Take bus #14 (brown beaver). Judy Jetson smoked way too many cancer sticks in this space-age lounge. The cutting-edge compress into dark booths and contemplate. One Bloody Mary ($4.50) will put you over the edge. Strictly cocktails. Open daily 6am-2:30am.

Other Neighborhoods

Satyricon, 121 NW 6th Ave. (243-2380). Alternarock rumbles in the glowing back room every night. PoMo bar and a chic new sister restaurant, **Fellini.** Step into this madly mosaiced space to rest your ears and taste an innovative cuisine (entrees start at $3). Or come just to loiter where (rumor has it) Courtney met Kurt. Cover $2-6. Food Mon.-Fri. noon-2:30am, Sat.-Sun. noon-4am; music 3pm-2:30am.

The Laurel Thurst Public House, 2958 NE Glisan St. (232-1504). A neighborhood crowd jams to the tune of local acoustic and electric acts. Two cozy intimate rooms allow for groovin', boozin' and schmoozin'. Breakfast until 3pm. Burgers and sandwiches $5-6. Microbrew pints $3.25, domestic $2.25. Cover $2-3. Free pool all day Sun., Mon.-Thurs. before 7pm.

BridgePort Brew Pub, 1313 NW Marshall (241-7179). The zenith of beer and pizza joints in a now defunct wood-beamed rope factory. The pizza is locally famous, and, though pricey ($19.75 for a 5-topping pie), it can feed a family of 4. Lotsa space for lotsa people. Tables cut from old bowling allies. The outdoor patio fills up during happy hour. Brews are all Bridgeport; $2 for 10oz, $3.25 for 20oz. Open Mon.-Thurs. 11:30am-11pm, Fri.-Sat. 11:30am-midnight, Sun. 1-9pm.

Embers, 110 NW Broadway at Couch St. (222-3082). This nightspot just hasn't been the same since Panorama's opening (see above). You can still follow the rainbows all the way onto the dance floor or the bustling bar. Mostly gay clientele; retro and house music. Nightly drag show at 10pm. Domestic bottled beer $2.25, mixed drinks $2.50. Open daily 11am-3am.

Gypsy, 625 NW 21st Ave. at Hoyt St. (796-1859). Take bus #17 (red salmon). This restaurant and lounge with sparkly red vinyl circular booths, looks like a 50s experiment gone awry. Bring your cool friends for moral support. Happy hour Mon.-Fri. 4-6:30pm and Sat.-Sun. 3-5:30pm features drinks for $1.50, appetizers at half-price. Pass through padded red velvet doors to the lounge where black lights and video poker rule the night. Open Mon.-Fri. 9am-2am, Sat.-Sun. 8am-2am.

EVENTS

Cinco de Mayo Festival (222-9807). The weekend closest to May 5th. Mexican Independence Day celebration with sister city Guadalajara complete with fiery food, entertainment, and crafts at Waterfront Park.

Rose Festival, 220 NW 2nd Ave. (248-7923 for recording, 227-2681 for the offices). Portland's premier summer event. During the 1st 3 weeks of June, U.S. Navy sailors flood the street while the city decks itself in all its finery. Waterfront concerts, art festivals, celebrity entertainment, auto racing, parades, an air show, Navy ships, and the largest children's parade in the world. Great during the day, at night women should exercise caution. Many events require tickets; call 224-4400.

Waterfront Blues Festival (973-FEST/3378). Early July. Outrageously good. International celebrities and some of the finest regional blues artists participate in this 3-day event. Suggested donation $3 and 2 cans of food to benefit Oregon Food Bank.

Oregon Brewers Festival (778-5917). Last weekend in July. The continent's largest gathering of independent brewers makes for one incredible party at Waterfront Park. Free admission, but $2 mandatory mug and $1 per taste.

Mt. Hood Festival of Jazz (666-3810). 1st weekend in Aug. at Mt. Hood Community College in Gresham. Expensive (tickets start at $29.50 per night and even more when you buy them by calling Ticketmaster at 224-4400), but this is the premier jazz festival of the Pacific Northwest. Wynton Marsalis and the late Stan Getz have been regulars. Reserve tickets well in advance. Write Mt. Hood Festival of Jazz, P.O. Box 3024, Gresham 97030. To reach the festival, take I-84 to Wood Village-Gresham exit and follow the signs, or ride MAX to the end of the line.

The Bite—A Taste of Portland (248-0600). 2nd week in Aug. in Waterfront Park. Food, music, stand-up comics, a wine pavilion and the 5k "Dine and Dash" race. Pricey, but Portland natives swear by it.

Artquake (227-2787). Labor Day weekend. Music, mime, food, and neo-situationist hoopla in and around Pioneer Courthouse Sq.

Portland Marathon (226-1111; www.teleport.com/~pdxmar). Late Sept. If you're in shape, join the thousands who run this 26.2-miler. Many shorter runs and walks also held (thank God). Remember, Phedippedes died.

Near Portland

Few Portland residents would consider relocating—not only is the city a cultural giant, but it is near some of America's most fantastic natural attractions. The burned-out, truncated shell of Mount St. Helens is a short drive north into Washington State; one edge of the Columbia River Gorge, full of world-class windsurfing and breathtaking views, is only a 30-minute drive up I-84; Mt. Hood is less than 60 mi. away and hosts skiers year-round. East along the Oregon Trail, the footprints of early pioneers carpet the Mount Hood National Forest, while the rugged rocks and cliffs lining the Pacific are just two hours west.

SAUVIE ISLAND

Twenty minutes northwest of downtown Portland on U.S. 30 (follow signs to Mount St. Helens from 405, Vaughn, or Yeon Ave.), Sauvie Island is a peaceful rural hideaway at the confluence of the Columbia and Willamette Rivers. The island offers great views of the city from its vast sandy stretches. On winter mornings, eagles and geese congregate along the roads, and in spring and summer, berries are everywhere. For many Portlanders, a summer trip to the island's **u-pick farms** (family operations announced by hand-lettered signs along the roads) is an annual tradition.

The island's beaches are another star attraction. Many visitors soak up the rays on the south side. Some bring fishing rods and bathing suits, but none swim in the Willamette's waters; factories and imperfect sewage systems upstream make sure of that. The best inland beach area is **Oak Island** on the south side of Sturgeon Lake, a 10-minute drive once on the island. Turn west onto Sauvie Island Rd. from the bridge, then take the first major right onto Reeder Rd. Continue onto Oak Island Rd. which turns into a gravel road after 3 mi. and ends in a parking lot. Wander the weedy road from there. A $3 parking permit is required for the whole island and is efficiently enforced. Pick one up at **Sam's Cracker Barrel Grocery,** along with a free map of the island and any supplies you may need. Plan ahead; Sam's is the only place that sells permits, and it's right by the bridge, a several mile backtrack from the beaches.

MOUNT HOOD

Magnificent, glacier-topped Mt. Hood is at the junction of U.S. 26 and Rte. 35, 90 minutes east of Portland and one hour from the Hood River. The 11,235 ft. active volcano may look dormant (it doesn't steam and has no crater because open vents keep internal pressure low), but the surrounding area is a hotbed of outdoor activity. Whether they be snowboarders, skiers, climbers, bikers, or hikers, Mt. Hood provides its suitors with endless opportunities for adventure.

Though Mt. Bachelor (see **Bend,** p. 485) is known as Oregon's best skiing, three respectable resorts are closer to Portland: **Timberline** and **Mt. Hood Ski Bowl,** off U.S. 26 at Government Camp, and **Mt. Hood Meadows,** 9 mi. east on Rte. 35. All three offer night skiing. Timberline, elevation 8540 ft. (272-3311 or 231-7979), a largely beginner and intermediate area, has the longest ski season in Oregon (until Labor Day). Rental equipment costs around $19. Snowboard rental is $33 with boots, $26 without (lift tickets $32, seniors and ages 7-12 $18). Winter night skiing, daily 4-10pm. Mount Hood Ski Bowl, 87000 E. U.S. 26 (222-BOWL/2695), in **Government Camp,** 2 mi. west of Hwy. 35, is smaller, but has the best night skiing and a snowboard park. Season is limited (Nov. to April), but 80-90% of the trails have night skiing (open Mon.-Tues. 1-10pm, Wed.-Thurs. 9am-10pm, Fri. 9am-11pm, Sat. 8:30-11pm, Sun. 8:30-10pm; ski rentals $17, ages 7-12 $11; snowboards $25; lift tickets $23 per day, $14 per night, $30 for both). **Mount Hood Meadows** (337-2222), 9 mi. east of Government Camp on Hwy. 35, is the largest and best resort in the area, offering an array of beginning, intermediate, advanced, and expert terrain. At a medium elevation (7300 ft.), it stays open through the July 4th weekend (ski rentals $18, juniors $13; lift tickets $35, juniors $21; night skiing Dec.-March Wed.-Sun. 4-10pm, $17). All three areas offer ski lessons averaging $35 per hour or $25 per person for groups.

Only Mt. Fuji draws more **climbers** each year than Mt. Hood; for adventurers who wish to tackle the mountain on foot, **Timberline Mountain Guides,** P.O. Box 23214, Portland (636-7704), in Government Camp, offers mountain, snow, and ice climbing courses. Climbs last one to three days, with one-day trips from $80. The best time for climbing is from May to mid-July; experience, wilderness permit and registration are necessary (more info available at Wy'east Day Lodge in Timberline). Or give your feet a break and take Timberline's **Magic Mile,** a lift that carries nonskiers above the clouds for spectacular views of the Cascades ($6, children $3; winter discounts with a coupon that just about any employee will happily hand out). Turn up the 6 mi. road just past **Government Camp** to the Depression-era **Timberline Lodge** (272-3311; for reservations 800-547-1406; rooms start at $65 per night), which starred in Stanley Kubrick's *The Shining* as the Overlook Hotel. The road to the lodge offers arresting views of the valley below, and the high Cascades to the south. Next door is the **Wy'east Day Lodge,** where skiers can store equipment without staying overnight, and the **Wy'east Kitchen,** a cafeteria alternative to Timberline's expensive dining (entrees $2-6; open daily summer 6:30am-4pm; winter 7:30am-4pm; 7:30am-10pm when there is night skiing). If you're there in the summer and the snow seems too soggy, Mount Hood Ski Bowl east offers an **Action Park,** complete with horseback rides ($22 per hr.), Indy Karts ($5 for 5min.), bungee jumping ($25), and an alpine slide ($10 for 3 slides). **Rent mountain bikes** on the west side of the Ski Bowl (mid-June to late Nov.; all day bike sky chair $15). The prices aren't nearly as steep as the trails. The bike rental cost does not include a $4 U.S. forest trail permit, required all over the mountain (park open Mon.-Fri. 11am-6pm, Sat.-Sun. 10am-7pm).

Hiking trails circle Mt. Hood. Simple maps are posted on a number of signs around Government Camp. The most popular dayhike is **Mirror Lake,** a 4 mi. loop (open June-Oct.) that starts from a parking lot off U.S. 26, 1 mi. west of Government Camp, and loops past a reflection of Mt. Hood's peak in the glassy lake. Stop by the **Hood River District Ranger Station,** 67805 Rte. 35, Parkdok 97041 (352-6002), or the **Zigzag District Ranger Station,** 70220 E. U.S. 26 (622-3191 or 666-0704 from Portland) for more detailed information (and some rolling papers?). The well-stocked **Mt. Hood Visitors Information Center,** 65000 E. U.S. 26, Welches 97067 (666-0704, ext. 684;

You Won't Find the Hendersons Here

John Lithgow has a new day job and **Sasquatch** fever has subsided of late, but the mystery members of this hominid family, their existence shrouded in murky lore, remain inscrutable to the scientific community. Mt. Hood marks the southern boundary of the Dark Divide, the area most associated with the sightings of these large, hirsute creatures who lurk in the forests and eat nuts and twigs. This fearsome beast was known even before the white man got his grubby hands on the New World. The Salish called the creature *saskehavas,* from which comes the English term "Sasquatch." Many dismiss the possibility of any such mysterious **ape-man.** Why, they query, hasn't conclusive evidence of its existence been adduced? Cryptozoologists (scientists who study undiscovered species) know better. They reply that numerous sightings and photographs *are* conclusive, and that naysayers are deluded by their own skepticism. If you do chance upon a **Bigfoot,** it will be easy to recognize. The big galoot stands roughly six to ten feet tall, wears size 23 Hush Puppies, weighs about 400 pounds, is covered in dark fur, and leaves behind a strong, fetid **odor.**

16 mi. west of Mt. Hood) also provides permits. It is a part of the **Mt. Hood Village** (622-4011 or 800-255-3069), a giant complex with everything from a dance hall to a heated pool (420 sites $23, full hookup $26).

Camping spots in the Mt. Hood National Forest cluster near the junction of U.S. 26 and Rte. 35. Less than 1 mi. below Timberline is **Alpine** (800-547-1406) accessible only in the summer. Choose one of 16 sites, all with water and toilets. Reservations are essential ($7). **Trillium Lake Campground,** 2 mi. east of the Timberline turnoff on U.S. 26, has trails around the clear lake and 57 paved sites with water and toilets. Pine trees offer some privacy ($10; premium lakeside site $12; doubles $20; all include a $3 parking fee). Just 1 mi. west of Trillium Lake, down a dirt road off U.S. 26, **Still Creek Campgrounds** has a quieter, woodsier, serene feel, unpaved sites, and a babbling brook ($9, premium creekside sites $11). On the other side of the action, 10 mi. north of U.S. 26 on Rte. 35, **Robinwood** and **Sherwood Campgrounds,** both $10, lie just off the highway beside a running creek. Reserve any Mt. Hood National Forest campsite by calling (800)-280-CAMP/2267.

■ Columbia River Gorge

Only an hour from Portland, the Columbia River Gorge stretches for 75 stunning miles. The Columbia River has carved a 1000 ft. canyon deep through rumpled hills and sheer, rocky cliffs. Mt. Hood and Mt. Adams loom nearby, and waterfalls plunge hundreds of feet over cliffs toward the Columbia. Traveling east along the gorge, heavily forested peaks give way to broad, bronze cliffs and golden hills. The river widens out and the wind picks up at the town of **Hood River.** The gorge is the confluence of Oregon's various identities. Once "as fast as a waterfall turned on its side," and so full of fish that Lewis and Clark joked that they could drive their wagons over fishbacks, the Columbia's waters are now slower and emptier due to dams and fishing. Surrounded by climates and habitats of all sorts, the gorge touches deserts, rain-soaked forests, mountains, and prairies.

Practical Information To follow the gorge, which divides Oregon and Washington, take I-84 east to Exit 22. Continue east uphill on the only road possible, and you will find yourself on Hwy. 30, a.k.a. the **Columbia River Scenic Highway.** This road follows the crest of the gorge walls and affords unforgettable views.

The largest town in the gorge is **Hood River,** at the junction of I-84 and Rte. 35. Take **Greyhound** from Portland ($10) or Seattle ($21.50) to Hood River; the **station** (386-1212 or 800-872-7245) is at 1205 B Ave., between 12th and 13th St. (open Mon.-Sat. and sometimes on Sun. 8:30am-7pm). **Amtrak** (800-872-7245) also runs trains from Portland to the foot of Walnut St. in Bingen, WA ($16). This **windsurfing mecca** is crammed with board-rental shops; boards are available for a range of abilities; contact the **Hood River County Chamber of Commerce,** 405 Portway Ave. (386-2000 or 800-366-3530), just off the City Center exit (#63), for info on Hood River (open Mon.-Thurs. 9am-5pm, Fri. 9am-4pm, Sat.-Sun. 10am-4pm; mid-Oct. to mid-April Mon.-Fri. 9am-5pm). Free publications, including *Visit the Gorge, Hood River County Four Season Fun,* and many for windsurfers, offer info on sights, camping, accommodations, history, and events; these are available at visitor centers along the gorge, as is the $3 US Forest Service **map** of the Columbia Wilderness, useful for backpackers. In an **emergency** call 911; for non-emergency needs call the **Hood River Police** at 386-3942. The **post office** is at 408 Cascade Ave. (open Mon.-Fri. 8:30am-5pm). The **area code** along the gorge in Oregon is 541 and in Washington is 509.

Accommodations and Camping Crash with boardsailers at the outdoorsy **Bingen School Inn Hostel** (509-493-3363), just across the Hood River Toll Bridge and 3½ blocks from the Amtrak stop in Bingen, WA. Take your third left after the yellow blinking light, and it's one block up the hill on Humbolt St. Sleep without guilt in front of blackboards in this converted school house in one of 48 hostel beds ($11) or five private rooms ($40; discounts for longer stays). **Mountain bikes** ($15 per day) and **sailboards** ($40 per day) are available for rent.

Beacon Rock State Park, across the Bridge of the Gods (Exit 44) then 7 mi. west on Washington Hwy. 14, has secluded sites for $10. The entrance to the park, directly across from the rock, is hard to miss. If you don't mind camping in a crowded yard by the road, the **Port of Cascade Locks Marine,** ½ mi. east off the bridge on the Oregon side, has a lawn on the river. They pack as many RVs and tents on it as they can ($10), but offer showers as compensation. **Ainsworth State Park** is also easily accessible (see **Portland: Accommodations and Camping,** p. 412).

Sights and Outdoors The mighty Columbia and its 30mph winds make Hood River a **windsurfing** paradise. Vibrantly colored sailboards decorate the Gorge, and engage in obsessive, zany competitions like the "Gorge Games" (all the outdoor games imaginable, expecting ESPN coverage). Everything stops in town on windy days, and folks gets antsy during calm stretches. Beginners sail at the **Hook,** a shallow, sandy cove, and experts try the **Spring Creek Fish Hatchery** on the Washington side, the place to watch the best in the business. The **Event Site,** the water off Exit 63 behind the visitor's center, is another hub. Parking all day is $3, but it's free if you just sit and watch. To fully experience Hood River, rent a board or take a lesson. A 2½-3 hour class at **Rhonda Smith Windsurfing Center** (386-WIND/9463)—take Exit 64 under the bridge and left after the blinking red light—will get you started ($65-75). Rentals (right on the water) start at $25-35 for a half-day, with discounts for longer. The gorge also has excellent mountain biking. **Discover Bicycles,** 1020 Wasco St. (386-4820), rents mountain bikes for $5 per hour and $25 per day, and can suggest routes (they also sell all sorts of **trail maps**). If you're staying at the hostel, try the 5 mi. roundtrip **Hospital Hill Trail,** which provides views of Mt. Hood, the Gorge, Hood River, and surrounding villages. To reach the unmarked trail, follow signs to the hospital, fork left to Rhine Village, park, and walk behind the Power Transformers through the livestock fence.

The Gorge also offers a panoply of sights that you don't have to get wet or dirty to enjoy. The famous **Vista House** (695-2230), completed in 1918 as a memorial to Oregon's pioneers, is now a visitors center in **Crown Point State Park** (open May 1-Oct. 15th daily 9am-6pm). Crown Point is 3 mi. east of eastbound Exit 22 off I-84. A three-dimensional model of the area illuminates various trails and waterfalls along the gorge, and maps are there for the taking. The house hangs on the edge of an outcropping, high above the river. A trail leaves the road a few yards down from the house, ending in a secluded view of both the house and the gorge. For an even loftier view, drive up the **Larch Mountain Road,** which splits from Hwy. 30 just above the Vista House and winds up 4000 ft. over 14 mi. to a picnic area that has views of Mount St. Helens, Mt. Rainier, Mt. Adams, Mt. Hood and Mt. Jefferson.

A string of waterfalls adorns the highway east of Crown Point. At **Latourell Falls,** 2½ mi. east of Crown Point, a jaunt down a paved path is sure to get you sprayed. Five miles farther east, **Wahkeena Falls** is visible from the road, winding 242 ft. down a narrow gorge. These falls (meaning "most beautiful") are a popular spot for picnicking and the start of hiking trails; a short, steep scramble over loose rock, or a ¼ mi. trip up a paved walk will put you right in the middle. Just ½ mi. east of Hwy. 30 is the granddaddy of them all, **Multnomah Falls,** which attracts two million visitors annually. From a viewing platform (just past the espresso cart, the gift shop, the dining room, and the info center), watch the falls crash 620 ft. into a tiny pool and then drain under the gracefully arching Benson Bridge into a lower falls. Exit 31, on I-84, takes you to an island in the middle of the freeway from which you can only see the upper falls. A quick hike that takes you to Benson Bridge shouldn't be missed. Those who push up the trail past the top will be rewarded with relative solitude and a series of smaller waterfalls. Hikers can follow other paths (including one that links up with Larch Mountain); the **information center** at the base of Multnomah Falls has free maps and great suggestions. **Oneonta Falls,** 2 mi. east, is a 1.1 mi. hike through Cold Creek in Oneonta Gorge (the trail *is* the creek). **Horsetail Falls,** another mile east, drops 176 ft.; a steep ½ mi. hike affords a closer look; a 1.3 mi. trail takes you past Horsetail Falls, upper Horsetail Falls and Oneonta Falls (start/park in Horsetail lot).

Two longer, sublime **hiking** experiences are the steep **Wyeth Trail** near the hamlet of Wyeth (Exit 51), which leads to a wilderness boundary after 4.4 mi. and to the road to Hood River after 7.3 mi.; and the long (13 mi.) but incredible **Eagle Creek Trail,** chiseled into cliffs high above Eagle Creek, passing four waterfalls before joining the Pacific Crest Trail. For info on trails and a friendly earful of local lore, call the Columbia **Gorge National Scenic Area Headquarters** (541-386-2333).

Forty-four miles east of Portland is the oldest of the Columbia River hydroelectric projects, the **Bonneville Dam** (Exit 40 off I-84). Woody Guthrie was working for the Bonneville Power Co. when he wrote "Roll On, Columbia," a salute to river development: "Your power is turning our darkness to dawn, so roll, on Columbia, roll on." You can make your way across one section of the river atop turbine powerhouses to the **Bradford Island Visitors Center** (503-374-8820), which has self-guided tours of the locks and fish hatcheries (open daily 9am-5pm).

One exit down off I-84 (#44), in Cascade Locks, stands the **Bridge of the Gods** (75¢ toll). The bridge was constructed at the site where, according to native legend, a natural bridge once stood. It collapsed when the two warrior gods, Klickitat and Wy'east, erupted in a fight for the honor of Loowit, the beautiful witch-woman in charge of fire. The chief of gods punished them by collapsing the bridge and turning them into Mt. Adams (12,307 ft.), Mt. Hood (11,235 ft.), and Mt. St. Helens (4,568 ft.) respectively. The bridge seems fragile even now; if you drive slowly, you can see through the grating to the river below.

About 7 mi. west of the bridge on the Washington side is **Beacon Rock,** the 848-ft.-high neck of an old volcano, the largest monolith in the U.S. (across the river from Exit 35 off I-84). You will know it when you see it, and you may long to climb it, but alas, it is not only a tough technical climb requiring a permit (contact the National Scenic Area Headquarters in Hood River at 541-386-2333). It is also closed to climbers in the summer, while the falcons roost at its crown. If you're up for an assertive incline, amazing views of the gorge, and, in June and July, an explosion of wildflowers, look for signs to **Dog Mountain.** A 2250 ft., 3½ mi. hike starts in a parking lot just east of Beacon Rock, and a series of switchbacks lead to the 2948 ft. summit.

In Stevenson, WA, 3 mi. east of the bridge, is the snazzy **Columbia Gorge Interpretive Center,** Box 396 (509-427-8211). Its highlights include an actual-size replica of the now-illegal fish wheels used to harvest millions of pounds of salmon, an enormous antique steam engine (that now runs on electricity), and a 12-minute multimedia show on the creation of the gorge (open daily 10am-5pm; $6, seniors and students $5, ages 6-12 $4, under 6 free).

Thirty miles east of Hood River, the **Maryhill Museum of Art,** 35 Maryhill Museum Dr. (509-773-3733), sits high above the Columbia on the Washington side. I-84 to

Biggs and the slightly more scenic Hwy. 14 both follow the river and will get you close enough to follow signs. Built by Sam Hill in the 20s, the mansion is named for his daughter. Peacocks stroll through the garden outside a gallery of European and American paintings, a collection of drawings and sculptures by Rodin (such as "Eve," "Youth Triumphant," and "Vase of Titans"), works by Native Americans, and nearly 150 intricately hand-made chess sets from around the world. If Bobby Fischer is hiding *anywhere,* it's here (open daily mid-March through mid-Nov. 9am-5pm; $5, seniors $4.50, ages 6-16 $1.50).

Nineteen miles east of Hood River on I-84, **The Dalles** (DALZ) was the last stop on the agonizing Oregon Trail. Lewis and Clark camped here at Fort Rock on Bargeway Rd. in 1805. French trappers named the area *Le Dalle* (the trough) after the rapids around that section of the river. For a free **map** and a walking tour of historical spots in town, go to the **Dalles Area Chamber of Commerce,** 404 W. 2nd St. (296-2231 or 800-255-3385; open Mon.-Fri. 8:30am-5pm, Sat. 10am-3pm, Sun. 10am-2pm; fewer winter hours). It's on your right, half a mile down Exit 84 off I-84. Up the hill, the **Fort Dalles Museum,** 500 W. 15th (296-4547), at Garrison, is housed in the original 1856 surgeon's quarters and displays memorabilia of the pioneer and military history of the region. Highlighting the dusty collection of old buggies and cars are an eight-passenger horse-drawn "bus" and two hearse carriages (open daily 10am-5pm; Nov.-Mar. closed Tues.-Wed.; $3, 18 and under free). The visitors center at the **Dalles Lock and Dam** (296-1181), the longest concrete dam in America, offers free one-hour tours that include a train ride to the dam, a view of the fish ladder, a glimpse of the generator, and a look at old Indian petroglyphs (open early June-Labor Day daily 9am-5pm; tours leave every 30min.; self-guided tours available the rest of the year).

OREGON COAST

If not for the renowned **U.S. 101,** Oregon's drippy beaches and dramatic seaside vistas would be only a beautiful rumor to those on the interior. From Astoria in the north to Brookings in the south, the highway hugs the shore along the Oregon Coast, linking endless resorts and fishing villages that cluster around the mouths of rivers feeding into the Pacific. Breathtaking ocean vistas spread between these towns, and hundreds of miles of state parks and national forests allow direct access to beaches and big surf. Wherever the windy two lanes leave the coast, even narrower beach-loop roads access long stretches of unspoiled coast, providing glimpses of the ocean's diverse sealife. Seals, sea lions, and waterfowl lounge on rocks just offshore, watching the human world whiz by on wheels.

GETTING AROUND

Gasoline and grocery **prices** on the coast are about 20% higher than in the inland cities. Motorists should try to stock up before reaching the coast. When searching for a site to pull into for the night, look to the small villages, as they tend to be cheaper and more interesting. From north to south, Nehalem, Wheeler, Depoe Bay, Winchester Bay, Charleston, and Bandon offer escape from the larger and more commercialized towns of Seaside, Tillamook, Lincoln City, Newport, and Coos Bay. There are 17 state parks along the coast offering major campgrounds with electricity and showers.

Travel down the coast by bike is both rewarding and exhausting. Cyclists should write to the **Oregon Tourism Commission** (see p. 407), or to virtually any visitors center or chamber of commerce on the coast for the free *Oregon Coast Bike Route Map;* it provides invaluable information on campsites, hostels, bike repair facilities, temperatures, and wind conditions. Remember that Portlanders head down the coast to vacation, so most traffic flows south of the city. In summer, prevailing winds blow south, keeping at the backs of cyclists, easing the journey. But beware: the shoulder of U.S. 101 and other coastal highways often narrows to nonexistent, and enormous log trucks lumber around tight turns. **Buses** run up and down the coast, stopping in most sizeable towns. Many local lines are affiliates of Greyhound (see p. 28) and make connections to major urban centers like Seattle, Portland, and Eugene.

Astoria

Lewis and Clark arrived in Astoria in 1805 at the end of their transcontinental trek; six years later, John Astor, scion of a famously wealthy 19th-century family, established a fur-trading post and left his name as a legacy, making Astoria the first permanent U.S. settlement west of the Rockies. Today, Astorians balance on the Oregon-Washington state line, making a living by fishing, surviving the same way Meriwether and William did almost two centuries ago.

Rows of Victorian homes (painted in pastel hues, perhaps to combat the area's perseverant cloud-cover), plenty of espresso bars and fast food, and a comfortable, working class atmosphere make this smallish town a Hollywood favorite: such classics of American cinema as *Kindergarten Cop, Goonies, Free Willy,* and *Teenage Mutant Ninja Turtles III* all shot footage in Astoria. Travelers heading up and down the coast (and Washingtonians shopping in sales-tax free Oregon) constantly filter through the town, crossing over the massive and scenic 4 mi. Astoria Bridge.

PRACTICAL INFORMATION AND ORIENTATION

Visitors Information: Astoria/Warrenton Area Chamber of Commerce, 111 W. Marine Dr. (325-6311), just east of the bridge to Washington. Pick up the free **map** of Astoria at this bastion of info on the Coast and southwest Washington. Open Mon.-Fri. 8am-6pm, Sat.-Sun. 9am-6pm; Oct.-May Mon.-Fri. 8am-5pm, Sat.-Sun. 11am-4pm.

Buses: Pierce Pacific Stages, Inc. (692-4437). A Greyhound affiliate. Pick-up at Video City, 95 W. Marine Dr., across from the Chamber of Commerce. To Portland (1 per day, $15) and Seaside (1 per day, $5). **Sunset Empire Transit** (325-0563), pick-up at the Greyhound bus station, Duane St. at 9th. To Seaside (7 per day, $2.25, seniors and disabled $1.75)

Public Transportation: Astoria Transit System, 364 9th St. (325-0563 or 800-452-2085). Local bus service Mon.-Sat. 6:50am-6:30pm. Makes a full city loop every hour (75¢, students 50¢).

Taxi: Yellow Cab (325-3131 or 861-2626). 24hr.

Car Club: AAA, 135 S. U.S. 101 (861-3118), at Warrenton. Open Mon.-Fri. 8am-5pm.

Laundromat: Coin Laundry, 823 W. Marine Dr. (325-2027), next to Dairy Queen. Wash $1.25, 8½min. dry 25¢. Open daily 7:30am-10pm.

Crisis Line: (325-3426). Open Mon.-Fri. 9am-5pm.

Women's Resource Center: 10 6th St. #205 (325-5735), at Marine Dr. 24hr.

Seniors Information Service: 800 Exchange St. (325-0123). Open Mon.-Fri. 8am-noon and 1-5pm.

Pharmacy: Astoria Pharmacy, 840 Exchange St. (325-1123). Open Mon.-Fri. 9:30am-5:30pm.

Hospital: Columbia Memorial, 2111 Exchange St. (325-4321 or 800-962-2407).

Emergency: 911. **Police:** 555 30th St. (325-4411). **Clatsop County Sheriff:** 325-2061. **Coast Guard:** 861-6228. **Fire:** 325-4237.

Post Office: 750 Commercial St. (325-2141), in the Federal Bldg. at 8th St. Open Mon.-Fri. 8:30am-5pm. **General Delivery ZIP Code:** 97103.

Area Code: 503.

Astoria is a convenient link between Washington and the Oregon coast. Two bridges run from the city: the **Youngs Bay Bridge,** to the southwest, where Marine Dr. becomes U.S. 101, and the two-lane, towering **Astoria Bridge,** which spans the Columbia River into Washington. The Astoria Bridge is so narrow that motorists might prefer to drive cyclists across rather than swerve around them and into incoming traffic. Many streets in downtown Astoria are one-way. Pick up a map from the

Chamber of Commerce (see above) before exploring downtown. All streets parallel to the water are in alphabetical order except for the first one, Marine Dr.

Warrenton lies a few miles west of Astoria. U.S. 30 runs to Portland, 96 mi. east of town. Astoria can also be reached from Portland via U.S. 26 and U.S. 101 at Seaside.

ACCOMMODATIONS AND CAMPING

Motels in the area cater to tourists heading south to Oregon's coastal resort towns, so rooms can be expensive and hard to come by during the summer. But the area has a marvelous, undiscovered hostel, and U.S. 101 south of Astoria is littered with clean and scenic campgrounds. **Fort Stevens State Park** is particularly nice.

Fort Columbia State Park Hostel (HI-AYH), Fort Columbia, Chinook, WA (360-777-8755), within the park boundaries. Cross the 4 mi. bridge from Astoria into Washington, then take a sharp left just after exiting the tunnel 3 mi. north of the bridge on U.S. 101. Take the 75¢ Astoria Transit System bus on weekdays and Saturday (see **Practical Information**). This 1896 military hospital-turned-hostel pampers guests with flowered bedsheets, shiny hardwood floors, and a cozy living room stocked with old *Let's Go*s (bless them) and board games. Hostel manager Marsha welcomes with free pancake breakfasts and fabulous facilities. The only difficult chore here is leaving. Despite all this and laundry facilities, the hostel rarely fills. Lockout 10am-5pm, check-in 5-10pm. $10, nonmembers $13, bicyclists $8, under 18 (with parent) $5. Open April-Sept.

Grandview Bed and Breakfast, 1574 Grand Ave. (325-0000 or 325-5555 for reservations). Cheery, fluffy, luxurious rooms. "Continental breakfast plus" includes fresh muffins, smoked salmon, and bagels. But there's a catch: the management says that unmarried couples may feel uncomfortable. A "love" poem by Emmet Fox woos visitors in the front hall, and "love" magnets make love to the refrigerators. Cheapest room $45, shared bath starts at $55, private bath at $73. Off-season, 2nd night is free.

Lamplighter Motel, 131 W. Marine Dr. (325-4051), between the Pig'n Pancake diner and the visitors center. Well-worn rooms with amenities and large bathrooms. Coffee in lobby, cable, and lamps to be lit. Singles $50, doubles $60; winter rates $15 less. Senior discounts. Reserve at least a week in advance during summer.

Fort Stevens State Park (861-1671), over Youngs Bay Bridge on U.S. 101 S., 10 mi. west of Astoria. A mammoth park (the largest state park in the U.S.!), with rugged, empty beaches and bike trails galore. This is the closest major campground to the resort towns of Seaside and Cannon Beach. 603 sites and hot showers. Facilities for the disabled. Call (800) 452-5687 to reserve for summer weekends ($6). Sites $17, $20 with full hookups; hiker/biker $4.50 per person; yurts—domed tents with sloping walls and plywood floors—$27.

FOOD

Escape expensive seafood and Whoppers at **Sentry Supermarket,** 3300 Leif Erickson Dr. (325-1931), and have the ultimate seaside experience while listening to nearby barking sea lions. Grab a latté ($1.75) at the drive-through and sit on the rocks to watch the animals (open daily 7am-10pm). A limited selection of natural foods and organic produce is available at the tiny **Community Store,** 1389 Duane St. (325-0027; open Mon.-Sat. 10am-6pm).

Columbian Cafe, 1114 Marine Dr. (325-2233). The charismatic chef's crêpe-flipping frenzy is the best show in town. The pasta and seafood dinners ($6-16), warm spinach salad ($3.50), and crêpes ($5-7) are divine. This crazy cafe is so popular, it recently took over a neighboring store for more santeria-style seating. There are sometimes waits for dinner, but local banter, the microbrew menu, and fantastic food make up for lost time. Order "Chef's Mercy"—he chooses your meal for you; you say how spicy ($7). One local has so much faith in the pretentious pancakes that he has begged for Mercy over 1200 times. Open Mon.-Tues. 8am-8pm, Wed.-Thurs. 8am-2pm and 5-8pm, Fri. 8am-2pm, 5-9pm, Sat. 10am-2pm, and 5-9pm.

Photo: R. Olken

Greetings from Let's Go Publications

The book in your hand is the work of hundreds of student researcher-writers, editors, cartographers, and designers. Each summer we brave monsoons, revolutions, and marriage proposals to bring you a fully updated, completely revised travel guide series, as we've done every year for the past 38 years.

This is a collection of our best finds, our cheapest deals, our most evocative description, and, as always, our wit, humor, and irreverence. Let's Go is filled with all the information on anything you could possibly need to know to have a successful trip, and we try to make it as much a companion as a guide.

We believe that budget travel is not the last recourse of the destitute, but rather the only way to travel; living simply and cheaply brings you closer to the people and places you've been saving up to visit. We also believe that the best adventures and discoveries are the ones you find yourself. So put us down every once in while and head out on your own. And when you find something to share, drop us a line. We're **Let's Go Publications,** 67 Mount Auburn St., Cambridge, MA 02138, USA (email: fanmail@letsgo.com; http://www.letsgo.com). And let us know if you want a free subscription to ***The Yellowjacket,*** the new Let's Go Newsletter.

Shark Rock Cafe, 577 14th St. (325-7720). This new cafe lurking in a baby blue Victorian gets a close second in Astoria's race for best food. Black and white Salem High yearbook photos from the 40s to the 70s peer out from wood tabletops, and a shark's-eye view of the Columbia River clear over to Washington helps diners relax with cinnamon french toast ($5), grilled chicken Caesar ($6), or wild mushroom rigatoni ($8.50). Open Wed. 8am-3pm, Thurs.-Sat. 8am-9pm, Sun. 10am-2pm; Sept.-May Tues.-Wed. 7am-3pm, Thurs.-Fri. 7am-9pm, Sat. 8am-9pm.

Someplace Else, 965 Commercial St. (325-3500). A family-style Italian restaurant that offers more than the Italian standards ($4-10). Every month, regulars vote on what specials they want, rotating among meat, chicken, fish, and veggie selections from, well, someplace else. The chick peas in tamarind sauce get rave reviews. Open Wed.-Mon. 11:30am-2pm and 4-9pm.

Ricardi Gallery, 108 10th St. (325-5450). Astoria's art collection is steadily improving thanks to this lovechild of a New York gallery and a Parisian cafe. The showroom displays all sorts of modern art and doubles as a hip coffeehouse. Cafe fare, with salads, soups, and copies of the *New Yorker* to boot. Open Mon.-Fri. 7:30am-5:30pm, Sat. 8:30am-5:30pm, Sun. 9am-4:30pm.

SIGHTS AND EVENTS

The **Astoria Column,** on Coxcomb Hill Rd., showcases a stupendous view of Astoria, cradled between views of Saddle Mountain in the south and the Columbia River estuary to the north—unless there are clouds (altogether too often). Completed in 1926, the column wraps around the 164 interior steps that pass newly repainted friezes depicting area history. Tableaux of historic Astoria include the discovery of the Columbia River by intrepid English sea captain Robert Grey, the arrival of Lewis and Clark, and the settling of Astoria. To troop up to the tower, follow the icons painted on Astoria's streets (open dawn-10pm; free).

The wave-shaped **Columbia River Maritime Museum,** 1792 Marine Dr. (325-2323), on the waterfront, makes waves with visitors and marine buffs. The prize of the model boat collection is Robert Grey's 1792 vessel, in which he "discovered" the mouth of the Columbia River. The cavernous museum is packed with marine lore, including displays on the salmon fisheries that once dominated Astoria. Tours of the *Columbia,* the last lightship to see active duty, are self-guided (museum open daily 9:30am-5pm; $5, seniors $4, ages 6-17 $2, under 6 free).

The **Astoria Regatta** (738-3430), held the second week in August, is one of the longest-running events in the Northwest and dates back to 1894. The tradition is still going strong and features food and craft booths, a watershow, scenic boat rides, fireworks, dances, and even a sailboat race or two. The **Scandinavian Festival** on the second weekend in June attracts a large following (admission for all 3 days $5, 6am-6pm $1, under 6 free). Contact the Chamber of Commerce (325-6311) for info.

Drinking with Paul

One block up from the Maritime Museum, Paul van der Velt, the eccentric owner of the **Shallon Winery,** 1598 Duane St. (325-5798), holds court, presiding over a fantasy kingdom of fantastic wines. He gives a tour of his minuscule viniculture facilities, complete with his interpretation of area history and the story behind his bizarre repertoire of wines, none made with grapes. A self-proclaimed connoisseur of fine food, he insists visitors call him "any time of day or night" before considering a meal at any restaurant within 50 mi. Samplers taste wines made from local berries and the only commercially produced **whey wines** (from Tillamook cheese) in the world. Approach the **cranberry** and whey wine with caution; its fruity taste belies its high alcohol content. Sampling **lemon meringue pie wine** is likely to be the highlight of any trip to the Oregon coast, and Paul's **chocolate orange wine** is more like a candy than a wine. Others have spent millions trying to reproduce this chocolate delicacy without success (of course you must be 21 to drink; gratuities and purchases appreciated; open almost every afternoon).

■ Near Astoria

Five miles south of Astoria, the **Fort Clatsop National Memorial** (861-2471) reconstructs the winter headquarters of the Lewis and Clark expedition from descriptions in their detailed journal. The log fort housed Lewis, Clark, their friend Charbonneau, his wife and interpreter Sacagawea, Clark's slave York, three officers, 24 enlisted men, several Northwest natives, and plenty of fleas. To find Ft. Clatsop, take the old Hwy. 101 exit (now the bus route) before the Youngs Bay bridge and make a left on Fort Clatsop Rd. Mimic the explorers' daily activities by sitting on beds covered in animal furs and hides, or attend a daily demonstration on such practices as quill pen writing and moccasin sewing by "living history" rangers swathed in feathers and leather.

Fort Stevens State Park (campground 861-1671, historical area 861-2000), off U.S. 101 on a narrow peninsula 10 mi. west of Astoria, has excellent swimming, fishing, boating facilities, beaches, and hiking trails. All equipment can be rented at the park, and a day use pass is $3. Fort Stevens was constructed in 1864 to prevent Confederate naval raiders from entering the Columbia; its sea of weapons included eight concrete gun batteries, nearly all of which remain (*sans* guns). These batteries are the primary focus of a self-guided walking tour (about 2hr.) that begins up the road from the day use and campground areas. A restored 1954 Army cargo truck takes visitors on narrated tours (daily in summer at 11am, 12:30, 2:30, and 4pm; $2.50, ages 12 and under $1.25). The tours leave from the **Fort Stevens Military Museum and Interpretive Center** (861-2000; open daily 10am-6pm; winter daily 10am-4pm).

Battery Russell (861-2471), in the park 1 mi. south of the historical area, bears the dubious distinction of being the only mainland American fort to fall under enemy fire since the War of 1812. At 11pm on June 21, 1942, a Japanese submarine surfaced offshore and shelled the fort with 17 rounds. The fort was undamaged and did not return fire. Today it is a military monument, and allows free access to visitors. Colorful kites offset the gloomy skeletal remains of the British schooner *Peter Iredale,* which ran aground in 1906. Bike paths weave through the park. If a dip in the ocean sounds a bit icy, try **Coffenbury Lake,** a warmer spot for swimming and fishing. The fee is included in the $3 day use fee, which is good for day use in any Oregon State Park until 10pm that evening.

Seaside

In the winter of 1805-6, explorers Lewis and Clark made their westernmost camp near Seaside. Were they to arrive today, they might just continue straight on into the Pacific in an attempt to avoid the hoards of baby strollers, bumper cars, and fried dough that have invaded the town. Built into a resort in the 1870s, 120 years of tourists have eroded Seaside's charm. With crowds, fast food, video arcades, and a developed beach, Seaside has Jersey shore ambitions; it lacks only sunshine, warm water, and a Trump casino. Seaside makes a good base for exploring the popular northern Oregon coast. Prices here are humbler than those in nearby Cannon Beach, and Seaside's hostel is one of the best in the Northwest.

PRACTICAL INFORMATION AND ORIENTATION

Visitors Information: Chamber of Commerce, 7 N. Roosevelt St. (738-6391 or 800-444-6740), on U.S. 101 and Broadway. Well-versed staff. Also a referral service for local motels; make reservations on a free phone. Open Mon.-Sat. 8am-6pm, Sun. 9am-5pm.; Oct.-May Mon.-Fri. 9am-5pm, Sat.-Sun. 10am-4pm.

Buses: Pierce Pacific Stages (717-1651), a Greyhound affiliate. Runs out of the hostel. To Portland (1 daily, $20) and Seattle (1 daily, $38). Buy tickets at the hostel (see **Accommodations,** below).

Public Transit: Sunset Empire Transit (325-0563). Runs between Astoria and Cannon Beach; stops at the hostel. 7 trips per day each direction Mon.-Sat. (roundtrip fares $1.50-6, senior/disabled $1-3.50, ages 6-12 $1-2). Tickets and info available at the hostel.

Taxi: Yellow Cab, 738-3131. 24hr.

Bike Rental: Prom Bike Shop, 622 12th Ave. (738-8251), at 12th and Holladay. Rents bikes, roller skates, in-line skates, beach tricycles, and surreys; most $6 per hr., $25 per day; tandem bicycles $10 per hr. ID held during rental. Open daily 10am-6pm. Also operates a rental shop at 80 Ave. A, downtown (open daily 7am-9pm) and **Seaside Surry,** a rental shop at 153 Ave. A (open daily 9am-6pm).

Laundry: Coin Laundry, 1150 N. Holladay Dr., 1 block north of hostel. $1.25 wash, 7½min. dry 25¢. Open daily 8am-9pm.

Library: 60 N. Roosevelt Dr. (738-6742). Open Tues.-Thurs. 9am-8pm, Fri.-Sat. 9am-5pm, Sun. 1-5pm.

Seaside Community and Senior Center: 1225 Ave. A (738-7393). Info and referral specialists. Open Mon.-Thurs. 8:30am-9:30pm, Fri. 8:30am-5:30pm.

Women's Crisis Service: 325-5735. 24hr.

Hospital: Providence Seaside Hospital, 725 S. Wahanna Rd. (717-7000).

Emergency: 911. **Police:** 1091 S. Holladay Dr. (738-6311). **Coast Guard:** 861-6228.

Post Office: 300 Ave. A (738-5462). Open Mon.-Fri. 8:30am-5pm, Sat. (for pickup only) 8:30-10am. **General Delivery ZIP Code:** 97138.

Area Code: 503.

Seaside lies 17 mi. south of Astoria and 8 mi. north of **Cannon Beach** along U.S. 101. The most direct route between Seaside and Portland is U.S. 26, which intersects U.S. 101 just south of Seaside near Saddle Mountain State Park. The **Necanicum River** runs north-south through Seaside, approximately two blocks from the coastline, paralleled by U.S. 101 and Holladay Dr. to the east. All three are bisected by **Broadway,** the town's main street, home to hundreds of arcade games, and a tourist-dollar black hole. Broadway is in walking distance of everything. "The Promenade" is a paved path that parallels the beach and is open to cyclists, roller skaters, and pedestrians.

ACCOMMODATIONS AND CAMPING

Seaside's expensive motel scene is hardly an issue for the budget traveler in Seaside, thanks to the large hostel on the south side of town. Reservations are essential at this godsend, as well as at all local motels. Motel prices are directly proportional to proximity to the beach; the cheapest rooms hover near $40 per night (less during the off-season). In summer, rooms are invariably full by 5pm; get ahead of the game and ask the Chamber of Commerce for availability listings. They won't reserve a room for you, but they'll offer advice.

Get ready to drive if you aim to camp. The closest state parks are **Fort Stevens,** 21 mi. north (see p. 432), and **Saddle Mountain** (861-1671), 9.5 mi. east, off U.S. 26 after it splits with U.S. 101. Drive 8 mi. northeast of Necanicum Junction, then another 7 mi. up a winding road to the base camp (10 campsites with potable water, $10). From there, **hike** 3 mi. to the Saddle summit, or just listen to rustling leaves and chirping birds. Sleeping on the beach in Seaside is illegal; police vigilantly enforce this rule.

Seaside International Hostel (HI-AYH), 930 N. Holladay Dr. (738-7911). In an office where attorneys once scribbled, friendly hostel employees now serve up lattés and cookies at the hostel's own espresso bar. Free movies shown nightly, a well-equipped kitchen, and a grassy yard along the river make this mega-hostel a pastoral wonderland. The management knows about everything there is to do in Seaside and filters the fun from the resort hysteria. Employees recommend "Off Broadway" options, map out local hikes, and rent kayaks and canoes to take out on the river (reasonable rates, but pricier for non-HI members). 48 large bunks $13, nonmembers $16; private rooms $36, nonmembers $55. Call well ahead.

Riverside Inn, 430 S. Holladay Dr. (738-8254 or 800-826-6151). Unique bedrooms, fresh flowers, and raftered ceilings with skylights make this B&B a secret garden amidst the Seaside motel-madness. And Riverside is, yes, beside the river. All rooms have private bath and TV. Take your homemade breakfast on the riverfront deck (included with price of rooms). Singles for 2 from $49, Oct.-April $45.

Mariner Motel, 429 S. Holladay Dr. (738-3690). Mauve-beige rooms, many newly recarpeted, with TVs and phones. Free coffee (8:30-10am) in the office. Heated outdoor pool. Singles $45, doubles $56. Call for reservations in summer. Sept. 15-June 11 $13-16 lower.

FOOD AND ENTERTAINMENT

Broadway, especially toward the beach, transforms from a madhouse to an insane asylum at lunch time. Prices are criminal. Try **Safeway,** 401 S. Roosevelt (738-7122; open daily 6am-midnight) for sane prices. The **Grocery Outlet,** 34 N. Holladay Dr. (717-1255), has close-out sales on packaged foods.

The Stand, 220 Ave. U (738-6592), at the south end of town, has the cheapest meals around and is frequented by locals—a good sign. Unassuming decor, loads of authentic Mexican food, enthusiastic service, and the company of local beach bums with permanently peeling noses transports this Oregon eatery to the beaches of Acapulco (burritos $1.50-3.25). Open Mon.-Sat. 11am-8pm.

Planet Zoe's Deli, 846 Ave. C (738-5286), across from Safeway. A world of its own for vegetarians and vegans, this shiny, happy deli serves fresh falafel and homemade hummus ($4.25), planet veggie burgers ($4), planet power bars with spirulina ($1) and juiced anything. Add to the collection of brown paper crayon drawings that adorn the wall. Open Tues.-Sat. 11pm-6pm, Sun. 11am-4pm.

Evergreen Lanes Coffee Shop, 3518 Hwy. 101 N. (738-5333), in Gearhart. The aura à la Denny's and attached bowling alley keep this local seafood favorite hidden from marauding Portlanders. The fish is just as fresh as on Broadway, but less expensive (halibut fish and chips $9). Again, locals swear by it. We promise. Don some polyester and bowl a few frames afterwards. Open daily 7:30am-10pm.

Cafe Espresso, 600 Broadway #7 (738-6169), on the Necanicum Walkway, makes a sublime cappucino ($2) and hosts the only palatable—if limited—Seaside nightlife. Live local jazz, blues, and acoustic rock light up the cafe's tapestried walls on Sat. at 8pm and on some other nights. Minimal cover, maximum atmosphere. Open Mon.-Tues. 8am-5pm, Thurs.-Fri. 8am-5pm, Sat. 9am-5pm, Sun. 10am-4pm.

Sam's Seaside Cafe, 104 Broadway (717-1725). Soups, salads, sandwiches, seafood, and suds in a simple central setting with smiling staff (food $1-12, microbrew pints $2.75, domestic pints $1.75). Open daily 11am-midnight, bar open later.

SIGHTS AND EVENTS

Seaside swarms around **Broadway,** a garish strip of arcades, shops, and salt water taffy running the ½ mi. from Roosevelt (U.S. 101) to the beach. Indoor mini golf, bumper cars, and those machines that squash pennies draw the big crowds. The **Turnaround** at the end of Broadway signals the "official" (read: arbitrary) end of the Lewis and Clark Trail. Seaside's beachfront is huge and hugely crowded. Lifeguards totter on overgrown beach chairs from Memorial Day to Labor Day (daily 10am-6pm) even though the Pacific is always too cold for swimming. There are strong undertows; exercise caution at all times. When red flags wave on the sand, the surf is too rough even to wade in. For a quieter beach, head to **Gearhart,** approximately 2 mi. north of downtown off U.S. 101, where long stretches of unmolested sand and dunes await exploration. This beach has no lifeguard, and town officials strongly discourage swimming. Brazen wave-weavers can try tearing up the surf with a board instead. **Cleanline Surf,** 710 1st Ave. (738-7888), rents surfing gear.

The tiny **Seaside Museum,** 570 Necanicum Dr. (738-7065), may be good for a rainy day (luckily, for the museum, there are plenty), specializing in the history of Seaside as Oregon's first resort community (open daily in summer 10:30am-4:30pm). The **Seaside Beach Run, Promenade Walk, and Sand Games** are held toward the end of July. The 8 mi. beach race leaves from Seaside's Turnaround. Contact Sunset Empire Park & Recreation, 1140 E. Broadway (738-3311), for more info on the race and **"Where the Stars Play,"** a free concert series every Saturday in July and August. At 2pm, musicians bust out everything from folk to Caribbean at Quatat Marine Park. The real kicker comes at the end of August, when runners tear up the trail in the **Hood to Coast Race,** which finishes in Seaside to the cheers of 50,000 spectators. Some 750 12-person teams run this two-day relay race from Mt. Hood in 5 mi. shifts.

Contact Bob Foote (292-4626) for more info. Seaside also hides little-known natural wonders behind its beach bungalows and cotton candy stands. The Necanicum River estuary picks up where the north end of the promenade ends and makes a dune-covered loop back into town. From the Seaside beach, head south to the **Tillamook Head** (see **Cannon Beach,** below) for a day-long hike amid uncrowded forests and along vertigo-inducing cliffs. This is the cheapest way to see Tillamook Head and the lighthouse, since the Cannon Beach entrance charges a fee.

Cannon Beach

Many moons ago, a rusty cannon from the shipwrecked schooner *Shark* washed ashore at Arch Cape, giving this town its name. Today, the only artillery in this beachfront town is its battery of boutiques, bakeries, and galleries. Nothing in Cannon Beach is cheap, but a traveler resigned to window shopping and gallery hopping can spend an enjoyable day dodging Saabs and drinking espresso with local surfers and Portland escapees. When the credit card-flashing crowds reach critical mass, head to the tide pools or trails of Ecola State Park.

PRACTICAL INFORMATION AND ORIENTATION

Visitors Information: Cannon Beach Chamber of Commerce, 207 N. Spruce St., P.O. Box 64 (436-2623), at 2nd St. Emblematic of the city, this visitors center sells everything: T-shirts, postcards, and brochures galore. Open Mon.-Sat. 10am-5:30pm, Sun. 11am-5pm.

Bus: Sunset Transit System (325-0563). To Seaside (75¢) and Astoria ($2.25).

Public Transportation: Cannon Beach Shuttle, a **free** natural gas powered bus service (50¢ donation requested). Traverses the downtown area; board at any point. Service daily 10am-6pm. Ask the chamber of commerce for a schedule.

Bike Rental: Mike's Bike Shop, 248 N. Spruce St. (436-1266 or 800-492-1266), around the corner from the chamber of commerce. Offers **maps** of routes along old logging roads. Mountain bikes ($6 per hr. or $30 for 24hr.), beach tricycles ($6 per 90min). Credit card deposit required. Open daily 11am-7pm.

Lifeguard Service: 436-2345. July-Aug. daily 10am-8pm.

Weather: 861-2722.

Hospital: Providence Seaside Hospital, 725 S. Wahanna Rd. (717-7000), in Seaside. Walk-in clinic in **Cannon Beach,** 171 Larch St. (436-1142), in Sandpiper Sq. Mon.-Fri. 9am-noon.

Emergency: 911. **Police:** 163 Gower St. (436-2811). **Fire Dept.:** 436-2949.

Post Office: 155 N. Hemlock St. (436-2822). Open Mon.-Fri. 9am-5pm. **General Delivery ZIP Code:** 97110.

Area Code: 503.

Cannon Beach lies 7 mi. south of Seaside and 42 mi. north of Tillamook on U.S. 101, and 79 mi. from Portland via U.S. 26. Hemlock, the town's main drag, connects with U.S. 101 in four places.

ACCOMMODATIONS AND CAMPING

Pleasant motels line Hemlock St., none of which costs under $40 in the summer, though family units sometimes end up being a good deal. Book early on summer weekends. In the winter, inquire about specials; most motels offer "two nights for one" deals in an effort to stay afloat. Real budget deals are only a short drive away. The Seaside International Hostel is only 7 mi. north (see p. 435), and **Oswald West State Park** (see p. 439), 10 mi. south of town, has a stunning campground.

The Sandtrap Inn, 539 S. Hemlock St. (436-0247 or 800-400-4106 from Portland). Picturesque rooms trap those hankering for a pretty place to stay. Working fireplaces, cable TV. Singles start at $55, off-season $45, 2-night min. stay on summer weekends. Off-season special 3 nights for the price of 2.

Blue Gull Inn, 487 S. Hemlock St. (436-2714 or 800-507-2714). Big, clean rooms with cable TV, free sauna, and laundry facilities to help wash the sand out of your suit. Set back from the street. Singles from $60; smaller (but comfortable) studio $45, doubles from $75. Oct.-May $4-10 less. Ask about winter specials; the 4-person family units are a good bulk deal (start at $80). 2-night min. stay July-Aug., weekends, and holidays.

Sea Ranch RV Park, 415 N. Hemlock St., P.O. Box 214 (436-2815). 55 tent sites and over 30 hook-up sights in a safe, tree-studded area with lots of grass and pebbles, right on the north edge of town. Sites $17, with full hook-up $20, any extra person over 2, $2, non-guest showers $4. Also offers a 1hr. horse ride for $25. Reservations recommended, 1-night deposit required.

FOOD

Soups, salads, and sandwiches have infected Cannon Beach eateries like a plague. For the best deals on food, avoid the strip and head farther down Hemlock to the midtown area. For the basics, **Mariner Market,** 139 N. Hemlock St. (436-2442), has a small, small-town, stock of groceries (open Sun.-Thurs. 8am-10pm, Fri.-Sat. 9am-11pm; Oct.-April Sun.-Thurs. 8am-9pm, Fri.-Sat. 8am-10pm.)

Midtown Cafe, 1235 S. Hemlock St. (436-1016), in the Haystack Sq. Everything in this cafe is home-made, from the hand-carved door to the jams and marmalades on the tables. Fill up on potatoes deluxe topped with spinach and melted Tillamook cheddar ($5.75), or a lentil burger ($7). The only problem with eating the mungo waffle breakfasts is that you'll be hungry again in a few days ($3.75). Open Wed.-Sat. 7am-2pm; in winter closed Wed.

The Homegrown Cafe, 3301 S. Hemlock (436-1803), just before the last exit back to U.S. 101. Decorated like a thrift store having a holiday party. Wolf down the ever-popular Homegrown burrito ($6-7.50) in front of the fireplace at any time of day. Fresh and fragrant veggie fare, most picked right out of the cafe's backyard. Open Mon. 11am-6pm, Tues. 11am-2pm, Fri. 11am-8pm, Sat-Sun. 3-5pm.

Bill's Tavern, 188 N. Hemlock (436-2202). This newly rebuilt brew-pub is *the* place to be. Well, unless you're somewhere else. Down-home pub grub $3-5, pints $1.75-2.75. Under 21 allowed only when food is served. Open Thurs.-Tues. 11:30am-midnight. Call for more info on hours and entertainment.

SIGHTS, EVENTS, AND OUTDOORS

Tourists in Cannon Beach beat the blues by leisurely shopping their way through a gauntlet of expensive and sporadically elegant galleries and gift shops. A more pedestrian stroll along the 7 mi. stretch of flat, bluff-framed beach is a less expensive option. Picnickers and hikers can follow the narrow, winding road to **Ecola State Park** (436-2844; $3 entrance fee). There, Ecola Point offers a view of hulking **Haystack Rock,** which is spotted with (and splattered by) gulls, puffins, barnacles, anemones, and the occasional sea lion. Follow the road 1½ mi., or hike the Indian Beach trail, to **Indian Beach** to see the **tide pools,** teeming with colorful and fragile sea life.

Ecola Point also affords views of the Bay's centerpiece, the **Tillamook Lighthouse,** which clings like a barnacle to a wave-swept rock. Construction of the lighthouse began in 1879 and continued for years in Sisyphean fashion as storms washed the foundations away. Decommissioned in 1957, the now privately owned lighthouse can be reached only by helicopter in order to deposit the ashes of the dead. From Indian Beach, take the 12 mi. round-trip hike to **Tillamook Head,** the mini-cape that separates Seaside Beach from Cannon Beach, to catch a glimpse of seasonally migrating whales. The trail is open year-round and offers access to the top of Tillamook Head (2 mi. up), where five hiker/biker sites await those willing to make the trek for **free camping**. To surf a set, rent boards from **Cleanline Surf,** 171 Sunset Blvd. (436-9726), which loans surfboards and boogieboards for $20 per day, or package deals for $35 per day. **Indian Beach,** in Ecola State Park, is a favorite among surfers.

Saddle Mountain State Park, 14 mi. east of Cannon Beach on U.S. 26, is named after the highest peak in the Coast Range. A 6 mi., four-hour hike to Saddle Mountain's 3283 ft. summit rewards the fit with an astounding view of the Pacific Ocean and Nehalem Bay to the west and the Cascades to the east (trail open March-Dec.).

To sate a hunger for high culture, call the **Coaster Theater,** 1087 N. Hemlock St. (436-1242), which stages theater productions, concerts, dance performances, comedy, and musical revues year-round (Fri. and Sat. at 8pm; tickets $12-15; by phone with Visa or MC or at the box office Tues.-Sat. 1-5pm, or 1hr. before showtime).

Summer excitement in Cannon Beach builds until the second Saturday in June, when the annual **Sand Castle Competition** towers over the rest of town. Contestants pour in from hundreds of miles and dig in early in the morning to construct ornate sculptures from wet sand. By evening, high tide washes everything away, leaving photographs as the sole testimony to the creative energy expended. Watch out, I.M. Pei! Call the Chamber of Commerce (436-2623) for more info.

■ Cannon Beach to Tillamook

In the summer of 1933, the "Tillamook Burn" reduced 500 sq. mi. of coastal forest near Tillamook to charcoal. While nature has restored Tillamook State Forest to health, coastal towns to the west seem to have sustained some nasty scars. Dime-a-dozen gift shops line the highway, hiding behind faded paint and crooked telephone poles. The coastline that these tiny towns flirt with, however, is much less crowded than Seaside and Cannon Beaches and attracts those in search of less populous sand. Tourist information for the area is available at the visitors information bureau in Tillamook (see **Tillamook: Practical Information**) or the **Rockaway Beach Chamber of Commerce,** 405 S. U.S. 101 (355-8108; open Mon.-Fri. 9am-noon, and 1-4pm).

Oswald West State Park, 10 mi. south of Cannon Beach, is a tiny headland **rainforest** with hefty spruce and cedar trees. Locals call this park "Short Sands Beach"; visitors blow their cover by using the park's official name. Although the beach and woodsy campsites are only accessible by a ¼ mi. trail off U.S. 101, campers here aren't quite "roughing it"—the park provides wheelbarrows for transporting gear from the parking area to the 36 campsites nestled in the forest. The campsites are just minutes away from the beach, balanced by a creek or nestled among the trees, all teeming with surfers. Fall asleep to the gentle babble of a stream or the chords of gently strumming Chris Isaak worshippers. These are the cheapest sites around, so an early arrival is essential (open mid-May to Oct.; sites $14). From the park, take the 4 mi. round-trip **Cape Falcon** trail over the headland, hike the 1661 ft. Neahkahnie Mt., or just follow the path from the campground to one of Oregon's few surfing beaches (which made a special appearance in the film *Point Break*).

Eight mi. south of Oswald State Park, a cluster of "made in Oregon"-type shops marshalled along U.S. 101 make up **Nehalem.** Stop in at **Bum Bee's Cafe,** 35845 7th St. (368-6495), for good ol' country-style cookin'. The biscuits and gravy ($2.75) are a local favorite, as are the plate of hotcakes ($3.25), the fish and chips ($6) and the old-fashioned milkshakes ($2.50; open daily 6am-8pm, breakfast served until 11am). Three miles away, south on U.S. 101 to Rte. 53, Nehalem hosts a sort of galactic, neverending party. The **Nehalem Bay Winery,** 34965 Hwy. 53 (368-WINE/9463), provides samples of local cranberry and blackberry wines (and many more local specialties), examples of small-town Oregon cheer, and one of the most entertaining evenings available on the coast. A major center of activity in the area, the winery sponsors performances in a small theater and an annual bluegrass festival, and is a general forum for bacchanalian revelry. Even if you're not up to tasting (or up to age 21), stop in to chat with owner Ray, who adores travelers and gives all sorts of valuable tips on free camping, local swimming holes, and the merits of a good time (open daily 9am-6pm; winter 10am-5pm, or later if you stop by and Ray's there).

Wheeler, a few mi. south of **Nehalem**, is a small coastal town with a wealth of ways to woo the water. **Wheeler on the Bay Lodge,** 580 Marine Dr. (368-5858), rents **kayaks** (open daily 8am-6pm; single boats $12 per hr., $28 per day; doubles $18 per hr., $40 per day; 3-person boat $20 per hr., $50 a day; includes a 10min. training session for beginners). Try your luck with **crabbing** on the bay south of Wheeler. Look for venders selling buckets off the docks. They'll often cook the crabs for you.

Tillamook

Although the word Tillamook (TILL-uh-muk) translates to "land of many waters," it means something else to Oregonians: cheese. Lazily grazing dairy cows that litter the hills around the town produce a nationally famous cheddar and lure a population of cheese fans almost as large as the herds themselves. Still a small farming town at heart, Tillamook gets its share of traffic and funnels it to the cheese factory, where tourists sample sharp, medium, or mild, or off to the coast, only 3 mi. away.

PRACTICAL INFORMATION AND ORIENTATION

Visitors Information: Tillamook Chamber of Commerce, 3705 U.S. 101 N. (842-7525), in the big red barn across the parking lot from the Tillamook Cheese Factory. Friendly folks, free **maps,** and a complete listing of places to camp in Tillamook County. Also 24hr. direct dial phone to local motels and eateries. Open Mon.-Fri. 9am-5pm, Sat. 10am-4:30pm, Sun. 10am-2pm.

Taxi: Tillamook Taxi (842-4567). 24hr.

Seniors' Information: (888-368-4200). Open Mon.-Fri. 8am-noon and 1pm-5pm.

Women's Crisis Center: 2215 11th St. (842-9486). 24hr.

Laundromat: 2525 U.S. 101 N. (322-3246), in **DeliMart** behind the Shell Station. Wash 75¢, 45min. dry 75¢. Open daily 6am-9:30pm, winter 6am-8:30pm.

Hospital: Tillamook County General Hospital, 1000 3rd St. (842-4444).

Emergency: 911. **Police:** (842-2522), in City Hall. **Fire:** 2310 4th St. (842-7587). **County Sheriff:** 201 Laurel St. (842-2561), in the courthouse. **Coast Guard:** 233-3246.

Post Office: 2200 1st St. (842-4711). Open Mon.-Fri. 8:30am-5pm. **General Delivery ZIP Code:** 97141.

Area Code: 503.

Tillamook lies 49 mi. south of Seaside, 74 mi. south of Portland, and 44 mi. north of Lincoln City on U.S. 101. From Portland, take U.S. 26 to Hwy. 6. Tillamook's main drag is U.S. 101, which splits into two one-way streets in the downtown area. Pacific Ave. runs north and Main Ave. runs south. The Tillamook Cheese Factory sits a mile or two north of the town proper.

OREGON

ACCOMMODATIONS AND CAMPING

When Tillamook flooded in February 1996, most businesses in the area had to do an interior overhaul, so while some motels may look washed-out on the outside, new beds and carpets glisten on the inside. The water has gone back down, but high rates still send budget travelers sailing into the area's finest campgrounds.

Tillamook Inn, 1810 U.S. 101 N. (842-4413), between the center of town and the Tillamook Cheese Factory. New carpets, coffee makers, and cable with HBO. Some bedrooms have kitchens in which to cook your mac' 'n' Tillamook cheese. Singles $43, doubles $51, with kitchen $59. Winter rates $3-5 lower. Call a few days ahead

MarClair Inn, 11 Main Ave. (842-7571 or 800-331-6857). Convenient location where Rte. 6 and U.S. 101 meet. Large, aqua-marine green rooms and outdoor pool hot tub, and sauna well shielded from the road. $2 AAA discount. Singles $62., doubles $64. Off-season less expensive. Credit card required.

Kilchis River Park (842-6694), 6 mi. northeast of Tillamook at the end of Kilchis River Rd., which meets U.S. 101 1 mi. north of the factory. 34 sites nestle between a forest of tall, mossy trees and the Kilchis River. Nifty swingset, small baseball field, volley court, horseshoes, swimming, and hiking trails. Water, flush toilets sinks. Tent sites $10. Hiker/biker $2. Open May-Oct.

Cape Lookout State Park, 13000 Whiskey Creek Rd. (842-4981), 15 mi. southwest of Tillamook on the Three Capes Loop (see p. 441). Some of these 201 sites are only 20 yd. from the beach, while others offer more privacy and shade. Tent sites $16; sites with full hook-ups $20; yurts $25; hiker/biker $4 per person; non-camper showers $2. Reserve with Oregon State Parks (800-452-5687).

FOOD

Tillamook is the cheese and ice-cream lover's paradise, but low-cholesterol food options don't come from the same land of milk and honey. Collect picnic supplies at **Safeway,** 955 U.S. 101 (842-4831; open daily 6am-midnight).

Blue Heron French Cheese Company, 2001 Blue Heron Dr. (842-8281), 1 mi. south of the Tillamook factory on U.S. 101 (still north of town). The Blue Heron focuses decidedly on brie; none of this provincial cheddar a la the Tillamook Cheese Factory here! Ooh la la. Much less a factory than a country-style family store. Deli serves up gourmet sandwiches ($5.50), fresh soups, and salads. Free tastings of local (and often unusual) dips, jams, jellies, honeys, syrups, mustards, wines, and, yes, brie. Open daily 8am-8pm, winter 9am-5pm.

La Casa Medello, 1160 U.S. 101 N. (842-5768). Eat like a *conquistador* under bull horns, a sombrero, and 2 mounted machetes. Good family dining, with mild Mexican food prepared to order. Small lunch specials $5.25-7. Massive 12 in. tacos ($7-9) and burritos ($6-9). Dinners ($7-12) come with rice, beans, and chips. Always hopping. Open Mon.-Fri. 11am-9pm, Sat.-Sun. noon-9pm.

Tillamook Cheese Factory, 4175 U.S. 101 N. (842-4481). The big cheese of cheese is fun just to see, less fun to stay and eat at. More than just hunks of cheddar and pepperoni by the foot (70¢)—loads of other visitors, too. Deli sandwiches featuring you-know-what $2-5. Breakfasts 8-11am. Divine melty ice cream $1.25. Mid-June to Aug. open daily 8am-8pm; Sept. to mid-June 8am-6pm.

SIGHTS AND ACTIVITIES

The **Tillamook Cheese Factory** (see **Food,** above), is a shrine to dairy delights and a surprisingly entertaining destination. The free self-guided tour kicks off with displays of antique churns and a video. **Learn** about the modern cowbell, a computer chip that monitors every bovine move. **Watch** as a milking machine tugs at a plastic cow. **See** the factory, including the cheddarmaster! **Find** the poor soul who has to wear a net on his beard while he watches blocks of cheese for eight hours a day. **Taste** a tidbit at the gift shop.

West of the highway, downtown, the **Tillamook County Pioneer Museum,** 2106 2nd St. (842-4553), at Pacific Ave., features all manner of household and industrial goods from pioneer days, set in mannequin-rich dioramas. But the accompanying collection of stuffed animals preserved by taxidermist Alex Walker (not to be confused with novelist Alice Walker, who is *not* a licensed taxidermist) is much more entertaining than the fake humans. See a head of oryx, horn of kudu, a pouncing bobcat, and an (ewww) unborn fawn (open Mon.-Sat. 8am-5pm, Sun. 11am-5pm; Oct.-Mar.15 closed Mon.; $2, seniors $1.50, ages 12-17 50¢, under 12 free, families $5).

Tillamook's bulkiest attraction is the **Tillamook Naval Air Station Museum,** 6030 Hangar Rd. (842-1130), 2 mi. south of Tillamook. This hulking hangar is the largest wooden clear-span structure in the world, covers seven acres, and is the only one of 16 built by the Navy in the 40s that has survived to the present. The chilly cavern contains functional WW II planes including an American P-51 Mustang, a British MK VIII Spitfire, and a German ME-109 Messerschmidt. The admission price is high, but airplane buffs get even higher off the exhibits (open summer daily 9am-6pm; winter 10am-5pm; $6, ages 7-12 $2.50).

■ Tillamook to Lincoln City

Between Tillamook and Lincoln City, U.S. 101 wanders east into wooded land, losing contact with the coast. The **Three Capes Loop,** a 35 mi. circle to the west of the straying U.S 101, connects a trio of spectacular promontories—**Cape Meares, Cape Lookout,** and **Cape Kiwanda State Parks**—and makes for a sweet Sunday drive, since the beaches here are quieter than those to the south. Cyclists and motorists beware: narrow twists and a rocky road make the trip tricky for those on two wheels.

Cape Meares State Park, at the tip of the promontory jutting out from Tillamook, protects one of the few remaining old growth forests on the Oregon Coast. The **Octopus Tree,** a gnarled Sitka spruce with six candelabra trunks, has made a park-wide name for itself as a climber's ultimate fantasy. The **Cape Meares Lighthouse** (842-4981), active from 1890 to 1963, operates as an illuminating on-site interpretive center. Struggle up 1½ flights of tiny stairs for sweeping views and a peek at the original lens of the big light (open May-Sept. daily 11am-4pm; Oct., March, April Fri.-Sat. 11am-4pm; free). From Cape Meares, squinters can see the three lonely **Arch Rocks** rising out of the water like the humps of a ghastly sea monster. These rocks are a federal refuge for sea lions and birds. Three miles south in **Oceanside,** Maxwell mountain gives better views of the sea lions (follow the signs to the House on the Hill Motel, then continue to the top on Maxwell Mt. Rd.). **Netarts** (NEE-tarts), 2 more mi. south, also offers better views overlooking Netarts Bay.

Another 12 mi. southwest of Cape Meares, **Cape Lookout State Park** (842-4981), offers picnic tables and access to the beach for drive-by dawdlers (day-use fee $3) as well as some overnight camping (see **Tillamook: Accommodations,** p. 440). Start here on the 2½ mi. Cape Trail to the end of the lookout to see a spectacular 360° view featuring **Haystack Rock.** The park provides more than 6 mi. of hiking trails.

South of Cape Lookout, the road undulates through sand dunes, where the sound of the rushing wind battles the roar of all-terrain vehicles. These ATVs are allowed in the dunes and specific beach areas. Alongside this sandy playground lies the U.S. Forest Service's popular **Sandbeach Campground** (follow signs to Sand Lake), where you might feel left out if you don't have a combustion engine toy of your own to play with. Arrive early in the summer or make a reservation at 800-280-CAMP/2267 (101 sites with toilets and potable water, $12). Or, camp in the sand at the edge of giant parking lots at **East Dunes** and **West Winds** just down the road ($5).

Cape Kiwanda State Park, the third promontory on the loop, saves itself for day use only (open 8am-dusk). On sunny, windy afternoons, hang gliders gather to soar over the wave-carved sandstone cliffs. But those winging it don't sail away with the best of the park—the sheltered cape also draws beachcombers, kite-flyers, beach volleyball players, fishers, and windsurfers. On this cape, barely north of Pacific City, massive rock outcroppings in a small bay mark the launching pad of the flat-bottomed **dory fleet,** one of the few fishing fleets in the world that launches beachside, directly from the sand to the surf. If you bring your own fishing gear down to the cape most mornings around 5am, you might convince someone to take you on board; the fee will probably be lower than that of a commercial outfitter.

Pacific City, a delightful town that most travelers on U.S. 101 never even see, is home to another **Haystack Rock,** just as impressive as its Cannon Beach sibling to the north (see p. 438). Anchor yourself at the **Anchorage Motel,** 6585 Pacific Ave. (965-6773 or 800-941-6250), which offers homey rooms with cable and coffee, but no phones (singles from $34, with kitchen unit $45; doubles from $37, with kitchen unit $60). Rates drop significantly in winter.

For so unpretentious a town, Pacific City hides away some startlingly good restaurants. The **Pelican Pub and Brewery,** 33180 Cape Kiwanda Dr. (965-7007), is the hands-down victor in the battle for most pastoral location. On the breezy patio, sippers and suppers see the sun setting between Cape Kiwanda and Haystack Rock. Before filling up on the view, pack away a generously stacked "Ham I Am" ($6) or salad ($3), a pint of pelican microbrew ($2.75) or a 22 oz. megapint ($3.50), then clamber up the sandy bank of the cape for even more view. For more memorable food, abandon the salt water and head east to the **Riverhouse Restaurant,** 34450 Brooten Rd. (965-6722), a tiny white house overlooking the Nestucca River. Stunning seafood ($14-19) and homemade desserts ($3-6) have earned the Riverhouse its reputation as the best restaurant in town (open Sun.-Fri. 11am-9pm, Sat. 11am-10pm). The **Grateful Bread Bakery,** 34805 Brooten Rd. (965-7337), comes in as a close second. Get anything from a black bean chili omelette ($6) and outstanding fresh squeezed OJ

($2) to a grilled salmon fillet with sauteed vegetables ($10; open Mon.-Tues. and Thurs.-Sat. 8am-6pm, Wed. and Sun. 8am-5pm; in winter closed Thurs.).

Back on U.S. 101 and 6 mi. north in **Hebo,** a **ranger station** for the **Siuslaw National Forest** at 31525 Hwy. 22 (392-3161), ¼ mi. east of U.S. 101, lists hiking and camping options in the forest (open Mon.-Fri. 7:30am-4:30pm). Five mi. up steep and twisty Forest Service Road #14 is **Hebo Lake Campground,** with 16 gorgeous, outhouse- and water-equipped sites bordering **Small Hebo Lake.** At only $6 per site, it's easy not to be a hobo at Hebo (open mid-April to mid-Oct.). Three and a half miles farther up the road, commune with microwave transmission towers at the summit of **Mt. Hebo.** Beyond the antennas, see excellent views of the coastline and, on clear days, Mt. Hood to the east. Other Forest Service campgrounds in the area include the **Rocky Bend Campground,** 15 mi. east of Beaver on paved Nestucca River Rd. (free; primitive; no drinking water).

About 1¼ mi. east on Hwy. 18 after its rendezvous with U.S. 101, the minuscule town of **Otis** (don't blink) covets the **Otis Cafe** (994-2813), across from the BP station. This source of local pride serves homestyle strawberry-rhubarb pie for $2.25 a slice and often has a line out the door. Patience is rewarded with sinful breakfast specials ($3.25-7). Two eggs and two rich waffles are a steal at $4.25. The cheese-smothered German potatoes are as legendary as they are huge (½ portion for $4.05, full for $5.20; open in summer Mon.-Thurs. 7am-3pm, Fri.-Sat. 7am-9pm, Sun. 8am-9pm).

A dozen wineries line Hwy. 18 on the way to Portland. A 9 mi. detour via Rte. 99 W and Hwy. 47 will take you far from the coast to **Carlton,** home of the **Chateau Benoit Winery** (864-2991), on Mineral Springs Rd. From Rte. 99 W near Lafayette turn north on Mineral Spring for 1¼ mi. Bring your own picnic for complimentary tasting at tables overlooking the vineyard (open daily 10am-5pm).

Lincoln City

OREGON

Lincoln City is actually five towns wrapped around a 7 mi. strip of motels, gas stations, and tourist traps along U.S. 101. Bicyclists will find Lincoln City hellish, and hikers should cut three blocks west to the seashore. Kite-flying and beach volleyball denizens flock to this coastal town, but nothing draws as many visitors (or as much money) as the new Chinook Winds Siletz Tribal Gaming Convention Center, where swingers gamble away days, nights, and life savings. This casino has only added to the town's extreme commercialism (Lincoln City boasts more than 1000 ocean-front motel rooms), but the crowds just keep coming.

PRACTICAL INFORMATION AND ORIENTATION

Visitors Information: Lincoln City Visitor and Convention Bureau, 801 SW U.S. 101 #1 (994-8378 or 800-452-2151), across from Burger King. Brochures covering Lincoln City and beyond. Sporty new 24hr. telephone board can connect you with local motels and restaurants at the (free) push of a button. Open Mon.-Fri. 8am-5pm, Sat. 9am-5pm, Sun. 10am-4pm.

Buses: Greyhound, 3327 NW U.S. 101 (265-2253), in Newport at the Circle K. To Portland (2 per day, $13) and Newport (2 per day, $6).

Car Rental: Robben-Rent-A-Car, 3232 NE U.S. 101 (994-5530 or 800-305-5530). $30 per day plus 15¢ per mi. after 50 mi. Must be 21 with major credit card and able to deposit $500. Reserve ahead. Open daily 8am-5pm.

Laundry: Coin Laundry, 2164 NE U.S. 101. Wash $1, 10min. dry 25¢. Open daily 9am-10pm.

Library: Driftwood Library, 801 SW U.S. 101 (996-2277), near the visitors center. Open Mon.-Thurs. 9am-9pm, Fri.-Sat. 9am-5pm, Sun. 1-5pm.

Swimming and Showers: Community Pool, 2150 NE Oar Place (994-5208). Pool use $1.75, teens $1.25, 12 and under $1, families $5; showers 75¢. Open daily for recreational swimming 1:30pm-3:30pm and 7-9pm, for laps 5:30-7:30am, noon-1:15pm, and 6-7pm; call for winter hours.

Senior Citizen Center: 2150 NE Oar Place (994-2722).

Hospital: North Lincoln Hospital, 3043 NE 28th St. (994-3661).

Emergency: 911. **Police:** 1503 SE Devils Lake Rd. (994-3636). **Fire:** 2525 NW U.S. 101 (994-3100).
Post Office: 1501 SE Devils Lake Rd. (800-275-8777), 2 blocks east of U.S. 101. Open Mon.-Fri. 9am-5pm. **General Delivery ZIP Code:** 97367.
Area Code: 541.

Lincoln City, situated 42 mi. south of Tillamook, 22 mi. north of Newport, 58 mi. west of Salem, and 88 mi. southwest of Portland, is a narrow strip of entrepreneurial achievement between the ocean and Devils Lake. Despite its oblong shape, Lincoln City follows a quadrant system: D River (marked "the smallest river in the world") is the north-south divide; the double yellow line of U.S. 101 divides the town east-west.

ACCOMMODATIONS

Camping near Lincoln City can be crowded, but may be worth the money saved. If high-and-dry is the priority, countless casino crowd-saturated motels yield nice rooms off the water along U.S. 101. (For more options, see **Tillamook to Lincoln City,** p. 441, and **Lincoln City to Newport,** p. 445).

Sea Echo Motel, 3510 NE U.S. 101 (994-2575). A single-story, stone-fronted building set back from the hwy. atop a steep driveway. Only an echo of a view visible over the tops of the trees. Pink sinks! Standard rooms, phones, cable TV. 1 bed $38, 2 beds $48.

Captain Cook Inn, 2626 NE U.S. 101 (994-2522 or 800-994-2522). Explorers will discover gracious, remodeled rooms with beautiful new checkered or flowered furniture in this well-maintained motel. Singles from $42, doubles from $48.

Budget Inn, 1713 NW 21st St. (994-5281) at U.S. 101. Fairly large, clean rooms with cable. Half the building faces the hwy., but the other half faces a quiet neighborhood. Much of the 3rd floor has a balcony facing the ocean. 2 blocks from the beach. Singles $40; doubles $47. Reserve at least 2 weeks in advance.

Devil's Lake State Park, off NW U.S. 101, then off N. 6th Dr. Spacious sites with picnic tables and easy access to Devil's Lake, a fishing and boating destination of its own. 68 tent sites $16; 32 full hookups $20; hiker/biker $4.50; non-camper showers $2. Call 800-452-5687 for July and Aug. reservations, or have a devil of a time getting a spot. 2 wheelchair accessible sites. Credit cards accepted.

FOOD

Lincoln City has a few classy joints if you can navigate the fast-food shoals, but head down to Depoe Bay or Newport for good seafood. Zip north to **Price Chopper Foods,** 4157 N. U.S. 101 (994-4246), in Lighthouse Square at the north end of town, for basic food items (open daily 7am-11pm). Across the street is a **Safeway,** 4101 NW Logan Rd. (994-8667; open daily 6am-midnight).

McMenamins Lighthouse Brew Pub, 4157 N U.S. 101 (994-7238), in Lighthouse Sq. Fresh-cut fries, phenomenal brews, and an upbeat atmosphere upstairs and down. The food is cheap and good—try a Communication Breakdown Burger ($5.50). After 9pm, selected prices drop $1-2 (cold sandwiches $2.75), and McMenamins becomes a beacon of good deals. Open Mon.-Sat. 11am-1am, Sun. 11am-midnight; call for winter hours.

Foon Hing Yuen, Inc., 3138 SE U.S. 101 (996-3831), at SW 30th St. Generous portions of good Chinese food. Lunches around $4; dinner specials $6-9. The *pork chow yuk* ($6.50) is delicious despite its name. This is one of few restaurants in town that doesn't close before 10pm. Take-out available. Bar and restaurant open Sun.-Thurs. noon-midnight, Fri.-Sat. noon-1:30am.

Kyllo's, 1110 NW First Ct. (994-3179), next to the D River Park; turn on NW 2nd. The town's biggest restaurant achieves maximum oceanfront sunset surface area and an elegant ambience. Elevated prices for prettily garnished but average food. Try 1 lb. Manilla clams in white wine ($9), but skip the forgettable crab cake ($9). Dinners $12-15. Open daily 7am-dark (breakfast served until 11am).

SIGHTS, ACTIVITIES, AND EVENTS

The windy beaches of Lincoln City host a fleet of annual kite festivals. The largest one is the **Fall International Kite Festival** in the beginning of October at D River Park, but the spring and summer festivals in early May and July stir up the sky with competitions like "best train." Check out hand-made wind toys at **Catch the Wind,** 266 SE U.S. 101 (994-9500). The folks here are rabid kite fans—just ask them about Wei Fong, Lincoln City's kite-flying sister city in China (open in summer daily 9am-9pm). The top-notch **Cascade Music Festival** comes to Lincoln City the last three weekends in June. International classical concerts ($15) take place at St. Peter the Fisherman Lutheran Church, 1226 SW 13th (994-5333).

You can enjoy coffee, food, and Oregon wines at the **Chateau Benoit Wine & Food Center,** 1524 E. Devils Lake Rd. (996-3981), in the **Factory Stores** (open Mon.-Sat. 9am-8pm, Sun. 9am-6pm; call for winter hours). Brave the crowded parking lots at the corner of E. Devils Lake Rd. and U.S. 101 for a chance to hunt bargains at 61 outlet stores (call 996-5000 or 888-SHOP/7467-333 for more info).

To finish off a day of spending, disappear into the black hole of **Chinook Winds Siletz Tribal Gaming Convention Center** (1777 NW 44th St.; 888-CHINOOK/244-6665), known around town as the "the casino." Check your budget at the door; your nickels (and dimes, and $50 bills) will doubtless disappear down a slot machine or into the pond by the escalator. Still, this Oregonian Vegas with glowing whales and cartoon wilderness is the perfect way to spend a rainy afternoon. Turn left at Lighthouse Sq. on NW Logan Rd. and look to your left; it's the hulking yellow stucco structure with red and blue tribal markings of dubious authenticity (open 24hr.). The casino also sponsors **Concerts-by-the-Sea** every other weekend during the summer (call 888-MAIN-ACT/624-6228 for more info).

OREGON

■ Lincoln City to Newport

Rest stops and beach-access parking lots litter U.S. 101 between Lincoln City and Newport. These puddles of pavement pop out every few mi., and one offers camping: The free **North Creek Campground,** a piece of the Siuslaw National Forest, is off County Rte. 229 on Forest Service Rd. 19. This campground is hard to find, but rewards the intrepid with secluded and scenic wooded camping (no drinking water).

A few mi. south on U.S. 101, diminutive **Depoe Bay** boasts opportune **gray whale viewing** along the seawall in town, at the **Depoe Bay State Park Wayside,** and at the **Observatory Lookout,** 4½ mi. to the south. Go early in the morning on a cloudy, calm day (Dec.-May during their annual migration) for the best chance of spotting the barnacle-encrusted giants. Several outfitters charter fishing trips from Depoe Bay. **Tradewinds Charters** (765-2345), on the north end of the bridge on U.S. 101 downtown, has two five-hour ($49 per person) and seven-hour ($65 per person) bottom-fishing trips per day (call for times, reservations, and info on other trips). **Dockside Charters** (765-2545 or 800-733-8915) offers similar trips for $49 (1 hr. whale-watching trip $10, teenagers $8, under 13 $6, and 6 hr. fishing and crabbing for $58). To find Dockside, turn east at the one and only traffic light in Depoe Bay; they're next to the Coast Guard station. Call for reservations.

Just south of Depoe Bay, take a detour from U.S. 101 on the famous **Otter Crest Loop,** a twisting 4 mi. drive high above the shore that affords spectacular vistas at every bend, including views of **Otter Rock** and the **Marine Gardens.** A lookout over **Cape Foulweather** has telescopes (25¢) for spotting sea lions lazing on the rocks below. Captain James Cook first saw the North American mainland here in 1778 when it greeted him with gale-force winds. Wind speeds at this 500 ft. elevation often reach 100 mph. Also accessible off the loop, the **Devil's Punch Bowl** drops out of the headlands. The bowl was formed when two seaside caves collapsed, leaving a hole in the sandstone terrace. During high tides when ocean water crashes through an opening in the side of the "bowl," the ocean inside becomes a frothing cauldron.

Just south of the punch bowl, the road returns to U.S. 101 and brings eager campers to the much-trafficked **Beverly Beach State Park,** 198 NE 123rd St. (265-9278), 7 mi. north of Newport, a year-round campground set in gorgeous, rugged terrain. Cold water and frequent riptides discourage even the most daring swimmers. Beverly Beach was one of the first parks in Oregon to sport the latest in outdoor accommodations, **YURTS** (Year-round Universal Recreational Tents), round tents with bunk beds modelled after Mongolian huts ($26.50; reserve ahead by calling 800-452-5687). Hot showers, facilities for the disabled, and a few hiker/biker spots are available (sites $16, hiker/biker $4.25, electrical $19, full $20; non-camper showers $2). Reservations are strongly advised in summer.

Just south of Beverly Beach is **Yaquina Head,** a lava delta formed by hot magma 14 million years ago, and the **Yaquina Head Lighthouse** (265-2863), a much-photographed coastal landmark. The top of the seven-story lighthouse can be reached only via free tours (every 30min. daily June to mid-Sept. 9-11:30am). The first 15 people get to go; arrive early to ensure a spot. The public can guide themselves through the ground-level kiosk of the lighthouse daily noon-4pm, but the **seabird colony** on the rocks below is just as spectacular. Large decks provide views of western gulls, cormorants, murres, guillemats, and, very rarely, the colorful **tufted puffin.** The tide pools along the low, flat rock to the south of the headland are home to harbor porpoises, sea lions, and other small intertidal life (the cement path through the rocky intertidal zone is wheelchair accessible). Gray whales sometimes sound in the waters beyond.

Newport

Newport is one part fishing village, one part logging town, and two parts tourist mill. Hordes of visitors flock to this coastal town to see Keiko, the orca-turned-icon of *Free Willy* fame, at the Oregon Coast Aquarium. Just beyond the miles of malls and gas stations of U.S. 101, Newport has a renovated waterfront area of restaurants and stores. Feel alive with pleasure away from kitschy shops and high admission fees at Nye Beach, a historic and relatively unspoiled sand-strip just north of the busy harbor.

PRACTICAL INFORMATION AND ORIENTATION

Visitors Information: Chamber of Commerce, 555 SW Coast Hwy. (265-8801 or 800-262-7844). Large new office with bus and theater schedules, free **maps,** guides, a 24hr. info board, and an on-the-ball staff. Open Mon.-Fri. 8:30am-5pm, Sat. 10am-4pm; Oct.-April Mon.-Fri. 8:30am-5pm. **Newport Parks and Recreation Office,** 169 SW Coast Hwy. (265-7783). Open Mon.-Fri. 7:30am-5:30pm.

Buses: Greyhound, 956 SW 10th St. (265-2253) at Bailey St. To: Portland (3 per day, $17); Seattle (3 per day, $38); and San Francisco (5 per day, $65). Open Mon.-Fri. 8-10am and 12:30-4:15pm, Sat. 8am-1pm.

Taxi: Yaquina Cab Company, 265-9552. 24hr.

Car Rental: Sunwest Motors, 1030 N. Coast Hwy. (265-8547). All cars $25 with 50 free mi. per day, 15¢ per extra mi. Must be 25 with a major credit card or able to hand over a $500 deposit, or must be 21 with a major credit card and proof of full coverage insurance. Reservations advised.

Bike Rental: Embarcadero, 1000 SE Bay Blvd. (265-5435). $4 per hour, $25 per day; $25 deposit or major credit card held. No helmets. Also rents crab rings ($6 per day), clam shovels ($3.50 per day), and skiffs ($13.50 per hr., 3hr. min.).

Public Library: 34 NW Nye (265-2153) at Olive St. Open Mon.-Thurs. 10am-9pm, Fri.-Sat. 10am-6pm, Sun. 1-4pm.

Laundry: Eileen's Coin Laundry, 1078 N. Coast Hwy. Wash $1, 10 min. dry 25¢. Open daily 6:30am-11pm.

Weather and Sea Conditions: 265-5511.

Crisis Line: CONTACT, 444 2nd St. NE (265-9234). Advice, referrals, and assistance for stranded travelers.

Senior Services: Senior Center, 20 SE 2nd St. (265-9617).

Hospital: Pacific Communities Hospital, 930 SW Abbey (265-2244).

Emergency: 911. **Police:** 810 SW Alder (265-5331). **Fire:** 245 NW 10th St. (265-9461). **Coast Guard:** 925 Naterlin Rd. (265-5381).

Post Office: 310 SW 2nd St. (265-5542). Open Mon.-Fri. 8:30am-5pm. **General Delivery ZIP Code:** 97365.
Area Code: 541.

U.S. 101, known in town as the Coast Highway, divides east and west Newport, while U.S. 20 (Olive St.) bisects the north and south sides of town. Corvallis lies 55 mi. east on U.S. 20, Lincoln City lies 22 mi. north on U.S. 101 and Florence lies 50 mi. south. Newport is bordered on the west by the foggy Pacific Ocean and on the south by Yaquina Bay. A suspension bridge ferries U.S. 101 traffic across the bay. Just north of the bridge, Bay Boulevard runs around the bay and through the heart of the port.

ACCOMMODATIONS AND CAMPING

The motel-studded strip along U.S. 101 provides plenty of affordable rooms with predictably noisy road-accompaniment. Weekend rates generally rise a couple of dollars, and winter rates plummet. Campers can escape to many state campgrounds along U.S. 101, with access to both beach and city. Just north of town, **Beverly Beach State Park,** 198 N. 123rd St. (265-9278), which has 151 sites specifically for tents ($16) and 53 full hookup sites ($20), makes almost every camper happy. **South Beach State Park,** 5580 S. Coast Hwy., South Beach 97366 (867-4715), 2 mi. south of town, has ten yurts ($27), 19 RV hookup sites ($19), 12 hiker/biker sites ($4.25), and showers ($2 for non-campers).

Brown Squirrel Hostel, 44 SW Brook St. (265-3729) off W. Olive St. This converted church has a few resident kittens and a neighborhood setting, but sorry, no squirrels. Bountiful basement kitchen, casually kept common space, and just 2min. from the beach. Coin laundry. 44 beds and neverending renovation. Doors open 7:30am-10:30pm. Beds $12; private rooms for families $25 (families should call ahead). No credit cards accepted.

City Center Motel, 538 SW Coast Hwy. (265-7381), across from the visitors center. Standard rooms with sparkling bathrooms. In summer, singles start at $40; doubles $48; renovated rooms cost much, much more. Call 800-628-9665 for reservations.

Summer Wind Budget Motel, 728 N. Coast Hwy. (265-8076). Old rooms are smallish with clean bathrooms and earthy tones. All rooms have HBO. Prices vary from room to room as quickly as the summer wind changes course. For now, singles $30; doubles $34. New rooms somewhat bigger, but audibly closer to the hwy. Singles $30; doubles $38.

Cuckoo for Keiko

Movie stars come in all colors, shapes, and sizes, but none as unusual as this one: **Keiko** is a giant Orca (*Orcinus orca*, often incorrectly called a "killer whale"), who achieved fame for his starring role as Willy in the childrens' film *Free Willy*. Despite 15 years of theme park stardom under his flippers, nothing could prepare Keiko for the fame that followed his movie debut. Soon after *Free Willy*, this 20-year-old, 9620 lb. movie star was relocated to the Oregon Coast Aquarium (see below) where visitors can watch his every stroke while he rehabilitates for possible release into the wild. If successful, this would be the first release of a tamed Orca into the sea. Aquarium employees warn, "Remember, Keiko does what he wants, so if you don't see him right away, move to another exhibit and come back," but star-struck adults and children alike sulk when he's sleeping out of view. Even while the Orca sleeps, Newport businesses replace him with thousands of Keiko keychains, sweatshirts, and handmade ceramic models. Rogue Ale Brewery (see above) pays profitable homage to the cetacean with Keiko Draft Root Beer ($4 per 6-pack). Local entrenpreneurs banking on the black-and-white beast fear the day when the Free Willy Foundation successfully petitions to release Keiko into ocean waters. But for now, the town is cuckoo for Keiko.

FOOD

Food in Newport is decent and not limited to bay-front restaurants where tourists cluster. **Oceana Natural Foods Coop,** 159 SE 2nd St. (265-8285), has a small selection of reasonably priced health foods and produce (open daily 9am-7pm). **J.C. Sentry,** 107 N. Coast Hwy. (265-6641), sells standard supermarket stock (open 24hr).

Mo's Restaurant, 622 SW Bay Blvd. (265-2979). Share a large wooden table in this small, crowded local favorite and slurp some of the best clam chowder on the coast until there's no mo' left (with fish 'n' chips $7). Open daily 11am-9pm.

Cosmos Cafe and Gallery, 740 W. Olive St. (265-7511). Celestial and marine scenarios send diners in this secluded cafe to a galaxy of cosmically good food. Great omelettes ($6), sumptuous black bean burrito ($6), and fresh pie ($2.50). Muffin flavors like rhubarb-applesauce and cranberry-peach ($1.25). Open Mon.-Wed. 8am-8pm, Thurs.-Sat. 8am-9pm; winter Mon.-Sat. 10am-8pm.

Rogue Ale & Public House, 748 SW Bay Blvd. (265-3188). All hail the local ale: plenty of brew on tap, beer cheese soup, and ale bread ($1.50) to boot. Walls explore beer as art. Pizza with Rogue Stout crust ($7-21) is delicious, but everyone orders the fish 'n' chips with Rogue Ale batter ($6.50). Locals pack it in for Fri. night trivia. Open Sun.-Thurs. 11am-11pm, Fri.-Sat. 11am-midnight.

Nye Beach Hotel and Cafe, 219 NW Cliff St. (265-3334), off W. Olive. Stylishly simple with high ceilings, a splendid view of the ocean, and 2 tropical Conures—exotic birds, that is. The fish-centric dinner menu ($11-15) is not aimed at the budget traveler, but the escape from tackiness and fried food may be worth the extra bucks. Breakfast until 2pm features Belgian waffles ($4.25). Roll off the back porch and onto the beach. Open Sun.-Thurs. 7:30am-10pm, Fri.-Sat. 7:30am-11pm.

SIGHTS, ACTIVITIES, AND EVENTS

The **Oregon Coast Aquarium,** 2820 SE Ferry Slip Rd. (867-3474) at the south end of the bridge, is at the top of Newport's greatest hits list. This world-class aquarium turned five just last year and is still celebrating the fairly recent arrival of Keiko the *Free Willy* Orca. The vast complex features 6 acres of wet and wild indoor and outdoor exhibits. Stroll through the galleries where anemones "stick" to your hands, and the "New Currents" changing exhibit...umm, changes. Under-appreciated sea otters and seals ham it up, vainly attempting to lure crowds away from Keiko's tank. Admission to the aquarium is worth the $8.50 (seniors $7.50, ages 4-13 $4.25; tickets can be ordered at home with a credit card up to 2 weekends in advance; handicap accessible) Lines are long but speedy. The recently reopened **Mark O. Hatfield Marine Science Center** (867-0100), at the south end of the bridge on Marine Science Dr., is a friendly, educational study of northwestern marine animals in their natural environment. This center is the hub of Oregon State University's coastal research (open daily 10am-6pm; admission by donation—fork it over, cheapskates!)

To sample local beer, cross the bay bridge, follow the signs to the Hatfield Center and turn off at the **Rogue Ale Brewery,** 2320 SE Oregon State University Dr. (867-3664). Taste their line of 20 brews—including the favorite Oregon Golden, American Amber, and Maierbock Ales—upstairs at **Brewer's on the Bay** (taster trays of four beers for $1), or at the pub in town (see **Food,** above; open daily noon-9pm).

If you've reached the bottom of the Newport entertainment barrel, **bottom-fishing** with one of numerous charter companies can be fun, if expensive. Salmon is no longer plentiful, but fishers net halibut in May and tuna mid-April to mid-October with **Newport Tradewinds,** 653 SW Bay Blvd. (265-2101). They run five, six, and eight-hour trips ($10 per hr.), a three-hour crabbing trip ($35), and a two-hour whale-watching trip daily at 1:30pm ($18). If you want to be near the water, but not in a boat, relax on **Nye Beach.** Follow Olive St. towards the water, then turn right on Coast St. and left on Beach Dr. and follow the road to the turnaround.

Observe more refined culture in the many elegant **art galleries** that populate Bay Blvd. by the harbor. Ask the chamber of commerce for help locating them, then pick up a schedule for the **Newport Performing Arts Center,** 777 W. Olive (265-2787).

Newport weekends turn out theater and dance performances, film festivals, and some excellent orchestral and band concerts. Tickets range from $4-18 with a few freebies (the box office is open Mon.-Fri. 9am-5pm and 1hr. before showtime).

Popular festivals in Newport include the **Newport Seafood and Wine Festival,** which showcases Oregon wines, food, music, and crafts in over 100 booths (last full weekend in Feb.; admission around $6) and the four-day **Lincoln County Fair and Rodeo** (265-6237) to the Newport Fairgrounds (3rd week in July; $6, ages 6-12 $3, under 6 free; adults $18 for all 4 days). Contact the chamber of commerce (see **Practical Information,** above) for info on all seasonal events.

■ Newport to Reedsport

From Newport to Reedsport, U.S. 101 slides through a string of small towns, passing beautiful campgrounds, spectacular stretches of beach, and a fair number of unsightly tourist snares flailing in their wake. The **Waldport Ranger District Office,** 1049 SW Pacific Hwy. (U.S. 101; 563-3211), in **Waldport,** describes hiking in the **Siuslaw National Forest,** a patchwork of three wilderness areas along the Oregon Coast. The office sells detailed **maps** of the district for $3 and of the National Forest for $4, on which they can point out the several campgrounds and trails (open Mon.-Fri. 8am-4pm).

Farther south, U.S. 101 passes through **Yachats** (YAH-hots), a perky town that offers a break from the many silk-screened t-shirt and seashell-earring centers of the Oregon Coast. Stop at the **New Morning Coffeehouse** (547-3848), at 4th and U.S. 101, a favorite coffee-stop for U.S. 101 travelers. Tantalizing pastries like blueberry cobbler ($1.50-3.50) make truckers smile in the morning, and the dinner-time pasta, fresh seafood, country beef, and veggie sausages ($9-13) make the rest of the day good, too (open daily 7am-8pm; in winter dinner Thurs.-Sun. only).

Cape Perpetua, 3 mi. south of Yachats, combines the highest point on the coast (803 ft.) with a few exciting sea-level trails. Take a break from perpetual highway driving and hop 2 mi. up to the **view point** for a heavenly vista overlooking the coast. The **Cape Perpetua Visitors Center,** 2400 S U.S. 101 (547-3289), just south of the viewpoint turnoff, has informative exhibits about the surrounding land (open 9am-5pm; Sept. Wed.-Sun. 9am-5pm; Oct.-May Sat.-Sun. 10am-4pm). Before you go, grab a free visitors guide that lists the many trails leading up through the hills and down to the rocks. Well-worn offshore attractions with names like **Devils Churn** (¼ mi. north of the visitors center down Restless Water Trail) and **Spouting Horn** (¼ mi. south of it down Captain Cook Trail), demonstrate the tremendous power of the waves hitting solid basalt.

Cape Perpetua Campground, at the viewpoint turn-off, has 37 sites that run straight back into a narrow valley along a tiny, fern-banked creek. It can accommodate rigs up to 30 ft. (all sites $12; drinking water, flush toilets). The **Rock Creek Campground,** 7½ mi. south, has 16 sites under mossy spruces by Rock Creek (drinking water, flush toilets, $12). A ½ mi. walk on the highway spits wanderers out at the unspoiled **Ocean Beach** day-use park. Five miles farther south, the **Sea Lion Caves,** 91560 U.S. 101 (547-3111), are a product of the clash of nature and capitalism. Visitors come here at all times of year to stare at **Steller** and **California sea lions,** while the "lions" completely ignore the visitors and yelp incessantly to keep themselves entertained. Stellers are more common here, coming in fall and winter for protection from the seas, and in spring and summer for breeding. Visitors can peep through a subterranean hole 200 ft. below ground into the populated sea cave, then use binoculars to gaze down at the mainland rookery (rock ledges that double as a breeding ground) over 200 ft. below. In order to see **the largest sea cave in the U.S.,** you've gotta pay a price ($6, ages 6-15 $4; open daily 9am-1 hr. before dark).

Florence is a far-too-long strip of fast-food joints and expensive motels. Fourteen miles east of Florence, at the junction of Hwy. 126 (to Eugene) and U.S. 36, is **Mapleton,** a tiny community (with a Ranger Station, 10692 Hwy. 126; 268-4473), that can offer tips to prospective hikers or bikers in the **Siuslaw National Forest** (open Mon.-

Fri. 8am-4:30pm). For a free experience in communal living, push 30 minutes east to **Alpha Farm** (964-5102), 7 mi. up Deadwood Creek Rd. The farm, in scenic Nowheresville, offers an unusual, distinctively communal alternative to the bourgeois tourism of the coast. In exchange for a day of labor on the farm, visitors can camp out or stay in the sparse but comfortable bedrooms. Visitors are welcome from Monday to Friday for stays of up to three days; call ahead. Be prepared to kiss the hands of your fellow diners in a warm pre-supper ritual. For a little less togetherness, the **Alpha Bit Cafe** (268-4311), in town on Hwy. 126, and owned and staffed by members of Alpha Farm, is part cafe, part book store and serves a mean *chai* (open Mon.-Thurs. and Sat. 10am-6pm, Fri. 10am-9pm).

Reedsport and the Dunes

Millennia of wind and water flow have formed the **Oregon Dunes National Recreation Area,** a 50 mi. grainy expanse between Florence and Coos Bay. Shifting mounds of sand rise 500 ft. and extend up to 3 mi. inland (often to the shoulder of U.S. 101), clogging mountain streams and forming small lakes. Hiking trails wind around the lakes, through coastal forests, and up to the dunes themselves. In many places, no grasses or shrubs grow, and the vista holds only sand, sky, and a few tire tracks. Campgrounds fill up early with dune buggy and motorcycle junkies, especially on summer weekends. The blaring radios, thrumming engines, and staggering swarms of tipsy tourists might drive you buggy. The dune-buggy invasion grows increasingly controversial, but the **National Recreation Area Headquarters** in Reedsport refuses to take sides.

OREGON

PRACTICAL INFORMATION AND ORIENTATION

Visitors Information: Oregon Dunes National Recreation Area Information Center, 855 U.S. 101 (271-3611), at Rte. 38 in Reedsport, just south of the Umpqua River Bridge. The Forest Service runs this center and will happily answer questions on fees, regulations, and hiking and camping. **Map** $4. Open daily 8:30am-5pm. **Reedsport/Winchester Bay Chamber of Commerce** (271-3495 or 800-247-2155) is now at the same location. Dune buggy rental info and motel listings. Same hours.

Buses: Greyhound (271-2690). To: Portland (3 per day, $24); Eugene (4 per day, $20); and San Francisco (3 per day, $58).

Taxi: Coastal Cab, 139 N. 3rd St. (271-2690). $7 to Winchester Bay, $3 more to the beach. Service daily 6am-3am.

Sand Buggy/ATV Rentals: Winchester Bay Dune Buggy Adventures, 881 U.S. 101 (271-6972), in Winchester Bay. Buggy rides $15 for 30min., $25 for 1hr. (3 person min.). ATVs $35 per hr., $30 each additional hr. Open daily 9am-6pm.

Laundromat: Coin Laundry, 420 N. 14th St. (271-3587), next to McDonald's in Reedsport. Wash $1, 8min. dry 25¢. Open daily 8am-9pm.

Library: 395 Winchester Ave. (271-3500). Open Mon. and Thurs. 2-8:30pm, Tues.-Wed. and Fri. 10am-6pm.

Emergency: 911. **Police:** 146 N. 4th St. (271-2109 or 271-2100), in Reedsport.

Coast Guard: (271-2137), near the end of the harbor, in Winchester Bay.

Post Office: 301 Fir Ave. (800-275-8777), off Rte. 38. Open Mon.-Fri. 8:30am-5pm. **General Delivery ZIP Code:** 97467.

Area Code: 541.

The dunes' shifting grip on the coastline is broken only once along the expanse, at **Reedsport,** where the Umpqua and Smith Rivers empty into Winchester Bay. One hundred and eighty-five miles southwest of Portland, 89 mi. southwest of Eugene, and 71 mi. south of Newport, at the junction of Rte. 38 and U.S. 101, Reedsport is a typical highway town of motels, banks, and restaurants. The older part of town flanks Rte. 38, just east of Hwy. 101 and south of the river.

ACCOMMODATIONS

The town of **Winchester Bay,** just south of Reedsport, has rooms for about $30; those in Reedsport average about $40.

Harbor View Motel (271-3352), 540 Beach Blvd. off U.S. 101 in Winchester Bay. Spitting distance from the boats. The turquoise and white exterior gives it a buoyant appearance reminiscent of pool floaties. Rooms are nice and tidy and have small refrigerators. Singles $31; doubles $34.

Fir Grove Motel, 2178 U.S. 101 (271-4848), in Reedsport. Attractive rooms with plaster walls and arched doorways. Outdoor heated pool is clean and lovely, but only inches from U.S. 101. Cable TV. Geraniums everywhere, coffee, donuts, and fruit in the lobby from 7-9:30am. Singles $40; doubles $49; in winter $10 less. $4-8 senior discount.

Tropicana Motel, 1593 U.S. 101 (271-3671 or 800-799-9970), in Reedsport off the parking lot of the Umpqua Shopping Center. A respectable, clean motel with comfortable rooms; no tropical fruit in evidence. Arrive early, when the parking lot is less than ½ full, and play "let's make a deal." Continental breakfast, TV with HBO and outdoor pool. Singles $40; doubles $50; 10% AAA discount.

CAMPING

The national recreation area is administered by Siuslaw National Forest. The campgrounds that allow dune buggy access, **Spinreel** (36 sites), parking-lot style **Driftwood II** (69 sites), **Horsfall** (69 sites, showers) and **Horsfall Beach** (34 sites), are generally loud and rowdy in the summer (all have flush toilets, drinking water and are open year-round; sites $11-13). Limited reservations for summer weekends are available; call 800-280-CAMP/2267 at least six days prior to arrival. **Carter Lake** (23 sites) and **Tahkenitch** (34 sites), both $14 per site, are quieter, designed for tenters and small RVs.

During the summer, RVs dominate all the campsites around Reedsport and Winchester Bay. Dispersed camping is allowed on public lands, but only 200 ft. from any road or trail. Ask at Dunes Information Center (see **Practical Information,** above) about legal overnight parking and camping. Summer campers with tents don't have much hope of finding a legal campground free of screaming children or screaming sand vehicles. Flee to Eel Creek and Carter Lake. At Eel Creek, you can slip away into the dunes (see **Outdoors,** below).

Carter Lake Campground, 12 mi. north of Reedsport on U.S. 101. Boat access to Carter Lake; some sites are lakeside. 23 well-screened sites, as quiet as it gets north of Reedsport. Nice bathrooms, but no showers. No ATVs. Open mid-May to mid-Sept. $14.

Eel Creek Campground, 10 mi. south of Reedsport on U.S. 101. The 52 sandy and spacious sites are well hidden from the road and each other by the tall brush. Quiet dunal adventures begin here at the trailhead for the 2½ mi. (1-way) **Umpqua Dunes Trail.** Flush toilets and drinking water; no hookups; no ATVs. $10.

William M. Tugman State Park (888-4902; reservations 800-452-5687), 8 mi. south of Reedsport on U.S. 101. 115 shady, manicured sites and pleasant smatterings of sand. Most of the sites are kept somewhat separate by bushes, but hiker/biker camp is the most private ($4). Very close to gorgeous Eel Lake. All sites ($17) have water and electricity; non-camper showers ($2); wheelchair access.

FOOD

Cheap, greasy options prevail in Winchester Bay and Reedsport; vegophiles should blaze a trail to **Safeway** (open daily 7am-11pm), in the Umpqua Shopping Center or **Price 'n' Pride** (6am-midnight) across the street, both in Reedsport along U.S. 101.

Back to the Best (271-2619), U.S. 101 at 10th St. Despite its turquoise and yellow exterior, this is one of the classiest spots in town. Sandwiches ($4.25) are piled high with fresh-cut fineries like smoked gouda and home roasted ham. Bowl of clam chowder $3.75. Open Mon.-Sat. 10:30am-6:30pm, Sun. 11am-5pm.

Seafood Grotto and Restaurant, 115 8th St. (271-4250), at Broadway in Winchester Bay. An unexpected find: excellent seafood in an average looking dining room. Sick of clam chowder? The cioppino soup ($5.45) is incredible, but prices float up after that. Lunches $4-11. Open Sun.-Thurs. noon-8pm, Fri.-Sat. noon-9pm.

OUTDOORS

When at the dunes, romp in them—there's nothing else to do. Even those with little time or low noise tolerance should at least stop at the **Oregon Dunes Overlook,** off U.S. 101, about halfway between Reedsport and Florence. Wooden ramps lead through the bushes for a peek at some untrammeled dunes and a glimpse of the ocean. The **Tahkenitch Creek Trail,** actually three separate loops, covers up to 4 mi. through forest, dunes, wetlands, and beach. It starts on U.S. 101 7 mi. north of Reedsport and is marked by blue-ringed posts. A free *Sand Tracks* brochure (available at the information center) has a detailed **map** of the dunes. The overlook is staffed daily from Memorial Day to Labor Day (10am-3pm). Guided hikes are available. An entire pamphlet on trails for dune-bound hikers is also available at the information center. An excellent walk is through the Umpqua Dunes, 2 mi. to the ocean. From the trailhead just south of Eel Creek Campground (see **Camping,** above), walk on or around the massive oblique dunes in bare feet. Be careful in the low, wet areas since there may be some quicksand.

For a silence-shattering dune experience, venture out on wheels. Plenty of shops between Florence and Coos Bay rent and offer tours. **Pacific Coast Recreation,** 4121 U.S. 101 (756-7183), in Hauser, has direct dune access and restored World War II army vehicles out front. Take a **sand dune tour** in an old transport ($12, under 14 $8) or rent ATVs ($30 per hr.). **Spinreel Dune Buggy Rentals,** 9122 Wild Wood Dr. (759-3313), on U.S. 101, 7 mi. south of Reedsport, rents Honda Odysseys ($20 30min., $30 1st hr., $25 2nd hr.). They also have dune buggy rides, a good alternative to the monster dune tours ($15 30min., $25 per person per hr.), and family tours in a VW "Thing" ($35 per 30min., $55 per hr.). Or rent from **Winchester Bay Dune Buggy Adventures,** in Winchester Bay (see **Practical Information,** above).

The Umpqua Lighthouse State Park has an excellent **gray whale viewing station.** The best times to see these massive creatures are during their migrations; they head north in two waves from March through May and south in late December and early January. Unfortunately, dune buggies cause a racket underneath this 100 ft. overlook.

Bird watching is also popular around Reedsport. Lists of rare and common species and their seasons are available at the National Recreation Area headquarters (see **Practical Information,** above). If you would rather catch animals than watch them, rent huge nets to nab crabs in Salmon Harbor. Around Labor Day, Winchester Bay merchants sponsor a crabbing contest. A $3000 reward goes out for catching the legendary **Cleo the crab.** More likely prizes are $50-100 for tagged crabs.

Coos Bay, North Bend, and Charleston

The largest city on the Oregon Coast, Coos Bay is making an economic turnaround in the face of environmental regulations that decimated the local lumber industry. Tourism has expanded economic opportunity, and businesses are returning to a once-deserted pedestrian shopping mall. Huge iron-sided tankers have begun to replace quaint fishing boats, and U.S. 101 barrels through a bustling strip of shops and espresso bars. The nearby town of North Bend blends immutably into Coos Bay, while tiny Charleston sits peacefully a few miles west on the coast. The beaches of Sunset Bay provide a sweet escape from the honkey-tonk mayhem of Coos Bay.

PRACTICAL INFORMATION AND ORIENTATION

Visitors Information: Bay Area Chamber of Commerce, 50 E. Central Ave. (269-0215 or 800-824-8486), off Commercial Ave. in Coos Bay, between the one-way thoroughfares of U.S. 101. Plenty of free brochures; comprehensive area **maps** cost 50¢-$3. Open Mon.-Fri. 8:30am-7pm, Sat.-Sun. 10am-4pm; mid-Sept. to May Mon.-Fri. 9am-5pm, Sat. 10am-4pm. **North Bend Information Center,** 1380 Sherman Ave. (756-4613), on U.S. 101, just south of the North Bend bridge. Open Mon.-Fri. 9am-5pm, Sat. 10am-4pm. **Charleston Information Center** (888-2311), at Boat Basin Dr. and Cape Arago Hwy. Open May-Oct. daily 9am-5pm. **Oregon State Parks Information,** 10765 Cape Arago Hwy., Charleston (888-8867). Open Mon.-Fri. 8am-5pm.

Buses: Greyhound, 275 N. Broadway, Coos Bay (267-4436). 3 per day to Portland ($26); 2 per day to San Francisco ($58). Open Mon.-Thurs. 9am-5pm, Fri.-Sat. 9am-4pm.

Car Rental: Verger, 1400 Ocean Blvd. (888-5594; ask for the rental department). Cars from $23 per day, 20¢ per mi. after 100. Open Mon.-Fri. 8am-5:30pm, Sat. 9am-5pm. Must be 22 or older with a credit card.

Taxi: Yellow Cab, 267-3111. 24hr. Senior discount.

Laundromat: Wash-A-Lot, 1921 Virginia Ave. (756-5439), in North Bend. Wash $1, 10min. dry 25¢. 24hr.

Public Library: 525 W. Anderson (269-1101), in Coos Bay. Open Mon. 10am-5:30pm, Tues.-Wed. 10am-8pm, Thurs.-Fri. noon-5:30pm, Sat. 1-5pm.

Crisis Line: 888-5911. 24hr. information and referral. **Women's Crisis Service:** 756-7000. 24hr.

Hospital: Bay Area Hospital, 1775 Thompson Rd. (269-8111), in Coos Bay. **Medical Emergency:** 269-8085.

Emergency: 911. **Police:** 500 Central Ave. (269-8911). **Fire:** 150 S. 4th St. (269-1191). **Coast Guard:** 4645 Eel Ave. (888-3266), in Charleston.

Post Office: 470 Golden Ave. (267-4514), at 4th St. Open Mon.-Fri. 8:30am-5pm. **General Delivery ZIP Code:** 97420.

Area Code: 541.

U.S. 101 jogs inland south of **Coos Bay,** rejoining the coast at Bandon. From Coos Bay, Route 42 heads east 85 mi. to I-5, and U.S. 101 continues north into dune territory. U.S. 101 skirts the east side of both Coos Bay and **North Bend,** and the Cape Arago Highway continues west to **Charleston,** at the mouth of the bay. Newark Street heads west from U.S. 101 and leads into the Cape Arago Highway.

ACCOMMODATIONS AND CAMPING

Non-campers should bunk-up at the affordable and lenient **Sea Star Hostel,** 23 mi. south on U.S. 101 in **Bandon** (347-9632; see p. 455). Campers, rejoice. The nearby state-run and private campgrounds allow full access to the breathtaking coast.

2310 Lombard, guess where (756-3857), at the corner of Cedar St. in North Bend. Two small, pleasant rooms with a smattering of African and Korean art on the walls. One with two twin beds ($35), one with a double bed ($40); shared bath. Full breakfast from a wonderful hostess. Reservations recommended.

Itty Bitty Inn Motel Bed and Breakfast, 1504 Sherman Ave. (756-6398). The exterior of this refurbished 5-room motel might not look like a B&B (more like an "inn" or a "motel," or perhaps even an "inn motel"), but the lavender doors lead to cozy, pastel rooms with wall hangings, cable, refrigerators, and microwaves. Breakfast voucher for the Virginia St. Diner is included. Singles $39; doubles $51.

Sunset Bay State Park, 10965 Cape Arago Hwy. (888-4902; reservations 800-452-5687), 12 mi. south of Coos Bay and 3½ mi. west of Charleston. Akin to camping in a well-landscaped parking lot; when it's full, the park is a zoo. Fabulous Sunset Beach makes it all worthwhile. Camping here wins you a free entrance to Shore Acres State Park. 138 sites with hot showers and wheelchair-accessible facilities. $16; electrical hookups $18; full hookups $19; yurts $25; hiker/biker sites $4. Non-camper showers $2. Open year-round.

Bluebill Campground, off U.S. 101, 3 mi. north of North Bend. Follow the signs to the Horsfall Beach area, then continue down the road to this U.S. Forest Service campground with flush toilets and 19 sites. Road leads ½ mi. to the ocean and dunes. Sites $10.

FOOD

Blue Heron Bistro, 100 W. Commercial St. (267-3933), at U.S. 101 in Coos Bay. Almost-upscale atmosphere with numerous skylights and a shiny tile floor. A tad more expensive than most, but the food's a tad better, too. Cajun and Tex-Mex dinners are $9-14, but you can have a Mexican grilled cheese with black beans for $6. Long beer list. Open daily 11am-10pm; in winter 11am-9pm.

Virginia Street Diner, 1430 Virginia St. (756-3475), 4 or 5 blocks north of U.S. 101 in North Bend. The booths are a festive, sparkly red, and the prices are right. A $1 bottomless coffee cup will keep you up as you move through town. The reliable tuna melt comes with a cup of soup ($4). Try the homemade meatloaf ($6.25) or the all-you-can-eat salad bar ($4.50). Open daily 6am-10pm.

Cheryn's Seafood Restaurant and Pie House (888-3251), at the east end of Charleston Bridge in Charleston. The menu boasts the widest selection of seafood in town. Any grilled or fried combo platter you could imagine, from $6 calamari to $20 steamed lobster. Diffuse awkward silences by staring at the rotating case of pre-cut pie slices ($2). Open daily 8am-9pm; winter daily 8am-8pm.

Kaffe 101, 134 S. Broadway St. (267-5894), in Coos Bay, next to the visitors center. The fireplace, chintz chairs, and book-strewn shelves echo an English tea house. Food is limited to the likes of fireside nibblettes like bagels (with cream cheese $1.35) and chocolate mint brownies ($1.50), but there is plenty of espresso ($1.50-3). Open Mon.-Thurs. 7am-9pm, Fri.-Sat. 7am-10pm; winter closes at 8pm.

Basin Cafe, 4555 King Fisher Dr. (888-5227), across the parking lot from the boats toward the end of the Charleston harbor. You can smell the sea breeze in the front, you can hear the grease spit in the back, and you can sit down to a $2.75 stack of 3 pancakes at 5am. Blow it all on the Denver omelette ($4.85), or save a dollar and take the burger basket spilling over with fries ($3.75). Open Sun.-Thurs. 5am-8pm, Fri.-Sun. 5am-9pm.

SIGHTS AND ACTIVITIES

Those who need to fill a rainy day or are simply tired of water should make a beeline for **Cranberry Sweets,** 1005 Newmark (888-9824), in Coos Bay. This sucrose wonderland is half-factory, half-shop. Free candy samples are tiny but abundant; nibble as you watch amorphous chocolate sludge miraculously transformed into shapely pieces of candy (open Mon.-Sat. 9am-5:30pm, Sun. 11am-4pm).

Coos Bay is one of the few places on the coast where life slows down as you near the shore. Escape industrial chaos by following Cape Arago Hwy. from the west end of Newmark St. in Coos Bay to rustic **Charleston,** a pleasant place to while away a coastal afternoon.

Fishing enthusiasts should hop on board with **Bob's Sportfishing,** P.O. Box 5018 (888-4241 or 800-628-9633), operating out of a small building at the west end of the Charleston Boat Basin, or **Betty Kay Charters,** P.O. Box 5020 (888-9021 or 800-752-6303), a stone's throw away on the water's edge, both of which run six-hour bottom fishing trips daily at 6am and noon ($55 with a $6.75 daily license). Betty Kay also rents crab rings for $4 each (with a $15 deposit).

OUTDOORS

Sunset Bay, 3½ mi. west of Bastendorff Beach on Cape Arago State Hwy., has been rated one of the top 10 American beaches, and for good reason. The beach is nestled between two low dirt cliffs that hook around to shelter the bay. The remaining ocean front is calmed by natural rock outcroppings. Water temperatures are a bit warmer than the frigid North Pacific norm, making Sunset Bay popular for swimming.

A mile beyond Sunset Bay on the Cape Arago Hwy. is the magnificent **Shore Acres State Park** (888-3732). Once the estate of local lumber lord Louis J. Simpson, the park contains elaborate botanical gardens that survived after the mansion was razed. The egret sculptures are a more recent addition, courtesy of artistically inclined inmates from the state penitentiary. A lovely rose garden boasting rows of award-winning strains lies hidden in the back. For all of December, the flowers are festooned with strings of over 150,000 lights, and the park serves complimentary cocoa and hot cider (open daily 8am-9pm; winter 8am-dusk; $3 per car; wheelchair accessible).

Farther south at the end of the highway is breezy **Cape Arago,** notable for its creature-encrusted **tide pools.** Paved paths lead out toward the tip of the cape and provide an excellent view of wildlife on **Shell Island,** ¼ mi. offshore. The island is a rookery for elephant and harbor seals. Paths here are closed to the public to prevent habitat destruction, but the island can be spotted from a pull-out ½ mi. before the cape. Bring binoculars. Blue whales, sea lions, and a number of noteworthy seabirds also make appearances.

Four miles south of Charleston up Seven Devils Rd., the **South Slough National Estuarine Research Reserve** (888-5558) is one of the most dramatic and underappreciated venues on the central coast. Spreading out from a small interpretive visitors center, almost 7 sq. mi. of mixed salt and fresh water estuaries protect wildlife, from sand shrimp to deer. Hiking trails weave through the sanctuary; take a lunch and commune with the blue heron. Maps are free at the visitors center and guided walks are given in the summer (Fri. 2-4pm). Canoe tours ($5) are available, if you have your own canoe. For a summer calendar, write P.O. Box 5417, Charleston 97420 (open daily June-Aug. 8:30am-4:30pm; Sept.-May Mon.-Fri.; trails open daily dawn-dusk).

EVENTS

For two weeks in mid-July, Coos Bay basks in the glory of the **Oregon Coast Music Festival,** P.O. Box 663, Coos Bay 97420 (267-0938), the most popular event on the coast. Art exhibits, vessel tours, and a free classical concert in Mingus Park triple cultural options in the area. This two-week music festival draws a variety of performances (ranging from Baroque to Country but skipping Rock and Roll) to Coos Bay, North Bend, Charleston, Bandon, and Reedsport. Tickets cost $11-15, or a few bucks more if bought by (269-2720 or 800-676-7563). Ask at the chamber of commerce (see **Practical Information,** above) about unreserved ticket outlets.

In the second week of August, Charleston hosts the **Seafood Festival** (888-9021) in the Boat Basin. In late August, Coos Bay celebrates a native fruit with the **Blackberry Arts Festival** (269-2720). Downtown rocks with square dancing, wine tasting, concerts, and crafts. In September, Oregon remembers one of its favorite native sons in the **Steve Prefontaine 10K Memorial Run** (269-1103), named after the great Olympic athlete who died in an automobile accident. The race draws dozens of world-class runners to the area (entrance $12-15).

■ Coos Bay to Brookings

BANDON

In spite of the steady flow of tourists in the summer, the small fishing town of Bandon (24 mi. south of Coos Bay on U.S. 101), has refrained from breaking out pink and turquoise paint and making itself up like Coney Island. **Greyhound** (267-4436) stops thrice daily at the **Sea Star Hostel,** once on the way north and twice going south. The **Bandon Chamber of Commerce,** 300 SE 2nd St., P.O. Box 1515 (347-9616), in the Old Town next to U.S. 101, gives out plenty of brochures and assistance (open daily June-Aug. 10am-5pm; Sept.-May 10am-4pm). The **post office** in Bandon is at 105 12th St. SE (800-275-8777; open Mon.-Fri. 8:30am-4:30pm). The **General Delivery ZIP Code** is 97411-9999, and the **area code** is 541.

The rambling **Sea Star Hostel (HI-AYH),** 375 2nd St. (347-9632), on the right as you enter Old Town from the north, gives Bandon a budget option. Comfortable bunkrooms, enclosed courtyard, kitchen, laundry room, noon check-out, and an open-24-hours policy make this hostel a relaxed and right-rocking place to pass a night ($13, nonmembers $16, ages 5-12 (can only stay in family rooms) $6; $28 for 2 members; nonmembers $34, additional person $13). Alternatively, find your way to the **Bandon Wayside Motel** (347-3421), on Hwy. 42 S, just off U.S. 101 (singles $32; 1 queen and 1 twin $40; 2 queens $44). Two miles north of town and across the bridge, **Bullard's Beach State Park** (347-2209), gives a home to the **Coquille River Lighthouse,** built in 1896. The park has 192 sites ($19, yurts $25, hiker/biker $4), tucked into the sand and pines. Although technically reserved for those with horses (or llamas, or elephants), the base camp, set off from the other sites, may be a peaceful place to park a tent. Campfire talks are given on summer evenings (Tues.-Sat.).

For a tasty and healthy morsel, step into **Mother's Natural Grocery and Deli**, 975 U.S. 101 (347-4086), near the junction with Rte. 42 S, to pick up four vegetarian *nori* rolls for $3 or a well-stuffed carrot hummus pita pocket ($3.50; open Mon.-Sat. 10am-6pm). The best seafood in town is at **Bandon Boatworks,** 275 Lincoln SW (347-2111), through Old Town and out South Jetty Rd. The dining room may be simple, but the splendid view of the ocean and the menu of sauteed, baked, and fried fish speak for themselves. Lunches ($6-8) are more affordable than dinners ($10-15), when the Boatworks breaks out the wine glasses for a fancier affair (open Mon.-Sat. 11:30am-2:30pm and 5-9pm, Sun. noon-8:30pm).

Outdoor activities abound near Bandon. Strolling around Old Town is pleasant, as is exploring the beaches on a horse from **Bandon Beach Riding Stables** (347-3423; 1 hr. trip $20). Or drive the beach loop road that leaves from Old Town and joins U.S. 101 5 mi. south. The loop is well marked and passes **Table Rock, Elephant Rock,** and **Face Rock,** some of the most impressive offshore outcroppings along the coast.

PORT ORFORD

Port Orford supports a funky and healthy community lifestyle, protected by the prosperity of its larger, more touristed neighbors. The town lies several miles south of **Cape Blanco,** the westernmost point in Oregon. **Cape Blanco State Park,** 5 mi. west of U.S. 101, has a campground high on the hill and a road leading down to the cape's beach. The very tip of the cape is capped with a functional lighthouse, open to the public (Thurs.-Mon. 10am-3:30pm). Port Orford is 26 mi. south of Bandon and 30 mi. north of **Gold Beach.** Some of the best views in the area are from **Battle Rock,** a seaside park in town where the whales pass close by during December and spring migrations. The beaches are littered with agate, easy to find at low tide when they sparkle in the sun.

Port Orford's **Chamber of Commerce,** P.O. Box 637 (332-8055), lazes in the parking lot overlooking the bay (open Mon.-Fri. 9am-5pm, Sat. and Sun. 10am-5pm). **Greyhound** stops at the Circle K, across from the Port Orford Motel, with one bus per day to Portland ($34) and two to San Francisco ($54). The **post office** is at 311 W 7th St. (332-4251), at Jackson (open daily Mon.-Fri. 8:30am-1pm and 2-5pm; **General Delivery ZIP Code:** 97465). The **area code** is 541.

For those traveling by bus, the **Port Orford Motel,** 1034 Oregon St. (332-1685), at U.S. 101, with its fluorescent green trim and convenient location, is hard to miss. The older, cramped rooms sport wooden walls and TVs (1 person $25-28, 2 people $35, 3 people $40). Several blocks south and around the bend, the **Shoreline Motel** (332-2903), on U.S. 101, sits across the road from dramatic Battle Rock and the bay. The bathrooms are small, but the rooms are big and well kept (1 person $36, 2 $38, 2 beds $42; winter rates drop $8). Two nearby campgrounds, one to the north and one to the south, offer the most peaceful and convenient access to the shore. **Cape Blanco State Park** (332-6774), 6 mi. north of Port Orford and 4 mi. west of U.S. 101, in a grove of pines just south of the lighthouse-dominated cape, has 58 sites ($16, full hookups $18, hiker/biker $4). Survivors of the 3 mi. hike up the mountain win a tremendous panorama of the entire area. Six miles south of Port Orford, where the highway ducks back behind mountains, **Humbug Mountain State Park** (332-6774) has 108 tightly packed sites in the crisp green shade of deciduous trees and no Scrooge in sight (showers and flush toilets; tents $16, water and electricity $18, hiker/biker $4).

Health food nuts are in luck in Port Orford. Beside the greasy seafood and breakfast joints, **Sisters Natural Grocery and Cafe,** 832 Hwy. 101 (332-3640), makes a case for itself with four lovely tables and plenty of granola. Come in the morning for garden sausage and a couple eggs from the chickens next door or have a vegetable sandwich on fresh sourdough rye (both $4.25) at lunch. The cafe is open Tuesday to Friday from 8am-3pm, the grocery store Monday to Friday from 10am-6pm and Saturday 10am-5pm.

Brookings

The southernmost stop on U.S. 101 before California, Brookings is one of the few coastal towns that remains relatively tourist-free. Here, trinket shops do not elbow out hardware stores and warehouses, making Brookings more of a stopover on the way to its surrounding beaches and parks than a destination in itself. The beaches are among the most unspoiled on the Oregon Coast, sitting in a region often called Oregon's "banana belt" due to its mild climate; warm weather is not rare in January, and Brookings' beautiful blossoms bloom early. Strictly speaking, there are two towns here, separated by the Chetco River—Brooking on the north side and **Harbor,** to the south. They share everything, including a chamber of commerce, and are referred to collectively as Brookings. Go figure. In town, U.S. 101 is called Chetco Avenue.

Practical Information The **Brookings Welcome Center,** 1650 U.S. 101 (469-4117), maintains an office just north of Brookings (open May-Sept. Mon.-Sat. 8am-6pm, Sun. 9am-5pm; April and Oct. Mon.-Sat. 8am-5pm). The town's **Chamber of Commerce,** 16330 Lower Harbor Rd. (469-3181 or 800-535-9469), is across the bridge to the south, a short distance off the highway. City **maps** are $1, but the Seaside Real Estate map is free (open Mon.-Fri. 9am-5pm and Sat. 9am-1pm, Dec.-Jan. closed Sat.). The **Chetco Ranger Station,** 555 5th St. (469-2196), distributes information on the neighboring part of the **Siskiyou National Forest** (open Mon.-Fri. 8am-4:30pm).

The **Greyhound** station, 601 Railroad Ave. (469-3326), at Tanburk, sends two buses north and two south each day (to: Portland, $37; San Francisco, $46; open Mon.-Fri. 8:45am-noon and 4-6:30pm, Sat. 8:45am-noon). The **Maytag Laundry** (469-3975), is known to locals as "The Old Wash House"; you'll find it in the Brookings Harbor Shopping Center (open daily 7am-11pm; wash $1, 10min. dry 25¢). The **post office,** 711 Spruce St. (800-ASK-USPS/275-8777), is open Monday to Friday 9am-4:30pm. The **General Delivery ZIP Code** is 97415, and the **area code** is 541.

OREGON

Accommodations and Camping Motel rooms and campsites alike are costly in Brookings except in winter, when motel rates tend to drop about $10. The **Bonn Motel,** 1216 Hwy. 101 (469-2161), is basic budget bedding. Its three low buildings have a row of hydrangeas lurking behind each room and a somewhat distant view of the ocean out front (singles $38, doubles $48; less in winter). Down the road, the **Beaver State Motel,** 437 Hwy. 101 (469-5361), provides spiffier accommodations for a few dollars more. Bedspreads actually match the curtains (one person $42, two people $49, two people, two beds $59; less in winter).

Harris Beach State Park (469-2021), at the north edge of Brookings, has 68 tent sites amid a grand natural setting. The beach looks across a narrow waterway toward a 21-acre hunk of uninhabited rock and pines known as **Goat Island.** The campground, set back in the trees behind the beach, is equipped with showers, hiker/biker sites ($4), and handicapped facilities (sites $16, with full hookup $19; open year-round). Make reservations (800-452-5687) for stays between Memorial Day and Labor Day. For campsites off the beaten path, travel 15 mi. east of Brookings on North Bank Rd. to the charming **Little Redwood Campground.** In a forest alongside a burbling, scurrying salamander-filled creek, the campground has 15 sites ($6), with drinking water and pit toilet. Several other campgrounds along that road are free but have no water. For information, contact the Chetco Ranger District (see **Practical Information,** above).

Food A fishing town at heart, Brookings can batter up a flounder with the best of 'em. A number of salty seafood spots can be found near the harbor, among them the local favorite **Marty's Pelican Bay Seafoods,** 16403 Lower Harbor Rd. (469-7971), just down the street from the chamber of commerce. Join loggers and fisherfolk for pancakes that truly fill the whole pan ($3.75). All servings are more than generous; for a delicious, if morbid-sounding treat, try the $2 bowl of "graveyard stew" (open Mon.-Thurs. 4am-8pm, Fri.-Sat. 4am-9pm, Sun. 5am-3pm). For serious Mexican food, stick to the highway and head for **Los Amigos,** 541 Hwy. 101 (469-4102). The plain, baby-blue exterior may not catch your eye immediately, but the $4.25 super burrito, $5.75 pork tamale, and 30¢ corn tortillas will startle your stomach, and domestic bottles are only $1.50 (open Mon.-Sat. 11am-8pm, Sun. noon-8pm).

Sights, Activities, and Events Brookings is known statewide for its beautiful flowers. In **Azalea Park,** downtown, large native and non-native azaleas, some more than 300 years old, encircle lawns, blooming between April and June. Two rare weeping spruce trees also grace the park's grounds. The pride of Brookings is its annual **Azalea Festival** (469-3181), held in Azalea Park during Memorial Day weekend. The **Chetco Valley Historical Society Museum,** 15461 Museum Rd. (469-6651), 2½ mi. south of the Chetco River, occupies the oldest building in Brookings and has exhibits on the patchwork quilts of settlers and Native American basketwork. The museum is hard to miss; just look for the **nation's largest cypress tree** in front (open March-Oct. Wed.-Sun. noon-5pm, Nov.-Feb. only Fri.-Sun.; $1, children 50¢).

If you're heading north from Brookings by bicycle, take scenic **Carpenterville Road,** the only highway out of town before U.S. 101 was built. The twisty, 13½ mi. road features beautiful ocean views. **Boardman State Park** enfolds U.S. 101 for 8 mi. north of Brookings; overlooks and picnic sites provide fantastic views of the coast. Thirty miles north of Brookings in **Gold Beach,** you can ride a mail boat up the **Rogue River. Mail Boat Hydro-Jets** (247-7033 or 800-458-3511) offers 64, 80, and 104 mi. daytrips. Whitewater trips last six to seven and a half hours and start at $30.

INLAND VALLEYS

While the jagged cliffs and coastal surf draw tourists to the Oregon coast, many Oregonians choose the lush inland Willamette and Rogue River Valleys for their vacation destinations. Vast tracts of fertile land here support agriculture and for decades the immense forest resources maintained a healthy timber industry, but in recent years a call to save what's left of Oregon's forest and wildlife has divided the population. A few years ago, Congress passed legislation to protect the endangered northern spotted owl, and a federal court injunction banned logging in the public forests of the Pacific Northwest. (In Oregon, over 50% of the forests are publicly owned.) Idle mills, unemployed loggers, and crippled local economies pushed the issue back into Congress in June 1994, and limited logging resumed under a complex new forest-use-and-protection plan created by the Clinton Administration. The issue of the spotted owl is still tense. But while the fortunes of the timber industry are uncertain, tourism is definitely a growth industry in small-town Oregon.

Interstate 5 runs north-south through Oregon to the west of the Cascades, traversing rolling agricultural and forest land punctuated by a few urban centers. Farther south, the Rogue River Valley, running from Ashland to Grants Pass, is hot and dry in the summer, bringing lucrative business to the whitewater rafting and kayaking outfitters. Eugene, Oregon's second-largest city and bawdiest college town, rests at the southern end of the temperate Willamette Valley. This carpet of agricultural land extends 20 mi. on either side of the river and continues 80 mi. north until it bumps into the bedroom communities of Portland. It is possible to drive Oregon's 305-mi.

stretch of I-5 from tip to toe in less than six hours, but lead-footed aliens be warned—most Oregonians obey speed limits, and fines have recently skyrocketed.

Ashland

With a casual, rural setting near the California border, Ashland mixes hippies and "Globe-al" history, making it the perfect stage for the world-famous **Shakespeare Festival.** From mid-February to October, drama devotees choose from a repertoire of 11 plays performed in Ashland's three elegant theaters. Over the festival's 60-year history, the town has evolved with it, giving rise to businesses like "All's Well Herbs and Vitamins," and a vibrant population of artists, actors, and Bard-buffs. Extravagant Shakespearean and contemporary productions draw both connoisseurs and casual observers. Ashland can be crowded in the summer, but the town has not yet sold its soul. Culture comes with a price, but low-cost accommodations and tickets reward those who investigate. And though all the world may know Ashland only as a stage, Oregonians also recognize Ashland's fabulous restaurants, art galleries, and concerts.

PRACTICAL INFORMATION AND ORIENTATION

Visitors Information: Chamber of Commerce, 110 E. Main St. (482-3486). A busy (but friendly) staff frenetically answers phones and dishes out free play schedules and brochures, several of which contain small but adequate **maps.** (Oddly, the best maps of Ashland are in the to-go menu at **Omar's,** 1380 Siskiyou Blvd., 482-1281. The chamber *does not sell tickets to performances.* Open Mon.-Fri. 9am-5pm. The chamber also staffs an **info booth** in the center of the plaza. Open in summer daily 9am-5pm. **Ashland District Ranger Station,** 645 Washington St. (482-3333), off Rte. 66 by Exit 14 on I-5. Hiking, mountain biking, and other outdoor info, including words of wisdom on the Pacific Crest Trail and area camping. Open Mon.-Fri. 8am-4:30pm.

Tickets: Oregon Shakespearean Festival Box Office, 15 S. Pioneer St., P.O. Box 158, Ashland 97520 (482-4331; fax 482-8045), next to the Elizabethan Theater. Rush tickets (½ price) occasionally available 30min. before performances not already sold out. Ask at the box office for more options; the staff is full of tips for desperate theatergoers. The best bet, though, is to write for tickets in advance.

Buses: Greyhound (482-8803; 779-2103 in Medford; 800-231-2222 departures). No depot in Ashland. Pick-up and drop-off at the BP station, 2073 Hwy. 99 N., at the north end of town. To: Portland (4 per day, $36); Sacramento, CA (3 per day, $40); and San Francisco, CA (3 per day, $47). **Green Tortoise** (800-867-8647) comes through at 4 inconvenient times per week, stopping at I-5 Exit 14 outside of the Copper Skillet Cafe on the east side of Hwy. 66. Northbound Tues. and Sat. 5:15am to Portland ($29), and Seattle, WA ($39); southbound Sun. and Thurs. 11:45 pm to San Francisco, CA ($39).

Public Transportation: Rogue Valley Transportation (779-2877), in Medford. Schedules available at the chamber of commerce. Base fare $1. Over 62 and ages 10-17 50¢, under 10 free. The #10 bus serving Ashland runs daily every 30min. 5am-6pm between the transfer station at 200 S. Front St. in Medford and the Plaza in Ashland. Also to Jacksonville 4 times daily (on bus #30, $1). Local buses loop through Ashland every 15min. (25¢).

Taxi: Yellow Cab, 482-3065. 24hr.

Car Rental: Budget, 3038 Biddle Rd. (488-7741 for reservations), in Medford (see **Medford: Practical Information,** p. 464).

Library: Ashland Branch Library, 410 Siskiyou Blvd. (482-1197), at Gresham St. Open Mon.-Tues. 10am-8pm, Wed.-Thurs. 10am-6pm, Fri.-Sat. 10am-5pm.

Laundromat: Main St. Laundromat, 370 E. Main St. (482-8042). Wash $1, 9min. dry 25¢. Ms. PacMan 25¢. Open daily 9am-9pm.

Equipment Rental: Ashland Mountain Supply, 31 N. Main St. (488-2749). Internal frame backpacks $7.50 per day ($100 deposit or credit card). External frame backpacks $5 per day ($50 deposit). Mountain bikes $10 per 2hr., $25 per day. Discounts for longer rentals. Open Mon.-Sat. 10am-6pm, Sun. 11am-5pm. **The Adventure Center,** 40 N. Main St. (488-2819 or 800-444-2819). Mountain bikes

$20 per 4hr., $25 per 8hr. Guided bike tours ($59 for 4hr. with lunch) and raft trips (4hr. $59, all day $110) also offered.

Crisis Intervention Services: 779-4357 or 888-609-HELP/4357. 24hr.

Emergency: 911. **Police:** 1155 E. Main St. (482-5211). **Fire:** 455 Siskiyou Blvd. (482-2770).

Post Office: 120 N. 1st St. (482-3986), at Lithia Way. Open Mon.-Fri. 9am-5pm. **General Delivery ZIP Code:** 97520.

Area Code: 541.

Ashland is located in the foothills of the Siskiyou and Cascade Ranges, 285 mi. south of Portland and 15 mi. north of the California border, near the junction of I-5 and Route 66, which traverses 64 mi. of stunning scenery between Ashland and Klamath Falls. Highway 99 cuts through the middle of town on a northwest-southwest axis. Its local name changes from N. Main St. to E. Main at the triangular plaza, where a medley of shops and restaurants form Ashland's downtown. Farther south, Main St. changes name again to Siskiyou St. **Southern Oregon State College** (SOSC), another few blocks down Siskiyou, is flanked by affordable motels and so-so restaurants.

ACCOMMODATIONS AND CAMPING

Now spurs the lated traveler apace to gain the timely inn.

—Macbeth, III.iii.6

In winter, Ashland is a budget traveler's paradise of vacancy and low rates; in summer, hotel and B&B rates double, and the hostel overflows with travelers. Only rogues and strumpets arrive without reservations. Midsummer nights see vacant accommodations in nearby Medford (see **Medford: Accommodations,** p. 465). At least part of Ashland's water supply contains dissolved sulfurous compounds. It is perfectly safe to drink and bathe in, but lends some bathrooms a repugnant and permanent odor.

OREGON

Ashland Hostel, 150 N. Main St. (482-9217). Well-kept and cheery, this hostel has an air of elegance worthy of the Bard himself. The Victorian parlor, sturdy bunks, and a front-porch swing play host to a mixed crowd of budget travelers and theater-bound families wise to money-saving ways. Laundry facilities and kitchen. Check-in 5-11pm. Curfew at midnight. Lockout 10am-5pm. $14 with any hostelling member card, $15 without. $3 discounts and free laundry for Pacific Crest Trail hikers or touring cyclists. Two private rooms (sleep 4 each, $37-40), and a private women's room ($22 for 1, $30 for 2). Reservations advised March-Oct.

Columbia Hotel, 262½ E. Main St. (482-3726 or 800-718-2530). A European-style home, 1½ blocks from the theaters. Spacious rooms with wood panelling, sepia-toned photos, and muted colors. No TVs. Bathroom and pay phone down the hall. Singles $49, 2 twins $59; Nov.-Feb. singles $30, 2 twins $34; March-May singles $42, 2 twins $46, 2 queens $49. 10% discount for HI-AYH members in the off season; children under 12 free. Call ahead.

Vista Motel, 535 Clover Lane (482-4423), just off I-5 at Exit 14, behind a BP station. Small rooms in a low red, white, and blue building resembling a Lego. Not center-stage, but there is cable, A/C, a small pool, and an amiable staff. Singles $37; doubles $45. Winter and spring discounts of about $10.

Ashland Motel, 1145 Siskiyou Blvd. (482-2561), across from the college. Fresh and tidy with a pale pink facade and an interior that puts little to no unique spin on the ubiquitous "motel brown" motif. Coin laundry, phones, cable, A/C, and a good-sized pool. Singles $43; doubles $63. Off-season rates $5-12 lower.

Mt. Ashland Campground, 9 mi. west of I-5 south at Exit 6. Follow signs to Mt. Ashland Ski Area and take the high road from the far west end of the lot (sign for Grouse Gap Snowpeak). Exquisitely placed on the side of a mountaintop, looking south across the valley to Mt. Shasta. Seven primitive sites set in the high grass. Fire pits and vault toilets, but no drinking water. Free, and seasonal.

Jackson Hot Springs, 2253 Hwy. 99 N. (482-3776), 2 mi. north of Ashland on Hwy. 99; from I-5 go west ½ mi from Exit 19 and turn right on 99. The nearest campground to downtown. Separate tent area in a grassy, open field encircled by RV sites. Laundry facilities, hot showers, and overpriced indoor mineral baths ($20 per person, $25 per couple). Tent and RV sites $10, with full hookup $15.

FOOD

Give them great meals of beef and iron and steel, they will eat like wolves and fight like devils.

—*Henry V*, III.vii.166

The incredible selection of eats 'n' mead available on North and East Main St. has earned the plaza a reputation independent of the festival. Even the ticketless come from miles around to dine in Ashland's fine restaurants. Beware the pre-show rush—a downtown dinner planned for 6:30pm can easily become a late-night affair. Many businesses close at 8:30 or 9pm, when the rush has receded into the theaters. **Ashland Community Food Store CO-OP,** 237 N. 1st St. (482-2237), at A St., has a lively spirit and a great selection of organic produce and natural foods (open Mon.-Sat. 8am-9pm, Sun. 9am-9pm; 5% senior discount). Standard, less expensive groceries are available at **Safeway,** 585 Siskiyou Blvd. (482-4495; open daily 6am-midnight).

Geppetto's, 345 E. Main St. (482-1138). The local favorite for late-night bite. The staff is fun, the walls covered in baskets, and the menu conversational, offering 6 feta and spinach wontons for $3.50. $15 dinner specials are enticing, but there are smaller ticket options, too, like a pile of sauteed vegetables ($3) or a marinated cucumber sandwich ($4.25). Lunches $4-6, breakfasts slightly more. Try the Pesto omelette ($7.50). Open daily 8am-midnight.

Greenleaf Restaurant, 49 N. Main St. (482-2808). Healthy, delicious food, right on the plaza with creekside seating out back. Omelettes and fritattas are a bargain in the morning for $5-6.50. Tremendous array of salads ($1.50-9.50), pastas ($5-9), and spuds that are meals in themselves ($2.25-6.50). Chomp inside or take it down the block for a picnic in nearby Lithia Park. Open daily 8am-9pm; off-season Tues.-Sun. 8am-8pm. Closed Jan.

Thai Pepper, 84 N. Main St. (482-8058), one level below the street. A hotspot in the coolest area of town, with decks in the leafy green shade over Ashland Creek. Delicious entrees, exotic and reasonably priced for Ashland ($10-14). The best deal is lunch, when you don't have to wait for a seat outside, and your choice of 3 small dishes (including curry, spring rolls, and satay) is a steal for $6.50. Open Mon.-Thurs. 5-9:30pm, Fri.-Sat. 5-10pm, Sun. 5-8:30pm.

Brothers Restaurant and Delicatessen, 95 N. Main St. (482-9671). A block off the trampled tourist track, this New York-style deli and cafe feeds more locals than most. Some offbeat selections like the zucchini burger ($4.25) join the more traditional deli fare. Sandwiches ($7); bagel and cream cheese ($2.25). Open Mon. and Wed.-Fri. 7am-2pm, Tues. 7am-8pm, Sat. and Sun. 7am-3pm.

Five Rivers, 139 E. Main St. (488-1883), one flight up from street level. Slip upstairs to the warm smells of eastern spices and delicious Indian cuisine. Elegant Indian artwork and music set an intimate tone. Entrees $5.50-11.50; vegetarian options all below $7. Daily lunch buffet $5.50. Open daily 11am-2:30pm and 5-10pm.

Evo's Java House, 376 E. Main St. (482-2261). Chill out away from the crowds with a bowl of coffee ($1) or a Zaffiro Smoothie (blackberries, blueberries, and OJ $2.50). College students and cool cats hang here. Live jazz every Sun. night attracts a crowd (open daily 7am-10pm).

THE SHAKESPEARE FESTIVAL

This is very midsummer madness

—*Twelfth Night*, III.iv.62

The **Shakespeare Festival,** the brainchild of local college teacher Angus Bowmer, began in 1935 with two plays performed in the Chautauqua Theater by schoolchildren as an evening complement to daytime boxing matches. Today, professional actors perform 11 plays in repertory. As the selections have become more modern, Shakespeare's share has shrunk to four plays; the other seven are classical and contemporary dramas. Performances run on the three Ashland stages from mid-February through October, and any boxing now is over the extremely scarce tickets ("Lay on, Macduff! And damned be him that first cries, 'Hold, enough!'" *Macbeth,* V.vii.62). On the side of the Chautauqua theater stands the 1200-seat **Elizabethan Stage,** an outdoor theater modeled after one in 18th-century London. Open only from mid-June through early October, the Elizabethan hosts three Shakespeare plays per season. The **Angus Bowmer** is a 600-seat indoor theater that stages one Shakespeare play and several classical dramas. The newest of the theaters is the intimate **Black Swan,** home to one Shakespeare play and other small, offbeat productions.

Due to the tremendous popularity of the festival, ticket purchases are recommended six months in advance. General mail-order ticket sales begin in January, but phone orders are not taken until February ($15-40 spring and fall, $18.75-45 in summer, plus a $3.50 handling fee per order for phone, fax, or mail orders; children under 5 not admitted to any of the shows). For complete ticket information, write Oregon Shakespeare Festival, P.O. Box 158, Ashland 97520 (482-4331; fax 482-8045; www.mind.net/osf). Spontaneous theatergoers should not abandon hope. The **box office** at 15 S. Pioneer St. opens at 9:30am on theater days; prudence demands arriving a few hours early. Local patrons have been known to leave their shoes to hold their places in line, and you should respect this tradition. At 9:30am, the box office releases any unsold tickets for the day's performances. If no tickets are available, limited priority numbers will be given out. These entitle their holders to a designated place in line when the precious few tickets that festival members have returned are released (1pm for matinees, and 6pm for evening performances). At these times, the box office also sells twenty clear-view standing room tickets for sold-out shows on the Elizabethan Stage ($10, obtained on the day of the show).

Unofficial ticket transactions also take place just outside the box office, "on the bricks," though scalping is illegal. ("Off with his head!"—*Richard III,* III.iv.75). Ticket officials advise those buying on the bricks to check the date and time on the ticket carefully, to pay only the face value, and to check with the box office before purchasing any tickets that have been altered. From March to May, half-price rush tickets are often available an hour before every performance that is not sold out. Additionally, in the spring and in October, some half-price student-senior matinees are offered. Spring and summer previews (pre-critic, full-performance shows) are offered at the Black Swan and Elizabethan Stage for a discounted price ($16-36).

Backstage tours provide a wonderful glimpse of the festival from behind the curtain. Tour guides (usually actors or technicians) divulge all kinds of anecdotes—from bird songs during an outdoor *Hamlet* to the ghastly events which take place every time they do "that Scottish play." Tours last almost two hours and usually leave from the Black Swan (Tues.-Sun. 10am; $8.50-9.50, ages 5-17 $6.30-7.10, children under 5 not admitted). Admission includes a trip to the **Exhibit Center** for a close-up look at sets and costumes (open Tues.-Sun. 10am-4pm, fall and spring 10:30am-1:30pm; without tour $2, children 5-17 $1.50). Further immersion in Shakespeare can be had at two-hour discussion **seminars** offered every Friday between Memorial and Labor Day (9:30-11:30am) by Southern Oregon State College ($5). Call 552-6331 for more information. The Shakespeare festival also includes special events, such as the **Feast of Will** in mid-June, a celebration honoring the annual opening of the Elizabethan Theater. Dinner and merry madness in Lithia Park start at 6pm (tickets $16; call 482-4331 for exact date).

SIGHTS AND ACTIVITIES

Mischief, thou art afoot, Take though what course thou wilt!

—*Julius Caesar,* III.ii.259

Before it imported Shakespeare, Ashland was naturally blessed with lithia water—water containing dissolved lithium salts, reputed to have miraculous healing powers.

(It is said that only 1 other spring in the world has a higher lithium concentration! Depression, be gone.) The mineral springs have given their name to the well-tended **Lithia Park,** west of the plaza off Main St. To quaff the vaunted water itself, hold your nose (the water contains dissolved sulfur salts) and head for the circle of fountains in the center of the plaza. Free concerts, readings, and educational nature walks happen early every day, in and around the park's hiking trails, Japanese garden, and the swan ponds by Ashland Creek. Events are listed in brochures at the chamber of commerce (see **Practical Information,** above).

If you have not yet perished from cultural overload, hang around Ashland even after the festival ends. ("Give me excess of it, that, surfeiting, the appetite may sicken and so die"—*Twelfth Night,* I.i.2-3.) Artists love to play to the town's characteristically enthused audiences, so there is always something to attend. The **Oregon Cabaret Theater,** P.O. Box 1149 (488-2902), at 1st and Hagardine St., stages light musicals in a pink former church with drinks, dinners, and optional Sunday brunch (tickets $11-18; box office open Mon. and Wed.-Sat. 11am-6:30pm, Sun. 11am-4pm). Small groups, such as **Actor's Theater of Ashland** (535-5250), **Ashland Community Theatre** (482-7532), and the theater department at Southern Oregon State (552-6346) also raise the curtains sporadically year-round. The travelling **Rogue Valley Symphony** and the **State Ballet of Oregon** perform at the Music Recital Hall at SOSC and in Lithia Park when they are in town. In July and August, the ballet strikes the stage on Mondays at 7:30pm; the Ashland City Band (488-5340) fires itself up at the same time on Thursdays in Lithia Park. The **Palo Alto Chamber Orchestra** (482-4331) performances in late June ($13) in the Elizabethan Theatre (weather permitting) are also a hit. Contact the chamber of commerce for a current schedule of events.

If your muscles demand a little abuse after all this theater-seat R&R, hop on the **Pacific Crest Trail** at Grouse Gap. Take Exit 6 off I-5 and follow the signs along the Mt. Ashland Access Rd. At the top of the 9 mi. road is **Mount Ashland,** a small community-owned ski area on the north face of the mountain with 23 runs (open Thanksgiving Day-April, daily 9am-4pm; night skiing Thurs.-Sat. 4-10pm; day ticket weekdays $20, children 9-12 and seniors $14, weekends $25, children and seniors $18; full rental $15; snowboard and boots $25). Contact **Ski Ashland,** P.O. Box 220 (482-2897). For **snow conditions,** call 482-2754. Over 100 mi. of free cross-country trails surround Mt. Ashland. **Bull Gap Trail,** which starts from the ski area's parking lot, is also good for skiing (and for biking after the snow has melted). It winds 2½ mi. down 1100 ft. to paved Tollman Creek Rd., 15½ mi. south of Siskiyou Blvd.

Join flocks of kids on the double-flumed, 280-ft. **waterslide** at **Emigrant Lake Park** (776-7001; 10 slides for $4 plus a $3 entry fee). The park is also a popular place for boating, hiking, swimming, and fishing. Although only 6 mi. east of town on Rte. 66, the lake is in a different geological region from Ashland. The parched hills that surround it are part of the Great Basin, where cows graze freely and render the lake water unsuitable to drink (open 10am-sunset, waterslide noon-6:30pm).

OREGON

BARS AND CLUBS

Come, come; good wine is a good familiar, if it be well us'd.

—*Othello,* II.iii.308

Catwork, 66 E. Main St. (482-0787). This nascent club and restaurant adds style and eccentricity to Ashland's post-show scene. Caters to the less traditional with DJs, live music, and assorted other entertainment (fashion shows!). Pacific Rim cuisine stars alongside a full bar and micropints. Open daily 11:30am-2am.

The Black Sheep, 51 N. Main St. (482-6414), upstairs on the Plaza. This English pub serves its brew in bulk: all pints are imperial (20 oz.) and cost $4. Food is fabulous. Freshly baked scones and jam ($3.50), salt and vinegar "chips" ($3), and herbs are grown in the British owner's bonny backyard. Open daily 11am-1am; minors welcome ("to dine") until 11pm.

Mark Antony Hotel, 212 E. Main St. (482-1721). Small and spare, with booths and a prominent stage. Live acts Mon.-Sat. have a $3-6 cover and include blues jams

Mon. and comedy Tues. Weekend dancing. Et tu, wet blankets? Daily happy hour brings microbrews and imports down from $3 to $2.25 and domestics from $2.25 to $1.50. Open Mon.-Thurs. 3pm-1am, Fri.-Sat. 11am-2am, Sun. 3-9pm.

Siskiyou Micro Pub, 31B Water St. (488-5061). Replacing the Rouge Brewery and Public House a mere 6 months after a severe creek flood destroyed it, this spacious "Hell or Highwater Pub" promises a bawdy time. Wooden tables inside, patio seating outside. Live music every Fri. and Sat. night at 9pm is usually free. 14 micros on tap (pints $3-3.50), bottled beers ($3), and full restaurant fare. Open Sun.-Thurs. 11am-midnight, Sat.-Sun. 11am-1am.

Medford

Once a mere Jacksonville satellite, Medford lured the 19th-century railroad barons with $25,000 in under-the-table cash and snagged the railroad lines and the county seat; Jacksonville was left in the dust with outmoded horse-and-buggy transport. Today, Medford is a rapidly expanding but nondescript community of motels and fast food. The visitor's center motto is "We Hug Visitors in Medford"—accept your hug, and then slip off to nearby Jacksonville or Ashland for some real action.

PRACTICAL INFORMATION

Visitors Information: 1314 Center Dr., Suite E. (776-4021 or 800-231-2222), in the Harry and David Country Village, just off I-5 at Exit 27. A plethora of free brochures. Staff is armed with fluorescent highlighters, the better to mark the **maps** they will give you. Open daily June-Sept. 9am-6pm, Oct.-May Mon.-Sat. 9am-5pm.

Buses: Greyhound, 212 N. Bartlett St. (779-2103; departures 800-231-2222), at 5th St. To: Portland (9 per day; $32); Sacramento, CA (8 per day; $42); and San Francisco, CA (6 per day, $48). Open Mon.-Sat. 5:30am-7:30pm and Sun. 5:30pm.

Public Transportation: Rogue Valley Transportation (RVTD), 3200 Crater Lake Ave. (779-2877). Connects Medford with Jacksonville, Ashland, and other cities. Buses leave from 200 S. Front St., at 10th St. (Mon.-Fri. 5am-6pm). Service to Ashland every 30min., hourly service to all other destinations. Fare $1, seniors and under 18 50¢, under 10 free.

Taxi: Metro Cab Co., 773-6665. 24hr.

Car Rental: Budget (773-7023 at the airport or 779-0488 at 3038 Biddle Rd.). Economy cars from $31 per day, $179 per week with unlimited mileage. 5% AAA, AARP discounts. Must be 21 with credit card; under 25 $7.50 extra per day. Open at airport Mon.-Fri. 8am-11pm, Sat. 8am-5pm, Sun. 9am-10pm; at Biddle Rd. Mon.-Fri. 8am-5:30pm, Sat. 8am-3pm.

Equipment Rental: McKenzie Outfitters, 130 E. 8th St. (773-5145), off Central Ave. Backpack rental: internal frame ($15 per 3 days, $25 per week) or external frame ($10 per 3 days, $15 per week); tents (2-person per 3 days, $20); kayak set ($40 per day). Open Mon.-Sat. 10am-6pm, Sun. 11am-4pm.

Public Library: 413 W. Main St. (776-7281), at Oakdale Ave. Open Mon.-Thurs. 9:30am-8pm, Fri.-Sat. 9:30am-5pm.

Crisis Intervention Services Helpline: 779-4357. 24hr.

Hospital: Providence Medford Medical Center, 1111 Crater Lake Ave. (773-6611). Emergency care 24hr.

Emergency: 911. **Police and Fire:** City Hall, 411 W. 8th St. (770-4783), at Oakdale.

Post Office: 333 W. 8th St. (776-1326), at Holly St. Open Mon.-Fri. 8:30am-5:30pm. **General Delivery ZIP Code:** 97501-9998.

Area Code: 541.

Medford straddles I-5 at its intersection with Route 238 in Southern Oregon. Main Street (I-5, in town) intersects Central Ave. in the heart of the city, then proceeds west to Jacksonville. Grants Pass is 30 mi. northwest, Ashland 12 mi. to the southeast. Both towns are accessible by I-5 or Hwy. 99.

ACCOMMODATIONS AND CAMPING

The small motels that line Central and Riverside Ave. are depressingly similar, but the prices will cheer up the weary visitor from overpriced Ashland or Jacksonville. Motels along the highway are kept in better condition, but tend to charge $8-10 more. Make sure to check with the **Ashland Hostel** (see **Ashland: Accommodations,** p. 459) for bed availability. For close-by camping, check out **Valley of the Rogue State Park,** just 10 mi. away. Ask at the visitors center for directions

Cedar Lodge, 518 N. Riverside Ave. (773-7361 or 800-282-3419). Spacious rooms, with complimentary coffee and fruit served in the office in the morning. Spiffy new section in back has microwaves and fridges (an extra $8). Cable, pool. Singles $40; doubles $45. 15% AAA and senior discounts.

Village Inn, 722 N. Riverside (773-5373). Clean, well-kept rooms with new red carpets. An old building, but a good price. Cable. Singles $32; doubles $45.

North Fork National Forest Campground, 34 mi. northeast of Medford on Rte. 140. Take the Crater Lake Hwy. Rte. 62 (Exit 30 off I-5) north 6 mi. to Rte. 140 E in White City. 9 lovely sites sit snugly in the woods on the north fork (fancy that) of Little Butte Creek. Serene surroundings. $4 suggested donation goes toward the new hand-pumped drinking water, pit toilets, and general upkeep.

FOOD

For a rapidly expanding city, Medford has surprisingly few attractive eateries. Other than the "downtown deli" concept, the only other dominant paradigms for Medford cuisine are 12 mi. away in Ashland, where locals go when they want something special. **Food 4 Less,** (779-0171), on Biddle Rd. near I-5 Exit 30, has mass quantities of every food imaginable and sells it 4 cheap (open 24hr.).

Harry and David's Original Country Store, 1314 Center Dr. Suite A (776-2277), in Harry and David's Country Village, next to the Visitors Center. The fruit and nut capital of the known universe. This L.L. Bean of the vegetable world sells produce, nuts, candies, and gift items (open Mon.-Sat. 11am-5pm, Sun. 10am-6pm).

C.K. Tiffins, 226 E. Main St. (779-0480). "Naturally good" health food and pastries served in a cafeteria-style space that just barely resembles the alleyway it once was. Great place to bring your newspaper for breakfast ($1.25-3.75). Downtown business crowds partake of $5 lunch specials that run the low-fat gamut from potato cakes and grilled chicken to feta, basil, and tomato pizza. The albacore tuna burger ($5) will rock your world. No red meat. Open Mon.-Fri. 7am-3pm.

Las Margaritas, 12 N. Riverside (779-7628). Feast on large portions of Mexican food amid Mediterranean murals and Jose Cuervo beer flags. Burritos range in price from the burrito vallarta ($10) down to the humble refried bean ($3). One of the few decent dinner places in town, serving nightly specials and festive cocktails like the Singapore Sling ($3.50). Open Sun.-Tues. 11am-10pm, Fri.-Sat. 11am-11pm.

SIGHTS AND ACTIVITIES

Medford's location on I-5 between Grants Pass and Ashland makes it the hub of southern Oregon. Many visitors use it as a gateway to the Shakespeare Festival or Jacksonville, but the town has little appeal on its own. The **Medford Railroad Park** (774-22400), on Berrydale Ave. by the fire station between I-5 and Table Rock Rd., offers Medford's closest brush with Disneyworld; for no charge, you can chug around in cars pulled by a miniature steam engine (open April-Oct. on the 2nd and 4th Sun. of each month, 11am-3pm). More glimpses of the past can be had at the **South Oregon History Center,** 106 N. Central Ave. (773-6536), at 6th St., where a new exhibit explores transportation starting in covered wagons and moving through the automobile ($3, seniors and children 6-12 $2; open Mon.-Fri. 9am-5pm, Sat. noon-5pm).

Next to Harry and David's and the visitors center is the most prolific rose grower in the world, **Jackson & Perkins,** 1310 Center Dr., Suite J (776-2388). Get your hands on a seasonal "ready-plant bare root" of a rose bush ($10-14) for your garden-happy grandma (open Mon.-Thurs 9am-8pm, Fri.-Sat. 9am-6pm, Sun. 10am-6pm; in winter Mon.-Sat. 9am-7pm and Sun. 10am-6pm). Second hand shoppers will be delighted by the **Value Village** in Bear Creak Plaza on Biddle Rd.

Jacksonville

The biggest of Oregon's gold rush boomtowns, Jacksonville played the role of rich and rowdy frontier outpost with appropriate licentious zeal. But the gold dwindled, the railroad and stagecoach lines took Jacksonville off their routes, and, in the final *coup de* (dis)*grâce,* the city lost the county seat to nearby Medford. On the brink of oblivion, Jacksonville was revitalized by nostalgia. Rehabilitated in the 50s, Jacksonville is the only town in Oregon designated a "National Historic Landmark City" by the National Park Service. A stroll through downtown passes century-old buildings: the United States Hotel, the Methodist-Episcopal Church, the old courthouse, and others. During the summer, visitors come just to catch some of the outdoor **Britt Festival** concerts.

Practical Information To reach Jacksonville (or "J-ville," as residents affectionately dub it), take Rte. 238, also called the Jacksonville Highway, southwest from Medford or take Highway 99 N, then follow the signs (15 mi.). Or, catch the #30 bus at 200 S. Front St. at 10th in Medford. (**Rogue Valley Transportation** runs 4 buses per day out of Medford Mon.-Fri. 5am-6pm; $1, seniors and under 18 50¢, under 10 free. See **Medford: Practical Information,** p. 464.) Rte. 238 becomes 5th St. in town and hangs a right on California.

Drop by the **visitors center** in the old railway station at 185 N. Oregon St. (899-8118), at C St., where you will be soused in directions and pamphlets (open daily 10am-4pm). The **post office** (800-ASK-USPS/275-8777) is next door at 175 N. Oregon St. (open Mon.-Fri. 8:30am-5pm; **General Delivery ZIP Code:** 97530-9999). The **area code** is 541.

Accommodations Avoid the many luxury B&Bs and lodges, and stay at the **Ashland Hostel** (see **Ashland: Accommodations,** p. 459), an easy 15 mi. southeast.

A number of campgrounds lie 25-30 mi. southwest of Jacksonville in the **Red Butte Wilderness.** Take Rte. 238 8 mi. west to Ruch, then turn left on Applegate Rd. The **Star Ranger Station,** 6941 Upper Applegate Rd. (899-1812), about 10 mi. past the turn, describes specific fees and amenities, but the campgrounds are another 7-12 mi. farther. **Latagawa Cove** requires a short hike and the forethought to bring water, but it's free and right on the edge of Applegate Lake.

Food For a classy but casual dining experience, head for the **Bella Union,** 170 W. California St. (899-1770). This revamped saloon serves American favorites like pizza, pasta, and chicken, at relatively high prices ($9-16), but the opportunity to dine beneath a canopy of vines out back may be worth the extra buck. A fine array of sandwiches ($6-8) come with salad, and appetizers include scrumptious spicy chicken wings ($3). The attached **Bella Union Saloon** hosts live bands Thursday through Saturday nights (restaurant open Mon.-Fri. 11:30am-10pm, Sat. 11am-10pm, Sun. 10am-10pm; saloon open until midnight). A cheaper and even more casual dining experience can be had at **The Mustard Seed,** 130 N. 5th St. (899-7144), a tiny cafe that made it past the turn of the century but got stuck in the 50s. Cushy red stools lined up at the speckled counter are ideal for sipping milk shakes made for two ($2.55). Veggie burgers ($4.75) may suit your fancy if the bacon cheeseburger ($5) isn't your style (open Mon.-Fri. 7am-6pm, Sat.-Sun. 8am-5pm; closed at 3pm in winter).

Sights and Events A walk down California St. is an instant flashback to the 19th century. The **Beekman Bank,** at the corner of 3rd and California, has not been touched since Cornelius Beekman, the town's most prominent figure, died in 1915. Down the street you can meet his "family" at the **Beekman House** (773-6536), on the

Eves in the Trees

For a decidedly unusual night's stay, head for **Out 'n' About,** a not-quite B&B in the southwestern town of Takilma, OR. The remnants of a commune built in the trees, those sturdy arboreal dwellings did not receive the county stamp of approval for business-status, perhaps because reticent authorities harbored no great trust for the former community, which celebrated its heyday in the 70s. Marijuana busts in the early 80s cast enough bad publicity on the area to cap the hippy utopia that once held 66 people, three dogs, and a cat. There is hope, however, for the tree-pees (tee-pee + tree = tree-pee). If you buy a $75-125 T-shirt and take an oath to "protect the treehouses and the trees," you will be made an official **Tree Musketeer.** An invitation to sleep over (head) will likely follow suit. Call (541) 592-2208 or (800) 200-5484 for info and directions.

corner of Laurelwood St. and California, where hosts, in character and costume, will be quite charmed, my dear, to guide you through the residence. The interactive tour lasts 35 minutes (open Memorial Day-Labor Day 1-5pm). If you see a well-dressed 19th-century gentleman in the middle of the street, it isn't a history-induced hallucination; "Mr. Beekman" often feels the urge to wander the streets of Jacksonville. The **Jacksonville Museum** at 206 N. 5th St., in the Old County Courthouse, is a treasure trove of history. As you explore the museum's fantastic collection of artifacts and historical photographs, leave the kids locked up in the jail next door (now the **Children's Museum**). Delightful, hands-on exhibits make it hard to obey the "no running" rule, resist an antique dentist's chair, or escape the exhibit on Jacksonville native **Bozo the Clown** (born 1892). Each site charges $3, $2 for seniors and ages 6-12. Multiple-site tickets, good for all of the above, are $7, $5 for seniors and ages 6-12. Both are open in summer daily 10am-5pm; in winter they are closed Monday.

Stan the Trolley Man (535-5617), a community legend, runs a 50-minute trolley-tour, which provides an excellent overview of the town's attractions and a chance to sit down out of the sun (runs from 3rd and California St. daily Memorial Day-Labor Day 10am-4pm on the hr.; $4, under 12 $2). Jacksonville is taken over every summer by the **Peter Britt Music Festivals,** P.O. Box 1124, Medford 97501 (773-6077 or 800-882-7488; fax 503-776-3712; http://www.mind.net/britt), named after the pioneer photographer whose hillside estate is the site of the fest. Now in its 36th year, the festivals feature jazz, classical, folk, country, and pop acts, as well as dance theater and musicals. 1997 saw the Indigo Girls, Little Richard, David Benoit, Bela Fleck and the Fleckstones, Booker T. Jones, and James Cotton perform in the 2200-seat outdoor amphitheater. Many listeners bring picnic dinners to eat as they watch. If you want a good space on the lawn get there early—150 seats are in front of the reserved seats, while the other 1400 are behind. Some fanatics even camp out for front seats. Gates open at 5:45pm for most night shows. (Reserved and lawn tickets for single events $9-46, 12 and under $6-15. Order tickets early in May; on performance days, tickets available at Main Pavilion at 1st and Fir St. $2 senior discounts for classical events.).

Grants Pass

Workers building a road through the Oregon mountains in 1863 were so overjoyed by the news of General Ulysses S. Grant's victory at Vicksburg that they named the town after the burly President-to-be. Grants Pass is a base to discover the Rogue River Valley and the Illinois Valley regions. The city itself sprawls awkwardly to fill the hot, flat valley with espresso stands, fast food joints, auto parts stores, and parking lots. Lofty mountains beckon from just beyond the city limits; heed their call.

PRACTICAL INFORMATION AND ORIENTATION

Visitors Information: Visitor and Convention Bureau, 1501 NE 6th St. (476-7717 or 800-547-5927), at 6th and Midland St. beneath the immense plaster caveman.

Covers all of Josephine County. A list of things to do in Grants Pass (you'll need it). Open Mon.-Fri. 8am-5pm, Sat. 9am-5pm, Sun. 10am-4pm; winter closed weekends.

Buses: Greyhound, 460 NE Agness Ave. (476-4513), at the east end of town. To: Portland (7 per day; $36); Sacramento, CA (5 per day; $42); and San Francisco, CA (5 per day; $50). A few storage lockers (75¢ per 24hr.). Open Mon.-Fri. 6:30am-6:15pm, Sat. 7am-3:30pm; winter closed Sat. at noon. Closed holidays.

Taxi: Grants Pass Cab, 476-6444. 24hr.

Car Rental: Discount Rent-a-Car, 1470 NE 7th St. (471-6411). Cars from $27 per day, unlimited mileage. Open Mon.-Fri. 7:30am-5:30pm.

Laundromat: MayBelle's Washtub, 306 SE I St. (471-1317), at 8th St. Wash $1, 10min. dry 25¢. Open Mon.-Fri. 7am-9pm, Sat.-Sun. 8am-8pm.

Crisis Hotline: (479-4357). 24hr. Helpline referral services.

Seniors' Information: Senior Community Center, 317 NW B St. (474-5440). **Senior Citizen Helpline** (479-4357). 24hr.

Information for Travelers with Disabilities: Independent Abilities Center, 290 NE C St. (479-4275). Open Mon.-Thurs. 9am-3pm, Fri. 9am-1pm.

Hospital: Three Rivers Community Hospital and Health Center, 715 NW Dimmick (476-6831).

Emergency: 911. **Police:** Justice Building at 101 NW A St. (474-6370), at 6th St. **Josephine County Sheriff:** 474-5123. **Oregon State Police:** 474-3174.

Post Office: 132 NW 6th St. (479-7526). Open Mon.-Fri. 9am-5pm. **General Delivery ZIP Code:** 97526.

Area Code: 541.

Interstate 5 curves around the northeast edge of Grants Pass on its way north to Portland. The Rogue River lies just south of the old downtown area, which is linked to Exit 58 off the highway by northbound 7th Street and 6th Street, the main southbound artery. 6th Street is the divider between streets labeled East and West, and the railroad tracks (between G and F St.) divide North and South addresses. U.S. 199 runs along the Rogue River before making the 30 mi. trip south to Cave Junction.

ACCOMMODATIONS AND CAMPING

The best, and most unusual, budget option is the **Fordson Home Hostel** near the Oregon Caves. Otherwise, Grants Pass supports one of every pricey franchise motel on earth. The one-of-a-kind cheapo motels are farther back from the interstate on 6th St. near A St. Since Grants Pass is a favorite highway and truckers' stop, rooms fill up quickly, especially on weekends and in August, when rates hit their peak. A few convenient campgrounds are an alternative, but even they are hardly cheap.

Fordson Home Hostel (HI-AYH), 250 Robinson Rd., Cave Junction 97523 (592-3203), 37 mi. southwest of Grants Pass on U.S. 199. Call for directions and availability. This rambling old house is secluded in the forests just 13 mi. from the Oregon Caves. The eccentric owner regularly gives tours of his 20 acres, which house 27 antique tractors, a hand built saw mill, several antique cars, a solar-powered shower, the (allegedly) tallest Douglas Fir tree, a vortex (!), and a few other hostel guests. Comfortable accommodations (2 double beds and a pull-out couch; a loft is under construction). Free bicycle loans. 33% discounted admission to the Oregon Caves National Monument. Camping available. $10; bicyclists, backpackers, and students with ID $8; nonmembers can buy temporary membership for extra $3. Reservations mandatory.

Hawk's Inn, 1464 NW 6th St. (497-4057), down the street from the visitors center. Although building is old, the sparkling pool out front is a blessed sight and it's the nicest $30 room around in the summer. Singles $30; doubles $40.

Knights' Inn Motel, 104 SE 7th St. (479-5595 or 800-826-6835), by the railroad tracks. Huge rooms are clean and freshly carpeted. Furniture is well-aged. Cable, A/C, the Holy Bible (but no Rocky Raccoon), and kitschy knight shields on the railings. Singles $43; doubles $45. Prices drop $10 in winter. Reservations advised.

Valley of the Rogues State Park (582-1118; 800-452-5687 for reservations), 12 mi. east of Grant's pass, off I-5 Exit 45B. Separate loops for tents ($15), electric ($17), and full hookups ($18) spread out along a 1 mi. stretch between the highway and river. Happy campers enjoy the thick green grass and the shade. Also Yurts ($25), non-camper showers ($2), and flush toilets.

FOOD

Dining in Grants Pass, if not inspiring, isn't that bad. For groceries, try **Safeway,** 115 SE 7th at G St. (479-4276; open daily 6am-midnight). **The Growers' Market** (476-5375), on C St. between 4th and 5th, is the largest open-air market in the state, granting everything a produce-lover lusts after (open Tues. 4-9pm and Sat. 9am-1pm).

The Square Nail, 2185 Rogue River Hwy. (479-5132). A down-home local favorite for low prices and large portions. Check the special board for the bargain of the moment, or stick with Hawaiian chicken, soup, salad, rice pilaf, and dessert, all for $5.75. Lunches hover around $4. Good diner breakfasts. Open Sun.-Wed. 5am-3pm, Thurs.-Sat. 5am-9pm.

Matsukaze, 1675 NE 7th St. (479-2961), at Hillcrest. Japanese food Americans will recognize in a simple and tasteful setting. Bonding opportunities in booths sunk into the floor. Daily lunch specials are $3.75-4.75—try the vegetable Tempura. California rolls (4 for $3.75) with crab and avocado are ever-so-tasty. Light dinners $6.50-7.50, full entrees like the Kalbi Ribs $9-15. Open Mon.-Fri. 11am-2pm; also open Mon.-Thurs. 5-9pm and Fri.-Sat. 5-9:30pm; winter closed 30min. earlier.

Pongsri's, 1571 NE 6th St. (479-1345). Sunlight struggles in through the hanging plants and trellises to illuminate a lengthy menu of Thai cuisine. 21 vegetarian dishes ($6.50), including spice mushroom broccoli. The pork spring rolls are greasy, but finger-licking good (4 for $5). Lunch special Tues.-Fri. $4. Open Tues.-Sun. 11am-3pm and 5-9pm.

SIGHTS AND OUTDOORS

The Rogue River is Grant's Pass' greatest attraction. One of the few federally protected rivers designated as a "Wild and Scenic River" can be enjoyed by raft, jetboat, mail boat, or simply by walking along its banks. If you fish, you'll be in good company—Zane Grey and Clark Gable once roamed the Rogue River with tackle and bait. Enterprising (and affluent) souls can hop on a two-hour scenic tour given by **Hellgate Excursions, Inc.,** 953 SE 7th St. (479-7204; $22, ages 4-11 $12). If you want to paddle the river yourself, head west off I-5 Exit 61 toward **Merlin** and **Galice,** where the outfitting companies cluster. A 35 mi. stretch of class III and IV rapids starting just north of Galice is the whitest water on the Rogue. It's a restricted area; to get on it, you have to go with guides and pay about $55 per person. Try **Rogue River Raft Trips,** 8500 Galice Rd. (476-3825 or 800-826-1963), in Merlin, for a full day trip ($60) with the best guides and equipment. **Orange Torpedo Trips,** 209 Merlin Rd. (479-5061 or 800-635-2925), runs more adventurous guided tours down the river in inflatable orange kayaks (full day $60; 4hr. $45; under 10 10% off).

Almost halfway from Medford to Grants Pass is the small town of **Gold Hill,** home of the **Oregon Vortex** and its own **House of Mystery,** 4303 Sardine Creek Rd. (855-1543). Take a right off Exit 43 (I-5 S) and follow signs 5 mi. east (over the tracks and up the hill). Here, the laws of physics take a siesta—balls roll uphill, pendulums hang at an angle, and people seem to vary in height depending on where they stand. The bizarre phenomena are supposedly caused by a local perturbation of the earth's magnetic field. The owners apologize for any crude imitations of this house that tourists may have seen across the country, and assure visitors that this is the *real* thing. Sure. Decide for yourself for a hefty charge (open June-Aug. daily 9am-6pm, March-May and Sept.-Oct. 9am-5pm; $6.50, ages 5-11 $4.50).

The **Oregon Caves National Monument** (592-3400) can be reached by heading 30 mi. south along U.S. 199 through lunar-like fields of stunted, dry pines to Cave Junction, and then following Rte. 46 as it slowly winds east for 20 mi. Here in the belly of the ancient Siskiyous, acidic waters carved out limestone later compressed into marble. Dissolved and redeposited, the limestone fills chilly cavernous chambers with exotic formations. Bring a jacket. Inside this series of caverns are soda straws, draperies, moonmilk, paradise lost, stalactites, and flow-stones. Wow. Tours last 75 minutes and are fairly strenuous, involving some ducking, twisting, and 500 stairs (tours given mid-May to Sept. daily 8am-7pm; mid-Sept. to mid.-Oct. 8:30am-5pm; mid-Oct. to April 9:30am-4pm; Dec.-Feb. call for hours; $7, under 11 $4.50). Children must be over 42 in. (107cm) tall and pass an ability test to take a tour.

Eugene

Eugene is a blender set to "liquefy," with students riding mountain bikes, hippies eating organically-grown food, outfitters making a killing off tourists, and rednecks wearing hunting boots, dodging each other on its streets. Tolerance defines Oregon's second-largest city, which straddles the Willamette River between the Siuslaw and Willamette National Forests. Home to the University of Oregon (U of O), Eugene gains much of its character from its students. City slickers happily shop and dine in the downtown pedestrian mall and Fifth St. Market or head to WOW Hall for an evening of entertainment. Outdoor types river raft along the Willamette and hike or bike in the many nearby parks. Fitness enthusiasts join the fleet of foot and free of spirit in this "running capital of the universe." Nike, founded in Eugene, sponsors the yearly "Bach Run," which accompanies the yearly Bach festival and culminates in a performance of the so-called "Sports Cantata" (based on Bach's "*Weinen, Klagen, Laufen,*" or "Weeping, Lamenting, Running").

PRACTICAL INFORMATION AND ORIENTATION

Visitors Information: Convention and Visitors Association of Lane County, 115 W. 8th Ave. #190 (484-5307 or 800-547-5445; http://www.cvalco.org), but the door is on Olive St. **Maps** and brochures line this office staffed by knowledgeable Eugenians and equipped with a courtesy phone. Open Mon.-Fri. 8:30am-5pm, Sat.-Sun. 10am-4pm; Sept.-April Mon.-Sat. 8:30am-5pm, closed Sun. **Willamette National Forest,** 211 E. 7th Ave. (465-6522), in the Federal Building. Beyond the metal detectors, lies info about the campgrounds, recreational areas, and wilderness areas in the National Forest; invest in a **forest map** ($4). Open Mon.-Fri. 8am-4:30pm. **University of Oregon Switchboard,** in Oregon Hall at 1585 E. 13th Ave. (346-3111). Referral for almost anything from rides to housing. Open Mon.-Fri. 7am-6pm.

Trains: Amtrak, 433 Willamette St. (800-872-7245), at 4th Ave. To: Seattle, WA (2 per day; $24.50-46); Portland (2 per day; $11.50-21); Berkeley, CA (1 per day; $61-112). 15% discount for seniors and people with disabilities; 10% AAA discount. No lockers, but you can check bags for $1.50 each per 24hr.

Buses: Greyhound, 987 Pearl St. (344-6265 or 800-231-2222), at 9th Ave. To: Seattle, WA ($30); San Francisco, CA ($51); and Portland ($15). Open daily 6:30am-10pm. Storage lockers $1 per day. **Green Tortoise** (800-867-8647), drop-off and pick-up at 14th and Kincaid St. To: San Francisco, CA ($39); Portland ($10); and Seattle, WA ($25). Reservations required for some routes. Open daily 8am-8pm.

Public Transportation: Lane Transit District (LTD) (687-5555), at 11th Ave. and Willamette St. Provides bus service throughout Eugene. Pick up a **map** and timetables at the visitors association or the LTD Service Center. Main route service Mon.-Fri. 5am-11:30pm, Sat. 7:30am-11:30pm, Sun. 8:30am-8:30pm. All routes are wheelchair-accessible. Fares 80¢, 50¢ Mon.-Fri. after 7pm; seniors and children 40¢.

Ride Board: Erb Memorial Union (EMU) Basement, University of Oregon. One block east of Kincaid, on the pedestrian section of 13th Ave. in the middle of campus. Housing bulletin board, too. Open Mon.-Thurs. 7am-7pm, Fri. 7am-5pm.

Taxi: Yellow Cab, 746-1234. 24 hr.

Car Rental: Enterprise Rent-a-Car, 810 W. 6th Ave. (683-0874). $30 per day; unlimited mileage within OR and WA. 10% county tax. Must be 21. Credit card required for non-local customers. Open Mon.-Fri. 7:30am-6pm, Sat. 9am-noon.

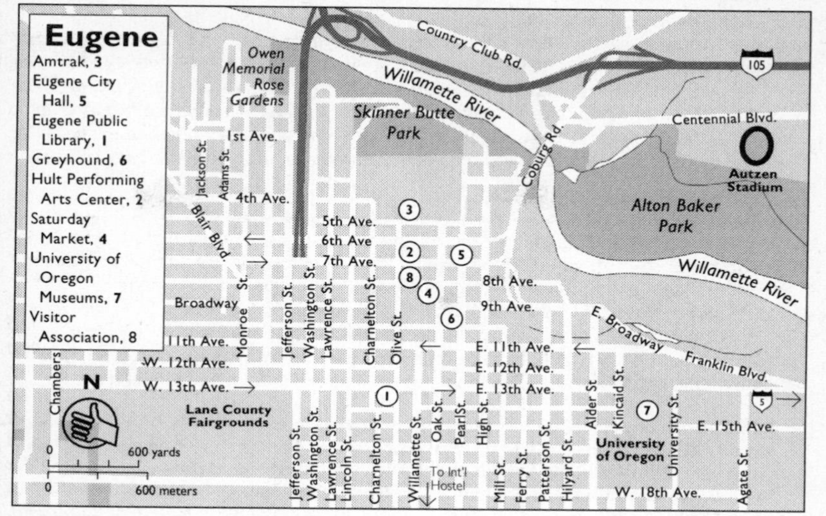

Auto Club: AAA, 983 Willagillespie Rd. (484-0661 or 800-AAA-HELP/222-4357), near Valley River Center Mall, 2 mi. north of the Univeristy of Oregon campus. Only members get goodies like maps. Open Mon.-Fri. 8am-5pm.

Laundromat: Club Wash, 595 E. 13th Ave. (431-1039), at Patterson. A TV almost the size of a movie screen, video games, beer on tap, and tanning facilities make this a lively laundry experience. Open daily 7am-2am. Wash $1, 10min. dry 25¢.

Bike Rental: Paul's Bicycle Way of Life, 152 W. 5th Ave. (344-4105). Friendly staff offers city bikes for $2 per hr., min. 4hr. Tandems $3 per hr., $30 per day. Major credit card or $100 deposit required. Open Mon.-Fri. 9am-7pm, Sat.-Sun. 10am-5pm. **Pedal Power,** 535 High St. (687-1775), downtown. 21-speeds $5 per hr., $20 per day. Mountain bikes $25 per 4hr., $40 per day. Tandems $10 per hr., $50 per day. Open Mon.-Fri. 9am-7pm, Sat. 9am-6pm, Sun. 10am-5pm; Sept.-May Mon.-Sat. 10am-6pm, Sun. 11am-5pm. Both shops also rent bike racks for cars ($5-7; racks hold up to 3 bikes).

Crisis Line: White Bird Clinic, 341 E. 12th Ave. (800-422-7558). Free 24hr. crisis counseling and low-cost medical care. Open Mon.-Fri. 8am-5pm.

Rape Crisis: Sexual Assault Support Services, 630 Lincoln St. (484-9791; 24hr. hotline 485-6700). Open Mon.-Fri. 8:30am-5pm.

Emergency: 911. **Police/Fire:** 777 Pearl St. #107 (687-5111), at City Hall.

Internet Access: Sip n' Surf, 43 W. Broadway (302-1581; http://www.sipn-surf.com). Buy any cybercafe item over $1 and get 15min. of Internet access free. 10¢ per min. Open mic Thurs. at 8pm, broadcast live over the Internet. Open Mon.-Fri. 8am-midnight, Sat.-Sun. 10am-midnight.

Post Office: 520 Williamette (800-ASK-USPS/275-8777), at 5th Ave. Open Mon.-Fri. 8:30am-5:30pm, Sat. 10am-2pm. **General Delivery ZIP Code:** 97401-9999.

Area Code: 541.

Eugene is 111 mi. south of Portland on I-5, just west of the town of Springfield. The **University of Oregon** campus lies in the southeast corner of Eugene, bordered on the north by Franklin Boulevard, which runs from the city center to I-5. First Avenue runs alongside the winding Willamette River; numbered streets go south. **Highway 99 W** is split in town—6th Avenue takes the northern route and 7th Avenue takes the southern one. **Willamette Avenue** intersects the river, dividing the city into east and west. It is interrupted by the pedestrian mall between 6th and 7th Ave. on Broadway downtown. **13th Avenue,** Eugene's main (student) drag, heads east to the U of O. The city is a motorist's nightmare of one-way streets, and free parking is virtually nonexistent downtown. The most convenient way to get around is by **bike**—the roads are flat and there are plenty of bike paths.

Most park hours are officially 6am-11pm, and while the University of Oregon has recently attempted to increase safety with ingenious schemes like the "yellow duck path" signifying better lit areas, locals still maintain that lone women should avoid the campus at night and be wary of Whittaker, the area around Blair Blvd. near 6th Ave.

ACCOMMODATIONS

Budget travelers stopping in Eugene will appreciate the recently opened **Hummingbird Hostel,** just minutes from downtown. The cheapest motels are on E. Broadway and W. 7th Ave. and tend toward the seedy side. Make reservations early; motels are packed on big football weekends. The closest legal camping is 7 mi. away, but tenters have been known to camp by the river (especially in the wild and woolly northeastern side, near Springfield). If you're committed to camping, the best bet is to camp in the surrounding **Willamette National Forest** and make daytrips into Eugene.

The Hummingbird (Eugene International Hostel) (HI-AYH), 2352 Willamette St. (349-0589). Take bus #24 or 25 and get off at 24th Ave. and Willamette, or park in back on Portland St. This graceful, old neighborhood home-turned-hostel is a wonderful addition to, and escape from, the city. A classy living room swathed in bookshelves, yard area with a picnic table, a tomato and lettuce garden, and warm-hearted managers (and their adorable 2-yr.-old son) make this a home away from home. 4 bedrooms sleep up to 20. Check-in 4-10pm; lockout 10am-4pm; kitchen open 7:30-9:30am and 5-10pm. Members $13, nonmembers $16; private rooms from $34. Cash or check only.

Downtown Motel, 361 W. 7th Ave. (345-8739 or 800-648-4366). Spacious rooms under a green terra-cotta roof. Art deco tiles and plaster walls enhance the architecture. Cable TV, A/C, phones, and free coffee and donuts in the morning. Singles $30; doubles $38. One of the few motels in the area that doesn't jack up prices during the summer; reserve early (credit card required).

Executive House Inn, 1040 W. 6th Ave. (683-4000). All rooms are not created equal; you're lucky if you get one with new carpet or a fridge (no extra charge). Rooms in back are cooled by fans instead of A/C and aren't quite as nice. TV. Proximity to country fairground; prices rise $5-10 when there are events. Singles $30; doubles $36.

CAMPING

Unfortunately, KOAs (Kampgrounds of America) and RV-only parks monopolize the Eugene camping scene. It is well worth it to head farther east on Rte. 58 and 126, where the immense **Willamette National Forest** is packed with campsites ($3-16). You can get info from the ranger station first (see **Practical Information,** above), but ample signs make things easy to find. A swamp gives the tree bark and ferns an eerie phosphorescence in the beautiful, mysterious **Black Canyon** campground, 28 mi. east of Eugene on Hwy. 58 ($8-16).

Pine Meadows, (942-8657). On the marshy shore of Cottage Grove lake. Take I-5 S to Exit 172, then head 3½ mi. east, turn left on Cottage Grove Reservoir Rd., and go another 2½ mi. Plenty of RV and jet ski traffic. Showers, shade, flush toilets, and 92 sites ($12). Venture down the road a bit to their 15 primitive sites for more privacy ($6; pit toilets). Both open just before Memorial Day-Labor Day.

Shwarz Park (942-1418), 5½ mi. off Exit 174 (I-5S). Turn right off the ramp and immediately left at the first stop light; go past the village green. The grounds are on Row River, about 2½ mi. below swimmable Dorena Lake on the dam spillway. Flat and quiet, with dry yellow grass and pine trees. Showers, flush toilets and drinking water. The better sites (all $10) are toward the back.

FOOD

Outdoor cafe dining and veggi-centric menus are common everywhere in Eugene. The downtown area specializes in gourmet food; the university hang-out zone at 13th Ave. and Kincaid has more grab-and-go options, and natural food stores encircle the city. A reliable option is **Sundance Natural Foods,** 748 E. 24th Ave. (343-9142), at 24th and Hilyard (open daily 7am-11pm). Right in town, **The Kiva,** 125 W. 11th Ave. (342-8666), supplies a smaller array of organic produce and natural foods (open Mon.-Sat. 9am-8pm, Sun. 10am-5pm). For American cheese singles and ground beef, head to the **Safeway,** 145 E. 18th Ave. at Oak (485-3664; open daily 6am-2am).

Ceres Hearth Cafe, 2495 Hilyard St. (431-3828). This enchanted forest offers nothing but organic vegetarian cuisine. The fountain, delicious flat bread, and crunchy staff add splendor to the roughage. Portions are as generous as they are tasty. Mediterranean mezze plate ($6); southwestern stir-fry ($9). Open daily 8am-10pm.

Keystone Cafe, 395 W. 5th St. (342-2075). The creative menu and strong local following give a true taste of Eugene. The incredible food is mostly meatless, some wheatless, and all bread is homebaked. A small kitchen makes for slow service during busy morning hours, but one mouthful of their famous plate-sized pancakes ($2.75, fruit or seeds on top 75¢) and all will be forgiven. Breakfast served all day. Open daily 7am-5pm.

Cafe Navarro, 454 Willamette St. (344-0943). Casual mood, but the Caribbean and Latin cuisine is served with a gourmet flare. Worldly selection of dishes from Jamaica, Ethiopia, and Peru. Challah french toast with mango syrup ($5.35) is sure to start the day off right. Lunch $5-8. Open Tues.-Fri. 11am-2pm and 5-9:30pm, Sat. 9am-2pm and 5-9:30pm, Sun. 9am-2pm.

New Day Bakery, 345 Van Buren St. (345-1695), at the corner of 3rd Ave. and Blair. Take bus #50 or 52. Far from downtown and the university, but definitely worth the trip. Heaps of goodies like raspberry hazelnut rolls ($1) fill the case in this sunlit cafe. Four kinds of soup ($2.75) that are perfect with fresh bread. Open Mon.-Sat. 7am-7pm, Sun. 7am-3pm.

Out of the Fog, 309 W. 3rd St. (302-8194), at Lincoln St. Hidden away and hard to find, this hippie hotspot is a gem of a coffeehouse. Organically grown and socially responsible coffee ($1.35 for 16oz.) to go with an organic veganberry muffin ($1.65). Or dare for "Da Bomb" and its 4 espresso shots, mocha, and flavored syrup ($3.25). Open Mon.-Thurs. 6:30am-midnight, Fri.-Sat. 7am-1am, Sun. 7am-8pm.

West Bros. Bar-B-Que, 844 Olive St. (345-8489). Grab a seat in the polished interior and relax with a beer ($3 per pint) from their microbrewery downstairs. Barbecue recipes collected on a journey across the U.S.; menu items like Memphis "dry-rubbed" baby-backs ($8.75) and blown-up photos tell the trip's tale. Except for the $2 sides, it's not cheap—lunch $6-11; dinner $7-16. Open Sun.-Thurs. 11:30am-9:30pm, Fri.-Sat. 11:30am-10pm.

Cafe Zenon, 898 Pearl St. (343-3005). If you have one night to splurge, this is the place. The Mediterranean and Northwest regional food is light and flavorful and the attitude is chic. Small plates $6.50; entrees climb to a $15.75 dinner peak. If nothing else, come for dessert ($4.25); the array is astounding and the quality superb. Open Mon.-Thurs. 8am-11pm, Fri.-Sat. 8am-midnight, Sun. 10am-11pm.

Glenwood Campus Cafe, 1340 Alder (687-0355). Locals relax on the brick patio, sipping coffee and watching the passers-by. The Blue Corn Waffles ($2.75) and Tomato Cheese Soup ($1.80-3.35) rival each other in local fame, and the Eggs Benedict ($5.50) is captioned "please forgive us if we sell out." Dinners $4-7. Open Mon.-Fri. 6:30am-2am, Sat. 7am-2am, Sun. 7am-10pm.

China Blue, 879 E. 13th Ave. (343-2832), upstairs. Sizable portions of Chinese food at college-kid prices. The mandarin chicken ($7) is tried and true. Want it all? Combination plates ($5-6.50) rescue the indecisive. Open Mon.-Thurs. 11am-9:30pm, Fri. 11am-10pm, Sat. 5-10pm, Sun. dim sum 11am-3pm, dinner 3-9:30pm.

Newman's Fish Company, 1545 Willamette St. (344-2371). A novel approach to dining in the Eugenest of Styles. This walk-up, bike-up window delivers the finest fish 'n' chips (salmon $5, cod $3.50, or halibut $5) east of the Cascades. Fries by themselves $1. Pre-ordered sushi by the piece ($1-2) and sushi rolls ($6) availabl on Fri. and Sat. Open Mon.-Fri. 11am-7pm, Sat. 11am-6:30pm.

SIGHTS AND ACTIVITIES

If you hanker for nature, **River Runner Supply,** 78 G. Centennial Loop (343-6883 o 800-223-4326), organizes outdoor experiences from fishing to whitewater rafting o the Willamette River. A four-hour rafting trip costs $45 per person (4-person min. They also rent kayaks ($25 per day), canoes ($20 per day), and rafts ($35-75 per day Reservations are recommended on weekends. The visitors information center sup plies a list of several other outfitters. Check local river conditions and **maps,** sinc there are some rough areas on the Willamette near Eugene, especially when th water is high. If you just have a free afternoon hour, canoe or kayak the **Millrac Canal,** which parallels the Willamette for 3 mi. Rent water craft from **The Wate Works Canoe Company,** 1395 Franklin Blvd. (346-4386), run by U of O student (open summer Mon.-Fri. 3pm-dusk, Sat.-Sun. noon-dusk; $5 per hr.; $15 for 24hr.; $3 deposit). Or join the ranks of cyclists and joggers at **Amazon Park.** Head south o Pearl St. and it will become Amazon Dr. just beyond E. 19th St. This small, peacefu park has paved and dirt trails along the river. To the northwest of the city just afte the I-5 overpass, the **Owen Memorial Rose Garden** is perfect for a picnic accompa nied by the sweet strains of rumbling traffic. Any frolicking should take place in fu daylight, because the surrounding Whittaker neighborhood is unsafe at night.

High-brow culture festoons the $26-million **Hult Performing Arts Center,** Eugene Center (687-5087 for info, 682-5000 ticket office, 682-5746 24hr. event info at 7th Ave. and Willamette St. The two theater halls host a wide variety of music fro blues to Bartók (free tours Thurs. and Sat. at 1pm). Locals young and old leave th Hult to the society types who can afford tickets and head instead to the Communit Center for the Performing Arts, better known as **WOW Hall,** 291 W. 8th Ave. (68 2746). For years WOW Hall, an old Wobblie (International Workers of the World meeting hall, has sponsored concerts by lesser-known artists. Flyers announcin these offbeat acts are everywhere. Tickets are available at WOW Hall (open Tues.-Fr 3-6pm), CD World (3215 W. 11th St.), and occasionally at the door for less ragin acts. The **Bijou Art Cinema,** 492 East 13th at Ferry St. (686-2458), is another favorit where obscure films show in the sanctuary of an old Spanish church ($2.50-6).

The University of Oregon is the centerpiece of Eugene. The people at the rece tion centers at **Oregon Hall** (346-3014), E. 13th Ave. and Agate St., and at the visito parking and information booth, just left of the main entrance on Franklin Blvd., giv tours and hand out **campus maps.** Take time to admire the ivy-covered halls that s the scene for National Lampoon's *Animal House*. Just off the pedestrian section c 13th St. between Kincaid and University St., the **University Museum of Art** (34 3027) houses a changing repertoire of Northwestern and American pieces not fe tured in *Animal House* and an extensive permanent collection from Southeast As (open Wed.-Sun. noon-5pm; tours Sat. by appointment and Sun. at 2pm; free). A fe blocks away, the **Museum of Natural History,** 1680 E. 15th Ave. (346-3024), a Agate, shows a collection of relics from indigenous cultures worldwide that include a 7000-year-old pair of shoes. A primitive "swoosh" logo is still visible (open Wed Sun. noon-5pm; free).

On the edge of town lurks the highly acclaimed **Fifth Street Market** (484-0383), a 5th Ave. and High St., an historic building that's been refurbished and ushered int mall-hood with a collection of exorbitantly priced boutiques and eateries (one unde the mystifying impression that British cuisine is "gourmet"). If your timing is righ you can easily find cheaper (often better) nourishment around the array of artist wares at the **Saturday Market** (686-8885), at 8th Ave. and Oak St., held weekly Ap to November (10am-5pm). The crafts, clothing, jewelry, artwork, and music provid a spectacular display.

CLUBS AND BARS

According to some, Eugene nightlife is the best in Oregon. Not surprisingly, the string of establishments by the university along 13th Street are often dominated by fraternity-style beer bashes. Refugees from this scene will find a diverse cross-section of nightlife throughout town. (Take a nap after dinner, then go out; Eugene parties through the wee hours.) Check out the *Eugene Weekly* for current bands.

Sam Bond's Garage, 407 Blair Blvd. (431-6603). Take bus #50 or 52. Supremely laid back gem of a cafe and pub in a soulful neighborhood. Entertainment every night and an ever-changing selection of Northwest microbrews ($2.50-3 per pint). Veggie fare is also fabulous. Rusting car parts in the haphazard flower beds speak the history of the 1918 garage. Take a bus or cab at night. Open daily 11am-1am.

High St. Brewery Cafe, 1234 High St. (345-4905). Proudly sells McMenamins and seasonal fruit ale. Toss on a pair of jeans and relax in this oriental rug-bedecked Victorian. Backyard deck and patio catch the overflow in this popular spot. Excellent ales brewed in the basement $2.85 a pint. Happy hour daily 4-6pm and food 'til midnight. Open Mon.-Sat. 11am-1am, Sun. noon-midnight.

Doc's Pad, 165 W. 11th St. (683-8101). Driven by the cocktail research team, the drinks are strong, the music loud, and the room smoky—take a deep breath and unbuckle your seat belt. Timothy Leary used to hang at this converted drive-thru. Classic rock until 9pm; "alternative" rock thereafter. Happy hour sees $2 micros, Mon.-Fri. 4-7pm. Open Mon.-Fri. 10:30am-2:30am, Sat.-Sun. 8:30am-2:30am.

Club Arena, 959 Pearl St. (683-2360). The only gay dance club in town. The huge, checkered dance floor gets kicking every night at 11pm to house and techno tunes. Sun. nights are retro, Mon. is men's night, Wed. is women's night, and Thurs. is packed for the $1 mixed drinks, popular with all genders. Cover Fri.-Sat. $2.50, Thurs. $1. Open daily 7pm-2:30am.

Jo Federigo's, 259 E. 5th Ave. (343-8488). A snazzy and pricey restaurant with New Orleans flair. Jazz 5 nights a week at 9:30pm. Wed. gets the blues, and the whole place rattles when the train goes by. Happy hour is 2:30-6:30pm. No cover, but $5 drink min. and an additional surcharge of 50¢ per drink after 9pm. Open Mon.-Thurs. 2pm-midnight, Fri. 2pm-2am, Sat. 5pm-2am, Sun. 5pm-1am.

John Henry's, 136 E. 11th Ave. (342-3358). In the heart of downtown, this warehouse-style venue hosts headliners and smaller potatoes drawing a mixed, slightly older crowd. Anything from alternative rock to country swing. Bits of abstract art give the high walls color; plenty of bar booths to hide in, but the action is on the dance floor. Microbrew pints $3. Cover usually $3-7. Call for a schedule. Free pool until 10pm; always free foosball. Open daily 4pm-1am.

EVENTS

The two-week **Oregon Bach Festival** (800-457-1486), at the Hult and U of O's Beall Concert Hall beginning the last week of June, brings Helmut Rilling, a world-renowned authority on Baroque music, to lead some of the country's finest musicians in performances of Bach's cantatas and concerti. (Contact the Hult Center Ticket Office, listed above, for info; tickets $8-37.50, senior and student discounts for selected events.) The **Art and the Vineyard** (345-1571), a four-day celebration of food, wine, and culture around the 4th of July comes close on the Bach Festival's heels. Alton Baker Park, on the north bank of the Willamette east of Coburg Rd., is taken over by West Coast artisans, food, and music (suggested donation $4).

By far the biggest event of the summer is the **Oregon Country Fair** (343-6554). It actually takes place in **Veneta,** 13 mi. west of town on Rte. 126, but its festive quakes can be felt in Eugene. For three days in mid-July, 50,000 people drop everything to go to the Fair. What started as a Renaissance Festival in 1969 has become a magical annual gathering of artists, musicians, misfits, and activists. Today, the 300 art, clothing, craft, herbal remedy, eco, furniture, spiritual, and food booths and the six stages-worth of show after show are only bits of the unique experience of the Country Fair. Lofty tree houses, all-consuming drum circles, parades of painted bodies, dancing 12-ft. dolls, and "fair-ies" offering free hugs transport travelers into an enchanted forest of frenzy. Word of this wonder has gotten out: a few thousand others will be partying with you. To alleviate the yearly traffic jams, free bus service is provided between a free parking area in Eugene (cross the river to Autzen Stadium) and the fairgrounds in Veneta. Buses run every 15 minutes starting around 10am and continuing until the fairgrounds close at 7pm. In 1997 no tickets were sold on site, and Saturday sold out early in the morning. Purchase in advance through Fastixx (800-992-8499), at the Hult Center, or at EMU (see **Practical Information,** above) on campus. (Advance tickets Fri. and Sun. $10, Sat. $15; day of $1 more.) No public camping or overnight parking is available; for camping info call 935-7870.

OUTDOORS

The Willamette Valley attracted waves of 19th-century pioneers with its fertile floor and forested hills. To see country that hasn't changed noticeably since their invasion, take Rte. 126 east from Eugene. The highway runs adjacent to the beautiful McKenzie River, and on a clear day the mighty snowcapped **Three Sisters** of the Cascades are visible. Just past the town of **McKenzie Bridge,** the road splits into a "scenic byway" loop; Route 242 climbs east to the vast lava fields of **McKenzie Pass,** while Route 126 turns north over Santiam Pass and meets back with Route 242 in Sisters.

Before McKenzie Bridge, 40 mi. east of Eugene on Rte. 126, **Blue River Lake** and **Cougar Lake,** river valleys dammed by the Army Corps of Engineers in the 60s, rest between heavily forested, steep mountain ridges. They are officially reservoirs and are only completely full April to mid-August. For info or free maps, stop in at the **Blue River District Ranger Station** (822-3317; open Mon.-Fri. 7:45am-4:30pm) off Rte. 126 in Blue River. Before heading to these hot spots, fill your belly at the **Whitewater Cafe,** 51578 Blue River Dr. (also Cascade St.; 822-3543). Located just off the Blue River Exit on the left hand side, this small-town cafe serves up a hearty meal. Store up on four pancakes ($4.25), a plate-sized omelette ($4.75-6.50), or a zucchini burger ($5). The larger and more popular Cougar Lake features the free pleasure of Terwilliger Hot Springs, known fondly by all as **Cougar Hot Springs.** To get there, go 4 mi. east of Blue River on Rte. 126, turn right onto Aufderheide Dr. (Forest Service Rd. #19), and follow the road 7.3 mi. as it winds on the right side of Cougar Reservoir. These five lovely rock pools have become the Willamette Forest's hippie hotspot. By convention, the springs (and the cove of the lake down the hill from them) are clothing-optional hangouts. Try to park in the area by the cove; otherwise there is no parking within 1 mi. of the hot springs. There is no regular attendant at the springs, but rangers do show up at dusk to enforce the area's **day-use only** policy. Other hot springs are scattered through the area; the Forest Service can suggest clothing-compulsory sulfur baths for the more modest. Continue down the road to camp on the other side of the lake at **Slide Creek** (16 sites, hand-pumped drinking water, $10) or along the south fork of the McKenzie and French Pete Creek at **French Pete** (17 sites, drinking water, $10).

Route 242 is often blocked by snow until the end of June. Wide enough for two cars to pass in places and kinked with tight turns in others, this Cascade Range route is off-limits to all vehicles over 35 ft. long. Trucks with trailers should not even try it. This stretch of Route 242 is an incredible drive, tunnelling its narrow, winding way between the Mt. Washington and the Three Sisters Wilderness areas before rising to the high plateau of McKenzie Pass, where lava outcroppings served as a training site for astronauts preparing for lunar landings. Decades earlier, the Civilian Conservation Corps left their mark on the land with a lava block lookout tower for all the world to use on clear days. Learn which of the peaks is which by squinting through the dozen square holes, each labelled with the mountain they frame.

Along the curviest section of Route 242, about 15 mi. east of the fork from Route 126, a number of trails begin that carry hikers above the treeline. As with all Oregon wilderness areas, biking is not allowed, and permits are required, but available free at the trailheads. For more info, call the **McKenzie Ranger Station** (822-3381; open daily 8am-4:30pm), 3 mi. east of McKenzie Bridge on Rte. 126. On the other side of the loop, the **McKenzie River Trail** winds 26½ mi. through thick, lush forest draped in moss, parallel to Rte. 126 and the river. It starts about 1½ mi. west of the ranger station (where you can pick up a map of the trail for $1 or a free faded copy) and ends up north at Old Santiam Road near the Fish Lake Old Growth Grove. The entire trail is now open to mountain bikers. The two most accessible parts of the trail are its first 6 mi., sandwiched between the highway and the river, and the spectacular 2 mi. section between **Koosah Falls, Sahalie Falls,** and **Clear Lake**. Camp at **Ice Cap Creek,** along the river, just below Koosah Falls and 16 mi. northeast of the ranger station (8 tent sites, 14 tent/trailer sites, drinking water faucets, $9) or the more picturesque **Coldwater Cove,** 1 mi. up the road at Clear Lake (35 tent/trailer sites, one handpump for drinking water, $10). The remarkable clarity of the water reveals 3000-year-old trees preserved on the lake bottom. A number of other Forest Service campgrounds cluster along this stretch of Rte. 126, including the riverside **Olallie** (9 mi. northeast of the ranger station, $6) and **Trailbridge** (11 mi. northeast of the ranger station, 26 campsites, drinking water, $6). More ambitious hikers can sign up for an overnight permit at the ranger station and head for the high country.

Corvallis

Unlike so many Oregon towns, this peaceful residential community in the central Willamette Valley assumes no "historic" pretensions. Home to **Oregon State University (OSU)** and a looming Hewlett-Packard plant, Corvallis lives smack-dab in the present. Mountain bikes rule the roads here, and those without wheels romp in several parks scattered throughout the city. Like any college town, Corvallis mellows during the summer, allowing time for a few choice festivals, down-time with OSU friends, and plenty of outdoor exploration.

PRACTICAL INFORMATION

Visitors Information: Chamber of Commerce (757-1505) and **Convention and Visitors Bureau** (757-1544 or 800-334-8118), both at 420 NW 2nd St., the first right past the bridge coming from the east. Free maps from the convention bureau, or pay $1 for more detailed maps from the chamber. Open Mon.-Fri. 8am-5pm. **Oregon State University** (737-0123 or 737-6445 for events info). Main entrance and info booth at Jefferson and 15th St. Get a free campus map here.

Buses: Greyhound, 153 NW 4th St. (757-1797 or 800-231-2222). To: Portland (4 per day, $13); Seattle (4 per day, $42); Newport (3 per day, $10); and Eugene (4 per day, $7). Lockers $1 for 24hr. Open Mon.-Fri. 7am-6:30pm, Sat. 7am-2pm, Sun. 11:30am-6:30pm.

Public Transportation: Corvallis Transit System (757-6998). Fare 50¢, ages 5-17, seniors, and disabled 25¢. Service Mon.-Fri. 6:45am-6:45pm, Sat. 9:45am-3:45pm. Schedule available free from chamber of commerce or City Hall.

Taxi: A-1 Taxi, 754-1111. $5 min. 24hr.

Laundromat: Campbell's Laundry, 1120 NW 9th St. (752-3794). Wash $1, 10min. dry 25¢. Open daily 6am-1am.

Library: 645 NW Monroe (757-6927 for recording, 757-6926 for further questions). Open Mon.-Fri. 9am-9pm, Sat. 9am-6pm, Sun. noon-6pm.

Peak Sports: 129 2nd St. NW (754-6444). Rents out mountain bikes ($15 per day) and 3-speed cruisers ($5 per day). Open Mon.-Thurs. and Sat. 9am-6pm, Fri. 9am-8pm, Sun. noon-5pm.

Medical Services: Corvallis Clinic, 3680 Samaritan Dr. (754-1150; walk-in service 754-1282). Open Mon.-Fri. 8am-9pm, Sat. 8am-6pm, Sun. 10am-6pm.

Emergency: 911. **Police:** 180 NW 5th St. (757-6924).

Post Office: 311 SW 2nd St. (758-1412). Open Mon.-Fri. 8am-5:30pm, Sat. 9am-4pm. **General Delivery Zip Code:** 97333.

Area Code: 541.

Corvallis is laid out in a checkerboard fashion that degenerates away from downtown; numbered streets run north-south and streets named for lesser-known presidents (Van Buren, Polk, Buchanan) run east-west. Highway 99W splits in town and becomes two one-way streets; 99W going north runs along 3rd St. while 99W going south runs along 4th St. College students and frat brats hang out along SW Monroe St. and the surrounding area when they aren't hitting the trails.

ACCOMMODATIONS AND CAMPING

Many of Corvallis' easily accessible campgrounds are *not* RV mini-cities, giving travelers a break from generators and Airstreams. Motels are reasonably priced, but are few and far between. In summer, most fill fast with pesky conventioneers.

C.E.W. Motel, 1705 NW 9th St. (753-8823). Who knows what C.E.W. stands for. Clean rooms with soft beds and an eclectic statue garden in the parking lot to boot. Upstairs rooms have tubs. 1 person $35.50; 2 people, one bed, $42; doubles $52. Reserve with a credit card 3 days in advance for weekends.

Budget Inn, 1480 SW 3rd St. (752-8756). Take 4th St. under the bridges. Bathrooms big enough for waltzing. Kitchen units available. Singles $35; doubles $45; senior discount $2. Reserve 2 weeks ahead. Credit cards accepted.

Benton County Fairgrounds, 110 SW 53rd St. (757-1521). Follow 34W, then turn right onto 53rd St. or take the Rte. 3 CTS bus. A pleasant campspot blessed with trees and showers. Sites $5; RV hookup $10. First-come, first-served. Call for info. Closed for fair and other events mid-July to early Aug.

Willamette Park (757-6918), on SE Goodnight Rd. Follow Rte. 99W toward Eugene, after 2 mi. turn left on Goodnight Rd. 15 closely spaced sites on a field near the Willamette River where the louder locals hang out and seemingly never say goodnight. Sites $8; no hookups. First-come, first-served.

OREGON

FOOD AND ENTERTAINMENT

Corvallis has a smattering of requisite collegiate pizza parlors and several variations on the Mexican theme. OSU students prowl Monroe St. for grub, influencing vendors with their limited finances. Their frugality pays off: cheap, tasty, filling food abounds in Corvallis. **First Alternative Inc.,** 1007 SE 3rd St. (753-3115) is a co-op run by volunteers who stock a range of well priced, natural products ranging from bountiful bulk foods to natural remedies (open Mon.-Sat. 9am-9pm, Sun. 10am-8pm. **Safeway,** 450 SW 3rd (753-5502), is open daily from 6am to 2am.

Nearly Normal's, 109 NW 15th St. (753-0791). This cottage combines large portions of everything except meat with low prices ($2-8.60) in a pleasant, arboreal aura. Dine under a live canopy of branches and surrounding kiwi vines, fuchsia plants, and rose bushes on the "porch." Sunflower seed burgers ($5) are as hearty as their cow-nterparts. Open Mon.-Fri. 8am-9pm, Sat. 9am-9pm.

McMenamins, 420 NW 3rd St. (758-6044). Some of the best pub fare in town, made from scratch and reasonably priced ($2-9). Fresh-cut fries ($1.15-4.50) are worth a trip themselves. All pints $2.85. Practice Dutch by reading the street signs that line the ceiling. Open Mon.-Sat. 11am-1am, Sun. noon-midnight.

Bombs Away Cafe, 2527 NW Monroe St. (757-7221). Where Mexican food and multicolored geometric art collide. Adventures in anti-authenticity end successfully in ricotta enchiladas and duck chimichangas (both $5.75). The enormous "Wet Burrito" ($6.25) has some loyal followers (go figure!), as does the tiny bar in back where tipplers down Tequila. Open Mon.-Fri. 11am-midnight, Sat. 4pm-midnight, Sun. 4-11pm. 21+ when kitchen closes (Mon.-Sat. at 10pm, Sun. at 9pm).

Clubs and Bars

Squirrel's Tavern, 100 2nd St. SW (753-8057). Few frat boys frolic at this older hippie bar where the bearded come to drink beer (domestics $2, microbrews $2.50), play pool (50¢ per game), and eat some of the best burgers in Corvallis (meat or veggie $3.25). Happy hour Mon.-Fri. 4:30-6:30pm ($1 domestic pints and $5.50 pitchers). Open Mon.-Thurs. 11:30am-1am, Fri.-Sat. 11:30am-1:30am, Sun. 5pm-midnight. Always 21+. Infrequent $2 cover.

Murphy's Tavern, 2740 SW 3rd St. (754-3508). OSU students and loggers drink together at this roadhouse. Live country music Fri. and Sat. during the school year. Brave the crowds for Mr. Bill's Traveling Trivia Night on Thurs. Domestic pints $2.25; beer 25¢ every Wed. 7-8pm. Open Mon.-Thurs. 10:30am-midnight, Fri.-Sat. 10:30am-1:30am, Sun. noon-8pm.

The Museum II, 137 SW 3rd St. (758-6641). An upbeat sports bar that attempts to cater to a more diverse crowd than its regular OSU Greek clientele. Bar food is affordable and comes with mystifying titles like "The Starker Arker" ($5 burger with sauteed mushrooms), or "The NW Fire Fighter" ($5 marinated chicken sandwich with jack). Pints $2.25; no hard alcohol. Young and friendly bar staff. Open Mon.-Wed. 10am-1am, Thurs.-Sat. 10am-2am, Sun. 10am-11pm. Always 21+.

EVENTS AND OUTDOORS

Mountain biking is a way of life in Corvallis, and all roads seem to lead to one bike trail or another. Many cyclists and sightseers sidle out to OSU's **McDonald Forest**; just drive west out of town on Harrison about 2 mi., then turn right on Oak Creek Rd. The pavement dead ends at OSU's lab, and multiple trails lead from there into the forest. Maps are available at Peak Sports for $4 (see p. 477).

On a clear day, **Chip Ross Park** offers splendid views of Cascade Valley from Mt. Hood to Three Sisters. Take 3rd St. north, turn left on Circle Blvd., right on Highland, and follow signs to the park. The vast campus of **Oregon State University,** marked by buildings of widely varying architectural styles, is worth exploring. Park behind the info booth at Jefferson and 15th (ask at the booth for a free permit).

The Corvallis heart rate picks up with the **da Vinci Days Festival** (757-6363 or 800-334-8118), during the third week in July. Renaissance men and women compete in the **Kinetic Sculpture Race,** in which people-powered, all-terrain works of art race for a crown. If your techno-interests extend no further than stereo equipment, don't despair: the festival brings nationally known bands, from jazz to rock ($5 each day, ages 3-12 $3, or all 4 days $15, $7). The **Fall Festival,** held in Central Park during the third weekend in September, combines food with music in one of the best arts and crafts fairs in Oregon. Performers have included Wynton Marsalis and James Cotton.

Ten miles east in **Albany** (off US 20 before I-5), thousands of jammers gather each Thursday night from mid-July through August for the **River Rhythms** concert series. Musical venues vary drastically from concert to concert, but they are always free, always at 7pm, and always held in the Monteith River Park. Each week in July, a special Monday night show features local performers and is also free at 7pm in Monteith River Park. Call the Albany Visitors Center (928-0911) for further info.

Salem

Although Salem is the state capital, the third-largest city in Oregon, and the home of Willamette University, this would-be big city struggles to register an urban pulse. What Salem lacks in metropolitan savvy, however, it makes up for in subtle, simple pleasures. This burg has an impressive capitol campus, some terrific breakfast cafes, impeccable streets, and is near the crashing waterfalls of Silver Falls State Park.

Practical Information and Orientation The **Salem Convention and Visitors Association,** 1313 Mill St. SE (581-4325 or 800-874-7012), in the Mission Mill Village complex, stocks brochures on Salem and the entire state (open Mon.-Fri. 8:30am-5pm, Sat. 10am-4pm).

Amtrak, 500 13th St. SE (588-1551 or 800-872-7245), is at 12th and Mill St. SE, across from the visitors center. Trains run daily to Portland ($6.50-12), Seattle ($19-35), and San Francisco ($76-140; open daily 6:30am-4:30pm). **Greyhound,** 450 Church St. NE (362-2428), at Center St., run buses north and south, with service to Portland (8 trips daily; $8 weekdays, $9 weekends; station open daily 6am-8pm; lockers $1 for 24hr.). For transport within Salem, the **Cherriots Customer Service Office,** 183 High St. NE (588-BUSS/2877), provides maps and multiple-day passes for

Salem's bus system. 20 routes originate from High St. between State and Court St. in front of the courthouse (runs every 30min. Mon.-Fri. 6:15am-9:35pm, Sat. 7:45am-9:35pm hourly; fare 75¢, under 18 50¢, seniors and disabled 35¢). For a taxi, call **Salem Yellow Cab Co.** (362-2411; 24hr.).

The **library** is on 585 Liberty St. SE (588-6315; open Tues.-Wed. 10am-9pm, Thurs.-Sat. 10am-6pm, Sept.-May also Sun. 1-5pm). Soap up duds at the **Suds City Depot,** 1785 Lancaster Dr. NE. (362-9845), at Market St. (open daily 7:30am-9pm; wash $1, Wed. 75¢, 17min. dry 25¢). Reach the **Women's Crisis Center** at 399-7722 (24hr.). The **Northwest Human Services Crisis and Info Hotline** is 581-5535 (24hr.). To reach the **Gay Resource Center,** call (800) 777-2437 (Mon.-Fri. 10am-9pm, Sat.-Sun. noon-6pm). The **Salem Hospital** is at 665 Winter St. SE (370-5200). In an **emergency,** dial 911 or find the **police** at 555 Liberty St. SE (588-6123), in City Hall. The **post office** is at 1050 25th St. SE (370-4700; open Mon.-Fri. 8:30am-5:30pm). The **General Delivery ZIP Code** is 97301. The **area code** is 503.

Salem is located in northwestern Oregon, 51 mi. south of Portland and 64 mi. north of Eugene on I-5. Willamette University and the capitol dominate the center of the city; the heart of downtown hovers several blocks northwest. Street addresses are arranged according to a quadrant system with State St. as the north-south divider and the Willamette River as the east-west divider.

Accommodations and Camping In the far, far away galaxy of Northwestern budget travel, Salem is the Death Star. Struggle valiantly against the tractor beam of commercialized RV parks like KOA and camp at Silver Falls State Park. Rent is high in this politician's playland, which pushes the price of modest motel rooms to $40 or $50. B&Bs, starting at $45 per room, provide a classier and often more comfortable setting for a comparable price; the visitors center has a list of area B&Bs. The **Cottonwood Cottage,** 960 E. St. NE (362-3979), between Capital St. and Summer St. is a prime example: this endearing old house close to downtown offers two quiet, sunny bedrooms with cable TV, A/C, and a shared bath (starts at $55). Reservations recommended for summer months. The **City Center Motel,** 510 Liberty St. SE (364-0121 or 800-289-0121; fax 581-0554), set across the tree-lined street from the downtown library and City Hall, is one of the most pleasant and convenient motels in Salem. The somewhat-worn rooms are clean and spacious (singles $45; doubles $52).

Fall in love with camping at **Silver Falls State Park,** 20024 Silver Falls SE (Rte. 214; 873-8681). Take Rte. 22E (Mission St.) for 5 mi., then take the exit for Silver Falls and Rte. 214 N. Follow 214 N. for about 20 mi. across rolling farmland. Oregon's largest inland state park sparkles with swimming holes, hiking trails, storytelling, horse rentals, and views of ten waterfalls, plus a trail that winds behind the watery curtain of three of them. The tallest, the magnificent Double Falls, crashes 178 ft. (60 tent sites $16; 44 RV hookup sites $20; showers, water, recycling center; reserve by calling 800-452-5687; credit cards accepted; wheelchair accessible sites available).

Food A global array of ethnic restaurants on Court St. nets yuppie dollars by day but shuts down at night when pedestrian traffic recedes to the 'burbs. On the other hand, one of the busiest roads in Oregon, Lancaster Dr. (just east of and parallel to I-5), woos burger lovers into the wee hours of the night with flashing fast food signs. For those with a market in mind, the local **Safeway,** 1265 Center St. NE (362-8511), is open daily 6am-midnight. Alternatively, **Heliotrope Natural Food,** 2809 Market St. NE (361-8845), has a healthy selection of bread and produce (open daily 8am-9pm).

The **Off-Center Cafe,** 1741 Center NE (363-9245), in a long, bluish-white one-story building, is a coffee shop with a liberal mindset, quick service, and scrumptious food. Start the morning off with a hearty dose of "bibble and squib" ($4.50) or scrambled tofu ($5.75). Or let witticisms on the wall tip your politics to the left while you balance out your diet with a boysenberry milkshake ($2.75; open Tues.-Fri. 7am-2:30pm, Sat.-Sun. 8am-2pm; dinner Thurs.-Sat. 6-9pm). **Tong King,** 989 12th St. SE (585-9932), two blocks past Mission St., stirs up some of the best Cantonese and Mandarin food in town. Try a generous combo lunch special ($4.25) or pea pods with mushrooms ($5.75). Vegetarians may want to wok out, though: most dishes have some sort of meat (open Mon.-Fri. 11:30am-2:30pm, 4:30pm-9:30pm, Sat. 4:30pm-9:30pm). Join locals in low, orange vinyl booths at the **Court Street Dairy,** 347 Court St. NE (363-6433), for a taste of the 30s and old-fashioned fountain fare. Burgers ($3) or shakes ($2.75) made from Curly's hard ice cream heal any hunger (open Mon.-Fri. 7am-2pm). **Rice Time,** 159 High St. SE (364-5512), stays true to its "fresh fast friendly" slogan. Make time for a heaping bowl of Korean noodles ($3.75), veggie *udon* ($4.25), or traditional *miso* soup ($1) while admiring the Korean lanterns and costumed dolls (open Mon.-Fri. 11am-7pm). Adjacent to The Arbor Garden Goods and Gifts, **The Arbor Cafe,** 380 High St. NE (588-2353), is upbeat and upscale, but down to earth—where Salem professionals take a break for panini sandwiches ($4.25), half salads ($2.95), or one of 20 tempting desserts ($2.75-4). Wine, beer, Italian sodas, and frozen coffee drinks are also available; sip them outside near the arbor during the summer (open Mon.-Thurs. 7:30am-10pm, Fri. 7:30am-11pm, Sat. 8am-11pm).

Sights and Events The **State Capitol,** 900 Court St. NE (986-1388), between W. Summer and E. Summer St., is presided over by a 23 ft. gold-leaf statue of the quintessential "Oregon Pioneer," perched upon its imposing pinnacle. This trailblazer seems to have commanded a presence inside the capitol, too: murals and sculptures depicting European expansion into Oregon and the West ornament the interior. Every 30 minutes, a free tour leaves for a 121-step climb to the top of the capitol rotunda and on into the bowels of the building (June-Aug. only). On weekday mornings, tours partake in a little legal voyeurism in the legislative chamber as Oregon lawmakers haggle (open Mon.-Fri. 7:30am-5:30pm, Sat. 9am-4pm, Sun. noon-4pm).

Across the street from the capitol, the sylvan campus of **Willamette University,** 900 State St. (370-6303) snuggles into the city. "Wil-AM-it, damn it!" is a favorite local tool to explain the pronunciation of the private school's oft-butchered name. Founded by Methodist missionaries in 1842, this is the oldest university in the West. Unfortunately it isn't the wealthiest; Willamette doesn't offer tours, but visitors are welcome to wander solo amid Willamette's ivied walls.

The Willamette Valley, basking in warm inland sun, is home to a bevy of successful wineries. **Willamette Valley Vineyards,** 8800 Enchanted Way SE, Turner, OR (588-9463), just off Exit 248 on I-5, is a publicly owned winery that boasts 75 acres, 35 of which are grapes. WVV not only produces fine wines, but offers tasters a view of the valley, unusual architecture, free wine tasting, and tours galore (open daily 11am-6pm). The Salem visitors association can provide info on many vintners.

The **Bush Barn Art Center and Museum,** 600 Mission St. SE (581-2228 or 800-874-7012), is one of Salem's gems. A tour unfolds the intricacies of the house museum ($2.50, seniors and students $2, 6-12 $1, under 6 free), but a stroll through the rose garden, greenhouse, and art center is free and equally fabulous. The art collection includes some entertainingly off-beat exhibits. During the third weekend of July, The Bush Barn hosts the free **Salem Art Fair and Festival** in Bush's **Pasture Park.** The festival showcases Northwestern art while bands strum away the afternoons. Anyone with extra energy can join the 5K **Run for the Arts,** held during the festival (contact the Bush Barn for more info and price of race registration).

Every year, Salem spends the summer gearing up for the annual **Oregon State Fair** at the **Expo Center,** 2330 17th St. NE (378-3247 or 800-833-0011). For 12 days in late August (ending on Labor Day), frolickers, farm animals, and chaos come hurtling into the city, all chaperoned by troops of rabbit-raising 4-Hers. The fair hosts fun for all sorts, from exhibits on macrame, to horse races, to live performances. In 1997, both Kathy Mattea and the Righteous Brothers performed here (concert tickets $15-30).

Nightlife and Entertainment Although Salem's nightlife leaves some charisma to be desired, plenty of sports bars, dart boards, and artsy movies await travelers. The **Ram Restaurant and Big Horn Brewery,** 515 12th St. SE (363-1904), at Bellevue St., serves an award-winning "Total Disorder Porter" (pints $3.25) to match the neon lights and framed jerseys that prove it is a bonafide sports bar (open daily

11am-2am; live DJ Thurs.-Sun.). **Tahiti Restaurant and Lounge,** 380 State St. (581-4978), at Liberty St., sports a dimly lit South Sea Islands decor and a full bar, specializing in tropical and blended drinks. If George mixes your drinks, the bamboo ceilings and wall engravings will transport you to the South Pacific (open Mon.-Fri. 11:30am-2:30am, Sat. 3pm-2:30am; mixed drinks $3-6.50, domestic pints $2, microbrews $3; happy hours Mon.-Fri. 4:30-7pm; all-you-can-eat buffet Mon. 5-7pm $3; 21+ in lounge). **The Salem Cinema,** 445 High St. SE (378-7676), in Pringle Plaza, offers relief from the repetitive college bar-scene with its independent and art film selection.

CENTRAL AND EASTERN OREGON

Most people picture Oregon as a verdant land of torrential rain and rich forests. This is true enough of western Oregon, where most Oregonians live, but the state's eastern half is actually a high desert region. The low evergreen Coast Range and the high, jagged, volcanic Cascades are natural rain barriers, trapping moisture from Pacific winds on their ocean sides. Consequently, the eastern basin is hot and arid.

For generations, this arid region has challenged its human inhabitants, from the Cayuse, Shoshone, Nez Perce, and others who first occupied it, to the pioneers who crossed it on foot and in wagons, to the modern farmers, ranchers, and loggers who live there today. Eastern Oregon is known as the High Desert, but the term "desert" is somewhat misleading. Central Oregon, on the eastern slope of the Cascades, is full of life, with high peaks, world-class skiing, volcanic flows, Crater Lake, and the rapidly growing, energetic town of **Bend.** The southeastern corner of Oregon, near **Burns,** is the driest, full of dramatic, desolate country: high mountains, expansive skies, vast grasslands, lava beds, desert, and its own share of marshes and lakes. Northeastern Oregon, near **Pendleton** and **Baker City,** offers the Wallowa Mountains, pine and fir forests, fossil beds, 8000-ft.-deep Hells Canyon, and a heap of Oregon Trail history. Despite all this opportunity for outdoor activity, eastern Oregon is sparsely populated and seldom visited. Recent attention is slowly attracting more visitors to this vast and largely undeveloped region where cars are almost a must; distances are great, and the few buses take roundabout routes.

Crater Lake and Klamath Falls

Mirror-blue Crater Lake, the namesake of Oregon's only national park, was regarded as sacred by Native American shamans who forbade their people to look upon it. Ice-less in winter, though snowbanked until late July, the flawless circular lake plunges from its 6176 ft. high shores to a depth of nearly 2000 ft., making it the nation's deepest lake and the seventh-deepest in the world. Klamath (kuh-LAH-math) Falls, one of the closest towns, is convenient for those making a pit stop, but time and money are much better spent at Crater Lake itself.

PRACTICAL INFORMATION AND ORIENTATION

Visitors Information: William G. Steel Center (594-2211, ext. 402), 1 mi. from the south entrance of the park. Pick up backcountry camping **permits** here or at Rim Village (free). **Crater Lake National Park Visitors Center** (594-2211, ext. 416), on the lake shore at **Rim Village.** A smaller center with advice regarding trails and campsites. Open daily June-Sept. 8:30am-6pm. The **Klamath County Department of Tourism** runs a visitors information center at 1451 Main St. (884-0666 or 800-445-6728) in Klamath Falls. Open June-Sept. Mon.-Sat. 9am-5:30pm; Oct.-May Mon.-Sat. 8am-4:30pm.

Park Admission: Prices doubled this past year, but now most of the profits go to the park itself. Cars $10, hikers and bikers $5, free with Golden Age Passport or Golden Eagle Passport. Free in winter.

Trains: Amtrak (884-2822 or 800-USA-RAIL/872-7245 for reservations), S. Spring St. depot, Klamath Falls. At the east end of Main St.; turn right onto Spring St. and immediately left onto Oak St. 1 train per day north, 1 per day south to Portland ($37.50-69). Open daily 6:45-10:15am and 9-10:30pm.

Buses: Greyhound, 1200 Klamath Ave., Klamath Falls (882-4616). To: Bend (1 per day, $21); Eugene (1 per day, $24); and Redding, CA (1 per day, $27). Lockers $1 per 24hr. Open Mon.-Fri. 6-10:30am and noon-5:30pm, Sat. 6am-noon.

Public Transportation: Basin Transit Service (883-2877), runs 5 routes around Klamath Falls Mon.-Fri. 6am-7:30pm, Sat. 10am-5pm. 80¢, seniors and disabled 40¢.

Taxi: AB Taxi, 885-5607. 24hr. 10% senior discount.

Car Rental: Budget (885-5421), at the airport. Take S. 6th St. and turn right on Altamonta. $34 per day on weekends, $50 weekdays. Open Mon.-Fri. 7:30am-7:30pm, Sat. 8am-3pm, Sun. 10am-5pm.

Laundromat: Main Street Laundromat, 1711 Main St. (883-1784). Clean and cool inside. Wash $1.25, 12min. dry 25¢. Open daily 8am-7pm.

Weather and Road Conditions: Broadcast continuously on **1610 AM** in Crater Lake.

Crisis: Poison Control, 800-452-7165. **Rape Crisis,** 884-0390). **Suicide/ Mental Health,** 800-452-3669.

Hospital: Merle West Medical Center, 2865 Doggett St. (882-6311). From U.S. 97 northbound, turn right on Campus Dr., then right on Doggett.

Emergency: 911. **Police,** 425 Walnut St. (883-5336). **Fire,** 143 N. Broad St. (non-emergency 885-2056).

Post Office: Klamath Falls, 317 S. 7th St. (884-9226). Open Mon.-Fri. 7:30am-5:30pm, Sat. 9am-noon. **Zip Code:** 97601. **Crater Lake,** in the Steel Center. Open Mon.-Fri. 10am-4pm, Sat. 10am-2pm. **Zip Code:** 97604.

Area Code: 541.

Crater Lake National Park is accessible from Rte. 62 and the south access road that leads up to the caldera's rim, but the park is not completely open until after the snow has melted. Crater Lake averages over 44 ft. of snow per year, and some roads could be closed as late as July; call the Steel Center for road conditions (see above). Route 62 skirts the southwestern edge of the park as it makes a 130 mi. arch northeast from Medford and back south to Klamath Falls (56 mi. southeast). To reach the park from Portland, take I-5 to Eugene, then Rte. 58 east to U.S. 97 south. During the summer you can take Route 138 west from U.S. 97 and approach the lake from the park's north entrance, but this route is one of the last to be cleared. Before July, stay on Hwy. 97 south to Rte. 62. *All of Crater Lake's services and operating hours are based on changing funding levels, which are not determined until April, and on weather conditions. Call the Steel Center to verify services and hours.*

OREGON

ACCOMMODATIONS AND CAMPING

Klamath Falls has several affordable hotels; you could sack out in town and make your forays to Crater Lake from there. For a more interactive visit, the national park contains **Mazama Campground,** and the smaller **Lost Creek Campground,** both of which are closed each year until roads are passable. Backcountry camping is allowed within the park; pick up free permits from Rim Village Visitors Center or at the Steel Center.

Fort Klamath Lodge Motel and RV Park, 52851 Rte. 62 (381-2234), 15 mi. from the southern entrance to Crater Lake National Park. The closest motel to the lake, the 6-unit lodge is in historic Fort Klamath, which consists of little more than a grocery store, post office, restaurant, and spring wildflowers. Cozy but aging countrified motel rooms with knotted-pine walls and orange carpet. TV; no phones in the rooms. 24hr. coin laundry. Singles $30; doubles $40. Closed Nov.-April.

Townhouse Motel, 5323 S. 6th St. (882-0924), 3 mi. south of Main, deep in the heart of strip-mall land. Off-beat furniture, but the price can't be beat. Cable, but none of the 16 units has phones. One double bed $25. Two bedrooms $32.

Lost Creek Campground, in Crater Lake National Park. 3 mi. off Rim Dr. on a paved road in the southeast corner of the park. Set amid thin, young pines. Only16 sites; try to secure one in the morning. Drinking water, flush toilets, and sinks. Tents only, sites $10. No reservations. Usually open mid-July to mid-Oct.

Mazama Campground, by the south entrance to Crater Lake National Park. RVs swarm into the 194 sites in this monster facility in midsummer, but fortunately a sprinkling of sites throughout are reserved for tents. **Loop G** has denser timber and more spacious sites, offering greater seclusion. Firewood for sale. No hookups, but flush toilets and showers. Pay laundry and telephone by the convenience store where you can get frozen burritos and beef franks. Tents $13, RVs $14. No reservations. Open June to mid-Oct. Wheelchair accessible.

FOOD

Eatin' cheap ain't easy in Crater Lake. The Crater Lake Lodge has a small dining room, and Rim Village establishments charge high prices for a skimpy food. There are several affordable restaurants in Klamath Falls and a number of large grocery stores, including a **Safeway** (882-2660), at Pine and 8th St., one block north of Main (open daily 6am-11pm). Stock up here; selection and prices only get worse towards the crater. If you're coming from the south, **Fort Klamath** is the final food frontier before a trek into the park. If you forgot the sweet gherkins, try **Crater Lake Grocery** (381-2263; open daily 8am-7pm, 6pm in winter).

Hobo Junction (882-8013), at 7th Ave. and Main St. This quiet, corner cafe in the center of Klamath Falls is working on its railroad motif. Sandwiches on the slim side, but the chili is hearty ($1.25), and there are 9 varieties of hot dogs. The poor Buff Dog ($1.50) has no bun. Open Mon.-Fri. 9am-4pm, Sat. 10am-3pm.

Cattle Crossing Cafe (381-9801), on Hwy. 62 in Fort Klamath. Step over the silver-plated cow pie into this spare restaurant. A perfect stop on your way to or from the park. Get a rib-sticking breakfast ($5.25) or burger ($4.25-5). Great selection of homemade pies ($2.25). Open April-Oct. daily 6am-9pm.

SIGHTS

Crater Lake initially looks unremarkable. As you ascend, however, the placid blue mirror becomes hypnotic. The fantastic depth of the lake (1932 ft.), combined with the clarity of its waters, creates the amazingly serene and intensely blue effect. About 7700 years ago, Mt. Mazama created this gentle scene in a massive eruption that buried thousands of square miles of the western U.S. under a thick layer of ash. The cataclysmic eruption left a deep caldera that gradually filled with centuries of rain. The lake has become the center of activity in the park.

Rim Drive, which does not open entirely until mid-July, is a 33 mi. loop around the rim of the caldera, high above the lake. The Park Service has carefully placed pull-outs at every point where a view of the lake might cause an awe-struck tourist to drive right off the road. A vast majority of visitors stay in their vehicles as they tour the lake, so it's relatively easy to get away from the shifting crowds. Just stop at any of the trailheads scattered around the rim and hike away from the road. **Garfield Peak** (1.7 mi. one-way), which starts at the lodge, and **Watchman Peak** (.7 mi. one-way), on the west side of the lake, are the most spectacular. The Steel Center (see **Practical Information,** above) has a handy photocopied map of the trails around the lake.

The hike up **Mt. Scott,** the park's highest peak (a tad under 9000 ft.), begins from the drive near the lake's eastern edge. Although steep, the 2½ mi. trail gives the persevering hiker a unique view of the lake and its surroundings that justifies the sweaty ascent. The steep **Cleetwood Trail,** 1 mi. of switchbacks on the lake's north edge, is the only route down to the water. From here, the **Lodge Company** (594-2511) offers popular two-hour boat tours (tour schedule varies; 3-9 tours per day usually mid-June to mid-Sept.; take Rim Drive clockwise from either park entrance to get there; fare $12.50, under 12 $7). Both **Wizard Island,** a cinder cone 760 ft. above the lake, and **Phantom Ship Rock** are fragile, tiny specks when viewed from above, but are startlingly large when seen from the surface of the water. If you take an early tour, you can be left on Wizard Island and picked up later. Picnics and fishing are allowed, as is swimming, but surface temperature reaches a maximum of only 50°F (10°C). Six species of fish have been introduced artificially into the lake, but the water is too pure to support much life; only rainbow trout and kokanee have survived. Park rangers lead free walking tours daily in the summer and periodically in the winter (on snowshoes). Call the Steel Center for schedules (see **Practical Information,** above).

If pressed for time, walk the easy 100 yd. from the visitors center at the rim down to the **Sinnott Memorial Overlook,** a stone enclave built into the slope. The view is the area's most panoramic and accessible, and in the summer, a ranger gives hourly talks on the area's geology and history. A similar talk is given nightly (July-Labor Day at 9pm) at the **Mazama Campground Amphitheater.**

A few hundred yards east of Sinnott Memorial Overlook is the **Crater Lake Lodge,** reopened July 7, 1995, after four seasons and $18 million worth of renovation. Rooms are booked a year in advance and start at $100, but you can have some fun in the lodge for free. Make a quick visit to the rustic "great hall," rebuilt from its original materials, and the observation deck, which affords great views from rocking chairs.

After you've seen the lake from every possible angle, consider a hiking trip into the park's vast **backcountry.** Leave all the exhaust and tourists behind and explore the **Pacific Crest Trail** where it passes through the park, or any of the other trails crossing the terrain. One excellent route starts at the **Red Cone** trailhead (on the north access road) and makes a 12 mi. loop of the Crater Springs, Oasis Butte, and Boundary Springs trails. Get info and permits (free) at the Steel Center (see **Practical Information,** above).

Bend

Nestled against the east slope of the Cascades, Bend is at the epicenter of a region with a kickin' array of accessible summertime activities. Defined by dramatic volcanic features to the south, Mt. Bachelor and the fish-rich Cascades to the west, and the Deschutes River through its heart, this area woos waves of skiers and nature-lovers.

Bend itself was settled as "Farewell Bend" in the early 19th century, a way station on a pioneer trail that paralleled the Deschutes. Oregon's biggest little city in the east is rapidly losing its small town feel to a stream of California, Portland, and Seattle refugees in search of the perfect blend of urban excitement, pristine wilderness, and some sun. Bend natives claim it has one of highest population growth rates *in the world!* This unexpected boom has wrought town controversy as to how to expand (up or out?), but newcomers just keep comin', promoting Bend's array of cultural, culinary, and athletic attractions. Although strip malls and chain stores along U.S. 97 make a bad first impression, the city's self-contained downtown area wins over most visitors. Cheap eats, a place to stay, and lively crowds are easy to find in Bend.

PRACTICAL INFORMATION AND ORIENTATION

Visitors Information: Bend Chamber and Visitors Bureau, 63085 N. U.S. 97 (382-3221). Read the State Park Guide, Events Calendar, National Forest info, and free **maps** while sipping a complimentary cup of coffee. Make plans on their **courtesy phone.** The *Attractions and Activities Guide* has a clear area map. Open Mon.-Sat. 9am-5pm, Sun. 11am-3pm. **Deschutes National Forest Headquarters,** 1645 E. U.S. 20 (388-2715). General forest, recreation, and wilderness info. Peruse the *Recreation Opportunity Guide* for each of the 4 ranger districts. Open Mon.-Fri. 7:45am-4:30pm. **Bend/Fort Rock District Ranger Station,** 1230 NE 3rd St. #A262 (388-5664), has more specific info on Deschutes National Forest. **Fish and Wildlife,** 61374 Parrell Rd. (388-6363), can fill you in on local regulations and permit requirements. Open Mon.-Fri. 8am-5pm.

Buses: Greyhound, 2045 E. U.S. 20 (382-2151), 1½ mi. east of town. 1 per day to Portland ($22) and Klamath Falls ($20). Open Mon.-Fri. 7:30-11:30am and 12:30-5:30pm, Sat. 7:30am-noon, Sun. 8-11:30am. Several other bus and van lines stop here, bound for different destinations; call the above number for info.

Taxi: Owl Taxi, 1919 NE 2nd St. (382-3311). 24hr.

Bicycle Rental: Hutch's Bicycles, 725 NW Columbia Ave. (382-9253). Mountain bikes $15 per day or $50 for 5 days. Open Mon.-Fri. 9am-7pm, Sat.-Sun. 9am-6pm.
Laundromat: Nelson's, 738 NW Columbia Ave. (382-7087). Attendant on duty Mon.-Fri. 8:30am-9:30pm. Wash 25¢, 10min. dry 25¢. Open daily 6am-9:30pm.
Library: Deschutes County Library, 507 NW Wall (388-6679). Open Mon., Wed., Fri. 10am-6pm, Tues. and Thurs. 10am-8pm, Sat. 10am-5pm.
Ben and Jerry's Peace Pops: Don't even think of buying them in this town. None to be found anywhere. This is a Peace Pop wasteland.
Central Oregon Battering and Rape Alliance (COBRA): 800-356-2369. 24 hr.
Poison Control: 800-452-7165. 24hr.
Hospital: St. Charles Medical Center, 2500 NE Neff Rd. (382-4321), for major emergencies only. For routine cuts, scrapes, fractures, and illnesses, go to **Mountain Medical Immediate Care Center,** 1302 NE U.S. 97 (388-7799). Open Mon.-Sat. 8am-8pm, Sun. 10am-6pm.
Emergency: 911. **Police:** 711 NW Bond (388-5550). **Fire:** 388-5533.
Post Office: 2300 NE 4th St. (388-1971), at Webster. Open Mon.-Fri. 8:30am-5:30pm, Sat. 10am-1pm. **General Delivery ZIP Code:** 97701.
Area Code: 541.

Bend is 160 mi. southeast of Portland either on U.S. 26 E through Warm Springs Indian Reservation to U.S. 97 S, or down 1-5S to Salem, then east on Rte. 22 E to Rte. 20 E through Sisters. Bend is also 144 mi. north of Klamath Falls on U.S. 97 N and 100 mi. southeast of Mt. Hood via U.S. 26 E and Rte. 97 S.

Bend is bisected by U.S. 97 (3rd St.). The downtown area lies to the west along the Deschutes River; Wall and Bond St. are the two main arteries. Watch out for curving streets with shifting names. From east to west, Franklin becomes Riverside, then Galveston, then Skyliner; Greenwood becomes Newport; and 14th St. becomes Century Dr. and is the first leg of the Cascade Lakes Hwy.

ACCOMMODATIONS AND CAMPING

Bend treats budget travelers right: The hostel and B&B provide phenomenal deals for tuckered-out travelers. Most of the cheapest motels line 3rd St. just outside of town, and rates are surprisingly low. **Deschutes National Forest** maintains a *huge* number of lakeside campgrounds along the Cascade Lakes Hwy. west of town. All have toilets; those with potable water cost $8-12 per night; those without water are free. Camping anywhere in the National Forest area is **free**. Contact the **Bend/Ft. Rock Ranger District Office** (see above) for more information.

Mill Inn, 642 NW Colorado (389-9198), on the corner of Bond St., 4 blocks from downtown. This B&B in a recently rebuilt hotel and boarding house is a labor of love for Ev and Carol Stiles, who keep the place sparkling. Hearty, home-cooked breakfast served in the open dining room. Free laundry, but the real treasure is the outdoor hot tub. $15 buys a bunk in a single-sex hostel room decorated with sports banners (sleeps 4), or spring for a trim, elegant private room (single $37; double $45, with shared bath). Rooms with private baths more expensive.
Bend Cascade Hostel, 19 SW Century Dr. (389-3813 or 800-299-3813). From 3rd St., take Franklin St. west, then follow the Cascade Lakes Tour signs to Century Drive (14th St.), just past the Circle-K. Foosball, coin laundry, and kitchen; linen rental available. Lockout 9:30am-4:30pm, curfew 11pm. 3 private rooms. 55 beds. $14; seniors, students, cyclists, and members $13; under 18 with parents ½ price.
Edelweiss Motor Inn, 2346 NE Division St. (382-6222), at Xerxes St. near the northern intersection with 3rd St. A worn building, with a hint of German heritage in soft beige and peach. Cable, microwave. No phones or A/C, but clean, and you won't find a cheaper room in Bend. Singles and studio rooms $25; doubles $36.
Royal Gateway Motel, 475 SE 3rd (382-5631). Clean and comfy, if close to the road. The bathrooms are not actually larger than the bedrooms; it's just a clever optical illusion. Free local calls and cable. Microwaves and fridges. Singles $30; doubles $38. Rates lower in winter; senior discounts.

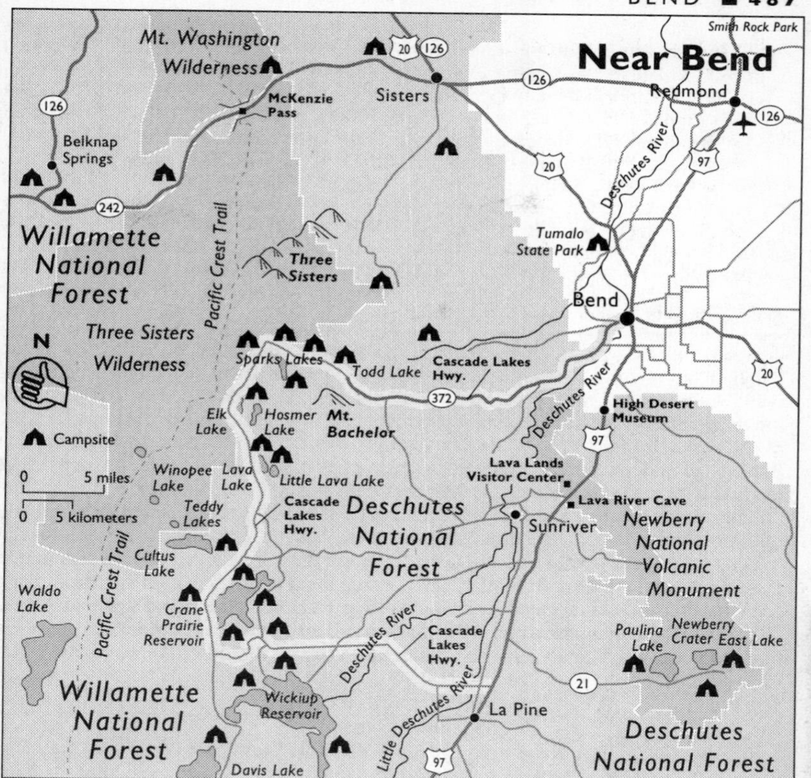

Tumalo State Park, 62976 OB Riley Rd. (388-6055 or 800-452-5687 for reservations). 4-5 mi. north of Bend off U.S. 20W. 67 tent sites $15; preferred river sites $17; 21 full hookups $19; teepees $25.

Cultus Lake Campground (389-5125, ext. 037244), 40 mi. west of Bend, 2 mi. off the Cascade Lakes Hwy. Get anything you need, including boat rentals, at the little resort across the lake. Well-shaded campground slopes to the shore, where cultists swim, sail, canoe, waterski, or just bask in the sun. A long drive from Bend, it is slow to fill up. Drinking water and vault toilets. $10.

FOOD

The diversity of food in Bend breaks the eastern Oregon beef-and-potatoes monotony. Bend's many restaurants maintain high standards, and the most interesting and exceptional are generally downtown. No fewer than four mega-markets line the east side of 3rd St. **Devore's Good Food Store and Wine Shop,** 1124 NW Newport (389-6588), peddles anything organic, including excellent wine, beer, and cheese (open Mon.-Sat. 8am-7pm, Sun. 11am-6pm).

Westside Bakery and Cafe, 1005 NW Galveston (382-3426). Feast on pastries beyond your wildest dreams (under $3). Bakers work around the clock to turn over more than 150 turnovers daily! Locally famous blackberry honeywheat pancakes ($4.50). Burgers and sandwiches ($4.75-6.25). Open daily 6:30am-3pm.

Taqueria Los Jalapeños, 601 NE Greenwood Ave. (382-1402). Narrow and delightfully simple space with a steady stream of devoted locals through the screen door. Bean and cheese burritos (a piddly $1.50), and chimichanga plates ($5, one of the priciest items). Open Mon.-Sat. 11am-8pm.

Deschutes Brewery and Public House, 1044 NW Bond St. (382-9242). The homemade sausage ($5), smoked salmon ($6), and smoked vegetable ($5) sandwiches are good, but 6 or 7 new specials a day ($5-7) render the menu moot. Imperial pints (20oz.) of ale, bitters, stout ($3), root beer and ginger ale ($1.75) brewed on the premises. Their Black Butte Porter is found on tap in bars all over Oregon. Open Mon.-Thurs. 11am-11:30pm, Fri.-Sat. 11am-12:30am, Sun. 11am-10pm.

Jo-Ol's Bento Bar, 114 NW Minnesota St. (385-9194; fax 385-9169), between Wall and Bond St. Fax in your order or make a personal appearance at this snappy little spot. Do the chicken, tofu, or vegetable skewer with rice ($3.75-4.15) or opt for a heap of *Yaki Soba* Noodles ($3); both come with any or all of 4 savory sauces. Open Mon.-Fri. 11am-5pm, Sat. 11am-4pm.

SIGHTS AND OUTDOORS

In Bend, you can get up close and personal with Canadian geese or enjoy a picnic lunch on the lawns of beautiful **Drake Park.** The park is sandwiched between Mirror Pond, a dammed part of the Deschutes River, and Franklin St., a block from downtown. The park is host to a number of events and festivals, most significantly the **Cascade Festival of Music** (383-2202), a 10-day series of classical concerts each year in late August under a tent by the river (tickets $12-20, $5 per family, ½ price for student rush. Call the festival office at 382-8381 or write 842 NW Wall St. #6.)

Seven miles south of Bend on U.S. 97, the **High Desert Museum** (382-4754) is one of the premier natural and cultural history museums in the Pacific Northwest. In the "Spirit of the West" exhibit, visitors walk through stunning life-size dioramas of life in the Old West, including mining tunnels straight out of *Indiana Jones.* The indoor "desertarium" presents seldom-seen animals like burrowing owls and collared lizards. Outside, paved paths wind past playful otters and docile porcupines, exhibits on birds of prey, a settler's cabin, sheepherder's wagon, and an old-time sawmill. The museum attracts 1200 visitors daily in summer, so arrive early to beat the crowds. The high price of admission is entirely worth it (open daily 9am-5pm; $6.25, seniors and ages 13-18 $5.75, ages 5-12 $3, under 5 free).

In November 1990, **Newberry National Volcanic Monument** was established to link and preserve the volcanic features south of Bend. For an introduction to the area, visit the **Lava Lands Visitor Center** (593-2421), 5 mi. south of the High Desert Museum on U.S. 97 (open daily 9:30am-5pm; April-Memorial Day and Labor Day-Oct. open Wed.-Sun. 9:30am-5pm). A mandatory $5 parking fee good for 5 days is required within ¼ mi. of the monument area (with Golden Age Passport $2.50). Immediately behind the visitors center is **Lava Butte,** a 500 ft. cinder cone from which much of the nearby lava flows. Between Memorial Day and Labor Day, take a shuttle bus ($2, seniors and children $1.50, under 6 free) that leaves every 30 minutes or walk the 1½ mi. In the off-season, visitors may drive their own cars up the spiralled incline. From the lookout point, gaze down at a 10 sq. mi. area leveled by the lava that flowed from the butte and the relatively rapid natural regeneration. On clear days, the point affords vistas of Mt. Bachelor, South Sister, and other Cascade peaks. Or, take the ¾ mi. **Trail of the Molten Land** through the lava fields behind the visitors center.

One mile south of the visitors center on U.S. 97 is **Lava River Cave** (593-1456), a 100,000-year-old, 1 mi. subterranean lava tube. The entrance is in a stand of ponderous ponderosa pines, perfect for a picnic. The cavern is 50 ft. high in places. Bundle up before descending and bring a lantern or rent one at the cave for $1.50 (open mid-May to mid-Oct. 9am-6pm; entrance $2.50, ages 13-17 $2, under 13 free).

The central component of the monument is **Newberry Crater,** 18 mi. south of Lava Butte on U.S. 97, then about 13 steep mi. east on Rte. 21. This diverse volcanic region was formed by the eruptions of Newberry Volcano over millions of years, the most recent of which was an estimated 7060 years ago, forming Lava Butte (Newberry is one of three volcanoes in Oregon most likely to erupt again "soon"). The caldera, or center of the volcano, covers about 500 sq. mi. and contains two lakes, **Paulina Lake** and **East Lake.** The most scenic campground is **Little Crater,** with 50 sites between Rte. 21 and the Paulina lakeshore. Over 150 mi. of trails cross the area,